PSYCHOTHERAPY RESEARCH: Selected Readings

PSYCHOTHERAPY RESEARCH

Selected Readings

Edited by   GARY E. STOLLAK
Indiana University

BERNARD G. GUERNEY, JR.
Rutgers—The State University

MEYER ROTHBERG
Rutgers—The State University

RAND McNALLY & COMPANY
Chicago

RAND McNALLY PSYCHOLOGY SERIES

Lloyd Humphreys, Advisory Editor

Preface

The amount of research aimed at understanding and controlling the variables involved in psychotherapy has increased in geometric proportions over the last fifteen years. Furthermore, as the graduate education of clinical students has become increasingly experimental in orientation, attention has become focused as much on methodology and design of research as on direct studies of process and outcome. Rather than attempting to answer the broad question, Does psychotherapy work?, research has come to emphasize more careful and specific exploration of those patient, therapist, and situational characteristics, and their interaction, that result in behavior change. The models, designs, and methods available to the researcher are no longer restricted to the traditional personality theory approaches, but come also from such areas as learning theory, communication analyses, interpersonal and group interaction process analyses, and so on.

The change from an anecdotal, subjective approach to one more objective and manipulative is best seen in the recognition of the importance of carefully controlled studies and of control groups. To this end, one significant advance, in attempting both to avoid or sidestep the "ethical" problem of using non-treated control groups and to make more explicit the possible "active" versus "inert" variables in psychotherapy, has been the extensive use of therapy analogues and quasi-therapy laboratory procedures. One result of the use of such techniques has been an increase in the degree of contact and communication between clinical and experimental psychology.

The most recent and comprehensive reviews of the literature in psychotherapy are found in the American Psychological Association conferences on psychotherapy held in 1958 and 1961.[1] The present editors have felt that there is a need for (1) presentation of more recent and more diverse material than that presented at these APA conferences and (2) specific details of the

[1] E. A. Rubinstein & M. B. Parloff (Eds.), *Research in psychotherapy,* Vol. 1 (Washington, D.C.: American Psychological Association, 1959); H. H. Strupp & L. Luborsky (Eds.), *Research in psychotherapy,* Vol. 2 (Washington, D.C.: American Psychological Association, 1962).

hypotheses, designs, and procedures, which the reviews must, of necessity, minimize in attempting to abstract and integrate the findings of this large body of research.

In the present volume, where feasible, we have included review articles which give the reader overviews of particular areas of research, and then followed these with what we regarded as the most interesting and informative research articles in those areas. If psychotherapy is ever to be considered a "science," it must meet the rigorous, operational standards characteristic of science. The editors feel that the stimulation to, and the conduct of, adequate research in the future will be greatly aided by examination of individual research articles of the past. We have also included, at the end of each section, a list of selected articles which we consider important and interesting but which could not be reprinted here because of space limitations.

Our goal, then, was to gather in one volume, for teachers, students, researchers, and practitioners, those articles which we felt represent the best work in the many areas of research. We have focused not only on those articles that report significant results, but more importantly, for stimulating future research, also on those articles that represent the multitude of therapy variants (e.g., individual, group, child, and family; client-centered and behavior), the unique and potentially heuristic ideas (e.g., "treatment" of "neurotic" computer programs, "autoanalysis," "experimenter-subject psychotherapy"), and the various experimental designs and methodologies that represent the current approaches to research in psychotherapy. We cannot, of course, claim to have included all deserving works, even in our lists of additional readings; we hope, however, that we have included a large portion and a diverse sample of them.

Acknowledgments are especially appropriate in a book of readings, and we would like to express our thanks to the authors and publishers who allowed us to reprint their works. Specific acknowledgments are included on the first page of each article. We would also like to take this opportunity to acknowledge the assistance and support of Dr. Kenneth Heller. Thanks are due also to Celicia Upper, Frances Oliphant, Barbara Kerr, and Martin Packard for their aid in preparing the manuscript, and to Louise Clempner for her interest and encouragement. Finally, Louise Guerney and Naomi Rothberg must be praised for their patience, suggestions, and sympathy.

G. E. STOLLAK
B. G. GUERNEY
M. A. ROTHBERG

Bloomington, Indiana
August, 1965

Contents

CONTENTS

CONTENTS

CONTENTS

CONTENTS

CONTENTS

CONTENTS

CONTENTS

Introduction:
The Problem

Psychotherapy Today or Where Do We Go from Here?*

CARL R. ROGERS

The germ of this paper started to develop more than four years ago, at the first workshop of the American Academy of Psychotherapists. I had, for many reasons, looked forward eagerly to this workshop. Among my reasons, as I realized later, was the implicit belief that experienced therapists, no matter how divergent their orientations, certainly had in common their *experience* of what constituted helpfulness. Hence if they could observe and participate together in a therapeutic *experience,* it would be a very important stride in the direction of ironing out their verbal and ideological differences. So it was very exciting that we were able to arrange to have patients interviewed by different therapists, the rest of us observing.

But then came the jolt. The very portions of those interviews which to me seemed obviously moments of "real" therapy, were experienced by other members as non-therapeutic or even anti-therapeutic.

Reprinted from *American Journal of Psychotherapy,* 1963, 17 (1), 5–16, with the permission of the Association for the Advancement of Psychotherapy and the author.

* Presented at the Sixth Annual Conference of the American Academy of Psychotherapists, New York City, October 14, 1961.

And the moments which some others regarded as clearly of a healing nature, I experienced as meaningless or ineffectual, or worse. At the time this was a hard blow to assimilate. It meant that our differences ran far deeper than I had presumed. I had supposed that we were all talking about the same *experiences,* but attaching different words, labels, and descriptions to these experiences. This was clearly not true. I have been mulling over this fact ever since.

I believe there is little question but that it *is* a fact. Let me mention some of the diverse and occasionally amusing incidents which support this statement—that what seems therapeutic to one seems anti-therapeutic to another.

Recently I participated in a diversified group of therapists in which a well-qualified analyst presented a portion of one of his cases. The central point was the way he had encouraged his patient to speak up to his boss and give the boss a solution to a problem which was troubling the company. To him, this encouragement seemed clearly therapeutic. The group felt, almost unanimously, that he had kept the man from making an important personal, existential choice, that he had robbed the incident of its therapeutic potential.

3

A prominent therapist, who would, I believe, term himself a practitioner of existential therapy, listened to a tape recording of a therapeutic interview conducted by two well-known members of the American Academy of Psychotherapists, which I am sure they regarded as helpful. Afterwards his comment was that the two therapists ought to refund the patient's money. "The only good elements in the interview were the bird songs in the background!"

This same existentialist played one of his taped therapeutic interviews and was particularly pleased with the way he had dissuaded his patient, a young woman, from going home for the weekend, a trip which he believed would have been regressive. I was surprised at his comments, for in listening to the interview I had felt that his persuasion was the one clearly anti-therapeutic portion of the interview.

A young therapist of my acquaintance was highly successful with a deeply disturbed hospitalized psychotic man. He feels that one of the crucial therapeutic moments occurred when he shouted at the man, who was engaged in rambling intellectualized incoherencies, the one word, "Bullshit!" Other therapists listening, however, have often been shocked, and feel not only that such a term is not proper therapeutic technique, but that it was not therapeutic in this instance.

Similarly unconventional, a serious paper was given at the recent Convention of the American Psychological Association on "The Dog as Co-Therapist" (1). The idea was born when the therapist's dog was by accident in his office and a very difficult problem child refused to return unless the dog was to be there. Since then he has found that his child clients use the dog as a confidant, fellow conspirator, companion, and scapegoat, and also as a "person" who may be loved, safely and without losing face. The dog can be the embodiment of "the bad me" which can be tolerated, then accepted, even loved. But curiously (or not

so curiously) some of those who listened to the paper thought this was ridiculous poppycock, and that his idea had no place among serious therapists.

Thus far I have spoken of these incidents as though they existed at arm's length. But in myself I have often had strong feelings when listening to tapes of therapeutic interviews, or even stronger feelings when, at workshops or in other situations, I have sat in on a therapy interview as an observer. My feeling in that situation has often been, "Move out of that chair and let me take over! This person needs therapy, not what you've giving him!" I suspected others among us have experienced similar feelings.

One more example. In the Standal and Corsini book on *Critical Incidents in Psychotherapy,* a therapist reports, anonymously, a critical or difficult situation in one of his cases, and a panel of experienced therapists give their individual reactions and comments in writing, each panel member ignorant of the comments being made by his fellows (2). The views expressed are often almost diametrically opposed. Here is one sample. A therapist describes a very difficult and dramatic episode in this therapy with a 19-year-old college girl. The content of the episode need not, for our purposes, concern us. Here are sample reactions, from five experienced therapists, to this interview:

The first has a completely negative reaction, and says, "It appears that the therapist realizes to some degree the serious implications of his seductiveness."

The second speaks very favorably, and says "This incident throws light on what therapy is —namely, living with a person on a real basis in an understanding relationship through the most awful moments of fear or disorganization."

The third indicates his attitude by saying, "Had I stumbled into such a predicament . . ." and adds, "This incident is an excellent example of what can happen when a therapist fails to perceive a schizophrenic's 'parataxic distortions.'"

The fourth says that this interview "I found most distressing to read about" and amplifies this negative statement.

The message of the fifth contains such statements as "This event was therapeutic"; "a lot of growth was demonstrated."

I hope I have made my point that our differences as therapists do not lie simply in attaching different labels to the same phenomenon. The difference runs deeper. An experience which is seen by one therapist as healing, growth-promoting, helpful, is seen by another as none of these things. And the experience which to the second therapist is seen as possessing these qualities is not so perceived by the first. We differ at the most basic levels of our personal experience.

Some people may feel that though we differ regarding specific incidents, as I have indicated, nevertheless in our goals and in our general directions there is much agreement, and much unity. I think not. To me it seems that therapists are equally divergent in these realms.

For the past two years I have encouraged my seminar of psychiatric residents to discuss goals of therapy, either in general, or in regard to a particular client we are considering. Such discussions reveal the most profound differences. We are not agreed on whether the goal is removal of symptoms, reorganization of personality, curing of a disease, or adjustment to the culture. When we try to pin down our goals to those specific behaviors in a specific client which we would regard as evidence of "success," the divergence is almost equally great. In my experience the only therapists who agree on goals of therapy are those who have been strongly indoctrinated in the same dogma.

Not only is there divergence in what we mean by success, but the conference of the American Academy of Psychotherapists, on "Failure in Psychotherapy," has demonstrated that we do not agree on what constitutes failure. There is even difference of opinion as to whether the suicide of a client or patient in therapy is necessarily a failure.

But what about the direction in which we should move? Is there agreement in this realm? A vigorous and growing group, particularly among psychologists, is the group which in one way or another bases its therapy upon learning theory as studied in the psychologic laboratory. They regard this as the only scientific direction in which to move, and look with scorn upon the so-called dynamic approaches. This scorn is returned by the majority of therapists who regard themselves as "dynamic." Each group feels positive that the other is moving in a fruitless, if not ridiculous, direction.

One of the more extreme forms of learning-theory approach is the operant conditioning carried on by B. F. Skinner and his group (3). Although as yet it has had little practical impact upon psychotherapy, it will be heard from. Fundamentally the hypothesis is that deviant human behavior can be "shaped up" into normal behavior by the same principle of properly scheduled immediate rewards which transform everyday pigeons into ping-pong players. Yet a large group of therapists would find this aim and this hypothesis definitely unacceptable.

In some ways closely related is the view of Eysenck that all "dynamic therapies," and their attempts to deal with "underlying complexes," are completely unfounded. His own theory is that "there is no evidence for these putative complexes, and symptomatic treatment is all that is required" (4). I feel sure that Wolpe (5) and various other therapists within the learning-theory stream of thought would join him in this statement. Yet at least an equal number of practicing therapists would hold a deeply opposed point of view.

In regard to the approach which has been developed by the so-called client-centered group, the situation is the same. Some therapists comment on the promise and significance of the direction in which we are moving. On the other hand, a serious-minded therapist and researcher said (privately) "Rogers has set back clinical psychology and psychotherapy by two decades!" And while I am deeply engaged in a research in client-centered therapy with psychotics, I come across a statement by a client-centered therapist in which he says, "I would question whether a clinic which uses a client-centered approach exclusively is prepared to accept psychotic clients" (6).

If we look at the new trends coming over the horizon—the growing development of a phenomenological existentialist point of view, the interest in Zen Buddhism, and the like—we find the same situation. The differences over such trends are just as strong as those I have cited. To some these appear to be important and promising directions, while others regard them as mystical dead ends. A reviewer, attempting to be objective, states that the effect of all such writings is "to obfuscate and impede the orderly development of a science."

Even within the fold of psychoanalysis, the original entrant in the field, there is the same divergence within the group, and about the group. There is strong evidence that though analysts may still talk in relatively orthodox terms, what they do in the practice of therapy in their offices bears little or no resemblances to classical analysis. *Time* magazine reports that "The original Freudian concept of analysis . . . is going out of style" (7). Some students of the professional culture believe that the analytic movement is well into its declining phase. Yet even in regard to psychotherapy of the psychoses a reviewer (with freudian background, to be sure) says "Psychoanalytic theory overshadows all other approaches, and appears to be most fruitful."

It is, I believe, clear that were I to close my paper at this point, a one-sentence summary would be, "The field of psychotherapy is in a mess." Therapists are not in agreement as to their goals or aims in therapy. They are in deep disagreement as to the theoretical structure which would contain their work. They cannot agree as to whether a given experience for a client is healing or destructive, growth-promoting or damaging. They are not in agreement as to what constitutes a succesful outcome of their work. They cannot agree as to what constitutes failure. They diverge sharply in their views as to the promising directions for the future. It seems as though the field is completely chaotic and divided.

I am sure that some must look back nostalgically to the situation which existed two or three decades ago. The small number of professionals who were then engaged in the field lived and worked within a comfortable and secure framework of freudian theory and practice. They knew what psychotherapy was, what its goals were, and the procedures by which to reach those goals. By contrast the field of psychotherapy today is fractionated in a hundred different ways, and the comfortable feeling of unified assurance has all but vanished.

In spite of the contradictions and confusions I have tried to describe, I find this a very exciting and hopeful period in the development of psychotherapy. It is a burgeoning period when new theories, new ideas, new methods of practice are being born at a startling rate. Psychotherapy is becoming a province of university departments, and hence its nature can be openly considered and discussed and criticized by professional workers whose daily livelihood does not depend upon defending a given point of view. Psychologists and psychiatrists are bursting forth with new conceptualizations of psychotherapy. I find this to be true even among graduate students. It is clear that the dogmatic views which held the profession in intellectual chains for many years have completely eroded and given way. Every worker in the field is now much more free to think his own thoughts, formulate his own views on the basis of his own experience, and put forth his own hypotheses. I regard this as a thoroughly healthy flowering of thought, even if a confusing one.

I believe I might bring this conceptual diversity alive if I try to indicate, even in over-simplified terms, the essence or core of the therapeutic experience as it seems to various therapists today. Suppose we were to ask today's wide variety of therapists, what is the essential moment of therapy? Granted that there are many background conditions and elements and procedures of therapy, what is the essence of the moment of change? What is the nature of those episodes in therapy where one feels that some real change has occurred, where it seems that one's client or patient has in some significant way altered in his personality, his self-organization, or his behavior? Recognizing that there is much that precedes such a moment, and much that must follow it if therapy is to be complete, what is the *crucial* core, without which no lasting change could take place?

Years ago one would have received primarily one answer to such a question. Now it seems to me there are dozens of answers, often overlapping answers to be sure, but still perceptibly different. I should like to give some of these answers as I have been able to understand them. I am sure no one individual will be satisfied with the formulation regarding his own point of view, both because it will be brief and oversimplified, and because of my own failure correctly to understand the nuances of each view. Nevertheless it may help to suggest the multiplying ways in which psychotherapy is now being perceived.

The traditional answer from the analytic group would, I believe, be this: That the moment of change is the moment in which there is an experience of insight or understanding of one's self in relation to one's past, usually following upon a well-timed interpretation.

But let us sample some of the many other answers. For the operant conditioning group I believe the statement would be something like this: The moment of change in therapy involves no necessary conscious element at all; it is simply a slight alteration of behavior which occurs when the subject's verbal or other behavior varies by chance to a form which is slightly closer to the goal which the experimenter has chosen, and is immediately rewarded. I do not call the participants therapist and client or patient, because I believe this group would prefer the more scientifically oriented term of experimenter and subject. I hope I have, however, satisfactorily described the essential unit of change as they perceive it. This is the way in which the individual's behavior would gradually be "shaped up."

Let us again choose a contrasting view. For the Atlanta group—Whitaker, Warkentin, Malone, and others (8)—the essence of therapy seems to be those moments in which the patient and therapist(s) live together in a deeply experienced fantasy relationship having little or nothing to do with the real world, but where the unconscious of one individual interacts with the unconscious of the other.

I trust it will be clear that the three formulations I have given are challengingly different. They cannot all be equally true, unless they represent three sharply different kinds of change, with sharply different outcomes. But let us add more.

Alexander (9) and many neo-Freudians would see the essential moment of change in therapy as a corrective emotional experience, in which some crippling experience from the past is newly experienced in a new context and with different meaning.

On the other hand, George Kelly (10) sees the key experience of therapy as one in which the individual recognizes that the way he has construed some aspect of his life is loosening or collapsing, and some reconstruing and some rebuilding of personal constructs is necessarily occurring.

The adlerian therapist would see the critical moment in a somewhat similar way—as one in which the patient, thanks to the interpretation and teaching of the therapist, sees the mistaken concepts he has had regarding himself and his life, and changes these erroneous conceptions.

With an even stronger cognitive emphasis, Ellis (11) sees the moment of change as being that moment when the individual is convinced by the therapist that the rational structure by which he has been functioning is in some respect erroneous, and that the structure suggested by the therapist is more correct.

For myself and the group that clusters around the client-centered focus, the moment of therapy is still differently defined (12). It is the immediate and complete experiencing by the client, in a psychologically safe relationship, of a feeling which has hitherto been too threatening to experience freely.

Many of the learning theorists would feel that the unit of change in psychotherapy is the counter-conditioning of anxiety. The moment in which the subject or patient experiences anxiety simultaneously with a comfort situation which is incompatible with anxiety is the moment of change.

Other psychologists whose views develop from Festinger's theory of cognitive dissonance (13) see it somewhat differently. For them the essence of change is the client's acceptance of the therapist's view of him, a view dissonant from his own, but made acceptable by the high status and credibility of the therapist. It is essentially a moment of reduction of cognitive dissonance in the client.

The psychotherapists who start from an existential base would have a sharply divergent view. For them the core of therapy is the instantaneous subjective encounter of two separate individuals, an event which cannot be planned for, but which can be *allowed* to occur—an I-Thou moment of relationship.

We could go on and on with these differing conceptions of the crucial moment in therapy. For those interested in family therapy, it is the reliving of the family relationship in a new context provided by the therapist. For the person interested in Zen, the crucial moment may be one of psychologic shock, as it was to the suicidal student who was enlightened and cured by the "thundering cry" of a Zen master (14).

Perhaps I have said enough to indicate that this rank growth of theory and practice in therapy has led to many diverging views as to what constitutes the essential moment of therapy, views which in some instances overlap, but in others seem quite completely irreconcilable. If there were "thirty-six therapies" when Robert Harper wrote his book (15), there seem to me to be closer to one hundred today.

What is the meaning and significance of all these variations in view, the confusion, the contradictions, the differences? What are the implications for the whole realm of psychotherapy? I should like to give my views on this, but with a clear recognition that I have no special gift of prophecy, and that I may be greatly mistaken.

It means, I believe, that we are backing off and taking a fresh look at the basic problem of our profession, with no inhibitions, few preconceptions, and no holds barred. We can ask again the central question, "How may constructive change in the behavior and personality of the troubled or deviant person be facilitated?" The variety of answers being given will, I believe, help us to open our minds to possibilities which we have not dreamed of before.

Another implication is that for the time being it will be a young man's field. The curiosity and skepticism, the vigor and creativity of younger minds are freed by this chaotic situation. No longer is it governed by the heavy hand of supposedly wise elders. Young men are free to go at the problems freshly, without the sense of being rebels.

I am sure that because of this situation of confusion, various means of altering human behavior will be proposed and tried which will seem to some of us as unethical, unsound, ineffective, and philosophically indefensible. In this respect it will be a difficult period for experienced therapists. But ways of working will also be proposed and tried which will stretch our imaginations, open new vistas of effectiveness, challenge our complacencies, cut through our verbal elaborations, and produce new means of assistance to human beings.

I believe that the present variations in thought and practice mean that the day of systems, of schools of thought, of dogma, is over. Institutions and organizations which indoctrinate therapists in one point of view only are pure anachronisms in today's situation. I do not say this casually. I believe that psychoanalytic institutes—of whatever brand—with their cultish type of training, are on the way out. I would say exactly the same about university departments which expose their students only to training in client-centered therapy, or in any other single approach to therapy. I know how hardy organizations are, and I am· well aware that such narrow institutions may continue to function for a long time, but I believe their day of vital influence on thoughtful individuals is past.

In this connection I believe that an organization such as the American Academy of Psychotherapists will increasingly come into its own. I think its instigators—and I can speak freely, because I was not one of that group—were even wiser than they knew. It is one of a very few organizations I know in this field in which a central purpose is to provide a forum for all points of view in therapy, with every approach equally welcome as long as the therapist himself is a broadly qualified professional person.† Certainly the distinc-

tive hallmark of our meetings and workshops has been the directness and deep honesty of our interchanges, whether we are in full agreement or profound and almost violent disagreement. This quality of communication is helping to set a pattern for the future in which free and open consideration can be given to every serious new way of working in this field.

There is one final implication of this flowering diversity in psychotherapy. I wish to examine several facets of this implication. It is that of necessity we must move toward looking at the *facts*. And to look at the facts means moving toward research. We are beyond the point where differences will be resolved by the voice of authority or by commitment to an essentially religious type of faith in one point of view as against another. To buttress our theory by quotations from Freud, or by pointing to the precision of our logic, or even by appealing to the depth of our own inner conviction, will not be enough. The public and the profession will want, in the words of the TV detective, "just the facts, please, ma'am, just the facts."

But how will we obtain these facts? First of all, perhaps, by a great extension of naturalistic observation. We need to *look* at therapy, in each of its various forms, and consider, openmindedly and thoughtfully, the events which are occurring. We need to do this individually, as we live with another person in a meaningful therapeutic relationship. We also need to do this as a profession. Here the Academy or some similar group might play a vital role. If the organization set as its goal one complete recorded case from each therapeutic point of view, what an astonishing difference this could make. The organization could furnish the recorder, the tapes, and a sympathetic person with the technical know-how to set up the recording in a satisfactory manner. Any serious therapist who was willing to have his work recorded, whether member or non-member, would receive this service.

† The Association for the Advancement of Psychotherapy, the parent organization of this Journal, is another such organization.

Perhaps some day one of the major requirements for membership would be the submission of a complete recorded case.

This material, available for thoughtful study by any qualified professional person, would be a great stride forward. Its value would be multiplied if it contained two follow-up interviews at least one year after the conclusion of therapy, one conducted by the therapist, and one conducted by an unbiased worker skilled in evoking responses to a series of survey questions which would be used with all clients.

Another way of getting at the facts is the empirical study of observed behaviors in therapy. This means the testing of theory-based hypotheses by means of pre-therapy and post-therapy tests, and by measures of in-therapy behaviors on the part of both therapist and client. Most psychotherapy research to date has been of this type, but such studies could be greatly extended.

A third way of getting at the facts will be the use of laboratory situations. When an issue regarding psychotherapy has been clearly identified in its essential form, it will often be possible to develop a laboratory situation which contains the issue in simplified form, and to test it at the laboratory level. Some very valuable beginnings have already been made along this line. "Conflicts" have been created by hypnosis, and then treated by differing procedures. In another study one group of clients talked to an understanding therapist, while another group talked to a tape recorder. In still another, clients were, under hypnosis, given different mind-sets as to the congruence or genuineness of their therapist. The differences in process under these different conditions have been studied. Such laboratory studies, much further developed, should teach us much about therapy.

But perhaps the most important means of getting at the facts will be an increasing skill and sophistication in measuring the subjective. A young psychologist (16) recently showed me a paper of his, as yet unpublished. Its title says a great deal. It is "Worknotes Toward a Science of Inner Experience." In this paper he describes the encouraging progress being made in coming to grips with the crucial problem of measuring the subjective feelings which occur in one's personal experience. Little by little the strictly behavioristic approach is modifying its rigid resistance to the study of inner subjective problems. Ways are being discovered—phenomenological descriptions, Q-sorts, semantic differentials— by which subjective feelings can be respectably and accurately put into operation and quantified. It is entirely possible that from this trend toward measuring the subjective will come not only new light on the complex processes of psychotherapy and personality change, but also a modification of our current philosophy of science. In any event this trend is already beginning to supply us with objective measurement of very subtle inner experiences. We can measure the changes which occur over therapy in the meaning of such concepts as mother, good, self, and therapist, as these concepts move in the "semantic space" of the client. We can reliably measure the degree of immediacy in the client's experiencing, or the perception of the therapist's genuineness by the client. Such beginnings are extremely promising for the future.

All of these various channels of fact-finding will, I believe, be called into service as we try to determine objectively the changes which occur in different modes of therapy, and the subtle pre-conditions which are associated with these changes. Such fact-finding processes are an inevitable part of the future of our field if it is to move forward. They need not interfere with the subjective personal quality of therapy itself—but they are essential if we are to find our way out of the present confusing Babel of voices, each with its own "truth."

SUMMARY

Psychotherapy at the present time is in a state of chaos. It is not however a meaningless chaos, but an ocean of confusion, teeming with life, spawning vital new ideas, approaches, procedures, and theories at an incredibly rapid rate. Hence the present is a period in which the most diverse methods are used, and in which the most divergent explanations are given for a single event. This situation makes inevitable the development of a new fact-finding attitude—a more objective appraisal of different types of change in personality and behavior, and a more empirical understanding of the subtle subjective conditions which lead to these changes. Only on the basis of such facts can the therapist of the future select the way of working which is most effective in achieving his own deeper aims and those of his client. Only out of such a fact-finding attitude can a reasonable order again emerge in this crucially significant area, and bring us again to some clarity in our understanding of ways by which constructive personality change may be facilitated.

REFERENCES

1. LEVINSON, B. M. The Dog as Co-Therapist. Paper given at convention of the American Psychological Association, Sept. 1961.
2. STANDAL, S. W., and CORSINI, R. J., Eds. *Critical Incidents in Psychotherapy.* Prentice-Hall, New York, 1959, pp. 38–63.
3. See LINDSLEY, O. R. Operant Conditioning Methods Applied to Research in Chronic Schizophrenia. *Psychiat. Research Reports,* 1956, No. 118–153.
4. EYSENCK, H. J. *Dynamics of Anxiety and Hysteria.* Praeger, New York, 1957, pp. 267–8.
5. WOLPE, J. *Psychotherapy of Reciprocal Inhibition.* Stanford University Press, 1958.
6. SNYDER, W. U. In Standal, S. W. and Corsini, R. J., *op. cit.,* p. 59.
7. *Time* magazine, May 19, 1961.
8. WHITAKER, C. A., WARKENTIN, J., and MALONE, T. P. The Involvement of the Professional Therapist. In *Case Studies in Counseling and Psychotherapy.* A. Burton, Ed., Prentice-Hall, New York, 1959, pp. 218–256.
9. ALEXANDER, F., and FRENCH, T. M. *Psychoanalytic Therapy.* Ronald Press, New York, 1946.
10. KELLY, G. A. *The Psychology of Personal Constructs* (2 vols.). W. W. Norton, New York, 1955.
11. ELLIS, A. *Reason and Emotion in Psychotherapy.* Lyle Stuart, New York, 1962.
12. LEWIS, M. K., ROGERS, C. R. and SHLIEN, J. M. Time-Limited, Client-Centered Psychotherapy: Two Cases. In *Case Studies in Counseling and Psychotherapy.* A. Burton, Ed., Prentice-Hall, New York, 1959, pp. 309–352.
13. FESTINGER, L. *A Theory of Cognitive Dissonance.* Row, Peterson, Evanston, Ill., 1957.
14. SATO, K. Implications of Zen Buddhism for Psychotherapy. *Psychologia, 1:* Dec. 1958.
15. HARPER, R. A. *Psychoanalysis and Psychotherapy: 36 Systems.* Prentice-Hall, New York, 1959.
16. BERGIN, A. Teacher's College, Columbia University, personal communication.

SECTION I Research Design, Strategy, and Philosophy

Like Carl Rogers' article, the following articles are overviews of psychotherapy research, and are also concerned with general but important methodological and theoretical problems.

Research designs and strategies are basically dependent upon the theoretical bias of the researcher, the kinds of questions asked, and the tools available. It had long been the rule rather than the exception that the early psychotherapy writers, when asking such broad questions as Does psychotherapy work? Which is better, psychoanalysis, or client-centered therapy? found themselves stifled and unable to come up with meaningful, reliable answers. Scientific questions must be posed in such a way as to be capable of being answered. And basic to this goal is the necessity for the words and concepts within the question (e.g., psychotherapy) to be operationally definable and manipulable. Unfortunately, for too long, this was not the case. More recent investigators, however, have been more sophisticated with respect to experimental methodology, and they have available to them more advanced equipment such as computers, tape recorders, and physiological apparatus, as well as a wider variety of theoretical approaches. As the following articles demonstrate, the result has been the asking and postulation of more narrowly circumscribed questions and hypotheses, capable of experimental testing and verification.

In a sense, this book deals with, and emphasizes, the multitude of strategies used by the psychotherapy researcher.

Intrapsychic Change:
Methodological Problems in
Psychotherapy Research[†]

HELEN D. SARGENT

Two quotations will provide a context for considering certain methodological problems of psychotherapy research. The first is a remark by Max Planck, founder of quantum physics: "There is scarcely any scientific principle that is not nowadays challenged by somebody."[1] The second is a recent statement by Gustav Bergmann, who writes: "Virtually every American psychologist, whether he knows it or not, is nowadays a methodological behaviorist."[2] Between the freewheeling spirit of the first and the arresting orthodoxy of the second are issues important for any of the disciplines now banded together under the designation "behavioral science," and for research into such frontier areas as psychotherapy.

Philosophically, methodological behaviorism, in Bergmann's sense, rests upon what Bakan has called "the postulate of epistemological loneliness."[3] Direct observation of the inner states of another is impossible, although, as Bergmann puts it, "commonsensically or, for that matter, clinically, we often attribute to a person a certain state of mind . . . nor is there any doubt commonsensically that we know what we mean. . . ."[4] The implied and familiar epistemological model is Behavior→Observation→Inference. Although definitions of behavior have been expanded to include ideas, affects, dreams, and verbal symbols, intrapsychic conditions are conceived of as intervening variables having only explanatory status.[5]

Reprinted from *Psychiatry* 1961, 24, 93–108, with the permission of the William Alanson White Psychiatric Foundation. A brief biography of the author has been omitted from these notes.

†. . . This paper is from the work of the Psychotherapy Research Project of The Menninger Foundation. The generous support of the Foundation's Fund for Research in Psychiatry and the Ford Foundation to this project is gratefully acknowledged.

[1] A. Stern, "Science and the Philosopher," *Amer. Scientist* (1956) 44:281–295; p. 282.

[2] Gustav Bergmann, "The Contribution of John B. Watson," *Psychol. Rev.* (1956) 63:265–276; p. 270.

[3] D. Bakan, "Clinical Psychology and Logic," *Amer. Psychologist* (1956) 11:655–662; p. 656.

[4] See footnote 2; p. 270.

[5] Kenneth MacCorquodale and Paul E. Meehl, "On a Distinction Between Hypothetical Constructs and Intervening Variables," *Psychol. Rev.* (1948) 55:95–107.

Since human beings can apprehend only through their five senses, and since only behavior is observable, the model seems so compelling as to be unalterable—as compelling, in fact, as the concept of three-dimensional space before Einstein. Other postulates and other models are, however, possible, carrying different implications for research, and different emphasis upon perceptual, constructional, experiential, empathic, and integrative aspects of the observational act. It is the purpose of this paper to review some consequences of the current orthodoxy, and to consider possibilities for redefinition, illustrated by reference to one project in which these are being tried out.[6]

METHODS AND DESIGN: TOOLS OR TENETS?

If, within the behavioral context, psychotherapy is regarded as a matter of learning and conditioning, outcome will be measured in terms of learned adaptations. If it is conceived of as a special case of social interaction, or of communication, change in interpersonal variables will be sought. If increased conscious comfort and self-acceptance are seen as the primary therapeutic goals, self-descriptions of feeling states will be prominent in the data. If theory recognizes such constructs as the ego, in which reorganization may come about with or without direct or immediate reflection in verbal report or behavior, dynamic balances and ego functions become the variables of interest, and methods suited to their study are needed. Bergmann concedes that the test of any

methodological position is its fruitfulness.[7] For psychology, the sophisticated modern version of Watson's behaviorist position has been highly productive, but one cannot deny that some problems are more amenable than others to exploration within its framework. In the phrase in the paragraph above, ". . . with or without direct or immediate reflection in verbal report or behavior," is a problem, crucial to evaluation of change in psychotherapy, too often by-passed. Bakan notes the paradox that even certain prominent animal psychologists have discovered that behavior observation is not the most productive source of behavior prediction.[8] A form of identification expressed in a variation of the old question, "If you were a horse (or a rat, or a patient), where would you go?," works better. In other words, to predict behavior, researchers must look at attitudes, intents, and motives, rather than acts. To the practicing therapist, the point is so much a truism as to be hardly worth discussion. Experienced clinicians are accustomed to discounting, for example, the verbalized euphoria of certain patients. Relatives of the man who committed suicide frequently report that he seemed "unusually cheerful" on the day of his death. By adjustment criteria the discharged patient with a job is considered "better" than the one who is only able so far, to return home for a trial visit. Yet the therapist may write confidently on the discharge summary of the first, "prognosis guarded," and on the chart of the second, "markedly improved." Such examples could be multiplied. Clinicians behave, at least, as if they perceive in these instances something which is obviously not behavior as such, regardless of what behavior observation has contributed to judgment. Clinical experience does not, however, make much headway against the prevalent behavioristic

[6] Robert S. Wallerstein, and others, "The Psychotherapy Research Project of The Menninger Foundation," *Bull. Menninger Clinic* (1956) 20:221–276; "The Psychotherapy Research Project of The Menninger Foundation: Second Report," *Bull. Menninger Clinic* (1958) 22:115–166; "The Psychotherapy Research Project of The Menninger Foundation: Third Report," *Bull. Menninger Clinic* (1960) 24:157–216.

[7] G. Bergmann and K. W. Spence, "The Logic of Psychological Measurement," *Psychol. Rev.* (1944) 51:1–24.

[8] See footnote 3.

position typified by the following quotation: "If the ultimate purpose of psychotherapy is to effect behavioral change (and it has to be) then behavior must be the criterion. This proposition not only makes sense, but gets us closer to the science of psychology."[9] Bergmann is right. Science, for most psychologists, is equated to the behaviorist doctrine. Even the psychoanalysts, in spite of primary interest in intrapsychic variables, abide by the B→ O→I schema, by expanding the definition of behavior to include reportable affects, dreams, conflicts, memories, and so forth.[10]

The published literature is crowded, on the one hand, with trivial studies of correlations between isolated variables, operationally redefined beyond recognition, and, on the other, with case studies, theoretical papers, and an occasional exploratory research program, distinguished more by the vitality of the questions asked than by the effectiveness of means suggested for finding definitive answers.[11] Perhaps

the reason is to be found in two different concepts of science itself. Science, for some, is conceived of as a body of knowledge. Freud's contribution needs, therefore, no supplement in the minds of many followers. At least there is little interest in what Kubie called "pallid laboratory demonstrations" of phenomena for which rich evidence is already at hand in the consulting room.[12] For those to whom the answer to a clinical question means more than the method of its derivation, a significant t means as little as the beauty of an apt interpretation does to an experimental psychologist; each views the other's most prized exhibit with indifference.

The majority of psychologists have, by training, incorporated another concept of science: Science is defined not by content but by method—'the' scientific method. Within this tradition, the structuralized—one might even say ossified—dictates of the behavioral premise exercise even more influence. Cattell argues for the method-centered view, citing the futility of inquiry into problems typified by the old scholastic question, "How many angels

---

[9] H. A. Murray, *Exploration in Personality;* New York, Oxford Univ. Press, 1938.

[10] David Rapaport, "The Structure of Psychoanalytic Theory (A Systematizing Attempt)," pp. 58–183; in *Psychology: A Study of a Science,* Vol. 3, *Formulations of the Person and the Social Context,* edited by Sigmund Koch; New York, McGraw-Hill, 1959.

[11] Winder, in a recent annual review of psychotherapy research (C. L. Winder, "Psychotherapy," pp. 309–330; in *Annual Rev. Psychol.,* Vol. 8; Palo Alto, Annual Reviews, 1957), regrets the paucity of systematic investigations of the outcome of psychoanalytic therapy, in which attempts to control relevant patient, treatment, and environmental factors are made. Not available for his survey were a psychoanalytic prediction study by Bellak (Leopold Bellak and M. Brewster Smith, "An Experimental Exploration of the Psychoanalytic Process," *Psychiatric Quart.* [1956] 25:385–414), an ambitious attempt by Gill and Leary to conceptualize the psychotherapeutic process according to the Leary system of level analysis (Timothy Leary, *Interpersonal Diagnosis of Personality;* New York, Ronald Press, 1957; and Merton Gill and Timothy Leary, "The Dimensions and a Measure of the Process of Psychotherapy," pp. 62–95; in *Research in Psychotherapy,* edited by Eli A. Rubinstein and Morris B. Parloff;

Washington, D.C., Amer. Psychological Assn., 1959), other studies in progress but not yet reported, such as Franz Alexander and Hedda Bolgar's investigation at Mt. Sinai Hospital in Los Angeles of the therapist as a factor in therapy, and the Psychotherapy Research Project of The Menninger Foundation (see footnote 6). The most extensive systematic program research in psychotherapy has been produced by Carl Rogers and his students, but its bearing upon the problems considered here is limited for the reason that the theory tested is confined to the levels of adjustive behavior and consciousness (see Carl R. Rogers and Rosalind F. Dymond, editors, *Psychotherapy and Personality Change;* Chicago, Univ. of Chicago Press, 1954; and William U. Snyder, "Psychotherapy," pp. 353–374; in *Annual Rev. Psychol.,* Vol. 9; Palo Alto, Annual Reviews, 1958).

[12] Lawrence S. Kubie, "Problems and Techniques of Psychoanalytic Validation and Progress," pp. 46–124; in *Psychoanalysis as Science;* edited by E. Pumpian-Mindlin; Stanford, Stanford Univ. Press, 1952; p. 64.

can dance on the head of a pin?"[13] Pleas for problem-centered research were sounded in the thirties by clinicians and personality theorists such as Murray and Maslow, later by MacKinnon and Shakow, and recently by that most distinguished of 'rat-men,' Skinner, who does "clinical" research with animals while some psychologists apply rat methods to men.[14] Method-centered research, however, maintains its popularity. A superscience known as *methods and design* began its development in the forties and has been flourishing ever since. The debt of psychological research—clinical research especially—to Fisher, Cronbach, Coombs, Edwards, Zubin, Gulliksen, and others is immense, but unfortunately factorial design and new applications of probability theory, which came on the scene as valuable tools, have become a discipline which intimidates many researchers whose specialties do not include higher mathematics or symbolic logic, and who abrogate, awefully, their methodological responsibilities to the experts. Consequently, much doctoral research today is by Vogue pattern. Even an American Psychological Association committee on research, a few years ago, conceived of its function as the production of a model study on the eye wink, an example for the isolated psychologist to follow, who might otherwise make the mistake of muddling through on his own original ideas. Stevens remarks that there seem to be "more people with a method who are looking for a problem to use it

on than there are searchers with a problem looking for a method."[15]

Confronted by the literature of psychiatry, psychology, and psychoanalysis, which offers convincing and useful, but scientifically unverified personality theory, together with neat proof of insignificant hypotheses, researchers may wonder if part of the trouble is not in a false dichotomy between the content of science and its method, and between problem-centered and method-centered research. If science is defined, instead, by purpose—the purpose of abstracting from the individual instance laws of broader application—then every clinician who seeks to learn and to generalize from single case experience is operating as a scientist, and all experimentalists who, while perfecting a method, envisage useful applications to individual problems, are functioning as clinicians. Problems, theories about them, and methods for their solution ought to be inseparable. Theories live by methods available for their exploration. Freud's theories without the technique of free association, or Pasteur's without Leeuwenhoek's microscope would have ended in speculative oblivion. The good theory implies the methods for its confirmation; the good method, likewise, is not only mothered by invention but sired by theory.

Problem-method-centered research in psychotherapy in the Planckian spirit can be an adventure, in which the search is not merely for applicable techniques but for more enabling principles. As the contributions of Vaihinger and Poincaré have shown, philosophical systems are "as if" positions, "conventions" or "conveniences" necessary to permit investigation. Research in quest of new "as ifs," taking nothing for granted except the problems given and the answers sought, is rather like a Lewis Carroll journey "through the looking glass," but is worth a certain amount of

[13] R. B. Cattell, "The Meaning of Clinical Psychology," pp. 3–16; in *An Introduction to Clinical Psychology* (2nd ed.), edited by D. A. Pennington and Irwin A. Berg; New York, Ronald Press, 1954.

[14] Murray, footnote 9. A. H. Maslow, "Problem-centering vs. Means-centering in Science," *Philosophy of Science* (1946) 13:326–331. Donald W. MacKinnon, "Fact and Fancy in Personality Research," *Amer. Psychologist* (1953) 8:138–146. David Shakow, "Clinical Psychology," pp. 449–482; in *Dynamic Psychiatry*, edited by Franz Alexander and Helen Ross; Chicago, Univ. of Chicago Press, 1952. B. F. Skinner, "A Case History in Scientific Method," *Amer. Psychologist* (1956) 11:221–233.

[15] S. S. Stevens, "On the Psychophysical Law," *Psychol. Rev.* (1957) 64:153–181; p. 178.

disorientation even if the only discovery is that "it can't go straight if you pin it all on one side," as Alice remarked to the Queen.

A PROJECT AND SOME ASSUMPTIONS

In the remainder of this paper, frequent reference will be made to one project which may be described as: (1) an outcome-process study of (2) intrapsychic change and its determinants in psychoanalytic psychotherapy, (3) assessed by impressions registered upon the clinician as an instrument, (4) 'calibrated' by theoretical constructs to which observations are ordered, and (5) subject then to quantitative and qualitative scientific methods for establishing reliability, validity, and predictive accuracy.

The project has been formulated in the above terms to emphasize a group of generic problems for consideration below, rather than to describe fully a particular program in all its aspects.[16] Details appear

elsewhere[17] and will be mentioned in sections to follow only when relevant to the problems of rationale and methodology which are the subject of this paper. Each of the numbered statements above refers to questions ranging from choice of a research model to epistemological issues by no means new, but reaching deep into the history of psychology, and wide into problems shared with other sciences. Outlined in more conventional terms, this illustrative project would probably arouse no more questions than others in the field. Methods-conscious critics will note, however, the absence of certain hallmarks of objective research as currently defined. Some will be disquieted by a relative de-emphasis upon behavioral data as "primary."[18] Disturbing, also, may be the substitution of routine clinical judgments for "standardized" ratings, and the omission of certain variables commonly assessed. For others, such criticisms will be outweighed by the richness of the material utilized, by the systematic effort to understand psychoanalytic psychotherapy naturalistically as practiced in a clinical setting through the interaction of theoretically defined *patient, treatment,* and *situational* variables, by the careful conceptualization of clinical-theoretical assessment categories, the introduction of clinically appropriate methods of quantification, the attempt to convert clinical appraisal and prognostication into testable predictions, and other features distinguishing multilevel exploratory research.

---

[16] In brief summary, this project, the Psychotherapy Research Project of The Menninger Foundation, is a naturalistic study of psychotherapy as undertaken in a hospital and outpatient setting. Clinical data collected at the initiation and termination, and from one to two years following termination of treatment, are studied by research teams of psychiatrists, psychologists, and social workers; and are ordered to psychoanalytic theoretical concepts, analyzed at several levels of qualitative and quantitative description, in terms of the interaction between patient, treatment, and situational variables. The aims of the project are to develop methods for the assessment of intrapsychic change in patients undergoing psychoanalysis and psychoanalytically oriented psychotherapy, as well as to refine and subsequently to test hypotheses regarding the nature of change and its determinants. In addition to the appraisal of patient status and change with respect to the major variables, the study includes an analysis of clinical predictions with reference to confirmation, refutation, and assumptive bases. Major focus is upon the development of methods for transforming clinical judgment into systematic instruments for the measurement of intrapsychic variables.

[17] See footnote 6.

[18] The term "primary data," like other terms to be considered later, has taken on meanings beyond its original use, which defined the basic data elected for study as reducible to sensory observation. In the project cited, the data are clinical observations and clinical inferences. Project researchers do not assume that behavior description can be purged of observer influence. Even the selection of what to observe is a function of observer assumptions. See footnote 6.

(1) Models and Methods:
Problems of Process and Outcome

In psychotherapy research, almost the first conventional question encountered, whether from visiting consultant, grant-dispensing benefactor, or bystanding colleague is apt to be, "Is this a process or an outcome study?" Since "process" is a series of emergent outcomes, and since "outcome" stops process at a point in time, understanding of process without reference to its outcomes is hardly conceivable; likewise, outcome studies which contribute nothing to knowledge of determinants would consist only in statistical summaries of judgments on gross change. The distinction appears, therefore, quite artificial unless certain semantic confusions and over-determining values are considered.

Process, in dictionary terms, has two meanings: First, process is something that continuously changes in time (as in the process of mountain formation). Second, process is the *way* in which something comes about, or is made, implying an *agent,* as in the process of manufacture. In psychotherapy research, process, in the first sense, may refer to intrapsychic processes, adaptive-behavioral processes, pathological processes, and so forth, or in the second sense may mean specifically the presumed agent of change, the psychotherapy itself, or the interaction between patient and therapist. Gill and Leary specifically define it as such.[19] More broadly, process research may be conceived of as concerned with the *how* of change, while outcome research attempts to identify *what* changes.

In addition to the above definitions, process research applied to psychotherapy has taken on other connotations, some derived from values attached to process as contrasted to outcome studies, others from methods which have become identified with each. Among clinicians and person-ality theorists, process research clearly has higher value status, which stems from recognition of the fallacy already noted: the inappropriateness of adjustment criteria as direct indices to intrapsychic change as theoretically conceived. Outcome studies, typically, have been of the kind surveyed by Eysenck and others, resulting in equivocal percentage counts of numbers "improved" or "unimproved" by variable standards,[20] which, as various critics have shown,[21] mask rather than contribute to understanding the *nature* of the change which presumably must take place —whether for better or for worse—as the result of the intensive experience of receiving, or even seeking, therapeutic help.

Agent-centered process research has become associated traditionally with two models. The first may be called the *seining* model, in which the fisherman drags a net to bring in everything from the river (one anecdote recounts that a typewriter was once caught by this method). The rationale for the seining model is that anything in the therapeutic interaction may be important, including an audible sigh or a lifted eyebrow. The best in modern electronics and photography are, therefore, used for collecting the full data of the therapeutic course on film and sound track, for later analysis by as yet indeterminate categories.

In contrast to the seining model, what may be called the *casting* model is also established. This model requires more knowledge of fish, hypotheses about their nature and habitat, construction of delicate lures, and skillful aim—knowledge and skill which those who advocate the seining model regard as not as yet avail-

---

[19] See Gill and Leary, footnote 11.

[20] H. J. Eysenck, "The Effects of Psychotherapy: An Evaluation," *J. Consult. Psychol.* (1950) 6:152–156.

[21] Lester Luborsky, "A Note on Eysenck's Article 'The Effect of Psychotherapy: An Evaluation,'" *Brit. J. Psychol.* (1954) 45:129–131. Saul Rosenzweig, "A Transvaluation of Psychotherapy: A Reply to Hans Eysenck," *J. Abnormal and Social Psychol.* (1954) 49:298–304.

able.[22] Translated back into research rationale, the casting model aims to collect data relevant to a few variables which seem to lend themselves to precise definition. Relevance to psychotherapy or any other problem is via confirmation or refutation of specific hypotheses derived from a theoretical framework. Painstaking research of this kind has been contributed by Rogers and his students.[23] Also in this category are not only experiments in psychotherapy but also research in processes such as perception and perceptual learning, basic to personality theory.[24] The import of all this, however, is still fragmentary and waits for a gigantic synthesizing effort to distinguish the trivial from the important. Its feedback into psychotherapy as practiced is as yet indeterminate.

An alternative model may more aptly be described by a shift in analogy from fishing to photography. This is the *zoom* model being tried out in The Menninger Foundation project. In zoom finding, the entire view is first surveyed—the ordinary data of routine evaluation—but with provision for magnifying and bringing into closer focus any area which, in the first sweep, appears to be of interest. Interchangeable lenses and special filters— by analogy the predefined concepts and theories which determine data selection and evaluation—are used to highlight selectively those areas which are potentially significant. To pursue the metaphor, shots may be taken at different distances, from different angles of view; developed film reveals which picture method is best. The zoom model asumes, in other words, that the choice of vantage point itself must be experimentally determined. To discover most about the construction of a house, is it possible to learn more by a view at the elbow of a carpenter as he drives each nail, or from across the street as the beams go up and the structure takes shape? Research in any process demands techniques to stop action for close inspection, but also preservation of movement as in the rapidly run movie.

Some processes in nature permit no choice of vantage point; the influence of the process of erosion in geological history, for example, must be understood from the position of the scientist's momentary presence on the planet Earth; multiple observations at each stage are ruled out. Other processes, such as the flash of lightning in the sky, are so rapid that only a brilliant hunch, guiding the crucial observation of a Benjamin Franklin, can reveal their nature. The process of psychotherapy is such that a range of perspectives and frequencies of observation is possible. To date, however, less attention has been paid to perspective than to the completeness of data demanded by the seining model, and the preselective aim of casting models.

If the important factors in psychotherapy are regarded as manifested by the frequency of their occurrence in conjunction with other factors in the patient or in the therapeutic interaction, frequent running observations are necessary to permit analysis by probability estimation statistics.[25] Lewin showed, however, in his discussion of Aristotelian versus Galilean modes of thought[26] that theoretically deduced propositions may be verified by single crucial observations rather than by frequency methods. In psychotherapy re-

---

[22] Shakow points out that the behavioral and social sciences have by-passed the long descriptive phase which other natural sciences have gone through. See Shakow, footnote 14.

[23] See Rogers and Dymond, footnote 11.

[24] George S. Klein, "The Menninger Foundation Research on Perception and Personality, 1947–1952: A Review," *Bull. Menninger Clinic* (1953) 17:93–99. Gardner Murphy, "Affect and Perceptual Learning," *Psychol. Rev.* (1956) 63:1–15.

[25] J. B. Chassan, "On the Unreliability of Reliability and Some Other Consequences of the Assumption of Probabilistic Patient-States," PSYCHIATRY (1957) 20:163–171.

[26] K. Lewin, *A Dynamic Theory of Personality*, translated by D. K. Adams and K. E. Zener; New York, McGraw-Hill, 1935.

search, the frequency approach might be illustrated by studies in which symptom reduction would be measured by decreasing occurrence of a symptom, such as hand-washing or overeating, and correlated with certain events in the therapy, such as interpretation of anal or oral material. Fluctuations in the transference, in which a patient alternately sees the therapist as a nurturant parent or as a punitive authority, might conceivably be related to the simultaneous presence in free association of certain memories, or might follow certain recognizable therapeutic maneuvers. To some investigators, however, it is questionable whether the crucial aspects of the psychotherapeutic process can be cast in the form of such correlated frequencies which when counted yield important results. Psychotherapy supervisors are familiar, also, with the fact that verbatim transcripts of therapy hours may mask problems and trends which emerge in spontaneous process notes. Characteristic of clinical experience is the fact that there are identifiable invariants: for example, the rigidity of defenses in a certain patient which appears as the determining factor in every relationship and in every means-end action, or an attitude of the therapist which constitutes the key problem of countertransference. *Pervasiveness, centrality,* and *pivotal significance* of factors affecting therapy can be deduced from a much smaller sample (clinical case conferences and supervisory hours could hardly operate otherwise), and, from the standpoint of design, this fact implies much greater attention to *perspective* than to completeness. Also independent of the frequency criterion are the dramatic turning points of therapy—the sudden insight, the single interpretation, which can markedly affect an entire course and outcome. It may be argued that full hour by hour and moment to moment data are necessary in order not to miss the key factors, and to support inferences drawn with regard to pervasive invariance, but this in itself is an assump-

tion. An equally tenable assumption is that spontaneous salience in material selected for special attention may serve as a criterion of significance. Ideally, full data —to whatever extent equipment and practical exigencies permit—should be available, together with provision for retrospective evaluation from strategic viewpoints.[27]

Problems of design and sampling so far considered refer to process research in the sense of *agent-centered* studies of the psychotherapeutic interaction, whether as reflected in overt behavior, subjective experience, or at the level of unconscious motivation and personality organization. When the term *process research* refers to investigation of postulated covert structures and functions, and to psychotherapeutic outcomes in terms of intrapsychic change, bold new concepts of design are badly needed. So-called mentalistic phenomena, ruled out by the early behaviorists as unsuitable topics for scientific attention, have been reinstated under a flag of truce bearing the inscription "intervening variables." MacCorquodale and Meehl's enlargement upon Tolman's earlier concept, and their definition of intervening variables and hypothetical constructs,[28] together with Cronbach and Meehl's conceptualization of construct validity,[29] have made possible the recognition of intrapsychic processes, but as variables having only explanatory

---

[27] Monthly progress reports are available for all the cases in the project mentioned here, and for about half, hourly notes are available on the process of therapy. In addition, information is gathered from the perspective of therapist, patient, supervisor, and, whenever possible, a relative. Information from these converging and diverging views is the basis for judgments on treatment, patient, and situational variables at the conclusion of psychotherapy.

[28] See footnote 5.

[29] Lee J. Cronbach and Paul E. Meehl, "Construct Validity in Psychological Tests," pp. 174–204; in *Minnesota Studies in the Philosophy of Science,* Vol. 1, edited by H. Feigl and M. Scriven; Minneapolis, Univ. of Minn. Press, 1956.

status[30] For the ultimate testing of psycho-analytic theory, a way must be found to treat its postulated intrapsychic variables as independent and dependent, not merely as intervening. Rapaport cites models in which such variables as structures, motivations, and even reality, as well as behavior, may be alternately cast in the above key roles.[31]

Departure from orthodoxy requires, however, a rationale beyond model building. More than one tenet in the psychologist's research creed requires reconsideration, if not revision. A few which have seemed to signal a dead end in vital aspects of psychotherapy research will be considered below. Hunt, loyal to 'science,' warns against changing ground rules to conform to problems.[32] Rules, however, are contrived operational means to scientific ends, and are not beyond improvement.

(2) Intrapsychic Variables and the Problem of Reality

The following completion test might be included as part of a graduate record examination or of a refresher course for behavioral scientists:

It is an obvious fact that no one has ever seen an (1)————, no one has ever weighed an (2)————, felt an (3)————, or in fact made any observation whatsoever of an (4) ————. What we have seen are (5)————, (6)————, (7)————, (8)————. By themselves they represent just a lot of observations having no particular connection with each other. But when we use the (9)———— equation . . . . we find that it is possible to get agreement between theory and experiment. Strictly speaking, an 10————

is merely that thing, that state of affairs, which is defined by the (11)———— theory.

Any well-trained group of graduate students in psychology would fill in a word such as "ego" in the first four blanks, and in the tenth. In the blanks numbered five to eight, such terms as "symptoms," "attitudes," "character traits," "actions," and so forth, would make sense. In the last blank the tenets of any psychological theory would serve, as, for example, "unconscious motivation," "Freudian," and the like.

The quotation was written, however, by Dancoff, a physicist. The original completions were "electron," "scintillations on a screen," "water droplets in a cloud chamber," "deflections on a dial," "spots on a photographic plate," "Schroedinger wave equation," and "Schroedinger-Dirac theory."[33]

The ego, then, is in powerful company. Its structures and processes are, like the structures and processes of the electron and the atom, constructs. Stern, quoting Dancoff, differs on the question of the 'reality' of constructs. For Dancoff, the question is irrelevant; for Stern it is important to preserve the anchorage of science in perceptual reality.[34] In psychology, there is an even greater compulsion to maintain a firm distinction between the objective and the subjective. An empirical fact has, however, been defined as beginning with an awareness[35] that can be communicated, hence confirmed or disconfirmed independently. Sharability and agreement, thus, become the crucial test of reality, rather than visibility or other sensory base.[36] One can, in other words,

---

[30] The dangers of reification are well known. Its heretical "as if" advantages have not been deliberately exploited, although these may be discerned in the early development of psychoanalytic theory.

[31] See footnote 10.

[32] William A. Hunt, The Clinical Psychologist; Springfield, Ill., Charles C Thomas, 1956.

[33] D. Dancoff, "Does the Neutrino Really Exist?," Bull. Atomic Sci. (1952) 8:139–141.

[34] See footnote 1.

[35] A. C. Benjamin, An Introduction to the Philosophy of Sicence; New York, Macmillan, 1937.

[36] See Bentley's famous commentary on "glorification of the skin," in A. F. Bentley, "The Human Skin: Philosophy's Last Line of Defense," Philosophy of Science (1941) 8:1–19. See also E. Brunswik,

perceive and compare one's own and others' awareness. The essence of objectivity is, in fact, thereby achieved. Of objectivity, philosopher Paul Schmidt writes: "To say that some scientific result is objective is to say that relative to some chosen frame of reference identical empirical descriptions will be given by trained scientists. Nothing more is needed for knowledge or possible. Objectivity does not refer to how nature really is but to how scientists find it in a given context."[37]

Psychology, still rooted in philosophy in spite of its relatively recent admission to the realm of natural science, remains preoccupied with the question, How can we know? This question is however, essentially an epistemological rather than a scientific one, unless formulated in a way to become itself a subject for scientific investigation, as in studies of the inferential process. The question, *What* do we know? (by the criterion of mutuality), and the further question, What are the empirical relationships and implications?, is more amenable, and more likely to result in delineating the boundaries and eventually the measurable dimensions of theoretical constructs. Whether the empirical datum is a shared awareness, such as agreement on the relative "ego strength" of two patients, or the observation that a gauge registers a certain figure, to the extent that either serves as a base for a verifiable prediction, the observation has reality status; the fact that the sensory source of the first is vague and complex and of the second explicit is a separate issue, as discerned below in connection with reliability and validity.

Historically, psychology as a science has advanced whenever new methodological approaches to its own peculiar subject

matter have superseded the epistemological concern with origins, elements, and physiological correlates. William James, to the delight of successive generations of graduate students, called psychophysics "that dreadful literature,"[38] and evaluated Fechner's search for the sensory counterparts of physical stimuli as coming to nothing. The dreadful literature has, however, become a fertile source for the development of methods of scaling applied to such subjective phenomena as attitudes and traits, for which no physical counterparts exist. Perception research took a new direction when the quest for sensory elements was abandoned. Gestalt theory took psychology away from myopic attention to lines, angles, and notes, shifting attention to the primary quality of squares and melodies. Little of clinical import was discovered about thinking and emotion while linkage to physiological processes was viewed as the basic problem. Freud's original attempt at a neurophysiological model[39] was set aside to make way for his theories of psychic functioning, which have had impact in almost every field of psychology.[40]

Separating problems of sensory origin and empirical base from problems of meaning and function involves no denial of the importance of the former. Perception depends upon sensation; thought without a nervous system is inconceivable; to think of apprehending psychological states of others without behavioral cues to judgment partakes of mysticism. Tolerance for doubt and ignorance of some unknown, together with willingness to start at the level of any empirical 'given' is, however, not only the essence of scientific advance,

"The Conceptual Framework of Psychology," pp. 655–760; in *International Encyclopedia of Unified Science*, Vol. 1; Chicago, Univ. of Chicago Press, 1955.

[37] P. S. Schmidt, "Models of Scientific Thought," *Amer. Scientist* (1957) 45:137–149; p. 148.

[38] Gardner Murphy, *Historical Introduction to Modern Psychology* (rev. ed.); New York, Harcourt, Brace, 1949; p. 90n.

[39] Sigmund Freud, *The Origins of Psychoanalysis; Letters to Wilhelm Fliess, Drafts and Notes: 1887–1902;* New York, Basic Books, 1954.

[40] Gardner Murphy, "The Current Impact of Freud upon Psychology," *Amer. Psychologist* (1956) 11:663–672.

but also the source of a new view of old problems.[41]

Reality-wise, researchers need only to contrast Mach's hope that the 'concept' *atom* might eventually disappear from the theory of heat,[42] with the threatening emergence of this 'concept' into present-day perceptual reality, to recognize that the constructs of today may become the percepts of tomorow. The task of science is not only to apply 'knowing operations' to 'sense' data, but also by instrumentation and construction to extend the range of empirical awareness. From the standpoint of systematic philosophy, the position taken in this paper finds a rationale in Bavink's realism[43] and in Whitehead's conception of the empirically given.[44] There are, of course, philosophical supports for almost any set of working premises, from which the scientist may choose without overconcern for strict adherence to a 'school.' Modern philosophy of science, under the leadership of logical positivism, has overridden the antithesis between science and philosophy by defining its own sphere of inquiry (as Robert Frost wrote, "good fences make good neigh-

bors"[45]), offering its services on a consultantship basis. The scientist, however, cannot quite afford to rely upon Schlick's concept of philosophy as the formulator of "meaningful questions" to be answered by science,[46] nor does the cogency of empirical statements and propositions rest upon formal characteristics alone. Bad questions die unanswered; good ones bear fruit; the philosophers may be able to say why.

The hypothetical construct *ego*, like the construct *atom*, must be measured not directly, but by its effect upon something else. At the point of measurement and demonstration, however, the reassuring companionship with physical science, so dependently sought by psychology since its late nineteenth-century break with philosophy, becomes less close. The "something else" for the physicist is eventually a dial-reading or an event. No matter how unnerving to the general population, the explosion of an atomic bomb must give to the nuclear scientist a consoling sense of reality. The unconscious, too, has its impressive demonstrations, sometimes also destructive and, if the new findings of subliminal perception research are verified, potentially no less controllable for benefit or exploitation.

(3) The Clinician as Recorder: The Epistemological Problem

What, in the study of postulated intrapsychic organization and structure, is the something else upon which ego conditions and functions are registered in a way

---

[41] Stevens, for example, re-examining psychophysics, advances a new "psychophysical law" which differs from Fechner's, but supports the original hope that a constant relationship between stimulus and sensation could be found (see footnote 15). Hebb's use of neurological models (D. O. Hebb, *The Organization of Behavior: A Neuropsychological Theory;* New York, Wiley, 1949), Bertalanffy's search for general system theory (L. von Bertalanffy, "The Theory of Open Systems in Physics and Biology," *Science* [1950] 3:23–29), and the work of Tinbergen and Lorenz on ethology (cited in Bertram Schaffner, editor, *Group Processes;* New York, Josiah Macy, Jr., Foundation, 1955; p. 9) keep hope alive for understanding the place of psychological phenomena within a comprehensive biological context.

[42] Ernst Mach, *Analysis of Sensations,* translated by C. M. Williams; Chicago, Open Court, 1914.

[43] B. Bavink, *The Natural Sciences;* New York, Century, 1932.

[44] A. N. Whitehead, *The Concept of Nature;* Cambridge, Cambridge Univ. Press, 1920. For an excellent brief summary of these and other viewpoints, see also Benjamin, footnote 35.

[45] Robert Frost, "Mending Wall," p. 548; in *The Oxford Book of American Verse;* New York, Oxford Univ. Press, 1950.

[46] Although Ekstein (R. Ekstein, "Concerning the Nature of Psychoanalytic Propositions," in Symposium on Philosophy of Science in Psychoanalysis; Beverly Hills, Calif., January, 1958; unpublished) advocates this division of labor, his own significant contributions to psychoanalysis show little dependence upon sources of questions beyond clinical data and hypotheses generated thereby.

which is observable, operationally definable, and subject to measurement? Behavior theory, by definition, assumes that this something else is the behavior of the individual in whom the ego is supposed to reside. According to the B→O→I schema, the ego is a set of inferences drawn from observations of behavior, which may be spontaneous or elicited clinically by tests and interviews, or by controlled experimental situations.

It may be enabling, however, to recognize that there is another something else upon which psychological states are registered—namely, another person, whether a peer in ordinary social intercourse, a rater who enters a check on a scale, a clinician who makes a diagnosis and treatment recommendation, or a psychoanalyst who offers an interpretation. The response of this other, without reference to its derivation, and regardless of the behavioral cues, the mediating operations, or the ideational transformations involved, then becomes a datum potentially measurable.

The use of the clinician as an 'instrument' is by no means new. Problems involved have not only been recognized, but have themselves been the subject of research. The crucial issues, however, lead back again into questions of epistemology and methodology: What faith can be placed in the data of subjective experience as describing others as objects; what corrections need be applied to insure accuracy? Acceptance of the clinical judgment as a primary datum brings from the logical positivist a reminder that, in such acceptance, the "object language" of judges rather than the "metalanguage" of science is in use.[47] The judge, not the subject, remains the object of study. Intrapsychic states and processes, like all experiences of others, by the "postulate of epistemological loneliness,"[48] are unknowable directly, hence not subject to measurement.

The magnitude of this problem is the incentive behind the whole brave effort of psychometrics to solve it. What psychological science has needed is not the telescope to bring far objects near, nor the microscope to make little things big, but the wrong end of an opera glass to render the near and the large remote enough for examination. Accordingly, by adoption of the B→O→I model, attention has been directed toward increasing the precision of the O factor by placing at the disposal of the observer tests and rating scales intended to serve as substitutes for the mediating instruments of the physical scientist, sharpening the boundary between O and I (observation and inference). Peak, for example, lists as the first canon of "objective" data collection the identification of the *behavior* (her italics) to be observed.[49] Next, the judge is given a list of criteria which define and limit what he is to make of his observation. Finally, an average of as many judges as possible is taken. By these operations, objectivity, at an uncomputed cost in discarding the full capacity of the observer-interpreter, is supposedly achieved.

Researchers might compare these careful instructions with Freud's adjuration to the analyst to pay "free floating" or "evenly suspended" attention,[50] and with instances of startlingly accurate prediction and postdiction reported by Reik,[51] and regularly duplicated in the experience of skilled therapists who "listen with the third ear," "see with the mind's eye," or make use of other little understood supplements to unaided sense. In spite of the flagrant errors of free observation and intuitive inference, these brilliant successes suggest that the effort to control

---

[47] See footnote 7.
[48] See footnote 3.

[49] Helen Peak, "Problems of Objective Observation," pp. 243–299; in *Research Methods in the Behavioral Sciences,* edited by Leon Festinger and Daniel Katz; New York, Dryden Press, 1953.
[50] Sigmund Freud, "Psycho-analysis," in *The Complete Psychological Works of Sigmund Freud* 18: 235–254; London, Hogarth, 1955.
[51] Theodor Reik, *Listening with the Third Ear;* New York, Farrar, Straus, 1948.

at the levels of perception and interpretation may be like placing a weight on the leg of a runner, or a governor on the balance wheel of a clock.[52]

Less dependent upon operational rules to transform research phenomena into data more easily managed by customary methods, and less anchored to what Bergmann has called the compelling common sense of methodological behaviorism,[53] psychological researchers might point out to the physicalistic philosopher that differences in the accuracy of pointer-readings and clinical judgments depend upon the purpose of measurement. The steps by which man constructs and reads rulers are reportable, but the end results are no more 'public' than empathic inferential response. The validity of measures rests not upon the process (which in the case of the pointer-reading deceptively appears to be a simple sensory matter) but upon implications and use of the results, and their demonstrable independence, comparability, repeatability, and potential for prediction, based on observed lawful relationships. What Bergmann extols as the "excellence of physical measurement"[54] is a questionable dictum when applied to human events, and depends upon what is measured. The waiting wife may misread

the clock by an hour, but may predict verbatim what her husband will say when he eases himself through the door. The B→O→I model suggests little 'scientific' use for such a successful prediction, unless the wife can point to the behavior on which her anticipation of subsequent behavior was based. If she cannot, the methodological behaviorist will designate the inference as intuition and press a rating scale into her hand to help her to become more 'objective.' Psychoanalysis, at least, has a theory of intuition referring to preconscious perception and association. Within behavior theory, in the narrow sense, intuition is simply a term for apprehension of the unknown and unknowable, hence scientifically negligible.

Signs of protest and returns to previously abandoned models now revamped are, as in the history of all thought, beginning to appear.[55] Bakan, after a telling critique of the postulate of epistemological loneliness, substitutes an alternate postulate which suggests that there may be little resemblance between the philosopher's model of "knowing operations" and the actual psychological processes of problem-solving. Bakan's postulate, "After all, we are all pretty much alike,"[56] has much to recommend it as a starting point for research which, if it is to be concerned with the data of clinical experience and the operations of clinical analysis, must begin with the clinical judgment as a point of departure. The *as if* advantages of the Bakan postulate are as follows: It avoids the defeatist emphasis on what is and is not 'knowable,' by which most ordinarily used clinical concepts and their implications are relegated to bias or error, or at best to unexplicated intuition. Somewhat paradoxically it avoids, simultaneously, the

---

[52] Even in studies limited in aim to selection or behavior prediction (rather than evaluation of intrapsychic change) inferential judgments based on complex and not easily identifiable cues have a way of coming out ahead. For example, in the Holt-Luborsky project (Robert R. Holt and Lester Luborsky, *Personality Patterns of Psychiatrists;* New York, Basic Books, 1958), among judgments, "liking" turned out to be one of the best predictors of success in psychiatry.

[53] See footnote 2. Alexander emphasizes the point that the great advances in modern physics have only become possible by the transcending of common sense (F. Alexander, "The Nature of Psychological Understanding," in Symposium on Philosophy of Science in Psychoanalysis; Beverly Hills, Calif., January, 1958; unpublished). Three dimensions make sense. Four are difficult to conceive. But the addition of the inconceivable dimension has led to the discoveries of the space age.

[54] See footnote 7; p. 23.

[55] David C. McClelland, "The Psychology of Mental Content Reconsidered," *Psychol. Rev.* (1955) 62:297–302.

[56] See footnote 3; p. 659. Alexander takes a similar position referring to the mechanisms of identification in interpretive observation (see footnote 53).

positive as well as the negative error. It does away with the scientifically naïve faith that the subjective factor, the participation of the observer in the observed, can be denied. When the last sigma is computed, and the most powerful statistic applied, it is the judge who decides where the rating should be entered. Rulers allow no such choice and demand no such decision.[57] The Bakan postulate offers a basis for accepting observer participation as a reality to be utilized and studied, rather than denied or 'corrected.' For clinical research, this shift is of stupendous importance, yet, as so often happens in the evolution of ideas, it may be less new than it seems; it may instead, represent a cycling back to earlier concepts and methods that had been consigned to disrepute but are being revived in a new context. Although Titchener would be shocked by the scientific 'impurity' and pragmatism of psychotherapy research, he would view as stimulus error (attention to the stimulus instead of to the sensory experience) the highly valued concentration upon 'objective' stimulus-defined data, and would advocate return to what he called "the psychological point of view." It is of considerable interest that his discarded method of introspection shows signs of revival, not for the purpose of analyzing the elements of sensory experience, but as an approach to the individual dynamics of concepts.[58]

(4) Calibration of the Judge: The Problem of Quantification

Since clocks tell only time, and rulers measure only inches, and since neither describes dimensions of people, with which psychotherapy is concerned, use of that most erratic and sensitive of instruments, the human observer, with or without supplementary devices, is forced upon the psychological scientist, whether or not he would prefer one more accurate. By what units, then, can this instrument be read in order to yield repeatable, independent, comparable measures by which to arrive at objective, identical empirical descriptions?

There are quantitative concepts in psychoanalysis as Rapaport notes,[59] as there are also in the derived assumptions and constructs of everyday clinical thinking, which abounds in comparisons of the more-or-less variety.[60] Even the language of the case history contains many references to magnitude, directional tendencies, relative weight, strain, and other mathematical concepts. Quantification itself is not a problem. Statistical techniques are available to correlate and test the significance of differences in anything which can be classified, counted, or numbered. The question is, rather, what to quantify and, to a greater degree than in any other science, whether to quantify at all. Since the purpose of science is to arrive at abstract laws of general application, progressing from full descriptive representation to abstractions which permit the formulation of laws from which predictions can be made with assurance, and since the more abstract the relationships the more they lend themselves to mathematical statement, to question the aim of quantification would be almost incomprehensible except for the paradox of clinical research. Here it must be recognized that the more general a scientific law becomes, applying to all instances, the less fully it describes the individual case; and, conversely, the more aptly an individual configuration is described, the less useful is its application to other simi-

[57] D'Arcy Wentworth Thompson, "On Magnitude," pp. 1001–1046; in *The World of Mathematics*, Vol. 2, edited by J. R. Newman; New York, Simon and Schuster, 1956.

[58] David Bakan, "A Reconsideration of the Problem of Introspection," *Psychol. Bull.* (1954) 51: 105–118.

[59] See footnote 10.

[60] A method for exploiting this fact is being tried in The Menninger Foundation project and will be reported in a paper in preparation.

lar, but never quite the same, instances. The clinician is primarily interested in the individual.

From the extreme clinical view, that which can be expressed quantitatively is of least importance. It may be easy to compare two patients as to 'amount' of anxiety, but what is more vital to the clinician is the tracking down of its source, its meaning, its management, and the defense against it, and these, of course, may be so different in two patients judged to have the same amount of anxiety, that a figure representing such an equivalent seems meaningless.

From the scientific standpoint, however, that which can be abstracted and counted is sought as the one little end in a tangled skein of yarn. If all else can be disregarded and a single thread followed, the snarl may be unwound. One fact which is often overlooked is that mathematics is capable of handling qualitative as well as quantitative relationships.[61] It is a long way from simple counting, and from the statistics of probability, to the mathematical expression of relationships, as in a logical system such as geometry.

In The Menninger Foundation project, the problem has been met by a design which aims to preserve full qualitative data for analysis at various levels of abstraction, and to select for quantification, however, crudely, those theoretically derived constructs in daily clinical use which lend themselves to quantitative comparisons. Among these, project members expect to encounter some basic constructs and many derivatives which, if systematically measured, might begin to describe in dimensional terms some of the postulates of basic psychoanalytic theory. A first step has been the definition of variables in use—in other words, the development of a nominal scale. Many of these variables remain at the categorical level and lend themselves only to simple counting, so far as inter-patient comparisons are concerned. Others

have clearly ordinal properties in that subjects can be ranked by a modification of the method of paired comparisons,[62] in terms of the degree to which a given characteristic in a given patient exceeds its judged presence in others. Finally, the resulting patient profiles may be examined for cardinal scalar properties of theoretical distributions implied by obtained distributions of choice scores.

Basic to the scaling of any phenomenon is the selection of appropriate units. The scalar units which apply to molecules are different from the light-years of astronomical space. Even within the measurement of three-dimensional space, the unit of surface measurement differs from that for volume. Basic to the theory of measurement are the concepts of magnitude and direction which, together, make up the concept of dimension. Rapaport points to the need for establishing the dimensions of psychoanalytic constructs, an achievement made particularly difficult by what he describes as the distance of constructs from observables.[63] It is, perhaps, exactly here that a break through the impasse is needed. It could be that this may require nothing more than a reconsideration of the behavioristic definition of what is observable. Measurement of constructs at the point of registration upon and organization by observers, instead of counting more exactly measurable but more remote and peripheral manifestations, is beset by well-known objections. But a fascinating set of equally formidable impossibles and unknowables has disturbed scientific progress very little, as Thompson has pointed out.[64]

(5) Reliability and Validity: Problems of Confirmation

Like the word *objectivity,* the terms *reliability* and *validity* connote, in psy-

---

[61] See footnote 57.

[62] See footnote 6.
[63] See footnote 10.
[64] See footnote 57.

chology, not only their basic meanings (consistency and soundness, respectively) but also definitions which embody customary rituals for establishing their application. Both terms were introduced to technical vocabulary via psychometrics. The consistency, or reliability, of a test measurement is represented by its self-agreement, demonstrated by congruent results from repeated administration of the same test in alternate forms, or by split halves of the same test. Carried over into rating techniques, in which judges become test surrogates, reliability came to be equated with agreement between judges using the same scale. An alogical reversal takes place here, however. Erroneously it is assumed that because reliability is measured by judge agreement, all judge agreement refers only to reliability, with no bearing on validity. The fact is sometimes overlooked that if judgments are separated in time, if one judgment is predicted from another, or if the conditions of judgment are systematically varied, judge agreement may signify independent confirmation, hence validity. For example, the research team undertaking the initial studies of The Menninger Foundation project has attempted to predict the judgments which will be made by clinicians who analyze the posttreatment data.

Validity, likewise, has undergone transition. In psychometrics it stands for the agreement of a test score with an independent measure of the same thing—another test, a rating, or other criterion. It represents, therefore, commitment to the basic rule of empirical science: independent confirmation. In usage, interchangeable with the term "independent criterion" is the concept "outside criterion." Too often, however, researchers forget to ask the question, Outside what? Ordinarily the implication is "outside the system," whatever the system may be, especially if it is a theoretical scheme in which constructs have only explanatory status until verified "outside." For physicalistic be-

haviorism, "outside" has come to mean, also, anchorage in operationally describable percepts—that is, in behavioral data as the only observables. Tolman, however, quoting an unnamed physicist, raises a pertinent question:

The fundamental concepts of psychoanalysis derive from scientific observations in exactly the same sense that concepts in any science are derived. The method of psychoanalysis, free association, is a definite, prescribed method which can be used by any qualified (analytically trained) experimenter and will, when used, yield consistent results. The experiment is repeatable by different experimenters (analysts) using precisely the same method. . . . It is folly to expect either to discover or to check psychoanalytic concepts by any other method. Why, he asks, is there such pressure to independently confirm (or rather to refute) psychoanalytic findings? Does anyone not trained in experimental physics ever say to Carl Anderson: "Look, I will not believe there is such a thing as a positron unless I can discover it for myself by some other independent method?" . . . In any other science, no one expects to step in without training in the specific method and verify or refute a finding.[65]

If researchers make the assumption that changes in psychotherapy may be manifest on different levels (behavioral as observed, subjective as experienced and reported, or intrapsychic as constructed), it becomes clear that intralevel validation must rest, first, upon measures appropriate to the levels studied. Bacteria, for example, can be seen only through a microscope. Intrapsychic phenomena, likewise, can be 'seen' only by application of the concepts and observations which gave rise to their discovery or formulation. If a bacteriologist wishes to observe increase or decrease in the number of organisms in a culture, microscopic examination must be repeated in spite of the fact that valua-

---

[65] Ruth S. Tolman, "Virtue Rewarded and Vice Punished," *Amer. Psychologist* (1953) 8:721–733; p. 726.

ble outside-the-system 'validation' may be obtained by taking note of the clinical effects of microorganisms in the course of disease in patients. Analogously, intrapsychic status following psychotherapy requires assessment by clinical judgments of the same nature as those used in the original assessment, whether based on test or clinical data. Interaction of intrapsychic change with behavioral change, and with defined treatment factors, is then possible to investigate.

An illustration of alternative approaches to the problem of validity and reliability may be found in the familiar Müller-Lyer illusion.[66] Physical, objective measurement by means of the inch ruler yields a one hundred percent reliable result, that the lines are equal. The human eye, with equally perfect reliability, reports that one line is longer than the other. In considering the source of disagreement, one can assume that the ruler is right and the eye wrong, in terms of reality, and proceed to test out various theories (eye movements, and so forth) to account for the error. Or, one may accept the verdict of the eye as confirmed within its own frame of reference or context[67] by agreement between independent observers, and test the implications in such significant areas as esthetics, advertising, learning, abnormal states, and so forth. This example is closely related to the role of the observer in psychological research and to the problem of objectivity discussed above. The point is that a subjective observation may be tested for reliability and validity within its own appropriate context.

Heretical as the proposal may seem, research in psychodynamics and psychotherapy might do well to return the terms *reliability* and *validity* to their original contexts, and to set up some other criteria by which to evaluate the empirical status of clinical observation. These might be *reality,* tested by agreement between observers; *relevance,* established by relationship of observations to other known facts; *import,* in terms of the hypotheses suggested by a given observation; and *utility,* gauged by hypotheses supported or confirmed. In The Menninger Foundation project, after preliminary definition of such variables as ego strength, anxiety tolerance, insight, and others admittedly vague and global, the first test applied has been that of agreement between clinical judgments on each variable. Correlations obtained so far have been almost startlingly high.[68] The question of relevance is being explored by a correlation study of the interrelationship of variables. The questions of import and utility await analysis of findings from the prediction study, and the final analysis of data.

THROUGH THE LOOKING GLASS

If a note of protest has been sounded here, this protest is not against methodological behaviorism, or behavioristic methodology as such, applied where its yield is good, but against equating this or *any* philosophy with empirical science itself. Empirical science rests upon independent observation (reportable, communicable, and sharable awareness), and upon confirmable predictions from demonstrated lawful relationships—this and nothing more. Theories, whether behavior, quantum, psychoanalytic, or evolutionary, live only by methods for their empirical confirmation. Methods, however, must be implied by and appropriate to the theories and the data which they are formulated to explain, before relationships to other theoretical systems can be established. Fortunately there are many angles from which to view precepts and problems, without

---

[66] The phenomenon in which the ends of two *equal* lines have arrows that point in opposite directions, so that one line invariably *appears* longer than the other.

[67] See footnote 37.

[68] Interjudge and test-retest results obtained in preliminary studies (see footnote 6) have been confirmed and will be described in later publications.

violating the basic tenets of empirical science; science offers more leeway than graduate students are permitted to realize, as also does philosophy. Even the most casual excursion into other fields shows that researchers in psychology are not as alone as they might think in their special problems, and that any position is at least debatable. Physicists, as I noted, are engaged in arguing the familiar question of the reality of constructs. In biology, the ideological morphologists have been on the defensive.[69] Quantum theory has faced the problem of accurate prediction for the individual instance.[70] Microphysics has had to recognize, as a limiting condition, breakdowns in the familiar partition between the observer and the observed,[71] the effect of measurement upon the measured. A century ago, astronomers survived the problem of the personal equation, by writing it into their formulae.

For psychology, the issue is no longer observation versus intuition, mediate versus immediate, objective versus subjective, science versus art, or even statistical versus clinical, the latest dichotomy.[72] As empirical scientists, psychologists are identified with the first in each pair, regardless of what use they may find for the second. The research problem lies in developing more psychologically sophisticated concepts of objectivity and of the levels at which controls should be applied in relation to different problems. Thurstone was

the first to discover the fallacy of stimulus standardization.[73] The projective methods next demonstrated the value, for certain purposes, of permitting unstructured response, reserving controls for the level of data analysis.[74] In psychotherapy research, judgments may be discovered to have increased predictive utility when released from strictures imposed by arbitrary unitization, the quest for unidimensionality, and control at the level of observation.

The position of methodological behaviorism may be analogous to the unquestioned status of Euclid's geometry until relativity theory demanded a different conception of space. Perhaps when a psychological Einstein comes along, he will need to turn from sensible Euclids to a Reimann—or to Freud. If such a revolution comes about, it need not be cataclysmic. Newton's laws, although they never taught man how to build an atom bomb, are as useful as ever in the realm of reality to which they apply. In fact, even the ancient Ptolemaic theory that the sun rises enables the fully accurate prediction of a daily experience, although the explanation is false. Behavior theory, likewise, is not likely to be replaced, but its sights need to be constantly reset. Its facts may turn out to be as confined to a limited vantage point as the law of gravity.

A nineteenth-century essayist, Thomas Huxley, wrote: "It is the customary fate of new truths to begin as heresies and to end as superstitions."[75] It is important to ask, occasionally, where psychology's truths are located on such a life continuum.

[69] F. Mainx, "Foundations of Biology," pp. 567–654; in *International Encyclopedia of Unified Science,* Vol. 1; Chicago, Univ. of Chicago Press, 1955.

[70] A. d'Abro, *The Evolution of Scientific Thought from Newton to Einstein* (2nd ed.); New York, Dover Publications, 1950.

[71] V. Lenzen, "Procedures of Empirical Science," pp. 281–339; in *International Encyclopedia of Unified Science,* Vol. 1; Chicago, Univ. of Chicago Press, 1955.

[72] Paul E. Meehl, *Clinical vs. Statistical Prediction;* Minneapolis, Univ. of Minn. Press, 1954.

[73] L. L. Thurstone, "The Stimulus Response Fallacy," *Psychol. Rev.* (1923) 30: 354–369.

[74] Helen Sargent, "Projective Methods: Their Origins, Theory, and Application in Personality Research," *Psychol. Bull.* (1945) 42:257–293.

[75] Thomas Henry Huxley, "Collected Essays, XII. The Coming of Age of 'The Origin of the Species' (1880)" in *Darwiniana Essays;* New York, Appleton, 1896, p. 229.

Critique and Reformulation of "Learning-Theory" Approaches to Psychotherapy and Neurosis

LOUIS BREGER
JAMES L. McGAUGH

A careful look at the heterogeneous problems that are brought to psychotherapy points up the urgent need for new and varied theories and techniques. While some new methods have been developed in recent years, the field is still characterized by "schools"—groups who adhere to a particular set of ideas and techniques to the exclusion of others. Thus, there are dogmatic psychoanalysts, Adlerians, Rogerians, and, most recently, dogmatic behaviorists.

It is unfortunate that the techniques used by the behavior-therapy group (Bandura, 1961; Eysenck, 1960; Grossberg, 1964; Wolpe, 1958) have so quickly become encapsulated in a dogmatic "school," but this seems to be the case. Before examining the theory and practice of behavior therapy, let us first distinguish three different positions, all of which are associated with the behaviorism or "learning-theory" label. These are: (a) Dollard and Miller (1950) as represented in their book, (b) the Wolpe-Eysenck position as represented

Reprinted from *Psychological Bulletin*, 1965, 63, (5), 338–358, with the permission of the American Psychological Association and the authors.

in Wolpe's work (1958; Wolpe, Salter, & Reyna, 1964) and in the volume edited by Eysenck (1960), and (c) the Skinnerian position as seen in Krasner (1961) and the work that appears in the *Journal of the Experimental Analysis of Behavior*.

Dollard and Miller present an attempt to translate psychoanalytic concepts into the terminology of Hullian learning theory. While many recent behavior therapists reject Dollard and Miller because of their identification with psychoanalysis and their failure to provide techniques distinct from psychoanalytic therapy, the Dollard-Miller explanation of neurotic symptoms in terms of conditioning and secondary anxiety drive is utilized extensively by Wolpe and his followers. Wolpe's position seems to be a combination of early Hullian learning theory and various active therapy techniques. He relies heavily on the idea of reciprocal inhibition, which is best exemplified by the technique of counterconditioning. In line with this Hullian background, Wolpe, Eysenck, and others in this group use explanations based on Pavlovian conditioning. They define neurosis as "persistent unadaptive habits that have been conditioned (that is, learned) [Wolpe et al., 1964, p. 9]," and their explanation of neurosis stresses the persistence of "maladaptive habits" which are anxiety reducing.

The Skinnerian group (see Bachrach in Wolpe et al., 1964) have no special theory of neurosis; in fact, following Skinner, they tend to disavow the necessity of theory. Their approach rests heavily on *techniques* of operant conditioning, on the use of "reinforcement" to control and shape behavior, and on the related notion that "symptoms," like all other "behaviors," are maintained by their effects.

Our discussion will be directed to the Wolpe-Eysenck group and the Skinnerians, keeping in mind that some of the points we will raise are not equally applicable to both. Insofar as the Skinnerians disavow a theory of neurosis, for example, they are not open to criticism in this area.

It is our opinion that the current arguments supporting a learning-theory approach to psychotherapy and neurosis are deficient on a number of grounds. First, we question whether the broad claims they make rest on a foundation of accurate and complete description of the basic data of neurosis and psychotherapy. The process of selecting among the data for those examples fitting the theory and techniques while ignoring a large amount of relevant data seriously undermines the strength and generality of the position. Second, claims for the efficacy of methods should be based on adequately controlled and accurately described evidence. And, finally, when overall claims for the superiority of behavioral therapies are based on alleged similarity to laboratory experiments and alleged derivation from "well-established laws of learning," the relevance of the laboratory experimental findings for psychotherapy data should be justified and the laws of learning should be shown to be both relevant and valid.

In what follows we will consider these issues in detail, beginning with the frequently voiced claim that behavior therapy rests on a solid "scientific" base. Next, we will examine the nature and adequacy of the learning-theory principles which they advocate. We will point out how their learning theory is unable to account for the evidence from laboratory studies of learning. That is to say, the laws or principles of conditioning and reinforcement which form the basis of their learning theory are insufficient explanations for the findings from laboratory experiments, let alone the complex learning phenomena that are encountered in psychotherapy. Then we will discuss how the inadequate conception of learning phenomena in terms of conditioned responses is paralleled by an equally inadequate conception of neurosis in terms of discrete symptoms. Within learning theory, conceptions of habit and response have been shown to be inadequate and are giving way to conceptions emphasizing "strategies," "plans," "programs," "schemata," or other complex central mediators. A central point of this paper is that conceptions of habit and response are also inadequate to account for neuroses and the learning that goes on in psychotherapy and must here too be replaced with conceptions analogous to strategies. Next we will turn our attention to an evaluation of the claims of success put forth by the proponents of behavior therapy. Regardless of the adequacy of their theory, the claims that the methods work are deserving of careful scrutiny. Here we shall raise a number of questions centering around the issue of adequate controls. Finally, we shall attempt a reformulation in terms of more recent developments within learning, emphasizing the role of central processes.

Science Issue

Claims of scientific respectability are made with great frequency by the behavior therapists. Terms such as laboratory based, experimental, behavioral, systematic, and control are continually used to support their position. The validity of a theory or method must rest on empirical evidence, however. Thus, their use of scientific sounding terminology does not make their approach scientific, but rather seems to obscure an examination of the evidence on which their claims are based.

Let us examine some of this evidence. Bandura (1961) provides the following account of a typical behavior-therapy method (Wolpe's counterconditioning):

On the basis of historical information, interview data, and psychological test responses, the therapist constructs an anxiety hierarchy, a ranked list of stimuli to which the patient reacts with anxiety. In the case of desensitization based on relaxation, the patient is hypnotized, and is given relaxation suggestions. He is then asked to imagine a scene representing the weakest item on the anxiety hierarchy and, if the relaxation is unimpaired, this is followed by having the patient imagine the next item on the list, and so on. Thus, the anxiety cues are gradually increased from session to session until the last phobic stimulus can be presented without impairing the relaxed state. Through this procedure, relaxation responses eventually come to be attached to the anxiety evoking stimuli [p. 144].

Without going into great detail, it should be clear from this example that the use of the terms stimulus and response are only remotely allegorical to the traditional use of these terms in psychology. The "imagination of a scene" is hardly an objectively defined stimulus, nor is something as general as "relaxation" a specifiable or clearly observable response. What the example shows is that counterconditioning is no more objective, no more controlled, and no more scientific than classical psychoanalysis, hypnotherapy, or treatment with tranquilizers. The claim to scientific respectability rests on the misleading use of terms such as stimulus, response, and conditioning, which have become associated with some of the methods of science because of their place in experimental psy-

chology. But this implied association rests on the use of the same *words* and not on the use of the same *methods*.

We should stress that our quarrel is not with the techniques themselves but with the attempt to tie these techniques to principles and concepts from the field of learning. The techniques go back at least as far as Bagby (1928), indicating their independence from "modern learning theory." Although techniques such as these have received little attention in recent years (except from the behavior therapists) they are certainly worth further consideration as potentially useful techniques.[1]

The use of the term conditioning brings us to a second point, that the claims to scientific respectability rest heavily on the attempts of these writers to associate their work with the prestigious field of learning. They speak of something called modern learning theory, implying that psychologists in the area of learning have generally agreed upon a large number of basic principles and laws which can be taken as the foundation for a "scientific" approach to psychotherapy. For example, Eysenck (1960) states:

Behavior therapy . . . began with the thorough experimental study of the laws of learning and conditioning in normal people and in animals; these well-established principles were then applied to neurotic disorders. . . . It may be objected that learning theorists are not always in agreement with each other and that it is difficult to apply principles about which there is still so much argument. This is only very partially true; those points about which argument rages are usually of academic interest rather than of practical importance. . . . The 10% which is in dispute should not blind us to the 90% which is not—disagreements and disputes

---

[1] Another early application of behavioral techniques has recently been brought to our attention: Stevenson Smith's use of the Guthrie approach to learning in his work at the children's clinic at the University of Washington. Guthrie's interpretation of reinforcement avoids the pitfalls we discuss shortly, and contemporary behaviorists might learn something from a review of his work (see Guthrie, 1935).

naturally attract more attention, but agreements on facts and principles are actually much more common. Greater familiarity with the large and rapidly growing literature will quickly substantiate this statement [pp. 14–15].

As we shall show in the next section, this assertion is untenable. "Greater familiarity with the large and rapidly growing literature" shows that the very core of "modern learning theory," as Eysenck describes it, has been seriously questioned or abandoned in favor of alternative conceptualizations. For example, the notion that the discrete response provides an adequate unit of analysis, or that reinforcement can be widely used as an explanation of both learning and performance, or that mediational processes can be ignored are being or have been rejected. Eysenck's picture of the field as one with 90% agreement about basic principles is quite simply untrue. The references that Eysenck himself give for this statement (Hilgard, 1956; Osgood, 1953) do not support the claim. Hilgard presented many theories, not one "modern learning theory," some of which (Gestalt, Tolman, Lewin) might just as easily be said to be in 90% disagreement with behavioristic conditioning approaches. In the same vein, Osgood's text was one of the first to give heavy emphasis to the role of mediation, in an attempt to compensate for the inadequacies of a simple conditioning or one-stage S-R approach. Eysenck seems largely unaware of the very problems within the field of learning which necessitated the introduction of mediational concepts, even by S-R theorists such as Osgood.

These inadequacies center, in part, around the problem of generalization. The problem of generalizing from the level of conditioning to the level of complex human behavior has been recognized for a long time (Lewin, 1951; Tolman, 1933). It is a problem that is crucial in simple laboratory phenomena such as maze learning where it has resulted in the introduction of a variety of mediational concepts, and it is

certainly a problem when complex human behavior is being dealt with. For example, Dollard and Miller (1950) began their book with an attempt to explain neurosis with simple conditioning principles. A careful reading of the book reveals, however, that as the behavior to be explained became more and more complex, their explanations relied more and more on mediational concepts, including language. The necessity for these mediators arises from the inadequacy of a simple *peripheral* S-R model to account for the generality of learning, the equivalence of responses, and the adaptive application of behavior in novel situations. We shall return to these points shortly; here we just wish to emphasize that the field of learning is not "one big happy family" whose problems have been solved by the widespread acceptance of a simple conditioning model. The claim to scientific respectability by reference back to established laws of learning is, thus, illusory.

Learning and Learning Theories

We have already noted the differences between the Wolpe-Eysenck and the Skinnerian approaches; let us now examine the similarities. Three things stand out: the focus on the overt response, the reliance on a conditioning model, and the notion of reinforcement. First, there is the belief that the response, consisting of some discrete aspect of overt behavior, is the most meaningful unit of human behavior. While this should ideally refer to a specific contraction of muscles or secretion of glands, with the possible exception of Guthrie (1935), traditional S-R theorists have tended to define response in terms of an effect on the environment rather than as a specific movement of the organism. The problems raised by the use of the response as a basic unit, both in traditional learning phenomena and in the areas of neuroses and psychotherapy will be discussed in the section entitled What is Learned?

A second common assumption is that the concepts taken from conditioning, either as described by Pavlov or the operant conditioning of Skinner, can be used as explanatory principles. The assumption in question here is that conditioning phenomena are the simplest kinds of learning and that all other behavior can be explained in terms of these "simple" principles. We shall deal with the problems that arise from this source in a second section. The third assumption is that rewards play an essential role in all learning phenomena. We shall consider the problems that stem from this assumption in a third section.

What Is Learned?

Since its inception in the early twentieth century, behaviorism has taken overt stimuli and responses as its core units of analysis. Learning, as the behaviorist views it, is defined as the tendency to make a *particular response* in the presence of a *particular stimulus;* what is learned is a discrete response. Almost from its inception, however, this view has been plagued by a number of problems.

First, findings from studies of perception, particularly the fact of perceptual constancy, provide embarrassment for a peripheral S-R theory. Perceptual constancy findings show, for example, that the stimulus is much more than peripheral receptor stimulation. For example, once we have learned a song in a particular key (i.e., particular stimulus elements), we can readily recognize it or sing it in other keys. We are amazingly accurate in recognizing objects and events as being "the same" or equivalent, even though the particular stimulation they provide varies considerably on different occasions (Gibson, 1950). Although the bases of perceptual constancies (size, shapes, brightness, etc.) are not yet well understood, the facts of perceptual constancy—invariance in percept with variation in perceptual stimulation—are not in question. The related phenomenon of transposition has received considerable attention in animal experimentation. Animals, infrahuman as well as human, respond to relations among stimuli (Köhler, 1929). For a number of years, transposition was not considered to pose a serious problem for a peripheral S-R theory since it was thought that it could be adequately handled by principles of conditioning and stimulus generalization (Spence, 1937). This view has not been supported by later experiments, however (Lawrence & DeRivera, 1954; Riley, 1958). It now appears more likely that stimulus generalization is but a special case of the more general complex phenomenon of stimulus equivalence. The absolute theory of transposition was important and instructive because it revealed in clear relief the nature and limitations of a peripheral S-R approach to behavior. The effective stimulus is clearly more "central" than receptor excitation. The chapters on learning in the recent Koch series make it clear that workers in this area have seen the need for coming to terms with the facts of perception (Guttman, 1963; Lawrence, 1963; Leeper, 1963; Postman, 1963).

Second, the facts of response equivalence or response transfer posed the same kind of problem for a peripheral S-R view. A learned response does not consist merely of a stereotyped pattern of muscular contraction or glandular secretion. Even within the S-R tradition (e.g., Hull, Skinner) there has been a tendency to define responses in terms of environmental achievements. Anyone who has trained animals has recognized that animals can achieve the same general response, that is, make the same environmental change, in a variety of different ways once the response is learned. "What is learned," then, is not a mechanical sequence of responses but rather, *what needs to be done in order to achieve some final event.* This notion is not new; Tolman stressed it as early as 1932 when he wrote of "purposive behavior," and it has been strongly supported by a variety of experimental findings (e.g., Beach, Hebb, Morgan, & Nissen, 1960; Ritchie, Aeschliman, & Peirce, 1950). As this work shows, animals somehow seem to be able to bypass the execution of specific responses in reaching an environmental achievement. They can learn to go to particular places in the environment in spite of the fact that to do so requires them to make different responses from trial to trial. The learning of relatively specific responses to specific stimuli appears to be a special case which might be called stereotyped learning (canalization) rather than a basic prototype on the basis of which all other learning may be explained.

It should be noted further that even the stereotyped learning that forms the basic model of S-R conditioning does not hold up under closer scrutiny. First, once a subject has learned a stereotyped movement or response, he is still capable of achieving a goal in other ways when the situation requires it. Thus, while we have all learned to write our names with a particular hand in a relatively stereotyped fashion, we can switch to the other hand, or even write our name with a pencil gripped in our teeth if we have to, in spite of the fact that we may not have made this specific response in this way before. Second, even a response that is grossly defined as constant, stable, or stereotyped does not appear as such a stereotyped pattern of muscular contractions when it is closely observed.[2] These findings in the area of response transfer indicate that a response seems to be highly variable and equipotential. This notion is, of course, quite old in the history of psychology, and it has been stressed repeatedly by numerous investigators including Lashley (see Beach et al., 1960), Osgood (1953), Tolman (1932), and Woodworth (1958).

The facts of both response transfer and stimulus equivalence seem much more adequately handled if we assume that what is learned is a *strategy* (alternatively called cognitive maps, programs, plans, schemata, hypotheses, e.g., Krechevsky, 1932) for obtaining environmental achievements. When we take this view, habits, in the traditional behaviorist sense, become a later stage of response learning rather than a basic explanation (building block) for later, more complex learning.

Perhaps this whole problem can be clarified if we look at a specific example such as language learning. As Chomsky (1959) has demonstrated in his excellent critique of Skinner's *Verbal Behavior* (1957), the basic facts of language learning and usage simply cannot be handled within an S-R approach. It seems clear that an adequate view of language must account for the fact that humans, at a rather early age, internalize a complex set of rules (grammar) which enable them to both recognize and generate meaningful sentences involving patterns of words that they may never have used before. Thus, in language learning, what is learned are not only sets of responses (words and sentences) but, in addition, some form of internal strategies or plans (grammar). We learn a grammar which enables us to generate a variety of English sentences. We do not merely learn specific English sentence habits. How this grammar or set of strategies is acquired, retained, and used in language comprehension and generation is a matter for serious research effort; but, it is clear that attempts to understand language learning on the basis of analogies from bar-pressing experiments are doomed before they start. To anticipate, we will argue shortly that if we are to make an attempt to understand the phenomena of neurosis, using analogies from the area of learning, it will be much more appropriate to take these analogies from the area of psycholinguistics and language learning rather than, as has typically been done, from studies of classical and operant conditioning. That is, the focus will have to

---

[2] G. Hoyle, personal communication, 1963.

be on response transfer, equipotentiality, and the learning of plans and strategies rather than on stereotyped response learning or habituation.

Use of a Conditioning Model

As we indicated earlier, when writers in the behaviorist tradition say "learning theory," they probably mean a conditioning theory; most of the interpretations of clinical phenomena are reinterpretations in terms of the principles of conditioning. Thus, a phobic symptom is viewed as a conditioned response, maintained by the reinforcement of a secondary fear drive or by a Skinnerian as a single operant maintained by reinforcement. Two types of conditioning are involved in these explanations by reduction. The first is Pavlovian or classical conditioning, frequently used in conjunction with later Hullian concepts such as secondary drive; the second is operant conditioning of the kind proposed by Skinner. The use of both of these models to explain more complex phenomena such as transposition, response transfer, problem solving, language learning, or neurosis and psychotherapy poses a number of difficulties.

The basic assumption that underlies the use of either kind of conditioning as an explanation for more complex phenomena is that basic laws of behavior have been established in the highly controlled laboratory situation and may thus be applied to behavior of a more complex variety. When we look at the way conditioning principles are applied in the explanation of more complex phenomena, we see that only a rather flimsy analogy bridges the gap between such laboratory defined terms as stimulus, response, and reinforcement and their referents in the case of complex behavior. Thus, while a stimulus may be defined as an electric shock or a light of a certain intensity in a classical conditioning experiment, Bandura (1961) speaks of the "imagination of a scene"; or, while a response may consist of salivation or a bar-press in a conditioning experiment, behavior therapists speak of anxiety as a response. As Chomsky (1959) puts it, with regard to this same problem in the area of language:

He (Skinner in *Verbal Behavior*) utilizes the experimental results as evidence for the scientific character of his system of behavior, and analogic guesses (formulated in terms of a metaphoric extension of the technical vocabulary of the laboratory) as evidence for its scope. This creates the illusion of a rigorous scientific theory with a very broad scope, although in fact the terms used in the description of real-life and of laboratory behavior may be mere homonyms, with at most a vague similarity of meaning [p. 30].

A second and related problem stems from the fact that the behavior-therapy workers accept the findings of conditioning experiments as basic principles or laws of learning. Unfortunately, there is now good reason to believe that classical conditioning is no more simple or basic than other forms of learning. Rather, it seems to be a form of learning that is in itself in need of explanation in terms of more general principles. For example, a popular but naive view of conditioning is that of stimulus substitution—the view that conditioning consists merely of the substitution of a conditioned stimulus for an unconditioned stimulus. Close examination of conditioning experiments reveals that this is not the case, however, for the conditioned response is typically *unlike* the unconditioned response (Zener, 1937). Apparently, in conditioning, a new response is learned. Most of the major learning theorists have taken this fact into account in abandoning the notion of conditioning as mere stimulus substitution.

More than this, the most important theoretical developments using essentially Pavlovian conditioning principles have not even stressed overt behavior (Osgood, 1953). Hull and the neo-Hullians, for example, have relied quite heavily on Tolman's (1932) distinction between learning and performance, performance being what is observed while learning (conditioning) is but one essential ingredient contributing to any instance of observed performance. The most important, and perhaps the most sophisticated, developments in Hullian and neo-Hullian theory concern the attempts to explain complicated goal-directed behavior in terms of the conditioning of fractional responses. Unobserved, fractional responses (already we see the drift away from the overt behavior criteria of response) are assumed to serve a mediating role in behavior. Once a fractional response is conditioned in a particular situation, it is assumed to occur to the stimuli in that situation when those stimuli recur. The stimulus consequences of the fractional response referred to as the r_g are assumed to serve as guides to behavior either by serving as a cue or by activating responses or by serving to reinforce other responses by secondary reinforcement. The latter-day proponents of a conditioning point of view (Bugelski, 1956; Osgood, 1953) have come to rely more and more heavily on concepts like the fractional response to bridge the gap between stimulus and overt behavior and to account for the facts of response transfer, environmental achievements, and equipotentiality. What this indicates is that a simple conditioning paradigm which rests solely on observable stimuli and responses has proved inadequate even to the task of encompassing simple conditioning and maze-learning phenomena, and the workers within this tradition have come to rely more and more heavily on mediational (central, cognitive, etc.) concepts, although they still attempt to clothe these concepts in traditional conditioning garb. To add to the problem, a number of recent papers (Deutsch, 1956; Gonzales & Diamond, 1960) have indicated that the r_g interpretations of complex behavior are neither simple nor adequate.

When we look again at the way conditioning principles have been applied to clinical phenomena, we see an amazing awareness of these problems that have been so salient to experimental and animal psychologists working with conditioning.

While the above discussion has been oriented primarily to classical conditioning, the general argument would apply equally well to those attempts to make the principles of learning derived from operant conditioning the basis of an explanation of neurosis and psychotherapy (as in Krasner, 1961). The Skinnerians have been particularly oblivious to the wide variety of problems that are entailed when one attempts to apply concepts and findings from laboratory learning experiments to other, and particularly more complex, phenomena. While we will deal more directly with their point of view shortly, a few comments might be in order now concerning their use of the operant-conditioning paradigm as a basis for the handling of more complex data. When Skinnerians speak of laws of learning, they have reference to the curves representing rate of responding of rats pressing bars (Skinner, 1938), and pigeons pecking (Ferster & Skinner, 1957) which are, in fact, a function of certain highly controlled contingencies such as the schedule of reinforcement, the amount of deprivation, the experimental situation itself (there is very little else to do in a Skinner box), and the species of animals involved. These experiments are of some interest, both as exercises in animal training under highly restricted conditions, and for what light they may shed on the more general question of partial reinforcement. It is dubious that these findings constitute laws of learning that can be applied across species (see Breland & Breland, 1961) or even to situations that differ in any significant way from the Skinner box.

Use of Reinforcement

Advocates of the application of learning theory to clinical phenomena have relied heavily on the "law of effect" as perhaps their foremost established principle of learning. We shall attempt to point out that a good deal of evidence from experimental animal studies argues strongly that, at the most, the law of effect is a weak law of performance.

Essentially, the controversy can be reduced to the question of whether or not reward is necessary for learning. The initial source of evidence indicating that it was not came from the findings of latent learning studies (Blodgett, 1929; Tolman & Honzik, 1930) in which it was found, for example, that rats who were allowed to explore a maze without reward made fewer errors when learning the maze than controls who had no opportunity for exploration. Thus, these early latent learning studies, as well as a variety of more recent ones (Thistlethwaite, 1951) indicate that learning can take place without reward but may not be revealed until a reward situation makes it appropriate to do so (or to put it another way, the reward elicits the performance but plays little role during learning). Other sources which point to learning without reward come from studies of perceptual learning (Hebb, 1949), imitation (Herbert & Harsh, 1944), language learning (Chomsky, 1959), and imprinting (Moltz, 1960).

Defenders of the point of view that reinforcement is necessary for learning have attempted to handle results such as these in a variety of ways. One has been by appealing to the concept of secondary reinforcement (e.g., a maze has secondary reinforcing properties which account for the learning during exploration). When this sort of thing is done, even with respect to experiments where attempts were made to minimize secondary reinforcements (Thistlethwaite, 1951), it seems clear that this particular notion of reinforcement has become incapable of disproof. Another way of handling these potentially embarrassing results has been by the invention of a new set of drives (curiosity drive, exploratory drive, etc.) but this too has a post hoc flavor to it, and one wonders what kind of explanation is achieved by postulating an "exploratory drive" to account for the fact that animals and humans engage in exploration. In fact, the assumption that exploration reduces an exploratory drive makes it difficult to explain why a rat's tendency to enter an alley of a maze *decreases* after he has explored the alley (Watson, 1961). Finally, there are those (particularly the Skinnerians) who tend to define reinforcement so broadly that neither the findings from latent learning nor any other source can prove embarrassing, since whenever learning has taken place this "proves" that there has been reinforcement. To better understand this problem, however, we had best look for a moment at the general problem of defining reinforcement in a meaningful way.

Obviously, if the view that reinforcement is necessary for learning is to have any meaning, what constitutes a reinforcement must be defined independently from the learning situation itself. There has been a great deal of difficulty in getting around a circular definition of the law of effect, and it might be worthwhile to examine some of the attempts that have been made in the past.

One of the best known was the attempt to relate the reinforcing properties of stimuli to their drive-reducing characteristics (Hull, 1951). The drive-reduction model has had to be abandoned, however, because of evidence from a variety of areas including latent learning, sensory preconditioning (Brogden, 1939), and novelty and curiosity (Berlyne, 1960). Other evidence such as that of Olds and Milner (1954) on the effect of direct brain stimulation have strengthened the conviction that the drive-reduction interpretation of reinforcement is inadequate; and, in fact, original adherents of this view have begun to abandon it (e.g., Miller, 1959).

The other most frequent solution to the circularity problem has been by way of the "empirical law of effect," an approach typified by Skinner's definition of reinforcement as any stimulus that can be demonstrated to produce a change in response strength. Skinner argues that this is not circular since some stimuli are found to produce changes and others are not, and they can subsequently be classified on that basis. This seems to be a reasonable position if it is adhered to; that is, if care is taken to define reinforcement in terms of class membership *independently* of the observations that show that learning has taken place. When we examine the actual use of the term reinforcement by Skinner (see especially *Verbal Behavior,* 1957) and by other Skinnerians (Lundin, 1961), we find that care is only taken in this regard within the context of animal experiments, but that when the jumps are made to other phenomena, such as language and psychotherapy, care is usually *not* taken to define reinforcement independently from learning as indicated by response strength. This leads to a state of affairs where any observed change in behavior is said to occur *because of* reinforcement, when, in fact, the change in behavior is itself the only indicator of what the reinforcement has been. Chomsky (1959) reviews the use of the concept of reinforcement by Skinner with regard to language and reaches the following conclusion:

From this sample, it can be seen that the notion of reinforcement has totally lost whatever objective meaning it may ever have had. Running through these examples, we see that a person can be reinforced though he emits no response at all, and the reinforcing "stimulus" need not impinge on the reinforced person or need not even exist (it is sufficient that it be imagined or hoped for). When we read that a person plays what music he likes (165), says what he likes (165), thinks what he likes (438–9), reads what books he likes (163), etc., *because* he finds it reinforcing to do so, or that we write books or inform others of facts *because* we are reinforced by what we hope will be the ultimate behavior of reader or listener, we can only conclude that the term "reinforce-

ment" has a purely ritual function. The phrase "X is reinforced by Y (stimulus, state of affairs, event, etc.)" is being used as a cover term for "X wants Y," "X likes Y," "X wishes that Y were the case," etc. Invoking the term "reinforcement" has no explanatory force, and any idea that this paraphrase introduces any new clarity or objectivity into the description of wishing, liking, etc., is a serious delusion [pp. 37–38].

This problem is exemplified in the area of psychotherapy by the attempts to use the studies of verbal conditioning (Krasner, 1958) as analogues to psychotherapy. First we should note that if these studies are taken at face value (i.e., if subjects are conditioned to increase the emission of certain responses because of reinforcement, without their awareness of this fact) it appears that a simple conditioning model is inadequate since subjects are presumably responding in terms of a class of responses (e.g., plural nouns, etc.) rather than in terms of a specific response (e.g., bar press), such classes implying response transfer and mediation. Second, and more to the point, a number of recent investigators (Eriksen, 1962) have begun to question whether verbal conditioning does occur without the subject's awareness. If it does not, the whole phenomenon begins to look like nothing more than a rather inefficient way to get subjects to figure out what the experimenter wants them to do (telling them directly to emit plural nouns would probably be much more efficient) after which they can decide whether they want to do it or not. In any case, there seems to be enough question about what goes on in verbal conditioning itself to indicate that it cannot be utilized as a more basic explanation for complex phenomena such as psychotherapy. Psychotherapists of many persuasions would agree that rewards of some kind are important in work with patients. Thus, the view that the psychotherapist is a "reinforcement machine" is trivial. The difficult problems are in specifying just what therapist activities are rewarding, in what ways, to what sorts of patients, and with what effects.

The above discussion should make clear that the use of the concept of reinforcement is only of explanatory usefulness when it is specified in some delimited fashion. As an empirical law of performance almost everyone in and out of psychology would accept it, including Lewin, Freud, Tolman, and others outside the traditional S-R movement. But this amounts to saying nothing more than that some events, when presented, tend to increase the probability of responses that they have followed. The hard job, but the only one that will lead to any meaningful use of the concept of reinforcement, is specifying what the various events called reinforcers have in common. Some have argued that since this is such a difficult task, we should restrict ourselves to listing and cataloging so-called reinforcers. But this is nearly impossible, in a general way, because reinforcers differ from individual to individual, from species to species, from situation to situation, and from time to time (the saying "one man's meat is another man's poison" is trite but true). Meaningful analysis must stem from a comprehensive study of the particular learning phenomena in question, whether it is language learning, the development of perceptual and perceptual-motor skills (Fitts, 1964; Hebb, 1949), the acquisition of particular species behavior patterns during critical periods of development (Scott, 1962), the learning of a neurosis, or the learning that takes place during pschotherapy. Experience with all of these phenomena has revealed that different kinds of events seem to be involved and that these can only be understood in the context of the phenomena in question. Lumping all these events together under the single term reinforcement serves to muddle rather than to clarify understanding.

The staunch reinforcement adherent might respond that all these complicated arguments may be true but we can ignore them, since all we are really interested in is predicting what the organism will do, and we can do this when we know the organism's reinforcement history. The answer to this is that the experimental literature does not support such a claim; rather, it shows that, in many instances, performance *cannot* be predicted on the basis of a knowledge of the history of reinforcement.

Latent learning studies indicate this quite clearly. Perhaps of more interest are the findings of discrimination-reversal learning studies (Goodwin & Lawrence, 1955; Mackintosh, 1963). Here we find that subjects that have been trained on a series of discrimination reversals learn to select the correct stimulus with very few errors even though they may have been rewarded *much more frequently and more recently for responding to another stimulus*. Similarly, in the double drive discrimination studies (Thistlethwaite, 1951) animals chose alleys leading to food when they were hungry and water when they were thirsty, even though they have been rewarded equally frequently on the alleys on previous trials. In other words, "what is learned" was not equivalent with "reinforcement history." The law of effect is not disproved by these studies; it is merely shown to be irrelevant.

To summarize: The "law of effect," or reinforcement, conceived as a *"law of learning,"* occupies a very dubious status. Like the principles of conditioning, it appears to be an unlikely candidate as an explanatory principle of learning. As a strong law of learning it has already been rejected by many theorists who previously relied on it. As an empirical "law of *performance*" it is noncontroversial, but usually so generally stated as to be of little explanatory value.

Conception of Neurosis

In this section we will explicate the conception of neurosis that forms the basis of the behavior-therapy approach (particularly of the Wolpe-Eysenck group) and attempt to demonstrate its inadequacies both in terms of learning theory and as a way of accounting for the observed facts of neurosis. Our argument in the first instance will be that the conception of neurosis in terms of symptoms and anxiety parallels the general conception of learning in terms of overt responses, conditioning, and secondary drives, and suffers from the same inadequacies that we have outlined in the preceding section. With regard to the facts of neurosis, we will argue that the behavior-therapy position is inadequate at a descriptive level as well as being conceptually incorrect. It should be pointed out again that we are discussing the explanation of theory of neurosis here and not the techniques used by the behavior therapists. The strict Skinnerian may excuse himself at this point if he adheres to a "no-theory" position and is only concerned with the effects of environmental manipulation. Furthermore, certain techniques themselves may be useful and have some of the effects attributed to them regardless of the theory.

In its essence, the conception of neurosis put forth by the behavior therapists is that neuroses are conditioned responses or habits (including conditioned anxiety) and *nothing else,* though it should be noted that they do not adhere to this argument when they describe the success of their methods. Wolpe, for example, while ostensibly treating overt symptoms, describes his patients as becoming more productive, having improved adjustment and pleasure in sex, improved interpersonal relationships, and so forth. The argument that removal of a troublesome symptom somehow "generalizes" to all of these other areas begs the question. Their conception is typically put forth as an alternative to a psychodynamic viewpoint, which they characterize as resting on a distinction between symptoms and underlying causes (unconscious conflicts, impulses, defenses, etc.). They stress the point that inferences about underlying factors of this sort are unnecessary and

misleading and that a more parsimonious explanation treats symptoms (which are typically equated with behavior or that which can be objectively observed) as the neurosis per se. They argue that by equating neurosis with symptoms, and symptoms, in turn, with habits (conditioned responses), they are able to bring "modern learning theory" with its "well-established laws" to bear on the understanding and treatment of neurosis.

As we have labored to show in the preceding section, the well-established laws of learning to which they refer have considerable difficulty within the area of simple animal behavior. More specifically, it seems clear that a wide variety of behaviors (from maze learning to more complex forms) cannot be adequately dealt with when the overt response and conditioned habit are the units of analysis. Furthermore, their learning position leads the behavior therapists into postulating an isomorphic relationship between antecedent learning and present behavior in which observed differences are accounted for in terms of principles of generalization. This is a key issue, and we shall explore it a little further at this time.

Much of the behaviorist conception of neurosis rests on a rejection of the distinction between symptoms and underlying causes (Eysenck, 1960) as typified by Yates' (1958) argument against "symptom substitution." By focusing attention on overt symptoms and banishing all underlying causes, however, the behavior therapists are faced with the same problem that has long confronted behaviorism; namely, the difficulty of explaining how *generality* of behavior results from specific learning experiences. The problem of *generality* (i.e., as exemplified by the facts of transposition and response transfer) has, in fact, brought about the downfall of peripheral S-R learning, of the conditioned habit as a basic unit, and tangentially, is leading to the dethroning of the law of effect. With regard to neurosis, this view has led the behavior therapists into the position where they must posit a specific learning experience for each symptom of a neurosis. They have partly avoided this problem by focusing their attention on those neuroses that can be described in terms of specific symptoms (bedwetting, if this is a neurosis, tics, specific phobias, etc.) and have tended to ignore those conditions which do not fit their model, such as neurotic depressions, general unhappiness, obsessional disorders, and the kinds of persistent interpersonal entanglements that characterize so many neurotics. This leaves them free to explain the specific symptom in terms of a specific learning experience, as, for example, when a fear of going outdoors is explained in terms of some previous experience in which the stimulus (outdoors) has been associated with (conditioned to) something unpleasant or painful and has now, through generalization, spread to any response of going outdoors. As our previous analysis should make clear, however, even a simple conceptualization such as this, in terms of stimuli, responses, and conditioning is extremely cumbersome and begs the important questions. Within an S-R framework, in which generalization occurs along the dimension of physical stimulus similarity, it is difficult, if not impossible, to show how a previous experience such as being frightened in the country as a child could generalize to the "stimulus" outdoors without a great deal of *mediation* in which the concept of "outdoors" carried most of the burden of generalization. As we have pointed out, most workers in the field of learning recognize this and rely heavily on mediational concepts in their explanations of complex behavior. Dollard and Miller (1950), for example, return again and again to mediational explanations once they move beyond the "combat neuroses" which lend themselves more readily to a simple isomorphic explanation.

A second important facet of the behaviorist conception of neurosis is the use of the concept of anxiety as a secondary drive.

Here, Wolpe and Eysenck and some others seem to follow the explanatory model laid down by Dollard and Miller. Anxiety is viewed as the main motivating force for symptoms and, in general, occupies a central place in their thinking. Briefly, it is worth pointing out that the concept of drive reduction, the distinction between primary drives and secondary drives, as well as the early thinking about the uniquely persistent qualities of fear-motivated behavior have had serious difficulty within learning theory (Watson, 1961; Solomon, 1964). The use of these concepts to explain clinical phenomena thus rests on an exceedingly shaky foundation.

Let us turn our attention now to the phenomena of neuroses. We shall try to point out that underlying the dispute over symptoms versus underlying causes is a real difference in definition that arises at the descriptive level, which, in a sense, antedates disagreements at the level of theory and explanation.

To keep the presentation simple, we will adopt the terms psychodynamic to refer to all those theorists and therapists, following Freud, whose view of neurosis and its treatment deals with motives (conscious and unconscious), conflict, etc. This covers a wide variety of workers, in addition to the more or less traditional followers of Freud, including Sullivan and his adherents (Fromm-Reichman, 1950), other neo-Freudians, and that broad group of psychiatrists and clinical psychologists who have been strongly influenced by the Freudian and neo-Freudian viewpoints even though they may not claim allegiance to any of the formal schools.

The point we wish to make here is that disagreement between the behaviorist and psychodynamic viewpoints seems to rest on a very real difference at the purely descriptive or observational level. The behaviorist looks at a neurotic and sees specific symptoms and anxiety. The psychodynamicist looks at the same individual and sees a complex intra- and interpersonal mode of functioning which may or may not contain certain observable fears [3] or certain behavioral symptoms such as compulsive motor acts. When the psychodynamicist describes a neurosis, his referent is a cohering component of the individual's functioning, including his characteristic ways of interacting with other people (e.g., sweet and self-effacing on the surface but hostile in covert ways), his characteristic modes of thinking and perceiving (e.g., the hysteric who never "remembers" anything unpleasant, the obsessive whose memories are overelaborated and circumstantial, etc.), characteristic modes of fantasy and dreaming, a variety of secondary gain features, and the like. Specific or isolatable symptoms may sometimes be a part of such an integrated neurotic pattern, but, even viewed descriptively, they in no sense constitute the neurosis per se.

So far, we have considered the behavior therapists' position at face value. In actuality, a good case can be made that they *behave* in a way which is quite inconsistent with their own position. A specific example, taken from one of Wolpe's own case descriptions, will illustrate this point, and, at the same time, show what the psychodynamicist sees when he looks at a neurotic. Wolpe (1960) presents the following case:

Case 5—An attractive woman of 28 came for treatment because she was in acute distress as a result of her lovers' casual treatment of her. Everyone of very numerous love affairs had followed a similar pattern—first she would attract the man, then she would offer herself on a platter. He would soon treat her with contempt and afer a time leave her. In general she lacked assurance, was very dependent, and was practically never free from feelings of tension and anxiety.

What is described here is a complex pattern of interpersonal relationships, psychological strategies and misunderstandings (such as the way she became involved with men, the way she communicated her availability to them, her dependency, etc.), expectations that she had (presumably that men would not react with contempt to her generosity, that being dependent might lead to being taken care of, etc.), and thoughts and feelings about herself (lack of assurance, acute distress, etc.). Many of the statements about her (e.g., the description of the course of her love affairs) are abbreviations for very complex and involved precesses involving two people interacting over a period of time. It is this, the psychodynamicist would argue, that *is* the neurosis. The tension and anxiety may be a part of it in this particular case (though there might be other cases in which there is no complaint of anxiety but, rather, its reverse—seeming inability to "feel" anything)—but it is secondary and can be understood only in relation to the other aspects of the patient's functioning. Wolpe's case histories are classic testaments to the fact that he cannot, and does not, apply the symptom approach when working with actual data. As a further example, consider the argument against a symptom-substitution point of view (Yates, 1958) in which it is implied that anything other than symptoms is some sort of metaphysical inference. While it may be true that theories such as psychoanalysis deal with a number of inferential and higher-order constructs in their attempts to integrate the complex mass of data that constitues a neurosis, it is also true that much more than symptoms exist at the level of observation. Secondary-gain features of a neurosis, in which it is apparent that a variety of goals may be served by a set of interchangeable symptoms are the rule in most neurotic individuals. We are not defending the view (attributed to psychoanalysis by Yates) that if one symptom is removed another pops up to take its place; rather, we are

---

[3] The term anxiety is frequently used as a theoretical inference, i.e., a patient deals with personal material in an overly intellectual fashion, and this is described as a defense mechanism—intellectualization—whose purpose is to ward off anxiety.

arguing that the empirical phenomena of neurosis does not fit the symptom or response theory, but is much more compatible with a theory built around central mediators. Whether unconscious conflicts and defense mechanisms are adequate ways of conceptualizing the problem is an entirely separate question. What is clear is that a view stressing central mediators in which specific responses are seen as equipotential means of reaching certain goals is necessary to encompass the data of neurosis just as it has proven necessary to encompass the phenomena of animal learning.

To sum up, it would seem that the behaviorists have reached a position where an inadequate conceptual framework forces them to adopt an inadequate and superficial view of the very data that they are concerned with. They are then forced to slip many of the key facts in the back door, so to speak, for example, when all sorts of fantasy, imaginary, and thought processes are blithley called responses. This process is, of course, parallel to what has gone on within S-R learning theory where all sorts of central and mediational processes have been cumbersomely handled with S-R terminology (e.g., Deutsch, 1956). Thus, we have a situation where the behavior therapists argue strongly against a dynamic interpretation of neurosis at some points and at other points behave as if they had adopted such a point of view. This inconsistency should be kept in mind in reading the next section in which we evaluate the claims of success put forth by the behaviorist group. Insofar as there is disagreement as to what constitutes the descriptive facts of neurosis, it makes little sense to compare the effectiveness of different methods. However, since the behaviorist group adopts very broad (or psychodynamic, if you will) criteria for improvement, and since their *techniques* may have some effectiveness, in spite of theoretical and conceptual inadequacies, it is crucial that we look carefully at the empirical results that they lay claim to.

Claims of Success

While much of the writing of the behavior therapists consists of arguments and appeals to principles of science and learning, the claims that are made for the success of the methods seem open to empirical analysis. No doubt a great deal of the appeal of behavior therapy lies right here. Here seem to be methods whose application can be clearly described (unlike such messy psychodynamic methods as "handling countertransference" or "interpreting resistance"), whose course is relatively short, and which seem to achieve a large number of practical results in the form of removal of symptoms. Wolpe (1960), for example, presents the following data: of 122 cases treated with behavioral techniques, 44% were "apparently cured," 46% were "much improved," 7% were "slightly or moderately improved," and 3% were "unimproved." Combining categories, he claims 90% "apparently cured or much improved," and 10% "improvement moderate, slight or nil." (Criteria of improvement consists of "symptomatic improvement, increased productiveness, improved adjustment and pleasure in sex, improved interpersonal relationships and ability to handle ordinary psychological conflicts and reasonable reality stresses.")

He compares this with data from the Berlin Psychoanalytic Institute (Knight, 1941) which shows 62–40.5% in the first category and 38–59.5% in the second. Wolpe concludes, as have others (Bandura, 1961; Eysenck, 1960; Lazarus, 1963), that this demonstrates the superiority of the behavior therapy methods. The fact that the psychoanalytic method showed as much as 62% improvement is explained as being due to whatever accidental "reciprocal inhibition" occurred during the therapy. (There is, however, no analysis or description of how this might have happened.) The behavioral methods achieve superior results presumably because of the more explicit application of these techniques.

It is fair to say that if these results can be substantiated they present a very strong argument in favor of behavioral *techniques*—even granting the theoretical and empirical inconsistencies we have discussed. However, we must ask if these claims are any better substantiated than those made by the practitioners of other methods of psychotherapy. Insofar as claims such as Wolpe's are based on uncontrolled case histories, they may reflect the enthusiasm of the practitioner as much as the effect of the method. History shows that new methods of therapy (ECS, tranquilizing drugs, as well as various schools of psychotherapy) have been oversold by their original proponents. Thus, a careful look at what lies behind the claims of the behavior-therapy group is in order.

The following does not purport to be a comprehensive review of the behavior-therapy literature. Rather, it is based on a survey of all the studies reported in the two reviews that have appeared (Bandura, 1961; Grossberg, 1964). The most striking thing about this large body of studies is that they are almost all case studies. A careful reading of the original sources reveals that only one study (Lang & Lazovik, 1963) is a controlled experiment, and here the subjects were not neurotics but normal college students. Thus, most of the claims (including those of Wolpe which have been widely quoted) must be regarded as no better substantiated than those of any other enthusiastic school of psychotherapy whose practitioners claim that their patients get better. Behavior therapy has appeared to differ on this score because of its identification with experimental psychology and with "well-established laws of learning." We have already dealt with this issue, so let us now turn to some problems in evaluating psychotherapy as a technique.

The problems here are essentially those of control, and they may be broken down into three areas: (*a*) sampling biases, (*b*) observer bias, and (*c*) problems of experimental control. While research in psycho-

therapy presents particular difficulties in controlling "experimental input," more sophisticated workers (Frank, 1959) have attempted to deal with at least the sampling and observer problems. It thus comes as somewhat of a surprise that the behavior-therapy workers, despite their identification with experimental psychology, base their claims on evidence which is almost totally lacking in any form of control. Let us examine these issues in greater detail.

Sampling biases. Obviously a claim such as Wolpe's of 90% success has meaning only when we know the population from which the sample of patients was drawn and the way in which they were selected. Ideally, a comparison of treatment techniques would involve the random assign of patient from a common population pool to alternative treatments. Since, in practice, this is rarely feasible, it is essential for anyone making comparisons of different treatment methods to, at the very least, examine the comparability of the populations *and* of the methods used in selecting from these populations. Neither Wolpe's data nor that of Lazarus (1963) contains this evidence. Wolpe reports, for example, that:

Both series (70 patients reported on in 1952 and 52 patients reported on in 1954 on which the 90% figure is based) include only patients whose treatment has ceased after they have been afforded a reasonable opportunity for the application of the available methods; i.e., they have had as a minimum both a course of instruction on the changing of behavior in the life situation and a proper initiation of a course of relaxation-desensitization. This minimum takes up to about 15 interviews, including anamestic interviews and *no patient who has had 15 or more interviews has been omitted from the series* [emphasis added].

We may conclude from this that some patients (how many we do not know) having up to 14 interviews have been excluded from the sample—a procedure highly favorable to the success of the method but which violates the simplest canons of sampling. Wolpe's final sample of 122 consists of those patients most likely to show improvement, since both they and he were satisfied enough with the first 14 (or less) interviews to warrant proceeding further. Those patients least likely to improve are those most likely to drop out early (14 sessions or less) and not be included in the computation of success rate. The fact that a large number of poor-prognosis patients would very likely be eliminated during these early sessions is supported by a variety of research findings (Strickland & Crowne, 1963), which show that most dropping-out of untreatable or unsuccessful cases occurs during the first 10 sessions. This serious sampling bias would be expected to spuriously inflate the percent showing improvement.

When we add this to whatever unknown factors operate to delimit the original population (presumably there is some self-selection of patients who seek out this form of treatment), it becomes apparent that little confidence can be given to the reports of success.

Observer bias. Psychologists have long been aware that human beings are fallible observers, particularly when they have predispositions or vested interests to protect. In controlled studies, we try to protect judges from their own biases by not acquainting them with the hypotheses, or with the nature of the groups they are judging, or by using blind and double-blind designs. This problem is particularly acute with regard to psychotherapy because both therapist and patient have investments of time, involvement, competence, and reputation to protect. For these reasons, workers in the area have become extremely skeptical of claims put forth for any method which rests on the uncontrolled observation of the person administering the treatment. At a minimum we expect some sort of external evidence. Beyond this minimum we hope for an independent judge who can compare differentially treated groups without knowing which is which.

In addition, there is the problem of the patient's freedom to report effects which may be seriously curtailed when all his reports go directly to the person who has treated him. It seems reasonable to assume that some patients are prevented from expressing dissatisfaction with treatment when they must report directly to the therapist, either because they do not want to hurt his feelings, or are afraid, or are just saying what they think is being demanded of them, or are being polite, or for some other reason. Again, it would be highly appropriate to provide the patients with the opportunity of reporting results in a situation as free from such pressure as possible.

Examination of the 26 studies reviewed by Bandura reveals a surprising lack of concern with these problems. Of the 26 studies sampled, only 12 report evaluation of results by persons other than the treating therapist; four of these use ratings of the hospital staff (who may be acquainted with the treatment), four use mothers or parents reporting on their children to the treating therapist, one is a wife reporting on her husband to the therapist, and three use a second observer. Obviously, whatever factors enter in to cause observer and reporter biases are allowed full reign in most of these cases. While we cannot conclude from this that the reported results are *due to* observer and reporter biases (as is clearly indicated with the sampling biases), it is impossible to rule them out. Furthermore, a great deal of evidence from many areas of psychology leads us to be very skeptical of claims in which biases of this sort go uncontrolled.

Experimental control. While control of sampling and observer effects are basic to a wide variety of research activities, including field and clinical research, more exacting control over experimental conditions has long been the sine qua non of the laboratory methods of experimental psychology. The power of the experimental method stems, in part, from keeping careful control over all but a few conditions, which are experimentally varied, with the subsequent effects of these variations being observed. Since psychotherapy is not a controlled experiment, it is probably unfair to expect this type of control. However, there are more and less accurate descriptions of what goes on during any form of therapy, and we can demand as accurate a description as possible in lieu of experimental control. Thus, while we are led to believe that methods, such as counterconditioning, extinction of maladaptive responses, methods of reward, and the like, are applied in a manner analogous to their laboratory counterparts—examination of what is *actually done* reveals that the application of the learning techniques is embedded in a wide variety of activities (including many of the traditional therapy and interview techniques) which make any attribution of effect to the specific learning techniques impossible. Let us consider a few examples. From Wolpe (1960):

Case 4—The patient had 65 therapeutic interviews, unevenly distributed over 27 months. The greater part of the time was devoted to discussions of how to gain control of her interpersonal relationships and stand up for herself. She had considerable difficulty with this at first, even though it had early become emotionally important to her to please the therapist. But she gradually mastered the assertive behavior required of her, overcame her anxieties and became exceedingly self-reliant in all interpersonal dealings, including those with her mother-in-law.

From Lazarus and Rachman (1957) on systematic desensitization:

Case 1—The patient was instructed in the use of assertive responses and deep (nonhypnotic) relaxation. The first anxiety hierarchy dealt with was that of dull weather. Starting from "a bright sunny day" it was possible for the subject to visualize "damp overcast weather" without anxiety after 21 densensitization sessions, and 10 days after the completion of this hierarchy, she was able to report that, "the weather is much better, it doesn't even bother me to look at the weather when I wake up in the morning" (previously depressing). . . . During the course of therapy, part of the reason for the development of the anxiety state in this patient was unearthed. When she was 17 years old she had become involved in a love affair with a married man 12 years her senior. This affair had been conducted in an extremely discreet manner for 4 years, during which time she had suffered from recurrent guilt feelings and shame—so much so, that on one occasion she had attempted suicide by throwing herself into a river. It was her custom to meet her lover after work *in the late afternoon.* The dull weather can be accounted for, as this affair took place in London.

From Rachman (1959):

Interview No. 12. The patient having received a jolt in her love relationship, this session was restricted to a sort of nondirective, cathartic discussion. No desensitizing was undertaken because of A.G.'s depressed mood and obvious desire to "just talk."

These excerpts have been presented because they seem representative of the practices of the behavioral therapists. As can be seen, the number and variety of activities that go on during these treatment sessions is great, including, in these few examples, discussions, explanations of techniques and principles, explanations of the unadaptiveness of anxiety and symptoms, hypnosis of various sorts, relaxation practice and training with and without hypnosis, "nondirective cathartic discussions," "obtaining an understanding of the patient's personality and background," and the "unearthing" of a 17-year-old memory of an illicit affair. The case reports are brief and presented anecdotally so that it is really impossible to know what else went on in addition to those things described. What should be abundantly clear from these examples is that there is no attempt to restrict what goes on to learning techniques. Since it seems clear that a great variety of things do go on, any attribution of behavior change to specific learning techniques is entirely unwarranted.

In summary, there are several important issues that must be differentiated. First, a review of both learning theory and of the empirical results of behavior therapy demonstrates that they can claim no special scientific status for their work on either ground. Second, there are important differences of opinion concerning the type of patient likely to be affected by behavior therapy. Grossberg (1964), for example, states that: "Behavior therapies have been most successful when applied to neurotic disorders with specific behavioral manifestations [p. 81]." He goes on to point out that the results with alcoholism and sexual disorders have been disappointing and that the best results are achieved with phobias and enuresis. He later states that "desensitization only alleviates those phobias that are being treated, but other coexisting phobias remain at high strength, indicating a specific treatment effect [p. 83]." Wolpe et al. (1964), on the other hand, argues that: "The conditioning therapist differs from his colleagues in that he *seeks out* the precise stimuli to anxiety, and finds himself able to break down almost every neurosis into what are essentially *phobic systems* [p. 11]." The best controlled study (Lang & Lazovik, 1963) indicates that "desensitization is very effective in reducing the intense fear of snakes held by normal subjects, though it can be questioned whether this is a phobia in the clinical sense."

Thus, there seems to be some evidence that these *techniques* (as techniques and not as learning theory) are effective with certain conditions.[4] We feel that this bears stressing because psychotherapy has come to be narrowly defined in terms of dynamic, evocative, and nondirective methods, placing unnecessary limitations on the

kind of patient suitable for psychotherapy. First, we must note that behavior techniques are not new (as Murray, 1964, points out in a recent article). Freud and Breuer used similar techniques prior to the development of psychoanalysis, Bagby described a number of these methods in 1928, and therapy based on techniques designed to eliminate undesirable responses was used for many years by Stevenson Smith at the University of Washington Clinic. While most of these techniques have been superseded by the various forms of dynamic psychotherapy, recent work (Frank, 1961) suggests that the time may be ripe for taking a fresh look at a variety of methods such as hypnosis, suggestion, relaxation, and other approaches of a more *structured nature* in which the therapist takes a *more active role*. Needless to say, this fresh look would best proceed unencumbered by an inadequate learning theory and with some minimal concern for control. As an example of a nondynamic approach to patient management, we refer to the work of Fairweather (1964) and his colleagues.

REFORMULATION

Up to this point our analysis has been primarily critical. We have tried to show that many of the so-called principles of learning employed by workers with a behaviorist orientation are inadequate and are not likely to provide useful explanations for clinical phenomena. In this section we will examine the potential value of ideas from different learning conceptions. Before proceeding, however, we would like to discuss briefly the issue of the application of "laws," principles, and findings from one area (such as animal experimentation) to another (such as neurosis and psychotherapy). The behaviorists have traditionally assumed that principles established under highly controlled conditions, usually with animal subjects, form a scientific foundation for a psychology of learning. Yet

---

[4] Just how many neurotics fit the phobia and/or specific symptom model is a complicated question, the answer to which depends in part on what one's own point of view leads one to look for. For example, an informal census of the first 81 admissions to the University of Oregon Psychology Clinic in 1964 revealed only 2 patients who could be so classified.

when they come to apply these principles to human learning situations, the transition is typically bridged by rather flimsy analogies which ignore crucial differences between the situations, the species, etc. Recently, Underwood (1964) has made the following comments concerning this problem:

Learning theories as developed in the animal-learning laboratory, have never seemed . . . to have relevance to the behavior of a subject in learning a list of paired associates. The emphasis upon the role of a pellet of food or a sip of water in the white rat's acquiring a response somehow never seemed to make contact with the human *S* learning to say VXK when the stimulus DOF was presented [p. 74].

We would add that the relevance is at least equally obscure in applications of traditional S-R reinforcement theory to clinical phenomena.

We do *not* wish, however, to damn any and all attempts to conceptualize clinical phenomena in terms of principles of learning developed outside the clinic. On the contrary, recent work in learning may suggest certain theoretical models which may prove useful in conceptualizing the learning processes involved in psychotherapy and the development of neuroses. Whether these notions can form the basis for a useful learning conceptualization of clinical phenomena will depend upon the ingenuity with which they are subsequently developed and upon their adequacy in encompassing the facts of neurosis and psychotherapy. Further, we would like to stress that their association with experimental work in the field of learning does not give them any a priori scientific status. Their status as explanatory principles in the clinical area must be empirically established within that area. In what follows, then, we will outline some ideas about learning and make some suggestions concerning their relevance to clinical problems.

Our view of learning centers around the concepts of information storage and retrieval. Learning is viewed as the process by which information about the environment is acquired, stored, and categorized. This cognitive view is, of course, quite contrary to the view that learning consists of the acquisition of specific responses; responses, according to our view, are mediated by the nature of the stored information, which may consist of facts or of strategies or programs analogous to the grammar that is acquired in the learning of a language. Thus, "what is learned" may be a system for generating responses as a consequence of the specific information that is stored. This general point of view has been emphasized by Lashley (see Beach et al., 1960), by Miller, Galenter, and Pribram (1960), in the form of the TOTE hypothesis, and by a number of workers in the cognitive learning tradition (Tolman, 1951; Woodworth, 1958). Recently it has even been suggested as a necessary formulation for dealing with that eminently S-R area, motor skills (Adams, 1964; Fitts, 1964).

This conception of learning may be useful in the clinical area in two ways: one, in formulating a theoretical explanation for the acquisition or development of neurosis, symptoms, behavior pathology, and the like, and, two, in conceptualizing psychotherapy as a learning process, and suggesting new methods stemming from this learning model.

A conceptualization of the problem of neurosis in terms of information storage and retrieval is based on the fundamental idea that what is learned in a neurosis is a set of central strategies (or a program) which guide the individual's adaptation to his environment. Neuroses are not symptoms (responses) but are strategies of a particular kind which lead to certain observable (tics, compulsive acts, etc.) and certain other less observable, phenomena (fears, feelings of depression, etc.). The whole problem of symptom substitution is thus seen as an instance of response substitution or response equipotentiality, concepts which are supported by abundant laboratory evidence.

Similarly, the problem of a learning conceptualization of unconscious phenomena may be reopened. Traditional S-R approaches have equated the unconscious with some kind of avoidance of a verbalization response. From our point of view, there is no reason to assume that people can give accurate descriptions of the central strategies mediating much of their behavior any more than a child can give a description of the grammatical rules which govern the understanding and production of his language. As a matter of fact, consciousness may very well be a special or extraordinary case—the rule being "unawareness" of the mediating strategies—which is in need of special explanation, rather than the reverse. This view avoids the cumbersome necessity of having to postulate specific fear experiences or the persistence of anxiety-motivated behavior, as has typically been done by S-R theorists with regard to unconscious phenomena. It also avoids equating the unconscious with the neurotic, which is a virtue since there is so much that goes on within "normal" individuals that they are unaware of. It further avoids the trap of attributing especially persistent and maladaptive consequences to painful experiences. As Solomon (1964) points out, the existing evidence does not support the view that punishment and pain lead unequivocally to anxiety and maladaptive consequences.

The view of learning we have outlined does not supply a set of ready-made answers to clinical problems that can be applied from the laboratory, but it indicates what sort of questions will have to be answered to achieve a meaningful learning conceptualization of neurosis and symptoms. Questions such as "What are the conditions under which strategies are acquired or developed?" stress the fact that these conditions may be quite different from the final observed behavior. That is to say, a particular symptom is not necessarily ac-

quired because of some learning experience in which its stimulus components were associated with pain or fear-producing stimuli. Rather, a symptom may function as an equipotential response, mediated by a central strategy acquired under different circumstances. As an example, consider Harlow's (1958, 1962) monkeys who developed a number of symptoms, the most striking being sexual impotence (a much better animal analogue of human neurosis than those typically cited as experimental neuroses [Liddell, 1944]). Their longitudinal record, or "learning history," indicates that the development of this abnormal "affectional system," as Harlow terms it, is dependent on a variety of nonisomorphic experiences, including the lack of a mother-infant relationship and the lack of a variety of peer-play experiences.

These brief examples are only meant to give a flavor of where a learning conception of neurosis which stresses the acquisition of strategies will lead. A chief advantage of this view is that it has *generality* built in at the core, rather than imported secondarily, as is the case with S-R concepts of stimulus and response generalization.

Let us now turn our attention to the very difficult problem of applying learning concepts to psychotherapy. Basically, we would argue that the development of methods and techniques is largely a function of the empirical skill and ingenuity of the individual-craftsman-therapist. Even a carefully worked-out and well-established set of learning principles (which we do not have at this time) would not necessarily tell us how to modify acquired strategies in the individual case—just as the generally agreed-upon idea that rewards affect performance does not tell us what will be an effective reward in any specific instance.

Bearing these cautions in mind, we might still address ourselves to the question of what applications are suggested by the learning approach we have presented. As a first suggestion, we might consider the analogy of learning a new language. Here we see a process that parallels psychotherapy insofar as it involves modifying or developing a new set of strategies of a pervasive nature. A careful study of the most effective techniques for the learning of a new language might yield some interesting suggestions for psychotherapy. Learning a new language involves the development of a new set of strategies for responding—new syntax as well as new vocabulary. Language learning *may or may not* be facilitated by an intensive attempt to make the individual *aware* of the strategies used, as is done in traditional language instruction which teaches old-fashioned grammar, and as is done, analogously, in those psychotherapies which stress insight. Alternatively, language learning sometimes seems most rapid when the individual is immersed in surroundings (such as a foreign country) where he hears nothing but the new language and where his old strategies and responses are totally ineffective.

Using this as a model for psychotherapy, we might suggest something like the following process: First, a careful study should be done to delineate the "neurotic language," both its vocabulary and its grammar, of the individual. Then a situation might be constructed (e.g., a group therapy situation) in which the individual's existing neurotic language is not understood and in which the individual must develop a new "language," a new set of central strategies, in order to be understood. The detailed working out of such a procedure might very well utilize a number of the techniques that have been found effective in existing therapies, both group and individual, and in addition draw on some new techniques from the fields of psycholinguistics and language learning.

These are, of course, but initial fragmentary guesses, and they may be wrong ones. But we believe that the conceptions on which these guesses are based are sufficiently supported by recent learning research to warrant serious attention. Although this reconceptualization may not lead immediately to the development of effective psychotherapeutic techniques, it may at least provide a first step in that direction.

REFERENCES

ADAMS, J. A. Motor skills. In P. R. Farnsworth (Ed.), *Annual Review of Psychology*, 1964, 15, 181–202.

BAGBY, E. *The psychology of personality*. New York: Holt, 1928.

BANDURA, A. Psychotherapy as a learning process. *Psychological Bulletin*, 1961, 58, 143–159.

BEACH, F. A., HEBB, D. O., MORGAN, C. T., & NISSEN, H. W. *The neuropsychology of Lashley*. New York: McGraw-Hill, 1960.

BERLYNE, D. E. *Conflict, arousal, and curiosity*. New York: McGraw-Hill, 1960.

BLODGETT, H. C. The effect of introduction of reward upon the maze performance of rats. *University of California Publications in Psychology*, 1929, 4, 113–134.

BRELAND, K., & BRELAND, M. The misbehavior of organisms. *American Psychologist*, 1961, 16, 681–684.

BROGDEN, W. J. Sensory preconditioning. *Journal of Experimental Psychology*, 1939, 25, 323–332.

BUGELSKI, B. R. *The psychology of learning*. New York: Holt, 1956.

CHOMSKY, N. Review of B. F. Skinner, *Verbal behavior. Language*, 1959, 35, 26–58.

DEUTSCH, J. A. The inadequacy of Hullian derivations of reasoning and latent learning. *Psychological Review*, 1956, 63, 389–399.

DOLLARD, J., & MILLER, N. E. *Personality and psychotherapy*. New York: McGraw-Hill, 1950.

ERIKSEN, C. W. (Ed.) *Behavior and awareness*. Durham, N. C.: Duke Univer. Press, 1962.

EYSENCK, H. J. (Ed.) *Behavior therapy and the neuroses*. New York: Pergamon Press, 1960.

FAIRWEATHER, G. W. *Social psychology in treating mental illness: An experimental approach*. New York: Wiley, 1964.

FERSTER, C. B., & SKINNER, B. F. *Schedules of reinforcement*. New York: Appleton-Century-Crofts, 1957.

FITTS, P. M. Perceptual-motor skill learning. In A. W. Melton (Ed.), *Categories of hu-*

man learning. New York: Academic Press, 1964. Pp. 244–285.

FRANK, J. D. Problems of controls in psychotherapy as exemplified by the psychotherapy research project of the Phipps Psychiatric Clinic. In E. A. Rubenstein & M. B. Parloff (Eds.), *Research in psychotherapy.* Washington, D.C.: American Psychological Association, 1959.

FRANK, J. D. *Persuasion and healing: A comtive study of psychotherapy.* Baltimore: Johns Hopkins Press, 1961.

FROMM-REICHMANN, FRIEDA. *Principles of intensive psychotherapy.* Chicago: Univer. Chicago Press, 1950.

GIBSON, J. J. *The perception of the visual world.* Boston: Houghton Mifflin, 1950.

GONZALES, R. C., & DIAMOND, L. A. test of Spence's theory of incentive motivation. *American Journal of Psychology,* 1960, 73, 396–403.

GOODWIN, W. R., & LAWRENCE, D. H. The functional independence of two discrimination habits associated with a constant stimulus situation. *Journal of Comparative and Physiological Psychology,* 1955, 48, 437–443.

GROSSBERG, J. M. Behavior therapy: A review. *Psychological Bulletin,* 1964, 62, 73–88.

GUTHRIE, E. R. *The psychology of learning.* New York: Harper, 1935.

GUTTMAN, N. Laws of behavior and facts of perception. In S. Koch (Ed.), *Psychology: A study of a science.* Vol. 5. New York: McGraw-Hill, 1963. Pp. 114–179.

HARLOW, H. F. The nature of love. *American Psychologist,* 1958, 13, 673–685.

HARLOW, H. F. The heterosexual affectional system in monkeys. *American Psychologist,* 1962, 17, 1–9.

HEBB, D. O. *The organization of behavior: A neurophysiological theory.* New York: Wiley, 1949.

HERBERT, M. J., & HARSH, C. M. Observational learning by cats. *Journal of Comparative Psychology,* 1944, 37, 81–95.

HILGARD, E. R. *Theories of learning.* New York: Appleton-Century-Crofts, 1956.

HULL, C. L. *Essentials of behavior.* New Haven: Yale Univer. Press, 1951.

KNIGHT, R. P. Evaluation of the results of psychoanalytic therapy. *American Journal of Psychiatry,* 1941, 98, 434.

KÖHLER, W. *Gestalt psychology.* New York: Liveright, 1929.

KRASNER, L. Studies of the conditioning of verbal behavior. *Psychological Bulletin,* 1958, 55, 148–170.

KRASNER, L. The therapist as a social reinforcement machine. In H. H. Strupp (Ed.), *Second research conference on psychotherapy.* Chapel Hill, N. C.: American Psychological Association, 1961.

KRECHEVSKY, I. The genesis of "hypotheses" in rats. *University of California Publications in Psychology,* 1932, 6, 45–64.

LANG, P. J., & LAZOVIK, A. D. Experimental desensitization of a phobia. *Journal of Abnormal and Social Psychology,* 1963, 66, 519–525.

LAWRENCE, D. H. The nature of a stimulus: Some relationships between learning and perception. In S. Koch (Ed.), *Psychology: A study of a science.* Vol. 5. New York: McGraw-Hill, 1963. Pp. 179–212.

LAWRENCE, D. H., & DeRIVERA, J. Evidence for relational transposition. *Journal of Comparative and Physiological Psychology,* 1954, 47, 465–471.

LAZARUS, A. A. The results of behaviour therapy in 126 cases of severe neurosis. *Behaviour Research and Therapy,* 1963, 1, 69–80.

LAZARUS, A. A., & RACHMAN, S. The use of systematic desensitization in psychotherapy. *South African Medical Journal,* 1957, 32, 934–937.

LEEPER, R. L. Learning and the fields of perception, motivation, and personality. In S. Koch (Ed.), *Psychology: A study of a science.* Vol. 5. New York: McGraw-Hill, 1963. Pp. 365–487.

LEWIN, K. *Field theory in social science.* New York: Harper, 1951. Ch. 4, pp. 60–86.

LIDDELL, H. S. Conditioned reflex method and experimental neurosis. In J. McV. Hunt (Ed.), *Personality and the behavior disorders.* New York: Ronald Press, 1944, Ch. 12.

LUNDIN, R. W. *Personality: An experimental approach.* New York: Macmillan, 1961.

MACKINTOSH, N. J. Extinction of a discrimination habit as a function of overtraining. *Journal of Comparative and Physiological Psychology,* 1963, 56, 842–847.

MILLER, G. A., GALANTER, E. H., & PRIBRAM, K. H. *Plans and the structure of be-*

havior. New York: Holt, Rinehart, & Winston, 1960.

MILLER, N. E. Liberalization of basic S-R concepts: Extension to conflict behavior, motivation, and social learning. In S. Koch (Ed), *Psychology: A study of a science.* Vol. 2. New York: McGraw-Hill, 1959. Pp. 196–292.

MOLTZ, H. Imprinting, empirical basis, and theoretical significance. *Psychological Bulletin,* 1960, 57, 291–314.

MURRAY, E. J. Sociotropic learning approach to psychotherapy. In P. Worchel & D. Byrne (Eds.), *Personality change.* New York: Wiley, 1964. Pp. 249–288.

OLDS, J., & MILNER, P. Positive reinforcement produced by electrical stimulation of septal area and other regions of rat brain. *Journal of Comparative and Physiological Psychology,* 1954, 47, 419–427.

OSGOOD, C. E. *Method and theory in experimental psychology.* New York: Oxford Univer. Press, 1953.

POSTMAN, L. Perception and learning. In S. Koch (Ed.), *Psychology: A study of a science.* Vol. 5. New York: McGraw-Hill, 1963. Pp. 30–113.

RACHMAN, S. The treatment of anxiety and phobic reactions by systematic desensitization psychotherapy. *Journal of Abnormal and Social Psychology,* 1959, 58, 259–263.

RILEY, D. A. The nature of the effective stimulus in animal discrimination learning: Transposition reconsidered. *Psychological Review,* 1958, 65, 1–7.

RITCHIE, B. F., AESCHLIMAN, B., & PEIRCE, P. Studies in spatial learning. VIII. Place performance and the acquisition of place dispositions. *Journal of Comparative and Physiological Psychology,* 1950, 43, 73–85.

ROTTER, J. B. *Social learning and clinical psychology.* New York: Prentice-Hall, 1954.

SCOTT, J. P. Critical periods in behavioral development. *Science,* 1962, 138, 949–958.

SKINNER, B. F. *The behavior of organisms: An experimental analysis.* New York: Appleton-Century-Crofts, 1938.

SKINNER, B. F. *Verbal behavior.* New York: Appleton-Century-Crofts, 1957.

SOLOMON, R. L. Punishment. *American Psychologist,* 1964, 19, 239–253.

SPENCE, K. W. The differential response in animals to stimuli varying within a single dimension. *Psychological Review,* 1937, 44, 430–440.

STRICKLAND, BONNIE R., & CROWNE, D. P. The need for approval and the premature termination of psychotherapy. *Journal of Consulting Psychology,* 1963, 27, 95–101.

THISTLETHWAITE, D. A critical review of latent learning and related experiments. *Psychological Bulletin,* 1951, 48, 97–129.

TOLMAN, E. C. *Purposive behavior in animals and men.* New York: Appleton-Century, 1932.

TOLMAN, E. C. Sign gestalt or conditioned reflex? *Psychological Review,* 1933, 40, 391–411.

TOLMAN, E. C. *Collected papers in psychology.* Berkeley: Univer. California Press, 1951.

TOLMAN, E. C., & HONZIK, C. H. Introduction and removal of reward and maze performance in rats. *University of California Publications in Psychology,* 1930, 4, 257–275.

UNDERWOOD, B. J. The representativeness of rote verbal learning. In A. W. Melton (Ed.), *Categories of human learning.* New York: Academic Press, 1964. Pp. 47–78.

WATSON, A. J. The place of reinforcement in the explanation of behavior. In W. H. Thorpe & O. L. Zangwill, *Current problems in animal behavior.* Cambridge: Cambridge Univer. Press, 1961.

WOLPE, J. *Psychotherapy by reciprocal inhibition.* Palo Alto: Stanford Univer. Press, 1958.

WOLPE, J. Reciprocal inhibition as the main basis of psychotherapeutic effects. In H. J. Eysenck (Ed.), *Behaviour therapy and the neuroses.* New York: Pergamon Press, 1960. Pp. 88–113.

WOLPE, J., SALTER, A., & REYNA, L. J. (Eds.) *The conditioning therapies.* New York: Holt, Rinehart, & Winston, 1964.

WOODWORTH, R. S. *Dynamics of behavior.* New York: Holt, 1958.

YATES, A. J. Symptoms and symptom substitution. *Psychological Review,* 1958, 65, 371–374.

ZENER, K. The significance of behavior accompanying conditioned salivary secretion for theories of the conditioned response. *American Journal of Psychology,* 1937, 50, 384–403.

Experimental Design for Research in Psychotherapy[*]

ALLEN L. EDWARDS
LEE J. CRONBACH

I

One way to evaluate experimental design in research in psychotherapy would be to consider completed studies. At this point, however, there are next to no studies which take advantage of formal experimental design. In the absence of such experience, we can obtain considerable guidance from experiments in psychology and education where similar complexities arise.

The problem of research in therapy is essentially one of evaluating the effect of a treatment, i.e., "How did this procedure change this individual?" Comparable questions are raised whenever a teacher seeks to evaluate the effectiveness of an educational method, and we have a generation of experience of educational research to teach us what mistakes to avoid. Psychology, whether studying the effect of food intake on maze running, the effect of varying amounts of practice on learning, or the effect of a group on an individual's reference frame, is continually examining the consequences of treatments. This cumulated experience with situations, some of which can be well controlled and easily replicated, is a welcome source of light on the present problem, for from the point of view of evaluating the effects of treatments, the problems of research in psychotherapy are fundamentally the same as those of psychology generally.

Special problems do arise in psychotherapy, one of which, for example, relates to the independent-variable complex. Either it is true that more variables interact in individual therapeutic treatment than is customary in experimental psychology, or that we are at present unable to specify the independent variables which account for response to treatment. Thus a study of psy-

Reprinted from *Journal of Clinical Psychology,* 1952, 8, 51–59, with the permission of Frederick C. Thorne and the authors.

* This paper originated in two separate efforts to state whether and how research on psychotherapy can profit from formal experimental design. One author prepared a statement of the advantages of experimental design; the other author developed, for the same symposium, the position that experimental designs had strictly limited usefulness. When, after presenting these statements before the Midwestern Psychological Association, April 27, 1951, the authors continued their discussion, they found themselves in basic agreement on both the positive argument and the warning regarding limitations and misuse, and therefore have collaborated on this joint treatment.

chotherapy cannot rule out a host of disturbing variables in order to concentrate on the significance of one or two. There is no prospect of rising to the level of the rat psychologist's control, where he gets rid of a great deal of genetic variability, for example, by drawing his animals from one purified strain. One of our concerns will be to state how, if at all, such special problems modify the use of formal design in research on therapy.

II

It will clarify the issues if we distinguish four kinds of research, for convenience designated as technique research, survey research, administrative research, and critical research.

Technique research is simply an attempt to get an instrument or operation for gathering data. Berg (1) deals with some of the developments leading to measures of therapeutic process or outcomes, and we need not be concerned with such studies here. Such work is preliminary to experimentation.

Some research can be described as survey research. Survey research often comes very early in the development of a given area. At this stage we are relatively ignorant of possible relationships among our variables and may even lack any knowledge concerning the pertinent variables. In survey research, we collect a lot of data on a lot of variables and then sit down and try to tease out some leads as to what might be important. At this stage we may rely on correlation techniques or on even more simple statistical methods such as counting the number of cases showing a certain behavior.

To illustrate the kind of research for which we use the term "survey," we may point to much of the early work in public opinion. Data were collected on age, sex, region of the country, economic status, religious background, political party affiliation, and what have you, and attempts were then made to determine whether any of these variables might possibly be related to the responses obtained in opinion polls. Comparable work in psychotherapy is seen, for example, when someone studies the records of psychoanalytic cases to see what background differences may exist between the improved and unimproved patients. Survey research is a necessary preliminary mapping stage, and not to be disparaged. It is, however, emphatically preliminary to the more delicate and enlightening analysis an experiment offers. It is one thing to find superior socio-economic status correlated with academic achievement, quite another and more difficult task to pursue this lead to more basic causes of the correspondence.

A third kind of research problem is administrative or applied research (although admittedly survey research is often practical in aim). Applied research is concerned with obtaining an answer to one or more specific practical questions upon which, usually, some administrative decision is to be based. Countless examples of this sort of research may be found in the volume on Mass Communication by Hovland and others (9). Administrative research often involves experimental design.

An even greater dependence on experimental design characterizes the fourth type of research which, for want of a better name, we call critical research. Critical research is research also designed to answer one or more questions. The nature of the questions, however, stems from theoretical considerations rather than from practical considerations. In critical research, theory should indicate to us the nature of the answers to the questions we raise before the experiment is actually conducted. The research itself is primarily a check upon the answers to which theory has led us, or shows the correct one among several explicit answers possible within the theory.

Studies of psychotherapy are usually intended to answer questions of the administrative or critical types, either to advise regarding a practical procedure or to unfold the causes of personality change. Such studies draw upon technique research for methods, and upon survey research for suggestions as to hypotheses. In each case, the investigation begins as a variant of the question: "Is Method A better than Method B?" If the question is stated so baldly, it is inappropriate for research. To obtain an answerable problem, the criterion must be carefully defined, the method must be specified, and the range of persons and conditions to be considered must be identified. As one specifies these variables he makes it clear whether he is doing administrative research on a local problem or more generalized critical research. And this in turn influences the experimental design.

III

The clinical investigator is convinced that his problems are unusually complex and this complexity is usually seen to lie in the large number of variables that may be relevant to a given problem. Perhaps some of the difficulties can be formulated in terms of three categories of variables: the stimulus variables, response variables and organismic variables. There should be no confusion of meaning over our use of *stimulus* and *response*—if you prefer substitute *situation* and *behavior*. By an organismic variable, we mean some property or attribute of the individual. Hair color, height, and age are convenient examples. Organismic variables may often be inferred from observations of previous response or from knowledge of previous experience. For example, in a given research problem, intelligence level may be considered an organismic variable, despite the fact that it is known from previous observations of response. Other examples will come to mind: We can classify individuals as Democrats and Republicans, as schizoids and manics, as men or women, and so on. Each of these, in a given investigation, may be an organismic variable. There would be no objection to the substitution of the term *person variable* for *organismic variable* (Wat-

son's "patient variables" (11) include variables which our approach forces us to divide between the *organismic* and *response* categories.)

Psychological research problems can now be viewed in terms of various permutations and combinations of one or more of these variables. To begin any research, the investigator first attempts to consider the variables which may be pertinent, including any in which he happens to be interested. He might then indulge in a little speculation and theorizing as to the nature of the relationships that exist among these variables. And before he begins any research he would, of course, have to face the very important problems of observing, recording, and if possible quantifying these variables. We should keep in mind, however, that some of the variables in which we are interested are not quantitative but instead qualitative, as for example when we are interested in two qualitatively different methods of teaching or in two methods of therapy.

At this point we can examine past studies for their lessons to the therapist. The first problems to consider relate to the organismic variables. Educators spent a generation on studies of the oversimplified "Is A better than B?" type. They sought to settle by experimentation whether large classes were better than small, lectures better than laboratories, frequent tests better than few. Their studies led to endless contradiction because, as you will notice, the question did not specify the organismic variables.

Now, one way to get past this problem is by delimitation. Suppose our investigator wishes to know which of two methods of teaching arithmetic is better. If we ask, we perhaps find that he will be content if he can answer the question as it relates to eighth graders. Granted unlimited resources, this might be investigated in a general way, but the question is not worth answering! For every study in education which has gathered sufficient data finds that the method which works best for some pupils is inferior for others. There is a thorough study by Brownell and Moser (3) who gathered enough data (1400 cases in 4 communities) to demonstrate what a tiny batch of responses usually conceals. They compared (*inter alia*) a meaningful method and a rote method for teaching borrowing in third grade subtraction. On the average the meaningful method was better; but in some schools the rote method proved superior because pupils had no general understanding of the number system, had never learned to reason in arithmetic, and could not follow the meanings presented. Only by organizing their design so that cases were classified on this organismic variable, i.e. nature of previous work in arithmetic, could Brownell and Moser get at the true relation. The relation had to be represented in the original design in the form of a stratifying or control variable. Another study by Anderson (10) showed that his Method A was better than B for bright, mediocre achievers, but that B was better for those of mediocre intelligence but good past achievement. The inclusion of both organismic variables in the design was essential if he was not to reach an oversimple, hence untrue, conclusion.

It follows that simple delimitation is often not enough, except for some administrative studies where we are content with an actuarial estimate that for the local sample one method tends to work better, on the whole, than the other. The proper proposal in the face of this difficulty is that cases should be described in terms of the largest possible number of organismic variables. Wherever possible these should be accurately measured. Second, the most promising (i.e., most likely to be relevant) variables should be built into the design so that gains can be assessed separately for each variable.

IV

Let us now consider an experimental design which will permit not only an answer to a question concerning the overall effectiveness of two methods of therapy, but also to the question of whether there is any differential in response of two groups of patients (say, those with a high degree of initial disturbance and those with a low degree) to the two methods of therapy. This type of design is called a factorial design. A factorial design is one in which we have two or more variables each varied in two or more ways and studied in all possible combinations.

If we use a factorial design for the problem at hand, the discrepancies in response between the two types of patients, if such discrepancies exist, will show up in a significant interaction. We set up a 2 x 2 table in which the top entries are Methods A and B. The side entries correspond to our high and low degrees of emotional disturbance. In each of the four cells of this table, we may enter the mean score on the response variable for a particular set of observations.

Method

	A	B
High disturbance	6	6
Low disturbance	12	8

Now a significant interaction might show up in a number of different ways. For example, we might find, as our hypothetical entries suggest, that the mean score for the more disturbed patients is much the same regardless of the method of therapy. For the less disturbed patients, perhaps Method A is the more effective. A different significant interaction might be found if, for example, the more disturbed patients respond very well to one of the methods, whereas the less disturbed patients respond very well to the other method. Various other possibilities might produce a significant interaction also. A factorial design permits a test of significance of any interactions in the variables investigated, as well as a test of significance of the main effects. It is for this reason that factorial designs should prove to be extremely useful in research in psychology and psychotherapy and superior to a simpler matched-group comparison in which all Method A cases are treated together.

This poses a new problem: how is the clinician to isolate effects among dozens of variables, many of them qualitative, when he usually has few cases to start with? If n variables are represented in the design, and each of these is represented as a dichotomy, then 2×2^n cases are required for a complete design. Hence 5 control variables call for 64 cases, 2 each of 32 specified types, assuming that all main effects and higher-order interactions are to be investigated.

There is some difference in the views of the writers here. Cronbach sees the number of relevant variables in the clinical study as likely to be so large that enough cases to account for them all will almost never be available. Edwards thinks a few well chosen organismic variables will clarify therapeutic conclusions and that in long range research the specified types to complete the cells of more complex factorial designs can be obtained. The writers agree that effort to isolate effects due to organismic variables can have only a beneficial effect and that cases should be selected to represent as much variation as can be. It is far more valuable to study ten cases, two each of five identifiable subtypes, than to study a pool of fifty undescribed and undifferentiated people.

The considerations that apply to organismic variables apply also to situational variables. It is well known that diagnoses vary with the hospital, and very likely so do the ways the treatments are applied. Educational studies have found it necessary to give constant attention to the interaction between the teacher's feeling about a new method and his effectiveness in using it. Surely the therapist is a significant variable to be used in building the design. Witness Dressel and Matteson (5), who found that counselees who interpreted their own tests gained more than those who were told what the scores meant—but this result was entirely accounted for by differences *between counselors* rather than by any differences between methods. This could never have been known except for care in including several cases per counselor (two, as before, being the minimum to consider).

It seems obvious at this point that simple comparisons of A *vs* B may often be relatively worthless, and that comparisons gain value as the design isolates the specific types of persons and situations for which A is superior. The investigator whose data are meagre should nonetheless organize them to search for such internal effects rather than test merely the overall difference, which, like any actuarial result, depends mostly on the composition of the sample. *If it is necessary to restrict a study to a single condition or situation, and to a few subjects, the results have maximum value when the situation is described in detail and the subjects are selected to be homogeneous on as many organismic variables as possible.*

V

Designs for research in psychotherapy call for more complex treatment of response variables than we have generally seen. Educational experience is again a case in point: studies that "prove" method A is superior to B may give different results if gains are evaluated in a different way. The classic idea of experimental design involves an experimental and control group which are compared on a single variable, but both the educator and the clinician are trying to alter a complex configuration in many ways. In evaluating guidance some investigator might propose to measure how the client feels about his problem after counseling. This is relevant evidence, but it is equally important to know if the client has learned new ways of thinking about himself that will help him solve later problems.

The necessity of evaluating change in many dimensions is well shown by Brownell and Moser (3), who found that limited evaluation resulted in prior investigators' recommending what actually turned out to be the poorer of two methods. For years the evidence had piled up that people who learned to substract by borrowing were slower than those who learned the so-called additive method. Brownell and Moser then taught children in Grade III in many schools by one of four methods: Borrowing-Rote, Borrowing-Meaningful, Additive-Rote, or Additive-Meaningful. The rote method meant that the skill was demonstrated and practiced, where the meaningful method put stress on analysis of reasons for the procedures. When they measured outcomes in terms of speed of substraction after training, Additive-Rote was as good as either Borrowing method. Additive-Meaningful gave poor results because the method could not be grasped by children. When the familiar speed test was supplemented by other measures, however, Borrowing-Meaningful came out well ahead of Additive- or Borrowing-Rote. This was true for delayed tests to measure retention, and for tests requiring transfer of the method to new types of problems like subtracting fractions. No doubt about it, Borrowing-Meaningful was the method which best set the stage for further learning, but this would never have been discovered if speed of performance had been the only criterion. A sidelight is that this method worked best in schools where previous arithmetic was taught meaningfully; it was hard to put over any method to those children by rote because they kept insisting on explanations. And the meanings were hard to introduce where all previous work had been by rote. Does this suggest that one experience in nondirective therapy establishes readiness for more such therapy, but that one directive treatment makes response to nondirective less likely? These are the sorts of conditions that must be considered in explaining results. Note, though, that Brownell and Moser would never have nailed down their conclusions by formal experiment if they had not, from thinking, reached these conclusions *before* doing the experiment.

Again one solution to the problem posed by multiple response variables is to delimit. The investigator is within his rights if he says he is concerned with one and only one type of change, leaving evaluation on the next variable to others. Unfortunately some investigators choose a single index without clearly realizing that other measures of movement would yield different conclusions. Where the investigator does not overgeneralize, the reader may be the one who assumes that the single index has demonstrated all-round improvement. There is an even stronger argument for multiple measurement. In research on counseling and therapy the costs of measurement are trival compared to other effort in setting up and carrying out the investigation. Finding enough cases of a certain type is often so hard that only a single study can be performed. Keeping the subjects for a long term, making transcriptions or extensive notes on therapy, and maintaining uniform conditions of treatment—these are so difficult and expensive that it is foolish to skimp on evaluation when a few more hours of testing are feasible. The information gained from an experiment mounts more or less in proportion to *factorial n,* where n is the number of uncorrelated response variables. By this estimate 5 tests can report 120 times as much knowledge as a single test in the same investigation!

Before examining how to treat multiple outcomes, we should mention another point, the importance of accuracy in assessment. When the outcomes are measured on a brief and unreliable test, or when subjective judgments of personality introduce inaccuracy, errors of measurement tend to obscure true differences. In this event, investigators are prone to accept the null hypothesis and not realize that a true difference may be concealed by their inadequate technique. Effort to refine measurement has the same beneficial effect on the power of an investigation as adding to the number of cases; the fanciest and largest study can be no better than the evaluating tools.

VI

Suppose an investigator is resolved to assess several response variables; how can his design be fitted to this intention? At this point the theory of experimental design necessitates treating a study with five assessed outcomes as five separate investigations, one for each variable.* Some investigators have tried to keep broad measures and yet stay within conventional statistics by pouring their data into a single overall index of adjustment. This is not recommended, for such an index blurs together the strengths and weaknesses of each method and provides no guide for improvement. Experience in predicting teacher success is a case in point. Hundreds of studies produced negligible correlations or contradictory results, so long as a global rating of success was the criterion. As soon as investigators went to more specific criteria which dealt with *aspects* of the teacher's performance, they began to get appreciable validities. A criterion of the teacher's rapport with pupils is predictable at a respectable level, where a mixed criterion lumping intellectual, emotional, and administrative contributions is not predictable. In therapy, an overall index is not a good criterion if the progress of a patient away from anxiety is concealed by negative scores assigned for an increase in expressed aggression.

The clinical investigator is frequently concerned with configurational changes: he wants to know if enhanced self-acceptance and greater obedience to social requirements go together in the same person, or whether the therapy increases one or the other. Either of these patterns could account for significant differences for the patients as a group in the two variables treated singly. Here an answer might be to define the configuration in advance as a pattern of two variables and measure that pattern as a single variable. The trouble is that the number of possibly important configurations is large, and that multiple significance tests raise the bogy of inflation of probabilities.

If there is one significance test, a P of .05 will arise 5 times per 100 experiments. If there are five such tests in an experiment, such a P arises 25 times in 100 experiments. The more tests that are made the more likely it is that some differences really due to sampling variations will seem to be significant. This requires the investigator to become more conservative in his inferences, and so he must now regard with suspicion a borderline-significant result which he would ordinarily accept if only one test had been given. The writers have separately discussed this problem elsewhere (4, 6). In effect, the introduction of more variables requires the investigator to use more cases to maintain the same sensitivity.

VII

All the foregoing comments point in the same direction: to take advantage of experimental design the investigator must have a clear idea in advance of the investigation as to what effects he expects to find. He must have some fairly sound insights as to what variables of all three types are relevant so that he can measure them and base the design on them. Wherever he ignores a relevant situation or organismic variable he increases his error term and hides significant effects. Wherever he includes a variable which is irrelevant, he unnecessarily inflates his probabilities and sacrifices the possibility of using the same effort on a more relevant variable. There is a paradox in this. The person who understands his phenomenon thoroughly can produce the best experimental design, but the

---

* Methods permitting treatment of several variables at once are beginning to be developed, a notable example being the procedure for treatment of patterns proposed by Block, Levine, and Mc-Nemar (2).

person who needs the experimental information is the one who does not understand his phenomenon. Thus the critical experiment, and even the applied experiment, depend for their effectiveness on the adequacy of the technique research and survey research which precedes them. The experiment confirms or denies specific hypotheses, but the experimental design does not produce hypotheses. An experiment designed to nail down a certain suspected effect can, however, be used for exploration and identification of hypotheses for the next experiment.

The statistical methods and formal tests of hypotheses are the tool of the cautious, tough-minded, hard-to-convince scientist. Every research worker has to have two personalities if he is to get the most good from his data. He must be the rigorous tester who believes nothing without conclusive evidence, when he is deciding what relations are to be admitted as proven facts. At this stage, he relies on significance tests and will not admit the validity of any hypothesis that does not yield a significant result. But if he proceeds to dismiss all such hypotheses, to conclude that "there is nothing in the idea", he makes what statisticians call an error of the second kind. The naive observer makes "errors of the first kind" by being too believing. The person who discards the unproven ideas makes the error of ignoring real relationships which his experiment is not powerful enough to bring out. So after the tough-minded half of the investigator's personality has accepted what it will from the study, he must turn loose the inquiring, speculative, and tender-minded half which is willing to entertain doubtful ideas. If this tender-minded soul is gullible, *believing* in what has met no significance test, he will end with a science stuffed with superstitions. But if he holds these yet-unproven ideas in the air, as notions which may guide him in the next experiment or the treatment of the next patient, he is more likely to be correct than the man who

casts the idea from his mind as soon as one experiment fails to provide significant confirmation.

A genuine relationship may yield a nonsignificant difference for several reasons. One is that too few cases were used in testing it, so that sampling errors obscured a real difference. Second errors of measurement have a similar effect. Thirdly, even when a new technique (say, of therapy) is based on a superior concept, it is likely to be used inefficiently in its first trials, so that its advantage over other approaches will be obscured by technical faults in its application. These are the factors our tender-minded, but not therefore unscientific, investigator bears in mind. He stresses that "not statistically significant"—like the Scotch verdict "not proven"—permits us to return the hypothesis on trial to the arms of those who love it, rather than at once chopping off its head.

VIII

So firmly have some investigators been convinced of the merit of statistical control that they regard their work as finished when the formally stated hypothesis has been fitted with a statement that P is or is not greater than .05. At the extreme, one psychological journal has the official policy of discouraging discussion of individual cases or other conditions not treated in the experimental design. But in research on psychotherapy, and in clinical problems generally, the time for such total reliance on formal analysis has not arrived. Once the significance tests are made on the hypotheses stated in advance, the investigator is ready to put his intelligence to work extracting new hypotheses from the data. The virtue of statistics, and their great defect, is that they are blind and unintelligent. They are therefore impartial and are not distracted by the broad scene; so they are marvelous for isolating and answering a narrow question. In a field where the significant narrow questions are unknown, we need explorers who go in with their eyes wide open, look at everything, and narrow their hypotheses in terms of what makes sense. Statistics never have to make sense. No amount of statistics could have done anything with the information that poured into Darwin's eyes on the voyage of the *Beagle*. Only after he had sifted it through a process much like clinical integration could biologists ask simple enough questions for statistics to be of help. Mathematical genetics is a later development, possible only after many important gross questions were cleared up.

There is the hope of including many of the relevant stimulus and organismic variables in the experimental plan, but literally thousands of such variables can be recorded in a case history and a transcript of therapy. These data are unused so far as the formal design is concerned, and go to waste unless the investigator looks through them with his eyes open. If the investigator studies the cases where the treatment worked better than usual for others of the same supposed type, he may discover a new factor, previously ignored, that facilitates treatment. Conversely, when some method works poorly, the question is, "What went wrong?" At this point a study of the process of the therapy, or of the subject's initial status, may show where difficulties and resistance came in. If the investigator can put his finger on a possible fault in the method, he is ready to do a new study in which the fault is corrected. Or he may find that conditions not under experimental control piled up in a way which handicapped the method under trial. If this happened, it would be important to repeat the experiment even if the statistical analysis indicated the method was a poor one. (An example of this sort of inspection of relevant data not in the original design is found in a study of the effect of thiamine on human learning (8). With 37 experimental subjects, there happened to be eight cases of traumatic difficulty during the study: sinusitis, boils on the writing arm, vomiting,

schizoid hallucination. Only one such interference appeared in the control group. The investigator properly saw this as a "levelling effect" to consider in interpretation.)

Some students seem to think it highly questionable to use "intuitive" (i.e., intelligent) methods to analyze data once the statistical ritual is completed. Perhaps this timidity can be allayed by demonstrating how a topnotch statistician does research. The problem was one in agriculture, and the investigator no less than R.A. Fisher (7). He had a fine criterion, yield of wheat in bushels per acre. He found that after he controlled variety, and fertilizer, there was considerable variation from year to year. This variation had a slow up-and-down cycle over a seventy-year period. Now Fisher set himself on the trail of the residual variation. First he studied wheat records from other sections to see if they had the trend; they did not. He considered and ruled out rainfall as an explanation. Then he started reading the records of the plots and found weeds a possible factor. He considered the nature of each species of weed and found that the response of specific weed varieties to rainfall and cultivation accounted for much of the cycle. But the large trends were not explained until he showed that the upsurge of weeds after 1875 coincided with a school-attendance act which removed cheap labor from the fields, and that another cycle coincided with the retirement of a superintendent who made weed removal his personal concern. Here we see a statistician accounting to his satisfaction for every systematic variation in his response variables, even if he has to consider the idiosyncracies of weed species and supervisors to do it. This is the way the clinical investigator should proceed if he is to get from the stage where he takes pride in *any* detectable difference to the stage where he can predict in advance the response of most patients to his treatment.

Now it is highly dangerous, having searched one's data for configurations and trends, to trust one's conclusions. Fisher could trust his because he had many confirming facts to support his final synthesis, and occasionally a clinician is in the same fortunate position. Because there are a huge variety of configurations in such a mass of data as the clinical researcher possesses, some plausible explanations will surely appear, but not all of them would be confirmed in a subsequent sample of cases. Hence what one arrives at by these intelligent explorations is *a posteriori* hypotheses in which the investigator may have faith but which require a new experiment before he can have scientific confidence. The experiment gives definitive results on the question it is designed to answer, but not on the questions that occur to you after you have peeked at the data.

IX

The writers differ to some degree on their view of the place of experimental design in therapy. Edwards is inclined to expect great advances to be made by identifying the major nomothetic organismic, stimulus, and response variables and then efficiently assessing therapeutic methods with formally designed experiments based on these. Cronbach is inclined to doubt that any limited number of nomothetic variables will account for much of the variation in response to therapy. We both feel that clinical research is now in need of good hypotheses to test, rather than of finer tests of hypotheses. But this is a question of timing, for early in a science finding hypotheses is primary; this exploratory stage has to be superseded by careful experimental confirmation.

On practical recommendations we are also agreed. Formal design has a major contribution to make when one has a good hypothesis. Even when the hypothesis is worthless, formal design organizes the data so that intelligent speculation can proceed faster. We are further agreed that it is grossly wasteful to close up shop, having once confirmed one's hypothesis, without

examining all the additional variation in the results which the hypothesis left unexplained. The graduate student doing a study is usually very much concerned about his significance tests. If he can report that A is better than B ($P < .05$) he is ready to pack up his degree and go home. In fact, since this finding asks no new questions, that is all he can do. If instead, he treats his data with more intelligence and looks beyond his statistics to see what the case records show, he will come out of the study with more questions than he went in with. And the highest function of research is to help us ask better questions in our next study.

By building a properly complex formal design around a limited number of presumably important stimulus, organismic, and response variables, the investigator may ask a certain number of specific questions regarding their interactions. The formal design asks these in a very efficient manner. Then if the records contain additional facts about other variables, the failure to include them in the design means that the investigator has not asked a scientifically answerable question regarding them. The exploratory phase which follows the planned significance test weighs these added variables to see if any of them, alone or in combination, seem important. Thus the exploratory phase of research is trying to find out what questions the next experiment should ask. Exploration and intelligent analysis are no substitute, however, for that next experiment which gives scientific legitimacy to the relationship suspected.

REFERENCES

1. BERG, IRWIN A. This symposium.
2. BLOCK, JACK; LEVINE, LOUIS, and MCNEMAR, QUINN. Testing for the existence of psychometric patterns. *J. abnorm. soc. Psychol.*, 1951, 46, 356–359.
3. BROWNELL, WILLIAM A. and MOSER, HAROLD E. *Meaningful vs. Mechanical Learning:* A Study in Grade III Subtrac-

tion. Duke University Research Studies in Education, No. 8. 1949, pp. xvi + 207.

4. CRONBACH, LEE J. Statistical methods applied to Rorschach scores: a review. *Psychol. Bull.*, 1949, 46, 393–429.

5. DRESSEL, PAUL L. and MATTESON, ROSS W. The effect of client participation in test interpretation. *Educ. Psychol. Meas.*, 1950, 10, 693–706.

6. EDWARDS, ALLEN. *Statistical Analysis for Students in Psychology and Education.* New York: Rinehart and Co., 1946, Pp. 201–202.

7. FISHER, R. A. Studies in crop variation. I. An examination of the yield of dressed grain from Broadbalk. *J. Agricultural Science,* 1920, 11, Pt. II, 107–135.

8. HARRELL, RUTH F. *Effects of Added Thiamine on Learning.* Teachers College Contributions to Education, No. 877. New York: Columbia University, 1943.

9. HOVLAND, CARL I., LUMSDAINE, ARTHUR A., and SHEFFIELD, FRED A. *Experiments on Mass Communication,* Vol. 3. Princeton: Princeton University Press, 1949.

10. SWENSON, ESTHER J., ANDERSON, G. LESTER, and STACY, CHALMERS L. *Learning Theory in School Situations.* Minneapolis: University of Minnesota Press, 1949, p. 103.

11. WATSON, ROBERT I. This symposium.

Toward an Integrated Program of Research on Psychotherapy[1]

J. McV. HUNT

It is generally agreed that the number of persons in English-speaking America who seek professional help for personal problems has been increasing rapidly. It is often argued that this increased seeking represents increased human need, that more people are unhappy, and that American life has become increasingly unsatisfying. On the contrary, one may also argue that this increased seeking for such help is based on a growing prevalence of the hope and belief that such professional persons as social workers, psychiatrists, and psychologists *can* help. From this standpoint, it is demand, in the economic sense, that is changing rather than the number of troubled people. Distinguishing with measuring operations between "need" and "demand" is an unsolved problem of considerable importance for social interpretations. Whether this increased seeking represents need or demand, however, it stresses the importance of understanding these personal problems, of increasing our knowledge of the techniques for helping people with them, and of the results obtained with existing techniques.

The most common helping method involves one person, a professional, consciously using his speech and gestures to develop a social relationship, a social relationship aimed at providing a corrective experience, with another person, his client. This is a broad definition for the helping techniques which may be subsumed under the general term psychotherapy. Their use is shared professionally by social work, guidance, the ministry, psychiatry, psychology, and occasionally by other professional groups. Needless to say here, this helping situation has provided much of our present information about personality development and dynamics. Psychotherapy has been and will continue to be a kind of window to the soul of man. But it is not with psychotherapy as a research tool that

Reprinted from *Journal of Consulting Psychology,* 1952, 16 (4), 237–246, with the permission of the American Psychological Association and the author.

[1] This paper, presented as the address of the president of the Division of Personality and Social Psychology at the meetings of the American Psychological Association in Chicago, September 1, 1951, was prepared while the author as director of the Institute of Welfare Research, Community Service Society of New York. He wishes to express his appreciation to the Community Service Society, the Rockefeller Foundation, the Carnegie Corporation, and the Davella Mills Foundation for support of the research program of the Institute. This research program provided him with the experience out of which the ideas expressed here were derived.

this paper is concerned. It outlines some thoughts about what we know and do not know about the psychotherapies as helping techniques and especially about their results. In it I wish (*a*) to outline the nature of our information and ignorance about their results, (*b*) to call attention to the segmental and piecemeal nature of nearly all of our current research concerning them, (*c*) to indicate what an integrated approach might be like, and (*d*) to point to both the difficulties and to the factors leading me to hope that an integrated approach may be feasible.

WHAT WE KNOW OF RESULTS

What we know about the "results" of the psychotherapies is very largely limited to attempts to answer what one may call the first evaluative question [10, p. 38], namely, is there improvement in the person associated with his receiving help? Our published information consists of percentages of the individuals improved or improved to various degrees. The most common measure of improvement is an evaluative judgment of change in the client or patient by a psychotherapist during the course of the therapeutic contact. This is true, for example, for psychoanalytic therapy with individuals diagnosed psychoneurotic. As surveyed by Knight [15] the percentage of at least "somewhat improved" is either 92 or 66 depending on whether or not one eliminates from the denominator those patients who discontinued treatment against the psychoanalyst's advice. Wilder [31] argues, and I would agree, that they should not be eliminated from the denominator. It is also true for psychotherapy in outpatient mental hygiene clinics. Wilder [31] reports the percentages of psychoneurotics improved at the time of discharge, for samples from different clinics, varying from 40 to 83 with the mode at approximately 50 per cent. For family casework, which by our definition is largely psychotherapy, the percentages improving range from 60 to somewhat more than 70 per cent [7, 10, 28]. For marriage counseling [8] the percentage improved approximates 67. It should be noted that a figure of about two-thirds improved is exceedingly common for the psychotherapies.

In a few instances our information consists of percentages of individuals showing improvement in their adjustive status as between the time they sought or were referred for help and the time of a follow-up study. Here again the measure is judgmental, but the judgment is usually made by the follow-up interviewer instead of the psychotherapist. An example is the group of follow-up studies of the results of child-guidance clinics supervised by Helen Witmer [33]. From these, the composite percentage of children judged to be improved approximates 75. For a third of *these improving* (25 per cent of the samples followed up), the original problem had disappeared and no new problems had appeared; the child had friends, his school work was consistent with his ability, he was a steady, reliable, and interested worker or student, and at home he was a friendly, cooperative member of the family. For the other two-thirds of those improving, the level of social adjustment at follow up was less desirable.

During the last decade, in what is probably the most vigorous research program in this area, but where the emphasis is more on process than results, Rogers [25, 26] and his students have devised several measures of change in the content of what a client says as nondirective or client-centered psychotherapy progresses. One example is a measure of change in what Raimy [24] calls the self-reference. This particular measure, deriving from phenomenological theory [30], has been shown by both Raimy [24] and Kogan and Horowitz [9] to be essentially the same as the Distress-Relief Quotient, devised by Dollard and Mowrer [3], which derives from learning theory. It is still an open question whether or not such measures of change in process will predict changes in social behavior, client reports of distress relieved, or change in social acceptability.

Recent years have also brought attempts to measure the change in persons associated with psychotherapy by means of such clinical tools as the Rorschach test. Witness, for example, Muench's [22] study of nondirective psychotherapy by means of the Rorschach. The validity of such measures for the purpose must also be established. Who knows how well changes in Rorschach will predict changes in social behavior, reports of distress relieved, and social acceptability?

WHAT WE DO NOT KNOW

This is an incomplete account designed only to indicate the general nature of what we know about results.[2] The variation in the percentages of clients improving may be related to several uncontrolled factors:

1. The unreliability or difference in the judgmental standards by which the various samples were judged;

2. The unreliability of diagnosis or the variety of persons-with-problems;

3. The nature and skill of the psychotherapists; and

4. Of no mean import, to the variety of ways in which the samples were limited, e.g., (a) to all those applying for help and undertaking to start psychotherapy [Heckman and Stone, 7], (b) to only those for whom psychotherapy was completed in the judgment of the psychotherapist [Knight, 15], or (c) to whatever intermediate between these two extremes.

But I wish to call your attention to the relatively obvious, but too frequently unrecognized, fact that were all these factors controlled, we should still have information only about the first evaluative question [10, p. 38], namely, is there change associated

with receiving psychotherapy? There need be no causal relationship, and the term *results* is logically an exaggeration.

In view of the infrequency with which one sees or hears it, perhaps elaboration of this argument may be useful. The fact that improvement is associated with receiving psychotherapy in a fairly high proportion of individuals (two-thirds appears to be the most repetitive figure) argues that psychotherapy *may* be getting some desired results. If, on the contrary, no one improved, we could conclude that there were no desired results. On the other hand, ever though neurotic and psychotic disorders tend to be seen theoretically as perversions of the normal adjustive process whereby distress from any source tends to set in motion processes that mitigate that distress, most of us have known both neurotics and psychotics (even schizophrenics) who appear to have recovered when no one was making any attempt to help them. Furthermore, Landis [17] has found that remission rates from psychopathic hospitals have changed very little during the last century even though the amount of psychotherapeutic effort has increased considerably. Thus, until we find out how frequently the changes associated with psychotherapy would occur *without* it, we cannot logically attribute them to psychotherapy.

THE NEED FOR CONTROL GROUPS

From a methodological standpoint, it is precisely here that the case method, indigenous to all psychotherapies, breaks down. For all the talk about idiographic and nomothetic psychology, I believe we must accept the dictum that it is impossible to repeat, and thereby test, the reproducibility of the psychotherapeutic action with one individual. We must, therefore, employ the statistics deriving from groups of individuals if we are to get any empirical test of hypotheses about causal relations between psychotherapy and change in clients or patients.

---

[2] More recent studies of the results of psychotherapy with methods not illustrated here are presented in *Psychotherapy: A symposium on theory and research* [21].

At this point, let me digress back to the importance of knowing to what degree the psychotherapies get results. I suspect that we psychologists may be responsible to a considerable degree for the increased demand for professional help with personal problems. More and more students are taking our courses. They hear our explanations of personality dynamics. They are exposed to case studies, all too often unconsciously selected because "the client lived happily ever after" treatment. From this standpoint, the college teaching of psychology becomes a mighty agency for advertising psychotherapeutic wares. Moreover, it is very easy to link these wares to our humanistic tradition. It then becomes the responsibility of society to supply psychotherapeutic aids. These wares of ours, which we share with our associated professions, are thereby removed from even the economic checks of the market place. These facts emphasize our professional responsibility to our society to know whether or not and to what degree the psychotherapies get results.[3] In finding out, we should be even more concerned to learn as much as we can about what kind of psychotherapy works best for what kind of client.

The impossibility of testing the reproducibility of psychotherapy with any single case, as I have just pointed out, forces us to depend methodologically upon the use of statistics deriving from groups. Control-group design is the most obvious answer, but it affords practical difficulties and its piecemeal nature leaves considerable to be desired. Ordinary control-group design cannot answer questions about what kinds of psychotherapy work best with what kinds of clients.

The practical difficulties abide in the conflict between our humanitarian desire to help the afflicted and the logical requirement that the experimental (psychotherapy receiving) and control groups be statistically equivalent. Any planned interference with giving help to those who are suffering and asking for help is contrary to our basic concern for the worth of each individual. Yet, is there any more suitable or feasible way to make groups statistically equivalent than to select them randomly from a population? Operationally this would mean withholding help by arbitrary turn from some previously decided proportion of those seeking.[4] The most serious attempt of this kind of which I know is that in the Cambridge-Somerville Youth Study. This attempt was concerned with help designed to prevent rather than to cure [23]. Moreover, it was not entirely successful because those in the control group all too often received help from other agencies. Withholding help appears especially bad to most psychotherapists because their very occupation almost demands that they be well convinced about the efficacy of the help they give. Thus, the desire of psychotherapists to be of help coupled with their professional convictions stand as a serious obstacle in the way of a direct experimental approach to increasing knowledge about the results of psychotherapy.

Nature, however, has provided ways to avoid this obstacle in research on psychotherapy that correspond somewhat with the circumstances used for the testing of hypotheses in such fields as astronomy and geology. For instance, seldom can the centers offering psychotherapy give the kind

---

[3] I am using the term *results* broadly. It need not be limited to so-called "cures" wherein the treated person becomes undistinguishable from healthy people of his social and work-group. It need not even be limited to discernible improvement in treated persons. It can also include absence of deterioration in those for whom deterioration was expected and for whom the treatment was aimed only as sustaining them through a crisis. I should want to detect this absence of deterioration, however, as less frequent deterioration among treated groups than among similar groups untreated.

---

[4] It is sometimes suggested that those who apply but do not return for psychotherapy after the intake interview be utilized as the control. This is not logically feasible because, in failing to return or in deciding not to return, these people are essentially different from those who continue "seeking help."

and amount of help they would wish to give to all the individuals who apply. At present, those who are judged to be most in need are given the best trained and most experienced psychotherapists, be they social caseworkers, psychologists, or psychiatrists. Or, those judged to be most in need receive the larger portions of the therapists' time. One need only turn skeptical of the validity of these diagnostic judgments of need to justify the process of randomizing, that is, assigning applicants to the various therapists in some arbitrary order.

In one general hospital, the medical social workers who face such a situation are considering a randomizing procedure whereby an arbitrary portion of patients selected by arbitrary turn will have the help of relatively untrained receptionists while the others will receive the help of the most skilled medical social workers obtainable. Here the independent variable will be the training and experience (presumably skill) of those attempting to help patients.

On the other hand, I see little chance of even such "natural" substitutes for the classical experiment getting done except in a few places where the administrator of the helping agency is imbued with the skepticism of a scientist and can thereby feel ethically free, or better, ethically bound to conduct such a procedure rigorously. I believe this will be done only seldom because the typical practitioner sees in such "control-group" design an answer only to a question for which he is convinced that he already has the answer, and no answer to the question for which he eagerly seeks one. To be concretely explicit, he tends already to be sure that the training and experience of the therapist make a difference to the patient. What he wants to know is: what kinds of therapeutic approaches work best with what kinds of clients or patients? To this last question he sees no answer forthcoming from classical control-group design. Control-group design can tell us, for each

given type of psychotherapy, to what degree it gets results on the whole. It is a clumsy design, however, for answering the question in which both psychotherapists and personality theorists are most interested, namely, what kind of therapeutic approach works with what kind of clients or patients?

A great deal of folklore now passes for psychological science in this area. All too commonly deductions are made from theoretical propositions which have little in the way of unequivocal confirmation from empirical observations. Because these propositions and deductions from them are often so stated that they scarcely permit empirical test, or because our current research designs do not test them, they can pass as dogma. In this sense, we are faced with what I should like to call our various "schools of conviction" in psychotherapy.[5]

Let me give you just one concrete example. In one of our student-training clinics where psychotherapists from various "schools of conviction" serve as supervisors, the convictions of the chief are of the orthodox psychoanalytic variety. He has dictated, on a priori grounds, that no patient exhibiting obsessive-compulsive trends is to be handled in nondirective fashion because "such an approach can only be damaging" to such people. Although my predilections, also deductive, would tend to agree with those of this chief, I have become highly skeptical about everything we think we know in this whole area. I have therefore asked some of my friends of nondirective conviction about any psychotherapeutic experience they may have had with clients showing obsessive-compulsive trends. Each reports some of his most outstanding therapeutic successes with obsessive-compulsive clients. Of course, this "I-cured-a-case" method proves nothing

[5] Shaffer [26] has already called attention to the manner in which the various explanatory theories indigenous to psychotherapy are constructed to protect the security of the psychotherapist and to serve as aids in training and indoctrination.

about the relative efficacy of psychoanalytic versus nondirective psychotherapy with obsessive-compulsive cases, but it does call into question any deductively derived conviction about the necessarily injurious nature of nondirective psychotherapy for such cases.

Let me ask just a few other still empirically unanswered questions.

1. Does psychotherapy aimed at the production of corrective experiences for specific, diagnostically determined personality defects produce improvement any more or less often than psychotherapy which aims only at providing the proper social-emotional atmosphere for healthy personal growth? And two corollary questions: (a) In what ways are these psychotherapies actually different in the discernible behavior of psychotherapists? (b) Are there distinguishable classes of clients for which one system works better than the other?

2. Do psychotherapists who exhibit in high degree the various characteristics and skills we try to teach get better results than those who do not? Or, a subquestion of this kind: Do psychotherapists who have more nearly ideal psychotherapeutic relationships with their clients, as defined by Fiedler's interesting theory and Q-technique, get better results than psychotherapists who have less ideal relationships with their clients?

3. Are the various schools of psychoanalytic conviction differentiated by either the proportion of clients in general or the proportions of the various kinds of clients, who show improvement?

These are hard questions, hard because they call simultaneously for statistically manageable data in three areas:

a. About the client and his characteristics;

b. About the psychotherapist; and

c. About the change in the client associated with his receiving psychotherapy.

Control-group design is poorly adapted for such questions. Yet these constitute the very kind of questions to which answers are most important from both the practical standpoint of practitioners and the theoretical standpoint. Research in this field demands that we develop first the methods of measurement for each of these areas and then that we develop a social and administrative organization such that we can have data from all three areas simultaneously.[6] This is the theme of my song.

THE PIECEMEAL NATURE OF MOST CURRENT RESEARCH IN PERSONALITY DIAGNOSIS AND PSYCHOTHERAPY

Our scientific development in personality diagnosis and psychotherapy has been increasing markedly in both volume and quality. Let me mention some of the specific developments.

The work of Carl Rogers and his students has demonstrated the feasibility and value of verbatim recording for research, provided methods of content analysis, yielded solid knowledge of process as psychotherapy is conducted nondirectively or in client-centered fashion, and lent a great impetus to research in psychotherapy. It has also contributed one indigenous theory of the psychotherapeutic process.

The development in the factor-analysis approach to personality description, especially the work of Cattell [1], Eysenck

---

[6] I do not wish to deprecate the role of the individual investigator working by himself on the problems close to his own heart and in his own way. The sciences of today are largely the cumulative result of such individual efforts. I believe that the frontiers of science will continue to be pushed back by such individual efforts. Moreover, the "way of life" of the individual investigator is one to be envied. But, as Marquis [19] has pointed out so well, certain problems do not lend themselves to solution by individual effort. Such problems seem especially prevalent in the area of human relations. I am saying that the problem of what kind of psychotherapy works with what kinds of patients is one of these which cannot be solved by individual effort.

[4], and Wittenborn [34] is of great interest although I question whether the proper measures have been analyzed as yet to provide us with factors controlling the variance in the results of psychotherapy.

The theoretical developments resulting from serious application of the principles of learning theory to this area by Dollard and Miller [2] by Mowrer [20, 21] and others [e.g., 30] provide a rich source of researchable hypotheses and a useful conceptual framework.

The attempts to assess the change in persons associated with their receiving psychotherapy are beginning to, be fruitful. Here I hope the work of our group at the Institute of Welfare Research of the Community Service Society may be pertinent to psychotherapy generally even though the methods were developed in a social work setting to measure the results of social casework [10, 11]. Somewhat related to this in one sense is the program of research by McQuitty [18] aimed at a measure of social adjustment.

In another area, there is the work of Fiedler [5, 6] which has the merit of comparing psychotherapists from three different schools of conviction on at least one variable in their practice which all agree is important, the quality of their relationships with clients. Here the empirical results show experts from different schools of conviction, as defined by reputation, to be more alike than experts and novices from the same schools. In view of the emotional heat engendered by our differences in conviction, it would be exceedingly interesting to compare the behavior of practitioners from different schools on other variables. I wonder whether the differences in the pattern of vocal noises they make about their practice may not be greater than the discernible differences in the practice itself.

A projected program about to start is Shakow's plan to make sound movies of psychotherapeutic interviews. These movies should be extremely useful. One use I particularly see for them is to determine how closely judgments of variables from sound recordings of interviews approximate judgments of the same variables from sound movies of interviews. If it should turn out that the visual cues add little, we could proceed with more confidence in the results obtained from the more readily obtainable sound recordings.

All these examples of work under way or projected are programmatic and extensive in nature. There are other programs and a good many fine studies that I cannot take time to mention and still others that I do not even know about. We psychologists may share professional pride in this work, but I have actually been motivated to mention these programs by a major shortcoming which they all share. They are too piecemeal and segmental to provide answers to the kind of questions I asked a moment ago. This criticism does not apply to the theoretical developments, but it does to all the empirical programs that I have mentioned.

Let me ask some questions to point up my meaning. Do the descriptions of the psychotherapeutic process found in the content analysis of consecutive nondirective interviews hold also for other types of psychotherapy? How well are the various measures of psychotherapeutic progress deriving from content analyses of interviews correlated with changes in social behavior? And do the subjective changes persist? Do they persist more in some kinds of clients than in other kinds? Such questions call for the combining of the excellent methods developed by Rogers' group with other measures.

Some of the factor analyses of personality variables are directed specifically toward testing the validity of our present clinical nosology [e.g., Wittenborn, 34] but much of it is isolated and appears to be done with the idea of discovering the basic nature of man [e.g., Cattell, 1]. I wonder whether the validity of any factors deriving from factor analysis will not have to be tested by means of the degree to which they predict something we want to know. In the context of this paper, we want to predict the variance in measures of the change associated with psychotherapy. I am prompted to recall for you at this point the title of a paper by the late John G. Jenkins, "Validity for What?" [12]. I would be the last to argue in this connection that there are no basic laws of behavior, but my intuition argues that the place to find them is not in descriptive dimensions of personality.

Let me turn to our own work on measuring movement in the clients of social casework. We have succeeded in standardizing the judgment of different workers to the extent that the judgments of individual workers trained on our Movement Scale show correlations of the order of +.9 with the averaged judgments of a group on a set of test cases. The mean interjudge correlation for individual case workers is of the order of +.8. We have thus begun to overcome the lack of a judgmental standard for assessing the change associated with casework. Use of this scale can tell us only about movement associated with casework, however; it cannot, strictly speaking, tell us about the results of casework until it is used either in connection with control-group design, or in conjunction with a proper system of diagnostic classification and proper description of caseworker or psychotherapist behavior.

In connection with Fiedler's measure of the quality of the psychotherapeutic relationship, do those psychotherapists who establish relationships approaching the ideal get improvement in a higher proportion of their clients than do those who establish relationships which fall far short of this ideal?

I have asked enough questions to indicate how even programmatic research may fall short if several kinds of variables are not measured and simultaneously taken into account in conjunction with one another. Only then can we begin to get solid answers to the complex yet basic questions about psychotherapy, about the results of psychotherapy, and about what kinds of people profit most from what kinds of psychotherapy. Such data would, I believe, contribute to personality theory as well as to our practical knowledge of the helping process.

THE NATURE OF AN INTEGRATED DESIGN

What would a design to answer these complex questions look like? As is common in science, in outline it is simple. In execution, however, it would be exceedingly complex, so complex, in fact, that I hesitate to present my thoughts for fear that they may be taken for delusions of grandeur. In outline, three kinds of data would be required for each psychotherapeutic situation, defined as a client applying for and getting psychotherapeutic help. These three kinds of data or measures are (a) diagnostic measures of the client, his problems, his attitudes about them and about seeking help, his social situation, etc., (b) records of the psychotherapeutic process to provide measures of therapist behavior and its interaction with client behavior, and (c) measures of change based on both psychotherapeutic process and direct evidence of change in client comfort, change in client behavioral productivity and change in the reactions of other persons toward the client.[7] The diagnostic measures and measures of therapist behavior would constitute in combination the independent variable, and change in the client the dependent variable. From the sampling standpoint, this design would call

___

[7] Discussion of the criteria of change here would take us too far afield. The three sources mentioned here are elaborated in the *After Comments* by Kogan and myself to the symposium on psychological theories and the evaluation of the results of psychotherapy [*Psychol. Serv. Center J.*, 1950, 2, p. 135ff].

for a broad cross-sectional sample of the people who came for help. One should also have several representatives of each of the various schools of psychotherapy as both novices and as highly experienced practitioners. The individuals seeking help should, ideally, go randomly to all kinds of practitioners. This in outline is one conception of an ideal, integrated, methodological approach to the study of the interrelated factors in psychotherapy. It is a conception that I have repeatedly come to whenever I have purposefully released myself from the restraints of everyday reality in order to dream about what the scientific method would mean in this area if it were taken seriously.

Anyone who has ever done a piece of psychological research can see difficulties: the task of developing and testing the reliabilities of a proper set of measures for each area, the file after file of process records, the enormous task of analyzing them, the nearly endless calculations. Such obstacles raise painful qualms in any responsible investigator. But these are relatively simple difficulties compared to those one can foresee on the social side. Think of the task of getting the cooperation of an adequate sample of psychotherapists from the various schools. Think of getting them to alter their practice sufficiently to get the necessary data about all their clients. Think of overcoming their ethical concern to follow their convictions about how the various kind of help seekers should be treated in order to permit a random distribution of all kinds of them to all kinds of psychotherapists. Think of the complexity of the administrative organization required to talk through these obstacles and to keep practitioners and research personnel in functional collaboration. Think of the problem of getting the large financial support necessary over a sufficient period of time.

On the other hand, as I see it, the stakes are high both in human welfare and in the amount of money involved in giving psychotherapeutic services. Moreover, there are glimmers of hope that something approximating such an ideal arrangement for an integrated program of research on psychotherapy may be gradually becoming feasible. It will mean the social and administrative organization of research on a large scale, but not so large as the Manhattan Project and perhaps not so very much larger than the VA project on the selection of clinical psychologists, a report of which has just been completed by Kelly and Fiske [14].

Moreover, such a program need not be organized, in fact, should not be organized on a large scale all at once. One can use even a single university clinic as a pilot plant, especially if one deliberately brings together to work in it psychotherapists from various schools. In such a setting the details of design and organization can be worked out on a small scale. The plan for a proper diagnostic study before treatment can be worked out. Here present practice would have to be modified so as to permit statistical manipulation of the diagnostic variables. The procedure of turning all diagnostic data into ratings, as used by Kelly and Fiske [14] in their VA selection study, has merit. Such a study should provide data with which other data from follow-up studies of the same individual may later be compared as one measure of the change associated with psychotherapy. Ways of short-cutting the immense labor of content analysis of verbatim records in order to measure therapist and client behavior in the psychotherapeutic situation should be explored. Intake workers or those who assign clients to therapists should work out both their philosophy and their procedures. It must be recognized, however, that such a pilot plant operation in a university clinic cannot answer the important questions by virtue of the limited nature of the sample of clients.

This is a major obstacle for I see little chance of organizing a chain of clinics in which randomizing of all kinds of clients to all kinds of psychotherapists would be carried out. On the other hand, I believe we can utilize what one might term the experiments of nature hereby getting the collaboration of existing clinics. These tend individually to be manned by given schools of psychotherapists. It is likely that each of these clinics attracts nearly the whole range of help seekers, although perhaps the distributions vary. If the collaboration of several clinics, in which the practitioners represent differing schools, could be obtained, and if they would alter their practice enough to utilize a standardized diagnostic study, provide verbatim records of at least proper samples of therapeutic interviews, apply standardized measures of change in clients and permit follow-up study by someone other than the psychotherapist or the person making the diagnostic study, we could go a long way toward answering the questions I have raised.

There are signs that getting such collaboration is not idle dreaming. There are administrators of a few clinics and social work agencies scattered over the country who really want to know what happens in and as a result of the service they offer. If someone would pay for the research procedures extraneous to their services, the diagnostic studies, the recording of interviews, and the follow-up studies, they would be glad to collaborate in such a program as outlined. I believe several of the foundations would be happy to pay toward the bill for such research procedures if their staffs of scientists were convinced that the plan and the tools developed promised just a fair chance of getting answers to some of these important questions.

There are also signs deriving much from research and practice now going on that the various parts of the integrated plan I have outlined are feasible. We already conduct diagnostic studies of clients in a large share of clinics before psychotherapy begins. It is merely a task of standardizing these diagnostic studies to yield in comparable form as broad a sample of relevant

behavioral data as feasible. The fact that judgments of movement in clients can be standardized by a process of scaling and training supports the hope that the same could be done for judgments by psychotherapists of a list of diagnostic and process variables. Psychotherapists commonly have qualms about client reactions to the electrical recording of interviews, but a study by Kogan [16] has shown that the amount of concern or resistance in an unselected sample coming for family casework service was exceedingly small. Concern for their clients leads psychotherapists to question the very idea of follow-up studies by persons other than themselves, yet our follow-up study of family casework at the Institute of Welfare Research has shown that, approached properly, nearly all ex-clients appear to accept and to approve being interviewed about the results of their experience. These signs lead me to be hopeful.

Recapitulation

To recapitulate,

1. The increasing use of professional help with personal problems, whether it derive from either need or demand, makes it important to understand both the problems and the psychotherapeutic helping process. This paper has been focused upon the results of the latter.

2. We know relatively little about the results of psychotherapy. Our present information consists largely of the percentages of clients or patients showing various degrees of improvement associated with their receiving help.

3. Control-group design, where the change is measured in randomly selected groups of help seekers who did *receive* and who did *not receive* help, could answer the question of results for each type of psychotherapy, but such a design would leave unanswered a major share of the important questions about what kind of psychotherapy gets best results with what kinds of people seeking help.

4. Several excellent programs of research in this area are now under way, but their limited nature makes it impossible for them to yield answers to many of the most important questions about psychotherapy.

5. Taking into account only the demands of logic and the scientific method, an ideal design for an integrated program of research on psychotherapy would include, in outline, getting

a. Diagnostic data about the person seeking help to permit the development of a system of classification.

b. Data on the process of psychotherapy appropriate to yield significant measures of therapist behavior, and

c. Measures of client change associated with psychotherapy. The first two of these may be interrelated to supply the independent variable while client-change may be taken as the dependent variable.

6. Finally, I have pointed out that the implementation of an integral program would be extremely difficult, but that there are considerations arguing that it may be feasible to achieve something approximating such an ideal, integrated design. It is in the hope of speeding that day that I have exposed you to my dream world for research in this area.

REFERENCES

1. CATTELL, R. B. Personality, a systematic theoretical and factual study. New York: McGraw-Hill, 1950.

2. DOLLARD, J., & MILLER, N. E. Personality and psychotherapy. New York: McGraw-Hill, 1950.

3. DOLLARD, J., & MOWRER, O. H. A method of measuring tension in written documents. J. abnorm. soc. Psychol., 1947, 42, 3–32.

4. EYSENCK, H. J. Dimensions of personality. London: Kegan Paul, 1947.

5. FIEDLER, F. E. The concept of an ideal therapeutic relationship. J. consult. Psychol., 1950, 14, 239–245.

6. FIEDLER, F. E. Factor analyses of psychoanalytic, nondirective, and Adlerian thera-peutic relationships. J. consult. Psychol., 1951, 15, 32–38.

7. HECKMAN, A. A., & STONE, A. Testing casework results: forging new tools. Surv. Midmon., 1947, 83, 267–270.

8. HOLLIS, FLORENCE. Women in marital conflict; a casework study. New York: Family Service Association of America, 1949.

9. HOROWITZ, FLORENCE. The relationship between a method of measuring tension and two methods of measuring the attitude toward the self in thirty-six electrically recorded initial social casework interviews. Boston University, School of Social Work; unpublished M.S. dissertation done under the direction of L. S. Kogan at the Institute of Welfare Research, Community Service Society of New York, 1951.

10. HUNT, J. McV., BLENKNER, MARGARET, & KOGAN, L. S. Testing results in social casework: a field-test of the movement scale. New York: Family Service Association of America, 1950.

11. HUNT, J. McV., & KOGAN, L. S. Measuring results in social casework: a manual on judging movement. New York: Family Service Association of America, 1950.

12. JENKINS, J. G. Validity for what? J. consult. Psychol., 1946, 10, 93–98.

13. KAUFFMAN, P. E., & RAIMY, V. C. Two methods of assessing therapeutic progress. J. abnorm. soc. Psychol., 1949, 44, 379–385.

14. KELLY, E. L., & FISKE, D. W. The prediction of performance in clinical psychology, Ann Arbor, Mich., Univer. of Michigan Press, 1951.

15. KNIGHT, K. P. Evaluation of the results of psychoanalytic therapy. Amer. J. Psychiat., 1941, 98, 434–446.

16. KOGAN, L. S. The electrical recording of social casework interviews. Soc. Casewk., 1950, 31, 371–378.

17. LANDIS, C. A statistical evaluation of psychotherapeutic methods. In L. E. Hinsie (Ed.), Concepts and problems of psychotherapy. New York: Columbia Univer. Press, 1937.

18. MCQUITTY, L. Implications of certain measures of personality integration for theories of social psychology. J. abnorm. soc. Psychol., in press.

19. MARQUIS, D. G. Research planning at the frontiers of science. *Amer. Psychologist,* 1948, 3, 430–438.

20. MOWRER, O. H. *Learning theory and personality dynamics.* New York: Ronald, 1950.

21. MOWRER, O. H. (Ed.) *Psychotherapy: a symposium on theory and research.* New York: Ronald, 1952.

22. MUENCH, G. A. An evaluation of nondirective psychotherapy by means of the Rorschach and other indices. *Appl. Psychol. Monogr.,* 1947, No. 13.

23. POWERS, E. An experiment in the prevention of delinquency, *Ann. Amer. Acad. polit. soc. Sci.,* 1949, 261, 77–78.

24. RAIMY, V. C. Self-reference in counseling interviews. *J. consult. Psychol.,* 1948, 12, 153–163.

25. ROGERS, C. R. *Counseling and psychotherapy.* Boston: Houghton Mifflin, 1942.

26. ROGERS, C. R. *Client-centered therapy.* Boston: Houghton Mifflin, 1951.

27. SHAFFER, L. F. The problem of psychotherapy. *Amer. Psychologist,* 1947, 2, 459–467.

28. SHIFFMAN, F. & OLSON, E. *A study in family casework: an attempt to evaluate service.* Evanston, Illinois: Family Welfare Association, 1939.

29. SNYDER, W. U. (Chm.) Group report of an integrated psychotherapy research program. Round table at Amer. Psychol. Assn., Chicago, Sept., 1951.

30. SNYGG, D., & COMBS, A. W. *Individual behavior.* New York: Harper, 1949.

31. WILDER, J. Facts and figures on psychotherapy. *J. clin. Psychopathol.,* 1945, 7, 311–347.

32. WITMER, HELEN L. Judging the results of the Cambridge-Somerville youth study. *Smith Coll. Stud. soc. Wk.,* 1949, 20, 1–15.

33. WITMER, HELEN L., *et al.* The later social adjustment of problem children: a report of thirteen follow-up investigations. *Smith Coll. Stud. soc. Wk.,* 1935, 6, 3–98.

34. WITTENBORN, J. R. Symptom patterns in a group of mental hospital patients. *J. consult. Psychol.,* 1951, 15, 290–302.

Problems of Controls in Psychotherapy as Exemplified by the Psychotherapy Research Project of the Phipps Psychiatric Clinic

JEROME D. FRANK

In the broadest sense, the purpose of controls is to answer the question: how sure are you that you really know what you think you know? Problems of control arise only after a researcher thinks he knows something—that is, after he has an hypothesis that certain variables are related in a certain way—and he wishes to determine whether he is right. The purpose of controls, in other words, is to exclude alternative hypotheses. The level of certainty at which the truth or falsity of an hypothesis can be established is a function of the accuracy with which the relevant variables can be identified, measured and manipulated. Therefore the degree of possible and desirable control in a particular field of study depends on its state of development. In its pre-scientific stage important insights may be achieved without the use of any controls worthy of the name.

Reprinted from E. A. Rubinstein & M. B. Parloff (Eds.), *Research in Psychotherapy* (Washington, D.C.: 1959), pp. 10–26, with the permission of the American Psychological Association and the author.

Even at this level, however, since the researcher only explores regions where he expects to find something, he is being guided by implicit hypotheses, and the use of crude controls may facilitate his search. Darwin, for example, used a kind of control when he made a special point of jotting down observed phenomena which seemed to refute his tentative hypotheses.

Research in psychotherapy attempts to set up and test hypotheses subsumed under the general question: what kinds of therapist activity produce what kinds of change in what kinds of patient. That is, the independent variables lie in the patient's state before the therapist's intervention and in the therapist's activity, the dependent variables in changes in the patients feelings and behavior. Since few of these variables are as yet adequately defined and the researcher can directly observe or manipulate only a few of those which are important, it is obvious that the field of psychotherapeutic research is still at a relatively primitive level. It is, however, pos-

sible to design studies which are controlled
at least to some extent in that they permit
planned, though crude, manipulations of
certain variables and randomization of
others.

For purposes of discussion of controls
in psychotherapy, the division suggested
by Edwards and Cronbach (6) into person variables, situation variables, and response variables seems especially convenient. The personal attributes of the therapist are situational variables from the patient's standpoint, and are therefore considered under this heading.

In order to give focus to the discussion,
I shall draw chiefly from a study of psychotherapy with psychiatric outpatients carried out at the Johns Hopkins Hospital, in
which we have barked our shins against
most of the major problems of control.[1]
The project took its origin from the lack
of demonstrable difference in improvement
rates reported by proponents of different
therapies (2), suggesting the likelihood
that all forms of therapy, including some
which are not called psychotherapy, have
much in common. The task we set ourselves was to try to identify attributes of
patients determining their responsiveness
to these common features of psychotherapy. This required the use of more than
one therapist and type of therapy and a
design which would make it possible to
determine if any attributes of patients were
related to improvement regardless of therapist or therapy. In addition, the design
permitted analysis of the data to discover
possible specific contributions of different

therapists and therapies to the obtained
results.[2]

The patients were selected for the project on their initial visits to the outpatient
department of the Johns Hopkins Hospital.
They were white, aged 18-55, and of both
sexes. Only those with organic brain disease, antisocial character disorders, alcoholism, overt psychosis, or mental deficiency were excluded. They were further
characterized initially by the usual clinical
diagnostic categories, by an inventory covering various aspects of their attitudes and
behavior deemed relevant to therapy, and
by initial scores on the scales used to
measure change, described below.

With respect to the situational variables,
the therapists were three members of the
psychiatric resident staff in the second year
of training. Each had done considerable
individual therapy and had conducted one
therapeutic group under supervision. Three
forms of therapy were used: group, individual, and "minimal." Group and individual therapy were guided by the therapeutic philosophy of the Phipps Clinic. In
general, the therapist's aim is to establish
a relationship with the patient which will
help him identify and correct current distortions in his interpersonal perceptions
and behavior. In the individual therapy
this implies relatively greater emphasis on
the present than the past; in group therapy,
emphasis on group interactions rather than
on events transpiring outside. Examination
of historical origins of these distortions is
seen as a means of clarifying them, when
appropriate, not as an end in itself. Patients
received group therapy one and one-half
hours once a week, individual therapy one
hour a week. Minimal therapy consisted
of a brief infrequent interview, not more
than one-half hour every two weeks, focused on the patient's complaints and how
he might best deal with them. The reasons
for the choice of these three forms of
treatment will be considered below.

[1] These studies were supported by the Veterans
Administration and by a research grant from the
National Institute of Mental Health, National Institutes of Health, United States Public Health Service.
The research staff consisted of Lester H. Gliedman,
M.D., Stanley D. Imber, Ph.D., Earl H. Nash, M.S.,
and Anthony R. Stone, M.S.S.W. in addition to the
writer. We wish to express our grateful acknowledgment to Dr. Morris B. Parloff for his crucial
contributions to the planning and early phases of
the project.

[2] For a more detailed account of the design see
Frank, Gliedman, Imber, Nash, & Stone (8).

The response variables were changes in the patient's subjective discomfort and his social ineffectiveness. These were chosen as representing the least common denominator of the aims of all the healing arts, including psychotherapy. However else a patient may change under treatment, unless he becomes more comfortable and more effective, it is hard to maintain that he has improved. Discomfort was defined in terms of forty-one symptoms or feelings which the patient reported as distressing. Ineffectiveness was defined in terms of fifteen types of behavior generally recognized as socially ineffective, rated by interviewers on the basis of information obtained from the patient and an informant. We attempted to measure decrease in discomfort and ineffectiveness rather than increase in comfort and effectiveness, because it proved much easier to define degrees of malfunctioning than of successful functioning. It is easier to define illness than health.

As to the research design, each psychiatrist conducted all three forms of treatment, and patients were assigned at random to each by the research staff. Each psychiatrist treated 18 patients, six in each of the three forms of treatment. Psychiatrists and patients were urged to remain in contact for at least six months, unless the psychiatrist felt that the patient had received maximum benefit before that time.

Each patient, whether he stayed in treatment or not, was re-evaluated six months after entering therapy (or when therapy terminated if this occurred between one and six months), again six months later, and at yearly intervals thereafter. In most cases a relative or close friend of each patient was interviewed separately at approximately the same time as the patient.

One of the major problems in attempting to do controlled studies in outpatient therapy is the difficulty in carrying through an experimental design. Because of the mobility of the American population, and the fact that psychotherapy competes with so many other activities in patients' lives,

attrition, missed appointments and the like create severe problems for maintaining any design which extends over time. Our design called for 54 patients to receive six months of treatment by three therapists. By starting with 91 patients and conducting the treatments over about 18 months, we finally succeeded in obtaining 54 patients, of whom 37 (68%) completed at least six months of treatment and 48 (90%) had four months or more of treatment. By expending considerable effort we obtained follow-up interviews on 53 of the 54 treated patients at one year and 48 at two years. Since then attrition has been marked.

With this example in mind, we may turn to consideration of some problems of control of patient, situational, and response variables.

CONTROL OF PATIENT VARIABLES

A problem which plagues all research with psychiatric patients is the adequate definition of the sample to be studied (25). The criteria used ideally should be communicable with sufficient clarity and precision so that other workers by using them can duplicate the sample. At the same time they must be relevant to psychotherapy. None of the customary criteria are adequate in these respects.

It is relatively easy to specify what may be termed actuarial characteristics of a research population, such as age, sex, race and so on, so that others can duplicate the sample. The relevance of many of these characteristics, however, is questionable. If to play safe, a large number of criteria are included, even though many are suspected of being irrelevant, it may be difficult to accumulate a sufficiently large research sample. On the other hand, if one bases selection of the sample on only a few criteria, one runs the danger of failing to include some that are relevant to therapy. For example, only recently has the importance of specifying social class in studies of psychotherapy been appreciated (20, 37).

Since characterization of a population in actuarial terms, however complete, seems insufficient, other modes of description must be considered. Of these perhaps the most obvious is clinical diagnosis. Unfortunately, clinical diagnoses are based on rather vague and overlapping criteria, so that a patient's proper diagnostic label is often in doubt. In one study three well-trained psychiatrists observing patients jointly showed agreement as to the patient's major diagnostic category in only 46% of the cases, and in only 20% with respect to the subcategory (3). An additional difficulty with descriptive diagnostic categories is that they are only loosely related to the major concerns of psychotherapy, the patient's underlying conflicts and his characteristic interpersonal behavior (10). They may even prove to be completely irrelevant for purposes of psychotherapy, although I do not share this view.

The limitations of the conventional diagnostic scheme suggest directions in which to look for more useful diagnostic criteria. One would be in terms of the patients' motivations and conflicts. Unfortunately, characterization of dynamics must be based on inferences, and these differ depending on the researchers' theoretical preconceptions, so such criteria lose in communicability what they gain in relevance.

Another possibility is to borrow a notion from drug studies and select patients in terms of the "target symptoms" which the particular form of psychotherapy hopes to modify (12), regardless of the clinical syndromes in which they occur. For example, one could study patients suffering from depression, anxiety, or visual hallucinations. Since these symptoms obviously can be expressions of various underlying states, however, the idea does not seem very promising in this form.

If the major target symptoms of psychotherapy are considered to be disturb-

ances in the patients' characteristic ways of perceiving others and behaving towards them, however, then this approach may prove to be very fruitful. A sophisticated and promising example is the scheme of interpersonal dimensions of personality devised by Leary and his co-workers (27).

Having selected the research population and described it as best we can, the next problem is how to divide it into experimental and control samples. There are four theoretically possible ways of doing this. Two exist only in fantasy, but should be mentioned for the sake of completeness. The perfect equivalent control group would consist of patients matched individually in all respects with those receiving psychotherapy. The matched patients would have identical heredity and life experiences up to the beginning of the experiment, an obvious impossibility. The second impossible method would be to match control and experimental populations, patient by patient, on certain variables believed to be significant, such as age, sex, educational level and so on. Since each additional matching variable greatly increases the size of the population which must be screened, this approach is hopelessly impractical in outpatient studies.

The third possibility is to match by stratified sampling. Groups can be matched with respect to the proportions of patients in certain categories without matching individuals. Even this procedure is ordinarily too cumbersome for an outpatient department, because one cannot wait for a sufficient population of patients to accumulate before starting some form of treatment.[3]

---

[3] Two potential ways of increasing the size of the population so as to make stratified sampling possible are by extending the project over time, or by drawing on the populations of several clinics as in the Veterans Administration Study (29). Each, however, introduces its own control problems. Extending the study over time rests on the assumption that time of year is not a significant variable; i.e. that patients presenting themselves for treatment at different times of year are essentially alike. This assumption may not be valid, as considered below.

The final resort is to match by random selection; that is, by assigning patients alternately to treatment and control groups. The assumption is that over the long pull all significant variables will be randomly distributed among both groups, so that differences found in therapy and control groups at the end of the experiment may safely be attributed to the therapeutic procedure rather than to an unequal distribution of patient variables in the two groups. Whether randomization has been achieved can be checked by simple statistical methods applied to measurable attributes of the populations such as actuarial indices and test scores.

All the methods of control of person variables described rest on the assumption that if the control and experimental groups are matched on known variables, or if these variables are found to be randomly distributed throughout both groups, then all other variables which might potentially account for the differences found between control and experimental sample would be similarly distributed. This assumption may not be valid, and this has occasionally resulted in scientific tragedy. To take an example from another field, vast amounts of biochemical work on hospitalized schizophrenics have come to grief because certain biochemical differences between the patients and matched nonhospitalized controls were attributed to schizophrenia, whereas they were really due to institutionalization, with its effects on activity, diet and so on. Recently high hopes were aroused by the discovery that the serum of schizophrenics oxidized adrenaline more rapidly than the serum of normal controls. The hopes were dashed when this phenomenon proved to be caused by vitamin C deficiency in the diets of the patients

(1). When this variable was controlled the difference between normals and schizophrenics disappeared. In this example, an unsuspected but crucial difference in situational variables invalidated the matching of person variables in control and experimental groups, leading to an erroneous explanation of the difference obtained.

With respect to control of the patient variable in studies of outpatient psychotherapy, it should be pointed out finally, that though complete matching of control and experimental groups may be practically impossible to achieve, certain differences between the experimental and control groups need not destroy their usefulness for all purposes. In our study, in spite of every effort to assign patients randomly to the three types of therapy, we found that more lower-class patients were placed in group therapy. The sampling bias made it difficult to interpret a finding that more patients dropped out of group than individual treatment, but did not affect other findings, for example that in all forms of treatment those who scored sickest initially improved most.

Another example of a biased control group in our study is that of patients who drop out of treatment within four sessions. These are self-selected and presumably differ systematically from those who remain in treatment, though the nature of the differences is unspecified. Nevertheless, the drop-outs served as a useful control of negative findings. For example, they showed the same drop in discomfort scores after six months as those receiving various forms of treatment over this period of time (9). This finding permits the conclusion that an improvement in discomfort is not a function of duration or type of psychotherapy received, or of differences in the nature of drop-outs and remainers.

In the Rogers and Dymond studies (15), the equivalent control group was unavoidably biased, in that it was selected from volunteers who were paid to participate in a "research on personality." They

---

If patients are drawn from many clinics, this increases the number of variables on which they must be matched, such as ethnic group, urban or rural, and so on, which tends to counteract the gain sought by increasing the size of the sample.

did not perceive themselves as sick or needing help—an obviously important difference from the clients in the therapy group.
Nevertheless they proved useful for certain
types of controls.

An ingenious way of circumventing the
whole matching problem is to use each patient as his own control. The patient is
observed before and after a time interval
in which he receives no therapy. He then
receives therapy, after which the same observations are repeated (15). Changes between the first and second readings are
compared with those between the second
and third; presumably, differences would
be due to the effects of therapy. Own-
control designs do not escape practical and
theoretical problems imposed by withholding therapy, which will be considered under situational variables. On the whole,
when they can be managed, they probably
represent a better control than use of an
equivalent group, except that they do not
control changes in patients related to passage of time. For example, it has often
been noted in a clinic that intake falls off
during vacation periods (28). Whatever
the reasons for this, it raises the possibility
that the condition of patients may be affected by factors connected with time of
year. If an own-control experiment happened to be set up so that the no-therapy
period was in the spring and the therapy
occurred in the summer, this would leave
open the possibility that differences in patient change in the no-therapy and therapy
periods were attributable to the season.

Obviously the proper selection of control groups in any study of psychotherapy
is difficult. There may be severe practical
restrictions on the researcher's freedom to
assign patients to therapy and control
groups. He must be alert lest unsuspected
bias creeps into these assignments, and
must search for important overlooked variables in which the control and experimental groups are not adequately matched or
randomized. Even inadequate selection
methods are better than none, however, as

a means of controlling for the patient variables in psychotherapy.

CONTROL OF SITUATIONAL VARIABLES

From the standpoint of situational controls, the first task is to control for the
eventuality that changes in patients observed in the course of a particular form
of psychotherapy are not due to intercurrent life experiences or spontaneous fluctuations in the patient's state. If this can
be shown, the question still remains as to
whether the changes are really attributable
to the aspect of therapy which the researcher hypothesizes to be responsible for
them. The chief problem of control in this
respect appears to be to distinguish the
effects of the therapist's personality or attitude, from the effects of his techniques.

Psychotherapy is only one of many influences which may produce changes in patients. For example, many psychiatric conditions seem to fluctuate spontaneously or
to be self-limited (39), and a patient is
most apt to seek treatment when he is in a
trough. The subsequent improvement may
be due to the natural course of his condition.
Treatment with younger persons may extend over a sufficient span so that processes
of growth and maturation may contribute
significantly to the changes observed. Improvement due primarily to extra-therapeutic occurrences, such as a change in job
or social relationships, may be erroneously
attributed to concomitant psychotherapy.
The task of untangling the roles of therapy and life changes is further complicated
by the fact that psychotherapy may have
contributed to the patient's ability to make
such changes.

An obvious way of controlling for
whether changes in patients are due to
therapy or something else is to compare
them with changes in an equivalent group
of patients who received no therapy. The
no-therapy group has just been considered
from the standpoint of control of patient

variables. We are now concerned with its use to control situational variables. With outpatients this presents formidable difficulties. The major problem is that an adequate no-therapy control would have to last the same length of time as therapy, to allow the same opportunity for the occurrence of significant extra-therapeutic events or spontaneous changes in both the control and treatment population. Since six months of therapy is usually considered to be the minimal requirement, a control group would have to go without therapy for six months. Patients present themselves to the clinic because they are in distress and want something done. It is hard to reconcile telling them to wait this long with one's professional conscience. But this is the least of the obstacles. Keeping a sizable number of patients without treatment for so long a period may have an adverse effect on the clinic's community relations. A possible source of a no-therapy control are patients on a waiting list for treatment, assuming that the clinic is so inefficient as to have a sufficiently large one. Experience has shown, however, that patients placed on waiting lists are apt to differ systematically from those who are taken promptly into treatment. Patients who seem more in need of help or who arouse the interest of the interviewer for other reasons tend to receive priority for treatment.

Another difficulty is that most patients who are told to go away and come back in six months for re-evaluation will not do so. In order to avoid a monumental attrition rate, the clinic would need to maintain some kind of regular contact with the patients over this period; and any contact may contain therapeutic components (33), so that the no-therapy control would be violated by this procedure. In addition, patients who are told that treatment at the clinic will not be available for some time, if they are in distress will inevitably seek treatment elsewhere, whether it be from a physician, faith healer, or corner druggist. By the same token, patients in psychother-

apy will be less likely to seek out other sources of help. Thus, we would not really have a no-treatment control group as against a psychotherapy group but two groups, receiving different kinds of treatment. Since the treatment received by the control group involves ingredients which may also be psychotherapeutic, interpretation of differences in the results obtained in the two groups may be very difficult. An additional potential source of error lies in the fact that rejection of a patient for immediate treatment may affect his attiude in such a way as to influence his scores on self-administered tests of change, a matter discussed more fully below.

The basic difficulty with the no-treatment control is that withholding treatment after interviewing a patient is, in a sense, a positive rejection of him. Psychotherapy is one form of interpersonal relationship, refusal of psychotherapy is another; it cannot be regarded as neutral.

For many purposes a more promising control than withholding treatment entirely is to offer the control group a form of psychotherapy differing in an essential ingredient from that received by the experimental group (42). Since patients in both populations, from their own standpoint, would be receiving therapy, this eliminates the problem of systematic differences in attitude towards the clinic and in the tendency to seek outside help. Since both types of treatment would be conducted for the same length of time, occurrence of spontaneous fluctuations or important intercurrent life experiences would be randomized in the two populations, so any obtained differences in results could be safely attributed to differences in the therapy used.

In this type of control, a major problem is to select and define the therapeutic ingredients in which experimental and control groups differ. Choice must be guided by two considerations: the probability that the variables are therapeutically significant and the ability to define them adequately.

However important one may suspect a variable to be, its usefulness for research is limited by the precision with which it can be described. Wittenborn points out that one of the common failings of research in psychotherapy is failure to define the independent variable. This permits the investigator only to say, "how infrequently his result could be ascribed to chance but the reader is uncertain as to precisely what the result can be frequently ascribed." (43, p. 35)

On the other hand, the researcher must not let himself be seduced into selecting aspects of therapeutic technique for study mainly because they can be easily described. Too often such aspects prove to be therapeutically unimportant, and the result is a beautifully designed and reported experiment which fails to disprove the null hypothesis. Precision has been gained at the expense of significance.[4]

In the Hopkins project we gained the impression from pilot studies that one important difference between therapies might be the amount of contact between psychiatrist and patient, so we incorporated this into our research design (19). Group and individual therapy were more nearly equated in amount of treatment contact than either was with minimal treatment. At the time of the first re-evaluation, patients in group and individual therapy had had approximately the same number of sessions, 15.8 and 17.7 respectively, as compared to 9.3 sessions for patients in minimal treatment. Since group therapy and individual therapy differed in at least one major definable way, namely that in the former several patients are present simultaneously, in the latter only one, the design also permitted determination of possible differences in effects of this variable. By our measure of social ineffectiveness, both group patients and individual therapy patients improved significantly more than minimally treated patients. This would seem to support the

hypothesis that amount of treatment contact, whether in a group or individually, significantly affects improvement in social ineffectiveness, although an alternative hypothesis cannot entirely be ruled out, as noted below.

The most important, and unfortunately the least understood, situational variable in psychotherapy is the therapist himself. His personality pervades any technique he may use, and because of the patient's dependence on him for help, he may influence the patient through subtle cues of which he may not be aware. Dr. David Rioch tells an amusing example of a patient of his who was always depressed in the treatment interviews except on five occasions when he seemed quite bright and alert. This puzzled Dr. Rioch until he reviewed his notes and realized that on these five mornings, and on no others, he himself had taken benezedrine.[5]

It is obvious that the therapist and therapy variables cannot be completely separated. It is unlikely that a therapist can conduct different types of treatment with precisely equal skill or that his attitudes towards them will be identical. Therefore, differences in results obtained by two forms of therapy conducted by the same therapist may be due to therapist rather than treatment variables, especially since the faith of a therapist in a form of treatment may account for much of its efficacy (7). In our psychotherapy study the psychiatrists disliked minimal treatment. They gave it reluctantly and felt that they were shortchanging the patients. The patients remained just as long in this type of treatment as in the other two, suggesting that they were not as lacking in confidence in it as the doctors. It is possible, however, that this difference in the doctors' attitudes may have contributed to the finding that patients improved less in social ineffectiveness under the minimal treatment conditions. This example illustrates how difficult it is to control ade-

---

[4] See, for example, (38).

[5] Personal communication.

quately for the influence of the therapist in the absence of fuller knowledge about the role of his personal attributes and attitudes in determining the outcome of treatment. Even though minimal treatment was less effective than group or individual treatment in the hands of three different therapists, we cannot be sure that this was not due to differences in their attitudes to the different approaches, though we believe this to be unlikely.

Evidence that the personal qualities of the psychiatrists were not irrelevant to the results of our study, however, is that one of the three showed a tendency, which did not reach acceptable statistical significance, to obtain better results than the other two with all three forms of treatment by both criteria—discomfort and ineffectiveness. Unfortunately, our project was not designed to elucidate aspects of therapists' personalities related to their therapeutic success.

It is clear that the achievement of better ability to identify and control therapist variables warrants a high priority in psychotherapeutic research. Two studies which represent promising beginnings in this regard are that of M. B. Parloff, who showed that of two therapists of roughly similar and equal training, the one who was able to establish better social relationships also established better therapeutic relations (31), and the series of studies of Whitehorn and Betz, who found that psychiatric residents of similar training could be placed in two classes on the basis of their relative degree of success with schizophrenic patients, and that these classes could be distinguished by certain patterns of scores on the Strong Interest Inventory (4).

CONTROL OF RESPONSE VARIABLES

Any attempt to consider control of the response variable in psychotherapy at once threatens to involve one in the tangle of questions as to what is meant by improvement in psychotherapy. For purposes of the present discussion I shall take the position, without attempting to defend it, that the aim of psychotherapy, as one of the healing arts, is to help the patient feel better and function better. The type of functioning which psychotherapy tries to improve is social behavior in its broadest sense; that is, the patient's ability to establish mutually satisfying relationships with others (32).

Before turning to considerations of these criteria, however, it may be well to pause a moment on another set of response variables. These are changes in the patient's behavior in the interview situation, including, for example, certain autonomic responses, the content of his verbalizations (30, 34), and formal aspects of his verbal behavior (35). Studies of changes in these variables as functions of the activities of the interviewer in a single interview circumvent many of the problems of control of situational factors discussed above. They eliminate problems of the role of intercurrent life experience, or outside therapy, or spontaneous long-term fluctuations in the patient's condition. Detailed studies of patients' responses in the interview situation are yielding much valuable information. The relevance of this information to psychotherapy, however, depends on the establishment of its relationship to long-term improvement in the patients' feelings and behavior, which is still far in the future.

Returning now to what I propose to regard as the ultimate criteria of improvement, let us first consider control problems connected with evaluation of the patients' social functioning. Since it is ordinarily impossible to observe the patient *in situ*, as it were, estimates of his social effectiveness must be inferences based on reports of patients and other informants, though impressions gained from these can be supplemented, confirmed, or called into question by observations of the patient in the treatment situation. Parenthetically, behavior of patients in therapeutic groups may be more useful for this purpose than their behavior in a private interview, since the group is closer to the interpersonal situations of everyday life (40).

The major control problem is how to minimize biases in the reports and in the observer. The former are best controlled by using at least one informant besides the patient. Presumably another informant will not have precisely the same attitude towards the patient and psychotherapy as the patient does. Comparing and contrasting the information from both sources should enable the raters to reach a more accurate evaluation of the actual state of affairs than relying on either alone.

With respect to rater bias, since the ratings are based on interviews, it is not practically possible to conceal from the raters the kind of treatment the patient has had since the previous rating. This could conceivably be done by transcribing the interviews, having one set of persons edit out all clues as to what treatment the patient had received, a second set check to make sure this has been done, and a third set make the ratings of change. In the present primitive state of our knowledge of psychotherapy, the enormous labor required to yield this level of control of rater bias can probably more profitably be expended in other ways. Moreover, it deprives the interviewer of face-to-face contact with the patient, and thus prevents his taking advantage of non-verbal cues, which may seriously handicap him. In our study we tried to guard against rater bias arising from knowledge of patients' treatment in three ways. The first was simply to keep this possibility always in mind. The second was to base the final global rating of social ineffectiveness on many sub-ratings of the patient's behavior in different situations, including the interview. Our social ineffectiveness scale permitted ratings on a maximum of fifteen types of ineffective behavior and nineteen categories of social situation, including the interview itself. Patients were only rated, of course, on the

behavior and situations for which data were available. As a final safeguard, each interview was rated independently by the interviewer and a concealed observer, and the joint rating was arrived at by a conference between the four raters, two having rated the patient and two the other informant.

The pros and cons of ratings arrived at by conference versus those arrived at by arithmetical combination of individual ratings are complex (18). In general, against the conference ratings is urged the danger that one person may unduly influence the total result, so that the conference would merely confirm the opinions of its most powerful member. We checked on this possibility in one of our studies by correlating ratings of individual conferees made before the conference with the conference rating. All correlations were within the same range, indicating that no one member dominated the group's judgment (24).

In favor of the conference method may be offered that it enables each participant to modify his impression in the light of information presented by the others, so that the rating finally reached by the group should be better than that of any individual in it. On the other hand, they may hear more information than they can digest and evaluate, which may impede their ability to make a valid collective judgment (23).

On balance we thought that conference ratings were probably more valid than those obtained by averaging individual ones. We did insist that each rater rate the patient before coming to the conference to help him withstand the pressures of the other members.

Turning to the other major criterion of improvement, change in the patient's feelings and attitudes, the only way of tapping these is through his reports, direct or indirect. If the patient can clearly perceive the significance of the information he gives, the question arises of controlling for factors influencing his statements other than his internal state. Indirect measures, which more or less conceal from the patient the significance of his response, shift the control problem to the validity of their interpretation.

In using scales which are relatively transparent to the patient such as a symptom check list or even Q-sorts which yield such measures as self-ideal discrepancy, one must always keep in mind the possibility that the patient is telling the rater what he wants him to hear, so that changes in scores may be due to changes in his attitude to the observer or to treatment than to genuine improvement. In Rogers and Dymond's study, for example, the own-control clients who were placed on a sixty-day waiting period of no therapy were divided into two groups: the attrition group who stayed for less than six sessions of therapy subsequently and those who stayed for more than six sessions. On all measures the attrition group showed more improvement over the wait period than those who later accepted therapy. This is interpreted to mean that the attrition group showed more tendency to spontaneous recovery (16). Another possibility exists, which is that at the second testing the remainers wanted to show that they still felt the need for treatment; the attrition group, that they did not want further treatment. Thus the remainers would tend to indicate that they still felt sick, and the attrition group that they did not. Needless to say, such distortion need not be deliberate or conscious. This interpretation would be consistent, I believe, with the Rogers and Dymond findings on the two Q-sort measures (self-ideal relationship and adjustment score), which do not fully disguise from the patient what the experimenter is looking for. I am not sure whether it could also account for the similar results on the TAT, but do not believe that even this highly indirect approach entirely excludes this possibility.

We found in our study that at the start of each evaluation period patients who remained in treatment until the next re-evaluation had higher discomfort scores on the average than those who dropped out before the next evaluation. This is similar to the results obtained by Rogers and Dymond, and suggests the same thing, namely that scores on a discomfort scale are partly the patient's means of communicating that he wishes further treatment.

Many indirect measures of the patient's subjective state have been devised in order to circumvent this type of problem. Projective tests such as the Rorschach or TAT permit measurements of changes in the patient's attitudes through the use of communications, the significance of which is hidden from him. Since projective tests yield permanent records, the points at which they were given can easily be concealed from the rater, eliminating bias based on knowledge of whether or not the patient has had treatment. An inescapable limitation of scores on projective tests is that they do not bear an obvious relationship to clinical improvement. Therefore, they must eventually be validated against other measures of patients' subjective state and behavior. For example, in the Rogers and Dymond study, scoring the TAT one way gave results consistent with other measures but scoring it in a different way, though it yielded another set of relationships to the treatment variables, gave results that bore no relationship to the other measures of improvement (5, 17).

Implicit in the discussion so far is that scores on measure of response variables may be influenced by the conditions under which they are measured, or by the measuring instrument itself. This problem, which exists even in the physical sciences, assumes major proportions in the evaluation of patients' reports of improvement. As already indicated, these may be affected by the patient's attitude towards therapy or the therapist. There remain to be considered the possible effects of the tester's expectancies, of the form of the test, and of its repetition.

With all measures except the strictly objective ones, and possibly even in these, the tester may influence the scores in accord with his expectations through a process which may be analogous to operant conditioning (14).[6] The cues which mediate this influence may be so subtle as to escape the awareness of both interviewer and subject. Although the limits of the effects of operant conditioning are not known, it certainly exerts more effect than has been generally realized. Examples are the way Freud's patients fabricated infantile memories to conform with his theory of the etiology of neuroses (11), the recent work by Salzinger and Pisoni who showed that within ten minutes it was possible significantly to increase the number of affective statements made by schizophrenic patients (34), and Murray's analyses of therapy protocols which demonstrated rapid shifts in frequency of certain content categories of the patients' productions in accordance with the therapists' values, even when the latter thought he was non-directive (30).

To complicate matters further, the patient may influence his own subjective state by hearing his report of it. If, in response to factors in the test situation, he says he feels better or worse than he "actually" does, his feelings may change to conform with his behavior, as William James observed long ago in a somewhat different context (22, p. 463).

The form of the test may influence the patients' scores. In our study the correlation between patients' global estimates of improvement and their scores on the discomfort scale was only 0.65. Apparently it made a difference whether the measure was itemized and written, or global and oral. An itemized scale perhaps makes the patient more cautious on the one hand and, on the other, reminds him of complaints which had slipped his mind.

The possible effects of mere repetition

of the test must also be considered, especially those due to the patients' greater unfamiliarity with the test and test situation on the first occasion than on subsequent ones (21). He may be puzzled by the test itself or made uneasy by other factors of the situation, which can adversely affect his scores. These influences are apt to be less strong the second time he takes the test, yielding "better" scores. We found that there was a marked average drop in discomfort scores the first time the scale was readministered, and that on the average this drop was maintained over the following two years. The most probable explanation of this phenomenon would be that the first scores on the Discomfort Scale were artificially heightened by the patient's general uneasiness in an unfamiliar situation, so that we were measuring not so much the effect of six months of treatment as the effect of greater familiarity with the test and the situation. It was possible to control for this by taking a group of patients at the two-year follow-up interval, giving them a placebo to take for two weeks, and then re-administering the Discomfort Scale. We found a drop of the same order of magnitude between this fourth and fifth administration of the scale, following the placebo, as there was between the first and the second, following psychotherapy (13). The drop in response to the placebo obviously could not be explained by increasing familiarity with the implement. This finding has implications for the relationship of psychotherapy to the placebo effect which are irrelevant here. In this context it is cited as an example of controlling for the effects of repetition of a test.

Discussion of control of response variables in psychotherapy would be incomplete without mention of the importance of follow-up studies to determine long-term effects of treatment. Evaluation of any form of treatment is obviously inadequate in the absence of information as to the duration of its effects. The longer the study

---

[6] Note a recent and relevant review of the literature: Krasner, L. Studies of the conditioning of verbal behavior. *Psychol. Bull.*, 1958, 55, 148–170.

continues, the greater is the problem posed by attrition of the sample. This is influenced by patients' attitudes towards the treatment received, and by the kind and amount of information sought by the investigator. The importance of the patients' attitudes may be illustrated by the fact that after two years we were able to obtain re-interviews with 90% of the patients who had originally accepted therapy, but on 33% of those who had dropped out of treatment. Presumably the feeling of the former group towards the Clinic was much more favorable.

The effect of the amount of information desired is suggested by the fact that our most strenuous efforts brought back only 56% of the treated patients for personal re-interviews after three years, whereas Saslow (36) reports a return of about 80% after four to six years, to written requests for limited information.

Thus the conductor of a follow-up study is faced with a variety of choices as to how best to expand his resources. He must balance considerations of completeness of sample against the relative value of various types of information obtained in different ways, and so on, but these questions need not concern us here.

DISCUSSION

In conclusion I should like briefly to review certain general considerations about controls, which seem to come up repeatedly in clinical research. The first concerns replication of findings. No findings, however striking, are more than tentative until they have been replicated. Replication, incidentally, need not involve actual repetition of the study. If the population is large enough, the same result can be achieved by dividing both experimental and control groups in half, and using one set as a test of the reliability of the findings obtained with the other.

Replication with a fresh sample tests the adequacy of the description of the variables in the original study and the accuracy of the original observations. This is particularly important in a field like psychotherapy where so much is still unknown. Thus it is not surprising, though perhaps a little disconcerting, to find that repetitions of studies at the same clinics, with presumably similar populations and therapists, have failed to reproduce certain findings that possessed high statistical reliability (29, 41). Failure of others to replicate a finding may lead the original researcher to discover that he had failed to make explicit an important experimental condition. Attempted replication by others also helps to establish the extent to which the original finding can be generalized to populations and settings differing in various ways from the original ones.

Perhaps the most important value of replication is that it guards against *ex post facto* reasoning. There is no limit to the ingenuity of the human mind. It seems to be literally impossible to present a person with a set of data that are so random that he will not be able to read a relationship into them.[7] In psychotherapy if an experiment seems to demonstrate a certain relationship between therapeutic variables and changes in the patient, the experimenter can always make an hypothesis to explain it. This is a necessary and desirable first step to further research. A common error, however, is to offer the observed relationship as proof of the hypothesis. This circular reasoning can be escaped only by making an explicit prediction on the basis of the hypothesis and then seeing if the prediction is borne out with a fresh sample.

While replication is ordinarily highly desirable, this is not to say that every finding should be replicated. Since, especially in research on therapy, replication may involve many months of work, and time and energy are limited, the investigator must ask himself whether the tentative relationship he thinks he has discovered is impor-

---

[7] Personal communication from Alex Bavelas.

tant enough to justify the effort of replication, or whether his time would not be better spent looking for more significant data. If he reaches the latter decision, is he justified in publishing the unreplicated finding? I believe he is, to make it available to others, as long as he does not present it as more than suggestive.

A general point about controls, which is obvious to statisticians but seems difficult for some clinicians to grasp, is that statistical methods of control can be applied to a relatively small sample. The size of the sample needed to achieve any given level of significance varies directly with the variability of the responses and the range of characteristics of the patients in the experimental and control groups, and varies inversely with the magnitude of the difference between the groups at the close of the experiment, assuming that they were matched at the beginning.[8] Also, it is possible validly to generalize findings obtained with a small population to a very large one, as demonstrated by public opinion polls. All that is required is that the small sample be truly representative of the larger one; that is, that important variables show the same relative frequency distributions in the two groups. Of course, the greater the discrepancy in size between the sample and the total populations, the greater the care needed to assure its representativeness.

Statistical measures of significance may be misleading in that a statistically significant finding need not be significant in the non-technical sense of the term. The discovery of a very low correlation between variables which achieves high significance because the groups involved are large, indicates, to be sure, that some relationship is present, but it may be so weak as to contribute practically nothing to an understanding of the phenomena under study.

The central question posed by such a finding is whether pursuit of the lead is likely to unearth a relationship of sufficient importance to justify the effort. An analogy might be the discovery of a low grade of ore. The decision as to whether to try to extract the metal from it would depend on the estimate of the work involved and the potential value of the metal. The Curies used tons of pitchblende to obtain a few grains of radium. They would not have made a similar effort to extract an equal amount of lead.

Failure to demonstrate a significant relationship between two variables does not prove the absence of such a relationship. The statement that a proposition has not been proven to be true is not the same as the statement that it has been proven to be false. Some of my colleagues accuse me of being a therapeutic nihilist when I point out that it has not yet been demonstrated that different forms of therapy lead to significantly different results. They hear this as an assertion that no such differences exist, instead of an attempt to point out an area requiring research.

Many factors may obscure the existence of a genuine relationship. Wittenborn (43) points out that if the sample is not normally distributed, this increases the standard error of estimate, decreasing the possibilities that the differences between experimental and control groups will meet a statistical criterion for significance. This may lead to a real difference being overlooked. He suggests statistical measures for testing and correcting for this error. Significant differences may also be obscured by insensitivities or errors of the measuring instruments. In research on psychotherapy, the therapist, through unfamiliarity with a new technique, may fail to get results, not because the technique is valueless, but because he uses it poorly. "These are the factors our tender-minded, but not therefore unscientific, investigator bears in mind. He stresses that 'not statisically significant'—like the Scotch verdict 'not

---

[8] Kramer and Greenhouse (26) have prepared tables indicating how large experimental and control groups must be in order that given amounts of differences between them will achieve given levels of significance.

proven'—permits us to return the hypothesis on trial to the arms of those who love it, rather than at once chopping off its head." (6, p. 57)

Though controls enable the investigator to state the level of confidence of his finding, they do not insure a correct interpretation of it. That the serum of hospitalized schizophrenics oxidizes adrenaline more rapidly than the serum of non-hospitalized controls was established with a high level of certainty and replicated, but this did not prove that the difference was due to schizophrenia. It turned out to be due to differences in the diet of the two populations. We can assert that the chances are better than 95 in 100 that patients will show more improvement in social effectiveness after six months of weekly individual therapy than after six months of minimal treatment, but the interpretation of this difference remains open. It would take another study to determine if the difference is best explained by the fact that patients in minimal treatment had less therapeutic contacts, or by some other factor, for example that minimal treatment was devalued by therapists and patients. These examples illustrate that often one cannot control for a variable until one thinks of it. The automatic use of controls is no substitute for thought.

Since controls are always relative, and since energy expended in establishing controls is diverted from that devoted to seeking new insights, their proper use is not solely a question of applying the correct methods, but involves exercise of judgment concerning what level of control should be attempted. How much control to strive for is determined by the state of development of the subject and the potential importance of the finding to be checked. Sometimes it may be better to accept a poorly controlled tentative finding as a source of leads for potentially more penetrating or definitive studies, than to divert time and energy to trying to increase its level of confidence. Efforts to use a level of control not warranted by the state of the problem may be as hampering to good research as failure to use controls that are possible.

Preoccupation with controls, moreover, is apt to guide the selection of questions for study, not by their significance, but by the ease with which they can be investigated. One is reminded of the familiar story of the drunkard who lost his keys in a dark alley but looked for them under the lamp post because the light was better.

What is most needed in research on psychotherapy is originality of thought and courage to grapple with important issues, setting up as much control as is feasible. Each experiment should lead to another which is an improvement over its predecessor. In this sense a bad experiment is better than none, and several are better than one. Unless one makes the original crude experiments, no progress is possible.

REFERENCES

1. ANGEL, C., LEACH, B. E., MARTENS, S., COHEN, M., & HEATH, R. Serum oxidation tests in schizophrenic and normal subjects. *Arch. Neurol. & Psychiat.*, 1957, 78, 500–504.

2. APPEL, K. E., LHAMON, W. T., MYERS, J. M., & HARVEY, W. A. Long term psychotherapy. In *Psychiatric treatment*. Baltimore: Williams & Wilkins, 1953. Pp. 21–34.

3. ASH, P. The reliability of psychiatric diagnoses. *J. abnorm. soc. Psychol.*, 1949, 44, 272–276.

4. BETZ, BARBARA J., & WHITEHORN, J. C. The relationship of the therapist to the outcome of therapy in schizophrenia. In N. S. Kline (Ed.), *Psychiatric Research Reports 5*. Washington: Amer. Psychiat. Assoc., 1956. Pp. 89–105.

5. DYMOND, ROSALIND F. Adjustment changes over therapy from thematic apperception test ratings. In C. R. Rogers and Rosalind F. Dymond (Eds.), *Psychotherapy and personality change*. Chicago: Univ. Chicago Press, 1954. Pp. 109–120.

6. EDWARDS, A. L., & CRONBACH, L. J. Ex-

perimental design for research in psycho-therapy. *J. clin. Psychol.,* 1952, 8, 51–59.

7. FRANK, J. D. The dynamics of the psychotherapeutic relationship, 1. determinants and effects of the therapist's influence. *Psychiat.,* in press.

8. FRANK, J. D., GLIEDMAN, L. H., IMBER, S. D., NASH, E. H., & STONE, A. R. Why patients leave psychotherapy. *Arch. Neurol. & Psychiat.,* 1957, 77, 283–299.

9. FRANK, J. D., GLIEDMAN, L. H., IMBER, S. D., STONE, A. R., & NASH, E. H. Patients' expectancies and relearning as factors determining improvement in psychotherapy. *Amer. J. Psychiat.,* in press.

10. FRANK, J. D., MARGOLIN, J., NASH, HELEN T., STONE, A. R., VARON, EDITH, & ASCHER, E. Two behavior patterns in therapeutic groups and their apparent motivation. *Human Relat.,* 1952, 5, 289–317.

11. FREUD, S. *A general introduction to psychoanalysis.* New York: Horace Liveright, 1920.

12. FREYHAN, F. A. Psychomotility and parkinsonian in treatment with neuroleptic drugs. *Arch. Neurol. & Psychiat.,* 1957, 78, 465–472.

13. GLIEDMAN, L. H., NASH, E. H., IMBER, S. D., STONE, A. R., & FRANK, J. D. The reduction of symptoms by pharmacologically inert substances and by short term psychotherapy. *Arch. Neurol. & Psychiat.,* 1958, 79, 345–351.

14. GREENSPOON, J. The reinforcing effect of two spoken sounds on the frequency of two responses. *Amer. J. Psychol.,* 1955, 68, 409–416.

15. GRUMMON, D. L. Design, procedures, and subjects for the first block. In C. R. Rogers & Rosalind F. Dymond (Eds.), *Psychotherapy and personality change.* Chicago: Univ. Chicago Press, 1954. P. 35–52.

16. GRUMMON, D. L. Personality changes as a function of time in persons motivated for therapy. In C. R. Rogers & Rosalind F. Dymond (Eds.), *Psychotherapy and personality change.* Chicago: Univ. Chicago Press, 1954. Pp. 238–255.

17. GRUMMON, D. L., & JOHN, EVE S. Changes over client-centered therapy, evaluated on psychoanalytically based thematic apperception test scales. In C. R. Rogers & Rosalind

F. Dymond (Eds.), *Psychotherapy and personality change.* Chicago: Univ. Chicago Press, 1954. Pp. 121–144.

18. HAMBURG, D. A., SABSHIN, M. A., BOARD, F. A., GRINKER, R. R., KORCHIN, S. J., BASOWITZ, H., HEATH, H., & PERSKY, H. Classification and rating of emotional experiences, *Arch. Neurol. & Psychiat.,* 1958, 79, 415–426.

19. IMBER, S. D., FRANK, J. D., NASH, E. H., STONE, A. R., & GLIEDMAN, L. H. Improvement and amount of therapeutic contact: an alternative to the use of no-treatment controls in psychotherapy. *J. consult. Psychol.,* 1957, 21, 309–315.

20. IMBER, S. D., NASH, E. H., & STONE, A. R. Social class and duration of psychotherapy, *J. clin. Psychol.,* 1955, 11, 281–284.

21. JACOBS, A., & LEVENTER, S. Response to personality inventories with situational stress. *J. abnorm. soc. Psychol.,* 1955, 51, 449–451.

22. JAMES, W. *The principles of psychology,* Vol. 2. New York: Holt, 1890.

23. KELLY, E. L., & FISKE, D. W. *The prediction of performance in clinical psychology.* Ann Arbor: Univ. Michigan Press, 1951.

24. KELMAN, H. C., & PARLOFF, M. B. Interrelations among three criteria of improvement in group therapy: comfort, effectiveness, and self-awareness. *J. abnorm. soc. Psychol.,* 1957, 54, 281–288.

25. KLINE, N. S., TENNEY, A. M., NICOLAOU, G. T., & MALZBERG, B. The selection of psychiatric patients for research. *Amer. J. Psychiat.,* 1953, 110, 179–185.

26. KRAMER, M., & GREENHOUSE, S. W. Determination of sample size and selection of cases. *Proceedings of the conference on the evaluation of pharmacotherapy, Washington, D. C., September 19–22, 1956,* in press.

27. LEARY, T. *Interpersonal Diagnosis of Personality.* New York: Ronald Press, 1957.

28. LHAMON, W. Time and rhythm in psychosomatic relationships. In P. Hoch and J. Zubin (Eds.), *Current problems in psychiatric diagnosis.* New York: Grune & Stratton, 1953, Pp. 244–255.

29. LORR, M. Progress and problems in research on psychotherapy. Paper read at VA-Univ.

Conf., Univ. Maryland, November 14, 1957.

30. MURRAY, E. J. A content-analysis method for studying psychotherapy. *Psychol. Monogr.*, 1956, 70, No. 13 (Whole No. 420).

31. PARLOFF, M. B. Some factors affecting the quality of therapeutic relationships. *J. abnorm. soc. Psychol.*, 1956, 52, 5–10.

32. PARLOFF, M. B., KELMAN, H. C., & FRANK, J. D. Comfort, effectiveness, and self-awareness as criteria of improvement in psychotherapy. *Amer. J. Psychiat.*, 1954, 111, 343–351.

33. ROSENTHAL, D., & FRANK, J. D. Psychotherapy and the placebo effect. *Psychol. Bull.*, 1956, 53, 294–302.

34. SALZINGER, K., & PISONI, STEPHANIE. Reinforcement of affect responses of schizophrenics during the clinical interview. *J. abnorm. soc. Psychol.*, 1958, 57, 84–90.

35. SASLOW, G., MATARAZZO, J. D., PHILLIPS, JEANNE S., & MATARAZZO, RUTH G. Test-retest stability of interaction patterns during interviews conducted one week apart. *J. abnorm. soc. Psychol.*, 1957, 54, 295–302.

36. SASLOW, G., & PETERS, ANN D. A follow-up study of "untreated" patients with various behavior disorders. *Psychiat. Quart.*, 1956, 30, 283–302.

37. SCHAFFER, L., & MYERS, J. K. Psychotherapy and social stratification: an empirical study of practice in a psychiatric outpatient clinic. *Psychiat.*, 1954, 17, 83–93.

38. SEMON, R. G., & GOLDSTEIN, N. The effectiveness of group psychotherapy with chronic schizophrenic patients and an evaluation of different therapeutic methods. *J. consult. Psychol.*, 1957, 21, 317–322.

39. SHEPHERD, M., & GRUENBERG, E. M. The age for neuroses. *Milbank Memorial Fund Quart.*, 1957, 35, 258–265.

40. STONE, A. R., PARLOFF, M. B., & FRANK, J. D. The use of "diagnostic" groups in a group therapy program, *Int. J. Group Psychother.*, 1954, 4, 274–284.

41. SULLIVAN, P. L., MILLER, CHRISTINE, & SMELSER, W. Factors in length of stay and progress in psychotherapy. *J. consult. Psychol.*, 1958, 22, 1–9.

42. WATTERSON, D. J. Problems in evaluation of psychotherapy. *Bull. Menninger Clin.*, 1954, 18, 232–241.

43. WITTENBORN, J. R. Critique of small sample statistical methods in clinical psychology. *J. clin. Psychol.*, 1952, 8, 34–37.

Psychotherapy as a Learning Process

ALBERT BANDURA

While it is customary to conceptualize psychotherapy as a learning process, few therapists accept the full implications of this position. Indeed, this is best illustrated by the writings of the learning theorists themselves. Most of our current methods of psychotherapy represent an accumulation of more or less uncontrolled clinical experiences and, in many instances, those who have written about psychotherapy in terms of learning theory have merely substituted a new language; the practice remains essentially unchanged (Dollard, Auld, & White, 1954; Dollard & Miller, 1950; Shoben, 1949).

If one seriously subscribes to the view that psychotherapy is a learning process, the methods of treatment should be derived from our knowledge of learning and motivation. Such an orientation is likely to yield new techniques of treatment which, in many respects, may differ markedly from the procedures currently in use.

Psychotherapy rests on a very simple but fundamental assumption, i.e., human behavior is modifiable through psychological procedures. When skeptics raise the question, "Does psychotherapy work?" they may be responding in part to the mysticism

Reprinted from *Psychological Bulletin*, 1961, 58, 143–159, with the permission of the American Psychological Association and the author.

that has come to surround the term. Perhaps the more meaningful question, and one which avoids the surplus meanings associated with the term "psychotherapy," is as follows: Can human behavior be modified through psychological means and if so, what are the learning mechanisms that mediate behavior change?

In the sections that follow, some of these learning mechanisms will be discussed, and studies in which systematic attempts have been made to apply these principles of learning to the area of psychotherapy will be reviewed. Since learning theory itself is still somewhat incomplete, the list of psychological processes by which changes in behavior can occur should not be regarded as exhaustive, nor are they necessarily without overlap.

COUNTERCONDITIONING

Of the various treatment methods derived from learning theory, those based on the principle of counterconditioning have been elaborated in greatest detail. Wolpe (1954, 1958, 1959) gives a thorough account of this method, and additional example of cases treated in this manner are provided by Jones (1956), Lazarus and Rachman (1957), Meyer (1957), and Rachman (1959). Briefly, the principle involved is as follows: if strong responses which are incompatible with anxiety reactions can be made to occur in the presence of anxiety evoking cues, the incompatible responses will become attached to these cues and thereby weaken or eliminate the anxiety responses.

The first systematic psychotherapeutic application of this method was reported by Jones (1924b) in the treatment of Peter, a boy who showed severe phobic reactions to animals, fur objects, cotton, hair, and mechanical toys. Counterconditioning was achieved by feeding the child in the presence of initially small but gradually increasing anxiety-arousing stimuli. A rabbit in a cage was placed in the room at some distance so as not to disturb the boy's eating. Each day the rabbit was brought nearer to the table and eventually removed from the cage. During the final stage of treatment, the rabbit was placed on the feeding table and even in Peter's lap. Tests of generalization revealed that the fear responses had been effectively eliminated, not only toward the rabbit, but toward the previously feared furry objects as well.

In this connection, it would be interesting to speculate on the diagnosis and treatment Peter would have received had he been seen by Melanie Klein (1949) rather than by Mary Cover Jones!

It is interesting to note that while both Shoben (1949) and Wolpe (1958) propose a therapy based on the principle of counterconditioning, their treatment methods are radically different. According to Shoben, the patient discusses and thinks about stimulus situations that are anxiety provoking in the context of an interpersonal situation which simultaneously elicits positive affective responses from the patient. The therapeutic process consists in connecting the anxiety provoking stimuli, which are symbolically reproduced, with the comfort reaction made to the therapeutic relationship.

Shoben's paper represents primarily a counterconditioning interpretation of the behavior changes brought about through conventional forms of psychotherapy since, apart from highlighting the role of positive emotional reactions in the treatment process, no new techniques deliberately designed to facilitate relearning through counterconditioning are proposed.

This is not the case with Wolpe, who has made a radical departure from tradition. In his treatment, which he calls reciprocal inhibition, Wolpe makes systematic use of three types of responses which are antagonistic to, and therefore inhibitory of, anxiety. These are: assertive or approach responses, sexual responses, and relaxation responses.

On the basis of historical information, interview data, and psychological test responses, the therapist constructs an anxiety hierarchy, a ranked list of stimuli to which the patient reacts with anxiety. In the case of desensitization based on relaxation, the patient is hypnotized and given relaxation suggestions. He is then asked to imagine a scene representing the weakest item on the anxiety hierarchy and, if the relaxation is unimpaired, this is followed by having the patient imagine the next item on the list, and so on. Thus the anxiety cues are gradually increased from session to session until the last phobic stimulus can be presented without impairing the relaxed state. Through this procedure, relaxation responses eventually come to be attached to the anxiety evoking stimuli.

Wolpe reports remarkable therapeutic success with a wide range of neurotic reactions treated on this counterconditioning principle. He also contends that the favorable outcomes achieved by the more conventional psychotherapeutic methods may result from the reciprocal inhibition of anxiety by strong positive responses evoked in the patient-therapist relationship.

Although the counterconditioning method has been employed most extensively in eliminating anxiety-motivated avoidance reactions and inhibitions, it has been used with some success in reducing maladaptive approach responses as well. In the latter case, the goal object is repeatedly associated with some form of aversive stimulus.

Raymond (1956), for example, used nausea as the aversion experience in the treatment of a patient who presented a fetish for handbags and perambulators which brought him into frequent contact with the law in that he repeatedly smeared mucus on ladies' handbags and destroyed perambulators by running into them with his motorcycle. Though the patient had undergone psychoanalytic treatment, and was fully aware of the origin and the sexual significance of his behavior, nevertheless, the fetish persisted.

The treatment consisted of showing the patient a collection of handbags, perambulators, and colored illustrations just before the onset of nausea produced by injections of apomorphine. The conditioning was repeated every 2 hours day and night for 1 week plus additional sessions 8 days and 6 months later.

Raymond reports that, not only was the fetish successfully eliminated, but also the patient showed a vast improvement in his social (and legal) relationships, was promoted to a more responsible position in his work, and no longer required the fetish fantasies to enable him to have sexual intercourse.

Nauseant drugs, especially emetine, have also been utilized as the unconditioned stimulus in the aversion treatment of alcoholism (Thirmann, 1949; Thompson & Bielinski, 1953; Voegtlen, 1940; Wallace, 1949). Usually 8 to 10 treatments in which the sight, smell, and taste of alcohol is associated with the onset of nausea are sufficient to produce abstinence. Of 1,000 or more cases on whom adequate follow-up data are reported, approximately 60% of the patients have been totally abstinent following the treatment. Voegtlen (1940) suggests that a few preventive treatments given at an interval of about 6 months may further improve the results yielded by this method.

Despite these encouraging findings, most psychotherapists are unlikely to be impressed since, in their opinion, the underlying causes of the alcoholism have in no way been modified by the conditioning procedure and, if anything, the mere removal of the alcoholism would tend to produce symptom substitution or other adverse effects. A full discussion of this issue will be presented later. In this particular context, however, several aspects of the Thompson and Bielinski (1953) data are worth noting. Among the alcoholic patients whom they treated, six "suffered from mental disorders not due to alcohol or associated deficiency states." It was planned, by the authors, to follow up the aversion treatment with psychotherapy for the underlying psychosis. This, however, proved unnecessary since all but one of the patients, a case of chronic mental deterioration, showed marked improvement and were in a state of remission.

Max (1935) employed a strong electric shock as the aversive stimulus in treating a patient who tended to display homosexual behavior following exposure to a fetishistic stimulus. Both the fetish and the homosexual behavior were removed through a series of avoidance conditioning sessions in which the patient was administered shock in the presence of the fetishistic object.

Wolpe (1958) has also reported favorable results with a similar procedure in the treatment of obsessions.

A further variation of the counterconditioning procedure has been developed by Mowrer and Mowrer (1938) for use with enuretic patients. The device consists of a wired bed pad which sets off a loud buzzer and awakens the child as soon as micturition begins. Bladder tension thus becomes a cue for waking up which, in turn, is followed by sphincter contraction. Once bladder pressure becomes a stimulus for the more remote sphincter control response, the child is able to remain dry for relatively long periods of time without wakening.

Mowrer and Mowrer (1938) report complete success with 30 children treated by this method; similarly, Davidson and Douglass (1950) achieved highly successful results with 20 chronic enuretic children (15 cured, 5 markedly improved); of 5 cases treated by Morgan and Witmer (1939), 4 of the children not only gained full sphincter control, but also made a significant improvement in their social behavior. The one child with whom the conditioning approach had failed was later found to have bladder difficulties which required medical attention.

Some additional evidence for the efficacy of this method is provided by Martin and Kubly (1955) who obtained follow-up information from 118 of 220 parents who had treated their children at home with this type of conditioning apparatus. In 74% of the cases, according to the parents' replies, the treatment was successful.

EXTINCTION

"When a learned response is repeated without reinforcement the strength of the tendency to perform that response undergoes a progressive decrease" (Dollard & Miller, 1950). Extinction involves the development of inhibitory potential which is composed of two components. The evocation of any reaction generates reactive inhibition (I_r) which presumably dissipates with time. When reactive inhibition (fatigue, etc.) reaches a high point, the cessation of activity alleviates this negative motivational state and any stimuli associated with the cessation of the response become conditioned inhibitors ($_sI_r$).

One factor that has been shown to influence the rate of extinction of maladaptive and anxiety-motivated behavior is the interval between extinction trials. In general, there tends to be little diminution in the strength of fear-motivated behavior when extinction trials are widely distributed, whereas under massed trials, reactive inhibition builds up rapidly and conse-

quently extinction is accelerated (Calvin, Clifford, Clifford, Bolden, & Harvey, 1956; Edmonson & Amsel, 1954).

An illustration of the application of this principle is provided by Yates (1958) in the treatment of tics. Yates demonstrated, in line with the findings from laboratory studies of extinction under massed and distributed practice, that massed sessions in which the patient performed tics voluntarily followed by prolonged rest to allow for the dissipation of reactive inhibition was the most effective procedure for extinguishing the tics.

It should be noted that the extinction procedure employed by Yates is very similar to Dunlap's method of negative practice, in which the subject reproduces the negative behaviors voluntarily without reinforcement (Dunlap, 1932; Lehner, 1954). This method has been applied most frequently, with varying degrees of success, to the treatment of speech disorders (Fishman, 1937; Meissner, 1946; Rutherford, 1940; Sheehan, 1951; Sheehan & Voas, 1957). If the effectiveness of this psychotherapeutic technique is due primarily to extinction, as suggested by Yates' study, the usual practice of terminating a treatment session before the subject becomes fatigued (Lehner, 1954), would have the effect of reducing the rate of extinction, and may in part account for the divergent results yielded by this method.

Additional examples of the therapeutic application of extinction procedures are provided by Jones (1955), and most recently by C. D. Williams (1959).

Most of the conventional forms of psychotherapy rely heavily on extinction effects although the therapist may not label these as such. For example, many therapists consider *permissiveness* to be a necessary condition of therapeutic change (Alexander, 1956; Dollard & Miller, 1950; Rogers, 1951). It is expected that when a patient expresses thoughts or feelings that provoke anxiety or guilt and the therapist does not disapprove, criticize, or withdraw interest, the fear or guilt will be gradually weakened or extinguished. The extinction effects are believed to generalize to thoughts concerning related topics that were originally inhibited, and to verbal and physical forms of behavior as well (Dollard & Miller, 1950).

Some evidence for the relationship between permissiveness and the extinction of anxiety is provided in two studies recently reported by Dittes (1957a, 1957b). In one study (1957b) involving an analysis of patient-therapist interaction sequences, Dittes found that permissive responses on the part of the therapist were followed by a corresponding decrease in the patient's anxiety (as measured by the GSR) and the occurrence of avoidance behaviors. A sequential analysis of the therapeutic sessions (Dittes, 1957a), revealed that, at the onset of treatment, sex expressions were accompanied by strong anxiety reactions; under the cumulative effects of permissiveness, the anxiety gradually extinguished.

In contrast to counterconditioning, extinction is likely to be a less effective and a more time consuming method for eliminating maladaptive behavior (Jones, 1924a; Dollard & Miller, 1950); in the case of conventional interview therapy, the relatively long intervals between interview sessions, and the ritualistic adherence to the 50-minute hour may further reduce the occurrence of extinction effects.

DISCRIMINATION LEARNING

Human functioning would be extremely difficult and inefficient if a person had to learn appropriate behavior for every specific situation he encountered. Fortunately, patterns of behavior learned in one situation will transfer or generalize to other similar situations. On the other hand, if a person overgeneralizes from one situation to another, or if the generalization is based on superficial or irrelevant cues, behavior becomes inappropriate and maladaptive.

In most theories of psychotherapy,

therefore, discrimination learning, believed to be accomplished through the gaining of awareness or insight, receives emphasis (Dollard & Miller, 1950; Fenichel, 1941; Rogers, 1951; Sullivan, 1953). It is generally assumed that if a patient is aware of the cues producing his behavior, of the responses he is making, and of the reasons that he responds the way he does, his behavior will become more susceptible to verbally-mediated control. Voluntarily guided, discriminative behavior will replace the automatic, overgeneralized reactions.

While this view is widely accepted, as evidenced in the almost exclusive reliance on interview procedures and on interpretative or labeling techniques, a few therapists (Alexander & French, 1946) have questioned the importance attached to awareness in producing modifications in behavior. Whereas most psychoanalysts (Fenichel, 1941), as well as therapists representing other points of view (Fromm-Reichmann, 1950; Sullivan, 1953) consider insight a precondition of behavior change, Alexander and French consider insight or awareness a result of change rather than its cause. That is, as the patient's anxieties are gradually reduced through the permissive conditions of treatment, formerly inhibited thoughts are gradually restored to awareness.

Evidence obtained through controlled laboratory studies concerning the value of awareness in increasing the precision of discrimination has so far been largely negative or at least equivocal (Adams, 1957; Erickson, 1958; Razran, 1949). A study by Lacey and Smith (1954), in which they found aware subjects generalized anxiety reactions less extensively than did subjects who were unaware of the conditioned stimulus provides evidence that awareness may aid discrimination. However, other aspects of their findings (e.g., the magnitude of the anxiety reactions to the generalization stimuli were greater than they were to the conditioned stimulus itself) indicate the need for replication.

If future research continues to demonstrate that awareness exerts little influence on the acquisition, generalization, and modification of behavior, such negative results would cast serious doubt on the value of currently popular psychotherapeutic procedures whose primary aim is the development of insight.

METHODS OF REWARD

Most theories of psychotherapy are based on the assumption that the patient has a repertoire of previously learned positive habits available to him, but that these adaptive patterns are inhibited or blocked by competing responses motivated by anxiety or guilt. The goal of therapy, then is to reduce the severity of the internal inhibitory controls, thus allowing the healthy patterns of behavior to emerge. Hence, the role of the therapist is to create permissive conditions under which the patient's "normal growth potentialities" are set free (Rogers, 1951). The fact that most of our theories of personality and therapeutic procedures have been developed primarily through work with oversocialized, neurotic patients may account in part for the prevalence of this view.

There is a large class of disorders (the undersocialized, antisocial personalities whose behavior reflects a failure of the socialization process) for whom this model of personality and accompanying techniques of treatment are quite inappropriate (Bandura & Walters, 1959; Schmideberg, 1959). Such antisocial personalities are likely to present *learning deficits,* consequently the goal of therapy is the acquisition of secondary motives and the development of internal restraint habits. That antisocial patients prove unresponsive to psychotherapeutic methods developed for the treatment of oversocialized neurotics has been demonstrated in a number of studies comparing patients who remain in treatment with these who terminate treatment prematurely (Rubenstein & Lorr,

1956). It is for this class of patients that the greatest departures from traditional treatment methods [are] needed.

While counterconditioning, extinction, and discrimination learning may be effective ways of removing neurotic inhibitions, these methods may be of relatively little value in developing new positive habits. Primary and secondary rewards in the form of the therapist's interest and approval may play an important, if not indispensable, role in the treatment process. Once the patient has learned to want the interest and approval of the therapist, these rewards may then be used to promote the acquisition of new patterns of behavior. For certain classes of patients such as schizophrenics (Atkinson, 1957; Peters, 1953; Robinson 1957) and delinquents (Cairns, 1959), who are either unresponsive to, or fearful of, social rewards, the therapist may have to rely initially on primary rewards in the treatment process.

An ingenious study by Peters and Jenkins (1954) illustrates the application of this principle in the treatment of schizophrenic patients. Chronic patients from closed wards were administered subshock injections of insulin designed to induce the hunger drive. The patients were then encouraged to solve a series of graded problem tasks with fudge as the reward. This program was followed 5 days a week for 3 months.

Initially the tasks involved simple mazes and obstruction problems in which the patients obtained the food reward directly upon successful completion of the problem. Tasks of gradually increasing difficulty were then administered involving multiple-choice learning and verbal-reasoning problems in which the experimenter personally mediated the primary rewards. After several weeks of such problem solving activities the insulin injections were discontinued and social rewards, which by this time had become more effective, were used in solving interpersonal problems that the patients were likely to encounter in their daily activities both inside and outside the hospital setting.

Comparison of the treated group with control groups, designed to isolate the effects of insulin and special attention, revealed that the patients in the reward group improved significantly in their social relationships in the hospital, whereas the patients in the control groups showed no such change.

King and Armitage (1958) report a somewhat similar study in which severely withdrawn schizophrenic patients were treated with operant conditioning methods; candy and cigarettes served as the primary rewards for eliciting and maintaining increasingly complex forms of behavior, i.e., psychomotor, verbal, and interpersonal responses. Unlike the Peters and Jenkins study, no attempt was made to manipulate the level of primary motivation.

An interesting feature of the experimental design was the inclusion of a group of patients who were treated with conventional interview therapy, as well as a recreational therapy and a no-therapy control group. It was found that the operant group, in relation to similar patients in the three control groups, made significantly more clinical improvement.

Skinner (1956b) and Lindsley (1956) working with adult psychotics, and Ferster (1959) working with autistic children, have been successful in developing substantial amounts of reality-oriented behavior in their patients through the use of reward. So far their work has been concerned primarily with the effect of schedules of reinforcement on the rate of evocation of simple impersonal reactions. There is every indication, however, that by varying the contingency of the reward (e.g., the patient must respond in certain specified ways to the behavior of another individual in order to produce the reward) adaptive interpersonal behaviors can be developed as well (Azran & Lindsley, 1956).

The effectiveness of social reinforcers in modifying behavior has been demonstrated repeatedly in verbal conditioning experiments (Krasner, 1958; Salzinger, 1959). Encouraged by these findings, several therapists have begun to experiment with operant conditioning as a method of treatment in its own right (Tilton, 1956; Ullman, Krasner, & Collins, in press; R. I. Williams, 1959); the operant conditioning studies cited earlier are also illustrative of this trend.

So far the study of generalization and permanence of behavior changes brought about through operant conditioning methods has received relatively little attention and the scanty data available are equivocal (Rogers, 1960; Sarason, 1957; Weide, 1959). The lack of consistency in results is hardly surprising considering that the experimental manipulations in many of the conditioning studies are barely sufficient to demonstrate conditioning effects, let alone generalization of changes to new situations. On the other hand, investigators who have conducted more intensive reinforcement sessions, in an effort to test the efficacy of operant conditioning methods as a therapeutic technique have found significant changes in patients' interpersonal behavior in extra-experimental situations (King & Armitage, 1958; Peters & Jenkins, 1954; Ullman et al., in press). These findings are particularly noteworthy since the response classes involved are similar to those psychotherapists are primarily concerned in modifying through interview forms of treatment. If the favorable results yielded by these studies are replicated in future investigations, it is likely that the next few years will witness an increasing reliance on conditioning forms of psychotherapy, particularly in the treatment of psychotic patients.

At this point it might also be noted that consistent with the results from verbal conditioning experiments, content analyses of psychotherapeutic interviews (Bandura, Lipsher, & Miller, 1960; Murray, 1956) suggest that many of the changes observed in psychotherapy, at least insofar as the patients' verbal behavior is concerned, can be accounted for in terms of the therapists' direct, although usually unwitting, reward and punishment of the patients' expressions.

PUNISHMENT

While positive habits can be readily developed through reward, the elimination of socially disapproved habits, which becomes very much an issue in the treatment of antisocial personalities, poses a far more complex problem.

The elimination of socially disapproved behaviors can be accomplished in several ways. They may be consistently unrewarded and thus extinguished. However, antisocial behavior, particularly of an extreme form, cannot simply be ignored in the hope that it will gradually extinguish. Furthermore, since the successful execution of antisocial acts may bring substantial material reward as well as the approval and admiration of associates, it is extremely unlikely that such behavior would ever extinguish.

Although punishment may lead to the rapid disappearance of socially disapproved behavior, its effects are far more complex (Estes, 1944; Solomon, Kamin, & Wynne, 1953). If a person is punished for some socially disapproved habit, the impulse to perform the act, becomes, through its association with punishment a stimulus for anxiety. This anxiety then motivates competing responses which, if sufficiently strong, prevent the occurrence of, or inhibit, the disapproved behavior. Inhibited responses may not, however, thereby lose their strength, and may reappear in situations where the threat of punishment is weaker. Punishment may, in fact, prevent the extinction of a habit; if a habit is completely inhibited, it cannot occur and therefore cannot go unrewarded.

Several other factors point to the futility of punishment as a means of correcting many antisocial patterns. The threat of punishment is very likely to elicit conformity; indeed, the patient may obligingly do whatever he is told to do in order to avoid immediate difficulties. This does not mean, however, that he has acquired a set of sanctions that will be of service to him once he is outside the treatment situation. In fact, rather than leading to the development of internal controls, such methods are likely only to increase the patient's reliance on external restraints. Moreover, under these conditions, the majority of patients will develop the attitude that they will do only what they are told to do—and then often only half-heartedly—and that they will do as they please once they are free from the therapists' supervision (Bandura & Walters, 1959).

In addition, punishment may serve only to intensify hostility and other negative motivations and thus may further instigate the antisocial person to display the very behaviors that the punishment was intended to bring under control.

Mild aversive stimuli have been utilized, of course, in the treatment of voluntary patients who express a desire to rid themselves of specific debilitating conditions.

Liversedge and Sylvester (1955), for example, successfully treated seven cases of writer's cramp by means of a retraining procedure involving electric shock. In order to remove tremors, one component of the motor disorder, the patients were required to insert a stylus into a series of progressively smaller holes; each time the stylus made contact with the side of the hole the patients received a mild shock. The removal of the spasm component of the disorder was obtained in two ways. First, the patients traced various line patterns (similar to the movements required in writing) on a metal plate with a stylus, and any deviation from the path produced a shock. Following training on the apparatus, the subjects then wrote with an electrified pen which delivered a shock whenever excessive thumb pressure was applied.

Liversedge and Sylvester report that following the retraining the patients were able to resume work; a follow-up several months later indicated that the improvement was being maintained.

The aversive forms of therapy, described earlier in the section on counter-conditioning procedures, also make use of mild punishment.

SOCIAL IMITATION

Although a certain amount of learning takes place through direct training and reward, a good deal of a person's behavior repertoire may be acquired through imitation of what he observes in others. If this is the case, social imitation may serve as an effective vehicle for the transmission of prosocial behavior patterns in the treatment of antisocial patients.

Merely providing a model for imitation is not, however, sufficient. Even though the therapist exhibits the kinds of behaviors that he wants the patient to learn, this is likely to have little influence on him if he rejects the therapist as a model. Affectional nurturance is believed to be an important precondition for imitative learning to occur, in that affectional rewards increase the secondary reinforcing properties of the model, and thus predispose the imitator to pattern his behavior after the rewarding person (Mowrer, 1950; Sears, 1957; Whiting, 1954). Some positive evidence for the influence of social rewards on imitation is provided by Bandura and Huston (in press) in a recent study of identification as a process of incidental imitation.

In this investigation preschool children performed an orienting task but, unlike most incidental learning studies, the experimenter performed the diverting task as well, and the extent to which the subjects patterned their behavior after that of the experimenter-model was measured.

A two-choice discrimination problem similar to the one employed by Miller and Dollard (1941) in their experiments of social imitation was used as the diverting task. On each trial, one of two boxes was loaded with two rewards (small multicolor pictures of animals) and the object of the game was to guess which box contained the stickers. The experimenter-model (M) always had her turn first and in each instance chose the reward box. During M's trial, the subject remained at the starting point where he could observe the M's behavior. On each discrimination trial M exhibited certain verbal, motor, and aggressive patterns of behavior that were totally irrelevant to the task to which the subject's attention was directed. At the starting point, for example, M made a verbal response and then marched slowly toward the box containing the stickers, repeating, "March, march, march." On the lid of each box was a rubber doll which M knocked off aggressively when she reached the designated box. She then paused briefly, remarked, "Open the box," removed one sticker, and pasted it on a pastoral scene which hung on the wall immediately behind the boxes. The subject then took his turn and the number of M's behaviors performed by the subject was recorded.

A control group was included in order to (a) provide a check on whether the subjects' performances reflected genuine imitative learning or merely the chance occurrence of behaviors high in the subjects' response hierarchies, and (b) to determine whether subjects would adopt certain aspects of M's behavior which involved considerable delay in reward. With the controls, therefore, M walked to the box, choosing a highly circuitous route along the sides of the experimental room; instead of aggressing toward the doll, she lifted it gently off the container.

The results of this study indicate that, insofar as preschool children are concerned, a good deal of incidental imitation of the behaviors displayed by an adult model does occur. Of the subjects in the experimental group, 88% adopted the M's aggressive behavior, 44% imitated the marching, and

28% reproduced *M*'s verbalizations. In contrast, none of the control subjects behaved aggressively, marched, or verbalized, while 75% of the controls imitated the circuitous route to the containers.

In order to test the hypothesis that children who experience a rewarding relationship with an adult model adopt more of the model's behavior than do children who experience a relatively distant and cold relationship, half the subjects in the experiment were assigned to a nurturant condition; the other half of the subjects to a nonnurturant condition. During the nurturant sessions, which preceded the incidental learning, *M* played with subject, she responded readily to the subject's bids for attention, and in other ways fostered a consistently warm and rewarding interaction with the child. In contrast, during the nonnurturant sessions, the subject played alone while *M* busied herself with paperwork at a desk in the far corner of the room.

Consistent with the hypothesis, it was found that subjects who experienced the rewarding interaction with *M* adopted significantly more of *M*'s behavior than did subjects who were in the nonnurturance condition.

A more crucial test of the transmission of behavior patterns through the process of social imitation involves the delayed generalization of imitative responses to new situations in which the model is absent. A study of this type just completed, provides strong evidence that observation of the cues produced by the behavior of others is an effective means of eliciting responses for which the original probability is very low (Bandura, Ross, & Ross, in press).

Empirical studies of the correlates of strong and weak identification with parents, lend additional support to the theory that rewards promote imitative learning. Boys whose fathers are highly rewarding and affectionate have been found to adopt the father-role in doll-play activities (Sears,

1953), to show father-son similarity in response to items on a personality questionnaire (Payne & Mussen, 1956), and to display masculine behaviors (Mussen & Distler, 1956, 1960) to a greater extent than boys whose fathers are relatively cold and nonrewarding.

The treatment of older unsocialized delinquents is a difficult task, since they are relatively self-sufficient and do not readily seek involvement with a therapist. In many cases socialization can be accomplished only through residental care and treatment. In the treatment home, the therapist can personally administer many of the primary rewards and mediate between the boys' needs and gratifications. Through the repeated association with rewarding experiences for the boy, many of the therapist's attitudes and actions will acquire secondary reward value, and thus the patient will be motivated to reproduce these attitudes and actions in himself. Once these attitudes and values have been thus accepted, the boy's inhibition of antisocial tendencies will function independently of the therapist.

While treatment through social imitation has been suggested as a method for modifying antisocial patterns, it can be an effective procedure for the treatment of other forms of disorders as well. Jones (1924a), for example found that the social example of children reacting normally to stimuli feared by another child was effective, in some instances, in eliminating such phobic reactions. In fact, next to counterconditioning, the method of social imitation proved to be most effective in eliminating inappropriate fears.

There is some suggestive evidence that by providing high prestige models and thus increasing the reinforcement value of the imitatee's behavior, the effectiveness of this method in promoting favorable adjustive patterns of behavior may be further increased (Jones, 1924a; Mausner, 1953, 1954; Miller & Dollard, 1941).

During the course of conventional psychotherapy, the patient is exposed to many incidental cues involving the therapist's values, attitudes, and patterns of behavior. They are incidental only because they are usually considered secondary or irrelevant to the task of resolving the patient's problems. Nevertheless, some of the changes observed in the patient's behavior may result, not so much from the intentional interaction between the patient and the therapist, but rather from active learning by the patient of the therapist's attitudes and values which the therapist never directly attempted to transmit. This is partially corroborated by Rosenthal (1955) who found that in spite of the usual precautions taken by therapists to avoid imposing their values on their clients, the patients who were judged as showing the greatest improvement changed their moral values (in the areas of sex, aggression, and authority) in the direction of the values of their therapists, whereas patients who were unimproved became less like the therapist in values.

FACTORS IMPEDING INTEGRATION

In reviewing the literature on psychotherapy, it becomes clearly evident that learning theory and general psychology have exerted a remarkably minor influence on the practice of psychotherapy and, apart from the recent interest in Skinner's operant conditioning methods (Krasner, 1955; Skinner, 1953), most of the recent serious attempts to apply learning principles to clinical practice have been made by European psychotherapists (Jones, 1956; Lazarus & Rachman, 1957; Liversedge & Sylvester, 1955; Meyer, 1957; Rachman, 1959; Raymond, 1956; Wolpe, 1958; Yates, 1958). This isolation of the methods of treatment from our knowledge of learning and motivation will continue to exist for some time since there are several prevalent attitudes that impede adequate integration.

In the first place, the deliberate use of the principles of learning in the modification of human behavior implies, for most psychotherapists, manipulation and control of the patient, and control is seen by them as antihumanistic and, therefore, bad. Thus, advocates of learning approach to psychotherapy are often charged with treating human beings as though they were rats or pigeons and of leading on the road to Orwell's *1984*.

This does not mean that psychotherapists do not influence and control their patients' behavior. On the contrary. In any interpersonal interaction, and psychotherapy is no exception, people influence and control one another (Frank, 1959; Skinner, 1956a). Although the patient's control of the therapist has not as yet been studied (such control is evident when patients subtly reward the therapist with interesting historical material and thereby avoid the discussion of their current interpersonal problems), there is considerable evidence that the therapist exercises personal control over his patients. A brief examination of interview protocols of patients treated by therapists representing differing theoretical orientations, clearly reveals that the patients have been thoroughly conditioned in their therapists' idiosyncratic languages. Client-centered patients, for example, tend to produce the client-centered terminology, theory, and goals, and their interview content shows little or no overlap with that of patients seen in psychoanalysis who, in turn, tend to speak the language of psychoanalytic theory (Heine, 1950). Even more direct evidence of the therapists' controlling influence is provided in studies of patient-therapist interactions (Bandura et al., 1960; Murray, 1956; Rogers, 1960). The results of these studies show that the therapist not only controls the patient by rewarding him with interest and approval when the patient behaves in a fashion the therapist desires, but that he also controls through punishment, in the form of mild disapproval and withdrawal of interest, when the patient behaves in ways that are threatening to the therapist or run counter to his goals.

One difficulty in understanding the changes that occur in the course of psychotherapy is that the independent variable, i.e., the therapist's behavior, is often vaguely or only partially defined. In an effort to minimize or to deny the therapist's directive influence on the patient, the therapist is typically depicted as a "catalyst" who, in some mysterious way sets free positive adjustive patterns of behavior or similar outcomes usually described in very general and highly socially desirable terms.

It has been suggested, in the material presented in the preceding sections, that many of the changes that occur in psychotherapy derive from the unwitting application of well-known principles of learning. However, the occurrence of the necessary conditions for learning is more by accident than by intent and, perhaps, a more deliberate application of our knowledge of the learning process to psychotherapy would yield far more effective results.

The predominant approach in the development of psychotherapeutic procedures has been the "school" approach. A similar trend is noted in the treatment methods being derived from learning theory. Wolpe, for example, has selected the principle of counterconditioning and built a "school" of psychotherapy around it; Dollard and Miller have focused on extinction and discrimination learning; and the followers of Skinner rely almost entirely on methods of reward. This stress on a few learning principles at the expense of neglecting other relevant ones will serve only to limit the effectiveness of psychotherapy.

A second factor that may account for the discontinuity between general psychology and psychotherapeutic practice is that the model of personality to which most therapists subscribe is somewhat dissonant with the currently developing principles of behavior.

In their formulations of personality functioning, psychotherapists are inclined to appeal to a variety of inner explanatory processes. In contrast, learning theorists view the organism as a far more mechanistic and simpler system, and consequently their formulations tend to be expressed for the most part in terms of antecedent-consequent relationships without reference to inner states.

Symptoms are learned S-R connections; once they are extinguished or deconditioned treatment is complete. Such treatment is based exclusively on present factors; like Lewin's theory, this one is ahistorical. Non-verbal methods are favored over verbal ones, although a minor place is reserved for verbal methods of extinction and reconditioning. Concern is with *function,* not with *content.* The main difference between the two theories arises over the question of "symptomatic" treatment. According to orthodox theory, this is useless unless the underlying complexes are attacked. According to the present theory, there is no evidence for these putative complexes, and symptomatic treatment is all that is required (Eysenck, 1957, pp. 267–268). (Quoted by permission of Frederick A. Praeger, Inc.).

Changes in behavior brought about through such methods as counterconditioning are apt to be viewed by the "dynamically-oriented" therapist, as being not only superficial "symptomatic" treatment, in that the basic underlying instigators of the behavior remain unchanged, but also potentially dangerous, since the direct elimination of a symptom may precipitate more seriously disturbed behavior.

This expectation receives little support from the generally favorable outcomes reported in the studies reviewed in this paper. In most cases where follow-up data were available to assess the long term effects of the therapy, the patients, many of whom had been treated by conventional methods with little benefit, had evidently become considerably more effective in their social, vocational, and psychosexual adjustment. On the whole the evidence, while open to error, suggests that no matter what the origin of the maladaptive behavior may be, a change in behavior brought about through learning procedures may be all that is necessary for the alleviation of most forms of emotional disorders.

As Mowrer (1950) very aptly points out, the "symptom-underlying cause" formulation may represent inappropriate medical analogizing. Whether or not a given behavior will be considered normal or a symptom of an underlying disturbance will depend on whether or not somebody objects to the behavior. For example, aggressiveness on the part of children may be encouraged and considered a sign of healthy development by the parents, while the same behavior is viewed by school authorities and society as a symptom of a personality disorder (Bandura & Walters, 1959). Furthermore, behavior considered to be normal at one stage in development may be regarded as a "symptom of a personality disturbance" at a later period. In this connection it is very appropriate to repeat Mowrer's (1950) query: "And when does persisting behavior of this kind suddenly cease to be normal and become a symptom" (p. 474).

Thus, while a high fever is generally considered a sign of an underlying disease process regardless of when or where it occurs, whether a specific behavior will be viewed as normal or as a symptom of an underlying pathology is not independent of who makes the judgment, the social context in which the behavior occurs, the age of the person, as well as many other factors.

Another important difference between physical pathology and behavior pathology usually overlooked is that, in the case of most behavior disorders, it is not the underlying motivations that need to be altered or removed, but rather the ways in which the patient has learned to gratify his needs (Rotter, 1954). Thus, for example, if a patient displays deviant sexual behavior, the goal is not the removal of the underlying causes, i.e., sexual motivation, but rather the substitution of more socially approved instrumental and goal responses.

It might also be mentioned in passing, that, in the currently popular forms of psychotherapy, the role assumed by the therapist may bring him a good many direct or fantasied gratifications. In the course of treatment the patient may express considerable affection and admiration for the therapist, he may assign the therapist an omniscient status, and the reconstruction of the patient's history may be an intellectually stimulating activity. On the other hand, the methods derived from learning theory place the therapist in a less glamorous role, and this in itself may create some reluctance on the part of psychotherapists to part with the procedures currently in use.

Which of the two conceptual theories of personality—the psychodynamic or the social learning theory—is the more useful in generating effective procedures for the modification of human behavior remains to be demonstrated. While it is possible to present logical arguments and impressive clinical evidence for the efficiency of either approach, the best proving ground is the laboratory.

In evaluating psychotherapeutic methods, the common practice is to compare changes in a treated group with those of a nontreated control group. One drawback of this approach is that, while it answers the question as to whether or not a particular treatment is more effective than no intervention in producing changes along specific dimensions for certain classes of patients, it does not provide evidence concerning the relative effectiveness of alternative forms of psychotherapy.

It would be far more informative if, in future psychotherapy research, radically different forms of treatment were compared (King & Armitage, 1958; Rogers, 1959), since this approach would lead to a more rapid discarding of those of our cherished psychotherapeutic rituals that prove to be ineffective in, or even a handicap to, the successful treatment of emotional disorders.

REFERENCES

ADAMS, J. K. Laboratory studies of behavior without awareness. *Psychol. Bull.*, 1957, 54, 393–405.

ALEXANDER, F. *Psychoanalysis and Psychotherapy.* New York: Norton, 1956.

ALEXANDER, F., & FRENCH, M. T. *Psychoanalytic therapy.* New York: Ronald, 1946.

ATKINSON, RITA L. Paired-associate learning by schizophrenic and normal subjects under conditions of verbal reward and verbal punishment. Unpublished doctoral dissertation, Indiana University, 1957.

AZRAN, N. H., & LINDSLEY, O. R. The reinforcement of cooperation between children. *J. abnorm. soc. Psychol.*, 1956, 52, 100–102.

BANDURA, A., & HUSTON, ALETHA C. Identification as a process of incidental learning. *J. abnorm. soc. Psychol.*, in press.

BANDURA, A., LIPSHER, D. H., & MILLER, PAULA E. Psychotherapists' approach-avoidance reactions to patients' expressions of hostility. *J. consult. Psychol.*, 1960, 24, 1–8.

BANDURA, A., ROSS, DOROTHEA, & ROSS, SHEILA A. Transmission of aggression through imitation of aggressive models. *J. abnorm. soc. Psychol.*, in press.

BANDURA, A., & WALTERS, R. H. *Adolescent aggression.* New York: Ronald, 1959.

CAIRNS, R. B. The influence of dependency-anxiety on the effectiveness of social reinforcers. Unpublished doctoral dissertation, Stanford University, 1959.

CALVIN, A. D., CLIFFORD, L. T., CLIFFORD, B., BOLDEN, L., & HARVEY, J. Experimental validation of conditioned inhibition. *Psychol. Rep.*, 1956, 2, 51–56.

DAVIDSON, J. R., & DOUGLASS, E. Nocturnal enuresis: A special approach to treatment. *British med. J.*, 1950, 1, 1345–1347.

DITTES, J. E. Extinction during psychotherapy of GSR accompanying "embarrassing" statements. *J. abnorm. soc. Psychol.*, 1957, 54, 187–191. (a)

DITTES, J. E. Galvanic skin responses as a measure of patient's reaction to therapist's permissiveness. *J. abnorm. soc. Psychol.*, 1957, 55, 295–303. (b)

DOLLARD, J., AULD, F., & WHITE, A. M. *Steps in psychotherapy.* New York: Macmillan, 1954.

DOLLARD, J. & MILLER, N. E. *Personality and psychotherapy.* New York: McGraw-Hill, 1950.

DUNLAP, K. *Habits, their making and unmaking.* New York: Liveright, 1932.

EDMONSON, B. W., & AMSEL, A. The effects of massing and distribution of extinction trials on the persistence of a fear-motivated instrumental response. *J. comp. physiol. Psychol.*, 1954, 47, 117–123.

ERIKSON, C. W. Unconscious processes. In M. R. Jones (Ed.), *Nebraska symposium on motivation.* Lincoln: Univ. Nebraska Press, 1958.

ESTES, W. K. An experimental study of punishment. *Psychol. Monogr.*, 1944, 57 (3, Whole No. 363).

EYSENCK, H. J. *The dynamics of anxiety and hysteria.* New York: Praeger, 1957.

FENICHEL, O. *Problems of psychoanalytic technique.* (Trans. by D. Brunswick) New York: Psychoanalytic Quarterly, 1941.

FERSTER, C. B. Development of normal behavioral processes in autistic children. *Res. relat. Child.*, 1959, No. 9, 30. (Abstract)

FISHMAN, H. C. A study of the efficiency of negative practice as a corrective for stammering. *J. speech Dis.*, 1937, 2, 67–72.

FRANK, J. D. The dynamics of the psychotherapeutic relationship. *Psychiatry*, 1959, 22, 17–39.

FROMM-REICHMANN, FRIEDA. *Principle of intensive psychotherapy.* Chicago: Univer. Chicago Press, 1950.

HEINE, R. W. An investigation of the relationship between change in personality from psychotherapy as reported by patients and the factors seen by patients as producing change. Unpublished doctoral dissertation, University of Chicago, 1950.

JONES, E. L. Exploration of experimental extinction and spontaneous recovery in stuttering. In W. Johnson (Ed.), *Stuttering in children and adults.* Minneapolis: Univer. Minnesota Press, 1955.

JONES, H. G. The application of conditioning and learning techniques to the treatment of a psychiatric patient. *J. abnorm. soc. Psychol.*, 1956, 52, 414–419.

JONES, MARY C. The elimination of children's fears. *J. exp. Psychol.*, 1924, 7, 382–390. (a)

JONES, MARY C. A laboratory study of fear: The case of Peter. *J. genet. Psychol.*, 1924, 31, 308–315. (b)

KING, G. F., & ARMITAGE, S. G. An operant-interpersonal therapeutic approach to schizophrenics of extreme pathology. *Amer. Psychologist*, 1958, 13, 358. (Abstract)

KLEIN, MELANIE. *The psycho-analysis of children*. London: Hogarth, 1949.

KRASNER, L. The use of generalized reinforcers in psychotherapy research. *Psychol. Rep.*, 1955, 1, 19–25.

KRASNER, L. Studies of the conditioning of verbal behavior. *Psychol. Bull.*, 1958, 55, 148–170.

LACEY, J. I., & SMITH, R. I. Conditioning and generalization of unconscious anxiety. *Science.* 1954, 120, 1–8.

LAZARUS, A. A., & RACHMAN, S. The use of systematic desensitization in psychotherapy. *S. Afr. med. J.*, 1957, 32, 934–937.

LEHNER, G. F. J. Negative practice as a psychotherapeutic technique. *J. gen. Psychol.*, 1954, 51, 69–82.

LINDSLEY, O. R. Operant conditioning methods applied to research in chronic schizophrenia. *Psychiat. res. Rep.*, 1956, 5, 118–138.

LIVERSEDGE, L. A., & SYLVESTER, J. D. Conditioning techniques in the treatment of writer's cramp. *Lancet*, 1955, 1, 1147–1149.

MARTIN, B., & KUBLY, DELORES. Results of treatment of enuresis by a conditioned response method. *J. consult. Psychol.*, 1955, 19, 71–73.

MAUSNER, B. Studies in social interaction: III. The effect of variation in one partner's prestige on the interaction of observer pairs. *J. appl. Psychol.*, 1953, 37, 391–393.

MAUSNER, B. The effect of one partner's success in a relevant task on the interaction of observer pairs. *J. abnorm. soc. Psychol.*, 1954, 49, 557–560.

MAX, L. W. Breaking up a homosexual fixation by the conditioned reaction technique: A case study. *Psychol. Bull.*, 1935, 32, 734.

MEISSNER, J. H. The relationship between voluntary nonfluency and stuttering. *J. speech Dis.*, 1946, 11, 13–33.

MEYER, V. The treatment of two phobic patients on the basis of learning principles: Case report. *J. abnorm. soc. Psychol.*, 1957, 55, 261–266.

MILLER, N. E., & DOLLARD, J. *Social learning and imitation*. New Haven: Yale Univer. Press, 1941.

MORGAN, J. J. B., & WITMER, F. J. The treatment of enuresis by the conditioned reaction technique. *J. genet. Psychol.*, 1939, 55, 59–65.

MOWRER, O. H. *Learning theory and personality dynamics*. New York: Ronald, 1950.

MOWRER, O. H., & MOWRER, W. M. Enuresis —a method for its study and treatment. *Amer. J. Orthopsychiat.*, 1938, 8, 436–459.

MURRAY, E. J. The content-analysis method of studying psychotherapy. *Psychol. Monogr.*, 1956, 70, (13, Whole No. 420).

MUSSEN, P., & DISTLER, L. M. Masculinity, identification, and father-son relationships. *J. abnorm. soc. Psychol.*, 1959, 59, 350–356.

MUSSEN, P., & DISTLER, L. M. Child-rearing antecedents of masculine identification in kindergarten boys. *Child Develpm.*, 1960, 31, 89–100.

PAYNE, D. E., & MUSSEN, P. H. Parent-child relationships and father identification among adolescent boys. *J. abnorm. soc. Psychol.*, 1956, 52, 358–362.

PETERS, H. N. Multiple choice learning in the chronic schizophrenic. *J. clin. Psychol.*, 1953, 9, 328–333.

PETERS, H. N., & JENKINS, R. L. Improvement of chronic schizophrenic patients with guided problem-solving motivated by hunger. *Psychiat. Quart. Suppl.*, 1954, 28, 84–101.

RACHMAN, S. The treatment of anxiety and phobic reactions by systematic desensitization psychotherapy. *J. abnorm. soc. Psychol.*, 1959, 58, 259–263.

RAYMOND, M. S. Case of fetishism treated by aversion therapy. *Brit. med. J.*, 1956, 2, 854–857.

RAZRAN, G. Stimulus generalization of conditioned responses. *Psychol. Bull.*, 1949, 46, 337–365.

ROBINSON, NANCY M. Paired-associate learning by schizophrenic subjects under conditions of personal and impersonal reward and punishment. Unpublished doctoral dissertation, Stanford University, 1957.

ROGERS, C. R. *Client-centered therapy*. Boston: Houghton Mifflin, 1951.

ROGERS, C. R. Group discussion: Problems of controls. In E. H. Rubinstein & M. B. Parloff (Eds.), *Research in psychotherapy*. Washington, D. C.: American Psychological Association, 1959.

ROGERS, J. M. Operant conditioning in a quasi-therapy setting. *J. abnorm. soc. Psychol.*, 1960, 60, 247–252.

ROSENTHAL, D. Changes in some moral values following psychotherapy. *J. consult. Psychol.,* 1955, 19, 431–436.

ROTTER, J. B. *Social learning and clinical psychology.* Englewood Cliffs, N.J.: Prentice-Hall, 1954.

RUBENSTEIN, E. A., & LORR, M. A comparison of terminators and remainders in outpatient psychotherapy. *J. clin. Psychol.,* 1956, 12, 345–349.

RUTHERFORD, B. R. The use of negative practice in speech therapy with children handicapped by cerebral palsy, athetoid type. *J. speech Dis.,* 1940, 5, 259–264.

SALZINGER, K. Experimental manipulation of verbal behavior: A review. *J. gen. Psychol.,* 1959, 61, 65–94.

SARASON, BARBARA R. The effects of verbally conditioned response classes on post-conditioning tasks. *Dissertation Abstr.,* 1957, 12, 679.

SCHMIDEBERG, MELITTA. Psychotherapy of juvenile delinquents. *Int. ment. hlth. res. Newsltr.,* 1959, 1, 1–2.

SEARS, PAULINE S. Child-rearing factors related to playing of sex-typed roles. *Amer. Psychologist,* 1953, 8, 431. (Abstract)

SEARS, R. R. Identification as a form of behavioral development. In D. B. Harris (Ed.), *The concept of development: An issue in the study of human behavior.* Minneapolis: Univer. Minnesota Press, 1957.

SHEEHAN, J. G. The modification of stuttering through non-reinforcement. *J. abnorm. soc. Psychol.,* 1951, 46, 51–63.

SHEEHAN, J. G., & VOAS, R. B. Stuttering as conflict: I. Comparison of therapy techniques involving approach and avoidance. *J. speech Dis.,* 1957, 22, 714–723.

SHOBEN, E. J. Psychotherapy as a problem in learning theory. *Psychol. Bull.,* 1949, 46, 366–392.

SKINNER, B. F. *Science and human behavior.* New York: Macmillan, 1953.

SKINNER, B. F. Some issues concerning the control of human behavior. *Science,* 1956, 124, 1057–1066. (a)

SKINNER, B. F. What is psychotic behavior? In *Theory and treatment of psychosis: Some newer aspects.* St. Louis: Washington Univer. Stud., 1956. (b)

SOLOMON, R. L., KAMIN, L. J., & WYNNE, L. C. Traumatic avoidance learning: The outcomes of several extinction procedures with dogs. *J. abnorm. soc. Psychol.,* 1953, 48, 291–302.

SULLIVAN, H. S. *The interpersonal theory of psychiatry.* New York: Norton, 1953.

THIRMANN, J. Conditioned-reflex treatment of alcoholism. *New Engl. J. Med.,* 1949, 241, 368–370, 406–410.

THOMPSON, G. N., & BIELINSKI, B. Improvement in psychosis following conditioned reflex treatment in alcoholism. *J. nerv. ment. Dis.,* 1953, 117, 537–543.

TILTON, J. R. The use of instrumental motor and verbal learning techniques in the treatment of chronic schizophrenics. Unpublished doctoral dissertation, Michigan State University, 1956.

ULLMANN, L. P., KRASNER, L., & COLLINS, BEVERLY J. Modification of behavior in group therapy associated with verbal conditioning. *J. abnorm. soc. Psychol.,* in press.

VOEGTLEN, W. L. The treatment of alcoholism by establishing a conditioned reflex. *Amer. J. med. Sci.,* 1940, 119, 802–810.

WALLACE, J. A. The treatment of alcoholics by the conditioned reflex method. *J. Tenn. Med. Ass.,* 1949, 42, 125–128.

WEIDE, T. N. Conditioning and generalization of the use of affect-relevant words. Unpublished doctoral dissertation, Stanford University, 1959.

WHITING, J. W. M. The research program of the Laboratory of Human Development: The development of self-control. Cambridge: Harvard University, 1954. (Mimeo)

WILLIAMS, C. D. The elimination of tantrum behaviors by extinction procedures. *J. abnorm. soc. Psychol.,* 1959, 59, 269.

WILLIAMS, R. I. Verbal conditioning in psychotherapy. *Amer. Psychologist,* 1959, 14, 388. (Abstract)

WOLPE, J. Reciprocal inhibition as the main basis of psychotherapeutic effects. *AMA Arch. Neurol. Psychiat.,* 1954, 72, 205–226.

WOLPE, J. *Psychotherapy by reciprocal inhibition.* Stanford: Stanford Univer. Press, 1958.

WOLPE, J. Psychotherapy based on the principle of reciprocal inhibition. In A. Burton (Ed.), *Case studies in counseling and psychotherapy.* Englewood Cliffs, N.J.: Prentice-Hall, 1959.

YATES, A. J. The application of learning theory to the treatment of tics. *J. abnorm. soc. Psychol.,* 1958, 56, 175–182.

Selected Additional Readings

ALEXANDER, F. Unexplored areas in psychoanalytic theory and treatment. *Behavioral Science.* 1958, 3, 293–316.

BUTLER, J. M., RICE, L. N., & WAGSTAFF, A. K. On the naturalistic definition of variables: An analogue of clinical analysis. In H. H. Strupp & L. Luborsky (Eds.), *Research in psychotherapy,* Vol. 2, Washington, D.C.: American Psychological Association, 1962. Pp. 178–205.

CHASSAN, J. B. Stochastic models of the single case as the basis of clinical research design. *Behavioral Science,* 1961, 6, 42–50.

COWEN, E. L. The experimental analogue—An approach to research in psychotherapy. *Psychological Reports,* 1961, 8, 9–10.

FINE, R. The measurement problem in psychology. *Psychoanalysis and the Psychoanalytic Review,* 1960, 47, 1–16.

FORD, D. H. Research approaches to psychotherapy. *Journal of Counseling Psychology,* 1959, 6, 55–60.

FOX, H. M. Effect of psychophysiological research on the transference. *Journal of American Psychoanalytic Association,* 1958, 6, 413–432.

GORDON, T., GRUMMON, D. L., ROGERS, C. R., & SEEMAN, J. Developing a program of research in psychotherapy. In C. R. Rogers & Rosalind F. Dymond (Eds.), *Psychotherapy and personality change.* Chicago: Univer. of Chicago Press, 1954. Pp. 12–34.

HELLER, K. Experimental analogues of psychotherapy: The clinical relevance of laboratory findings of social influence. *Journal of Nervous and Mental Diseases,* 1963, 137, 420–426.

HELLER, K. A broader perspective for interview therapy. Paper presented at the symposium "Implications of Conditioning Techniques for Interview Therapy," Midwest Psychological Association, Chicago, 1965.

KANFER, FREDERICK H. Comments on learning in psychotherapy. *Psychological Reports,* 1961, 9, 681–699.

KOGAN, W. S., QUINN, R., AX, A. F., & RIPLEY, H. S. Some methodological problems in the quantification of clinical assessment by Q array. *Journal of Consulting Psychology,* 1957, 21, 57–62.

LUBORSKY, L. & STRUPP, H. H. Research problems in psychotherapy: A three-year follow-up. In H. H. Strupp & L. Luborsky (Eds.), *Research in psychotherapy,* Vol. 2. Washington, D.C.: American Psychological Association, 1962. Pp. 308–329.

MURRAY, E. J. Learning theory and psychotherapy: Biotropic versus sociotropic approaches. *Journal of Counseling Psychology,* 1963, 10, 250–255.

RAMZY, I. Research aspects of psychoanalysis. *Psychoanalytic Quarterly,* 1963, 32, 58–76.

STRUPP, H. H. Some comments on the future of research in psychotherapy. *Behavioral Science,* 1960, 5, 60–71.

WALLERSTEIN, R. S., & ROBBINS, L. L. The psychotherapy research project of the Menninger Foundation. Third report. Operational problems of psychotherapy research: I. Initial studies. *Bulletin of the Menninger Clinic,* 1960, 24, 164–189.

WITTENBORN, J. R. Contributions and current status of Q methodology. *Psychological Bulletin,* 1961, 58, 132–142.

SECTION 2 Research on Outcome and Methods of Evaluating Outcome

Outcome research in psychotherapy has been an especially controversial issue since 1952, when H. J. Eysenck[1] published his summary of the psychotherapy literature, drawing the conclusion from the material available that patients treated with psychotherapy showed no more improvement than untreated populations of patients. This study came under intense attack on both emotional and scientific grounds.[2] The scientific criticism, in most cases, was just, the most cogent points being that the criteria for improvement in the "untreated" control groups were unrelated to those used for the "treated" groups, and that the "untreated" groups actually received an indeterminate amount of treatment. However, Eysenck's work was of value in that it called into question the effectiveness of psychotherapy and demonstrated clearly that some recovery occurs without intensive professional treatment.

Perhaps stimulated in part by critics such as Eysenck, outcome research in more recent years has graduated from reports of percentages of success, with the exact nature of "success" left undefined, to carefully controlled and well designed studies. The results of these studies have not been consistent, but many of them have demonstrated statistically significant differences between treated and untreated patient groups, using the same improvement criteria in judging both. Additionally, as A. E. Bergin points out in the first article of this section, some of the studies which do not show differences between the *mean* change

---

[1] H. J. Eysenck, The effects of psychotherapy: An evaluation. *Journal of Consulting Psychology,* 1952, 16, 319–324.

[2] S. Rosenzweig, A transvaluation of psychotherapy: A reply to Hans Eysenck. *Journal of Abnormal and Social Psychology,* 1954, 49, 298–304. A. E. Bergin, The effects of psychotherapy: Negative results revisited. *Journal of Counseling Psychology,* 1963, 10, 244–250.

scores of treated and untreated groups do show increased *variance* within the treated, as compared with the untreated, group. Bergin calls this a "deterioration effect" and presents a valuable discussion of its possible importance to psychotherapy research.

All-important in these studies is the absolute necessity for a control condition. The most frequently used control condition is a no-therapy group. Some investigators, however, have used a waiting period, equal to the duration of therapy, and compared changes which occur after therapy to those occurring at the end of the waiting period. Another type of control condition involves the variable of "amount of treatment." Clearly, if it can be shown that a greater amount of treatment results in more change, there is a sufficient demonstration that psychotherapy does produce changes. Some studies that employ the "amount of treatment" variable to examine the effects of psychotherapy are included in this section. Also included are studies demonstrating degrees of change produced by different therapeutic methods. In the case of this type of study, also, if it can be shown that one particular type of therapy results in significantly more change than another, this is again sufficient demonstration that psychotherapy does produce a change of some kind.

If the results of psychotherapy outcome studies are to be generalized to the particular discipline employed by the therapists used for that study, and ultimately to psychotherapy in general, it is important that the experimental conditions be appropriate. This is to say that the therapists should be fully trained in and confident about the discipline they employ. One cannot conclude anything about orthodox psychoanalysis as such unless the therapist is an orthodox psychoanalyst. Additionally, if comparisons are to be made between two types of therapy, the therapists should be equally trained and motivated in their approaches.

The measures used for the evaluation of changes due to psychotherapy are, of course, also critical. They must demonstrate reliability. Additionally, since the changes are expected to be more or less permanent and generalized, follow-up studies and "field" observation of the patient's behavior outside the clinical setting—or valid correlates thereof—are necessary. Through the use of sets of diverse criteria, rather than single measures, in evaluating psychotherapy outcome, much can be learned about the nature of change beyond a simple "effect–no effect" result.

Research on the various methods of evaluating outcome is also included in this section. A promising approach to this problem is that offered by factor analysis. In this way, major factors of change can be defined, and those tests and measures that represent them can be identified. Additionally, one can determine the interrelationships among change variables as measured by tests, therapists, clients, and independent observers. Knowledge accumulated from this type of research will allow investigators to evaluate outcome efficiently and intelligently. It should direct them toward using sets of measures that are comparable and that cover the major factors of change associated with psychotherapy.

Another area of research included in this methodology section utilizes a psychotherapy analogue situation. In these studies, "symptoms" are induced in the experimental subjects, and then a "therapeutic" treatment is used in an attempt to remove the induced symptoms. This type of laboratory simplification of the psychotherapy situation is valuable because it avoids the very complicated, varied disturbances and extraneous variables encountered in regular clinical practice. This approach also allows study of the entire process that psycho-therapy deals with, from symptom acquisition to symptom reduction. However, as with any laboratory research, generalization of results must be made with caution and qualification.

Some Implications of Psychotherapy Research for Therapeutic Practice[1]

ALLEN E. BERGIN

The material to follow is a digest of research findings which have implications for practice and research in psychotherapy. It has been formulated in terms of six conclusions and implications which appear justifiable and defensible. This catalogue of conclusions is based upon a comparative handful of research reports which have been carefully selected from the present empirical chaos for their adequacy of conceptualization, design, and outcome. Conclusions have been drawn only in those areas where the results have substance and where they have been replicated.

THE DETERIORATION EFFECT

Conclusion 1: Psychotherapy may cause people to become better- or worse-adjusted than comparable people who do not receive such treatment.

[1] Based in part on a paper presented at the Pre-Convention Institute of the Ontario Psychological Association, London, Ontario, February 1964. Presented at a symposium: "Implications of empirical research for innovations in therapeutic practice and research." American Psychological Association Convention, Los Angeles, September 1964. [Reprinted with the permission of the author.]

Two years ago a curious and provocative finding occurred in the preliminary results of the large psychotherapy research project at the University of Wisconsin conducted by Rogers, Gendlin, and Truax (Rogers, 1961; Truax, 1963; Truax and Carkhuff, 1963) It was that the subjects in psychotherapy tended to become either better or worse in adjustment than their matched control-group counterparts.

At that time (Bergin, 1963) two earlier studies were analyzed (Barron and Leary, 1955; Cartwright and Vogel, 1960; Cartwright, 1956) in which similar findings had occurred, but being incidental to other results, they had not been emphasized in proportion to their true import. Since then, we have found four additional studies of excellent design which suggest the same thing (Fairweather et al., 1960; Mink, 1959; Powers and Witmer, 1951; Rogers and Dymond, 1954). In all seven of these studies, although there tends to be no difference in the average amount of change between experimentals and controls, there tends to be a significant difference in *variability* of change. The criterion, or change, scores for treatment groups attain a much wider dispersion than do those of control groups, even though the mean change in both groups is quite similar. Typically, control subjects improve somewhat, with the varying amounts of change clustering about the mean. On the other hand, experimental subjects are typically dispersed all the way from marked improvement to marked deterioration. Now frequently documented, this information is alarming to say the least. Psychotherapy can and does make people worse than their control counterparts! Because of the controversial nature of this conclusion, the following material is presented as detailed substantiating evidence in support of it.

Table 1 is reproduced from Cartwright's re-analysis (1956) of the well-known Barron and Leary study (1955).

TABLE 1

VARIANCES OF DISCREPANCY SCORES ON MMPI SCALES FOR INDIVIDUAL PSYCHOTHERAPY AND NONTREATMENT GROUPS

MMPI Scale	Individual psychotherapy (N = 42) V*	Nontreatment group (N = 23) V	F	p
1. Lie	19.89	23.43	1.18	...
2. F	215.21	22.94	9.38	.01
3. K	55.95	31.70	1.76	...
4. Hs	127.46	64.16	1.99	.05
5. D	244.30	93.32	2.62	.01
6. Hy	113.21	87.80	1.29	...
7. Pd	155.00	89.68	1.73	...
8. Pa	111.94	68.06	1.64	...
9. Pt	208.51	73.27	2.85	.01
10. Sc	272.91	74.13	3.68	.01
11. Ma	126.79	75.34	1.68	...
12. Es	43.56	14.82	2.94	.01

*Variances computed from SD data reported by Barron and Leary (2, p. 243).

He comments as follows on the data:

For many scales the variance results suggest that mean differences between the groups are absent because differences of two kinds, opposed in sign, are present. It seems that some

therapy patients *deteriorated* to a greater extent than did the waiting-list controls, while some therapy patients *did improve* significantly more than the controls. It should be noted that this occurred only for individual and not for group therapy.

It is a fascinating fact that Cartwright's observation has lain unattended in the literature for years, while implicit in his statement is a clear means of resolving much of the controversy over negative results in therapy outcome studies. It is even more fascinating that Cartwright himself participated in a study (Rogers and Dymond, 1954) in which a similar phenomenon occurred, but just as the data in the Barron and Leary study it was never emphasized in proportion to its true import. The classic features in this study, reported under the editorship of Rogers and Dymond, apparently overshadowed the passing references to a *client deterioration phenomenon*. While the study is properly famous for other reasons, it provides supporting bits of evidence for our thesis that negative change in therapy is not an isolated or chance occurrence. A careful reading of the report indicates that of 25 therapy subjects, 6 or 24% declined in self-ideal correlation between pre-therapy and follow-up testing. A quick computation of the mean change in self-ideal correlation indicates that those who increased averaged an increment of .49 in their correlations, whereas those who declined averaged a decrement of −.40, a difference that is clearly significant. The mean pre-therapy correlations were not different for these two groups, whereas the follow-up means were .43 and −.26 respectively. Analyzing the change scores of the decliners alone, we find that the mean change of −.40 yields a t-ratio of 1.74 which is not significant at the .05 level; thus the firmness of the general conclusion regarding self-ideal deterioration must be attenuated somewhat. While the authors do not examine these possibilities in the data, they do allude to them in passing: "It is of interest, though it does not bear directly upon the hypothesis, that there has also been a marked increase in the degree of variation of correlations [self-ideal] over this period" (Butler and Haigh, 1954).

In another section of the same volume, an analysis of behavior observations made of the clients is summarized by Rogers (p. 228) as follows:

During the whole period from pre-therapy to follow-up, observers saw a definite increase in the maturity of behavior of those clients whose therapy was rated as successful and a sharp decrease in the maturity of behavior of those clients rated as unsuccessful. The relationship was statistically significant.

While there are additional fragmentary evidences of deterioration phenomena in the book, these suffice to illustrate our point.

In a controlled study of counseling with high school students, Mink (1959, p. 14) observes the same phenomenon: "Counseling affected the expression of social adjustments of the California Test of Personality. The forms of expression indicate both improvement and recession."

The excellent multi-factor design executed by Fairweather et al. (1960) yielded similar results:

Generally, significantly different variances occurred on most instruments between treatments and diagnoses. The control group usually had the smallest variance and the three psychotherapy groups the largest (p. 24). . . .In these three interactions, one or all of the three long-term psychotic groups in psychotherapy demonstrated changes in the maladaptive scale direction [MMPI] while the controls remain relatively the same or change in the adaptive direction (p. 9).

Cartwright and Vogel (1960) discovered the same type of differential effect in a neurotic sample using different criterion measures:

Thus, as measured by the Q score, adjustment changes, regardless of direction, were sig-nificantly greater during a therapy period than during a no-therapy period (p. 122). . . . The post-therapy tests showed those in therapy with experienced therapists to have improved significantly on both tests, whereas those in therapy with inexperienced therapists not to have improved . . ., in fact, they bordered on a significant decrease in health on the TAT (p. 127).

Turning back several decades to the Cambridge-Somerville youth study (Powers and Witmer, 1951) which was initiated in 1937, we find the same phenomenon with a group of pre-delinquent boys:

. . . when the Study Services were effectual most of the boys did function better than their C-twins. This conclusion can be accepted, however, only if its opposite is also accepted: that some of the boys who were not benefited may have been handicapped in social adjustment by the organization's efforts. If this is true, we can conclude that the apparent chance distribution of terminal adjustment ratings . . . was due to the fact that the good effects of the Study were counterbalanced by the poor (p. 455).

Elsewhere the authors indicate that in a significant proportion of cases where the counselor's efforts were judged as poor, the boys "were more socially maladjusted than their control twin" (p. 509). It is unfortunate that this excellently designed and executed study is one leaned upon most heavily by Eysenck (1960) in his bold denial of the usefulness of psychotherapy, for while the study shows no difference between experimentals and controls, it demonstrates the efficacy of treatment as well as its deteriorative effect.

Finally, we cite the recent Wisconsin project on therapy of schizophrenia which has been published thus far only in tempting bits and pieces:

. . . high levels of therapist-offered conditions during therapy are related to patient improvement, but . . . low levels . . . are related to patient deterioration, so that if all therapy combined is indiscriminately compared to control conditions there is little average change. Thus psychotherapy can be for better or for worse . . . (Truax, 1963, p. 256).

Fortunately, these various data indicate that psychotherapy can make people considerably better off than control subjects. Therefore, contrary to the notions of some critics, psychotherapy can produce improvement beyond that which may occur due to spontaneous remission alone. Consistently replicated, this is a direct and unambiguous refutation of the oft-cited Eysenckian position (Eysenck, 1960). An additional refutation is, of course, contained in the remarkable fact that some studies even demonstrate greater mean change for experimentals than controls (Rogers and Dymond, 1954; Shlien, Mosak and Dreikurs, 1962).

A general paradigm is suggested by the double-edged effect observed in the studies cited which may be schematized as shown in Figure 1. Such a startling phenomenon certainly deserves a name, and we suggest *The Deterioration Effect.*

Implication No. 1. (a) We should not give up the practice of psychotherapy as some have advocated; (b) We should be more cautious and critical of our own practices, carefully eliminating any dangerous influences. We should find out whom we are making worse or better and how with all due speed. (c) We should find out whether some therapists make people better and some make them worse or whether individual therapists do both. After that, we have the ticklish business of making changes in technique, personality, or personnel as may be necessary to eliminate negative influences and accentuate positive ones.

NATURAL THERAPEUTIC CONDITIONS

Conclusion 2: (a) It has been frequently replicated and is now a well-established fact that control subjects who do not receive psychotherapy change positively as a group with the passage of time. This is the so-called spontaneous remission effect. (b) Three studies (Frank,

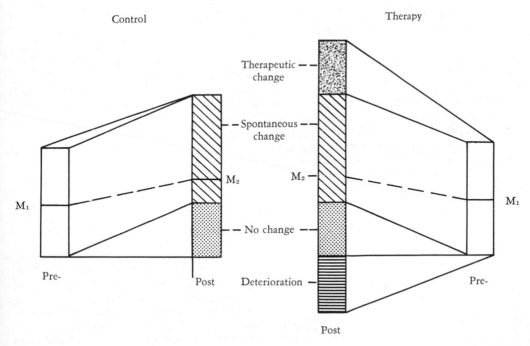

Figure 1.

1961; Gurin, Veroff and Feld, 1960; Powers and Witmer, 1951) indicate that these disturbed persons who receive no psychotherapy seek and obtain help from various professional and non-professional sources such as friends, clergymen, physicians, teachers, and even psychotherapists (Bergin, 1963). All this has typically been unknown to the researchers who were depending upon these so-called controls to be a baseline for comparison with their treatment cases.

It seems clear that this aid has an ameliorative effect since the people improve; although it would be impossible to substantiate this fully without further study of the influences upon control subjects in their "natural" habitat. To the extent that this position is correct it further undermines the Eysenck-type position, because it shows that control subjects often change due to the influence of therapy or therapy-like procedures. Thus, "spontaneous remission" is just another name for the effects of non-specific therapy.

Implication No. 2. (a) Researchers who utilize control groups should carefully ascertain that these groups are indeed controls, or, if necessary, should directly measure the effects of non-experimental influences which they cannot control. (b) The fact that some of these previously uncontrolled influences are much like therapy but frequently occur outside of a professional setting implies that non-professional help can stimulate positive personality change. It would be surprising, in fact, if society did *not* have built into its structure some stop-gap remedies for everyday neuroses. This notion could lead us to presume that society provides only a stop-gap and that professional treatment provides a better cure; but I should like to submit a different proposition. I would hypothesize that there exist naturally in everyday life powerful therapeutic agents which are as yet not fully recognized. These may consist partly of individuals who have "therapeutic personalities" and who are sought out for counsel and catharsis by many people; but

I would suggest that there are also numerous relationships, organizational structures, events, activities, and even belief systems that sustain personality integration and promote personality growth.

Just as cures for various physical disorders have been discovered by studying health, so it may be possible to discover antidotes for some of the mental disorders that confront us by discovering conditions in "nature" which support or promote our desired ends. Such knowledge could be a great stimulus to prevention. Our field has been largely inclined to derive solutions for the problems of living from clinical experience with people who are not functioning well in life. The evidence accumulating from psychotherapy research reemphasizes the notion that we should reverse this trend and devise methods of treatment from examples of positive functioning that occur in everyday life. Such a movement would clearly be in keeping with modern trends toward the use of milieu therapy and community mental health procedures and it would add a significant dimension to them.

A far reaching implication of this conclusion is that we may need to modify our treatment procedures in the direction of actually implementing social changes, such as in institutions, families, schools, neighborhoods, etc. The implication is one of social engineering to develop "healthy" social interactions and social structures. It is an implication that would move us toward significantly less reliance upon one-to-one consulting room relationships.

INGREDIENTS OF THERAPY

Conclusion 3. Therapeutic progress varies as a function of therapist characteristics such as warmth, empathy, adequacy of adjustment, and experience.

As was indicated in relation to conclusion 1, it is urgently essential that we identify and differentiate characteristics of therapist behavior and personality which facilitate or retard personality growth.

In a review published a few weeks ago, Gardner (1964) cited a smattering of positive results to the effect that the more a therapist has an attitude of *liking and warmth,* the more likely he is to obtain positive change in his clients. While some of the studies enumerated are of questionable design or generalizability, they are relatively consistent when compared with many other areas of research.

A recent questionnaire study of patients' retrospective reports regarding their therapeutic experience (Strupp, Wallach and Wogan, 1964), which was not reported by Gardner, further confirms this general finding. While the study is uncontrolled and appears to be contaminated by artifactually inflated correlations, it is of interest that it strongly emphasizes the importance of therapist warmth and genuineness in relation to patient-perceived outcome (r. = .53).

The most substantial additional data on this point come from the client-centered group in a series of studies with neurotics and psychotics. It should be noted that some of the therapists studied were *not* client-centered. These studies are consistent in discovering a significant relationship between operational measures of Rogers' concept of positive regard and independent indices of therapeutic progress or outcome (Truax and Carkhuff, 1963; Barrett-Lennard, 1962). Measures of the therapist's attitudes have included ratings by both the therapist himself and the patient. Three types of analysis have resulted in similar results and in different studies with different samples of clients and therapists. It has thus become increasingly clear that a therapist's ability to be warm and positively inclined toward his patients is an effective therapeutic ingredient.

Empathy is one of those variables which has been exhaustively studied with little growing out of the effort that has been of consequence. Its unfortunate use as a blanket term for innumerable different operations has made clarity and useful consequences especially difficult to obtain (Al-lerand, 1964). Acknowledging the past confusion and contradiction involved in this area, we submit that the recent data summarized at Chicago (Barrett-Lennard, 1962) and Wisconsin, (Truax, 1961a; Truax and Carkhuff, 1963) offer a healthy antidote to our empathic dis-ease. Again, analyses of recorded therapist behavior and ratings by clients during the process of treatment yield consistently significant data revealing a positive relationship between empathic understanding and outcome.

The strength of these findings appears to lie in the excellence of the research designs (Rogers, 1961), in the analysis of therapist behavior "in vivo" which is quite unusual in this area of research, and in the care with which empathy has been defined and operationalized (Truax, 1961b). It is defined generally as accurate ". . . sensitivity to current feelings *and* the verbal facility to communicate this understanding in a language attuned to the patient's current being." (Truax and Carkhuff, 1963, p. 8).

The third characteristic, *adequacy of adjustment,* has not been studied as thoroughly as we would like, but thus far the data are relatively consistent. Those therapists who are more anxious, conflicted, defensive, or "unhealthy" are least likely to promote change in their cases.

Several studies have indicated that supervisor and client ratings of the therapists' competence are negatively related to his degree of anxiety or maladjustment (Bandura, 1956; Bergin and Solomon, 1963; Arbuckle, 1956). Other studies have yielded similar findings when the therapist's actual in-therapy behavior and the patient's response to it was evaluated and used as a criterion of competence. Bandura, Lipsher and Miller (1960), e.g., found that therapists' hostility anxiety was directly associated with avoidance responses to patients' expressions of hostility toward them. The more hostility conflict a therapist had, the more likely he was to avoid his patients' hostility and consequently the patients' self-exploration in this area diminished and his conflicts remained unresolved. A practically identical result was found by Winder, Ahmad and Rau (1962) with regard to dependency anxiety.

In one of our own studies (Bergin and Solomon, 1963) which is still in process, we have thus far found that measures of the therapists' degree of personal disturbance correlate negatively with his level of empathy as measured by ratings of tape-recorded psychotherapy interviews. Independent measures of personality strength, on the other hand, correlate positively with degree of "live" empathy.

Additional data comes from the various client-centered researches at Chicago and Wisconsin on therapist congruence. Congruence (Rogers, 1957; 1959) means essentially the healthiness of the therapist in his relationship with his client—his own spontaneity, non-defensiveness, openness, or genuineness. Like positive regard and empathy, this variable has also been clearly related to therapeutic progress, and further confirms the general finding of a direct connection between level of therapist adjustment and therapeutic effectiveness.

The three elements of warmth, empathy, and congruence have been found, in the Wisconsin studies which have been directed by Rogers, Truax, and Gendlin, to vary directly with outcome in both negative and positive directions. That is, when these therapist characteristics were at a low level, the patients were getting worse (Truax and Carkhuff, 1963). These studies thus provide us with a partial answer to the question we raised earlier as to how negative change occurred in the outcome studies reviewed. The other studies cited here in the same realm further clarify the point; although none of the data are elaborate enough to make practical decisions possible.

With regard to the much debated variable of *therapist experience,* we feel secure in asserting that in general more experienced therapists are more effective and successful. We base this on four studies (Fiedler, 1950a, 1950b, 1951; Chance,

1959; Cartwright and Vogel, 1960; Barrett-Lennard, 1962), one of which suggests that highly inexperienced therapists may actually cause patient deterioration (Cartwright and Vogel). This latter study is, in fact, one of the outcome studies we cited earlier as indicating that negative change can occur as a result of treatment.

Implication No. 3. (a) Since psychotherapists are effective partly as a function of personal adjustment, they should be selected for this quality and not solely on the basis of academic and intellectual abilities. Future practice of therapy should therefore be modified by new selection procedures which will bring healthier personalities to bear upon problems of pathology, and by closer self-scrutiny and exposure of one's work among present practitioners. There is presently no evidence that personal therapy for the therapist can in any way qualify him on these grounds for practice and should not be depended upon until such evidence is provided. There are no studies in which treated neurotics have improved to a level of functioning which is similar to that of control normals; therefore, treatment should not be counted upon to take care of errors in selection. The behavior ratings and personality inventories used in the studies reviewed could provide a beginning in research geared specifically toward the selection problem.

(b) Given the necessary personal attributes, therapists should develop their abilities in the realm of warmth and empathic communication, particularly in the case of empathy which is known to be subject to training and experience influences. Further study should be conducted so that clear, measurable standards of performance can be required of aspirants to professional status before they are permitted to practice. As an example, the Truax Empathy Scale (Truax, 1961b) could be used as a beginning to assess one's level of functioning via analysis of recorded interviews.

(c) Inexperienced potential therapists should be very carefully introduced to practice with clients, perhaps with much more stringent care than is now commonly exercised. Since all beginners make many mistakes, it may be more useful and ethical to have them see more resilient, normal people until they reach a criterion level of interview performance, measured perhaps on dimensions such as warmth and empathy.

Conclusion 4. To date, the only school of interview-oriented psychotherapy which has consistently yielded positive outcomes in research studies is the client-centered approach (Rogers and Dymond, 1954; Shlien, Mosak and Dreikurs, 1962; Truax and Carkhuff, 1963).

The fact that other schools have not subjected their methods to systematic study of this sort is important but it should not deter us from accepting the fact that client-centered treatment is efficacious. The implications for practice seem quite clear, particularly in light of the consistently dismal reports on percentages of improvement in psychoanalytic therapy. It should be noted before moving on, however, that one technique which has developed from the analytic tradition has shown important potentiality for being therapeutically significant. This is what Speisman (1959) has called "moderate interpretation." Its definition is very similar to that given for "good" interpretation by various analysts (Fenichel, 1941) and it is related to productive patient self-exploration. It consists of responding to client affect just below the surface and labeling, identifying or emphasizing it. This does not involve making connections between past and present, being diagnostic or theoretical, nor telling the patient about feelings he "really has" when he's not experiencing them. It is, rather, an instance of good empathy. If one looks carefully at the definitions and operations for identifying accurate empathy and moderate or good interpretation, it is very difficult to distinguish between them. As a consequence, it seems likely that some analysts are effective but when they are they are probably doing client-centered therapy! Truax and Carkhuff (1963) refer to this notion in an interesting comment:

As can be seen from the examples, "accurate empathy" has much in common with the "good psychoanalytic interpretation," in that it makes use of both verbal and nonverbal cues presented by the patient. It differs from some good psychoanalytic interpretations in its insistence that the therapist's empathic response focuses upon feelings and experiences of the patient's own unique viewpoint. Still, it should be recognized that virtually all responses at stages 7, 8 and 9 would be considered by most psychoanalysts as "good" interpretations.

Conclusion 5. In spite of all that we have said so far about the possibilities for substantially improving our consulting room effectiveness, there are some stubborn facts that still confront us. One is that even when the various sources of slippage and inadequacy are accounted for, we still do not produce very dramatic changes in people by means of interviews. Another is the now well-known fact that many types of people simply are not helped at all by this procedure.

Studies of the relationship between client qualities and therapeutic outcome indicate consistently and clearly that positive outcome is limited or nil with many personality types. It is common for private practitioners and even clinics to either refuse to treat or reluctantly accept for treatment cases that do not fit their conception of psychotherapy. To a great extent this is realistic because traditional methods do not work with these cases. These "rejects" tend to be less intelligent, less anxious, less educated, less verbal and insightful, more concrete and action-oriented, more severely disturbed, more impulsive in the sociopathic sense, and often find the typical consulting room procedure rather meaningless (Barron, 1953; Cartwright, 1955; Fulkerson and Barry, 1961; Garfield and Affleck, 1961; Hollingshead and Redlich, 1958; Kirtner and Cartwright, 1958a, 1958b). This general observation has been made fairly frequently by various clinicians and is currently rather well-substantiated by the research literature.

Implication No. 5. The implication of these data, which only confirm an already widely believed idea, is that we must develop novel or modified techniques for dealing with a vast population whose problems are not amenable to standard methods. The importance of novel approaches is further emphasized by the fact that standard methods are not dramatically effective even in those cases where they are applicable.

There are three primary sources of possible innovation that might help us out of this predicament. One is creative work in the clinical setting; another is naturally existing conditions in society; and another is that general area of research which is concerned with personality and behavior change such as studies of learning, attitude change, and personality development.

THE PROMISE OF BEHAVIOR THERAPY

Conclusion 6. Studies of learning have thus far been most fruitful in generating principles and methods for promoting personality change. The work by Wolpe (1958), Lazarus, Lang, Lindsley and others has been both provocative and fruitful. In the cases presented and research studies reported we find more positive evidence of the usefulness of these methods than is the case in any form of traditional interview or dynamic psychotherapy.

They involve clinical adaptation of learning principles, such as counter-conditioning or extinction of anxiety symptoms, positive reinforcement in shaping adaptive responses and developing appropriate discriminations, aversive conditioning of maladaptive approach responses, etc. It is the *effects* of these methods which are important for our purposes. Wolpe (1964) cites over 200 cases of neurosis in which he has obtained substantial recovery in 89%. Lazarus (1963), in England, reports 408 cases

with a similar improvement rate. The striking aspect of these results is that they have been achieved with difficult symptom pictures in brief periods of time. A study by King, Armitage, and Tilton (1960) indicated that substantial changes could be effected even in schizophrenic cases by operant conditioning procedures. They were able to produce clinically observable improvement in cases so treated which was greater than the changes occurring in conventional interview therapy, recreational therapy or no therapy. Lang and Lazovik (1963) were able to significantly alter snake phobias with brief desensitization procedures. A comparison group being treated by traditional interpretive group therapy showed considerably less improvement, only two of seventeen cases becoming symptom free after 22 sessions. These same cases were subsequently treated by group desensitization and after a mean of ten sessions each, two-thirds were symptom free.

In spite of the fact that the evidence is certainly in their favor, these techniques have been criticized as simply removing symptoms and as being applicable only to very simple neuroses. Both criticisms are, however, quite theoretical and are not based upon examinations of the evidence. Neither are true. In a summary of 86 cases, Wolpe (1964) cites the following data on successfully treated complex cases:

TABLE 2

COMPARISON OF NUMBERS OF SESSIONS IN COMPLEX AND SINGLE NEUROSES. THE TOTAL IS ONLY 86 BECAUSE 2 CASES THAT TURNED OUT TO BE SCHIZOPHRENIC ARE EXCLUDED

	Number	Median Number of Sessions	Mean Number of Sessions
Complex	65	29	54.8
Simple neuroses	21	11.5	14.9
Whole group	86	23	45.4

In addition to the obvious fact that difficult cases show improvement in a short time, these reports indicate that significant relapses are rare. This is perhaps the most persuasive evidence that behavior therapists are right when they assert that "symptoms" are not symptoms of analytic style pathology, but that they are learned behaviors subject to modification via re-learning.

Implication No. 6. The implications of this work seem quite clear. Since these techniques are considerably more useful for many types of symptomatology than standard methods, they should be used. With regard to some of the more complex and difficult problems, behavior therapists argue that it would be better to spend time developing more complex social learning paradigms for treatment than to expend equal energy modifying traditional interview methods. It appears that special effort should be devoted to integrating these methods with others and in some cases substituting them for the other methods.

CONCLUSION

In conclusion, it is only regrettable that we have had to exclude comment upon so many topics of research. Suffice it to say that the results in many of these not mentioned are as yet not synthesizable. A good example is the material on the patient-therapist relationship. Nearly all of this research really pertains to therapist qualities and has nothing to do with an actual analysis of interactional factors. An unusual exception is the work of Barrett-Lennard which was cited briefly in our discussion of the client-centered research on therapist qualities. The few other useful facts in this domain were also included in the section on therapist characteristics. A promising line of investigation in this area is that on patient-therapist similarity; but the meaning of the data to date is too vague to get excited about (Sussman, 1964).

In spite of the fact that much of what is called psychotherapy research is appalling in its inadequacy, we are delighted to have found a handful of reliable conclusions. The groundwork seems well laid for some initial steps at productive innovation in therapeutic treatment.

REFERENCES

ALLERAND, ANNE-MARIE. Empathy in and out of psychotherapy. Unpublished manuscript, Teachers College, Columbia University, 1964.

ARBUCKLE, D. S. Client perception of counselor personality. *J. counsel. Psychol.*, 1956, 3, 93–96.

BANDURA, A. Psychotherapist's anxiety level, self-insight, and psychotherapeutic competence. *J. abnorm. soc. Psychol.*, 1956, 52, 333–337.

BANDURA, A. LIPSHER, D. H., and MILLER, PAULA E. Psychotherapists' approach-avoidance reactions to patients' expressions of hostility. *J. consult. Psychol.*, 1960, 24, 1–8.

BARRETT-LENNARD, G. T. Dimensions of therapist response as causal factors in therapeutic change. *Psychol. Monogr.*, 1962, 76, No. 43 (Whole No. 562).

BARRON, F. Some test correlates of response to psychotherapy. *J. consult. Psychol.*, 1953, 17, 235–241.

BARRON, F., and LEARY, T. Changes in psychoneurotic patients with and without psychotherapy. *J. consult. Psychol.*, 1955, 19, 239–245.

BERGIN, A. E. The effects of psychotherapy: negative results revisited. *J. counsel. Psychol.*, 1963, 10, 244–250.

BERGIN, A. E., and SOLOMON, SANDRA. Personality and performance correlates of empathic understanding in psychotherapy. *Amer. Psychol.*, 1963, 18, 393. (Abstract)

CARTWRIGHT, D. S. Success in psychotherapy as a function of certain actuarial variables. *J. consult. Psychol.*, 1955, 19, 357–363.

CARTWRIGHT, D. S. Note on "changes" in psychoneurotic patients with and without psychotherapy. *J. consult. Psychol.*, 1956, 20, 403–404.

CARTWRIGHT, ROSALIND D., and VOGEL, J. L. A comparison of changes in psychoneurotic patients during matched periods of therapy and no-therapy. *J. consult. Psychol.*, 1960, 24, 121–127.

CHANCE, ERIKA. *Families in treatment.* New York: Basic Books, 1959.

EYSENCK, H. J. The effects of psychotherapy.

In H. J. Eysenck (Ed.), *Handbook of abnormal psychology*. New York: Basic Books, 1960. Pp. 697–725.

FAIRWEATHER, G., SIMON, R., GEBHARD, M. E., WEINGARTEN, E., HOLLAND, J. L., SANDERS, R., STONE, G. B., and REAHL, J. E. Relative effectiveness of psychotherapeutic programs: a multicriteria comparison of four programs for three different patient groups. *Psychol. Monogr.*, 1960, 74, No. 5 (Whole No. 492).

FIEDLER, F. E. The concept of the ideal therapeutic relationship *J. consult. Psychol.*, 1950, 14, 239–245. (a)

FIEDLER, F. E. A comparison of therapeutic relationships in psychoanalytic, nondirective, and Adlerian therapy. *J. consult. Psychol.*, 1950, 14, 436–445. (b)

FIEDLER, F. E. Factor analyses of psychoanalytic, nondirective and Adlerian therapeutic relationships. *J. consult. Psychol.*, 1951, 15, 32–38.

FRANK, J. D. *Persuasion and healing*. Baltimore: Johns Hopkins Press, 1961.

FENICHEL, O. *Problems of psychoanalytic techniques*. Albany, N.Y.: Psychoanal. Quart., 1941.

FULKERSON, S. D., and BARRY, J. R. Methodology and research on the prognostic use of psychological tests. *Psychol. Bull.*, 1961, 58, 177–204.

GARDNER, G. GAIL. The psychotherapeutic relationship. *Psychol. Bull.*, 1964, 61, 426–437.

GARFIELD, S. L., and AFFLECK, D. C. Therapists' judgments concerning patients considered for psychotherapy. *J. consult. Psychol.*, 1961, 25, 505–509.

GURIN, G., VEROFF, J., and FELD, SHEILA. *Americans view their mental health*. New York: Basic Books, 1960.

HOLLINGSHEAD, A. B., and REDLICH, F. C. *Social class and mental illness*. New York: Wiley, 1958.

KING, G. F., ARMITAGE, S. G., and TILTON, J. R. A therapeutic approach to schizophrenics of extreme pathology. *J. abnorm. soc. Psychol.*, 1960, 61, 276–286.

KIRTNER, W. L., and CARTWRIGHT, D. S. Success and failure in client-centered therapy as a function of client personality variables. *J. consult. Psychol.*, 1958, 22, 259–264. (a)

KIRTNER, W. L., and CARTWRIGHT, D. S. Success and failure in client-centered therapy as a function of initial in-therapy behavior. *J. consult. Psychol.*, 1958, 22, 329–333. (b)

LANG, P. J., and LAZOVIK, A. D. Experimental desensitization of a phobia. *J. abnorm. soc. Psychol.*, 1963, 6, 519–525.

LAZARUS, A. A. An evaluation of behavior therapy. *Behav. Res. Ther.*, 1963, 1, 69–79.

MINK, O. G. A comparison of effectiveness of nondirective therapy and clinical counseling in junior high school. *School Counselor*, 1959, 6, 12–14.

POWERS, E., and WITMER, HELEN. *An experiment in the prevention of delinquency*. New York: Columbia University Press, 1951.

ROGERS, C. R., and DYMOND, ROSALIND F. *Psychotherapy and personality change*. Univer. of Chicago Press, 1954.

ROGERS, C. R. The necessary and sufficient conditions of therapeutic personality change. *J. consult. Psychol.*, 1957, 21, 95–103.

ROGERS, C. R. A theory of therapy, personality, and interpersonal relationships, as developed in the client-centered framework. In S. Koch (Ed.), *Psychology: a study of a science*, Vol. III. New York: McGraw-Hill, 1959. Pp. 184–256.

ROGERS, C. R. A theory of psychotherapy with schizophrenics and a proposal for its empirical investigation. In J. G. Dawson and N. P. Dellis (Eds.), *Psychotherapy with schizophrenics*. Baton Rouge: Louisiana State Univer. Press, 1961. Pp. 3–19.

SHLIEN, J. M., MOSAK, H. H., and DREIKURS, R. Effect of time limits: a comparison of two psychotherapies. *J. counsel. Psychol.*, 1962, 9, 31–34.

SPEISMAN, J. C. Depth of interpretation and verbal resistance in psychotherapy. *J. consult. Psychol.*, 1959, 23, 93–99.

STRUPP, H. H., WALLACH, M. S., and WOGAN, M. Psychotherapy experience in retrospect: questionnaire survey of former patients and their therapists. *Psychol. Monogr.*, 1964, 78, No. 11 (Whole No. 588).

SUSSMAN, ALICE. Patient-therapist similarity as a factor in psychotherapy. Unpublished manuscript, Teachers College, Columbia University, 1964.

TRUAX, C. B. The process of group psychotherapy. *Psychol. Monogr.*, 1961, 75, No. 14 (Whole No. 511). (a)

TRUAX, C. B. A scale for the measurement of

accurate empathy. *Psychiatric Institute Bull.,* Wisconsin Psychiatric Institute, Univer. of Wisconsin, 1961, 1, No. 10. (b)

TRUAX, C. B. Effective ingredients in psychotherapy. *J. counsel. Psychol.,* 1963, 10, 256–263.

TRUAX, C. B., and CARKHUFF, R. R. For better or for worse: the process of psychotherapeutic personality change. In *Recent advances in behavioral change.* Montreal: McGill Univer. Press, 1963.

WINDER, C. L., AHMAD, FARRUKH Z., BANDURA, A., and RAU, LUCY. Dependency of patients, psychotherapists' responses, and aspects of psychotherapy. *J. consult. Psychol.,* 1962, 26, 129–134.

WOLPE, J. *Psychotherapy by reciprocal inhibition.* Stanford: Stanford Univer. Press, 1958.

WOLPE, J. Behavior therapy in complex neurotic states. *Brit. J. Psychiat.,* 1964, 110, 28–34.

Interpersonal Assessment of Play Therapy Outcome*

JULIUS SEEMAN
EDYTH BARRY
CHARLOTTE ELLINWOOD

Research in outcomes of psychotherapy has begun to gain a secure scientific footing. However, most of the research developments concern therapy with adults, and the province of therapy with children has seen much less research advance. This paper reports a study of therapy with children.

A study by Cox (1953) appears to be the first in which the concept of controls was fully realized. Cox chose two equivalent groups of children living within an institutional setting and provided play therapy for the children in one of the groups. Pretest-posttest comparisons on TAT and sociometric measures showed significant changes in favor of the experimental group.

Controlled studies by Bills (1950) and by Seeman and Edwards (1954) investigated the effect of play therapy upon reading performance. Both studies showed positive effects of therapy upon performance.

Dorfman (1958) studied personality outcomes of client-centered play therapy, using both the own control and matched control techniques. Her results indicated significant positive changes associated with therapy.

Three reviews have summarized research in play therapy (Dorfman, 1951; Lebo, 1953; and Levitt, 1957). Levitt used Eysenck's method of deriving a base point of improvement without therapy and then comparing reported changes brought about by therapy. He found that the proportion of children reported as improved by therapy was no higher than the proportion reported as improved in the nontherapy groups. There are a number of weaknesses conceded in this method, most of which concern questions about comparability of the groups and adequacy of the criterion measures. The issue, however, is a basic research issue.

The history of therapy research reveals that most studies founder on the problem of adequate controls. The variables of self-initiated request for therapy, motivation for

Reprinted from *Psychotherapy: Theory, Research and Practice*, 1964, 1 (2), 64–66, with the permission of Psychologists Interested in the Advancement of Psychology and the authors.

* Appreciation is expressed to Lois DeLattre, Leonard Hersher, Sophie Fox Kirtner, and Leo Subotnik for their help in the study.

Thanks are due to the U.S. Public Health Service, Institute of Mental Health (projects M-593 and M-707), for grants in support of this study.

change, and personality organization have not often been adequately accounted for, and have risen to obscure the effect of the therapeutic process itself. The present study was designed to come to terms with these variables.

From the standpoint of criterion measures, the study chose to utilize interpersonal assessment of change. These criteria make sense on both practical and theoretical grounds. Interpersonal judgments have a demonstrated validity (Gronlund, 1959); they are readily interpretable; and they are in accord with predictions from the theory of therapeutic outcome.

METHOD

Selection of Samples

The locale of the study was a predominantly upper middle class school in a large city. The second and third grades, consisting of about 150 children, were given a modified version of the Tuddenham reputation test (Tuddenham, 1952), and the teachers completed a teacher rating scale (Radke-Yarrow, 1946) for each child. Both of these instruments contain behavior ratings of a personality assessment type, and permit classification of the children into categories of high adjustment, aggression, and withdrawal.

All scores were converted to standard scores so that a composite adjustment rating could be devised. The sixteen children rated lowest in adjustment on these scales comprised the children in the study. Eight children were designated as the therapy children and eight as the controls. There was equal representation in the groups among boys and girls, and among aggressive and withdrawn children. The experimental and control groups were thus equivalent in age, sex, total adjustment scores, and type of maladjustment. There was no differential selection in terms of the crucial variable, motivation for therapy, since the subgroups were selected randomly.

During the course of the experiment, two children each in the experimental and control groups transferred out of the neighborhood; all data analyses omit these children. By a fortunate coincidence all of these children were from the withdrawn groups. The experimental vs. control balance thus remained intact.

Procedure

Each child in the experimental group was brought to a clinical facility once a week for individual play therapy. Length of therapy was determined by therapist judgment of need in conjunction with the children's attitudes toward continuing, without reference to test data. Median length of therapy for the group was 37 sessions.

In order to provide for a clear-cut test of the effect of therapy upon the children, no differential contact was made with the parents of the experimental and control groups. Mothers of the experimental group were seen once before therapy and once after therapy. Control group mothers were also seen twice, at time intervals equivalent to those of the experimental group.

Testing Intervals

The teacher rating scale and reputation tests were administered on three occasions: once before therapy, once at the end of the school year (seven months after the first administration), and finally one year after the second testing. The interval from first to last testing was thus 19 months.

By the time of follow-up testing, the classes had been reorganized and were taught by different teachers, so that we may consider this testing period the most removed from the experiment. Although the second testing interval is referred to in Table 1 as *posttest,* two of the children had not completed therapy at that point. For these children might be considered a "late therapy" testing point.

A priori directional hypotheses specified that score changes for the experimental group would exceed significantly those of the control group.

RESULTS

Table 1 presents the results. Difference scores were derived by comparing directly the standard scores of a given child at each testing interval.

It will be noted from the table that score changes on the reputation test favored the experimental group. On the teacher rating scale the experimental group showed marginally significant improvement as compared to the control group on the posttest vs. follow-up. However, the overall teacher rating scores conceal more decided differences between the groups. Since the aggressive experimental and control subgroups re-

mained intact throughout the study, it was possible to compare the two groups with respect to changes in aggression scores, according to *a priori* hypotheses. Table 2 presents the results. It will be seen that at pretherapy time all children had positive aggression Z scores, indicating that all of them were more aggressive than the class average. This is of course to be expected, since they were chosen on this basis. By follow-up time, all children in the experimental group had lower aggression scores than the average child in the class, while all control children still had higher-than-average aggression scores.

Statistical comparison of the two groups with respect to change scores yielded a t ratio of 4.86, thus indicating a significant contrast between the groups.

TABLE 1

Score Changes for the Groups

| | Teacher Rating | | | | | | |
| | Experimental | | Control | | | | |
Interval	$\overline{D}$	Sigma	$\overline{D}$	Sigma	Diff.	t	p[a]
Pretest vs. posttest	− .33	8.71	.83	8.57	−1.16	.23	n.s.
Pretest vs. follow-up	5.17	13.24	−1.00	8.85	6.17	.95	n.s.
Posttest vs. follow-up	5.50	10.18	−1.83	3.54	7.33	1.67	$10 > P > .05$
	Reputation Test						
Pretest vs. posttest	2.67	5.89	2.00	10.12	.67	.14	n.s.
Pretest vs. follow-up	9.17	5.88	−1.83	7.71	11.00	2.78	$< .05$
Posttest vs. follow-up	6.50	6.32	−3.83	10.38	10.33	2.08	$< .05$

[a] $t_{.05} = 1.81$ for 10 d.f. on one-tailed test of directional hypothesis.

TABLE 2

Teacher Rating of Aggressive Behavior

Experimental Aggressive Group Z scores*				Control Aggressive Group Z scores			
Child	Pretherapy	Follow-up	Difference	Child	Pretherapy	Follow-up	Difference
A	2.87	− .67	−3.54	W	1.94	2.28	.34
B	.47	−1.29	−1.76	X	.87	1.74	.87
C	1.38	− .52	−1.90	Y	.17	1.56	1.39
D	1.60	− .23	−1.83	Z	1.79	1.37	−.42

* Negative Z scores denote aggression ratings lower than the class mean.

It is clear from the foregoing results that children who are involved in a therapy experience are perceived by others as significantly less maladjusted after therapy. Comparable shifts in interpersonal judgments do not occur in the absence of therapy.

It is pertinent to point out one incidental statistical finding here. When groups are chosen from the extremes of a distribution, as these groups were, a statistical regression effect may complicate the results. It is of interest to note that in none of the control group analyses does a regression effect appear.

DISCUSSION

Two points may be worthy of special note in this study. The first point relates to the findings with regard to the aggressive groups. Parents and educators sometimes express concern at the behavior latitude permitted in play therapy, particularly with regard to aggressive children. The view sometimes expressed is that such children need a controlled environment rather than a permissive one. The findings in this study are of interest in this connection, since they indicate that a striking reduction in aggressiveness may result from a permissive therapeutic climate. Such an outcome is predicted from therapeutic theory. The second point is that behavior changes occurred without work with the parents. This finding suggests that children as young as seven or eight years old may change even in the absence of systematic environmental alteration. There may be implications here for degree of autonomy in children of this age level.

The final point concerns the cumulative implications of this study when taken in conjunction with the ones previously cited by Cox, Bills, Dorfman, and Seeman and Edwards. All of these studies of therapy used control techniques and all showed that the experimental groups registered changes not observable in the control groups. It seems reasonable to state that the conclusions of Levitt concerning the absence of evidence for change due to therapy no longer hold categorically.

SUMMARY

Two equivalent groups of children relatively low in adjustment were selected from a larger sample. Members of the E group came for individual play therapy. Reputation test scores for the E group showed significant positive contrasts with the control group. Overall teacher rating changes were marginal. Teacher ratings of aggression for the aggressive therapy group were significantly lower than those for the control groups at follow-up.

REFERENCES

BILLS, R. E. Nondirective play therapy with retarded readers. *J. consult. Psychol.*, 1950, 14, 140–149.

COX, F. N. Sociometric status and individual adjustment before and after play therapy. *J. abnorm. soc. Psychol.*, 1953, 48, 354–356.

DORFMAN, ELAINE. Play therapy. In C. R. Rogers, *Client-centered therapy*. Boston: Houghton Mifflin, 1951. Pp. 235–277.

DORFMAN, ELAINE. Personality outcomes of client-centered child therapy. *Psychol. Monogr.* 1958, 72, No. 3 (Whole No. 456).

GRONLUND, N., *Sociometry in the classroom*. New York: Harper & Bros., 1959.

LEBO, D. The present status of research in nondirective play therapy. *J. consult. Psychol.*, 1953, 17, 177–183.

LEVITT, E. E. The results of psychotherapy with children. *J. consult. Psychol.*, 1957, 21, 189–196.

RADKE-YARROW, MARIAN J. *The relation of parental authority to children's behavior and attitudes*. Minneapolis: Univer. Minnesota Press, 1946.

SEEMAN, J., & EDWARDS, BENNER. A therapeutic approach to reading difficulties. *J. consult. Psychol.*, 1954, 18, 451–453.

TUDDENHAM, R. D. Studies in reputation. *Psychol. Monogr.*, 1952, 66, No. 1 (Whole No. 333).

Evaluating Therapy in a Delinquency Prevention Program

HANS-LUCAS TEUBER
EDWIN POWERS

This is a report on work done during our association with a unique social experiment: the Cambridge-Somerville Youth Study, originally conceived and endowed by the late Dr. Richard C. Cabot (24). For approximately eight years, from 1937 to 1945, this large-scale treatment effort was directed at the prevention of delinquency, by guidance, counseling, and therapy, in a group of several hundred underprivileged boys. The uniqueness of the Study, however, did not so much lie in the scope of its treatment efforts, nor in the outcome, as in its avowed purpose to serve the ends of evaluative research.

By setting up a control group, and by keeping unusually detailed records, the Study made provisions for quantitative measurement of the effects of therapy, and for systematic attempts at an objective description of the therapeutic relationships. Probably the most outstanding feature of the program, as envisaged by Cabot, was the existence of an untreated control group, whose members had been matched individ-

Reprinted from *Psychiatric Treatment*, 1953, 21, 138–147, with the permission of The Williams & Wilkins Co. and the authors.

ually, at the outset, with the members of the treatment group. As far as we can ascertain, the only study of therapy which approximates such controlled experimentation has been Denker's survey (5). The results of the Cambridge-Somerville Youth Study, as you shall hear, have not been too different from those reported by Denker.

PROCEDURES

As in any ordinary instance of experimental therapeutics, the basic design of the Cambridge Study was simple. The program began with the selection of subjects from the underprivileged areas of Cambridge and Somerville (Massachusetts). The names of the boys, between six and ten, and rated as likely to become delinquent, were solicited from school teachers, policemen "on the beat," and settlement workers. A smaller number of boys without any apparent delinquent tendencies was also included. A list of 650 boys was obtained, and these boys were individually matched, in pairs, according to a large number of variables; such as age, intelligence quotient, school grade, delinquency rating, ethnic and socioeconomic background, and other factors.

The decision which boy in each pair should be treated was made by the toss of a coin. By this matching process the original group of 650 was split into two equal groups of 325: a treatment group (T) and a control group (C).

As soon as a boy had been selected and matched, he was assigned to one of the original ten counselors employed by the Study, and "treatment" was initiated. Treatment activities ranged from a friendly relationship of the big-brother variety to increasingly formal therapeutic interviews according to principles of psychiatric social work. With the turnover in the treatment staff enforced by World War II, and the employment of an analytically trained treatment supervisor, the Study's approach became gradually more similar to that of other, more orthodox guidance centers. To the end of the treatment period, however, there remained some of the orginal emphasis on directed "friendship" as a means of delinquency prevention, and the staff's attitudes seemed clearly divided between apostles of "friendship," and those of professional counseling.

Regardless of the individual counselor's predilection, all treatment consisted of individual, face-to-face contacts. These individual relationships between counselors and boys thus served as the independent variable: they represented "treatment" as originally planned by Cabot; they were restricted to the treatment group and consistently withheld from the control group. By the end of the treatment period, in 1945, one of us (E.P.) compared treatment and control groups with regard to the number of offenses committed, and three years later a similar statistical comparison was made. Treatment, by 1945, had lasted for 2 to 8 years in individual cases, with a median duration of 4 years and 2 months.

EVALUATING OUTCOME

The total number of court appearances from the beginning of treatment to July 1, 1948, for the T and C groups, respectively, was

	T	C
Number of boys	96	92
Number of offenses	264	218

A similar picture is given by the number of appearances before the Crime Prevention Bureau, from 1938 to 1946, inclusive:

	T	C
One Time	49	49
Two or three times	65	52
Total	114	101

Such an outcome of the delinquency prevention program of the Study appears to be not only negative, but paradoxical. Instead of confirming the expectation that the treatment group would be less delinquent than the matched control group, there is a slight difference in favor of the control group. This apparent advantage of the control group may be offset, however, by other factors which more detailed statistics seem to reveal. There is a slightly greater incidence of serious recidivism (if defined as three or more offenses per boy) in the control group, and a rating of all offenses according to "seriousness" likewise shows a slight advantage of the treatment cases over the controls: there is a tendency on the part of the controls to commit a proportionately greater number of the more serious offenses.

None of these trends, however, are as yet significant. Unless further developments change the picture (as they well might) the direct comparison between T and C groups fails to show that the major hypothesis can be sustained: treatment did not, so far, reduce the incidence of adjudged delinquency in the treatment group.

We think this outcome is especially revealing in view of the rather different expectations of the counselors themselves. They believed that the Study's program had "substantially benefited" about two-thirds of the boys whom the Study served. Moreover, slightly more than half of the boys, when interviewed systematically after the close of the treatment period, volunteered that they had been helped by their association with the Study.

These findings illustrate the importance of the control group, and the peculiar difficulty one has in interpreting the counselor's (or the counselee's) "own story" unless objective behavioral indices for treatment success are available. Quantitative indices of behavior, of course, are not infallible; and evaluation in terms of court appearances might suggest some of the crudity of market research. Yet, quantitative indices, where available, are better than professions of faith bolstered by the therapist's prestige and the skillful use of the illustrative case.

EVALUATING RELATIONSHIPS BETWEEN COUNSELORS AND BOYS

A control group design is indispensable as a basis for demonstrating tangible results of treatment; but it does not yield any definition of the independent variable: the treatment process itself (12). The task of analyzing the treatment relationships fell to one of us (H.L.T.) at the suggestion of Gordon W. Allport, the Study's principal scientific advisor.

The traditional approach to analysis of therapy has been the psychiatric case study: an historical and interpretive commentary on the therapist's activities, as recalled by the therapist himself at the time of recording. As a form of historiography, the case study is the more persuasive the greater the artistic skill of its author (1, 13). As a source for an objective analysis of what happened in the course of the therapeutic relationship, however, the therapist's report should be supplemented by complete phonographic records and other objective material, a practice convincingly advocated by Carl Rogers and his school (4, 27, 28, 34).

In the Cambridge-Somerville Youth Study, completely transcribed interviews came into use only after the end of the formal treatment period, that is after 1945.

The available sources for analyzing the relationships between counselors and boys were, as usual, the counselor's own records, kept in the form of (often daily) logs of the treatment process. By 1945, these records of interviews, visits and similar activities had grown into an aggregate of 22,000 single-spaced typewritten pages, referring to individual interaction between 19 counselors and a varying number of boys (325 in 1939, and 75 by the end of the treatment, in 1945). Such massive evidence would seem sufficient to discourage even the hardiest social scientist, if called upon to analyze treatment relationships and to relate this analysis to the total outcome of the Study.

What is more, these records, despite their bulk, were incomplete: they presented only the counselor's side of the picture. As a description of the relationship between counselor and boy, the counselor's "own story" was inadequate. Rather than follow the usual method of accepting the therapist's view, we proceeded therefore as if faced with the task of a cultural anthropologist: that of describing a social system different from one's own (3, 25, 39). As in anthropological field work—and we hope, without malice—we consistently made a distinction between what the partners did, and what they said they did (14, 15, 18). We further compared what A said about B (the counselor's account of the boy's relationship with the counselor), with what B said about A (the boy's account of the counselor's relationship with the boy) (16, 35, 36).

Data were accordingly gathered, both during and after the treatment period, concerning 1) the counselor's conceptions of the relationship ascertained by means of questionnaires, rating scales, and focused interviews; 2) the boys' conceptions of the relationship ascertained primarily by means of focused interviews with 135 boys, and by modified sociometric procedures (17, 19, 22); 3) the facts pertaining to the counseling relationship as far as they could be ascertained independently of the partners' interpretations, including a record of frequency of face-to-face meetings, place of meetings, and types of joint activities.

The results of these surveys have been described elsewhere (37); they do not lend themselves readily to any summary presentation. It turned out, for instance, that counselors differed consistently in the articulation or stereotypy of their relationships; in the degree of accuracy with which they estimated the boy's reaction to themselves (the counselors); and in their ability in maintaining strong relationships (high "rapport") with many boys or with few. The principal features of the analysis, however, can be characterized; they were determined by the conceptual scheme which we adopted for the purpose of interpreting our data.

First of all, the counselor-counselee relationship was considered as a miniature social system (9, 20, 21): a group consisting of two participants (dyad) (10, 11, 32, 33, 41). Analysis of social interaction in such dyadic groups is notoriously difficult, since sociological concepts are ordinarily applicable only to larger systems, and psychology deals either with the individual, or with the individual and the group, but rarely with groups consisting of only two participants. The dyad as a problem for social science thus falls into the gap between psychology and sociology, and the difficulties of communicating about the psychiatric treatment process, between adherents of different schools of therapy, will not be overcome until we have a descriptive scheme which can be applied to all types of therapy. Given a formal conceptual scheme we can communicate about miniature social systems, such as dyads, and we can describe the therapeutic process in terms that are both quantifiable and neutral with regard to therapeutic doctrines.

Considered as minimal social systems, or dyadic groups, the individual counseling relationships could be ordered along a number of dimensions. Dyads, we concluded, could be classified to the extent to which they appeared to be "generic" or "unique," i.e., the extent to which the partners considered each other as replaceable or irreplaceable in their relationship (33). Dyadic groups could further be classified into "embedded" and "isolated" dyads—according to the extent to which the partners were able or unable to maintain their relationships within a matrix of other social relations. (Such distinctions may appear unnecessarily formal and theoretical, but their value lies, we repeat, in their universal applicability (20, 21, 38, 39, 41).)

In the setting of the counseling program "dyads" could be classified finally as "parataxic" or "integrated," according to the extent to which the partners failed or succeeded in grasping each other's conception of their relationship. For the concept of parataxis we are indebted to H. S. Sullivan (35, 36).

Of particular interest were occasional instances of marked discrepancy in the partners' interpretations of their relationship. While a counselor might describe a boy's attitude toward him as affectionate, or depending and trusting, the boy might assert that the counselor functioned as a detective, or a hostile social investigator. Such discrepant interpretations, if persistent, were considered as indicative of parataxis.

Parataxis was found to be either unilateral or bilateral. If unilateral, A "misinterpreted" the attitude of B toward himself (A), but not vice versa. In bilateral parataxis, A misjudged B's attitude toward A, and B misjudged A's attitude toward B. Longitudinal analysis of a stratified sample of 65 counselor-boy relationships suggested that relationships that had become parataxic did so almost from the start, and that the partners' mininterpretations, in this setting, were surprisingly persistent. Seemingly sudden shifts towards hostility in the counseling dyads frequently could be traced back to initial inadequacies in the partners' conceptions of the relationship.

Although outright parataxis seemed to appear in only about one third of the counselor-boy relationships analysed, their possible relation to failures of "treatment" prompted further studies of those counselors who were high in parataxis as against those (the majority) whose counseling relationships appeared to be predominately integrated (non-parataxic). Following the example of earlier studies by Frenkel-Brunswik (6) and by Sears (29, 30, 31), all counselors were asked to rate each other, as well as themselves, on a number of scales referring to personality traits and to professional competence. By analysing the ratings one could discover the extent to which counselors departed in their self-ratings from the pooled ratings given to them by their colleagues. We could furthermore quantify the extent to which a counselor agreed, in rating his colleagues, with the pooled ratings given them by the staff as a whole.

From these analyses it appeared that counselors with frequent parataxis exhibited a number of related tendencies: 1) they patterned the descriptions of their relationships with excessive uniformity; 2) they were poor judges of themselves; 3) although not necessarily poor judges of others, they tended to judge by projection; 4) they considered their counseling relations as a highly effective tool in producing changes in their charges. All these tendencies can be considered as instances of lack of articulation in social perception (7, 8, 40). Counselors with integrated dyads tended toward high degrees of articulation; counselors with parataxic dyads toward low degrees of articulation.

Parataxis was discovered by comparing the counselors' accounts of their relationships with the boys' "own story" (interviews with boys). Transcripts of these interviews held by members of the research staff with the boys, were submitted to four judges who rated each interview with respect to "rapport" and "perspective" manifested in the boy's account of his relationship with his counselor. "Rapport" was defined as the value which a boy seemed to attach to the relationship with his counselor. "Perspective" denoted the boy's apparent insight into the purpose of the relationship. The ratings on rapport were validated by an order-of-preference procedure in which the boys ranked their counselors on the same scale as their friends and associates. A further check on the validity of the ratings was made by counting the frequency of a boy's spontaneous visits to his counselor.

Contrary to the belief of counselors who stressed the professional aspects of their relationships, rapport and perspective turned out to be higher among the adherents of "friendship." In cases of low rapport, the counselors were found to misjudge the situation by overestimating their success in achieving rapport. But generally, a counselor's estimate of a boy's liking for him was less valid, as an indication of "true" rapport (judges' ratings), than the counselors' rating of his own liking for the boy.

Analysis of additional sources of information on counselors and boys revealed that, on the part of the counselors, ability to maintain rapport was unrelated to the amount and kind of professional training. On the boys' part, there was evidence for a particular "friendship proneness": boys who had many friends and who preferred contemporary playmates, responded better to their counselors than those who had few friends or were rejected at home. Boys who had been adjudged delinquent by the courts responded better than "unofficial" delinquents. Rapport and perspective were highest wherever the boy himself took the initiative, and wherever a definite goal common to counselor and boy was adopted.

The usefulness of these descriptions of the counseling process would have been greater, if the outcome had revealed differences between treatment and control groups. In the absence of such differences, the descriptions retain some value: they represent the trial application of a conceptual scheme which might be found useful in other settings were therapeutic relationships are to be described.

We insist particularly on our conclusion that an adequate empirical description of minimal social groups (such as therapeutic dyads) cannot be accomplished by relying exclusively on, either, the partners' conceptions of the relationship, or on the conception of the relationship held by outside observers; both are necessary sources of data. Further experimental studies of the effects of therapy should consider the potential usefulness of such a formal approach to their material, in which sociological theory and anthropological field work methods are combined into a framework of universal applicability.

DISCUSSION

The results of the Cambridge-Somerville Youth Study, as presented thus far, are neither final nor unequivocal. Gordon Allport (2) in particular, has stressed that future surveys comparing T and C groups might reveal a gradual unmatching of the two groups, in the direction of an increasing tendency to law-abiding behavior among the "Ts." Such an instance of "delayed" results is not precluded by the data now available. Nor can we extend our conclusions beyond the unique features of the Study and assert that delinquency prevention, in general, is impossible. Conceivably, a program using different methods, or merely operating in a different setting, might have greater or more immediate results. But all this is not the point at issue. We believe that the Study should rather be considered as a paradigm for research in the effects of therapy.

Before the data derived from the control group had become known, all but two members of the treatment staff predicted significant success. An evaluation in the usual style, based on the counselor's own story, and devoid of objective indices of altered behavior would have resulted in merely another report on eminently successful therapy (23).

In fact, one of the most remarkable features of the Study was this willingness, on the therapists' part, to submit their work to the scrutiny of an independent research staff, whose functions could have easily been misinterpreted as those of efficiency experts or company spies (26). To be sure, some frictions did arise, but they were overcome through the joint effort of the treatment and research staff. An analysis of those tensions that did develop from time to time is instructive, since similar difficulties are likely to appear in other agencies in which treatment and research staff members have to interact.

To some of the counselors, the whole control group idea, and our insistence on an objective description of the counseling process, seemed slightly blasphemous, as if we were attempting a statistical test of the efficacy of prayer. Theirs was an "ethics of sentiments" rather than an "ethics of consequences" (39). They insisted that the relationships established had their value in themselves, irrespective of their possible effect on the boys' behavior, and they were not perturbed when the seemingly negative results of the delinquency prevention program became known. Other counselors reacted differently; they felt that research was superflous, since all the necessary rules of conduct in therapy were already known. When they were informed of the outcome of the Study, they reacted in a characteristic fashion: those who were analytically trained and oriented asserted that the results would have been positive, had analytic principles been applied by all staff members, consistently, throughout the course of the treatment period. Conversely, those counselors, who were followers of Carl Rogers' non-directive approach averred that a systematic use of non-directive methods would have produced more definite success.

Patently, our data do not bear on any

of these questions. The varied and eclectic approach to treatment in the Study precluded a fair test of any specific form of therapy. We submit, however, that the data yield one definite conclusion: that the burden of proof is on anyone who claims specific results for a given form of therapy. It is admittedly difficult to provide for expensive control settings similar to that of the Cambridge-Somerville Youth Study. But the objective evaluation of therapeutic processes is of such importance that similar studies, in many areas of therapy, are indicated.

REFERENCES

1. ALLPORT, G. W. *The Use of Personal Documents in Psychological Science.* New York, Social Science Research Council, Bull. 49, 1942.

2. ALLPORT, G. W. Foreword to: POWERS, E. AND WITMER, H. *An Experiment in the Prevention of Delinquency,* pp. v-xxx. New York, Columbia University Press, 1951.

3. BATESON, G. *Naven: a Survey of the Problems Suggested by a Composite Picture of a New Guinea Tribe Drawn from Three Points of View.* Cambridge, Cambridge University Press, 1936.

4. COVNER, B. J. Studies in phonographic recording of verbal material. III. The completeness and accuracy of counseling interview reports. *J. gen. Psychol.,* 30, 181–203, 1944.

5. DENKER, P. G. Results of treatment of psychoneuroses by the general practitioner: a follow-up study of 500 cases. *N. Y. State J. Med.,* 46, 2164–2166, 1946.

6. FRENKEL-BRUNSWIK, ELSE, Mechanisms of self-deception. *J. soc. Psychol.,* 10, 509–520, 1939.

7. HEIDER, F. Social perception and phenomenal causality. *Psychol. Rev.,* 51, 358–374, 1944.

8. HEIDER, F. Attitudes and cognitive organization. *J. Psychol.,* 21, 107–112, 1946.

9. HENDERSON, L. J. Physician and patient as a social system. *New Engld. J. Med.,* 212 (18), 819–823, 1935.

10. HENNING, H. Der Mehrpersonen- und Partnerversuch. Bericht ueber den 10. Kongress fuer experimentelle Psychologie in Bonn, 1927.

11. HENNING, H. Ziele und Moeglichkeiten der experimentellen Charakterpruefung. *Jb. Charakterol.,* 6, 213–274, 1929.

12. HUNT, J. McV. A program of research in psychotherapy. Presidential address, Division of Personality and Social Psychology, American Psychological Association, Chicago, Illinois, September 1, 1951.

13. KLUCKHOHN, C. The personal document in anthropological science. In L. GOTTSCHALK ET AL. (eds.): *The Use of Personal Documents in History, Anthropology, and Sociology.* New York, Social Science Research Council, Bull. 53, 1945.

14. KLUCKHOHN, C. Patterning as exemplified in Navajo culture. In: SPIER, L. (Ed.): *Language, Culture, and Personality.* Menasha, Wisconsin, Sapir Memorial Publication Fund, 1941.

15. LASSWELL, H. D. A provisional classification of symbol data. *Psychiatry,* 1, 197–204, 1938.

16. MEAD, G. H. *Mind, Self, and Society from the Standpoint of a Social Behaviorist.* Chicago, University of Chicago Press, 1934.

17. MORENO, J. L. *Who Shall Survive?* Washington, Nervous and Mental Disease Publishing Co., 1934.

18. MORRIS, C. M. Foundations of the theory of signs. *Int. Encycl. Unif. Sci.,* 1, 2. Chicago, Univ. of Chicago Press, 1938.

19. NORTHWAY, MARY L. A method for depicting social relationships obtained by sociometric testing. *Sociometry,* 3, 144–150, 1940.

20. PARSONS, T. *The Structure of Social Action.* New York, London, McGraw-Hill, 1937.

21. PARSONS, T. AND SHILS, E. A. (Eds.). *Toward a General Theory of Action.* Cambridge, Mass., Harvard University Press, 1951.

22. POTASHIN, REVA. A sociometric study of children's friendships. *Sociometry,* 9, 48–70, 1946.

23. POWERS, E. An experiment in prevention of delinquency. *Annals Amer. Acad. Pol. Soc. Sci.,* 261, 77–88, 1949.

24. POWERS, E. AND WITMER, HELEN. *An Experiment in the Prevention of Delinquency: The Cambridge-Somerville Youth Study,* pp. xliii and 649. New York, Columbia Univ. Press, 1951.

25. RADCLIFFE-BROWN, A. R. *The Andaman Islanders: a Study in Social Anthropology.* Cambridge, Cambrige Univ. Press, 1922.

26. ROETHLISBERGER, F. AND DICKSON, W. J. *Management and the Worker.* Cambridge, Harvard Univ. Press, 1943 (6th printing).

27. ROGERS, C. R. *Counseling and Psychotherapy.* New York, Houghton, Mifflin & Co., 1942.

28. ROGERS, C. R. Significant aspects of client-centered therapy. *Amer. Psychologist,* 1, 415–422, 1946.

29. SEARS, R. R. Experimental studies of projection. I. Attribution of traits. *J. soc. Psychol.,* 7, 151–163, 1936.

30. SEARS, R. R. Experimental studies of projection. II. Ideas of reference. *J. soc. Psychol.,* 8, 389–400, 1937.

31. SEARS, R. R. *Survey of Objective Studies of Psychoanalytic Concepts.* New York, Social Science Research Council, Bull. 51, 1943.

32. SIGHELE, SCIPIO. *Le crime à deux: essai de psychologie morbide.* Paris, F. Alcan, 1893.

33. SIMMEL, G. *Soziologie; Untersuchungen ueber die Formen der Vergesellschaftung,* 3rd Ed. München and Leipzig: Duncker and Humblot, 1923. Partly translated in: *The Sociology of Georg Simmel,* Ed. by Kurt H. Wolff. Glencoe, Illinois, Free Press, 1950.

34. SNYDER, W. U. An investigation of the nature of nondirective psychotherapy. *J. gen. Psychol.,* 33, 193–223, 1945.

35. SULLIVAN, H. S. A note on the implications of psychiatry and the study of interpersonal relations for investigation in the social sciences. *Amer. J. Sociol.,* 42, 848–861, 1937.

36. SULLIVAN, H. S. Psychiatry: Introduction to the study of interpersonal relations. *Psychiatry,* 1, 121–134, 1938.

37. TEUBER, H. L. The Dyadic Group: A Study in Counseling Relationships, pp. iv and 549, Ph.D. Thesis, 1947, Harvard University. Widener Library, Harvard University, Cambridge, Massachusetts.

38. TÖNNIES, F. *Fundamental Concepts of Sociology (Gemeinschaft und Gesellschaft).* Transl. and supplemented by C. P. LOOMIS. New York, Cincinnati, American Book Co., 1940.

39. WEBER, M. *The Theory of Social and Economic Organization.* (Translated by A. M. HENDERSON AND T. PARSONS). New York, Oxford University Press, 1947.

40. WERTHEIMER, M. Laws of organization in perceptual forms, pp. 71–88 in: *A source book of Gestalt psychology* (W. D. Ellis, Ed.). New York, Harcourt, Brace & Co., 1939.

41. WIESE, L. VON. *Systematic Sociology, on the basis of the Beziehungslehre and Gebildelehre of Leopold von Wiese,* adapted and amplified by HOWARD BECKER. New York, J. Wiley & Sons, 1932.

An Intensive Five-Year Follow-up Study of Treated Psychiatric Outpatients[1]

ANTHONY R. STONE
JEROME D. FRANK
EARL H. NASH
STANLEY D. IMBER

INTRODUCTION

Follow-up studies of psychiatric patients have been concerned primarily with evaluation of the efficacy of various forms of therapy, and collection of data on the long-term course of psychiatric illness. Both of these topics have proved to be extraordinarily refractory, largely because we still cannot adequately describe patients, treatments or types of improvement, and because patients undergo so many experiences outside of therapy and subsequent to it that may affect them for better or worse. Hastings rightly says, "A review of the literature of prognosis in psychiatric illness is a lesson in humility, for it is difficult to obtain a clear picture either of

spontaneous remission rates or how the rates differ from spontaneous when some treatment is used" (9, p. 1057). As will be seen, even this seemingly simple statement incorporates a knotty problem by using the adjective "spontaneous." Goldstein's recent paper criticizing the widespread use of the word "spontaneous" (7) lends support to the search for evidence which may clarify what Frank and his co-workers (3) have noted concerning patient-response to nonspecific activity of culturally defined healers. They have found evidence that reduction of symptoms is partially a function of the potentiation and activation of the patient's expectancies regarding such improvement.

This paper deals with long-term improvement, patient experiences subsequent to a treatment program, and relationships between these two factors. It is the report of a five-year follow-up study of a group of adult psychiatric patients who had originally received approximately six months of psychotherapy to which they were assigned

Reprinted from *Journal of Nervous and Mental Disease*, 1961, 133, 410–422, with the permission of The Williams & Wilkins Co. and the authors. Note 2, containing the authors' affiliation, has been omitted.

[1] This study was supported in part by grants from the U.S. Public Health Service and the Ford Foundation.

in accordance with requirements of an ongoing research study. Subsequent treatment was uncontrolled but was ascertained at periodic follow-up evaluations. Results are considered from the standpoints of the long-term course of psychiatric illness and the effects of psychotherapy.

PROCEDURE

The patients were 54 white outpatients of the Phipps Clinic of The Johns Hopkins Hospital, diagnosed as having a psychoneurosis or personality disorder. Their ages ranged from 18 to 55 years, and about two-thirds were women.

Three forms of treatment were used: individual therapy, in which the patient was seen privately for one hour once a week; group therapy, in which groups of five to seven patients were seen for one and one-half hours once a week; and minimal contact therapy,[3] in which they were seen individually for not more than one-half hour once every two weeks. The first two therapies differed from the third in the amount of treatment time available to the patients, and differed from each other in the use of individual or group sessions.

Patients were assigned sequentially to one of the three types of treatment. Three second-year psychiatric residents each conducted the three types of treatment, with six patients assigned to each type. These therapists had nothing to do with the assignment of patients or with evaluation of patient progress. The design called for each patient to receive six months of treatment, and, although this goal was not quite achieved, it was reasonably approached. Of the 54 patients included in the study, 48 (89 per cent) had four or more months of treatment during the experimental phase.

Patients were evaluated at the end of

the six-month experimental period of treatment (or when treatment was terminated, if this occurred prematurely). Subsequently, an attempt was made to retain contact with the total group of 54 patients for four more re-evaluations, which took place six months after termination of treatment, one year following that, a year later, and two years later—that is, five years after the first treatment contact. Thirty patients returned for the five-year evaluation, and they comprise the sample presented in this paper.

Changes in personal discomfort and social ineffectiveness were selected as a means of gauging therapeutic efficacy (4). Change in discomfort was measured by a scale on which the patient indicated which symptoms he had and how much they distressed him. Measurement of change in social ineffectiveness was more difficult, since adequacy in interpersonal functioning cannot be determined simply by a person's behavior. The meanings of his actions to himself and others must be taken into account before socially pertinent judgments can be made.

The solution was to devise a social ineffectiveness scale, consisting of 15 social interactional categories, such as over-dependent, over-independent, officious, withdrawn, impulsive, cautious and so on.[4] The patient was rated on each category on the basis of two observed interviews, one

---

[3] Minimal contact therapy as described in this paper is labeled Continued Treatment Clinic (CTC) at the Outpatient Department of the Henry Phipps Psychiatric Clinic.

[4] The following are examples of definitions of social ineffectiveness scale categories:

2) *Superficially-sociable:* Seeks many superficial acquaintanceships. Breaks off relationships before they become intimate and/or refuses to form close relationships. N.B. Does not apply to relationships forced on patient, *e.g.,* family or necessities of occupation.

6) *Hyper-reactive:* Tends to over-react emotionally; behaves in an uncontrolled manner.

10) *Intra-punitive:* Self-critical; tends to blame, criticize and hold himself responsible for his difficulties, frustrations and failures. Over-apologetic.

Copies of this scale are available on request.

with him and one with a relative. Interviewer and observer in each case met following the session, resolved differences by consensus, and produced a combined rating. Finally, the four staff members (two for the patient and two for the relative) met for a staffing, during which differences again were resolved by consensus and a final rating was established for the patient. Though rather cumbersome, this procedure was considered to be necessary to minimize bias.

Throughout the five-year period the amount of formal help patients continued to receive was impressive. This treatment was obtained at the Phipps Clinic and elsewhere, either in parallel with clinic treatment or independently. Stimulated by the thinking of Hinkle *et al.* (10) concerning the possible role of life stress in the production of all types of illness, we gathered data which appeared to be pertinent to this question at each follow-up period. Events such as births, deaths, job changes, catastrophic events, illness of self or close friends and relatives, and seasonal fluctuations in symptoms and ineffectiveness were recorded. However, patient status could not be related directly to these intercurrent events, partly because of our difficulty in evaluating the *meanings* of these experiences to the patient, and partly because of the problem of disentangling changes produced by therapy from those produced by environmental events. For example, advancement on the job could be the *result* of improvement in behavior produced by therapy, or the *cause* of such improvement. The familiarity of these methodologic problems had not made them easier to solve. It was decided finally to limit the analyses to intercurrent illnesses and treatment.

At each follow-up evaluation the interviewer completed a questionnaire with the patient. This was supplemented by another staff member's administration of the same questionnaire to a relative of the patient to record the relative's observations of these events in the patient's life for the same evaluation period. Information obtained included illnesses or treatments the patient had had during the follow-up period. These data were later categorized as follows:

1) Type of illness (medical, psychologic, or psychologically based somatic complaints).
2) Duration of illness (chronic or acute).
3) Severity of illness (major or minor).
4) Treatment resource (medical excluding psychiatric, psychologic including psychiatric, social work or religious counseling; or a medical resource for psychologic help).
5) Type of medication (for medical complaints or for psychologic complaints, *e.g.,* tranquilizers).

A special category under each heading was reserved for illnesses and treatments not clearly classifiable into one of the categories.

The data obtained were classified into the above categories by two independent judges, and differences between them were later resolved by consensus. It is acknowledged that the data are imprecise, in part because of the inadequacy of information on which the ratings were based, and in part because certain categories are not mutually exclusive. As an example, the same illness could be classified under two categories if the patient reported both psychic and somatic symptoms. On the other hand, each category was checked only once at any one evaluation point, regardless of how many different illnesses in that category the patient reported. Similarly, only one tally was made for a contact with a given category of treatment resource in a single evaluation period, no matter how many visits were made.[5]

---

[5] The records did not yield information as to the number of visits to a given treatment resource in any one evaluation period. If a patient visited the same resource in more than one evaluation period, the visit was tallied once in each period.

The variation in the length of intervals between evaluations may also have been a source of inaccuracy, though the duration of the interval did not seem to be related to the *amount* of illness reported. The patient reports seemed to be based on a "psychologic present" which was relatively unaffected by the actual interval between evaluations. For this reason, no corrective factor was applied for intervals of differing time periods. Even in the face of these inadequacies, certain trends were apparent and will be presented in the section to follow.

RESULTS

The 30 patients who returned for the five-year evaluation did not differ in any important dimension from the original total group of 54 patients. That is, the initial test scores, diagnoses, types of treatment received and certain demographic characteristics of the five-year returnees seemed to be representative of the total original sample, which, in turn, was similarly representative of the general population of psychoneurotic white outpatients seen at the Phipps Clinic.

For the purposes of studying improvement and its correlates, the discomfort and social ineffectiveness data were analyzed independently. This was mainly because of an earlier finding (13)—that improvement is not a unitary phenomenon—and also because of our intrinsic interest in the two criteria and their components. There is some evidence that they might have been combined, with most improved and least improved patients categorized on the basis of ordering averaged ranks, as was done to study intercurrent illness and treatment. (See below.) For example, actual status (as opposed to change status) on one measure was positively correlated with actual status on the other at the five-year point ($r = .61, p < .001$). There was also some association between *change* on each of the two measures at the fifth re-evaluation ($r = .38, p < .05$). However, if

the measures had been combined to study improvement, this would have limited our opportunity to examine the subscales of the discomfort scale, as well as the different categories of the social ineffectiveness scale.

Discomfort Improvement

With respect to discomfort, at the five-year point 23 patients (77 per cent of the 30 returnees) showed improvement from their initial level, two were unchanged, and five (17 per cent) were worse. At the time of the first re-evaluation, immediately following the six-month experimental treatment program, 19 (63 per cent) of these 30 patients were improved and the remaining 11 (37 percent) were worse. Thus, at the five-year point, the gains reported immediately following the formal treament program had been maintained or increased.[6]

The mean status of the 30 patients as a group, at each of the evaluation points, supported the above finding. Figure 1 indicates that the group showed its greatest improvement between successive evaluations at the time of the first re-evaluation, immediately following the experimental treatment period. The mean symptom drop of 8.3 was significant ($t = 2.52, p < .05$). Thereafter the symptom level was generally maintained or showed a continuing slight drop, except for the third re-evaluation, when a slight increase occurred. The mean differences of 16.2 and 8.0 from the initial to five-year, and the six-month to five-year points, respectively, were both significant ($p = < .05$).

Five subscales of the discomfort scale

---

[6] Of the 16 patients who failed to return after the third evaluation, 12 were in the "most improved" category of the total sample, which is consistent with an earlier finding on the same population—that patients who showed most improvement at each evaluation were less likely to return for subsequent ones. This suggests that the improvement over time of a group of psychoneurotic patients is probably even greater than the figures in the text indicate.

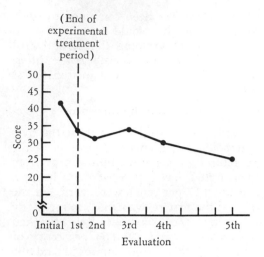

Fig. 1. Mean discomfort scale scores at each evaluation of follow-up returnees (*N* = 30).

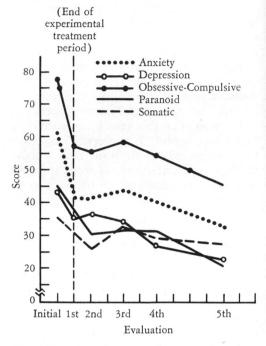

Fig. 2. Mean discomfort subscale scores at each evaluation of follow-up returnees (*N*=30).

were examined separately. These consisted of statements to evaluate anxiety, and depressive, obsessive-compulsive, paranoid or somatic symptoms. Figure 2 demonstrates that all of the subscales showed significant improvement over five years (*ps* for all differences < .05). The anxiety and depression subscales showed rapid initial improvement and were the only ones to show significant change at six months (*p* < .02). The obsessive-compulsive and the paranoid subscales changed more slowly, but showed about as much change as did anxiety and depression between six months and five years. The somatic subscale showed the least improvement.

The total initial symptom level was found to be only moderately related to amount of change reported at five years. The correlation (*r* = .41, *p* < .02) between initial scores and five-year change scores indicated the somewhat limited prognostic value of initial discomfort level for status at five years.

To study improvement, the change scores (initial to five years) were dichotomized at the median, providing a group of 15 most improved patients and a group of 15 least improved patients. The correlation between initial and change scores was moderately high (*r* = .66, *p* < .01) for the most improved patients, but about zero for the least improved. The scattergram in Figure 3 presents these data. With respect to initial scores, the most improved were relatively homogeneous, whereas the least improved fell into two discrete groups, one of which had high initial scores and the other low initial scores. This finding is discussed below.

Although demographic (age, sex, etc.) and treatment (length, type) variables did not differentiate the dichotomized groups, certain other differences were apparent. The most improved had significantly[7] higher mean initial discomfort levels (49.6 to 33.9). They also presented more psychologic complaints on the average than did

[7] All differences (unless otherwise specified) were significant at less than the .05 level using appropriate statistical tests.

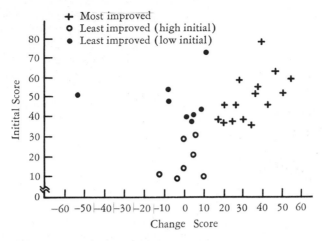

Fig. 3. Scattergram of discomfort scale scores: initial and change
(to five years) of follow-up returnees ($N = 30$).

the least improved (37.7 to 21.8), but about the same average number of somatic complaints (11.9 to 12.1). In other words, the proportion of the total discomfort score which resulted from somatic complaints was much higher for the least improved than for the most improved. With respect to change at five years, all types of symptoms (*e.g.,* anxiety, depression) were significantly reduced in the most improved, whereas none was in the least improved. In fact, there was a tendency ($p < .20$) for the low improvers to have slightly greater scores at five years in the depression subscale, perhaps reflecting despondency over the relative lack of improvement. Two further findings were the lower mean age of the most improved (28.5 years to 33.7 years), and the tendency ($p < .20$) for the most improved to include more persons of the Catholic and Lutheran religious groups. Two-thirds of the most improved were Catholic or Lutheran, but only one-third of the least improved were. Another finding related religion and type of complaint. Nearly all patients whose initial complaints were exclusively or predominantly psychologic were Catholic or Lutheran, whereas the reverse was true for patients whose complaints were heavily weighted with somatic symptoms. Among the ten patients ranked highest on a psychic/somatic index, nine were Catholic or Lutheran; among the ten ranked lowest, only one was.

As noted above, the most improved were relatively homogeneous in terms of initial discomfort, which was high, as opposed to least improved, whose initial discomfort was either high or low. Patients who had not improved or were worse, who also had high initial scores, had a very high proportion of somatic symptoms. Incidentally, only two categories contained in the scale used to evaluate social ineffectiveness distinguished most- from least-improved initially. The most improved tended to be rated initially as less officious in their dealings with other people, and more intrapunitive.

Ineffectiveness Improvement

By the five-year evaluation, 29 (97 per cent) of the 30 returnees had improved in social ineffectiveness; one was worse. This surpasses improvement in ineffectiveness immediately following the six-month ex-

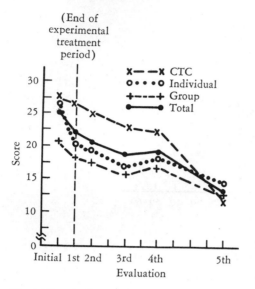

Fig. 4. Mean ineffectiveness scale scores at each evaluation by type of treatment of follow-up returnees ($N = 30$).

perimental treatment period, when only 20 (67 per cent) were improved, nine (30 per cent) were worse, and one was unchanged.[8]

Inspection of the mean scores over the five-year period reveals a steady downward trend (Figure 4). However, as reported elsewhere (3), there were treatment differences at six months favoring individual treatment in which patients improved significantly, whereas patients in group therapy and minimal contact therapy (CTC) had not changed significantly. By five years, the outcome differences between treatment forms had disappeared.

Of the 15 ineffectiveness-scale categories, eight were infrequently used (withdrawn, officious, over-cautious, impulsive, overly-independent, unsystematic, irresponsible, and superficially-sociable), on each of which at least half of the sample had initial scores of zero, and less than one-

_____
[8] The relation between improvement and failure to return was similar to that found with discomfort (cf. footnote 6).

quarter had scores of three or more (on a five-point scale). On four of the more frequently used categories (sexually maladjusted, constrained, intra-punitive and hyper-reactive), at least 60 per cent of the group received scores of three or more initially. On the remaining three categories (overly-systematic, extra-punitive and over-dependent), about half of the patients had scores of three or more. These distributions illustrate the kinds of social ineffectiveness characteristic of a group of neurotic out-patients that contained no severely ill individuals.

As with discomfort, the ineffectiveness change scores were dichotomized at the median for the purpose of studying improvement. Of the demographic factors, only religion, where there was a tendency ($.20 > p > .10$) for more Catholics and Lutherans to be among the most improved patients, distinguished the two groups. With respect to initial test scores, the only finding was the tendency ($.20 > p > .10$) for least improved patients to have a higher proportion of somatic symptoms (as was the case with the least improved in discomfort). Those patients who had changed the most in social ineffectiveness at five years were initially more ineffective than were those who changed the least.

Degree of sexual maladjustment clearly differentiated the two improvement groups initially. Those patients who were most improved had higher scores (least well adjusted) in this category. Three other social ineffectiveness categories were predictive. Irresponsible and over-cautious were more characteristic of the most improved patients, as was superficially sociable of the least improved. However, these categories were so infrequently scored that little confidence can be placed in this result.

Four ineffectiveness ratings changed significantly in the total patient sample, regardless of improvement status. They were: extra-punitive, intra-punitive, hyper-reactive and constrained. These changes are in line with those usually attributed to psychotherapy.[9] Three additional high-change categories (overly-systematic, over-dependent and sexual maladjustment) showed significant change only in the 15 patients who improved most.[10] This means that the difference between most improved and least improved in ineffectiveness was attributed chiefly to these.

Intercurrent Illness and Treatment

The following results are based on information gathered beginning with the second re-evaluation, six months after the completion of the experimental treatment period, since primary interest was in illnesses and treatments subsequent to that period. The total time span over which the reported data were gathered is four and one-half years. Ideally, 120 evaluations should have been recorded for the 30 patients during this time; however, not every patient kept his scheduled appointment. A total of ten evaluations were missed at various points among the 30 patients over the study period, leaving a total of 110 evaluations available.

To consider first the amount of illness as determined by patients' complaints, of the total of 110 *evaluations,* no illnesses at all were reported in only 12 (11 per cent). However, every patient reported at least one illness in the four and one-half year period.

With respect to type of complaint, medical complaints were many times more frequent than were psychologic. Of 142 classifiable entries of illnesses, only about one-third were clearly psychologic, the rest being about equally divided between strictly medical, and medical with a psychologic component. Results were similar when tabulations were made per patient. Twenty-

three patients reported psychologic illnesses at least once, 26 reported medical illness, and 21 reported medical complaints which had a probable psychologic involvement. Since there were only 30 patients, it is apparent that illness was frequently tabulated under more than one category. Twenty-seven patients were scored in more than one category, and 13 of these were scored in at least three. Only three patients were checked in just one category.

The patients sought help quite frequently. A visit to a helper was checked at least once in 92 (84 per cent) of the 110 evaluations. Twenty-seven patients (90 per cent) visited a helper in all or in all but one of the evaluation intervals, and every patient made at least one such visit in the four and one-half years.

The type of help sought and type of medication received reflect the type of illnesses reported. Of 103 classifiable entries, one-third were contacts with a psychologic helper (including psychiatrists); the remainder were with non-psychiatric physicians,[11] half for relief of emotionally based symptoms. All but three patients went at least once to a general practitioner, and nine went *only* to this type of physician, but almost two-thirds of the 30 patients got help for emotionally based symptoms from these physicians. Of 21 patients who sought help from a counselor or psychiatrist at least once during the four and one-half years, 19 also visited a general practitioner at least once. Two-thirds of the total sample went to more than one helper in an evaluation period at least once during the total time span, and five reported these multiple visits on three or more evaluations.

In terms of medication received, of 59 classifiable entries, 41 were sedatives or stimulants, and 18 were medications for

---

[9] These items had not changed at the six-month evaluation. Actually, for the group of 30 patients there were no significant item changes at six months.

[10] Of these items, only sexual maladjustment had changed at six months in this group of 15 patients.

[11] For ease of exposition, these will be referred to hereafter as general practitioners, although actually a few medical or surgical specialists are included.

specific medical illnesses. Most of the 32 unclassifiable entries represented aspirin or vitamins, which in most cases probably could have been included in the psychologic category. Twenty patients took sedatives or stimulants at least once, and ten took other medications. Sixteen patients took more than one type of medication, and 16 reported taking medicines on all or on all but one evaluation, whereas ten received medication during no more than one evaluation period.

With respect to severity, illnesses were classified as "major" if they caused a severe impairment of the patient's usual functioning, including illnesses requiring hospitalization; as "minor" if this was obvious from the notation (e.g., "colds"), or if there were no visits to a physician, or little or no medication taken. On this basis, there were 13 major illnesses among ten patients, all of whom also had minor or not clearly definable illnesses. At the other extreme, six patients had minor illnesses only. The remaining 14 had at least one illness of indeterminable severity, and all but one of these also had at least one minor illness.

With respect to duration, the number of chronic illnesses was probably over-represented in our tallies, since if a chronic illness was reported at more than one evaluation, it was checked each time, although it might have represented a single continuing illness. On the other hand, no matter how many acute illnesses a patient reported for one evaluation period, the category was scored but once. It is of interest, however, that 27 patients were checked for chronic illness at least once, and 23 for both chronic and acute illnesses.

To summarize, this sample had few obviously severe illnesses, but many minor or questionable ones which tended to be chronic and were regarded by the patients as medical, though a physician would see most as having major psychologic components. Patients tended to seek a lot of help, primarily from local medical doctors, and to take medicines for relief. The overall picture also suggests frequent inability to define clearly the illness or the type of help needed. All but three patients had more than one type of illness, and most visited general medical practitioners as the primary source of help at least once. However, the most common reason for doing this seemed to be for relief of psychologically based complaints. In the same connection, about two-thirds visited more than one treatment source in a given evaluation period, and about one-half took more than one kind of medication.

To investigate the relationship between improvement and intercurrent medical history, the patients were dichotomized on the basis of their combined rank orders of improvement in discomfort and ineffectiveness.[12] The least improved reported more illnesses (88 to 66) and more treatment contacts (83 to 55) than did the most improved. Of the 15 patients who visited a help-giver in *each* evaluation period, ten were in the least improved group; of the 15 who did not see such a person during at least one interval, only five were in this group. (These findings can be seen as an independent validation of the improvement measures—that is, patients who were sicker on the criterion measures had more illnesses and treatments than did those who were less sick.)

With respect to clarity of definition of illnesses noted above, some especially interesting differences appeared in the nature of the complaints reported by the least and most improved, and in the pattern of help-seeking. Clearly psychologic and clearly medical illnesses were noted with about equal frequency in the two groups. However, the greater number of illnesses among least improved patients was accounted for almost completely by illnesses perceived by the patients as bodily but by the raters as

---

[12] The two scales were analyzed separately, producing essentially the same results. For reasons of economy, only the results of the combined criteria are presented.

having a psychologic basis, or by illnesses which the raters could not classify clearly from the patients' reports of their complaints. The least improved had 24 entries of medical complaints on a psychologic basis; the most improved, 16. The least improved had 11 entries of unclassifiable illness among six patients; the most improved, only one. Also, all five patients who had two or more notations of this type of illness were among the least improved.

Consistent with the findings, the least improved made contact with general medical practitioners over twice as often as did the most improved (47 to 20). The preponderance of contacts for the least improved was for illnesses they apparently regarded as medical but the raters regarded as psychologic or unclassifiable. This tends to explain why they went to general medical practitioners more often for help with emotional problems than did the most improved. These findings suggest that the least improved were inclined to define their complaints in such a way that they could not get adequate help, either because they went to the wrong resource or because the complaints were so poorly expressed. Confirmation of this assumption is suggested by the finding that the least improved did more "shopping around" than did the most improved. All five patients who reported using every type of treatment resource (medical, psychiatric, non-medical, psychologic) during the four and one-half year period were among the least improved.[13]

To check this impression further, a special tally was made when the record indicated that a patient had had more than one treatment contact in a given evaluation period. Over the four re-evaluations, this was noted 21 times for the least improved and 14 times for the most improved. Of the ten patients who were in contact with more than one help resource within more than one of the four evaluation periods, seven were among the least improved.[14]

The relationship between difficulty in obtaining appropriate help and lack of improvement was found also with respect to resources for psychologic help. Consistent with the equal frequencies of illnesses classed as clearly psychologic for both groups, the most and least improved were also noted almost equally often as seeking help from a psychologic treatment resource (23 to 26). On the other hand, if these resources are grouped as "psychiatrists" and "other,"[15] the most improved, in contrast to the least improved, went to psychiatrists much more often (18 to five, respectively). Again it appears that, even when the least improved reported their complaints as clearly psychologic, they were unsure about, or unaware of, the psychiatric resources available in the community.

DISCUSSION

In any attempt to interpret these findings, it must be kept in mind that the analysis has disregarded individual differences among patients. In all probability, certain patients are concealed in the statistical results who responded unusually well or poorly to treatment. A detailed study of them would undoubtedly provide important information concerning psychotherapy which investigations of this type cannot yield. Furthermore, the initial period of therapy was very brief, and was conducted by relatively inexperienced psychiatrists. It

[13] In the same connection, all three contacts with chiropractors were made by members of the "least improved" group.

[14] When the 45 patients who returned for the third evaluation (at two years) were dichotomized into most and least improved, the relationship between ambiguity and failure to improve did not appear; nor was it noted in the five-year sample at the two-year evaluation. Apparently this tendency emerges only over a long period of time.

[15] Thirteen of the 20 contacts with non-psychiatric resources for psychologic help were with clergymen, the rest having been social workers and psychologists.

is possible that longer treatment by more mature practitioners might have yielded different results. Nevertheless, the consistency of many of our findings with those reported by others suggests that they possess some validity.

As a group, these run-of-the-mill adult psychiatric outpatients improved over the five-year observation period, despite the fact that they continued to report intercurrent illnesses. Improvement in discomfort occurred rather early, whereas improvement in social ineffectiveness, though more pronounced at five years, occurred less rapidly. Symptoms of anxiety and depression are characteristically relieved by expectation of help, and from previous studies it may be surmised that the improvement noted at six months actually occurred much more promptly (6). The apparently more gradual improvement in other types of symptoms suggests that other processes must be involved that probably also account for the continuing improvement in anxiety and depression after six months. What these processes are remains to obscure. The least changed symptoms at five years were somatic ones, and these symptoms were especially characteristic of least improved patients throughout the study. This is in accord with general experience.

With respect to social effectiveness, the group as a whole became less hyper-reactive, less constrained, less intra-punitive and less extra-punitive. These changes may simply reflect general alleviation of subjective distress, enabling patients to achieve more spontaneity of emotional expression within a narrower range, and giving them less occasion to assign blame either to themselves or to others. This may also reflect greater acceptance of the desirability of objectivity—a value implicit in psychotherapy.

Diminution in overly-systematic behavior, over-dependency and sexual maladjustment was significant only in the patients who improved most. The first change is compatible with greater spontaneity; the second has also been reported by Lorr (12), and the third accords with general experience. It probably results in part from improvement in anxiety and depression (which tend to inhibit sexual interest and activity), and may also reflect a greater capacity to integrate intimate relationships.

For the group as a whole, the improvement at five years was so great as to obscure the differences in improvement related to different forms of psychotherapy noted immediately at the close of the experimental period. Similarly, Levitt (11) found that three-quarters of a population of treated neurotic children reported improvement at a one- to ten-year follow-up, as compared to only two-thirds immediately at the close of treatment, and that improvement was a function of time. Denker (2) found that 45 per cent of his sample of adults treated by insurance company physicians for emotionally based complaints were discharged as recovered at the end of one year, 91 per cent at the end of five years. Whitehorn (16) found that after five to ten years the improvement rates of schizophrenic patients of the less successful psychiatrists had overtaken those of the more successful ones.

Similar results have been found with physical treatments. Thus Scoville (15) reported that various series of psychiatric patients who had undergone orbital undercutting showed marked benefit in from six to 64 per cent immediately after treatment. Four to 11 years later the rate was appreciably increased in every series, the incidence of marked benefit ranging from 38 per cent to 100 per cent. Zubin's (17) statistical studies of hospitalized patients showed that, after five years, results were no better for those who had received treatment than for those who had "spontaneously" recovered. In view of the amount and variety of help obtained by patients in this study, it seems plausible that much of their long-term improvement may be attributable to non-specific treatment (7), offered chiefly by physicians.

It has been generally assumed that the

evaluation of the effectiveness of different forms of psychotherapy depends ultimately upon follow-up studies. The findings of this study raise serious questions as to the validity of this premise. The cumulative effect of the life experiences of psychiatric patients after the termination of treatment, coupled with the impossibility of determining what part of these experiences should be attributed to changes in the patients' behavior resulting from therapy, would make it well-nigh impossible to determine what features of the end state can be attributed to a course of treatment years before (1). The problem is identical with that of evaluating different methods of child-rearing in terms of the finished adult products.

A more nearly valid evaluation of different forms of psychotherapy might be in terms of their ability to accelerate improvement. Even if the results of all forms of therapy prove to be statistically indistinguishable after a sufficient lapse of time, the better therapy would be the one which achieved the greatest amount of improvement most rapidly. A prompt and sizable reduction in the duration of a patient's suffering and disability would be sufficient justification for psychotherapy. If this view is correct, evaluation of different forms of psychotherapy should be primarily in terms of their immediate results.

That younger patients improve more than older ones is compatible with general experience, though this relationship did not appear with respect to improvement in social ineffectiveness. The relationship of symptomatic improvement to religious affiliation, however, was quite unexpected, and we would be inclined to dismiss it as a chance result were it not that it also appears to be related to responsiveness to placebo.[16] A possible explanation is that Catholics and Lutherans, as members of relatively authoritarian denominations, may be more prone to respond favorably to the prestige and authority of physicians, especially as agents of an institution with status in the community. Why they have a greater proportion of psychic complaints than the remainder of the sample, however, is obscure.

This paper has presented certain features of the intercurrent illnesses and treatments, and their relation to improvement. In the absence of a control group we cannot say how the health record of these patients compares to that of the population at large. The variety of illnesses reported, however, supports the finding of Hinkle et al. (10), that stress increases the incidence of all types of illness.

In accord with general experience, it was found that patients who express their psychologic problems in bodily terms and seek medical treatment for them do less well than do those who recognize the psychic causation of their difficulties. It will be recalled that the least improved patients compared to the most improved had a much larger percentage of illnesses classified by the raters as bodily complaints on a psychologic basis. The least improved also much more often reported their complaints in ambiguous terms than did the most improved, went to general medical practitioners for them, and visited more different kinds of treatment resources. Since these findings appeared only at the five-year re-evaluation, the extent to which they can be generalized is not certain. They do, however, appear to be related to certain findings reported by Freedman et al. (5) with ambulatory schizophrenics who were receiving placebos. In their work, they found that patients who denied mental illness were more likely to be driven out of treatment by physicians with an active, "warm" attitude than by those with a detached attitude. Those who accepted the fact they were mentally ill remained in treatment with warm physicians but promptly terminated contact with detached ones. That is, whether a patient remained in treatment depended upon the consistency of his expectations with the type of

---

[16] Unpublished data from studies now in progress by the authors.

relationship offered·by the physician. Furthermore, an inconsistent doctor-patient relationship militated against a favorable response to placebo (8).

Taken in conjunction, these findings suggest that failure to improve is related to inadequate communication between sufferer and helper. There may be several reasons for this. If patient and doctor cannot clearly define what is wrong, this in itself creates anxiety. If the patient goes to a general physician, he fails to gain relief for psychologically based symptoms because the treatment is inappropriate. If a patient who somatizes his problems goes to a psychologic resource he fails to get help because psychotherapy operates by words; such patients typically have difficulty verbalizing their problems, and these cannot be readily modified by the words of others (14). Furthermore, to the extent that psychotherapy is a form of problem-solving, unless patient and therapist can agree on the nature of the problem little progress can be made. The patient's inability to express himself clearly obviously impedes reaching such an agreement. Failure to gain relief causes the patient to go from one resource to another, which aggravates his distress by heightening his conviction that no one really understands what to do for him.

Thus ability to profit from treatment seems to be related to the clarity of the patient's perception and communication of his symptoms, and the ability of patient and therapist to agree on their nature and treatment.

SUMMARY

In this five-year follow-up study of adult psychiatric outpatients, the focus has been on the long-term course of psychiatric illness, as well as on the effects of psychotherapy. To evaluate the long-term course, special attention was given to intercurrent illnesses and treatments. The major findings were as follows:

Improvement in discomfort immediately following treatment was primarily in anxiety and depressive symptoms. By five years, all types of symptoms were substantially reduced.

Patients found to be most improved in discomfort at five years were younger, more likely to be Catholic or Lutheran, and more likely to have been sicker initially on the criterion measure. Those least improved had many somatic symptoms, both initially and at five years.

Improvement in social ineffectiveness, though less than discomfort change, was marked at five years. Differential effects of treatment forms found immediately after the initial six-month treatment period had disappeared by five years.

Patients most improved in social ineffectiveness seemed to have gained greater spontaneity in their intimate relationships, and this was associated with greater personal comfort.

As a group, though they steadily improved, patients reported a great deal of intercurrent illness and treatment throughout the follow-up period. Much of the illness was reported as medical and was treated by a general medical practitioner, but often with sedatives and stimulants.

At five years the least improved patients were more likely than the most improved to define their illnesses in bodily terms, or to express them ambiguously. Consistent with this, they sought more different kinds of treatment resources, which, in turn, may have aggravated their condition by increasing their confusion. Thus, ability to respond to treatment may be a function of the patient's success in communicating his difficulties to the therapist, and the acceptance by patient and therapist of a course of action.

REFERENCES

1. COWEN, E. L. AND COMBS, A. W. Follow-up study of 32 cases treated by nondirective psychotherapy. *J. Abnorm. Soc. Psychol.,* 45, 232–258, 1950.
2. DENKER, P. G. Results of treatment of psy-

choneuroses by the general practitioner. *New York J. Med.,* 46, 2164–2166, 1946.

3. FRANK, J. D., GLIEDMAN, L. H., IMBER, S. D., STONE, A. R. AND NASH, E. H. Patients' expectancies and relearning as factors determining improvement in psychotherapy. *Amer. J. Psychiat.,* 115, 961–968, 1959.

4. FRANK, J. D., GLIEDMAN, L. H., IMBER, S. D., NASH, E. H. AND STONE, A. R. Why patients leave psychotherapy. *A.M.A. Arch. Neurol. Psychiat.,* 77, 283–299, 1957.

5. FREEDMAN, N., ENGELHARDT, D. M., HANKOFF, L. D., GLICK, B. S., KAYE, H., BUCHWALD, J. AND STARK, P. Drop-out from outpatient psychiatric treatment. *A.M.A. Arch. Neurol. Psychiat.,* 80, 657–666, 1958.

6. GLIEDMAN, L. H., NASH, E. H., IMBER, S. D., STONE, A. R. AND FRANK, J. D. Reduction of syptoms by pharmacologically inert substances and by short-term psychotherapy. *A.M.A. Arch. Neurol. Psychiat.,* 79, 345–351, 1958.

7. GOLDSTEIN, A. P. Patient's expectancies and non-specific therapy as a basis for (un)spontaneous remission. *J. Clin. Psychol.,* 16, 399–403, 1960.

8. HANKOFF, L. D., ENGELHARDT, D. M., FREEDMAN, N., MANN, D. AND MARGOLIS, R. The doctor-patient relationship in a psychopharmacological treatment setting. *J. Nerv. Ment. Dis.,* 131, 540–546, 1960.

9. HASTINGS, D. W. Follow-up results in psychiatric illness. *Amer. J. Psychiat.,* 114, 1057–1066, 1958.

10. HINKLE, L. E., PLUMMER, N., METRAUX, R., RICHTER, P., GITTINGER, J. W., THETFORD, W. N., OSTFELD, A. M., KANE, F. D., GOLDBERGER, L., MITCHELL, W. E., LEICHTER, H., PINSKY, R., GOEBEL, D., BROSS, I. D. AND WOLFF, H. G. Studies in human ecology, factors relevant to the occurrence of bodily illness and disturbances in mood, thought and behavior in three homogeneous population groups. *Amer. J. Psychiat.,* 114, 212–220, 1957.

11. LEVITT, E. E. The results of psychotherapy with children: An evaluation. *J. Consult. Psychol.,* 21, 189–196, 1957.

12. LORR, M. Relation of treatment frequency and duration to psychotherapeutic outcome. Paper presented at the Second Research Conference in Psychotherapy sponsored by the American Psychological Association, Chapel Hill, North Carolina, May, 1961.

13. PARLOFF, M. B., KELMAN, H. C. AND FRANK, J. D. Comfort, effectiveness and self-awareness as criteria of improvement in psychotherapy. *Amer. J. Psychiat.,* 111, 343–351, 1954.

14. RUESCH, J. The infantile personality. *Psychosom. Med.,* 10, 134–144, 1948.

15. SCOVILLE, W. B. Late results of orbital undercutting. *Amer. J. Psychiat.,* 117, 525–529, 1960.

16. WHITEHORN, J. C. Studies of the doctor as a crucial factor for the prognosis of schizophrenic patients. *Int. J. Soc. Psychiat.,* 6, 71–77, 1960.

17. ZUBIN, J. Evaluation of therapeutic outcome in mental disorders. *J. Nerv. Ment. Dis.,* 117, 95–111, 1953.

Comparison of Results with Different Forms of Psychotherapy

JOHN M. SHLIEN

One of the most valuable research efforts to be made in the fact-thirsty field of psychotherapy is the comparison of different forms of treatment, the variation of important conditions within the same form of treatment, or both. An attempt to execute such research will be described here, with some comments upon the way in which the choice of the criterion, and the method of its measurement, may both uncover similarities and mask differences in outcomes of different forms of therapy.

THE DESIGN

The *structure* being varied in these researches is that of duration of treatment. Under special conditions, time limits are imposed before therapy begins contrasted with the usual mode of end-setting by the therapist, through voluntary termination, or by some form of joint decision (1). The two types of treatment are adlerian,

Reprinted from *American Journal of Psychotherapy*, 1964, 18 Suppl. 1, 15–22, with the permission of the Association for the Advancement of Psychotherapy and the author.

and client-centered (or rogerian, if a personal title is desired). These forms are being compared in a multivariate study of which only a part has yet been evaluated and reported by Shlien, Dreikurs and Mosak (2). The *criterion* under discussion here is that called self-esteem (3, 4) and the *method of measurement* is the self-ideal correlation using the Q-sort technique (5).

To place this research in its over-all context, here is a graphic illustration of the design of the experiment. Figure 1 shows the divisions of the total population into four segments. All clients or patients are tested before therapy and at equal ten-week intervals, during which the suggested rate of interviews is two per week. There are really two basic divisions in this design. One is length of therapy, since we are trying to study the effects of total duration or number of interviews. The other is the presence or absence of time limits arbitrarily set before therapy begins. These two divisions create a combination of four segments in the total research population: (1) Brief therapy, time-limited to 20 interviews; (2) longer therapy, unlimited and voluntarily terminated; (3) longer therapy but time-limited to 40 interviews; and (4) brief therapy, unlimited and voluntarily terminated after approximately 20 interviews. Segment III is designed to show effects of a "no-therapy" period when some therapy has been experienced and more can be expected. This no-therapy period can be compared with other equivalent amounts of time both before and after therapy. In the present discussion, only Segments I and II will be considered.

In order to structure the time limits for patients in Segment I, a group of applicants for therapy were told that they would be limited to a maximum of 20 interviews, because of the clinic's long waiting list and short supply of available therapists. This group was not especially selected, and no special resistance to the limits was encountered at the time of the preliminary interview. Segment II is composed of a group of applicants who received no instructions regarding termination, so that the end of therapy was determined by each one's own decision, when he chose to make it. Again, there was no special selection, and as a matter of fact, the data on Segments I and IV were collected before

the time-limited cases were begun. The theoretical and practical background for the study of predetermined endings has been discussed in a survey by Shlien (6) covering the ideas of Freud, Jung, Rank and Taft, and Rogers.

SOME RESULTS

Only one of several criteria will be presented for discussion. That criterion is called the self-ideal correlation, considered to be a measure of self-esteem. The measure is made up of a Q-sort, which is in many ways like that described by Dr. Weiss in this symposium. The Q-sort consists of descriptive statements, an empirically derived set of traits taken from positive and negative things patients say about themselves. Eighty of such statements are sorted by the patient in a forced normal distribution as being "most like him" or "least like him." These sorts are made according to two instructions: First, "describe yourself as you see yourself" and second, "describe your ideal, the person you would most like to be." Then, unknown to the subject, these two sorts are mechanically correlated in a simple statistical manipulation, and the resulting "self-

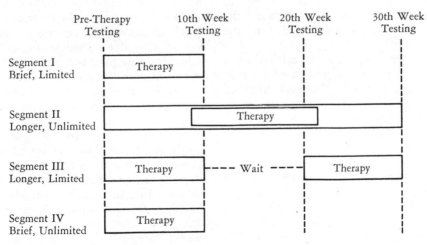

Fig. 1 Flow chart for experiment.

ideal correlation" becomes a score, a measure of the degree to which one is what one wants to be. This is called a measure of self-esteem with some justification: William James used the ratio between pretensions and success to derive self-esteem; Kurt Lewin used the ratio between level of aspiration and level of achievement. The idea of self-esteem as a prime criterion of psychotherapy stems, I should like to remind you, from Karen Horney rather than Carl Rogers, whose work with the self-concept has often been confused with the measures of congruence between self and ideal. The method of the Q-sort was developed, as you learned from Dr. Weiss, by Dr. William Stephenson (5).

It is true that this is a "subjective" criterion, being a form of self-evaluation. As such, it is of course subject to distortion, as is the MMPI or any other form of self-reporting. One simply has to recognize that there is the possibility of distortion and error on the part of the patient, and then to recognize further that the same possibilities of error and liabilities of distortion exist in the judgment of any outside and supposedly "objective" observer —therapist, friend, spouse, social worker, or whoever, so that in fact, one simply has to choose the subjectivity one wishes to deal with, and in this case, we choose the source closest to the subject, that is, the person himself.

Using this self-ideal correlation as a score, Fig. 2 shows the results of a rather unique experiment in the evaluation of psychotherapy. This chart shows the group means, the averages, for five different groups of people, two "control" groups and three "experimental" treatment groups. The vertical axis shows the range of S-I correlations and the horizontal axis the number of interviews. The range of scores is large for *individuals,* who vary from + .90, where the self and ideal descriptions are nearly identical, through the zero point of no relation, to − .75, where the self is almost the opposite of the ideal.

The *group averages* are, naturally, in a smaller range. The interviews are numbered at 0, 7th (after which there was a Q-sort testing point), 20th (the end of time-limited therapy), and 37th (the average of the unlimited voluntarily terminated cases). The shaded area indicates a follow-up period about 12 months beyond the post-therapy point.

CONTROLS

There are two control groups, which, taken together, strongly suggest that passage of time, without therapy, does not change the average "score" of self-esteem. The so-called "matched normal controls" are a group of people who had not applied for therapy, but who were asked (and paid) to take part in some "personality research." As one person was taken into therapy, one of these "controls," matched for age, sex, socioeconomic status, was tested, and as his counterpart terminated therapy, the control was "post-tested," (although he had received no therapy). Two points should be made before proceeding to the next control group. The matching for such gross variables as age, and so forth, is not really effective matching. To match for what matters, would require that we equate the psychologic status of the matching person, not on one variable only but on *all* criteria used in the battery of tests. Not only that, but we would have to know the *potential rate* of change for each person. For instance, if the treatment were a particular diet, and the question were its effect on growth, we not only need to know initial height and weight, and to match for those, but we would need to know the ultimate size of the subjects, since some will grow faster than others of equal starting size. Such information is not available for psychologic measures, and even if it were, an army of prospective subjects would be required for only a few cases so well matched. The limitations of the matching in the present experiment are

Mean Correlation Chart

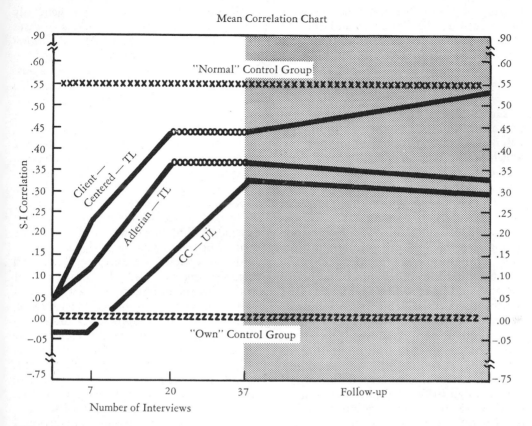

Number of Interviews

Figure 2.

many, and well known, yet the control group serves a useful purpose.

The second point is that the "no-therapy" condition appears to be related to a "no change" consequence. For the group average, there is indeed a remarkable stability over time without therapy, but this does not mean that individuals are absolutely stable. There is in fact a fair degree of individual fluctuation in the absence of therapy, perhaps due to plus and minus factors in life experience, but it cancels out to zero change for the group as a whole. Again, this does not destroy the value of the control method. The fact remains that these people who did not see themselves as needing therapy had a very stable "score," at a high average level, over time, without therapy.

The second group is called "own-controls." Here the method is to obtain an exact match by using each person as his own control. As they apply for therapy, some individuals are asked to take the pre-therapy tests, wait for 60 days, take the tests again, and *then* begin therapy. They then become their own controls, perfectly matched. The difficulty is that they have been asked to wait, which may carry a suggestion (an unintended effect) that no change is expected for this period. These two control groups, taken together, provide a framework for the treatment groups, since they describe the levels of people seeking therapy and those not feeling the need of it. They also tell us, as the designers intended (7) that neither group, on the average, changes as a result of mere

passage of time. The difference between
the groups at the .00 level and the .55
level is of course statistically significant,
well beyond the .01 level.

THE THERAPY GROUPS

Three groups represent the results of
treatment. One is composed of unlimited,
voluntarily terminated cases of therapy,
which on the average ended after 37 interviews. It has no great relevance in this discussion except for the demonstration of a
proved outcome in the ordinary sequence
of events, where patients (in this case
called clients, since it is a demonstration
of rogerian therapy) are permitted to continue until they wish to stop. The trend
begins with a zero order correlation before
therapy, and ends with a significant gain,
which proves to be stable in the follow-up
period.

The other two treatment groups are
those in the special structure, earlier referred to, limited in time to a maximum
of 20 interviews. One is a group of patients treated in the Alfred Adler Institute
of Chicago, the other a group treated in
the Counseling Center at the University
of Chicago (2). The tests, and the structure of limits, were the same for both
groups. The two groups of therapists
were, I think, about equally competent
and homogeneous in their own styles,
though the Adlerians probably had longer
experience, on the average. Both groups
of patients begin at the same point, again
a zero order correlation. So far as the outcome is concerned, they are indistinguishable, statistically. Both make significant
gains, again stable in the follow-up period.
Both show that time-limited therapy, according to this single criterion, at least, is
effective and efficient, since it accomplishes
in roughly half the time the same outcome
achieved by the longer unlimited therapy.
There is also the special characteristic upward trend within the first seven interviews, so far seen as an acceleration effect

of the time-limited structure, and generally
predictive of only the most successful cases
in the unlimited structure. At the follow-
up period, both adlerian and client-
centered therapies maintained their gains.

The interesting thing about these two
therapies in the present comparison is that
they appear to be very similar—in fact
almost identical and interchangeable. This
does not fit some of the other facts as I
know them. The two orientations have a
good many theoretical similarities, and it is
good to find them both producing like
appearing and salutory results. But, knowing the practical differences in treatment
methods, differences which seem to be
easily apparent when one listens to recorded interviews, the picture of identical
therapies seems false. It could be, of
course, that the differences in the theories or
the practitioners are of no real consequence,
or are of consequence only to the practitioners themselves, while to the patients the
conduct of therapy feels much the same.
This may be partly, but not wholly true.

Another possibility is that we see here
only a "placebo effect," either because that
is all there is, or because that is all we have
measured. The most likely construction I
can put upon the situation is that we have
uncovered some true similarities of the two
truly different types of therapy *when both
are operating under the same structure of
time limits,* and moreover, that the method
of measurement—that is, the self-ideal correlation, is a very high level of abstraction
in measurement. This has been discussed
elsewhere (4), and it is a problem to be
reckoned with in this and any comparative
study of different forms of therapy. The
correlation is, in effect, similar to a rating,
and we know that while two ratings may be
identical, what went into the making of
them might, if partialed out, show important differences.

Fortunately, we will not have to settle
finally for a guess on this score. It will be
remembered that the component parts of
the Q-sort are specific items of description.

Two people might have identical self-ideal correlations with very different arrays of the items as they arranged their own descriptive sortings. This makes it possible to review the data through an item analysis, or a "cluster of items" analysis. The technique to be used is that of factor analysis, and this is not yet completed, but from an inspection of some preliminary steps, it is clear that while the adlerian and rogerian populations appeared to be identical on the gross aspects of outcome, they do differ when the details are examined. That is to say, for instance, that they may have become equally "well adjusted," but they are equally adjusted in different ways. In a rather idealized fashion, extrapolating from results of other studies (8) the present inspection of our data suggests this prediction: at pre-therapy, there will be three factors with much overlap between the two therapy populations; at post-therapy, four major factors appear, with one unique to each type of therapy and two common to both; at the follow-up point, five factors, with two unique to each type of therapy and one common to both. It is certain that the similarity between adlerian and rogerian results, though it is a fact, is not the only fact and that upon closer inspection differences in outcome will also appear. It is also likely that the two patient populations spread apart and differentiate further as they pass later stages of therapy and post-therapy.

One more problem should be mentioned. In this particular experiment, there was too much success. According to the criterion discussed here and to a combination of others, the percentage of success cases ran to between 70 and 85. That is good for the patients, but not necessarily best for research. Without intending to belittle the effectiveness of the therapies, one suspects that a very high percentage of success may mean that we have dealt with a large number of people who have a strong, natural regenerative power. The problem is that in some sense, these are not really a good test of psychotherapy. A more critical test would be to take the predicted failure or difficult cases. This is now becoming possible, since there are in development methods which will distinguish predicted successes and failures. Using measures of expectation, social class, personality variables and early in-therapy behavior, poor and good prognosis can be made with a high degree of confidence. When therapeutic orientations can be studied and their effectiveness compared on poor prognosis cases, rotating and transferring them when desirable, a truly convincing evaluation will be accomplished. Not only will the potency of the therapeutic agents be established, but such a study will tell us whether there are modes of therapy better fitted to some personality types than others, and if, indeed, there are some people who are really inaccessible to any present-day form of therapy.

Finally, we may be able to discover, through the study of the difficult or poor prognosis cases, the real process of therapy. The objective of science is not simply to observe and verify the phenomena, as this research has done, but to find the mechanisms by which these observed phenomena are brought about. Problems of evaluation are not yet settled, but questions of process will become primary as evaluations of outcomes make it absolutely clear that a process is indeed in operation.

REFERENCES

1. TAFT, J. Dynamics of Therapy in a Controlled Relationship. Macmillan, New York, 1933.

2. SHLIEN, J. M., MOSAK, H. H., AND DREIKURS, R. Effect of Time Limits: A Comparison of Client-centered and Adlerian Psychotherapy. J. Counsel. Psychol., 9, 318, 1962.

3. BUTLER, J. M. AND HAIGH, G. V. Changes in the Relation between Self-concepts and Ideal Concepts Consequent upon Client-centered Counseling. In Psychotherapy and Personality Change. ROGER, C. R. AND

DYMOND, R. F., Eds. University of Chicago Press, Chicago, 1954.

4. SHLIEN, J. M. Toward what Level of Abstraction in Criteria? In *Research in Psychotherapy.* STRUPP, H. H. AND LUBORSKY, L., Eds. American Psychological Association, Washington, D.C., 1962.

5. STEPHENSON, W. *The Study of Behavior: Q-Technique and its Methology.* University of Chicago Press, Chicago, 1953.

6. SHLIEN, J. M. Time-limited Psychotherapy: An Experimental Investigation of Practical Values and Theoretical Implications. *J. Counsel. Psychol.,* 4, 318, 1957.

7. ROGERS, C. R. AND DYMOND, R. F., Eds. *Psychotherapy and Personality Change.* University of Chicago Press, Chicago, 1954.

8. BUTLER, J. M. Factorial Studies of Client-centered Psychotherapy: A Preliminary Report. Univ. Chicago Lib. Counsel. Cent. Discussion Papers, 1956.

Interaction and Insight in Group Psychotherapy[1]

W. H. COONS

All major schools of psychotherapy have encountered difficulty in explaining how and why therapeutic changes occur during psychotherapy. Since Freud's development of psychoanalysis the primary stress in all systematic psychotherapies has been on insight as the core of adjustment. However, no unequivocal relationship between degree of insight and level of adjustment has yet been demonstrated. If insight is considered to be a cognitive act by which the significance of some pattern of relations is understood (12), clinical experience does not wholly support its use as an explanatory concept. Improved adjustment occurs in persons who have not shown evidence of increased insight; other persons who are thought to have gained insight remain seriously maladjusted. This suggests that there is a more basic explanation for behavioral changes which occur during psychotherapy.

The literature reveals two lines of evidence which converge to support the assumption that insight is not the crucial condition for change in behaviour. All major psychotherapeutic systems recognize that insight alone is ineffective and make careful provision for interpersonal interaction (1, 2, 5, 11, 13, 15). At the same time, current research on personality development suggests that understanding is not enough to assure adaptive learning, and that adjustment to reality depends on opportunities for the repeated trial and check of an individual's expectations (7, 10, 14). Both these trends suggest that opportunity for interpersonal interaction in a consistently warm and accepting social environment is central to psychotherapy.

From this theoretical orientation it was hypothesized that interaction, rather than insight, is responsible for therapeutic improvement. Therefore, it was predicted that a technique of psychotherapy which stressed interpersonal interaction in the absence of insightful content would be superior, in effecting improved adjustment, to a technique which stressed insight with minimal interaction.

Reprinted from the *Canadian Journal of Psychology,* 1957, 11, 1–8, with the permission of The Canadian Psychological Association and the author.

[1] Adapted from part of a thesis submitted in 1955 in partial fulfillment of the requirements for the degree of Doctor of Philosophy at the University of Toronto. The author is indebted particularly to Dr. J. N. Senn and Dr. C. R. Myers for their assistance in the conception and development of this study.

The present study was designed to test this hypothesis experimentally by comparing the effects on adjustment of two techniques of group psychotherapy. One of these (Interaction Therapy) fostered group interaction in the absence of the usual concern for imparting insight; the other (Insight Therapy) strove to impart insight while holding group interaction to a minimum. A control group which received no group psychotherapy was included in the study as an index of the absolute efficacy of the two therapeutic techniques.

METHOD
The Measures of Adjustment

For reasons outlined in the original report of the study (4), the Rorschach Technique of Personality Diagnosis (8) and the Wechsler-Bellevue Adult Intelligence Scales (16, 17) were chosen as the best available indices of adjustment.

The Rorschach. The Rorschach was administered to each of 64 research subjects before and after the period of therapy. Pre- and post-therapy protocols for each subject were analyzed "blind" by an experienced Rorschach examiner.[2] The examiner knew only that each pair of protocols was from the same subject, and that one of the protocols was the pre-therapy, the other the post-therapy record. He did not know which was which, nor did he know in which type of group the subject had been. This procedure eliminated any personal biases due to acquaintance with the subject or active espousal of either therapeutic technique.

The examiner was instructed to select in each pair the protocol which represented the better level of adjustment. When the protocol which he judged to be "better" was the post-therapy record, that subject was considered to have shown improved adjustment during the therapy period. The examiner was unable to distinguish differences between the protocols of eight patients. These patients were considered to have shown no improvement.

As a reliability check, another experienced Rorschach examiner[3] independently examined 20 of the 64 pairs of Rorschach protocols. His selections correspond with those of the first examiner in 19 out of the 20 pairs.

The Wechsler-Bellevue Adult Intelligence Scales. Pre- and post-therapy intellectual efficiency was measured with forms I and II of the Wechsler-Bellevue (16, 17). Since available evidence shows no significant difference between the Verbal Scale, Performance Scale, and Full Scale Intelligence Quotients of these two scales (6, 17), they were treated as equivalent, the two forms being administered alternately to each patient, i.e., when one form of the scale was used for the pre-therapy assessment, the other was used for the post-therapy assessment.

Research Design

The research involved the operation of two experimental units (one male, one female), each of which was composed of three different types of group:

1. Interaction groups. Members of this type of group were subject to the usual hospital routines with the addition for three hours each week of a type of group experience which will be referred to as interaction group psychotherapy. The technique used was designed to create a warm, acceptant, and permissive atmosphere in which patient-to-patient interaction was encouraged. Interaction was considered to be any type of verbal communication on any subject. There was little or no reference to the content usually associated with psychotherapy, and discussion ranged from the price of fur coats to the progress of industrial expansion in Newfoundland. Thus the interaction groups were characterized

---

[2] K. G. Ferguson, Westminster Hospital, London, Ontario.

[3] F. W. Burd, Westminster Hospital, London, Ontario.

by emphasis on maximum interaction in the absence of insightful material.

2. Insight groups. Members of this type of group were subject to the usual hospital routines with the addition three times each week of a type of group experience which will be referred to as insight group psychotherapy. The technique involved directed discussion of the aetiology, manifestations, and control of psychological disturbances. Personal involvement on the part of each group member was encouraged. Each member was directively encouraged to examine his personal difficulties, their origins, and their solution. Emotional catharsis was common. The therapeutic climate might best be described as benignly authoritarian. Interaction was restricted to that between patient and therapist. Thus the insight groups were characterized by maximum emphasis on insight with minimum interaction.

3. Control groups. Members of the control groups received no planned group psychotherapy, but were subject to the usual hospital routines. They did not realize that they were considered as a group.

To ensure that the two types of therapy groups actually showed the difference in amount of interaction required by the research design, all available transcripts of the recordings of the therapy sessions were analyzed after the method of Bovard (3) to derive "interaction ratios." These ratios confirm that the interaction group sessions were characterized by a high proportion of patient-to-patient interaction, and that this was largely absent in the insight group sessions. (The difference in ratios is highly significant: C.R. 12.8, P.001.)

Subjects

A total of 66 patients at the Ontario Hospital, Hamilton, were used as research subjects. These were all the patients for whom complete, or nearly complete pre- and post-therapy data was available.

Selection. Each subject was selected on the basis of suitability for group psychotherapy. The selection procedures took no account of psychiatric nosology. The majority of the patients chosen turned out to be classified as Schizophrenic.

To reduce the possibility that any one group might be formed of patients with an especially favourable prognosis, patients selected for therapy were randomly assigned to each group of each unit. Comparison of the groups on such factors as economic status, occupational classification, nosological grouping, educational level, I.Q., age, duration of illness, and hospitalization, number of E.C.T., etc., indicated that the randomization procedures were successful in producing comparable groups (4).

Replacement. Initially 21 patients were selected for each unit and randomly assigned to the three groups comprising it. However, group members were subject to the ordinary hospital routines, including those regarding discharge. Thus, when a group member was considered suitable for release by the physician in charge, or when relatives insisted on taking him home, he was discharged from the hospital.

Replacements were taken in sequence as required, from a reserve of patients considered suitable for group psychotherapy. When a vacancy occurred in any group of a unit it was filled with the patient whose name headed the reserve list.

Procedure

The experimental procedure lasted for fifteen months, during which the composition of the six groups altered as patients were released and replaced by others (see above). At any given time there were seven members in each group, 21 in each experimental unit (male and female). Each psychotherapy group had three group sessions, each of one-hour duration, each week. Two therapists were involved, one working with the male unit, the other with the female unit. All group sessions were recorded electrically and transcripts of samples made at regular intervals.

Duration of therapy. Owing to the fluid membership of the groups, duration of therapy was not the same for all subjects. However, no member was used as a research subject unless he had a minimum of eight hours of psychotherapy. The maximum number of hours for any subject was ninety. In this respect, members of the control groups were dealt with as though they were members of a group receiving therapy. That is, at any time they were considered to have had the number of sessions which they would have had if they had actually been assigned to a psychotherapy group when first included as a "control" subject. The average number of group sessions of patients in the Interaction Group was 27 (Range: 8–60), the Insight Group 32 (Range: 9–87), and the Control Group 47 (Range: 12–90).

Testing. The Rorschach and Wechsler tests were administered individually before and after therapy by members of the psychological staff at the Ontario Hospital, Hamilton.

Statistical Analysis

The study was designed to permit comparison of the effects of three different types of experience: interaction group psychotherapy, insight group psychotherapy, and no group psychotherapy. Differences were held to be significant when they made possible the rejection of the null hypothesis at the 5 per cent level of confidence. Techniques, and methods of reporting results, follow McNemar (9). The devices used are: standard error of the difference between percentages, and analysis of variance for small samples. No t-scores are considered significant unless they occur in the context of significant over-all F-ratios.

RESULTS
Rorschach

As is shown in Table I, 16 out of 23 subjects in the Interaction Group, 10 out of 23 subjects in the Insight Group, and 7 out of 19 subjects in the Control Group were rated as showing improved adjustment following the therapy period.

TABLE I

NUMBERS OF SUBJECTS IN EACH GROUP RATED AS IMPROVED AND UNIMPROVED AFTER THERAPY

Group	Improved	Unimproved	Total
Interaction	16	6	19
Insight	10	13	22
Control	7	12	23

Table II shows that the percentage of improved subjects in the Interaction Group was significantly greater than the percentages of improved subjects in either the Insight Group ($P = .04$) or the Control Group ($P = .02$). The difference between the Insight and Control Groups was not significant.

TABLE II

DIFFERENCES IN PERCENTAGES OF SUBJECTS SHOWING IMPROVEMENT IN INTERACTION, INSIGHT, AND CONTROL GROUPS

Groups compared	Difference in per cent	D_r	CR	P
Interaction-Insight	31	14.7	2.1	0.04
Interaction-Control	37	15.5	2.4	0.02
Insight-Control	12	15.2	0.8	N.S.

Wechsler-Bellevue

Table III indicates that significant intergroup differences in the amount of change in Wechsler Full Scale IQ occurred during the therapy period ($F = 5.3$, $P = .01$). The Interaction Group showed improvement which was not approached by either the insight Group ($t = 3.14$, $P = .003$) or the Control Group ($t = 2.63$, $P = .01$). The difference in mean changes in IQ between the Insight and Control Groups was not significant.

TABLE III

DIFFERENCES BETWEEN PRE- AND POST-THERAPY WECHSLER-BELLEVUE IQ'S OF (a) INTERACTION, (b) INSIGHT AND (c) CONTROL GROUPS

| | Mean change in I.Q. | | | | t-scores of differences between means | | |
	(a)	(b)	(c)	F-ratio †	(a)&(b)	(a)&(c)	(b)&(c)
Verbal IQ	4.4	−0.5	1.7	2.0*	2.0	1.0	0.9
Performance IQ	7.6	2.1	1.0	2.2	1.7	1.9	0.3
Full IQ	9.0	0	1.0	5.3**	3.1**	2.6**	0.3

† With 2 and 62 degrees of freedom.
* Significant at the 5% level.
** Significant at the 1% level.

No significant intergroup differences in change on the Verbal and Performance Scales of the test are evident. This suggests that the change in intellectual efficiency was a function of a general improvement on all sub-tests. For confirmation of this suggestion, the significance of the intergroup differences of mean changes on subtest weighted scores was tested. The results show only two exceptions, the Comprehension and Digit Symbol sub-tests. The Interaction Group showed improvement on Comprehension which was significantly greater than that shown by the Insight Group (t = 2.57, P = .01). The change in performance of the Insight and Control Groups on this sub-test was not significant. On Digit Symbol also, the Interaction Group showed greater improvement than did the Insight Group (t = 2.23, P = .03) or the Control Group (t = 2.21, P = .03).

In summary, the Interaction Group showed a generally greater improvement in intellectual efficiency which was most marked in the areas of general comprehension and new learning ability.

DISCUSSION

We have found two indications that the interaction technique was more effective in producing improved adjustment than the insight technique. This evidence supports the hypothesis that it is interaction rather than insight that is the basis of psychotherapeutic change; it casts serious doubt on the generally accepted belief that the chief purpose of psychotherapy is to facilitate insight. It suggests that the interpersonal interaction which characterizes both individual and group psychotherapy may, in itself, be the crucial factor in the production of therapeutic change. If this is true, explicit recognition of interaction as the prime therapeutic agent would require reorientation of our therapeutic efforts.

Psychotherapists from Freud onward have found it necessary to deviate in practice from those parts of their theoretical systems which stressed insight as the medium of therapeutic change. While insight has been retained as the explanatory concept , actual practice has moved progressively towards techniques which maximize patient-to-therapist or patient-to-patient interaction, in special types of acceptant atmospheres. Modern group therapy has been the culmination of this trend. Rational man is loath to surrender voluntarily any aspect of his behavior to a noncognitive process, since this implies that he is not complete master of his fate. In theory, psychotherapists have (with some difficulty) resisted surrender; in practice, the surrender is becoming ever more complete. Practical considerations have thus resulted in the modification of therapeutic techniques along the lines suggested by the present study. Explicit recognition of interaction as basic to therapeutic changes could provide the foundation for further and much need technical advances.

SUMMARY

Sixty-six hospital patients were divided at random into three groups:

(a) A group which experienced a technique of group psychotherapy which stressed interpersonal interaction in a warm, permissive, therapeutic climate and made no reference to personal difficulties;

(b) A group which experienced a technique of group psychotherapy which stressed cognitive understanding of personal difficulties (insight) in a benignly authoritarian therapeutic climate;

(c) A control group which experienced no group psychotherapy.

The first group showed significantly greater improvement than did either of the two other groups.

From these results the following conclusions were drawn:

(1) In group psychotherapy, greater improvement results from a technique which stresses interaction than from a technique which stresses insight.

(2) Therapeutic change can and does occur as a result of controlled interaction in the absence of traditional insight methods of psychotherapy.

(3) Since there were no apparent differences in results between an insight technique and "no treatment," interaction rather than insight seems to be the essential condition for therapeutic change.

REFERENCES

1. ADLER, A. *The practice and theory of individual psychology.* (Trans. by P. Radin.) London: Kegan Paul, Trench, Truber & Co., 1927.
2. BACH, G. R. *Intensive group psychotherapy.* New York: Ronald Press, 1954.
3. BOVARD, E. W. Interaction record. Personal communication, 1954.
4. COONS, W. H. Interaction and insight in group psychotherapy. Unpub. doctor's dissertation, Univer. of Toronto, 1955.
5. FREUD, S. *Collected papers.* Vol. II. (Transl. by JOAN RIVIERE). London: Hogarth Press, 1924.
6. GIBBY, R. G. A preliminary survey of certain aspects of Form II of the Wechsler-Bellevue Scale as compared to Form I. *J. clin. Psychol.,* 1949, 5, 165–169.
7. HILGARD, E. R. The role of learning in perception. In BLAKE, R. R. & RAMSEY, C. V. (Eds.), *Perception: An approach to personality.* New York: Ronald Press, 1951.
8. KLOPFER, B., & KELLEY, D., *The Rorschach technique.* New York: World Book Co., 1942.
9. MCNEMAR, Q. *Psychological statistics.* London: Chapman & Hall, 1949.
10. PARSONS, T., & SHILS, E. A. (Eds.) *Toward a general theory of action.* Cambridge, Mass.: Harvard Univer. Press, 1951.
11. RANK, O. *Will therapy and truth and reality.* (Transl. by JESSIE TAFT). New York: Knopf, 1945.
12. REID, J. R., & FINESINGER, J. E. The role of insight in psychotherapy. *Amer. J. Psychiat.,* 1952, 108, 726–734.
13. ROGERS, C. R. *Client-centered therapy.* Boston: Houghton Mifflin, 1951.
14. ROGERS, C. R. Perceptual reorganization in client-centered therapy. In BLAKE, R. R., & RAMSEY, G. V. (Eds.), *Perception: An approach to personality.* New York: Ronald Press, 1951.
15. WASSERMAN, M. B. *The psychology of C. G. Jung.* Mimeographed lectures delivered to the Institute of Psychology, Univer. of Ottawa, 1953.
16. WECHSLER, D. *The measurement of adult intelligence.* Baltimore: Williams and Wilkins, 1944.
17. WECHSLER, D. *The Wechsler-Bellevue intelligence scale: Form II.* New York: Psychological Corporation, 1946.

Improvement and Amount of Therapeutic Contact: An Alternative to the Use of No-treatment Controls in Psychotherapy[1]

STANLEY D. IMBER
JEROME D. FRANK
EARL H. NASH
ANTHONY R. STONE
LESTER H. GLIEDMAN

One of the most formidable problems for researchers in psychotherapy is the use of control groups for the evaluation of treatment effects. The difference in results obtained from a no-treatment control group and an experimental (treatment) group should provide the crucial test of the efficacy of a psychotherapeutic method. For both ethical and practical persons, however, the utilization of this paradigm has in general not proved feasible.[2] From an ethical point of view, it is not considered proper to deny a sick patient available therapeutic facilities, even for the sake of scientific certainty. In this light, it may seem inconsistent that no-treatment controls are appearing with increasing frequency in pharmacological (as well as electro-shock and lobotomy) studies although there remains a relative dearth of these controls in studies of psychotherapy. This is true despite the

Reprinted from *Journal of Consulting Psychology,* 1957, 21 (4), 309–315, with the permission of the American Psychological Association and the authors.

[1] This study is part of a larger research project supported by Research Grant No. M-532 (C-2) from the National Institute of Mental Health, United States Public Health Service.

[2] There are exceptions to this generalization, e.g., the work of Rogers and his colleagues (6) and Barron and Leary (1). The great preponderance of psychotherapy studies, however, have no control provisions at all, at least in the sense in which we are concerned with control design in this paper.

fact that both drug and psychotherapy investigations may use similar nonhospitalized patient samples, with comparable diagnoses and levels of illness. There are, however, important differences in the conditions under which studies in these two areas are conducted. To begin with, there is the matter of the length of the control period. Where a drug is being tested, the control patient ordinarily is denied therapeutic intervention for only a few weeks, rarely more than a month. This relatively brief time interval is considered sufficient for evaluating the potency of the drug, and hence, the control period is adequate. Unfortunately, the efficacy of psychotherapy cannot be assessed in so short a time. Psychotherapy controls would have to undergo a no-treatment period of at least six months, possibly much longer, if they are to match the average time most patients spend in treatment. Few psychotherapists are willing to expose patients to this condition, if some treatment form is available.

Furthermore, there is the very practical problem of retaining control patients in the experimental design. Should a large number of patients deliberately withdraw or drop out prior to completion of the experiment, a biased sample may remain which differs in important characteristics from that population which was the original focus of investigation. The likelihood of a large dropout is much greater in psychotherapy than in drug studies, primarily because of the differential in control time described above. It is a rare case where a distressed patient is willing to wait six months or longer for professional help, as would be the situation for the therapy control. Moreover, the motivation and degree of illness of the patient who does accept this limitation becomes a matter of conjecture.

There is still another distinction between drug and therapy controls which bears comment. Theoretically, a control patient should have no contact with the clinic or treatment source during the control period since even brief contact may be equated with treatment. This restriction is frequently violated in drug studies where control patients sometimes receive placebos and usually maintain clinic contact over the control period, at least for "prescription renewal" purposes. These patients are given to understand and believe that they are being "treated." Furthermore, there is evidence that placebos alone can effect significant changes in the physical and emotional status of patients (7). It is a moot question, therefore, whether placebo patients may be accurately described as receiving "no treatment." On the other hand, no-treatment controls in psychotherapy ordinarily have no clinic contacts at all and are fully aware that they are not receiving formal treatment. Under such conditions it is not surprising that these controls are harder to collect and retain in a study, and that their use is more often challenged on ethical grounds.

Psychotherapy studies are also done, of course, on hospitalized patients. With this "captive" population, the problem of retaining patients in the design is less crucial. Yet, even in institutional settings psychotherapy studies, with or without control provisions, have been rather unsatisfactory. Partly this is because it is difficult to collect a sufficiently large sample of treated patients, let alone controls, due to the paucity of trained psychotherapists and the long treatment periods required. However, this does not explain the relative absence of controls for those psychotherapy studies that are done in hospitals. The use of controls is a quite common practice for evaluating electro-shock and lobotomy procedures in the same settings. This discrepancy may have something to do with the fact that, compared to the latter two types of treatment, psychotherapy may be considered more tried, less radical, and of no great potential danger to patients. That is, a more cautious design specifically including controls may be thought prudent where more "controversial" treatments are being examined. Unfortunately, the designs used in typical studies of shock and lobotomy are hampered by other complications. For example, although the controls in these studies are excluded from a clearly defined experimental condition, strictly speaking they are not no-treatment controls since usually the patients are exposed to other treatment influences, e.g., the general therapeutic atmosphere of the hospital plus occupational therapy, recreational therapy, or other special activities.

It seems, then, that although the use of no-treatment controls would improve the elegance of experimental designs, their application to the evaluation of psychiatric treatments has encountered serious ethical and practical obstacles. These obstacles have been particularly prominent in investigations of psychotherapy where, as a consequence, no-treatment controls are used only infrequently. The most common type of design in current psychotherapy studies consists of the comparison of the pre- and posttherapy status of a single treatment group or the comparison of two or more groups, differing in techniques or methods of treatment. One method or technique may be found superior to the others although all of them may produce change in patients, at least from their initial baseline. The failure to include control groups, however, leaves crucial questions unanswered.

Some investigators have attempted to circumvent the problem by utilizing modified types of control. These fall into two categories, in terms of the populations used: (a) "Dropout" patients (or terminators) and (b) "Wait-list" patients.

1. Dropout patients are those individuals who applied for treatment but either deliberately, or for reasons beyond their control, did not keep any treatment appointments, or terminated treatment very early, usually without the approval of the therapist. The flaw involved in the use of these patients as controls is that they represent an obviously self-selected sample whose motivation for help, on a behavioral basis alone, is quite different from patients accepting and receiving treatment. In the dropout sample there are usually a few patients who are unable to keep treatment appointments for "accidental" reasons, seemingly unrelated to any otherwise negative attitudes toward treatment. Closer examination of the reasons offered often reveals that these reasons simply have provided convenient opportunities for avoiding and rejecting treatment (3). In short, these patients generally differ from treated patients in one significant respect, their unwillingness to accept treatment. In the case of those few patients whose reasons for rejecting treatment appear quite plausible (e.g., family suddenly moved to another state), the unavailability of the patients for treatment generally means that re-evaluations of such patients at later periods are also impossible.

2. Most treatment centers are unable to offer therapy immediately to new patients and, except for acute cases, routinely require wait periods of varying lengths before the beginning of formal treatment. In using these wait-list patients as controls, the investigator has the advantage of the availability of individuals presumably not different from those presently in treatment but who, for reasons not determined by themselves, must undergo an interval of time without access to formal treatment. A study utilizing these patients must make certain that the wait-list represents an unbiased sample and is reduced systematically, i.e., that patients are not assigned differentially from the wait-list to a particular kind of psychotherapy or a particular therapist. It is not uncommon for patients with more acute symptoms, or with especially "interesting" or unique problems, to receive priority in assignment, thus making the wait-list a repository of "superficial" or unwanted cases.[3]

Recently, the rather ingenious device of

---

[3] Grummon, for example, placed a client "in the own-control group only if it seemed that waiting was not likely to cause him serious discomfort or harm . . . (and) assignment to the wait group was occasionally changed to the no-wait group if . . . the client developed anxiety during the waiting period . . ." (4, p. 46).

"own-controls" has been adopted to obviate the difficult matter of matching control and treated groups (4). Here the changes in a patient during the wait interval are compared with the changes in that same patient during treatment. The one serious drawback in this approach is that the wait period almost invariably is shorter than the treatment period itself. The lack of equivalence of the two periods reduces the validity of comparisons. Aside from the temporal inequality, the own-control design has another shortcoming, which is shared by all wait-list approaches: the largely undetermined influence of the promise of treatment on the patients' status (1). The knowledge that treatment is in the offing may work to improve or worsen the condition of some patients, but to what extent, if at all, is a question that only recently has received some attention (6).

Because of the many complicating factors found in the efforts to use traditional and even modified controls, Watterson (8) has suggested another possible solution. "When we test the efficacy of a given drug, we give tablets of the actual drug to the experimental group and control group. Neither the therapist . . . nor the patients themselves know which are the real and which the dummy pills. It is possible and logical to think about psychotherapy in a parallel way; the patient receives a unit of supposed treatment, but this unit may contain the necessary ingredients or it may not. There is nothing fanciful or unusual about such a point of view. We are quite used to judging a kind of psychotherapy as being likely to succeed or to fail because it contains or fails to contain this or that ingredient" (8, p. 239). Watterson adds that a test of this approach will require the precise statement of hypotheses relative to the significant elements in the treatment and consequent changes in the patient. In this way, testable predictions may be made concerning patient change as a function of some specific element or technique. Experimental and control groups would be used, but neither patient nor therapist would be aware of what hypotheses were being tested. The study reported herein serves as an illustration of this alternative design suggested by Watterson.

Previous unpublished data accumulated by the authors in a series of pilot studies indicated that the amount of contact between patient and psychotherapist is an important factor influencing improvement rate. Because this factor appeared so consistent over several criteria, and seemed to account for so much of the variance between improved and unimproved patients, it was felt that it should be controlled in the next sequence of studies. In the present experiment, therefore, a group of patients was formed in which patients were to have minimal contact with their therapists, in contrast to the more traditional techniques. The limitation was imposed in terms of both number of appointments over a period of time and the amount of time which each of these separate appointments consumed. The specific hypothesis to be tested was that patients who have fewer and briefer sessions of psychotherapy will show significantly less improvement in the effectiveness of their social relationships than patients with measurably more and longer psychotherapeutic sessions, over approximately the same period of time.

PROCEDURE

A total of 54 psychiatric patients[4] who appeared at the Henry Phipps Psychiatric Clinic Outpatient Department between

---

[4] The total sample actually was 91 patients, but those patients ($N = 28$) who had three or less psychotherapy sessions were excluded from the present study. The design required a sample of 54 patients who had at least 4 treatment sessions. To make allowance for anticipated "dropouts" (arbitrarily set at 3 or less sessions), extra patients were assigned initially and, consequently, 63 patients were treated in the program. Nine patients were omitted from the present analysis to balance the design and simplify statistical computations. The major condition for omission was poor attendance at therapeutic sessions. Criterion test scores were not appreciably altered in any of the cells or groupings affected by removal of the 9 patients.

June, 1953 and October, 1954 were included in this study. Most patients were psychoneurotic, diagnosed mainly as anxiety and depressive reactions, and the remainder had personality disorders. Patients with diagnoses of organic brain disease, antisocial character disorder, alcoholism, overt psychosis, or mental deficiency were excluded. The patients were assigned to one of three different forms of psychotherapy:

a. Analytically oriented group therapy, in which patients were seen in groups of five to eight once a week for about one and one-half hours;

b. Analytically oriented individual therapy in which patients were seen at least one hour a week;

c. Minimal contact therapy in the Continued Treatment Clinic (CTC) of the Phipps Outpatient Department where patients were seen individually no more than half an hour once every two weeks.

Three psychiatrists participated in the study. They were in the second year of their residency, and had approximately equivalent experience in both group and individual treatment. Each psychiatrist treated a roster of eighteen patients, six in each of the three forms of treatment. Assignment of patients to form of treatment and to therapist was made on a random basis by the research staff. Neither patient nor psychiatrist, therefore, could influence either choice of treatment or choice of therapist (or patient). Patients in the three treatment forms showed no significant differences in age, sex, diagnosis, social class, length of illness, or marital status.

Prior to treatment assignment, each patient was given a structured interview by the research psychiatrist, and the interview was observed through a one-way screen by the research psychologist. The focus of the interview was the patient's day-to-day relationships with each significant individual in his life (e.g., spouse, siblings, children, parents, boss, co-workers, male and female peers, etc.). The extent of the patient's ineffective behavior with each individual during the four-week period immediately preceding the interview was rated on a six-point scale in each of 15 categories: overly-independent, superficially sociable, extrapunitive, officious, impulsive, hyperreactive, overly-systematic, overly-dependent, withdrawn, intrapunitive, irresponsible, overcautious, constrained, unsystematic, and sexual adjustment. The interviewing psychiatrist and the psychologist-observer made separate ratings on the patient, and then in conference, after comparing differences in ratings,[5] completed a series of joint ratings based on the consensus of their conference discussion. A similar interview was also conducted with a relative (or close friend) of each patient by the research social worker and a second psychologist-observer, the interview similarly focusing on the patient's ineffective social behavior. The independent ratings of interviewer and observer were also conferenced, resulting in a set of joint ratings. Finally, the two interviewing teams met to pool their accumulated information and make a single final series of ratings in each of the 15 categories. The ratings for all categories were summed, resulting in a total Social Ineffectiveness score.

The experimental design required re-evaluation of all patients six months after treatment commenced, again after twelve and twenty-four months, and periodically thereafter. Data from the first (six-month) re-evaluation is reported in this paper.

RESULTS

Table 1 indicates that up to the time of the first re-evaluation, all three categories of patients had been in treatment over approximately the same period of time (from 5.0 to 5.5 months),[6] but there was a difference between them in terms of aver-

---

[5] Reliability studies indicate that interrater correlation over the 15 categories of the Ineffectiveness scale is approximately .69.

[6] A few patients in each type of treatment terminated before the 6-month evaluation, reducing the mean number of months of treatment in each category to less than six.

TABLE 1

MEAN NUMBER OF MONTHS AND SESSIONS OF PSYCHOTHERAPY FOR GROUP, INDIVIDUAL, AND CTC PATIENTS ($N = 54$)

Treatment	Month	Sessions
Group	5.0	15.8
Individual	5.1	17.7
CTC	5.5	9.3

age number of therapeutic sessions attended over this period. The number of sessions for group patients was 15.8, for individual patients 17.7, and for CTC patients only 9.3. On the average per month, then, group patients had 3.2 sessions, individual patients 3.5 sessions, and CTC patients 1.7 sessions. In short, over the same period of time patients in individual treatment and those in group treatment had approximately twice as many therapeutic contacts as patients assigned to the Continued Treatment Clinic.

Patient change (or "improvement") was measured by the algebraic difference between the initial (pretherapy) Ineffectiveness scores and the first re-evaluation Ineffectiveness scores. These difference or change scores were analyzed to determine the relative efficacy of the three forms of therapy, the influence of the three psychiatrists, and the importance of the interaction between therapy and psychiatrist. As a statistical control for certain differences between types of treatment due to differential dropout rates, and for a small correlation between initial and change scores, the analysis of covariance was applied. The results summarized in Table 2 indicate a highly significant difference between types of treatment. Group patients improved more than CTC patients ($p < .01$), and individually treated patients also improved more than those treated in CTC ($p < .05$). No difference was found between group and individually treated patients. There was, however, some slight evidence of a difference in the influence of the psychiatrists ($p < .20$).

DISCUSSION

The hypothesis that fewer and briefer sessions of psychotherapy reduce improvement has been confirmed within the framework of the paradigm suggested by Watterson. An assumed "necessary ingredient" of treatment was diluted or restricted for certain patients whose improvement rate was thereby adversely affected. A step by step

TABLE 2

ANALYSIS OF COVARIANCE OF THE INEFFECTIVENESS SCALE SCORES FOR TREATED PATIENTS ($N = 54$)

Source	df	ΣX^2	ΣXY	ΣY^2	Adj. ΣY^2	df	Adj. MS	F
Therapist	2	100.48	42.83	169.00	151.65	2	75.83	2.19**
Therapy	2	615.82	−14.12	294.70	354.79	2	177.40	5.11*
Interaction	4	39.63	−13.10	92.60	105.81	4	26.45	
Within	45	2309.33	785.83	1827.00	1559.59	44	35.44	
Total	53	3065.26	801.44	2382.30				
Pooled Error	49	2348.96	772.73	1919.60	1665.40	48	34.70	
Therapist + Pooled Error	51	2449.44	815.56	2088.60	1817.05	50		
Therapy + Pooled Error	51	2964.78	758.61	2214.30	2020.19	50		

* $p < .01$.
** $p < .20$.
Note.—X and Y refer to Initial and Difference scores, respectively.

verification of other supposed necessary ingredients of psychotherapy might well proceed in analogous fashion.

Specifically, the present study indicates that reduction of interpersonal ineffectiveness is more dependent on the number and extent of contacts between therapist and patient than on the particular psychotherapeutic technique used. CTC patients had measurably less contact with their therapists than did other patients, and they derived significantly less benefit in terms of the criterion employed.[7] The difference in treatment results between the three psychiatrists is only suggestive rather than conclusive. Since the general background, training, and experience of all therapists were similar, personality differences between therapists would seem to warrant further study.

The exact significance of the ingredient of treatment identified in this study is not entirely clear. Perhaps the most parsimonious explanation is that there is an optimum "dosage" of psychotherapy, in terms of amount of patient-therapist contacts, but the minimal amount of dosage received by CTC patients was inadequate, at least by comparison with the more conventional amounts received by the other patients in the study. There are, however, other possible interpretations of our results. Recently, it has been pointed out that the "placebo effect" observed in pharmacological studies may have direct implications for psychotherapy (7). In this context, the placebo effect was defined as those changes in the patient produced primarily "by the patient's faith in the efficacy of the therapist

---

[7] Other criteria utilized in the larger study, of which this is a part, did not reflect similar changes. Improvement, however, is by no means a simple, unitary phenomenon and it may vary depending on the criterion of change (5). Social ineffectiveness was selected for exposition in the present paper because the scale measuring that factor is much the same as the original one used in the pilot studies where the tentative findings concerning amount of contact and improvement were made. The other criteria have undergone considerably greater revision from their original forms.

and his technique" (7, p. 301). It was suggested that the adequate evaluation of any treatment form requires that it be compared with another treatment form in which patients have equal faith. Admittedly, the present study meets this requirement only indirectly, if at all. The conviction with which the patients accepted the different types of treatment and the therapists was not investigated. Yet there appears to be no compelling reason why patients should have the least faith in the CTC treatment. To most patients who come to a public clinic, this kind of brief intermittent contact with a physician is similar to their other medical experiences, and presumably it was what they expected and sought when they requested psychiatric help. At least initially, therefore, there seems little reason to consider the CTC patients as not having confidence in the treatment form to which they were assigned. On the other hand, the therapists themselves may have had unequal faith in the efficacy of the three treatments, especially viewing the limited contact form as inferior, and conceivably could convey this attitude in quite subtle ways to the CTC patients. However, if we can assume that rate of dropout (or early termination) is an inverse measure of faith in treatment, the CTC patients cannot be said to have possessed less of this attribute. Other studies by the authors have shown that the dropout rate for the patients in group therapy was appreciably higher than for patients in CTC (2).

Finally, it might be suggested that number and extent of therapeutic contacts are themselves crucial for instilling faith in a therapist and his techniques. That is, a patient's conviction that he will be helped is not necessarily something that he brings to treatment initially, but is a kind of confidence that is built up through fairly intensive and frequent therapeutic contacts. Hence, the inferiority of the CTC treatment might simply reflect the less amount of faith of patients assigned thereto, as a consequence of their limited therapeutic contacts. If this interpretation is correct, the experiment may be said to confirm the validity of the concept of placebo effect as it operates in psychotherapy.

SUMMARY

The unavailability of nontreatment control groups to test the efficacy of psychotherapy and dissatisfaction with the use of dropout and wait-list groups as substitute procedures, has prompted the use of an alternate experimental design. This design requires the precise statement of hypotheses relative to the presence or absence of an assumed significant element of treatment and the consequent changes in patients. Adopting this scheme, the present study specified that patients having fewer and briefer sessions of psychotherapy will show significantly less improvement than patients with more and longer sessions, over the same period of time. Fifty-four psychiatric patients were assigned at random to three psychiatrists, each of whom treated an equal number of patients in group therapy and two different forms of individual therapy. In one of these latter forms, the patients were able to have only one-half as many psychotherapy sessions and the sessions lasted only one-half as long as patients treated in the other two forms. Over a six-month experimental period the patients with restricted therapeutic contacts showed less improvement on the criterion of change used. The significance of amount of therapeutic contacts is discussed.

REFERENCES

1. BARRON, F., & LEARY, T. F. Changes in psychoneurotic patients with and without psychotherapy. *J. consult. Psychol.*, 1955, 19, 239–245.
2. FRANK, J. D., GLIEDMAN, L. H., IMBER, S. D., NASH, E. H., JR., & STONE, A. R. Why patients leave psychotherapy. *Arch. Neurol. and Psychiat.*, 1957, 77, 283–299.
3. GLIEDMAN, L. H., STONE, A. R., FRANK, J. D., NASH, E. H., JR., & IMBER, S. D. Incentives for treatment related to remaining or improving in psychotherapy. *Amer. J. Psychother.*, in press.
4. GRUMMON, D. L. Design, procedures, and subjects for the first block. In C. R. ROGERS & ROSALIND F. DYMOND (Eds.), *Psychotherapy and personality change.* Chicago: Univer. of Chicago Press, 1954. Pp. 35–52.
5. PARLOFF, M. B., KELMAN, H. C., & FRANK, J. D. Comfort, effectiveness, and self-awareness as criteria of improvement in psychotherapy. *Amer. J. Psychiat.*, 1954, 3, 343–351.
6. ROGERS, C. R., & DYMOND, ROSALIND F. (Eds.) *Psychotherapy and personality change.* Chicago: Univer. of Chicago Press, 1954.
7. ROSENTHAL, D., & FRANK, J. D. Psychotherapy and the placebo effect. *Psychol. Bull.*, 1956, 53, 294–302.
8. WATTERSON, D. J. Problems in evaluation of psychotherapy. *Bull. Menninger Clin.*, 1954, 18, 232–241.

Measurement of Personality and Behavior Changes Following Psychotherapy[1]

MELVIN ZAX
ARMIN KLEIN

In his general review of the area of psychotherapy in 1946, Snyder (1947) expressed optimism and foresaw that this field was at least in the early stages of becoming a science. He saw as a "commendable trend" the fact that the scientific approach was being more widely used in the study of all methods of therapy and pointed out that the measurement of outcome was undergoing objectification. Since the time of that paper at least 400 studies have been published in which some effort was made to evaluate the effects of psychotherapy. Despite this extensive research activity, there are some (Eysenck, 1952) who have questioned whether anyone has adequately demonstrated that psychotherapy is effective.

Evaluatory research in psychotherapy is a most complex activity but an extremely important one if we are to understand more about the nature of what can bring about personality change. The practical and theoretical problems involved in acquiring Ss, developing meaningful controls, and making measurements are enormous. Add to these the question of what one should measure, that is, what criterion should be used, and the complexity is increased many times over.

It is the purpose of this paper to summarize and evaluate some of the approaches which have been used to deal with the problem of the criterion. This is based largely on an exhaustive survey of the many experiments, proposals for experiments, theoretical papers, and some reports of case studies involving the evaluation of individual or group psychotherapy which have appeared in the major American psychological and psychiatric journals between 1946 and 1959 (Zax & Klein, 1958). In this context Snyder's (1947) definition of psychotherapy has been adopted which rules out studies devoted to educational procedures and guidance activities emphasizing the giving of information, as well as social activities, occupa-

Reprinted from *Psychological Bulletin,* 1960, 57 (5), 435–448, with the permission of the American Psychological Association and the authors.

[1] The authors are grateful to E. L. Cowen of the University of Rochester for reading the manuscript and offering many pertinent criticisms and suggestions.

tional therapy, shock therapy, chemotherapy, etc.

The present review is divided into two major sections devoted to (a) criteria based on client behavior in the therapy situation or his personal report and (b) criteria based on the client's behavior outside of the therapy situation. The studies cited in this paper are selected as being illustrative of these two approaches. Phenomenological measures and indices of client behavior within the therapy situation have been used in some of the major systematic programs for evaluating psychotherapy (Rogers & Dymond, 1954; Snyder, 1953). Measures of extratherapeutic behavior represents logically a most important yardstick. In addition to these two major approaches, psychological tests have also found frequent use as criteria, but, because of space limitations, it was felt that they might better be reviewed separately.

INTRATHERAPEUTIC BEHAVIOR AND PHENOMENOLOGICAL CRITERIA

Criteria based on S's self-experience and his behavior within the therapy situation have stemmed largely from the work of the client centered group who have actively studied their treatment approach. In their research program, they have developed a few instruments which were directly intended to serve as outcome criteria and several indices which have important inplications for outcome.

Seeman (1954) constructed a measure which has found considerable use both as a criterion of therapeutic outcome and as a validating instrument for other indices (Rogers & Dymond, 1954). It consists of 10 nine-point scales, several of which required the counselor to evaluate some aspect of the client's experience. This instrument was applied to 23 therapy cases, and it was found that for all items but one there was significant change in the direction of improvement from the beginning to the end of treatment. Also, correlations between ratings on individual items and an item which referred simply to success of outcome revealed that when a client was judged to be successfully treated he was rated highly on scales measuring the extent to which he used therapy as an emotional experience, used it for personal rather than situational exploration, liked and respected his therapist, moved in the direction of both personal integration and situational adjustment, and was satisfied with the outcome of therapy. While this appears as a validation of the instrument it seems likely that the changes measured by many of these individual scales are implicit dimensions of the global judgment of success to which it was compared.

The other instrument which has been used as a criterion in a number of studies (Snyder, 1953) was developed by Tucker (1953) who termed it the "multiple criterion." This involved a Client Post Therapy Scale which was essentially a self-assessment device in which the client was asked to rate his feelings toward such things as the possibility of having problems in the future, the status of the problem which brought him to treatment, relationship with immediate family, sexual adjustment, relationship to others, etc. Another measure as part of the criterion was the Counselor Post Therapy Check List which involved 29 items referring to the client's behavior during therapy and was based on a careful review of therapy notes and interview recordings. This check list was filled out by both the therapist and in each case by one other of a group of trained raters who also used transcribed interview material. Finally, the first and last interviews in each case were analyzed as to the number of positive and negative emotional statements made by the client and an index derived by dividing number of negative statements by the sum of negative and positive ones.

The client's self-report which was an integral part of Tucker's "multiple criterion" has been used as the sole criterion at times and represents the most direct phenomenological measure of therapy outcome. Investigations using such measures have ranged from those employing elaborate rating devices, with some effort at standardizing the procedure, to ratings based on relatively unstandardized interviews in which the S is asked to describe his present state or changes which may have occurred as the result of therapy. Fiedler's study (1949) serves as an example of the former. He had Ss fill out a 10-item self-rating scale with each item scaled from 0 to 12. The items referred to emotional tensions related to the stress of taking academic examinations and to changes as the result of psychotherapy.

In studies using less systematic self-evaluative techniques, like that of Lipkin (1948), general questions have been asked such as, "What seemed to go on during your visits here?" "How do things look to you now?" Responses were evaluated subjectively and the clients' descriptions of their experience in therapy and its effect on them were seen to confirm the expectations of Rogerian theory.

Cowen and Combs (1950) used a third approach for eliciting the client's evaluation of therapeutic progress. They conducted open-ended follow-up interviews which were recorded and evaluated by three judges as being "successful, progress, or failure" cases.

Other instruments have been developed which elicit self-descriptions from the client. While such descriptions have not been a direct evaluation of the therapy experience itself, they have implications for the effects of therapy and have been used as outcome measures. In one study, Butler and Haigh (1954) used a Q sort involving 100 self-referent statements which had been randomly selected from available therapy protocols. Ss were required to sort these to describe themselves as they were at the time on a "like-me" to "unlike-me" continuum. They were further asked to make sortings which would describe their own ideal on a "like-ideal" to "unlike-ideal" continuum. The investigators reported significant increases in the correlation between self and ideal sorts of clients who underwent therapy despite the fact that the same clients failed to show such changes on the same sorts made before and after a waiting period prior to the beginning of therapy. A no-therapy control group also failed to demonstrate such changes. Cartwright (1957) found a significant relationship between success in treatment as rated by the therapist and an increased consistency in the sorting of the Butler-Haigh items when three self-sorts were made each using different people as interacting reference points.

Rosenthal (1955) constructed a Morals Value Q-Sort comprising 100 statements which the S sorted into two piles as being relatively more or less descriptive of himself. This was administered to the patients in his sample before and after treatment and the therapists involved also made the sort. His findings were that patients judged as improved tended to revise more values in the direction of those of the therapist than the unimproved.

Dymond (1953) selected 74 of the Butler and Haigh items which two non-client-centered psychologists had sorted into two equal piles as being characteristic of the well adjusted on the one hand and of the poorly adjusted on the other. These in turn were given to four other judges who sorted them independently in a similar fashion and a high degree of agreement was found. Ss were then given an adjustment score based on how many of either kind of statement appeared on the "like-me" or "unlike-me" sides of their sortings. She found scores on this Q-adjustment scale, as it was termed, to move toward good adjustment following therapy (1953, 1954). Cartwright and Roth (1957) found the correlation of a client's self and ideal sorts to be related to the Q-adjustment sort and the client's self-rating on the Willoughby

Emotional Maturity scale. Although Dymond (1953) had not found differences in the Q-adjustment scores after a two-month interval during which her Ss were waiting to enter therapy and ultimately did, Grummon (1954) did find significant changes in this type of score among Ss who requested treatment but then decided against it when it was available. In this case a two month interval had also elapsed between tests. Dymond (1955) re-examined the Q sorts of Grummon's Ss and concluded that

although positive adjustment changes appear to take place in maladjusted persons in the absence of psychotherapy, these are not identical with the changes which occur in equally maladjusted persons who complete therapy (p. 107).

She denied that any "deep" reorganization takes place and saw the improvement as characterized by "a strengthening of neurotic defenses and a denial of the need for help."

A number of studies of personality change as seen in the therapeutic interaction have implications for criteria, especially insofar as these changes have often been related to direct evaluations of outcome. Snyder (1945), following a pioneer investigation of the therapy process by Porter (1943), made the earliest of such studies. He classified client statements into four major categories along the dimension of content significance: descriptions of problems, simple responses asking for advice or accepting or rejecting clarification of feeling, responses showing insight into remedies for a problem, and responses which were unrelated to the principal problem of the client. A second dimension for clients' statements was identified as expressions of feeling and nine categories were set up to classify them. These described attitudes expressed in clients' statements as being positive, negative, or ambivalent with reference to the self, the counselor, or other persons or situations. As a result of his analysis of nearly 10,000 client responses

in the 48 interviews he used, Snyder concluded that there was a marked tendency for the client's feelings to change in affective tone from negative to positive. Further he noted that in his attitude toward the counselor the patient was slightly rejecting at first, and indifferent during most of the treatment; but in the last interview or so, there was a marked increase in positive attitudes. He also interpreted his findings as indicating that "clients approaching the end of treatment show an excellent amount of insight into the nature of their problem."

In another of the early studies of personality change with psychotherapy, Raimy (1948) was concerned with changes in self-concept. He analyzed client responses in a set of 14 cases by classifying statements into six catagories. These involved self-references which were positive, negative, ambivalent, and ambiguous; statements which did not involve self-references; and nonrhetorical questions. He found that in cases considered successfully treated on the basis of the judgments of the counselor, the supervisor of most of the cases, and Raimy himself, the client went from a preponderance of negative and ambivalent self-references to a preponderance of positive self-references. This was taken to support the hypothesis that in successful therapy a positive change in self-concept took place.

Several measures of client experience were developed in a series of studies of the process of psychotherapy in a single sample of 10 cases at the University of Chicago. Changes in the clients' experience reflected by these measures were found by Raskin (1949) to be associated with success in therapy as judged by the counselor. Thus, in the more successful cases clients showed an increase in acceptance of, and respect for, self as measured by a scale developed by Sheerer (1949); an increase in positive and objective attitudes directed toward the self as measured by a scale developed by Stock (1949); a tendency toward more mature behavior as judged from the client's own verbalizations in therapy (Hoffman, 1949); and a decrease in defensiveness as measured by Haigh (1949).

In a later study of his own, Raskin developed a four-step scale, illustrated at each point by three examples of client statements, on the basis of which judges estimated whether the client, in what he said, was being governed largely by the expectations of others or by his own values and standards. Ratings on this "locus of evaluation" scale were found to correlate significantly with therapists' ratings as to the success of treatment and with the five parallel interview measures described in the previous study, but not with rated change on the Rorschach.

In a later study of the changes in personality in successful psychotherapy, seen phenomenologically, Vargas (1954) measured self-awareness in three ways and related increase on his measures to a number of criteria of outcome. He summarized his findings by saying:

The conclusion which seems to follow from these observations is that the hypothesis—increasing self-awareness during therapy correlated with success in therapy—is confirmed when success is measured by instruments which rate highly those changes and states deducible from client centered theory (p. 165).

It should be noted that nearly all of these studies relating personality change in psychotherapy to judgments of the general outcome of treatment involve a certain circularity. In nearly all cases the judgment as to outcome was made by people holding theoretical viewpoints similar to those of the researchers who developed the scales for measuring change. It is, therefore, likely that the two measures were not completely independent.

A few measures of changes in clients' verbal behavior within the therapy interaction have been developed outside of the client-centered framework. One of these was the Discomfort Relief Quotient (henceforth referred to as DRQ) which was first proposed by Dollard and Mowr-er (1953). This measure classifies words, clauses, or sentences as to whether they signify discomfort, relief from discomfort, or a neutrality of emotion. To arrive at the quotient the number of discomfort words, clauses, or sentences are divided by the same number plus the number of relief words, phrases or clauses. Thus, the quotient may vary from zero to one, with scores nearer zero representing a preponderance of expressions of relief and those approaching one indicating considerable expression of discomfort. Dollard and Mowrer made no claim that the DRQ measured "success" in treatment. To do this they felt that it must first be related to a reliable measure of "real life success."

Several attempts have been made to validate the DRQ as a measure of success in therapy. Hunt (1949a, 1949b) applied it in a social casework setting and found that changes in DRQ failed to correlate significantly with judgments of improvement made by case workers. Other studies (Assum & Levy, 1948; Cofer & Chance, 1950; Murray, Auld, & White, 1954) reported analyses of the published protocols of cases presented by the therapist as successful, with two finding the predicted change and the third finding no relationship.

Kauffman and Raimy (1949) derived a related measure from Raimy's self-concept categories (described above). It consisted of the number of negative self-references plus the number of ambivalent self-references divided by the number of negative self-references plus the number of ambivalent self-references plus the number of positive self-references (more conveniently termed the PNAvQ). Using this quotient, they analyzed 17 verbatim interviews and compared their analysis with an analysis of the same protocols using the DRQ. They concluded that both methods traced changes from maladjustment to adjustment in a similar fashion. They also noted that PNAvQ judgments were obtained in about one-third the time required for DRQ judgments.

Another study of the nature of personality change was recently reported by Berg (1958). He analyzed an eight-interview protocol of a case published by Rogers as successful and proposed that early in treatment, clients are preoccupied with self and move in the direction of a more empathic concern for others. He made a frequency count of "ego" words (I, me, my, myself, mine), "empathic" words (we, our, they, us, you, your), "negative" words and "expletive-bombastic sounds" at various points in treatment. It was found that empathic words did indeed increase while ego, negative, and expletive-bombastic expressions decreased with succeeding interviews.

Most recently, Rogers (1958) has developed and given a preliminary report on a scale of process levels in psychotherapy which bears considerable significance for the measurement of the effects of successful psychotherapy. Again, his goal was a further understanding of the nature of change in personality from a theoretical framework rather than measurement of outcome. He conceived that clients move "not from fixity or homeostasis through change to a new fixity . . . but much the more significant continuum is from fixity to changingness. . . ." He hypothesized that the naure of clients' immediate relationship to their feelings at any point in the therapeutic interaction might indicate their position on a seven-stage continuum.

BEHAVIORAL CRITERIA

In many instances, studies of the results of psychotherapy have used criteria which depend on an evaluation of the way the patient actually behaves without inference as to its personal meaning for him. Such indices were generally developed directly as criteria for use in a given situation and were not related to a theoretical framework about personality change.

Of the many studies which have used behavioral criteria, certain ones have been particularly noteworthy in that they dealt with crucial aspects of behavior which can be objectively established. The simplest of such criteria focused on relatively circumscribed individual behaviors which were seen to be central to the person's difficulty in living. The more complex criteria attempted to assess wide, more representative areas of functioning through the use of elaborate rating scales.

A study by Friedman (1950) is typical of those employing criteria emphasizing delimited behaviors which are central to the person's difficulty in living. His Ss were 50 patients complaining of a "phobia of travel," which can be objectively measured. Evaluation was based on their ability to travel after treatment and it was found that 12 patients were unimproved, 15 showed some improvement, and 23 were completely recovered. Another example of a study utilizing a single symptom which bore implications for a much wider range of behavior was that of Teuber and Powers (1951). They simply totaled the number of court appearances among a large group of potential juvenile delinquents who had received treatment and made comparisons with a matched control group which had received no treatment. No significant differences were found between groups on this measure.

A variation in the use of an important individual behavior as a criterion was introduced by Thetford (1952) who derived an automatic measure of frustration tolerance This study stands out in that the behavior which was measured was not a specific complaint but depended on the theoretical consideration that therapy should reduce anxiety and tension so that the manner in which one responds to stress as reflected in the autonomic nervous system should be altered. He developed a "Recovery Quotient" based on various Galvanic Skin Response measures and found significant changes as the result of psychotherapy which indicated the development of a higher frustration threshold.

The criterion used by Pascal and Zax

(1956) likewise involved objective behavioral measures, but these varied with the individual patient, reflecting presenting complaints. These complaints were evaluated for 30 cases which had undergone various types of treatment. In 28 of these, changes in the predicted direction were found.

Institutional settings have made it possible to study wider samples of behavior objectively. In such settings Cowden, Zax, Hague and Finney (1956); Fox (1954); and Ludwig and Ranson (1947) have used multiple but individually significant behaviors as their criteria. Cowden et al. (1954) considered the number of times hospitalized patients required neutral wet packs, electroconvulsive maintenance shock, or engaged in fights, in addition to such indications of improvement as transfer to a ward requiring a higher level of integration or discharge from the hospital. They concluded that patients who received group psychotherapy in addition to tranquillizing drugs showed more improvement than various control groups. To evaluate the effects of counselling programs in a prison, Fox (1954) used such behavioral criteria as work stability, school stability, financial budgeting, reports from chaplain, block officers, and work supervisors, successful discharge from parole, and return to prison as a parole violator; he found counseled groups had significantly higher adjustment scores on such indices than similar uncounseled groups In a report of results of psychiatric treatment among soldiers, Ludwig and Ranson (1947) reported that relatively high percentages of treated patients were able to return to duty stations and that ratings of commanding officers indicated that most of them were able to perform their services adequately.

Many studies have made use of longer and more elaborate rating scales which attempted to assess the extratherapy functioning of the individual on the basis of diverse behavioral observations. One of the older instruments of this type which was used in the evaluation of treatment with children (Gersten, 1951; Mehlman, 1953) is the Haggerty-Olson-Wickman Behavior Rating Schedules (Jones, 1941). This consists of two separate schedules (A and B) the first of which (A) lists 15 problems such as cheating, lying, defiance of discipline, speech difficulties, sex offenses, obscene notes, talk, or pictures, etc. Raters checked in one of four columns according to the frequency of occurrence of each for a given individual. Standardized weights were assigned according to the frequency and seriousness of a given problem. The other schedule (B) comprised a series of 35 graphic five-point rating scales covering traits which may be classified according to intellectual, physical, social, and emotional traits. On the basis of ratings made before and after group therapy with juvenile delinquents, Gersten (1951) reported progress in emotional security and social maturity among his subjects. Mehlman (1953), who used the scale to rate mentally retarded children before and after group therapy, found significant increases in adjustment at the time of the second rating.

Of the many devices which have been used to evaluate change in hospitalized patients, perhaps the most promising and certainly the most searching are Palo Alto Hospital Adjustment Scale (McReynolds & Ferguson, 1953) and the Lorr Multidimensional Scale (Lorr, 1953). The Palo Alto scale consists of 90 descriptive statements applicable to psychiatric patients. Examples of these statements are, "the patient ignores the activities around him" or "the patient's talk is mostly not sensible." Each one is marked as true, not true, or does not apply, for a particular patient and is keyed in such a manner that a general hospital adjustment score can be obtained. The scale was designed to be filled out at intervals by ward personnel who are familiar with the patient's behavior. On this measure, schizophrenics were seen to improve with group psychotherapy (Semon

& Goldstein, 1957). In another study (Wilcox & Guthrie, 1957) items from this scale were combined with others suggested by personnel in an institution for defective children, and by this index group therapy was found to be effective.

The Lore scale consists of 62 brief rating scales which are directed toward observable or inferable patient behavior. Many of the items refer to relatively objective behaviors concerning which judgments should be quite reliable, such as bizarre postures, speech peculiarities, orientation, eating, sleeping, assaultiveness. On the other hand many other items refer to aspects of behavior which are probably less reliably rated such as emotional responsiveness, attitude toward himself, suspiciousness, recurrence of useless thoughts, etc. The use of this scale was reported in a study with long term schizophrenic patients who were seen by this measure to have improved significantly more than a control group (Funk, Shatin, Freed, & Rockmore, 1955).

The scales used to evaluate outpatients have as a rule been more difficult to apply and often have been more complex. This is due to the obvious fact that the behavior of the nonhospitalized patient is less limited by the structured aspects of institutional life so that he functions in a much wider range. Observation is thereby also made more difficult. Hunt (1949a, 1949b) has attempted to measure "movement" in social casework by developing a criterion to evaluate the DRQ. Movement was defined as "the change which appears in an individual client and/or his environmental situation between the opening and closing of his case" (Hunt, 1949b, p. 76). His scale was set up in seven steps ranging from minus two, through zero, to plus four with anchoring illustrations at each of these three points. It was found that experienced workers could use the scale reliably, but no relationship was found between movement and DRQ changes in the course of the therapy.

The Willoughby Emotional Maturity Scale (1931) has been used by Rogers (1954) to evaluate changes in psychotherapy. It consists of 60 statements descriptive of varying levels of maturity of functioning. The levels had been determined by 100 clinicians who sorted a large number of statements along a nine-step continuum. The 60 items selected for the scale were representative of the nine levels of maturity and were ones on which there was high agreement among judges. In Rogers' study, each client was rated by himself and two personal friends whom he designated. Although intrarater reliability was high, interrater reliabilities were low. Conceivably, this scale might have higher reliability in the hands of trained observers although this might limit its use to a somewhat standardized setting such as a dormitory or school setting.

Miles, Barrabee, and Finesinger (1951) developed a series of five-point scales covering the general areas of (a) symptoms; (b) social adjustment including functioning in the areas of occupation, marriage, interpersonal relations, and sex; (c) insight; and (d) life situation since hospitalization. As a group, the scales were comprehensive and individual steps were well described. On the basis of these instruments, overall evaluations were made of patients and summarized in the categories "apparently recovered, much improved, improved, slightly improved, unimproved, and worse." In using this measure to assess a group of 62 cases two years after treatment, they found that 58% had improved in varying degrees while 42% were unchanged. Imber, Frank, Nash, Stone, and Gliedman (1957) derived a Social Ineffectiveness score on the basis of a series of six-point scales which applied to each of 15 behavioral categories concerning the patient's relationships with the significant individuals in his life (spouse, sibs, children, parents, boss, etc.). Some of the categories were overly independent, withdrawn, superficially sociable, extrapunitive, officious, impulsive, etc. Using this scale they investigated the relationship between improvement and amount of therapeutic contact, and they found less improvement for patients with restricted therapy contacts than for those with more frequent ones.

Raush, Dittman, and Taylor (1959) have made a recent contribution to the methodology of making observations and developing behavioral criteria to assess change with treatment. Working in a residential treatment setting for children, they standardized their observations of six male Ss and systematically studied samples of their behavior in a variety of settings including mealtimes, play periods, and an arts-and-crafts period. One set of observations was made early in the children's stay at the center and another 18 months later focusing on interpersonal behavior at these two points in time. Objective observations were recorded and later rated on a scale based on two polar coordinates: love (affiliate, act friendly) to hate (attack, act unfriendly) and dominate (command, high status action) to submit (obey, low status action). More striking changes were found in the relationships of these children to adults than in their relationships to their peers.

DISCUSSION

As is the case with any measure of personality, a criterion for evaluating the effects of psychotherapy must satisfy the requirements of reliability and validity. The latter usually poses the more serious problem in that no absolute state of complete validity exists as a standard. In dealing with this problem we generally conclude that a given measure is valid for certain specified purposes and not necessarily valid for others. Therefore, we may have a variety of "valid" measures of the outcome of psychotherapy. The judgment of whether these are useful measures, however, must be based upon our evaluation of the purposes for which they are valid. The criteria which have been reviewed will be considered in the light of such issues.

Perhaps the simplest and most direct means of assessing a client's progress in treatment is to ask him to evaluate his own status. Such a phenomenological approach has often been used. Unfortunately, on close analysis, this deceptively simple procedure is seen to be fraught with serious pitfalls. Standards for such assessments will vary both among clients and between client and researcher; clients will vary in the extent to which they can report what they feel; the reports of many clients will be subject to various unconscious distortions; finally, the client's evaluation of his condition may be affected by conscious or semiconscious motives. In positing the "hello-goodbye" effect, Hathaway (1948) has warned of the subtle social influences which limit the reliability of many of the phenomenological measures which have been made. On entering treatment the client is under the conventional pressure to justify his appeal for help so that problems are discussed freely. When seeking to terminate, however, he feels an obligation, out of courtesy toward one who has attempted to help, to express gratitude and satisfaction. A fundamental weakness of the phenomenological approach would, therefore, seem to reside in the difficulty in obtaining reliable assessments. It seems likely that the content of such assessments depends greatly upon who asks for it and the circumstances under which it is requested.

Intratherapy behavior, usually verbal behavior, lends itself to measurement and has been used often as a criterion. In many of the studies reporting the use of such criteria a single theoretical system, that of Rogers, has guided the expectations of researchers. As a result many of these studies relate to each other in a more systematic fashion than is usually the case with outcome studies. The aspects of verbal behavior which have been studied by the client-centered group have usually been carefully defined and found to be reliably measured. Designed to explore personality changes during psychotherapy rather than to be evaluators of psychotherapy, their significance for outcome measures is mostly by implication for they remain unvalidated, not yet having been compared to an independent criterion. Used for the purpose of exploring changes, they were compared in the published studies only to a judgmental criterion of the therapist who shared the same theoretical point of view as the researcher and whose global judgment could have included the concept under study.

Those intratherapy criteria which have not stemmed from the work of the client centered group have found relatively infrequent use and the one attempt to relate change in DRQ to an independent, external criterion (Hunt, 1949a, 1949b) resulted in an insignificant correlation.

The most serious failing at this time in the use of phenomenological measures and measures of intratherapy behavior as criteria of outcome is that neither has yet been related to everyday, externally observable behaviors in the life space of the Ss. Unless phenomenological changes and changes in verbal behavior in therapy can be related to concomitant behavioral changes in the family and the community their significance remains unclear.

External measures of clients' behavior stand out as potential criteria having validity for purpose which are extremely important. However, when one attempts to use such criteria he is beset by a host of measurement problems which are much more difficult to resolve than is the case with phenomenological and intratherapy indices. The central problem here is the development of criteria of sufficient breadth that they are meaningful and representative of a wide range of functioning and yet, at the same time, circumscribed enough to be measured with reliability.

The present review would seem to indicate that the development of such criteria is in the stage of infancy. Many workers have been able to reliably observe narrow aspects of functioning which had implications for a wider range of behavior. In

such cases, however, the possibility remains that one circumscribed symptom was abandoned in favor of another which was equally or even more disabling. The assessment of broader areas of functioning has been carried on primarily within the confines of institutional settings where the patients' range of functioning is limited. Perhaps the most glaring weakness in the way such criteria have been developed and applied is that there has been no unifying set of principles to guide observations. Consequently, the results which have been reported are fragmented. We are told of a variety of behavioral changes which take place as the result of therapy but very few of these appear in any one study and even fewer are observed in more than one study. It would seem that the present need is for the development of a theory or even a set of loose hypothetical notions about "normal" behavior to guide our observations and systematize our thinking.

It seems likely that one of the obstacles to the development of such a theory has been the reluctance of many psychologists to become embroiled in the philosophical issues of the desirability of different behaviors. Actually, the problem of making value judgments when one conducts research cannot be avoided. The very selection of the phenomena which will be observed and measured is in itself a judgment depending upon the values one holds. Indeed then, the further development of criteria for evaluating the effects of psychotherapy awaits the clarification, resolving, and communication of the values we hold.

One approach to the development of a systematic set of values which may clarify our thinking about what behavior is generally considered "psychologically desirable" would be to formalize the notion of the client's relationship to social norms which was discussed by Pascal and Zax (1956). Their concern was with the behaviors on the part of the person presenting himself for treatment which were notably deviant from expected social norms (i.e., overt homosexual acts, frequent crying spells, few friends) and the extent to which such behaviors were changed. Other writers have suggested that the clinician does generally function with a concern for such social norms. As the result of his work in the area of personality assessment, Edwards (1957) has suggested that the notions of the clinician about what constitutes disturbance in patients may correspond essentially to an operational definition of what is socially undesirable. Cowen (in press) who was investigating the social desirability variable in personality assessment actually provided data which lends support to this idea. He found a correlation of $-.917$ between the published ratings of a group of clinicians on 77-trait descriptive terms scaled for abnormality and the social desirability ratings of the same terms by 67 undergraduate students of psychology.

This approach suggests that the person considered most psychologically handicapped is the one who is unable to function in the way in which it is expected that he should in his social group. Furthermore, it suggests that phenomenological reports of how one feels are characteristically considered in the light of such evidence about how he functions in the same way that the felt experience of physical comfort or discomfort is evaluated on the basis of various measures of bodily function.

While this approach, which is probably implicit in the thinking and functioning of most clinicians, may provide a useful beginning to the development of criteria of what therapy should accomplish, it is unlikely that any single set of norms would apply to all. In essence, we are proposing that there are, contentwise, many "normal" or "healthy" personalities. That which is common to each is the ability to function in relation to the norms of his particular social setting. The uniqueness of each individual's social setting makes this a complex area of study and is undoubtedly discouraging. It may well develop, however, that what people have in common is important

enough to permit the development of a relatively limited number of norms reflecting basic interpersonal environments which can be useful. At any rate, it would seem that what is now needed is a series of broad normative studies of a personal-social psychological nature. In addition to providing norms which can be used as a foundation for behavioral criteria of "normality," they would provide a basis for determining just which dimensions of social group membership have significance for actual functioning. The availability of a criterion based on such indices would also provide a context in which to evaluate the significance of changes in the experiencing of Ss, either reported directly or reflected in their intra-therapy verbal behavior. Ultimately, a combined measure of related changes in observed behavior and experiencing might facilitate a common, communicative frame of reference among workers of different orientations and be a basis for delineation of dimensions of personality change.

REFERENCES

Assum, A. L., & Levy, S. J. Analysis of a nondirective case with followup interview. *J. abnorm. soc. Psychol.*, 1948, 43, 78–89.

Berg, I. A. Word choice in the interview and personal adjustment. *J. counsel. Psychol.*, 1958, 5, 130–135.

Butler, J. M., & Haigh, G. V. Changes in the relation between self concepts and ideal concepts consequent upon client-centered counseling. In C. R. Rogers & R. F. Dymond (Eds.), *Psychotherapy and personality change*. Chicago, Ill.: Univer. Chicago Press, 1954.

Cartwright, D. S., & Roth, I. Success and satisfaction in psychotherapy. *J. clin. Psychol.*, 1957, 13, 20–26.

Cartwright, Rosalind D. Effects of psychotherapy on self consistency. *J. counsel. Psychol.*, 1957, 4, 15–22.

Cofer, C. N., & Chance, June. The discomfort-relief quotient in published cases of counseling and psychotherapy. *J. Psychol.*, 1950, 29, 219–224.

COWDEN, R. C., ZAX, M., HAGUE, J. R., & FINNEY, R. C. Chlorpromazine: Alone and as an adjunct to group psychotherapy in the treatment of psychiatric patients. *Amer. J. Psychiat.*, 1956, 112, 898–902.

COWEN, E. L. The social desirability of trait descriptive terms: Preliminary norms and sex differences. *J. soc. Psychol.*, in press.

COWEN, E. L., & COMBS, A. W. Follow-up study of 32 cases treated by nondirective psychotherapy. *J. abnorm. soc. Psychol.*, 1950, 45, 232–258.

DOLLARD, J., & MOWRER, O. H. A method of measuring tension in written documents. In O. H. Mowrer (Ed.), *Psychotherapy theory and research*. New York Ronald, 1953.

DYMOND, ROSALIND F. An adjustment score for Q sorts. *J. consult. Psychol.*, 1953, 17, 339–342.

DYMOND, ROSALIND F. Adjustment changes over therapy from self-sorts. In C. R. Rogers & R. F. Dymond (Eds.), *Psychotherapy and personality change*. Chicago, Ill.: Univer. Chicago Press, 1954.

DYMOND, ROSALIND F. Adjustment changes in the absence of psychotherapy. *J. consult. Psychol.*, 1955, 19, 103–107.

EDWARDS, A. E. *The social desirability variable in personality assessment and research.* New York: Dryden, 1957.

EYSENCK, H. J. The effects of psychotherapy: An evaluation. *J. consult. Psychol.*, 1952, 16, 319–324.

FIEDLER, F. E. An experimental approach to preventive psychotherapy. *J. abnorm. soc. Psychol.*, 1949, 44, 386–393.

FOX, V. The effects of counseling on adjustment in prison. *Soc. Forces,* 1954, 32, 285–289.

FRIEDMAN, J. H. Short-term psychotherapy of "phobia of travel." *Amer. J. Psychother.*, 1950, 4, 259–278.

FUNK, I. C., SHATIN, L., FREED, E. X., & ROCKMORE, L. Somato-psychotherapeutic approach to long-term schizophrenic patients. *J. nerv. ment. Dis.*, 1955, 121, 423–437.

GERSTEN, C. An experimental evaluation of group therapy with juvenile delinquents. *Int. J. group Psychother.*, 1951, 1, 311–318.

GRUMMON, D. L. Personality change as a function of time in persons motivated for therapy. In C. R. Rogers & Rosalind F. Dymond (Eds.), *Psychotherapy and personality change*. Chicago, Ill.: Univer. Chicago Press, 1954.

HAIGH, G. Defensive behavior in client-centered therapy. *J. consult. Psychol.*, 1949, 13, 181–189.

HATHAWAY, S. R. Some considerations relative to nondirective psychotherapy as counseling. *J. clin. Psychol.*, 1948, 4, 226–231.

HOFFMAN, A. E. A study of reported behavioral changes in counseling. *J. consult. Psychol.*, 1949, 13, 190–195.

HUNT, J. McV. The problem of measuring the results of psychotherapy. *Psychol. Serv. Cent. J.*, 1949, 1, 122–135. (a)

HUNT, J. McV. A social agency as the setting for research. *J. consult. Psychol.*, 1949, 13, 68–91. (b)

IMBER, S. D., FRANK, J. D., NASH, E. H., STONE, A. R., & GLIEDMAN, K. H. Improvement and amount of therapeutic contact: An alternative to the use of no-treatment controls in psychotherapy. *J. consult. Psychol.* 1957, 21, 309–315.

JONES, H. E. Haggerty-Olson-Wickman Behavior Rating Schedules. In O. K. Buros (Ed.), *The 1940 mental measurements yearbook*. Highland Park, N. J.: Mental Measurements Yearbook, 1941. Pp. 1222–1223.

KAUFMAN, P. E., & RAIMY, V. C. Two methods of assessing therapeutic progress. *J. abnorm. soc. Psychol.*, 1949, 44, 379–385.

LIPKIN, S. The client evaluates nondirective psychotherapy. *J. consult. Psychol.*, 1948, 12, 137–146.

LORR, M. Multidimensional scale for rating psychiatric patients. *VA tech. Bull.*, 1953, TB 10-507, 1–44.

LUDWIG, A. O., & RANSON, S. W. A statistical follow-up of effectiveness of treatment of combat-induced psychiatric casualties: I. Returns to full combat duty. *Milit. Surg.*, 1947, 100, 51–62.

McREYNOLDS, P., & FERGUSON, J. T. *Clinical manual for the Hospital Adjustment Scale.* Stanford, Calif.: Stanford Univer. Press, 1953.

MEHLMAN, B. Group therapy with mentally retarded children. *J. abnorm. soc. Psychol.*, 1953, 48, 53–60.

MILES, H. W., BARRABEE,, EDNA L., & FINESINGER, J. E. Evaluation of psychotherapy. *Psychosom. Med.*, 1951, 13, 83–105.

MURRAY, E. J., AULD, F., JR., & WHITE, ALICE M. A psychotherapy case showing progress but no decrease in the discomfort-relief quotient. *J. consult. Psychol.*, 1954, 18, 349–353.

PASCAL, G. R., & ZAX, M. Psychotherapeutics: Success or failure. *J. consult. Psychol.*, 1956, 20, 325–331.

PORTER, E. H., JR. The development and evaluation of a measure of counseling interview procedures: II. The evaluation. *Educ. psychol. Measmt.*, 1943, 3, 215–238.

RAIMY, V. C. Self reference in counseling interviews. *J. consult. Psychol.*, 1948, 12, 153–163.

RASKIN, N. J. An analysis of six parallel studies of the therapeutic process. *J. consult. Psychol.*, 1949, 13, 206–221.

RAUSH, H. L., DITTMAN, A. T., & TAYLOR, T. J. The interpersonal behavior of children in residential treatment. *J. abnorm. soc. Psychol.*, 1959, 58, 9–26.

ROGERS, C. R. Changes in the maturity of behavior as related to therapy. In C. R. Rogers & Rosalind F. Dymond (Eds.), *Psychotherapy and personality change*. Chicago, Ill.: Univer. Chicago Press, 1954.

ROGERS, C. R. A process conception of psychotherapy. *Amer. Psychologist*, 1958, 4, 142–149.

ROGERS, C. R., & DYMOND, ROSALIND F. (Eds.) *Psychotherapy and personality change*. Chicago, Ill.: Univer. Chicago Press, 1954.

ROSENTHAL, D. Changes in some moral values following psychotherapy. *J. consult. Psychol.*, 1955, 19, 431–436.

SEEMAN, J. A study of the process of nondirective therapy. *J. consult. Psychol.*, 1949, 13, 157–169.

SEEMAN, J. Counselor judgments of therapeutic process and outcome. In C. R. Rogers & R. F. Dymond (Eds.), *Psychotherapy and personality change*. Chicago, Ill.: Univer. Chicago Press, 1954.

SEMON, R. G., & GOLDSTEIN, N. The effectiveness of group psychotherapy with chronic schizophrenic patients and an evaluation of different therapeutic methods. *J. consult. Psychol.*, 1957, 21, 317–322.

SHEERER, ELIZABETH T. The relationship between acceptance of self and acceptance of others. *J. consult. Psychol.*, 1949, 13, 169–175.

SNYDER, W. U. An investigation of the nature of nondirective psychotherapy. *J. gen. Psychol.*, 1945, 33, 193–223.

SNYDER, W. U. The present status of psychotherapeutic counseling. *Psychol. Bull.*, 1947, 44, 297–386.

SNYDER, W. U. *Group report of a program of research in psychotherapy*. State College, Pa.: Pennsylvania State Coll., 1953.

STOCK, DOROTHY. The self concept and feeling toward others. *J. consult. Psychol.*, 1949, 13, 176–180.

TEUBER, H. L., & POWERS, E. Evaluating therapy in a delinquency prevention program. *Res. Publ. Ass. Nerv. Ment. Dis.*, 1951, 31, 138–147.

THETFORD, W. N. An objective measurement of frustration tolerance in evaluating psychotherapy. In W. Wolff & J. A. Precker (Eds.), *Success in psychotherapy*. New York: Grune & Stratton, 1952.

TUCKER, J. E. Measuring client progress in client-centered therapy. In W. U. Snyder (Chmn.), *Group report of a program of research in psychotherapy*. State College, Pa.: Pennsylvania State Coll., 1953.

VARGAS, M. J. Changes in self-awareness during client-centered therapy. In C. R. Rogers & Rosalind F. Dymond (Eds.), *Psychotherapy and personality change*. Chicago, Ill.: Univer. Chicago Press, 1954.

WILCOX, G. & GUTHRIE, G. Changes in adjustment of institutionalized female defectives following group psychotherapy. *J. clin. Psychol.*, 1957, 13, 9–13.

WILLOUGHBY, R. R. A scale of emotional maturity. *J. soc. Psychol.*, 1931, 3, 131–136.

ZAX, M., & KLEIN, A. The criterion in evaluation studies of psychotherapy. Unpublished manuscript, Univer. of Rochester, 1958.

Method Factors in Changes Associated with Psychotherapy[1]

DESMOND S. CARTWRIGHT
WILLIAM L. KIRTNER
DONALD W. FISKE

The practice of client-centered therapy has been accompanied by various persistent research efforts to document and to understand therapeutic process and outcomes. Within these various efforts, one stream of work has concentrated on detailed examination of the varieties of personality change

Reprinted from *Journal of Abnormal and Social Psychology*, 1963, 66 (2), 164–175, with the permission of American Psychological Association and the authors.

[1] This study was supported largely by a grant from the Ford Foundation to the Counseling Center, University of Chicago. The Social Sciences Research Committee of the University of Chicago also made several small grants to the principal investigators to assist in collection and analysis of data.

The authors would like to express their appreciation to the staff of the Counseling Center, University of Chicago, for their extensive support and collaboration in making this research possible. The authors are particularly indebted to Jane Blare, Rosalind Dymond Cartwright, and Sophie Fox Kirtner who served as diagnosticians, and to Raleigh Lyles, Donald Peterson, and Richard Robertson who provided valuable assistance in the collection and processing of the data.

concomitant with psychotherapy (Cartwright & Roth, 1957; Gibson, Snyder, & Ray, 1955; Rogers & Dymond, 1954). Throughout this stream of work, the evidence requires the conclusion that certain important questions about personality change itself should be directly raised and investigated: Is such change a global modification of an entire personality, or is it a series of modifications of essentially separate parts or aspects of a personality? Using the language of traits, one may fomulate the question as follows: Do all relevant personality traits change together, or are there groups of traits such that changes in one group are uncorrelated with changes in other groups? Answers to these questions are essential both to the understanding of psychotherapeutic change and to research seeking the correlates of such change.

Answers to the questions as posed above may be sought through the application of factor analytic methods. Somewhat analogous to the Spearman-Thurstone controversy about the nature of intelligence, the present dilemma may be stated as a question: Are the personality changes concomitant with client-centered therapy best described by a single general factor or by a multiple-factor representation?

This question is further complicated, however, by the finding that different variables measured by the same instrument (e.g., MMPI) show concomitant changes (Gibson et al., 1955). Moreover, available evidence indicates that different variables arising from self-report instruments tend to change together; that the same is true for different variables arising from therapist ratings; and that little relation is indicated between the self-report and rating variables (Cartwright & Roth, 1957).

The foregoing discursive considerations and research results lead to several specific questions about personality changes associated with psychotherapy:

1. Is such personality change general over all variables (i.e., is such change single-dimensional)?

2. If not single-dimensional, then is each factor specific to the variables from a single measuring instrument?

3. Or, is each factor specific to the variables from a single viewpoint or class of observer, such as therapist or client?

4. Or, is each factor specific to a defined personality variable as measured by each of several observer-instrument combinations?

5. Or, is each factor specific to a group of such personality variables, each measured by several observer-instrument combinations?

Pointedly and directly, these questions concern the nature of the domain of personality changes associated with psychotherapy. And further questions immediately follow: Is personality change during psychotherapy similar to or different from personality change after the termination of psychotherapy? Before the start of a course of psychotherapy, is prediction of personality change possible? What relation, if any, has length of therapy with personality change? Can certain variables that describe the personality and behavior of the thera-

pist be shown to influence critically personality changes in the clients?

Questions 1–5 and related further questions imply a certain research design: Question 1 requires that a large sample of clients be tested before and after therapy on a wide selection of personality variables. Question 2 requires several measuring instruments, each of which would yield measurements of a set of conceptually distinct personality variables. Question 3 requires that several classes of observers each generate measurements on a variety of personality variables. Question 4 requires that several observer-instrument combinations be used to measure the same defined personality variable. Requirements for Question 5 may be met through fulfillment of those for the first four questions.

The question concerning personality change after the termination of therapy requires that the same battery of tests be administered at some follow-up date. A point 18 months after termination was selected.

Except for the question of therapist influence, the design of the present research was dictated by the requirements of all foregoing questions. Table 1 gives a schematic outline of the design.

In the present paper, only material pertaining to the nature of personality changes will be reported. Other aspects of the total research, some questions about which have been raised in the preceding paragraphs, will be reported in subsequent papers.

METHOD
Fourteen Behavioral Adequacy Scales

The rating scales used in this study were designed to give maximum coverage of variables investigated in previous research. The literature on personality changes associated with psychotherapy was reviewed (Cartwright, 1957a, 1957b), and variables were classified according to conceptual content. For example, decreasing Depression in the MMPI (Gallagher, 1953), increas-

TABLE 1

SCHEMATIC OUTLINE OF RESEARCH DESIGN

Observer source	Instrument	Data collection points		
		Pretherapy	Posttherapy	Follow-up
Clients	Preliminary interview form	+		
	Posttherapy questionnaire		+	
	Follow-up questionnaire			+
	MMPI	+	+	+
	Q sort (Butler & Haigh, 1954)	+	+	+
	Social attitude scales (O'Neil & Levinson, 1954)	+	+	+
	14 Behavioral Adequacy self-rating scales[a]	+	+	+
	Marginality questionnaire			+
Therapists	14 Behavioral Adequacy rating scales[a]	+	+	
	Rating of integration	+	+	
	Rating of liking for client	+	+	
	Posttherapy questionnaire		+	
Diagnosticians	14 Behavioral Adequacy rating scales[a] on TAT protocols	+	+	+
	14 Behavioral Adequacy rating scales on therapy interview recordings	+	+	
	14 Behavioral Adequacy rating scales on structured interview recordings			+
	Ratings of liking for client by TAT and interview diagnostician	+	+	+
	Typology ratings on therapy interview recordings	+	+	
	Sentence completion test	+	+	+
	Rorschach	+[b]		
Other	WAIS	+[b]		
	Number of weeks pre- to posttherapy		+	
	Number of interviews		+	

[a] The Behavioral Adequacy scales are described in the text.

[b] Due to testing load it was decided to administer the Rorschach and the WAIS each to only half of the total sample.

ing positive self-reference (Raimy, 1948), and increasing self-ideal correlation (Butler & Haigh, 1954) were, among other variables, deemed categorizable under the notion of "increasing contentedness with self."

Fourteen such categorizing conceptions were elaborated to encompass as completely as possible the range of previous research variables; ratings, test scores, clinical judgments, etc. A 10-point rating scale was then developed for each conceptual variable.

Each scale had five anchor positions, each anchor position ranging over two scale points. The positions ranged from an extremely low level of adequacy (anchor at Scale Points 1 and 2) to optimal functioning (anchor at Scale Points 9 and 10). Several different modes of inadequate behavior were described for each of the numerically lower anchor positions on the scales, on the assumption that the same level of inadequate behavior may be expressed in a variety of ways.

The following are two sample anchors from the low end and one anchor from the high end of one scale (Scale II, Adequacy of Contentedness re Relationships with Others, Roles, etc.).[2]

1 and 2 (a): The person feels extremely uncomfortable with others, feels that relationships with others are strained, never flow easily and relaxedly, are devastating to a sense of contentment. Relating to others is a source of great discomfort and dissatisfaction to him. Being around others, functioning in a role toward or with them, dealing and communicating with them—social and interpersonal exchange—are a continuing and very great strain upon him. "I don't like the way relationships go." "I feel awful around people." "I just feel completely nervous in social gatherings." "I simply don't know what to do around people." "People just bother me so much." "People are so difficult to get along with, just impossible."
"I feel extremely uncomfortable in relationships with others."
"I feel a kind of awful strain when I'm with other people."
1 and 2 (c): The person is extremely unquestioning of and unconcerned with his relationships with others, role functions, etc. Relationships are occurrences or experiences which happen as they do and go on or cease as they do. With respect to relationships there is an unmoving unconcern, an utter ignoring or disregard of them. Elaboration upon them is minimally sparse.
"I rarely think about relationships with other people."
"I almost never pay any attention to relationships with other people."
9 and 10: The person expresses a basic contentment with respect to relationships with others. In general, his experience of interaction is of a smooth interpersonal flow—an experience of comfort and satisfaction in his personal and social exchanges. The person is calm around others, enjoys being around others. Interactional discomforts, role discomforts, interpersonal dissatisfactions, are transient experiences; for, in dealing with others, whatever the momentary situation, the person indicates his continuing interpersonal functioning as experienced with much that is satisfying and much that is comfortable, with a very obvious sense of contentment in that functioning.
"I feel relaxed and comfortable with people in general."
"I feel pretty much at ease with people and get a good deal of satisfaction out of my relationships with others."

Below each main paragraph of an anchor may be seen two single statements (e.g., "I feel a kind of awful strain when I'm with other people"). While scales containing complete anchors as shown were used by diagnosticians, clients and therapists used scales having only such single statement anchors. All raters were instructed to consider all anchors for a given scale and to choose the one most appropriate and the one next most appropriate anchor for describing the particular subject. Nomograph scoring was achieved through giving double weight to the first choice, single weight to the second choice and summing. The resulting scores could range between 1 and 13 points for each scale as used by any rater.

Names of the 14 scales are shown in Table 3. Clients rated themselves at the pretherapy and posttherapy testing sessions. Therapists rated their clients immediately after the first and after the last interview. Diagnostician ratings were obtained for two kinds of material: TAT transcripts and therapy interview recordings. The TAT protocols were based on 12 cards: 1, 2, 3BM, 4, 5, 6BM, 10, 11, 13MF, 16, 17BM, 19. The interviews were the first and last interviews of a given client's series of therapy sessions.

---

[2] The full scale, "Adequacy of Contentedness re Relationships with Others, Roles, etc.," has been deposited with the American Documentation Institute. Order Document No. 7336 from ADI Auxiliary Publications Project, Photoduplication Service, Library of Congress; Washington 25, D.C., remitting in advance $1.25 for microfilm or $1.25 for photocopies. Make checks payable to: Chief, Photoduplication Service, Library of Congress.

Other Instruments Referred to in the Present Study

Clients:

1. Posttherapy Questionnaire. This form sought biographical data and also included a series of items about the client's experience in therapy and reasons for terminating. A typical item was:

1. In general how satisfied are you with what your therapy accomplished? (not satisfied, somewhat satisfied, pretty well satisfied, very well satisfied)

Since the several questions about the experience in therapy yielded highly correlated answers, a single composite score was computed from them.

2. MMPI. The full-scale Minnesota Multiphasic Personality Inventory was taken by the client at home. After a testing session, he was given the MMPI booklet and furnished with instructions to complete it in privacy without discussion with others. He was provided with a stamped addressed envelope for return of the material. The tests were scored on the standard scales and four others.

3. Q Sort. The sort was the same as that used in previous studies at the Counseling Center (Butler & Haigh, 1954). The sort consists of 100 statements drawn from counseling protocols. It includes such statements as: "I put on a false front"; "I am a failure"; "I feel adequate"; "I can usually make up my mind and stick to it." The measure obtained was the Q adjustment score (Dymond, 1953).

4. Social Attitude Scales. These include the Ethnocentricism (E), Traditional Family Ideology (TFI), and Religious Conservatism (RC) scales developed by Levinson and others (O'Neil & Levinson, 1954). A single form contained items for all three scales, with items from each randomly dispersed throughout. The form was entitled "Attitudes to Social Issues." Subjects were instructed:

Mark each statement in the left margin according to how much you agree or disagree with it. *Please mark every one.* Write in: +1, +2, +3; or −1, −2, −3, depending on how you feel in each case.

+1: I agree a little   −1: I disagree a little
+2: I agree pretty   −2: I disagree pretty
      much   much
+3: I agree very   −3: I disagree very
      much   much

There were 39 items altogether. Typical items were:

(E) One trouble with Jewish businessmen is that they stick together and prevent other people from having a fair chance in competition.

(TFI) A child should never be allowed to talk back to his parents, or else he will lose respect for them.

(RC) Every explanation of man and the world is incomplete unless it takes account of God's will.

The relation of social attitude measures to changes in psychotherapy has been shown in several studies (e.g., Gordon & Cartwright, 1954).

Therapists:

1. Rating of Integration. Attached to the therapist form of the 14 Behavioral Adequacy scales was a 10-point rating scale. Raters were asked to rate "the present psychological adjustment" of the client. The scale had anchors throughout. At Point 1 the anchor was: "Most extreme maladjustment"; at Point 10 the anchor was: "Optimal adjustment (fully functioning, optimal maturity)."

2. Rating of Liking. Also attached to the 14 Behavioral Adequacy scales was a 10-point scale for rating of the extent to which the therapist liked the client. The scale ranged from 1, "I dislike him very much" to 10, "I like him very much." Verbal anchors were given for each point.

3. Posttherapy Questionnaire. With slight changes in wording, this form matched the client posttherapy questionnaire. A typical item was:

In general how satisfied are you with what therapy has accomplished for this client? (not satisfied, somewhat satisfied, pretty well satisfied, very well satisfied)

Once again, a composite score was derived from these questions since the responses were highly correlated. In addition, the therapist was asked to rate the outcome of therapy using the nine-point success rating scale from several previous studies (Rogers & Dymond, 1954).

Diagnosticians:

1. Sentence Completion Test. This test was adapted from one devised and used by Thelen and his coworkers (Thelen, Stock, Ben-Zeev, Gradolph, Gradolph, & Hill, 1954). Originally it had been planned to have the 14 Behavioral Adequacy scales applied also to the SCT protocols. In pretesting, however, the obtained interjudge reliabilities were extremely low; consequently it was decided to utilize the original Thelen-Stock variables. Ultimately we included only those variables which had substantial interjudge reliability: these variables refer mainly to interpersonal attitudes of Fight, Flight, Dependency, Pairing, and Work. The subject may "accept" an item such as "When Hal felt angry with the group, he . . ." by completing with a response such as "came out and told them." The score would be 1 point for the variable "Accept fight." Thirteen such variables were included in our analysis.

2. Ratings of Liking for Client. These scales were identical in form with that used by the therapists. The diagnosticians (TAT and interview) rated on the basis of their reaction to the protocol. These ratings were included so that we might judge the influence of the rater's overall affective response upon his 14 Behavioral Adequacy ratings.

Psychometric considerations:

1. Ordering of Scale Points. Diagnosticians were given the full scales. Since the ordering was explicit, we may assume there were no special problems about the ratings or about change scores obtained by subtracting pretherapy scores from posttherapy scores.

The clients and the therapists were given each scale in the form of a set of 11 to 19 statements. The several statements for each modality were consecutive but the blocks were randomized so that there was no systematic progression (e.g., from low to high) in the total listing for each of the scales. Hence the accuracy of the scale positioning of each statement is of importance. For any one modality, there would be little difficulty: the several successive statements rather obviously progress from low to moderate adequacy. However, the matter of correspondence between modalities presents possible difficulties: e.g., does the statement for Point 3 for Modality *a* represent the same degree of inadequacy as the statement for 3 for Modality *b*? This correspondence between modalities was reviewed by the group of three investigators who developed the scales. It was also checked by having independent judges scale the statements in terms of adequacy. While the scale positions determined from these latter judgments differed in some instances from those we had established originally, the fundamental ordering was supported. The occasional discrepancy did not appear to justify departing from the basic a priori structure. It will be noted that our focus was on intraindividual comparisons between pre- and postscores, not on interindividual comparisons which would more frequently be across modalities.

2. Reliability of the Scales. For a group of 30 students tested twice with an interval over 2 weeks, the median of the stability coefficients for the 14 scales was .68. Evidence for internal consistency was obtained by testing our assumption that a subject's first and second choices would have equal or adjacent values. For several groups (students, clients, and therapists), the analyses of such correspondence between first and second choices yielded medians between 75 and 85%.

3. Ratings by Diagnosticians. It was

financially impossible to have each TAT protocol and each interview rated by two diagnosticians. Hence we had one person rate all the TAT's, pre and post, and a separate judge rate all the interviews. Thus while a particular change score might be influenced by idiosyncrasies of the single judge, it would not be accentuated by inter-judge differences. The TAT protocols were censored to eliminate cues indicating whether they were pre or post and were given to the judge in random groups which included both pre- and postprotocols. It was not possible to conceal from the inter-view rater whether an interview was early or late. However, the early and late inter-views were randomized in the order in which recordings were rated, with the re-striction that the ones for any single case were well separated in the sequence.

Before each diagnostician began to rate, she studied the scales until she was fully familiar with them. Practice materials were rated by each diagnostician and by another judge, the ratings being compared and dis-cussed to maximize consensus of the inter-pretation and application of the scales.

4. Change Scores. Change scores, the basic data of this study, have an inherent source of unreliability, above and beyond those sources associated with the level or status scores at pre- and posttherapy. The reliability of a change or difference score is equal to the mean of the reliabilities of the two compared scores when these scores are not correlated with each other. The higher the correlation between these scores, the lower the reliability of the change score (cf. Gulliksen, 1950, pp. 351–355). In a study where the two scores are obtained from the same person at different times, some degree of correlation can be expected. While no attempt was made to estimate the reliability of our change variables di-rectly, it must be emphasized that these reliabilities are undoubtedly no better than fair.

The analysis of change scores depends more heavily upon the validity of the as-sumption of equal intervals than do some other operations. Consider a variable which may appear to be an equal-interval scale but which actually is stretched out at one end (e.g., raw reaction time). While such a condition may have little effect on a prod-uct-moment correlation between two such variables, it will bias change scores: an in-terval of two steps at one end of the scale may not be equal to a two-step interval at the other.

Another problem arises from the fact that a change score is correlated with the two level scores from which it is derived. In our case, we would expect a positive correlation with posttherapy score and a negative correlation with initial score (cf. Lord, 1956, 1958; McNemar, 1958). We have quite intentionally made no adjust-ment of change scores for differences in initial level. We have formulated our goal as the determination of the factors in raw change scores, regardless of the role of such components as initial scores. The de-termination of the correlates or predictors of change is being deferred for later in-vestigation.

There are substantive reasons for not correcting change scores for initial level. Insofar as the objectives of both therapist and client are to make the client more ade-quate in the areas of his greatest relative deficiencies, both are concerned, in effect, with raising his low (unfavorable) scores and have little or no concern with raising his moderate or high (favorable) scores. Therefore partialing out initial scores may also partial out the very effects that are sought in the study.

Subjects

The sample for this study is composed of 93 subjects. A summary of certain char-acteristics of the sample is given in Table 2. The subjects represent a major portion of the applicants seeking psychotherapy at the University of Chicago Counseling Cen-ter between November 1956, and March

TABLE 2

CHARACTERISTICS OF THE SAMPLE

Student or community		Age		Sex		Marital status		Length of therapy[a]	
Student	45	Range	17–52	Male	52	Married	36	Range	3–181
		Mean	28.8			Single	50		
Community	39	Median 27		Female	41	Divorced	2	Median	26
						Separated	5		

[a] Number of interviews.

1958. The Counseling Center provides client-centered therapeutic service to students of the university and to residents of the Chicago area, on a mainly self-referral basis.

Only two restrictions were placed upon subject participation in the present study: he must have had not more than six interviews of formal psychotherapy, of any kind, within the 3 years prior to his present application for therapy; and he must be willing to participate in research. The restrictions on participation introduced no significant selection bias, since approximately 95% of those applying to the Counseling Center for therapy during the project intake period met these criteria, and were thus eligible as subjects in this study.

A total of 106 subjects was accepted into the project and given the battery of pretherapy tests. Of this total, 12 were attrition cases: 1 subject did not appear for therapy after completing the pretherapy testing; 3 subjects terminated with only one interview; 8 subjects had more than one interview but did not complete the battery of posttherapy tests. The range in number of interviews for the attrition cases was 0–13, inclusive. The sample was reduced to the final number of 93 complete cases by the death of one subject during the course of psychotherapy. (To complete the collection of data, 6 of these 93 clients were posttested after at least 71 interviews but before they terminated therapy.)

With respect to social status, the sample may be characterized as predominantly middle class, a rather large proportion of the subjects occupying white-collar and professional positions. A few subjects occupied very high status positions, senior executive or managerial roles. Another few subjects occupied skilled and unskilled labor positions.

In terms of presenting problems, or clinical characteristics, the present sample appears to be typical of the population of clinical subjects described for the Counseling Center by Rogers and Dymond (1954).

Therapists

Of the 30 therapists, all trained in client-centered therapy, 22 were males, 8 were females. Therapists ranged in experience from 1 year through 24 years. The 5 most experienced therapists (more than 5 years of experience) saw 18 cases; the 14 least experienced therapists (first year interns with at least 6 months of training beyond the practicum level) saw 36 cases. The 11 therapists with intermediate experience saw 39 cases. The range of cases seen per therapist was 1–8, with a median of 3.

Procedure

For each of the 79 measures taken at pretherapy and again at posttherapy, the pretherapy score was subtracted from the posttherapy score, yielding a difference or change score. In addition, there were the three scores from the clients' and the therapists' posttherapy evaluation of change, obtained through questionnaires, and two measures of length of therapy. (The log of the number of interviews and the log of the number of weeks between first and last interviews.)

Each of these 84 change measures was transformed to standard scores which were analyzed on UNIVAC by a program yielding Eigenvectors of principal axes directly from the scores. Extraction was stopped after the sixteenth factor, the last several factors extracting about the same amount of variance (2%) from the data. These factors were then rotated on ILLIAC by a varimax program, yielding an orthogonal simple structure.[3]

The rotations yielded a relatively good simple structure. Examination of the rotated factor matrix with the aid of representative plots of pairs of factors supported the judgment that the orthogonal structure provided a satisfactory solution. While small moves on some factors might have been carried out to produce a somewhat tighter but slightly oblique structure, the interpretations of the factors would not have been changed. (Such rotations would have produced small correlations between Factors 1 and 3, and between Factors 1 and 4. At a later time, the same procedures were carried out on UNIVAC for the 79 pretherapy scores. Once again, 16 factors were extracted and rotated. Subsequent to these analyses, the ratings of the first and last interviews by a diagnostician were completed. These ratings on the 14 scales and on Liking were then added to the other scores and two correlation matrices were computed, one for the 94 pretherapy measures and one for the 99 change measures.)

RESULTS

Table 3 shows the rotated factor matrix for change variables. Only the first five

[3] We are indebted to Henry Kaiser and J. H. Snyder of the University of Illinois for their assistance in carrying out this analysis.

factors are reported here as being clearly interpretable.

Major Change Factors

The first factor reflects the change in the client's perception of his adjustment, the degree to which he moves, in his reports, from feeling upset and in difficulties to feeling comfortable and adjusted. Most of the high loadings are for MMPI scales: Social Desirability, Ego Strength, and K scores go up; Manifest Anxiety, Social Introversion, and D go down. Several of the 14 scales as reported by the client also go up, as does his Q sort adjustment score. This factor may be tentatively labeled Change in Favorableness of Client Self-Evaluation.

The second factor is clearly Change in TAT Adequacy. The change scores derived from the TAT diagnostician's ratings on the 14 scales and on Liking have, with one exception, loadings between .65 and .86 on this factor. No loading for other measures exceeds .33; the great majority are below .10.

On the third factor, all of the high loadings are derived from the several judgments made by the therapist, each of these variables having a loading of at least .32 and the majority being above .50. The only other appreciable loadings are for the composite index from the client's posttherapy questionnaire and the client's self-ratings on Scales 1 and 3, these three being in the low 30s. This factor obviously represents the Therapist's Perception of Change.

Factor 4 is largely a doublet involving the Hs and Hy scales from the MMPI but including loadings in the 30s and 40s for other MMPI scales: F, Sc, L, Pt, K, Pd, and D. Change in reported symptomatology, especially somatic, seems to be the core of this Hs-Hy Factor.

The fifth factor is primarily a doublet characterizing Length of Therapy. No other variable has a loading greater than .24

with the exception of the two scores based on the therapist's posttherapy evaluation of change or success (cf. Cartwright, Robertson, Fiske, & Kirtner, 1961).

Remaining Factors

The first five change factors are strong in terms of amount of variance accounted for and appear to be clear-cut as to meaning; four of them also resemble in form or content the factors found in previous studies. The remaining factors are more difficult to evaluate. On the one hand, each accounts for an appreciable part of the total variance (in the order of 2% each). On the other hand, there are a number of reasons for questioning their significance.

1. Since the basic data, change scores, presumably have relatively low reliability, one must guard against overinterpretation.

2. While the first four factors are also factors in the initial scores, no other shows any close correspondence to any initial factors.

3. For each of the first four factors, the mean change for each variable loaded highly on the factor is generally considerable and the changes are toward the optimal ends of their scales. For the last 11 factors, the mean changes are typically smaller, often being close to zero for variables loaded only on the given factor. In such cases, the changes are more bidirectional than unidirectional. While the possibility exists that meaningful changes on one variable may occur in both directions in different clients, the pattern approaches that expected on retest without intervening effects.

4. For the first five factors, the variables with major loadings intercorrelate substantially (all r's but one are above .21, the value required for significance at the .05 level). For the last 11, the corresponding intercorrelations never exceed .45 and frequently are less than .21. The median intercorrelation among the variables for each of the latter factors is typically below .21. (These correlations may of course be de-

pressed by the dissimilarity of their loadings on other factors.)

5. Most of the latter 11 factors have a pattern characterized by high loadings for one or at most two variables, all other loadings being moderate or low. It appears likely that this peaking results in part from the extraction of factors by a method equivalent to factoring a correlation matrix with unity in the diagonal cells.

6. Separate intensive analyses of Factors 8 and 12 failed to support the hypothesis that each of these factors emerged because a few clients made substantial gains on the relevant variables while the great majority did not.

Interview-Diagnostician Ratings

As mentioned above, the ratings by the diagnostician who listened to the first and last interviews are included in the intercorrelations but not in the factor analyses completed at an earlier date. Examination of the intercorrelations makes it quite evident that the interview-diagnostician's ratings would have formed a separate factor if they had been included in the analysis of change scores. The 15 change measures derived from these ratings have consistent positive correlations with each other, with a mode in the 30s. The intercorrelations between these change measures and those from other sources are systematically near zero, with but occasional exceptions: a couple of other variables might have small loadings on this conjectured factor. It is also quite clear that this cluster would be entirely independent of Factors 4 and 5 (Hs-Hy and Length).

Pretherapy Factors

The factor analysis of the pretherapy scores yielded a series of factors, the first four corresponding almost exactly with those found for the change scores, but in different order; TAT Diagnostician's Perception of Adequacy, Favorableness of Self-

TABLE 3

ROTATED FACTOR MATRIX

Source	Variable	Factors and loadings				
		1	2	3	4	5
Client self-ratings	Contentedness with Self (Impulses, Emotions)	51	—01	34	03	05
	Contentedness with Relationships to Others	45	03	24	—20	—15
	Evaluation of Own Capacity	25	03	30	—16	—24
	Evaluation of Own Behavior	—12	—02	03	18	—14
	Evaluations of Others	28	05	—01	—08	11
	Quality of Anticipations	21	—09	12	—01	11
	Choice Process for Courses of Action	68	—07	00	00	—01
	Goals-Means Consideration in Courses of Action	40	—03	—05	—09	—21
	Energy Deployment over Courses of Action	21	—06	10	—09	—07
	Personal and Interpersonal Considerations	45	—01	06	03	04
	Interpretation as to Source of Felt Disturbance	06	00	—06	—04	—07
	Differentiation of Own Feelings, Tensions, etc.	36	—06	02	—18	18
	Perception of Other People	20	—12	—01	14	—01
	Quantity and Range of Emotional Response	34	—06	12	—03	—17
	Q sort adjustment score	66	—07	22	01	—04
	Social attitudes: Ethnocentrism	—05	—16	—06	06	—01
	Social attitudes: Traditional Family Ideology	—10	—11	—11	—17	—01
	Social attitudes: Religious Conservatism	20	—13	—07	—19	—11
	Client posttherapy questionnaire: Composite	26	17	32	02	15
	MMPI: "?"	—15	—06	—03	02	02
	MMPI: L	—25	03	12	40	01
	MMPI: F	36	10	00	44	06
	MMPI: K	65	07	07	—37	—03
	MMPI: Hs	09	—15	02	84	06
	MMPI: D	69	—09	20	35	—05
	MMPI: Hy	23	—12	01	79	—04
	MMPI: Pd	10	14	14	37	—03
	MMPI: Pa	16	05	—03	11	04
	MMPI: Pt	52	04	24	40	—07
	MMPI: Sc	44	07	03	41	—16
	MMPI: Ma	—18	12	—17	—01	10
	MMPI: Si	74	—04	21	04	05
	MMPI: Es	61	02	10	19	00
	MMPI: MA	82	08	22	13	—10
	MMPI: SD	83	03	18	11	—10
	Log weeks in therapy	—06	—03	—03	—03	88
	Log number of interviews	—13	—04	16	03	90
Therapist ratings	Contentedness with Self (Impulses, Emotions)	19	04	66	—08	02
	Contentedness with Relationships with Others	21	02	76	08	03
	Evaluation of Own Capacity	33	16	64	04	03
	Evaluation of Own Behavior	11	—13	47	—06	—17
	Evaluations of Others	06	—07	65	—05	—06
	Quality of Anticipations	03	—03	76	12	—15
	Choice Process for Courses of Action	—14	—10	71	04	—06
	Goals-Means Consideration in Courses of Action	05	05	75	02	03
	Energy Deployment over Courses of Action	11	02	59	—12	02
	Personal and Interpersonal Considerations	13	33	47	02	—11

TABLE 3—*Continued*

ROTATED FACTOR MATRIX

Source	Variable	Factors and loadings 1	2	3	4	5
Therapist ratings— *Continued*	Interpretation as to Source of Felt Disturbance	02	01	49	−14	23
	Differentiation of Own Feelings, Tensions, etc.	−02	01	56	16	−02
	Perception of Other People	16	00	44	02	00
	Quantity and Range of Emotional Response	03	00	32	−09	−02
	Liking	−10	−09	32	−01	23
	Integration	15	06	71	07	22
	Posttherapy questionnaire: Composite	12	16	64	11	46
	Success	12	20	65	00	42
TAT ratings	Contentedness with Self (Impulses, Emotions)	15	82	05	02	03
	Contentedness with Relationships to Others	04	80	−02	−05	07
	Evaluation of Own Capacity	06	77	06	02	08
	Evaluation of Own Behavior	−08	86	00	−01	−07
	Evaluations of Others	−02	76	−04	−07	−19
	Quality of Anticipations	00	83	−01	06	20
	Choice Process for Courses of Action	06	78	12	−06	−09
	Goals-Means Consideration in Courses of Action	12	82	03	−03	−03
	Energy Deployment over Courses of Action	03	27	10	06	−14
	Personal and Interpersonal Considerations	09	71	02	−01	02
	Interpretation as to Source of Felt Disturbance	02	65	02	−10	−02
	Differentiation of Own Feelings, Tension, etc.	−07	77	01	−06	04
	Perception of Other People	−18	69	00	−01	−10
	Quantity and Range of Emotional Response	−07	74	05	13	09
	Liking	−02	77	−03	−03	00
Sentence completion variables	Accept: Fight	−04	−02	−02	−08	23
	Accept: Dependency	−10	−08	−02	−14	−15
	Accept: Pairing	10	15	−02	−09	21
	Accept: Work	16	−09	05	−05	06
	Overt fight	−17	03	04	−21	−06
	Overt flight	02	−21	16	−05	01
	Overt dependency	09	10	−01	02	−01
	Overt pairing	−01	03	04	−14	−12
	Overt work	19	04	15	00	−03
	Overt emotionality	−07	00	−15	−15	18
	Total covert	−27	17	04	27	−09
	Total fight	−12	−08	−03	00	03
	Ideation	−18	−09	−04	−10	25

Note.—Decimal points and plus signs omitted.
The change scores were obtained by subtracting the pretherapy scores from the posttherapy scores. However, the signs for all MMPI variables except K, Es, and SD were reflected because the majority of clients had lower numerical scores after therapy on these variables.

Evaluation, Therapist's Perception and Adequacy, and Hs-Hy. The remaining factors tended to be associated largely with technique or instrument: there were two from the Sentence Completion and one from the three Social Attitude scores. The others typically had one loading of .6 or .7 and several between .3 and .5. None of these latter 12 factors closely corresponded to any of the factors in the change analysis.

DISCUSSION

Results of this study are highly consistent with previous findings. Change factors tend to be associated with point of view or role (e.g., Cartwright & Roth, 1957), with type of data (e.g., Gibson et al., 1955), or combinations of these (e.g., Nichols & Beck, 1960). With the possible exception of the Gibson et al. results, the ratings from any one person other than the client load on only one factor, and typically on a factor specific to that source. On the other hand, in at least two studies (Nichols & Beck and the present one), the client scores yield more than one factor. Table 4 shows suggested similarities, where possible, of present factors with those of previous studies.

TABLE 4

SUGGESTED MATCHING OF PRESENT FACTORS WITH THOSE OF PREVIOUS STUDIES

	Factor				
	1	2	3	4	5
Present					
Gibson, Snyder, and Ray (1955)	3	—	1	6	—
Cartwright and Roth (1957)	P	—	Q	—	—
Nichols and Beck (1960)	A	—	B	D	—

Our study yielded no clear discriminant validation of our 14 scales (Campbell & Fiske, 1959). Even when the same variable was being assessed by different persons, there were only minimal tendencies for the correlations for the same variable to be high compared to those between different variables. While this finding may indicate deficiences in these scales, the overall finding of these four studies is the predominance of method factors over substantive factors drawn from more than one method.

It must be noted that all four studies involved clients in university of counseling centers. The mean number of interviews was roughly 10–40 in the several groups. Although method factors predominated in these four analyses, it seemed possible that a somewhat different picture would emerge for a group of subjects who had undergone much longer therapeutic experiences.

We took a first step toward investigating the possibility that the findings might be different for a group with substantial therapy. We isolated a subgroup of 28 cases who completed a course of therapy with 37 or more interviews. We selected two variables providing relatively pure representations of each of the first four factors and of the Interview-Diagnostician cluster. A majority of the possible intercorrelations between these variables were computed. The results were quite comparable with those for the entire sample: there was no evidence suggesting that change variables might be more highly intercorrelated for a population undergoing a considerably longer course of therapy.

The phrase "method factor" has been used above to indicate that several of the factors tend to be associated with specific methods of measurement. In these four studies, each method utilizes a particular body of data, such as a kind of protocol, and an observer-respondent playing a special role. Thus the TAT-diagnostician worked from the transcribed TAT protocols and was a disinterested party. The interview-diagnostician listened to selected interviews and was also disinterested. The therapist heard all interviews and saw the client during them, and was in the role of helper to the client. The client had all these data, plus all of his other experiences, outside the therapy and testing rooms, but was a deeply involved participant. We believe that these differences in role and in available data are responsible for the essential independence of the change factors. We also believe that each factor has some degree of validity: each represents some aspect of the changes that occurred during the course of therapy. The preponderant influence of method, however, makes impossible at this time any confident delineation of substantive dimensions of change, with the possible exception of that suggested by the *Hs-Hy* factor.

It has been suggested to us that all of the changes we analyzed depend on client statements which in turn stem from his perception of himself. Such an interpretation would require some communality among the diverse measures of change and therefore among the several factors. The evidence is to the contrary. The intercorrelations among the change scores are typically near zero: they do not yield a positive manifold. The factors are orthogonal and their plots indicate that an oblique solution would produce only minimal correlations between factors. Specifically, it should be recalled that the *Hs-Hy* factor is clearly differentiated from the factor indicating Change in Favorableness of Client Self-Evaluation even though the latter has high loadings for several other MMPI scales.

The interpretation suggested to us does call attention to the fact that all of our measures were derived from the psychotherapeutic interviews or from the testing situation. How promising are other sources of data and other observer-respondents? Such factual data as changes in the client's job or job responsibilities and changes in avocational and recreational activities could be analyzed although their significance would be problematical. Professional evaluations could be made on the basis of special interviews or other diagnostic procedures. Lay opinions could be obtained from significant others or from associates less involved with the client. It is quite likely that the change measures from each of these three sources would yield an additional factor: each source would involve a separate type of data and a distinct viewpoint subject to potential distorting influences. Since the judgments of others before and after therapy would usually be made with knowledge that psychotherapy had taken place, they could provide only relative, not absolute, measures of change.

The problem of obtaining adequate assessments of the effects of psychotherapy may have to wait further developments in the measurement of personality. The recent work of Cattell (1957) and of Cattell and Scheier (1961) promises substantial improvement through the application of prefactored objective test measurements. In the meantime, the presence of method factors seriously impedes any attempt to determine the specific substantive changes occurring in any given client.

Moreover, even the application of prefactored objective test batteries would still require concomitant use of precisely such clinical and real-life sources of evidence as the client himself, the therapist, clinical diagnosticians, friends, and so on. The business of neurosis and recovery exists and is exhibited only in the contexts of the self, family, friends, employers, and clinical practitioners. We feel that our data were obtained in such manner as to maximize the possibility for persons in some of these various roles to agree about what they saw in a client's changes. Yet there was generally little agreement. Nor was there systematic disagreement, however: e.g., client's ratings did not correlate negatively with diagnosticians' ratings.

The absence of systematic agreement or disagreement might suggest that none of the conceptual variables employed in our research attains a degree of interent meaningfulness such that persons in different roles can agree or disagree systematically. If this suggestion is correct, then it has an important implication precisely for the lines of further development in the measurement of personality. Specifically, it means that the conceptual variables themselves must be radically revised. A desirable conceptual varible in the domain of neurosis and recovery through psychotherapy would likely have at least one principal quality: observers in different roles can systematically agree or disagree about it. A second prerequisite would be that of inherent meaningfulness. All observers might easily agree, that, following a sudden loud noise, a patient's galvanic skin response has changed in a certain direction and amount. But what such a change might signify would be unclear. In particular, its relevance to daily functioning in ordinary interaction with others is in doubt. Yet it is precisely for such daily functioning that the appropriate conceptual variables must have inherent meaningfulness.

What might be the nature of at least one such conceptual variable? It must permit systematic agreement or disagreement between different classes of observers, and also have the same degree and nature of inherent meaningfulness to all of them. We find it impossible, on the basis of existing research, to think of even one such variable. The search for such variables would seem to be the next important task for research in the field of theory evaluation.

On the more positive side of present interpretive possibilities however, it appears that changes in psychotherapy may be viewed in the manner suggested by Leary and others (e.g., Leary & Coffey, 1955) with regard to diagnosis. Our Factor 1 is similar to their Level II—patients' self-descriptive ratings on check list and MMPI; our Factor 2 is similar to their Level III—interpersonal themes attributed to heroes in TAT stories; our Factor 3 is similar to their Level I—ratings of patient's behavior by therapist. (Another interpretation in terms of levels is made by Gibson et al., 1955.)

The total picture from all the studies of change in psychotherapy has clear implications for the experimenter planning a study to compare two types of treatment or some other investigation requiring a criterion for change associated with treatment. Such a person must choose between: a composite criterion based in some fashion on changes assessed from several points of view by different methods; and a set of separate criteria, each derived from a single instrument or source. No single test score, no one rater's rating can be considered adequately representative of the diversity of measured changes accompanying psychotherapy.

One implication for goal setting and evaluation of outcome by therapists seems warranted. It appears that there are important dimensions of change which are not ordinarily attended to by the therapist. In the present study these dimensions are reflected in the viewpoints of the client and of the two diagnosticians. For the therapist to make a more complete evaluation of his case, it would seem necessary that he somehow gain access to these other dimensions.

REFERENCES

BUTLER, J. M., & HAIGH, G. V. Changes in the relation between self-concepts and ideal concepts consequent upon client-centered counseling. In C. R. Rogers & Rosalind F. Dymond (Eds.), *Psychotherapy and personality change.* Chicago: Univer. Chicago Press, 1954. Pp. 55–75.

CAMPBELL, D. T., & FISKE, D. W. Convergent and discriminant validation by the multitrait-multimethod matrix. *Psychol. Bull.,* 1959, 56, 81–105.

CARTWRIGHT, D. S. Annotated bibliography of research and theory construction in client-centered therapy. *J. counsel, Psychol.,* 1957, 4, 82–100. (a)

CARTWRIGHT, D. S. Methodology in counseling evaluation. *J. counsel. Psychol.,* 1957, 4, 263–267. (b)

CARTWRIGHT, D. S., ROBERTSON, R. J., FISKE, D. W., & KIRTNER, W. L. Length of therapy in relation to outcome and change in personal integration. *J. consult. Psychol.,* 1961, 25, 84–88.

CARTWRIGHT, D. S., & ROTH, I. Success and satisfaction in psychotherapy. *J. clin. Psychol.,* 1957, 13, 20–26.

CATTELL, R. B. *Personality and motivation: Structure and measurement.* New York: World Book, 1957.

CATTELL, R. B., & SCHEIER, I. H. *The meaning and measurement of neuroticism and anxiety.* New York: Ronald, 1961.

DYMOND, ROSALIND F. An adjustment score for Q sorts. *J. consult Psychol.,* 1953, 17, 339–342.

GALLAGHER, J. J. MMPI changes concomitant with client-centered therapy. *J. consult. Psychol.,* 1953, 17, 334–338.

GIBSON, R. L., SNYDER, W. U., & RAY, W. S. A factor analysis of measures of change following client-centered therapy. *J. counsel. Psychol.*, 1955, 2, 83–90.

GORDON, T., & CARTWRIGHT, D. S. The effect of psychotherapy upon certain attitudes toward others. In C. R. Rogers & Rosalind F. Dymond (Eds.), *Psychotherapy and personality change*. Chicago: Univer. Chicago Press, 1954, Pp. 167–195.

GULLIKSEN, H. *Theory of mental tests*. New York: Wiley, 1950.

KIRTNER, W. L., & CARTWRIGHT, D. S. Success and failure in client-centered therapy as a function of client personality variables. *J. consult. Psychol.*, 1958, 22, 259–264.

LEARY, T., & COFFEY, H. S. Interpersonal diagnosis: Some problems of methodology and validation. *J. abnorm. soc. Psychol.*, 1955, 50, 110–124.

LORD, F. M. The measurement of growth. *Educ. psychol Measmt.*, 1956, 16, 421–437.

LORD, F. M. Further problems in the measurement of growth. *Educ. psychol. Measmt.* 1958, 18, 437–451.

MCNEMAR, A. On growth measurement. *Educ. psychol. Measmt.*, 1958, 18, 47–55.

NICHOLS, R. C., & BECK, K. W. Factors in psychotherapy change. *J. consult. Psychol.*, 1960, 24, 388-399.

O'NEIL, W. M., & LEVINSON, D. J. A factorial exploration of authoritarianism and some of its ideological correlates. *J. Pers.*, 1954, 22, 449–463.

RAIMY, V. C. Self-reference in counseling interviews. *J. consult. Psychol.*, 1948, 12, 153–163.

ROGERS, C. R., & DYMOND, ROSALIND F. (Eds.) *Psychotherapy and personality change*. Chicago: Univer. Chicago Press, 1954.

THELEN, H. A., STOCK, DOROTHY, BEN-ZEEV, S., GRADOLPH, IDA, GRADOLPH, P., & HILL, W. F. *Methods for studying work and emotionality in groups*. Chicago: University of Chicago, Human Dynamics Laboratory, 1954.

Immediate and Long-term Symptomatic Course of Psychiatric Outpatients[1]

JEROME D. FRANK
EARL H. NASH
ANTHONY R. STONE
STANLEY D. IMBER

Almost all patients come to treatment for the relief of distress. The distress may take the form of bodily discomfort or disturbing psychic states—especially fear and depression. Ideally, the physician attempts to relieve this distress by discovering and removing its cause, whether it be a pathogenic bodily process, a traumatic memory, or inability to fulfill a social role. It is common knowledge, however, that the physician's activities may powerfully counteract the patient's distress, even when they appear unrelated to its cause. In fact, until recent years, since many pharmaceuticals were

Reprinted from *The American Journal of Psychiatry*, 1963, 120 (5), 429–439, with the permission of the American Psychiatric Association and the authors. Footnotes 2 and 3 have been omitted.

[1] Read at the 119th annual meeting of The American Psychiatric Association, St. Louis, Mo., May 6–10, 1963.

This study was supported in part by grants from the U.S. Public Health Service and the Ford Foundation, whose aid is gratefully acknowledged.

either worthless or harmful, the physician's prestige in our society, based on his success in relieving patients' distress, must have been based on these non-etiological remedies (1).

A deliberate way of relieving patients' distress without attacking its supposed etiology is the administration of a placebo—a medication that the patient believes is potent but which the physician knows to be inert. Placebos have long been known to have powerful beneficial effects, not only on psychic states but also on bodily processes.

On the basis of several drug studies in which placebos were used as controls, as well as a study of psychotherapy (2), it seemed to us that administration of a placebo offered a good means of exploring the non-specific component in all forms of therapy, including psychotherapy. Knowledge of the determinants and effects of this non-specific factor is a prerequisite to identifying the specific effects of different forms of psychotherapy (3).

This paper reports some findings concerning the immediate and long-term symptomatic course of 2 groups of psychiatric outpatients, totalling 109, who were administered placebos. The patients were selected according to the same criteria as in our study of psychotherapy (4), except that Negroes were not excluded and comprised ¼ of each population.

Each patient received a variety of personality tests and measures of autonomic activity, then was given a placebo and observed for about ½ hour while he took other tests. He was then asked to take the medication for a week, returned for re-examination, and was again examined 1 or 2 weeks later. A little over half the patients were re-examined after 2 to 3 years, at which time some were again given a placebo to take for a week and evaluated once more.

Each patient's level of discomfort was determined at the beginning of the initial interview, after the initial tests—but before receiving the placebo—at the end of the interview, and at the beginning of each subsequent visit.

METHOD

The first population (Population I) comprised 49 outpatients, all of whom had a psychoneurosis diagnosis. They were between 18 and 55 years of age, had at least a fifth-grade education, including ability to read and write, and were not currently receiving medication.

On the first research day the patient was seen by a psychologist who administered the criterion measures—a Discomfort Scale (5) and the Feeling, Energy, and Outlook sub-scales of the Hildreth Feeling and Attitude Scales (6). The Discomfort Scale consisted of 41 symptoms commonly found in psychiatric patients, each of which the patient rated as present or absent. If present, he then rated its severity on a 3-point scale. The psychologist also administered a battery of other tests and measures.[4] These procedures took about 1½ hours.

The patient then saw the research psychiatrist who took some readings of the patient's autonomic functions, then had him fill out a Hildreth Scale again and a short form of the Discomfort Scale.[5] He offered the patient a pill, presented as a new medication not yet on the market but found to help others with complaints similar to the patient's. During the 15 to 20 minutes in which the pill was "working" the patient filled out some personality tests, following which he completed a form indicating whether he felt the same, better, or worse. The psychiatrist then repeated the autonomic measures, prescribed a week on the pill, and asked the patient to return in a week to evaluate the results of treatment. Finally, the patient was seen again by the research psychologist, and again completed the Hildreth Scale (administration #3) and the short Discomfort Scale. He then took the patient to the receptionist, who gave him a week's supply of pills and an appointment to return in a week.

On the second research day, the patient completed the Hildreth and Discomfort Scales and saw the psychiatrist who got a statement from him concerning improvement and recorded certain physiological levels. The patient was prescribed another week of medication. This time (unbeknown to the patient) the pill was either placebo or active medication, depending on the patient's reaction during the previous week. The physical characteristics (size, shape, color, etc.) of the active and the inert pills were the same as the pills received by the patient during the previous week, but the patients who now received the ac-

---

[4] Personality tests and physiological measures are not further described since this report is not concerned with them.

[5] The Scale comprised 24 symptoms which could reflect rapid change. Symptoms that could not change within a single interview (e.g., insomnia) were eliminated.

tive drug were told that it was a more potent medication.[6] Finally, the patient completed a personality inventory, was given a supply of the prescribed pills and an appointment for the following week.

The procedure for the third research visit by the patient was similar, except that the psychiatrist's interview served both to evaluate the patient and to disengage him. In disengaging, the psychiatrist discussed further treatment in the psychiatric outpatient department with the patient when this was deemed necessary.

In the second study (N = 60), designed primarily as a replication, the general paradigm of the first was followed, with modifications not pertinent to this report. Two psychiatrists, rather than one, were used, the interval between the second and third visits was 2 weeks instead of 1, and all patients remained on placebo, with dosage levels set at the psychiatrist's discretion. Some tests were eliminated and new ones included.[7]

Twenty-eight patients (59%) of Population I were reinterviewed after 3 years and 34 members (60%) of Population II after 2 years, at which time the Hildreth and Discomfort Scales were administered and patients interviewed extensively about intercurrent illnesses, treatment, and current status.[8] Ten patients of Population I and 7 of Population II were also given medication. These patients were selected on the psychiatrist's judgment that their degree of distress warranted the treatment: a week's supply of placebo, with the information that they were receiving again the original medication or a "different" one, depending on which instruction the psychiatrist expected to be more effective. Pa-

tients were re-evaluated after one week and referred to the outpatient department.

RESULTS

Although the 2 populations were quite closely matched on such demographic variables as sex and race distribution, age, marital status, and education, population II scored considerably lower initially on both the Discomfort and Hildreth Scales than Population I—that is, they reported less subjective distress. Consistent with this, clinical diagnoses of anxiety or depressive reactions were made in 60% of Population I, but only 33% of Population II. This was counterbalanced by a higher rate of personality disorders (33% to 18%) and obsessive phobic reactions (12% to 4%) in Population II. Despite these differences, however, results presented below will demonstrate that the general trends in placebo responsiveness were comparable in the two populations, although the extent of change was less in Population II.

1. *Over-all Changes in Distress.* Regardless of criterion used or the interval measured, considerably more patients report improvement than worsening. This can be illustrated in Population I. If a 1-point change in discomfort score is the criterion, after a week about 80% of the patients are improved and 20% are worse. Using a change of 10 points, about 50% are improved but only 8% worse. With respect to patients' subjective global reports after 1 week on placebo, 55% said they felt better, and 12% said they felt worse.

After 2 to 3 years, and using the criterion of 1-point change in mean discomfort, 66% of Population I were better and 27% worse. The improvement rate was more striking when change was measured within the first interview, as described below.

These percentage findings, also quite similar for Hildreth scores, were reflected in mean scores for the total populations, and subsequent results will be reported in these terms. The mean changes in discom-

---

[6] For purposes of this report, responses of patients to placebos or to active medication during the second week are combined. The justification for this is given in another paper (7).

[7] For details see Reference 7.

[8] If further treatment was indicated, the patient was referred to the outpatient department.

fort in Populations I and II during the initial experimental period are given in Figure 1. Differences between the initial scores and the scores after a week were statistically significant (<.01) for each population. Further change after another week was significant (<.05) for Population I but not after 2 weeks for Population II. It should be noted that the absolute and relative declines in mean discomfort were less in Population II than Population I, confirming a repeated finding that amount of improvement is positively related to initial level of distress (2, 8).

2. *Relative Sensitivity of Different Symptoms.* Anxiety-Depressive and Somatic Subscales were constructed from the total Discomfort Scale.[9] As will be seen from Table 1, for both populations the former were scored higher initially and showed more positive responses than the latter, a finding consistent with earlier reported results (2).

3. *Changes in Distress within a Single Interview.* As already indicated, members of Population I received an abbreviated Discomfort Scale (limited to items that could change promptly) at the end of the initial testing period, just before receiving the placebo, and again at the end of the interview, approximately ½ hour after placebo was administered. The mean scores were compared with the means of the same items abstracted from the total scale given

[9] Ten and 16 items respectively were selected from the total scale and weighted by dividing the mean score on each subscale by the number of items in that subscale.

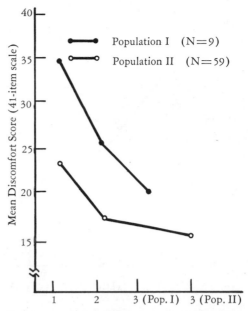

Figure 1. Mean discomfort scores at weekly evaluations for populations I and II.

before the initial interview, and again 1 and then 2 weeks later. Results are graphed in Figures 2 and 2a. Comparison of Figure 2 with Figure 1 indicates that, with respect to changes over the first week, the short form behaved like the full-scale in that scores showed an appreciable drop. In contrast to the full scale, however, no further significant decline occurred between the second and third weeks.

Figure 2a, which charts the course of distress change within the first day only, reveals that a precipitous decline in discom-

TABLE 1

WEIGHTED MEANS OF ANXIETY-DEPRESSION AND SOMATIC SUBSCALES
BEFORE AND AFTER PLACEBO

	N	AD (Weighted) *			SO (Weighted) *		
		Day 1 (Init.)	Day 2	Day 3	Day 1	Day 2	Day 3
Population I	49	1.26	.87	.71	.67	.57	.46
Population II	60	.92	.64	.58	.40	.36	.33

* AD ÷ 10, SO ÷ 16.

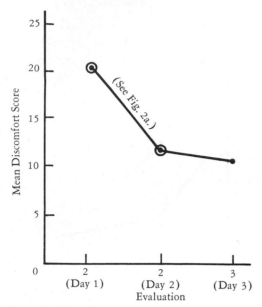

Figure 2. Mean discomfort score (24-item scale) at weekly evaluation for population I, (circled dots indicate corresponding points in Figure 2a.)

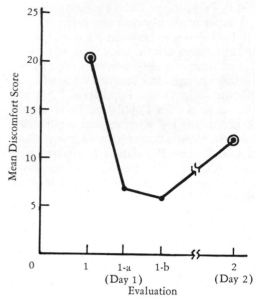

Figure 2a. Population I discomfort scores (24-item scale) within day 1 and on day 2, (circled dots indicate corresponding points in Figure 2.)

fort occurred on that day but that most of the decline took place even *before* the administration of the placebo. Over the subsequent week, some of the gain is lost, but the general effect persists to a statistically significant degree.

We did not repeat this particular use of the Discomfort Scale (short form) with Population II but instead relied solely on the Hildreth. Since this always taps the patient's immediate mood, its repetition at short intervals seems justified.

Figures 3a and 3b graph Hildreth Scale results of the 2 populations. It will be noted that an additional Hildreth reading was obtained from 34 Population I and 55 Population II patients in the outpatient department prior (usually by 3 or 4 days) to the first Research Day.[10] Figure 3a shows that mean improvement in mood starts with the patient's visit to the outpatient de-

partment and continues at a fairly constant rate throughout the 3-week period of observation. Population II showed less initial distress (higher Hildreth scores) throughout than did Population I and less response following clinic contacts, a finding congruent with Discomfort results.

The difference between the outpatient department and the first research day scores was quite similar to that between the latter and the second research day (after a week on placebo). Since the outpatient visit was regarded as solely diagnostic by those who conducted it, its effect on the Hildreth score, apparent at the very next clinic visit, suggests that any type of contact with a member of the hospital staff may be followed by relatively long-term symptomatic relief.

This possibility is supported by the changes in Hildreth score within the first research day, shown on Figure 3b. In both populations the mean Hildreth score registers considerable improvement even *before* administration of the placebo, as well

---

[10] The outpatient department routinely had most patients complete this scale and therefore those data were conveniently available for an additional evaluation of patient status prior to research intervention.

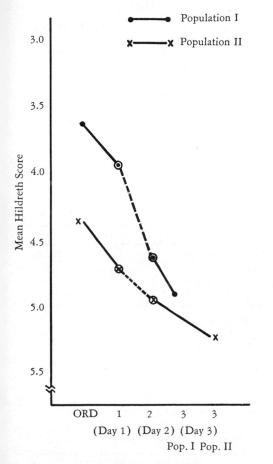

Figure 3a. Mean Hildreth scores by research day, (circled points in the two graphs correspond.)

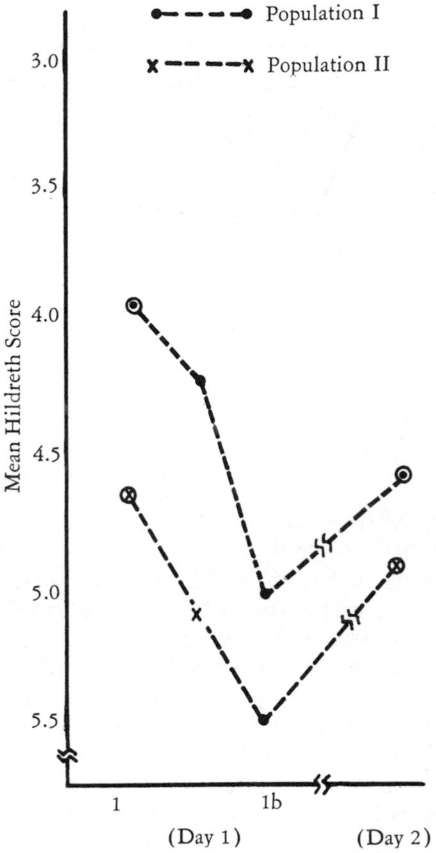

Figure 3b. Mean Hildreth scores during day 1.

as after. In short, the Hildreth Scale confirms the findings with the Discomfort Scale that relief of distress may be produced by activities not viewed as specifically therapeutic by the treatment staff, and that this relief need not be transient.

4. *Follow-up Results.* Twenty-eight patients (57%) from Population I and 34 patients (67%) from Population II returned upon request for follow-up evaluations. The follow-up interval was 3 years for Sample 1 (Population I returnees) and 2 years for Sample 2 (Population II returnees).

a. Mean changes in Discomfort scores at follow-up. As will be seen from Figure 4, changes in discomfort in the follow-up samples over the 1- or 2-week placebo period are not significantly different from those in the total population. The discomfort curves exhibit trends similar to the original populations, and both samples held their gains over the long-term period. Similarly anxiety and depression showed more change than the somatic symptoms.[11]

---

[11] These results also confirm those of the earlier study (9).

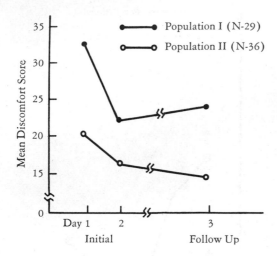

Figure 4. Discomfort scores of follow-up samples initially, at one week, and after 2-3 years.

Scrutiny of the scores of the individual follow-up patients shows that in both samples, those who improved most at the time of their initial placebo experience tended to relapse, but not to their initial level; those who improved least (most of whom got slightly worse) showed as much or more improvement at follow-up than they had initially. If the groups are trichotomized with respect to initial change, the number of shifts in each direction at follow-up are shown in Table 2. The corresponding mean discomfort scores for the upper and lower thirds are given in Table 3.

b. Results of administration of placebo at follow up. These data are summed up in Figure 5, which also includes comparable results from the psychotherapy study. Only the results with the Population I sample are considered here because, as was the case with other findings, Population II results were less impressive although showing similar trends. Comparison with Figure 4 reveals that those Population I patients who had relatively high discomfort scores at follow-up (and therefore received a placebo) tended to have higher scores initially than the full original population. They had, as a group, responded promptly

TABLE 2

CHANGE IN DISCOMFORT SCORES DURING FOLLOW-UP PERIOD OF PATIENTS WHO CHANGE DIFFERENT AMOUNTS DURING WEEK ON PLACEBO

Population I			
D1-D2 Change		D2-FU 1 Change	
	N	+ (Less (Discomfort)	− (More) (Discomfort)
Upper 1/3	10	2	8
Middle 1/3	9	6	3
Lower 1/3	10	6	4
Total	29	14	15
Population II			
D1-D2 Change		D2-FU 1 Change	
	N	+ (Less (Discomfort)	− (More) (Discomfort)
Upper 1/3	11	2	9
Middle 1/3	13	7	6
Lower 1/3	11	9	2
Total	35	18	17

TABLE 3

MEAN DISCOMFORT SCORES AT FOLLOW-UP OF PATIENTS WITH MOST AND LEAST PLACEBO RESPONSES AT FIRST WEEK

Mean Discomfort Scores			
	Upper Third		Follow-up
	N	Init.	1 Week	up
Sample 1	10	46	20	34
Sample 2	11	28	15	23
	Lower Third		Follow-up
	N	Init.	1 Week	up
Sample 1	10	22	28	20
Sample 2	11	14	19	7

to the placebo, but over the follow-up interval their discomfort climbed back approximately to its initial height. A re-administration of the placebo produced a drop of almost precisely the same order of magnitude as the initial one. The findings

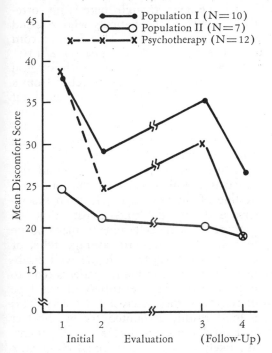

Figure 5. Discomfort scores of patients receiving placebo at 2-3 year follow-up visit.

Note: In the placebo studies, the interval between 1st and 2nd readings is one week, in the psychotherapy study, six months.

from the psychotherapy population are included since they show a pattern of response practically identical with that of Population I, even though the interval between first and second evaluations was 6 months instead of 1 week.

Despite the almost identical amount of discomfort drop in Population I on the first and second administrations of the placebo, no consistency was found with respect to individual patients. That is, many patients who responded the first time did not respond the second, and vice versa.

c. Patterns of intercurrent illnesses and treatment over follow-up interval. The type, severity, and duration of intercurrent illnesses and treatment received were obtained from the follow-up patients by a structured interview, and then categorized

by the interviewer and another rater on the basis of the recorded information, following the method of an earlier study(9). Because of the unknown reliability of the procedure, only the grossest findings seem worth considering. The findings are of interest in their similarity to those reported with psychiatric outpatients followed for 5 years in the previous study(9).

Most patients reported at least one illness for which they sought treatment during the follow-up period—82% of Sample 1 and 65% of Sample 2. Patients in both samples averaged about 2 distinguishable illnesses during the follow-up interval. In both samples the illnesses were about equally divided between chronic and acute (the former defined as of more than 1 month's duration, the later as a month or less), but the preponderance was minor. Only 20% of the illnesses reported by Sample 1 and 14% reported by Sample 2 were recurrences of illnesses for which the patient initially sought treatment. Eighty-five per cent of the visits of Sample 1 and 92% of the visits of Sample 2 were to non-psychiatric physicians. As reported by the patients, all but one of them took some sort of medication—if only aspirin—at least once during the follow-up period, and over half the drugs prescribed were sedatives, stimulants, or medications to counteract "functional" disturbances, such as carminatives or aspirin.

In short, psychiatric outpatients who appear for a follow-up seem representative of a mildly ailing population who define their complaints as caused by bodily disturbances and seek and receive medical treatment for them.

DISCUSSION

This study of placebo reactivity with over 100 psychiatric outpatients has confirmed other studies of this phenomenon in yielding a paradoxical result. On the one hand, reaction to a placebo seems to depend largely on properties of the situation in which it is administered. The degree of response varies with the nature of the criterion used to measure it, and individual patients show little consistency of response to placebo at different times. Enduring personality attributes related to placebo responsiveness, if such there be, are largely obscured by variables that change from one situation or time to the next.

Yet despite the will-o'-the-wisp quality of the placebo response on any one criterion, groups of patients receiving placebos show certain statistical regularities with respect to relief of distress that appear repeatedly. These regularities also appear in patients receiving psychotherapy, as well as in psychiatric outpatients followed over longer intervals, during which they have presumably been exposed to a variety of help-givers, many of whom do not offer formal treatment.

The major regularities follow:

1. No matter what the criterion, or the interval between the initial and later measures, considerably more patients report improvement than worsening.

2. The amount of improvement reported is related to the level of initial distress.

3. Anxiety and depressive symptoms contribute more to the level of initial distress and are affected more than somatic ones.

4. Maximal response occurs very promptly—within the initial day—and is due to the total situation rather than to the administration of the placebo. Patients showed as much or more relief of distress in the interval of examination and testing before receiving the pill than in the interval after it.

5. Over a period of time there is a trend for the total group of patients to maintain symptomatic improvement, but less than that shown in the initial interview.

6. On readministration of a placebo to patients who had initially responded favorably to it (or to psychotherapy) and relapsed, the group shows average response of the same order of magnitude as the initial one, even though there is no correlation between the patients who respond on the two occasions. This is in accord with the findings of Lasagna, et al.(10) that only 14% of patients with surgical pain consistently experienced relief from a placebo, though 55% reported significant relief on at least one occasion. It is at variance with Jellinek's patients with headaches, most of whom were either always relieved or never relieved by a placebo(11).

In attempting to interpret these findings, it seems useful to consider the long-term decline of distress separately from the response during the initial visit, although some of the same determinants may operate in both. The long-term average relief of distress is consistent with the well established fact that psychiatric patients tend to improve over time regardless of the type of treatment they receive(9, 12, 13). This is most readily accounted for by the fact that psychic distress fluctuates and patients are likely to make their initial psychiatric contact during an exacerbation or in the middle of a crisis. Hence any cohort would be expected to be more distressed, on the average, at their first clinic visit than subsequently. Thus, the final average Discomfort score in our patients was not below the level of those patients who initially showed least distress (and were unresponsive to placebo), as if this were the baseline that the whole population tended to approach.

In the same connection, patients sought the Clinic on their first visit but were sought by it at follow-up, so it would be expected that fewer of them at follow-up would be in a period of exacerbation, a finding reflected in their generally lower mean distress scores.

In attempting to account for the drop in discomfort during the first interview, it is useful to distinguish determinants of the initial discomfort from determinants of its rapid drop. The patient's initial report of discomfort is, of course, partly determined by his interpretation of his own internal state. Here two sources of distress may be distinguished—the stress that led him to seek the clinic's aid, considered above, and the stress of the clinic visit itself. It is scarcely necessary to describe in detail factors creating emotional turmoil at a first visit to a psychiatric clinic, such as the conflict between hope of relief and fear that nothing can be done or that one will be adjudged insane, the tense family interactions of which the clinic visit is the outcome, and so on. The novelty of the visit itself should not be overlooked. As Fishman, et al.(14), have shown, a novel situation arouses apprehension, and patients would be expected to have some anticipatory anxiety on this basis alone.

The patient's report of initial distress is also affected by the impression he wishes to make. He may, for example, exaggerate his distress to win sympathy or demonstrate his need for help, or minimize it to gain the Staff's respect for his fortitude. On balance, we could expect that in most patients factors increasing initial reported discomfort would be more powerful than those lowering it, so that the initial score would tend to be higher than the "base" level before the appointment was made.

Part of the drop in discomfort in the first interview, then, might be attributed to neutralization of the patient's anticipatory apprehension as the strangeness of the situation wears off and his initial fears are not realized. A further determinant of lowered scores on repetition of the Discomfort or Hildreth Scales may be the "demand characteristics" of the situation(15). If a test is repeated after the patient has been subjected to any type of procedure, the implication is that he is expected to give a different response the second time than the first. Since the clinic is supposed to be of help, the implicit expectation is that the patient will be "better" at the end of a visit than at the beginning. The patient's response to this expectation might account in part for the drop in distress scores, although this does not seem to explain the

fact that depression and anxiety improve most, except possibly on the assumption that the demand character of a psychiatric clinic is that psychic symptoms should show more improvement than bodily ones.

A final determinant of the initial drop in discomfort is probably that the patient perceives himself as receiving help; that is, his expectation of help is being met. Support for this assumption is found in Friedman's finding(16) of a relationship between a patient's expectancy of relief and his reported relief after the initial interview.[12]

The fact that the positive responses were at least as strong before receiving the placebo as after it is evidence that patients invest the hospital itself with a healing function, and assume that whatever goes on within its walls is done to help them. Reider(17) has described this phenomenon as transference to an institution, and Wilmer(18) refers to it as an "edifice complex."

Favorable responses of psychiatric patients to research procedures, especially in a hospital setting, have been frequently noted(19, 20), and have usually been attributed to the fact that the introduction of a research project increases the attention paid to patients by the staff. This would be expected to heighten the patient's expectation of help. That is, they may view the research procedures as treatment, and, in fact, some refer to them by this term.[13]

A finding that does not seem adequately accounted for by the above speculations is that patients who report the most distress initially improve most, both relatively and absolutely. One contributing factor may be that patients who show little distress on

[12] A detailed consideration of the role of expectancy in psychotherapy is found in Goldstein (21).

[13] Rashkis(19) has suggested that the introduction of order and reduction of randomness in the environment may also play a part. The confrontation of the patient with a battery of highly organized tests and measures in our studies may have a comparable effect.

the Discomfort or Hildreth Scales are either unwilling to communicate it, or the Scales may not be tapping the kind of distress that led to their coming to the clinic. In either case, even if their distress were relieved, this would not appear on our criteria.

Assuming that with many patients the criteria do reflect actual distress, two lines of thinking proposed by Gliedman, *et al.* (22) seem relevant to the tendency of the most distressed to show the greatest response. According to one, distress signifies both a state of disequilibrium and an effort to restore equilibrium. When a person fails to react to a noxious agent, like carbon monoxide or the bacillus of leprosy, or when he gives up the fight, he experiences little if any subjective distress. Suffering is the expression of an active struggle to cope with a harmful agent—it signalizes that recovery processes are already at work. Under these circumstances, slight environmental influences can tip the balance, and it seems reasonable to include among these anything the suffering patient perceives as potentially helpful, including placebos.

Perhaps one can go even further with Gliedman, *et al.* (22) and accept their analogy between placebo responsiveness and a conditioned response. In conditioning experiments it has been found that the intensity of the elicited conditional response varies exponentially with the size of the stimulus eliciting the unconditional response. In placebo studies, the unconditional stimulus may be whatever is causing the patient's distress, the conditional one the offer of help implicit in the treatment situation, including the placebo; hence the greater the distress, the greater the response.[14]

The ready responsiveness of symptoms of anxiety and depression to a clinic visit, the difficulty in finding strong relationships between this response and enduring personality traits of patients, and the marked inconsistency of response of the same patients at different times highlight the extent to which it is determined by properties of the immediate situation. It is consistent with the increasing body of work showing that a person's subjective experience is a function of the interaction of his perception of his bodily state with cognitive cues in his environment. A commonplace example is the hurt child who starts to cry—and presumably actually feels worse—when mother comes into view. Nowlis and Nowlis(24) found that a subject's descriptions of the feelings induced in him by a drug depended on whether others in the same face-to-face group received the same or different drugs. Schachter and Singer(25) in an elegant experiment demonstrated that subjects who received an injection of epinephrine without knowing what it was described themselves as feeling happy if exposed to an amusing situation and angry if placed in one that called for an angry response. From this standpoint, complaints of anxiety and depression are demands for help. Hence a given internal state of disequilibrium may be more likely to be perceived by the patient as anxiety or depression when he is in a situation that he perceives as containing potential for help than when in one that does not.

If perceptions of internal states are intimately bound up with cognitive cues in the situation, it becomes understandable why the placebo response is so inconstant. For example, on a follow-up visit the patient is asked to come to the clinic instead of coming on his own or being referred by an outside source, and he meets a different physician than he had originally. These differences in the cognitive aspects of the situation, as well as many possible others, might lead him to interpret his internal state, both before and after receiving a pill,

---

[14] In tangential support of the hypothesis that the placebo effect may be simply a conditioned response, Hermstein (23) reports that after rats have received repeated injections of scopolamine hydrobromide, which disrupts learned behavior, physiological saline mimics the effect to some extent. That is, they seem to show a placebo response to the saline, albeit a negative one.

quite differently than on his first visit; yet they are too subtle and complex to have been captured by our crude measuring instruments.

In short, a patient's report of his distress is a communication that depends at least on the following five interacting factors: 1) his actual internal state; 2) the form of the report he is asked to give; 3) his perception of the situation as a source of help or harm—his expectations from it; 4) his perception of its "demand characteristics"; and 5) the ends he seeks.

In view of this welter of determinants of the placebo response, the persistent difficulty in establishing clearcut relationships between it and personality traits or previous experiences is hardly surprising.

SUMMARY

Two populations of psychiatric outpatients totalling 109 were given placebos and the effect on their reported level of distress noted immediately and after 1 and 2 weeks on the placebo. Patients in both populations received special tests and measures before and after receiving placebo. Over half the patients in each group were re-examined after 3 and 2 years respectively, at which time some again received a placebo.

In both groups, whatever the criterion used or the time interval, a greater proportion of patients reported improvement than reported getting worse. The mean discomfort score dropped sharply during the first interview, before as well as after administration of the placebo, then tended to increase, but not back to the initial level. Maintenance on placebo did not increase the effect. The amount of improvement was related to amount of distress reported initially, and symptoms of anxiety and depression showed more improvement than somatic ones.

Patients showed little consistency in their responsiveness to placebo at different administrations, and we have been unable definitely to relate their responses to personality variables.

Various hypotheses to account for these findings are examined, with special reference to the role of cognitions in emotional distress and its relief.

BIBLIOGRAPHY

1. SHAPIRO, A. K.: *Am. J. Psychiat.,* 116, 298, 1959.
2. GLIEDMAN, L. H., *et al.*: *A.M.A. Arch. Neurol. Psychiat.,* 79, 345, 1958.
3. ROSENTHAL, D., and FRANK, J. D.: *Psychol. Bull.,* 53, 294, 1956.
4. FRANK, J. D., *et al.*:*Am. J. Psychiat.,* 115, 961, 1959.
5. KELMAN, H. C., and PARLOFF, M. B.: *J. Abnorm. Soc. Psychol.,* 54, 281, 1957.
6. HILDRETH, H. M.: *J. Clin. Psychol.,* 2, 214, 1946.
7. NASH, E. H., *et al.*: Selected Effects of Inert Medication on Psychiatric Outpatients. *Am. J. Psychother.* In press.
8. UHLENHUTH, E. H.: Trans. Fifth Res. Conf. Coop. Chemother. *Studies Psychiat. Res. Appr. Ment. Illness,* 5, 209, 1960.
9. STONE, A. R., *et al.*: *J. Nerv. Ment. Dis.,* 133, 410, 1961.
10. LASAGNA, L., *et al.*: *Am. J. Med.,* 16, 770, 1954.
11. JELLINEK, E. M.: *Biomet. Bull.,* 2, 87, 1946.
12. EYSENCK, H. J.: *J. Consult. Psychol.,* 16, 319, 1952.
13. ZUBIN, J.: *In* Cole, J. O., and Gerard, R. (Eds.); *Psychopharmacology: Problems in Evaluation.* Washington: Nat. Acad. of Sciences-Nat. Res. Council, 1959.
14. FISHMAN, J. R., *et al.*: *Arch. Gen. Psychiat.,* 6, 271, 1962.
15. ORNE, M. T.: *Am. Psychol.,* 17, 776, 1962.
16. FRIEDMAN, H. J.: *Arch. Gen. Psychiat.,* 8, 61, 1963.
17. REIDER, N.: *J. Hillside Hosp.,* 2, 23, 1953.
18. WILMER, H. A.: *Calif. Med.,* 96, 173, 1962.
19. RASHKIS, H. A.: *Arch. Gen. Psychiat.,* 2, 612, 1960.
20. FRANK, J. D.: *In* Brody, E. B., and Redlich, F. C. (Eds.): *Psychotherapy with Schizophrenics.* New York: International Universities Press, 1952.

21. GOLDSTEIN, A. P.: *Therapist-Patient Expectancies in Psychotherapy.* New York: Pergamon Press, 1962.

22. GLIEDMAN, L. H., GANTT, W. H., and TEITLEBAUM, H. A.: *Am. J. Psychiat.,* 113, 1103, 1957.

23. HERRNSTEIN, R. J.: *Science,* 138, 677, 1962.

24. NOWLIS, V., and NOWLIS, H. H.: *Ann. N. Y. Acad. Sci.,* 65, 345, 1956.

25. SCHACHTER, S., and SINGER, J. E.: *Psychol. Rev.,* 69, 379, 1962.

An Experimental Analogue of Psychotherapy for Anxiety Reduction

PETER K. LEVISON
MELVIN ZAX
EMORY L. COWEN

In an earlier paper (Cowen, 1960) an argument for the potential usefulness of an analogue approach to psychotherapy research was developed. Through such an approach, we strive to set up laboratory paradigms of complex psychotherapeutic interactions, hoping thereby to achieve greater precision of research control, as well as greater breadth and flexibility of measurement than is possible in the "natural" setting. While there are important limitations, notably in the area of generalization from results, inherent in the method, it is seen primarily as a complement to, rather than a substitute for, existing approaches to psychotherapy research.

"Outcome" analogues such as the present study presume the presence of an established "deficit" in functioning, whether due to natural conditions or to experimental induction. The analogue therapeutic interaction becomes the independent variable

Reprinted from *Psychological Reports*, 1961, 8, 171–178, with the permission of Southern Universities Press and the authors. Note 1, giving Peter Levison's affiliation, has been omitted.

and the impaired function becomes the criterion or dependent measure.

In the relatively brief history of the analogue method, we have witnessed the use of a variety of therapeutic techniques, ranging from simulation of broad systems such as psychoanalysis or client centered therapy (Kesner, 1954; Keet, 1948) to utilization of specific and delimited techniques (Haggard, 1947; Grossman, 1952; Wiener, 1955; Gordon, 1957; Dinoff, Rickard, Salzberg, & Sipprelle, 1960), and a wide variety of criterion deficit functions including word block (Keet, 1948), maze performance (Pomeroy, 1950), test behavior (Cowen, 1952; Grossman, 1952; Kesner, 1954; Wiener, 1955) and physiological function (Haggard, 1947; Gordon, Martin, & Lundy, 1959; Martin, Lundy, & Lewin, 1960).

Because of the widespread recognition of the central importance of the anxiety variable in psychotherapeutic transactions (O'Kelley, 1953), the present investigators were attracted to the possibility of setting up a laboratory paradigm of learned anxiety responses and to the exploration of the effectiveness of certain simulated psychotherapeutic functions with respect to "anxiety reduction." As our criterion measure of anxiety we selected an autonomic index [galvanic skin response (GSR)], not only because of the widespread prior use of this measure for such a purpose (e.g., Haggard, 1947; Thetford, 1952; Martin, 1956; Dittes, 1957a; Dittes, 1957b; Gordon, et al., 1959; Martin, et al., 1960), but also because of its inherent face validity as an indicator of physiological activity. While it is true that GSR may reflect on-going processes other than anxiety, and hence may be regarded by some simply as an index of autonomic activity, our experimental set-up, involving continuous physiological recording, was such as to make defensible the assumption that GSR changes did, for most Ss, reflect an emotional state akin to anxiety. In any case anxiety as we are using the term is operationalized in this study in terms of GSR response.

Our basic plan involved the establishment of a conditioned GSR (anxiety) response, which, on the basis of prior experimental evidence, we believed would remain stable for a substantial period of time (Diven, 1937). Next, Ss were to be assigned either to a "therapy" group, focussing technique-wise on the reinstatement of cues associated with the anxiety producing situation and the provision of opportunities to express affect connected with the aversive situation, or to a control group, in which Ss merely rested for a comparable period of time. However, since it was our intent that the therapist's demeanor be one of warmth, permissiveness, and encouragement of free expression, we were faced with the potential problem of trying to separate, after the fact, the "beneficial" effects of "therapy," if any, into components attributable to specific therapeutic techniques and those attributable to the general nature of the interpersonal interaction. For this reason we considered it desirable to initiate a "talk-control" group,

holding constant the nature of the interaction (i.e., its warmth, encouragement of expression, etc.), but confining the content to matters unrelated to the prior anxiety-producing experience and, in that sense, therapeutically inert. This type of control has been used elsewhere in therapeutic research (Mehlman, 1953; Wiener, 1955).

Underlying the study was the hypothesis that experimentally induced anxiety may be alleviated by a verbal interaction (simulating therapy) built upon the opportunity to explore cues and to cathart cue-related affect. Thus, we anticipated greatest anxiety reduction in our therapy group, and least in our control-group. Our expectation was that the "talk-control" group would, as a result of the beneficial effects of the understanding interpersonal interaction, fall between the therapy and the "time-control" groups in terms of our criterion of anxiety reduction.

METHOD AND PROCEDURE

The experimental procedure for all Ss, regardless of assigned group, consisted of three distinct phases lasting a total of $1\frac{1}{2}$ hrs. The first of these was the conditioning series, followed for each S by the assigned treatment condition (i.e., therapy, time-control, or talk-control), in turn followed by the extinction trials. One E ran all Ss through the conditioning and extinction trials. The other two Es, both PhDs in clinical psychology with considerable postdoctoral experience in psychotherapy, did the therapy and talk-control interviews alternately.

Subjects. Fifty-four undergraduate females, volunteers enrolled either in an introductory or an advanced (junior) level psychology course served as Ss.

Apparatus. Stimulus words were presented visually by a modified Phipps and Bird paired-associate learning apparatus. In this instrument a horizontal drum functions as a drive sprocket to move a continuous paper belt, on which two lists of stimulus words are printed. The belt is powered by an electric motor through a cam; each revolution of the cam moves the belt a specified distance. At each movement of the belt a new stimulus word is presented in each of a pair of small windows in the face of the box enclosing the apparatus. A pair of shutters raised by two other cams control the exposure time of the words. In this experiment only one word was exposed at a time. A complete list of words was presented through one window; then a second list was presented through the other. The instrument was regulated so that the belt moved a word into position every 10 sec.; the shutters were lifted exposing the word for 3 sec.

The unconditioned stimulus (UCS) was the activation of a loud buzzer attached to one of a pair of earphones worn by S. The buzzer proved to be an effective stimulus for eliciting a GSR, and is considerably easier to use than electric shock. The occurrence of the buzzer stimulus was automatically programmed by the closing of a circuit through holes punched in the paper belt. The interval between the appearance of the conditioned stimulus (CS), the word CHAIR, and the onset of the buzzer was 1.5 sec.; the buzzer fired for .5 sec. These durations were automatically controlled by a pair of Hunter Model 111A and 111B electronic timers. The timers and the relays in the circuit were enclosed in a sound resistant box and "white" noise constantly played into S's earphones to mask any extraneous cues.

A continuous measure of S's palmar skin resistance was obtained with a Hunter GSR amplifier (Model No. 731). A graphic record of the output from the amplifier was produced on an Esterline-Angus continuous ink-writing recorder (Model AW). A stimulus artifact representing the onset of the CS was included on the record. The palmar electrode and a padded box securing S's hand were constructed from the description of Haggard and Gerbrands (1947). Their method provides firm, continuous electrode contact without discomfort to S. The jelly used in the electrode cup by Haggard and Gerbrands was replaced by a sponge soaked in a 2.4% zinc sulphate solution. The ground electrode was of similar construction to the palmar one; it was strapped to the dorsal surface of the ipsilateral forearm following an application of electrode paste to the skin. The GSR circuit maintained a current of a constant value of approximately 40 micro-amp. through S.

Stimulus materials. Each list contained 74 five lettered words considered by Es to be emotionally neutral. The CS, *CHAIR,* occurred 21 times and appeared in the same ordinal positions on both lists. All the other words ("buffer" words) were included only once among the two lists.

Procedure. S was seated in a comfortable chair facing the windows of the stimulus presentation apparatus. A shield was fastened behind S's head to screen her view of the E and of the rest of the apparatus during the conditioning and extinction trials. The electrodes were attached to S and a trial "balance" of the GSR circuit was obtained. S was assured that no electric shock was used. She was then told that her task was to read aloud each word as it appeared in a window, but that it was not necessary to remember the words. Then the white noise was turned on and adjusted appropriately if S found it to be painfully loud.

Conditioning trials. The second and third exposure of *CHAIR* and every third presentation of the CS therafter were reinforced by the buzzer stimulus. S was considered conditioned when her GSR record met the following criteria: (a) a GSR was elicited by five of six consecutive presentations of the unreinforced CS; (b) within six consecutive presentations of the unreinforced CS there was not more than one instance in which a GSR to an unreinforced CS was smaller than one or more GSRs to a buffer word. If S failed to condition to the criterion by the end of the first list, that list was blocked and the second one was uncovered and presented. The two lists were presented in the same order for all Ss. Those Ss who still failed to meet the criterion by the end of the second list were dropped from the experiment ($N = 12$). After S was conditioned to criterion she was removed from the apparatus and told that there would be a 15 to 20 min. delay before the experiment could be resumed.

GSR measures. The measures taken were the differences in basal resistance between the low point within the 3-sec. interval when a word appeared and the following highest point within that interval. A transformation called the *square root of conductance change* described by Obrist (1958) was then applied to these data. This transformation has been found to act similarly to log transformations with the advantages that: (a) zero scores can be used, (b) it is simpler to compute, and (c) it yields smaller, more easily manipulated values. It involves multiplying the reciprocal of the GSR by 10^6 (thus eliminating decimals) and taking the square root of the resulting figure.

Treatment conditions. The *time control Ss* ($N = 11$) were merely escorted by E to an empty room nearby where they remained for 20 min. They were free during that time to read or to rest, as they chose. In no case did these Ss have an opportunity to have contact with another person during this waiting period.

Both the *therapy* ($N = 17$) and *talk-control Ss* ($N = 14$) were individually escorted to the nearby office of one of the two therapist Es, and were asked to talk with Dr. ——————— for a little while. An attempt was made by the therapist E to disassociate the treatment phase of the experiment from the prior and subsequent conditioning and extinction trials. Each therapy group S was told that we were interested in learning about reactions of individuals to various experiments in the psychology department and that we would like to find out about her reactions to the experiment in which she had just been an S. For

the talk-control Ss the comparable lead was that we would like to learn a little bit more about the background of individuals who were volunteering for our various psychological experiments; hence we had a series of questions to explore with her. From that point on except for the constant factor of a warm, interested orientation by the therapist E, the two types of interviews departed sharply.

With our therapy Ss the interview was conducted in an essentially open-ended style, taking off from the following question, posed immediately after the initial structuring remark: "Perhaps you could tell me how you feel about the experiment in which you've just participated." Ss were permitted to discourse spontaneously on this lead at whatever length they chose within the time limits imposed. There were, however, several specific points which had to be covered during the course of the contact. If these were not dealt with spontaneously, the therapist E gradually narrowed and made more specific the focus of the interview, so that each S would have an opportunity to react in each area. The specific coverage "musts" included: description of the actual conditioning procedure with emphasis on S's on-going feelings and anticipations, speculation as to the purpose of the experiment, feelings about E and the experimental room, mention of the words that were used in the observed list, and the function of the buzzer. Throughout, emphasis was placed on S's *reactions* and *feelings* with respect to the component cues in the conditioning situation.

In the talk-control situation E asked a series of specific questions, in a pleasant and interested manner, and each was pursued to the extent that the given S was responsive thereupon. The topics raised, in sequence, were as follows: What is your major area of concentration? What do you intend to do after graduation? What are your major extra-curricular activities? Where do you come from (home town and background and interests)? Contrast high school life with college life. How do you think college life might be made better?

All of the therapy and talk-control interviews were approximately 20 minutes in length (ranging from 17 to 23 min., comparable to the rest period for the control group). Whenever, in either of the two interview situations, an S requested specific information about the prior conditioning experience, E responded with a pleasant but firm refusal, indicating that such information would be provided by Mr. ——— upon completion of the experiment. A standard closing comment was made at the end of each of the two interview situations, as follows. "The information you have given us has been very helpful. We really appreciate your co-operation. I think Mr. ——————— is probably ready to complete the final part of his experiment now." The interviewer then escorted the S back to the original room in which the conditioning trials had taken place.

Rating scales. At the end of each interview, while Ss were being run on the extinction trials, the therapist Es rated them on a series of *crude* five-point rating scales. Five such scales were applicable to the therapy Ss: (1) extent to which S was able to perceive the basic purposes of the experiment spontaneously; (2) extent to which S was able to talk about her feelings coming from the experiment; (3) extent to which S was able to socialize and verbalize freely; (4) extent to which S ultimately was able to identify basic elements of the experience and basic cues involved; (5) estimated degree of anxiety of S during interview. In the case of the talk-control Ss only scales three and five were applicable. Finally, the "therapist" E wrote a narrative, clinically-oriented summary of the interview, this culminating in a prediction about what, in his opinion, was likely to happen on the extinction runs. Regrettably, the rating scales, narrative summary and prediction were something of a last minute after-thought in the experiment. Hence no reliability data are available for

the former, while the latter two leave much to be desired with respect to objectivity of data recording.

Extinction trials. After the intervening session S returned for the extinction trials. The same basic procedure was used as during conditioning except for the following changes: (a) the buzzer stimulus was never activated; (b) the entire first list presented during the conditioning trials, but none of the second, was exposed, regardless of the number of trials previously required for S to condition to criterion.

Finally, the purposes of the experiment were explained to S in detail, and she was strongly urged not to discuss it with anyone.

RESULTS AND DISCUSSION
Comparison of Groups

Our primary concern was with the determination of the effectiveness of the experimental therapeutic experience on the GSR. In order to do this we compared our three groups with respect to differences in anxiety level between the conditioning and extinction trials. For each S we computed a difference score (D-score) between the mean of the last six converted conditioned GSR's given to the CS *CHAIR* during the conditioning trials and the mean of the first six GSRs to the same stimulus during the extinction run. The grand mean D-scores for the three groups were $- 0.75$, $+ 1.36$, and $+ 6.30$, respectively, for the Therapy, Talk-Control, and Time-Control groups. In the relative sense, then, our three groups ordered themselves as anticipated; absolutely, however, this reflected only a modest decrease in anxiety for the Therapy group, a slight increase for the Talk-Controls and a fairly substantial increase for the Time-Controls.

These data were subjected to a simple analysis of variance in which the main effect of groups yielded an F ratio of 1.77 (non-significant). Thus, although our groups fall in the expected pattern, we must conclude that there are no significant differences among them with respect to change in anxiety level following the several treatment conditions. Inspection of the actual data reveals immediately that very considerable inter-subject variability was operating to reduce the likelihood of a significant F ratio. It is quite possible, following the argument raised by Lacey (1959) that our failure to obtain significant group differences may reflect an oversimplification in the selection of our outcome criterion, the GSR. Lacey argues that these are profound inter-individual differences in autonomic reactive systems, and that whereas some individuals might react very sensitively on GSR measures, others, similarly activated, may show their response primarily through another autonomic measure such as heart rate for example. The implication from Lacey's position is that their is merit in using multiple autonomic indices so that measures optimally sensitive to each S's response balance may be obtained. We would consider this to be a worthwhile probing point in further work with the type of paradigm explored in the present investigation.

Rating Scales and Clinical Predictions

In hopes of obtaining some further understanding of factors potentially relating to decreasing anxiety level following interview interactions, we undertook a series of empirical analyses, correlating post-interview rating scale scores for the five selected items with the GSR D-score. In the case of Items 1, 2, and 4 which were relevant only to the Therapy group the N for these correlations was 17. However, since Items 3 and 5 applied both to the Therapy and Talk-Control groups. It was possible to pool Ns for these analyses, yielding a total of 28 Ss.[2] With but one exception these rating scale scores failed to correlate with postinterview change in anxiety level. That

---

[2] Three Ss were lost for these analyses because we did not initiate the procedure until after they had been seen.

exception was Item 3 where a .408 correlation ($p < .05$) was obtained. This suggests that the greater S's ability to socialize and to verbalize freely during the post-traumatic interview the greater was her anxiety reduction likely to be during the extinction trials.

Our clinical predictions about the likelihood of drop in anxiety during the extinction trials were, as noted earlier, originally formulated in literary, narrative style. In order to utilize these data for purposes of statistical analysis, considerably greater objectification was needed. Accordingly, we set up an objective five-point scale ranging from "marked drop in anxiety expected," at one extreme, to "no change" at the other, and applied it to the prediction protocols. Considering the *post hoc* nature of this venture, the scale proved to be remarkably reliable, the correlation of the ratings of two judges for the pooled sample of 28 Ss being .945. We then correlated the predicted change scores with the actual GSR D-score. The resultant r of .334 barely falls short of significant at the .05 level.

We are somewhat intrigued by the implications of these two findings (i.e., the correlations between Item 3, the clinical predictions and GSR D-score). Though each represents a highly empirical, almost after the fact, datum they mesh consistently and dovetail well with E's observations. In our view the crucial component in both of these findings was S's ability freely to express affect. The conditioning procedure was definitely an unpleasant experience for most Ss, and quite probably instigated them toward the expression of negative affect and resentment. On the other hand, because Ss were undergraduates and Es college professors, we might say that there were situational determinants which represented barriers to free verbalization and socialization. Those Ss who, in spite of these situational obstacles, were able to socialize and to verbalize freely and spontaneously, appeared to derive the greatest benefit from the interview experience, at least insofar as our particular criterion is concerned. By contrast those Ss who tended to deny, to rationalize or to intellectualize their feelings (e.g., "That's a very ingenious experimental set-up Mr. ——— has devised") showed little GSR improvement. Thus it seems that the ability to verbalize easily and to express affect, including negative feelings and hostility, realistically prompted by the noxious experimental situation, may be a crucial factor in tension reduction as measured by GSR. The ability to react in this way may well be a favorable prognostic precondition to focal anxiety reduction following therapy. The present findings point to the desirability of further study of this subsidiary phase of the original problem in its own right.

SUMMARY AND CONCLUSIONS

An experimental analogue of psychotherapy designed to reduce anxiety level was described. A conditioned GSR (anxiety) response to the word *CHAIR* was established in 42 female undergraduates. These Ss were then assigned to one of three treatment conditions: *Time-Control*—in which they merely rested; *Therapy*—in which they interacted with a clinical psychologist in a paradigmatic therapy interview focussing on the reinstatement of cues associated with anxiety and the expression of affect thereupon; and *Talk-Control*—in which they spoke with professionally qualified clinicians about topics deemed to be therapeutically inert. Each of the treatment conditions lasted approximately 20 minutes, after which all Ss were run on a series of extinction trials. A GSR D-score was computed for each S based on differences between the last six conditioning trials and the first six extinction trials. Although the groups ordered themselves as predicted, with greatest drop in anxiety for the Therapy group and least for the Time-Controls, these differences failed to reach statistical significance. The greater S's ability to socialize and to verbalize freely in the inter-

view situation, the greater was the likelihood of drop in anxiety level on the extinction series.

REFERENCES

COWEN, E. L. Stress reduction and problem solving rigidity. *J. consult. Psychol.,* 1952, 16, 425–428.

COWEN, E. L. The experimental analogue: an approach to psychotherapy research. *Psychol. Rep.,* 1961, 8, 9–10.

DINOFF, M., RICKARD, H. C., SALZBERG, N., & SIPPRELLE, C. N. An experimental analogue of three psychotherapeutic approaches. *J. Clin. Psychol.,* 1960, 17, 70–73.

DITTES, J. E. Extinction during psycotherapy of GSR accompanying "embarrassing" statements. *J. abnorm. soc. Psychol.,* 1957, 54, 187–191. (a)

DITTES, J. E. Galvanic skin response as a measure of patient's reaction to therapist's permissiveness. *J. abnorm. soc. Psychol.,* 1957, 55, 295–303. (b)

DIVEN, K. Certain determinants of the conditioning of anxiety reactions. *J. Psychol.,* 1937, 3, 291–308.

GORDON, J. E. Leading and following psychotherapeutic techniques with hypnotically induced repression and hostility. *J. abnorm. soc. Psychol.,* 1957, 54, 405–410.

GORDON, J. E., MARTIN, B., & LUNDY, R. M. GSRs during repression, suppression and verbalization in psychotherapeutic interviews. *J. consult. Psychol.,* 1959, 23, 243–251.

GROSSMAN, D. An experimental investigation of a psychotherapeutic technique. *J. consult. Psychol.,* 1952, 16, 325–331.

HAGGARD, E. A. Some conditions, determining adjustment during and readjustment following experimentally induced stress. In S. D. Tompkins (Ed.), *Contemporary psychopathology.* Cambridge, Mass.: Harvard Univer. Press, 1947. Pp. 529–544.

HAGGARD, E. A., & GERBRANDS, R. An apparatus for the measurement of continuous changes in palmar skin resistance. *J. exp. Psychol.,* 1947, 37, 92–98.

KEET, C. D. Two verbal techniques in a minature counseling situation. *Psychol. Monogr.,* 1948, 62, No. 7 (Whole No. 294).

KESNER, L. S. A comparison of the effectiveness of two pschotherapy techniques in the resolution of a posthypnotic conflict. *J. clin. exp. Hypnosis,* 1954, 2, 55–75.

LACEY, J. I. Psychophysiological approaches to the evaluation of psychotherapeutic process and outcome. In E. A. Rubenstein and M. B. Parloff (Eds.), *Research in psychotherapy.* Washington D. C.: Amer. Psychol. Assn., Pp. 160–208.

MARTIN, B. Galvanic skin conductance as a function of successive interviews. *J. clin. Psychol.,* 1956, 12, 91–94.

MARTIN, B., LUNDY, R. M., & LEWIN, M. H. Verbal and GSR responses in experimental interviews as a function of three degrees of "therapist" communication. *J. abnorm. soc. Psychol.,* 1960, 60, 234–240.

MEHLMAN, B. Group play therapy with mentally retarded children. *J. abnorm. soc. Psychol.,* 1953, 48, 53–60.

OBRIST, P. A. An investigation of the claim of autonomic discrimination without awareness and the relationship of GSR conditioning to measures of skin conductance. Unpublished doctoral dissertation, Univer. of Rochester, 1958.

O'KELLEY, L. I. Physiological changes during psychotherapy. In O. H. Mowrer (Ed.), *Psychotherapy: theory and research.* New York: Ronald, 1953. Pp. 641–656.

POMEROY, D. S. The ameliorative effects of "counseling" upon maze performance following experimentally induced stress. *Amer. Psychologist,* 1950, 5, 327. (Abstract)

THETFORD, W. N. An objective measurement of frustration tolerance in evaluating psychotherapy. In W. Wolff and J. A. Precker (Eds.), *Success in psychotherapy.* New York: Grune & Stratton, 1952, Pp. 26–62.

WIENER, M. The effects of two experimental counseling techniques on performances impaired by induced stress. *J. abnorm. soc. Psychol.,* 1955, 51, 565–572.

Leading and Following Psychotherapeutic Techniques with Hypnotically Induced Repression and Hostility[1]

JESSE E. GORDON

Psychotherapy research has in general been refractory to experimental methods. A set of procedures is needed by means of which laboratory research into the influence of a variety of patient, therapist, and outcome variables may be conducted. These procedures, however, must be such that results may be generalized to clinical practice. The ecological validity required of such research makes it necessary that subjects be permitted a wide range of responses, as are patients in therapy. Such requirements make experimental control and direct behavioral measurement difficult.

These problems are not so acute when the experimental vairables are global ones

Reprinted from *Journal of Abnormal and Social Psychology*, 1957, 54, 405–410, with the permission of the American Psychological Association and the author. Note 2, containing the author's affiliation, has been omitted.
[1] This article is based upon a thesis submitted in partial fulfillment of the requirements for the degree of Doctor of Philosophy at the Pennsylvania State University. The writer wishes to acknowledge his indebtedness to Dr. George M. Guthrie and Dr. William U. Snyder.

such as directive vs. nondirective therapy, therapeutic success as defined by various criteria, and patient "maladjustment." However, systematic investigation aimed at building up a body of knowledge regarding therapeutic practices, instead of simply "proving" one school of thought to be superior to another, requires more refined control and manipulation of discrete, unitary variables rather than global ones. When a body of knowledge has been acquired in which the relationships among particular therapeutic practices and specific responses by patients are known, then a therapist may decide what effect he wishes to have on a particular patient and select his therapeutic techniques accordingly. Although this state of affairs may be an unattainable goal, it seems to be the only possible ideal at which the scientific therapist can aim.

With these considerations in mind, a set of experimental procedures was developed which seemed to possess ecological validity, which permitted a measure of control over the major client, therapist, and outcome variables, and which permitted the use of direct behavioral measures as well as psychometric methods. The experimental procedures involve the use of hypnosis to make normal subjects believe and act as if they had undergone a standard, mildly upsetting experience. The Ss have freedom to react to the experience in their own indiosyncratic ways. Reviews by Weitzenhoffer (9), Hull (5), and Rapaport (8) present much direct and indirect evidence to support the validity of generalizing from such hypotically stimulated reactions to reactions actually encountered in clinical patients.

The use of a standard mildly upsetting experience, hypnotically induced, puts control over an important patient variable into the hands of the experimenter. This kind of control is practically and theoretically impossible in field research in psychotherapy. The acquisition of such control by the experimenter represents the major advantage of this type of research over therapy research conducted in the clinic with a patient population.

Instructions to the hynotized Ss were designed to make them believe that they had been bumped into by a physical education teacher in high school and unjustly blamed for the incident. These instructions were patterned after those used successfully by Counts and Mensh (1). In addition, it was suggested to S that the therapist who was to interview him after he awakened bore some resemblance to the physical education teacher. Posthypnotic amnesia for the upsetting experience was also induced. These hypnotic instructions are based on a neurosis model which characterizes neurotically inappropriate behavior as resulting from an unconscious identification of the patient's present situation with an unpleasant and often unremembered experience in the patient's past.

The independent variables of this experiment were therapist's Leading (asking questions, making suggestions, etc.) and the therapist's Following (restating, reflecting, clarifying). These two kinds of therapist verbal behavior were selected for ex-

perimental comparison on the basis of investigations which indicate that they reflect a basic split among schools of psychotherapy (2, 4, 7). Roughly paralleling this split regarding the use of Leading and Following behaviors is a split in what is regarded as the important outcomes of therapy. Those who use Leading techniques tend to regard the lifting of repressions as the aim of therapy. Those who use Following techniques generally disclaim interest in the historical approach to therapy and focus instead on improvement in the patient's present interpersonal functioning as the aim of therapy. It seems appropriate, therefore, to employ measures of both types of outcome variables, repression and interpersonal functioning. The hypnotic instructions to forget the "traumatic" experience produce behavior analogous to repression, making possible the measurement of the lifting of represssion. The inclusion in the hypnotic instructions of a suggested similarity between the teacher in the traumatic experience and the therapist provides a situation analogous to transference, and thus makes possible some measurement of the inappropriate, "neurotic" interpersonal behavior of S.

The specific purpose of the present research, then, was to test a set of procedures for the experimental investigation of psychotherapy by applying them to a study of the effects of therapist Leading and therapist Following on hypnotically induced repression and on neurotic interpersonal functioning.

METHOD
Procedure

Sixty-two male college students volunteered to participate in "an experiment on hypnosis." Two group and then one individual training and screening sessions were held, out of which 26 of the volunteers emerged as susceptible enough to obey a hynotic suggestion to be amnesic for trance events. Of this group, the data on eight subjects were lost as a result of faulty recordings of the interviews. Thus, 18 Ss remained in the two experimental conditions, Leading and Following.

The Ss were appointed for the individual experimental sessions following the third training and screening session. During this third session they were instructed, while hypnotized, to imagine themselves in a situation in high school in which a physical education teacher accidently bumped into the S in a hallway, then blamed S for clumsiness and threatened reprisal. The S was instructed not to remember the incident after he was awakened and was told to have a daydream about it upon a signal. This served as a check on the acceptance of the hypnotic suggestions and as practice in covertly playing the role of an unjustly blamed person. Following this test, the graduate student "therapist" to whom S had been assigned was introduced to the subject. The S was then rehypnotized and told that the incident with the physical education teacher had actually occurred. In addition, it was specified that the physical education teacher looked "something like Mr. ————, the man who will be interviewing you soon." The instructions used to induce belief that the incident had actually occurred were those used with success by Erickson (3). In addition to Erickson's instructions, it was further specified that though S would not be able to recall the experience when he awoke, it would bother him, and he could spend the interview hour trying to figure out what was bothering him. The instructions made it permissible to recall the experience during the course of the interview. Before being awakened, Ss were made amnesic for the entire session, including the introduction of the therapist.

The S was then awakened and brought into the interview room for a 50-minute interview, which was tape recorded. Following the interview, S was again rehypnotized, permitted to recall the content of the previous hypnosis, and disabused of the experience.

The therapists were nine advanced graduate students in clinical psychology at the Pennsylvania State University. Each therapist was in possession of a statement describing the acceptable therapist verbal behaviors in the Leading and Following conditions. These were explained and discussed more fully in a group meeting with the therapists. However, the therapists were not told the nature of the dependent variables or that a paramnesia had been induced in the Ss. Each therapist appeared twice, once in each condition, in an effort to control intertherapist differences. The order in which each therapist appeared in the conditions was counterbalanced.

Typescripts were prepared from the tape recordings of the interviews. Therapist statements on all even-numbered typescript pages were categorized by the E as Leading, Following, and Miscellaneous as a check upon the extent to which the experimental conditions were realized.

Repression. The content of the experimental "traumatic experience" had been broken down into meaning units, and criteria for scoring recall of the units were prepared. Three independent graduate student judges scored the typescripts, using these criteria to obtain scores for an Amount Recalled measure of the extent to which repression had been lifted. The means of the recall scores assigned by the judges constituted the scores on this variable. Agreement among the judges was high ($r = .94, .98, .93$).

The judges were also asked to indicate the statement in each typescript containing each S's third scorable recall item. By locating these S recall statements on the tape recordings, it was possible to record the amount of elapsed time from the beginning of the interview, thus yielding a Recall Time score of the speed with which successful lifting of repression began to occur.

One other measure related to the lifting of repression was designated Recognition Time. To obtain this measure, the judges

TABLE 1

MEAN FREQUENCY AND PROPORTION OF
THERAPIST LEADING AND FOLLOWING STATE-
MENTS IN THE LEADING AND FOLLOWING
CONDITIONS

Measure	Leading Condition		Following Condition	
	Leading	Follow-ing	Leading	Follow-ing
Frequency:				
Mean	26.88	10.22	10.55	27.22
Sigma	12.22	8.48	10.93	13.64
Proportion				
Mean	.64	.21	.20	.65
Sigma	.21	.16	.14	.19

were asked to check the first *S* statement in each typescript which contained a verbalized awareness that the therapist, or someone like him, was familiar to *S*. Again, by locating the checked *S* statement on the tape recordings, it was possible to measure the elapsed time from the beginning of the interview to the point at which this kind of insight began to develop.

Hostility. Hostility related behavior of the *S*s was measured by means of rankings. Verbal descriptions of three aspects of hostility were given to three graduate students in a course in therapeutic interviewing at the University of Wisconsin, who then ranked the typescripts on each aspect. These hostility variables were (*a*) Extrapunitiveness, in which *S* attempted to convey his hostility to the interviewer in a direct manner, (*b*) Passive Hostility, in which hostility was expressed through negativism, uncooperativeness during the interview, and general resistance to the therapist, and (*c*) Disguised Hostility, in which *S*'s hostility was communicated in symbolized or other indirect fashion, such as discussion of hostile dreams, overemphasis on aggressive feelings toward others, etc. Coefficients of concordance revealed significant agreement among the judges in their rankings on the first two variables but not on Disguised Hostility,

which was therefore not included in further statistical analyses. Each *S*'s rank on the two hostility variables was the mean of the ranks assigned to him by the three judges. Kendall's tau was computed between the rankings on Extrapunitiveness and on Passive Hostility and was found to be nonsignificant. The two indexes were therefore regarded as independent.

RESULTS

The results of the classification of the therapists' verbal behaviors are presented in Table 1 in terms of frequencies and proportions.

Repression

Amount Recalled. Significance testing was in terms of the differences between each therapist's Leading and Following interviews. Six differences showed greater Amount Recalled in the Leading condition with two differences favoring the Following condition and one of zero value. A randomization test of the differences, described by Moses (6), indicates that this distribution of differences just falls short of significance at the 5 per cent level with a two-tailed test.

Recall Time. Analysis of Recall Time was again in terms of the differences between each therapist's Leading and Following interviews. Three differences showed faster recall in the Leading condition; five differences favored the Following condition, and one difference was zero. A randomization test of the differences indicates that this distribution does not depart significantly from chance ($p > .05$).

Recognition Time. The differences in Recognition Time between each therapist's Leading and Following interviews indicated more rapid recognition in the Leading condition five times, three differences favoring the Following condition, and one difference of zero. A randomization test of the differences indicates that this distribution does not depart significantly from chance ($p > .05$).

The correlation between Amount Recalled and Recall Time was $-.78$, between Amount Recalled and Recognition Time $-.55$, and $+.50$ between Recall Time and Recognition Time. All three correlations are significant at the .05 level. The very high correlation between Amount Recalled and Recall Time probably represents the extent to which these variables measure S's ability to repress and to conform to the hypnotic suggestions. On this assumption, an analysis of variance of errors of estimate in the regression of Amount Recalled on Recall Time was carried out. In effect, this procedure partialed out intersubject variability in conformity to the hypnotic suggestion. The results of this analysis are presented in Table 2.[3]

Table 2 indicates that the errors of estimate in the regression of Amount Recalled on Recall Time were significantly larger in the Following condition when differences among therapists are eliminated from the comparison. It would appear that in the Leading condition, Ss tended to verbalize the "repressed" material more nearly to the limits of their ability to recall; whereas in the Following condition, other variables be-

---

[3] It is important to recognize that this analysis is not an analysis of covariance. In this analysis, the matching variable (Recall Time) was obtained under the experimental conditions and was presumable affected by the conditions. In covariance analysis, the matching variable must be measured before the experimental conditions are imposed. The analysis of variance of errors of estimate as carried out here is, in effect, a test of the significance of the difference between the correlation between Amount Recalled and Recall Time in the Leading condition and in the Following condition. The analysis demonstrates that the correlation is very high in the Leading condition ($-.93$), thus the interpretation that Ss are recalling to the limits of their abilities in this condition; it is much lower in the Following condition ($-.63$), thus yielding larger errors of estimate and indicating that other factors have influenced the Amount Recalled, reducing it below the limits of the S's ability to recall as this ability is estimated from the Recall Time variable.

TABLE 2

ANALYSIS OF VARIANCE OF ERRORS OF ESTIMATE IN THE REGRESSION OF AMOUNT RECALLED ON RECALL TIME

Source	df	Mean Square	F
Between Treatment	1	62.94	12.87**
Among Therapists	8	17.66	3.61*
Residual	8	4.89	
Total	17		

* Significant at .05 level.
** Significant at .01 level.

yond the basic recall factors entered into the determination of how much recalled material was verbalized, thus producing larger errors of estimate and less verbalized recall. Differences among therapists were also found to be significant, which probably reflects differences in therapeutic skill.

The interviews were divided into those which were the therapists' first interviews and those which were second, and then analyzed in order to test the effect of therapist experience in this sense. Randomization tests of the differences indicate that first interviews produced significantly more recall than second interviews ($p < .05$), but Recall Time and Recognition Time variables were not significantly different from first to second interviews.

All interviews were then combined and ranked in terms of the number of Leading statements, the proportion of Leading statements, and on the three repression variables. Kendall's tau statistic was computed between all pairs of independent and dependent variables. The only relationship found that approximated significance was expressed by a tau coefficient of .31, with an associated probability of .075, between Amount Recalled and proportion of Leading statements.

Hostility

Mann-Whitney U tests indicate that there was no significant tendency for Leading or Following interview Ss to be ranked higher on either hostility variable. Chi square was computed between classification of the interviews as above or below the median rank on Extrapunitiveness and their classification in the same terms on Proportion Leading. The value obtained after correction for continuity was 3.56, just short of significance at the .05 level. Similar analyses between Extrapunitiveness and Amount Leading, and between Passive Hostility and Amount and Proportion Leading, yielded definitely nonsignificant results.

The rank order correlation between rankings on Extrapunitiveness and on Recognition Time was .44, which is significant beyond the .05 level. Passive Hostility was not significantly correlated with Recognition Time, and neither of the two hostility variables was found to be significantly related to the other repression variables. The relationship between Extrapunitiveness and Recognition Time would be expected on the basis of the nature of the experimental instructions regarding the similarity between the therapist and the teacher. An S who quickly "recognized" his interviewer would be expected to be, and was, more hostile toward him than one whose recognition was delayed. One cannot decide, on the basis of these data, whether the recognition led to the hostile expression or *vice versa*.

As in the analysis of the repression variables, the typescripts were divided into those for the therapists' first interviews and those for their second, and analyzed for any relationships between sequence and hostility. A Mann-Whitney U test yielded a probability of less than .01, including that Ss were significantly more extrapunitive in the therapists' second interviews than in their first. It will be remembered that there was also significantly less recall in these interviews.

DISCUSSION

The results of this experiment indicate that Leading therapist behaviors tended in the samples used to be more efficient in obtaining as much verbalization of "repressed" material as S was capable of. A review of the typescripts lends support to this interpretation; in the Following interviews one notes several instances in which Ss failed to pursue what appeared to be a productive line of thought, ostensibly because of the lack of stimulation from therapist.

The finding that therapists' first interviews were more productive than second interviews, in terms of the amount of recall, appears contrary to what one might expect. Second interviews should have reflected the insights gained by the therapists in their first interviews, and therefore might have been expected to be more productive. A suggested explanation for the findings is that the poorer results in the second interviews arose as a result of generally incorrect hypotheses developed by the therapists on the basis of their experiences in the first interviews. None of the therapists were able correctly to identify the nature of the experiment or the role of hypnosis after the first interview. Considering the many things about which Ss spoke in the interviews, it was highly probable that therapists would give undue weight to irrelevant verbalizations in forming hypotheses about the experiment and the Ss. This may be a function of the relative lack of experience of the graduate students who served as therapists. If this interpretation is valid, the danger of premature diagnostic hypotheses becomes apparent.

The significantly greater Extrapunitiveness of Ss in the therapists' second interviews is of interest. The relationship between Extrapunitiveness and Recognition Time indicates that the hostility is at least in part a product of the experimentally induced negative transference. The data do not permit a clear understanding of the relationship between this negative transference and the serial position of the interviews. It will be recalled that Ss in the therapists' second interviews had significantly lower Amount Recalled scores. Possibly the direct hostility in these interviews inhibited the recall, but it appears equally plausible that the unresolved repressions in the second interviews produced tensions in Ss expressed as Extrapunitiveness. Neither of these hypotheses was supported by the nonsignificant correlations between Amount Recalled and Extrapunitiveness. However, the experimental design used in the present research provides a method for testing these hypotheses more systematically in the future.

Many of these suggested conclusions stem from inferences drawn from relatively unreliable data. However, the experimental technique employed in the present study has demonstrated its usefulness in studying psychotherapy variables and generating new hypotheses. That these procedures bear striking similarities to clinical practice is demonstrated by the behaviors of the Ss, who appeared genuinely anxious about the "repression." They seemed highly motivated yet natural in their associations, defenses, topics of conversation, etc.

Of incidental interest in reviewing the typescripts are the chains of associations by which Ss approached and eventually resolved the repression. These associations were natural, involving the telling of past experiences in the Ss' lives related to the "repressed" incident. For example, one S began the interview by describing his hostility and guilt when, as a small boy, his mother had punished him unjustifiably. She later overheard him expressing his anger toward her to a playmate. The relevance of this memory to the induced experience is obvious. It is interesting that this S eventually recalled most of the induced experience but could not correctly identify the relationship between the therapist and the physical education teacher. However, he did manufacture a plausible though incorrect reason for his feelings toward the therapist and experienced a real sense of relief when he hit upon this "reason." This observation suggests that true insight may not be a necessary prerequisite for relief

from anxiety. It is quite possible that reasonable rather than accurate schematizations of experience contribute most to therapeutic effectiveness. Other interesting phenomena encountered in the interviews were dynamic determiners in word choice ("I'm sure we've *bumped into* each other somewhere or other") and the many ways in which hostility toward the therapists was expressed.

Other examples of realism in the interviews are provided by one S who spent the entire interview time "spontaneously" discussing difficulties in controlling frequent and intense anger. Another S experienced much embarrassment in relation to the therapist, whom he eventually discovered reminded him of his high school physical education teacher. He described the teacher as a father figure who disappointed him by not always behaving in the perfect way in which the S idealized him. The specific incident which S finally described as support for his disappointment was the induced one. Thus, there is considerable clinical evidence that the reactions of the Ss to the induced experience were idiosyncratic and clinically realistic.

The procedures used here appear to be practicable, and they potentially provide reliable and quantifiable information on a number of important psychotherapeutic issues: the relationships between the lifting of repressions and transference and hostility, the effects of therapist experience, the interaction of therapist and client personalities, the effects of therapists' sex on male and female Ss, etc. The procedures in their present form, however, are not without their limitations. The use of hypnotically susceptible Ss places an important restriction on the extent to which experimental results may be generalized. The restriction of this kind of study to a single interview with each S makes it difficult to study such procedures as the free association method, which requires fairly extensive training of S. Further, the traumatic neurosis model implied in the experimental design does not take into account the observation that neuroses occur only as a result of many such experiences in persons of particular personality structures.

Finally, there are problems in controlling therapist behavior. It is fundamental to the present study that the independent variable is a unitary, easily defined verbal response of the interviewer. An attempt was made to select for study a verbal response similar to those frequently made during psychotherapy. However, psychotherapy cannot be defined strictly by such limited verbal behaviors. The purpose of the present research was *not* to study psychotherapy; rather it was to provide a framework for studying variables involved in psychotherapy. This is an important distinction, and one which makes it necessary to select meaningful but well-defined variables while controlling as many associated contaminating variables as possible. As long as experimental research is concerned with different kinds of therapy, it will suffer from such problems as those involved in having therapists artificially change their professional styles, difficulties related to the experience of therapists, etc. Such problems may be largely avoided when research is conceived as chiefly concerned with particular classes of verbal response in face-to-face interactions.

The considerations emphasize the apparently essential limitations of experimental research in psychotherapy in that complexity and richness may be sacrificed in order to obtain reliable answers. However, there is still much to be profitably learned about the kinds of variables included within the relatively wide limitations of these experimental procedures. Inasmuch as this method makes possible the reliable measurement of fairly discrete variables, it has value for current investigators. It may be important to find answers for the questions that can be confidently answered at present before going on to find less reliable answers to more difficult questions.

SUMMARY

A set of experimental procedures for use in psychotherapy research was tested. These procedures involved the use of hypnosis for the induction of miniature neuroses in normal individuals. Therapist Leading and Following, operationally defined, were studied for their effects on hostility and on the lifting of repressions in one-hour therapeutic interviews.

The findings indicate that Therapist Leading is more effective than Following for lifting repressions. It was also found that therapist experience which might lead to the formation of incorrect hypotheses about a client has a deleterious effect on the lifting of repression and is also associated with stronger expression of transference hostility by the client. The usefulness and limitations of the experimental procedures in providing possibilities for better control and measurement of psychotherapy variables were emphasized.

REFERENCES

1. COUNTS, R. M., & MENSH, I. N. Personality characteristics in hypnotically-induced hostility. *J. clin. Psychol.*, 1950, 6, 325–330.
2. DANSKIN, D. G., & ROBINSON, F. P. Differences in "degree of lead" among experienced counselors. *J. counsel. Psychol.*, 1954, 1, 78–83.
3. ERICKSON, M. H. The method employed to formulate a complex story for the induction of an experimental neurosis in a hypnotic subject. *J. gen. Psychol.*, 1944, 31, 67–84
4. GUMP, P. V. A statistical investigation of one psychoanalytic approach and a comparison of it with nondirective therapy. Unpublished master's dissertation, Ohio State Univer., 1944.
5. HULL, C. L. *Hypnosis and suggestibility.* New York: Appleton-Century, 1933.
6. MOSES, L. E. Non-parametric statistics for

psychological research. *Psychol. Bull.*, 1952, 49, 122–143.

7. PORTER, E. H. The development and evaluation of a measure of counseling interview procedures. II. The evaluation. *Educ. Psychol. Meas.*, 1943, 3, 321–350.

8. RAPAPORT, D. *The organization and pathology of thought.* New York: Columbia Univer. Press, 1951.

9. WEITZENHOFFER, A. *Hypnotism: An objective study in suggestibility.* New York: Wiley & Sons, 1953.

Selected Additional Readings

OUTCOME

ANKER, J. M., & WALSH, R. P. Group psychotherapy, and a special activity program, and group structure in the treatment of chronic schizophrenia. *Journal of Consulting Psychology,* 1961, 25, 476–481.

BAEHR, G. O. The comparative effectiveness of individual psychotherapy, group psychotherapy, and a combination of these methods. *Journal of Consulting Psychology,* 1954, 18, 179–183.

BARRON, F. B., & LEARY, T. F. Changes in psychoneurotic patients with and without psychotherapy. *Journal of Consulting Psychology,* 1955, 19, 239–245.

BERGIN, A. E. The effects of psychotherapy: Negative results revisited. *Journal of Counseling Psychology,* 1963, 10, 244–250.

CARTWRIGHT, D. S. Note on "Changes in psychoneurotic patients with and without psychotherapy." *Journal of Consulting Psychology,* 1956, 20, 403–404.

CARTWRIGHT, D. S., & VOGEL, J. L. A comparison of changes in psychoneurotic patients during matched periods of therapy and no therapy. *Journal of Consulting Psychology,* 1960, 24, 121–127.

CROSS, H. J. The outcome of psychotherapy: A selected analysis of research findings. *Journal of Consulting Psychology,* 1964, 28, 413–417.

ENDLER, N. S. Changes in meaning during psychotherapy as measured by the semantic differential. *Journal of Counseling Psychology,* 1961, 8, 105–111.

ENDS, E. J., & PAGE, C. W. Group psychotherapy and concomitant psychological change. *Psychological Monographs,* 1959, 73, No. 10 (Whole No. 480).

EYSENCK, H. J. The effects of psychotherapy: An evaluation. *Journal of Consulting Psychology,* 1952, 16, 319–324.

FAIRWEATHER, G. W., & SIMON, R. A further follow-up comparison of psychotherapeutic programs. *Journal of Consulting Psychology,* 1963, 27, 186.

FAIRWEATHER, G. W., SIMON, R., GEBHARD, M. E., WEINGARTEN, E., HOLLAND, J. L., SANDERS, R., STONE, G. B., & REAHL, J. E. Relative effectiveness of psychotherapeutic programs: A multicriteria comparison of four programs for three different patient groups. *Psychological Monographs: General and Applied,* 1960 Vol. 74, No. 5 (Whole No. 492).

JENSEN, M. B. Consultation versus therapy in the psychological treatment of neuropsychiatric hospital patients. *Journal of Clinical Psychology,* 1961, 17, 265–268.

KING, G. F., ARMITAGE, S. G., & TILTON, J. R. A therapeutic approach to schizophrenics of extreme pathology: An operant interpersonal method. *Journal of Abnormal and Social Psychology,* 1960, 61, 276–286.

LEVITT, E. E. Psychotherapy with children: a further evaluation. *Behavior Research and Therapy,* 1963, 1, 45–51.

LORR, M., McNAIR, D. M., MICHAUX, W. W., RASKIN, A. Frequency of treatment and change in psychotherapy. *Journal of Abnormal and Social Psychology,* 1962, 64, 281–292.

ROSENZWEIG, S. A transvaluation of psychotherapy: A reply to Hans Eysenck. *Journal of Abnormal and Social Psychology,* 1954, 49, 298–304.

SEMON, R. G., & GOLDSTEIN, N. The effectiveness of group psychotherapy with chronic schizophrenic patients and an evaluation of different therapeutic methods. *Journal of Consulting Psychology,* 1957, 21, 317–322.

SHLIEN, J. M., MOSAK, H. H., & DREIKURS, R. Effect of time limits: A comparison of two psychotherapies. *Journal of Counseling Psychology,* 1962, 9, 31–34.

OUTCOME RESEARCH—METHODOLOGY

BERG, I. A. Measures before and after therapy. *Journal of Clinical Psychology,* 1952, 8, 46–50.

BLOCK, J., & THOMAS, H. Is satisfaction with self a measure of adjustment? *Journal of Abnormal and Social Psychology,* 1955, 51, 254–259.

CARTWRIGHT, D. S. Effectiveness of psychotherapy: A critique of the spontaneous remission argument. *Journal of Counseling Psychology,* 1955, 2, 290–296.

FORSYTH, R. P., & FAIRWEATHER, G. W. Psychotherapeutic and other hospital treatment criteria: The dilemma. *Journal of Abnormal and Social Psychology,* 1961, 62, 598–605.

LEARY, T., & HARVEY, J. S. A methodology for measurement of personality changes in psychotherapy. *Journal of Clinical Psychology,* 1956, 12, 123–132.

LOEVINGER, JANE, & OSSORIO, A. Evaluation of therapy by self-report: A paradox. *Journal of Abnormal and Social Psychology,* 1959, 58, 392–394.

NICHOLS, R. C., & BECK, K. W. Factors in psychotherapy change. *Journal of Consulting Psychology,* 1960, 24, 388–399.

ROSENTHAL, D., & FRANK, J. D. Psychotherapy and the placebo effect. *Psychological Bulletin,* 1956, 53, 294–302.

THORNE, F. C. Rules of evidence in the evaluation of the effects of psychotherapy. *Journal of Clinical Psychology,* 1952, 8, 38–41.

SECTION 3 Methods to Predict the Course of Psychotherapy

Because the need for trained psychotherapists exceeds the available supply, it is important for the practicing clinician to know early in the treatment, or, if possible, before it begins, what his probability of success is with a particular patient. In this way, he can select patients whom he is likely to help and, perhaps, refer others to different therapists or different types of treatment.

The prediction researcher's ultimate goal is to forecast the success or failure of psychotherapy on the basis of information available to the therapist before he has made a large investment in the treatment. This problem is generally approached through retrospection, that is, the researcher attempts to determine which, if any, of the variables describing the pretherapy and early therapy situation are significantly related to the outcome of therapy. He then hopes to use such variables to predict success or failure in other cases.

The variables which researchers have attempted to relate to success—the predictor variables—have been diverse. They have involved both patient and therapist characteristics. Patients have been grouped according to demographic data, personality test data, case histories, interview data, and expectations in regard to therapy. Therapists have been categorized along such dimensions as sex, therapeutic orientation, experience, and personality.

The nature of what is meant by "success" or "failure" in this area of research also varies greatly. Some investigators have used as a criterion of failure, for example, the termination of therapy by the patient before the therapist feels the patient is ready, or termination before some designated number of sessions has been attended. Others have used psychometric measures as criteria for success, e.g., the difference between pre- and posttherapy scores on personality tests.

In a review article included in this section, Lewis W. Brandt indicates that the predictor variables and criteria of termination used in studies of psychotherapy "dropouts" have been both inexact and not comparable from study to study. Samuel C. Fulkerson and John R. Barry, in another review article, find that the prognostic use of psychological tests has not yet been successfully demonstrated, and they suggest a more sophisticated approach to the problem than has yet been utilized.

Since prediction research is aimed at the predetermination of outcome, the research in the latter area is crucial to it. The results of outcome research will decide whether the clinician is predicting which of his patients is likely to recover spontaneously or which will respond to, or at least continue in, psychotherapy. In this sense, it would appear that a no-therapy control group could clarify the meaning of prediction research results, as well as contribute to knowledge concerning the effects of psychotherapy. Prediction studies ideally should also include follow-up data and evaluation of patient adjustment in his outside environment. As with any study that involves the outcome of psychotherapy, it is important to determine the duration and extent of changes occurring in the patient.

Improvement on the predictor variable side should come with increased knowledge in the general area of psychometrics, or, more specifically, from some of the directions suggested by Fulkerson and Barry. Content and linguistic analyses of pretherapy interviews or initial in-therapy behavior seem promising sources of prediction data. Predicting psychotherapy outcome from behavior which closely matches behavior in psychotherapy seems quite sensible. Such analyses have been used increasingly in studies of process and progress in psychotherapy.

Finally, it is possible that specific forms of therapist behaviors may prove differentially effective in treating different symptoms and complaints of patients. Should this prove to be true, prediction research would be a necessary step in determining which types of therapy are most effective for individual patients.

Methodology and Research on the Prognostic Use of Psychological Tests

SAMUEL C. FULKERSON
JOHN R. BARRY[1]

There has not been a general review of the use of psychological tests in prognosis since Windle's review in 1952. At that time Windle concluded that, (*a*) it appeared to be some characteristic of the patient rather than the therapy given which determined the outcome of mental illness; (*b*) most studies in the area were difficult to interpret due to inadequate specification of one or more of the following: the sample characteristics, the treatment schedule, the criteria of improvement, and the degree of control imposed on variables influencing outcome; (*c*) the necessary step of cross-validation was usually omitted; and (*d*) personality tests, including the projective tests, had shown little promise in predicting outcome.

The purpose of the present article is to bring the review of the research on the prognostic use of tests up-to-date and to deal with some related methodological issues. The scope and organization will depart from that used by Windle. Firstly, the present review covers a wider range of criteria. Windle considered primarily the problem of predicting improvement. However there seems to be a complex of criteria which are closely related, logically and in practice, and so articles have been included dealing with a variety of criteria other than improvement. Secondly, the organization will differ from Windle's. He centered his review around individual tests, taking each test in turn and citing all prognostic studies where it had been used. The present paper is organized around the predictive problem rather than the individual test, since in practice the clinician wants to know how to come to a decision about a patient rather than what can be done with a given test. It is hoped that this emphasis will help to point up which questions are involved in the area of prognosis, and the relative attention each has received in research. And finally, the emphasis on decisions reflects an interest in decision theory (Luce & Raiffa, 1957), which has recently been

Reprinted from *Psychological Bulletin,* 1961, 58 (3), 177–204, with the permission of the American Psychological Association and the authors.

[1] Acknowledgment is due the criticism and additions of Charles Windle and Joseph Zubin.

suggested (Cronbach & Gleser, 1957) as a promising frame of reference from which to regard psychodiagnostic testing.

Windle included studies from as early as 1926 through 1951. The present review mainly covers the period from 1952 through June 1959. The coverage is more complete for those sections dealing explicitly with the prognostic use of tests than for the sections on methodological problems. Only the major psychological and psychiatric journals have been reviewed exhaustively.

METHODOLOGY

The methodological difficulties in research on prognosis concern the researcher's decisions as to what samples he will use, what selection instruments he will apply to the sample, and what criteria seem most appropriate.

Sample Attributes

One of the primary methodological difficulties has been the definition of the sample. Psychiatric diagnosis appears to have been the predominant basis of sample definition in spite of the known unreliability of these categories. Attributes of the sample such as age, education, sex, or socioeconomic status are usually listed. However, little attention has been paid in most of the studies reviewed to achieving homogeneous samples or subsamples. Some investigators have worked with only one diagnostic group, mainly schizophrenics. Since schizophrenia is a diagnosis given to over 50% of unspecified functional psychotic disorders, the difference between the results from such studies and those using psychotics sampled at random are hard to determine.

The need for homogeneous samples is clearly pointed up by a consideration of the question of base rates. Meehl and Rosen (1955) said "a psychometric device, to be efficient, must make possible a greater number of correct decisions than could be made in terms of the base rate alone" (p. 194). Studies of base rate as a function of diagnostic category (Langfeldt, 1956; Pascal, Swensen, Feldman, Cole, & Bayard, 1953; Rennie, 1953) indicate wide fluctuation in outcome between categories. Examination of these base rates indicates that a sample of psychotic patients with a preponderance of manic-depressives would have a higher base rate of improvement (approximately 68%) than a sample consisting of schizophrenics (approximately 50%). A predictor, even though its actual validity was zero, could do much better predicting outcome in the first sample than in the second if the cutting point of the predictor was adjusted to take advantage of the percentage of improvement. The optimal chance percentage of correct prediction in the first sample (achieved by calling everyone improved) would be 68%, which is equal to the base rate. With a sample of any size this would differ significantly from 50%, the value likely to be designated as chance if one did not know the base rate. And if the relative effectiveness of a predictor in the two samples were tested it could appear, spuriously, that the predictor was 68% correct within one sample but only gave 50% correct prediction in the other. Thus, prognostic research designs which compare the results in the experimental group against statistical chance, or which compare two small groups that are not sufficiently matched on variables related to base rates, cannot result in useful information. Since effective handling of the problem of sample homogeneity is uncommon in the prognosis studies reviewed by Windle and ourselves, the generality of findings is low, or at best difficult to determine.

It has been assumed that homogenous sampling represents an effective way of solving the problem of sample definition. However there is one danger. If the basis on which the homogeneity is established is highly related to the criterion variable, the variability of the criterion will be restricted. This can of course obscure a relationship that might exist between a predictor and criterion. It has been tacitly assumed that adequate randomization is not easily achieved in prognosis research, considering the usual sample size and the biases of the clinical populations from which they are drawn; otherwise random sampling would be an efficient way to select, and thus operationally define, the sample.

Another difficulty with diagnosis as a basis for the definition of the samples is that it represents clinical judgments which are based upon an often uncertain weighting of situational and response variables. For instance, the diagnosis of depressive reaction typically requires a differentiation as to whether the affective response reflects anxiety or depression, and a decision concerning the degree to which the affective response is related to a currently stressful situation. Clearly clinicians can vary as to the relative emphasis they place on these variables; and, as several studies (Glass, Ryan, Lubin, Reddy, & Tucker, 1956; Gleser, Haddock, Starr, & Ulett, 1954) have shown, they do vary in their weighting procedures. Therefore, despite the convenience of using diagnosis as a sample-defining operation, it is weak in that the researcher loses some control over the basic stimulus and response elements upon which the judgment is based. Studies of the effects of these elements on test validity and on the efficiency of cutting scores are called for; this kind of research, frequent in personnel psychology, seldom appears in the clinical journals.

Tests

Here the primary difficulty has been to define that universe of test behavior related to outcome. The majority of studies cited in Windle's earlier review used standard tests,, e.g., Rorschach, TAT, MMPI. It is likely that these tests tap only a small part of the response spectrum. With the welter available, it is still far from clear how many separate functions they sample, and no definitive taxonomy of tests exists. Zu-

bin and his co-workers (Burdock, Sutton, & Zubin, 1958; Burdock & Zubin, 1956; Zubin, 1958, 1959) have proposed five broad categories of activity to which test behavior can be assigned: physiological, sensory, perceptual, psychomotor, and conceptual. Each of these five categories has been further subdivided into classes of stimuli and responses. For the most part, the prognostic measures which Zubin has selected to use within each category are simpler than such tests as the Rorschach, in the sense that they present fewer stimulus dimensions and require less elaborate and lengthy responses. Such systems of categorization may indicate a range of tests available, but within each category there is a degree of complexity which at this time is largely unknown. However, factor analyses have been carried out in the areas of perception (Thurstone, 1944), psychomotor tests (Fleishman & Hempel, 1954, 1956; Hempel & Fleishman, 1955; Seashore, Buxton, & McCollum, 1940), and cognition (Guilford, 1956, 1959). Such analyses afford at least a partial basis for rational test selection.

Since a number of studies (e.g., Conrad, 1954) indicate that severity of mental illness is a significant prognostic variable, researchers looking for simple tests for prognostic studies may find it of value to consider studies in the area of differential diagnosis. H. E. King (1954) was able to differentiate between chronic schizophrenics, subacute behavior disorders, and normals using psychomotor tasks; and Eysenck, Granger, and Brengelmann (1957), with groups similar to those used by King, found a large number of both simple and complex perceptual tests which discriminated between their groups. Rabin and G. F. King (1958) reviewed studies dealing exclusively with schizophrenia, and concluded that "relatively high discriminatory power . . . has been obtained with simple experimental tasks. In many cases it has been as good as or better than that found with more complex tasks" (p. 253).

Criteria

There are three broad aspects of prognosis in mental illness: duration, course, and outcome. Studies predicting duration have used criteria such as length of hospital stay, the amount of time spent on the admitting or disturbed ward before transfer to a less disturbed ward (Gordon, Lindley, & May, 1957), and length of treatment.

Criteria involving the course of illness include measures of termination and relapse. In inpatient settings premature termination has been defined as leaving the hospital against medical advice; in outpatient settings it has been variously defined as not appearing for the initial interview after making an appointment, dropping out of therapy before some stipulated minimal number of contacts, or dropping out of therapy against the wishes of the therapist.

All criteria of improvement have been classified in this paper as measures of outcome. It could be argued that change over time is a measure of the course of illness, but this category has been reserved for specific qualitative aspects of change. Current criteria of improvement present the same difficulties in definition, and for this reason it is convenient to deal with them together, and to separate them from termination and relapse criteria. Because there is no universally agreed upon definition of the term "mental illness" (Jahoda, 1958; Scott, 1958), there has been a concomitant lack of clarity about how to measure its alleviation. Three sources of improvement criteria are common: (a) ratings of improvement made by the therapist, the patient, or other persons in contact with the patient such as relatives, professional staff other than therapist, or even fellow patients; (b) changes in objective measures of functioning such as physiological changes, or improvement in psychological test performance; and (c) follow-up data of a behavioral nature, such as whether patient is able to get and hold a job, to get or remain married, or, in whatever way, to resume a minimally independent social existence.

There have been several attempts to systematize these various outcome measures. An early breakdown of the separate areas of behavior which should be evaluated was made by Knight (1941). He suggested that therapists look for change in these five areas of adjustment: the disabling symptoms or problems, the interpersonal relations, the sexual adjustment, the productivity (i.e., the ability to work effectively and to utilize available energy), and the ability to handle stress. In Zubin's classification of tests, the ability to handle stress is viewed as a general parameter which might apply to the other four areas.

Barron (1953b) listed five similar criteria of improvement: (a) the patient feels better—indicated by introspective comments by the patient; (b) the patient relates better to others—requiring a follow-up at work, school, or home, and often based on reports of members of the patient's social group; (c) the patient's symptoms clear up—as measured by psychiatric ratings of improvement at discharge, as well as indirectly by measures of duration, e.g., length of hospital stay and speed of transfer to minimum security wards; (d) the patient makes decisions in a health-tending direction; and (e) the patient's verbal behavior shows increased "insight."

A few other criteria have occasionally been proposed to supplement these. Winder (1957) has suggested changes in the adjustment of children of the patient, and Morse (1953) has proposed accessibility to psychotherapy. Reznikoff and Toomey (1959) list in detail a variety of attempts to provide a taxonomy of outcome criteria.

There are measurement problems in all of these approaches. Scott (1958) has pointed out several conceptual and methodological difficulties in the various definitions of mental health. His discussion can be applied to Barron's criteria of improvement in mental health: (a) apparent change in subjective feelings or symptomatology can be a function of change in environmental conditions or can be distorted by defense mechanisms; (b) difficulties in social relationships can be a function of the differing requirements of socioeconomic and cultural systems, and can change as the patient changes his community or his contacts in the community; (c) there can be disagreement over which is a health-tending direction, since value systems are frequently involved; and (d) changes in insight may be a function of the degree to which the patient is willing to conform to the theory and values of the therapist. It should be noted that these points need not be regarded as criticisms of the definitions. If, for instance, changes in subjective feelings are considered important in their own right, then changes in feelings, whether due to environment or defense mechanisms, are still of interest. However, when used as criteria, such changes are meant to reflect specific intra-individual changes that are independent of environmental or irrelevant personal factors. Despite this, most of the research in prognosis seems designed to demonstrate only that characteristics of the patient exist which relate to outcome, without controlling sufficiently for the above mentioned environmental and personal factors.

On a less general level, Parloff, Kelman, and Frank (1954) have listed several common sources of ambiguity in improvement criteria: (a) improvement is often treated as a unitary concept, but this may be erroneous; (b) the emphasis of the rater can interact with aspects of the treatment—for instance, symptoms typically disappear before insight occurs, so that a rater who requires signs of insight before he gives a rating of improvement will judge fewer patients to be improved than one who accepts symptom alleviation as improvement; and (c) improvement is likely to be overestimated, since patients fluctuate in behavior, and at any given time signs of improvement in one or more specific areas are likely to be present and thus over-

valued by a judge being asked to make a global, subjective rating. Pascal and Zax (1956) criticize the usual gross "improved-unimproved" criterion on the grounds that it is not sufficiently tailored to the specific desired changes of the patient. They reject all nonbehavioral criteria of improvement, and essentially appear to feel that symptom-change should be the primary criterion of improvement.

It would be valuable to know the factorial structure of the above course, duration, and outcome measures. While no study was found which attempted to do this, several reported intercorrelations between two or more prognostic criteria. These will be described separately for the kinds of criteria involved.

Correlations between outcome measures. Kelman and Parloff (1957) intercorrelated a number of measures, including ratings of comfort and self-awareness made by the patient, and social effectiveness ratings made by persons close to the patient as well as professional observers. The change in rating from pretherapy to 20 weeks after the initiation of therapy was determined, Only 1 of 21 intercorrelations between these measures of change was found to be significant. However, the correlations were based on an N of only 15, and the period of time was perhaps too short to expect more than minimal changes.

Storrow (1959, 1960) compared ratings of improvement made by therapists, patients, relatives of the patient, and a psychiatrist who had access only to abstracted material. Two related rating clusters were found: the patient's self-rating, the relative's rating, and the rating made by inexperienced therapists ('third year medical students) formed one cluster; with the experienced therapist and the nontherapist psychiatrist forming the other. The correlations within clusters ranged from .61 to .79; between clusters, .32 to .57. These two clusters seemed to reflect primarily a dichotomy between patient and experienced therapist, since the relatives, and apparently the inexperienced therapists, gained their impression from hearing the patient's views of his progress, while the nontherapist psychiatrist obtained his knowledge from the file written by the therapist. Storrow had the ratings made separately for each of Knight's (1941) five areas, and the average intercorrelation between areas was approximately .60. Ellsworth and Clayton (1959) found that a measure of ward adjustment at discharge correlated significantly (.47) with a 3-month follow-up rating of community adjustment. However, amount of psychotherapy at discharge had no relationship to the follow-up criterion. Their finding can be compared with the intercorrelation of .57 reported between two simultaneous ratings of adjustment made on different scales (Stilson, Mason, Gynther, & Gertz, 1958).

Patient expressions of positive and negative feelings have been used as evidence of improvement (see Auld & Murray, 1955, for a review of these measures). Barry (1950) found low but significant correlations between these so-called internal or feeling criteria and global judgments of improvement in adjustment. Rogers and Dymond (1954) have found that changes in patient self-ratings on Q sorts correlated with ratings and other criteria of improvement. In an analogous group research program Snyder (1953) reported that self-rating changes correlated significantly with judgments of improvement. The same results have been reported by Kalis and Bennet (1957). Taylor (1955) found that self-ratings (Q sorts) tend to become increasingly positive simply with the passing of time. This suggests that it is imperative to control for time in treatment in order to evaluate the actual extent of the relationship between self-ratings and other improvement criteria.

Correlations between duration and outcome. Ullman (1957) reported that a measure of length of hospital stay correlated .36 ($N = 72$) with a measure of adequacy of interpersonal relationships (Palo Alto Group Therapy Scale), those

rated most adequate after a period of group therapy being the ones with the shortest hospital stay. Pascal et al. (1953) found a correlation of .37 ($N = 486$) between length of hospital stay and ratings of improvement made a year after discharge; again, the greater the improvement, the shorter the hospital stay.

A significant positive relationship has been frequently reported (Bailey, Warshaw, & Eichler, 1959; Myers & Auld, 1955; Seeman, 1954; Sullivan, Miller, & Smelser, 1958) in which greater length of psychotherapy in outpatient settings is accompanied by judgments of greater improvement. An interesting exception to this is the phenomenon called the "failure zone."

D. S. Cartwright (1955) found a grossly linear relationship between the number of psychotherapy sessions and success of outcome as noted by the therapists; but the mean success rating dropped sharply for those whose therapy lasted from 13 to 21 interviews. Cartwright was reporting on cases treated by nondirective techniques. Taylor (1956) validated this "failure zone" in a psychoanalytically oriented setting. Standal and van der Veen (1957) obtained the same drop in a counseling center sample. Vosburg (1958), in an examination of treatment charts, found evidence that from the fifteenth to twentieth hour was a period where outpatients tended to be preoccupied with their relationship with the therapist, suggesting that treatment which ended in this period might often be due to a desire on the part of either the patient or therapist to avoid the close, dependent relationship which was developing. Perhaps supplementing this, Ends and Page (1959) reported that the "flight into health" reaction occurred in group psychotherapy uniformly around the fourteenth session.

Correlation between duration and course. Crandall, Zubin, Mettler, and Logan (1954) found a significant relationship between the duration of initial hospitalization and rehospitalization; patients who stayed in the hospital a short time were most likely to still be out of the hospital on 1 to 4 year follow-up.

To summarize these intercorrelations, patient self-ratings and therapist ratings appear to covary to a high degree. Although measures of duration and course of illness have some relationship to improvement ratings, they seem also to tap different sources of variance.

Reliability. The reliability of outcome criteria has received attention; the duration and course measures are objective enough so that their reliability has been taken for granted. Miles, Barrabee, and Finesinger (1951) reported low interjudge but high test-retest intrajudge reliability of global judgments of improvement. Ten cases were rated by four judges on a six-point scale. There was complete agreement for only 20% of the judgments, though no disagreement was by more than two points. Test-retest figures showed 70% to 74% complete agreement between ratings taken 6 to 8 months apart. The ratings were based on structured interview material, and probably represent the lower bounds of interjudge agreement, if it is assumed that ratings made after a long period of observation of the patient would show more stability than ratings made on the minimal information contained in a structured interview. These investigators felt that changes in psychiatric status over time cannot be discriminated any more finely than in terms of three gross classes: unchanged or worse, improved, and markedly improved. Levitt (1957) presented data suggesting that judged improvement rate tends to increase as a function of the number of points on the scale. The greatest discrepancy was due to studies using a two-point "improved-unimproved" scale, where the mean percentage improved was 51. Studies using three- to five-point scales had mean improvement rates of 73% to 76%.

A possible source of unreliability in judgments of improvement lies in the fact that they may confound the amount of change with the absolute level of terminal adjustment. Thus it seems likely that the reason initial severity of illness correlates with improvement (Conrad, 1954) is to some extent due to the fact that those who are high on a measure of adjustment initially will be high on adjustment terminally, though the change may be far from being as dramatic as for patients who are admitted in a state of confusion and disorientation, and discharged without these symptoms. Since each judge can combine amount of change and absolute level as he chooses, in most studies, a lowering of interjudge agreement is to be expected. This may be involved in the much higher interrater reliabilities reported by Morton (1955) than by Miles, Barrabee, and Finesinger (1951). Morton developed seven-point scales of absolute level of adjustment in 12 different areas. After training, the interrater reliability coefficients ranged from .79 to .91 when the ratings were based only on transcriptions of a terminal interview; and the reliability of the improvement score (the difference between ratings of an initial and terminal interview) ranged from .59 to .78.

Tests as criteria. A possible criterion of outcome is performance as measured by tests. The present review uncovered no studies which used changes in test scores as primary prognostic criteria but it remains a reasonable possibility. The primary requisite for this use of tests would be evidence that the tests covary with the changes in patients that go to make up the concept of improvement. A number of studies have been published which tackle this question, and in general they support the assumption of covariation.

Pascal and Zeaman (1951) found that the Bender-Gestalt, color-naming, noun-naming, and serial subtraction, for a larger battery of tests, correlated with the course of progress as judged clinically, for four patients getting electroconvulsive therapy.

Hybl and Stagner (1952) reported a significantly greater decrease in the amount of disruption of performance brought about by a frustration experience, for patients rated by their therapists as improved. The tasks were three psychomotor tests: the Ferguson Form Boards, Digit Symbol from the Wechsler-Bellevue, and the Minnesota Rate of Manipulation Test.

Vinson (1952) administered a mirror drawing test before and during electroshock therapy to 18 patients. Change in the mirror drawing score correlated .72 with change in orientation as evaluated by the clinical staff.

Several studies (Hozier, 1959; Wechsler, 1958) indicate that as psychotic patients improve there is a decrease in variability of both the quality and the quantity of test performance.

The MMPI has been used in a number of studies of change: several studies (Carp, 1950; Feldman, 1951; Schofield, 1950, 1953) have reported that hospitalized patients treated with somatic therapies show an average drop on all of the MMPI scales of from 8 to 13 T-scale points. The acutely ill changed more than the chronically ill, and the affective disorders showed a greater change than the schizophrenics. Feldman (1951, 1952) found that improved patients' MMPI profiles dropped more than unimproved patients' profiles, and that the averaged profiles of these two groups showed greater differences after therapy than before. Work with predominantly psychoneurotic samples (Barron & Leary, 1955; Kaufman, 1950; Schofield, 1950) has indicated a larger drop on most scales for improved patients than for those rated unimproved. Changes taken without regard to sign (decreases as well as increases) were significantly greater in an individually treated group than in a group treated by group-therapy methods (Barron & Leary, 1955; Leary & Harvey, 1956).

Harris (1959) has summarized such MMPI studies to date as follows:

scores on the MMPI show little change in normals and in untreated psychiatric patients over extended periods of time; somatic therapy, which is known to be effective at least in readying patients for discharge from the hospital, is accompanied by sizeable drops in test scores; patients in psychotherapy show smaller changes, perhaps not much larger than those produced by the passage of time alone; and the magnitude of change in test scores is related to clinical estimates of improvement (p. 519). (Quoted by permissions of National Academy of Sciences–National Research Council)

Extraneous effects in test-retest comparisons need to be kept in mind, and Windle (1954) has reviewed these in reference to questionnaires. He presents evidence for a general tendency toward less deviant answers on retest, irrespective of external factors. This tendency is less, the greater the time period between test administrations. But even taking these artifactual sources of error into account, there appears to be evidence that a variety of test responses change in a manner consistent with therapist judgments of change in mental health.

RESEARCH IN PROGNOSIS

This section is organized around the three elements that seem most prominent in any treatment: the treatment itself, the person administering the treatment, and the patient who receives the treatment. Duration, of course, or outcome of illness can potentially be affected by any one of these. The practical need to determine the prognosis of a patient implies that some selection is possible concerning the most appropriate treatment for that patient, or the most appropriate patient for a given treatment. Thus in the headings below we use the terms: treatment selection, therapist selection, and patient selection.

Treatment Selection

Ideally, the basic problem in prognosis is the assignment of patients to treatments in such a way as to maximize the total ratio of improved to unimproved patients.

In decision theory terms, the prognostic judgment is a case of decision-making under conditions of certainty, which implies that the relationships between treatments and effects or outcomes are known. However, it has not been demonstrated that different treatments have different effects. To quote an authority,

One is reluctantly forced to admit that we simply do not possess the factual knowledge as of 1957 which permits us to say that we have any treatment procedure in psychiatry which promises a better outlook for a particular illness than does nature left to her own devices (Hastings, 1958, p. 1057). (Quoted by permission of the *American Journal of Psychiatry*)

Several attempts have been made to survey the literature on treatment effects, all of them hampered by the difficulties in comparing studies with different diagnostic groups, and different criteria for improvement. Eysenck (1952) selected 24 studies on the effect of psychotherapy with psychoneurotics, and concluded that these relatively homogeneous studies did not offer any evidence that improvement rate for those receiving psychotherapy was greater than for those getting only custodial care. Methodological weaknesses in his survey were pointed out by Rosenzweig (1954) and DeCharms, Levy, and Wertheimer (1954).

Levitt (1957) surveyed 30 articles evaluating psychotherapy with children. He compared the improvement rate on discharge and follow-up for treated cases with that reported for children accepted for therapy who never appeared for a first interview. The results were similar to those found by Eysenck, and did not demonstrate any facilitation for recovery due to psychotherapy.

Appel, Myers, and Scheflen (1953) summarized the results of studies which met a list of what they felt were minimal standards. They broke down the findings separately for schizophrenic, affective, and psychoneurotic disorders. Their survey indicated that none of the treatments studied —insulin coma, eltroconvulsive shock, electronarcosis, lobotomy, or psychotherapy— gave recovery rates significantly greater than that reported for groups receiving only routine hospital care, in any of the three disorder categories. A more recent review by Staudt and Zubin (1957) covering the somatotherapies indicated that insulin and electroconvulsive shock temporarily increase the improvement rate, but after 3 years the increase has dissipated. This conclusion would seem to fly in the face of the fact that most of the studies reviewed by Staudt and Zubin reported significantly greater recovery for the treated group than for the control group at all periods of follow-up. However, the groups were equally different before treatment was begun; in most instances the control groups "seem to be highly selected and loaded with patients of apparently poor prognosis. Their improvement rates fall far short of the 'spontaneous improvement rates' " (Zubin, 1959, p. 344). This bias in selection of control groups is also likely to be operating in studies of psychotherapy unless matching procedures are possible, since there seems to be a feeling in many clinics that ethical considerations make it mandatory that patients who appear treatable be given treatment as quickly as possible.

Kramer and Greenhouse (1959) discuss a point which bears directly on the adequacy of studies in this area. They show the statistical implications of the common sense notion that the less dramatic the effect one is looking for, the larger the sample necessary to show that it is significant. Their tables indicate that if one is interested in identifying in the experimental group as slight an improvement as 5% over the control group (at the .05 level of significance) for base rate improvement of 40% (which is close to that found in schizophrenia) it would take at least 569 cases in each group. For a base rate improvement of 70% (typical of the psychoneurotic) 472 cases per group would be needed to demonstrate a 5% increase under ideal conditions. These estimates further assume perfect reliability of the improvement criterion. Kramer and Greenhouse point out that very few states have a large enough population of mentally ill to do a study with a sample sufficient to detect slight but significant effects. Thus all the studies on the effect of treatment using small samples implicitly assume no interest in detecting anything less than extremely large differences. This is why it has been emphasized that treatment effects seem to be negligible relative to other variables in determining outcome; in view of the size of samples for research in this area it would not be fair to say that slight treatment effects may not exist.

How do patients regard psychotherapy? Stotsky (1956a) found that only 10% of a VA sample mentioned psychotherapy when asked to list any treatments which helped them. If asked directly whether they felt psychotherapy was the most important part of their treatment, over 50% said yes. These patients came predominantly from a lower socioeconomic class which, as will be discussed later would bias the results in the direction of more negative answers.

Two final points can be made. It first should be said that clear-cut effects of psychotherapy seem to have been demonstrated using the patient's verbal behavior, rather than judgments of improvement, as the criterion measure (Rogers & Dymond, 1954; Rosenthal, 1955).

Secondly, it might be pointed out that the inconclusive state of affairs regarding the effects of treatment is not necessarily discouraging from the restricted point of view of the researcher. If treatment effects are currently less important than effects due to other sources of variance, then the researcher can ignore treatment differences in his samples and in the formulation of

his hypotheses, thus considerably simplifying the research design.

Therapist Selection

A special aspect of treatment selection is the question of what kind of therapist does best with what kind of patient in psychotherapy. In the years surveyed in this review the pertinent articles in this area dealt with such therapist variables as sex, vocational interests, professional affiliation, and experience.

Irrespective of cause, are there differences between therapists as to treatment results? Imber, Frank, Nash, Stone, and Gliedman (1957) compared three therapists, each of whom worked with 18 patients. No significant differences were found between therapists, against a criterion of ratings of improvement in social effectiveness. Sullivan, Miller, and Smelser (1958) found neither sex, experience, nor profession (psychiatrist, psychologist, or social worker) to be related to either length of stay in therapy or to ratings of improvement. Hiler (1958a) reported significant differences in number of responses on the Rorschach between six groups of patients (14 per group), each group subsequently treated by a different therapist. He interpreted this as indicating that the therapists differed in their ability to keep unproductive patients in therapy. Stieper and Wiener (1959) found significant differences between therapists as to the length of time they kept patients in therapy. The differences seemed to be related to personality variables in the therapist, such as having high goals concerning very sick patients, and needing to feel appreciated. They took a negative view toward this minority of therapists who keep patients in therapy for long periods:

It seems to us likely that psychotherapeutic practice today contains self-defeating concepts which may not only be hampering to the success of treatment, but potentially harmful to its clients (p. 241).

Betz and Whitehorn (1956) found differences in treatment between therapists who had a cumulatively high improvement rate with schizophrenics and therapists with a low improvement rate. The successful therapists were more active, emphasized utlization of assets, understood the meaning of the patient's behavior, and engendered more trust and confidence. They also differed from unsuccessful therapists in their scores on the Strong Vocational Interest Test.

Myers and Auld (1955) found that the experienced staff in an out-patient clinic had fewer patients quit against the therapist's wishes, and more patients who improved, than the residents in the same clinic. Katz and Solomon (1958) concluded that in their sample the less experienced therapists tended to lose more patients, but if the patient continued treatment, the improvement rate was as high as for the more experienced therapists. Strupp (1958) had 134 residents and psychiatrists respond to a sound film of an initial interview. He interpreted his data as showing two types of therapists. Type I was positive in his feelings toward the patient, optimistic about prognosis, and permissive and passive in therapy—and relatively inexperienced. Type II was more experienced, was negative toward the patient, pessimistic about prognosis, and active in therapy (giving orders and advice, and venting his irritations). Strupp quotes Kubie (1956) on reasons for this increasing pessimism: Kubie mentions his disappointment, saying it is one shared by other psychoanalysts, to find that with increasing experience he did not seem to have increasing success.

Several studies (Katz, Lorr, & Rubinstein, 1958; Sullivan et al., 1958) have reported that the more experienced the therapists, the larger the percentage of cases rated by him as improved; and the

less severe the illness, the greater the likelihood of a patient's having an experienced therapist. Clearly, it is advisable to control for severity of illness in research on therapy. Differences in socioeconomic level also appear to interact with experience. Schaffer and Myers (1954) studied all cases accepted for treatment in an out-patient clinic during 1 year and found that

the higher a patient's social class position . . . in the community, the greater were his chances of being accepted for psychotherapy, of being assigned to a relatively experienced therapist occupying a high status within the clinic, and of maintaining contact with the clinic (p. 88). (Quoted by permission of *Psychiatry*)

It is apparently also likely (Winder & Hersko, 1955) that the higher the social position, the higher the likelihood that the therapist will decide on analytic rather than supportive procedures.

Since the above studies did not control for these contaminating factors, it must be concluded that demonstration of between-therapist effects on outcome has not been conclusively obtained. This is not particularly surprising, in view of the fact that therapist selection is just a special case of treatment selection. Again, though, it can be said that effects can probably be shown, against other than improvement criteria. For instance, Rosenthal (1955) found that the amount of benefit a client said he obtained from therapy correlated .68 with the degree of shift in moral values toward those held by the therapist, if the values had been talked about during psychotherapy. This change would appear to be related to those obtained in laboratory studies on verbal conditioning (Krasner, 1958).

Patient Selection: Outcome Criteria

We turn now to the question of the relationship of intra-individual variables to prognostic criteria. The studies will be grouped along two dimensions. They will be considered according to the kind of criterion used—outcome, duration, or course—and further broken down, where possible, in terms of the type of test used —projective, questionnaire, or performance (including cognitive tests).

Nontest indicators. Before turning to the research using tests as predictors of outcome, it is of interest to survey briefly what has been found using nontest variables. Huston and Pepernik (1958) reviewed prognostic variables in schizophrenia, and presented evidence that only these variables had been firmly established as going with favorable outcome: acute onset, short duration of illness prior to hospitalization, a precipitating stress, and the absence of flat or inappropriate affect. A series of studies under the direction of Pascal investigated the interrelationships of these variables within a sample of varied psychotics. It was found that acute onset (Swensen & Pascal, 1954b) and aggression directed toward oneself (Feldman, Pascal, & Swensen, 1954) related significantly to favorable outcome when other prognostic variables were controlled. However, precipitating stress (Cole, Swensen, & Pascal, 1954), affective expression (Bayard & Pascal, 1954), and duration of illness (Swensen & Pascal, 1954a) did not relate to outcome in their sample when the effect of other prognostic variables was held constant. The generality of their findings is not clear, since their method of balancing groups for control purposes led to their using only a small portion of the total sample, thus allowing for the possible introduction of unknown biases.

Eskey, Friedman, and Friedman (1957) could not find support for the notion that disorientation relates to duration of illness; however, they restricted their sample on the criterion variable by not using patients who were unimproved at discharge. Several studies (Eskey & Friedman, 1958; Phillips, 1953) indicate that intact cognitive processes and a mature premorbid

social and sexual life go with favorable outcome. Zubin (1959) presents the results to date of an uncompleted survey of prognostic indicators for schizophrenia, which suggests that the variables defining reactive schizophrenia go with favorable prognosis, and those defining process schizophrenia go with unfavorable prognosis. He presents a valuable count of articles supporting or negating the postulated relationship for almost every if not every prognostic indicator that has been investigated. There have been several attempts to combine these variables into a scale. Thorne (1952) intuitively combined five into a quantified prognostic scale. More recently Lindemann, Fairweather, Stone, and Smith (1959) have developed a somewhat similar scale and cross-validated it against a criterion of duration of hospital stay. An eight-point scale (Schofield, Hathaway, Hastings, & Bell, 1954) developed to predict a follow-up criterion of adjustment in schizophrenia could not be cross-validated by Stone (1959). Becker and McFarland (1955) developed and cross-validated a 16-item scale against a criterion of improvement in a lobotomized sample.

The above studies have dealt with psychotics, or samples predominantly psychotic. Miles, Barrabee, and Finesinger (1951) reported that in a hospitalized psychoneurotic sample, age of onset, duration of illness prior to hospitalization, and a number of symptoms were unrelated to outcome. Patients with symptoms associated with autonomic discharge were most likely to remit. Rosenbaum, Friedlander, and Kaplan (1956), studying an outpatient sample, found improvement occurred in patients with good premorbid history whose environment offered many supports; and improvement was mainly in marital and work adjustment. Comparison of results on inpatient and outpatient samples suggests some reason for dealing separately with psychotics and psychoneurotics in prognosis research.

An important question is how well the clinician, using these nontest indices, can do in predicting outcome. Clow (1953) obtained a majority opinion of prognosis at the staff conference which was held 2 months after admission on each of 100 female schizophrenics. The prognoses were 73% correct in predicting a dichotomous improved-unimproved criterion obtained at discharge. More studies of this kind would be helpful in evaluating the practical usefulness of adding tests to current prognostic procedures.

Projective tests. Several Rorschach studies have used a configurational score, the Prognostic Rating Scale (PRS) (Klopfer, Kirkner, Wisham, & Baker, 1951). Kirkner, Wisham, and Giedt (1953) found a correlation of .67 between PRS and improvement ratings obtained by evaluating the terminal closure note, on a sample of 40 receiving psychotherapy. Mindness (1953) obtained a correlation of .66 (*N* of 70) between PRS and a diagnostic criterion running from normal through neurotic to psychotic, obtained 6 months after initiation of psychotherapy. Filmer-Bennett (1952, 1955) did not obtain significant results with either the PRS or global judgments based on the total Rorschach protocol. His criterion was a dichotomous improved-unimproved rating of the degree to which the patient was making a satisfactory social and vocational adjustment a year after discharge from the hospital. Rosalind D. Cartwright (1958) presented a review of several successful studies using the PRS, and described further positive results from her own study. The criterion was ratings of success of psychotherapy made by the counselor after termination of therapy. In an appended discussion of her paper Snyder argued that other tests might do as good a job with much less time needed for testing. Bloom (1956) added an interesting modification to his design. He divided his 46 subjects into two groups, an unproductive group (less than 11 Rorschach responses) and a productive group (11 or more responses). The PRS differentiated a dichotomous criterion of outcome of psychotherapy significantly in the productive group, but not in the unproductive. He further assessed 11 other scores, and found none which were either significant or nonsignificant for the total sample as a whole; all discriminated significantly in one or the other of his groups —four for the productive group, and seven for the unproductive. His results suggest the operation of an interaction similar to the one Zubin and co-workers (see below) have reported between chronicity and outcome, and deserve further investigation.

Rogers and Hammond (1953) and Roberts (1954), both working with VA outpatients, tried a sign approach on the Rorschach with negative results. Dana (1954) hypothesized that Card IV, assumed to be most likely to pick up attitudes to authority, would give responses related to improvement in psychotherapy, if the authority relationship was crucial to outcome. The responses were placed in three categories—"adequate," "inadequate," "negative"—and there was a significant tendency for those with "adequate" response to improve, and those with "inadequate" responses to remain unimproved. Hammer (1953) felt that his review of the literature suggested that those patients whose Rorschach protocols look sicker than their H-T-P protocols have a good prognosis, while a poor prognosis is associated with giving more negative feelings on the H-T-P than on the Rorschach.

Ullman (1957) found two highly related measures—clinical judgments of TAT protocols and a social perceptions test—to be correlated significantly with two criteria of improvement: the Palo Alto Group Therapy Scale and hospital status after 6 months (hospitalized vs. discharged). S. Rosenberg (1954) developed and cross-validated eight prognostic

signs based on the Wechsler-Bellevue,
Sentence Completion, and on the Rorschach. Grauer (1953) found more Rorschach indices of anxiety in an improved
group of schizophrenics than in an unimproved. Organic signs did not discriminate. The welter of signs which these
studies find related to improvement shows
no clear pattern. Obviously most of these
positive findings with projective techniques
should be further validated before they
can be accepted as more than promising
leads.

Questionnaires. Barron (1953b) reported lower pretherapy MMPI and Ethnocentrism scores for an improved outpatient
group than for an unimproved group. The
criterion was judgments of change in psychotherapy made by professionals who had
not been involved in the treatment. At least
some of these relationships were due to
differences in IQ between the groups. Rosen (1954) was not able to verify Barron's
finding with the E Scale. Barron developed a special ego strength scale from the
MMPI (Barron, 1953a), which he successfully cross-validated against improvement
criteria in three disparate samples. Wirt
(1955, 1956) found the ego strength scale
significantly discriminated an unimproved
from a greatly improved group, the groups
being extremes drawn from a hospitalized
sample receiving psychotherapy. The scale
did a better job of discrimination than experienced clinicians who based their judgments on the total MMPI profile.

Feldman (1951, 1952, 1958) explored
the validity of the MMPI for the prediction of outcome after electroshock therapy.
He found that items dealing with hostility
and interpersonal relationships were predictive of outcome, while items dealing
with symptomatology reflected the amount
of improvement. Pumroy and Kogan
(1958) were unable to cross-validate Feldman's prognostic scale in a small VA sample. Dana (1954) also obtained negative
results with the MMPI, attempting to predict improvement after electroshock.

Performance tests. Stotsky (1956b)
gave vocational aptitude and interest tests
to a group of schizophrenics most of whom
had been in the hospital for a year or more.
The aptitude tests predicted later work success, but the interest tests did not. Swensen
and Pascal (1953) reported that the Pascal-
Suttell Z score on the Bender-Gestalt test,
was significantly lower for a group of inpatients judged to be improved on follow-
up a year and a half later, than for those
judged unimproved. Landis and Clausen
(1955) found efficient performance on
critical flicker fusion, reaction time, finger
dexterity, auditory acuity threshold, and
tapping speed was predictive of improvement in an inpatient sample receiving a
variety of treatments. A variability score of
palmar sweating (Ellsworth & Clark,
1957) predicted changes in a behavioral
adjustment scale concurrent with the administration of tranquilizing drugs. Keehn
(1955) took 12 measures from simple
cognitive and psychomotor tests that had
been shown to discriminate between normals and psychotics, and found only one
score that predicted outcome in a group of
inpatients receiving insulin coma therapy;
he concluded that initial degree of psychoticism was not prognostic of outcome.

Vinson (1952) used a mirror drawing
test to predict the prognosis made at discharge—a dichotomous "favorable-unfavorable" prognostic judgment made by the
staff. His sample consisted of 18 hospitalized patients who received electroshock
therapy. He tested before and during
treatment, and the difference between
these scores predicted the prognostic criterion at the .02 level of significance.

The most promising findings made in
prognosis in the last 10 years have been
reports coming out of the Columbia-Greystone project of two interaction effects. The
first interaction dealt with the relation of
chronicity to outcome. Windle and Hamwi
(1953) reported that chronic patients who
were discharged after treatment had poorer
admission scores on a complex reaction
time test than chronic patients who were
not discharged. However, for acute pa-

tients, those whose illness was of short duration, the reverse was true, namely, poor admission scores were associated with poor outcome. Zubin, Windle, and Hamwi (1953) rechecked data on other tests, using chronic patients from the same study, and found four other tests which gave the same results. An independent validation was provided by Sonder (1955) using different tests. In all of these studies the results were most clear-cut for the chronic group, probably due to the fact that among the acute patients were some who were potentially or actually chronic.

The second interaction emerged from the study by Zubin, Windle, and Hamwi (1953) who found that the chronic patients who did well on conceptual tasks (intelligence, memory, personality tests) but poorly on perceptual tasks (learning and perception tests) had a poorer prognosis than chronic patients who showed conceptual confusion but perceptual clarity. Williams and Machi (1957), also working with the chronic sample from the Columbia-Greystone project, factor analyzed the test data, and found some support for this conceptual-perceptual differentiation. However, this finding is not yet as clearly supported by the evidence as the chronicity-outcome interaction. Zubin and Windle (1954) reviewed a number of independent prognostic studies, and reported that a consideration of the two interaction effects accounted for much of the conflicting findings. In the light of this work, further attempts to investigate these interactions cannot help but be of value.

Patient Selection: Duration Criteria

Projective tests. Stotsky (1952), working only with schizophrenics, compared a group of patients who in a 2-year period had not left the hospital with a group which in the same period of time had been discharged and remained outside for at least 6 months. His hypothesis was that the prognosis would be best for patients with the best pretreatment emotional and intellectual integration. Of 19 Rorschach signs, 5 were significantly cross-validated in a second sample. Also, all of the 19 signs except *R* were found to be in the predicted direction in both samples.

Questionnaires. Grayson and Olinger (1957), in a VA inpatient sample, reported that those who were given early trial visits were able to give improved MMPIs when asked to respond in "the way a typical, well-adjusted person on the outside would do" to a greater extent than those still hospitalized after 3 months. Rapaport (1958) was not able to validate this finding, using a military sample, although the change on most of the scales was in the correct direction. Stieper and Wiener (1959) found a group of VA outpatients who were seen in psychotherapy for an average of 5.3 years had higher pretherapy scores on the MMPI scales, *Hs* and *Hy,* than a group who were discharged after 14 months.

A demographic study (Lindemann et al., 1959) found an index using marital status, diagnosis, degree of incapacity, legal competence, and alcohol intake as variables, was related to length of hospital stay. Ellsworth and Clayton (1959) found a rating scale of psychotherapy filled out at admission did not correlate significantly with length of hospital stay, but a behavioral adjustment scale did correlate, patients with the best admission adjustment tending to remain in the hospital the shortest length of time.

Performance tests. Venables and Tizard (1956b) found "short-stay" schizophrenics performed better on a repetitive psychomotor task than did chronic schizophrenics. Reaction time differences (Venables & Tizard, 1956a) occurred on initial testing, but disappeared on retest.

Patient Selection: Course Criteria

Under criteria measuring the course of illness we have placed two broad questions: who will relapse, and who will terminate treatment.

Relapse. The broad question here is one of predicting who will get worse over time. It is of course the reverse of the question of who will improve. However, the prediction of improvement and its opposite may not necessarily be most effectively accomplished with the same test. It can not be assumed that the prediction of relapse or hospitalization can be made from the same tests which predict improvement. This is consistent with the assumption that change of mental status need not be a unitary concept.

Peterson (1954b) used the MMPI, Wechsler-Bellevue, Rorschach, and nontest data to predict who would require admission to the hospital from patients being seen on an outpatient basis in a VA mental hygiene clinic. Considering the base rates, the predictive power of the tests was slight, but the results suggested that the person who gets worse in therapy is single, has been previously hospitalized, is diagnosed psychotic, and has an MMPI profile strongly elevated on the psychotic scales. Using a six-point scale based on signs of psychosis on the MMPI developed by Meehl, Peterson (1954a) was able to achieve 75% correct discrimination. Briggs (1958) was able to cross-validate this scale to a certain extent. He took patients who were already in the hospital when they received the MMPI. On follow-up he found the Peterson score differentiated those who were rehospitalized from those who were not only for patients originally diagnosed psychoneurosis or mixed psychoneurosis. This is consistent with Peterson's finding that in his study similar outpatient diagnoses were most often given to the cases which were later hospitalized.

Schofield and Briggs (1958) related several measures of improvement previous to initial discharge to rehospitalization, the median follow-up period being 5.8 years. Improvement in behavior ratings made by nurses was not related to rehospitalization, but a combination of ratings based on pre- and posttreatment MMPIs and psychiatric evaluations of improvement made at the time of discharge allowed 75% correct prediction for the 66% of cases on which the two ratings agreed. Since knowledge of the base rate alone would allow 66% correct prediction, this was only slightly better than chance.

Cowden, Deabler, and Feamster (1955), using a criterion of whether patient was re‹ hospitalized within 90 days after discharge, reported judgments of change from admission to discharge on Sentence Completion and the H-T-P Test predicted the criterion. An "ego" score obtained from combining the Binet Vocabulary with Cards I, III, and VIII of the Rorschach predicted relapse within a 2-year period for a sample of discharge patients (Orr, Anderson, Martin, & Philpot, 1955), but did not predict discharge for a sample of nondeteriorated admissions. Working with a special group (outpatients considered interminable) Wiener (1959) studied return to psychotherapy over a 6-month period after initial psychotherapy was arbitrarily terminated. In his sample of 48, 37 returned for further therapy within this period. The MMPI did not discriminate returnees from nonreturnees. Months in treatment appeared to be a promising measure, with the returnees having a longer history of psychotherapy.

A study that fits under neither of our two course criteria is one by Rioch and Lubin (1959). They obtained lengthy follow-up data on 93 patients, sufficient to allow an assessment on an 11-point scale of how consistently the patient had moved upward or downward in his social adjustment over several years. Both the Wechsler-Bellevue IQ and a global rating based on the Rorschach correlated significantly with this criterion, mainly due to discrimination at the low end of the scale: all of the patients who deteriorated steadily had low scores on the predictors.

Termination of treatment. The criterion involved in the prediction of length of therapy is more objectively determined than improvement, but there are some difficulties in its determination nonetheless.

One question is how to measure length of therapy. Most studies have used the number of interviews as the measure. Number of weeks in treatment would appear to be an equivalent measure. However, Lorr, Katz, and Rubinstein (1958) found that the number of interviews correlated only .60 with number of weeks in treatment, and they argued that number of interviews is likely to be the less reliable of the two.

Another problem springs from the research design used in most of the studies of termination. The total sample is usually divided into two groups, terminators and remainers, and test scores are related to this dichotomous criterion. The question becomes one of where to cut the distribution. Terminators have been defined as those remaining less than 4 sessions (Gliedman, Stone, Frank, Nash, & Imber, 1957), less than 10 sessions (Auld & Eron, 1953; Kotkov & Meadows, 1953), or less than 20 sessions (Gibby, Stotsky, Hiler, & Miller, 1954). Gibby et al. (1954) found that those terminating between 5–19 sessions resembled in their test responses those who terminated earlier rather than those continuing on for more than 19 sessions. Our previous discussion of the "failure zone" (Taylor, 1956) suggests that a variety of factors are operating in the first 20 weeks. When these factors have not been controlled, they can influence the findings in termination studies.

A further criticism has been made by Gundlach and Geller (1958) who suggest that termination rate and duration of illness are partly administrative artifacts, and partly a reflection of "the kind of personality problems that the staff are interested in, or skilled at, handling." This criticism can be taken as indirect support for the common practice of defining termination in terms of the distribution of the length of therapy measures, since in any given setting, the median or mean length takes some account of the effects of policy and staff interests.

Research on the prediction of termination by the use of *projective tests* shows a familiar, monotonous pattern: initial positive results with subsequent negative or indeterminate cross-validation. Kotkov and Meadow (1952, 1953) began with 12 formal scores, and validated one of these (FC/CF). They applied a formula based on three scores ($FC/CF, R, D\%$) to another sample, and $D\%$ washed out. When these same signs are examined in an earlier study (Rogers, Knauss, & Hammond, 1951), none were significant, and only R was in the predicted direction. Auld and Eron (1953) tried a further validation of the Kotkov and Meadow formula, and obtained insignificant results. They found the Wechsler-Bellevue IQ accounted for the one Rorschach variable, R, which held up in their sample.

Starting anew, Gibby et al. (1954; Gibby, Stotsky, Miller, & Hiler, 1953) found 9 of 31 Rorschach signs promising. Taking the 9 to a second sample, 3 held up (R, K, m) and a predictive formula based on these variables was applied to a further independent sample, and afforded 68% correct prediction. However, knowledge of the base rate would have allowed 60% correct prediction, so the results were not strong enough to be of practical use. In their sample the Kotkov and Meadow formula did no better than chance, and IQ was not related to the criterion. Affleck and Mednick (1959) used an equation based on $R, M,$ and H to predict who would remain for longer than three interviews. Their equation allowed 71% correct prediction in a validation sample. Their terminators were lower in IQ than the continuers (significant at .06 level). This is consistent with the findings of Auld and Eron (1953).

All of the above Rorschach studies except for Auld and Eron used equivalent VA males being seen on an outpatient basis, so in some respects sample homogeneity was better from study to study than is true of most validation research in this area. Of all the Rorschach signs only R seems to have maintained its promise in these studies. More recent work (Gallagher, 1953, 1954; Taulbee, 1958) supports the conclusion that the number of Rorschach responses (R) relates to termination. However the Rorschach is probably an unnecessarily cumbersome way of measuring this variable; for instance, Gallagher (1954) found that the number of words used on the Mooney Problem Check List to describe the clients' problems was a better predictor than R.

Libo (1957) used a TAT-type test to predict the number of patients who would return the week after the test was administered. For 40 subjects he was able to make a significant prediction based on an "attraction score": the number of references in the stories to a desired move toward the therapist, or of anticipated satisfactions from therapy.

Three studies dealt with the prediction of termination in a tuberculosis hospital. Vernier, Whiting, and Meltzer (1955) were able to differentiate patients who left the hospital against medical advice from those who continued treatment to the end, using the Rorschach and H-T-P tests. The TAT did not discriminate. Moran, Fairweather, and Morton (1956), using a biographical inventory and an attitude questionnaire found that only prehospital life adjustment predicted who would leave the hospital prematurely, with those leaving having a long history of being unable to adjust to their life situations. Calden, Thurston, Stewart, and Vineberg (1955) developed and cross-validated a scale from the MMPI to predict premature discharge.

Taulbee (1958) developed a key based on the MMPI and the Rorschach to predict continuation of outpatient psychotherapy beyond the thirteenth interview. His results, not cross-validated, led him to conclude that those who continue in therapy are less defensive, and more persistent, dependent, anxious, and introspective than the terminators. Sullivan et al. (1958) reported no significant difference between MMPI scores of terminators, and continuers on a VA male sample. Of a number of variables only ed-

ucation and occupation related to the criterion. Conrad (1954) had therapists fill out a check list covering positive mental health, social conformity, and behavior pathology on VA outpatients with differing lengths of stay in psychotherapy. Continuers tended to look least disturbed initially, and to be at the median rather than at either extreme on social conformity.

Rubinstein and Lorr (1956) found differences between extreme groups (patients in psychotherapy for over 6 months vs. patients who had come less than six times and had terminated against the wishes of the therapist), on the authoritarian F Scale, and a vocabulary test. However, a later study (Lorr et al., 1958) which defined termination as having less than 7 weeks of psychotherapy, did not give significant results, though the scales were in the predicted direction. They combined a number of scales in a further attempt, and obtained a significant multiple correlation in a validation sample. However, the scales allowed no better prediction than interviewer's judgment.

A large recent project on termination was carried on at Johns Hopkins University (Frank, Gliedman, Imber, Nash, & Stone, 1957; Gliedman et al., 1957; Imber, Frank, Gliedman, Nash, & Stone, 1956; Imber, Nash, & Stone, 1955; Nash, Frank, Gliedman, Imber, & Stone, 1957). Their prognostic battery included an inventory and a Sway test. Those who stayed in therapy more than three interviews were more suggestible on the Sway test, were more sociable, of higher socio-economic status, and more likely to see treatment as a means of maintaining status in their immediate social environment, than the terminators. When they compared group versus individual psychotherapy they found an interaction between treatment and termination: in group therapy, the terminators were more socially ineffective than the continuers, while the relationship was reversed for those getting individual therapy. This intriguing finding may have been related to an unequal distribution of social levels in the two groups—

most of the lower class patients ended up in group psychotherapy, while most of the middle class patients were assigned to individual psychotherapy.

Hiler (1959) studied intial complaints, and concluded that continuers come to a clinic with typical psychoneurotic symptoms —obsessions, phobias, anxiety, depression, poor concentration—while early terminators are more likely to list purely organic symptoms, antisocial acts, or schizoid feelings. His continuers also obtained higher scores on the Wechsler-Bellevue with a subtest pattern characterized by Similarities being higher than Digit Span or Digit Symbol (Hiler, 1958b).

How much overlap is there between predictors of termination and improvement? Sullivan et al. (1958) investigated the relationship of MMPI scores and demographic variables to both improvement and termination criteria. Only occupational level was related significantly to both. Katz et al. (1958) found none of their predictors of length of stay correlated with therapist ratings of improvement. Frank et al. (1957) reported that a past history of social activity and a fluctuating course of illness was associated with continuation and improvement. A short duration of illness was associated with termination as well as improvement. Gallagher (1954) found the Taylor Manifest Anxiety Scale predicted continuation as well as improvement. In general the results suggest little overlap. This is somewhat unexpected, since as was mentioned earlier, there appears to be a positive relationship between criteria of duration of treatment and improvement. The most tenable assumption would seem to be that the variance shared by the two criteria is different from the variance shared by predictor and criterion. Possibly the correlation between criteria is due to rater bias.

DISCUSSION

The previous sections of this paper have included the word "selection" in order to underline the fact that the practical need to predict to any of these criteria exists only when some sort of selection is necessary. For example, if the waiting list of an outpatient clinic is too long, selection of cases to receive treatment can be made on the basis of predicted probability of improving or terminating. If there is no need to deny treatment to anyone, knowledge of these prognostic probabilities is of no practical use. In most mental treatment centers today administrative procedures probably do not involve rejection of the patient as an alternative action, except in some outpatient clinics. Prognosis would be indispensable in the question of treatment selection, if differential effects of treatment were known; our survey has suggested that such effects have not yet been demonstrated. Thus it could be argued that prognosis is a sleeping giant at the present time, awaiting a future chance to be of service. Several other uses can be made of prognostic information, of course. Knowledge of the variables which relate to changes in duration, course, or outcome of mental illness is of theoretical importance, an aid to understanding. A second promising use has been proposed by Feldman (1952) and Zubin (1959). They recommend that in nonprognostic research prognostic status be tried as a method of classifying patients into homogeneous categories, in place of diagnosis.

Is such a suggestion tantamount to substituting a measure of severity of illness for one of type of illness? The literature survey indicates a wide variety of tests have shown positive results, with no discernible common characteristic except that they measure adequacy of functioning, directly or indirectly. The fact that the same measures do not predict for all patients may be due to differences in the type and etiology of symptoms from patient to patient; but such differences do not vitiate the possibility that when prediction occurs it is largely because the dimension of severity of illness has been accurately assessed by the test. In any case, the effect of matching groups on prognostic variables would be to control for base rate differences in improvement, a procedure which is imperative for many kinds of evaluational studies, though rarely invoked in research on therapy.

As with all predictive questions, the primary problem in prognosis is the definition of the criterion. From the point of view of decision theory, the general notion of "outcome of illness" involves assigning utility values to specific outcomes; and since cost of achieving any given outcome may be a factor, an explication of the treatment strategies is also necessary. The low interjudge reliabilities which obtain in judgments of improvement indicate that utility of outcome may differ from judge to judge. A program for achieving a more objective ranking of treatments, outcomes, or treatment-outcome combinations seems called for. Cronbach and Gleser (1957) offer a possible framework for such a program, and most of the points they make, although dealing with personnel selection, can be easily generalized to prognosis.

A frequent misinterpretation of empirical research is that it is based on no theory. In the sense of a content theory—i.e., a theory stating relationships between tangibles or concepts related to tangibles—empirical research is usually weak, though in the selection of measures some sort of rough theory has to be involved. However, empirical research often is strongly tied to a mathematical model. In prognosis the guiding model has been the linear regression model. The studies have assumed that a measurable quality exists which is linearly related to outcome. The findings in respect to performance differences between acute and chronic patients (Burdock et al., 1958) suggest that this linear model probably will have to take account of interaction effects. If so, almost all studies to date are too simple in design. They involve a one-stage decision: look at one final score per person (the final score may of course be a combination of several subsidiary scores) and assign the patient to an outcome (criterion category) by whatever rule of operation is being applied to the score. The work of Zubin's group indicates that at least a two-stage de-

cision process is needed: (a) a score is obtained to decide which of several operations will be applied to a second score, and (b) the second score is used to assign patients to the criterion category. Indeed there is no reason why tests should not be useful as a basis for deciding what operational rule to apply to other data. The variables which appear to have the strongest relationship to outcome have been nontest variables: severity and duration of illness, acuteness of onset, degree of precipitating stress, etc. A possible direction of research might be to use tests to increase the validity of the nontest variables, either by trying to find tests which tap interactions, or which correlate with the error term in the psychiatric predictor. This latter approach has not been tried in prognosis, but it has been used with some success in personnel selection (Fulkerson, 1959; Ghiselli, 1956). A third suggested avenue of research would be to apply nonlinear or configurational models to prognostic data. The general point to be made is that prognosis research seems to require a different, more complex, mathematical model, and thus a more complex research design, than has been generally used so far. Specifically the one-stage design, where a predictor is correlated with an outcome measure, would appear to be inadequate in this field.

REFERENCES

AFFLECK, D. C., & MEDNICK, S. A. The use of the Rorschach test in the prediction of the abrupt terminator in individual psychotherapy. *J. consult. Psychol.*, 1959, 23, 125–128.

APPEL, K. E., MEYERS, J. M., & SCHEFLEN, A. E. Prognosis in psychiatry. *AMA Arch. Neurol. Psychiat.*, 1953, 70, 459–468.

AULD, F., JR., & ERON, L. D. The use of Rorschach scores to predict whether patients will continue psychotherapy. *J. consult. Psychol.*, 1953, 17, 104–109.

AULD, F., JR., & MURRAY, E. J. Content-analysis studies of psychotherapy. *Psychol. Bull.*, 1955, 52, 377–395.

BAILEY, M. A., WARSHAW, L., & EICHLER, R. M. A study of factors related to length of stay in psychotherapy. *J. clin. Psychol.*, 1959, 15, 442–444.

BARRON, F. An ego-strength scale which predicts response to psychotherapy. *J. consult. Psychol.*, 1953, 17, 327–333. (a)

BARRON, F. Some test correlates of response to psychotherapy. *J. consult. Psychol.*, 1953, 17, 235–241. (b)

BARRON, F., & LEARY, T. F. Changes in psychoneurotic patients with and without psychotherapy. *J. consult. Psychol.*, 1955, 19, 239–245.

BARRY, J. R. The relation of verbal reactions to adjustment level. *J. abnorm. soc. Psychol.*, 1950, 45, 647–658.

BAYARD, JEAN, & PASCAL, G. R. Studies of prognostic criteria in the case records of hospitalized mental patients: Affective expression. *J. consult. Psychol.*, 1954, 18, 122–126.

BECKER, W. C., & McFARLAND, R. L. A lobotomy prognosis scale. *J. consult. Psychol.*, 1955, 19, 157–162.

BETZ, BARBARA J., & WHITEHORN, J. C. The relationship of the therapist to the outcome of therapy in schizophrenia. *Psychiat. res. Rep.*, 1956, No. 5, 89–105.

BLOOM, B. L. Prognostic significance of the underproductive Rorschach. *J. proj. Tech.*, 1956, 20, 366–371.

BRIGGS, P. F. Prediction of rehospitalization using the MMPI. *J. clin. Psychol.*, 1958, 14, 83–84.

BURDOCK, E. I., SUTTON, S., ZUBIN, J. Personality and psychopathology. *J. abnorm. soc. Psychol.*, 1958, 56, 18–30.

BURDOCK, E. I., & ZUBIN, J. A rationale for the classification of experimental techniques in abnormal psychology. *J. gen. Psychol.*, 1956, 55, 35–49.

CALDEN, G., THURSTON, J. R., STEWART, B. M., & VINEBERG, S. E. The use of the MMPI in predicting irregular discharge among tuberculosis patients. *J. clin. Psychol.*, 1955, 11, 374–377.

CARP, A. MMPI performance and insulin shock therapy. *J. abnorm. soc. Psychol.*, 1950, 45, 721–726.

CARTWRIGHT, D. S. Success in psychotherapy as a function of certain actuarial variables. *J. consult. Psychol.*, 1955, 19, 357–363.

CARTWRIGHT, ROSALIND D. Predicting response to client-centered therapy with the Rorschach *PR* scale. *J. counsel. Psychol.*, 1958, 5, 11–15.

CLOW, H. E. The use of a prognostic index of capacity for social adjustment in psychiatric disorders. In P. H. Hoch & J. Zubin (Eds.), *Current problems in psychiatric diagnosis.* New York: Grune & Stratton, 1953. Pp. 89–106.

COLE, MARY E., SWENSEN, C. H., & PASCAL, G. R. Prognostic significance of precipitating stress in mental illness. *J. consult. Psychol.*, 1954, 18, 171–175.

CONRAD, DOROTHY C. The duration of the therapeutic relationship and therapists' successive judgments of patients' mental health. *J. clin. Psychol.*, 1954, 10, 229–233.

COWDEN, R. C., DEABLER, H. L., & FEAMSTER, J. H. The prognostic value of the Bender-Gestalt, H-T-P, TAT, and Sentence Completion Test, *J. clin. Psychol.*, 1955, 11, 271–275.

CRANDALL, A., ZUBIN, J., METTLER, F. A., & LOGAN, N. D. The prognostic value of "mobility" during the first two years of hospitalization for mental disorder. *Psychiat. Quart.*, 1954, 28, 185–210.

CRONBACH, L. J., & GLESER, G. *Psychological tests and personnel decisions.* Urbana: Univer. Illinois Press, 1957.

DANA, R. H. The effects of attitudes towards authority on psychotherapy. *J. clin. Psychol.*, 1954, 10, 350–353.

DeCHARMS, R., LEVY, J., & WERTHEIMER, M. A note on attempted evaluations of psychotherapy. *J. clin. Psychol.*, 1954, 10, 233–235.

ELLSWORTH, R. B., & CLARK, L. D. Prediction of the response of chronic schizophrenics to drug therapy: A preliminary report on the relationship between palmar sweat and the behavioral effects of tranquilizing drugs. *J. clin. Psychol.*, 1957, 13, 59–61.

ELLSWORTH, R. B., & CLAYTON, W. H. Measurement of improvement in "mental illness." *J. consult. Psychol.*, 1959, 23, 15–20.

ENDS, E. J., & PAGE, C. W. Group psychotherapy and concomitant psychological change. *Psychol. Monogr.*, 1959, 73(10, Whole No. 480).

ESKEY, A., FRIEDMAN, GLADYS M., & FRIEDMAN, I. Disorientation as a prognostic criterion. *J. consult. Psychol.*, 1957, 21, 149–151.

ESKEY, A., & FRIEDMAN, I. The prognostic significance of certain behavioral variables. *J. consult., Psychol.,* 1958, 22, 91–94.

EYSENCK, H. J. The effects of psychotherapy: An evaluation. *J. consult. Psychol.,* 1952, 16, 319–324.

EYSENCK, H. J., GRANGER, G. W., & BRENGELMAN, J. C. *Perceptual processes and mental illness.* London: Institute of Psychiatry, 1957.

FELDMAN, DOROTHY A., PASCAL, G. R., & SWENSEN, C. H. Direction of aggression as a prognostic variable in mental illness. *J consult. Psychol.,* 1954, 18, 167–170.

FELDMAN, M. J. A prognostic scale for shock therapy. *Psychol. Monogr.* 1951, 65(10, Whole No. 327).

FELDMAN, M. J. The use of the MMPI profile for prognosis and evaluation of shock therapy. *J. consult. Psychol.,* 1952, 16, 376–382.

FELDMAN, M. J. An evaluation scale for shock therapy. *J. clin. Psychol.,* 1958, 14, 41–45.

FILMER-BENNETT, G. Prognostic indices in the Rorschach records of hospitalized patients. *J. abnorm. soc. Psychol.,* 1952, 47, 502–506.

FILMER-BENNETT, G. The Rorschach as a means of predicting treatment outcome. *J. consult. Psychol.,* 1955, 19, 331–334.

FLEISHMAN, E. A., & HEMPEL, W. E. A factor analysis of dexterity tests. *Personnel Psychol.,* 1954, 7, 14–32.

FLEISHMAN, E. A., & HEMPEL, W. E. Factorial analysis of complex psychomotor performance and related skills. *J. appl. Psychol.,* 1956, 40, 96–104.

FRANK, J. E., GLEIDMAN, L. H., IMBER, S. D., NASH, E. H., & STONE, A. R. Why patients leave psychotherapy. *AMA Arch. Neurol. Psychiat.,* 1957, 79, 283–299.

FULKERSON, S. C. Individual differences in response validity. *J. clin. Psychol.,* 1959, 15, 169–173.

GALLAGHER, J. J. The problem of escaping clients in nondirective counseling. In W. U. Snyder, *Group report of a program of research in psychotherapy.* State College: Pennsylvania State College, Psychotherapy Research Group, 1953. Pp. 21–38. (Mimeo)

GALLAGHER, J. J. Test indicators for therapy prognosis. *J. consult. Psychol.,* 1954, 18, 409–413.

GHISELLI, E. E. Differentiation of individuals in terms of their predictability. *J. appl. Psychol.,* 1956, 40, 374–377.

GIBBY, R. G., STOTSKY, B. A., HILER, H. W., & MILLER, D. R. Validation of Rorschach criteria for predicting duration of therapy. *J. consult. Psychol.,* 1954, 18, 185–191.

GIBBY, R. G., STOTSKY, B. A., MILLER, D. R., & HILER, H. W. Prediction of duration of therapy from the Rorschach test. *J. consult. Psychol.,* 1953, 17, 348–354.

GLASS, A. J., RYAN, F. J., LUBIN, A., REDDY, C. V. R., & TUCKER, A. C. Factors influencing psychiatrists in the prediction of military effectiveness. *Walter Reed Army Inst. Res. res. Rep.,* 1956, No. WRAIR-186–56.

GLEIDMAN, L. H., STONE, A. R., FRANK, D. D., NASH, E., JR., & IMBER, S. D. Incentives for treatment related to remaining or improving in psychotherapy. *Amer. J. Psychother.,* 1957, 11, 589–598.

GLESER, GOLDINE, HADDOCK, J., STARR, P., & ULETT, G. A. Psychiatric screening of flying personnel: Inter-rater agreement on the basis of psychiatric interviews. *USAF Sch. Aviat. Med. proj. Rep.* 1954, No. 10.

GORDON, M. H., LINDLEY, S. B., & MAY, R. B. A criterion measure of within-hospital change in psychiatric illness. *J. clin. Psychol.,* 1957, 13, 145–147.

GRAUER, D. Prognosis in paranoid schizophrenia on the basis of the Rorschach. *J. consult. Psychol.,* 1953, 17, 199–205.

GRAYSON, H. M., & OLINGER, L. B. Simulation of "normalcy" by psychiatric patients on the MMPI. *J. consult. Psychol.,* 1957, 21, 73–77.

GUILFORD, J. P. The structure of intellect. *Psychol. Bull.,* 1956, 53, 267–293.

GUILFORD, J. P. Three faces of intellect. *Amer. Psychologist,* 1959, 14, 469–479.

GUNDLACH, R. H., & GELLER, M. The problem of early termination: Is it really the terminee? *J. consult. Psychol.,* 1958, 22, 410.

HAMMER, E. F. The role of the H-T-P in the prognostic battery. *J. clin. Psychol.,* 1953, 9, 371–374.

HARRIS, R. E. The prediction and measurement of drug-induced psychological change. In J. O. Cole & R. W. Gerard (Eds.), *Psychopharmacology: Problems in evaluation.* (NAS-NRC Publ. No. 583) Washington, D.C.: National Academy of Sciences–National Research Council, 1959. Pp. 514–528.

HASTINGS, D. W. Follow-up results in psychiatric illness. *Amer. J. Psychiat.*, 1958, 114, 1057–1066.

HEMPEL, W. E., & FLEISHMAN, E. A. A factor analysis of physical proficiency and manipulative skills. *J. appl. Psychol.*, 1955, 39, 12–16.

HILER, E. W. An analysis of patient-therapist compatibility. *J. consult. Psychol.*, 1958, 22, 341–347. (a)

HILER, E. W. Wechsler-Bellevue intelligence as a predictor of continuation in psychotherapy. *J. clin. Psychol.*, 1958, 14, 192–194. (b)

HILER, E. W. Initial complaints as predictors of continuation in psychotherapy. *J. clin. Psychol.*, 1959, 15, 244–245.

HOZIER, ANN. On the breakdown of the sense of reality: A study of spatial perception in schizophrenia. *J. consult. Psychol.*, 1959, 23, 185–194.

HUSTON, P. H., & PEPERNIK, M. C. Prognosis in schizophrenia. In L. Bellak (Ed.), *Schizophrenia: A review of the syndrome.* New York: Logos, 1958. Pp. 531–546.

HYBL, A. R., & STAGNER, R. Frustration tolerance in relation to diagnosis and therapy. *J. consult. Psychol.*, 1952, 16, 163–170.

IMBER, S. D., FRANK, J. D., GLIEDMAN, L. H., NASH, E. H., & STONE, A. R. Suggestibility, social class and the acceptance of psychotherapy. *J. clin. Psychol.*, 1956, 12, 341–344.

IMBER, S. D., FRANK, J. D., NASH, E. H., STONE, A. R., & GLIEDMAN, L. H. Improvement and amount of therapeutic contact: An alternative to the use of no-treatment controls in psychotherapy. *J. consult. Psychol.*, 1957, 21, 309–315.

IMBER, S. D., NASH, E. H., & STONE, A. R. Social class and duration of psychotherapy. *J. clin. Psychol.*, 1955, 11, 281–284.

JAHODA, MARIE. *Current concepts of positive mental health.* New York: Basic Books, 1958.

KALIS, BETTY L., & BENNETT, LILLIAN F. The assessment of communication: The relation of clinical improvement to measured changes in communicative behavior. *J. consult. Psychol.*, 1957, 21, 10–14.

KATZ, J., & SOLOMON, REBECCA Z. The patient and his experiences in an outpatient clinic. *AMA Arch. Neurol. Psychiat.*, 1958, 80, 86–92.

KATZ, M. M., LORR, M., & RUBINSTEIN, E. A. Remainder patient attributes and their relation to subsequent improvement in psychotherapy. *J. consult. Psychol.*, 1958, 22, 411–413.

KAUFMAN, P. Changes in the Minnesota Multiphasic Personality Inventory as a function of psychiatric therapy. *J. consult. Psychol.*, 1950, 14, 458–464.

KEEHN, J. D. An investigation into the value of "objective test psychoticism" in predicting response to insulin coma therapy. *J. ment. Sci.*, 1955, 101, 871–877.

KELMAN, H. C., & PARLOFF, M. B. Interrelations among three criteria of improvement in group therapy: Comfort, effectiveness, and self-awareness. *J. abnorm. soc. Psychol.*, 1957, 54, 281–288.

KING, H. E. *Psychomotor aspects of mental disease.* Cambridge: Harvard Univer. Press, 1954.

KIRKNER, F. J., WISHAM, W. W., & GIEDT, F. H. A report on the validity of the Rorschach Prognostic Rating Scale. *J. proj. Tech.*, 1953, 17, 465–470.

KLOPFER, B., KIRKNER, F. J., WISHAM, W., & BAKER, G. Rorschach Prognostic Rating Scale. *J. proj. Tech.*, 1951, 15, 425–428.

KNIGHT, R. P. Evaluation of the results of psychoanalytic therapy. *Amer. J. Psychiat.*, 1941, 98, 434–446.

KOTKOV, B., & MEADOW, A. Rorschach criteria for continuing group psychotherapy. *Int. J. group Psychother.*, 1952, 2, 324–333.

KOTKOV, B., & MEADOW, A. Rorschach criteria for predicting continuation in individual psychotherapy. *J. consult. Psychol.*, 1953, 17, 16–20.

KRAMER, M., & GREENHOUSE, S. W. Determination of sample size and selection of cases. In J. O. Cole & R. W. Gerard (Eds.), *Psychopharmacology: Problems in evaluation.* (NAS-NRC Publ. No. 583) Washington, D.C.: National Academy of Sciences–National Research Council, 1959. Pp. 356–371.

KRASNER, L. Studies of the conditioning of verbal behavior. *Psychol. Bull.*, 1958, 55, 145–170.

KUBIE, L. S. Some unsolved problems of psychoanalytic psychotherapy. In F. Fromm-Reichman & J. L. Moreno (Eds.), *Progress in psychotherapy 1956.* New York: Grune & Stratton, 1956. Pp. 87–102.

LANDIS, C., & CLAUSEN, J. Changes in sensory and motor performances induced by active psychiatric treatment. *J. Psychol.*, 1955, 40, 275–305.

LANGFELDT, G. The prognosis in schizophrenia. *Acta psychiat. neurol. Scand., Kbh.*, 1956, Suppl. 110, 1–66.

LEARY, T., & HARVEY, J. S. A methodology for measuring personality changes in psychotherapy. *J. clin. Psychol.*, 1956, 12, 123–132.

LEVITT, E. E. The results of psychotherapy with children: An evaluation. *J. consult. Psychol.*, 1957, 21, 189–196.

LIBO, L. M. The projective expression of patient-therapist attraction. *J. clin. Psychol.*, 1957, 13, 33–36.

LINDEMANN, J. H., FAIRWEATHER, G. W., STONE, G. B., & SMITH, R. S. The use of demographic characteristics in predicting length of neuropsychiatric hospital stay. *J. consult. Psychol.*, 1959, 23, 85–89.

LORR, M., KATZ, M. M., & RUBINSTEIN, E. A. The prediction of length of stay in psychotherapy. *J. consult. Psychol.*, 1958, 22, 321–327.

LUCE, R. D., & RAIFFA, H. *Games and decisions.* New York: Wiley, 1957.

MEEHL, P. E., & ROSEN, A. Antecedent probability and the efficiency of psychometric signs, patterns, or cutting scores. *Psychol. Bull.* 1955, 52, 194–216.

MILES, H. H. W., BARRABEE, E. L., & FINESINGER, J. E. Evaluation of psychotherapy with a follow-up study of 62 cases of anxiety neurosis. *Psychosom. Med.*, 1951, 13, 83–105.

MINDESS, H. Predicting patients' responses to psychotherapy: A preliminary study designed to investigate the validity of the Rorschach Prognostic Rating Scale. *J. proj. Tech.*, 1953, 17, 327–334.

MORAN, L. J., FAIRWEATHER, G. W., & MORTON, R. B. Some determinants of successful and unsuccessful adaptation to hospital treatment of tuberculosis. *J. consult. Psychol.*, 1956, 20, 125–131.

MORSE, P. W. A proposed technique for the evaluation of psychotherapy. *Amer. J. Orthopsychiat.*, 1953, 23, 716–731.

MORTON, R. B. An experiment in brief psychotherapy. *Psychol. Monogr.*, 1955, 67(1, Whole No. 386).

MYERS, J. K., & AULD, F. Some variables related to outcome of psychotherapy. *J. clin. Psychol.*, 1955, 11, 51–54.

NASH, E. H., JR., FRANK, J. D., GLIEDMAN, L. H., IMBER, S. D., & STONE, A. R. Some factors related to patients remaining in group psychotherapy. *Int. J. group Psychother.*, 1957, 7, 264–274.

ORR, W. F., ANDERSON, R. B., MARTIN, M. P., & PHILPOT, D. F. Factors influencing discharge of female patients from a state mental hospital. *Amer. J. Pspchiat.*, 1955, 111, 576–582.

PARLOFF, M. B., KELMAN, H. C., & FRANK, J. D. Comfort, effectiveness, and self-awareness as criteria of improvement in psychotherapy. *Amer. J. Psychiat.*, 1954, 111, 343–351.

PASCAL, G. R., SWENSEN, C. H., FELDMAN, D. A. COLE, M. E., & BAYARD, J. Prognostic criteria in the case histories of hospitalized mental patients. *J. consult. Psychol.*, 1953, 17, 163–171.

PASCAL, G. R., & ZAX, M. Psychotherapeutics: Success or failure. *J. consult. Psychol.*, 1956, 20, 325–331.

PASCAL, G. R., & ZEAMAN, JEAN B. Measurement of some effects of electroconvulsive therapy on the individual patient. *J. abnorm. soc. Psychol.*, 1951, 45, 104–115.

PETERSON, D. R. The diagnosis of subclinical schizophrenia. *J. consult. Psychol.*, 1954, 18, 198–200. (a)

PETERSON, D. R. Predicting hospitalization of psychiatric outpatients. *J. abnorm. soc. Psychol.*, 1954, 49, 260–265 (b)

PHILLIPS, L. Case history data and prognosis in schizophrenia. *J. nerv. ment. Dis.*, 1953, 117, 515–525.

PUMROY, D. K., & KOGAN, W. S. A validation of measures that predict the efficacy of shock therapy. *J. clin. Psychol.*, 1958, 14, 46–47.

RABIN, A. I., & KING, G. F. Psychological studies. In L. Bellak (Ed.), *Schizophrenia: A review of the syndrome.* New York: Logos 1958. Pp. 216–278.

RAPAPORT, G. M. "Ideal self" instructions, MMPI profile changes, and the prediction, of clinical improvement. *J. consult. Psychol.*, 1958, 22, 459–463.

RENNIE, T. A. C. Prognosis in the psychoneuroses: Benign and malignant developments. In P. H. Hoch & J. Zubin (Eds.), *Current problems in psychiatric diagnosis.* New York: Grune & Stratton, 1953. Pp. 67–79.

REZNIKOFF, M., & TOOMEY, L. C. *Evaluation of changes associated with psychiatric treatment.* Springfield: Charles C. Thomas, 1959.

RIOCH, MARGARET J., & LUBIN, A. Prognosis of social adjustment for mental hospital patients under psychotherapy. *J. consult. Psychol.,* 1959, 23, 313–318.

ROBERTS, L. K. The failure of some Rorschach indices to predict the outcome of psychotherapy. *J. consult. Psychol.,* 1954, 18, 96–98.

ROGERS, C. R., & DYMOND, ROSALIND F. (Eds.) *Psychotherapy and personality change.* Chicago: Univer. Chicago Press, 1954.

ROGERS, L. S., & HAMMOND, K. R. Prediction of the results of therapy by means of the Rorschach test. *J. consult. Psychol.,* 1953, 17, 8–15.

ROGERS, L. S., KNAUSS, JOANNE, & HAMMOND, K. R. Predicting continuation in therapy by means of the Rorschach test. *J. consult. Psychol.,* 1951, 15, 368–371.

ROSEN, E. Ethnocentric attitude changes and rated improvement in hospitalized psychiatric patients. *J. clin. Psychol.,* 1954, 10, 345–350.

ROSENBAUM, M., FRIEDLANDER, JANE, & KAPLAN, S. M. Evaluation of results of psychotherapy. *Psychosom. Med.,* 1956, 18, 113–132.

ROSENBERG, S. The relationship of certain personality factors to prognosis in psychotherapy. *J. clin. Psychol.,* 1954, 10, 341–345.

ROSENTHAL, D. Changes in some moral values following psychotherapy. *J. consult. Psychol.,* 1955, 19, 431–436.

ROSENZWEIG, S. A transvaluation of psychotherapy: A reply to Hans Eysenck. *J. abnorm. soc. Psychol.,* 1954, 49, 298–304.

RUBINSTEIN, E. A., & LORR, M. A comparison of terminators and remainers in outpatient psychotherapy. *J. clin. Psychol.,* 1956, 12, 345–349.

SCHAFFER, L., & MYERS, J. K. Psychotherapy and social stratification: An empirical study of practice in a psychiatric out-patient clinic. *Psychiatry,* 1954, 17, 83–93.

SCHOFIELD, W. Changes in response to the Minnesota Multiphasic Personality Inventory following certain therapies. *Psychol. Monogr.,* 1950, 64(5, Whole No. 311).

SCHOFIELD, W. A further study of the effects of therapies on MMPI responses. *J. abnorm. soc. Psychol.,* 1953, 48, 67–77.

SCHOFIELD, W., & BRIGGS, P. F. Criteria of therapeutic response in hospitalized psychiatric patients. *J. clin. Psychol.,* 1958, 14, 227–232.

SCHOFIELD, W., HATHAWAY, S. R., HASTINGS, D. W., & BELL, DOROTHY M. Prognostic factors in schizophrenia. *J. consult. Psychol.* 1954, 18, 155–166.

SCOTT, W. A. Research definitions of mental health and mental illness. *Psychol. Bull.,* 1958, 55, 29–45.

SEASHORE, R. A., BUXTON, C. E., & McCOLLUM, I. N. Multiple factorial analysis of fine motor skills. *Amer. J. Psychol.,* 1940, 53, 251–259.

SEEMAN, J. Counselor judgments of therapeutic process and outcome. In C. R. Rogers & R. F. Dymond (Eds.), *Psychotherapy and personality change.* Chicago: Univer. Chicago Press, 1954. Pp. 99–108.

SNYDER, W. U. *Group report of a program of research in psychotherapy.* State College: Pennsylvania State College, Psychotherapy Research Group, 1953. (Mimeo)

SONDER, SYLVIA L. Perceptual tests and acute and chronic status as predictors of improvement in psychotic patients. *J. consult. Psychol.,* 1955, 19, 387–392.

STANDAL, S. W., & VAN DER VEEN, F. Length of therapy in relation to counselor estimates of personal integration and other case variables. *J. consult. Psychol.,* 1957, 21, 1–9.

STAUDT, VIRGINIA, M., & ZUBIN, J. A biometric evaluation of the somatotherapies in schizophrenia. *Psychol. Bull.,* 1957, 54, 171–196.

STIEPER, D. R., & WIENER, D. N. The problem of interminability in outpatient psychotherapy. *J. consult. Psychol.,* 1959, 23, 237–242.

STILSON, D. W., MASON, D. J., GYNTHER, M. D., & GERTZ, B. An evaluation of the comparability and reliabilities of two behavior rating scales for mental patients. *J. consult. Psychol.,* 1958, 22, 213–216.

STONE, BETH. Prognostic factors in schizophrenia. *J. consult. Psychol.,* 1959, 23, 279.

STORROW, H. A. The measurement of change in psychotherapy. *Scientific Papers of the 115th Annual Meeting of the American Psychiatric Association,* 1959, 41–42. (Abstract)

STORROW, H. A. The measurement of outcome in psychotherapy. *AMA Arch. gen. Psychiat.,* 1960, 2, 142–146.

STOTSKY, B. A. A comparison of remitting and non-remitting schizophrenics on psychological tests. *J. abnorm. soc. Psychol.,* 1952, 47, 489–496.

STOTSKY, B. A. How important is psychotherapy to the hospitalized psychiatric patient. *J. clin. Psychol.,* 1956, 12, 32–36. (a)

STOTSKY, B. A. Vocational tests as measures of performance of schizophrenics in two rehabilitation activities. *J. clin. Psychol.,* 1956, 12, 236–242. (b)

STRUPP, H. H. The psychotherapists' contribution to the treatment process. *Behav. Sci.,* 1958, 3, 34–67.

SULLIVAN, P. L., MILLER, CHRISTINE, & SMELSER, W. Factors in length of stay and progress in psychotherapy. *J. consult. Psychol.,* 1958, 22, 1–9.

SWENSON, C. H., & PASCAL, G. R. A note on the Bender-Gestalt test as a prognostic indicator in mental illness. *J. clin. Psychol.,* 1953, 9, 398.

SWENSEN, C. H., JR., & PASCAL, G. R. Duration of illness as a prognostic indicator in mental illness. *J. consult. Psychol.,* 1954, 18, 363–365. (a)

SWENSEN, C. H., JR., & PASCAL, G. R. Prognostic significance of type of onset of mental illness. *J. consult. Psychol.,* 1954, 18, 127–130. (b)

TAULBEE, E. S. Relationship between certain personality variables and continuation in psychotherapy. *J. consult. Psychol.,* 1958, 22, 83–89.

TAYLOR, D. M. Changes in the self concept without psychotherapy. *J. consult. Psychol.,* 1955, 19, 205–209.

TAYLOR, J. W. Relationship of success and length in psychotherapy. *J. consult. Psychol.,* 1956, 20, 332.

THORNE, F. C. The prognostic index. *J. clin. Psychol.,* 1952, 8, 42–45.

THURSTONE, L. L. *A factorial study of perception.* Chicago: Univer. Chicago Press, 1944.

ULLMAN, L. P. Selection of neuropsychiatric patients for group psychotherapy. *J. consult. Psychol.,* 1957, 21, 277–280.

VENABLES, P. H., & TIZARD, J. Paradoxical effects in the reaction time of schizophrenics. *J. abnorm. soc. Psychol.,* 1956, 53, 220–224. (a)

VENABLES, P. H., & TIZARD, J. Performance of functional psychotics on a repetitive task. *J. abnorm. soc. Psychol.,* 1956, 53, 23–26. (b)

VERNIER, C. M., WHITING, J. F., & MELTZER, M. L. Differential prediction of a specific behavior from three projective techniques. *J. consult. Psychol.,* 1955, 19, 175–182.

VINSON, D. B., JR. Response to electroshock therapy as evaluated by mirror drawing. *J. clin. exp. Psychopath.,* 1952, 13, 201–210.

VOSBURG, R. Some remarks on psychotherapy as reflected in hospital charts. *Psychiat. Commun.,* 1958, 1, 151–160.

WECHSLER, D. *The measurement and appraisal of adult intelligence.* Baltimore: Williams & Wilkins, 1958.

WIENER, D. N. The effect of arbitrary termination on return to psychotherapy. *J. clin. Psychol.,* 1959, 15, 335–338.

WILLIAMS, R. J., & MACHI, V. S. An analysis of interperson correlations among thirty psychotics. *J. abnorm. soc. Psychol.,* 1957, 55, 50–57.

WINDER, A. E., & HERSKO, M. The effect of social class on the length and type of psychotherapy in a Veterans' Administration mental hygiene clinic. *J. clin. Psychol.,* 1955, 11, 77–79.

WINDER, C. L. Psychotherapy. *Annu. Rev. Psychol.,* 1957, 8, 309–330.

WINDLE, C. Psychological tests in psychopathological prognosis. *Psychol. Bull.,* 1952, 49, 451–482.

WINDLE, C. Test-retest effect on personality questionnaires. *Educ. psychol. Measmt.,* 1954, 14, 617–633.

WINDLE, C., & HAMWI, VIOLET. An exploratory study of the prognostic value of the Complex Reaction Time Test in early and chronic psychotics. *J. clin. Psychol.,* 1953, 9, 156–161.

WIRT, R. D. Further validation of the ego-strength scale. *J. consult. Psychol.,* 1955, 19, 444.

WIRT, R. D. Actuarial prediction. *J. consult. Psychol.,* 1956, 20, 123–124.

ZUBIN, J. A biometric model for psychopathology. In R. A. Patton (Ed.), *Current trends in the description and analysis of behavior.* Pittsburgh: Univer. Pittsburgh Press, 1958. Pp. 22–47.

ZUBIN, J. Role of prognostic indicators in the evaluation of therapy. In J. O. Cole & R. W. Gerard (Eds.), *Psychopharmacology: Problems in evaluation.* (NAS-NRC Publ. No. 583) Washington, D.C.: National Academy Sciences–National Research Council, 1959. Pp. 343–355.

ZUBIN, J., & WINDLE, C. Psychological prognosis of outcome in the mental disorders. *J. abnorm. soc. Psychol.,* 1954, 49, 272–281.

ZUBIN, J., WINDLE, C., & HAMWI, V. Retrospective evaluation of psychological tests as prognostic instruments in mental disorders. *J. Pers.* 1953, 21, 342–355.

Studies of "Dropout" Patients in Psychotherapy: A Review of Findings

LEWIS W. BRANDT

The increase in mental health clinics since the late forties has led to a number of studies aiming to identify dropout patients as early as possible. Levinger (1960) summarized a number of those studies. The present report shows that findings from the various studies can be compared only to a very limited degree because of the great variations in both dependent and independent variables.

Morris and Soroker (1953), Fanshel (1958), and Lake and Levinger (1960) studied dropouts from family agencies and child guidance clinics. There, the decision to begin and to end treatment is generally made by a parent. Dropout of children thus differs basically from that of adult patients.

Another group of dropout studies, hardly comparable to studies in mental health clinics, are those on group psychotherapy (Kotkov and Meadow, 1952) and on private practice (Crowley, 1950).

One also must distinguish between short-term counseling (Kirk and Headley, 1950; Bartlett, 1950), client-centered therapy (Gallagher, 1951; Kirtner and Cartwright, 1958), and long-term psychoanalytic treatment. Patients' expectations are basically different in short and long-term therapies, and, therefore, *dropout* has very different meanings (Gundlach and Geller, 1958). Freedman *et al.* (1958), Heine (1960), and Kadushin (1962) actually reported a correlation between patients' expectations of and their continuation in therapy.

"Dropout" is widely taken to refer to the patient's decision, not the therapist's. However, both kinds of termination are mixed together in most studies. Garfield and Affleck (1959) state that "the reasons for termination fall into two primary groups: those in which the patient initiates termination and those in which termination is largely guided by the therapist." Yet, later in the same paper, they combine the two groups in their statistical analyses. The same is true of the otherwise extremely detailed studies by Rosenthal and Frank (1958) and Lief *et al.* (1961), as well as in briefer ones by Auld and Myers (1954), Taylor (1956), and Gundlach and Geller (1958).

Reprinted from *Psychotherapy: Theory Research and Practice,* 1965, 2, 6–13, with the permission of Psychologists Interested in the Advancement of Psychotherapy and the author.

Yet, the distinction is an important one as can be seen from a statement by Myers and Auld (1955):

The patient was discharged by the therapist as an unsuccessful case. The doctor felt the therapeutic relationship was unsatisfactory and that the patient was not able to profit from it. In essence, the therapist gave up on the case, even though the patient may have desired to continue.

Myers and Auld found 8% of terminations within the first nine, and 17% during the following ten sessions to fall into this category.

The reason for the common omission of this distinction may be (Myers and Auld, 1955) "the manner in which therapy was terminated was not noted officially at any specific place in the record, but it was possible to determine it by examining the entire record."

None of these studies, except Myers and Auld, note which of the non-dropouts (patients who continued treatment after a specified number of sessions) terminated treatment a little later with or without the concurrence of the therapist. Now, Gundlach and Geller (1958) reported a median number of 44 sessions for all patients, and Lief et al. (1961) reported a similar average number. Psychoanalytically oriented therapists frequently recommend three or six-month "trial periods" at three to five weekly sessions. As Burnham (1951) showed, patients rated optimal as well as those rated poorest by their respective therapists frequently remained in treatment for several years. Continuation beyond even the twentieth session, then, is not an indication of the patient's "motivation for psychotherapy" nor of his "remaining in therapy."

It would seem more meaningful to disregard the number of sessions and distinguish instead between "ceased keeping appointments" and "discharged" as Goucher (1949), Feldman, Barba, and Sell (1950), and Weinberger and Gay (1951) did. Exactly because they had no cut-off point, these studies cannot be compared, however, with other dropout studies (except on broken appointments before the sixth interview).

IN-THERAPY DROPOUT STUDIES REVIEWED

Twenty-five dropout studies of adult patients in individual long-term psychotherapy at outpatient clinics who terminated clearly without therapist concurrence were found in the literature.

As can be seen from Table I, these studies differed in type of clinic, fee, sex, cut-off point (varying for remainers between 4 sessions and 6 months), population size (ranging from 24 to 2,478), and also in the amount of information they supplied.

A few studies contained no reference to the clinic where they were undertaken. Only one-third mentioned the kind of therapy given. Most of those which did mention an orientation reported "psychoanalytically oriented psychotherapy." Only a fourth mentioned treatment fees. Half the studies were from Veterans Administration Mental Hygiene Clinics, which charge no fee. The authors apparently assumed that readers knew this fact.

Less than half the studies gave the percentage which dropouts represented in terms of the total patient population. Kurland (1956) stated the difficulty of interpreting dropouts in the "absence of base-line or generalized information about how long patients stay in treatment in various settings." Table I shows that the more recent studies have not included this information.

Figure I shows how dropouts varied from one clinic to the other. Pre-therapy dropout varied between 3% and 35%. The time when 50% of dropouts occurred varied between the third and the forty-fourth session. These figures were contaminated by the inclusion of therapist-terminations in the case of 44 sessions and by the probable exclusion of pretherapy dropouts by the majority of the studies. Thus, dropout rates even when stated were usually not comparable. Some of

TABLE I

Summary of Data Presented in Various Dropout Studies

Year	Senior Author	Type	Clinic Orien-tation	Fee	% Drop out[1]	Fre-quency[2]	Cutoff[3]	N	Sex	Diag-nosis	Prev. Therapy[4]
1949	Staiman	VA	disr.[5]	x[6]	x		5/14	100	M	x	x
	Kennedy	VA			x		3	40	M	x	
	Weinberger	VA			x		5				
1951	Rogers	VA			x		4	109			
1953	Gibby	VA	x			x	5/6m[7]	66	M	x	
	Kotkov	VA					8	52	M	x	
	Auld	x		x			8	33		x	
1954	Gibby	VA	x	x	x		5/19	269	M	x	
	Hiler	VA	x	x	x		5/19	302		x	x
1955	Myers		x		x		9/19	63			
1956	Imber	x			x		3	57		x	
	Kurland	VA			x		4/6	2478	x[8]		x
	Rubinstein	VA	x			x	5/6m[7]	128	M	x	x
1957	Frank	x			x	x	3	91	x	x	x
	Gliedman	x	disr.				3	91	"see Frank '57"[9]		
1958	Freedman	x	x				9	54	x	x	
	Hiler	VA	x				5/19	133	"see Gibby '54"		
	Kadushin	x	x		x		4	110		x	x
	Lorr	VA				x	6w/25w	230	M	x	x
1959	Affleck			x	x		3	100	M	x	
	Hiler	VA	x					95	"see Gibby '54"		
1960	Heine	x					6w	46			
1961	Affleck						7	46	x		
	Garfield						17	24	x		
	Quaytman	x		x			5/19	100	F	x	

[1] Percentage of patients who left treatment without therapist's concurrence is mentioned.
[2] Frequency of sessions is mentioned.
[3] A single number indicates the last session kept by dropouts and beyond which patients were classified as remainders. Two numbers separated by a diagonal line indicate the last session kept by dropouts and the session beyond which patients were considered remainers. "w" indicates that instead of session number, number of weeks were taken as differentiating factor.
[4] Previous psychotherapy was taken into account and mentioned.
[5] The authors mention that they disregarded this variable.
[6] The variable is mentioned only.
[7] Dropouts did not stay beyond the fifth sessions, remainers stayed at least 6 months.
[8] There is only some reference to patients' sex.
[9] The authors refer the reader for these data to another study.

the differences in percentage of dropout may reflect differences in patient populations or in the clinics themselves, their intake procedures, selections, fees, therapists, or all of these. The differences in base-lines make it impossible to decide which variables may be responsible for the differences in reported dropout rates.

Frequency of sessions was mentioned by only 4 out of the 25 studies. In these 4 studies frequency varied: for Gibby et al. (1953), "between one and three times per week"; for Frank et al. (1957), "at least one hour per week," or "not more than one-half hour every two weeks" (which two groups are combined furthermore with pa-

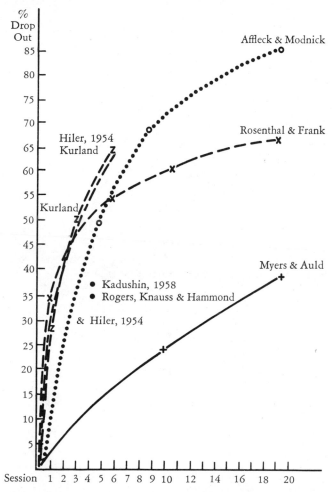

Figure I. Cumulative percentages of dropout before given number of psychotherapy sessions according to different studies.

tients in group therapy); and patients in the study of Lorr, Katz, and Rubinstein (1958) received "an average of at least one treatment every four weeks."

The meaningfulness of cut-off points has already been questioned. It is even more questionable to compare studies whose cut-off point varies from 3 sessions to 6 months. If the differences in frequencies of sessions are combined with the differences in cut-off points, the following picture results: 3 sessions spread over 3 months could be equated

with 3 sessions within the same week. Six sessions in 6 months might have been equated with 78 sessions in the same period.

Table I also shows that the largest sample used in these studies was just 100 times as large as the smallest one. It seems doubtful that even careful statistical procedures permit comparisons between such divergences.

As Table I indicates, in one-fourth of the studies no diagnostic categories were given to describe the population. About half of those which did used very broad terms, e.g.,

TABLE II

VARIABLES FOUND IN DROPOUT STUDIES TO DIFFERENTIATE (d), NOT TO DIFFERENTIATE (0) BETWEEN REMAINERS AND TERMINATORS OR HELD CONSTANT (c) FOR BOTH GROUPS

	Kurland	Kennedy	Kotkov	Rogers	V. A. Detroit[1]	Staiman	Lorr	Rubinstein	Heine	Phipps Clinic[2]	Freedman	Auld	Kadushin	Quaytman	Affeck 59	Affeck 61	Garfield	Myers
Sex		c	c		c	c	c	c		0	c			c	c	0		
Age		0			0	0	0	0		0				d		0		
Education					d	d	d	d		d				c		0		
Religion		0					d	0		c				c				
Race		c					d			c				0				
Income		0			d	d	0	d		d				0		0		
Occupation		0				d	0	0		0				0		0		
Marital Status					d	0	0	d		d						0		
Social Class						d					c							
Referral Source		d			d	d	0	c		d				0				
Previous Therapy	d	0				0	0	d		0				d				
Statement of Problem		d			d	d			0	d	d			d			0	
Intake Data, History		0				0	0	d		d	c		d					
Diagnosis					d	d		0		0								
Prognosis					0			d		d								
Personality characteristics		d		0	d	d	d	d		d	d			d			d	
Therapist's Sex					d		c	c		c								
Therapist's Discipline		c			d		c	c		c	c			c				
Therapist's Experience					d		c	c		c								
Therapist's Personality					0		c	c		d	d				d			
Patient's Expectations					0						d	0			0	0	d	d
Rorschach			d	d		d						d						
Wechsler-Bellevue						0												
Sentence Completion										0								
Bender Gestalt																		
Draw-A-Person																		
Self-rating Scales							d	d		0								
Sway-test										d								
Max. % prediction[3]		69			71	71	71	68			73			73	67	$\frac{52}{87}$[4]		

[1] Combined data from Gibby, 1953 and 1954, and Hiler, 1954, 1958 and 1959, which were based on subsamples of the same population.
[2] Combined data from Frank, 1957, Gliedman, 1957, and Imber, 1956, which were based on subsamples of the same population.

by excluding cases of service-connected brain damage or psychosis. Quaytman (1961), on the other hand, whose subjects were all neurotic women, presented a detailed breakdown of the two comparison groups into subcategories of neurosis. Yet, he did not make any further analysis although his two groups were not matched on those subcategories.

FINDINGS

Findings concerning the relationship of diagnosis to dropout differed (Table II). While the Detroit and Phipps researchers found diagnosis related to dropout, a number of other researchers did not.

Similar differences in findings exist on the relationship between dropout and previous therapy. Yet, only a minority of studies took previous psychotherapy into account (Table I).

Discrepancies in findings far outweighed agreements. Of the 29 criteria investigated by 18 researchers and research teams, only sex, age, and marital status consistently did not differentiate between dropouts and remainers. The only criterion which consistently differentiated between the two groups was "personality characteristics." However, the specific personality characteristics and the methods for determining them differed from one study to the next.

Before concluding this comparison of dropout studies, we should mention the only study found in the literature which attempted to decrease the number of dropouts. This is the study by Weinberger and Gay (1949), not included in Table II because it mentioned none of the variables on that table.

Weinberger and Gay used a new dual intake procedure: each new patient was seen by both the psychiatrist and a social worker for intake. They then compared the monthly number of patients ceasing to keep appointments and of discharged patients in the old and new intake procedure. The terminations of patients who ceased keeping appoint-

ments dropped from 57.5% and 76.5% to 39.6%. They seem to have demonstrated that intake procedure is related to dropout.

In summary, there is very little uniformity in the data presented, the controlled variables, the variables investigated, the baselines, the definitions, and the findings reported.

PRE-THERAPY DROPOUT STUDIES

The number of variables involved in pre-therapy dropout is smaller than for in-therapy dropout: type of therapy and therapist and frequency of sessions are excluded by definition. Yet, on a number of variables these studies also differ.

Weinberger and Gay began an "Analysis of Factors Involved in the Rejection of Treatment by Patients at the Point of Intake," but never completed it because of the difficulty of tracing persons who had had such limited contact with their clinic.* These difficulties also confronted the writer (Brandt, 1963). They may explain why an extensive literature search did not reveal a single follow-up study of pretherapy dropout.

A number of general dropout studies quoted percentage figures for pre-therapy dropout as related to total clinic applicants. These percentages appear in Figure I as dropouts before the first interview. Only applicants who were not rejected by the respective clinic but who rejected treatment at the clinic are included in Figure I.

Kurland (1956) compared "work-up only" dropout, *i.e.,* dropout during intake under two conditions: (1) without, and (2) with an intake team. He found a slightly higher percentage of pre-therapy dropout in the second instance. He pointed out that this may be because under the first condition "veterans began treatment with the second visit to the clinic," whereas under the second condition "actual treatment

---

* Personal communication by Dr. Jerome L. Weinberger on March 8, 1963.

might not begin until the third to fifth visit." He reported no further comparisons concerning pre-therapy dropout.

Gibby *et al.* (1953) found smaller differences between pre-therapy dropouts and those who dropped out in the first five sessions than between the latter group and those who remained in treatment for at least six months. Differences between the first two groups were found only on a few Rorschach criteria and on race. Nine of the 33 "refusers" were Negro as compared to 2 and 3 Negroes respectively in the other two groups.

Rosenthal and Frank (1958) reported that "of the 384 patients referred for psychotherapy, 130 or 35 per cent failed to accept it when it became available." They found differences between rejectors and acceptors in terms of education, annual income, referral source, and motivation, but not in terms of waiting time, sex, age, race, or diagnosis. Their rejectors had less education, income, and motivation than their acceptors; fewer rejectors than acceptors had been referred by physicians, psychiatrists, courts, and themselves, but more by social agencies.

Goucher (1949) compared veterans who ceased keeping appointments in and after intake with those who were seen by a psychiatrist, a psychologist, and a social worker respectively. She tried to relate "the reasons for breaking treatment" with "the points at which treatment was broken." She found "no striking correlation" (and no differences among disciplines). She suggested that intake and later dropout reasons do not differ because (contrary to the view of the administration) the patient does not distinguish between intake and therapy interviews since in both he has to reveal himself.

Only percentage figures of pre-therapy dropout were quoted by several authors. Lief *et al.* (1961) found among 1,291 applicants "thirty (who) withdrew their applications before being seen," and of those accepted for treatment, another 7% who "did not start treatment", Quaytman's fig-

ure (1961), when converted into percentages, is 14%; Kurland (1956) quoted 27%. None of these authors compared these rejectors with acceptors on any demographic or personality variables.

The present author recently compared rejectors** and acceptors of psychotherapy who were matched by age, sex, education, and previous psychotherapy, and who all belonged to the lowest income group of the middle class (Brandt, 1963). Rejectors tended to present problems as lying in the environment rather than within themselves, and when presenting the problems in writing used fewer words and less verbs than acceptors. Contrary to the findings by Rosenthal and Frank (1958), rejectors had slightly more education, and fewer had previous therapy, than acceptors. The identification of rejectors from written statements of problems reached statistical significance, but there were too many misidentifications to make prediction clinically useful. Perhaps the distinction between rejectors, early terminators, and those who remain in treatment until some desired changes have occurred, is an artifact: persons who have applied for psychotherapy are at various stages of a complex decision-making process (Kadushin, 1958).

CONCLUSION

A great deal of research effort has gone into various attempts to identify prospective dropouts. So far, these attempts have been so different that no clear-cut conclusions can be drawn as to who are the premature terminators or even whether they represent a distinct group.

The findings presented in this review of the literature suggest a need for greater attention to the many different variables involved. Since past studies did not prove to

---

** "Rejectors" were defined as pre-therapy dropouts who did not enter therapy elsewhere. They represented only 37% of all pre-therapy dropouts. Sixty-three per cent reported on follow-up that they had entered treatment elsewhere (Brandt, 1964).

be comparable with each other, it seems necessary to duplicate the best of them in terms of population, treatment setting, therapist, length of stay, and test variables. Valuable information could be gained from a project following the lines of that at the outpatient clinic of the University of Heidelberg, Germany, where demographic, clinical, and other data from all treated and untreated patients were collected over a ten-year period and analyzed (Boor and Künzler, 1963).

It was the purpose of this discussion of the literature to serve as a basis for such future validation studies.

REFERENCES

AFFLECK, D. C., & GARFIELD, S. L. Predictive judgments of therapists and duration of stay in psychotherapy. *J. clin. Psychol.*, 1961, 17, 134–137.

AFFLECK, D. C., & MEDNICK, S. A. The use of the Rorschach Test in the prediction of the abrupt terminator in individual psychotherapy. *J. consult. Psychol.*, 1959, 23, 125–128.

AULD, F., & ERON, L. D. Use of Rorschach scores to predict whether patients will continue psychotherapy. *J. consult. Psychol.*, 1953, 17, 104–109.

AULD, F., & MYERS, J. K. Contribution to a theory for selecting psychotherapy patients. *J. clin. Psychol.*, 1954, 10, 56–60.

BARTLETT, M. P. A six month follow-up of the effects of personal adjustment counseling of veterans. *J. consult. Psychol.*, 1950, 14, 393–394.

BOOR, C. DE & KÜNZLER, E., *Die psychosomatische Klinik und ihre Patienten. Erfahrungsbericht der psychosomatischen Universitätsklinik Heidelberg*. Bern: Hans Huber, & Stuttgart: Ernst Klett, 1963.

BRANDT, L. W. *Psycholinguistic analysis of statements of problems from applicants for psychotherapy. A comparison of a group who rejected and a group who accepted treatment at three outpatient mental health clinics*. Ph.D. dissertation, New York University, 1963.

BRANDT, L. W. Rejection of psychotherapy. The discovery of unexpected numbers of pseudo-rejectors. *Arch. Gen. Psychiat.*, 1964, 10, 310–312.

BURNHAM, C. A. *Reliability and validity of psychologists' evaluation of therapy readiness*. Unpublished Ph.D. dissertation, New York University, 1951.

CARTWRIGHT, D. S. Success in psychotherapy as a function of certain actuarial variables. *J. consult. Psychol.*, 1955, 19, 357–363.

CROWLEY, R. A. A low cost psychoanalytic service. *Psychiat. Quart.*, 1950, 24, 462–482.

DENGROVE, E., & KUTASH, S. Why patients discontinue treatment in a mental hygiene clinic. *Amer. J. Psychother.*, 1950, 4, 457–472.

FANSHEL, D. A study of caseworkers' perceptions of their clients. *Soc. Casewk.*, 1958, 39, 543–551.

FELDMAN, H. W., BARBA, N., & SELL, C. *A study of appointment breakages in the Social Service Section of the Mental Hygiene Unit, Boston Regional Office Veterans Administration, during 12-week period October 9 to December 30, 1950*. Unpublished research paper, Boston, 1951.

FRANK, J. D., *et al*. Why patients leave psychotherapy. *A.M.A. Arch. Neurol. Psychiat.*, 1957, 77, 283–299.

FREEDMAN, N., *et al*. Drop-out from outpatient psychiatric treatment. *A.M.A. Arch. Neurol. Psychiat.*, 1958, 80, 657–666.

GALLAGHER, J. J. *An investigation into factors differentiating college students who discontinue nondirective counseling from college students who continue counseling*. Unpublished Ph.D. dissertation, Pennsylvania State College, 1951.

GARFIELD, S. L., & AFFLECK, D. C. An appraisal of duration of stay in outpatient psychotherapy. *J. nerv. ment. Dis.*, 1959, 129, 492–498.

GARFIELD, S. L. Therapists' judgments concerning patients considered for psychotherapy, *J. consult. Psychol.*, 1961, 25, 505–509.

GARFIELD, S. L., & KURZ, M. Evaluation of treatment and related procedures in 1,216 cases referred to a mental hygiene clinic. *Psychiat. Quart.*, 1952, 26, 414–424.

GIBBY, R. G., *et al*. Prediction of duration of therapy from the Rorschach Test. *J. consult. Psychol.*, 1953, 17, 348–354.

GIBBY, R. G. Validation of Rorschach criteria for predicting duration of therapy. *J. Consult. Psychol.*, 1954, 18, 185–191.

GLIEDMAN, L. H., *et al*. Incentives for treatment related to remaining or improving in psychotherapy. *Amer. J. Psychother.*, 1957, 11, 589–598.

GOUCHER, E. L. *Why do veterans break treatment?* Unpublished thesis for Master of Science, Simmons College, 1949.

GUNDLACH, R. H., & GELLER, M. The problem of early termination. *J. consult. Psychol.*, 1958, 22, 410.

HEINE, R. W., & TROSMAN, H. Initial expectations of the doctor-patient interaction as a factor in continuance in psychotherapy. *Psychiatry*, 1960, 23, 275–278.

HILER, E. W. *An investigation of psychological factors associated with premature termination of psychotherapy.* Ph.D. Dissertation, University of Michigan, 1954.

HILER, E. W. Wechsler-Bellevue intelligence as a predictor of continuation in psychotherapy. *J. clin. Psychol.*, 1958, 14, 192–194.

HILER, E. W. The sentence completion test as a predictor of continuation in psychotherapy. *J. consult. Psychol.*, 1959, 23, 544–549.

IMBER, S. D., *et al.* Suggestibility, social class and the acceptance of psychotherapy. *J. clin. Psychol.*, 1956, 12, 341–344.

KADUSHIN, C. Invividual decisions to undertake psychotherapy. *Administr. Science Quart.*, 1958, 3, 379–411.

KADUSHIN, C. Social distance between client and professional. *Amer. J. Sociol.*, 1962, 67, 517–531.

KENNEDY, J. *Factors relating to breaking treatment.* Unpublished M.S.S. thesis. Smith College School for Social Work, 1949.

KIRK, B. A., & HEADLEY, R. R. Factors related to voluntary discontinuance of contact during counseling. *J. Counsel. Psychol.*, 1950, 14, 386–392.

KIRTNER, W. L., & CARTWRIGHT, D. S. Success and failure in client-centered therapy as a function of initial in-therapy behavior. *J. consult. Psychol.*, 1958, 22, 329–333.

KOTKOV, B., & MEADOW, A. Rorschach criteria for continuing group psychotherapy. *Int. J. Group Psychother.*, 1952, 2, 324–333.

KOTKOV, B., & MEADOW, A. Rorschach criteria for predicting continuation in individual psychotherapy. *J. consult. Psychol.*, 1953, 17, 16–20.

KURLAND, S. H. Length of treatment in a mental hygiene clinic. *Psychiat. Quart. Supple.*, 1956, 30, 83–90.

LAKE, M., & LEVINGER, G. Continuance beyond application interviews at a child guidance clinic. *Soc. Casewk.*, 1960, 41, 301–309.

LEVINGER, G. Continuance in casework and other helping relationships. *Soc. Wk.*, 1960, 5, 40–51.

LIEF, H. I., *et al.* Low dropout rate in a psychiatric clinic. *Arch. gen. Psychiat.*, 1961, 5, 200–211.

LORR, M., KATZ, M. M., & RUBINSTEIN, E. A. The prediction of length of stay in psychotherapy. *J. consult. Psychol.*, 1958, 22, 321–327.

MORRIS, D. P., & SOROKER, E. P. A follow-up study of a guidance-clinic waiting list. *Ment. Hyg.*, 1953, 37, 84–88.

MYERS, J. K., & AULD, F. Some variables related to outcome of psychotherapy. *J. clin. Psychol.*, 1955, 11, 51–54.

QUAYTMAN, W. *Motivation for psychotherapy.* Ph.D. dissertation, New York University, 1961.

ROGERS, L. S., KNAUSS, J., & HAMMOND, K. R. Predicting continuation in therapy by means of the Rorschach test, *J. consult. Psychol.*, 1951, 15, 368–371.

ROSENTHAL, D., & FRANK, J. D. The fate of psychiatric clinic outpatients assigned to psychotherapy. *J. nerv. ment. Dis.*, 1958, 127, 330–343.

RUBINSTEIN, E. A. & LORR, M. A comparison of terminators and remainers in outpatient psychotherapy. *J. clin. Psychol.*, 1956, 12, 345–349.

SIEGEL, N. H., & FINK, M. The disposition of applications for psychotherapy in an outpatient clinic. *Soc. Casewk.*, 1962, 43, 515–517.

STAIMAN, M. G. *Comparative study of psychoneurotic veterans who continue and discontinue psychotherapy.* Unpublished Ph.D. dissertation, New York Universtiy, 1949.

SULLIVAN, P. L., MILLER, C., & SMELSER, W. Factors in length of stay and progress in psychotherapy. *J. consult. Psychol.*, 1958, 22, 1–9.

TAYLOR, J. W. Relationship of success and length in psychotherapy. *J. consult. Psychol.*, 1956, 20, 332.

WEINBERGER, J. L., & GAY, E. Utilization of psychiatrist and social worker as an intake team. *Amer. J. Psychiat.*, 1949, 106, 384–388.

Characteristics of
Terminators and Remainers in
Child Guidance Treatment

ALAN O. ROSS
HARVEY M. LACEY

Caseload statistics at Pittsburgh Child Guidance Center indicate that 28% of all families accepted for treatment terminate their contact unilaterally and at a time which the clinic staff considers premature. This experience seems similar to that of other clinics, for Levitt (1958) states that some report a dropout rate of more than 30%. Premature termination is costly because as many as 15 hours of scarce professional time may have been spent in diagnostic study and related activities before the family decides to discontinue the contact. This poses a practical problem. At the same time these families are of theoretical interest because, though carefully selected, they are unable to make use of collaborative treatment, the traditional approach of child guidance clinics.

Some families seem to derive benefit even from a truncated contact (Inman, 1956) so that the professional time may not be wasted completely, but if potential terminators could be identified early in the proceedings,

Reprinted from *Journal of Consulting Psychology,* 1961, 25, (5), 420–424, with the permission of the American Psychological Association and the authors.

they might be provided with a modified service, more suited to their needs. The staff time thus freed could then be made available to other families better able to use the traditional child guidance approach.

This study was designed to explore variables which might help differentiate between terminators and remainers. A number of investigators have attempted to identify characteristics of families who remain in treatment and of those who terminate prematurely. Levitt (1958) found that judgments of clinicians, made on the basis of diagnostic information, did not identify "defectors" successfully; nor did judgments of motivation for treatment and severity of symptoms differentiate between the two groups.

Hofstein (1957) has pointed out that in a child guidance clinic, assessment of a child's treatability must rest on the evaluation of the parents' capacity to involve themselves in the treatment process and to work toward a change in their relations to each other as well as to their child. The important contribution of parental attitudes to contin-

277

uance in child guidance treatment has also been stressed by Inman (1956) and Smigelsky (1949).

Lake and Levinger (1960) found differences in parental attitudes when they compared 50 continuers with 50 discontinuers. The parents of continuers tended to be more aware of the child's disturbance and of their own contribution to it. They were more inclined to see the problem as something for which the family as a whole was responsible and accepted that they themselves had to participate in finding a solution. They also displayed greater cooperation during interviews and tended to agree with the worker on the nature of the child's disturbance.

Levitt (1957) compared defectors with remainers on 61 variables and found 5 which seemed to differentiate between the two groups. The variables did not form a meaningful cluster, nor did there appear to be "any theoretical reason to expect them to be differentiating." In addition, the probability of finding 5 analyses out of 61 significant at the .05 level is very nearly .25. These considerations led Levitt to ascribe his results to chance. The present study attempted to anticipate this dilemma by testing a priori predictions made on the basis of logical and theoretical considerations.

METHOD

This center prepares an IBM punch-card record at the time each case is closed. The record is coded on 67 categories, ranging from objective background descriptions of the child and the family, to items dealing with developmental and health history, presenting symptoms, diagnosis, and clinic procedures.[1] The system includes every case closed since 1943 and, at the time of this investigation, contained 2,400 records. A

[1] This system was instituted by William F. Finzer, Director of the center, and is maintained by Sallie Churchill. To them, and to David S. Lepson, who assisted with the analysis, the authors express their appreciation.

study by Gilbert (1957) suggests that girls referred to child guidance clinics do not come from the same population as boys. Therefore, only boys' records were used for the present analysis. There were 1,497 boys among the cases. Terminators and remainers were drawn from this population.

Terminators were defined as families who had entered treatment but discontinued therapy on their own decision before five treatment interviews with the child had taken place. A total of 107 cases met these criteria.

Remainers were defined as families who had entered treatment, continued for more than 16 treatment interviews with the child, and terminated either by mutual or clinic decision. A total of 154 cases met these criteria.

Of the 67 categories of information available on each case, 27 were chosen for analysis. Those categories were selected in which the information was specific enough for research purposes and relevant to aspects of parental attitudes toward the clinic or toward the child. Specific predictions of the relations between the variables and the continuance dichotomy were made and recorded before analysis of the data. In four of the categories more than 1 prediction was made so that a total of 32 discrete predictions was put to test.

Some predictions were based on results of studies reported in the literature (Affleck & Mednick, 1959; Lake & Levinger, 1960; Levitt, 1957; Rubenstein & Levitt, 1957; Tuckman & Lavell, 1959). Other predictions were based on parent's ability to participate in treatment, which seemed relevant on the basis of clinical experience.

RESULTS

Of the 32 predictions, 9 could not be tested because insufficient information precluded a meaningful analysis. These hypotheses related to infantile behavior, tomboy or effeminate behavior, father's employment status, mother's employment status, nature of family residence, and three others related to diagnostic categories. Five of the 32 predictions were confirmed at better than the .02 level of significance. When 32 comparisons are possible, the probability of obtaining five differences, significant below the .02 level, by chance is less than .0001 ($CR = 5.51$). This calculation is based on the approximation described by Brožek and Tiede (1952).

For the remaining 18 predictions the results failed to reach a satisfactory level of statistical significance, although the differences were in the predicted direction in all but five of the comparisons.

Confirmed Predictions

Compared to terminators, remainers have a greater proportion of histories of developmental difficulties (complications in weaning, toilet training, delayed speech, reduced social responsiveness) ($\chi^2 = 10.12$, $p < .01$).[2]

The classification "Unusual Behavior" (confusion, disorientation, panic reactions, unpredictable, meaningless, and self-destructive acts) was found more frequently among the remainers than among the terminators ($\chi^2 = 11.49$, $p < .001$).

There was a higher incidence of marital disharmony (excluding divorce and separation) among the remainers than among the terminators ($\chi^2 = 5.96$, $p < .02$).

Compared to terminators, remainers contained more cases where, in addition to the child's individual therapy, both parents were seen individually for treatment. Among the terminators only one parent (usually the mother) tended to be in concurrent treatment ($\chi^2 = 15.25$, $p < .001$).

Termination was positively related to obtaining clinic service immediately after application, without having to wait for the intake interview; remainers tended to be families who had to wait for service ($\chi^2 = 29.16$, $p < .001$).

---

[2] $df = 1$ unless otherwise indicated.

In addition to the results which confirmed specific predictions, two findings for which no hypotheses had been formulated emerged as the data were analyzed. Not having been specifically predicted, however, they are somewhat less convincing than the results cited above.

Compared to terminators, remainers have a higher incidence of specific somatic disorders (asthma, eczema, stuttering) as opposed to nonspecific somatic disorders (undiagnosed pains, sweating, tension) ($\chi^2 = 10.19$, $p < .01$).

When truancy was compared with other educational problems (reading and other learning difficulties, school phobia, school behavior problems) it was found more often among terminators than among remainers ($\chi^2 = 11.04$, $p < .001$).

Unconfirmed Predictions

The following relations, although not statistically significant, were in the predicted direction: The older the child, the greater the tendency to remain ($t = .25$). Families previously known to other social agencies tend to remain ($\chi^2 = .63$). Families known to juvenile court tend to terminate ($\chi^2 = 1.27$). Children with runaway problems tend to be among the terminators ($\chi^2 = 2.08$). Antisocial behavior is high among the terminators ($\chi^2 = .07$). The more advanced the mother's education, the greater the tendency to remain ($\chi^2 = 2.68$). The lower the child's intelligence, the greater the tendency to terminate ($\chi^2 = .15$). The middle income group, as opposed to the low income and high income groups, tends to remain ($\chi^2 = 3.79$).

The following comparisons were found to be in the opposite direction of predictions, but none reached a statistically significant level. It had been predicted that Negro families would tend to terminate ($\chi^2 = .99$); that fee paying cases would remain ($\chi^2 = .005$); that children with all types of somatic disorders would be among the remainers ($\chi^2 = .19$); that children with all kinds of educational problems would tend to remain ($\chi^2 = .95$); and that the more advanced the father's education the greater the tendency to remain ($\chi^2 = .04$).

DISCUSSION

Studies of abrupt termination in adult psychotherapy have shown that a patient's motivation is one factor which differentiates the terminator from the remainer (Affleck & Mednick, 1959). In child guidance therapy it is the parents' motivation which is the determining factor, but the parents must not only have the motivation to bring the child and support his treatment experience, but they must also have the capacity to involve themselves actively in the therapy program. Premature termination tends to occur when either of these important conditions is not met.

Length of time on the waiting list between application and intake seems to be one measure of parental motivation. The parent with low motivation would not be expected to remain in clinic contact if he had to wait for any length of time. When treatment is finally started the group still on the waiting list may be assumed to contain a high proportion of well motivated individuals. Thus, there is a significantly greater proportion of waiting list cases among the remainers than among the terminators. There was a similar relation, although below the adopted level of significance, when the groups are compared on waiting from intake to diagnostic study ($\chi^2 = 1.37$, $p > .20$) and on waiting from diagnostic study to beginning of treatment ($\chi^2 = 1.79$, $p > .10$). While a waiting list is an undesirable feature of a clinic's operation, delay does, in many instances, serve as a screening device which eliminates poorly motivated patients before they get to the point of treatment.

The comparison which bears most directly on the parents' ability to involve themselves in treatment is that between families where only one parent was in concurrent treatment and those where both parents were being seen individually. When only one parent is in concurrent treatment, it is almost always the mother. The results clearly show that when the father, as well as the mother, can be involved in the treatment plan the chances that the case will terminate prematurely are greatly reduced.

It has become more universally recognized that the father plays an important and often crucial role in the treatment of children (Rubenstein & Levitt, 1957). The findings here reported lend strong support to this trend. They suggest that when the father is not in treatment, he may either actively sabotage treatment efforts or, by failing to support the mother and the child in their treatment experiences, materially undermine the process. This may be especially true in the treatment of boys, the subjects in the present study.

Parental motivation might be expected to be a function of the distress which the child's symptoms cause the parents. Hiler (1959), studying adults in individual psychotherapy, found that patients who complain only of somatic symptoms are likely to terminate, probably because the symptom enables them to "bind" their anxiety In child guidance therapy, the reverse seems to be true. The bizarre behavior of the mentally ill child and such specific somatic disorders as asthma may be assumed to be distressing to the parent, who would be very much aware of the disturbance and motivated to obtain help. The results of relevant comparisons strongly suggest that the more apparent the symptom, the more likely the case is to continue in treatment.

Another indirect reflection of parental involvement and motivation may be the fact that remaining was positively related to histories of developmental difficulties. A child with such a history may be assumed to have a psychological problem of long standing so that his parents might be more aware of it, more distressed by it, and thus more highly motivated to remain in treatment. In addition, a mother's report of difficulties in her child's early years may represent her awareness of her own contribution to the problem, an awareness Lake and Levinger (1960) report as a factor in continuance.

The confirmed prediction that remainers would contain proportionately more cases with marital disharmony also bears on a parent's personal involvement. The finding reflects the parents' ability to talk about a problem which concerns them. In addition, marital disharmony is a distressing personal problem for parents and one for which they might hope to find some relief through the clinic contact.

On the basis of studies reported from adult outpatient clinics (Hollingshead & Redlich, 1958; Rubinstein & Lorr, 1956), it had been predicted that certain sociocultural factors would be related to continuance in child guidance therapy. While there was a trend for the remainers to contain proportionately more Jewish than Catholic families ($\chi^2 = 2.92$, $p = < .10$), no difference between remainers and terminators in fathers' occupational class was found ($\chi^2 = 3.72$, $df = 5$, $p = < .70$). Tuckman and Lavell (1959), who compared social status at all stages of clinic contact, also found that higher status patients were no more likely to maintain contact with the clinic than lower status patients. This would suggest that child guidance clinics are more successful than adult outpatient clinics in helping patients from the lower socioeconomic levels to remain in treatment.

It has been reported that a higher proportion of the continuers perceive the child's problem themselves, rather than through the demands made by the community, and that they desire change in themselves, as well as in their child and in their spouse (Lake & Levinger, 1960). The present results are consistent with these findings. Terminators were more often referred by an authority, such as juvenile court or school, while remainers were more often referred by friends, social agencies, or themselves ($\chi^2 = 3.77$, $p < .10$).

The incidence of truancy is significantly higher among terminators than among remainers when compared with other school problems. This result had not been specifically predicted. It seems that truancy is an expression of pathological family behavior patterns where avoidance of anxiety-arousing situations takes the form of physical departure. A family which abruptly and unilaterally terminates clinic contact and a child who truants from school may be manifesting the same basic reaction to stress.

While we were able to confirm a significant number of a priori predictions, this investigation shares the weakness of all ex post facto research on closed cases. A specific fact only becomes a research datum if the patient reports it accurately, the interviewer records it fully, and the person responsible for coding codes it correctly. It is hoped that a projected long range study will not only overcome these difficulties but also address itself to the question of treatment outcome and to the problem of parental attitudes toward the child which Lake and Levinger (1960), among others, have suspected to be an important variable in continuance of treatment contact.

SUMMARY

Families who terminated child guidance contact before the fifth treatment session were compared with families who continued treatment for a minimum of 16 interviews. Remainers had significantly more developmental difficulties, unusual behavior, marital disharmony, and specific somatic disorders. They contained significantly more cases where both parents were in concurrent treatment. Terminators had significantly more school truancy, and they had less often experienced a waiting period between application and intake. The results were discussed in terms of the importance of the parent's motivation and their ability to involve themselves in the treatment process.

REFERENCES

AFFLECK, D. C., & MEDNICK, S. A. The use of the Rorschach test in the prediction of the abrupt terminator in individual psychotherapy. *J. consult. Psychol.*, 1959, 23, 125–128.

BROŽEK, J., & TIEDE, K. Reliable and questionable significance in a series of statistical tests. *Psychol. Bull.*, 1952, 49, 339–341.

GILBERT, G. M. A survey of "referral problems" in metropolitan child guidance centers. *J. clin. Psychol.*, 1957, 13, 37–42.

HILER, E. W. Initial complaints as predictors of continuation in psychotherapy. *J. clin. Psychol.*, 1959, 15, 344–345.

HOFSTEIN, S. Social factors in assessing treatability in child guidance. *Children*, 1957, 4, 48–53.

HOLLINGSHEAD, A. B., & REDLICH, F. *Social class and mental illness.* New York: Wiley, 1958.

INMAN, ANN C. Attrition in child guidance: A telephone follow-up study. *Smith Coll. Stud. soc. Wk.*, 1956, 27, 34–73.

LAKE, MARTHA, & LEVINGER, G. Continuance beyond application interviews at a child guidance clinic. *Soc. Casewk.*, 1960, 91, 303–309.

LEVITT, E. E. A comparison of "remainers" and "defectors" among child clinic patients. *J. consult. Psychol.*, 1957, 21, 316.

LEVITT, E. E. A comparative judgmental study of "defection" from treatment at a child guidance clinic. *J. clin. Psychol.*, 1958, 14, 429–432.

RUBENSTEIN, B. O., & LEVITT, M. Some observations regarding the role of fathers in child psychotherapy. *Bull. Menninger Clin.*, 1957, 21, 16–27.

RUBINSTEIN, E. A., & LORR, M. A comparison of terminators and remainers in outpatient psychotherapy. *J. clin. Psychol.*, 1956, 12, 345–349.

SMIGELSKY, EVA. Why parents discontinue child guidance treatment. *Smith Coll. Stud. soc. Wk.*, 1949, 19, 118–119.

TUCKMAN, J., & LAVELL, MARTHA. Social status and clinic contact. *J. clin. Psychol.*, 1959, 15, 345–348.

Patient and Therapist Influences on Quitting Psychotherapy

DOUGLAS M. McNAIR
MAURICE LORR
DANIEL M. CALLAHAN

Many studies in the past decade have aimed at predicting premature termination of psychotherapy. Fulkerson and Barry (1961, pp. 194–197) have presented a review and bibliography of the principal studies of the problem. Lorr, Katz, and Rubinstein (1958) reported the development and cross-validation of a test battery (TR battery) to predict early termination of psychotherapy. Results of a double cross-validation provided substantial evidence that the test battery identified a high proportion of patients who terminated psychotherapy after a few interviews without their therapists' advice or consent. The TR battery predicted termination with significantly greater accuracy than base-rate predictions and contrary to the statement in Fulkerson and Barry's review, with significantly higher accuracy than predictions by an interviewer. The characteristics assessed by the TR battery indicated,

Reprinted from *Journal of Consulting Psychology,* 1963, 27 (1), 10–17, with the permission of the American Psychological Association and the authors.

The Terminator is either not anxious or does not admit to being anxious and self-dissatisfied. He is likely to have a history of antisocial acts, he admits to being undependable and impulsive, and may be authoritarian or rigid in his social attitudes (Lorr et al., 1958, p. 326).

One aim of the present study was to attempt to increase the predictive accuracy of the TR battery and to obtain greater knowledge of Terminator response patterns by including additional patient measures in a study of premature termination of treatment. A corollary aim was to perform a second cross-validation of the TR battery.

Studies of termination have emphasized patient variables related to dropping out of therapy. Few studies systematically assessed the influence of nonpatient variables on premature termination of therapy, although some investigation suggested the unexplained criterion variance might be due to variables such as therapist behavior and the setting in which treatment takes place. Lorr et al. (1958) reported that therapist sex, profession, and experience did not relate significantly to termination. They also noted that setting factors such as scheduled treatment frequency, length of interview, and type of therapy (group versus individual) did not correlate significantly with the Terminator-Remainer criterion. Recently, however, Hiler (1958) presented evidence that the type of patient terminating related to characteristics of the therapist. Briefly, he reported that therapist sex, warmth, and psychotherapeutic competence were associated with whether therapists retained predicted Quitters or predicted Stayers in treatment ("Quitter" and "Terminator," "Stayer" and "Remainer" are used synonymously.) He typed his patients as Stayers or Quitters on the basis of total Rorschach responses—an index with some cross-validational evidence. It should be noted that Hiler reported an interaction effect between therapist characteristic and patient type on outcome—not an association between therapist characteristic and actual termination rate. Thus his findings do not necessarily disagree with Lorr's.

Hiler's (1958) study provided the interesting lead that therapist-patient compatibility influenced premature termination, and his results suggested that the interaction between the therapist and patient "type" might be crucial. His findings, however, were based on small samples from a single clinic and there was no cross-validation of the interaction. Since no data were presented giving the correlations between sex, warmth, and competence, their relative independence could not be judged. Some of Hiler's one-tailed test findings (e.g., competence and patient type) would not be significant if two-tailed tests had been used. One-tailed tests seem questionable in such an unexplored area. Finally, certain relevant data were not presented by Hiler. He reported an interaction of therapist warmth and patient type among Remainers; no comparable test for Terminators was mentioned. He reported the interaction of therapist competence and patient type among his Terminators but cited no com-

parable test for Remainers. While he reported data relevant only to stated hypotheses, it is unclear why comparable (or converse) hypotheses were not tested for both Terminators and Remainers. Thus a third aim of the current report was to investigate the effect of the therapist on termination and to attempt confirmation of Hiler's interactions between therapist characteristics and patient type.

Terminators were operationally defined as patients who refused or stopped therapy in less than 16 weeks without the advice or consent of their therapists. The study hypotheses, based on surveys of previous findings in the area, were:

1. The TR battery predicts better than chance and better than the base rate those patients who will terminate therapy prematurely.

2. Terminators have more poorly developed verbal behavior than Remainers.

3. Terminators have less formal education—the crucial component of most social class indices (Freeman, 1961)—than Remainers.

4. Terminators admit less anxious and "neurotic" behaviors than Remainers.

5. Compared with Remainers, Terminators have a history of more impulsive and antisocial behavior, more difficulties with the law, and lack close interpersonal relationships.

6. Terminators are less interested than Remainers in participating in verbal psychotherapies.

7. Compared with Remainers, Terminators admit less dissatisfaction with their own characteristics and behavior.

8. Terminators more frequently than Remainers endorse rigid, authoritarian, irrational social attitudes, and opinions.

9. When patients are classified in advance as probable Terminators or Remainers on the basis of a predictively valid test, interaction effects on outcome will appear between patient type and characteristics of the therapist such as sex and competence.

METHOD

The sample consisted of 282 psychotherapy outpatients in seven Veterans Administration Mental Hygiene Clinics.[1] All patients satisfied these criteria for inclusion in the study: males under age 51; without evidence of CNS damage; less than 12 hours of therapy during the preceding 90 days; acceptable to the clinic for "intensive" psychotherapy—defined as weekly interviews lasting about 1 hour, aimed at changing personal adjustment patterns, and excluding supportive or maintenance therapy. Clinics added research procedures to their customary prepsychotherapy processing routines. The assessment included a research test battery, evaluation by a social worker, and appraisal by the therapist. When a patient terminated prior to the 16-week evaluation date, a data sheet was completed giving the date and reason for termination. There were 176 Remainers and 106 Terminators. Patients who terminated for reality reasons—e.g., moving, requiring hospitalization—were excluded from analysis. Within 6 weeks or less, 74 of the Terminators quit therapy—confirming the observation of Lorr et al. (1958) that most premature terminations occur during the first few weeks of treatment.

Only 2 of the 7 clinics involved were among the 13 in the Lorr et al. (1958) study. All clinics in both studies are located in large cities widely distributed geographically and all clinics had 10–40 staff members. Most therapists in both studies had Freudian or Rogerian orientations. The present data were collected throughout

[1] We are grateful to the following psychologists and to other staff members at their stations for participating in the study: R. W. Boyd (Boston), L. Hemmendinger (Bridgeport), P. W. Morse (Hartford), L. Rutledge (Denver), J. E. Tucker (Albany), H. H. Weiss (Chicago), and B. B. Yorman (Buffalo).

The data were collected in collaboration with a larger Veterans Administration Cooperative Project (Lorr, McNair, Michaux, & Raskin, 1962).

1957 and 1958; the Lorr et al. data in 1955–56. World War II veterans comprised more than 90% of both samples. The remainder were Korean veterans. A separate study (McNair, Callahan, & Lorr, 1962) of the effect of the therapist on response to psychotherapy involved 40 of the current Remainers.

The Terminator-Remainer criterion in the present study differed from those of Lorr et al. (1958) and Hiler (1958). Lorr's Terminators and Remainers were defined, respectively, as patients remaining in therapy 6 weeks or less and patients remaining 6 months or longer. Hiler's Terminators had 5 or fewer interviews; his Remainers had 20 or more interviews. Both studies excluded the middle group from analysis. Inclusion of the middle group in the current project probably made for a more severe test of the hypotheses, especially Hypothesis 1. Obvious Terminators were probably excluded from the present sample since the criteria for inclusion were more rigorous than the usual clinic criteria for acceptance into psychotherapy. The 16-week termination rate (38%) is much lower than the usual 6-week base rate (about 50%) in Veterans Administration clinics.

Predictor Variables

Patient predictor variables are briefly described below. The arabic number in parentheses indicates the hypothesis tested by each predictor(s). In addition to those below, 10 other patient measures, which proved unrelated to the Terminator-Remainer criterion, were included as tests of Hypotheses 2–8.

Patients predictors. (1) TR-A, TR-BD, and TR-F are, respectively, six-, eight-, and seven-item subtests which constitute the TR Battery. They are taken from the longer Manifest Anxiety (MA) scale, Behavior Disturbance (BD) scale, and F Scale described below; (2) a 30-item multiple-choice vocabulary test adapted from the Cooperative English Test, Form Z, Educational Testing Service; (3) a nine-point scale of formal education completed; (4) a slightly modified form of Taylor's (1953) *MA* scale and a Sociability scale abbreviated from a scale in the Guilford-Zimmerman (1949) Temperament Survey; (5) BD: 50 questionnaire items adapted from an inventory by Applezweig, Dibner, and Osbourne (1958) to measure antisocial behavior and psychopathic tendencies; (6) Motivation for Treatment: rating by the therapist on a four-point graphic scale of the patient's interest in obtaining psychotherapy; (7) Ideal-Actual Self-Discrepancy: a discrepancy score between ratings of the actual self and the ideal self on 21 five-point scales designed to measure self-satisfaction; (8) F Scale: 25 items from the Adorno, Frenkel-Brunswik, Levinson, and Sanford (1950) measure of authoritarianism.

Therapist predictors. Eight therapist predictors were included to test Hypothesis 9. These were: sex; profession; years of experience as a therapist; amount of personal psychotherapy; competence; liking for the patient; interest in the type of problem presented by the patient; and therapist A or B "type." Competence ratings were obtained by having three clinical psychologists with 5 or more years experience audit tape recordings of psychotherapy sessions conducted by the therapists (interrater agreement was .68[2]). Liking and Interest were rated on graphic scales by therapists at the conclusion of the initial therapy hour. Therapists were typed as A's or B's on the basis of their scores on 23 items from the Strong Vocational Interest Blank. Whitehorn and Betz (1960) found these items discriminated between groups of therapists who obtained different success rates (A's were more successful) with hospitalized schizophrenics. McNair et al. (1962) found that A and B therapists also obtained significantly different results with outpatients (but B's were more successful).

---

[2] Interclass correlation coefficient.

RESULTS
Cross-Validation of the TR Battery

Ten patient predictors significantly differentiated Terminators and Remainers (Table 1). All three tests in the TR battery significantly discriminated the two groups of patients. As in previous studies, the TR battery subtests discriminated more clearly than their parent tests. The point biserial correlations of TR-A and TR-F with the criterion were slightly higher than for the

TABLE 1

DIFFERENCES BETWEEN REMAINERS AND TERMINATORS ON 10 CHARACTERISTICS

| | M | | |
| | Re-main-ers | Ter-mi-nators | |
Variable			*t*
TR-BD	5.9	5.3	3.10**
TR-A	3.3	2.8	2.97**
TR-F	4.0	3.1	3.84**
MA scale	29.6	27.1	2.39*
F scale	24.5	23.1	3.26**
Sociability	7.3	9.0	3.70**
Ideal-Actual Self	34.6	30.9	2.61**
Education[a]	5.3	4.8	3.31**
Vocabulary	22.4	20.2	3.44**
Motivation	2.7	2.3	4.93**

[a] Score of 5 on education indicates high school graduation.
* $p < .05$.
** $p < .01$.

MA scale and the F scale, while Terminators and Remainers did not differ significantly on the total BD inventory. The product-moment correlation between TR-A and *MA* scale for the entire sample was .83. The correlation is somewhat inflated, as the TR-A items are in the *MA* scale. Even so, the correlation is as high as the *MA* scale reliability and indicates TR-A can be considered an abbreviated *MA* scale.

The configural prediction approach suggested by Lorr et al. (1958) was applied to the pattern of scores on the TR battery.

Using cutting scores from the original study, patients' scores on each subtest were classified as either Terminator or Remainer scores. The eight resulting patterns of scores on the three subtests in the battery were then classified as Terminator or Remainer predictor patterns. Table 2 presents the outcome of treatment for patients with the two classes of patterns. Chi square for the accuracy of prediction was highly significant. Overall accuracy of prediction was 66% with 64% of the actual Terminators and 68% of Remainers identified.

TABLE 2

OUTCOME OF TREATMENT FOR PATIENTS
PREDICTED TO REMAIN AND TERMINATE

Configural prediction	Outcome		
	Remain	Terminate	Total
Remain	119	38	157
Terminate	57	68	125
Total	176	106	282

Note.—$x^2 = 27.05$; $df = 1$, $p < .001$.

Lorr's original beta weights [3] were used to find the multiple correlation (R) of the TR battery with the criterion for the current sample. The R obtained was .44 ($p < .001$), a value that compares favorably with Rs of .67 in Lorr's original sample and .39 in his cross-validation sample. The difference between $R = .44$ and the beta of .36 between the configural scores and the criterion was tested (Osburn & Lubin, 1957), and R is significantly larger. The cutting score based on the multiple regression equation yielding maximum accuracy identified 72% of the Remainers, 64% of the Terminators, with 69% overall accuracy. Compared with the configural approach, use of the multiple regression equation increased accuracy of identifying Remainers with no loss of accuracy among the Terminators.

[3] Beta weights and cutting scores are available upon request.

Use of the configural scores increased accuracy of predicting Remainers 6% above the sample base rate, while R increased accuracy 10%. Only the latter represented a significant increase ($\chi^2 = 4.10$, $p, < .05$). Judgment of the actual utility of the TR battery should consider the facts that these patients had to meet rather rigorous criteria for inclusion, that the criterion groups were defined differently, and that the analysis was not confined to extreme groups. It should also be noted that the TR battery increased accuracy of identifying Terminators by almost the same percentage as Lorr et al. (1958) found. Here the increase was from 38% to 64%; their sample included 55% Terminators, and 80% were accurately identified.

Additional Patient Predictors

The findings in Table 1 support the hypotheses that Remainers have a history of less impulsive and less antisocial behavior, admit more anxious behavior, are more critical of themselves, and are less likely to endorse rigid, irrational beliefs. They are also more retiring in interpersonal relationships, better educated, have better vocabularies, and therapists consider them more highly motivated for psychotherapy.

Do any combinations of the measures of these characteristics offer potentialities for increasing the accuracy of predicting termination of therapy? The Lubin-Summerfield (1951) square root method was applied to the 10 significant variables in Table 1. The procedure selects the minimum number of variables which yields the highest possible R with the criterion. Variables are added in order of decreasing proportion of criterion variance accounted for. Five variables were added to the minimum set in the following order: Motivation, TR-BD, TR-A, TR-F, and Sociability. The multiple R for the five variables with the criterion was .48. The five variables accounted for little more criterion variance than the TR battery alone, using the original beta weights.

Therapist and Duration

Patients were divided into two groups or types—predicted Quitters and Stayers—on the basis of the duration predicted by applying the multiple regression equation to their TR battery scores. Effects of therapist variables were tested by determining if actual duration for the two groups related to the therapist variable operating. Table 3 presents the proportion and number of predicted Quitters and Stayers who remained in

TABLE 3

NUMBER AND PROPORTION OF PREDICTED QUITTERS AND STAYERS WHO REMAINED UNDER DIFFERENT THERAPIST CONDITIONS

Therapist characteristic	Quitters		Stayers	
	N	p	N	p
Sex				
Male	49	.45	84	.79
Female	8	.62	27	.93
Profession				
Psychiatrist	11	.41	28	.82
Psychologist	28	.44	53	.82
Social Worker	18	.53	31	.82
Experience				
Four years or less	26	.41	46	.81
Over four years	30	.52	67	.87
Personal psychotherapy				
Some	25	.43	59	.80
None	32	.50	54	.81
Competence				
High	11	.46	24	.89
Average	35	.52	48	.75
Low	7	.35	31	.83
Liking				
High	17	.47	51	.88
Low	40	.45	60	.76
Interest				
High	26	.59	63	.88
Low	31	.39	48	.74
"Type"				
A	17	.49	57	.88
B	20	.56	41	.89

treatment with therapists who differed on eight characteristics. The Ns in Table 3 are smaller than in the preceding analyses because Terminators who kept no therapy appointments were omitted; Ns in Table 3 are variable, depending on availability of data.

Statistical analyses of the Table 3 data were similar for all variables. An overall χ^2 test for the four or six groups (depending on the therapist variable) was highly significant due to the association of predicted and actual duration. Each contingency table was divided into two smaller tables and comparisons made to test for association of each therapist characteristic with length of therapy among the predicted Quitters and Stayers separately (Cochran & Cox, 1957, pp. 103–105). If results for the two groups differed, an interaction effect of therapist characteristic and patient type on duration would be suggested.

Therapist sex did not relate significantly to duration among predicted Quitters ($\chi^2 = 2.00$, $df = 1$, $p > .10$) or among predicted Stayers ($\chi^2 = 2.12$, $df = 1$, $p > .10$) For the combined patient groups, there appeared to be a relation between therapist sex and duration. However, the $\chi^2 = 6.40$, $p < .05$, is not exact as it is based on a comparison made after seeing the data. The results merely suggest that women therapists in this study held higher proportions of patients in therapy.

Profession of the therapist did not relate significantly to duration either among Quitters or Stayers; nor did his experience. There was, however, some suggestion of an experience effect. For the combined patient groups, the association of experience and duration yielded $\chi^2 = 3.99$, $p < .05$. Unless confirmed, the association also should be regarded as tenuous because it is based on a post hoc comparison and the correlation between experience and length of treatment is low ($\phi = .12$).

Therapists with personal psychotherapy had a median of 13 months of treatment (range = 4–40 months). They did not differ significantly from therapists with no psychotherapy in the extent to which they held either Quitters or Stayers in therapy. Likewise, judged therapeutic competence, therapist "type," and liking for the patient did not relate significantly to duration among Quitters or Stayers. (Chi square = 4.07, $p < .05$, for the association of liking and duration for the combined groups, but, again, the reservation concerning post hoc comparisons applies.)

Remaining in therapy related to the degree of interest the therapist expressed in the type of problem presented by the patient. The relationship was consistently significant both among predicted Quitters ($\chi^2 = 4.73$, $df = 1$, $p < .05$) and among predicted Stayers ($\chi^2 = 4.14$, $df = 1$, $p < .05$). The correlations of interest and outcome among Quitters ($\phi = .20$) and among Stayers ($\phi = .17$) are so similar as to offer little suggestion of an interaction effect.

Some additional analyses were performed to explore for suggestions that any therapist characteristics interact with patient type. All therapists who saw at least two predicted Quitters or Stayers were categorized as obtaining predicted or unpredicted results. A therapist was considered to have achieved a predicted result if he retained at least 50% of his Stayers or lost at least 50% of his Quitters. Two or more predicted Stayers were assigned to 36 therapists. Only 3 therapists failed to retain at least 50% of them. Two or more predicted Quitters were assigned to 29 therapists; 9 of these therapists retained more than 50% of them (actual range = 67%–100%). The proportion (.31) of therapists obtaining unpredicted results with Quitters was significantly greater ($p < .05$) than the proportion (.08) obtaining unpredicted outcomes with Stayers. Stayers appeared to respond as predicted with most therapists in the sample, but there was a distinct group of therapists who somehow retained potential Quitters in therapy.

The above finding does not indicate a significant interaction between therapist char-

acteristics and patient type. It would be necessary to show that Stayers respond differently than Quitters to the nine therapists identified as retainers of Quitters. These nine therapists were assigned 26 Quitters, and only 4 actually terminated. They were also assigned 15 Stayers, 6 of whom terminated prematurely. The proportions of Stayers (.60) and Quitters (.77) remaining with these therapists did not differ significantly (.10 > p > .05), although the trend is suggestive.

A final analysis indicated a highly significant association between the type of patient a therapist most effectively retained and the type of patient assigned to him for treatment. The 16 therapists in the study who retained 100% of their predicted Stayers were initially assigned 47 Stayers and 18 Quitters. The 9 therapists who retained Quitters were assigned 26 Quitters and 15 Stayers. Chi square = 13.21, $df = 1$, $p < .001$, for the association between type of patient assigned and type retained. Since, typically, the individual therapist had considerable freedom in rejecting or accepting a specific patient, he was a major factor in the assignment decision. Thus the evidence on patient-therapist compatibility offered no substantial support for the hypotheses that Stayers and Quitters responded differently to the same therapist characteristic. It did, however, uncover two distinct groups of therapists who appeared able to recognize the two patient types, who showed differential preferences in selecting them as patients, and who were unusually successful in retaining the preferred type in therapy.

DISCUSSION

In three separate studies, the TR battery has demonstrated useful predictive validity. All three studies have involved veteran populations, and the results may not be generalizable to other populations. Nevertheless, there is reason to believe that the characteristics measured by the TR battery are not unique to veterans and that these characteristics are incompatible with the behavior required in conventional, verbal, insight-oriented psychotherapy interviews. If so, it would appear worthwhile to try the test in other settings as a means of screening out patients for whom ordinary psychotherapy is likely to be simply a waste of time and effort.

While this study revealed that a sizable number of patient characteristics are related to premature termination, few of these added significantly to the predictive power of the TR battery. The one which added most, the therapist's rating of patient motivation for psychotherapy, is not available until the conclusion of 1 therapy hour. Most clinics would prefer to have a prediction in advance in order to treat the patient appropriately. A sizable proportion of Terminators do not keep their first therapy appointment, and most patients wait 2–4 weeks for their first therapy appointment. It would be preferable to obtain a comparable rating from an intake interviewer, such as the social worker, and to rely on the predictor patterns previously published (Lorr et al., 1958). Addition of the Sociability scale to the predictive battery should await cross-validation, especially since it increases predictive accuracy very little.

The evidence did not confirm Hiler's (1958) report that Quitters and Stayers reacted differently to similar therapist qualities. Therapists who had "more than ordinary" interest in the problems of the patients were more likely to hold each type of patient in treatment. There was suggestive evidence that women therapists, more experienced therapists, and therapists with strong liking for their patients retained higher proportions of both types in treatment. The finding concerning therapist sex seems sample specific. A significant relationship was suggested in the present study, but Lorr et al. (1958) found no such relation, and, in Hiler's sample, women kept proportionately more Quitters and lost proportionately more Stayers. Sample specificity may also account for the experience relation-

ship, as Lorr et al. found no relation between experience and outcome. While the basis for predicting which patients will quit or stay differed from Hiler's, the present method certainly qualifies as a rigorously cross-validated classification scheme based on large samples of cases widely distributed geographically. The liking and interest measures in the present study are not directly comparable to Hiler's peer ratings of therapist warmth. Raush and Bordin (1957), however, have discussed the multidimensionality and unreliability of global assessments of warmth.

The current findings point to an interaction possibility with a distinctly different interpretive significance than Hiler's (1958). There appeared to be subgroups of therapists who somehow selected unusually high proportions of Quitters or Stayers as their therapy patients. They were quite successful in retaining the preferred type of patient in treatment, whereas the nonpreferred type patient responded to these therapists about as would be predicted from his TR score. Thus the interaction suggested is that different groups of therapists respond differently to the two types of patients rather than the converse. The interaction appears to take place when patients are selected for therapy.

At this time, the sum of the evidence suggests that Remainers and Terminators are two distinct patient populations who generally react differently to what is offered them in the conventional, verbal, psychotherapy setting. Patient characteristics can be assessed which identify large proportions of these two populations. While therapists' reactions to their patients have some influence on the proportions of both populations, they can hold in treatment, there is little evidence that this is a marked effect.

We are at a stage where the potential Terminator can be identified readily and accurately before psychotherapy need be tried as the treatment of choice. Since Terminators constitute a large proportion of patients seeking treatment from clinics and reject verbal psychotherapy as a method of treatment long before it could conceivably modify behavior, it appears there is an urgent need to stop wasting time and effort on a foredoomed treatment procedure. As Bandura (1961) suggests, the time is ripe for exploring and experimenting with other, perhaps drastically different and largely nonverbal, treatment techniques and methods for modifying the symptomatic and problem behavior of these patients.

REFERENCES

ADORNO, T. W., FRENKEL-BRUNSWIK, ELSE, LEVINSON, D. J., & SANFORD, R. N. *The authoritarian personality.* New York: Harper, 1950.

APPLEZWEIG, M .H., DIBNER, A. S., & OSBOURNE, R. L. PEAQ: A measure of psychopathic behavior. *J. Psychol.,* 1958, 14, 26–30.

BANDURA, A. Psychotherapy as a learning process. *Psychol. Bull.,* 1961, 58, 143–159.

COCHRAN, W. G., & COX, GERTRUDE M. *Experimental designs.* New York: Wiley, 1957.

FREEMAN, H. E. Attitudes toward mental illness among relatives of former patients. *Amer. sociol. Rev.,* 1961, 26, 59–66.

FULKERSON, S. C., & BARRY, J. R. Methodology and research on the prognostic use of psychological tests. *Psychol. Bull.,* 1961, 58, 177–204.

GUILFORD, J. P., & ZIMMERMAN, W. *The Guilford-Zimmerman Temperament Survey.* Beverly Hills, Calif.: Sheridan Supply. 1949.

HILER, E. W. An analysis of patient-therapist compatibility. *J. consult. Psychol.,* 1958, 22, 341–347.

LORR, M. KATZ, M. M., & RUBINSTEIN, E. A. The prediction of length of stay in psychotherapy. *J. consult. Psychol.,* 1958, 22, 321–327.

LORR, M., MCNAIR, D. M., MICHAUX, W. W., & RASKIN, A. Frequency of treatment and change in psychotherapy. *J. abnorm. soc. Psychol.,* 1962, 64, 281–292.

LUBIN, A., & SUMMERFIELD, A. A square root method of selecting a minimum set of variables in multiple regression: II. A worked example. *Psychometrika,* 1951, 16, 425–437.

MCNAIR, D. M., CALLAHAN, D. M., & LORR, M. Therapist "type" and patient response to psychotherapy. *J. consult. Psychol.,* 1962, 26, 425–429.

OSBURN, H. G., & LUBIN, A. The use of configural analysis for the evaluation of test scoring methods. *Psychometrika,* 1957, 22, 359–371.

RAUSH, H. L., & BORDIN, E. S. Warmth in personality development and psychotherapy. *Psychiatry,* 1957, 20, 351–363.

TAYLOR, JANET A. A personality scale of manifest anxiety. *J. abnorm. soc. Psychol.,* 1953, 48, 285–290.

WHITEHORN, J. C., & BETZ, BARBARA J. Further studies of the doctor as a crucial variable in the outcome of treatment with schizophrenic patients. *Amer. J. Psychiat.,* 1960, 117, 215–223.

Are Psychotherapeutic Changes Predictable?[1]

DONALD W. FISKE[2]
DESMOND S. CARTWRIGHT
WILLIAM L. KIRTNER

A factor analysis of changes during psychotherapy yielded factors predominately associated with methods of measurement (Cartwright, Kirtner, & Fiske, 1963). That analysis was part of a project which had as its original objective a comprehensive attempt to establish variables that predict changes during psychotherapy. The present paper reports findings on the relationship between several pretherapy measures and several criteria. In the analyses of both pretherapy measures and change measures, the obtrusive role of method variance became so apparent that our earlier plans and hopes had to be modified substantially.

Reprinted from *Journal of Abnormal and Social Psychology,* 1964, 69 (4), 418–426, with the permission of the American Psychological Association and the authors.

[1] This study was supported by a grant from the Ford Foundation to the Counseling Center, University of Chicago, and by a Ford Behavior Research grant from the Social Sciences Research Committee of the University of Chicago.

[2] We are indebted to Naomi Berne, Robert Meyer, Pamela Pearson, and Robert Williams for their assistance in this study.

METHOD
Sources of Data

Since a full description of the procedures is given in the previous article, only a brief statement of the study and of the sources of materials utilized in the analyses reported below is necessary. Ninety-three clients counseled by 30 therapists at the University of Chicago Counseling Center were tested before and after therapy. (The median number of interviews was 26.) Each client rated himself on 14 Behavioral Adequacy (BA) scales and was given the MMPI and the TAT. The therapist rated the client after the first interview and at the end of the therapy on the same 14 scales. He also rated the success of the therapy. The two TAT protocols of each client were independently rated on the 14 scales by one diagnostician, and the first and last interviews were rated by another diagnostician on the same scales.

Criteria

Most of our criteria were based on the change factors reported in the earlier paper.

To obtain a factor score for each factor, we tried to select variables which had high loadings on the factor and essentially zero loadings on each of the other factors. The variables chosen are listed below under each factor.

Factor 1: Change in Favorableness of Client Self-Evaluation

Choice Process for Courses of Action (BA scale Number 7)

Client Q Sort Adjustment Score

MMPI Social Introversion scale (direction reversed)

(Although some variables had slightly higher loadings on this factor than the first two listed above, these two were selected to provide a diversity of instruments. The last two variables had loadings of .22 and .21, respectively, on C_3, the therapist factor. These are the only instances in which a selected variable had a loading above .15 on another factor.)

Factor 2: Change in TAT Adequacy (ratings by diagnostician)

Contentedness with Self (BA scale Number 1)

Evaluation of Own Behavior (BA scale Number 4)

Goals-Means Consideration in Courses of Action (BA scale Number 8)

Factor 3: Therapist's Perception of Change

Evaluations of Others (BA scale Number 5)

Quality of Anticipations (BA scale Number 6)

Goals-Means Consideration in Courses of Action (BA scale Number 8)

Factor 4: Change (decrease) on MMPI Hs-Hy

Hs (Hypochondriasis) scale

Hy (Hysteria) scale

Factor L: Length of Therapy

Log weeks

Log interviews

The preceding factor is given a different type of identifying symbol from the other four because it is clearly not a direct index of change and can hardly be considered in itself as an ultimate objective of psychotherapy. Two other scores were included as criteria:

Factor ID: Interview-Diagnostician's Perception of Change

Contentedness with Self (BA scale Number 1)

Contentedness with Relationships to Others (BA scale Number 2)

Evaluation of Own Capacity (BA scale Number 3)

Factor S: Therapist's Rating of the Outcome of the Therapy ("Success" scale)

The ID score represented the change in the ratings of the diagnostician who listened to the first and last interviews. While these change measures were not available for the factor analysis of change measures, subsequent inspection of their intercorrelations and their correlations with change measures from other sources strongly suggested that they could appropriately be considered a separate cluster or "factor." Although the therapist's rating of success had a high loading on the therapist factor, it was given separate treatment because it has received considerable attention in research on psychotherapy, many people viewing it as the best single measure of psychotherapeutic effects. This variable correlated .32, .43, and .47, respectively, with the three variables representing the therapist's perception of change (Factor 3).

Types of Gain Scores

The measurement of change, growth, or gain presents many psychometric difficulties (cf. Lord, 1956, 1958; McNemar, 1958; Manning & DuBois, 1962). On the substantive side, a strong case can be made for measuring psychotherapeutic gain in terms of observed or raw change scores because of the particular and perhaps individualized objectives of psychotherapy. Both the therapist and the client are primarily concerned with effecting gains in those areas where the client is relatively deficient. The greater the deficiency, the greater the interest of both participants in producing such gains. (In contrast, teachers in a typical learning situation seek to maximize learning both in pupils who have low initial knowledge or skill and also in pupils at high initial levels.) Thus in studying psychotherapy, we would predict that the largest gains on any one variable would be found in clients whose initial status was low.

On the other hand, it is a well-established fact that raw gain scores have undesirable psychometric properties. Such scores are less reliable than initial and final level scores, and ordinarily will be less reliable than residual gain scores (Manning & DuBois, 1962). They can be expected to have negative correlations with initial levels.

Residual gain scores provide a criterion based on posttreatment status with the effect of initial status partialed out. By using such a measure, the experimenter can estimate the relationships which he would have observed if it had been feasible to utilize subjects equated for initial status. Such an approach might be preferable where one is concerned primarily with adequacy of functioning within a single area, and with the relative effectiveness of two treatments for remedying the particular type of inadequacy. On the other hand, the population of clients entering therapy have differing patterns of inadequacy. In the present study, the focus was on the extent to which therapeutic gains in such a diverse population are predictable, regardless of factors producing the gains.

Thus both raw gains and residual gains have merits and limitations as criteria for psychotherapeutic change. Since neither is completely satisfactory, we used both in the hope that by examining and comparing the two sets of results, we could estimate the possibilities of predicting criteria derived from changes as opposed to criteria based solely on posttherapy status or on subjective estimates of gains.

The first type of gain score was the observed or raw change score, posttherapy score minus pretherapy score. (These are subsequently identified by the prefix C.)

For Factors 1–4 and ID, the raw change scores for the two or three variables selected for each factor were combined, giving equal weight to each variable by converting its array to standard scores and then adding the standard scores. For Factor L, the log values were used. The intercorrelations among the components in each of these factor scores were all above .40 with the median being .58.

The second type was the residual gain score (labeled "RG"), the posttherapy score with the influence of the pretherapy score eliminated from it. Using the same variables indicated above and again converting to standard scores, a posttherapy factor score and a pretherapy factor score were computed for each factor. Then the contribution of the pretherapy score was partialed out of the posttherapy score. For computational convenience, this elimination was carried out by subtracting from the posttherapy score the pretherapy score times the regression coefficient (the correlation between pre- and postscore multiplied by the standard deviation for post over that for pre). This operation yielded sets of residual gain scores with arbitrary means and variances.

Predictors

Approximately 100 pretherapy variables were available as potential predictors. However, most of them had been included in a factor analysis which yielded four factors clearly corresponding to the first four factors found in the change measures. Each of these four pretherapy factors formed the basis for a single score obtained by combining separate variables in standard score form. To simplify the interpretation of the results, we used the same variables that were used to obtain the criterion composite scores. Inspection of the loadings from the pretherapy factor analysis indicated that these variables were satisfactory representatives of the several factors. (These composite predictor scores were labeled P_1 to P_4, the numerals corresponding to those for the equivalent criterion scores.) On the same basis, a score was obtained to represent the interview-diagnostician's ratings. The intercorrelations within the set of two or three variables representing each factor were all above .40, the median being .68.

In addition, we included several predictors which had seemed promising on the basis of reports in the literature prior to 1956 when the study was designed. Half of the clients were given four subtests of the WAIS at the pretherapy testing: Similarities, Comprehension, Digit-Symbol, and Block Design. Our sample was generally above average in intelligence: the mean scaled score per subtest was 13.3. Probably as a consequence of the special characteristics of the sample, the intercorrelations of these subtests were somewhat lower than for the general population. The four weighted scores were, nevertheless, summed to provide an estimate of intelligence. The other half of the group were given the Rorschach to obtain scores on the Kolpfer Prognostic Rating Scale (Klopfer, Ainsworth, Klopfer, & Holt, 1954, Ch. 19). The scores ranged from 0 to 10, most scores falling in the top three of Klopfer's six groups. Time did not permit giving both tests to all clients.

Two other predictors were included. The Ego Strength (Es) scale (Barron, 1953a) was treated separately, even though it had a high loading on the general Client Self-Evaluation factor (P_1), because of its frequent previous use as a predictor. The Kirtner Typology (Kirtner & Cartwright, 1958) was also used to classify each client, on the basis of the first therapeutic interview. (All prediction variables are identified by the letter P.)

Reliabilities

No uniform estimates of reliability were computed. However, the intercorrelations among the variables combined in each score can be used as a rough lower-bound estimate. On this basis, the observed change criterion scores C_1 through C_4 can be judged to have reliabilities above .72. As estimated by the formula for reliability of differences, the values are somewhat lower, .51 to .85. The measurement of length is obviously quite reliable. It seems likely that the success rating has reasonable reliability because it correlates with several other criteria (see below) and it has a number of high correlations with specific change measures: it correlates .46 with C_3, the change score based on therapist ratings.

The first four pretherapy scores and P_{ID} can be estimated to have reliabilities above .69. The reliability of the WAIS appears to be established. We can provide no estimate of the reliability of the Klopfer Prognostic Rating Scale in this context. Some impression of the consistency of the diagnostician's classifications into the typology can be obtained from the fact that, in her independent classification of the last therapeutic interviews, two-thirds of the group were placed in the same type (three-quarters of the changes being toward a more favorable type).

Analyses

For the intercorrelations among predictor and criterion variables, Pearson r's were used with one exception. Since the Kirtner Typology was viewed as an ordered set of categories for which the assumption of equal intervals could not be made with confidence, the rank-correlation coefficient (rho) was used to determine the relationship between this classification and each of the other 15 variables.

RESULTS
Observed Change Scores

Intercorrelations among criteria. Although 17 of the 21 correlations between criteria are positive, many are quite low (see the lower right quadrant of Table 1). Since the therapist's success rating, C_s, is related appreciably to all other criteria except *Hs-Hy,* it appears to be the most representative

TABLE 1

INTERCORRELATIONS OF PRETHERAPY AND CHANGE CRITERION MEASURES

Variable	Pretherapy							Criteria						
	P_2	P_3	P_4	P_{ID}	P_{WAIS}	P_{KPRS}	P_T	C_1	C_2	C_3	C_4	C_{ID}	C_S	L
P_1 Client Self-Evaluation	.14	.33**	.30**	.23*	.25	.01	.22*	-.60**	.03	-.01	-.27**	-.03	-.06	-.12
P_2 TAT Adequacy		.06	.21*	.29**	.33*	-.10	.01	.01	-.46**	-.12	.02	-.18	.01	.01
P_3 Therapist's Evaluation			.13	.22*	.06	.01	.05	-.20	.04	-.52**	-.09	-.07	-.10	.03
P_4 Hs-Hy (MMPI; reversed)				.21*	.16	-.10	.12	.02	.01	-.05	-.60**	-.01	.08	-.10
P_{ID} Interview-Diagnostician					.23	-.09	.47**	.03	-.01	.00	-.07	-.30**	.18	-.08
P_{WAIS} Four WAIS scales							.09	-.13	.16	.09	-.12	.13	.04	-.11
P_{KPRS} Klopfer Prognostic Rating Scale						-.12	-.11	-.14	-.08	-.10	-.03	-.26	-.19	
P_T Kirtner Typology							-.05	.19	.09	-.16	.14	.35**	.12	
C_1 Change in Favorableness of Client Self-Evaluation								-.01	.20	.14	.10	.22*	-.07	
C_2 Change in TAT Adequacy									.07	-.18	.23*	.20	-.03	
C_3 Therapist's Perception of Change										.08	.32**	.46**	.01	
C_4 Change (decrease) on Hs and Hy scales (MMPI)											.09	.04	.06	
C_{ID} Interview-Diagnostician												.36**	.23*	
C_S Therapist's Rating of Success													.36**	
L Length														

Note.—All coefficients are Pearson r's except those involving the Kirtner Typology, for which rho was used.
N = 93 except for correlations involving P_{WAIS} (N = 48) and P_{KPRS} (N = 42).
No subject received both the Wechsler and the Rorschach.
* p ≤ .05, two-tailed.
** p ≤ .01, two-tailed.

single criterion. On the other hand, the correlation of C_8 with C_3, the score based on therapists' pre- and posttherapy differences, is low enough to indicate that the success rating made at the end of therapy is based on some considerations in addition to the therapist's perception of change. Since C_8 correlates significantly with length but C_3 does not, it would appear that the judgment involved in C_8 is influenced by the duration of treatment (cf. the significant correlation between length and the therapist change factor in Nichols & Beck, 1960).

The C_8 rating is correlated with the interview-diagnostician's perception of change (C_{ID}), the latter being based on two of the various interviews conducted by the therapist. The C_{ID} also has a significant correlation with length, unlike the scores based on the TAT and on direct reports from the clients.

This set of intercorrelations among criteria serves to reemphasize the conclusion of the previous paper (Cartwright et al., 1963) that no one measure and no one score based on a single method appears to provide in itself an adequate index of psychotherapeutic change.

Intercorrelations among pretherapy measures. Inspection of the top left quadrant of Table 1 shows that all of the Pearson r's among the pretherapy measures are positive with the exception of three involving the Klopfer score (KPRS). Based on a distinct type of protocol and an independent rationale, this KPRS measure is unrelated to any other potential predictor.

The significant relationship between the Typology and P_{ID} scores is presumably a consequence of the fact that both ratings were made by the same person. The other significant rho involves the client self-evaluation score (P_1); this value appears to be significant because those in the least favorable type have a distinctly low mean on self-evaluation.

Correlations between pretherapy scores and criteria. Each of the five boldfaced correlations is between a pretherapy measure

and the corresponding change criterion. These values are considered in the Discussion section. It will also be noted that the off-diagonal correlations among these variables tend to be negative. The significant negative value between P_1 and C_4 probably falls in the same general class as the diagonal values, since both come from the client, although the correlation between P_4 and C_1 is essentially zero.

The KPRS score has consistently negative correlations with all criteria but none reach significance. The WAIS has no significant correlations. The relationship between the typological classification and C_8 is significant. Both variables are based on the interviews. Hence none of these criteria is predicted significantly by a measure from a completely independent source.

In addition, separate attention was given to two other potential predictors. Since the *Es* scale was originally developed from items differentiating rated improvement from psychotherapy (Barron, 1953a), the association between scores on this scale and each of the criteria was determined. The pattern of correlations was the same as that for P_1, a result which had been anticipated since *Es* had a high loading on the P_1 factor.

Therapist experience was also used as a predictor. This variable was represented by the square root of the number of clients the therapist had seen, this transformation seeming to represent experience better than the raw number. None of the seven correlations with raw gain criteria approached significance.

Residual Gain Scores

Intercorrelations among criteria. The bottom half of Table 2 presents the intercorrelations among the residual gain criteria. The Interview-Diagnostician score has significant relationships with two other scores; the more prominent value is that with the Therapist's Evaluation, for which the interviews were also the basis for judg-

TABLE 2

RESIDUAL GAIN SCORES: INTERCORRELATIONS AND CORRELATIONS WITH PREDICTORS

Predictors		Residual gain criteria				
		RG_1	RG_2	RG_3	RG_4	RG_{ID}
P_1	Client Self-Evaluation	.00	.12	.10	−.15	−.02
P_2	TAT Adequacy	.05	.00	.00	.23*	−.12
P_3	Therapist's Evaluation	.07	.08	.00	−.03	−.02
P_4	Hs-Hy (MMPI; reversed)	.20	.18	.04	.00	.05
P_{ID}	Interview-Diagnostician	.18	.13	.24*	.02	−.01
P_{WAIS}	Four WAIS Scales	.00	.36*	.10	.04	.24
P_{KPRS}	Klopfer Prognostic Rating Scale	−.06	−.23	−.13	−.13	−.14
P_T	Kirtner Typology	−.05	.19	.23*	.12	.39**
Residual gain criteria						
RG_1	Client Self-Evaluation		.04	.22*	.17	.19
RG_2	TAT Adequacy			.12	−.04	.26*
RG_3	Therapist's Evaluation				.02	.43**
RG_4	Hs-Hy (MMPI; reversed)					.17
RG_{ID}	Interview-Diagnostician					
Other criteria						
C_s	Therapist's Rating of Success	.21*	.25*	.58**	.03	.46**
L	Length	−.21*	−.06	.05	.02	.17

Note.—All coefficients are Pearson r's except those involving the Kirtner Typology, for which rho was used.
$N = 93$ except for correlations involving P_{WAIS} ($N = 48$) and P_{KPRS} ($N = 42$).
* $p \leq .05$, two-tailed.
** $p \leq .01$, two-tailed.

ment. The only other significant correlation is that between RG_1 and RG_3, the clients' and therapists' evaluations. In general, the total set of intercorrelations is positive and, as would be expected, resembles the pattern for the raw change scores.

The only significant correlation with length of therapy is a negative one for RG_1 (Client Self-Evaluation). While the Therapist's Rating of Success is, of course, associated with the Therapist's Evaluation, it is also associated with the Interview-Diagnostician score, the TAT Adequacy score, and the Client Self-Evaluation score.

Correlations between pretherapy scores and criteria. Each of the boldfaced correlations in the top half of Table 2 involves a pair of variables derived from the same source of data. These correlations will be considered in the Discussion section. In contrast to Table 1, the predictor-criterion correlations in Table 2 are generally posi-

tive and several are statistically significant.

The only predictor significantly associated with TAT Adequacy is the set of WAIS subtests. To see whether this value was determined primarily by verbal ability, a composite of the Comprehension and Similarities scores was correlated with RG_2 and other residual gain scores. All the resulting r's were not significant and were lower than the corresponding values for the total of the four subtests, presumably as a consequence of reduced reliability.

The Therapist's Evaluation criterion is predicted by the Interview-Diagnostician's ratings and by the Typology. The residual score for Hs-Hy is predicted by initial TAT Adequacy. The Interview-Diagnostician criterion has a positive association with the Typology as classified by this judge on the basis of the first therapy interviews.

None of the residual gain criteria had

significant correlations with either Es or therapist experience.

DISCUSSION
Technical Considerations

The five significant and negative values along the diagonal of Table 1 were expected: it is well known that gain scores tend to be negatively correlated with the initial score which is subtracted to obtain the index of raw gain. The absolute values would be even greater for separate variables than the observed ones for composite scores. Such negative correlations are even more likely when the larger, later-in-time scores crowd the ceiling of the scale. In these data, however, this effect would be attenuated by the use of three measures; also the ceiling on the scales appears to have had little restrictive effect on these ratings.

We recognize that the other correlations in the first five rows of Table 1 are about what would be expected on technical grounds. These criterion measures were based on five independent factors (although the measures are not as separate as the factor structure might have led one to expect). The same is true for the corresponding pretherapy measures. Hence there would be little reason to anticipate any significant off-diagonal correlations. The generally negative tendency of these latter values reflects the associations among pretherapy measures and among criteria.

These considerations illuminate Gallagher's (1954) findings that clients judged as more improved by a multiple criterion had higher pretherapy scores on the MMPI Taylor Anxiety and Depression scales. Both of these scores were highly loaded on our P_1 factor, .88 and .71, respectively. Gallagher's multiple criterion included a client self-rating of improvement, a therapist rating, and an interview-judge rating.

The generally positive picture in the top of Table 2 is to be expected when the pretherapy measures are positively related. The technical basis for this expectation is given by Lord (1958). The correlations between pretherapy scores and the corresponding residual gain scores (the boldfaced values in Table 2) are necessarily zero (except for grouping error) because the contribution of the pretherapy scores was partialed out of the posttherapy scores.

Substantive Findings

The overall pattern of our results is distinctly unpromising. Neither raw gain nor residual gain criteria appear to be predictable by measures derived from methods that are independent of the criterion measures. The rare exceptions are best interpreted as results of sampling fluctuations. No potential predictor has much success in our sample (except possibly the Kirtner Typology).

The failure of the KPRS was a distinct surprise. An earlier study at the Counseling Center had reported a significant positive relationship with therapists' ratings of success (Cartwright, 1958). Although the range of KPRS scores was comparable to that for the present study, the N for the earlier study was much smaller (13) and the Rorschachs were scored by different raters in the two studies. While other studies (e.g., cf. Butler & Fiske, 1955; Novick, 1962) have reported positive predictive values for the KPRS, the usual criterion has been rated improvement rather than a change score. In the present study, rated improvement is represented by the C_s variable. We would expect to find at least a positive correlation between KPRS and C_s. All correlations between KPRS and criterion variables were negative, however. Three possible explanations may be offered. First, since most of the present scores fell into the top three of Klopfer's six groups, the variability or the range represented may have been insufficient. Second, the diagnostic rater of the Rorschach may have had some unique biases in his scoring procedures. Third, the balance of components representative of ego strength may be markedly different in a sample of persons applying for client-centered therapy, as found by Cartwright (1959) for a sample of 13 clients compared with a sample of 40 outpatients attending a Veterans Administration clinic.

Within the restricted range of intelligence in our sample, the composite of four WAIS subtests offers very slight promise as a predictor of two residual gain scores. It should be noted that the WAIS was unsuccessful in predicting criteria derived from judgments of the therapist in the present study. However, Barron (1953b) found a positive relation between scores on the same four WAIS subtests and clinically judged improvement. Rosenberg (1954) also found Full-Scale WAIS scores positively correlated with psychiatrist's judgment of improvement. In the present study, only the residual gain in TAT Adequacy was significantly positively related to the WAIS. The next highest correlation, however, was for residual gain in the Interview-Diagnostician's ratings. Since client-centered therapists, on principle, make no diagnostic evaluations of their clients, it is conceivable that the WAIS is a better predictor for primarily diagnostic appraisals of improvement.

The absence of significant relationships between all criteria and therapist experience is puzzling. One would expect that an important concomitant of greater experience is a greater ability to provide benefit for the client. Myers and Auld (1955) found that more experienced therapists had a greater percentage of improved patients. Nichols and Beck (1960) found two change factors positively related to skill of therapist as judged by supervisors. Both factors were composed of changes as rated at the termination of therapy, one by the therapist, one by the client. The only comparable criterion in the present research is the C_S variable. But it, too, had a nonsignificant correlation with experience.

The fault may lie in our measure of experience: perhaps number of clients should be combined with number of therapeutic interviews conducted, or with number of years as a therapist. (Number of years and number of clients are highly correlated in this group of therapists.) Again, the difficulty may be that experience is a poor index of skill. Finally, before concluding that therapist experience is unrelated to therapeutic effectiveness, one would have to establish that the clients seen by each therapist were comparable with respect to potentiality for benefiting from psychotherapy.

It is noteworthy that length is positively related only to C_{ID} and C_S. The relationship to the therapist's Success Rating was reported in a previous paper (Cartwright, Robertson, Fiske, & Kirtner, 1961). There it was also shown that posttherapy ratings of improvement in personal integration had higher correlations with two measures of length of therapy than did computed differences between pretherapy and posttherapy ratings of current level of integration. In the present research we find that neither raw differences nor residual gain scores from therapist ratings correlate significantly with length of therapy, while the posttherapy Success Rating does correlate significantly. Nichols and Beck (1960) also found that, out of six factors of change, only one correlated significantly with length of therapy: the factor of therapist ratings of improvement, judgments which were made at the end of therapy. In regard to the relation between length and C_{ID}, we note a similarity with the findings of Frank, Gliedman, Imber, Stone, and Nash (1959). In their study, changes in self-rated Discomfort (like our C_1) were unrelated to amount of therapy contact while decreases in diagnostically rated Social Ineffectiveness (like our C_{ID}) were positively related to amount of contact. On the side of prediction, yet another similarity is noted between the present results and those of an earlier study by the same group (Frank, Gliedman, Imber, Nash, & Stone, 1957). They found no relation between length and initial scores on their Discomfort scale (like our P_1), and no relation between length and their Social Ineffectiveness scale (like our P_{ID}). While length of treatment has previously been found related to intelligence (e.g., Rubinstein & Lorr, 1956), the absence of such relation in the present study may well be due to the relatively small variance in WAIS scores for our population.

No one of our criteria is predicted appreciably better than any other. Furthermore, no one criterion appears to be sufficient by itself. While the criteria based on the Interview-Diagnostician's ratings do share variance with other criteria, they cannot be said to represent these other measures well. Even though the posttherapy rating of success made by the therapist also has consistently positive and sometimes significant correlations with other criteria, it would be unsatisfactory as a sole criterion. On the one hand, different therapists (or other judges) may have different perceptions of what constitutes improvement, especially for clients with markedly different initial levels of adjustment. On the other hand, such judgments appear to be inappropriately influenced by the amount of time and effort that the therapist has spent on the client, or by the therapist's expectation that duration will be related to improvement, an expectation which is hardly supported by our data.

How can this generally negative picture be interpreted? The lack of significant correlations cannot be attributed to unreliability: as noted earlier, it is clear that the various measures had sufficient reliability to permit quite sizable intercorrelations to emerge. Perhaps the population is to blame. It probably differs in both intelligence and severity of illness from many of the outpatient groups that have been used on previous prediction studies.

It seems clear that there are reliable changes associated with psychotherapy but that none of our measures of initial status or initial assets accounts for any very appreciable proportion of the variance in such changes. Where else should one look for predictors? The belief structures or expectancies of the client regarding therapy? The specific dyadic relationships between each therapist and his client? Untapped dimensions of therapist behavior?

An entirely different approach may be necessary. From among a large population of clients, one might be able to isolate small groups who were homogeneous with respect to the specific change or changes which were observed. For each such group, gains might be found to be associated with certain competences and initial liabilities or adaptive difficulties defined in much narrower terms than the broad variables used in this study. But such an approach must overcome the serious obstacles resulting from the substantial method variance found in measures of gains and in assessments of initial status.

REFERENCES

BARRON, F. An ego-strength scale which predicts response to psychotherapy. *J. consult. Psychol.,* 1953, 17, 327–333. (a)

BARRON, F. Some test correlates of response to psychotherapy. *J. consult. Psychol.,* 1953, 17, 235–241. (b)

BUTLER, J. M., & FISKE, D. W. Theory and techniques of assessment. *Annu. Rev. Psychol.,* 1955, 6, 327–356.

CARTWRIGHT, D. S., KIRTNER, W. L., & FISKE, D. W. Method factors in changes associated with psychotherapy. *J. abnorm. soc. Psychol.,* 1963, 66, 164–175.

CARTWRIGHT, D. S. ROBERTSON, R. J., FISKE, D. W., & KIRTNER, W. L. Length of therapy in relation to outcome and change in personal integration. *J. consult. Psychol.,* 1961, 25, 84–88.

CARTWRIGHT, ROSALIND D. Predicting response to client-centered therapy with the Rorschach *PR* Scale. *J. counsel. Psychol.,* 1958, 5, 11–17.

CARTWRIGHT, ROSALIND D. A note on the Rorschach Prognostic Rating Scale. *J. counsel. Psychol.,* 1959, 6, 160–162.

FRANK, J. D., GLIEDMAN, L. H., IMBER, S. D., NASH, E. H., JR., & STONE, A. R. Why patients leave psychotherapy. *Arch. Neurol. Psychiat.*, 1957, 77, 283–299.

FRANK, J. D., GLIEDMAN, L. H., IMBER, S. D., STONE, A. R., & NASH, E. H. Patients' expectancies and relearning as factors determining improvement in psychotherapy. *Amer. J. Psychiat.*, 1959, 115, 961–968.

GALLAGHER, J. J. Test indicators for therapy prognosis. *J. consult. Psychol.*, 1954, 18, 409–413.

KIRTNER, W. L., & CARTWRIGHT, D. S. Success and failure in client-centered therapy as a function of initial in-therapy behavior. *J. consult. Psychol.*, 1958, 22, 329–333.

KLOPFER, B. AINSWORTH, MARY, KLOPFER, W., & HOLT, R. *Developments in the Rorschach technique.* Vol. 1. New York: World Book, 1954.

LORD, F. M. The measurement of growth. *Educ. psychol. Measmt.*, 1956, 16, 421–437.

LORD, F. M. Further problems in the measurement of growth. *Educ. psychol. Measmt.*, 1958, 18, 437–451.

MCNEMAR, Q. On growth measurement. *Educ. psychol. Measmt.*, 1958, 18, 47–55.

MANNING, W. H., & DUBOIS, P. H. Correlational methods in research on human learning. *Percept. mot. Skills,* 1962, 15 (Monogr. Suppl. No. 15), 287–321.

MYERS, J. K., & AULD, F., JR. Some variables related to outcome of psychotherapy. *J. clin. Psychol.*, 1955, 11, 51–54.

NICHOLS, R. C., & BECK, K. W. Factors in psychotherapy change. *J. consult. Psychol.*, 1960, 24, 388–399.

NOVICK, J. I. Effectiveness of the Rorschach Prognostic Rating Scale for predicting behavioral change in children following brief psychotherapy. *Amer. Psychologist,* 1962, 17, 359–360. (Abstract)

ROSENBERG, S. The relationship of certain personality factors to prognosis in psychotherapy. *J. clin. Psychol.*, 1954, 10, 341–345.

RUBINSTEIN, E. A., & LORR, M. A. A comparison of terminators and remainers in outpatient psychotherapy. *J. clin. Psychol.*, 1956, 12, 345–349.

Success and Failure in Client-Centered Therapy as a Function of Client Personality Variables[1]

WILLIAM L. KIRTNER
DESMOND S. CARTWRIGHT

Cartwright (5) has presented evidence for the existence of a "failure-zone," ranging between 13 and 21 interviews, in client-centered therapy. In a subsequent paper, Taylor (25) presented closely comparable evidence with respect to psychoanalytically oriented psychotherapy.

Cartwright demonstrated that therapeutic outcomes were divided by the failure-zone and suggested that there may be two forms of therapeutic process, identifying these processes as "short" (1–12 interviews) and "long" (13–77 or more interviews). He further hypothesized (5, p.

362) "that certain individual differences between clients give rise to different kinds of therapeutic process."

On the basis of these results and hypotheses, five client groups were distinguished: short success, 1–12 interviews; short failure, 1–12 interviews; failure-zone, 13–21 interviews; long success, more than 21 interviews; and long failure, more than 21 interviews. Utilizing this schema, Kirtner (12) hypothesized that therapy length-by-outcome is related to the personality structures of clients at the beginning of therapy. The present paper reports an investigation of this hypothesis.

METHOD AND PROCEDURE
Subjects

From the research files of the Counseling Center, University of Chicago, all clients were selected for whom the following four conditions held: (a) the therapists' rating of outcome on a 9-point success

Reprinted from *Journal of Consulting Psychology,* 1958, 22 (4), 259–264, with the permission of the American Psychological Association and the authors.
[1] This investigation is based upon a dissertation submitted by the senior author to the University of Chicago in partial fulfillment of the requirements for the degree of master of arts. It was supported in part by research grants from the National Institute of Mental Health, National Institutes of Health, U.S. Public Health Service, and from the Ford Foundation.

rating scale (22) fell either between 7 and 9 inclusive ("success") or between 1 and 4 inclusive ("failure"); (*b*) the exact number of interviews was recorded; (*c*) a pretherapy Thematic Apperception Test (TAT) protocol was available; and (*d*) a recorded or transcribed first therapy interview was available. Twenty-four clients fulfilled all conditions. Two clients who fulfilled conditions (*a*), (*b*), and (*c*), but not (*d*), were also included, yielding *n* = 26 for this study. All clients were seen by experienced therapists (25 male and 1 female) between 1949 and 1954. The sample included 12 males, 14 females; 10 students, 16 nonstudents; the mean age was 27.5 years and the range 19 to 41 years.

Instruments

Rating scales were developed to measure twelve personality variables. These variables were selected to comprehend: (*a*) some of those variables widely referred to as designating level or pattern of personality integration, e.g., sex role and identification, motivation, impulse life; (*b*) some of those variables particularly relevant to the phenomenological basis of client-centered therapy, e.g., decision-making, rule usage, sense of self as a causative agent (16; 17, pp. 4–5); and (*c*) some of those variables especially associated with previous research in client-centered therapy, e.g., sensitivity to others (23, 24, 26), intrapunitive feelings (9). Upon analysis of the results derived from the application of the 12 scales, 6 scales were eliminated due to functional overlap with the remainder. Numerical ratings made by an independent judge on the 12 scales were intercorrelated. The resulting matrix was inspected for clusters from each of which one scale was selected, yielding four relatively independent scales, numbered I, IV, X, and XI. Scale VIII, while substantially correlated with Scale I, was uncorrelated with the other three selected scales and is therefore reported upon. Scale XII, highly correlated with Scale XI

on numerical ratings, is also reported upon because of its distinctive qualitative differentiation between clients. Over the six scales, the range of intercorrelations was − .24 to .77. The median correlation was .29.

Following are brief descriptions of the six scales reported in this study. In complete form, all are 5-point, fully anchored scales.[2] A rating of 1 indicates minimal disturbance (optimal adjustment), and a rating of 5 indicates maximal disturbance.

Scale I—Impulse Life

From free flow and expression of generative impulses and ideas, to extreme:
a. fright about impulses but with expression;
b. control or repression;
c. distortion of impulses.

Scale IV—Sense of Capability

From a sense of felt capacity to cope adequately with situations, to a sense of helplessness and lack of internal resources to cope with situations.

Scale VIII—Sex-role and Identification

From direct and open expression of sexuality with good control of feelings, to extreme conflict, uncertainty, and confusion about sex.

Scale X—People—Object Orientation

From the ability to relate deeply both to people and in activities, to:
a. a desperate need for people;
b. avoidance of relating to people with concomitant desperate need for activities;
c. immobilization.

Scale XI—Sense of Comfort and Satisfaction

From a sense of self-comfort and satis-

---

[2] Copies of the complete scales and of the raw data from both judges may be obtained without charge from William L. Kirtner, Counseling Center, University of Chicago, 5737 Drexel Avenue, Chicago 37, Illinois or for a fee from the American Documentation Institute. Order Document No. 5585, remitting $1.75 for microfilm or $2.50 for photocopies.

faction with the ability to locate problem sources both internally and externally in good balance, to:

    a. intensely driven to search himself for causes of discomfort and dissatisfaction;

    b. intensely driven to search outward for causes of discomfort and dissatisfaction;

    c. intense hopelessness to locate causes.

Scale XII—Punitive Feelings

From a self-appraising person who is not self-reproachful, to:

    a. extremely self-punishing person;

    b. extreme anticipation of punishment from external source;

    c. vacillation between "*a*" and "*b*."

It will be noted that some of the scales include alternate descriptive anchors, indicated by letters *a, b, c.* Such letter ratings occur only in connection with numerical ratings of 3 or more. As the level of disturbance increases in a given area (as the numerical rating is higher on these scales), the behavior displayed may take on one of several modal characteristics. Salient nonreactive, explosive, or other features of behavior become usual and representatively distinguishing attributes of the person rated. Such salient characteristics or modal patterns of behavior must be discretely described in order to obtain a fully anchored scale of levels of disturbance. As the level of disturbance decreases (as the numerical rating is lower on these scales), the behaviors displayed do not require multiple discrete descriptions; salient nonreactive, explosive, or other features of behavior are neither usual nor representatively distinguishing attributes of the person rated.

While the foregoing paragraph presents the descriptive (i.e., scale-making) problem, the existence of the problem invites explanation. The authors hold the working hypothesis that the individual adopts certain specifiable modes or techniques of behavior in order to control his internal disturbance or anxiety with respect to a given segment of his experience. As anxiety or disturbance intensifies, the techniques required for control of the disturbance, or for maintenance of personality organization, become more drastic and more representatively typical of the individual.

Ratings

Ratings of each client, on each of the six scales, were made on the basis of the pretherapy TAT protocol in conjunction with the recorded or transcribed first therapy interview. In two cases, the recorded first interview was not available, and the TAT protocol alone was used.

Ratings were made independently by the senior author and by another judge. The latter ("Judge II") knew neither the length nor the success rating of any case.

Reliability

Reliability of the therapist rating of outcome on the 9-point scale has been previously reported (5, 22) as slightly better than $r = .80$. To determine reliability for the numerical ratings on the six scales, all ratings by the two independent judges were correlated using Kendall's tau for ties in both rankings (10). The computational procedure employed was that developed by Cartwright (3). Corrections for continuity were made using Schaeffer and Levitt's (21) modification of Whitfield's correction (27). The routine for computing corrections for continuity and p values was that described by Cartwright (4). Table 1 presents these reliability data, which were considered adequate throughout.

Letter ratings occurred on four out of the six scales. Since such ratings are associated only with numerical ratings of 3 or more on these scales, a long and tedious problem in combinatorics would have to be solved to obtain an exact estimate of reliability, which did not seem justifiable. A fortiori, it did not seem justifiable to work

TABLE 1

RELIABILITY COEFFICIENTS (TAU) FOR
NUMERICAL RATINGS ON SIX SCALES

Scale	Tau	p
I. Impulse life	.65	.01
IV. Sense of capability	.62	.01
VIII. Sex-role and identification	.53	.01
X. People-object orientation	.73	.01
XI. Sense of comfort and satisfaction	.85	.01
XII. Punitive feelings	.83	.01

on a solution for the reliability of joint numerical-plus-letter ratings. Instead, simple percentages of agreement were computed for all cases where both judges employed a letter rating, and regardless of numerical rating. Table 2 presents these data and includes, for the reader's information, the number of cases where neither judge used a letter rating.

TABLE 2

PERCENTAGES OF AGREEMENT FOR LETTER
RATINGS ON FOUR SCALES

Scale	Number of cases for which letter ratings were used by		Agreements	
	Neither judge	Both judges	Number	%
I.	3	22	20	91
X.	0	26	23	88
XI.	0	26	25	96
XII.	1	25	22	88

No statistical analysis of results from letter ratings was made. However, the authors judge the data of Table 2 to warrant descriptive characterization of modal behaviors displayed by subjects rated on the four scales referred to.

Analysis

The sample of 26 cases was divided into length-by-outcome groups according to the schema given. Table 3 summarizes descriptions of the resulting groups.

Regrettably for the research, only one long-failure case was among those available. This group was therefore eliminated from subsequent analysis. The remaining groups were examined in all possible pairs on each of the six scales as numerically rated by Judge II. All comparisons were made using tau for a dichotomy in one ranking as described by Kendall (10, pp. 32–34). The significance of differences between groups was computed in the manner previously indicated for the reliability analysis. In order to show the direction of differences between pairs of groups, mean values for each group on each scale were also computed.

RESULTS
Numerical Ratings

Table 4 presents means for groups on each of the six scales and the p values of the differences between groups.[3]

_____
[3] See footnote 2.

TABLE 3

SUMMARY DESCRIPTION OF GROUPS

Group	Number of interviews	Range of outcome ratings	N	Male	Female	Student	Non-student
Short failures	<13	1–4	10	4	6	4	6
Short success	<13	7–9	4	0	4	3	1
Failure-zone	13–21	1–4	7	5	2	1	6
Long failure	>21	1–4	1	1	0	1	0
Long success	>21	7–9	4	2	2	2	2

TABLE 4

SIGNIFICANCE LEVELS OF DIFFERENCES BETWEEN GROUPS ON SIX SCALES, AND
MEANS INDICATING DIRECTION OF DIFFERENCES

| | Means of Groups[b] | | | | p of Differences[a] | | | | | |
Scale	SS	LS	SF	FZ	SS vs. LS	SS vs. SF	SS vs. FZ	LS vs. SF	LS vs. FZ	SF vs. FZ
I.	2.00	3.00	4.10	4.43	<.10	<.01	<.01	<.01	<.01	>.20
IV.	3.00	3.25	4.30	3.71	>.20	<.02	>.20	<.03	>.20	<.07
VIII.	2.50	3.75	3.80	4.57	<.07	<.02	<.02	>.20	<.10	<.02
X.	3.50	3.75	4.10	4.00	>.20	>.20	>.20	>.20	>.20	>.20
XI.	3.75	4.50	3.90	3.57	<.15	>.20	>.20	>.20	<.08	>.20
XII.	3.25	4.25	3.80	3.85	<.19	>.20	>.20	>.20	>.20	>.20

[a] Two-tailed tests throughout.
[b] SS—short success; LS—long success; SF—short failure; FZ—Failure-zone.

Rejecting the null hypothesis if $p < .05$, each success group shows a lesser degree of disturbance than either failure group on Scale I. Also, the short-success group shows a lesser degree of disturbance than either failure group on Scale VIII.

Of special interest are results setting a given group apart from the other three groups. We reject sets of three null hypotheses if in each instance $p < .10$. On this basis, Table 4 contains the following results: the short-success group shows less disturbance than any other group on Scales I and VIII; the short-failure group shows more disturbance than any other group on Scale IV; and the failure-zone group shows more disturbance than any other group on Scale VIII.

Letter Ratings

Table 5 presents the number of letter ratings agreed upon by both judges for

TABLE 5

LETTER RATINGS AGREED ON BY BOTH JUDGES

| | Short success | | | Long success | | | Short failure | | | Failure zone | | |
Scale	a	b	c	a	b	c	a	b	c	a	b	c
I.			4							2 3 4		5 1
X.	4					4				1 4 4		2 1 2
XI.	3					4				8 2		6 1
XII.	3					4				8 1		4 1

four scales with respect to the four groups.

The most interesting feature of Table 5 is that success groups appear to differ from failure groups on Scales X, XI, and XII. While there were no differences on these scales as numerically rated for degree of disturbance, differences in typical mode of controlling inner disturbance were observed by both judges.

Distinguishing Descriptions

The results and observations mentioned in connection with Tables 4 and 5 are given embodiment in descriptions distinguishing the groups. Descriptions employ the language of those scales, and only those scales, for which either statistically significant differences or clear qualitative observations have been made.

The short-success group shows a generally higher level of personality integration than that descriptive of other groups. In particular, they are rather open to their impulse life (I), and, while showing some distortion and uncertainty, they are a good deal less confused about their sex role than other groups (VIII).

Though similar to the short-success group in many respects, the long-success group shows a somewhat lower level of personality integration in general. In particular, they are rather anxious about their impulse life (I) and rather confused about the meaning and place of sex in their identity (VIII).

Both success groups differ from each failure group in showing less disturbance in their impulse life (I). Letter ratings show the success groups typically displaying a strong need for people to relate to in order to feel worthwhile (X), seeking internally for the cause and resolution of felt discomfort (XI), and rather strongly condemning, berating, and disvaluing themselves (XII).

The short-failure group shows a generally low level of personality integration. Especially distinguishing is their extreme underlying sense of incapacity to deal with their life situations (IV).

The failure-zone group also shows a generally low level of personality integration. Especially distinguishing is their extreme conflictedness about and rejection of their sex role (VIII).

Both failure groups show greater disturbance than either success group on several scales. They are extremely disturbed in their impulse life (I), with expressions frequently occurring in over-controlled or distorted modalities, as indicated by letter ratings. Over-control seems somewhat more typical for the failure-zone group. Letter ratings show the failure groups typically looking outward for the cause and resolution of their discomfort (XI), and typically anticipating punishment from external sources (XII).

DISCUSSION

The foregoing results seem unambiguously consistent with the general hypothesis motivating the study: that therapy length-by-outcome is related to the personality structure of clients at the beginning of therapy. While caution must be invoked due to the small sizes of the groups studied, the results add to the growing body of knowledge about factors which favor or limit therapeutic change in client-centered

therapy. Earlier work in this area has been summarized by Rogers (17, pp. 423–424, 427–428).

It may be noted that the present approach constitutes a synthesis of two trends in previous work on the general problem. One trend has dealt with the relations between pretherapy characteristics of clients and eventual ratings of improvement or outcome (e.g., 1, 2, 8, 11, 15, 19, 26). The other trend has dealt with the relations between pretherapy characteristics of clients and their length of stay in treatment (e.g., 7, 13, 14, 18, 20). To our knowledge, only one previous investigator, Dana (6), has attempted to predict improvement and length of treatment jointly. Due to the findings of Cartwright (5) and Taylor (25), a fusion of the two main trends into systematic emphasis upon length-by-outcome groupings now seems necessary. More generally, it is necessary to predict both amount and rate of change constituting improvement. While something of a beginning has been made in this direction by Dana's results and by those of the present study, much more needs to be done.

SUMMARY

Twenty-six clients, who had completed a course of client-centered therapy at the Counseling Center, University of Chicago, were divided into five groups on the basis of length-by-outcome:

Short success (1–12 interviews)—N equals 4

Short failure (1–12 interviews)—N equals 10

Failure-zone (13–21 interviews)—N equals 7

Long success (more than 21 interviews)—N equals 4

Long failure (more than 21 interviews)—N equals 1

Twelve personality variables were selected, and 5-point rating scales were constructed to describe both intensity and mode of behavior with respect to each of the 12 variables. These scales were applied independently by two judges to the pre-therapy Thematic Apperception Test protocol in conjunction with the recorded or transcribed first therapy interview in each case. Interjudge agreement was deemed adequate throughout.

The ratings made by an independent judge were intercorrelated, and the resulting matrix was inspected for clusters from each of which one scale was selected, yielding four relatively independent scales. Two further scales were reported upon because, though substantially correlated with one of the four selected scales, they are uncorrelated with the others and point up interesting and distinctive differences between client personality structure.

It was thus found that therapy length-by-outcome is related to the personality structure of clients at the beginning of therapy. The most marked differences found on these scales were those between success groups and the failure groups.

REFERENCES

1. BARRON, F. An ego-strength scale which predicts response to psychotherapy. *J. consult. Psychol.*, 1953, 17, 327–333.

2. BARRON, F. Some test correlates of response to psychotherapy. *J. consult. Psychol.*, 1953, 17, 235–241.

3. CARTWRIGHT, D. S. A computational procedure for tau correlation. *Psychometrika*, 1957, 22, 97–104.

4. CARTWRIGHT, D. S. A note concerning Kendall's tau. *Psychol. Bull.*, 1957, 54, 423–425.

5. CARTWRIGHT, D. S. Success in psychotherapy as a function of certain actuarial variables. *J. consult. Psychol.*, 1955, 19, 357–363.

6. DANA, R. H. The effects of attitudes towards authority on psychotherapy. *J. clin. Psychol.*, 1954, 10, 350–353.

7. GALLAGHER, J. J. A comparison of clients who continue with clients who discontinue

client-centered therapy. In Psychotherapy Research Group (Ed.), *Group report of a program of research in psychotherapy.* State College, Pa.: Pennsylvania State College, 1953. Pp. 21–38.

8. GALLAGHER, J. J. Test indicators for therapy prognosis. *J. consult. Psychol.*, 1954, 18, 409–413.

9. HAIMOWITZ, NATALIE R., & HAIMOWITZ, M. L. Personality changes in client-centered therapy. In Werner Wolff (Ed.), *Success in psychotherapy.* New York: Grune & Stratton, 1952. Pp. 63–94.

10. KENDALL, M. G. *Rank correlation methods.* London: Griffin, 1948.

11. KIRKNER, F, J., WISHAM, W. W., & GIEDT, F. H. A report on the validity of the Rorschach Prognostic Rating Scale. *J. proj. Tech.*, 1953, 17, 465–470.

12. KIRTNER, W. L. Success and failure in client-centered therapy as a function of personality variables. Unpublished master's thesis, Univer. of Chicago, 1955.

13. KOTKOV, B., & MEADOW, A. Rorschach criteria for predicting continuation in individual psychotherapy. *J. consult. Psychol.*, 1953, 17, 16–20.

14. LUTES, B. C. A factorial study of an attrition group in client-centered therapy. Unpublished master's thesis, Univer. of Chicago, 1952.

15. MINDESS, H. Predicting patients' responses to psychotherapy: A preliminary study designed to investigate the validity of the Rorschach Prognostic Rating Scale. *J. proj. Tech.*, 1953, 17, 327–334.

16. ROGERS, C. R. *Client-centered therapy.* Boston: Houghton Mifflin, 1951.

17. ROGERS, C. R., & DYMOND, ROSALIND F. (Eds.), *Psychotherapy and personality change.* Chicago: Univer. of Chicago Press, 1954.

18. ROGERS, L. S., KRAUSS, JOANNE, & HAMMOND, K. R. Predicting continuation in therapy by means of the Rorschach test. *J. consult. Psychol.*, 1951, 15, 368–371.

19. ROSENBERG, S. The relationship of certain personality factors to prognosis in psychotherapy. *J. clin. Psychol.*, 1954, 10, 341–345.

20. RUBINSTEIN, E. A., & LORR, M. A. comparison of terminators and remainers in

outpatient psychotherapy. *J. clin. Psychol.,* 1956, 12, 345–349.

21. SCHAEFFER, M. S., & LEVITT, E. E. Concerning Kendall's tau, a nonparametric correlation coefficient. *Psychol. Bull.,* 1956, 53, 338–346.

22. SEEMAN, J. Counselor judgments of therapeutic process and outcome. In C. R. Rogers & Rosalind F. Dymond (Eds.), *Psychotherapy and personality change.* Chicago: Univer. of Chicago Press, 1954. Pp. 99–108.

23. SHEERER, E. T. An analysis of the relationship between acceptance of and respect for self and acceptance of and respect for others in ten counseling cases. *J. consult. Psychol.,* 1949, 13, 169–175.

24. STOCK, D. An investigation into the interrelations between the self-concept and feelings directed toward other persons and groups. *J. consult. Psychol.,* 1949, 13, 176–180.

25. TAYLOR, J. W. Relationship of success and length in psychotherapy. *J. consult. Psychol.,* 1956, 20, 332.

26. TOUGAS, R. R. Ethnocentrism as a limiting factor in verbal therapy. In C. R. Rogers & Rosalind F. Dymond (Eds.), *Psychotherapy and personality change.* Chicago: Univer. of Chicago Press, 1954. Pp. 196–214.

27. WHITFIELD, J. W. Rank correlation between two variables, one of which is ranked, the other dichotomous. *Biometrika,* 1947, 34, 292–296.

Selected Additional Readings

CARTWRIGHT, D. S. Success in psychotherapy as a function of certain actuarial variables. *Journal of Consulting Psychology*, 1955, 19, 357–363.

CARTWRIGHT, D. S., & LERNER, BARBARA. Empathy, need to change, and improvement with psychotherapy. *Journal of Consulting Psychology*, 1963, 27, 138–144.

IMBER, S. D., FRANK, J. D., GLEIDMAN, L. H., NASH, E. H., & STONE, A. R. Suggestibility, social class, and the acceptance of psychotherapy. *Journal of Clinical Psychology*, 1956, 12, 341–344.

KIRTNER, W. L., & CARTWRIGHT, D. S. Success and failure in client-centered therapy as a function of initial in-therapy behavior. *Journal of Consulting Psychology*, 1958, 22, 329–333.

LORR, M., KATZ, M. M., & RUBINSTEIN, E. A. The prediction of length of stay in psychotherapy. *Journal of Consulting Psychology*, 1958, 22, 321–327.

PARLOFF, M. B. Therapist-patient relationships and outcome of psychotherapy. *Journal of Consulting Psychology*, 1961, 25, 29–38.

RICE, LAURA N. Therapist's style of participation and case outcome. *Journal of Consulting Psychology*, 1965, 29, 155–176.

RIOCH, M. J. & LUBIN, A. Prognosis of social adjustment for mental hospital patients under psychotherapy. *Journal of Consulting Psychology*, 1959, 23, 313–318

STRICKLAND, B. R., & CROWNE, D. P. Need for approval and the premature termination of psychotherapy. *Journal of Consulting Psychology*, 1963, 27, 95–101.

TAULBEE, E. S. Relationship between certain personality variables and continuation in psychotherapy. *Journal of Consulting Psychology*, 1958, 22, 83–89.

TUCKMAN, J., and LAVELL, M. Social status and clinic contact. *Journal of Clinical Psychology*, 1959, 15, 345–348.

SECTION 4 Research on Process and Methods of Evaluating Process

Studies of the process of psychotherapy concern themselves with such questions as the following: Does psychotherapy follow a typical course which can be defined objectively? What occurrences in therapy are apt to reflect psychotherapeutic progress? What sorts of variables are useful in describing the therapist's behavior within the therapeutic hour? What is the effect on clients of variations along such dimensions of therapist behavior? Do some types of therapist responses seem to facilitate the client's ability to come to grips with his problem more than others? What sorts of content seem most related to the client's progress in therapy? What is the relationship between occurrences in the interview and the emotions of the client? In the area of process research, the editors have selected studies which represent attempts to answer a variety of such questions through the analysis of actual psychotherapy sessions.

Obviously, it is frequently necessary to accumulate much experience and to devote a great deal of work to developing the ideas and methods that will be useful in answering such questions, by trying them out with small numbers of therapists and clients. And, at times, the most feasible or desirable way to study the questions raised by the process of psychotherapy is to reformulate them so that they become amenable to experimental manipulation, and to test them with more accessible, clearly defined populations than are typically found in a clinic or hospital. Works representing these aspects of the problem of studying the process of psychotherapy are presented in the methodological research section.

Dependent variables to choose from in process research are many, and the choice presents the investigator with certain decisions of research strategy. One

313

choice is whether he wishes to rely on some of the more traditional and well developed types of measurement in the psychologist's armamentarium, by using or developing attitude scales, Q sorts, and so on, or whether he wishes to analyze the actual *behavior* manifested by therapist and client during the sessions themselves. In the former instance, he has a more tried type of tool, and his data collection is far simpler. In fact, he may be interested in reactions he could not hope to get in any other way. But the price paid is that he moves away from the behavior actually transpiring in time—by collecting his data after the session—and he must accept his data through the filters of abstractions and selective perception of the subject. If he decides to study the behavior of the therapist or client—and to simplify matters, most of this discussion concentrates on the client rather than the therapist—he must still face other difficult choices.

Type of variable represents one such choice. If the investigator relies on the traditional working knowledge and experience of practicing therapists and wishes to study variables that are critical from this point of view, he will, for example, want to study variables on the order of "insight" and "defensiveness." Such variables are very frequently difficult to define precisely and to measure reliably. Very elaborate care needs to go into defining them in such a way as to maintain the essentials of their clinical usage, while at the same time precisely specifying the cues necessary to distinguish them from other variables, so that judges or coders can measure them reliably and so that the measuring procedures may be replicated by other scientists. Unfortunately, this is a difficult state of affairs to achieve. The necessity of reliable measurement is obvious to any student in all disciplines. The communicability of the system is an equally important goal, but it is frequently overlooked in psychotherapy research. That is, co-workers can achieve reliability because of their common outlook or because of discussion involved in their training procedure, which they may unwittingly attribute to the operational definitions they have used. If that is the case, and they have achieved positive results in relating a variable to other variables, they may only have demonstrated their own clinical ability and not have established anything that can enter the realm of scientific fact. Replicability of procedure by other investigators is even more necessary in this kind of research than in others. Yet, as Gerald Marsden notes in one of the following selections, the area of process research is one in which a number of very elaborate systems of coding have been developed, but these have been used only by their authors and not carried into new investigations by others; often, in fact, they are abandoned by their authors as well. The difficulty of spelling out systems in enough detail so that they can be used by others is only part of the problem. The time- and money-consuming nature of detailed study of the process of psychotherapy acts as another rein on this sort of investigation.

On the other hand, the advantage possessed by this sort of choice is that the work is usually tied at the outset to knowledge and theory acquired and developed by those who have grappled with problems in actual practice for many decades. This is a good starting point for research. As has been pointed out, the task of developing and testing the system used to judge the events being studied is usually a trying and expensive one. But it can be done first. If it does not meet the necessary standards, one need spend no further time and money. If it does meet the requirements, the researcher is in the comfortable position of working with variables whose importance is already felt and which are likely to bear obvious relevance to a great many theoretical and applied questions. The expensiveness of such research in time and money may continue to be a problem.

Some investigators are attracted to the alternate choice: process variables, such as time variables and formal elements of speech, that are not part of the working theoretical system and vocabulary of most psychotherapists, but are easier to communicate, replicate, and quantify, and tend to devour less time and money. The choice of this type of variable has the advantage of almost built-in reliability and replicability. The training of coders or observers tends to be easier, and, with the advent of computers, the work can perhaps be done even more easily and efficiently than it has been in the past. Attempting to show the relevance of the variables to theoretical and applied problems can often begin more quickly and be carried out less expensively (although process research is never likely to be an inexpensive form of research). The problems here tend to begin at this latter point, in trying to relate such variables to a theoretical framework. Just as the investigator making the first choice runs the risk of never achieving adequate reliability and replicability, the investigator choosing the second runs the risk of never seeing his work arrive at a meaningful relationship to a theoretical framework. A possibility not to be overlooked, however, is that the latter investigator need not rely only on traditional theories of psychotherapy; he may be able to work from a theoretical framework—communication theory, or small-group processes, for example—drawn from other realms of psychology, with the resulting research being both theoretically meaningful and precise.

Thus, it is not a matter of good or bad research, but a matter of differing, but equally legitimate, research strategies. Ideally, of course, the investigator searches for variables that are reliable and replicable on the one hand, and rich in clinical or theoretical meaning on the other. And researchers have been reaching for, and will doubtless continue to approach, this ideal from both directions.

Independent variables to choose from are also many and varied. Since process research is essentially to answer the question, What goes on and why? in psychotherapy, its position in a diagram of psychotherapeutic research would logically be in the center of the circle. It touches on and is touched by everything of relevance to psychotherapy. The *client* or patient is of a certain age, had a certain syndrome of problems, certain particular personality traits, a certain amount of intelligence and education, and so forth. All such individual differences could logically be related to the way people are going to react and to behave under a given psychotherapeutic experience. Similarly, the *therapist* has personal mannerisms and individual ways of utilizing a given therapeutic method and interacting with his clients. Presumably, such individual differences on the part of the therapist are related to his interests, attitudes, personality traits, degree of experience with a given method, and so forth. These could be related not only to the relationship between client and therapist *per se,* but to the process itself, particularly the behavioral events that transpire in the course of therapy.

Finally, and of central interest with respect to the process, is the effect of type of therapy (kind of statements made, timing, and so on) on the client's experience and behavior. Many of the same strategic choices face the investigator as were outlined with respect to the type and level of dependent variable, with a similar array of advantages and disadvantages; it therefore seems unnecessary to spell them out again in detail. There is one factor, however, which does seem particularly important with respect to the effect of specific technique upon the psychotherapeutic process. It is the fact that experimental procedures —by which we mean actual manipulation as opposed to selection or description of variables—are more feasible in the investigation of the comparative effects of different techniques of therapy than they are with the types of independent variables previously discussed. Such an experimental procedure, as opposed to a correlational procedure, affords the experimenter a better opportunity to pin down and specify the important variables at work in a process. A major criticism of most process research is that the independent variable is not clearly specified, so that we don't really know what produced the effect. For example, it isn't sufficient to report that ten therapists of age A, experience level B, participated in client-centered therapy for 15 sessions. We still would not know what went on—or what exactly produced the therapeutic effect. Clearer and more precise specification of independent variables would certainly benefit process research.

Related to the central position of process research in psychotherapy research and the place of experimental methodology within it are what we believe are two emerging trends. One is a growing ability and willingness of therapists to vary their approach systematically in the real therapy situation so that the effects of their behavior may be studied. The other, and perhaps more important and stronger, trend is the reformulation of problems for more adequately controlled studies outside the actual therapy situation. This trend is seen as a highly desirable one. It enables the investigator to use larger, more homogeneous, and more clearly specified populations, and it frees him to manipulate variables systematically in ways that are not often feasible in the real therapeutic situation. It permits the therapy researcher to study questions about process in more "pure" terms, just as researchers in other areas of science have often studied problems of the real world under less "real" but better defined and controlled laboratory conditions. Knowledge gained in this way can then be tested in actual practice.

The area of process research seems a particularly appropriate arena for such cross-movement between the laboratory and the therapist's office. Perhaps more than the other aspects of therapy research, it provides a bridge between psychotherapy and more general psychological research in such areas as attitudes, attitude change, personality, physiological correlates of overt behavior, communication, and, of course, learning.

Content-Analysis Studies
of Psychotherapy

FRANK AULD, Jr.
EDWARD J. MURRAY[1]

It is only sixty years since Freud developed psychoanalysis (40, p. 252) and thereby originated dynamic psychotherapy. Although psychoanalysts and other investigators have learned a great deal about psychotherapy in these sixty years, studies of psychotherapy have suffered from three hindrances:

1. The basic data of psychotherapy were transient. Furthermore, they were accessible only to the therapist; others had to take his word for what happened in the interviews. The consequences of this lack of adequate recording are eloquently set forth by Kubie (44).

2. Conclusions stemming from investigations were matters of impression and opinion, because there was no technique for studying the verbal materials objectively.

3. The data could not be fitted into a suitable theoretical framework because the psychologies of the day (for example, Wundt's and Brentano's) had little relevance to the phenomena observed. To appreciate this, one might imagine oneself in Freud's place in 1895 and ask, "How could I explain the things I've observed?"

Recent methodological and theoretical developments seem to justify the hope that these three obstacles to scientific research on psychotherapy can be overcome. The new methods are sound recording and content analysis; the new theoretical developments are the recent attempts to develop a general science of behavior.

Sound recording of interviews has made a common set of data available to scientists, a set that can be preserved and be studied as many times as necessary (7, 26, 76). Pioneers in the recording of psychotherapy interviews include Zinn, Lasswell (45, 46, 47), Rogers (80, 81), Robinson (79), Covner (14, 15, 16), and Porter (70, 71). All of the studies reviewed in this article, with one excep-

Reprinted from *Psychological Bulletin,* 1955, 52 (5), 377–395, with the permission of the American Psychological Association and the authors.

[1] The authors wish to thank Professor John Dollard for his guidance and support of their research. Professor Dollard read this paper and made helpful suggestions. This paper is a product of research project M-648, "Development of quantitative methods for detailed study of psychotherapy," supported by the National Institute of Mental Health, U.S. Public Health Service.

318

tion, derived their data from sound recordings.

Content analysis is a method for studying the content of communication in an
obective, systematic, and quantitative way
(Berelson, 4, p. 18). "Content" is what
is said. Lasswell (48, 49) pioneered the
application of content analysis to social
science problems. In the past decade content analysis has been widely used for
studying therapeutic interviews. All the
studies reviewed in this paper are content-
analysis studies.

General theories of behavior, which
have been developed in recent years, provide possible frameworks for explaining
the data of psychotherapy and for guiding
investigators toward studies that will advance our understanding of human behavior as well as give answers to specific
questions (32). The fusion of psychological theory with psychotherapeutic research is exemplified in the work of
Dollard and Miller (20). Although the
nondirective group at first had no comprehensive theoretical platform, in recent
years these investigators have shown a
growing tendency to state explicit theories
and to design their investigations to test
hypotheses derived from the theories (83,
84). And, of course, it cannot be forgot-
ten that the psychoanalysts, building on
their clinical experience, constructed a
comprehensive psychological theory. Despite its vagueness and lack of rigorous
formulation, it has served as a guide for
a number of investigators.

In this paper we attempt to review the
considerable body of literature on content
analysis of recorded interviews.

A SURVEY OF THE STUDIES

The content-analysis studies of psychotherapy fall into three general classes:
(*a*) Methodological studies, in which the
aim was principally to develop measures,
(*b*) Descriptive studies of cases, and (*c*)
Theoretically guided studies of therapy

(i.e., studies of cause-and-effect relationships). Although it is admitted that the
third kind of study, if well done, contributes the most to our understanding, studies of the first type are necessary to
develop methods and studies of the second type may provide hunches that can
be rigorously tested later by a theoretically
oriented study.

Methodological Studies

In these studies, the emphasis is on development of new measures rather than
on testing of hypotheses. Nevertheless,
the inventor of a measure always has
some theoretical presuppositions; and
these are what influence him to measure
one kind of thing rather than another.
Porter (70, 71), for instance, developed
a classification of therapist responses. His
classification emphasizes the degree to
which the therapist takes responsibility
for the interview, which Porter considers
an important variable in therapy (72, pp.
45–60). Among the nondirective therapists, Royer (87), Snyder (91), Curran
(17), Raimy (73), Hogan (34), Haigh
(31), Stock (93), Hoffman (33), Kahn
(41), and others have developed measures of various kinds. We shall choose
several measures for special comment, because they illustrate the problems involved in such classifications.

Snyder's system. Snyder's system (91)
has been especially influential. Seeman
(88), Aronson (1), Rakusin (74),
Tucker (96), Gillespie (27), and Blau
(6) have made use of it in their investigations. In Snyder's system, the therapist's
responses are classified according to a
modification of Porter's categories. The
categories designate the technique which
the therapist uses: restating content, clarifying feeling, interpreting, structuring,
leading, suggesting, questioning, persuad-
ing, accepting, reassuring, approving, disapproving. The client's responses are
classified under these headings: problems,

simple responses (questions, answers, acceptance, disagreement), insight, planning. Notice that Snyder, like Porter, considers the degree of responsibility assumed by the therapist to be an important variable in the therapist's behavior. On the side of the client, Snyder's classification implies that it is important to notice whether the client is discussing problems or showing understanding. Presumably in successful cases problems dominate at the beginning and insight and plans dominate at the end.

Curran's two systems. Curran (17) has reported a detailed analysis of a single case. His study is of special interest for two reasons. First, he measured "insight" by noting instances of the client's connecting two different problems. Also of interest is Curran's classification of the problems discussed by the client. The problems discussed by the client included: hostility, dependency, insecurity, unhappiness, conflict, discouragement, withdrawal, daydreaming, feelings of inferiority, sex, sin, younger brother, school work, and war. The special interest of this classification lies · in the fact that while most researchers have only noted whether the client talked about a problem or about something else, Curran described *what* the problems were that the client talked about.

Haigh's measure of defensiveness. Haigh (31) developed a measure of defensiveness, building on previous work by Hogan (34). Haigh defined defensive behavior as behavior that shifts attention away from an inconsistency that, if perceived, would threaten the client.[2] It may

be noted, by the way, that in order to judge a remark as defensive according to Haigh's system one must make the judgment that two of the statements of the client are incongruent or that the client "ought" to be exploring some aspect of his emotional life and is avoiding it (31, p. 182).

Interaction Process Analysis.—The theory behind this system, which was developed by Bales (3), is that problem solving involves a series of steps: getting information, making decisions, carrying out actions. At each stage of problem solving, the participants interact with each other. One participant, for instance, asks for information; another gives information; then a third member of the group may offer an opinion of the correctness of this information; the individual who gave the information may then proceed to defend his views with some heat. As applied to therapy, the Bales system is used to score both the remarks of the therapist and those of the client.

Discomfort-Relief Quotient.—The Discomfort-Relief Quotient, or D.R.Q., was suggested by behavior theory. Behavior theory states that responses are incited by drives and reinforced by drive reduction. The learning of new habits is, according to this theory, accompanied by drive reduction. The new learning that occurs in successful therapy ought, therefore, to be accompanied by a reduction in drive. Guided by these theoretical notions, Dollard and Mowrer (21) attempted to measure the amount of drive borne by the client. They did this by classifying each word as a drive, reward, or neutral word according as the word seemed to represent discomfort (suffering, tension, pain, unhappiness) or relief (comfort, satisfac-

---

[2] This definition seems essentially the same as the psychoanalytic definition of "resistance." Colby, for example, defines resistances as "those defenses that operate in and against the therapeutic process to prevent an uncovering and a dissolution of the neurotic conflict" (12, p. 8). Haigh's definition differs from the analytic one, however, in this respect: He notes only those resistances that can be easily inferred from the content of the client's speech, i.e., from the client's denials, rationalizations, and pro-

jections. Analysts, on the other hand, note not only these but also such evidences of resistance as: silences, avoidance of obvious topics, lateness in keeping appointment, and various transference responses · (12, pp. 95–106).

tion, enjoyment) or neither. The D.R.Q. is obtained by dividing the number of discomfort words by the total number of discomfort *and* relief words. The authors demonstrated very satisfactory reliability of D.R.Q. scores. Dollard and Mowrer, employing other units besides words, found that sentences and "thought units" could also be reliably scored.

Dollard and Mowrer intended the D.R.Q. as a measure of the tension *experienced* by the client. We know, however, that the client's verbal responses do not always accurately label his drives (20). It is possible that: (*a*) A verbal response may indicate a drive when the drive is not present, as when a client makes an insincere complaint in order to enlist the sympathy of the therapist. (*b*) A drive may be present with no verbal response describing it, as when a client denies having sexual wishes while his other behavior convinces us that he does have them. (*c*) A verbal response may describe a conflict different from the one the patient is actually experiencing, as when talk about vocational problems replaces talk about an unconscious homosexual conflict. It is also possible that the importance of a drive is not accurately reflected by the *frequency* of occurrence of sentences about it. It is the task of empirical research to discover whether clients accurately label their drives or whether these possible distorting factors interfere with accurate labeling to such a degree that verbal responses cannot be used as indices of drive.

In a study of interviews from six recorded psychotherapy cases, Mowrer *et al.* (62) found a moderately high relationship between the D.R.Q. scores for interviews and measures of palmar sweating made after the same interviews. For five of these cases, the *r* between D.R.Q. and palmar sweating was .57; in the sixth case, for which the correlation was computed separately, the *r* was only .30. To the extent that palmar sweating is itself

an adequate measure of "tension," this finding somewhat strengthens the case for considering the D.R.Q. a measure of tension. Meadow *et al.* (53), studying psychotic patients, found no significant relationship between D.R.Q. score in a special interview and a psychiatrist's rating of tension made on the basis of other interviews with the patient. In interpreting this result one should note, first, that the rating of tension was not made in the same situation in which the D.R.Q. score was obtained; second, that the result of a study of psychotic patients, who as a group are likely to make verbal responses without showing "appropriate" emotional reactions, may not predict very well what will be found when normal and neurotic subjects are studied; and, finally, that the validity of the psychiatrist's ratings is not known.

The problem of how the verbal behavior of the client, which is taken note of in content analysis, is related to his nonverbal behavior, is a difficulty not only for the D.R.Q. but also for every other system of content analysis.

Positive-Negative-Ambivalent Quotient. A measure independently developed by Raimy (73) has a strong family resemblance to the D.R.Q. Raimy's PNAvQ is a quotient, as the D.R.Q. is; and, like the D.R.Q., it is an indication of positive and negative emotional reactions of the client. It differs from the D.R.Q. in focusing attention on the statements of the client about himself (whereas the D.R.Q. includes all statements of the client, whether they are self-referential or not). In some cases, the two measures would be expected to give similar results, which is what Kauffman and Raimy (43) found to be true in a study of 17 counseling interviews. These authors also found the PNAvQ to be somewhat lower, on the average, than the D.R.Q.

Horwitz (35), however, found only a low correlation ($r = .38$) between the D.R.Q. and PNAvQ in 36 initial casework interviews. It is possible that the low correlation should be attributed to unreliability of scoring; but this seems unlikely, since investigators using these measures in other studies have found them to be reliable. It is more likely that the correlation is low because the D.R.Q. includes all statements of the client, whether about himself or about others, while the PNAvQ includes only statements referring to the client. If the client talks a great deal about other persons, these statements will affect the D.R.Q. but not the PNAvQ—with a resulting drop in agreement between the two measures.

Doubting that a measure of the "self concept" would be much related to the D.R.Q. if the "self concept" were narrowly defined, Horwitz also investigated the correlation between the D.R.Q. and a "self-approval quotient." The self-approval quotient is the same as the PNAvQ except that statements which indicate that the client is happy, glad, or improving, or fearful, anxious, or unsuccessful are not included. (Such statements *are* included in the PNAvQ.) The only statements included in the self-approval quotient are those in which the client evaluates himself. The D.R.Q. was not significantly correlated with the self-approval quotient ($r = .14$).

A system in terms of motivation and conflict. E. J. Murray (63, 64), in devising a system for the study of motivation and conflict in psychotherapy, was influenced by psychoanalysis and learning theory. Murray wished to designate underlying motivations of the client; but, at the same time, he wanted the system to be objective, i.e., to have explicit rules for inferring the underlying motives. In keeping with the wish to have an objective system, Murray chose categories that require relatively little inference by the scorer and reflect chiefly manifest content. The category system designates statements expressing a need, statements expressing anxiety about a need, and statements expressing hostility on account of frustration of a need. The drives included are: sex, affection, dependence, independence, and "unspecified" drive. The system also requires the scorer to designate the person who is the object of the need, e.g., the person who is loved or hated.

Murray (63, 64) also devised categories for describing the therapist's behavior, building on the theoretical work of Dollard and Miller (20). Remarks of the therapist were classified according to activity-passivity and according to their function as rewards, punishments, labels, discriminations, generalizations, instructions concerning free association, directions, or probes.

The reliability of scoring these categories was studied (63, 64) and found to be fairly high. It was found that reliability decreased as a greater number of simultaneous discriminations were required of the scorer. This finding agrees with the experience of Kaplan and Goldsen (42).

Lasswell's general purpose system. Lasswell (48) has suggested a scheme for classifying interview materials under very general headings, so that the system can be applied to interviews differing widely in topic. The classification tells who makes the statement (talker-listener-another), whom the statement refers to (talker-listener-another), and what attitude is expressed (favorable-unfavorable). To our knowledge this scheme has not been applied to psychotherapy cases, except apparently in a recent study by Rosenman (85).

Other measures.—Other proposed measures include: Collier's (13) scale for the degree of "uncovering" used by the therapist, Helen E. Miller's (54) measure of "acceptance," Raskin's (75) "locus-of-evaluation" rating, Elton's (22) responsibility rating, Carnes and Robinson's (9) talk ratio, the various measures used by Lewis in her pioneering study (50), and

White's (97) frustration-satisfaction ratio, a measure similar to the D.R.Q.

Descriptive Studies

Movement from problems to insight. Snyder (91) has described how the content of the client's speech changes during the course of nondirective therapy. According to Snyder, first there is a statement of a problem or problems; then discussion of these problems, with increased insight; and finally, formulation of plans for new responses. Studying four "successful" cases and one "unsuccessful" case, Snyder (92) found that the successful cases showed a trend from problems to plans; the unsuccessful case failed to show this trend. Seeman (88) repeated Snyder's study, using a larger sample of cases, and confirmed his results. Results reported by Snyder (91), by Seeman (88), and by Blau (6) also indicate that in the cases that were believed successful, the client talked less about problems and more about insights and plans at the end of treatment than at the start; similarly, he expressed more positive feelings and fewer negative feelings than he did at the beginning. Such a change was not observed in unsuccessful cases. This result is hardly an independent confirmation that the cases judged to be successful *were* successful, since the judges undoubtedly reacted to just such changes in the client's verbalizations when deciding whether cases were successful. While these studies do not give independent confirmation, they are nevertheless valuable because they specify some ways in which the client's speech behavior changed, and they provide reliable measures for these changes.

Attitudes toward self.—Raimy (73) studied the kinds of attitudes toward self expressed by the client at various times in the course of therapy. He found that in cases that were judged to be successful, positive statements about self increase and negative statements decrease during the course of treatment. Seeman (88) studied all attitudes of the client, both about self and about other people, and found that positive expressions increase and negative expressions decrease during therapy. He found no significant correlation between the change from negative to positive attitudes and the counselor's rating of success of the case, if all statements of attitude were considered; but when he examined only statements expressed in the present tense, he found a significant correlation between changes in these statements and the counselor's rating ($r = .66$). Bugental (8) has used Raimy's scales and somewhat modified them.

Studies using the D.R.Q.—Still another way of describing the course of psychotherapy is to note changes in the degree of tension expressed in the client's sentences. A measure of verbal tension (the D.R.Q.) has already been described in the preceding section, and the theoretical considerations that guided its invention were presented there. Results with the use of the D.R.Q. will be briefly presented here. Hunt (36, 37, 38, 61) found little agreement between changes in the D.R.Q. (scored from caseworkers' summaries) from the beginning to the end of casework and the degree of movement or progress in the case as judged by experienced caseworkers. When these judgments of experienced caseworkers were quantified and made highly reliable, by use of a scale of "movement," there was still little agreement between movement and drop in D.R.Q. Assum and Levy (2), studying one case, found a drop in D.R.Q. accompanying success. Natalie Rogers (61) studied three cases, one judged as very successful, one as moderately successful, and one as unsuccessful. The successful cases showed a drop in D.R.Q., but the unsuccessful one did not. Cofer and Chance (10) computed the D.R.Q. for each hour of five published cases—four nondirective cases and the case in Lindner's *Rebel Without a Cause* (51). All the cases were judged as successful by the therapists, and all showed a drop in D.R.Q. Mowrer (61) reported one of his own cases which showed a drop in D.R.Q. and was believed to be a successful case.

On the evidence so far, there is no clear relationship between the change in D.R.Q. from beginning to end of a case and the success of the case. Some investigators have reported a drop in D.R.Q. accompanying success (these investigators studied, in total, verbatim transcripts of 10 cases); others (who studied case workers' notes of 38 cases) found no relationship between drop in D.R.Q. and success of the cases. It may be noted that no evidence for the reliability of the judgments of "success" was reported for those 10 cases showing positive results; but reliability of the judgments of "movement" in the 38 cases was established.

Murray, Auld, and White (65) have reported a "partly successful" case showing no drop in D.R.Q. Their paper includes a discussion of the reasons for absence of any change in the D.R.Q.

The critical issue here, it seems to the present authors, is that we have no adequate measure of "success." Until such a measure has been devised, it makes little sense to ask whether a drop in D.R.Q. is related to success.

Relations of problems to each other. Curran (17), studying 20 recorded interviews of a single case, described changes in the client's perceptions of relationships between his problems. At the beginning of therapy, the client discussed a large number of problems and talked about them separately; at the end of therapy he discussed a smaller number of problems, tending to combine problems that had previously been separate. Curran's contribution to methodology is his idea of studying "insight" by noting the client's discovery of relationships between previously separate problems.

Differences between different therapies. Porter (70, 71) described differences between "directive" and "nondirective" counselors. The directive counselors studied by Porter talked much more than the nondirective counselors and took more responsibility for guiding the interview by questioning, explaining, probing, and advising. Gump (30) compared responses of the therapists in one psychoanalytic and five nondirective cases and noted differences in technique. No generalizations about analytic or nondirective therapy should be made, however, on the basis of only six cases.

Strupp (94) has compared the verbal responses of Rogerian and non-Rogerian therapists when they were asked what they would say after various statements by a client. Answers of the therapists were classified according to Bales' system, with fairly high reliability (78% agreement between two scores). As would be expected, there were differences between the answers of Rogerian and non-Rogerian therapists. Variation within the two groups of therapists was also large. Strupp (95) further classified the non-Rogerian therapists according to whether they had received a personal analysis. Those who had been analyzed were more likely to give answers classified as "disagrees" and "shows antagonism" and less likely to give answers coded as "agrees, shows passive acceptance." The analyzed therapists less often indicated that they would say nothing at all after the client's statement.

Group psychotherapy. Coffey *et al.* (11) have presented a description of the content of group psychotherapy interviews with college students. The nuclear conflict of students in these groups was described by the authors as follows: "High standards and intellectualized ideals are often associated with passivity and inhibition of emotions. The constricted feelings find distorted expression in intellectualization and isolated fantasy resulting in varying amounts of guilt, immobilization, and affective sterility" (11, p. 58). A classification of what the groups talked about yielded the following results: Sexuality, 27% of total time; vocational problems, 14%; attitudes toward psychotherapy, 12%; attitudes toward and perception of self, 11%; society and the individual, 10%; interpersonal and social relations, 9%; relations to authority, 6%; family relations, 6%; handling of hostile feelings, 4%.

Roberts and Strodtbeck (78) applied the Bales system (Interaction Process Analysis) to group therapy interviews of depressive and schizophrenic patients. They expected that the paranoid schizophrenic patients would use relatively more of the negative responses ("shows aggression" and "disagrees") and would make fewer responses to each other and more to the leader. The depressed patients were expected to make fewer responses per minute than the schizophrenic patients. All three of these predictions of differences between the groups were borne out by the data.

Gorlow *et al.* (28) studied nondirective group therapy sessions, using a system of categories similar to that developed by Snyder.

Application of Bales system to student counseling. Perry and Estes (69), with the collaboration of Bales, applied the Interaction Process Analysis system to four counseling interviews with a student. In this counseling case, the therapist shifted from responses categorized as "gives orientation" to responses falling in the categories "giving opinion" and "asks for opinion" The student showed a falling off, during the four interviews, in the percentage of responses classified as "shows tension, asks for help, withdraws out of the field." The authors interpreted the shift in therapist responses as documenting their belief that the counselor used nondirective techniques at the start of counseling, then shifted to responses that defined the counseling process as a collaborative venture.

The drop in the client's "asks for help" responses was interpreted as showing his acceptance of a collaborative view of therapy and his giving up expectations that the therapist would play an authoritarian role.

Studies of linguistic characteristics. It is beyond the scope of this paper to discuss here studies of the grammatical structure of clients' speech during therapy. Pertinent studies include those of Roshal (86), Zimmerman and Langdon (99), and Grummon (29). These studies and others have been reviewed by Mowrer (60).

Theoretically Guided Studies

Lasswell's pioneering work. Lasswell was a pioneer not only in making sound recordings of analytic interviews, but also in applying content-analysis methods to their study. His earliest report on the analysis of transcribed interviews (45) indicates that he classified the client's utterances according to whether they referred to the interviewer or not. He proposed the hypothesis that *conscious affect* is indicated by references to the interviewer and that *unconscious tension* is indicated by slow speech, pauses, etc. If this hypothesis is correct, then tension as shown by slow speech should be correlated with other measures (e.g., physiological measures) of tension. In the cases studied Lasswell found a correlation between verbal indices of tension (slow speech) and physiological indices (high conductivity of the skin). On the other hand, conscious affect (indicated by references to interviewer) was correlated with increased heart rate. It is not clear to us why this latter relationship should have been found. Lasswell, however, interpreted it as supporting his hypothesis concerning the meaning of references to the therapist. The measures of unconscious tension (slow speech and high skin conductance) were negatively correlated with the measures of conscious affect (references to therapist and increased heart rate.)

In another study (47) Lasswell obtained similar results. In this later study he included measures of blood pressure before and after each hour and of gross bodily movements during the hour. He found that unconscious affect (defined as above) decreased in the course of the interviews and conscious affect increased, as would be expected to occur in successful psychoanalytic treatment.

Is clarification of feeling the best technique? Rogers (82) has asserted his belief that progress in therapy always follows "recognition of feeling" by the therapist. Analytic therapists take a quite different view, believing that interpretation of resistance and labeling of previously unlabeled emotions are essential therapeutic techniques (Freud [23, 24], Dollard and Miller [20], Colby [12]). The available evidence from content-analysis studies concerning effectiveness of various techniques of the therapist is summarized in this section.

Snyder (91) studied the client responses following various kinds of responses by the therapist. He found that "insight" and "discussion of plans" by the client were more likely to follow nondirective than directive responses of the therapist.

Sherman (90) in a study of student counseling interviews found that "tentative analysis" by the therapist was most likely to be followed by client responses rated high on her "working relationship" scale; "interpretation" and "clarification" were moderately likely to be followed by good "working relationship"; and "urging" was the therapist tehnique least likely to be followed by good "working relationship." In discussing her study Robinson (79, p. 130) points out, however, that "a primary technique can have just about every degree of effect. Part of this range is due to the unreliability of rating scales, but in great part this range shows that at times each technique was a highly effective way of handling a particular unit or, in the case of poor outcomes, that the particular tech-

nique was the wrong one to use or that, with the interview conditions as they were, no particular technique could have worked." Sherman also investigated the effect of technique used by the therapist on degree of insight shown by the client in the following response. In "adjustment-problem" units, clarification was most likely to be followed by a response rating high in "insight"; "interpretation" and "tentative analysis" were next most likely to be followed by "insight"; and "urging" was least likely to be so followed. It should be noted that the "insight" spoken of here is *insight-as-judged-by-Snyder's-or-Sherman's-judges*—and that other investigators might not have agreed with these authors concerning what is or is not insight. Psychoanalysts, for example, might require the patient to discover unconscious motivations before crediting him with the achievement of insight. Snyder and Sherman were dealing with something other than this.

In another study bearing on this point, Bergman (5) reached the conclusion that "reflection of feeling" was the only technique that led to insight or continued exploration. According to Bergman, interpretation by the therapist led to the abandonment of self-exploration. Contradictory results were obtained by Gillespie (27), who found that "verbal signs of resistance tend to be proportional to the number of counselor statements regardless of the counselor category" (27, p. 119). Hostile expressions toward the therapist and therapy were more likely to occur after interpretation or "inaccurate clarification of feeling" by therapist than after "restatement of content" and "accurate clarification of feeling." Other signs of "resistance" noted by Gillespie, however, were not significantly associated with interpretative activity by the therapist. These other signs included: client-initiated long pauses, short answers, stereotyped repetition of the problem, changing the subject being discussed, excessive verbalization and intellectualizing, and emotional blocking. These signs of "resistance" are exactly those which psychoanalysts take as indicating resistance (12, pp. 96–98). Analytic therapists, however, apparently do not worry so much about the client's attacks and disagreements as the nondirective therapists do, except when these client responses threaten to interrupt communication.

In a study of a single case, Dittmann (18) noted what kinds of therapist responses were likely to be followed by client behavior that was judged to indicate progress. Client responses indicating "progress" were most likely to come after therapist responses that were slightly more interpretive than pure "reflection."

What can we learn from these studies? We learn, especially from the work of Robinson and his students, that there is no single type of response by the therapist that works best under all circumstances. Effectiveness of a response by the therapist probably depends on the expectations of the client (e.g., whether he expects the therapist to give advice or not), on the particular circumstances of the situation, and on the client's ability to tolerate increased self-knowledge at that particular time. We also learn that judgment about the effectiveness of a technique depends on having some measure of effect and that different measures of "effect" yield different judgments about what produces effectiveness. Measures of effectiveness (e.g., of "insight") that are considered appropriate by nondirective therapists may not necessarily be considered appropriate by analytic therapists—and vice versa.

Differences in therapist responses. Reid and Snyder (77) investigated the differences between counselors in their responses to identical client statements. Phonographically recorded client statements were replayed to a group of 15 clinical psychologists. After each statement the psychologists were allowed 15 seconds to write down the principal feelings they believed the client had expressed. Reid and Snyder found, first, that the same client response evoked a variety of responses from the counselors. They reported, further, that the counselors who were judged by their instructors to be more skillful were more likely to label the client's feeling in the way that a majority of the group labeled it. The authors also observed that some counselors consistently tended to label clients' feelings in a preferred way, e.g., some counselors were likely to perceive the clients as reporting feelings of insecurity, while other counselors labeled the same client responses as indicating hopefulness and ambition. This study shows a promising way to apply experimental methods to the study of the therapist's behavior.

Haigh's study of defensiveness. Haigh (31), believing that "defensiveness" (incorrect perception of one's behavior) should decrease during successful psychotherapy, identified instances of defensive behavior in 10 client-centered therapy cases, counting the number of these defensive responses in each interview. Haigh found that the clients had fewer defensive responses in the second half of treatment than in the first half. Seven of the clients had fewer defensive responses during the second half; two had more defensive responses during the second half; one had no identified defensive responses during either half. The present authors have applied the exact test of significance to these data, and find that the first and second halves of therapy do not differ significantly ($p = .30$).[3] A larger number of subjects must be studied before a definite conclusion concerning the course of defensiveness throughout therapy can be drawn.

A further aim of Haigh's study was to

---

[3] Haigh's statistical analysis, which resulted in a significant value of chi square, is inappropriate. The chi-square test requires the assumption that the items included in the table are independently selected. But the responses have not been independently selected from a population of responses; instead, if one response of a particular client was included in the sample, all his responses were included.

show that awareness of defensiveness caused a decrease in defensiveness. According to Haigh, the client would at the beginning of therapy present a number of defensive opinions. As the nondirective therapist reacted to the client with acceptance, lack of moral evaluation, and willingness to have the client make his own decisions, the client would have progressively weaker motives to present defensive opinions. He would become aware of inconsistencies in his opinions, actions, and emotions; in the benign atmosphere of therapy, he would be able to abandon these inconsistencies.[4] According to this account of therapy, increased awareness of defensiveness should be followed, in successful therapy, by a decrease in defensiveness. Haigh did not make the detailed analysis that would be necessary to test the adequacy of this construction, but he did report whether awareness-of-defensiveness showed any change, on the whole, throughout therapy. Haigh found that defensive behavior of which the client was unaware declined in the six cases that showed a drop in total defensive behavior; "unaware" defensive behavior increased in the three cases that showed an over-all increase in defensive behavior. Remembering that these results are derived from a very small sample of cases, we can make the tentative interpretation that clients in nondirective therapy who are unaware of their defensive behavior cannot change it; clients who become aware of it, can and do change it. We would like, however, to see the process of increased awareness studied in greater detail.

A study of hostility and defenses. An exploratory study making use of his content-analysis system has been reported by Murray (63). The hypotheses tested in this

study were suggested by N. E. Miller's work on learning theory (55, 57, 58, 59, 67) and by psychoanalytic theory. Murray found that in the course of the psychotherapy case studied, defensive sentences of the client decreased and hostile sentences increased. He also found that interviews which contained a large number of defensive sentences had a relatively small number of hostile sentences ($r = -.73$). Intellectualization and physical complaints comprised the defensive sentences; statements of frustration and resentment comprised the hostile sentences.

The results were interpreted in terms of learning theory as follows: The defenses were assumed to be motivated by anxiety. When the client uttered a defensive sentence instead of a hostile sentence, he thereby escaped the anxiety which would have been aroused by utterance of the hostile sentence. During the psychotherapy the therapist interpreted one form of defense (physical complaints), while maintaining a permissive attitude toward the expression of hostility. These acts of the therapist resulted in a weakening of the defenses and extinction of the anxiety motivating them and thereby permitted an increased expression of hostility.

Murray also tested the hypothesis that the various hostile sentences would appear in a sequence which might be predicted by the theory of displacement (56, 58). His expectation was that the client would first express hostility about the less significant persons in his life and would gradually proceed to express hostility toward more important persons—for example, his mother. An examination of the data showed a sequence in the expression of hostility toward various persons, but not the sequence that had been predicted. Hostility was expressed first toward the more significant persons, then toward less significant persons. This finding led to a re-examination and reformulation of the displacement theory. Murray and Berkun made certain ex-

---

[4] Note the parallelism between this account of therapy and the account given by Dollard, Ault, and White (19). Dollard *et al.* believe, however, that the therapist must react with doubt and incredulity to elements of the client's account that do not make sense.

tensions of Miller's displacement theory and verified them in an animal experiment (66).

It was also discovered that the two defenses, intellectual discussion and physical complaints, seemed to operate as alternative members of a habit-family hierarchy. When one defense declined, the other tended to rise. Additional evidence for the hypothesis that the defenses functioned as members of a habit-family hierarchy is given by the fact that in the later stages of therapy, when anxiety was increasing following the greatly increased expression of hostility, the previously uninterpreted defense (intellectualization) increased much more than the defense that had been interpreted.

Attitudes toward self and others. Researchers of the nondirective group have investigated the changes in attitudes toward self and toward others that occur during psychotherapy. They believe that positive attitudes toward self and others are desirable, and they have been interested to discover what actions of the therapist can cause a change in these attitudes. One hypothesis is as follows: The therapist's warm, accepting attitude toward the client enables the client to recognize his own wishes more fully and evaluate his own behavior with greater acceptance (Rogers, 83, p. 41). A second hypothesis is this: To the degree that client has positive feelings about himself, he can have positive feelings toward other people. A third hypothesis is this: A person who feels affirmatively about other people gets along with them better than a person who reacts negatively. From these three hypotheses it follows that the therapist by a warm, accepting attitude toward the client can cause the client to feel positive about other people and to get along better with them (Rogers, 83, pp. 160, 520).

So far as we know, there has been no content study bearing on the first hypothesis. The second hypothesis was tested by Sheerer (89) and by Stock (93), who both found a correlation between positive opinions about self and positive opinions about others. The third hypothesis was investigated by McIntyre (52), who found no evidence that persons with high scores on an "acceptance-of-others" questionnaire were themselves accepted by others (as judged by a sociometric questionnaire). One must conclude that these three hypotheses have not yet been proved.

Prognostic studies. Can outcome of therapy be predicted from early clues in the case? There seem to be only two content-analysis studies bearing on this question. Lasswell (46) investigated whether certain measures of speech and of physiological responses, made in early hours, could be used to predict the success of treatment. He reported that a combination of measures taken during the first 10 or 12 hours permitted accurate prediction of the client's progress. Lasswell reported of his subjects: "Those who adjusted themselves readily to the situation (and who made progress in insight) showed rising skin resistance curves. Our interpretation is that they were finding satisfactions in the interview experience against which they did not maintain a strong inner defense. Unconscious tension was diminishing, even though active conscious affect might rise" (46, pp. 246–247). Since the number of cases studied by Lasswell was small, this promising exploratory work needs to be repeated with larger samples.

The other study of prognostic indicators is that of Page (68), who found that measures of variability of the content and feeling of the client's speech in the first interview were not correlated with outcome of treatment. The amount of talk by the client in the first interview had a small ($r = .30$) but statistically significant correlation with the criterion of success. It should be noted that Lasswell, Page, or any investigator who tries to find prognostic signs is hampered by the lack of any fully adequate definition or any adequate measure of "success" of therapy.

CHOICE OF A CONTENT-ANALYSIS SYSTEM

In choosing a content-analysis system, one faces all the problems of choosing a topic that deserves scientific investigation *plus* the problems involved in choosing appropriate methods after one has decided on the topic. A few comments will be made on each of these tasks.

Experience has shown that the most fruitful scientific investigations are those that bear some relation to a general theory or, at least, to a well-thought-out hypothesis (Wilson, 98, p. 2). What hypotheses, then, might best be investigated? A large amount of attention has been focused on the immediate effects of various techniques used by the therapist and on the positive and negative opinions of patients. Little or no study by content-analysis methods has been made of such questions as these: What is the function of transference responses in psychotherapy? What is the effect of the therapist's giving love to the client? What is the role of childhood memories—must they be recaptured in successful therapy? How does the client learn new verbal units? What cues in the client's behavior does a good therapist respond to? These questions are relevant to a general theory of psychotherapy and thus, in our opinion, are worthy of study.

Once the investigator has chosen his field of inquiry, he must select appropriate techniques. If there are extant content-analysis systems which bear on his topic of inquiry, how can he decide whether to use one or more of them? This is the problem of validity. If the investigator is interested in the emotions of the client, he will want to know whether the D.R.Q. measures emotion. If he is interested in the influence of the therapist on the client, he may ask, "Does Porter's classification of therapist responses adequately measure this influence?" If he wants to assess therapeutic progress, he might ask, "Do measures of 'self-attitude' such as Raimy's PNAvQ really re-flect better adjustment of the client? Do these measures neglect unlabeled emotional conflicts? Do they give equal weight to changes in fundamental psychological conflicts and to resistant escape sentences?"

Janis (39) has proposed that the validity of a content system be judged by the number of relationships found by investigators who have used the system. As Janis points out, this does not mean that a valid measure is related to every other valid measure. For instance, intelligence may not be very important in determining the success of psychotherapy. If such be the case, we will not call the Wechsler-Bellevue Scale invalid if it fails to correlate with measures of success in therapy. But the intelligence-test score *should* be related to other measures of intelligence, e.g., to success in school work. Similarly, content measures are valid if they are correlated with other measures, when we have reason to believe they *should* be correlated. Admittedly, it is hard to designate which variables ought to be related to each other, and so it is difficult to determine when a lack of correlation implies lack of validity.

In our opinion, the content-analysis systems so far developed are not adequate to the task of marking out the main variables in therapy. Most of them rely too much on the opinions presented by clients and neglect clients' unconscious motives. Some investigators have assumed that an increase in favorable opinions about himself indicates improvement in the client. While we believe that this is sometimes true, we are aware that clients can change their opinions in response to stimuli other than improved psychological well-being. For instance, a client having an unconscious motive to escape the anxiety evoked by therapy may offer the opinion that he feels much better and has been enormously helped. Therefore, the client says, he is ready to quit psychotherapy. Again, a client motivated by the desire to please the therapist may say that he has been greatly benefited. He would feel ungrateful if he did not acknowledge benefit. These two motives, used as illustrations, are only two of many possible motives, both conscious and unconscious, that can influence the client's expression of an opinion about himself. Our knowledge that such motivations exist warns us not to rely too much on these opinions.[5]

Content systems are inevitably criticized for what they leave out. The practicing clinician often feels that the measured part of the therapeutic transaction is pitifully small alongside the complex of stimuli that he senses as a participant observer. Yet it seems unfair to expect any single content-analysis system to describe all of this complex situation. We would probably make a fairer appraisal of content systems if we expected each system to deal with only a part of this complexity. An adequate descriptive and causal analysis of psychotherapy will most likely require a large number of measures, each of them shown to be reliable and valid for its limited purpose. Measures of the content of clients' and therapists' utterances will undoubtedly be supplemented by measures of other, nonverbal responses of client and therapist. By the combination of a variety of measures, each useful in its own domain, we may in time construct an adequate science of psychotherapy.

SUMMARY

Research on psychotherapy has been hampered until recently by the lack of permanent records of the transaction, by absence of objective measures, and by lack of an appropriate theoretical framework. The advent of sound recording of interviews, the widespread application of content-analysis methods, and the development of psychological theories such as learning theory have opened up new possibilities for research on psychotherapy. This paper surveys some of the first fruits of the new developments.

Studies are here classified as methodological (development of measures), descriptive, or theoretically oriented. An attempt has been made to include representative and important studies of each type. It is believed that the value of studies in this field must finally be assessed in terms of relevance to theory. Studies that only result in the development of new measuring instruments or in the publication of a description of some type of therapy are less valuable than studies that test some hypothesis. The methodological and descriptive investigations may be valuable, however, if they provide the tools and the hypotheses that make later theoretically guided investigation possible.

---

[5] We believe that an objective system of content analysis need not neglect unconscious motives. The therapist who attributes unconscious motives to his patient is, when he does this, reacting to cues provided by the patient's behavior. It should be possible to teach other persons to react similarly to the patient's behavior. If the responses of the patient that reveal unconscious motivation are verbal, it would be possible to designate these unconscious reactions by the content-analysis method. For example, if overconcern about another person's health indicates unconscious hostility toward that person, any sentence expressing overconcern can be scored as "unconscious hostility."

REFERENCES

1. ARONSON, M. A study of the relationships between certain counselor and client characteristics in client-centered therapy. In W. U. Snyder (Ed.), *Group report of a program of research in psychotherapy.* State College, Pa.: Pennsylvania State Coll., 1953. Pp. 39–54.

2. ASSUM, A. L., & LEVY, S. J. Analysis of a nondirective case with followup interview. *J. abnorm. soc. Psychol.,* 1948, 43, 78–89.

3. BALES, R. F. *Interaction process analysis.* Cambridge: Addison-Wesley, 1950.

4. BERELSON, B. *Content analysis in communication research.* Glencoe, Ill.: Free Press, 1952.

5. BERGMAN, D. Counseling method and client responses. *J. consult. Psychol.,* 1951, 15, 216–224.

6. BLAU, B. A. A comparison of more improved with less improved clients treated by client-centered methods. In W. U. Snyder (Ed.), *Group report of a program of research in psychotherapy.* State College, Pa.: Pennsylvania State Coll., 1953. Pp. 120–126.

7. BRODY, E. B., NEWMAN, R., & REDLICH, F. C. Sound recording: the problem of evidence in psychiatry. *Science,* 1951, 113, 379–380.

8. BUGENTAL, J. F. T. A method for assessing self and not-self attitudes during the therapeutic series. *J. consult. Psychol.,* 1952, 16, 435–439.

9. CARNES, E. F., & ROBINSON, F. P. The role of client talk in the counseling interview. *Educ. psychol. Measmt,* 1948, 8, 635–644.

10. COFER, C. N., & CHANCE, JUNE. The discomfort-relief quotient in published cases of counseling and psychotherapy. *J. Psychol.,* 1950, 29, 219–224.

11. COFFEY, H. S., FREEMAN, M., LEARY, T., & OSSORIO, A. Community service and social research—group psychotherapy in a church program. *J. soc. Issues,* 1950, 6, 1–65.

12. COLBY, K. M. *A primer for psychotherapists.* New York: Ronald Press, 1951.

13. COLLIER, R. M. A scale for rating the responses of the psychotherapist. *J. consult. Psychol.,* 1953, 17, 321–326.

14. COVNER, B. J. Studies in phonographic recordings of verbal material: I. The use of phonographic recordings in counseling practice and research. *J. consult. Psychol.,* 1942, 6, 105–113.

15. COVNER, B. J. Studies in phonographic recordings of verbal material: III. The completeness and accuracy of counseling interview reports. *J. gen. Psychol.,* 1944, 30, 181–203.

16. COVNER, B. J. Studies in phonographic recordings of verbal material: IV. Written reports of interviews. *J. appl. Psychol.,* 1944, 28, 89–98.

17. CURRAN, C. A. *Personality factors in counseling.* New York: Grune & Stratton, 1945.

18. DITTMANN, A. T. The interpersonal process in psychotherapy: development of a research method. *J. abnorm. soc. Psychol.,* 1952, 47, 236–244.

19. DOLLARD, J., AULD, F., & WHITE, ALICE M. *Steps in psychotherapy.* New York: Macmillan, 1953.

20. DOLLARD, J., & MILLER, N. E. *Personality and psychotherapy.* New York: McGraw-Hill, 1950.

21. DOLLARD, J., & MOWRER, O. H. A method of measuring tension in written documents. *J. abnorm. soc. Psychol.,* 1947, 42, 3–32.

22. ELTON, C. F. A study of client responsibility: counselor technique or interview outcome? *Educ. psychol. Measmt.,* 1950, 10, 728–737.

23. FREUD, S. Further recommendations in the technique of psychoanalysis. On beginning the treatment. The question of the first communications. The dynamics of the cure. In *Collected papers,* Vol. 2. London: Hogarth and the Institute of Psychoanalysis, 1924. Pp. 342–365.

24. FREUD, S. Further recommendations in the technique of psychoanalysis. Recollection, repetition, and working through. In *Collected papers,* Vol. 2. London: Hogarth and the Institute of Psychoanalysis, 1924. Pp. 366–376.

25. GELLER, A., KAPLAN, D., & LASSWELL, H. D. An experimental comparison of four ways of coding editorial content. *Journ. Quart.,* 1942, 19, 362–370.

26. GILL, M., NEWMAN, R., & REDLICH, F. C. *The initial interview in psychiatric practice.* New York: International Universities Press, 1954.

27. GILLESPIE, J. F. Verbal signs of resistance in client-centered therapy. In W. U. Snyder (Ed.), *Group report of a program of research in psychotherapy.* State College, Pa.: Pennsylvania State Coll., 1953. Pp. 105–119.

28. GORLOW, L., HOCH, E. L., & TELSCHOW, E. F. *The nature of nondirective group psychotherapy: an experimental investigation.* New York: Teachers Coll., Columbia Univer., 1952.

29. GRUMMON, D. L. An investigation into the use of grammatical and psycho-grammatical categories of languages for the study of personality and psychotherapy. Unpublished doctor's dissertation, Univer. of Chicago, 1950. (Not seen; cited by Mowrer [60].)

30. GUMP, P. V. A statistical investigation of one psychoanalytic approach and a comparison of it with non-directive therapy. Unpublished master's thesis, Ohio State Univer., 1944.

31. HAIGH, G. Defensive behavior in client-centered therapy. *J. consult. Psychol.*, 1949, 13, 181–189.

32. HILGARD, E. R. Experimental approaches to psychoanalysis. In E. Pumpian-Mindlin (Ed.), *Psychoanalysis as science.* Stanford, Calif.: Stanford Univer. Press, 1952. Pp. 3–45.

33. HOFFMAN, A. E. Reported behavior changes in counseling. *J. consult. Psychol.*, 1949, 13, 190–195.

34. HOGAN, R. A. A measure of client-defensiveness. In W. Wolff and J. A. Precker (Eds.), *Success in psychotherapy.* New York: Grune & Stratton, 1952. Pp. 112–142.

35. HORWITZ, FLORENCE S. The relationship between a method of measuring tension and two methods of measuring the attitude toward self in thirty-six electrically recorded initial social casework interviews. M.S. thesis, Boston Univer. Sch. of Soc. Work, 1951.

36. HUNT, J. MCV. Measuring the effects of social casework. *Trans. N. Y. Acad. Sci.,* 1947, 9, 78–88.

37. HUNT, J. MCV. Measuring movement in casework. *J. soc. Casewk.,* 1948, 29, 343–351.

38. HUNT, J. MCV. A social agency as a setting for research—the Institute of Welfare Research. *J. consult. Psychol.,* 1949, 13, 69–81.

39. JANIS, I. L. The problems of validating content analysis. In H. D. Lasswell, N. Leites, *et al., Language of politics.* New York: Stewart, 1949. Pp. 55–82.

40. JONES, E. *The life and work of Sigmund Freud,* Vol. 1. New York: Basic Books, 1953.

41. KAHN, M. W. The role of perceptual consistency and generalization change in Rorschach and psychotherapy behavior. In W. U. Snyder (Ed.), *Group report of a program of research in psychotherapy.* State College, Pa.: Pennsylvania State Coll., 1953. Pp. 115–134.

42. KAPLAN, A., & GOLDSEN, J. M. The reliability of content-analysis categories. In H. D. Lasswell, N. Leites, *et al., Language of politics.* New York: Stewart, 1949. Pp. 83–112.

43. KAUFFMAN, P. E., & RAIMY, V. C. Two methods of assessing therapeutic progress. *J. abnorm. soc. Psychol.,* 1949, 44, 379–385.

44. KUBIE, L. S. Problems in clinical research. *Amer. J. Orthopsychiat.,* 1947, 17, 196–203.

45. LASSWELL, H. D. Verbal references and physiological changes during the psychoanalytic interview: a preliminary communication. *Psychoanal. Rev.,* 1935, 22, 10–24.

46. LASSWELL, H. D. Certain prognostic changes during trial (psychoanalytic) interviews. *Psychoanal. Rev.,* 1936, 23, 241–247.

47. LASSWELL, H. D. Veraenderungen an einer Versuchsperson waehrend einer Kurzen Folge von psychoanalytischen Interviews. *Imago,* 1937, 23, 375–380.

48. LASSWELL, H. D. A provisional classification of symbol data. *Psychiatry,* 1938, 1, 197–204.

49. LASSWELL, H. D., LEITES, N. *et al. Language of politics.* New York: Stewart, 1949.

50. LEWIS, VIRGINIA W. Changing the behavior of adolescent girls. *Arch. Psychol.,* 1943, No. 279.

51. LINDNER, R. M. *Rebel without a cause.* New York: Grune & Stratton, 1944.

52. MCINTYRE, C. J. Acceptance by others and its relation to acceptance of self and others. *J. abnorm. soc. Psychol.,* 1952, 47, 624–625.

53. MEADOW, A., GREENBLATT, M., LEVINE, J., & SOLOMON, H. C. The Discomfort-Relief Quotient as a measure of tension and adjustment. *J. abnorm. soc. Psychol.,* 1952, 47, 658–661.

54. MILLER, HELEN E. "Acceptance" and related attitudes as demonstrated in psychotherapeutic interviews. *J. clin. Psychol.,* 1949, 5, 83–87.

55. MILLER, N. E. Experimental studies of conflict. In J. McV. Hunt (Ed.), *Personality and the behavior disorders.* Vol. 1. New York: Ronald Press, 1944. Pp. 431–465.

56. MILLER, N. E. Theory and experiment relating psychoanalytic displacement to stimulus response generalization. *J. abnorm. soc. Psychol.,* 1948, 43, 155–178.

57. MILLER, N. E. Comments on theoretical models, illustrated by the development of a theory of conflict behavior. *J. Pers.,* 1951, 20, 82–100.

58. MILLER, N. E., & KRAELING, DORIS. Displacement: greater generalization of approach than avoidance in a generalized approach-avoidance conflict. *J. exp. Psychol.,* 1952, 43, 217–221.

59. MILLER, N. E., & MURRAY, E. J. Displacement and conflict: learnable drive as a basis for the steeper gradient of avoidance than of approach. *J. exp. Psychol.,* 1952, 43, 227–231.

60. MOWRER, O. H. Changes in verbal behavior during psychotherapy. In O. H. Mowrer (Ed.), *Psychotherapy, theory and research.* New York: Ronald Press, 1953. Pp. 463–545.

61. MOWRER, O. H., HUNT, J. McV., & KOGAN, L. S. Further studies utilizing the Discomfort-Relief Quotient. In O. H. Mowrer (Ed.), *Psychotherapy, theory and research.* New York: Ronald Press, 1953. Pp. 257–295.

62. MOWRER, O. H., LIGHT, B. H., LURIA, ZELLA, & ZELENY, MARJORIE P. Tension changes during psychotherapy with special reference to resistance. In O. H. Mowrer (Ed.), *Psychotherapy, theory and research.* New York: Ronald Press, 1953. Pp. 546–640.

63. MURRAY, E. J. A case study in a behavioral analysis of psychotherapy. *J. abnorm. soc. Psychol.,* 1954, 49, 305–310.

64. MURRAY, E. J. A method for studying psychotherapy. Unpublished doctor's dissertation, Yale Univer., 1955.

65. MURRAY, E. J., AULD, F., JR., & WHITE, ALICE M. A psychotherapy case showing progress but no decrease in the Discomfort-Relief Quotient. *J. consult. Psychol.,* 1954, 18, 349–353.

66. MURRAY, E. J., & BERKUN, M. M. Displacement as a resolution of conflict. *J. abnorm. soc. Psychol.,* 1955, 1, 47–56.

67. MURRAY, E. J., & MILLER, N. E. Displacement: steeper gradient of generalization of avoidance than of approach with age of habit controlled. *J. exp. Psychol.,* 1952, 43, 222–226.

68. PAGE, H. A. An assessment of the predictive value of certain language measures in psychotherapeutic counseling. In W. U. Snyder (Ed.), *Group report of a program of research in psychotherapy.* State College, Pa.: Pennsylvania State Coll., 1953. Pp. 88–93.

69. PERRY, W. G., & ESTES, S. G. The collaboration of client and counselor. In O. H. Mowrer (Ed.), *Psychotherapy, theory and research.* New York: Ronald Press, 1953. Pp. 95–119.

70. PORTER, E. H. The development and evaluation of a measure of counseling interview procedures. I. The development. *Educ. psychol. Measmt,* 1943, 3, 105–126.

71. PORTER, E. H. The development and evaluation of a measure of counseling interview procedures. II. The evaluation. *Educ. psychol. Measmt,* 1943, 3, 215–238.

72. PORTER, E. H. *An introduction to therapeutic counseling.* Boston: Houghton Mifflin, 1950.

73. RAIMY, V. C. Self reference in counseling interviews. *J. consult. Psychol.,* 1948, 12, 153–163.

74. RAKUSIN, J. M. The role of Rorschach variability in the prediction of client behavior during psychotherapy. In W. U. Snyder (Ed.), *Group report of a program of research in psychotherapy.* State College, Pa.: Pennsylvania State Coll., 1953. Pp. 60–74.

75. RASKIN, N. J. An objective study of the locus-of-evaluation factor in psychotherapy. In W. Wolff and J. A. Precker (Eds.), *Success in psychotherapy.* New York: Grune & Stratton, 1952. Pp. 143–162.

76. REDLICH, F. C., DOLLARD, J., & NEWMAN, R. High fidelity recording of psychotherapeutic interviews. *Amer. J. Psychiat.,* 1950, 107, 42–48.

77. REID, DOROTHY, & SNYDER, W. U. Experiment in "recognition of feeling" in non-directive psychotherapy. *J. clin. Psychol.,* 1947, 3, 128–135.

78. ROBERTS, B. H., & STRODTBECK, F. L. Interaction process differences between groups of paranoid schizophrenic and depressed patients. *Int. J. group Psychother.,* 1953, 3, 29–41.

79. ROBINSON, F. P. *Principles and procedures in student counseling.* New York: Harper, 1950.

80. ROGERS, C. R. *Counseling and psychotherapy.* Boston: Houghton Mifflin, 1942.

81. ROGERS, C. R. Electrically recorded interviews in improving psychotherapeutic techniques. *Amer. J. Orthopsychiat.,* 1942, 12, 429–435.

82. ROGERS, C. R. The development of insight in a counseling relationship. *J. consult. Psychol.,* 1944, 8, 331–341.

83. ROGERS, C. R. *Client-centered therapy.* Boston: Houghton Mifflin, 1951.

84. ROGERS, C. R., & DYMOND, ROSALIND F. (Eds.) *Psychotherapy and personality change.* Chicago: Univer. of Chicago Press, 1954.

85. ROSENMAN, S. Changes in interpersonal relations in the course of non-directive counseling. Unpublished doctor's dissertation, Harvard Univer., 1953.

86. ROSHAL, JEAN J. G. The type-token ratio as a measure of changes in behavior variability during psychotherapy. In W. U. Snyder (Ed.), *Group report of a program of research in psychotherapy.* State College, Pa.: Pennsylvania State Coll., 1953. Pp. 94–104.

87. ROYER, ANNE E. An analysis of counseling procedures in a non-directive approach. Unpublished master's thesis, Ohio State Univer., 1943. (Not seen; cited by Snyder [91].)

88. SEEMAN, J. The process of non-directive therapy. *J. consult. Psychol.,* 1949, 13, 157–168.

89. SHEERER, ELIZABETH T. An analysis of the relationship between acceptance of and respect for self and acceptance of and respect for others in ten counseling cases. *J. consult. Psychol.,* 1949, 13, 169–175.

90. SHERMAN, DOROTHY. An analysis of the dynamic relationship between counselor techniques and outcomes in larger units of the interview situation. Unpublished doctor's dissertation, Ohio State Univer., 1945. (Not seen; cited by Robinson [79].)

91. SNYDER, W. U. An investigation of the nature of non-directive psychotherapy. *J. gen. Psychol.,* 1945, 33, 193–223.

92. SNYDER, W. U. A comparison of one unsuccessful with four successful non-directively counseled cases. *J. consult. Psychol.,* 1947, 11, 38–42.

93. STOCK, DOROTHY. The self concept and feelings toward others. *J. consult. Psychol.,* 1949, 13, 176–180.

94. STRUPP, H. H. An objective comparison of Rogerian and psychoanalytic techniques. *J. consult. Psychol.,* 1955, 19, 1–7.

95. STRUPP, H. H. An objective study of certain psychotherapeutic operations; the effect of the therapist's personal analysis upon his verbal techniques. *Amer. Psychologist,* 1954, 9, 479–480. (Abstract)

96. TUCKER, J. E. Measuring client progress in client-centered therapy. In W. U. Snyder (Ed.), *Group report of a program of research in psychotherapy.* State College, Pa.: Pennsylvania State Coll., 1953. Pp. 55–59.

97. WHITE, R. K. *Black boy:* A value analysis. *J. abnorm. soc. Psychol.,* 1947, 42, 440–461.

98. WILSON, E. B., JR. *An introduction to scientific research.* New York: McGraw-Hill, 1952.

99. ZIMMERMAN, W., & LANGDON, J. A preliminary attempt to establish criteria for measuring progress in psychotherapy. Unpublished manuscript, Univer. of Illinois. (Not seen; cited by Mowrer [60].)

Content-Analysis Studies of Therapeutic Interviews: 1954 to 1964[1]

GERALD MARSDEN

Content analysis denotes a research technique for the systematic ordering of the content of communication processes. Typically it involves procedures for division of content into units, for assignment of each unit to a category or to a position on a metric, and for summarizing coded units and arriving at inferences concerning the significance of the summations. The basic contribution of content analysis is that it makes public the bases on which an investigator makes inferences about the significance of a body of communication. The purpose of this review is to discuss the applications of content analysis to data derived from counseling and psychotherapy interviews in the period from 1954, when they were last reviewed (Auld & Murray, 1955), to 1964, and, within this context, to offer a framework for conceptualizing

the variety of research efforts that might be considered content-analysis studies. To this end, the studies reviewed are divided into three broad procedure families called models: the classical, the pragmatic, and the nonquantitative.[2]

MODELS OF CONTENT ANALYSIS

The classical model was exhaustively explicated by Berelson (1952) in a book which undertook to survey the field of content analysis, clarify its assumptions, codify its procedures, and summarize methodological refinements. On the basis of his study, Berelson offered the following definition: "Content analysis is a research technique for the objective, systematic, and quantita-

Reprinted from *Psychological Bulletin,* 1965, 63 (5), 298–321, with the permission of the American Psychological Association and the author.

[1] The author wishes to gratefully acknowledge the assistance of Raymond C. Hummel who made helpful suggestions during the preparation of the paper and offered useful criticisms of an earlier draft.

[2] Auld and Murray's article reviewed some papers published during and after 1954, but their coverage is far more complete through 1953. In the present paper, studies involving comparison of interview content variables with physiological variables, and studies involving the use of content-analysis procedures to evaluate operant conditioning studies, are not treated systematically because they are considered beyond its scope and have been recently and well reviewed elsewhere.

tive description of the manifest content of communication [p. 18]." Berelson discusses in detail several important assumptions underlying this definition. Two of these are of particular interest here because their necessity is challenged by the nonclassical models to be discussed below. These are the assumptions regarding the limitation to manifest content, and the use of quantitative methods.

The aim of those who developed the classical model was to achieve objective (i.e., reliable) and systematic results. They felt this could best, or perhaps only, be done through the use of quantitative methods. Berelson explicitly assumed that it is useful to quantify communication content and that the frequency of appearance of content characteristics is an important dimension of the communication process. Quantification is, for him, an essential part of content analysis.

Berelson's restriction to manifest content derived from his desire to assure a common meeting ground for the communicator, the person with whom he is communicating, and the content analyst. Yet the implications of the phrase "manifest content" have not always been understood as Berelson intended. He stated explicitly that he considered musical, pictorial, plastic, and gestural systems of communication, as well as lexical systems, appropriate for content-analysis investigation (p. 13). Similarly, the common distinction between formal characteristics of a communication and a narrower definition of its content (e.g., lexical content), though useful in some situations, seems unsatisfactory in any generic definition of content analysis. But more important is Berelson's use of the word "manifest," by which he intended to limit content analysis to the semantic and syntactic aspects of communication, and to prevent its extension to the pragmatic aspect— to the relationship between the communication symbol and its user. The restriction is *not* intended to rule out the use of inference in coding relevant syntactic and semantic content units to the categories of the content-analysis system.

The pragmatic model challenges this requirement that content analysis be restricted *from* the pragmatic aspect of communication, and *to* the semantic and syntactic aspects. While, in the classical model, units are coded to categories descriptive of the content itself, in the pragmatic model, units are coded to categories descriptive of some condition of the communicator or of the relationship between him and his communication. In the classical model, once the units are coded, the analyst may make further inferences about the internal state of the communicator, and these inferences are the point at issue, subject to validation only by other procedures. In the pragmatic model, this kind of inference is made initially, at the time of coding, and is the basis of the coding. This procedure is usually chosen when the behavioral cue for the internal condition in question (on which the classical model depends) cannot be specified satisfactorily.

This difference in research strategy provides one focus for argument of the more generic controversy of clinical versus statistical prediction (Gough, 1962). The classical model places a premium on objectivity and is designed so that workers with minimal special training can reliably perform the analysis, maximizing his (and his reader's) ability to specify just what configuration of data led to the investigator's inference. The price paid for this precision is often a superficiality of results. The pragmatic model attempts to realize psychological meaningfulness by working directly with complex clinical constructs. It represents an effort to utilize the skills and understanding of the clinician, while formalizing the conditions under which these skills are used to insure, insofar as possible, procedural rigor suitable to a scientific undertaking. Those who place little stock in the power of clinical skills as instruments of science consider the compromise with objectivity unwarranted (Leary, 1960), while clinicians who deny the identity of predictive ability with the understanding of human behavior disparage what they consider the empty formalism of their detractors. The strategy selected appears to hinge, often, on which compromise implies a greater sacrifice to a given worker and is determined by his personality, his data, and the questions he seeks to answer.

Unlike the classical and pragmatic models, the nonquantitative model lacks methodological homogeneity. The studies representing it share the purpose of attempting to develop alternatives to the frequency approach of measuring intensity in communication materials. The classical model and many pragmatic model systems measure intensity in terms of the frequency of occurrence in accord with Berelson's assumption of the value of quantification. That is, the assumption is made that frequency of occurrence of units in a category is highly correlated with the intensity of that category in the communication. This assumption has been a major target of criticism directed at classical content analysis. Advocates and antagonists alike have asked how much of the variance this correlation could be expected to explain. They have wanted to know what factors other than frequency of occurrence are significant carries of intensity, and in what situations they become important. Above all, they have asked how might they be measured (Mahl, 1959a, p. 90; Salzinger, 1962; Strupp, 1962a, pp. 590–591; Strupp & Luborsky, 1962, pp. 292–298)?

Viable answers to these questions have not yet appeared, but some promising beginnings have been made. Some investigators have attempted to measure both frequency and nonfrequency aspects of intensity by using rating scales within categories, or weighted units. More rigorously formulated nonquantitative approaches, though not yet applied to analysis of therapeutic interviews, include George's (1959a, 1959b) "nonfrequency analysis" and Osgood's (1959) work on evaluative asser-

tions. The most highly developed nonquantitative content-analysis technique accounting for intensity, and the only one thus far extensively applied to therapeutic interview data, is linguistic analysis.

Linguists, and many content analysts as well, will be distinctly uneasy at the characterization of linguistic analysis as a type of content analysis. But it seems appropriate in terms of the applications of linguistic analysis in therapeutic interview research reviewed here. Like other types of content analysis, the goal of linguistic analysis in these studies is the systematic ordering of the communication content to provide a public basis for inference.

Linguistics has been put on a scientific footing within the present century, and is methodologically far in advance of other content-analysis techniques (Firth, 1956; McQuown, 1954b, 1957; Saporta & Sebeok, 1959). It commands rigorous, valid, and highly reliable[3] procedures for explicating the total structure of language, making accessible to the observer all the functioning parts and their mutual dependencies (Carroll, 1955; McQuown, 1954a, 1954b, 1957). These methods are traditionally nonquantitative, that is, they have been used to indicate the presence or absence of linguistic phenomena rather than their frequencies of occurrence. Only recently have linguists become interested in the application of statistical techniques to linguistic data (Carroll, Agard, Dulany, Newman, Newmark, Osgood, Sebeok, & Solomon, 1951; Pool, 1959, pp. 224–225; Saporta & Sebeok, 1959, p. 139).

Writers discussing the relation of content analysis and linguistics have stated that they are different precisely in that content analysis is primarily concerned with meanings, while linguistic analysis is concerned with the properties of language as a code for the transmission of communication (Pool, 1959, pp. 224–225; Saporta & Se-

---

[3] For a dissent regarding reliability see Boomer (1964).

beok, 1959, p. 135). But if linguists have pursued a strategy of emphasizing structural considerations, linguistics is nonetheless ultimately concerned with meaning (Carroll, 1955, pp. 23–29). Moreover, it is entering a phase of development in which its methods are being applied to extralinguistic problems in cooperation with specialists in other disciplines, one result of which is a more immediate concern with the problems of meaning (Carroll et al., 1951, pp. 27–29; Firth, 1956, p. 133; Hoijer, 1954; McQuown, 1957; Pittenger & Smith, 1957). Recent applications of linguistic analysis to therapeutic interview material is one manifestation of this development.

CLASSICAL MODEL STUDIES

The lion's share of content-analysis studies of therapeutic interviews has been conducted within the classical model. Because of the great number of these studies, they are arranged here so as to bring together studies bearing on the same general research problem. There are four such areas: characteristics of patients, of therapists, of patient-therapist interactional systems, and of internal, psychodynamic states. A fifth group of studies based on a relatively recent advance in content-analysis methodology called analysis of contingent relationships is treated separately.

Patient Characteristics

One focus of content-analysis research on patient characteristics has been the assessment of change or movement toward greater psychological "health" as a result of treatment (Auld & Murray, 1955; Dittes, 1959). Vargas (1954) reported a study in this tradition designed to test the hypothesis that judged success of therapy is positively correlated with changes in self-awareness reflected in client verbal behavior. A content-analysis system was used to measure various aspects of self-aware-

ness. Unfortunately the methodology was poorly reported; the scoring unit [4] was not even described. A strong positive correlation between self-awareness and success in therapy was found when the criterion of success was the therapist's rating. However, three other success criteria yielded low positive, near zero, and negative correlations with increasing self-awareness. Braaten (1961) achieved similar results using a related but more sophisticated content-analysis system to test the hypothesis that success in client-centered therapy is correlated with increasing expression of feelings referent to self as opposed to nonself material. Again, therapists' rating of success was the criterion best related to the measure.

Based on a more recent formulation of the process of personality change, Rogers and his associates developed a content-analysis system for measuring the degree of change during treatment (Rogers, 1959, 1961; Walker, Rablen, & Rogers, 1960). Rogers viewed personality on a continuum with one end representing stasis, fixity, and rigidity, and the other end looseness and flexibility. This continuum was comprised of seven aspects of psychological functioning which Rogers called "strands." He conceptualized these as being discrete and

---

[4] Dollard and Auld (1959, pp. 10–12) are the only analysts working in the period covered by this paper, to the writer's knowledge, who made a formal distinction between scoring, contextual, and summarizing units. The scoring unit is the entity that is actually coded and counted. The contextual unit is the communication material surrounding the scoring unit that is considered before the latter is assigned to a category. The summarizing unit is the group of scoring units about which some statement is made. For example, the number of nouns in 2-minute segments of an interview are counted, and judgment as to whether a word is a noun is based on its use in the sentence in which it occurs. The 2-minute segments represent summarizing units. The nouns themselves are the scoring units and the sentences in which the nouns appear are the contextual units. These distinctions, made by Berelson in 1962, are necessary and important; the failure of content analysts working with therapeutic interview material to make them has, at times, led to conceptual confusion and ambiguous results.

separate at the rigid end, but merging and only artificially separable at the other.

Each of these strands represented one category in the content-analysis system. Within each, a system of subcategories in the form of a 7-point rating scale was used to locate the patient on the continuum with respect to that category. The system is not wholly faithful to its theoretical model in that the categories did not merge in the upper range. Scores for all categories can be combined to produce a score indicating the patient's over-all position on the continuum. Arithmetic procedures for their combination were not described. Nor have clear-cut scoring units been defined, though this issue was examined empirically in one study (Kiesler, Mathieu, & Klein, 1964) with respect to one of the seven strands.

Studies employing this system have demonstrated its power to differentiate between cases judged more and less successful at a high level of statistical significance by a variety of clinical criteria of success. Findings indicated that successful cases began and terminated at a significantly higher level on the scale than did less successful ones, and that there was greater movement along the scale during therapy in successful cases. There appeared to be intrainterview changes in the direction of higher scores, reaching statistical significance in the more successful cases (Rogers, 1961; Tomlinson & Hart, 1962).

Smith, Bassin, and Froehlich (1960) examined the relationship between verbal productivity and improvement in two groups of adult probationers. They found no statistically significant relationships. Shellhase (1960) examined relationships between improvement in group psychotherapy, role acceptance, and activity in treatment. His study lacks adequate statistical analysis.

Outcome-oriented studies continue to suffer (Auld & Murray, 1955) from limitations induced by failure to reach consensus on what constitutes adequate and independent criteria of success.

Other investigators have explored patient characteristics unrelated to treatment outcome. Matarazzo, Saslow, and their associates conducted a series of studies using a content-analysis system based on the work of Chapple. Chapple believes that a scientific theory of personality should be based on the time relationships in observable human interaction. He developed the "interaction chronograph," a recording and computing instrument operated by an observer, to facilitate measurement of various behaviors and their time relationships. These procedures represent a highly sophisticated content-analysis system in which both units and categories are derived from theoretical notions about personality and human interaction. An overview of his theoretical position and a detailed discussion of the interaction chronograph is presented in J. D. Matarazzo, Saslow, and Matarazzo (1956).

In most of their work, Matarazzo and associates have used a structured interview which has the effect of standardizing interviewer behavior along certain formal, nonlexical dimensions and sharply varying other dimensions during different phases of the interview, thus treating the interviewer as an independent variable. In a series of five studies, this group demonstrated high levels of reliability in the interview's behavior (J. D. Matarazzo, Saslow, & Guze, 1956; Saslow, Matarazzo, & Guze, 1955), in the observers' recording (Phillips, Matarazzo, Matarazzo, & Saslow, 1957), in scoring the final interaction chronograph record (Saslow et al., 1955), and in the interaction patterns of the interviewee from one interview to another over varying periods of time (Saslow, Matarazzo, Phillips, & Matarazzo, 1957; Saslow & Matarazzo, 1959; Tauson, Guze, McClure, & Beguelin, 1961). They have examined various aspects of the system's validity in cross-validational and replication studies (Ruth G. Matarazzo, Matarazzo, Saslow, & Phillips, 1958; J. D. Matarazzo, Saslow, & Hare, 1958; Saslow & Matarazzo, 1959), in correlational studies with variables measured by other content-analysis systems (Hare, Waxler, Saslow, & Matarazzo, 1960; Phillips, Matarazzo, Matarazzo, Saslow, & Kanfer, 1961) and psychosociological variables (Ruth G. Matarazzo et al., 1958; Saslow & Matarazzo, 1959), in a factor analytic study (J. D. Matarazzo, Saslow, & Hare, 1958), and in studies testing the system's capacity to differentiate between nosological groups and normal subjects (J. D. Matarazzo, 1962, pp. 479–490; J. D. Matarazzo & Saslow, 1961). They also generated normative data on the action and silence behavior of subjects (J. D. Matarazzo, Hess, & Saslow, 1962).

Matarazzo and his associates found repeatedly that while interviewee behavior was stable from one interview to another, there were significant changes in the behavior of the interviewee from one period to another within the same interview. These changes corresponded to the planned changes in the behavior of the interviewer. They found, further, that this stability and modifiability in individuals and groups across interviews was maintained even with different interviewers so long as they operated within the rules of the standardized interview (J. D. Matarazzo, Saslow, & Guze, 1956; J. D. Matarazzo, Saslow, Matarazzo, & Phillips, 1958; J. D. Matarazzo, Weitman, Saslow, & Wiens, 1963; Saslow et al., 1955; Saslow et al., 1957; Saslow & Matarazzo, 1959). Interviewee response duration appears to be independent of the lexical content of the interview (J. D. Matarazzo, Weitman, & Saslow, 1963), but it varies with the nature of the interviewer's statement. For example, they found that interpretive interviewer statements could be differentiated from exploratory or information-seeking statements in terms of interviewee response duration (Kanfer, Phillips, Matarazzo, & Saslow, 1960).

Timmons, Rickard, and Taylor (1960) tested the hypothesis that the interviewer can be treated as an independent variable in a group therapy situation. They used a structured interview suggestive of Matarazzo and his associates, and similar, though less elegant, measures of frequency and duration of verbal behavior derived from tape recordings. Initial findings supported their hypothesis, but a replication confounded these results. Taking their lead from this, they (Dinoff, Kew, Rickard, & Timmons, 1962) next examined the stability of individual verbal behavior in a group setting. The findings indicated that as a function of group interaction, group members tend to establish a persistent hierarchy of verbal response behavior analogous to the pecking-order phenomena in chickens.

Block (1964) developed a content-analysis system to investigate the relationship between patient affect, motivation, and expectations regarding psychotherapy. His purpose was to perform a critical test of two formulations of the discrepancy hypothesis in achievement-motivation theory. This hypothesis states that there is "a primary affective reaction attending the patient's evaluation of a discrepancy between past expectations (as governed by the adaptation level . . . of prior expectations) and the given therapeutic event such that an appropriate motive is redintegrated [p. 268]." His findings support the formulation which holds that the direction, rather than the size, of the discrepancy from the prevailing expectancy level determines primary affect and secondary motive. He concluded that his findings support the applicability of adaptation-level theory to psychotherapy research.

Rosenman (1955) explored the theoretical divergence between Freudian libido theory, which asserts that ego cathexis occurs in inverse proportion to cathexis of objects, and the views of Fromm, Sullivan, and some client-centered theorists that one's hatred or love for others is in direct proportion to one's hatred or love for self. He compared successful with unsuccessful client-centered counseling cases at the beginning and end of treatment in a content analysis of client verbal behavior. His system contained 48 categories designed to facilitate analysis of the representation of self- and other-directed action and evaluation in such a way that these categories were not contaminated by the effects of the representation of the self-other interaction. He found that positive evaluation of others decreased while positive self-evaluation, self-to-self actions, and actions directed toward others increased in successful cases during treatment. Similar changes occurred in the unsuccessful cases, but the magnitude of change was not as great. Unfortunately, Rosenman did not provide data pertaining to the statistical significance of these changes.

Berg (1958) investigated lexical-grammatical characteristics of patients' verbal behavior and found that self-references, negative words and words with "expletive and explosive (initial) sounds" decreased in frequency over therapy, while "empathetic words" increased. He failed, however, to test for the significance of these changes. Weintraub and Aronson (1962, 1964) report a method, based largely on word-count procedures, for analyzing aspects of patient speech for evidence from which the use of specific defense mechanisms might be inferred. Lorenz and Cobb (1954) and Lorenz (1955) also used word-count procedures and found that major diagnostic groups and "normal" subjects could be differentiated on the basis of intergroup differences in patterns of word usage. Conrad and Conrad (1956) applied similar techniques to a study of group therapy. Colby (1960) used a classical system to investigate aspects of the effects of the psychoanalyst's presence on the free associations of the analysand during psychoanalytic sessions.

A system devised by Leary and Gill (1959) is relevant here, as well as at other points in this discussion of classical model studies, for it is an omnibus system designed to allow for coding almost all verbalization of both patient and therapist in what is probably the most complex category structure offered to date. It was designed primarily to facilitate analysis and comparison of clinicians' summaries of psychotherapy and the therapy protocols themselves. Aside from a brief preliminary demonstration application, this system has not been used in published studies of therapeutic interview material.

Therapist Characteristics

Bandura, Lipsher, and Miller (1960) explored therapist behavior in the face of patient hostility, and the effect on the patient of the therapist's reaction. A patient statement, the therapist response, and the next patient statement were studied. The first patient statement in this sequence (first scoring unit) was judged as being hostile or nonhostile. If nonhostile, the total segment was not considered further. If judged hostile, this scoring unit was further subcategorized as to the object of hostility. Next the therapist response (second scoring unit) was judged as being one of avoidance or approach. Each of these categories had several subcategories facilitating the analysis of avoidance and approach techniques. Finally, the second patient statement (third scoring unit) was judged hostile or nonhostile in the same way as the first.

There were no differences among therapists when patient hostility was directed toward the therapist himself. In this situation therapists were more likely to emit an avoidance response than they were when patient hostility was directed elsewhere. However, therapists rated by their colleagues as expressing hostility directly and rated low in need for approval were found more likely to make approach responses to patient hostility directed toward objects having little to do with therapy than were therapists rated high on approval-seeking behavior or low on direct expression of hostility. When patient hostility was approached by the therapist there was a high probability that the hostile expression would continue in the next patient statement. But when the therapist reacted with avoidance the patient was likely to change the object of his hostility or drop the hostile expression altogether.

Using the same general method in a second study, Winder, Ahmad, Bandura, and Rau (1962) examined the effect of therapists' approach or avoidance of patients' dependency expressions on continuation versus termination of therapy. The correspondence between dependency expressions primarily avoided and termination, and dependency expressions primarily approached and continuation was very marked, particularly when the therapist was the object of dependency. There was a clear tendency for approached dependency expressions to be followed by a continuation of such expression, and for avoided dependency expression to be discontinued.

Salzberg and associates conducted four studies on the effect of therapist verbal behavior on interaction in group therapy. In the first (Salzberg, 1961), he attempted to ascertain what type of therapist verbalization elicits general group interaction as opposed to responses directed to the therapist. The findings showed that group member interaction varied inversely with the frequency of therapist verbalizations, particularly when the therapist responded directly to a patient rather than directing him to another member of the group. These results were elaborated in a second study (Heckel, Froelich, & Salzberg, 1962). Salzberg (1962) next turned to the question of whether therapist silence or redirection most facilitated group interaction and their effect on patient responses in group psychotherapy. The study's design called for a structured interview in which the therapist varied his verbal behavior through four conditions. The results suggested that while silence appeared to facilitate interaction, it also facilitated patient verbalization about nontherapeutic aspects of their environment. Redirection, on the other hand, while not leading to significantly more interaction, did lead to more group-directed patient response. Salzberg, Brokaw, and Strahley (1964) have now employed these silence-redirection strategies to investigate the development of spontaneity and problem-relevant discussion in a new psychotherapy group which lacked membership stability, and to compare this group with an older, more stable group on these variables.

Perhaps the most comprehensive content-analysis investigation of therapist characteristics and behavior was undertaken by Strupp. After three initial studies (Strupp, 1955a, 1955b, 1955c) using Bales' interaction process analysis system, he developed one of his own based on an explicitly stated theoretical rationale (Strupp, 1957c). This system was intended to be sufficiently general to make possible valid comparisons across theoretical orientations and to be relevant to psychotherapy as a special kind of communication (Strupp, 1960). Strupp's system employed five major dimensions, each of which contained a category structure or rating scale. These tapped the gross behavior of the therapist, the degree of inference and of warmth implicit in his communication, the degree to which he channeled the patient's communication, and whether he worked from within the patient's frame of reference or his own. The somewhat arbitrary scoring unit consisted of all therapist communication occurring between two patient statements. However, he noted that it was sometimes necessary to subdivide a therapist communication into two or three units but offered no criteria for this division. All units were coded to each of the five dimensions. The contextual unit was the prior material in the interview series.

Strupp published two papers demonstrating the usefulness of this system. One (Strupp, 1957a) reported the analysis of interviews from a published case of brief psychotherapy by Wolberg. A second (Strupp, 1957b) compared the results of the first with a similar analysis of a published case by Rogers. The findings showed that Rogers' behavior was fairly consistent over the course of his interviews, while Wolberg's varied systematically. Wolberg was more inferential and he exerted stronger guidance in the middle and terminal interviews. In three papers, Strupp (1958a, 1958b, 1958c) presented the findings of a study in which his system of content analysis was part of a larger design. The study attempted an exploration of the therapist's perceptions and evaluations of therapeutic problems, and the relation of these to his treatment plans, and of both to his actual behavior in the therapy sessions. The major finding showed a clear interaction between the therapist's clinical observations, his treatment recommendation, his attitude toward the patient, and the nature of his communication to the patient. This interaction was patterned in some respects according to the training and experience of the therapist. (For a critical discussion of the design of this study and its justification, see Strupp, 1962b.) Other applications of this system are Strupp (1961) and Auerbach (1963).

Several other studies have attempted to delineate various aspects and effects of therapist style. Cutler (1958) has investigated countertransference phenomena. Dipboye (1954) showed that counselor style varied with topics of discussion, and that within each topic they tended to resemble each other in style. Danskin and Robinson (1954) investigated the degree of lead used by counselors at five universities. Danskin (1955) attempted to ascertain whether the roles played by a counselor in the course of a series of interviews could be inferred reliably from the typescripts and whether these roles were related to certain other interview variables. Raters unitized the contents of 30 interviews in terms of transitions from one role to another. Scoring units corresponded to the material between two role-transition points. These units were then coded to 11 role categories. All the material in an interview representing a role was subsequently considered a "role unit," and rated on a scale of working relationship. In addition, each counselor remark within each role unit was used as a scoring unit and coded on a scale of degree of lead. Counselor remarks within role units were also coded to four categories of discussion topics. Danskin was able to show, among other things, that 71% of the transition points between role units occurred with a change in topic, that the amount of counselor lead was related to the counselor's role (and by implication, to the topic being discussed), and that the quality of the working relationship between client and counselor was similar across roles. Hoffman (1959) used a similar method of analysis to examine the frequency with which various roles were employed by experienced counselors, and the similarities of role patterning and range of roles used by counselors with different clients and from different counseling centers. Campbell (1962) applied Hoffman's procedures to protocols of interviews conducted by inexperienced counselors to compare their role behavior with Hoffman's experienced counselors, and to examine personality and background correlates of counselor role behavior.

Few variables used in content-analysis studies of therapeutic interviews have been subject to prior examination of their conceptual purity or the impact of changes in the conditions of their use. Perhaps as a testament to therapists' concern with their own role, only variables descriptive of therapist behavior have been so singled out (Bordin, Cutler, Dittmann, Harway, Raush, & Rigler, 1954; Bordin, 1955). The concept of "depth of interpretation" is a case in point. Scales for its measurement have been developed, sometimes empirically (Harway, Dittmann, Raush, Bordin, & Rigler, 1955), and examined regarding use with different scoring and contextual units and with different methods of presentation to judges (Cutler, Bordin, Williams, & Rigler, 1958; Harway et al., 1955). Their unidimensionality (Raush, Sperber, Rigler, Williams, Harway, Bordin, Dittmann, & Hays, 1956) and semantic structure characteristics (Howe, 1962b) have been explored and used to investigate other therapeutic process correlates of depth (Fisher, 1956; Howe, 1962a).

Speisman (1959) used the depth of interpretation scale developed and investigated by Harway et al. (1955) to test the hypothesis that deep interpretations lead to more resistance than superficial interpretations, and that these lead in turn to more resistance than moderate interpretations. Resistant behavior was coded to a system of categories using a patient response as the scoring unit. In the depth of interpretation scale, the therapist statement was used as the scoring unit and the preceding patient response as the contextual unit. Ratings on each scale were made independently by different groups of judges. The results supported Speisman's hypothesis and indicated that the level of resistance suggested by a patient's response does not significantly influence the depth of the immediately following therapist interpretation. Frank and Sweetland (1962) also obtained similar results with respect to the selective influence of therapist statements on patient responses.

Howe and Pope (1961b) developed scales for measuring therapist activity level and investigated their unidimensionality characteristics (Howe, 1964; Howe & Pope, 1961a). In an application of their scale (Howe & Pope, 1962), they failed to support the hypothesis that the activity level of therapist responses was inversely related to the diagnostic utility of the following patient response. When the covariance contributed by verbal productivity was partialed out, the net correlations between activity level and diagnostic util-

ity ratings failed to reach significance.

Pope and Siegman (1962) examined the relationship between activity level and specificity in therapist behavior on the one hand, and productivity and speech disturbance in patient behavior on the other. The specificity scale, developed by Lennard and Bernstein (1960), consisted of eight categories concerning the extent to which the therapist's statement "tends to place limits upon the array of verbal responses from which the patient may choose a reply [p. 43]." Specificity is the reverse of ambiguity, and ambiguity is one of the three attributes of the activity-level scale along with lead and inference. The two scales should, therefore, correlate highly and yield similar results when compared with patient productivity and speech disturbance. Patient productivity was measured by counting the number of clauses in patient responses, while speech disturbance was measured by the Speech-Disturbance Ratio developed by Mahl (1956). Pope and Siegman hypothesized negative relationships between the therapist scales and patient measures. No support was found for their hypothesis with the activity-level scale, but the specificity scale was significantly negatively related to both patient productivity and speech disturbance. Further analysis indicated that the variance shared by both scales was only moderate. Subsequently, Siegman and Pope (1962) developed an empirical scale for measuring therapist specificity in initial therapeutic interviews.

Truax and Carkhuff (1964) examined a similar variable which they called concreteness. Unfortunately they did not discuss the relationship of concreteness to the specificity variable, though they appeared to use the terms interchangeably. Nor is it clear from their report whether, and to what extent therapist concreteness was investigated, or how he contributed to the concreteness of the interview. They found concreteness significantly related to criterion measures of therapeutic process and concluded that, as a variable largely under therapist control, it plays an important role in successful treatment.

Interactional Systems

A number of classical content-analysis systems have been developed to facilitate investigation of patient-therapist interaction, applying the same categories to both participants in an effort to investigate their characteristics as a communication system, and to avoid the information loss inherent in conceptualizing them as independent organisms whose behavior is determined primarily by factors external to their interaction (Gottschalk, 1961, p. 163; Scheflen, 1963). While the relatively few studies of this type vary in the degree to which they have explicitly articulated and achieved this goal, they have already demonstrated their fruitfulness in both the substantive and methodological realms.

A general purpose content-analysis system, called interaction process analysis, was developed by Bales (1950). It was based on a theory of small group behavior which conceived of interaction as problem-solving activity distributed across members and over time. Its 12 categories represented the dimensions of instrumental-adaptive, and social-emotional behavior. The scoring unit was the act, defined as the smallest discriminable segment of verbal or nonverbal behavior which can be coded. Coding was done by trained workers observing the interaction, though alternative coding procedures have been suggested (Psathas, 1961). Each act was coded to a single category, and judgments were based on the context surrounding the act in question.

Bales and his associates found a marked phasing tendency over the course of experimental group sessions, from a relative emphasis on acts of orientation, to acts of evaluation, to acts of control. Group discussion was also found to progress in cycles beginning with the introduction of a disturbance and ending with its resolution, thus achieving successive states of equilibrium (Bales, 1950, 1953; Bales & Strodtbeck, 1951). Talland (1955) reasoned that groups engaged in group psychotherapy differed from Bales' experimental groups in several important respects affecting these phase and equilibrium characteristics. With some deviations in procedure, and using a different statistical technique than that of Bales and Strodtbeck (1951), Talland found no evidence in his data suggesting the operation of either the control-oriented phase sequence or the cyclical tendency to equilibrium. Smith, Basin, and Froelich (1962) reached the same conclusions in a study essentially duplicating Talland's. These results were confounded by Psathas (1960b) who followed the Bales and Strodtbeck coding and statistical procedures. His findings clearly support Bales' formulations. Other more or less related studies are Fine and Zimet (1956), Noble, Ohlsen, and Proff (1961), and Psathas (1960).

Lennard and Bernstein (1960) and their associates sought to delineate in quantitative terms the expectation- and communication- interactional systems of patient and therapist (Lennard, 1962; Lennard, Calogeras, & Hendin, 1957; Palmore, Lennard, & Hendin, 1959). Drawing on Bales' formulations concerning phase movement and equilibrium in problem-solving groups and on other social science concepts, they developed a complex and sophisticated program of research anchored in theoretical notions of small group behavior. Their methodology was two-pronged, involving the use of questionnaires administered to both patient and therapist at several points prior to and during treatment, and a multidimensional, multilevel system of classical content analysis of therapist and patient verbal behavior. The content-analysis system involved the use of three sizes of scoring units, each one appropriate to one or more of five groups of categories. The use of multiple scoring units represents a new departure in content analysis of therapeutic interviews. The findings were complex. In brief, they discovered a great and increasing similarity between patient-therapist pairs in the longitudinal development of the interaction despite major differences in behavior and expectations. They also found that the therapist-patient interactional system contained built-in mechanisms for maintaining system equilibrium. For example, sessions exhibiting more than usual amounts of silence tended to be followed by those in which the therapist emitted more evaluative behavior and behavior of greater informational specificity.

This provocative research is marred by inadequate statistical analysis of data. Tests of significance are either lacking or of questionable appropriateness. Its usefulness is further limited by the authors' apparent unfamiliarity with research already conducted on therapeutic interviews which employ the same or similar concepts to those the authors believe they are introducing *de novo* to therapeutic interview research.

Jaffe (1961b), too, has insisted that the therapist and patient coming together in therapeutic sessions are appropriately regarded as a single interpersonal system. He called this system the "dyad" and developed a procedure for investigating its verbal behavior within the framework of the classical model of content analysis. His approach was simply to regard the speech of patient and therapist as if it emanated from one person, that is, to subject it to content analysis without regard to change of speaker. To this stream of communication Jaffe has applied several content-analysis systems.

Gottschalk (1961, pp. 205–206) has expressed skepticism about the utility of the dyad for many questions, in part because it masks the degree to which the two participants share the time of the interview. This information only becomes available if some other system of analysis is used in conjunction with dyadic analysis. In fact, most of Jaffe's applications of this technique to therapeutic interview material were accom-

panied by additional analyses which provided such information. The approach is also open to criticism precisely on grounds that data on the individual is lost in dyadic analysis. Jaffe (1961b) argued that these data are recoverable since the speech samples in which one of the participants talked maximally or minimally can be analyzed separately. However, this manner of breaking the dyad into its components rests on the assumption that speech samples dominated by one of the speakers are equivalent to those in which there is more nearly equal interaction.

Most of Jaffe's work employed a content-analysis system known as the Type-Token Ratio (TTR). (See Mowrer, 1953, for a review of earlier studies applying the TTR to the speech of individuals.) This scheme used the word as the scoring unit, and consisted of the ratio of different words occurring in a summarizing unit (types) to the total number of words in that unit (tokens). Any size summarizing unit may be used, although its size determines the natural arithmetic limits of the ratio. TTR values of given speech samples are determined, in part, by the syntactic patterns of the language, but also by factors idiosyncratic to the speaker, or in this case, the dyad (Jaffe, 1961b). The TTR is thus an indicator of redundant word usage. Pilot research by Jaffe showed a normal frequency distribution of dyadic TTR values in integrated conversation (Jaffe, 1958). Departures from the normal pattern or central tendency of TTR values for a given dyad can be considered indicative of changes in the pattern of communication taking place.

Dyadic analysis of pre- and posttreatment interviews and of a third interview at time of discharge of a successfully treated psychotic patient showed TTR changes at critical points both within interviews and over a series of interviews (Jaffe, 1957). Within the interviews dramatic shifts in mean TTR levels or variation about these means appeared to mark the natural phasing of the interviews (Jaffe, 1961b). Jaffe speculated that these shifts may correlate with such clinical constructs as defensive maneuvering and stressful disorganization. The trend over the interview was toward such diminished variability accompanied by a general rise in mean values. Thus the communication of the dyad became more succinct with clinically judged recovery from psychosis. Other aspects of TTR validity have been examined in two experimental studies (Fink, Jaffe, & Kahn, 1960; Jaffe, Fink, & Kahn, 1960).

In the past few years the direction of Jaffe's research efforts has turned to pioneering investigations of the language behavior of the dyad and its members through development of computer-mediated techniques of lexical and nonlexical content analysis (Cassotta, Feldstein, & Jaffe, 1962; Jaffe, 1962). One such procedure involved transcription of the verbal material to punch cards or tape in computer language. Given this raw material, the computer can be programed to perform a variety of analyses (Jaffe, 1963). This procedure was demonstrated in an unpublished paper (Jaffe, 1962), the results of which seem to corroborate the findings discussed above. It also revealed a complicated pattern of stabilization in interactions, most notably a curious "tracking" phenomenon not wholly attributable to either member of the dyad. This tracking characteristic may well represent an independent manifestation of the equilibrium mechanisms found by Lennard and Bernstein (1960).

Analysis of Contingent Relationships

Some analysts working with the classical model have begun to focus on the contingent relationships between categories within summarizing units. Such a procedure enables one to make a different inference when Category A is associated with Category B than when it is associated with Category C. Used with appropriate summarizing units, this method yields infor-

mation concerning the associational structure of the communicator (Osgood, 1959; Pool, 1959).

This important recent advance largely overcomes a long-standing criticism of classical content analysis—that in ignoring transitional in favor of simple probabilities, content analysts fail to account systematically for the context in which the scoring unit occurs, and consequently each unit is assigned an inappropriately invariant meaning (Carroll et al., 1951, p. 27; McQuown, 1954; Pool, 1959, pp. 196–197). A related argument holds that scoring units are coded traditionally on the basis of their representational meanings rather than their instrumental meanings when, in fact, information bearing on the instrumental characteristics of the verbal behavior is required for the kind of inference the analyst wishes to make. Analysis of contingent relationships is one approach to dealing more directly with instrumental meanings in verbal behavior (Mahl, 1959b; Pool, 1959, pp. 206–212).

One such method, called "contingency analysis," was developed by Osgood (1959), but, to the writer's knowledge, has not been applied to therapeutic interview material in formal studies. A similar method was used by Rosenberg (1962) in an analysis of the contingencies of topics discussed in group therapy. A study of contingent relationships by Auld and White (1959) is discussed below among studies based on another content-analysis model.

Laffal developed a method called "analysis of contextual associates," which is rooted in recent word-association research which shows, in part, that word associations appear in clusters corresponding to semantic superordinate structures or categories, and that common factors underlie single and continuous word associations (Laffal, 1964; Laffal & Feldman, 1962). Using the word as the scoring unit, Laffal developed a category system representing possible superordinates for most of the words appearing in English language samples. Words were coded to categories on the basis of synonymity or denotative closeness. This procedure reduces the diversity of meaning in a speech sample, thereby facilitating comparison of categories across summarizing units (Laffal, 1961, 1963, 1964).

This system was first applied to the examination of certain key words in the autobiography of a psychotic patient, Daniel Paul Schreber, in an effort to throw light on the symbolic meaning of the sun and God in his delusional system (Laffal, 1960). In a second study (Laffal, 1961), the verbal behavior of a schizophrenic patient was analyzed and compared with the results of a similar analysis of a second psychotic patient and with the language of Schreber's autobiography. The results showed that the coding reliability was high, that the method discriminated clearly the spoken and written language of different individuals, and that the language of a patient in one psychological state (unimproved) could be sharply differentiated from his language in another (markedly improved). Watson and Laffal (1963) have also explored the coherence of therapists' verbal behavior with different patients. The language categories used by patients were uncorrelated, while those used by the therapists in describing one patient were significantly correlated with their language in describing another.

A strikingly similar system has been developed by Harway and Iker (1964, in press). It differs in that the analysis was conducted largely by computer. A detailed description of the computer programs involved appears in an unpublished paper by Iker and Harway.[5]

Investigation of Internal States

A number of workers have used classical content-analysis methods to study the emo-

tional and other internal states of participants in therapeutic interviews. This was one of the earliest applications of content analysis to therapeutic interview research (Auld & Murray, 1955; Lasswell, 1935). Many early studies sought to establish, for a given individual, a more or less permanent level of the state in question. In the period covered by this paper, this aim has largely given way to the investigation of momentary changes. One focus of these efforts has been to specify changes in both lexical and nonlexical communication content. Such changes are then interpreted as indicative of changes in internal states.

The Discomfort-Relief Quotient (DRQ) is a lexical measure introduced by Dollard and Mowrer (1947) and assumed to tap drive-tension levels. It is computed by dividing the number of discomfort expressions (pain, unhappiness) by the number of discomfort plus relief expressions (happiness, pleasure, satisfaction). A series of such quotients, calculated periodically, yields a record of change in relative frequencies of discomfort and relief expressions, presumably reflecting differential handling of drive tension, and thus indicating movement in treatment. Research prior to 1954 investigating the relation of the DRQ to therapy movement and success yielded mixed results (Auld & Murray, 1955; Mowrer, Light, Luria, & Zeleny, 1953). More recently, Murray, Auld, and White (1954) compared DRQ ratings with the results of a content analysis in which patient material was coded in terms of motivation and conflict. While the DRQ showed no decrease in discomfort levels over the course of treatment, the other content analysis showed very real movement. The authors concluded that the DRQ is not as useful as other content measures for assessing therapeutic progress. However, a study by Proff (1952) and discussion of his findings by Callis, Polmantier, and Roeber (1957) suggested that the DRQ may reflect movement "toward problem solution" if it is computed on the basis of

[5] H. P. Iker and N. I. Harway. A computer approach toward the analysis of content. Submitted for publication.

patient discussion of feeling-laden material rather than "cognitive" material.

Lebo and Applegate (1958) and Callis et al. (1957) found that DRQ ratings depended in part on the topic of discussion. The former concluded that to the extent that therapists influence topics of discussion, DRQ ratings reflect an interaction effect between therapist and patient rather than a purely internal state of the patient. Auld and Mahl (1956) compared DRQ ratings with the results of another content-analysis scheme designed to yield a measure of drive tension as manifested in the variables anxiety, hostility, and dependency. Correlations between the DRQ and global ratings of these three variables, taken separately and together, were positive but small. The authors concluded that if the combined criterion variables are measures of drive tension the DRQ is not a very good measure of individual differences in drive tension.

Mahl developed a nonlexical method of investigating momentary anxiety in patients. He examined two general aspects of patients' speech: hesitancies and longer silences, and disturbances in speech. These phenomena, Mahl argued, can be considered either defensive behaviors designed to ward off or delay anxiety-provoking material, or as the disruptive, nondefensive consequences of anxiety on complex forms of behavior such as language production (Mahl, 1956, 1959a). Silence was measured in terms of a quotient yielded by dividing the number of seconds of silence during 2-minute segments of interview time by the number of those seconds during which the patient might have spoken (i.e., seconds not filled by therapist talk). Relatively little research using this measure has been reported, and Mahl (1956, 1961; Kasl & Mahl, 1956) has discussed complications in its use.

Far more work has been reported with Mahl's measure of speech disturbance. He identified eight types of speech disruption in interview protocols, among them the "ah" sound, repetitions, stuttering, tongue slips, and omissions. Analysis of a variety of speech materials indicated such disturbances are ubiquitous in spoken English, though they pass largely unnoticed. The occurrence of these, as identified from tape recordings and typescripts, was used to calculate a Speech-Disturbance Ratio for 2-minute summarizing units of patient speech. The ratio represents the number of speech disturbances divided by the number of words spoken by the patient. Subsequently, Mahl found that the "ah" sound, unlike other disruptions, did not vary with other measures of anxiety, and he has excluded it from the ratio, now called the Non-Ah Ratio (Kasl & Mahl, 1958; Mahl, 1958, 1959a, 1959b). This finding has been disputed by Panek and Martin (1959), and by Boomer. Boomer (1963) found that when Mahl's original Speech-Disturbance Ratio was divided into three types of speech-disruption phenomena, and their occurrence correlated with simultaneous nonpurposeful body movements (considered an independent indicator of anxiety), the resulting positive correlations differed markedly in magnitude and statistical significance. The "ah" and repetitions type were most highly correlated ($.42$, $p < .01$). Still, Mahl (1959a, 1959b) has summarized several investigations, providing evidence for the validity of the Non-Ah Ratios as measures of anxiety. An attempt by Boomer and Goodrich (1961) to replicate and extend one of these studies yielded inconclusive results.

In two investigations, Jaffe (1961a) and Feldstein and Jaffe (1962a) attempted to relate the Non-Ah Ratio, as on indicator of anxiety, to the TTR, as a measure of vocabulary diversity indicating general affective arousal including anxiety. In the first, a significant negative relationship obtained, but the data were derived from only two interviews with a single patient. In the second, 30 nonpsychiatric patients were compared with 30 schizophrenics on their responses to stimulus pictures. In this study a significant inverse relationship resulted for the nonpsychiatric patients, but the relationship, while negative, was not significant for the schizophrenic patients who were, however, on tranquilizing drugs. In another study, Feldstein and Jaffe (1962b) found that neither the Non-Ah Ratio, nor the occurrence of "ahs" was related to experimentally induced anger.

As part of a larger study, Pope and Siegman (1962) tested the hypothesis that patient speech disruption (anxiety) is negatively related to their measure of therapist activity level and to Lennard and Bernstein's measure of therapist specificity in the preceding therapist utterances. Using the original Speech-Disturbance Ratio, they found that the hypothesis with respect to therapist activity level was not confirmed, but that as therapist specificity increased, patient speech disturbances decreased in the following patient response.

In several studies Mahl found evidence to confirm his judgment that nonlexical content-analysis systems provide a better route to the study of emotional states than systems based on lexical content only (Mahl, 1960b; Schulze, Mahl, & Murray, 1960). Low correlations between his speech-disturbance and silence measures and Gottschalk's anxiety scale based on the same two interviews (Mahl, 1961) confirmed his belief and provided fuel for a spirited methodological debate in the volume in which this study appeared. In a recent paper, Mahl (1960a) analyzed speech-disturbance findings in relation to the lexical behavior of the patient, demonstrating the idiosyncratic manner in which defensive and anxious behavior manifests itself in lexical content. Other internal state studies, some of them relevant to the anxiety construct, include Dibner (1956, 1958), Eldred, Hamburg, Inwood, Salzman, Meyersburg, and Goodrich (1954) and Kanfer (1959, 1960).

Thus, classical model content-analysis studies of internal, psychodynamic states have shifted from an emphasis on exploring drive tension with the DRQ, a measure based on lexical indicators, to examination of constructs such as anxiety with measures using nonlexical indicators. It is not clear whether this trend reflects the changing interests of content analysts, or a change in their judgment about which methods are most fruitful for content-analysis investigation, or both. Many writers, but perhaps most pointedly Mahl (1959a), Strupp (1962a, pp. 590–591, 1962b, pp. 35–36), and Gottschalk (1961, p. 161), have discussed the fundamental philosophical and methodological problems facing those who investigate emotional and other internal states through classical content analysis. Mahl attempted to resolve these issues by remaining within the fold, forswearing work with lexical aspects in favor of the nonlexical, expressive dimensions of verbal behavior. Others, notably Matarazzo and associates and Jaffe, made a similar choice. Still others responded by departing from the classical model in favor of the pragmatic model of content analysis.

PRAGMATIC MODEL STUDIES

Gottschalk and his associates have developed one such system. After early research on psychogrammatical categories of word types (Gottschalk, Gleser, & Hambidge, 1957; Gottschalk & Hambidge, 1955; Gottschalk, Kaplan, Gleser, & Winget, 1962) their attention turned to psychodynamic trends in thematic material (Gottschalk, Gleser, Daniels, & Block, 1958; Gottschalk & Kaplan, 1958; Kaplan & Gottschalk, 1958), resulting most notably in the development of scales considered sensitive to both conscious and unconscious material for measuring anxiety (Gleser, Gottschalk, & Springer, 1961; Gottschalk, Gleser, Springer, Kaplan, Shanon, & Ross, 1960), hostility (Gottschalk, Gleser, & Springer, 1963; Gottschalk et al., 1960; Kaplan, Gottschalk, Magliocco, Rohovit, & Ross, 1961), and severity of schizophrenic disorganization (Gottschalk et al., 1958;

Gottschalk, Gleser, Magliocco, & D'Zmura, 1961). Recently these scales have been applied to the analysis of successive 5-minute intervals of two psychotherapeutic interviews (Gottschalk, Springer, & Gleser, 1961) and 5-minute samples from psychoanalytic sessions (Gottschalk et al., 1963).

The fundamental assumptions underlying these scales were derived from psychoanalytic theory of defense mechanisms, affects, and primary and secondary process thought. The category structures, varying from scale to scale, consisted of themes found in the verbal content. The scoring unit used in recent years is the grammatical clause, and each unit was coded to all categories to which it was relevant. Relevance is a highly inferential matter, requiring a clinical judgment concerning the suppressed or repressed meanings of the unit to the patient. It is precisely for these kinds of analyses, where more objective methods are considered deficient, that the pragmatic model was developed. Coding reliability has averaged in the low to mid-80's. Validity studies of the hostility and anxiety scales are summarized in Gottschalk et al. (1963), and Gleser et al. 1(961) and Gottschalk et al. (1962), respectively, while validity data on the schizophrenic disorganization scale can be found in Gottschalk and Gleser (1962) and Gottschalk et al. (1958, 1961).

Murray developed a pragmatic system rooted in psychoanalytic and learning theory which focused on internal emotional processes. Recognizing the complexity of the relationship between verbal behavior and underlying drive structure, his strategy was to infer the patient's needs, motivations, and conflicts from conscious or "face-value" meanings of the patient's speech. While he subsequently elaborated his category structure, his scoring unit, the grammatical clause or simple sentence, has remained unchanged. He is one of few content analysts of therapeutic interviews to take the problem of unit definition and rationale seriously (Murray, 1954; Murray, Auld, & White, 1954).

Two years later Murray (1956) published a description of his system as it was then formulated, together with summaries of studies bearing on its reliability and validity. There were four major patient drive categories: sex, affection, dependence, and independence. Each of these contained three subcategories of drive components: approach, anxiety, and frustration. In addition, there were special categories for residual patient units. Therapist categories, introduced for the first time, facilitated coding active and passive remarks and certain other aspects of therapist behavior. Murray applied this system to a published case of client-centered therapy. His hypotheses were that patient categories containing statements followed by therapist remarks having mild approval value would increase in frequency in the course of therapy, and that patient categories containing statements followed by therapist remarks having mild disapproval value would diminish in frequency over the course of therapy. Both hypotheses were supported. In another study (Schulze, Mahl, & Murray, 1960), Mahl's Speech-Disturbance Ratio was negatively related to Murray's measure of anxiety in one case and showed no relationship in several others. Speech disturbance was related to some of Murray's other categories, however, in ways specific to the individual patients. Application of a modified version of Murray's system to two cases of Rosen's direct analysis has also been reported (Murray, 1962).

Stimulated by Murray's work, Dollard and Auld (1959) developed a complex content-analysis system which constitutes the most thoroughgoing current example of the pragmatic model. Developed empirically out of the mix of their psychoanalytic and learning-theory orientation, their clinical sensitivity and their data, the category system ranged across the area of overt behavior, symptoms, and aspects of the therapeutic process. But its essential focus was on the dynamic motive states of the patient. These could be either conscious or unconscious. Motives were considered conscious if the patient could name them as his own. Unconscious motives were those that the patient never learned to label appropriately. They are nonetheless recognizable, the authors asserted, and can be coded (Dollard & Auld, 1959, pp. 2–3, 4). There were also categories for processes associated with motives and for motive referents. In contrast to the complexity of the 78 patient categories, there were only 6 broad therapist categories. For both patient and therapist categories the scoring unit was the statement or simple sentence used by Murray, but more adequately discussed and defined (Auld & White, 1956). In addition, in those patient categories depending on nonverbal overt behavior temporal scoring units of 5 seconds were used. The contextual unit for both sets of categories was the material in the case preceding the unit in question.

Dollard and Auld discussed at length the reliability of their coding system, together with the rationale for the study of reliability of content-analysis data. They presented their own reliability data broken down to make possible study of a case profile, one category over a series of interviews, and single-unit coding. Some of their categories were found to be quite reliable, others were not. They provided a useful discussion of the possible reasons for these problems and their implications.

Thus far, relatively little work has been done on the validity of the system, though an argument for its construct validity was presented by Auld (1961). Preliminary work (Dollard & Auld, 1959) suggested that certain categories may differentiate between neurotic and psychotic patients. Theory-based predictions about relationships between certain categories were significantly supported in four cases and were in the predicted direction in several others. Auld and White (1959) applied the sys-

tem to four cases of psychoanalytically oriented psychotherapy. Using a method of sequential dependency analysis modification, they found that patients' speech was likely to persist in the same category to which the previous unit was coded, that psychoanalytically oriented therapists were more likely to intervene after resistances than at other times, that interpretations were not followed by heightened resistance in the following patient units, and that silence and speech judged resistant tended to occur in units that followed one another, thus providing a basis for the authors' conclusion that these are equivalent forms of resistance. To check on the possibility of bias in the classification of "resistant speech," Goldenberg (1961; cited in Auld, 1961) repeated this portion of the Auld and White study with methodological improvements. His results strongly confirmed theirs. White, Fichtenbaum, and Dollard (1964) successfully used a modification of this system to predict continuation in treatment of psychiatric outpatients from an analysis of initial interviews.

Sklansky, Isaacs, and Haggard (1960) devised a pragmatic model system based on psychoanalytic concepts designed to elucidate the verbal interaction of psychotherapy and its therapeutic effect by studying the manifest and latent meanings of the patient's communication in relation to certain aspects of the therapist's responses. The scoring unit for the patient was the topical segment, defined as the conversation occurring between two successive points at which the patient changes the topic. The scoring unit for the therapist was each therapist response within each topical segment. The contextual unit for both patient and therapist scoring units was the preceding therapy sessions.

Patient units were read by experienced psychotherapist judges who interpreted them at as many meaning levels as seemed useful, ranging from the manifest to the deeply unconscious. Three or four levels were usual. Each patient unit was stated as if the patient had uttered it explicitly in the language of the level to which it had been assigned. Then each therapist response within the topical segment in question was coded as being either ego syntonic or egodystonic for the patient and either a direct, indirect, or irrelevant response to the patient at each of these meaning levels. The authors carefully pointed out the methodological difficulties concerning the reliability of the operations performed on the patient units; meaning levels are a function of rater sensitivity and theoretical orientation, and agreements on unconscious meanings are noted for their unreliability. Their best solution to this problem was to work for consensual validation among several experienced judges of similar theoretical persuasions.

The method was found to differentiate among patients in terms of their manner of response and among therapists in terms of their therapeutic style. It also differentiated early and late sessions for a given patient-therapist pair. They found that when the therapist's response was direct at the manifest level and irrelevant at deeper levels the topic tended to be dropped by the patient at all levels. When the therapist's responses were direct at the manifest level and indirect at latent levels the topic continued to be discussed even if the therapist made occasional responses irrelevant at all levels. When the therapist responded directly at the manifest and at some of the latent levels, therapeutic activity seemed to be facilitated, but when the therapist's responses were directly pitched to latent-meaning levels and only indirectly dealt with the manifest level, there was a tendency for the patient to change the topic after a short time. Ego-syntonic responses facilitated therapeutic work while ego-dystonic responses impeded it, though occasional direct but ego-dystonic responses sometimes had the effect of shocking the patient into more intensive therapeutic work.

Others have used the pragmatic model in whole or in part. Ashby, Ford, Guerney, and Guerney (1957) used several pragmatic variables as part of a larger study, as have Glad and Glad (1964) who used their system to study the relationship of patient behavior in group psychotherapy to therapist behavior and to certain patient personality variables (Glad, Hayne, Glad, & Ferguson, 1963). Frostig and Horne (1963) used a pragmatic model system to evaluate the treatment of psychotic children. Several other studies discussed elsewhere in this paper employed pragmatic model elements (Bandura et al., 1960; Cutler, 1958; Eldred et al., 1954; Speisman, 1959; Strupp, 1960; Winder et al., 1962).

NONQUANTITATIVE MODEL STUDIES: LINGUISTIC ANALYSIS

If pragmatic model systems facilitate work with dynamic constructs for which behavioral cues cannot be specified, linguistic analysis holds forth hope of making possible identification of these cues through a basically nonquantitative approach or through its combination with appropriate statistical techniques. Many studies treated elsewhere in this paper have been enriched by the work of linguists, particularly those involving various forms of speech disruption which the linguist knows as paralinguistic phenomena. The studies treated in this section, however, are those utilizing or critically testing the techniques of linguistics, particularly microlinguistics, as the basis of analysis.

The conventions and rationale of linguistic analysis were presented to workers in therapeutic interview research after 1957 in papers by Pittenger and Smith (1957) and Pittenger (1958). The first of these discussed several interview-research applications of linguistic analysis. Among them were identification of the specific linguistic cues which are the source of hunches and impressions achieved in traditional clinical work, development of more useful descriptive analyses of interaction patterns, and more precise understanding of differences in communication patterns believed to have diagnostic significance such as "flattened affect" in schizophrenia. Such questions were explored by Pittenger, Hockett, and Danehy (1960) in an exciting and incredibly rich examination of the first 5 minutes of an initial psychiatric interview. This study combined the tools of linguistic and paralinguistic analysis and clinical inference in an effort to generate as much data as possible about this brief interlude in the lives of two people. Their skillful weaving together of these various kinds and levels of analysis demonstrated clearly that linguistic techniques applied to interview materials can produce insights quite impossible without them.

McQuown (1957) performed a classical content analysis on the data resulting from a linguistic analysis of the first half hour of an interview. His categories were designed to distinguish the cultural background norm of linguistic and paralinguistic behavior from the personality-defining departures from this norm. From the frequencies of linguistic phenomena in these categories, he developed personality profiles of both the psychoanalyst and the patient.

Eldred and Price (1958) attempted to explore the relationships between four dimensions of the paralinguistic phenomena called "vocalization" and the clinical impression of certain affect states in the patient. They characterized each passage judged as expressing one of five affective states in terms of the vocalization pattern it reflected. They also characterized the patient's normal speaking voice in each interview. The findings showed alterations in the relatively stable patterns of normal voice over the period of 12 months from which the interviews were drawn. Affect states were characterized differently than the normal voice material in the rest of the interview in which an affect passage occurred. Furthermore, each of the affect

states, except anxiety, was characterized by a different vocalization pattern.

An unfortunate weakness in this provocative study is the absence of any statistical reliability measures of the various judgments made, or of the significance of results. This is particularly regrettable in light of a study by Dittmann and Wynne (1961) investigating the relationship between linguistic phenomena and the clinical impression of affect. This study was broader in scope, including both linguistic and paralinguistic features, and applied more appropriate statistical tests. The results indicated that the paralinguistic features could not meet statistical reliability standards. The linguistic features could be identified reliably, but were unrelated to affect.

Other developments in this area too recent to evaluate at this time, include the work of Scheflen (1963) described in a recent paper and to be elaborated in a forthcoming book (Scheflen, English, Hampe, & Auerbach, in press) in which linguistic, paralinguistic, kinesic, tactile, and other modes of communication are studied separately and in relation to each other. Another forthcoming volume (McQuown, in press) uses linguistic and kinesic data in the analysis of a therapeutic interview. A few studies based on kinesic data have begun to appear (Birdwhistell, 1960; Boomer, 1963; Dittman, 1962; Ekman, 1964).

CONCLUSION

Two general comments are in order. Discussions of content-analysis methodology tend to treat the problem of unit and category selection as relatively unrelated issues. This tendency is manifest in most of the studies considered in this paper. While specific category systems were developed, presumably because of their relation to the research problem, choice of units has often reflected only the need to divide communication material into segments in a systematic fashion. Infrequently have investigators argued for their choice of a unit in terms of its logical or psychological relation to either the category structure or the questions under investigation.

Despite the burgeoning of content-analysis studies of therapeutic interviews in the past two decades (Auld & Murray, 1955), one is struck by the relative infrequency with which any of these systems has resulted in more than an initial thrust at a given research problem. System after system has been developed and presented in one or two demonstration studies, only to lie buried in the literature, unused even by its author, Moreover, few variables or notions about therapeutic interviews have received anything approaching programmatic or extensive content-analysis investigation. This has resulted in redundancy; systems were developed with apparent unawareness that other approaches to the same problem, or efforts to apply the same approach to other problems, had already been reported. Happily, some recent studies suggest that this pattern may be changing.

REFERENCES

ASHBY, J. D., FORD, D. H., GUERNEY, B. G., JR., & GUERNEY, LOUISE F. Effects on clients of a reflective and a leading type of psychotherapy. *Psychological Monographs*, 1957, 71(24, Whole No. 453).

AUERBACH, A. H. An application of Strupp's method of content analysis to psychotherapy. *Psychiatry*, 1963, 26, 137–148.

AULD, F., JR. Emotions in the interview: Can they be measured? *Psychological Reports*, 1961, 8, 239–242.

AULD, F., JR., & MAHL, G. F. A comparison of the DRQ with ratings of emotion. *Journal of Abnormal and Social Psychology*, 1956, 53, 386–388.

AULD, F., JR., & MURRAY, E. J. Content-analysis studies of psychotherapy. *Psychological Bulletin*, 1955, 52, 377–395.

AULD, F., JR., & WHITE, ALICE M. Rules for dividing interviews into sentences. *Journal of Psychology*, 1956, 42, 273–281.

AULD, F., JR., & WHITE, ALICE M. Sequential dependencies in psychotherapy. *Journal of Abnormal and Social Psychology*, 1959, 58, 100–104.

BALES, R. F. *Interaction process analysis.* Cambridge: Addison-Wesley Press, 1950.

BALES, R. F. The equilibrium problem in small groups. In T. Parsons, R. F. Bales, & E. A. Shils, *Working papers in the theory of action.* Glencoe, Ill.: Free Press, 1953.

BALES, R. F., & STRODTBECK, F. L. Phases in group problem solving. *Journal of Abnormal and Social Psychology*, 1951, 46, 485–495.

BANDURA, A., LIPSHER, D. H., & MILLER, PAULA E. Psychotherapists' approach-avoidance reactions to patients' expressions of hostility. *Journal of Consulting Psychology*, 1960, 24, 1–8.

BERELSON, B. *Content analysis in communications research.* Glencoe, Ill.: Free Press, 1952.

BERG, I. A. Ford choice in the interview and personal adjustment. *Journal of Counseling Psychology*, 1958, 5, 130–135.

BIRDWHISTELL, R. L. Critical moments in the psychiatric interview. Paper read at the Tenth Anniversary Symposium, Galesburg State Research Hospital, Galesburg, Illinois, October, 1960.

BLOCK, W. E. A preliminary study of achievement motive theory as a basis of patient expectations in psychotherapy. *Journal of Clinical Psychology*, 1964, 20, 268–271.

BOOMER, D. S. Speech disturbance and body movement in interviews. *Journal of Nervous and Mental Disease*, 1963, 136, 263–266.

BOOMER, D. S. Linguistics and speech behavior. In, *Monograph series on language and linguistics.* (No. 17) Washington, D.C.: Georgetown Univer. Press, 1964. Pp. 149–154.

BOOMER, D. S., & GOODRICH, D. W. Speech disturbance and judged anxiety. *Journal of Consulting Psychology*, 1961, 25, 160–164.

BORDIN, E. S. Ambiguity as a therapeutic variable. *Journal of Consulting Psychology*, 1955, 19, 9–15.

BORDIN, E. S., CUTLER, R. L., DITTMANN, A. T., HARWAY, N. I., RAUSH, H. L., & RIGLER, D. Measurement problems in process research on psychotherapy. *Journal of Consulting Psychology*, 1954, 18, 79–82.

BRAATEN, L. J. The movement from non-self to

self in client-centered psychotherapy. *Journal of Counseling Psychology*, 1961, 8, 20–24.

CALLIS, R., POLMANTIER, P. C., & ROEBER, E. C. Five years of research on counseling. *Journal of Counseling Psychology*, 1957, 4, 119–123.

CAMPBELL, R. E. Counselor personality and background and his interview subrole behavior. *Journal of Counseling Psychology*, 1962, 9, 329–334.

CARROLL, J. B. *The study of language.* Cambridge: Harvard Univer. Press, 1955.

CARROLL, J. B., AGARD, F. B., DULANY, D. E., NEWMAN, S. S., NEWMARK, L. D., OSGOOD, C. E., SEBEOK, T. A., & SOLOMON, R. L. Report and recommendations of the interdisciplinary summer seminar in psychology and linguistics. Unpublished manuscript, Harvard Graduate School of Education Library, 1951.

CASSOTTA, L., FELDSTEIN, S., & JAFFE, J. A device for automatic extraction and quantification of vocal behavior in interviews. Based on paper read at Eastern Psychological Association, Atlantic City, April 1962.

COLBY, K. M. Experiment on the effects of an observer's presence on the imago system during psychoanalytic free-association. *Behavioral Science*, 1960, 5, 216–232.

CONRAD, DOROTHY C., & CONRAD, R. The use of personal pronouns as categories for studying small group interaction. *Journal of Abnormal and Social Psychology*, 1956, 52, 277–279.

CUTLER, R. L. Countertransference effects in psychotherapy. *Journal of Consulting Psychology*, 1958, 22, 249–256.

CUTLER, R. L., BORDIN, E. S., WILLIAMS, JOAN, & RIGLER, D. Psychoanalysts as expert observers of the therapy process. *Journal of Counseling Psychology*, 1958, 22, 335–340.

DANSKIN, D. G. Roles played by counselors in their interviews. *Journal of Counseling Psychology*, 1955, 2, 22–27.

DANSKIN, D. G., & ROBINSON, F. P. Differences in "degree of lead" among experienced counselors. *Journal of Counseling Psychology*, 1954, 1, 78–83.

DIBNER, A. S. Cue-counting: A measure of anxiety in interviews. *Journal of Counseling Psychology*, 1956, 20, 475–478.

DIBNER, A. S. Ambiguity and anxiety. *Journal of Abnormal and Social Psychology*, 1958, 56, 165–174.

DINOFF, M., KEW, J. K., RICKARD, H. C., & TIMMONS, E. O. The stability of group verbal behavior. *Psychological Record,* 1962, 12, 323–325.

DIPBOYE, W. J. Analysis of counselor style by discussion units. *Journal of Counseling Psychology*, 1954, 1, 21–26.

DITTES, J. E. Previous studies bearing on content analysis of psychotherapy. In J. Dollard & F. Auld, Jr., *Scoring human motives: A manual.* New Haven: Yale Univer. Press, 1959. Appendix A.

DITTMANN, A. T. The relationship between body movements and moods in interviews. *Journal of Counseling Psychology*, 1962, 26, 480.

DITTMANN, A. T., & WYNNE, L. C. Linguistic techniques and the analysis of emotionality in interviews. *Journal of Abnormal and Social Psychology*, 1961, 63, 201–204.

DOLLARD, J., & AULD, F., JR. *Scoring human motives: A manual.* New Haven: Yale Univer. Press, 1959.

DOLLARD, J., & MOWRER, O. H. A method of measuring tension in written documents. *Journal of Abnormal and Social Psychology*, 1947, 42, 3–32.

EKMAN, P. Body position, facial expression, and verbal behavior during interviews. *Journal of Abnormal and Social Psychology*, 1964, 68, 295–301.

ELDRED, S. H., HAMBURG, D. A., INWOOD, E. R., SALZMAN, L., MEYERSBURG, H. A., & GOODRICH, GENEVA. A procedure for the systematic analysis of psychotherapeutic interviews. *Psychiatry.* 1954, 17, 337–345.

ELDRED, S. H., & PRICE, D. B. A linguistic evaluation of feeling states in psychotherapy. *Psychiatry*, 1958, 21, 115–121.

FELDSTEIN, S., & JAFFE, J. A note about speech disturbances and vocabulary diversity. *Journal of Communication*, 1962, 12, 166–170. (a)

FELDSTEIN, S., & JAFFE, J. The relationship of speech disruption to the experience of anger. *Journal of Consulting Psychology*, 1962, 26, 505–509. (b)

FINE, H. J., & ZIMET, C. N. A quantitative method of scaling communication and interaction process. *Journal of Clinical Psychology*, 1956, 12, 268–271.

FINK, M., JAFFE, J., & KAHN, R. L. Drug induced changes in interview patterns: Linguistic and neurophysiologic indices. In G. J. Sarwer-Foner (Ed.), *The dynamics of psychiatric drug therapy*. Springfield, Ill.: Charles C. Thomas, 1960. Pp. 29–37.

FIRTH, J. R. Linguistic analysis and translation. In, *For Roman Jakobson: Essays on the occasion of his sixtieth birthday*. The Hague: Mouton, 1956. Pp. 133–139.

FISHER, S. Plausibility and depth of interpretation. *Journal of Counseling Psychology*, 1956, 20, 249–256.

FRANK, G. H., & SWEETLAND, A. A study of the process of psychotherapy: The verbal interaction. *Journal of Counseling Psychology*, 1962, 26, 135–138.

FROSTIG, MARIANNE, & HORNE, D. Changes in language and behavior in psychotic children during successful therapy: Method of evaluation and findings. *American Journal of Orthopsychiatry*, 1963, 33, 734–737.

GEORGE, A. L. *Propaganda analysis: A study of inferences made from Nazi propaganda in World War II*. Evanston, Ill.: Row, Peterson, 1959. (a)

GEORGE, A. L. Quantitative and qualitative approaches to content analysis. In I. Pool (Ed.), *Trends in content analysis*. Urbana: Univer. Illinois Press, 1959. Pp. 7–32. (b)

GLAD, D. D., & GLAD, VIRGINIA B. *Interpersonality synopsis*. New York: Libra, 1964.

GLAD, D. D., HAYNE, M. L., GLAD, VIRGINIA B., & FERGUSON, R. E. Schizophrenic factor reactions to four group psychotherapy methods. *International Journal of Group Psychotherapy*, 1963, 13, 196–210.

GLESER, GOLDINE C., GOTTSCHALK, L. A., & SPRINGER, KAYLA J. An anxiety scale applicable to verbal samples. *Archives of General Psychiatry*, 1961, 5, 593–605.

GOLDENBERG, G. M. Silence as a form of resistance. Unpublished master's thesis, Wayne State University, 1961.

GOTTSCHALK, L. A. (Ed.) *Comparative psycholinguistic analysis of two psychotherapeutic interviews*. New York: International Universities Press, 1961.

GOTTSCHALK, L. A., & GLESER, GOLDINE C. Distinguishing characteristics of the verbal communications of schizophrenic patients. *Proceedings of the Association for Research in Nervous and Mental Disease on Disorders of Communication*. Baltimore: Williams & Wilkins, 1962.

GOTTSCHALK, L. A., GLESER, GOLDINE C., DANIELS, R. S., & BLOCK, S. The speech patterns of schizophrenic patients: A method of assessing relative degree of personal disorganization and social alienation. *Journal of Nervous and Mental Disease*, 1958, 127, 153–166.

GOTTSCHALK, L. A., GLESER, GOLDINE C., & HAMBIDGE, G., JR. Verbal behavior analysis. *Archives of Neurology and Psychiatry*, 1957, 77, 300–311.

GOTTSCHALK, L. A., GLESER, GOLDINE C., MAGLIOCCO, E. B., & D'ZMURA, T. L. Further studies on the speech pattern of schizophrenic patients. *Journal of Nervous and Mental Disease*, 1961, 132, 101–113.

GOTTSCHALK, L. A., GLESER, GOLDINE C., & SPRINGER, KAYLA J. Three hostility scales applicable to verbal samples. *Archives of General Psychiatry*, 1963, 9, 254–279.

GOTTSCHALK, L. A., GLESER, GOLDINE C., SPRINGER, KAYLA J., KAPLAN, S. M., SHANON, J., & ROSS, W. D. Effects of perphenazine on verbal behavior patterns. *Archives of General Psychiatry*, 1960, 2, 632–639.

GOTTSCHALK, L. A., & HAMBIDGE, G., JR. Verbal behavior analysis: A systematic approach to the problem of quantifying psychologic processes. *Journal of Projective Techniques*, 1955, 19, 387–409.

GOTTSCHALK, L. A., & KAPLAN, S. A quantitative method of estimating variations in intensity of a psychologic conflict or state. *Archives of Neurology and Psychiatry*, 1958, 79, 688–696.

GOTTSCHALK, L. A., KAPLAN, S. M., GLESER, GOLDINE C., & WINGET, CAROLYN M. Variations in magnitude of emotion: A method applied to anxiety and hostility during phases of the menstrual cycle. *Psychosomatic Medicine*, 1962, 24, 300–311.

GOTTSCHALK, L. A., SPRINGER, KAYLA J., & GLESER, GOLDINE C. Experiments with a method of assessing the variations in intensity of certain psychologic states occurring during two psychotherapeutic interviews. In L. A. Gottschalk (Ed.), *Comparative psycholinguistic analysis of two psychotherapeutic interviews*. New York: International Universities Press, 1961. Ch. 7.

GOUGH, H. G. Clinical versus statistical prediction in psychology. In L. Postman (Ed.),

Psychology in the making. New York: Knopf, 1962. Ch. 9.

HARE, A. P., WAXLER, NANCY, SASLOW, G., & MATARAZZO, J. D. Simultaneous recording of Bales and Chapple interaction measures during initial psychiatric interviews. *Journal of Consulting Psychology,* 1960, 24, 193.

HARWAY, N. I., DITTMANN, A. T., RAUSH, H. L., BORDIN, E. S., & RIGLER, D. The measurement of depth of interpretation. *Journal of Consulting Psychology,* 1955, 19, 247–253.

HARWAY, N. I., & IKER, H. P. Computer analysis of content in psychotherapy. *Psychological Reports,* 1964, 14, 720–722.

HARWAY, N. I., & IKER, H. P. Objective content analysis of psychotherapy by computer. In K. Enslein (Ed.), *Data acquisition and processing in biology and medicine. Proceedings of the 1964 Rochester Conference.* New York: Pergamon Press, in press.

HECKEL, R. V., FROELICH, R. E., & SALZBERG, H. C. Interaction and redirection in group therapy. *Psychological Reports,* 1962, 10, 14.

HOFFMAN, A. E. An analysis of counselor subroles. *Journal of Counseling Psychology,* 1959, 6, 61–67.

HOIJER, H. (Ed.) *Language in culture.* Chicago: Univer. Chicago Press, 1954.

HOWE, E. S. Anxiety-arousal and specificity: Rated correlates of the depth of interpretive statements. *Journal of Consulting Psychology,* 1962, 26, 178–184. (a)

HOWE, E. S. A study of the semantic structure of ratings of interpretive responses. *Journal of Consulting Psychology,* 1962, 26, 285. (b)

HOWE, E. S. Three-dimensional structure of ratings of exploratory responses shown by a semantic differential. *Psychological Reports,* 1964, 14, 187–196.

HOWE, E. S., & POPE, B. The dimensionality of ratings of therapist verbal responses. *Journal of Consulting Psychology,* 1961, 25, 296–303. (a)

HOWE, E. S., & POPE, B. An empirical scale of therapist verbal activity level in the initial interview. *Journal of Consulting Psychology,* 1961, 25, 510–520. (b)

HOWE, E. S., & POPE, B. Therapist verbal activity level and diagnostic utility of patient verbal responses. *Journal of Consulting Psychology,* 1962, 26, 149–155.

JAFFE, J. An objective study of communication in phychiatric interviews. *Journal of the Hillside Hospital,* 1957, 6, 207–215.

JAFFE, J. Language of the dyad: A method of interaction analysis in psychiatric interviews. *Psychiatry,* 1958, 21, 249–258.

JAFFE, J. Discussion. In L. A. Gottschalk (Ed.), *Comparative psycholinguistic analysis of two psychotherapy interviews.* New York: International Universities Press, 1961. Pp. 162–173. (a)

JAFFE, J. Dyadic analysis of two psychotherapeutic interviews. In L. A. Gottschalk (Ed.), *Comparative psycholinguistic analysis of two psychotherapeutic interviews.* New York: International Universities Press, 1961. Ch. 5. (b)

JAFFE, J. Computer analysis of verbal behavior in psychiatric interviews. Paper read at Association for Research in Nervous and Mental Disease, New York, December 1962.

JAFFE, J. Electronic computers in psychoanalytic research. In J. H. Masserman (Ed.), *Science and psychoanalysis.* Vol. 6. New York: Grune & Stratton, 1963. Pp. 160–170.

JAFFE, J., FINK, M., & KAHN, R. L. Changes in verbal transactions with induced altered brain function. *Journal of Nervous and Mental Disease,* 1960, 130, 235–239.

KANFER, F. H. Verbal rate, content, and adjustment ratings in experimentally structured interviews. *Journal of Abnormal and Social Psychology,* 1959, 58, 305–311.

KANFER, F. H. Verbal rate, eyeblink, and content in structured psychiatric interviews. *Journal of Abnormal and Social Psychology,* 1960, 61, 341–347.

KANFER, F. H., PHILLIPS, JEANNE S., MATARAZZO, J. D., & SASLOW, G. Experimental modification of interviewer content in standardized interviews. *Journal of Consulting Psychology,* 1960, 24, 528–536.

KAPLAN, S. M., & GOTTSCHALK, L. A. Modifications of the oropharyngeal bacteria with changes in psychodynamic state. II. A validation study. *Psychosomatic Medicine,* 1958, 20, 314–320.

KAPLAN, S. M., GOTTSCHALK, L. A., MAGLIOCCO, E. B., ROHOVIT, D. D., & ROSS, W. D. Hostility in verbal productions and hypnotic "dreams" of hypertensive patients: Studies of groups and individuals. *Psychosomatic Medicine,* 1961, 23, 311–322.

KASL, S. V., & MAHL, G. F. A simple device for obtaining certain verbal activity measures during interviews. *Journal of Abnormal and Social Psychology*, 1956, 53, 388–390.

KASL, S. V., & MAHL, G. F. Experimentally induced anxiety and speech disturbance. *American Psychologist*, 1958, 13, 349. (Abstract)

KIESLER, D. J., MATHIEU, PHILLIPA L., & KLEIN, MARJORIE H. Sampling from the recorded therapy interview: A comparative study of different segment lengths. *Journal of Consulting Psychology*, 1964, 28, 349–357.

LAFFAL, J. The contextual associates of sun and God in Schreber's autobiography. *Journal of Abnormal and Social Psychology*, 1960, 61, 474–479.

LAFFAL, J. Changes in the language of a schizophrenic patient during psychotherapy. *Journal of Abnormal and Social Psychology*, 1961, 63, 422–427.

LAFFAL, J. The use of contextual associates in the analysis of free speech. *Journal of General Psychology*, 1963, 69, 51–64.

LAFFAL, J. Linguistic field theory and studies of word association. *Journal of General Psychology*, 1964, 71, 145–155.

LAFFAL, J., & FELDMAN, S. The structure of single word and continuous word associations. *Journal of Verbal Learning and Verbal Behavior*, 1962, 1, 54–61.

LASSWELL, H. D. Verbal references and physiological changes during the psychoanalytic interview: A preliminary communication. *Psychoanalytic Review*, 1935, 22, 10–24.

LEARY, T. Huck and Jim in their interpretive balloon. *Contemporary Psychology*, 1960, 5, 337–338.

LEARY, T., & GILL, M. The dimensions and a measure of the process of psychotherapy: A system for the analysis of the content of clinical evaluations and patient-therapist verbalizations. In E. A. Rubinstein & M. B. Parloff (Eds.), *Research in psychotherapy*. Washington, D.C.: American Psychological Association, 1959. Pp. 62–95.

LEBO, D., & APPLEGATE, W. The influence of instructional set upon the discomfort-relief quotient. *Journal of Clinical Psychology*, 1958, 14, 280–282.

LENNARD, H. L. Some aspects of the psychotherapeutic system. In H. H. Strupp & L. Luborsky (Eds.), *Research in psychotherapy*.

Vol. 2. Washington, D.C.: American Psychological Association, 1962. Pp. 218–236.

LENNARD, H. L., & BERNSTEIN, A. *The anatomy of psychotherapy*. New York: Columbia Univer. Press, 1960.

LENNARD, H. L., CALOGERAS, R., & HENDIN, HELEN. Some relationships between verbal behavior of therapist and patient in psychotherapy. *Journal of Psychology*, 1957, 43, 181–186.

LORENZ, MARIA. Expressive behavior and language patterns. *Psychiatry*, 1955, 18, 353–366.

LORENZ, MARIA, & COBB, S. Language patterns in psychotic and psychoneurotic subjects. *Archives of Neurology and Psychiatry*, 1954, 72, 665–673.

McQUOWN, N. A. Analysis of the cultural content of language materials. In H. Hoijer (Ed.), *Language in culture*. Chicago: Univer. Chicago Press, 1954. Pp. 20–31. (a)

McQUOWN, N. A. Cultural implications of linguistic science. *Monograph series on language and linguistics*. (No. 7) Washington, D.C.: Georgetown Univer. Press, 1954. Pp. 57–61. (b)

McQUOWN, N. A. Linguistic transcription and specification of psychiatric interview materials. *Psychiatry*, 1957, 20, 79–86.

McQUOWN, N. A. (Ed.) *The natural history of an interview*. New York: Grune & Stratton, in press.

MAHL, G. F. Disturbances and silences in the patient's speech in psychotherapy. *Journal of Abnormal and Social Psychology*, 1956, 53, 1–15.

MAHL, G. F. On the use of "ah" in spontaneous speech: Quantitative, developmental, characterological, situational, and linguistic aspects. *American Psychologist*, 1958, 13, 349. (Abstract)

MAHL, G. F. Exploring emotional states by content analysis. In I. Pool (Ed.), *Trends in content analysis*. Urbana: Univer. Illinois Press, 1959. Ch. 3. (a)

MAHL, G. F. Measuring the patient's anxiety during interviews from "expressive" aspects of his speech. *Transactions of the New York Academy of Sciences*, 1959, 21(Ser. 2), 249–257. (b)

MAHL, G. F. The expression of emotions on the lexical and linguistic levels. Paper read at American Association for the Advancement of Science Symposium, New York, December 1960. (a)

MAHL, G. F. Speech disturbances and emotional verbal content in initial interviews. In G. F. Mahl, The expression of emotions on the lexical and linguistic levels. Paper read at American Association for the Advancement of Science Symposium, New York, December, 1960. (b)

MAHL, G. F. Measures of two expressive aspects of a patient's speech in two psychotherapeutic interviews. In L. A. Gottschalk (Ed.), *Comparative psycholinguistic analysis of two psychotherapeutic interviews*. New York: International Universities Press, 1961. Ch. 6.

MATARAZZO, J. D. Prescribed behavior therapy: Suggestions from interview research. In A. J. Bachrach (Ed.), *Experimental foundations of clinical psychology*. New York: Basic Books, 1962. Ch. 14.

MATARAZZO, J. D., HESS, H. F., & SASLOW, G. Frequency and duration characteristics of speech and silence behavior during interviews. *Journal of Clinical Psychology,* 1962, 18, 416–426.

MATARAZZO, J. D., & SASLOW, G. Differences in interview interaction behavior among normal and deviant groups. In I. A. Berg & B. M. Bass (Eds.), *Conformity and deviation*. New York: Harper, 1961. Ch. 9.

MATARAZZO, J. D., SASLOW, G., & GUZE, S. B. Stability of interaction patterns during interviews: A replication. *Journal of Consulting Psychology,* 1956, 20, 267–274.

MATARAZZO, J. D., SASLOW, G., & HARE, A. P. Factor analysis of interview interaction behavior. *Journal of Consulting Psychology,* 1958, 22, 419–429.

MATARAZZO, J. D., SASLOW, G., & MATARAZZO, RUTH G. The interaction chronograph as an instrument for objective measurement of interaction patterns during interviews. *Journal of Psychology,* 1956, 41, 347–367.

MATARAZZO, J. D., SASLOW, G., MATARAZZO, RUTH G., & PHILLIPS, JEANNE S. Stability and modifiability of personality patterns manifested during a standardized interview. In P. H. Hoch & J. Zubin (Eds.), *Psychopathology of communication*. New York: Grune & Stratton, 1958. Ch. 8.

MATARAZZO, J. D., WEITMAN, M., & SASLOW, G. Interview content and interviewee speech

durations. *Journal of Clinical Psychology,* 1963, 19, 463–472.

MATARAZZO, J. D., WEITMAN, M., SASLOW, G., & WIENS, A. N. Interviewer influence on duration of interview speech. *Journal of Verbal Learning and Verbal Behavior,* 1963, 1, 451–458.

MATARAZZO, RUTH G., MATARAZZO, J. D., SASLOW, G., & PHILLIPS, JEANNE S. Psychological test and organismic correlates of interview interaction patterns. *Journal of Abnormal and Social Psychology,* 1958, 56, 329–338.

MOWRER, O. H. Changes in verbal behavior during psychotherapy. In O. H. Mowrer (Ed.), *Psychotherapy theory and research.* New York: Ronald Press, 153. Ch. 17.

MOWRER, O. H., LIGHT, B. H., LURIA, ZELLA, & ZELENY, MARJORIE. Tension changes during psychotherapy, with special reference to resistance. In O. H. Mowrer (Ed.), *Psychotherapy theory and research.* New York: Ronald Press, 1953. Ch. 18.

MURRAY, E. J. A case study in a behavioral analysis of psychotherapy. *Journal of Abnormal and Social Psychology,* 1954, 49, 305–310.

MURRAY, E. J. A content-analysis method for studying psychotherapy. *Psychological Monographs,* 1956, 70(13, Whole No. 420).

MURRAY, E. J. Direct analysis from the viewpoint of learning theory. *Journal of Consulting Psychology,* 1962, 26, 226–231.

MURRAY, E. J., AULD, F., JR., & WHITE, ALICE M. A psychotherapy case showing progress but no decrease in the discomfort-relief quotient. *Journal of Consulting Psychology,* 1954, 18, 349–353.

NOBLE, F., OHLSEN, M., & PROFF, F. A method for the quantification of psychotherapeutic interaction in counseling groups. *Journal of Counseling Psychology,* 1961, 8, 54–60.

OSGOOD, C. E. The representational model and relevant research methods. In I. Pool (Ed.), *Trends in content analysis.* Urbana: Univer. Illinois Press, 1959. Ch. 2.

PALMORE, E., LENNARD, H. L., & HENDIN, HELEN. Similarities of therapist and patient verbal behavior in psychotherapy. *Sociometry,* 1959, 22, 12–22.

PANEK, D. M., & MARTIN, B. The relationship between GSR and speech disturbances in psychotherapy. *Journal of Abnormal and Social Psychology,* 1959, 58, 402–405.

PHILLIPS, JEANNE S., MATARAZZO, J. D., MATARAZZO, RUTH G., & SASLOW, G. Observer reliability of interaction patterns during interviews. *Journal of Consulting Psychology,* 1957, 21, 269–275.

PHILLIPS, JEANNE S., MATARAZZO, RUTH G., MATARAZZO, J. D., SASLOW, G., & KANFER, F. H. Relationships between descriptive content and interaction behavior in interviews. *Journal of Consulting Psychology,* 1961, 25, 260–266.

PITTENGER, R. E. Linguistic analysis of tone of voice in communication of affect. *Psychiatric Research Reports,* 1958, 8, 41–54.

PITTENGER, R. E., HOCKETT, C. F., & DANEHY, J. J. *The first five minutes: A sample of microscopic interview analysis.* Ithaca, N.Y.: Paul Martineau, 1960.

PITTENGER, R. E., & SMITH, H. L., JR. A basis for some contributions of linguistics to psychiatry. *Psychiatry,* 1957, 20, 61–78.

POOL, I. Trends in content analysis today: A summary. In I. Pool (Ed.), *Trends in content analysis.* Urbana: Univer. Illinois Press, 1959. Ch. 7.

POPE, B., & SIEGMAN, A. W. The effect of therapist verbal activity level and specificity on patient productivity and speech disturbance in the initial interview. *Journal of Consulting Psychology* 1962, 26, 489.

PROFF, F. C. A validity study of the distress-relief quotient as a measure of movement within the topical discussion unit. Unpublished doctoral dissertation, University of Missouri, 1952.

PSATHAS, G. Interaction process analysis of two psychotherapy groups. *International Journal of Group Psychotherapy,* 1960, 10, 430–445. (a)

PSATHAS, G. Phase movement and equilibrium tendencies in interaction process in psychotherapy groups. *Sociometry,* 1960, 23, 177–194. (b)

PSATHAS, G. Alternative methods for scoring interaction process analysis. *Journal of Social Psychology,* 1961, 53, 97–103.

RAUSH, H. L., SPERBER, Z., RIGLER, D., WILLIAMS, JOAN, HARWAY, N. I., BORDIN, E. S., DITTMANN, A. T., & HAYS, W. L. A dimensional analysis of depth of interpretation.

Journal of Consulting Psychology, 1956, 20, 43–48.

ROGERS, C. R. A tentative scale for the measurement of process in psychotherapy. In E. A. Rubinstein & M. B. Parloff (Eds.), *Research in psychotherapy.* Washington, D.C.: American Psychological Association, 1959. Pp. 96–107.

ROGERS, C. R. A process conception of psychotherapy. In C. R. Rogers, *On becoming a person.* Boston: Houghton Mifflin, 1961. Ch. 7.

ROSENBERG, PEARL P. Methodology for an objective analysis of the content of a group protocol. *International Journal of Group Psychotherapy,* 1962, 12, 467–475.

ROSENMAN, S. Changes in the representations of self, other, and interrelationship in client-centered therapy. *Journal of Counseling Psychology,* 1955, 2, 271–277.

SALZBERG, H. C. Manipulation of verbal behavior in a group psychotherapeutic setting. *Psychological Reports,* 1961, 9, 183–186.

SALZBERG, H. C. Effects of silence and redirection on verbal responses in group psychotherapy. *Psychological Reports,* 1962, 11, 455–461.

SALZBERG, H. C., BROKAW, J. R., & STRAHLEY, D. F. Effects of group stability on spontaneity and problem-relevant verbal behavior in group psychotherapy. *Psychological Reports,* 1964, 14, 687–694.

SALZINGER, K. Some problems of response measurement in verbal behavior: The response unit and intraresponse relations. Paper read at Conference on Methods of Measurement of Change in Human Behavior, Montreal, September 1962.

SAPORTA, S., & SEBEOK, T. A. Linguistics and content analysis. In I. Pool (Ed.), *Trends in content analysis.* Urbana: Univer. Illinois Press, 1959. Ch. 4.

SASLOW, G., & MATARAZZO, J. D. A technique for studying changes in interview behavior. In E. A. Rubinstein & M. B. Parloff (Eds.), *Research in psychotherapy.* Washington, D.C.: American Psychological Association, 1959. Pp. 125–159.

SASLOW, G., MATARAZZO, J. D., & GUZE, S. B. The stability of interaction chronograph patterns in psychiatric interviews. *Journal of Consulting Psychology,* 1955, 19, 417–430.

SASLOW, G., MATARAZZO, J. D., PHILLIPS, JEANNE S., & MATARAZZO, RUTH G. Test-retest stability of interaction patterns during interviews conducted one week apart. *Journal of Abnormal and Social Psychology,* 1957, 54, 295–302.

SCHEFLEN, A. E. Communication and regulation in psychotherapy. *Psychiatry,* 1963, 26, 126–136.

SCHEFLEN, A. E., ENGLISH, O. S., HAMPE, W. W., & AUERBACH, A. H. *Research in psychotherapy: A study of the Whitaker-Malone method,* in press.

SCHULZE, G., MAHL, G. F., & MURRAY, E. J. Speech disturbances and content analysis categories as indices of underlying emotional states of patients in psychotherapy. *American Psychologist,* 1960, 15, 405. (Abstract)

SHELLHASE, L. J. Acceptance of role and resultant interaction in the group psychotherapy of schizophrenia. *Group Psychotherapy,* 1960, 13, 208–229.

SIEGMAN, A. W., & POPE, B. An empirical scale for the measurement of therapist specificity in the initial psychiatric interview. *Psychological Record,* 1962, 11, 515–520.

SKLANSKY, M. A., ISAACS, K. S., & HAGGARD, E. A. A method for the study of verbal interaction and levels of meaning in psychotherapy. In J. S. Gottlieb & G. Tourney (Eds.), *Scientific papers and discussions, divisional meeting, Mid-West Area District Branches.* Detroit: American Psychiatric Association, 1960. Pp: 133–148.

SMITH, A. B., BASSIN, A., & FROEHLICH, A. Changes in attitudes and degree of verbal participation in group therapy with adult offenders. *Journal of Consulting Psychology,* 1960, 24, 247–249.

SMITH, A. B., BASSIN, A., & FROEHLICH, A. Interaction process and equilibrium in a therapy group of adult offenders. *Journal of Social Psychology,* 1962, 56, 141–147.

SPEISMAN, J. C. Depth of interpretation and verbal resistance in psychotherapy. *Journal of Consulting Psychology,* 1959, 23, 93–99.

STRUPP, H. H. The effect of the psychotherapist's personal analysis upon his techniques. *Journal of Consulting Psychology,* 1955, 19, 197–204. (a)

STRUPP, H. H. An objective comparison of Rogerian and psychoanalytic techniques. *Journal of Consulting Psychology,* 1955, 19, 1–7. (b)

STRUPP, H. H. Psychotherapeutic technique,

professional affiliation, and experience level. *Journal of Consulting Psychology,* 1955, 19, 97–102. (c)

STRUPP, H. H. A multidimensional analysis of technique in brief psychotherapy. *Psychiatry,* 1957, 20, 387–397. (a)

STRUPP, H. H. A multidimensional analysis of therapist activity in analytic and client-centered therapy. *Journal of Consulting Psychology,* 1957, 21, 301–308. (b)

STRUPP, H. H. A multidimensional system for analyzing psychotherapeutic techniques. *Psychiatry,* 1957, 20, 293–306. (c)

STRUPP, H. H. The performance of psychiatrists and psychologists in a therapeutic interview. *Journal of Clinical Psychology,* 1958, 14, 219–226. (a)

STRUPP, H. H. The performance of psychoanalytic and client-centered therapists in an initial interview. *Journal of Consulting Psychology,* 1958, 22, 265–274. (b)

STRUPP, H. H. The psychotherapist's contribution to the treatment process. *Behavioral Science,* 1958, 3, 34–67. (c)

STRUPP, H. H. *Psychotherapists in action.* New York: Grune & Stratton, 1960.

STRUPP, H. H. An analysis of therapist activity in two psychotherapeutic interviews. In L. A. Gottschalk (Ed.), *Comparative psycholinguistic analysis of two psychotherapeutic interviews.* New York: International Universities Press, 1961. Ch. 4.

STRUPP, H. H. Patient-doctor relationships: The psychotherapist in the therapeutic process. In A. J. Bachrach (Ed.), *Experimental foundations of clinical psychology.* New York: Basic Books, 1962. Ch. 17. (a)

STRUPP, H. H. The therapist's contribution to the treatment process: Beginnings and vagaries of a research program. In H. H. Strupp & L. Luborsky (Eds.), *Research in psychotherapy.* Vol. 2. Washington, D.C.: American Psychological Association, 1962. Pp. 25–40. (b)

STRUPP, H. H., & LUBORSKY, L. (Eds.), *Research in psychotherapy.* Vol. 2. Washington, D.C.: American Psychological Association, 1962.

TALLAND, G. A. Task and interaction process: Some characteristics of therapeutic group discussions. *Journal of Abnormal and Social Psychology,* 1955, 50, 105–109.

TAUSON, V. B., GUZE, S. B., MCCLURE, J., & BEGUELIN, J. A further study of some features of the interview with the Interaction Chronograph. *American Journal of Psychiatry*, 1961, 118, 438–446.

TIMMONS, E. O., RICKARD, H. C., & TAYLOR, R. E. Reliability of content-free group verbal behavior. *Psychological Record*, 1960, 10, 297–305.

TOMLINSON, T. M., & HART, J. T., JR. A validation study of the process scale. *Journal of Consulting Psychology*, 1962, 26, 74–78.

TRUAX, C. B., & CARKHUFF, R. R. Concreteness: A neglected variable in research in psychotherapy. *Journal of Clinical Psychology*, 1964, 20, 264–267.

VARGAS, M. J. Changes in self-awareness during client-centered therapy. In C. R. Rogers & Rosalind F. Dymond (Eds.), *Psychotherapy and personality change.* Chicago: Univer. Chicago Press, 1954. Ch. 10.

WALKER, A. M., RABLEN, R. A., & ROGERS, C. R. Development of a scale to measure process changes in psychotherapy. *Journal of Clinical Psychology*, 1960, 16, 79–85.

WATSON, D. L., & LAFFAL, J. Sources of verbalizations of psychotherapists about patients. *Journal of General Psychology*, 1963, 68, 89–98.

WEINTRAUB, W., & ARONSON, H. The application of verbal behavior analysis to the study of psychological defense mechanisms: Methodology and preliminary report. *Journal of Nervous and Mental Disease*, 1962, 134, 169–181.

WEINTRAUB, W., & ARONSON, H. The application of verbal behavior analysis to the study of psychological defense mechanisms: II. Speech pattern associated with impulsive behavior. *Journal of Nervous and Mental Disease*, 1964, 139, 75–82.

WHITE, ALICE M., FICHTENBAUM, L., & DOLLARD, J. Measure for predicting dropping out of psychotherapy. *Journal of Consulting Psychology*, 1964, 28, 326–332.

WINDER, C. L., AHMAD, F. Z., BANDURA, A., & RAU, LUCY C. Dependency of patients, psychotherapists' responses, and aspects of psychotherapy. *Journal of Consulting Psychology*, 1962, 26, 129–134.

Evaluation of Topics in
Therapy Group Discussion*

GEORGE A. TALLAND
DAVID H. CLARK

INTRODUCTION

The literature of group therapy, though extensive, includes few systematic studies of the topics of discussion. Reports tend to deal with overt content only in relation to inferred needs and motives. Frank (3) discussing the problem of research in this field advocated the study of the "more or less permanent issues about which patients are concerned and about which they are trying to do something," the study of *themes* perceived by the therapist though not necessarily by the patients themselves. One research included a time sampling analysis of a list of topics, but the authors dismissed the findings obtained by this method as being of minor importance in comparison with their subjective impressions of what the group discussion had been about. (1) Plank (4) made an at-

Reprinted from *Journal of Clinical Psychology*, 1954, 10 (2), 131–137, with the permission of Frederick C. Thorne and the authors.

* The research of which this study forms a part has been facilitated by a grant from the Bethlem Research Fund, made available to one of the authors (G. A. T.) by the Governors of the Royal Bethlem and Maudsley Hospitals, London.

tempt to tabulate the frequencies of certain 'types of utterances' over a series of meetings at a V.A. clinic, but his list so far from being comprehensive omits certain topics precisely because they tended to be raised at each meeting.

It is hardly surprising that content analysis in therapeutic group discussion should have produced no significant results. On the one hand, psychoanalytically oriented therapists tend to hold the view that for the purposes of group psychotherapy any topic is as useful as any other, that it is not what patients say that matters, but how or in what context they say it. On the other hand, actuarial reports are obviously of limited intrinsic interest, for the composition of the group membership determines the choice of topics to a large extent. Plank's veterans will certainly talk more about occupational problems, students about religious or philosophical doubts than a group consisting of six housewives troubled by marital maladjustments.

PROBLEM

Our object was to investigate the significance of different topics of discussion as seen by the patients themselves, and more particularly to test whether they support the view held by the so-called dynamic school of psychotherapy, which dismisses the importance of overt content. We predicted, on the strength of casual remarks made by group patients, that they would not agree with the dictum that any topic is as useful as any other, and formulated also several additional hypotheses to test some general psychotherapeutic propositions: (1) group patients distinguish various topics of discussion according to their value in therapy, and generally agree in their evaluations; (2) in well integrated groups, patients will not markedly distinguish between the relative value of a topic to themselves individually and to the group as a whole; (3) topics judged to be disturbing are also thought to be helpful; (4) no topic is judged entirely useless, wasting the group's time or hindering its progress; (5) those topics will be considered most helpful, which can be openly talked about in the group therapeutic setting but not elsewhere.

SUBJECTS

The research was carried out on seven groups of patients undergoing treatment at the Maudsley Hospital, London. The groups were conducted according to the principles of *group analytic psychotherapy* described by Foulkes (2) and Taylor (6), which agree in most essentials with the technique of other psychoanalytically oriented group therapeutic procedures, e.g. Slavson's (5). In membership the groups varied from 5 to 8, some were mixed, others consisted entirely of men or of women. The subjects were out-patients who were suffering from the various classes of psychoneuroses and in a few instances from less severe psychoses. The age range was from 17 to 45; of the 17 men and 26 women in the sample, 28 were married. Most of the patients were office and shop workers, though a fair proportion of the women had no employment outside

their homes; they were all of high average or higher intelligence. The meetings took place in consulting rooms once weekly for periods of 90 minutes.

PROCEDURE

The material for the research was obtained by asking the subjects to rank items of a set list of topics on various criteria. It was essential for the purpose of analysis to deal with a standard list of topics, though its compilation involved us in attempting to satisfy two conflicting demands. The list had to be comprehensive enough to be reasonably representative of the varied subject matter raised in therapeutic discussion, yet not so wide as to become unmanageable for the task of ranking. It had to include most topics central to the average group patient's problems, but also some more peripheral ones so that we could test in its literal sense the statement that 'any topic is as useful as any other.' The final selection was based on the records of some forty group meetings and on the advice of several experienced group therapists. The topics were defined in words or phrases drawn from the patients' own vocabulary so as to avoid the theoretical preconceptions of any particular psychotherapeutic school, and also in order to be certain that the items to be ranked would be all meaningful to the subjects. The list consisted of the following 15 items: Childhood memories; dreams; reactions to others in the group; feelings and thoughts about the group doctor; people outside the group; is illness due to physical or psychological causes?; marriage problems; money troubles; problems at work; quarrels, angry feelings; children, bringing up children; symptoms, anxieties; social position, class feelings; sex; shame, guilt.

Our object was to discover which of these items the patients thought to be helpful or unhelpful in discussion, which disturbing, which—if any—to hinder treatment. Apart from absolute choices we were also interested in the ranks assigned to the topics under each heading. Choices were therefore limited to five on each criterion, and these had to be ranked. Each task of choice and ranking was performed separately, first with a view to the group as a whole, and again with a focus on the subject himself. Complete rankings of 15 items were constructed for each subject by combining the two partial rankings made for 'helpfulness' and 'unhelpfulness,' and by taking the remaining items as tied in the mid-rank position. This procedure was adopted in order to simplify the task set to the patients, and was justified by the very high negative correlations between ranked frequency scales of 'helpful' and 'unhelpful' items. Thus complete rankings were obtained from each patient for helpfulness, and partial rankings on the disturbing and hindering effects of the topics, all with a view to the group and again with a focus to the subject himself.

Patients were interviewed while in a group, following a therapeutic meeting. The therapist was not present. Scoring sheets with two rows of four columns each, blank but for being numbered from 1 to 5, were issued to the subjects with a set of 15 cards. In the middle of each card was printed one of the 15 topics, and in the top right corner its code letter. Subjects selected five cards for each task, placed them in rank order, and noted down the code letters in the appropriate column in the same order. Introducing them to the task the experimenter pointed out that in group therapy the content of discussion was not regarded as being of primary importance, that their therapists had told the patients to discuss anything they wished to bring up and that this would help them no matter what the topic. None the less, the experimenter added, they had probably found that discussion of some topics had been more helpful than on others. If that were the case, they were asked to select on the basis of their experience in the group the five topics which had proved most help-

ful in the progress of the entire group. The instruction to consider the progress of the entire group and not just their own, was twice stressed and repeated in the introduction of each subsequent task. In order of performance, these were selection and ranking of the five least helpful items out of the remaining batch of ten cards, then of the five most disturbing topics from the entire pack, and lastly any number of topics up to five which had been not merely unhelpful but actually interfering with, hindering the progress of the group. On completion of these four tasks subjects were asked to fold back the scoring form so that they could not see what they had written down, and the entire procedure was repeated, this time each patient selecting and ranking the topics with a view to his own progress. Throughout, subjects were allowed to choose fewer items if they could not think of five fitting the category or any number up to ten, and to rank these.

In order to test the hypothesis that those topics would be judged more helpful which could be discussed in the therapeutic setting but not outside, the research included a panel of 35 judges recruited from psychologists working at the Institute of Psychiatry, none of whom had had any direct contact with group therapy. Some of the topics were slightly re-worded for this purpose so as to have more general terms of reference, and the judges were instructed to consider them being discussed as the speaker's personal problem. They had to perform two tasks: first to mark those items which in their opinion could be brought up in an intimate setting only, secondly to rank the entire list starting with the topic most emphatically suitable for discussion among close friends and ending with that which could be talked about in any situation. Judges performed their task individually, working with a printed list and not cards. They were asked to break down the ranking into three sections, beginning with the top five and ending with the middle five items.

Hypothesis I was tested by the concordances of the patients' group-focused total rankings for helpfulness; hypothesis II by correlating each patient's group-focused and self-focused rankings for helpfulness; hypothesis III by tabulating the association of individual choices for helpfulness and disturbing effect separately on the group-focused and self-focused tasks, and calculating chi square on the entire samples; hypothesis IV by inspection of the total number of choices made for 'uselessness' or hindering effect; hypothesis V by correlating the judges' scale for 'intimacy' with the patients' scale for 'helpfulness,' and by examining the association between the topics most highly chosen for 'helpfulness' and the frequency of their judgment on 'intimacy.'

RESULTS

All subjects were highly co-operative. The patients, with no exception, took readily enough to stating their preferences; none regarded himself as unqualified to judge the topics for their helpfulness, nor did any one question the meaning or validity of the task. A few could not think of five topics which were definitely helpful, some more were unable to select as many unhelpful or disturbing items, but many of them could not think of several or even one topic which was entirely useless in or actually hindered the discussion.

The patients' response to the task thus itself confirmed the principal argument of our first hypothesis: they all easily distinguished the topics according to their usefulness in therapeutic discussion. They also showed considerable consensus in their rankings which gave an average rank correlation coefficient of .32. This consensus thus transcends group barriers, and remains significantly higher than could happen by chance at the .01 level of confidence even after the exclusion of the four topics which are generally judged as least helpful. Concordances of rankings, measured by Kendall's W coefficient, are significant

within 6 groups at the .01, in the seventh at the .05 level of confidence. Sex and married status account for only minor variations in the rank order; product moment correlations between the summated rankings of men and women is .82, of married and unmarried patients .86. Correlations based on frequencies of choices of the items under the two sets of four headings in table 1 are given below:

Helpful and unhelpful to group —.95
Helpful and unhelpful to self —.89
Helpful to group and self   .78
Unhelpful to group and self   .91
Helpful and disturbing to group .78
Helpful and disturbing to self .79
Unhelpful and hindering to group .78
Unhelpful and hindering to self .53

The high negative correlations between helpfulness and unhelpfulness are a most satisfactory proof of the validity of the procedure by which rankings under these two headings were combined into a single scale. Correlations between group-focused and self-focused rankings of frequencies confirm the findings based on correlating each subject's individual complete rankings for helpfulness which averaged .59 with a standard deviation of .10. Except for three patients, these coefficients were all positive, ranging from .30 to .95. From the high correlations between ranked frequencies on helpfulness and disturbing effect, it is evident that there is a general tendency to place the same topics either high or low on both criteria. Several patients remarked that having chosen and ranked five topics for helpfulness it was unnecessary to put them down again under the heading of 'disturbing.' Taking the subjects individually, the topics were tabulated according to frequencies of being judged helpful, moderately helpful or unhelpful and disturbing or not disturbing. These categories are, of course, relative: helpfulness stands for the most helpful five, unhelpful for the least helpful five, moderately for the re-

TABLE 1

FREQUENCIES OF CHOICES

Topics	Group-focused				Self-focused			
	Help.	Unhelp.	Dist.	Hind.	Help.	Unhelp.	Dist.	Hind.
Childhood memories	25	3	14	1	25	6	11	1
Dreams	12	11	12	2	9	14	7	5
Others in group	21	7	23	4	13	7	17	0
Group doctor	9	13	14	5	12	18	10	3
People outside group	2	31	4	4	16	20	7	2
Shame and guilt	24	6	23	1	21	2	22	2
Illness physical?	11	15	1	5	13	12	6	3
Marriage problems	10	9	10	0	16	10	11	1
Money troubles	1	32	2	8	0	28	3	2
Problems at work	10	21	6	6	7	23	10	3
Quarrels	22	5	23	1	14	7	24	2
Children	7	18	8	5	4	25	6	4
Symptoms, anxieties	26	2	19	3	31	6	23	1
Social position	3	26	7	8	1	27	3	5
Sex	30	5	30	0	25	7	29	3

maining items. Likewise 'not disturbing' may include some disturbing topics other than the five most upsetting. The frequency tabulations are given in table 2. Chi square values are significant at the .001 level of confidence, both for data based on group focused and self focused choices. It is therefore evident that judgments of helpfulness are not independent from those made for disturbing effect.

In selecting topics hindering the progress of treatment the subjects varied widely between some who chose five items to others who could not think of one. The latter numbered 18 judging for the group, 24 judging for themselves individually. Altogether 53 entries were made under this heading with the group, 37 with self in

view, giving averages of 1.23 and .86. These totals rendered a quantitative analysis of the data impracticable, and also account for the comparatively low correlation between self-focused choices for unhelpfulness and hindering effect, as computed from ranked frequencies.

Table 3 gives the mean ranks of the 15 items computed from the patients' rankings for helpfulness and their mean ranks computed from the judges' rankings for intimacy, as well as the frequencies with which they were assigned to be fit for discussion in an intimate setting only. Product moment correlation between the two arrays of mean ranks gives a coefficient of .69. Of the five topics judged most helpful by the patients, however, only two were re-

TABLE 2

ASSOCIATION OF CHOICES FOR HELPFULNESS AND DISTURBING EFFECT

Topic	Group-focused			Self-focused		
	Helpf.	Moder.	Unhelpf.	Helpf.	Moder.	Unhelpf.
Disturbing	113	75	12	110	65	18
Not disturbing	102	150	193	95	163	194

TABLE 3

Mean Ranks of Helpfulness and Intimacy

Topics	Helpfulness Rank	Intimacy Rank	Frequency
Sex	4.06	5.03	21
Symptoms, anxieties	5.18	5.23	15
Shame and guilt	5.68	3.30	30
Childhood memories	5.79	10.55	1
Quarrels	5.86	6.55	14
Others in group	6.35	5.47	22
Marriage problems	7.94	3.92	27
Group Doctor	8.38	7.42	11
Illness psysical?	8.46	10.28	1
Dreams	8.74	9.73	5
Children	9.21	12.52	1
Problems at work	9.75	10.34	2
Social position	10.98	10.37	2
People outside	11.63	11.08	—
Money troubles	11.96	8.20	8

garded as suitable only for discussion in an intimate setting, while the other two items so rated, though above the mean, are not in the top range of helpfulness.

DISCUSSION

The results tend to confirm our hypotheses, though they do not provide conclusive evidence in support of the fifth. Patients do show marked preferences when asked to rank topics of discussion for their helpfulness in group therapy. They also agree among themselves to a considerable extent on which topics are more, which less helpful. In fact, they do not confirm the dictum that 'any topic is as useful for therapeutic discussion as any other.' The statistically significant concordances of their rankings within single groups and over the entire sample is not an artifact caused by the inclusion of several topics which are almost unanimously ranked low. As would be expected discussion of problems most directly relating to manifest maladjustments is thought to be most helpful and the attempt to relate these to childhood experiences.

A high measure of group identification is evident from the finding that sex and marital status have little bearing on the rank order in which the topics are held to be useful to the group, although some of them are necessarily of more direct interest to one category of patients than to the other. The high correlation between individual subjects' group and self-focused rankings provides further confirmation of this conclusion. The three patients whose two rankings for helpfulness correlate negatively were known to be isolated in their groups; one attended irregularly, another hardly ever participated in the discussion, the third deliberately dissociated her problems from those of her fellow patients. None the less, the comparatively wide scatter of the correlation coefficients suggests that individual problems are not entirely or uniformly identified with group problems. It is also worth noting that while discussion about 'others in the group' and 'quarrels' is thought to help the group, these topics are not held to be particularly helpful to individual patients personally. On the other hand, many patients believe to have benefited by talking about their relatives or friends outside the group, but not by their colleagues' discussion of their relatives and friends.

The finding that the topics judged as disturbing by a patient matched closely the list of items he had found helpful, confirms a basic tenet of psychotherapy. It is also evident from the results that, although the patients do not regard all topics as equally helpful, they believe that the discussion of any one may be of some value, that none would actually hinder the progress of treatment.

Although the overall trend is to rank topics for helpfulness in the same order in which they are judged to be suitable for discussion in an intimate setting only, the results do not provide a definite confirmation of the principle that the chief value of group therapy is in the opportunity it affords for bringing into the open problems which cannot be aired in other situations. By more closely matching the judges with the patients for their cultural background, perhaps, stronger evidence might have been furnished to support this hypothesis. It is also likely that the two types of subjects had entirely different childhood memories in mind.

SUMMARY AND CONCLUSIONS

By means of asking members of seven analytic psychotherapy groups to select items and rank them on several criteria and by analysing the data, the following hypotheses were tested and confirmed:

Group patients distinguish different top-ics of discussion for their contribution to the progress of therapy, and are considerably agreed in their preferences, whether they belong to the same group or have had no experiences in common.

They tend to judge the topics alike whether they have their own personal progress or that of the entire group in mind. Topics which cause them greater disturbance are thought to be more helpful. The discussion of no topic is held to be entirely useless or hindering the group in its work.

There is strong, though not conclusive, indication that topics which cannot be discussed outside the intimate atmosphere of the therapeutic situation, are thought to be the most valuable items in clinical discussion.

REFERENCES

1. COFFEY, H. S., FREEDMAN, M. B., LEARY, T. F. AND OSSORIO, A. Community service and social research: Group psychotherapy in a Church program. *J. Soc. Iss.*, 1950, 6.

2. FOULKES, S. H. *Introduction to Group-analytic Psychotherapy*. London: Wm. Heinemann Medical Books, 1948.

3. FRANK, J. D. Some problems of research in group psychotherapy. *Int. J. Psychotherapy*, 1951, 1, 78–81.

4. PLANK, R. An analysis of a group therapy experiment. *Human Organization*, 1951, 10, 5–21 and 26–36.

5. SLAVSON, S. R. *Analytic Psychotherapy with Children, Adolescents and Adults*. New York: Columbia University Press, 1950.

6. TAYLOR, F. K. The therapeutic factors in group-analytical treatment. *J. ment. Sci.*, 1950, 96, 967–997.

Therapist Attendance as a Variable in Group Psychotherapy[1,2]

JOHN E. EXNER, Jr.

Much has been written concerning the usefulness of group psychotherapy as an effective treatment technique. While these writings often manifest confusion concerning the definition of group psychotherapy, the most effective method of group selection, group direction, and the theoretical constructs which underline the process, it is generally conceded that the therapist is a necessary component in the successful operation of any group. Even in those methods where the therapist is passive such as suggested by Bion (1961) in the "leaderless group" and McCann (1953) in the "round table technique," presence of a therapist or "power figure" is accepted. In the "leaderless group" the therapist is defined as being a passive-observer whereas in the round table technique the therapist has a ten minute interview with all group members at which time direction

is offered. Cartwright and Zander (1958) have implied that the power or leadership role in a group has a significant relevance to the direction of the group and is pertinent to the establishment of group interpersonal relationships. Luchins (1964) has pointed out that failure was experienced in an attempt to start a leaderless group with schizophrenics. He adds however that after groups are underway the therapist can physically absent himself or can specify a non-participating role and in either instance, some value is derived in that patients are forced to consider their relation to the therapist.

The purpose of this investigation was to evaluate the effects of attendance in group psychotherapy sessions by a trained therapist. It was hypothesized that the rate of improvement would increase and number of sessions to discharge would decrease as a function of regular attendance in the group by the therapist.

PROCEDURE

Thirty female patients, 14 of whom were diagnosed as psychoneurotic and 16

Reprinted with the permission of the author.

[1] A paper based on parts of this investigation was presented at the meetings of the Midwestern Psychological Association, May 1, 1965.

[2] This investigation was supported in part in an institutional research grant from Bowling Green State University.

diagnosed as personality disorder, were selected randomly from a treatment waiting list of a community mental health clinic. They were randomly divided into five groups of 6 patients each. Two of these groups were assigned to each of two therapists, one male and one female. No therapist was assigned to the fifth group. Therapists attended the sessions of one group regularly, (Group I-Female therapist; Group II-Male therapist) and the second group irregularly (Group III-Female therapist; Group IV-Male therapist). The number of sessions in the irregular group attended by the therapist totaled a random half of the meetings. Prior to group assignment all patients were rated on a 15 item scale concerning symptoms, and prognosis by two staff members neither of whom had any direct involvement in the investigation. These ratings were repeated by the same staff members at discharge or on the termination of the investigation. At the beginning of the study all patients received orientation instructions in which they were told they could terminate treatment at any time or request further evaluation at any time. The investigation was terminated after 42 weeks.

If during the 42 week period a patient was discharged, hospitalized, or transferred to individual treatment, another patient was added to the group selected from the waiting list so as to keep all groups at a constant size. All sessions were recorded with the original intent of analyzing the verbalization time for each patient per session and for the more subjective purpose of evaluating the general content of each session. The complexities of computing times for verbalization were found to be such that this portion of the investigation was not completed although all tapes were subjectively evaluated for content. Each group met weekly for a one and one-half hour period. At any time a patient requested evaluation or discharge staff evaluation was arranged immediately and a decision concerning the request evolved

within the matter of a few days. The final choice concerning the recommendations of the staff was always left to the patient.

RESULTS

Data comparing the groups on the rating scale are presented in Table 1. It will be noted from examination of Table 1 that the analysis of variance on first rating yields a non-significant F ratio suggesting no differences between groups, whereas a similar analysis concerning the second rating yields an F ratio significant beyond the .01 level. It will also be noted in Table 1 that a reduction in the mean rating, indicating improvement, occurred in all four of the groups in which a therapist participated but an increase in mean rating occurred in the no-therapist group. It should be noted that the largest differences between first and second ratings occurred in the two groups in which the therapist attended irregularly.

Table 2 gives data concerning the number of sessions to discharge. In this respect, the maximum number would be 42. Patients who during the course of the investigation, were transferred to hospitalization or individual psychotherapy were given the score of 42 so as to provide a base for statistical analysis. It should also be noted that none of the patients in Group I or Group IV participated for a full 42 sessions. Only 4 of the 12 patients in groups II and III continued for a full 42 sessions whereas 5 of the 6 patients in group V continued through the 42 weeks or were transferred to hospitalization or individual therapy prior to that time. Analysis of variance on the number of sessions to discharge yields an F ratio of 6.10 which is significant at .01.

Table 3 indicates the number of subjects in each of the groups who were discharged, transferred to hospitalization or individual treatment or who continued on to the end of the investigation in group therapy. This Table also indicates the di-

TABLE 1

COMPARISON OF FIVE GROUPS ON SYMPTOMATIC-PROGNOSTIC RATING SCALE
AT PRE AND POST THERAPY INTERVALS*

	X 1st Rating	X 2nd Rating	Diff.	Total Grp 1st Rating	Total Grp 2nd Rating	Diff.
Grp 1 (Reg. Ther.)	55.5	42.1	−13.4	333	253	− 80
Grp II (Reg. ther.)	57.3	37.1	−20.2	344	223	−121
Grp III (Irr. ther.)	59.6	26.8	−32.8	358	161	−197
Grp IV (Irr. ther.)	57.0	23.3	−33.7	342	140	−202
Grp V (No. ther.)	55.0	64.3	+ 9.3	330	380	+ 50

1st Rating

	SS	df	MS
Bet.	80.4	4	20.1
With.	5,202.3	25	208.1

F = .096 not significant

2nd Rating

	SS	df	MS
Bet.	6,290.4	4	1,572.6
With.	7,395.0	25	295.8

F = 5.316 significant beyond .01

* Maximum possible rating per subject = 75.0.

TABLE 2

COMPARISON OF FIVE GROUPS FOR NUMBER OF SESSIONS TO DISCHARGE*

	Grp I (Reg. Th.)	Grp II (Reg. Th.)	Grp III (Irr. Th.)	Grp IV (Irr. Th.)	Grp V (No. Th.)
X	33.66	34.16	26.33	18.83	40.0
Range	21–42	20–42	16–42	13–27	30–42

Analysis of Variance

	SS	df	MS
Bet.	1591.3	4	397.8
With.	1630.2	25	65.2

F = 6.10 significant beyond .01

**Highest possible number is 42.

TABLE 3

DISPOSITION AND RATING CHANGES OF PATIENTS IN FIVE GROUPS

	N	Disch.	Hosp.	Tran. To Ind. Th.	Remained In Group Th.	Rated Improv.	Rated Not Improv.
Reg. Grps	12	7	1	2	2	10	2
Irr. Grps	12	11	0	1	0	12	0
No. Ther. Grp	6	1	1	1	3	2	4

rection of rating change for the total number of subjects in each of the group categories. It will be noted from examination of Table 3 that 11 of the 12 patients in the irregularly attended groups were discharged by staff recommendation, 10 prior to the 30th week. Seven of the 12 patients in the regularly attended groups were similarly discharged, while only 1 of the 6 patients in the no-therapist group was discharged. A median test comparing the number discharged from the regularly attended groups with the number of the irregularly attended groups yields $\chi^2 = 8.668$ which is significant beyond the .01 level suggesting that the patients in the irregularly attended groups fared better. It should also be noted that, with regard to rating changes, all 12 of the patients in the irregularly attended groups showed improvement as manifest by ratings whereas only 10 of the 12 patients in the regularly attended group showed this type of improvement and only 2 of the 6 patients in the no-therapist group showed such an improvement.

DISCUSSION

It is necessary to reject the hypothesis that rate of improvement would increase and number of sessions to discharge decrease as a function of regular attendance in the group by the therapist. While rate of improvement does increase and number of sessions to discharge does decrease as some function of therapist attendance in the group, it is apparently not a function of regular attendance. Even though small samples have been used, irregular attendance by the therapist appears to be a variable in group psychotherapy more conducive to patient improvement than either regular attendance by a therapist or no attendance whatsoever by a therapist. Regular attendance by the therapist does appear to be more conducive to improvement than no attendance at all.

At first glance it might be suggested

that the principles of irregular reinforcement are applicable. However, after considering this postulate more thoroughly in light of the content evaluations of the sessions it is probably not the best explanation. Also the suggestion of Luchins that those sessions in which the therapist is absent are utilized by patients to clarify their feelings and relationship to the therapist is not supported from analysis of the recordings of the sessions in which the therapists were absent. Quite the contrary, the content provided in these sessions appears to have been more direct to the patient's problems than in the sessions where the therapist actually attended. The discussions in the therapist-absent sessions seemed to be more "revealing" on the part of each patient. When no authority or "power" figure was present to manifest a control or limit on depth of discussion, "secrets" seemed to be revealed more frequently. All patients were aware that every session was recorded but in the "therapist-absent" sessions this fact seems to have been ignored and the patients often interacted much more freely and much more emotionally. The productions of one patient in particular are worth noting as an example. In the therapist-attended sessions this patient offered material that was usually superficial, well organized, and with avoidance of sexual content. In the therapist-absent sessions this same patient talked much more freely of sexual matters in a spontaneous manner. This particular event becomes even more remarkable when it is pointed out that the therapist attending this group was also female and thus sex differences should not have been of significance.

A subjective comparison of the content of the groups in which the therapist attended regularly with the content of the therapist-absent sessions of the irregularly attended groups may give some clue concerning the differences found. In the regularly attended group sessions the group generally seemed to be more reserved and dependent upon the therapists even though the initial instructions were those similar to that used by Bion in defining the therapist role as a passive-observer. In other words, these groups appeared to feel some control from the therapist even though the therapist participation was minimal. A subtle dependency phenomena seemed to appear from one session to the next in which the therapists as unspeaking group leaders somehow maintain a power role. The attitude of the patients in the irregularly attended groups seemed quite different. They were much more able to define the group as a group minus the therapist, in which the dependency relationships were obviously contained among the patients themselves. Group leaders became manifest after four or five sessions in all five of the groups but in the irregularly attended groups these leaders were perceived with less importance. Rather than having a professional role they were regarded more as a private friend, i.e., a person of one's own sex to whom secretive personal emotional information could be offered much in the same way that we might suspect housewives are prone to talk over midmorning coffee. This type of dependency or power relationship also appears to have less permanency in the group in that whenever a patient leader offered advice or made comments which were inconsistent with the group orientation, she was immediately chided thus losing some "power" importance. In contrast, there were very few times when the patients in the regularly attended groups were similarly critical of each other or of the therapist and in general seemed much more conservative in changing their attitudes toward each other.

If these data are a result of differences in patient dependency on the therapist then there is cause to re-evaluate the therapist-patient relationship not only in group situations but also in individual treatment. Several writers including Bion, Luchins, and others have noted that transference in a group situation is similar to the individual treatment case. If irregular attendance by the therapist diminishes or prohibits the development of such transference relationships to the therapist and in turn creates a greater pressure on the patient for emotional independence it would appear to be a worthwhile approach.

Naturally there are many unanswered questions arising from this study. Among these is the possibility that the differences between the irregularly and regularly attended groups could have been precipitated by some unperceived artifact. Even should this be the case the data still would be important to reflect on the notion that regular attendance by a therapist offers no notable gain when contrasted with irregular attendance. Also, the value of the differences in ratings should be considered cautiously as the rating scale was unique and devised specifically for this study and has no validation or reliability data. The number of sessions to discharge, however, are more concrete data, and may have the most significant meaningfulness. There is no question that replication is required with a number of variables more adequately controlled. In general, however, it may well be that group therapy is most useful when the patients are not given the opportunity for the establishment of a "behavioral habit routine" which is protected by the presence of the "omnipotent" therapist.

REFERENCES

BION, W. R. *Experiences in groups.* New York: Basic Books, 1961.

CARTWRIGHT, D. AND ZANDER, A. (Eds.) *Group Dynamics.* Evanston, Ill.: Row Peterson, 1960.

LUCHINS, A. H. *Group Therapy.* New York: Random House, 1964.

McCANN, W. H. The round table technique in group psychotherapy, *Group Psychoth.,* 1953, 5, 233–239.

Galvanic Skin Response Correlates of Different Modes of Experiencing[1]

EUGENE T. GENDLIN
JEROME I. BERLIN[2]

INTRODUCTION

In a recent theory (2, 3), the term "experiencing" is applied to the individual's stream of directly felt data. Personality change during psychotherapy is held to involve many brief periods during which the individual refers his attention directly, and in a continuous way, to these immediately felt data of experiencing. Rogers (5, 6, 7) in his most recent formulation, cites the client's direct reference to experiencing as an index of therapeutic movement.

During the hours of psychotherapy the

Reprinted from *Journal of Clinical Psychology,* 1961, 17, (1), 73–77, with the permission of Frederick C. Thorne and the authors.

[1] A preliminary report of this study was presented at the American Psychological Association Convention, 1959. The study was supported in part by grants from the National Institute of Health and the Society for the Investigation of Human Ecology.

[2] The authors are indebted to Mrs. Irene Waskow for her generous assistance in producing this paper.

client's reference to his experiencing is indicated by voice quality, verbal context, and certain characteristic forms of expression. For example, the use of the demonstrative pronoun for feelings ("This feeling," "this all-tied-up way I feel"), and the client's often difficult search for words, may show that he is referring *directly* to felt data the character of which he seeks to convey. Periods of silence are often preceded and followed by words that indicate that the client has been directly and continuously referring to his experiencing during the silence.

The theory considers experiencing to be an aspect of the physiological life of a unitary organism. Therefore, if periods of continuous reference to experiencing are therapeutic, physiological tension - reduction should be measurable during them.

The present study attempts to define and produce "continuous reference to experiencing" in the laboratory, and to contrast its autonomic correlates with those found during other modes of attention. The study thus predicts differences for different *modes of process,* rather than for different verbal or affective *contents.*

METHOD

The subjects were 17 male and female college undergraduates previously not known to the experimenter. They received credits for participation in the experiment.

The subject was taken into a room controlled for temperature ($73° \pm 1°$) and humidity ($45\% \pm 5\%$) and seated on the couch. Yellow Springs Zinc Sulfate paste electrodes were then placed on the palmar surface of the left hand. The galvanic skin resistance was measured by the use of a Grass DC1A preamplifier which passed a 50 microampere current through the electrodes. The subject's responses were recorded on the Model 5A Grass polygraph chart driven at a speed of 2.5 millimeters per second.

The experimenter remained seated and silent in the room throughout the experiment. After a five minute accommodation period, seven tape recorded instructions were played. Exactly two and one half minutes separated the conclusion of one instruction and the beginning of the next.

Instructions for continuous reference to experiencing ("a") are contrasted with instructions ("b") during which the individual was either asked to attend *continuously* to an *external* object, or *discontinuously* (self-interruptedly) to a number of different *internal* data. Instructions ("c") asked the subject to speak, speech to an unfamiliar experimenter being held to involve both *discontinuity and external attention.* All three types of conditions were duplicated[3] for personally disturbing ("–1") and undisturbing ("–2") verbal content. The instructions were:

---

[3] Eight experimental conditions are implied. However, there was no practical method of presenting a *continuous external* personally disturbing object, hence "b-3" is not duplicated for threat. This omission made it impossible to employ a complete factorial design.

c-2   For the first instruction, I'd like to ask you to talk out loud about anything at all. Please talk about various different things, not just one. You might talk about how difficult it is to find something to talk about, or anything at all. All right.

b-2   All right. For the second instruction, please continue to *think* about the same sort of things you were talking about, only this time don't speak, just think to yourself. Do be sure to think about various things, not just one. All right.

b-3   All right. Now please concentrate your attention on this table. Try to get all involved in what you see. Pretend that you want to draw the table afterwards and that you want to notice exactly what it looks like. All right.

a-2   All right. Now, silently to yourself, try to remember as many of your school mates in the early grades of school as you can. Try to remember them, and, if you can, their names. All right.

b-1   All right. Again in this next instruction, please just think silently to yourself. Please, just to yourself, choose some situation or problem about which you have some strong troublesome feelings. When you have decided which problem feelings to choose, please wait until you hear how I'd like you to think about it. All right.

a-1   O.K. Please think about some one specific aspect of the problem. As you think about it, try to feel it as specifically as you can. If you find yourself thinking about many different things, please again choose one feeling from among these and continue thinking about one feeling as much as possible. All right.

c-1   All right. Now, in this experiment you are *not* going to be asked to communicate anything personal. But we would like to ask you to speak in some very general way about the problem you have been thinking about. For example, you might say whether it has to do with other people or just with yourself, whether it happens often or rarely or why it is difficult to talk about. All right.

The choice of specific GSR indices was based on the pilot observations which gave rise to the study. GSR was observed during psychotherapy as well as under other circumstances. A strikingly linear increase in resistance was often noted during silences of which the individual later asserted that he was referring to deeply and immediately felt data. Since our theory and the study itself attempt to define this variable, and since no rigorous theoretical basis exists for choosing among the many possible GSR indices, these pilot observations determined the choice. The GSR indices were:

Linearity (the absence of deflections) is defined as an inverse function of the number of deflections (of 1250 ohms or more, each occurring during two seconds or less).

Increment is defined as the increase in resistance between the beginning and the end of each experimental period.

There are thus two separate GSR measures for each comparison of experimental periods. Three hypotheses were formulated as follows:

Hypothesis 1: The "a" as well as the "b" silences will be associated with greater GSR linearity and increment than will periods of speech "c."

Hypothesis 2: Type "a" silences will be associated with greater GSR linearity and increment than will type "b" silences.

Hypothesis 3: There will be no significant difference on the GSR variables between experimental periods numbered "1" and those numbered "2."

RESULTS

For each subject, the means for each type of experimental period were computed and used as raw scores. Tables 1 and 2 show the results of the analyses of variance run in order to test for differences between silences type *a*, type *b*, and speech, on both linearity and increment. F's were significant at better than the .01 level in both analyses. The Duncan Range Test was applied to the results.

Type "a" silences were significantly higher than speech "c" on increment and linearity (both .01). Type "b" silences were significantly different from speech only on the linearity variable (.01). Type "b" silences differed significantly from type "a" silences only on the increment variable (.05). In both GSR indices, the means for "b" fell betwen those of "a" and "c" (Table 3). Comparison of periods "1"

TABLE 1

ANALYSIS OF VARIANCE FOR INCREMENT DIFFERENCES OF TYPE *a* VS. TYPE *b* VS. SPEECH

Source	df	SS	ms	f
Instructions	2	639,290,098.86	319,645,049.43	7.084**
Subjects w/in	16	834,503,302.04	52,156,456.38	1.156
Residual	32	1,443,945,411.14	45,123,294.10	
Total	50	2,917,738,812.04		

** .01 level of significance.

TABLE 2

ANALYSIS OF VARIANCE FOR LINEARITY DIFFERENCES OF TYPE *a* VS. TYPE *b* VS. SPEECH

Source	df	SS	ms	f
Instructions	2	189.61	94.81	12.140**
Subjects w/in	16	1,329.70	83.11	10.641**
Residual	32	250.06	7.81	
Total	50	1,769.37		

and "2" yielded no significant differences on either GSR index. The third hypothesis appears supported.

The hypotheses were further examined in terms of comparisons between individual experimental periods. Tables 4 and 5 present the results of an analysis of variance between individual scores. F's were at .01 for both GSR variables. Duncan Range Tests concerning individual experimental periods showed that 23 of the 32 differences which would be implied by hypotheses 1 and 2 were found to be significant in the predicted direction. Table 6 shows these results.

These findings tend to support the hypotheses that both kinds of silence are dif-

TABLE 3

MEANS OF INCREMENT AND LINEARITY

	Increment	Linearity*
"a"	9986.76	5.62
"b"	4778.47	6.94
"c"	1377.35	10.21

* Linearity is measured as the inverse of variability.

TABLE 4

ANALYSIS OF VARIANCE OF INCREMENT DIFFERENCES BETWEEN INSTRUCTIONS

Source	df	SS	ms	f
Instructions	6	1,619,173,440.34	269,862,240.06	35.88**
Subjects w/in	16	1,798,223,969.75	112,388,998.11	14.94**
Residual	96	722,060,759.66	7,521,466.24	
Total	118	10,638,000,169.75		

** .01 level of significance.

TABLE 5

ANALYSIS OF VARIANCE OF LINEARITY DIFFERENCES BETWEEN INSTRUCTIONS

Source	df	SS	ms	f
Instructions	6	451.40	75.23	5.46**
Subjects w/in	16	3,108.89	194.31	14.11**
Residual	96	1,321.46	13.77	
Total	118	4,881.75		

** .01 level of significance.

TABLE 6

DUNCAN RANGE TEST OF SIGNIFICANCE OF DIFFERENCES BETWEEN INDIVIDUAL INSTRUCTIONS

	A1 > C1	A1 > C2	A2 > C1	A2 > C2		
Linearity	.01	.01	.01	.01		
Increment	.01	.01	.01	.01		

	B1 > C1	B1 > C2	B2 > C1	B2 > C2	B3 > C1	B3 > C2
Linearity			.01	.01	.01	.01
Increment	.01		.01	.05	.01	

	A1 > B1	A2 > B1	A1 > B2	A2 > B2	A1 > B3	A2 > B3
Linearity	.05					
Increment	.01	.01	.01	.01	.01	.01

ferent from speech, and that "b" (self-interrupted or externally focused) silences differ from "a" silences (continuous reference, as defined by these instructions). Type "b" silences do not show the extremely high increment found in "a," nor the many deflections found in speech, ("c").

DISCUSSION

The instructions were presented in the same order to all subjects. This was unavoidable, since some instructions depend upon previous ones. (One cannot refer to a single feeling, as in "a-1" without first going through the quite different mode of process involved in choosing one feeling from among many, as in "b-1.")

The effect of time alone is ruled out in the findings themselves, since much increment occurred in the second, fourth and sixth periods, while the fifth and seventh showed little. However, the order of speech, threat, and time, in combination, requires that we limit the generalization of these findings to these conditions presented in this order.

Another limitation on the generality of the findings lies in the relationship between theory and laboratory conditions. While the instructions arose from the theory, other instructions are conceivable. Especially "discontinuity" and "external attention" could be called for in many ways other than those used here. Hence predictions for quite different laboratory conditions must be made cautiously, even if they were to seem in accord with the general theory. The study predicted and found differential GSR patterns for just these contrasted laboratory conditions. Even so, the implications are striking:

1. Silence seems to involve significantly more linear increase in resistance, than speech. This difference should be considered in the design and controls used in psychophysiological experiments.

2. Silences during which subjects were instructed to refer directly to *troublesome* personal feelings showed *tension-reduction*

patterns. The implication is that—as in psychotherapy—there may be a mode of psychological process in which troublesome content is referred to in a tension-reductive way. Of course, theoretical interpretations of such a process may differ. Auld (1) reports, "Typically, when a patient is basking in regressive thoughts and appears relaxed, there are no GSRs." Would he consider instructions "a" as engendering a basking in regressive thoughts? Direct reference to experiencing during psychotherapy may similarly be considered "regressive thoughts." Another interpretation might consider continuous reference as a light, self-induced hypnotic trance. Linear resistance increase during such a time would not be surprising. Whatever one's theoretical interpretation, it does appear that linear resistance increase (tension-reduction) accompanies a certain mode of psychological process, even when the contents attended to are troublesome feelings.

Such a conclusion may also clarify previously contradictory findings. Contents (such as "hostility") have been found associated with autonomic tension increase in some studies, while other studies (4) find tension reduction. The present findings imply that predictions of GSR pattern cannot be made on the basis of the threat value of content alone. The *manner* of the psychological *process* must be considered. As defined by laboratory instructions, continuous reference to directly felt experiencing (during silence and in the absence of interruptions) is associated with linear increase in galvanic skin resistance. The findings are consistent with the theory (among others) that the mode of psychological process termed "continuous reference to experiencing" is an organismic tension-reduction process. In other words, emersion in ones ongoing feeling process appears to be organismically adaptive.

SUMMARY

The study attempted to define and produce in the laboratory a phenomenon observed in psychotherapy and theoretically formulated as "continuous reference to experiencing." Organismic tension-reduction was theoretically predicted as a physiological correlate.

Seventeen subjects were given seven tape recorded instructions, each followed by an experimental period of two and one half minutes. Number of GSRs and resistance rise were measured during each period. Following the laboratory instructions for silent continuous reference to experiencing significantly fewer GSRs and greater resistance increase occurred, than during experimental periods that involved speech, or silent external or self-interrupted attention.

REFERENCES

1. AULD, F. JR., DREYER, H. W. AND DOLLARD, J. Measurement of electrical skin resistance during interviews. *Psychological Reports*, 1958, 4, 1.

2. GENDLIN, E. Experiencing: A variable in the process of therapeutic change. *Amer. J. Psychotherapy*. In press.

3. GENDLIN, E. AND ZIMRING, R. The qualities or dimensions of experiencing and their change. Counseling Center Discussion Papers, University of Chicago, Counseling Center, 1955, 1, 3.

4. LACEY, J. I. Psychophysiological approaches to the evaluation of psychotherapeutic process and outcome. In *Research in Psychotherapy*. Proceedings of a conference, Washington, D.C.: American Psychological Assn., 1959, p. 174.

5. ROGERS, C. R. A process conception of psychotherapy. *Amer. Psychologist,* 1958, 13, 4.

6. ROGERS, C. R. A tentative scale for the measurement of process in psychotherapy. *In Research in Psychotherapy*. Proceedings of a conference, Washington, D.C.: American Psychological Assn., 1959.

7. WALKER, A. M., RABLEN, R. A. AND ROGERS, C. R. Development of a scale to measure process changes in psychotherapy. *J. clin. Psychol.,* 1960, 16, 1.

Modification of Behavior Through Verbal Conditioning: Effects in Group Therapy[1]

LEONARD P. ULLMANN
LEONARD KRASNER
BEVERLY J. COLLINS

A recent conference on research in psychotherapy (Rubinstein & Parloff, 1959) pointed up the difficulties of validating the effectiveness of psychotherapy by the current methods of assessing change in behavior. The number of relevant variables in the therapy situation is such that even random assignment of cases to treatment or no treatment groups (Fairweather, Simon, Gebhard, Weingarten, Holland, Sanders, Stone, & Reahl, 1960; Rogers & Dymond, 1954) does not guarantee that differences obtained may be reasonably associated with the form of *treatment* as distinct from either the *practitioner* or the unique interaction among the variables in the situation. Rather than attempting to assess the value of the total therapy situation, it seems more efficient first to isolate the behaviors of the therapist and the patient which are characteristic of the psychotherapy situation. Then these characteristic behaviors may be systematically manipulated in order to test hypotheses about the psychotherapeutic process. Among these hypotheses are: (*a*) that one person can influence the behavior of another in a predictable direction; (*b*) that this change has a desirable effect on behavior in a second, criterion situation; and (*c*) that as far as possible, the changed behavior in the criterion situation is associated with a specific aspect of the already circumscribed behavior of the experimenter.

The first point, that one person can influence another person's verbal behavior in a specifiable manner, may be accepted as reasonably well established by the studies of operant verbal conditioning reviewed by Krasner (1958) and Salzinger (1959). It is primarily to the second point, the change of subjects' behavior in a situation other than the experimental one, that this article

Reprinted from *Journal of Abnormal and Social Psychology,* 1961, 62 (1), 128–132, with the permission of the American Psychological Association and the authors.

[1] From the Psychology Research Laboratory, Veterans Administration Hospital, Palo Alto, California. This investigation was supported in part by Research Grant M-2458, National Institute of Mental Health, United States Public Health Service.

is addressed. Relevant studies in which behavior has been manipulated in one situation and the effect of this manipulation has been measured in a second may be roughly categorized into three types: motor operant conditioning, verbal operant conditioning, and "psychotherapy."

Motor operant conditioning techniques as a means of deliberate "therapeutic" manipulation of patient behavior has been employed in a series of recent investigations (King, Merrell, Lovinger, & Denny, 1957; Lindsley & Skinner, 1954; Peters, 1952; Peters & Jenkins, 1954; Tilton, 1957). In these studies, motor operant conditioning was purposefully used as a therapeutic technique to bring patients into more active contact with reality.

In the verbal conditioning literature, reports on generalization effects are infrequent. The usual procedure has been to present a series of test-like tasks prior to and immediately following a verbal conditioning session, and then to ascertain changes in these tests. For example, Williams (1959) used as his pre- and postmeasures an "interpersonal check-list" and the Osgood Semantic Differential Scale. In one of his experimental groups, "feeling statements" were reinforced; in a second experimental group, "nonfeeling statements" were reinforced. The experimental situation itself was presented to the subjects as "psychotherapy." Although use of the reinforced verbal classes was increased during the experimental sessions, there were no significant differences between groups on the pre- and posttest measures. Using a similar design, Rogers (1960) also reported significant effects of conditioning but failure to obtain generalization as measured by a battery of four personality tests. However, Sarason (1957) did report significant generalization effects as measured by a "free word naming" situation before and after a verbal conditioning situation.

The "psychotherapy" studies generally involve the use of a series of psychological measures before and after a stated "treatment" period (Rogers & Dymond, 1954). Some studies (Grossman, 1952; Keet, 1948) make use of a specified number of experimental sessions to test the effectiveness of a given therapeutic technique. There have been several discussions (Berg, 1952; Leary & Harvey, 1956; Miller 1954) of the rationale of the use of such tests as projective techniques, rating scales, and Q sorts as measures of therapeutic effectiveness. Using a different criterion and one closer to the present study, Brown (1957), working with "chronic ward patients," used as his dependent measure responsiveness to an avoidance conditioning situation (paired tone and light stimuli alternately reinforced by a painful faradic shock). After the pre-experimental measures, half the patients were subjected to various psychotherapeutic manipulations, principally group therapy. The group that had received therapy was significantly more responsive to conditioning after therapy than before, whereas the control (no therapy) group showed no significant increase after the same period of time.

Where Brown used responsiveness to conditioning as a dependent variable, the present study used verbal operant conditioning sessions as the independent variable and ratings of behavior in group therapy as the dependent variable. The purpose of this design was the attempt to test two hypotheses basic to psychotherapy: that interpersonal interaction can lead to change in a desirable manner in a second, nonexperimental situation, and that the observed change may be associated with a specific aspect of the experimenter's behavior.

METHOD

Three groups, each consisting of 10 male "continued treatment" patients at a VA neuropsychiatric hospital, served as subjects. At the start of the experiment the median age of the subjects was 35 (range: 21–47), the median education was 12 years (range: 7–16 years), and the median length of current hospitalization was 5 months (range: 1–133 months). On admission, 28 of the subjects had been diagnosed as schizophrenic reaction, one had been diagnosed as manic depressive, and one as depressive reaction. Each group was given the same experimental task, the experimenter's response being varied. All subjects were rated by group therapists before and after the experimental sessions.

Experimental task. Subjects were seen for two sessions per week for 2 weeks. The situation was structured to the patient as "a study into how people make up stories about pictures shown to them." In each session, the patients were shown four pictures and asked to make up stories to last for 5 minutes each. If responses lagged, the usual TAT instructions and encouragement were used by the experimenter. The picture stimuli used were line drawings of situations common to the experiences of patients in hospitals and were scenes such as buying a tie, mowing a lawn, fishing, buying a movie ticket, ordering a meal in a restaurant. The situations were selected to be commonplace and not emotionally arousing in themselves. This procedure minimized differential "card-pull" (Gurel & Ullmann, 1958; Ullmann, 1957a) and reduced the possibility that emotionally toned stimuli would alter verbal production in a schizophrenic sample (Ullmann, 1958). The use of less direct stimuli is in line with Krasner and Ullmann's (1958) suggestion that minimal cues (e.g., "mmm-hmm") about which the schizophrenic subject is less aware may be less threatening and therefore more effective in increasing and guiding his verbal behavior than overt examiner responses (e.g., "good-bad,"' "right-wrong," "true-false") which the schizophrenic may perceive as evaluative of his behavior.

Experimental groups. Each subject was assigned, in the manner described below, to one of three conditions. Once in a condition, the same examiner behavior was maintained throughout the four story-telling sessions, each of which involved four stories. That is, the pattern of examiner reinforcement started on the first trial of the first session. In the first condition, the *positive-personal* reinforcement group, the examiner responded to the verbal class to be reinforced by a head nod and the approving sound "mmm-hmm." In the second group, the *impersonal-unstructured* reinforcement group, the examiner responded by pushing a button attached to an electric counter which emitted a loud click. The dial of the counter faced the patient, and he saw an increase in the number on the dial. At the end of each story, the counter was reset to zero. Questions about the meaning of the counter were answered with the phrase that it was one of the experimental measures. In the third group, the *no reinforcement* group, the experimenter made no responses to the stories told by the subjects.

Verbal class reinforced. The verbal class reinforced was "emotional words" as defined by Ullmann and McFarland (1957). There were two reasons for the selection of this group of words. The first was the relevance of such words to group therapy ratings. Ullmann (1957b) found that ability to express feeling resulting from social premises presented in a projective test was significantly correlated with group therapy scale ratings. Similarly, Ullmann and McFarland (1957) found that the number of emotional words used in response to TAT cards was highly correlated with the group therapy ratings. In terms of relevance, then, emotional words represent the sort of material that is produced in therapy and is of particular interest to psychotherapists. An increase in the use of emotional words in the experimental situation may be therapeutic in itself, or the practice of these words during experimental sessions may lead to an increase in their use in the group therapy situation. If either or both of these possibilities were the case, it could be hypothesized that an improvement in group therapy ratings would result.

A second reason for the use of emotional words was the high rater reliability previously obtained in the use of this class of verbal behavior. In the original work with TAT protocols (Ullmann & McFarland, 1957), rater reliability was .92. Using a single "hearing" of 16 nonreinforced 4-minute tapes of college students, three raters (including the examiner in this study) obtained a coefficient of concordance significant beyond the .001 level (Weiss, Krasner, & Ullmann, 1960).

Dependent criterion measure. The dependent measure used was the Palo Alto Group Therapy Scale (GTS) (Finney, 1954). The GTS is an 88-item scale, checked by therapists for the patient's behavior during the most recent four therapy sessions. Finney (1954) reported that for 18 groups in a neuropsychiatric hospital a median rank order correlation of .84 was obtained between scale scores and global rankings of patients by group leaders. In the same study, a rank order correlation of .80 was obtained between the average ratings by 10 ward personnel of adequacy of interpersonal relationships throughout the hospital and the patients' GTS scores.

In the present study, five group therapists [2] on two wards completed GTS forms about their patients. The therapists knew

[2] The authors wish to express their thanks to George Fairweather, Ben Finney, Ralph Forsyth, Sidney Gelfand, and Donald Lim for making the criterion ratings.

that a number of conditions were involved in the experiment but not to which one the specific patient would be assigned. One of the authors scored the ratings and then assigned patients to the three experimental groups. A restriction on absolute randomness of patient assignment was that the means and standard deviations of the pre-ratings for the three groups were kept as equal as possible. Another of the authors (BJC) was the examiner in all cases and did not know the subjects' GTS scores. Immediately after the last experimental session, the group therapist rerated the patient.[3] In all cases, the same therapist made both the pre- and post-GTS ratings.

RESULTS

The major results of the experiment are presented in Table 1. The means and standard deviations of the pre-experimental groups were not significantly different. The average gain ($\bar{x}_1 - \bar{x}_2$) for the positive-personal reinforcement group was 5.70 GTS points; for the impersonal-unstructured reinforcement group, it was 1.00 GTS points, and for the no reinforcement group, it was 0.50 GTS points. Finally, the own-control change was at the .05 level (one-tailed test) for the positive-personal reinforcement group ($t = 1.83$), whereas it was not significant ($t = 0.34$ and 0.15) for the other two groups.

[3] The time between pre- and postratings averaged 14.80 days with a standard deviation of 3.31 days.

TABLE 1

MEANS AND STANDARD DEVIATIONS OF GROUP THERAPY RATINGS BEFORE AND AFTER STORY-TELLING UNDER THREE DIFFERENT REINFORCEMENT CONDITIONS

Type of Reinforcement	N	Pre-experimental		Post-experimental		r_{12}	$\bar{x}_1 - \bar{x}_2$	t
		$\bar{x}_1$	σ_1	$\bar{x}_2$	σ_2			
positive-personal	10	58.2	20.6	63.9	25.5	.94	5.70	1.83
impersonal-unstructured	10	56.8	18.4	57.8	21.1	.91	1.00	0.43
no reinforcement	10	61.0	20.0	61.5	21.1	.89	0.50	0.15

Clinically, these results may be presented in the following manner: Five of the 10 subjects in the positive-personal reinforcement group gained 10 or more GTS points; whereas 2 of the 10 subjects in the impersonal - unstructured reinforcement group gained this much, and only 1 of the 10 subjects in the no reinforcement group gained 10 or more GTS points.

DISCUSSION

The results of this study will be discussed in terms of hypotheses that are basic to interpreting psychotherapeutic interactions. One of these hypotheses is that the effect of such an interaction is measurable in an independent criterion situation. The frequency of use in projective situations of the verbal class conditioned in this study, emotional words, had previously been demonstrated to be significantly correlated with GTS scores (Ullmann & McFarland, 1957). The relevance of the use of emotional words to group therapy ratings may explain why positive results were obtained in this study. Further, the evidence for the validity of the criterion used in this study (Finney, 1954) and the fact that the ratings depended on actual interpersonal behavior add to the pertinence of the criterion as a measure of the effectiveness of interpersonal interactions.

In terms of amount of change, it is interesting to note the relatively brief period of time (80 minutes) involved in the experiment itself. In addition, these results were obtained within an ongoing hospital treatment program which may well have increased within-group variance.[4] Despite

this evidence for the therapeutic effectiveness of verbal conditioning, however, there are considerations that limit the generalizations to be drawn. On the one hand, the technique is not pertinent to regressed patients who cannot tell stories. Such patients are ones who might have been successfully approached by motor operant conditioning techniques (King et al., 1957; Lindsley & Skinner, 1954). With highly verbal or more "normal" subjects—college students, for example—it is possible to hypothesize that the practice of speech in general and emotional words in particular would be less effective because these subjects have less need for additional practice in emotional expressiveness. It is therefore hypothesized that the effectiveness of verbal conditioning as a "therapeutic" technique may well be useful only with people in a particular segment of the continuum of mental health.

The results of this study also lend support to the proposition that the changes in criterion measures ascribed to psychotherapy may be associated with specifiable therapist behaviors. Evidence for this concept stems from the three experimental groups used. In both the no reinforcement and the impersonal-unstructured reinforcement groups, the amount of additional personal contact with the patients matched that of the positive-personal reinforcement group. The use of the clicker-counter in the impersonal-unstructured reinforcement group matched the additional attention called to emotional words. Such additional cuing, by itself, did not yield a significant gain in group therapy scale ratings. Therefore, within the limits of the present design, there is evidence that positive-personal re-

---

[4] An idea of the uncontrolled variation present within an ongoing treatment program may be obtained by considering why subjects on whom pre-experimental ratings had been made did not complete the experiment: Eight of the men either failed to come to appointments, or when they came, were not cooperative in story-telling; four moved to different wards; three left the hospital; two men underwent extensive and painful dental work that interfered with story-telling; two were lost to the

study when the group therapist moved to a different ward, and procedures were not completed with one man because the examiner broke her leg. In terms of the criterion pre-experimental ratings, these 20 men were not significantly different from the 30 who did complete the experiment. The average GTS rating of the 20 men who did not complete the experiment was 61.4 with a standard deviation of 20.9.

inforcing behavior of the examiner was an important factor associated with the significant change in group therapy scores.

It is possible to hypothesize that the amount and direction of change measured by the criterion should be positively correlated with change in the experimental situation in the use of the reinforced verbal class. The design of the present study did not permit a test of this hypothesis. All experimental trials were reinforced, that is, there were no nonreinforced operant trials. This was done to avoid the extinction effect on schizophrenics of unreinforced trials which might have decreased the chance of obtaining change on the dependent measure. Other reasons for the decision made in this study were the failure of Rogers (1960) and Williams (1959) to obtain generalization effects after having obtained significant conditioning, and the attempt to design an analogue of psychotherapy in which the therapist is likely to give immediate reinforcement to the patient's first emission of the desired verbal behavior. Finally, the hypothesis of the positive correlation between change in use of the verbal class during experimental sessions and change on the criterion may be over-simplified. It may well be that the important thing learned was the permissibility of spontaneously using emotional words in an interpersonal situation rather than practice in the use of the words per se.

Beyond the evidence for specific hypotheses which underlie psychotherapy, the present paper illustrates the use of verbal conditioning as a miniature situation for the study of interpersonal behavior (Krasner, 1955). Verbal conditioning may be used both as a dependent variable to measure the effects of various experimental conditions on responsiveness to reinforcement, or, as in this study, as the independent variable. In either case, the verbal conditioning situation permits the reduction and isolation of interpersonal variables with a resultant increase in the opportunity for their systematic study.

SUMMARY

This study used a verbal conditioning situation to investigate hypotheses relevant to psychotherapeutic interactions. Neuropsychiatric patients who were receiving group therapy participated in four story-telling sessions during which emotional words were reinforced in one of the following three ways: a positive-personal manner, an impersonal-unstructured manner, and not reinforced at all. Ratings made by group therapists before and after the experimental story-telling sessions indicated a significant gain in adequacy of interpersonal relationships in group therapy for the group receiving positive-personal reinforcement. There was no significant gain for the other two groups on this criterion measure. The results support the hypotheses that one person can influence another person in a positive way and that this change may be measurable by an independent criterion situation. Further, this change in the subject's behavior may be demonstrated to be associated with specific behavior on the part of the experimenter.

REFERENCES

BERG, I. Measures before and after therapy. *J. clin. Psychol.*, 1952, 8, 46–50.

BROWN, C. C. Changes in avoidance conditioning following psychotherapeutic treatment. *J. nerv. ment. Dis.*, 1957, 125, 487–489.

FAIRWEATHER, G. W., SIMON, R. GEBHARD, M. E., WEINGARTEN, E., HOLLAND, J. L., SANDERS, R., STONE, G. B., & REAHL, J. Relative effectiveness of psychotherapeutic programs: A multicriteria comparison of four programs for three different patient groups. *Psychol. Monogr.*, 1960, 74(5, Whole No. 492).

FINNEY, B. C. A scale to measure interpersonal relationships in group therapy. *Group Psychother.*, 1954, 7, 52–66.

GROSSMAN, D. An experimental investigation of a psychotherapeutic technique. *J. consult. Psychol.*, 1952, 16, 325–331.

GUREL, L., & ULLMANN, L. P. Quantitative differences in response to TAT cards: The relationship between transcendence score and number of emotional words. *J. proj. Tech.,* 1958, 22, 399–401.

KEET, C. D. Two verbal techniques in a miniature counseling situation. *Psychol. Monogr.,* 1948, 62(7, Whole No. 294).

KING, G. F., MERRELL, D. W., LOVINGER, E., & DENNY, M. R. Operant motor behavior in acute schizophrenics. *J. Pers.,* 1957, 25, 317–326.

KRASNER, L. The use of generalized reinforcers in psychotherapy research. *Psychol. Rep.,* 1955, 1, 19–25.

KRASNER, L. Studies of the conditioning of verbal behavior. *Psychol. Bull.,* 1958, 55, 148–170.

KRASNER, L., & ULLMANN, L. P. Variables in the verbal conditioning of schizophrenic subjects. *Amer. Psychologist,* 1958, 13, 358. (Abstract)

LEARY, T., & HARVEY, JOAN S. A methodology for measuring personality changes in psychotherapy. *J. clin. Psychol.,* 1956, 12, 123–132.

LINDSLEY, O. R., & SKINNER, B. F. A method for the experimental analysis of the behavior of psychotic patients. *Amer. Psychologist,* 1954, 9, 419–420. (Abstract)

MILLER, J. G. Criteria and measurement of change during psychiatric treatment. *Bull. Menninger Clin.,* 1954, 18, 130–137.

PETERS, H. N. An experimental evaluation of learning vs. therapy in schizophrenia. *Amer. Psychologist,* 1952, 7, 354. (Abstract)

PETERS, H. N., & JENKINS, R. L. Improvement of chronic schizophrenic patients with guided problem-solving motivated by hunger. *Psychiat. Quart. Suppl.,* 1954, 28, 84–101.

ROGERS, C. R., & DYMOND, ROSALIND F. (Eds.) *Psychotherapy and personality change.* Chicago: Univer. Chicago Press, 1954.

ROGERS, J. M. Operant conditioning in a quasi-therapy setting. *J. abnorm. soc. Psychol.,* 1960, 60, 247–252.

RUBINSTEIN, E. A., & PARLOFF, M. B. (Eds.) *Research in psychotherapy.* Washington, D.C.: American Psychological Association, 1959.

SALZINGER, K. Experimental manipulation of verbal behavior: A review. *J. gen. Psychol.,* 1959, 61, 65–94.

SARASON, BARBARA R. The effects of verbally conditioned response classes on post-conditioning tasks. *Dissertation Abstr.,* 1957, 12, 679. (Abstract)

TILTON, J. R. The use of instrumental motor and verbal learning techniques in the treatment of chronic schizophrenics. Unpublished doctoral dissertation, Michigan State University, 1957.

ULLMANN, L. P. Productivity and the clinical use of TAT cards. *J. proj. Tech.,* 1957, 21, 399–403. (a)

ULLMANN, L. P. Selection of neuropsychiatric patients for group psychotherapy. *J. consult. Psychol.,* 1957, 21, 277–280. (b)

ULLMANN, L. P. Clinical correlates of facilitation and inhibition of response to emotional stimuli. *J. proj. Tech.,* 1958, 22, 341–347.

ULLMANN, L. P., & McFARLAND, R. L. Productivity as a variable in TAT protocols: A methodological study. *J. proj. Tech.,* 1957, 21, 80–87.

WEISS, R. L., KRASNER, L., & ULLMANN, L. P. Responsivity to verbal conditioning as a function of emotional atmosphere and pattern of reinforcement. *Psychol. Rep.,* 1960, 6, 415–426.

WILLIAMS, R. I. Verbal conditioning in psychotherapy. *Amer. Psychologist,* 1959, 14, 388. (Abstract)

An Analysis of Therapist-Child Interaction in Play Therapy

CLARK E. MOUSTAKAS
HENRY D. SCHLALOCK[1]

The present investigation purposed to examine the nature of the interaction of therapist and child in a play therapy situation, with particular reference to two groups of children, one with serious emotional problems, the other without such problems. The study involved the analysis of one therapist's behavior, and is therefore essentially exploratory.

Several studies (1, 2, 3, 6, 7) have attempted to measure discrete aspects of therapist-child interaction, especially the child's responses to the therapist. In general, however, they have not analyzed the child's influence on the therapist's responses to the child, nor are they based on a measure of the minute-by-minute interaction between therapist and child. This study sought to provide information concerning such interaction in the play therapy situation.

THE MEASURING DEVICE

A system of categories has been devised (6) that permits a comprehensive quantitative measurement of adult-child interaction and provides an objective basis for studying the play therapy situation. A total of 82 adult and 72 child categories are included in the schedule. These categories were constructed on the assumption that adult-child interaction involves reciprocal stimulation: that the child's behavior is potentially as significant in influencing the adult's behavior as the converse. The measuring instrument is therefore focused equally on adult and child interactional behavior.

This concept of interaction makes no inference about the motivation of specific behavioral acts. The categories are interchangeable; that is, the categories for measuring adult and child behavior are essentially the same. In addition, a hostility

Reprinted from *Child Development,* 1955, 26 (2), 143–157, with the permission of the Society for Research in Child Development and the authors.

[1] Clark E. Moustakas, psychologist, was the play therapist for this study; Henry D. Schlalock, a graduate student at the Merrill-Palmer School in 1953–54, . . . was the observer.

or anxiety rating accompanies all category entries. A report (6) now in preparation lists, describes, and discusses the categories. The behavior of both child and adult (in this instance, the therapist) is recorded at five-second intervals in terms of the categories and ratings involved.

Reliability of Observations

Reliability was determined by findings and agreement between two independent observers on simultaneous observational records. Reliability, computed on the basis of an item-by-item comparison of these independent simultaneous records, is reported in terms of percentage of agreement. For two observers, recording approximately 90 minutes of therapist-child interaction, it was 96.41 for the behavioral categories, 98.27 for the anxiety-hostility ratings, and 92.44 for a combined score in each five-second interval. Another report (6) gives reliability scores on the individual categories.

PROCEDURES

The subjects, selected from four-year-old children enrolled in the Merrill-Palmer Nursery School, were each rated as having or not having emotional problems of sufficient severity to impair personal and social relations in the nursery school. Three independent ratings of the children were made: one on the basis of home and school longitudinal records, one by the nursery school teacher, a third by a student teacher. No child was included in the study unless there was complete agreement as to the presence or absence of severe emotional problems. Such agreement was reached on 10 of the 16 children aged four. This criterion prevented matching the children on the basis of sex. However, all came from similar socio-economic and educational backgrounds, that is, from middle-class, professional families. Group A (without emotional problems) included

three girls and two boys; group B, four boys and one girl.

With the exception of one child in each group who was seen only once because of withdrawal from the school, each subject was seen by the same therapist for two 40-minute play sessions, usually with an interval of three days between the sessions.

Observations were made from a room equipped with a one-way vision mirror and sound amplifiers. The therapist endeavored to avoid obstructing the view of the observers.[2]

Observational data were not discussed between therapist and observer. The observer was not familiar with the subjects or with the ratings of the children. Since approximately a thousand items were recorded during each session, and the sessions were held at three-day intervals for any particular child, it is unlikely that the observer had any preconceived ideas about the expected behavior of either therapist or child.

The Therapist's Rule

In accordance with the child-centered orientation (5), the role and purpose of the therapist were to convey to the child attitudes of faith, acceptance, and respect throughout the session. He attempted to achieve these goals by maintaining a listening attitude and sympathetic responsiveness and by creating a warm, permissive relationship. His function was so to structure the relationship as to give the child a clear understanding of his freedom, to encourage him to express himself in his own way, to reflect his feelings and thus show him that he was understood and accepted, and to set limits, helping the child to feel secure, to move safely, and to tie the experience to reality.

RESULTS

The data obtained from observations of therapist and child behavior were arranged

---

[2] After reliability had been established, one observer continued the observations.

in two master tables (not included in this report), and the results were summarized in terms of the information they provide with reference to certain specific questions.

I. *What is the nature of the therapist's behavior as he interacts with the child in a play therapy setting? Are there differences in this behavior when he interacts with* (a) *a child not having emotional problems and* (b) *a child with emotional problems?*

Data relevant to the first part of the question were summarized and analyzed in terms of rank order of frequency. A total of 9,084 observations and an equal number of anxiety-hostility ratings of the therapist's behavior were made, based on five-second periods. The five categories appearing most frequently, and accounting for about 85 per cent of the therapist's interaction with the children, were: Attentive Observation (the therapist observes and listens while the child plays); Recognition of Stimulation (the therapist shows recognition overtly, e.g., by saying, "Um hm," or "I see,"); Giving Information Verbally; Interpretation by Restating Verbalized Feelings; and Seeking Information of an Impersonal Nature (e.g., the therapist asks the child if he noticed the crayon under the chair).

Certain categories seldom used by the therapist were: Restriction with an Explanation, Enthusiastic Cooperation, Reassurance, Directing with a Threat, Noncooperation Accompanied by an Explanation, Seeking Personal Information, Seeking Permission, and Giving Qualified Permission.

Categories not used at all by the therapist included: Seeking Help, Seeking Reassurance, Seeking Reward, Orienting Roles by use of status and power, and most "Restricting" and "Forbidding" categories. The therapist did not employ "Criticism" or "Disciplinary Action" of any kind. Threat of Attack and Rejection by changing the subject, denying the validity of a statement, or rejecting the child as a person

were not used. Other categories that did not appear in the therapist's behavior were: Expressions of Affection, Reward, Compliance, Noncooperation, and two categories of "Interpretation," namely, Interpretation by Associating Current and Past Events, and Interpretation by Giving an Account of Reality or Translation of Symbolic Behavior.

Data relevant to the second part of the question show little difference between the two groups with respect to the five most frequently used categories, totaling about 85 per cent for each group. The category used most often, Attentive Observation, represented 57 per cent of the therapist's interaction with the children of group A (children without emotional problems), 62 per cent with group B, a difference significant at the .05 level. Recognition of Stimulation represented 10 per cent of the interaction with group A, 8 per cent with group B; Giving Information Verbally, approximately 8 per cent with each group; Interpretation by Restatement of Verbalized Feelings, 4 per cent with each group; Seeking Impersonal Information, 4 per cent with group A, 3 per cent with group B.

The difference between the groups in Giving Help—used less than 1 per cent of the time with group A, about 2 per cent with group B—was not statistically significant. Interpretation by Clarification of Verbalized Feelings was used significantly more often with group B (at the .05 level). Straightforward Cooperation appeared approximately 1 per cent of the time with group A, 2 per cent with group B, an insignificant difference.

In summary, most of the differences in the therapist's approach to the two groups were not statistically significant. Differences in frequency, however, show some interesting patterns, which may be summarized as follows:

Giving Help. The therapist gave help to group B, children with emotional problems, more than twice as often as to group

A, namely, 85 times as compared with 34 times.

Giving Information by Demonstration. Another indication that group B received more aid than group A appeared in this category: the therapist used it 22 times with group B, only twice with group A.

Forbidding. Though the frequencies for all "Forbidding" categories were small, they showed that the therapist consistently used them more with group B than with group A. Thus he used Forbidding with an Explanation with group B 9 times, compared to 4 times with group A; Forbidding with a Direct Statement was used 8 times with group B, never with group A; Forbidding by Use of Physical Restraint was used 3 times with group B, never with group A.

Directing. Directing by Command was used 16 times with group B, only 6 times with group A. In contrast, Directing by Suggestion was used 30 times with group A, only 11 times with group B.

Discussion

Viewing the therapist's behavior from an all-around approach, we find primary emphasis on *being there,* that is, interacting with the child by observing, listening, and making statements of recognition. Since this behavior occurs so frequently, it must provide an important basis for the therapy experience. The five major categories of the therapist's interaction behavior were responses to clues from the child, and served primarily to help the child further explore his behavioral expressions. The category Seeking Impersonal Information, though seemingly a directive, was actually a means of gaining a clearer understanding of the child and of stimulating the child to further exploration of his behavior.

Expressions of affection and approaches involving support or rewards were strikingly absent from the therapist's behavior. Punishing and criticizing methods were not used at all, nor were interpretation categories that departed from the child's immediate expression. When these factors are considered, along with the relatively small amount of forbidding, structuring, restricting, directing, and anxiety on the therapist's part, it appears that the child was left to operate on his own terms, in a nonjudgmental atmosphere, while the therapist attempted to understand the child on the basis of the child's own expressions.

In an overall sense, the therapist's behavior toward the two groups of children, and with one child as compared with another, was essentially the same, whether or not the children exhibited emotional problems. This observation is supported by the finding of a rank order correlation of .886, when the therapist's behavior with the two groups is compared. The few major differences occurred because the two groups initiated different types of interaction behavior. Thus the therapist attentively observed children of group B significantly more than those of group A, because the children with emotional problems more often sought a considerable amount of contact with the therapist which did not require a response from him. Similarly, they were more involved in their own individual play.

II. *What is the nature of the interaction behavior of children not having emotional problems (group A) and children with emotional problems (group B) in a play therapy setting?*

On the basis of 4,610 observations and an equal number of anxiety-hostility ratings of group A and 4,934 observations and ratings of group B, seven categories are found to appear most frequently in both groups, representing approximately 95 per cent of the interaction behavior. They are: Nonattention, Attentive Observation, Statement of Condition or Action, Seeking Information, Giving Information Verbally, Recognition of Stimulation, and Nonrecognition of Stimulation.

The most frequent category for group B

was Nonattention, which appeared 47 per cent of the time, while group A showed this category 33 per cent of the time, a difference significant at the .01 level. Statement of Condition or Action was a basic approach in group A, involving 34 per cent of their total interaction behavior, compared to 23 per cent in group B. This difference is not statistically significant. No other difference between the two groups in the major categories was statistically significant.

Categories not used by either group of children were: Giving Information by Demonstration and Explanation, Giving Reassurance, Seeking Affection, Seeking Reward, Directing by Command Accompanied by Threat, all "Restricting" categories, most "Forbidding" and "Criticism" categories, all "Disciplinary Action" categories (except Punishment by Attacking the Therapist's Objects), Rejection of the Therapist as a Person, Giving Permission, Praise, Affection, Reward, and most "Noncooperation" categories.

Some interesting, though minor, differences in the approach of group A and group B to the therapist are revealed. Thus group A used the following categories of behavior oftener than did group B: Joint Participation in Activity, Seeking Help, Orienting the Role of the Therapist in Play, Directing by Suggestion, Seeking Permission, and Rejection by Changing the Subject and Rejection by Denying the Validity of the Therapist's Statement. Group B used more frequently all categories of "Forbidding" and "Physical Attack" and all categories of "Threat of Attack."

A significant difference (.005 level of confidence) appeared in the hostility ratings of the two groups. In group B (children with emotional problems) there were 418 episodes of the presence of some hostility; in group A, only 23. The children of group B also showed 72 instances of severe hostility; those of group A showed none—a difference significant at the .05 level. A reversed, though not significant

trend, appeared in the data on anxiety ratings. Here group A had a total of 32 ratings; group B had only 8.

Discussion

Perhaps the most interesting result was that the children with serious emotional problems were more like than different from the children without such problems in terms of interaction behavior. The scores of the two groups showed a correlation of .694. In general, their behavior patterns were similar.

The differences in behavior between the groups appeared to be related to the problems of the children in group B. These children spent much of their time in noninteractive behavior—in fantasy, play, and other activity that excluded the therapist— or they responded to him in a way that did not encourage interaction. In contrast, the children of group A showed considerable verbal interaction with the therapist, talking about friends, school, home, and other conditions in their lives, explaining their behavior, and giving the therapist clues to an understanding of their behavior. Though, when combined, the categories of Nonattention and Statement of Condition account for approximately 70 per cent of all behavior in both groups, further examination of the data shows that group A is much more verbal in a social sense, while group B is more often nonattentive, that is, does not interact with the therapist, or interacts in a way that does not elicit interactive responses from him.

The large number of hostile feelings conveyed by group B is the second major difference between the two groups; group A showed only a small number of such feelings. This finding would be expected, since all the children in group B were described as having serious problems of hostility interfering with their personal and social effectiveness in the nursery school. The fact that all were disturbed, in the sense of having hostile attitudes, probably explains the marked absence of overt anxiety in this group. Mention of overt fears and anxieties was lacking in both the teachers' descriptions and the longitudinal records. Actually, though the difference was not a large one, the children without problems expressed more anxiety than did the children with emotional problems.

Certain minor differences between the two groups reinforced group B's pattern of more frequent hostile behavior. These children tended to be more forbidding, more prone to attack and threaten to attack, and more likely to use physical barriers to block or restrain the therapist. There was also some indication that dependency, often associated with hostility, was more frequently expressed by group B, in the sense of frequently asking questions and in the assertive quality of their behavior. Along with the tendency of group A children toward more verbal interaction on a friendly, social level, there was more Joint Participation in Activity with the therapist and more Seeking Permission. These children were also more assertive in the sense of orienting the therapist to his role and function, directing by suggestion, and denying the validity of the therapist's statements or actions when his behavior did not satisfy the child.

Both groups of children devoted at least one third of their time to behavior that did not directly involve interaction with the therapist. By choice, all the children spent much of their time playing alone and working through their ideas and feelings, without seeking the support or help of the therapist. This fact seems to emphasize the value to children of being free to operate on their own in the therapy setting. It also shows that had recorded transcriptions of verbal exchange been used as the basis for this study, approximately 47 per cent of the behavior of children in group B and 33 per cent of the behavior of children in group A would have been lost.

The data seem to indicate that such approaches as reward, praise, affection, giving reassurance, and so on have been overemphasized in such interaction. In the nearly 10 thousand observations made in this study, the children did not once seek reward or affection; they looked for praise only once and for reassurance only three times. Only rarely, or not at all, did the therapist find these methods useful or necessary in his approach to the children.

In terms of time, approximately 1 per cent only of the disturbed child's behavior was spent in the destructive expressions—such as physical attack on the therapist or play materials—so frequently associated with children having severe emotional problems. Hostile feeling, great or little, was indicated in only about 8 per cent of all the expressions of the group with emotional problems; 92 per cent showed little or no hostility. These children exhibited considerable positive behavior; such behavior is sometimes overlooked, while the more dramatic negative expressions are stressed.

III. *Do certain kinds of behavior in the therapist consistently produce certain reactions in children in therapy?*

In addition to analyzing therapist behavior in play therapy interaction in terms of its basic components and the child's behavior in a similar fashion, we attempted to view behavior episodes involving child-therapist interaction as a unit; that is, the initiating category of the therapist and the child's response to it. This unit is here called an "interaction sequence."

A total of 1,882 interaction sequences initiated by the therapist were analyzed. The criterion for selecting categories upon which the analysis was made were: (*a*) having a frequency of 35 or more, and (*b*) having high stimulus properties. Analyses of the categories follow.

Offering Verbal Information. The therapist initiated an interaction sequence with this type of behavior a total of 688 times. There were five major kinds of responses from the children: Attentive Observation, Statement of Condition or Action, Seeking

Information, Recognition of Stimulation, and Rejection by Ignoring or Evading of Stimulation. When the therapist gave verbal information, both groups responded approximately the same number of times by expressing a Statement of Condition or Action, by seeking Further Information, or by Rejection. The group without problems responded nearly three times as often by simply watching or listening. Group B used twice as many Recognition of Stimulation responses. However, these are not real differences, since watching and listening are nonverbal forms of recognition.

Orienting the Child to Time. The therapist initiated interaction by structuring time a total of 51 times. The children's primary responses to this approach were: Statement of Condition or Action, Recognition of Stimulation, Rejection by Ignoring or Evading Stimulation, and Rejection by Changing the subject. Each of these responses occurred approximately the same number of times in both groups. In both groups rejection by nonrecognition was the most frequent response to the therapist's structuring of time.

Orienting the Child to His Role by Leaving the Responsibility of Decision to the Child. This analysis is based on data obtained with group B only, since the therapist used this category only 6 times with group A. On the basis of 36 episodes with group B, the responses were equally divided among Statement of Condition or Action, Recognition, and Rejection by Nonrecognition.

Directing by Suggestion. In a total of 41 interaction sequences involving this category, both groups responded in almost the same way, in the great majority of instances by Straightforward Cooperation.

Interpretation. A total of 964 episodes of interpretation were analyzed, involving the first six subcategories of interpretation; that is, by restating the content of a remark, by stating the content of motor behavior, by restating verbalized feelings, by recognizing feelings of motor behavior, by clarifying feelings present in the child's total behavior. Three type of responses dominated: Statement of Condition or Action, Recognition, and Rejection by nonrecognition of stimulation. When the therapist used interpretation by simple restatement, the responses were Recognition 54 per cent of the time, Statement of Condition or Action 23 per cent of the time, and Rejection by Nonrecognition 23 per cent of the time. When the therapist interpreted by restating the content of motor behavior, the responses were Recognition 56 per cent of the time, Nonrecognition 30 per cent of the time, and Statement of Condition or Action 14 per cent of the time. When the therapist interpreted by restating verbalized feelings, recognizing feelings of motor behavior, or clarifying verbalized feelings, the children's responses were similar; that is they responded with Recognition about 60 per cent of the time, Rejection by Nonrecognition about 25 per cent of the time, and Statement of Condition or Action about 15 per cent of the time. The therapist interpreted by clarifying feelings present in the child's total behavior only 16 times throughout the course of the play sessions. The response was Recognition in 8 instances, Nonrecognition in 4, and Statement of Condition or Action in 2. In addition to these major types of response to the therapist's interpretations, the children occasionally responded by watching and listening, seeking information, and rejection.

Frequencies too low to be meaningful were found in a sequential analysis of several other categories: Offering Information by Demonstration and Explanation, Reassurance, Forbidding and Restricting (all categories), Directing by Command with a Threat, and Directing by Command.

Discussion

It should be pointed out that no sequential analysis was made of several categories representing major aspects of the therapist's behavior. Thus, Attentive Observation was not analyzed because it is primarily a response category; that is, the child either played alone while the therapist observed or responded in a way that made it difficult to determine the relationship between the child's response and the therapist's behavior. Statement of Condition or Action and Recognition were also omitted, as essentially response categories. Seeking Information about an ongoing activity was omitted on the basis of the finding that most of the children's responses to this category were in the nature of giving verbal information.

Whenever the therapist gave verbal information the children in both groups responded by exploring the information further, simply recognizing it, or failing to recognize it. Approximately 80 per cent of the responses led to some kind of recognition or further exploration. Apparently this form of therapist behavior is generally accepted and used by the child in his therapy experience. Such information concerned the child's immediate experience in play therapy; information regarding the therapist's view of the meaning of the child's behavior was considered under an Interpretation category.

Orienting the Child to Time is apparently not well received by either group of children. Approximately 50 per cent of all the children rejected it, and in addition the children of group B expressed hostility to the structuring of time in the play session. Neither group, apparently, wished to leave the play situation, but group B perhaps found it more difficult than group A to accept its termination, and therefore expressed hostility toward the therapist.

In this study the therapist structured the experience by leaving decisions to the children of group B more often than to those of group A, owing to the greater tendency of the children with emotional problems (group B) to ask the therapist to make decisions for them and to be unresponsive when asked to make such decisions.

The therapist's use of suggestion as a way of directing the child was well accepted. The children consistently responded with Straightforward Cooperation. Interestingly enough, the children with emotional problems almost always accepted the therapist's suggestions These suggestions did not restrict or order behavior; rather, they encouraged children to carry out their ideas, to feel free to move about in the situation, and to find alternatives for impossible goals.

The relationship between therapist and child behavior in response to Interpretation was particularly interesting. Within the first six types of this category (see above), the children's responses were of approximately the same number and kind, with acceptance of the therapist's interpretation leading all other responses. As the therapist's interpretation departed further from the child's concrete activity or verbal expression, there was a slight tendency toward increased acceptance and decreased nonrecognition. When the therapist attempted to respond to a totality of behavioral clues, rather than simply to verbal content or motor expression, a greater percentage of the total responses of the children involved acceptance. Interpretation that departed from the immediate experience of the child in therapy, that was based on past history or previous child associations, was not used at all by the therapist. It is therefore impossible to say, on the basis of this study, whether the child would accept or reject this type of interpretation.

Sequential analysis of the Interpretation categories revealed no essential differences in group A and group B in response to this technique. The one exception was in responses to Interpretation by Restating Verbalized Feelings; here the recognition responses of group A were nearly twice those of group B. Apparently the presence of emotional problems is not a relevant factor in influencing the child's response to interpretation that is based on immediate behavior.

IV. *Do certain types of child behavior consistently produce certain reactions from the therapist?*

A total of 771 interaction sequences initiated by the child were analyzed. The same criteria were used in selecting child categories for sequential analysis as in selecting therapist categories, namely, a frequency of at least 35 and high stimulus value. Only three categories met these criteria: Seeking Information, Directing by Suggestion, and Directing by Command.

Seeking Information. The therapist responded in three major ways when children sought information: with Attentive Observation, Giving Verbal Information, and Seeking Information. In about 73 per cent of instances the therapist gave the information requested; in 14 per cent he responded with a question—that is, himself sought information; and in 13 per cent he simply listened and observed. There were no important differences in responses to the two groups. Occasionally the response of the therapist was to orient the child or make an interpretation.

Directing by Suggestion. The therapist responded to this form of child behavior with Straightforward Cooperation, in approximately the same number of instances with both groups. Occasionally he responded by Attentive Observation and Seeking Information.

Directing by Command. Again, the therapist's predominant response was to cooperate. In response to 18 per cent, he sought information; in response to 11 per cent, he made an interpretation No particular differences appeared in relation to the two groups. Occasionally the therapist responded by Attentive Observation, Statement of Condition or Action, Giving Verbal Information, Recognition, and Noncooperation.

A sequential analysis on several other categories showed frequencies too small to give meaningful results. Such analyses were made on all categories of Forbidding, Criticism, Attack, Threat of Attack, and some

categories of Seeking Help, Seeking Reassurance, Seeking Praise, Seeking Permission, Seeking Attention, and Command Accompanied by a Threat.

Discussion

The therapist's general response to the child's seeking of information was to give the information requested. This response accounted for about 75 per cent of instances. The remaining responses left the child to cope with the problem. From the therapist's point of view, information was given mainly when it was not easy for the child to obtain it on his own. Most requests for information from the child involved simple, factual matters. Usually the child asked the location of particular toys or other materials in the room. When it was possible for the child to obtain this information on his own, the therapist encouraged him to explore the environment for himself; but in most instances the therapist felt that simply giving the information requested served the purpose better and allowed the child to make better use of his energies in using the material and exploring the play experience. Thus the therapist aimed to help the child get started in his play experience, rather than to create a dependency relationship. When he felt that it was better to encourage the child to use his own resources in finding the solution, he simply listened to the child's request, responding with a question, or leaving the responsibility of making a decision to the child (Orienting the Child's Role).

Directing by Suggestion from the child was answered almost always by cooperation with both groups of children. In a small number of instances the therapist paused, in Attentive Observation, or sought information, before cooperating, thus giving the child time to explore the play situation on his own.

When the children used Directing by Command, the therapist generally accepted this behavior and responded by cooperating. Most of these commands were simple, such as "Hand me the darts," or "Give me the ball," rather than attempts to direct the therapist with more dynamic implications for control of the relationship. Several other responses were used, particularly when the therapist felt it important for the child to operate on his own Whenever the command involved some issue in the relationship as the therapist perceived it, he left the resolving of the situation to the child; this he did by delaying a direct response to the child's request, seeking information, making an interpretation, observing attentively, stating a condition or action, giving information, recognizing the command, and, occasionally, refusing to cooperate.

SUMMARY AND CONCLUSIONS

The development of a comprehensive predetermined category system for measuring adult-child interaction was the basis for an objective analysis of therapist-child interaction in play therapy. A total of 82 adult and 72 child categories in the schedule were accompanied by anxiety-hostility ratings. The behavior of both child and therapist, in terms of these categories and ratings, was recorded every five seconds. Reliability, based on percentage of agreement between two independent observers, was 92.44 for the combined recording of the behavioral categories and the anxiety-hostility ratings. The observer, who was not familiar with the children in the study, was in an observation room fitted with sound amplification and a one-way vision mirror.

Two groups of nursery school children, similar in age and in socio-economic backgrounds, were observed in 18 play therapy sessions. The children were classified in two groups of five each: group A, without serious emotional problems, and group B, with emotional problems serious enough to interfere with effective personal and social relations in the nursery school. Children

were placed in one of these groups on the basis of complete agreement among three judges—a nursery school teacher, a student teacher, and a psychologist—who used observation and data in the Merrill-Palmer longitudinal records as the basis for their judgment. With one exception in each group, observed for one session only, each child was observed for two 40-minute play sessions, scheduled three days apart, providing a total of 18 play therapy sessions. The same therapist saw all the children. The conclusions were as follows:

1. Data obtained from 9,084 observations of the therapist's behavior and an equal number of anxiety-hostility ratings were summarized. The five categories appearing most frequently were: Attentive Observation, Recognition of Stimulation, Offering Verbal Information, Interpretation by Restating Verbalized Feelings, and Seeking Impersonal Information. Together, they accounted for 84 per cent of the therapist's interaction with the children. The therapist's primary emphasis was on *being there,* interacting with the child by observing, listening, and making statements of recognition. His behavior lacked supportive or reward approaches to the child, expressions of affection or punishment, criticism, and evaluation, and seldom showed use of forbidding and restricting. He responded in nearly the same way to both groups of children (rank order correlation, .886)

2. Data obtained from 9,544 observations of the children's interactive behavior and an equal number of anxiety-hostility ratings, summarized for the two groups, showed more similar than divergent behavior in the two groups of children (rank order correlation, .694). The behavior categories appearing most frequently in both groups, accounting for about 95 per cent of responses, were: Nonattention, Attentive Observation, Statement of Condition or Action, Seeking Information, Giving Information Verbally, Recognition of Stimulation, and Nonrecognition of Stimulation. The most significant difference in behav-

ioral categories (.01 level) between the two groups was in Nonattention: group B, with emotional problems, showed such behavior 47 per cent of the time; group A, without emotional problems, 33 per cent of the time.

Differences between the groups were probably related to the kinds of emotional problems in group B. These children spent considerable time in noninteractive behavior; that is, in fantasy, play, or other activity that excluded the therapist; or they responded in a way that discouraged interaction. In comparison, the children of group A interacted significantly more often by talking about friends, school, home, and other conditions in their lives. They also explained their behavior more often and gave the therapist more clues to an understanding of their behavior.

The children of group B showed a significantly greater number of hostile feelings, tended to be more forbidding, more prone to attack and threaten to attack, and to block or restrain the therapist. However, such behavior was infrequent in both groups. Dependency behavior was expressed more often by the children of group B, while the children of group A tended to be more assertive.

Both groups spent about one third of their time in behavior that did not directly involve interaction with the therapist; that is, in playing alone and working through ideas and feelings without support or help. None of the children sought reward or affection; they looked for praise only once and reassurance only three times.

The disturbed children (group B) spent only 1 per cent of their time in destructive behavior. About 8 per cent of their expressions involved some or much hostility, while 92 per cent conveyed little or none. Thus, these children significantly more often expressed positive, accepting behavior than negative, rejecting behavior.

3. A total of 1,882 interaction sequences initiated by the therapist and the children's responses to them were analyzed. When the therapist gave information, the children in both groups responded by exploring the information further, by simply recognizing it, or by failing to recognize it. About 80 per cent of their responses involved some kind of recognition or further exploration. Structuring of time resulted in some kind of rejection 50 per cent of the time. Suggestions were well received, and were responded to almost consistently by cooperation. Acceptance led all child responses to the therapist's use of interpretation. As the interpretation departed further from the child's concrete activity or verbal expression, the number of acceptances increased and the number of rejections decreased. Interpretation based on past history or associations with the child from previous play sessions was not used by the therapist. However, the more holistic interpretations, based on total behavioral clues rather than isolated expressions, resulted in more acceptance and less rejection.

4. A total of 771 interaction sequences initiated by the child were analyzed. When the child sought information, the therapist gave it about 75 per cent of the time and left the child to cope with the problem the remaining 25 per cent. Information was given mainly when it involved the location of particular toys or materials. In general, the therapist responded by cooperation to the child's suggestions. Similarly, he generally responded to simple commands by acceptance and cooperation. Briefly, when the child's request did not tend to create a dependency relationship or to dominate or control the therapist, the response was generally acceptance and cooperation.

REFERENCES

1. FINKE, HELENE. Changes in the expression of emotionalized attitudes in six cases of play therapy. Unpublished master's thesis, Univer. of Chicago, 1947.

2. LANDISBERG, SELMA, & SNYDER, W. U. Nondirective play therapy. *J. clin. Psychol.,* 1946, 2, 203–214.

3. LEBO, D. The relationship of response categories in play therapy to chronological age. *J. child Psychiat.*, 1952, 2, 330–336.

4. MOUSTAKAS, C. E. *Children in play therapy.* New York: McGraw-Hill, 1953.

5. MOUSTAKAS, C. E. The frequency and intensity of negative attitudes expressed in play therapy: A comparison of well-adjusted and disturbed young children. *J. genet. Psychol.*, in press.

6. MOUSTAKAS, C. E., SIGEL, I. E., & SCHALOCK, H. D. An objective method for the measurement and analysis of adult-child interaction. (In preparation)

7. SEEMAN, J., *et al.* The development of empirical criterion measures in the study of play therapy. (Unpublished manuscript)

Effects of Silence and Redirection on Verbal Responses in Group Psychotherapy[1]

H. C. SALZBERG

In recent years, there has been growing interest in the process of small group behavior. This interest has come from several major sources. One source has been described by Glanzer and Glaser (1961) regarding the structure of small groups. Another source has been Moreno's work (1947) in psychodrama. A third source of this interest has been in verbal conditioning and the relating of learning theory to psychotherapy. The latter lends itself well to application in the practical situation for the modification or manipulation of behavior in a systematic fashion. Krasner (1961) has written an excellent comprehensive review of the therapist as a verbal reinforcer. Most of the studies on verbal conditioning have had the therapist reinforce certain

Reprinted from *Psychological Reports,* 1962, 11, 455–461, with the permission of the Southern Universities Press and the author.

[1] The assistance of Robert V. Heckel and the other members of the Psychology Staff and trainees at VA Hospital, Augusta, Georgia, is gratefully acknowledged. They supplied constant encouragement and helped in the preparation of the study and editing of the manuscript.

content categories, e.g., expressions of hostility, dependency, etc., which require a judgment in order to classify a response. The individual psychotherapeutic situation rather than the group psychotherapeutic situation has often been the unit of investigation.

Timmons, Rickard, and Taylor (1960), modifying a standardized interview technique introduced by Saslow and Matarazzo (1959), found that content-free measures of group behavior were unusually stable under a standardized interview. Different Es using the standardized interview technique, on different occasions, obtained highly similar responses from the same patient.

Dinoff, Horner, Kurpiewski, and Timmons (1960) were able to condition psychiatric patients to respond to different aspects of their environment. This was accomplished in a group situation where a therapist reinforced personal responses, environmental responses, group responses, or responses about the therapist. The therapist's behavior was only controlled in reinforcing a certain response class. It did establish a reliable and scorable index of patient behavior. Salzberg (1961) found that silence on the part of the therapist was highly correlated with patient verbal interaction in a group psychotherapeutic situation. In a follow-up study Heckel, Froelich, and Salzberg (1962) found that redirecting patients to talk to one another in a group induced more interaction than speaking directly to patients.

The present study has attempted systematically to measure the effects of silence and redirection by the therapist on interaction and type of response in group psychotherapy. Hopefully, this could be an aid in obtaining a method of eliciting maximum interaction about pertinent problems in group psychotherapy in an atmosphere where there would be generalization outside of the group psychotherapeutic setting. It seems that the most desirable response in group psychotherapy is one in which a patient shows an interest in another patient's personal problems. This constitutes a maximum of social interaction. The least desirable response seems to be a response about the environment (talking about the weather) directed to the therapist. If silence and redirection have a significant effect on the direction of a response and type of response a patient makes in a group, the patient's behavior can then be shaped to respond most desirably and a therapist can be trained to bring out this desired response.

METHOD

Subjects. The subjects for the experiment were all psychiatric inpatients on a privileged ward. These patients had been voluntarily participating in group psychotherapy for varying periods of time. As the experiment progressed some members were discharged and other members were admitted to the group. The group varied from 7 to 12 members during the experimental treatment. In all, there were 19 Ss of whom 4 attended all sessions.

Apparatus. The group was seen in a sound-shielded room with a one-way mirror. There were two standing microphones in the room and all sessions were tape recorded. The patients were seated in a circle with E. No seating order was maintained.

Procedure. The group was seen for two hourly sessions each week. The experimental treatment lasted for 10 weeks and 20 sessions. E varied his responses in four ways, silence, talking, redirecting, and directing. During silence E refrained from speaking except when silence would have been extremely awkward and artificial. During talking, E spoke whenever conversation lagged, eliminating silences almost completely. During redirection if S_1 asked E a question, E would either mention S_2 and/or S_3 in answering S_1 or would respond to S_2 and/or S_3 referring to S_1. Each statement by E, therefore, included more than one member of the group. During direction, E spoke directly to a patient making no reference to any other member of the group. Below is the schedule[2] E used in varying these four responses. Four combinations were used: Silence-Redirection (SR), Silence-Direction (SD), Talking-Redirection (TR) and Talking-Direction (TD). SR and SD are not very different in practice because of the few comments E makes in each case. The other categories are quite different experimentally.

Sessions	0-15 min.	16-30 min.	31-45 min.	46-60 min.
1 - 5	SR	TD	TD	SR
6 - 10	TD	SR	SR	TD
11 - 15	SD	TR	TR	SD
16 - 20	TR	SD	SD	TR.

Measures of the dependent variable were the patients' responses to the four treatments. A response consisted of a statement made by a patient until he was interrupted by either E or another patient. Frequency was found to reflect almost the same func-

[2] Later studies will use all four conditions throughout.

tion as a time measure of responses. Because frequency is also easier to obtain, it was used as the only measure. The patients' responses were scored along two dimensions. A response was either environmental (E), personal (P), or a group (G) response and it was also either an interaction (I) or a non-interaction (N) response. Hence, two scores were given to each response. One score indicated the quality of a response and the other indicated the direction of a response. A response was scored "E" when the patient spoke about an object or person other than himself or any other group member. A response was scored "P" when the patient spoke about himself. A response was scored "G" when a patient referred to another member of the group.

A response was scored "I" when a patient spoke to a member of the group other than E. A response was scored "N" when a patient spoke to E. Six scorable responses emerged, environment interact, environment non-interact, personal interact, personal non-interact, group interact, and group non-interact.

The patients were aware that all sessions were being tape recorded but they had no knowledge that E was scoring each session. They also were not consciously aware of E's differential responding. Silence, talking, direction, and redirection were interspersed in every session so that the patients would not be able to recognize E's changes in behavior. The therapeutic goal of the group did not seem to be hampered by the experimental treatment.

RESULTS

Six analyses of variance were performed to ascertain the differential effects of silence and talking, redirecting and directing, and their interaction for each of six response variables. Table 1 presents the analysis for total responses. There were no significant differences between silence and talking, redirecting and directing or their interaction for total responses, despite the fact that E's mean number of responses during the treatments varied from 4.1 to 99.1 responses in a half-hour unit. Under each condition, the group gave about the same mean number of responses.

Table 2 presents the analysis for E responses. There was no significant interaction nor was there a significant difference

TABLE 1

TOTAL RESPONSES: MEANS AND ANALYSIS OF VARIANCE

	Redirect	Direct	Source	df	MS	F	p
Silence	213.6	236.6	Silence-Talking	1	921	0.29	NS
			Redirect-Direct	1	449	0.14	NS
			Interaction	1	8821	2.81	NS
Talking	233.7	197.3	WSS	36	3136		

TABLE 2

ENVIRONMENT RESPONSES: MEANS AND ANALYSIS OF VARIANCE

	Redirect	Direct	Source	df	MS	F	p
Silence	64.2	76.3	Silence-Talking	1	10240	12.91	< .001
			Redirect-Direct	1	230	0.29	NS
			Interaction	1	533	0.67	NS
Talking	39.5	37.0	WSS	36	793		

between redirecting and directing but there was a highly significant difference between silence and talking. There were significantly more E responses when E was silent.

Table 3 presents the analysis for P responses. TD elicited the greatest number of P responses and is significantly different from SR, SD, and TR. There were no significant differences between SR, SD, and TR.

Table 4 presents the analysis for G responses. Redirecting elicited a significantly greater number of G responses than directing but this was true only when E was talking. There was no difference when E was silent because the therapist made very few comments during both SR and SD which made them almost indiscriminable experimentally.

Table 5 presents the analysis for I responses. Silence elicited more I responses than talking. There was no significant difference between redirecting and directing. However, TD elicited significantly fewer responses than TR.

Table 6 presents the analysis for N responses. Talking elicited a significantly larger number of N responses than did silence. Directing elicited a significantly larger number of N responses than redirecting. The combination of talking and directing elicited the greatest number of N responses.

The results indicate that there is in no case a significant difference between SR and SD. The major reason for this result is that the two variables do not differ very much experimentally. When E was silent and redirecting, he only made an average of 5.9 responses per each half-hour unit.

TABLE 3

PERSONAL RESPONSES: MEANS AND ANALYSIS OF VARIANCE

	Redirect	Direct	Source	df	MS	F	p
Silence	67.6	72.2	Silence-Talking	1	6631	8.78	< .01
			Redirect-Direct	1	5688	7.53	< .01
			Interaction	1	4473	5.92	< .05
Talking	70.3	117.2	WSS	36	755		

TABLE 4

GROUP RESPONSES: MEANS AND ANALYSIS OF VARIANCE

	Redirect	Direct	Source	df	MS	F	p
Silence	81.8	88.1	Silence-Talking	1	21	0.02	NS
			Redirect-Direct	1	13876	11.54	< .001
			Interaction	1	18966	15.78	< .001
Talking	123.9	43.1	WSS	36	1202		

TABLE 5

INTERACTION RESPONSES: MEANS AND ANALYSIS OF VARIANCE

	Redirect	Direct	Source	df	MS	F	p
Silence	196.3	225.7	Silence-Talking	1	77176	20.93	< .001
			Redirect-Direct	1	5929	1.61	NS
			Interaction	1	28891	7.84	< .01
Talking	162.2	84.1	WSS	36	3687		

TABLE 6

NON-INTERACTION RESPONSES: MEANS AND ANALYSIS OF VARIANCE

	Redirect	Direct	Source	df	MS	F	p
Silence	17.3	10.9	Silence-Talking	1	61231	181.69	< .001
			Redirect-Direct	1	3115	9.24	< .01
			Interaction	1	5784	17.16	< .001
Talking	71.5	113.2	WSS	36	337		

When he was silent and directing he made an average of 4.1 direction responses per half-hour unit. On the other hand, when he was talking and redirecting he made an average of 55.5 responses per half-hour unit and when he was talking and directing he made 99.1 responses per half-hour unit. Therefore, the major three variables that are being differentiated are silence, talking-redirection, and talking-direction.

DISCUSSION

The results were, in general, in the expected direction. Silence led to significantly more interaction than talking as had been found previously (Salzberg, 1961). Talking led to less interaction. Redirecting did not lead to significantly more interaction but did lead to significantly more G responses. This indicates that a combination of silence and redirecting would probably bring out the most I and G responses. A finding that had not been expected was that silence elicited a significantly greater number of E responses than talking. This can be be explained by the fact that silence on the part of a therapist creates a much less structured situation than talking. Dinoff, Rickard, Salzberg, and Sipprelle (1960) found that in an unstructured situation the most comon response was an E response. Since this the least desirable response, it would be somewhat non-therapeutic for a therapist to remain silent all of the time.

E observed that, in order for G responses to be sufficiently meaningful, P responses have to be emitted initially. In this way each member of the group becomes acquainted with one another. A therapist talking and directing elicits the greatest number of P responses. It seems then that, when a group is new and the members are unfamiliar with each other, a therapist might structure the situation more and talk and direct so that patients could become familiar with each other's problems. After this, a therapist could reduce the number of his responses and begin redirecting.

Some questions may be raised as to how well interaction and group response in psychotherapy will generalize to the milieu of the individual and how well they will contribute to the outcome of psychotherapy. This can be ascertained by focusing on individual patient's response changes in a group situation and by evaluating his progress following group psychotherapy.

Other steps might be taken toward discovering more refined measures of both the therapist's behavior and the patients' behavior. More stable and reliable parameters of verbal and non-verbal responsivity in group psychotherapy are necessary so that we can better understand the process. Because of the grossness of the measures used here, a good deal of important behavioral data is omitted. It is hoped that further investigation will add refinement of measurement.

It has become increasingly evident to E that patient behavior in a group psychotherapeutic situation appears to follow lawful principles. Psychotherapy, although it has existed in one form or another for many years, has always been considered more of an art form than a scientific procedure. Tough-minded psychologists have avoided systematic investigations of the psychotherapeutic process because of the difficulty in instituting controls. The recent developments in learning theory have opened several avenues of controlled investigation of the psychotherapeutic process. A great deal can also be uncovered concerning more complex principles of behavior than we have been studying in the animal laboratories.

SUMMARY

An investigation was undertaken to ascertain the effects of silence and redirection on the verbal responses of patients in group psychotherapy. It was found that both of these classes of responses significantly influenced the interaction and the quality of response of group members. The magnitude of the effects indicated that verbal behavior, at least as measured grossly, follows lawful principles. It is hoped that this report will help to interest other investigators in refining measuring techniques and in studying the process of group psychotherapy with the goal of making it a more efficient technique.

REFERENCES

DINOFF, M., HORNER, R. F., KURPIEWSKI, B. S., & TIMMONS, E. O. Conditioning verbal behavior of schizophrenics in a group therapy-like situation. *J. clin. Psychol.*, 1960, 16, 367–370.

DINOFF, M., RICKARD, H. C., SALZBERG, H., & SIPPRELLE, C. N. An experimental analogue of three psychotherapeutic approaches. *J. clin. Psychol.*, 1960, 16, 70–73.

GLANZER, M., & GLASER, R. Techniques for the study of group structure and behavior: II. Empirical studies of the effects of structure in small groups. *Psychol., Bull.*, 1961, 58, 1–27.

HECKEL, R. V., FROELICH, R. E., & SALZBERG, H. C. Interaction and redirection in group therapy. *Psychol. Rep.*, 1962, 10, 14.

KRASNER, L. The therapist as a social reinforcement machine. Paper presented at Second Conference on Research in Psychotherapy, Univer. of North Carolina, May, 1961.

MORENO, J. L. *The theatre of spontaneity: an introduction to psychodrama.* New York: Beacon House, 1947.

SALZBERG, H. C. Manipulation of verbal behavior in a group psychotherapeutic setting. *Psychol. Rep.*, 1961, 9, 183–186.

SASLOW, G., & MATARAZZO, J. D. A technique for studying changes in interview behavior. In E. A. Rubenstein & M. B. Parloff (Eds.), *Research and psychotherapy.* Washington, D.C.: American Psychological Association, 1959. Pp. 125–159.

TIMMONS, E. O., RICKARD, H. C., & TAYLOR, R. E. Reliability of content-free, group verbal behavior. *Psychol. Rec.*, 1960, 10, 297–305.

The Process Equation of Psychotherapy

CARL R. ROGERS

For many years now I have been trying to formulate for myself the process by which change in personality and behavior is achieved in psychotherapy. These formulations change in various ways as my experience as a therapist increases. They continue to change as little by little we gain a more exact knowledge of the process through research. Sometimes I feel that our progress in gaining understanding is discouragingly slow. At other times, when I look back to what was known about psychotherapy thirty years ago, when I first became a therapist, then I feel that we have made very considerable strides.

I have been encouraged in recent years by our ability to write some crude equations. We can formulate statements which are comparable to crude chemical equations. We can say that given a person desiring help, and a second person providing a relationship with elements a, b, and c, then a process of change occurs which involves elements x, y, and z. We can specify rather definitely the nature of each of these elements. We have acquired, in other words,

Reprinted from *American Journal of Psychotherapy,* 1961, 15 (1), 27–45, with the permission of the Association for the Advancement of Psychotherapy and the author.

408

more objective knowledge of cause and effect in psychotherapy.

I would like in this paper, to present my current formulation of the process of therapy which incorporates some of this more recently acquired knowledge.

THE EFFECTIVE RELATIONSHIP

There are two recent studies in which the findings excite me because they represent a considerable step forward in defining objectively the effective elements which bring about therapeutic change.

The Relationship as Perceived by "Judges"

The first study I wish to report is one completed by Halkides (1). She began with a theoretical formulation of mine regarding the necessary and sufficient conditions for therapeutic change (2). She hypothesized a significant relationship between the extent of constructive personality change in the client and four therapist variables, four subtle attitudinal characteristics: (a) the degree of empathic understanding of the client manifested by the therapist; (b) the degree of positive affective attitude (unconditional positive regard) manifested by the therapist toward the client; (c) the extent to which the therapist is genuine or congruent, his words matching his own internal feeling; and (d) the extent to which the therapist's response matches the client's statement in the intensity of affective expression.

To investigate these hypotheses she first selected, by multiple objective criteria, a group of 10 cases which could be classed as "most successful" and a group of 10 "least successful" cases. She then took an earlier and a later recorded interview from each of these cases. On a random basis she picked nine client-counselor interaction units—a client statement and a counselor response—from each of these interviews. She thus had nine early interaction units and nine late interaction units from each case. This gave her several hundred units in these interview samples, which were now placed in random order. The units from an early interview of an unsuccessful case might be followed by the units from a late interview of a successful case, etc.

Three judges, who did not know the cases, or their degree of success, or the source of any given unit, now listened to this material four different times. They rated each unit on a seven-point scale, first as to the degree of empathy, second as to the degree of the counselor's positive attitude toward the client, third as to the counselor's congruence or genuineness, and fourth as to the degree to which the counselor's response matched the emotional intensity of the client's expression.

I think all of us who knew of the study regarded it as a very bold venture. Could judges listening to single units of interaction possibly make any reliable rating of such subtle qualities as I have mentioned? And even if suitable reliability could be obtained, could 18 counselor-client interchanges from each case—a minute sampling of the hundreds or thousands of such interchanges which occurred in each case—possibly bear any relationship to the therapeutic outcome? The chance seemed slim.

The findings are surprising. It proved possible to achieve high reliability between the judges, most of the inter-judge correlations being in the .90's except on the last variable. It was found that a high degree of empathic understanding was significantly associated, at an .001 level, with the more successful cases. A high degree of unconditional positive regard was likewise associated with the more successful cases, at the .001 level. Even the rating of the therapist's genuineness or congruence—the extent to which his words matched his feelings—was associated with the successful outcome of the case, and again at the .001 level of significance. Only in the investigation of the matching intensity of affective expression were the results equivocal and inconclusive.

It is of interest, too, that high ratings of these variables were not associated more significantly with units from later interviews than with units from earlier interviews. This means that the counselor's attitudes were quite constant throughout the interviews. If he was highly empathic, he tended to be so from first to last. If he was lacking in genuineness, this tended to be true in both the earlier and later interviews.

Another finding of interest is that three of the four variables investigated show a high degree of relatedness. The measures of empathy, unconditional positive regard, and genuineness or congruence correlate highly, from .72 to .89. Evidently all of these three are very much tied together, or may represent three measures of one more underlying factor. The matching of the client's affective intensity by the therapist did not correlate significantly with the other three, any more than it did with success.

Halkides findings may be expressed very simply. The quality of the therapist's interaction with his client may be reliably judged on the basis of a very small sampling of his behavior. There is a strong probability of an effective helping relationship if the therapist is congruent, his words matching his feelings; if the therapist likes and accepts the client, unconditionally; and if the therapist understands the feelings of the client as they seem to the client, communicating this understanding.

The Relationship as Perceived by Clients

A second study of the therapeutic relationship has been completed by Barrett-Lennard (3). He too wished to investigate the theory I had proposed as to the essential qualities in a relationship which produces therapeutic change. Instead of using objective judges, however, he studied the manner in which the relationship was perceived by the client and by the therapist. He developed a Relationship Inventory which had different forms for client and therapist, and which was designed to study five dimensions of the relationships. Thus far he has analyzed only the data from the client's perceptions of the relationship, and it is these findings which I shall report. Barrett-Lennard studied a fresh series of cases, in which he knew that he would have various objective measures of degree of change. He gave his Relationship Inventory to each client after the fifth interview. In order to give more of the flavor of his study, I will elaborate with regard to each variable.

He was interested, first, in measuring the extent to which the client felt himself to be empathically understood. He therefore included items pertaining to the therapist which were evaluated by the client on a 6-point scale which ranged from very true to very strongly not true. It will be evident that these represent different degrees of empathic understanding.

He appreciates what my experience feels like to *me*.
He understands what I say from a detached, objective point of view.
He understands my words but not the way I feel.

Second, he wished to measure the *level* of regard, the degree of liking of the client by the therapist. To measure this there

were items such as those listed below, each one again rated from strongly true to strongly not true.

He cares about me.
He is indifferent to me.
He disapproves of me.

To measure the unconditionality of the regard, the extent to which there were "no strings attached" to the counselor's liking, items of this sort were included.

Whether I am expressing "good" feelings or "bad" ones seems to make no difference to the way he feels toward me.
His interest in me depends on what I am talking to him about.

In order to measure the congruence or genuineness of the therapist in the relationship, items of this sort were used.

He behaves just the way that he *is,* in our relationship.
He pretends that he likes me or understands me more than he really does.
He is playing a role with me.

He also wished to measure another variable which he regarded as important—the counselor's psychologic availability, or willingness to be known. To measure this, items of this sort were used.

He will freely tell me his own thoughts and feelings, when I want to know them.
He is uncomfortable when I ask him something about himself.
He is unwilling to tell me how he feels about me.

Barrett-Lennard's findings are of interest. The more experienced of his therapists were perceived as having more of the first four qualities than the less experienced therapists. In "willingness to be known," however, the reverse was true.

In the more disturbed clients in his sample, the first four measures all correlated significantly with the degree of personality change as objectively measured, and with the degree of change as rated by the therapist. Empathic understanding was most significantly associated with change, but genuineness, level of regard, and unconditionality of regard were also associated with successful therapy. Willingness to be known was not significantly associated.

Thus we can say, with some assurance, that a relationship characterized by a high degree of congruence or genuineness in the therapist; by a sensitive and accurate empathy on the part of the therapist; by a high degree of regard, respect, liking for the client by the therapist; and by an absence of conditionality in this regard, will have a high probability of being an effective therapeutic relationship. These qualities appear to be primary change-producing influences on personality and behavior. This statement holds whether these elements are rated by an impartial observer who listens to the recorded interviews, or whether they are evaluated by the client as he perceives them. It seems clear from both studies that these qualities can be measured or observed in small samples of the interaction, relatively early in the relationship, and can be used to predict the outcome of that relationship.

These elements appear necessary to successful therapy of a client-centered type. Whether they are necessary for *any* constructive personality change is unknown, but I would hypothesize that this is true. Whether they represent *all* the necessary conditions is likewise unknown, but it is of interest that two other relationship qualities which were measured proved *not* to be related to degree of change in therapy.

A Tentative Equation

Thus we can phrase our crude equation in several ways. Given a relationship between therapist and client we can say:

Genuineness plus empathy and unconditional positive regard for the client equals successful therapy for the client.

More accurately we can phrase it this way:

Perception by the client of genuineness, empathic understanding and unconditional positive regard in the therapist equals successful therapy for the client.

Or perhaps still better:

The more the therapist is perceived by the client as being genuine, as having an empathic understanding, and an unconditional regard for him, the greater will be the degree of constructive personality change in the client.

I am sure that this question will be modified and rewritten as we are better informed through further study. That we have enough empirical knowledge to write it at all is to me a striking advance.

THE PROCESS IN THE CLIENT

I have tried to spell out the left hand or causal side of the equation of therapy. Is it possible to give, in equally factual detail, the right hand or effect side of the equation? What happens in the client? What is this process of change, of learning, of therapy, which is set in motion? Here it seems to me the formulations have been even more varied, and our knowledge is even more tentative. Yet beginnings have been made. We are identifying various types of learnings which occur, the sequential events which characterize the process.

During the past three years I have especially concerned myself with the process of sequential events which occur in the client (4). I have immersed myself in recordings of psychotherapeutic sessions. In these I have tried to discern the characteristic changes or learnings which occur when therapy is helpful. From this experience has come a somewhat different formulation of a continuum of psychologic functioning. I should like to present it in a very tenta-

tive form. I see it as a long, uphill pathway
of change and development. A given client
begins therapy at some point on this pathway and, if he is helped, moves a variable
distance up the slope.

I hope that the nature of this pathway
will become more clear in what follows. It
should be sufficient for the present to say
that it commences at one end with a rigid,
static, undifferentiated, unfeeling, impersonal type of psychologic functioning. It
evolves through various stages to, at the
other end, a level of functioning marked by
changingness, fluidity, richly differentiated
reactions, by immediate experiencing of
personal feelings, which are felt as deeply
owned and accepted. In any successful therapy, I would hypothesize, the client moves
upward on this pathway from whatever
point he initially finds himself.

A group of us at Wisconsin have tried
to take the observations of this sequential
process and turn them into an operational
scale (5, 6). We have at least succeeded to
the point where, given a segment of a recorded interview we can say, with satisfactory objectivity and reliability, that it is
characteristic of a given point on the continuum. I would like to try to give you
some feeling for the qualities of personal
expression which are characteristic of different stages in the process, and also for
the different strands out of which the process appears to be woven.

The Change in Relationship to Feelings

Let me speak first of the manner in
which the client relates to the feelings and
personal meanings which exist within himself. Brief examples may help. In these excerpts, it is not the content but rather the
quality of expression which is important
for our present purposes. A patient in a
state hospital says, "Voices keep bothering
me all the time, saying filthy things, and I
can't stop them." Notice that these are not
owned as her feelings at all. They are completely unowned, out of her control, un-

recognized as being related to her. If she
were able to say, "I am troubled by my
sexual feelings," she would be much further along on the continuum.

Or take another example, characteristic
of a somewhat higher point on the scale.
A man says "It discourages me to feel dependent because it means I'm kind of helpless about myself." Here he is freely describing his feelings as objects existing in
the present, and to some degree owned by
himself. He is not expressing them, but he
is describing them. He determines the
meaning and significance of his feeling by
an intellectual process rather than by sensing the meaning in himself.

Still further up the scale, we find statements of this sort. The client is quite per-
plexed as to what she is feeling and finally
voices it this way, "It feels like I sort of
have—I don't know—I have a feeling of
strength, and yet I have a feeling of realizing it's so sort of fearful, of fright." Here
it is clear that she is expressing the feelings
she is having in the moment, living them,
sensing them, differentiating them and
owning them at the same time that she is
expressing them.

Thus if I were to try to describe briefly
the way in which this strand changes from
the lowest point on the continuum to the
highest, it would go something like this.
At the lowest end the individual does not
recognize or own his feelings. This changes
to a description of feelings as remote, unowned objects not now present, usually existing in the past. Then they are described
as present objects, with some sense of own-
ership. Then feelings are fearfully expressed—not described—in the immediate present. Feelings which have been
denied in the past now bubble painfully
through into awareness. Finally the person
comes to live in the process of experiencing
a continually changing flow of feelings. He
is no longer remote from the feelings and
personal meanings which are continually
occurring in him. He is freely and acceptantly living them.

Change in the Manner of Experiencing

What I have been saying can be formulated in a different way, with reference to the client's manner of experiencing, as that concept has been developed by Gendlin and Zimring (7, 8). The client moves toward living in his experiencing, and using it as the referent for guiding himself in his encounter with life. He is no longer characterized by remoteness from his experiencing nor does he discover its meaning only long after it is past. Thus typical of a low point on the continuum is a client who, trying to tell of the problem which brought him to the therapist, says, "The symptom was—it was just being very depressed." We may assume that at some point he experienced deep depression, but the closest he can come to this experiencing is to conceptualize it in the past, and to remove it from himself. It is not he who was depressed. It was simply a symptom which existed.

As clients move in therapy they come closer to their own experiencing, become less fearful of it. They recognize that it may have value as a referent, as a basis for discovering meanings. Thus a client says, in regard to something going on within him, "I really don't have my finger on it. I'm just kinda describing it." Here he realizes that he is not entirely *in* his experiencing but he wishes that he were. Still further up the continuum a client says "I feel stopped right now. Why is my mind blank right now? I feel as if I'm hanging on to something, though I've been letting go of other things; and something in me is saying, "What more do I have to give up?" In this bit he is acceptantly living in his immediate experiencing. He recognizes that if he can symbolize what is going on in him at the moment, it will provide meaning for him, will serve as a useful guide. This is the kind of reaction characteristic of the person who has moved far toward the upper end of the continuum.

Change in Personal Constructs

Another strand of learning which is woven into this continuum is a change in the way the client construes his experience. At the lower end of the continuum his personal constructs, to use Kelly's term, are rigid, and are unrecognized as constructs, but are thought of as facts. Thus a client says "I can't *ever* do anything right—can't ever finish it." Here this seems to be a description of a fact—this is the way things are. As he learns, in the safety of therapy, he begins to question this rigid construct. A client at this higher stage says "I don't know how I got this impression that being ashamed of myself was such an *appropriate* way to feel." Here he is doubting and changing a personal construct which has always seemed to him unchangeable. At the upper end of the continuum experience is never given more than a tentative construction, and the construing is recognized as something "I" am doing, not a quality inherent in the situation. The client learns that meaning is something he gives to an experience. It is not a fact inevitably fastened to the experience.

Change in Communication of Self

Still another strand of learning in this total continuum is the client's learning of the satisfaction involved in communicating himself. In the lower portion of the pathway there is a real unwillingness to communicate self. We find clients making statements like this: "Well, I'll tell you, it always seems a little bit nonsensical to talk about one's self except in times of dire necessity." Communication is only about externals and non-self material. Gradually the client learns that it is safe and satisfying to talk about himself as an object. Then he learns to own and express his self feelings. An example from the upper half of the continuum: "The real truth of the matter is that I'm not the sweet, forebearing guy that I try to make out I am. I get irritated at things. I feel like snapping at people, and I feel like being selfish at times; and I don't know why I should pretend I'm *not* that way." At the upper end of the continuum self, as an object, tends to disappear. The individual loses consciousness of self. He finds satisfaction in being and expressing the complexity of his feelings of the moment. He is continually in process of discovering himself.

Braaten (9) has provided corroboration of this kind of movement in therapy. He finds that when early and late interviews from more successful cases are compared with early and late interviews from less successful cases, the more successful cases show a significantly greater increase in the amount of self-reference. Even more interesting they show a greater increase in expression of the immediately present self. Further, when one compares the expression of the private self—the internal communication within the individual, his awareness of being and functioning—this too increases significantly more in the successful than in the less successful cases.

Change in Relationship to Problems

There are at least two more strands in this continuum which I would like to describe briefly. The first has to do with the client's relationship to his problems. Kirtner (10) was the first to observe this and to formulate the different ways in which clients present and approach their problems, and the correlation of these approaches with outcome. Put in my own terms, we might say that at the lowest point on the continuum the client recognizes no problems, or perceives them only as entirely external to himself. A state hospital patient summarizes his problems this way. "I sleep here a little too much. I have a bad tooth problem and a couple of others like that." Here we find no recognition of the real problem nor any involvement in it. As the client loosens up in therapy, there is more recognition of problems and more

feeling of self responsibility for problems. Gradually the client is able to face the fact that the most pressing issues are problems of feeling-in-relationship-to-others, and there is a desire to examine the inner reactions which may be contributing to these difficulties. Gradually he learns to live these problem feelings in the relationship with the therapist, and comes, through accepting them, to utilize them more constructively.

Change in Interpersonal Relationships

Finally, there is the strand of relating to others. At a lower point on the continuum the person is fearful of close personal contact, and avoids it through many devices, including intellectualization. He asks questions of the therapist. He wants to play the proper role. But he does not wish to enter, as a person, this dangerous and unknown world of relating. Gradually he learns that it is safe to risk himself occasionally on a feeling basis. Thus one client dares to say to his therapist, "Oh, all right, I *don't* trust you." Increasingly he dares to live openly in relationship to the therapist, as an ever-changing but integrated flow of feelings. He can express freely his fear of the therapist, his love for the therapist, his anger also. He finds he can live a relationship on the basis of his feelings.

Example of the Upper Portion of the Continuum

In the upper ranges of the scale, all these different strands which I have described tend to merge together and become one. Here is a very brief example of one of the "moments of movement" in therapy which illustrate this. Notice the qualities in his excerpt. The client is experiencing something right now, in this moment, and trying to sense the meaning of what is going on within him. He is changing a personal construct which he has always held—"I am not likable." He is communicating himself deeply, not withholding himself or talking about himself but *being* the internal communication going on within himself. Finally he is doing all this in a very open and fluid relationship with the therapist. Here is the excerpt:

I could even conceive of it as a possibility that I could have a kind of tender concern for me—but how could *I* be tender, be concerned for *myself,* when they're one and the same thing? But yet I can *feel* it so clearly. You know, like taking care of a child. You want to give it this and give it that. I can kind of clearly see the purposes for somebody else, but I can never see them for myself—that I could do this for me, you know. Is it possible that I can really want to take care of myself, and make that a major purpose of my life? That means I'd have to deal with the whole world as if I were guardian of a most cherished and most wanted possession, that this *I* was between this precious *me* that I want to take care of, and the whole world. It's almost as if I *loved* myself—you know—that's strange—but it's true.

This is a good example of a higher stage on the continuum.

The Process Summarized

Let me summarize these learnings which I see as involved in the process of therapy, using a segment of an earlier paper. "I have tried to sketch, in a crude and preliminary manner, the flow of a process of change which occurs when a client experiences himself as being received, welcomed, understood as he is. This process involves several threads, separable at first, becoming more of a unity as the process continues.

"This process involves a loosening of feelings. From feelings which are unrecognized, unowned, unexpressed, the client moves toward a flow in which everchanging feelings are experienced in the moment, knowingly and acceptingly, and may be accurately expressed.

"The process involves a change in the manner of experiencing. From experiencing which is remote in time from the organic event, which is bound by the structure of experience in the past, the client moves toward a manner of experiencing which is immediate, in which he senses and conceptualizes meaning in terms of what *is,* not what was.

"The process involves a loosening of the cognitive maps of experience. From construing experience in rigid ways which are perceived as external facts, the client moves toward developing changing, loosely held construings of meaning in experience, constructions which are modifiable by each new experience.

"The process involves a change in the self. From being a self which is not congruent with experience, the client moves through the phase of perceiving self as an object, to a self which is synonymous with experience, being the subjective awareness of that experience.

"There are other elements, too, involved in the process: movement from ineffective to effective choice, from fear of relationships to freely living in relationship, from inadequate differentiation of feelings and meanings to sharp differentiation.

"In general, the process moves from a point characterized by fixity, where all these elements and threads are separately discernible and separately understandable, to the flowing peak moments of therapy in which all these threads become inseparably woven together. In the new experiencing with immediacy which occurs at such moments, feeling and cognition interpenetrate, self is subjectively present in the experience, volition is simply the subjective following of a harmonious balance of organismic direction. Thus, as the process reaches this point, the person becomes a unity of flow, of motion. He has changed; but, what seems most significant, he has become an integrated process of changingness." (4, p. 149)

EMPIRICAL CORROBORATION

Is the foregoing description simply another speculative, unverifiable, clinical for-

mulation? I believe not. We have, as
mentioned earlier, built an operational
"Scale of Process in Psychotherapy" out of
these ideas. Several investigations have
been made, using this Scale and others are
in process. Some of the current findings of
an investigation being conducted by Hart
and Tomlinson (11) may be reported.

These investigators took cases unknown
to themselves or the judges who helped
them, cases in which various criteria of success were available. Nine two-minute samples were taken from the recordings of the
second and next to last interview in each
case. These samples were randomized and
presented to three judges who worked independently. The task of the judges was to
rate each interview segment on a 70-point
continuum as outlined in the Scale. When
their ratings were completed they were
compared with the case outcome, the cases
having been divided into more and less
successful cases on the basis of objective
criteria.

They found the Scale of Process in Psychotherapy to be a reasonably reliable instrument. Interjudge correlations range
from about .60 to .85 depending upon the
experience of the raters and the auditory or
visual presentation of the material.

Two studies (6, 11) have shown that
the Scale distinguishes sharply between
more and less successful cases in early interviews. The less successful cases begin and
end at a significantly lower point on the
Scale than do the more successful cases.
This was an unexpected finding.

This tends to confirm the earlier study by
Kirtner and Cartwright (10), and shows
that we have little success in helping,
through psychotherapy, those clients who
initially rate low on this Process Scale. This
means that with further refinement of the
instrument, we may be able to predict
which clients we are going to be able to
help, and which we are not, given the present state of our knowledge.

The studies indicate a sobering fact. The
change in the direction of fluidity is modest, even in the more successful cases. Thus
the average change in the more successful
cases in terms of the Process Scale, is usually less than the difference which we
found between the less and more successful
cases. Perhaps the changes due to therapeutic learning are always relatively small,
even though important. At least this is suggested by these findings.

Probably the major finding of these
studies is that we have uncovered another
dimension of the process of therapy. Some
of our earlier research indicated that change
in the concept of self was one such dimension (12). Now we can say with some assurance that in therapy which by objective
measures is shown to be successful, there is
a significant degree of movement away
from fixity and rigidity and toward a quality of changingness. This movement is not
found in unsuccessful cases (6, 11).

THE WHOLE EQUATION

From what I have described as the process of therapy, I think I can now spell out
the whole equation as it stands today in its
crude and tentative form.

The more the client perceives the therapist as
real or genuine, as empathic, as having an
unconditional regard for him, the more the
client will move away from a static, unfeeling,
fixed, impersonal type of functioning and the
more he will move toward a way of functioning
which is marked by a fluid, changing, acceptant
experiencing of differentiated personal feelings.

IMPLICATIONS

I have presented some of the knowledge
we have recently gained about the causal
aspect of psychotherapy, the relationship. I
have presented some recent knowledge of
the sequence of events which the relationship sets in motion. I have tried to formulate the equation. What are the implications
of what I have been saying? I should like
to spell out a few.

It seems to me that we are making a
solid beginning on cause and effect in psy-

chotherapy. This knowledge, as it is refined and improved, can have vast importance. It will mean that we answer questions regarding psychotherapy by recourse to factual studies, rather than on the basis of theoretical dogma or clinical hunch.

We are acquiring more detailed knowledge of one process of constructive personality change, of one equation which we can write in this field. We may learn that there are many processes of change, each with its antecedent conditions. Perhaps each therapeutic orientation produces its own distinctive changes. We do not know. This makes it imperative to discover the equation in other therapies.

The facts seem to suggest that personality change is initiated by *attitudes* which exist in the therapist, rather than primarily by his knowledge, his theories, or his techniques.

It seems to be clear that very small samples of our interaction with our clients can reveal the quality of the relationship we have established, and the likelihood of its being therapeutic.

It appears probable from our findings that we can soon identify, very early in the relationship, the individuals whom we are not likely to help by means of psychotherapy as it is today. This constitutes a tremendous challenge to all of us to develop new approaches which will help these individuals.

The studies suggest that it may be a new way of experiencing, experiencing in a more immediate, more fluid way, with more acceptance, which is the essential characteristic of therapeutic change, rather than, for example, the gaining of insight or the working through of the transference relationship, or the change in the self-concept.

The studies suggest a clearer picture of the goal or end-point of therapy. Therapy seems to be moving toward a full living in the moment—and away from a rigid intellectualized conforming to built-in expectations. It is a harmonious actualizing of all the sensitivities which the organism possesses, so that the individual can be fully alive to what is going on in him at this moment, and equally alive to all of the demands and realities of his environment, personal and impersonal. Behavior is then the sensitive and harmonious adaptation to all of the inner and outer stimuli.

This clearer picture of the end-point, of the right hand side of the equation, gives society the right to accept or reject this way of living as a suitable goal. Certainly many people would be frightened by the fluidity and changingness which I have pictured, and would not choose to move in this direction.

Finally these findings mean to me that therapy is a relationship which challenges the therapist to be, as sensitively as he is able, the person he is in this moment, knowing that it is his transparent realness, together with the liking and empathic understanding which are fostered by that realness, which can be of help to his client. To the extent that he can be a person in this moment, he can relate to the person, and the potential person, in his client. This I believe is the healing, growth-promoting, essence of psychotherapy.

EPILOGUE

So then what is the process of counseling and therapy? I have spoken of it objectively, marshalling the facts we have, writing it as a crude equation in which we can at least tentatively put down the specific terms. But let me now try to approach it from the inside, and without ignoring this factual knowledge, present this equation as it occurs subjectively in both therapist and client.

To the therapist, it is a new venture in relating. He feels, "Here is this other person, my client. I'm a little afraid of him, afraid of the depths in him as I am a little afraid of the depths of myself. Yet as he speaks, I begin to feel a respect for him, to feel my kinship to him. I sense how frightening his world is for him, and how tightly he tries to hold it in place. I would like to sense his feelings, and I would like him to know that I understand his feelings. I would like him to know that I stand with him in his tight, constricted little world, and that I can look upon it unafraid. Perhaps I can make it a safer world for him. I would like my feelings in this relationship with him to be as clear and transparent as possible, so that they are a discernible reality for him, to which he can return again and again. I would like to go with him on the fearful journey into himself, into the buried fear, and hate, and love which he has never been able to let flow in him. I recognize that this is a very human and unpredictable journey for me, as well as for him, and that I may, without even knowing my fear, shrink away within myself, from some of the feelings he discovers. To this extent I know I will be limited in my ability to help him. I realize that at times his own fears may make him perceive me as uncaring, as rejecting, as an intruder, as one who does not understand. I want fully to accept these feelings in him, and yet I hope also that my own real feelings will show through so clearly that in time he cannot fail to perceive them. Most of all I want him to encounter in me a real person. I do not need to be uneasy as to whether my own feelings are 'therapeutic.' What I am and what I feel are good enough to be a basis for therapy, if I can transparently *be* what I am and what I feel in relationship to him. Then perhaps he can be what he is, openly and without fear."

And the client, for his part, goes through far more complex sequences which can only be suggested. Perhaps schematically his feelings change in some of these ways. "I'm afraid of him. I want help, but I don't know whether to trust him. He might see things which I don't know in myself— frightening and bad elements. He seems not to be judging me, but I'm sure he is. I can't tell him what really concerns me, but I can tell him about some past experiences which are related to my concern. He seems to understand those, so I can reveal a bit more of myself.

"But now that I've shared with him some of this bad side of me, he despises me. I'm sure of it, but it's strange I can find little evidence of it. Do you suppose that what I've told him isn't so bad? Is it possible that I need not be ashamed of it as a part of me? I no longer feel that he despises me. It makes me feel that I want to go further, exploring *me,* perhaps expressing more of myself. I find him a sort of companion as I do this—he seems really to understand.

"But now I'm getting frightened again, and this time deeply frightened. I didn't realize that exploring the unknown recesses of myself would make me feel feelings I've never experienced before. It's very strange because in one way these aren't new feelings. I sense that they've always been there. But they seem so bad and disturbing I've never dared to let them flow in me. And now as I live these feelings in the hours with him, I feel terribly shaky, as though my world is falling apart. It used to be sure and firm. Now it is loose, permeable and vulnerable. It isn't pleasant to feel things I've always been frightened of before. It's his fault. Yet curiously I'm eager to see him and I feel more safe when I'm with him.

"I don't know who I am any more, but sometimes when I *feel* things I seem solid and real for a moment. I'm troubled by the contradictions I find in myself—I act one way and feel another—I think one thing and feel another. It is very disconcerting. It's also sometimes adventurous and exhilarating to be trying to discover who I am. Sometimes I catch myself feeling that perhaps the person I am is worth being, whatever that means.

"I'm beginning to find it very satisfying, though often painful, to share just what it is I'm feeling at this moment. You know, it is really helpful to try to listen to myself, to hear what is going on in me. I'm not so frightened any more of what *is* going on in me. It seems pretty trustworthy. I use some of my hours with him to dig deep into myself to know what I *am* feeling. It's scary work, but I want to *know*. And I do trust him most of the time, and that helps. I feel pretty vulnerable and raw, but I know he doesn't want to hurt me, and I even believe he cares. It occurs to me as I try to let myself down and down, deep into myself, that maybe if I could sense what is going on in me, and could realize its meaning, I would know who I am, and I would also know what to do. At least I feel this knowing sometimes with him.

"I can even tell him just how I'm feeling toward him at any given moment and instead of this killing the relationship, as I used to fear, it seems to deepen it. Do you suppose I could be my feelings with other people also? Perhaps that wouldn't be too dangerous either.

"You know, I feel as if I'm floating along on the current of life, very adventurously, being me. I get defeated sometimes, I get hurt sometimes, but I'm learning that those experiences are not fatal. I don't know exactly *who* I am, but I can feel my reactions at any given moment, and they seem to work out pretty well as a basis for my behavior from moment to moment. Maybe this is what it *means* to be *me*. But of course I can only do this because I feel safe in the relationship with my therapist. Or could I be myself this way outside of this relationship? I wonder. I wonder. Perhaps I could."

What I have just presented does not happen rapidly. It may take years. It may not, for reasons we do not understand very well, happen at all. But at least this may suggest an inside view of the factual picture I have tried to present of the process of psychotherapy as it occurs in both the therapist and his client.

BIBLIOGRAPHY

1. HALKIDES, GALATIA: *An Experimental Study of Four Conditions Necessary for Therapeutic Change.* Unpublished Ph.D. dissertation, Univ. of Chicago, 1958.

2. ROGERS, C. R.: The Necessary and Sufficient Conditions of Therapeutic Personality Change. *J. Consult. Psychol.,* 21: 95–103, 1957.

3. BARRETT-LENNARD, G. T.: *Dimensions of Perceived Therapist Response Related to Therapeutic Change.* Unpublished Ph.D. dissertation, Univ. of Chicago, 1959.

4. ROGERS, C. R.: A Process Conception of Psychotherapy. *Am. Psychologist,* 13: 142–149, 1958.

5. ROGERS, C. R. & RABLEN, R. A.: *A Scale of Process in Psychotherapy.* Unpublished manual, Univ. of Wisconsin, 1958.

6. WALKER, A., RABLEN, R. A., & ROGERS, C. R.: Development of a Scale to Measure Process Changes in Psychotherapy. *J. Clin. Psychol.,* 16: 79–85, 1959.

7. GENDLIN, E. T.: *The Function of Experiencing in Symbolization.* Unpublished Ph.D. dissertation, Univ. of Chicago, 1958.

8. GENDLIN, E. T., & ZIMRING, F.: The Qualities or Dimensions of Experiencing and Their Change. *Counseling Center Discussion Papers,* Univ. of Chicago Counseling Center, 1, No. 3, 1955.

9. BRAATEN, L. J.: *The Movement from Non-Self to Self in Client-Centered Psychotherapy.* Unpublished Ph.D. dissertation, Univ. of Chicago, 1958.

10. KIRTNER, W. L., & CARTWRIGHT, D. S.: Success and Failure in Client-Centered Therapy as a Function of Initial In-Therapy Behavior. *J. Consult. Psychol.,* 22: 329–333, 1958.

11. HART, J., & TOMLINSON, T., et al.: *Research Investigations Using the Process Scale* (in process at Univ. of Wisconsin).

12. ROGERS, C. R. & DYMOND, ROSALIND F., Eds.: *Psychotherapy and Personality Change.* Univ. of Chicago Press, 1954.

GSRs During Repression, Suppression, and Verbalization in Psychotherapeutic Interviews

JESSE E. GORDON
BARCLAY MARTIN
RICHARD M. LUNDY

The relationship between anxiety and the process whereby a psychotherapy patient becomes aware of and eventually verbalizes repressed material is a matter of both theoretical and practical interest to the therapist. The present status of psychological theory with respect to this problem allows for several different and contradictory predictions about this relationship.

It is perhaps reasonable to assume that when certain material is repressed, the repressor experiences anxiety associated with this material to the extent that the repression is incomplete. That is, with complete repression, internal anxiety-producing cues are not present and, accordingly, an anxiety

response is not made. As repression becomes less complete (more and more anxiety-producing cues appear), more and stronger anxiety responses are made. From this point on, it is possible to pose reasonable but alternative predictions as to the relationship between anxiety and the process of "lifting" a repression.

On the one hand is the view implied in some psychoanalytic writings that the achievement of full realization ("insight") into the repressed material results in relief or anxiety reduction.

On the other hand, one might expect that the increased number and clarity of the anxiety-producing cues, associated with less and less complete repression, leads to even greater anxiety as the individual approaches complete awareness of the formerly repressed material. Further, overt verbalization of the repressed material should

Reprinted from *Journal of Consulting Psychology*, 1959, 23 (3), 243–251, with the permission of the American Psychological Association and the authors. Note 1, containing information about the senior author's affiliation, has been omitted.

420

involve even more fully constituted anxiety-producing cues and, accordingly, greater anxiety than is present during awareness without overt verbalization.

To complicate the problem further, one must introduce the possibility of extinction of the learned association between cue and anxiety response. Such extinction is likely to begin shortly after awareness or overt verbalization has occurred in psychotherapy.

In view of the above considerations it does not seem appropriate to state directional hypotheses in the present study, which was designed to explore empirically the relationship between anxiety and the "lifting" of a repression, as the threatening material moves from a state of repression through awareness without verbalization (suppression) to overt verbalization.

Research which might clarify this relationship has been made difficult by the nature of repression. An experimenter cannot know what is repressed until it is no longer repressed, at which time it is too late to measure anxiety associated with it. However, a set of procedures used in an earlier study (Gordon, 1957) has been modified to make possible measurement of anxiety in a situation in which repression and suppression of known content is experimentally induced. Thus measurement of anxiety during repression, suppression, and verbalization of experimenter-controlled material is possible.

A state of repression is assumed to exist when a person fails to produce either overt or covert cues (usually verbal) to which anxiety responses have been attached, where where the production of such cues is appropriate. For the purposes of this research, posthypnotic instructions were used for inducing this condition. Posthypnotic amnesia was created by the instruction to "not think about" a particular area of experience. The area of experience selected was that of conflict with one or both parents. It was assumed that anxiety is usually associated with such experiences, so that the

words used to symbolize such experience also serve as cues for anxiety.[2]

Suppression is defined as an awareness of an area of experience together with the motivation to not verbalize about it overtly. The experimental manipulations involved hypnotic instructions that the subject would think about and recall her conflicts with her parents, but would not want to talk about them.

Verbalization was defined as conversation about parents and/or conflicts with parents with the interviewer. The experimental manipulations involved hypnotic instructions to want to talk about conflicts with parents with the interviewer.

Anxiety was defined in terms of galvanic skin conductance. Although there is disagreement about the nature of anxiety and the most valid measures of it, there is considerable evidence that skin conductance, which reflects changes in sympathetic nervous system activation, is associated with states of general emotional arousal or mobilization (Schlosberg, 1954). Emotional arousal may be a somewhat broader concept than anxiety, but lacking precise operational distinction between anxiety and this

---

[2] One may question these procedures as satisfying the definition of Freud's concept of repression as a defensive maneuver. The instructions to "not think about," while omitting specific mention of avoidance motivation, however, do presumably produce a phenomenon in which previously "conscious" material is no longer verbalizable (i.e., because "unconscious") even though this material later becomes available for verbalization. Thus we are not dealing with forgetting or extinction. The process in the subject by which material is for a time rendered unconscious is better described by the term "repression" than any other term in current usage. As far as defensive motivation is concerned, it is assumed that because the conflict material used in this study is usually unpleasant to most people, then anxiety is assumed to be associated with the verbal conflict symbols. There is reason to regard such associated anxiety as a drive or motivational factor, the reduction of which can reinforce the responses which led to the anxiety reduction. In this sense, the instructions to "not think about" an unpleasant experience are considered to be analogous to defensively motivated repression.

more general concept, the skin conductance measure was accepted as the operational definition of anxiety in this study.

PROCEDURE

Subjects. Ss were 12 female undergraduate students at the University of Wisconsin. These Ss were selected from a group of 20 females who had already been trained and screened for hypnotic susceptibility, who agreed to serve in this research. The group of 20 from which they came was screened from an initial group of 44 females who volunteered for "an experiment on hypnosis." Training and screening procedures consisted of three successive hypnotic sessions, in each of which a more "difficult" posthypnotic suggestion was given, and the response tested. The final criterion for selection of Ss was complete posthypnotic amnesia by the end of the third training and screening session.

Control. After the third session, appointments were made with Ss for a control interview. Immediately preceding this interview, S was told that electrodes would be attached to her fingers in order to record "changes in the electrical activity" of the skin, and S was reassured that she would experience no electrical shock. S was then introduced to the interviewer who attached the electrodes to S seated in a chair at the interviewer's desk. Control interviews consisted of 15-minute nondirective interviews conducted by a trained clinical psychologist. Ss were told that they could talk about anything they cared to, that the topic of conversation was completely up to them The purpose of this interview was to provide a period of adaptation to the GSR device, and to obtain a measure of base level conductance against which to compare the conductance measure obtained under the experimental conditions.

At the conclusion of the control interview, each S was again seen by the principal investigator, who asked her to fill out the Psychotherapy Reaction Questionnaire,

a scale developed by Ford (Ashby, Ford, Guerney, & Snyder, 1957) to tap defensive reactions and positive or negative attitudes toward the therapist.

Experimental conditions. Two experimental groups were formed. The only difference between these groups was in the order of the experimental conditions. One group, designated RVS, was to receive instructions designed to produce repression, verbalization, and suppression in that order. The other group, designated RSV, was to be given instructions designed to produce repression, suppression, and verbalization in that order.

Following the control interviews, Ss were appointed in random order to the two groups for the fifth and final sessions. Ss were hypnotized and given the following instructions:

> Now, as you continue to sleep, I want you to recall in your imagination some of the occasions on which you have come into conflict with either or both of your parents. Think of times when you might have had arguments, or when you felt either your mother or your father were too strict, or when you might have felt that you were unfairly treated or not being understood. Review some of these occasions in your memory. See them in your mind's eye. You don't need to tell me about them—just think about them yourself. I'll give you a minute or two in which I'll be silent to give you a chance to envision yourself in those situations. Feel just exactly the way you felt at those times. Kind of relive those experiences in your imagination now. Just think about them for a little while.

Conflict with parents was selected as the area of experience for this research because it is a fairly universal experience, and thus likely to be realistic for each S, and is one which is usually attended by anxiety. The procedures thus have the advantage over artificially induced neuroses of permitting some control over a true and meaningful experience in S's past.

Following these instructions, Ss in the RVS group were instructed as follows:

Now, when you wake up, all those experiences you've been thinking about will have completely left your mind. You won't be thinking of them at all. They'll be the farthest things from your mind. In the beginning of your interview with Dr. _____, he'll click a key three times. Just ignore that. It doesn't mean anything. But later on, when he clicks the key again, all these thoughts and experiences with your father or mother or both, and your feelings about those experiences, will come to mind. You'll begin to think about them again. You can talk about the feelings and experiences that are on your mind. You'll want to talk them over with Dr. _____. Later on, Dr. _____ will click the key again. When he does, it'll occur to you that you shouldn't really talk to him about your experiences and feelings toward your parents, and you won't want to talk about them anymore, although they will still be on your mind.

These instructions were then summarized, posthypnotic amnesia for the instructions induced, and *S* awakened.

For the RSV group, the instructions were substantially the same, except that instructions for suppression were given before the instructions for verbalization.

Upon awakening, *S* was told that she was to be interviewed by Dr. ——, and that throughout the course of the 45-minute interview, she would have electrodes strapped to two fingers. *S* was told that, as in the control interview, she could talk about anything she cared to. *S* was then brought to the interview room, introduced to Dr. ——, and the electrodes attached. The interviews began in a standard manner, with the interviewer telling *S* that the interview would be about the same as the one she had before and that she might start off by telling something about herself. From that point on, the interview remained within the nondirective framework. All interviews were tape recorded. At the conclusion of the interview, *S* returned to the experimenter who again administered the Psychotherapy Reaction Questionnaire, disabused *S* of the hypnotic instructions, and told her of the purpose of the study.

The interviewer did not know beforehand whether an *S* was in the RVS or RSV group.

GSR recording. Skin conductance measures were obtained by using an AC circuit designed by Grant (1946) and dry silver electrodes bound to the palmar surfaces of two fingers of *S*'s left hand. Continuous ink recordings of *S*'s resistance throughout the session were obtained by feeding the output of the GSR apparatus into a General Electric Photoelectric Recorder. Resistance scores were obtained by halving the difference between the low and high points in one-minute sections of the ink recordings, and adding this to the low point within each one-minute interval. The conductance scores for data analysis were reciprocals of these resistance measures.

RESULTS

As a check on the validity of the experimental procedures, the interview tape recordings were scored in 30-second intervals for the presence of reference to parents, and to conflict with parents. Each interval was scored plus or minus for the presence or absence of such references during that interval. No attempt was made to score for magnitude of references, or to frequency within intervals. Figure 1 shows the distribution of plus scores for the RVS and RSV

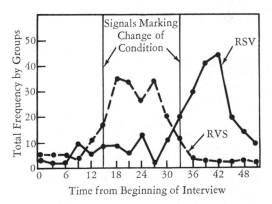

Fig. 1. Distribution of references to parents and conflict with parents

groups. It is apparent from Fig. 1 that the Ss did follow the hypnotic instructions, as far as verbalizing is concerned.[3] One S in each group failed to follow the instructions; neither made any reference to parents, with or without conflict, throughout the course of her interview. These two Ss were therefore dropped from further analysis.

Figure 2 presents the conductance scores of both groups over all conditions.[4] The abscissa represents number of two-minute intervals from the beginning of the particular experimental condition. As noted above, the GSR records were scored in one-minute intervals. These data were collapsed into

two-minute intervals by adding the scores together in successive pairs of one-minute intervals. The height of the curves therefore represents the RVS and RSV means of conductance scores (in micromhos) summed over two-minute intervals.

It may be seen from Fig. 2 that there is a general increase in conductance across the entire time period. The levelling-off of the conductance, usually interpreted as adaptation, which is commonly found in GSR records after the first 15 minutes of recording, is not present in these data. That the over-all increase in height is not a function of the particular order of the experimental conditions is suggested by the data on Suppression and Verbalization. The conductance curve for the last experimental condition is higher than for the next to last, regardless of whether the last was Suppression or Verbalization.

The GSR data were therefore analyzed for differences in shape of the conductance curves, rather than for differences in mean conductance levels. It is thus possible to draw conclusions about the relationship between the independent variables and the growth of anxiety, although level of anxiety at any particular point must be ignored. Figure 3 presents the conductance curves of all Ss, combined by experimental conditions. The units are the same as in Fig. 2.

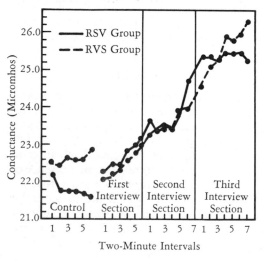

Fig. 2. GSR curves over time.

[3] The lines marking the boundaries of the experimental conditions are approximate. The interviewer varied somewhat in his timing of the signals, so as not to interrupt an S in a flow of conversation. The interview sections are therefore not strictly comparable from S to S in terms of length. The boundary lines in this figure are drawn at the times when the signals were most frequently given.

[4] As was noted in connection with Fig. 1, the length of the experimental conditions varied somewhat from S to S. The number of intervals reported in this figure and used in the statistical analyses was the maximum number of intervals common to all Ss. For several Ss, therefore, the last one or two intervals in some conditions were dropped from the analyses.

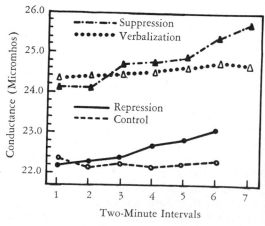

Fig. 3. GSR curves of all Ss combined, by conditions.

Grant's (1956) extension of Alexander's trend test was applied to these data. For each *S*, a difference was found between her conductance levels in two-minute intervals of one condition and the comparable two-minute intervals in a comparison condition. Thus a set of difference curves was generated for each pair of conditions which were to be compared with each other. Each difference curve was tested for the significance of its difference from a curve of zero slope. This then tells one whether there is a difference in the slopes of the curves representing the different conditions to be compared. Tables 1, 2, 3, and 4 report the results of these analyses.

TABLE 1

ANALYSIS OF VARIANCE OF
TREND OF DIFFERENCES
BETWEEN REPRESSION AND CONTROL[a]

Source	df	Mean Square	F
Between ind. slopes	8	1.46	
Between ind. quadratics	8	.18	
Between ind. cubics	8	.28	
Over-all slope	1	6.96	4.77*
Over-all quadratic	1	.10	.56
Over-all cubic	1	.12	.43

* *p* < .05.
[a] Owing to error in recording, control GSR level of one *S* was useless for statistical analysis. Therefore this analysis is based on 9 Ss.

TABLE 2

ANALYSIS OF VARIANCE OF
TREND OF DIFFERENCES
BETWEEN REPRESSION AND SUPPRESSION

Source	df	Mean Square	F
Between ind. slopes	9	.86	
Between ind. quadratics	9	1.13	
Between ind. cubics	9	.06	
Over-all slope	1	.67	.78
Over-all quadratic	1	.24	.21
Over-all cubic	1	.02	.33

TABLE 3

ANALYSIS OF VARIANCE OF
TREND OF DIFFERENCES
BETWEEN REPRESSION AND VERBALIZATION

Source	df	Mean Square	F
Between ind. slopes	9	1.63	
Between ind. quadratics	9	.32	
Between ind. cubics	9	.89	
Over-all slope	1	1.78	1.09
Over-all quadratic	1	.001	—
Over-all cubic	1	.001	—

TABLE 4

ANALYSIS OF VARIANCE OF
TREND OF DIFFERENCES
BETWEEN SUPPRESSION AND VERBALIZATION

Source	df	Mean Square	F
Between ind. slopes	9	1.23	
Between ind. quadratics	9	1.79	
Between ind. cubics	9	.15	
Over-all slope	1	7.20	5.85*
Over-all quadratic	1	.27	—
Over-all cubic	1	.20	1.33

* *p* < .05.

Table 1 indicates that under the Repression condition, Ss' conductances were increasing at a faster rate than they were during the Control interviews. It appears that anxiety increases as *S* approaches the point of awareness, and the repression mechanism becomes less effective.

Tables 2 and 3 compare Repression with Suppression and Verbalization. The results do not reveal any significant differences between the conductance curves in Repression and Suppression. The Repression-Verbalization difference curve also does not yield a significant slope, although there is a tendency for the Repression curve to be somewhat steeper than the Verbalization curve.

Table 4 reports the comparison of Suppression and Verbalization. The significant difference found indicates that conductance measures obtained under Suppression increase at a greater rate than those obtained during Verbalization. Figure 3 reveals that the Verbalization slope is almost flat, whereas the Suppression slope is one of the steeper slopes obtained. Thus it is found that anxiety accumulates or builds up at a faster rate during Suppression than during Verbalization of disturbing material.

The differences between the RSV and RVS groups in the questionnaire of attitudes toward the therapist yield $t = 1.64$ ($p > .05$). The mean change in the RSV group was $+3.6$, which is in the direction of more positive attitudes; the mean change in the RVS group was -5, which is in the direction of more negative attitudes; $\sigma_{\bar{x}-\bar{y}} = 5.25$. Although the differences are not significant, due to the great variability among the Ss, the results suggest a tendency for RSV Ss to feel more positively toward the therapist than the RVS Ss. This suggests that Ss whose most recent experience has been one in which they revealed, rather than hid from the therapist, some personally threatening material may feel more positively toward the therapist.

DISCUSSION

The most striking outcome of this study is the finding that there is never a downward turn in the absolute measure of anxiety during the 45-minute experimental session. This suggests that the lifting of a repression, whether it included Suppression or Verbalization, or both, is accompanied by a fairly consistent rise in anxiety. An absolute reduction in anxiety, for whatever reason, does not seem to occur during the first 30 minutes or so after the S first becomes aware of the repressed material. It is of interest to note that the two Ss who failed to comply with the posthypnotic instructions by never verbalizing about parents in any fashion were the only two Ss who did not show this over-all increase in conductance. One of these Ss had a decreasing conductance curve, and the curve of the

other S was about level. Experience with GSR indicates that this upward trend is not necessarily characteristic of interviews of comparable length. This phenomenon thus appears to be associated with the effects of the hypnotic instructions. One possible explanation of the continuing rise in conductance may be that anxiety associated with parental conflict accumulates throughout the time that the Ss are forced by the hypnotic instructions to deal with this aspect of their experience. The over-all upward trend does tend to level off during Verbalization. One may account for this by assuming that extinction of the association between cue and anxiety response occurs when anxiety-producing material is verbalized in an accepting atmosphere. From this point of view, we might expect the curve eventually to turn downward if sufficiently long periods of Verbalization were maintained until the verbal cue-anxiety association is extinguished. Perhaps the 15-minute period was not sufficient to get a full indication of the degree to which extinction could occur during Verbalization.

A simpler account of the change in slope during Verbalization might be that the increase in anxiety is retarded only when the S is talking about the anxiety-arousing material. In this sense, the anxiety curve begins to level off only when there is congruence between the Ss' experiencing of the material, their awareness of the material, and their verbalization of it. This account also suggests that, had there been more time in which S could experience this congruence, the anxiety might have reduced. When there is not this complete congruence, as in the Repression and Suppression conditions, anxiety consistently increases.

Given this over-all increase in conductance, which appears to be unrelated to the particular experimental conditions, except possibly for Verbalization, one may still compare the conditions in order to discover which ones contribute most heavily to the growth of the anxiety. The results of such comparisons indicate that repressing Ss generate anxiety at a faster rate than they do in the nonrepressing control condition. One cannot decide from these data whether the increasing slope in repression is caused by the imminent cessation of repression, or by a simple anticipation of the signal denoting the start of another condition. The control interview was not followed by another condition, as was the case with the Repression section. However, an examination of the curves in Fig. 2 suggests that increases in conductance may not be solely determined by anticipation; the RVS group does not have as rapid an increase in conductance as the RSV group during the second interview section, even though there is still a third interview section for both groups to anticipate. It is suggested that what is being anticipated plays at least some part in the anticipation response. This further suggests that some anxiety-arousing cues are being produced in the Ss even 'though they are repressing, as defined by the hypnotic instructions, and that these cues increase as the point of awareness approaches. Since the Ss are not overtly verbalizing about the induced threat or about the signal which they may be anticipating, it must be assumed that the anxiety-arousing cues are being produced covertly. If we assume that the Ss were not thinking about the threat or the approaching signal, according to the hypnotic instructions, we must conclude that the anxiety-producing cues were being produced without the Ss' awareness.

This raises some questions about the nature of awareness. According to Dollard and Miller (1950), repression exists when an individual fails to think (produce verbal cues, usually) because of the association between these cues and anxiety. This is essentially a learned avoidance response. If such were the case, one would expect little or no anxiety in repressing Ss. This, of course, is not what was found. Our data, indicating increasing anxiety during Repression, suggest that some anxiety-arousing cues were being produced when the Ss

are assumed, on the basis of the hypnotic instructions, to be unaware of the threat. Thus there is evidence for the presence of anxiety-producing cues without awareness. Dollard and Miller's hypothesis that unawareness or unconsciousness is defined in terms of the absence of such cues is therefore inconsistent with the analysis based on our data. It is suggested that awareness be defined in terms of some other secondary response to the covert (verbal) anxiety cue-producing responses which the unaware Ss appear to be making, and that it is these other responses (perhaps self-related evaluations) which are not being made by repressing Ss. That is, awareness may be defined in terms of some self-related evaluations which the individual may or may not make as responses to internal, usually verbal cue-producing responses, rather than in terms of the cue-producing responses themselves.

Hypnosis may be thought of as an indirect way of producing the condition of not being aware of the covert cues associated with anxiety. There is no guarantee that the Ss were indeed unaware of the anxiety-producing cues, namely, thoughts about parental conflict. If one is willing to accept the validity of the posthypnotic instructions in this respect, then the rather interesting conclusion must be drawn that anxiety increases with equal rapidity whether S is aware of the covert anxiety-producing cues or not, since the conductance curves for Repression and Suppression do not differ in slope. This finding that anxiety continues to rise in the Suppression condition suggests that awareness or insight, of itself, is not sufficient to reduce anxiety.

At the same time, an account of the relationship between anxiety and the lifting of repression which would predict a direct relationship between anxiety and availability of anxiety-producing cues would have some difficulty with these data. With initial verbalization and its profusion and clarity of cues, we should expect an even greater increase in the anxiety measure. In contrast we find that it is only during Verbalization that the increase in anxiety tends to slow down.

This reduction in anxiety increase during Verbalization may have a counterpart in the positive feelings toward the therapist which the RSV Ss tend to show to a greater extent than the RVS Ss. It seems probable that the verbalization section, occurring last for the RSV Ss, leaves the S with a more positive feeling because the S has been experiencing a lessening of the anxiety increase just prior to her rating of the therapist. In contrast the increase in anxiety associated with the last condition—Suppression—for the RVS Ss may be associated with the tendency of these Ss to feel less positive toward the therapist.

Certain qualitative aspects of the Ss' behavior in the interviews may provide a clearer picture of the nature of these interview sessions. In all respects, Ss' verbal behavior was natural; it is doubtful that the most insightful psychologist would discover, from listening to the tape recordings, that Ss were performing according to hypnotic suggestions. Of particular interest is the manner in which Ss responded to the signal denoting the beginning of a new experimental condition. In no case was there a verbal response relating to the signal itself. Some Ss lapsed into silence for a few seconds, and then began verbalizing, usually with a change to subject matter appropriate to the new condition. A frequent remark from Ss who had been in the Verbalization condition when the signal was given marking the beginning of Suppression was "Well, let's talk about something pleasanter," or "I guess I shouldn't bore you with these personal problems." During Suppression sections, particularly in the RSV group, one notes frequent references to the parental conflicts of others—friends, relatives, etc., and occasionally a spontaneous denial of personal conflicts with parents.

One recording was particularly illuminating in the manner in which it reveals the development of associations to the threatening material. The S was in the RSV group. The major topic of conversation during Repression was S's interest in a film on intellectual deficiency and brain pathology she had recently seen in psychology lecture. This film reminded her of her friend's mother, who suffers from multiple sclerosis. This conversation was continued in the Suppression section, where the major emphasis was on the emotional climate of the friend's home, in relation to the mother's illness. S stressed the frequent conflicts between her friend and her friend's father, growing out of the continual stress at home. This continued until the Verbalization section began, in which S discussed her own conflicts with her parents. She introduced the topic by saying, "Of course, lots of people have problems with their parents, even when there isn't that kind of sickness and tension." Thus the discussion of the psychology film seems to have been closely associated with, or at least led directly to, a discussion of S's own problems. This may suggest that therapists be cautious in deciding that any particular topic is as irrelevant as a discussion of a film on brain damage at first appears. It is the ability to produce behaviors such as these which become intelligible only when the experimenter has knowledge and control of the antecedent conditions, that makes the experimental procedures used in this research of particular value.

SUMMARY

An experiment was performed to study the effects on anxiety, as measured by GSR recording, of repression, suppression, and verbalization of threatening material. Ten selected and trained undergraduate female Ss were stimulated to recall conflicts with their parents under hypnosis, and were given posthypnotic suggestions to "not think about" (Repression), "think about but not talk about" (Suppression), and "talk about" (Verbalization) conflicts with parents to the interviewer, who conducted a nondirective type interview for 45 minutes with each *S*. Each condition occupied 15 minutes of the interview, with *S* responding to signals demarcating the beginning of each condition as instructed under hypnosis. Skin conductance was recorded continuously throughout the interviews, and a scale of attitudes toward the therapist given once at the end of a 15-minute control interview and again at the end of the 45-minute interview, constituted the dependent variables. Skin conductance measures were analyzed in terms of differences in slope. The findings were as follows:

1. There was a consistent over-all increase in conductance throughout the experimental session, indicating a continuous growth in anxiety regardless of the order of conditions.

2. The increase in conductance was more rapid under Repression than during the control interview.

3. Conductance slopes during Repression and Suppression were not found to differ significantly.

4. The conductance slopes during Suppression were significantly steeper than during Verbalization, in which the slopes tended to flatten.

5. *S*s whose last interview section was Verbalization showed a tendency toward more positive shift in attitudes toward the therapist than *S*s whose last interview section was Suppression. However, this difference was not significant.

REFERENCES

ASHBY, J. D., FORD, D. H., GUERNEY, B. G., GUERNEY, LOUISE F., & SNYDER, W. U. Effects on clients of reflective and a leading type of psychotherapy. *Psychol. Monogr.*, 1957, 71, No. 24 (Whole No. 453).

DOLLARD, J., & MILLER, N. *Personality and psychotherapy.* New York: McGraw-Hill, 1950. Pp. 198–221.

GORDON, J. E. Leading and following psychotherapeutic techniques with hypnotically induced repression and hostility. *J. abnorm. soc. Psychol.*, 1957, 54, 405–410.

GRANT, D. A. A convenient alternating current circuit for measuring GSR's. *Amer. J. Psychol.*, 1946, 59, 149–151.

GRANT, D. A. Analysis of variance tests in the analysis and comparison of curves. *Psychol. Bull.*, 1956, 53, 141–154.

SCHLOSBERG, H. Three dimensions of emotion. *Psychol. Rev.*, 1954, 61, 81–88.

A Multidimensional Comparison of Therapist Activity in Analytic and Client-centered Therapy[1]

HANS H. STRUPP

"In science we need flexible minds and rigid concepts, but in psychoanalysis we have rigid minds and flexible concepts" (13, p. 233). This statement by a leading analyst, which is equally applicable to other forms of psychotherapy, epitomizes a growing awareness among research-minded psychotherapists that the fluidity of concepts, the ambiguities of language, and the idiosyncratic frames of reference espoused by competing schools represent serious barriers against furthering our knowledge of the psychotherapeutic process. From numerous quarters in recent years has come the cry for simpler concepts, for operational definitions, and for identifying the common denominators underlying all psychotherapeutic procedures. This trend implies, among other things, that differences in theory are meaningless if they fail to carry over into practice, and that focus upon the actual operations may be more fruitful for testing theoretical differences than prolonged controversy about the uniqueness of a given system.

The analysis of therapeutic protocols has occupied the time of researchers for some years, but rarely has an attempt been made to go outside a school of thought and to compare the techniques of, say, a nondirectivist with those of an analyst. Yet, such comparisons will inevitably play a part in future attempts to evaluate the relative effectiveness of competing approaches to psychotherapy.

Reprinted from *Journal of Consulting Psychology*, 1957, 21 (4), 301–308, with the permission of the American Psychological Association and the author.

[1] This research is part of a larger project which is supported by a research grant (M-965) from the National Institute of Mental Health, of the National Institutes of Health, U.S. Public Health Service. Grateful acknowledgment is made to Winfred Overholser, M.D., under whose general direction this work was carried out, and to Leon Yochelson, M.D., project consultant. In addition, I am greatly indebted to my former research associate, Rebecca E. Rieger, A.M., who contributed materially to the execution of this study. A slightly different version of this paper was presented at the 1956 Annual Meeting of the American Psychological Association in Chicago.

This paper presents a preliminary descriptive analysis of two varieties of psychotherapeutic techniques: insight therapy with reeducative goals based on psychoanalytic principles, and client-centered therapy. The analysis is mediated by a multidimensional system, designed to quantify the common denominators in the verbal operations of therapists irrespective of their theoretical orientation. The data obviously do not permit an evaluation of the respective merits of short-term analytic and client-centered therapy.

THE TWO CASE HISTORIES

The first case history, published by Wolberg (12, pp. 688–780),[2] comprises nine treatment sessions with a retired business woman, a widow in the middle years of life, who had become progressively depressed, and retreated from her customary social contacts. Concerning his technique, the therapist (Wolberg) mentions that the work proceeded almost entirely on a characterologic level, and that the effect of treatment was mostly of a reeducative nature, despite the fact that he interpreted some of the patient's defenses. A follow-up indicated that the results of treatment had been durable.

The second case history is that of Mary Jane Tilden, counseled by Rogers in a series of eleven interviews (9, pp. 128–203). Unfortunately, the author was not aware that this case is available in its entirety, which necessitated the selection of reasonably complete interviews from the beginning, middle, and terminal phases of treatment from the published portions.

Miss Tilden was described as a 20-year-old attractive young woman brought to the clinic by her mother, who complained that the patent was sleeping all the time, brooding, and ruminating. Miss Tilden seemed to be withdrawing progressively—she had given up her job and lost interest in her

social life. Miss Tilden was treated by non-directive therapy. Rogers felt that the eleven counseling hours were followed by a period of improved adjustment; nevertheless, the evaluation of final outcome remained somewhat in doubt since, shortly after a year had elapsed, there seemed to be a recurrence of the earlier symptomatology.[3]

THE SYSTEM OF ANALYSIS

The system of analysis whose development and operational characteristics have been delineated in another publication (10), yields five measures relative to any therapist communication. There are two sets of categories (*Type of Therapeutic Activity* and *Dynamic Focus*), and three intensity scales (*Degree of Inference, Initiative,* and *Therapeutic Climate*). These components may be briefly characterized as follows:

Type of Therapeutic Activity. The categories specified the outer form or structure of a therapeutic intervention and provide a gross analysis of the therapist's techniques. The major categories were:

00 Facilitating Communication (Minimal activity).
10 Exploratory Operations.
20 Clarification (Minimal interpretation).
30 Interpretive Operations.
40 Structuring.
50 Direct Guidance.
60 Activity not clearly relevant to the task of therapy.
70 Unclassifiable.

Sixteen subcategories served to refine the primary rating.

Degree of Inference. This intensity scale was based on the conception that inference is an integral part of all therapeutic communications and that it is always present to some degree. Each communication was rated by means of a five-point scale

---

[2] This case, particularly the therapist's activity, has been more fully discussed (11).

[3] Although one cannot be sure, this case may pertain to that period in the evolution of client-centered therapy in which Rogers (7) detects "vestiges of subtle directiveness."

ranging from low to high inference. Scale points were defined a priori rather than via empirical judgments, but examples of typical communications were used to define each scale point.

Dynamic Focus. Dynamic Focus referred to the frame of reference adopted by the therapist at a particular juncture, and characterizes the manner in which he focuses the therapeutic spotlight. Two major sectors were used to differentiate whether the therapist "goes along" with the patient (A) or whether he introduces a different focus (B). Communications assigned to Sector B were further analyzed in terms of five subcategories:

B-1   Requests for additional information.

B-2   Focus on dynamic events in the *past.*

B-3   Focus on dynamic events in the *present.*

B-4T Focus on dynamics of the therapist-patient relationship (analysis of the transference).

B-4   Focus on the therapist-patient interaction in terms of the therapist's role as an expert, authority, etc.

Initiative. The second intensity scale measured the extent to which the therapist assumes responsibility for guiding the patient's communications in a given channel. Initiative was conceived as ranging from low to high, and ratings were made on a four-point continuum. As in the case of *Degree of Inference,* scale points were defined by reference to appropriate examples.

Therapeutic Climate. Emotional overtones discernible in a communication were quantified by means of a bipolar scale: $0 =$ neutral; $+1 =$ mild degree of warmth; $+2$ strong degree of warmth; -1 mild degree of coldness; -2 strong degree of coldness. A "warm" communication is one in which the therapist empathizes, shows understanding, or supports; a "cold" communication is one in which the therapist rejects, withdraws support, or punishes.

PROCEDURE

Seven of the nine Wolberg interviews and three representative interviews from the Miss Tilden case were scored jointly by two raters from the printed scripts. Two of the Wolberg interviews were rated independently by the same raters to obtain a measure of rater agreement.

RESULTS
Rater Agreement

Table 1 presents results based on a unit-by-unit analysis of two interviews scored independently by two raters. Agreement on

TABLE 1

AGREEMENT BETWEEN
TWO INDEPENDENT RATERS[a]

System Component	Wolberg Interview VII ($N = 114$)	Wolberg Interview IX ($N = 154$)
Type	80.7%	80.5%
Degree of Inference	86.0% ($r = .86$)	94.0% ($r = .885$)
Dynamic Focus	80.7%	85.7%
Initiative	87.7% ($r = .87$)	93.5% ($r = .93$)
Therapeutic Climate[b]	—	—

[a] All percentages and correlation coefficients are significant beyond the .01 level.
[b] Nonzero scores too infrequent.

a unit (therapist communication) means that both raters assigned it to the same category (on *Type* and *Focus,* respectively), or that they gave it an intensity score (on *Degree of Inference* or *Initiative,* respectively) no more than one-half step apart. For the last two scales, product-moment coefficients were computed in addition.

The Wolberg Case

The therapist's activity, as mirrored by the multidimensional system of analysis, is presented in Figures 1, 2, 3, and 4. Within each interview, frequencies have been converted into percentages. In the case of *Degree of Inference* and *Iniative,* the designation Level 1, 2, and 3 signifies that scores have been grouped; Level 3 refers to the most intense scores. Chi squares computed for each component of the system were significant beyond the .01 level, indicating that the fluctuations in therapist activity for the interview series are not attributable to chance.

The therapist's techniques show systematic variations on all components over the course of therapy.[4] The initial interview is devoted largely to an exploration of the patient's problem; the next two interviews reveal an intensification of therapeutic activity, both in terms of inferential operations and *Initiative;* Interviews IV and VII emerge as interpretive ones, the intervening sessions as less "dramatic"; data for the remaining sessions point to a phasing out of interpretive activity, but *Initiative* remains at a relatively high level.

The therapist's interpretations are geared to the patient's current interpersonal relations, with relatively little emphasis on the therapist- patient relationship or on genetic antecedents. Throughout treatment, but especially in the second half, the therapist stands out as a person who, in the role of an expert, gives guidance, states opinions, and engages in procedures which may be labeled reeducative. He is clearly more ac-

[4] *Therapeutic Climate* had to be omitted because there were very few nonzero scores.

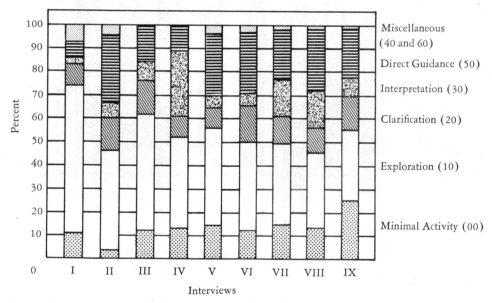

Fig. 1. Therapist activity in the Wolberg case in terms of *Type of Therapeutic Activity.* (Interviews: I, N = 108; II, N = 79; III, N = 108; IV N = 174; V, N = 123; VI, N = 85; VII, N = 114; VIII, N = 130; IX, N = 154. Total number of therapist interventions: N = 1,075.)

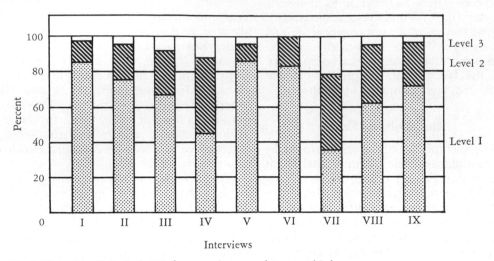

Fig. 2. Therapist activity in the Wolberg case in terms of *Degree of Inference*.

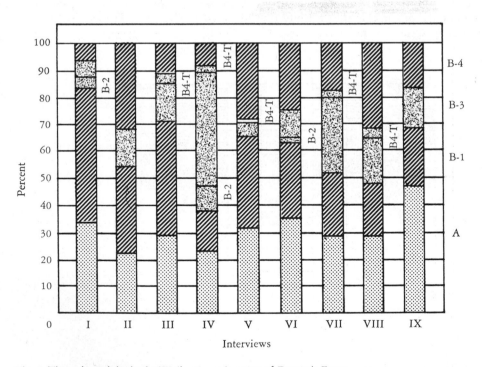

Fig. 3. Therapist activity in the Wolberg case in terms of *Dynamic Focus*.

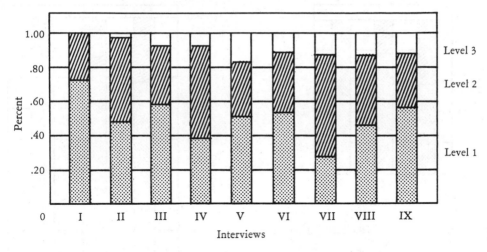

Fig. 4. Therapist activity in the Wolberg case in terms of *Initiative*.

tive than passive, both in terms of frequency of intervention and in directing the course of therapy. Wolberg's own descriptive label "insight therapy with re-educative goals" appears to be corroborated by the quantitative analyses.

The most noteworthy single result is perhaps the *phasing* of therapeutic activity. It seems as if the therapist gradually prepares the patient for more inferential formulations which he advances in the fourth session. Then he waits for a consolidation of insight before renewing his interpretive efforts in Interview VII. Thereafter, he diminishes his interpretive activity while maintaining a degree of therapeutic pressure till the end.

The Case of Miss Tilden

The analysis comprises three selected interviews; they are, however, separated in time and they presumably represent different stages of therapy.

Reference to Figures 5, 6, 7, and 8 indicates that the profiles of therapist activity are quite similar from interview to interview. As might be expected, reflections of feeling account for a large percentage of all

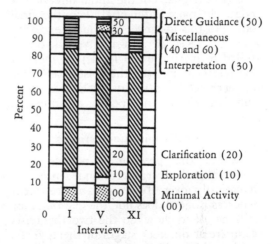

Fig. 5. Therapist activity in the Miss Tilden case in terms of *Type of Therapeutic Activity*. (Interviews: I, $N=57$; V, $N=23$; XI, $N=53$. Total number of therapist interventions: $N=133$.)

interventions (75%); interpretations are virtually absent; explorations are used minimally in the initial session and are almost nonexistent later on; direct guidance is equally rare. The data on *Degree of Inference* and *Initiative* corroborate these findings: neither maximal *Degree of Inference* nor maximal *Initiative* is used to any ap-

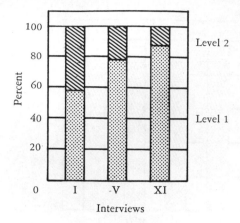

Fig. 6. Therapist activity in the Miss Tilden case in terms of *Degree of Inference*.

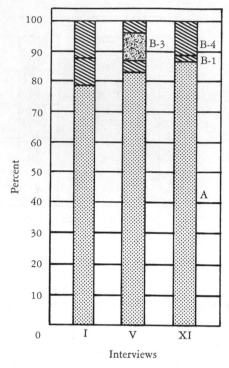

Fig. 7. Therapist activity in the Miss Tilden case in terms of *Dynamic Focus*.

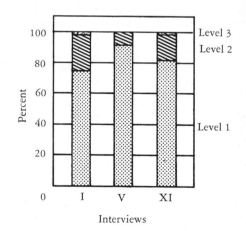

Fig. 8. Therapist activity in the Miss Tilden case in terms of *Initiative*.

preciable degree, but the initial interview is relatively more inferential than the final one. (In this instance, chi square exceeded the .01 level of probability; all others failed to reach the .05 level.) In most of his interventions, the therapist accepts the patient's focus; only very rarely does he assume the role of an expert or an authority.

Intertherapist Comparisons

While the preceding analyses have shown that Wolberg's technique varies systematically over the course of treatment whereas Rogers' does not, the question may still be asked, how do the two therapists compare at different stages of therapy? To explore this problem, three interviews from the beginning, middle, and terminal phases of the Wolberg series were selected and compared with the Miss Tilden case. Since the distributions of the categories within *Type* and *Dynamic Focus* vary so greatly for the two therapists, the only meaningful comparisons concern the continua of *Degree of Inference* and *Initiative*. The results of this analysis are presented in Table 2.

In the case of *Degree of Inference*, a significant chi square indicates that Wolberg's technique is significantly more inferential than Rogers'; with respect to *Initiative*, Wolberg exerts stronger guidance in the middle and terminal interviews, but not in

TABLE 2

CHI-SQUARE COMPARISONS OF
THERAPIST ACTIVITY IN
INITIAL, MIDDLE, AND TERMINAL INTERVIEWS

	Wolberg I (N = 108) vs. Rogers I (N = 57)	Wolberg IV (N = 174) vs. Rogers V (N = 23)	Wolberg IX (N = 154) vs. Rogers XI (N = 53)
Degree of Inference	19.32***	9.39**	4.66*
Initiative	.19	22.79***	9.85**

* Significant between the .02 and .05 level.
** Significant at the .01 level.
*** Significant at the .001 level.

the initial one. The latter finding is accounted for by the fact that Wolberg employs a great many exploratory questions of a diagnostic character in his first session, which in terms of *Initiative* receive scores similar to the reflection-of-feeling technique, which Rogers employs throughout.

DISCUSSION

A multidimensional system of analysis has been applied to the therapist's communications in two forms of therapy in an effort to measure aspects which may be common to both. With respect to the Miss Tilden case, the system of analysis yields data which are substantially in agreement with other analyses which have been performed on interviews conducted by nondirective counselors. By and large, these results also agree with Rogers' recommendations on therapeutic technique. Wolberg's technique, too, is in agreement with his descriptive account but, to my knowledge, no comparable quantitative studies have been published. While not crucial, such evidence attests indirectly to the validity of this system of analysis. Of at least equal importance, however, is the tentative demonstration that the method facilitates the comparative treatment of therapeutic techniques—a treatment which is quantitative and highly objective, and which does not

prejudge a particular communication as desirable or undesirable on a priori grounds.

To be sure, the present two case histories are comparable only in superficial respects and they do not lend themselves to a rigorous evaluative comparison. However, they suggest a number of questions which appear to be basic to all psychotherapy research. Consider the following two points.

We know that both patients entered psychotherapy seeking alleviation of their emotional problems. Did their difficulties have any common basis? What was the relative degree of their disturbance? Even if both had been diagnosed as "depressed," or by any other label, we would know but little about the common denominators of the underlying dynamics. As Kubie (6) has pointed out, the time is ripe for fresh attempts to identify the common principles of the "neurotic process." It is clear that studies in which patients are matched with experimental "controls" remain largely meaningless unless this Herculean research task can be accomplished.

Secondly, what transpired in the therapeutic sessions that led both therapists to evaluate the outcome as "successful?" Both therapists are highly experienced men in their field; both had a rationale for their respective procedures which on the evidence of this study differed quantitatively (*Degree of Inference* and *Initiative*) and perhaps qualitatively, *Type* and *Dynamic Focus*). Rogers, in keeping with his theory, consistently reflected the patient's feelings, whereas Wolberg, combining analytic principles with reeducative techniques, attempted to effect therapeutic changes in his patient mainly by means of interpretation and guidance. But even if the patients could be equated it would not be possible to attribute differences in therapeutic outcome (whose measurement is another staggering problem) to variations in technique as long as relevant factors in the therapist's personality are left out of account. Certainly, Wolberg was more "directive" (by Rogerian standards). But both therapists conveyed an attitude of respect for their patients and implied their right to self-direction; both appeared to be warm, accepting, and noncritical; both encouraged the patient's expression of feelings; and both, by their therapeutic performance, seemed to engender a feeling of greater self-acceptance in their patients. These attitudes on the part of the therapist—he may have them in common with the mature person who can also be a good parent[5]—are as yet largely unexplored by objective research, but they may be the touchstone of *all* therapeutic success, regardless of the theory.[6] Given the "basic therapist personality" it may still be possible that some therapeutic techniques or combinations of techniques

catalyze the therapeutic process whereas others are relatively inert; contrariwise, no amount of training in technique may compensate for deficiencies in the therapist's "basic attitudes." To approach these problems by research is difficult, but by no means impossible.

It seems that altogether too little attention has been paid by researchers to the therapist and his contribution to the therapeutic process. In keeping with this conviction, I have focused upon one facet—the therapist's techniques—and attempted to abstract common denominators from the therapist's verbal operations. The isolation and measurement of common denominators in varying therapeutic techniques appears to be a needed research task which must be expanded by research on the therapist's personality, from which technique seems to be inseparable.[7]

SUMMARY

In an effort to compare the therapist's activity in two forms of psychotherapy, a multidimensional system for analyzing therapeutic communications has been applied to two published case histories: a case treated by short-term therapy based upon psychoanalytic principles, and a case treated by client-centered therapy.

The therapist's activity in analytically oriented therapy showed statistically significant variations over the course of treatment in terms of *Type of Therapeutic Activity, Degree of Inference, Dynamic Focus,* and *Initiative.* The data point to an intensification of therapeutic activity from the first to the fourth interview, at which time a number of relatively more inferential interpretations were advanced. In the seventh session, a similar intensification occurred, followed by a phasing out to the end of

---

[5] I have in mind Fromm's "productive character" (5).

[6] There is increasing evidence that the therapist's attitude may "cut across" theoretical orientations. For a comprehensive statement of the client-centered position, see Rogers' discussion (8, pp. 19–64). On the other hand, Wolberg's transcript offers evidence that respect for the patient, his capacities, his right to self-direction, and his worth as a human being can be conveyed even when the therapist makes interpretations. Fiedler's studies (2, 3, 4) suggest that "experts," irrespective of whether they subscribe to the analytic, Adlerian, or client-centered viewpoint, create highly similar "ideal therapeutic relationships" but, as Bordin (1, pp. 115–116) has pointed out, Fiedler's findings cannot be regarded as evidence for or against the question of the importance to be attached to differences among theories.

[7] A three-year investigation, currently nearing completion, deals with the techniques, therapeutic formulations, and attitudes of more than 200 therapists who responded as vicarious interviewers to a sound film of an initial interview.

treatment. Interpretations dealt principally with the patient's current interpersonal situation; in addition, the therapist's verbalizations were designed to achieve a degree of reeducation in the patient.

As predictable from theory, the client-centered therapist's activity consisted principally of reflections of feeling. This therapeutic technique was sustained, with minor fluctuations, throughout treatment.

Intertherapist comparisons showed that the analytically oriented therapist used techniques which were generally more inferential and which showed greater *Initiative* than those of his client-centered counterpart. While the initial interviews did not differ significantly in terms of *Initiative*, the approach of the two therapists was nevertheless divergent on other dimensions.

The primary implications of this preliminary comparison relate to the comparative study of therapeutic techniques, which is considered one of the most important frontiers of research in psychotherapy. The isolation and measurement of common denominators in the techniques of therapists adhering to different schools should lead to more definitive studies of the therapist's personality, particularly of those attitudes which, wittingly or unwittingly, he brings to bear upon the therapeutic interaction.

REFERENCES

1. BORDIN, E. S. *Psychological counseling.* New York: Appleton-Century-Crofts, 1955.

2. FIEDLER, F. E. The concept of an ideal therapeutic relationship. *J. consult. Psychol.,* 1950, 14, 239–245.

3. FIEDLER, F. E. A comparison of therapeutic relationships in psychoanalytic, nondirective, and Adlerian therapy. *J. consult. Psychol.,* 1950, 14, 436–445.

4. FIEDLER, F. E. Factor analyses of psychoanalytic, nondirective, and Adlerian therapeutic relationships. *J. consult. Psychol.,* 1951, 15, 32–38.

-5. FROMM, E. *Man for himself.* New York: Rinehart, 1947.

6. KUBIE, L. S. Some unsolved problems of psychoanalytic psychotherapy. In Frieda Fromm-Reichmann & J. L. Moreno (Eds.), *Progress in psychotherapy 1956.* New York: Grune & Stratton, 1956. Pp. 87–102.

7. ROGERS, C. R. Significant aspects of client-centered therapy. *Amer. Psychologist,* 1946, 1, 415–422.

8. ROGERS, C. R. *Client-centered therapy.* Boston: Houghton Mifflin, 1951.

9. SNYDER, W. U. (Ed.) *Casebook of nondirective counseling.* Boston: Houghton Mifflin, 1947.

10. STRUPP, H. H. A multidimensional system for analyzing psychotherapeutic techniques. *Psychiatry,* in press.

11. STRUPP, H. H. A multidimensional analysis of technique in brief psychotherapy. *Psychiatry,* in press.

12. WOLBERG, L. R. *The technique of psychotherapy.* New York: Grune & Stratton, 1954.

13. WOLFF, W. *Contemporary psychotherapists examine themselves.* Springfield, Ill.: Charles C. Thomas, 1956.

Extinction During Psychotherapy of GSR Accompanying "Embarrassing" Statements[1]

JAMES E. DITTES

Although changes in the electrical conductivity of the palmar surfaces of the hand are known to accompany emotional responses in general (2, 5) and palmar sweating has been found correlated with other measures of general tension during psychotherapy (4), little is known about which, if any, specific emotions or attitudes are accompanied during therapy by measurable galvanic skin responses. Unless the variables which it supposedly measures can be more precisely specified, the GSR is unlikely to prove useful in research on psychotherapeutic problems.

Reprinted from *The Journal of Abnormal and Social Psychology,* 1957, 54 (2), 187–191, with the permission of the American Psychological Association and the author.

[1] This study was done as part of a psychotherapy research program supervised by Dr. John Dollard and supported by United States Public Health Service Grant M-648. Appreciation is due Dr. Frank Auld, Jr., and Dr. Dollard for their suggestions and assistance. The data used here had all been previously obtained by them in other phases of the research program. Mr. Harry W. Dreyer, electronics engineering consultant to the project, designed and built some of the apparatus used. Mrs. Ann C. Byler served as a judge of the verbal material.

An emotion with which psychotherapy is centrally concerned is fear, especially when associated with patient reports of certain thoughts or behavior which have been historically punished, particularly by the parents. Because such thoughts or behavior are reported by the patient to the therapist without ensuing punishment, the associated fear should extinguish. Extinction also should generalize to any existing fear which may be evoked by simply thinking such thoughts, as well as that evoked by reporting them (1).

One type of thought commonly supposed to arouse such transferred fear is a report of personal sexual wishes or activity. This study attempts to discover whether the GSR can be used to trace the arousal and extinction of fear connected with making such "embarrassing" sex statements to the therapist.

Two interpretations might be offered for the coincidence of a galvanic skin response and a statement describing sexual behavior or wishes. One is that the emotion indicated by the GSR is the fear of making the statement to another person or the fear evoked by acknowledging the sexual impulse or wishes to oneself. Another explanation is that the GSR represents the "re-experienced" emotion which is reported, that sexual feelings themselves are aroused in the reporting and that this sexual mobilization produces the GSR. However, this second interpretation would not predict the extinction of the GSR during therapy, since extraclinical situations are presumably continuing to reinforce the evocation of sexual mobilization in response to sexual thoughts as much during the period of therapy as previously. A finding, then, that statements reporting sexual behavior and wishes are not accompanied by GSR late in therapy as frequently as in early hours affords some basis for determining whether the GSR reflects a particular emotion indicated in the contents of a patient's remarks or the feelings of fear associated with making the report. The hypothesis proposed here is that the GSR more readily measures the latter.

METHOD

This study is based on the records of a 35-year-old, white, male, neurotic patient seen by an experienced therapist weekly for an hour and a half for 30 sessions. All sessions were electrically recorded, and verbatim transcripts were typed.

A continuous record of the patient's palmar skin conductance was made during each session after the first two (except for hours 18 and 22, during which the equipment failed) with the following apparatus:

1. Small electrodes in a Bakelite holder were taped to the palmar surface of the patient's finger. The electrodes were made of analytic reagent silver .001 inch thick and approximately 1 cm. wide and 2 cm. long. An electrode paste made of bentonite, glycerine, and isotonic saline solution was used.

2. A dry-cell voltage source, including a variable voltage so that the voltage drop across the patient's basic resistance level can be balanced out, allowed an amplifier to be used in its most sensitive range and

also provided a measure of the basic level.

3. A Sanborn model 126 DC amplifier was used.

4. A Sanborn model 127 galvanic recorder recorded changes in conductance on a continuously moving, calibrated paper.

5. A device was employed which periodically produces characteristic pips on the recording paper simultaneously with beeps on the sound tape. This device could also be manually operated to produce an identifying pattern of pips and beeps at the beginning and any other point to insure absolute synchrony for subsequent playback.

Judging embarrassing sex statements. The typed transcript of each session was read independently by two judges, who picked out statements judged to be embarrassing sex statements (subsequently abbreviated ESS), according to a definition summarized as follows: An ESS is (*a*) a detailed description of a specific occasion of personal sexual behavior, including details of the patient's own or his partner's body or mention of orgasm and implying his responsibility for the event at least in part; or (*b*) a positive and emphatic statement of strong sex desires, apart from any particular episode; or (*c*) use of vulgar sex vocabulary. A statement was considered to be an ESS if both judges independently selected it. One judge was ignorant of the specific hypothesis being tested. Hours were judged in random order, except that all the odd-numbered hours were judged before the even-numbered.

The unit of a "statement" was not defined more objectively than as a verbalization of a single thought or topic. However, the reliability of the implicit units used may be assessed in part by noting that each judge indicated the line of the typescript in which the statement was judged to begin and that the average difference between the judges, for those statements which both selected, was .48 of a line. They selected the same line of typing in well over half of the cases and differed by only one line on most of the others.

TABLE 1

COMPUTATION OF PHI COEFFICIENT
OF RELIABILITY
OF ESS JUDGMENTS FOR HOUR 15

		Judge A	
		Sex speeches judged as ESS	Sex speeches not judged as ESS
Judge B	Sex speeches judged as ESS	6	1
	Sex speeches not judged as ESS	1	21
Total number of sex speeches as selected by Judges C and D			29
Phi coefficient of reliability			.81

A phi coefficient of correlation was used to assess the reliability of the judging of ESSs. There were available, as an estimate of the population of sex statements from which the ESSs were selected, judgments of sex content which had been made by other judges in connection with another study using the same material.[2] Table 1 illustrates, for Hour 15, the median hour, how the phi coefficient was calculated, based on the number of those statements selected as an ESS by both judges, and the number selected by only one or the other of the judges, from the total population of sex speeches, as determined independently by other judges. Table 2 reports, for each hour, the phi coefficient and the actual number of ESS judgments.

Scoring of GSR record. A GSR was scored whenever the continuous record of

[2] For purposes of obtaining this reliability estimate, a unit of "speech" was objectively defined as all the remarks of the patient between statements by the therapist or between pauses of at least five seconds, or else ten typed lines if the speech was otherwise more than that. Since this unit of a "speech" is larger and therefore less numerous than the unit of a "statement" used in the actual judging, the reliability coefficient is biased in a conservative direction.

TABLE 2

NUMBER OF ESS AND RELIABILITY
COEFFICIENTS OF ESS JUDGMENTS
FOR EACH HOUR

Hour*	Number of Embarrassing Sex Statements			Phi Coefficient
	Judge A	Judge B	Agreed	
3	1	1	1	1.00
4	1	2	1	.67
5	1	1	0	—
7	14	13	7	.41
8	13	13	10	.63
9	14	15	10	.56
10	8	8	7	.82
11	20	21	16	.52
13	11	10	7	.49
15	7	7	6	.81
16	8	10	5	.44
17	4	5	4	.85
19	14	15	14	.95
20	25	26	23	.86
21	5	4	4	.88
25	7	5	5	.81
29	6	9	6	.74
30	7	5	5	.63

* No ESS was found by either judge for hours 6, 12, 14, 23, 24, 26, 27, or 28, which are omitted from this table.

conductance met one of the following criteria: (*a*) a rise at the rate of 4,000 or more ohms per second with an amplitude of at least 6,500 ohms; or (*b*) a rise of at least 10,000 ohms amplitude at a rate of 1,333 or more ohms per second. Such a rise represented a change of the order of 3 per cent of the basal level. These criteria were selected after an independent study of the GSR record indicated that they differentiated fairly clearly between clear-cut abrupt rises in conductance and smaller fluctuations. There were few borderline observations close to the criteria. These values were easily distinguishable with the calibrated paper used.

Despite indications (5) that the GSR actually varies in proportion with the basic resistance level, the criteria for the GSR were kept standard for all sessions because the variation of basic resistance level was not great. The mean basic level for the start of the hour was 360,400 ohms, with the particular apparatus used, and the series

of hours varied with a standard deviation of 88,000 ohms, less than one-fourth the mean.

RESULTS

The solid line in Fig. 1 shows for each therapy session the percentage of ESS on which a GSR rise occurred. No data are given for hours 5, 6, 12, 14, 23, 24, 26, 27, and 28, during which no ESS was found. To test the decline in percentage of GSR from early to late hours, a division into four quadrants at the median hour and median percentage yielded a chi square of 7.42, significant beyond the .01 level. Estimation of the correlation between sequence of hours and the GSR percentage resulted in a rho of .85 and a tau of .71, significant beyond the .0001 level.[3]

---

[3] Although generally yielding a lower absolute figure than rho for comparable data, tau is used in the analysis because it permits partial correlation and a test of significance involving fewer assumptions (3).

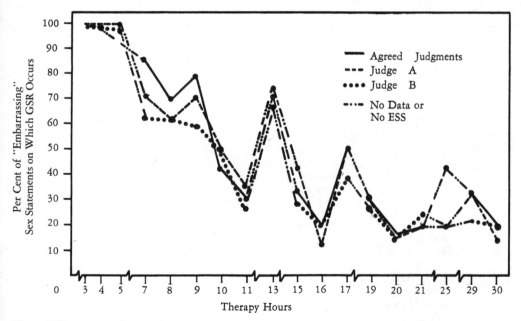

Fig. 1. GSR accompanying "embarrassing" sex statements in successive therapy hours. No GSR data are available for hours 1, 2, 18, and 22. No ESS was found by judges for hours 6, 12, 14, 23, 24, 26, 27, and 28.

Various types of analysis were made in order to rule out possible alternative explanations of the results. To test the possibility that the results could be a consequence of biases in judging ESS by the one judge who was aware of the hypothesis, the percentage of rises on statements selected by each judge are shown by the broken lines in Fig. 1. The trend is similar whether the agreed upon or the separate judgments are used.

To test the possibility that the lack of an objective definition for the unit of statement allowed for bias in determining whether or not a GSR occurred during a particular statement, three analyses, were made. First, results were calculated using as an arbitrary objectively defined unit a "speech" of the patient, defined as all his remarks occurring between remarks by the therapist or between pauses of at least five seconds, or ten typed lines if the speech was otherwise longer than that. Such a "speech" would ordinarily include several "statements." Using any GSR which occurred within the same speech as an ESS, the results still show an over-all decline. With a division at the median hour and the median percentage, chi square was 4.58, significant at beyond the .05 level.

Second, it was noted that the average dis-crepancy, in typed lines, between the beginning of an ESS as determined, on the average, by the judges and the beginning of the GSR was .8. No GSR which occurred within one line of the judged beginning of an ESS was excluded. This figure of .8 can be compared with the average of 4.3 lines discrepancy between ESS and the nearest non-scored GSR occurring within the same "speech" as previously defined.

Third, the average discrepancy in typed lines between GSR and ESS was .86 for the first half of the series of hours and .79 for the second half, a difference hardly great enough to suggest any systematic bias in scoring the correspondence of GSR and ESS.

Table 3 presents tau coefficients of rank correlation among variables which might be suspected of producing an artifactual relationship between sequence of hours and GSR percentage of ESS. None of these relationships approaches significance except the predicted one and that between number of ESS and number of sex speeches, which is hardly unexpected and which suggests a certain utility in the judgments of ESS. The partial rank correlation of sequence and GSR percentage with number of ESS partialled out is .70, and the same correlation with number of GSR partialled out is .73.

TABLE 3

RANK-ORDER INTERCORRELATIONS
AMONG VARIABLES*

	Percentage of GSR on ESS	Total Number of ESS	Total Number of GSR	Number of Sex Speeches
Sequence	.71	− .05	.19	.02
Percentage of GSR on ESS		− .21	.17	− .24
Total Number of ESS			− .09	.48
Total Number of GSR				− .09

* Tau coefficient used.

DISCUSSION

The results support the hypothesis proposed on the basis of the two assumptions that the GSR is associated with feelings concerning the immediate interpersonal relationship and that such feelings should extinguish in the course of therapy. The GSR can be interpreted as an index of transferred embarrassment over reporting sexual material in therapy. Whether the GSR could be similarly used to indicate other feelings towards the therapist remains to be determined. It seems likely that most aspects of "negative" transference would show the same kind of relationship with GSR as that reported here.

Study of the three serious exceptions to the general declining trend shown in Fig. 1 offers incidental support to the argument that the GSR measures transferred feelings. The patient's parents lived in a different city; during the course of his therapy, the patient visited them twice, once between Hours 11 and 12 and once between Hours 26 and 27. Each visit home was followed by one or more hours in which he produced no ESS and then an hour in which ESSs are accompanied by an increased percentage of GSR. The first two-thirds of Hour 17 were devoted to sustained recollections of early home life in association to a dream, the only hour in the series in which such concentrated reminiscences occurred. The few ESSs in the last part of this hour were accompanied by an increased percentage of GSR. These facts suggest that the real or fantasied contacts with his parents restored in some degree the transferred feelings which had been partially extinguished during therapy.

Two interpretations of these results have not been sharply distinguished in this study. The feelings apparently measured by the GSR may simply be the fear aroused by acknowledging certain thoughts to oneself, rather than the fear connected with reporting them to another person such as the therapist. However, just as the fear of thinking these thoughts is probably acquired by generalization from fear of reporting them, so the extinction of fear during therapy would be expected to generalize from fear of reporting to fear of thinking. The two would probably covary, and for present purposes, it seems unnecessary to insist on the distinction. It is simply suggested that the fear of reporting, being the one which therapy primarily affects, provides the more likely interpretation of the results, but the alternative interpretation is not excluded by the design of this study.

SUMMARY

Statements by a therapy patient acknowledging personal sexual behavior or desires were frequently accompanied during early hours of therapy with galvanic skin responses, but not during later hours, following a progressive decline. This finding is taken as evidence that the GSR is associated with such feelings as fear or embarrassment in the interpersonal relationship with the therapist and that such feelings extinguish during therapy.

REFERENCES

1. DOLLARD, J., & MILLER, N. E. *Personality and psychotherapy.* New York: McGraw-Hill, 1950.
2. FULTON, J. F. *Physiology of the nervous system.* New York: Oxford, 1943.
3. KENDALL, M. G. *Rank correlation methods.* London: Griffin, 1948.
4. MOWRER, O. H., LIGHT, B. H., LURIA, A., & ZELENY, M. P. Tension changes during psychotherapy with special reference to resistance. In O. H. Mowrer (Ed.) *Psychotherapy: theory and research.* New York: Ronald, 1953, Pp. 545–640.
5. WOODWORTH, R. S., & SCHLOSBERG, H. *Experimental psychology.* New York: Holt, 1954.

Verbal and GSR Responses in Experimental Interviews as a Function of Three Degrees of "Therapist" Communication

BARCLAY MARTIN
RICHARD M. LUNDY
MARK H. LEWIN[1]

The present study deals with the tendency of a subject in an experimental pschotherapy interview to approach or avoid coming to grips with therapeutically significant material as a function of the amount of communication he receives from the therapist. The process of psychotherapy is formulated in terms of an approach-avoidance model similar to the conceptions of Miller (1944) and Murray and Berkun (1955), in which it is conceived as a situation where the client alternately approaches significant ma-

Reprinted from *Journal of Abnormal and Social Psychology,* 1960, 60 (2), 234–240, with the permission of the American Psychological Association and the authors.

[1] The authors wish to thank Irene Waskow, Vilma Ginsberg, and Jack Hokanson for their helpful assistance on this study, and the University of Wisconsin Graduate School for providing financial support for research leave for one of the authors.

terial and retreats from it. No single motive is postulated to account for the approach behavior, but rather several motives that vary in nature from client to client. Thus, the long range goal of relief from psychological distress may motivate a person to endure the momentary increases in discomfort usually associated with approach behavior. There are also more immediate motives, such as a desire to please and gain approval from the therapist, a desire to obtain advice and reassurance, etc. Avoidance behavior, on the other hand, is motivated by the anxiety, embarrassment, or (more generally) the negative affect associated with approaching therapeutically significant material. It is postulated that, as a client alternately approaches and retreats from such material and experiences the resultant negative affect in a therapeutic atmosphere of noncritical acceptance, understanding, etc., the negative affect associated with these sensitive areas tends to extinguish. It is also assumed that this extinction of negative affect generalizes to some extent beyond the therapy session, and that, accordingly, this process is in part responsible for what is therapeutic about psychotherapy.

A question that naturally follows from these considerations is, "What are some of the factors which facilitate or impede approach behavior?" The factor that was introduced experimentally into the present study was the amount of communication or feedback that the S received from the therapist. Three groups were employed that were thought to represent points along this dimension. In one group, the S talked to a tape recorder with no therapist present, and accordingly received virtually no communication from the therapist. In a second group, the therapist was present but responded by nonverbal means only. In the third group, the therapist responded in an essentially client-centered fashion, thus providing a maximum of communicative feedback compared with the other two treatment groups.

It was thought that an S in Group 1 who received no communication from the therapist when he engaged in approach behavior would soon extinguish and show an increasing tendency to avoid therapeutically significant material. This was predicted because there would be no positive reinforcement from the nonpresent therapist for approach attempts, nor would the S have any way of knowing to what extent the nonpresent therapist might be implicitly responding in a critical, judgmental fashion. The nonverbal therapist condition, by providing some communication, was expected to result in more approach behavior than in Group 1, but less than in the "regular" therapy condition of Group 3.

These expected relationships were to be analyzed in terms of approach and avoidance behavior trends over the five experimental sessions. Thus, the research can be

viewed in a more restricted sense as a study of the reinforcing effects of three degrees of experimenter communication upon affectively toned verbalizations in the Ss. In addition, changes in tension or anxiety level, both within and between sessions, were assessed by continuous GSR recordings. Since various alternative predictions with respect to increasing or decreasing tension levels among the treatment groups seemed reasonable, no specific hypothesis was proposed with respect to this part of the study.

METHOD
Subjects

The Forced Choice Manifest Anxiety Scale (Heineman, 1953) was given to the 240 students in a course on the Psychology of Adjustment. At the same time, the students were asked to indicate on their IBM answer sheets if they would be interested in participating in a brief psychotherapy experience as part of a research project. From the students who volunteered, (about 80% of the class) the 44 who scored highest on the anxiety scale were contacted for 15-min. preliminary interviews. At the end of each interview, the interviewer rated S on a 5-point scale of severity of disturbance and a 5-point scale of defensiveness. No Ss were eliminated because of the possible eminence of a psychotic break; one S was eliminated because she was already on the waiting list at another clinic. None of the Ss had experienced psychotherapy within the last two years.

The first step was to select the 27 Ss who were relatively high on disturbance and low on defensiveness. Next, Ss were divided into groups of three, with the 3 Ss in each group matched as well as possible on their disturbance and defensiveness ratings. Within each triad, they were then randomly assigned to one of the three major treatment groups. For each treatment group, 5 Ss were assigned to therapist A, 3 to therapist B, and 1 to therapist C. Ten Ss were male, 17 female.

The Treatment Procedures

Tape recordings and continuous GSR recordings were obtained for all Ss in all sessions, including the preliminary session. The GSR apparatus consisted of an ac circuit designed by Grant (1946) which fed into a G.E. Photoelectric Recorder. Dry silver electrodes were attached to the palmar surfaces of two of S's left hand fingers, which rested comfortably on a low table beside the S. The GSR and tape recordings were synchronized by a timer which operated a marker pen on the GSR record and simultaneously made an audible click in the tape recorder every 37 sec.[2]

Ss were seen for five 30-min. sessions one week apart. At the beginning of the first experimental session, Ss were given instructions that varied with the treatment condition as described below:

Tape Recorder Group. We are asking the subjects in different parts of the study to do different things. As you know, we are interested in studying various factors which affect the process of psychotherapy, and in one group, the group you are in, we want to study the effects of not having a therapist present in the room at all. We would like for you to imagine that you are a client in psychotherapy, but instead of talking to a therapist we want you to talk into this tape recorder. This may seem a little strange, but try to talk about the things that you would expect to in a regular therapy session. People ordinarily talk about things that are emotionally important to them and how they get along with the important people in their lives. But in general, feel free to talk about whatever comes to mind. There may be times when nothing comes to mind, and that's O.K. too. You can just wait until something does, and then talk about that. In general, though, try to keep talking as much as you can. After each session I will listen to the tape recording of your session. I will not talk with you about the session, though. I will just start you going each time, but will not talk with you about

what you say on the tapes, although I will be listening to them after each session.

Nonverbal Group. These instructions were the same except for the following modification:

. . . We want to study the effects of having you talk to a therapist who remains silent. So that, as the therapist in this situation, I will be listening carefully to what you have to say, but will respond by nonverbal means only. In other words, I will indicate that I understand what you are saying by nodding my head, or saying 'uh-huh', etc., but I will not be able to say anything out loud.

Regular Group. These instructions were similar to the above except that the S was told that the therapist would be responding as he would in ordinary psychotherapy.

Although outcome assessment was not the primary focus of the study, a forced-choice adjective check list, hereafter referred to as the Feeling Inventory, was obtained on all Ss after the preliminary interview and again at the end of the fifth session. This inventory consisted of 41 sets of three adjectives each with one adjective in each set representing a tension or anxiety dimension. S is asked to indicate which adjective is most and which is least like the way he feels. Some evidence for the sensitivity of this inventory to changes in anxiety level had been previously established (Martin, 1959).

Ss were instructed to answer the Feeling Inventory before the experimental sessions in terms of how they had been feeling during the past month. They were instructed at the end of the sessions to answer in terms of how they had been feeling during the last several days. A fourth group of nine Ss who were matched roughly on initial score on this inventory with the other groups, but who did not attend any experimental sessions, were retested after the same amount of time had elapsed.

The Content Ratings of the Interviews

The following rating scheme was developed after considerable trial-and-error prac-

[2] The 37-sec. interval has no particular significance. By mistake, the timer was set for this interval rather than 30 sec., and had to be continued at this interval throughout the study.

tice on other tapes. Each 74-sec. interval of an interview was rated individually for two major categories of behavior: Approach and Avoidance. If approach behavior occurred during an interval, a check was placed under the Approach column on the rating sheet; if avoidance behavior also occurred during the same interval, a check was placed in the Avoidance column.

In addition to this rather arbitrary time interval and the dichotomous scoring of approach-avoidance behavior, an additional rating of the extent of approach behavior based on more meaningful units of behavior was made. To this end, a four-point scale was developed for assessing degree of approach to therapeutically meaningful material. Raters were required to classify the approach behaviors checked under the Approach Column according to meaningful themes and to make a rating on the four-point scale for each of these "meaning units."

Some examples of the kinds of behavior representing avoidance and approach behavior at the four levels of the rating scale are given below. An attempt was made to make the four-point scale appropriate to the range approach behaviors expected in this particular study and sample, and it is likely that some modifications would be necessary before applying this scheme to the process of longer, regular psychotherapy.

Avoidance behavior. General discussion of course work, campus activities, and other ordinary school-related topics without relation to their own personal-emotional conflicts; abstract philosophical or psychological discussion; description of other people and their personalities for at least one 37 sec. interval without relating this to their own problems; description of only positive or success experiences for at least one 37 sec. interval; any blanket and categorical denial of negative feelings with respect to a given person or situation.

Approach behavior, Level 1. In general, indications of approach were inferred

both from signs of increasing negative affect resulting from the approach, and signs of verbal approach based upon the raters' preconceptions about therapeutically significant material. The following are examples of Level 1 approach: (*a*) talks in generalities about self, (*b*) describes interpersonal relationships including those with parents; (*c*) describes historical background material; (*d*) no feeling or strong personal involvement is expressed; (*e*) may specify negative feelings, but qualifies with instances of positive or success experience and does not indicate strong conflicts.

Approach behavior, Level 2. Describes clear cut psychological "symptom" or problem area, for example: (*a*) impotency, nervous vomiting, or specific situations in which handicapped by shyness, anxiety, hostility, etc.; (*b*) does not necessarily experience much feeling while describing symptom; (*c*) employs less qualification and less emphasis on positive or success experiences than for Level 1; (*d*) problem may be externalized to large extent.

Approach behavior, Level 3. Considers interpersonal aspects of symptoms or problem with some specificity accompanied by feeling; this feeling may relate to emotional reactions associated with the particular conflict area or may relate to feelings of discomfort and anxiety about going into the area; highly charged expression of feeling without much content exploration also scored here.

Approach behavior, Level 4. Shows strong, unequivocal expression and experiencing of feeling associated with approach to conflict area with considerable specificity. Level 4 represents an extension and intensification of Level 3 behavior.

The 27 Ss were assigned in groups of nine to each of three judges for rating purposes. Two of these judges were therapists in the research and were assigned Ss they had *not* seen in the interviews. Whenever a judge rated an interview, another person set the tape recorder up for him so that he would not know which interview in the sequence was being rated. If there were initial comments in the interview that would provide a clue as to the sequence of the interview, the tape was set so that the rating began after this point. The first, second, fourth, and fifth interviews were rated with all those for a given S done at one time. It was not possible to keep the raters blind with respect to the treatment condition, but they were blind with respect to sequence.

Reliability estimates of the scores obtained from these ratings were obtained as follows. Judges A and B jointly, but independently, rated interviews for five Ss selected randomly; judges B and C, likewise, rated five other Ss. The three basic scores used were: (a) Meaning Unit Rating, based upon the products of meaning unit rating (1–4), times the number of the 74-sec. intervals involved in the meaning unit and summed for all meaning units for a given interview; (b) Approach Behavior, the number of intervals during which approach behavior was checked in an interview; (c) Avoidance Behavior, the number of intervals during which avoidance behavior was checked in an interview. A fourth score, change in Meaning Unit rating from the first half to the last half of each interview, was also obtained. As an estimate of reliability, the three basic scores were correlated for the two judges for *each* S over the four interviews, because it was changes within Ss with which the study was concerned. Thus, for judges A and B, there would be a correlation based on four pairs of scores for each of the five Ss for each measure. These correlations were averaged, using Fisher's z transformation; the averages ranged from .80 to .94.

RESULTS

Curves for the average Meaning Unit ratings and intra-interview change in Meaning Unit ratings as a function of the four rated interviews are shown in Fig. 1. These curves depict the Regular group as showing

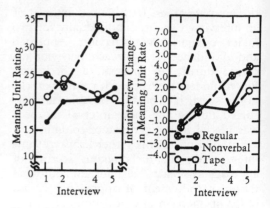

Fig. 1. Meaning unit ratings as a function of successive interviews.

the greatest increase in both average Meaning Unit ratings and in intra-interview change in Meaning Unit ratings as the interviews progressed. The Tape group showed a slight tendency to decrease in both these measures, and the Nonverbal group revealed an intermediate amount of change.

The results for the Approach and Avoidance ratings showed similar between-group trends, but because statistical analysis showed no significant between-group effects, the curves for these variables are not presented.

For purposes of statistical analysis of the trends shown in Fig. 1, the ratings for interviews one and two and those for interviews four and five were averaged. Differences between these two sets of averages were then computed, and an analysis of variance was performed to see if the treatment groups differed significantly in their average change scores. An orthogonal polynomial trend test was not performed on these data because the assumption of equal intervals was not met, interview three not having been rated. The between-group changes for the average Meaning Unit ratings did not reach statistical significance. The between-group changes in intra-interview change in Meaning Unit ratings, however, were significantly different ($p <$

.05). A Multiple Range Test (Duncan, 1955) indicated that the Regular and Tape groups were significantly different from each other, but neither differed significantly from the nonverbal group. Thus, if one considers the change from the first half to the last half of an interview in approach to therapeutically significant material, one finds that the Regular group showed a progressively increasing tendency to approach further than did the Tape Group.

The means and standard deviations for the pre- and postexperiment results on the Feeling Inventory are shown in Table 1. Although the initial mean score for the Regular group is higher than the means for

TABLE 1

MEANS AND SIGMAS FOR THE PRE- AND POST-ANXIETY SCORES ON THE FEELING INVENTORY

Group	Preexperiment		Postexperiment	
	Mean	Sigma	Mean	Sigma
Regular	19.6	5.4	14.1	4.2
Nonverbal	16.3	7.2	11.2	6.1
Tape	16.6	5.9	14.3	3.8
Control	16.7	3.3	17.6	3.4

the other groups, it was not significantly so as tested by the Multiple Range Test. These Feeling Inventory scores were converted into pre- and postexperiment difference scores, and the Multiple Range Test was then performed. The Nonverbal and Regular groups both showed significantly greater decreases in reported anxiety than did the Control group, whereas the Tape group was not significantly different from the Control group on this score.

The skin conductance recordings were scored both in terms of general level of conductance and in terms of reactivity. Median log conductance scores were obtained for all five interviews for each S. A change in log conductance score was also obtained for each interview by subtracting the median log conductance score for the

first half of the interview, from the last half of the interview. A reactivity score was obtained for each interview by marking off four equally spaced 4-min. intervals in each interview, obtaining the average of the three largest GSR deflections within each log conductance units, and then averaging these four values for an over-all estimate of reactivity. A change in reactivity score was obtained by subtracting the average reactivity score in the first 4-min. period from that in the last 4-min. period. Trends of these four scores as a function of the five sessions were tested for statistical significance by orthogonal polynomial trend tests (Grant, 1956). A significant between-groups trend was found only for the intra-interview change in conductance scores, where a significant between-groups quadratic component emerged. Inspection of the curves in Fig. 2 shows that the Regular group showed an initial rise and then a fall in the variable, whereas the Tape group showed an initial fall and then a sharp rise in this variable, with the Nonverbal group lying in between.

DISCUSSION

It is perhaps not altogether appropriate to refer to these experimental sessions, even those of the Regular group, as psychotherapy. The conditions and Ss were rather special and not necessarily representative of psychotherapy or psychotherapy clients. The more restricted problem of studying factors that affect the extent to which a person openly discusses emotionally important aspects of his life is, however, certainly one that has direct implications for the more complex therapeutic process.

The intra-interview change in Meaning Unit ratings showed significant between-group changes from the first two to the last two interviews. Stated otherwise, the Regular group showed a marked increase in approach to emotionally important material from the first to the last half of an interview as the five interviews progressed,

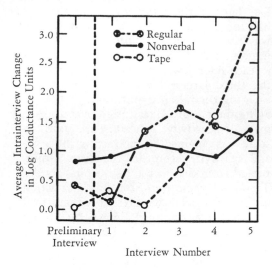

Fig. 2. Intrainterview change in log conductance as a function of successive interviews.

creasingly higher approach ratings in the last half of the interviews.

The Feeling Inventory results indicate that the Regular and Nonverbal groups were inclined to report themselves as having experienced a larger decrease in anxiety after the five sessions than the Control group. An obvious possibility is that this self-report is not tapping "real" changes in anxiety level so much as S's belief, that he should be less anxious, or that the experimenters expect him to be less anxious. On the other hand, the consistency of these results with the change in Meaning Unit rating scores and the GSR data suggest that they may be due to more than superficial changes in verbal report.

The only significant GSR finding was the between-groups quadratic component for the intra-interview change in skin conductance, which is illustrated in Fig. 2. This finding suggests that the Tape group showed an increasing tendency to become more anxious within interviews as the five sessions progressed, with this intra-interview increase in anxiety being especially marked in the last two sessions. The Regular group, on the other hand, showed increasing intra-interview changes in anxiety through the third session and thereafter showed progressively less of an increase in anxiety within interviews.

If this interpretation of the GSR data in terms of the hypothetical anxiety state of the individual is correct, it raises some interesting questions when one compares the GSR results with the Meaning Unit ratings of the verbal behavior. First, it should be noted that for both kinds of data it is the intra-interview changes that are significant, not the mean scores for the interviews. Second, there appears to be in part an inverse relationship between the GSR data and the Meaning Unit ratings. Thus, in the fourth and fifth sessions, the Regular group showed a decreasing amount of intra-interview change in anxiety at the same time that this group was showing the greatest amount of intra-interview increase in

whereas the Tape group, although rather erratic, showed a slight tendency to decrease on this measure over the interviews. Perhaps these results reflect the reinforcing effect of an attentive, responding therapist who communicates not only positive reinforcement for approach behavior, but also by his accepting, noncritical attitude aids in the extinction of the negative affect associated with the approach behavior. For this short series of experimental interviews, this "learning" appears more pronounced within interviews than when between-interview means are compared. Since it is not possible to tell from the difference scores whether changes are due to increases or decreases in the first or last halves of the interviews, the means for the first and last halves were plotted separately as a function of the successive sessions, and it was quite apparent that the between-group trends resulted almost entirely from changes in the last half of the interviews. In other words, the increasing tendency for the Regular group to approach further within interviews was not due to these Ss starting off at a lower level of approach in the succeeding interviews, but from their obtaining in-approach to emotionally important material. The Tape group, on the other hand, in these last two sessions showed a striking increase in intra-interview change in anxiety, at the same time that it was showing a decrease in the tendency to approach emotionally significant material. At first glance, these observations suggest that approaching emotionally important material is less anxiety arousing than avoiding it. But the situation is probably much more complex than that.

Ss in the Regular group, as they began to verbalize emotionally important content, did indeed show increasing degrees of intra-interview increase in anxiety. These results suggest that the Tape Ss were not completely withdrawing from the psychological field, but were experiencing concerns about which they were progressively more reluctant to talk. This suppressing behavior was apparently accompanied by a great deal of anxiety. If avoidance behavior on the part of the Tape group Ss came to be associated with greater increases in anxiety, then one would expect a negative correlation between intra-interview changes in Meaning Unit ratings and skin conductance scores for these Ss in the later interviews. The correlations between these two variables for interviews 4 and 5 were $-.47$ and $-.31$ respectively, which for an N of 9 are not significant but are in the expected direction.

This interpretation, as well as the empirical findings are consistent with evidence from a different study. Gordon, Martin, and Lundy (1959) induced conflict areas hypnotically, and then by posthypnotic suggestion caused the Ss in one group in a subsequent interview first to "repress," then to suppress, and then to verbalize overtly the conflict material. In a second group, order was partly controlled by having them first "repress," then overtly verbalize, and then suppress. When skin conductance for the suppressing condition was compared with skin conductance for the verbalizing condition for the combined groups, it was found that Ss showed a greater increase in

conductance when suppressing than when overtly verbalizing. Both studies, then, support the hypothesis that approaching and verbalizing conflict areas is associated with less of an increase in anxiety than when overt discussion of troubling material is avoided.

More light may be shed on this relationship if a more refined analysis of the data were carried out. There is considerable evidence that the GSR is positively related to momentary changes in the therapy behavior of patients (Dittes, 1957; Panek & Martin, 1959), and it is doubtful if the present findings should be interpreted as indicating a negative relationship between momentary changes in approach behavior and GSR measures. It may be that there is some initial rise in conductance or reactivity as S first approaches a new therapy theme, followed then by an overshadowing decrease.

SUMMARY

From a population of college students who scored high on the Forced-Choice Manifest Anxiety Scale and who also volunteered for a brief psychotherapy experience, 27 Ss were selected on the basis of an initial screening interview and assigned to three treatment groups. One group talked to a tape recorder with no therapist present; a second group experienced a therapist who responded by nonverbal means only, and a third group received regular psychotherapy.

Ss were seen for five sessions with continuous tape and GSR recordings being obtained. A self-report index of anxiety, the Feeling Inventory, was also obtained before and after the five sessions. The verbal content of the interviews was rated in terms of degree of approaching or avoiding emotionally important areas.

The major significant findings were that the Regular group showed a tendency to increase in their intra-interview approach to emotionally important material as the five interviews progressed, whereas the Tape group showed the opposite trend, with the Nonverbal group lying in between. The GSR data indicated that the Regular group showed concomitant increases in anxiety as they approached emotionally important material in the first three sessions, but in the last two sessions their even further approach behavior was accompanied by less and less of an increase in anxiety. The Tape group, on the other hand, while showing a decreasing amount of intra-interview approach behavior as the sessions progressed, showed a marked increase in intra-interview change in anxiety as the sessions progressed. The Nonverbal group showed intermediate trends. The Feeling Inventory results indicated that the Regular and Nonverbal groups reported a greater decrease in reported anxiety than a Control group, but the Tape group did not differ significantly from the Control group on this variable.

REFERENCES

DITTES, J. E. Extinction during psychotherapy of GSR's accompanying "embassassing sex statements," *J. abnorm. soc. Psychol.*, 1957, 54, 187–191.

DUNCAN, D. B. Multiple range and multiple *F* tests. *Biometrics*, 1955, 11, 1–9.

GORDON, J. E., MARTIN, B., & LUNDY, R. M. GSR's during repression, suppression, and verbalization in psychotherapeutic interviews. *J. consult. Psychol.*, 1959, 23, 243–251.

GRANT, D. A. Analysis-of-variance tests in the analysis and comparison of curves. *Psychol. Bull.*, 1956, 53, 141–154.

GRANT, D. A. A convenient alternating current circuit for measuring GSR's. *Amer. J. Psychol.*, 1946, 59, 149–151.

HEINEMAN, C. E. A forced choice form of the Taylor Anxiety Scale. *J. consult. Psychol.*, 1953, 17, 447–454.

MARTIN, B. The validity of a self-report measure of anxiety as a function of the time interval covered by the instructions. *J. consult. Psychol.*, 1959, 23, 468.

MILLER, N. E. Experimental studies of conflict. In J. McV. Hunt (Ed.), *Personality and the Behavior Disorders*. Vol. I. New York: Ronald, 1944.

MURRAY, E. J., & BERKUN, M. M. Displacement as a function of conflict. *J. abnorm. soc. Psychol.*, 1955, 51, 47–56.

PANEK, D. M., & MARTIN, B. The relationship between GSR and speech disturbances in psychotherapy. *J. abnorm. soc. Psychol.*, 1959, 58, 402–405.

Characteristics of
Interactional Behavior in
a Psychotherapy Analogue[1]

FREDERICK H. KANFER
ALBERT R. MARSTON

In recent research on the psychotherapy process most progress has been made in the exploration of gross, molar factors. For example, the contributions of the therapist's personality, experience, and technique have been carefully examined (Strupp, 1960). Personality variables in patients (Luborsky, 1962) have been shown to relate to progress, and many studies have reported new methods. Relatively few studies (Auld & White, 1959; Bandura, Lipsher, & Miller, 1960) have attempted to examine the momentary changes of the therapeutic process in detail. In summarizing current research problems in psychotherapy Luborsky and Strupp (1962, p. 318) phrase the basic question: How does the therapist influence the patient? They suggest that it is vital to

know how patients interpret therapeutic operations, and whether therapist activities can be reduced to operations and roles which are shared with other members of the culture.

It is reasonable to propose that, prior to elaborate theorizing about therapeutic operations, an effort be made to ascertain whether subjects can discriminate at all among therapist response classes which are assumed to effect changes in the patient, and to examine the effects of specified variables on the patient's interactional behavior. Only systematic study of the specific effects of therapist responses on patient behavior can provide the knowledge needed for a functional classification of therapist responses. This knowledge, in turn, may eventually permit the "programing" of therapist behavior to achieve a desired outcome and thus become the basis of psychotherapy practice.

In the present studies an experimental laboratory analogue was devised to explore changes in S's interactional behavior as a function of (a) the content of interviewer's comments; (b) the participation of an in-

Reprinted from *Journal of Consulting Psychology*, 1964, 28 (5), 456–467, with the permission of the American Psychological Association and the authors.

[1] This study was supported in part by research grants MH 6921-02 and MH 6922-02 from the National Institutes of Mental Health, United States Public Health Service, to F. H. Kanfer, principal investigator. The authors wish to acknowledge the assistance of K. Craig and D. Slavin.

terviewer as a speaker or listener; (*c*) the structure of the interviewer's role; and (*d*) the *S*'s tendency to conform, as measured by the Social Desirability Scale (Crowne & Marlowe, 1960). Three aspects of the *S*'s interactional behavior were selected for their apparent significance in maintaining a therapy system: (*a*) *S*'s attitude toward the interviewer; (*b*) *S*'s tendency to seek information, i.e., invite the interviewer to comment; and (*c*) *S*'s tendency to continue the flow of communication.

The three separate experiments reported in this paper share a general procedure. College student *S*s were instructed to talk without interruption about a topic presented to them. They had available switches permitting them to control the participation of the interviewer (*E*). In Experiment I, *S*s selected one of two *E*s who would respond at the end of their discussion of a topic; in Experiment II, prior to discussing a topic *S* could choose whether or not he wished to hear any comment at all from the *E* at the end of the topic; in Experiment III they were free to ask for comments from *E* throughout their discussion.

As all experimental analogues, the present one sacrificed the natural setting of psychotherapy for improved control over the independent variables and precise measurement of some dimension of the response. In particular, in psychotherapy a patient may use a wide range of verbal and kinesic responses to invite therapist participation, or to refute, or avoid a therapist intervention. In the present studies *S*s were restricted to a simple motor response which functioned to control the interviewer's behavior. There are further differences between psychotherapy and the present analogue. College *S*s participate because of curiosity or an achievement orientation. They are probably not as highly motivated as neurotic patients in therapy. The relationship between *S* and *E* is different by structure, and probably less favorable toward major changes than the therapist-patient relationship. Finally, there are pop-

ulation differences between well-adjusted college *S*s and patients in therapy, in personality and in the history of previous psychological and medical treatment for their "condition." These factors should attenuate the effects of therapist operations in normal college *S*s. In addition, the increased simplicity in the analogue may be obtained only at the cost of omission of critical variables. Therefore analogues provide a poor basis for rejection of a theoretical formulation of psychotherapy. However, the results from analogue research are useful in focusing attention on general relationships which ultimately have to be substantiated in the psychotherapy situation itself.

EXPERIMENT I

The purpose of this experiment was to compare the differential effects of reflections and interpretations by *E* on *S*'s attitudes toward *E* and on the temporal characteristics of *S*'s talk. In all groups *S*s selected either of two switches to obtain a comment from two *E*s after their discussion of a topic for a fixed time interval. In two groups both *E*s made the same type of response, either interpretations (Group I-I) or reflections (R-R). In a third group (I-R) the two switches yielded different interviewer responses, one switch yielded interpretations, the other yielded reflections. It was hypothesized that interpretations function as punishing stimuli (Murray, 1954; Kanfer, Phillips, Matarazzo, & Saslow, 1960) and therefore *S*s in the I-I group would spend less of their time in talking, would show longer latencies before starting to talk, and would have a less favorable attitude toward *E* than *S*s in the R-R group. For the group which had a free choice between the two types of responses the assumption of some aversive consequences of interpretations leads to the expectation of preference for reflections. Further, it can be expected that preference for either type also might correlate with personality variables.

METHOD

Subjects. All students from a class in abnormal psychology volunteered to serve in this study. There were 13 females and 24 males. An additional 13 volunteer Ss served in the replication.

Procedure. Prior to conducting the experiment Ss took the MMPI, the Bass ORI Inventory (1962) and the Marlowe-Crowne Social Desirability (SDS) Scale (1960) in class. In subsequent class hours the instructor passed out a sign-up sheet for appointments. The instructor never served as E.

When S arrived at the experimental room he was told that he was participating in a study in which graduate students in clinical psychology were compared in their ability to describe personality. With the information obtained from the previous tests and from a brief interview the graduate students would evaluate S and conduct a clinical interview. With two Es behind the curtain, S was then asked a series of brief questions by a third E about his status, e.g., age, size of family, parents, etc. This E recorded S's answers and then gave instructions to S which described the experimental procedure.

Ss were instructed to press a switch labeled "ready" to produce a topic in a window, and then to select one interviewer by pressing one of the switches on either side of the ready button. When they pressed an interviewer switch a light would go on above it and Ss had to continue talking until the light went off. The interviewer then made a comment. E also told the Ss that they were to come to prefer one of the interviewers. The interviewers would be evaluated on their understanding of S's personality, and on the amount of information they could get from S.

Each S was given 50 trials. The initial five trials served as a warm-up period on which Es made no response. On the last 5 trials the Es also made no response. The topics consisted of statements taken from the MMPI.

For alternate Ss, each E was assigned either the left or right switch position, and either an interpretive or reflective role. For these roles both Es were pretrained on a series of pilot Ss. They were instructed that the *interpretations* role should (*a*) lead the S (be directive), (*b*) probe for dynamic causation, (*c*) may be historical, relating S's statements to earlier experiences, (*d*) be sometimes speculative about possible dynamic relationships. For the *reflecting* roles Es were told to (*a*) follow the S, (*b*) essentially rephrase what S had said in a preceding comment, (*c*) restrict themselves to current material. The level of interpretation approximates levels (*h*) and (*i*) of the depth of interpretation scale proposed by Harway, Dittmann, Raush, Bordin, and Rigler (1955).[2] The Es also practiced the duration of their comments on each trial; a 5-second delay was introduced before E began his response.

During the session the E who had instructed S sat next to the responding Es and recorded latencies. After completion of the experimental session this E conducted S to a desk outside the experimental room and gave him a postexperimental questionnaire. The questionnaire contained 50 items, modified from Snyder's (1961) form for evaluation of the therapist. For each statement S was instructed to rate his agreement (1) or disagreement (0) for each E separately. For 23 statements an answer of "true" indicated a positive attitude, for the remaining 27 statements

---

[2] To contrast the effects of interpretations and reflections only extreme levels along a scale of depth were selected. Use of intermediate levels of depth of interpretation might have produced different results, as Speisman (1959) reported differences in verbal resistance following interpretations of moderate and deep levels. No criterion was available for a test of the accuracy of E's interpretations and the effect of the veridity of interpretations was not under consideration here. The statements were more arbitrary and farfetched than those encountered in therapy, due to E's brief acquaintance with S.

"true" showed a negative reaction to E. Replies were scored by summing the score on the positive statements minus the score on the negative statements. Thus, the scores could range from $+23$ to -27. The items were clustered into six areas: (a) accuracy and adequacy of E's responses, (b) effect of E on S's comfort or insight, (c) attitude toward E "as a person," (d) attention value of E, (e) S's behavior as a function of E's comments, and (f) general attitude toward the experimental procedure.

Apparatus. The S's requests for E's responses were mediated by activation of the appropriate switches. Before each S on a table was a black box containing three switches, with a red jewel light above the right switch, a green jewel light above the left switch and the label "ready" above the center switch. Behind a black screen the two Es faced a similar box with switches for each E. When S pressed the ready switch a chronoscope was activated. The E exposed the topic in the exposure window and the clock was stopped by S's selection of either switch. This clocked interval yielded a latency measure of S's selection of either E plus a fixed time used for card presentation. Activation of the left or right switch also turned on the light above the switch and activated a Hunter timer for 30 seconds, and a corresponding light above the switch in front of the Es. When this light went off, it indicated to S that he was to stop talking. After a 5-second interval E began to talk and at the same time relighted his identifying jewel light for S. When E stopped talking he released his switch, thereby turning off the light and activating a second chronoscope which ran until S again pressed the ready switch. This circuit permitted measurement of the following temporal intervals: (a) the latency between S's indication of readiness and his selection of interviewers (*choice time*), and (b) the posttrial delay from the end of the interviewer's comment to the ready signal (*incubation time*). The latter was used to evaluate S's tendency to attend to and think about the preceding comment before turning to the next trial.

In addition, the following measures were obtained from the tape recording of each interview: (a) *starting latency,* the time from interviewer selection to the start of S's verbal utterances and (b) *talk time,* the duration of S's verbal output during the 30-second period. This measure was converted to *silence* by subtracting talk time from 30 seconds and is reported to reflect S's failure to use the available time.

Experimental design. The Ss were assigned randomly to the following groups: (a) R-R, both switches yielded reflective statements ($N = 12$), (b) I-I, both switches yielded interpretive comments ($N = 12$), and (c) I-R, one switch yielded interpretive, the other reflective comments ($N = 13$). Since individual differences in E's ability to carry out the respective roles may have affected S responses, two Es were alternately assigned to either role in group I-R and to left and right positions in groups R-R and I-I. Thus the effects of content could be separated from E characteristics and position preferences. The design allowed for two separate comparisons on all variables. First, a comparison of the effect of reflection versus interpretation in groups R-R and I-R. Secondly, a comparison of subjects who preferred either interpretations or reflections in group I-R. Since initial findings on the I-R group appeared promising but went beyond the specific hypotheses of this study, a replication was carried out for the I-R groups. In the replication 13 Ss were given the same personality tests and the same experimental procedures. However, the second group of students came from a different college and Ss were volunteers from introductory psychology classes.[3] No differences between the original and replication I-R groups were obtained by t tests on the MMPI scales, the ORI, and the Marlowe-Crowne SDS.

---
[3] The first sample was obtained at Purdue University. The replication used Ss from Portland State College.

RESULTS

Differences among Es and Discriminability of Statements

Both Es had been instructed to comment with reflections in group R-R and with interpretation in Group I-I. Therefore, any differences between preferences for either switch can be attributed to individual differences manifested in the manner in which Es executed their role. In the R-R group a t of 1.34 ($p > .10$) and in the I-I group a t of less than 1 indicated that there were no significant differences in selection of either E in either group. To assure that E's statements could be reliably classified in the appropriate categories 40 statements were randomly selected from the tape recordings from all groups and were transcribed. The typed statements were given to three clinical psychologists who were not acquainted with the study. The judges were asked to assign the statements to the category "reflection" or "interpretation." These categories were defined for the judges as described above. There was 100% agreement among judges on 36/40 statements in assigning the statements to the same class as E had intended them.

Reflection Group versus Interpretation Group

In order to examine the differences of attitudes between Ss in groups R-R and I-I, a t test was run on mean attitude scores. A t of 5.18 ($p < .005$) indicated a significantly more positive attitude toward Es when they used reflection than when they delivered interpretations.

Groups I-I and R-R were compared by an analysis of variance on silence. The amount of silence did not significantly differ between groups. However, in both groups Ss tended to stop earlier as trials progressed (F for blocks = 13.83, $p < .001$). Further, a significant block by group interaction showed that Ss in the I-I group tended to increase less in silence

than Ss in the R-R groups. The latter used almost all their time at first, but tended to stop earlier as the session progressed.

Groups I-I and R-R did not differ significantly on starting latency nor choice time when compared by analyses of variance.

An analysis of variance on incubation time for Groups I-I and R-R indicated that all Ss showed decreased incubation time over blocks ($F = 3.92$, $p < .001$). A significant groups effect ($F = 4.27$, $p < .05$) indicated that the I-I group had a longer overall delay subsequent to E's comments.

The comparison between Groups I-I and R-R suggests some differences in the relative effect of interpretive and reflective statements with regard to S's attitude toward the interviewer, his total amount of verbal output during a fixed time, and the delay following E's response.

Reflection versus Interpretation, Simultaneous Choice Groups

The analysis of data from this group consisted of an analysis of the temporal measures, and attitutdes toward Es. Results from the original group and the replication were pooled, since no differences were found on any of these variables between the two samples. On the analysis of the relationships between personality variables and choice for interpretation or reflection, however, the two groups were kept separate because the significant findings, despite the small size of the first sample, had led to the decision to replicate in order to cross validate the findings.

All Ss in the combined I-R group ($N = 26$) were classified as I- or R-preferrers on the basis of their preference for either interviewer on the last block. In the first group, nine Ss consistently (four or five times during the last five trial blocks) chose interpretations (I-preferrers), and four consistently chose reflections (R-preferrers). In the replication group there were eight I-preferrers and five R-preferrers. Thus, in both groups preference for interpretations was shown approximately in a ratio of two to one.

On a postexperimental questionnaire, I-preferrers ($N = 17$) yielded a mean score of 12.5 for E who gave interpretations and 3.7 for E who gave reflections. Those Ss who preferred reflections, on the other hand, yielded a score of 11.5 for the E giving reflections and 3.4 for the E giving interpretations. Analysis by t tests indicated that Ss showed a significantly more positive attitude toward the E whom they eventually selected consistently, whether he gave reflections or interpretations.

An analysis of variance on the amount of silence yielded no significant difference between I- and R-preferrers, nor was there a tendency to decrease amount of talk over blocks. This finding contrasts with a tendency of the I-I and R-R groups to increase in silence as trials progressed. The choice time, the duration between the ready signal and S's choice of an interviewer, was analyzed over blocks by a repeated measures analysis of variance. Neither groups nor blocks revealed significant differences in the time taken to select interviewers. Similarly, an analysis of variance yielded no significant differences in incubation time between I- and R-preferrers. However, as in the I-I and R-R groups, all Ss decreased incubation time over blocks ($F = 3.90$, $p < .01$).

To evaluate the ease with which Ss made their choices for one or the other type of E response, an analysis of variance was carried out on the mean frequency of choices of the preferred response over all blocks. As shown in Figure 1, both I-preferrers and R-preferrers eventually reached the criterion, as they were instructed to do. However, I-preferrers appeared to do so much more smoothly, with increasing increments over trials, while R-preferrers seemed to shift more. An analysis of variance on repeated measures yielded no differences in choice frequencies of preferred response

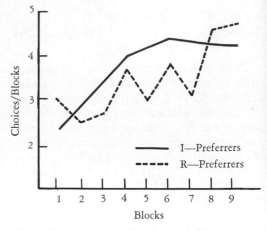

Fig. 1. Mean frequency of choices over blocks for the preferred interviewer by Ss in Group I-R.

for the treatments. Choices increased significantly over blocks ($F = 15.57$, $df = 7/168$, $p < .01$). A significant blocks $\times$ groups interaction ($F = 3.59$, $df = 7/168$) indicated that the manner with which choices were made differed for the I- and R-preferrers. An analysis of this interaction by Edwards' trend analysis (1960) yielded a significant linear trend for both interpretation and reflection preferrers. Interpretation preferrers also showed a significant quadratic trend ($F = 12.8$, $p < .05$), while reflection preferrers showed none. The analyses substantiate the visual impression from Fig. 1 of a constant increment in choices in the I group while the R group mainly shows a linear trend and suggests much vacillation in Ss' choices from block to block.

Although the number of Ss obtained by the split into I- and R-preferrers was rather small in the original group, several analyses were run to determine whether preferences for either type of comment were related to personality variables. In the original group I-preferrers showed a significantly higher score on the self-orientation scale of the ORI ($M = 29.0$ versus 19.5; $t = 3.8$, $p < .01$); they also showed a significantly lower score on the Marlowe-Crowne SDS

($M = 10.8$ versus 18.2; $t = 2.76$, $p < .05$) than R-preferrers. Consistent differences between I-preferrers and R-preferrers on the MMPI were shown on all scales except the F and L scales of the MMPI. The differences between the groups were significant at $p < .05$ for the K scale and the Sc scale. I-preferrers showed a trend ($p < .10$) toward higher scores on the Hs scale, the D scale, and the Pd scale. The mean scores for the I- and R-preferrers, respectively, were: K, 50.1 and 60.0; Sc, 64.8 and 50.6; IIs, 53.4 and 47.2; D, 62.6 and 50.2; Pd, 62.5 and 54.1. Examination of these tendencies suggests that I-preferrers tended toward more introspection and self-awareness with consistently higher scores on all the clinical scales and a lower score on the K scale. This finding necessitated cross validation because of the small number of Ss on whom it was obtained. If supported, correlation of preferences for interpretations with lower defensiveness and slightly higher tendencies toward self-awareness and introspection would suggest the differential effects of therapeutic operations and techniques with different personality patterns, even within the narrow range of variability found in college students.

On replication the differences are not as clear-cut. None of the subscales of the ORI yielded significant differences. On the Marlowe-Crowne SDS I-preferrers again showed significantly lower scores than R-preferrers ($M = 12.2$ versus 18.9; $t = 2.35$; $p < .05$). On the MMPI, scores on the Sc scale were again significant in the same direction ($M = 63.2$ and 53.6). However, on the K scale the differences were no longer significant, on the Hs scale the trend was still in the same direction but weaker. On the D and Pd scales the trends in the second group were reversed. The cross validation then suggests that the significant findings in the original group with regard to personality differences among I- and R-preferrers may have been partially based on sampling errors. Never-

theless, the Ss who preferred interpretations showed significantly higher scores on the Sc scale and lower social conformity scores on *both* samples. In order to assess the extent of the relationship between the preference criterion and MMPI scores, point-biserial correlations were run for each of the scales, dichotomizing at the mean of the combined original and replication group, I- versus R-preferrers. The highest correlations were obtained for the Sc scale with an r_{pb} of 0.48 and for the K scale with an r_{pb} of -0.36. These findings suggest further that preference for interpretation versus reflections may be associated to a moderate degree with scores on these two MMPI scales. Since our Ss may have been motivated by curiosity and had limited personal involvement with E, the effects of situational and attitudinal variables also require further study. Nevertheless, considering the narrow range of MMPI scores in this normal college population and the nature of the setting in which these broad interpretations or reflections were given, further investigation of the differential preference for therapeutic operations as a function of personality variables seems warranted.

EXPERIMENT II

One dimension along which schools of psychotherapy have often been ordered is the degree of activity by the therapist. The therapist's theoretical orientation may determine whether his behavior falls at one extreme of the activity dimension, i.e., minimal participation as in free association, or whether he continuously participates and intervenes, as in directive therapy (Strupp, 1960). In this study the focus was on the "patient's" response to this therapist activity. What are the variables which affect S's preferences for having E participate either as a listener or as a speaker? It was hypothesized that the content of the material under discussion (neutral or emotional), the content of E's comments (agreement or disagreement), and the general structure of the influencing aspects of the two-person relationship would affect *S*'s attempt to maintain a two-way communication system or to engage primarily in one-way communication. The purpose of this study was to determine the effect of these three variables on *S*'s request for participation by *E* and on the temporal characteristics of *S*'s verbal utterances.

METHOD

Subjects. 48 male undergraduate volunteers from elementary psychology classes served as *S*s.

Apparatus and Procedure. The apparatus was essentially the same as in Experiment I. Each *S* had before him a black box with three switches. The center switch was labeled "ready," as before. The other switches were now labeled "Interviewer" and "No-Interviewer," with jewel lights above each. The trials were timed as before by a Hunter timer. Chronoscopes were used to obtain the same dependent variables as in Experiment I.

The procedure differed in that the *S*s in this experiment were not given prior personality tests. The *S*s were told that this was a study of interview procedures. "We are interested in examining an individual's ability to express his feelings on various topics in a situation similar to real-life psychotherapy." They were shown a card with a statement for discussion on each trial. Half of the *S*s received statements designated as "Emotional," and half received "Neutral" topics. The emotional topics were designed to have more personal and more taboo content in order to produce greater anxiety than neutral topics. They included such statements as: "I sometimes get irritated by my mother's overconcern about me"; " I think it would be hard to be faithful to one woman"; "Sometimes I feel like smashing someone who has made me real angry." Neutral topics included statements as "The fraternity system does more harm than good for the student";

"The faculty here is not really interested in teaching, they would rather do research or write books"; "The world is better today than it was 50 years ago." The *S*s were asked to speak for 100 seconds on each of 15 statements. Duration of the trial was controlled by flashing a light to indicate length of a trial.

The *S*s were instructed to press the ready switch in order to procure a card containing an interview topic in the exposure window. After reading the topic silently, they were to press either the Interviewer or No-Interviewer switch to choose "whether or not you want to talk with an interviewer." The *S*s were told that choosing an interviewer would yield occasional comments from *E*. If *S*s chose the other switch they would talk on their own. As in Experiment I *S*s were instructed to press the ready switch, to decide whether they wanted an interviewer to comment, to talk as long as the light indicated that the trial was on and to use the switch to indicate readiness for the next trial.

Half of the *S*s were also given information concerning the role of the interviewer. They were told that the interviewer's role was to try to influence the conversation and to guide *S* to talk about important and useful matters. Those *S*s who received these additional instructions will henceforth be called *Informed S*s, those who did not will be called *Noninformed*.

The *E*'s response content compared an agreeing, supportive *E* with one who was disagreeing. This same *E*, a male graduate student, ran all *S*s and played both roles. During each 100-second period he interjected five comments, three of approximately 5 seconds duration and two of 2 seconds duration. These comments were spaced roughly 20 seconds apart and were given when there was a natural pause in *S*'s talk. For the *Agree* groups the longer statements consisted of rephrasing *S*'s comments, reflection of feeling, or reassuring statements, as "I agree" or "I understand." The shorter responses included "Mm-hmm," "I agree," "yes," and "that's right." In the *Disagree* groups these longer comments were obvious negative reactions to S's previous statements, following the phrase "I disagree." The shorter responses included "I don't know about that," "Huh-uh," and "I disagree." The responding E was never seen by S, a second E gave instructions and then sat behind the partition to record the latencies. At the end of each session S again filled out a 50-item evaluation form patterned after Snyder and used in Experiment I in this study.

Experimental Design. The design consisted of a $2 \times 2 \times 2$ factorial design: Emotional versus Neutral topics; Informed versus Noninformed Ss; and Agree versus Disagree E responses. Fifteen trials were grouped into three blocks of five trials in a repeated measures analysis.

RESULTS

Table 1 presents a summary of the analysis of variance of the frequency with which S chose a "No-Interviewer" switch on each block. There was a significant interaction ($F = 5.86$, $p < .025$) between the E response variable and the information variable. When S was informed that E's role was to influence him, he avoided the interviewer more frequently if E disagreed with his statements. Noninformed Ss showed more interviewer participation choices than informed Ss under disagreement. Thus, when Ss were aware of the interviewer's role and his attempt to influence them, they showed less willingness to listen to a disagreeing interviewer than when they were unaware. There were no significant effects due to the topics, nor did

TABLE 1

ANALYSIS OF VARIANCE ON MEAN FREQUENCY OF "NO-INTERVIEWER" CHOICES, AND MEAN INCUBATION TIMES OVER BLOCKS IN EXPERIMENT II

Source	df	Frequency		Incubation	
		MS	F	MS	F
Interviewer response (A) (Agreement versus Disagree)	1	0.45		8.07	1.15
Information (B) (Informed versus Noninformed)	1	3.36	1.23	1.96	
Topics (C) (Emotional versus Neutral)	1	0.45		1.57	
AB	1	15.99	5.86**	2.05	
AC	1	0.05		2.20	
BC	1	2.24		2.01	
ABC	1	0.71		0.61	
Subjects in groups	40	2.73		7.00	
Blocks (D)	2	0.53	1.00	34.96	16.89***
AD	2	0.42		12.19	5.89**
BD	2	0.05		0.89	
CD	2	0.54	1.02	0.42	
ABD	2	0.41		1.55	
ACD	2	0.16		2.89	1.40
BCD	2	1.54	2.91	3.27	1.58
ABCD	2	0.69	1.30	5.84	2.82
Blocks × subjects in groups	80	0.53		2.07	

** $p < .025$.
*** $p < .01$.

the overall frequency of No-Interviewer requests change over trials.

Table 1 also summarizes the analysis on Incubation time, the time between the end of one trial and S's pushing the Ready switch for the next trial. While there were no significant differences between groups, Incubation time decreased significantly over blocks ($F = 16.89$, $p < .01$) and the interaction of the E response variable and blocks was significant ($F = 5.89$, $p < .025$). Disagreement resulted in longer Incubation times during Block 1 (F for E response at Block $1 = 15.21$, $p < .01$), and approximately the same latencies in Blocks 2 and 3 (F's < 1.0). There was an overall tendency for Incubation time to decrease over blocks ($F = 16.89$, $p < .01$). If Incubation time is viewed as reflecting S's interest in E's responses, whether this interest be simply curiosity or anxious hesitation, one sees a reduction in this interval over time and a greater initial reaction on S's part to disagreement by the interviewer. An analysis of Choice time also indicated a significant decrease over blocks ($F = 4.81$, $p < .025$) but no significant effects between groups or groups $\times$ blocks. There was a trend ($F = 4.81$, $p < .10$) for agreement by E to produce longer latency with Emotional topics and shorter latency with Neutral topics.

An analysis of the questionnaire showed a tendency for Agreement to produce a more positive mean attitude toward E ($F = 3.48$, $p < .10$). For Agreement on a 50-point scale M was 30.83; for Disagreement M was 26.38. There was a Pearson r correlation of 0.28 between total frequency of No-Interviewer requests and attitude scores. Because of the significant group differences in the requests for E, and attitude scores, the correlations were run separately for the groups. The only significant correlation was found in the Informed groups (0.46, $p < .025$), indicating that the attitude toward E was more negative the more often he had been asked to respond. Thus, it appears that for Ss who were told that

the E would try to influence them, the more they allowed themselves to be influenced, the more negative their attitude toward the influencer. Instructions and content of E's response not only affected S's tendency to seek E participation, temporal speech characteristics, and attitudes separately, but there seem to be additional effects shown by the relationship among the dependent variables.

EXPERIMENT III

In Experiment II S's opportunity to request a response from E was limited. The S had to make this decision prior to his own discussion therefore he had no control over the *specific* statements on which he could request a comment. In this experiment S was allowed to ask for E's comment any time *during* the trial. This procedural modification more closely approximates the clinical interview and promised to yield a more sensitive measure of S's tendency to solicit comments from E. Further, the effects of topics and S's conformity measured by the Marlowe-Crowne SDS (1960) were studied as independent variables, using the same temporal measures of S responses as in the previous experiments.

METHOD

Subjects. Thirty male undergraduates who were students in an abnormal psychology class served as volunteer Ss.

Apparatus. The previously used apparatus was modified to allow S the opportunity for free requests of E participation. One of the two choice switches in the panel before the S was eliminated. One of the remaining switches was labeled "Ready," as before, and activated a chronoscope when S pressed it to receive a stimulus card. The second switch was labeled "Start." When pressed, the Start switch activated a jewel light above it for 110 seconds. When the jewel light went off, a second chronoscope was activated and stopped by the next activation of the Ready switch. The session was tape recorded and silence was later recorded from the tapes. In addition to the two switches, S was given a microswitch to press whenever he wished to hear a comment from the interviewer. The E who gave instructions also recorded latencies and requests for E participation.

Prodecure. The procedure was essentially the same as in Experiment II, with the exception that S controlled the occurrence of the interviewer response. The following are the instructions explaining the procedure to S:

This is a study on interview procedures. We are interested in examining an individual's ability to express his feelings on various topics in a situation similar to real-life psychotherapy. You will see a series of topics in this window. For each one you are to express yourself as best you can during the time allotted. If you are having difficulty an interviewer behind the screen will be available for comments. Over there on the table is a black box that has two buttons. When you press the center *Ready* button a topic will appear in the window. When you are ready to begin talking press the *Start* button on the left. The *Start* button will turn on this light which will remain on for a short period during which you are to continue talking on the topic in the window, elaborating on it as you wish. In order to hear the interviewer at any time while the light is on, press the *Interviewer* button on the right. Most people are able to talk on their own and occasionally wish to hear the interviewer. When the light goes out the topic will be removed. When you are ready for the next topic, press the *Ready* button again and then the *Start* button when you want to begin talking.

Fifteen of the Ss received the Emotional topics used in Experiment II, and 15 the Neutral topics. The E responded with a reflective statement of approximately 5 seconds in length whenever he was asked for his comment. Completing a 2×2 design, half of the Ss in each topic group had scored in the high range on the M-C SDS and half in the low range. The students were given the M-C SDS in a class prior to

the experimental session. The 30 male student's scores were divided at the median (10.42); and those above and below the median assigned to the High SD and Low SD groups, respectively. Each of these groups was then split randomly, with half receiving Emotional and half Neutral topics.

RESULTS

Table 2 presents a summary of the analysis of variance on frequency of requests in blocks of five trials each. The analysis shows a significant decrease in frequency over blocks ($F = 15.59$, $p < .001$) and a significant differential decrease with respect to the Personality variable ($F = 3.57$, $p < .05$). A test for Blocks effects within each group showed that the High SD group did not change significantly in frequency of requests for E comments over blocks ($F = 2.34$), while the low SD group decreased significantly ($F = 16.82$, $p < .001$). The groups were also compared on a difference score taken between the frequency of requests in the first and second halves of each trial. While none of the

TABLE 2

ANALYSIS OF VARIANCE ON
MEAN FREQUENCY OF REQUESTS FOR
E COMMENTS OVER BLOCKS IN EXPERIMENT III

Source	df	MS	F
Topic (A) (Emotional-Neutral)	1	135.37	1.41
Personality (B) (Social desirability)	1	40.04	
AB	1	40.05	
Ss in groups	26	95.83	
Blocks (C)	2	40.54	15.59****
AC	2	1.63	
BC	2	9.29	3.57*
ABC	2	2.04	
Blocks × subjects in groups	52	2.60	

* $p < .05$.
**** $p < .001$.

group differences were significant (highest $F = 1.36$), a t test of the overall significance of this difference indicated that over all groups and trials Ss asked for E's comments significantly more often in the second half of a trial ($t = 5.43$, $p < .01$).

The results of the difference score analysis suggest that frequency of requests may relate to the silence measure. As the trial progressed S relied more and more on the interviewer to carry the burden of the interaction. However, examination of the frequency over trials indicated a decrease during the later trials. The Ss scoring low on the SD scale showed this decrease while the High SD group maintained an even rate of asking for E's comments, indicating that the latter group, being more concerned with the opinions of others, continued to seek the social response of the interviewer. Therefore, from these two analyses it is not clear whether the increase within trials indicated decreased interest in the interview or increased reinforcement value of E's response.

The analyses of Start time and Incubation time yielded significant effects only with respect to an overall decrease over blocks ($Fs = 11.93$ and 18.63, $p < .001$ for Start and Incubation times, respectively). These findings indicate a decrease in concern or interest in the task as trials progressed. There were no significant effects in the analysis of silence.

The analysis of the attitude questionnaire (Table 3) yielded a significant interaction

TABLE 3

SUMMARY OF ANALYSIS OF VARIANCE ON MEAN POSTQUESTIONNAIRE ATTITUDE SCORE IN EXPERIMENT III

Source	df	MS	F
Personality (A)	1	7.67	
Topic (B)	1	73.02	1.81
A × B	1	172.70	4.29*
Subjects in groups	24	40.21	

* $p < .05$.

between the personality and optic variables ($F = 4.29$, $p < .05$). An analysis of simple effects showed that Topics were significant ($F = 5.85$, $p < .025$) in the High SD group but not in the Low SD group ($F < 1.0$). In the High SD group, those receiving Emotional topics had a mean attitude score of 25.50 and those receiving Neutral topics a mean of 33.17. The findings suggest that Ss with high SD who are conforming individuals tend to resent any encouragement for talking about personal topics which would reveal their individuality.

The correlation of frequency of requests for E comments and attitude showed a relationship similar to the results of Experiment II. Over all groups the Pearson r was $-.45$, $p < .025$, indicating a more negative attitude in Ss who had asked E to participate more frequently. The correlations calculated separately for the four groups yielded a significant r only for the High SD group receiving Emotional topics ($-.94$, $p < .005$). Thus, the effect of the interviewer's responses on these Ss was not to reduce their approach to E but to produce a more negative attitude. They seemed to wish continued E support for talking on the Emotional (anxiety-arousing) topics, but the more E responded to them the more negative became their attitude.

DISCUSSION

The results emphasize the multiplicity of determinants affecting the temporal speech characteristics and attitudes of a subject in a psychotherapy analogue. Although the specific procedures varied somewhat in the three studies, the results suggest some general trends. There is evidence that the nature of the interviewer's comments affects both S's attitudes toward him and the particular way in which S talks. The interviewer's response differed in each of the studies, with the first and last experiment providing some groups which received only reflective statements and the second experiment providing E responses of agreement and disagreement. With regard to amount of information one might suggest that E agreement is closer to reflection, in that no new information is provided. Disagreement, on the other hand, might be more similar in its effect to interpretations.

The preference for interpretations in the I-R group of Experiment I was contrary to the assumption that interpretations function as aversive stimuli. However, in an initial interview under laboratory conditions Ss discussed relatively nonthreatening matters. Because they were students in a psychology course, their interest in hearing E's comments and getting feedback might have exceeded the aversive nature of the interpretations. The preference for either class of E responses is only one index of S's discrimination. Differences in S's attitudes toward E and consistency of choices over blocks also reflect the multiple consequences which follow such a complex operation as interpreting or reflecting. Thus, prediction of the effects of these quasi-therapeutic operations requires evaluation of total patterns of dependent variables. In psychotherapy, for example, an unfavorable attitude may result in termination, even while the patient appears to respond to treatment when he seems interested in the therapist's interpretations.

When S could control the intertrial interval, he tended to spend progressively less time between trials (Incubation time) under all conditions. However, Incubation time was longer when interpretations were forthcoming on subsequent trials (Experiment 1) and was initially longer when E disagreed with S (Experiment 2). These results would suggest that both disagreement and interpretations tend to prolong the amount of time spent by S in either stalling or considering the content of these comments before embarking on a new trial. Alternately, if decrease in Incubation time over blocks is interpreted as evidence for adaptation of Ss to the experimental situation, disagreement and interpretations would be considered to have interfered with this adaptation process.

When S knew that E was attempting to influence him, he tended to call on E less frequently when disagreement was forthcoming than under conditions of E agreement. When uninformed of E's attempt to influence him, disagreements appeared to result in more frequent invitations for E to participate (Experiment 2). Further, interpretations were favored by Ss who were higher on the Sc scale of the MMPI, and less conforming to socially desirable response patterns (Experiment 1). The tendency to involve E in a two-way communication system was also affected by S's personality. When E makes reflective statements (Experiment 3) only those Ss who have low SD scores tend to decrease in their invitations for E participation. Only in Experiment 1 was there a difference in amount of silence attributable to the independent variables.

The current procedures are not very similar to psychotherapeutic operations because of the differences of emotional involvement of both parties, the differences between college student and patient populations, and the differences in the purposes of these interactions. Even in the experimental situation, however, it becomes clear that attitudes toward E vary as a function of E's behavior and are not always correlated with S's attempts to engage E in more extensive communication exchanges. Subject attitudes were measured in the present study by post-experimental questionnaires; in psychotherapy the same responses may have far-reaching effects. The patient's attitudes may, in fact, be manifested by his termination of psychotherapy, or by the degree to which his behavior is modified as a consequence of therapist activity. While Ss in Experiment 1 picked interpretation-yielding Es when they had a choice, they were more favorably inclined toward reflection-yielding Es. In Experiment 2 they were more favorable toward agreeing Es, and in Experiment 3 they were more favorable when they were high on the M-C SDS and the content of communication was neutral. These results strongly support the findings that favorable attitudes are related to the therapist's ability to conduct psychotherapeutic interviews with minimal threat (Bandura, 1956). The differential effect of a therapist response upon his client would have important implications for psychotherapy. A therapist, by agreement, support, or avoidance of threatening material, may increase his patient's dependence on him and the patient's tendency to solicit advice or information. At the same time, however, such responses may also build up negative attitudes toward the therapist so that the long-range effects of such therapist behavior may result in termination rather than successful treatment. Further, highly conforming repressed individuals in discussing emotional topics may tend to seek support and reassurance from a therapist but at the same time develop negative attitudes toward him. It is plausible from the present data and earlier research (Kanfer, Phillips, Matarazzo, & Saslow, 1960) that the proper timing of interpretations, as suggested intuitively by early psychoanalysts, may reflect the fact that similar therapist operations would differentially affect the patient's attitudes as well as his momentary behavior in the interview. Of course, the relative freedom from serious emotional disturbance in the present population also suggests that the need for seeking additional information, such as offered by interpretations or E disagreement, may not be equal for Ss with serious emotional disturbances.

The results in Experiment 2 emphasize the importance of structuring the therapeutic relationship and the effect of therapist responses. They suggest that Ss oriented toward the influencing aspect of the interaction are much less susceptible to disagreeing responses, and much more likely to resent the therapist's apparent effort to change him. As suggested on the basis of an earlier study (Kanfer & Marston,

1961), a therapist may be wise in leaving the situation unstructured at the beginning, allowing for reinforcement of responses which had earlier aversive consequences without development of sufficient hostility to result in premature termination of therapy.

REFERENCES

AULD, F., JR., & WHITE, ALICE MARSDEN. Sequential dependencies in psychotherapy. *J. abnorm. soc. Psychol.*, 1959, 58, 100–104.

BANDURA, A. Psychotherapist's anxiety level, self-insight, and psychotherapeutic competence. *J. abnorm. soc. Psychol.*, 1956, 52, 333–337.

BANDURA, A., LIPSHER, D., & MILLER, P. E. Psychotherapists approach-avoidance reactions to patients' expressions of hostility. *J. consult. Psychol.*, 1960, 21, 1–8.

BASS, B. M. *The orientation inventory*. Palo Alto, Cal.: Consulting Psychologists Press, 1962.

CROWNE, D. P., & MARLOWE, D. A new scale of social desirability independent of psychopathology. *J. consult. Psychol.*, 1960, 24, 349–354.

EDWARDS, A. L. *Experimental design in psychological research*. New York: Holt, Rinehart, & Winston, 1960.

HARWAY, N. I., DITTMANN, A. T., RAUSH, H. L., BORDIN, E. S., & RIGLER, D. The measurement of depth of interpretation. *J. consult. Psychol.*, 1955, 19, 247–253.

KANFER, F. H., & MARSTON, A. R. Verbal conditioning, ambiguity, and psychotherapy. *Psychol. Rep.*, 1961, 9, 461–475.

KANFER, F. H., PHILLIPS, J. S., MATARAZZO, J. D., & SASLOW, G. Experimental modification of interviewer content in standardized interviews. *J. consult. Psychol.*, 1960, 24, 528–536.

LUBORSKY, L. The patient's personality and psychotherapeutic change. In H. H. Strupp & L. Luborsky (Eds.), *Research in psychotherapy*, Vol. 2. Baltimore, Md.: French-Bray, 1962. Pp. 115–133.

LUBORSKY, L., & STRUPP, H. H. Research problems in psychotherapy: A three-year follow-up. In H. H. Strupp & L. Luborsky (Eds.), *Research in psychotherapy,* Vol. 2. Baltimore, Md.: French-Bray, 1962. Pp. 308–329.

MURRAY, E. J. A case study in a behavioral analysis of psychotherapy. *J. abnorm. soc. Psychol.,* 1954, 49, 305–310.

SNYDER, W. U. Summary report: Therapist's contribution (B). In H. H. Strupp & L. Luborsky (Eds.), *Research in psychotherapy.* Vol. 2. Baltimore, Md.: French-Bray, 1962. Pp. 308–329.

SPEISMAN, J. C. Depth of interpretation and verbal resistance in psychotherapy. *J. consult. Psychol.,* 1959, 23, 93–99.

STRUPP, H. H. *Psychotherapists in action.* New York: Grune & Stratton, 1960.

Relationships Between Descriptive Content and Interaction Behavior in Interviews[1]

JEANNE S. PHILLIPS
RUTH G. MATARAZZO
JOSEPH D. MATARAZZO
GEORGE SASLOW
FREDERICK H. KANFER

This study was undertaken in order to explore possible relationships between two different general approaches to the description and measurement of verbal interview behavior. One widely applied frame of reference directs attention to the communication aspects of verbal behavior, that is, to some symbolic dimension of the content of the words spoken, using content analysis to

Reprinted from *Journal of Consulting Psychology,* 1961, 25 (3), 260–266, with the permission of the American Psychological Association and the authors.

[1] This investigation was supported by a research grant (M-735) from the National Institute of Mental Health, of the National Institutes of Health, United States Public Health Service. This paper is based in part on a dissertation, under the direction of Frederick H. Kanfer, submitted by the senior author in partial fulfillment of the requirements for the degree of doctor of philosophy at Washington University. The data were collected while all of the investigators were at Washington University.

define and quantify its variables. A second frame of reference focuses upon quantitative *temporal* characteristics of interview interactions, utilizing measures such as number and duration of utterances, duration of silences, etc.

The few studies which have incorporated measures of *both* content *and* temporally defined variables have usually indicated the greater discriminatory power of the latter. For example, Page (1953), Lennard (1955), Goldman-Eisler (1952) and others have found that quantity or tempo of verbal output is both more stable and more highly correlated with various criteria of personal adjustment or psychotherapeutic success than are content-derived variables.

Lundy (1950) found that a single patient seen concurrently by two therapists differing in therapeutic technique showed no difference in his responses to the two therapists in measures of content (Distress

Relief Quotient, Raimy's self-references, etc.) However, differences in *tempo* of interaction in the two sets of therapeutic interviews were apparent in the protocols. As a secondary aspect of a subsequent study, Lundy (1955) compared the temporal variables with clinical estimates of occurrence of significant emotional and topical content in "key" interviews. The results indicated that the contentual and temporal variables were related.

The present study involves the direct investigation of relationships between more precisely measured content variables and the temporal measures of the Interaction Chronograph. This instrument and Chapple's underlying interaction theory (Chapple, 1949; Chapple & Arensberg, 1940) constitute an extensive, systematically developed attempt to describe temporal phenomena in verbal behavior and to investigate their significance. Definitions of the Interaction Chronograph variables involved in the present study are given in Table 1. Without more extensive knowledge on our part of the subtle differences in "meaning" of the several intercorrelated Interaction Chronograph variables (Matarazzo, Saslow, & Hare, 1958), precise hypotheses as to specifically which content and interactional variables would be related could not be formulated. However, tentative hypotheses regarding the general types of relationships to be expected on a "face validity" basis were obviously the determinants of the kinds of content categories selected for use, and are illustrated below in the description of the content system.

PROCEDURE

Forty patients randomly selected from new referrals to the Psychiatric Outpatient Clinic of a large urban medical center were interviewed by the same psychiatrist according to the published rules of the partially standardized interview which is used with the Interaction Chronograph in order that the interviewer may serve as a partially

TABLE 1

INTERACTION CHRONOGRAPH VARIABLES

Pt.'s Units	The number of times the patient acted
Pt.'s Tempo	The average duration of each action plus its following inaction (silence), as a single measure
Pt.'s Silence	The average duration of the patient's silences
Pt.'s Adjustment	The durations of the patient's interruptions minus the durations of his latencies in responding, divided by Pt.'s Units
Pt.'s Initiative	The percentage of times, out of the available number of opportunities (usually 12) in Period 2, in which the patient acted again (within a 15-second limit) following his own last action
Pt.'s Quickness	The average length of time in Period 2 that the patient waited before taking the initiative following his own last action
Pt.'s Dominance	The number of times in Period 4 that the patient "talked down" the interviewer minus the number of times the interviewer talked down the patient, divided by the number of Pts.'s Units in that period

controlled or independent variable during each of five predefined subperiods of the interview (Matarazzo, Saslow, & Matarazzo, 1956; Saslow & Matarazzo, 1959). Each interview was observed from an adjoining room through a one-way mirror by the same observer, who recorded the ongoing interaction on an Interaction Chronograph and made a verbatim sound recording on a Gray Audograph. Ten of the 40 patients were omitted from the final experimental sample because of deficiencies in the sound recordings, or, in a few cases, because of the presence of acute psychosis which resulted in confused, incoherent interview content. The 30 remaining patients served as the subjects of the present study. Of these, 17 were female, 13 were male. Their ages ranged from 20 to 61 years, with a median age of 35.5. The most frequent diagnoses were: hysteria (eight cases), anxiety neurosis (seven cases), depression (six cases) and schizoid personality (four cases).

The sound recordings were carefully and repeatedly monitored by the typist and a judge, until a high degree of recording transcription fidelity was achieved. Since the reliability of the content scoring process had been demonstrated on an independent sample of transcripts shortly before (Phillips, 1957), the final transcripts were unitized and then categorized, unit by unit, by one experimenter.

The content aspects of the verbal interview behavior were defined and quantified according to the category system schematically diagrammed in Table 2. The system

TABLE 2

CONTENT CATEGORY SYSTEM

I. Description (units which "tell about" an event)
  A. Actor (subject [person] of unit)
    1. Patient himself
    2. Patient's family
    3. Patient's spouse, date, fiancee
    etc.
  B. Time (of occurrence of described event)
    1. Present
    2. Past
    3. Future
    4. Subjunctive
  C. Interpersonal Acts (overt motor behavior involving two or more people, e.g., telling, hitting, leaving someone)
         OR
  C'. Interpersonal States (nonovert states, thoughts, attitudes, etc., involving two or more people; e.g., thinking of, being angry at, or afraid of someone)
    1. Interpersonal System Categories to 16
    17. Neutral, unscorable

         OR
  D. Noninterpersonal Acts (overt motor behavior involving only one person, e.g., eating, bathing, walking, etc.)
         OR
  D'. Noninterpersonal States (nonovert states, thoughts, attitudes, etc. involving only one person, e.g., feeling ill, being sleepy, poor, happy, etc.)
    1. Positive (welcome, pleasant, etc. to patient)
    2. Neutral (neutral or indeterminant in significance to patient)
    3. Negative (disliked, unpleasant, etc. to patient)
  E. Object (person acted on or with, in interpersonal units)
    (As for A above)
  F. Topical Area (of general life experience)
    1. Financial
    2. Marital—Sexual
    3. Religious—Philosophical
    4. Educational
    etc.
II. Direct Interaction (units dealing directly with current interview interaction)
  A. Agrees, expresses compliance with interviewer
  B. Disagrees, expresses noncompliance with interviewer
  C. Asks for information, repetition, clarification, etc., from interviewer
  etc.
III. Unscorable

and its development have been described in Phillips (1957). It represents an adaptation and extension of the Interpersonal System devised by Freedman, Leary, Ossorio, and Coffey (1951), C and C' in Table 2, which consists of a circular continuum of 16 categories, representing qualitative blendings of two orthogonal dimensions, love-hate and dominance-submission. A seventeenth category was added for coding of units unscorable or neutral within the Interpersonal System.

In addition to the Interpersonal System, several other dimensions were coded in order to achieve completeness of coverage and more general applicability. These other dimensions were operationally defined by: (*a*) coding of units without interpersonal reference, D and D′ in Table 2, such as "I sat down and ate," "My head aches," etc.; (*b*) coding of the actor or subject of a description and of the receiver of action or attitude, if any, A and E in Table 2; and (*c*) coding of the general topic discussed, e.g., marriage, finances, symptoms, etc. Provision was also made for differentiation of descriptions of *motor acts,* C and D, from description of *nonmotor states* of being, thinking, feeling, etc., C′ and D′. For example, "I yelled at her" is an interpersonal act, C, while "I was angry at her" is coded as an interpersonal state, C′; "I ate dinner" is a noninterpersonal act, D, while "I felt sick" is a noninterpersonal state, D′. Those units which referred directly to the ongoing interview interaction and had no referent outside of the current situation (e.g., "Thank you, doctor," "I agree with you") were classified separately, according to their function, within categories adapted from Bales (1950), II in Table 2. A residual category was utilized for unscorable units, III.

The resulting system is of a pyramidal nature, involving several series of mutually exclusive categories. It was considered particularly suited to the purposes of this study because of its interpersonal interactional emphasis and its use of content variables seemingly parallel to the temporal variables of the Interaction Chronograph. For example, it was expected that one or more of the Interaction Chronograph measures of verbal "output" (number and duration of utterances, etc.) would be related to the frequency of content describing the self as physically *active,* Self C + D in Table 2. Since the former measures of verbal output in the interview have been described by Chapple[2] as involving both a physical high energy aspect *and* an out-going, interaction seeking aspect, it was further expec-

ted that one or more of them would be related to the degree of emphasis which the patient's content placed on interacting with others, Self C + C′ in Table 2. Since the degree to which a patient takes the initiative in speaking, when the interviewer deliberately remains silent, has been proposed by Chapple as a measure of both the "drive" aspect of behavior and of the independence and scope of a person's interpersonal relationships, it was tentatively expected that Patient's (Pt.'s) Initiative would covary with content measures of breadth of interests (number of different persons and topics mentioned) and with description of the self in dominant interpersonal roles. It was such expectations as these, then, which guided the choice of dimensions of content to be included with the overly narrow Leary System in satisfying our goal of a comprehensive and multilevel content system.

The specific content scoring procedures include the stipulations that the categories are to be applied by the judges with a minimum degree of inference, and from the point of view of the patient. That is, all coding under this system is performed according to the relationship to or impact on the patient of the events as he describes them, without consideration of possible interpretations of psychological defenses or mechanisms, etc.

The content unit utilized for dividing verbalizations into countable and codable segments was basically defined as the minimal verbal statement which consensus of raters indicates to be understood as expressing an independent communication or thought. Although it was developed and tested independently, this unit is very similar to that of Auld and White (1956) and of Murray (1956).

Both the content unitizing and categorizing processes have been shown to have adequate reliability when applied independently by trained judges according to detailed definitions and rules (Phillips, 1957).

---

[2] E. D. Chapple. *Manual for the Interaction Chronograph,* personal communication, undated.

Raw frequency scores (number of content units coded for each category) were converted into percentages so that intersubject comparisons would be unaffected by differences in absolute numbers of unitized items. The percentage scores were transformed by the arc-sine transformation (Snedecor, 1946) for purposes of statistical analysis. The major content scores were then correlated (Pearson r) with 12 temporal Interaction Chronograph variables. Means and other statistics, when obtained, were converted back to percentages.

RESULTS

Table 3 presents the major findings. In order to conserve space, only those relationships which reached statistical significance, and those approaching significance (given in parentheses), are included. Table 3 also does not include content categories which are essentially reciprocals of those presented, nor some Interaction Chronograph variables which have been shown to be highly correlated with those included and whose correlations with content categories essentially duplicated these results.[3]

Pt.'s Units

Because of the relatively fixed length of the interview and of the interviewer's utterances, Pt.'s Units is highly correlated in a negative direction with measures (Pt.'s Action, Pt.'s Tempo, and Pt.'s Activity) of the duration of the patient's utterances. In the present sample it correlates —.70 with

[3] The complete matrices for content vs. Interaction Chronograph correlations have been deposited with ADI. Order Document No. 6641 from ADI Auxiliary Publications Project, Photoduplication Service, Library of Congress: Washington 25, D.C., remitting in advance $1.25 for microfilm or $1.25 for photocopies. Make checks payable to: Chief, Photoduplication Service, Library of Congress.

TABLE 3

CORRELATIONS BETWEEN CONTENT CATEGORIES AND INTERACTION CHRONOGRAPH VARIABLES

Content	Interaction Chronograph						
	Pt.'s Units	Pt.'s Tempo	Pt.'s Silence	Pt.'s Adj.	Pt.'s Init.	Pt.'s Quick.	Pt.'s Domin.
Description (I)			—.42	(—.34)		—.40	
Self Subject (A)				.48			.36
Self Acts (D + C)	—.38			—.40			
Self Interpersonal (C + C')	(—.34)						
Self Dominant-Hostile Quad.		.38					
Self Submissive-Hostile Quad.				(.33)			
Self Dominant-Positive Quad.							.37
Self Submissive				.41			
Self Positive							(.33)
Self Noninterpersonal (D + D')	.37			(.35)			
Self Noninterpersonal Negative (D + D' — 3)				—.36			
Other Interpersonal (C + C')				—.38			
Other Noninterpersonal (D+D')			(—.33)	—.46			.36
All Interpersonal (C + C')	—.40						
Direct (II)	(.34)	(—.31)	.39	(.32)		.38	
Number Topics (F)	(—.31)			(—.31)	.46	—.36	
Number Persons (A + E)					—.52	(.28)	(—.34)

Note.—$r = .36$ for $p = .05$. $r = .46$ for $p = .01$. Parenthetical values approach significance at .05 level.

Pt.'s Action and may be assumed to be one of the more stable and representative measures of the general level of the patient's verbal output because, as a *frequency* measure, it is less affected by a few extremely short or long utterances than are the duration measures.[4] The results shown in the first column of Table 3 reveal that the patient who has fewer Pt.'s Units, that is, who speaks relatively infrequently (but with longer durations per utterance), is shown by these correlations with content measures to describe himself as relatively: more active in his daily living, more oriented toward interactions with other people, less concerned with his own solitary experiences, interested in a wider variety of events in daily living, and less prone to evade description of himself in general.

Pt.'s Tempo

This is highly related to Pt.'s Units ($r = -.84$ in this sample) since the less frequently a patient speaks in the standardized interview, the longer *of necessity* will be his Tempo or "cycle" of speaking. Hence the relationships shown for Pt.'s Tempo should be considered in close conjunction with those for Pt.'s Units. As indicated in Table 3, the longer the average duration of a patient's Tempo, the more he describes himself as dominant-hostile in his dealings with and attitudes toward other persons.

Pt.'s Silence

This is negatively related to the percentage of content units which are *descriptive* in nature and is positively related to the relative frequency of direct interaction with

[4] The fact that these highly related measures of verbal activity level do, however, at times differ somewhat in their relationships with external behavior points out the necessity for retaining all of the Interaction Chronograph variables despite some high intercorrelations, until the areas of their overlap and independence have been more completely defined and explored.

the interviewer. One might hypothesize that both silence behavior and remarks made to the interviewer represent "resistance" or avoidance tactics, since the questions asked of the patients are nondirective ones calling for description of their general life patterns and do not deal with events within the interview. This hypothesis is also supported by the tendency noted above for the number of (short) utterances to be inversely related to such direct discussion with the interviewer, as well as by the trend for longer silences to be accompanied by the introduction of fewer different topics.

Pt's Adjustment

Since all patients hesitated before responding for longer durations than they interrupted, in analyzing the data, the minus sign was omitted, so that high scores for Pt.'s Adjustment indicate greater relative latency of response. The results in Table 3 show that patients with high Pt.'s Adjustment scores can be considered to be almost opposite to those with fewer (but longer) Pt.'s Units. Thus, "maladjustment" is *negatively* related to the relative frequency of description of the self as active and to the number of different other persons mentioned, while it is positively related to the relative amount of talk about the self. Further, the "slow responders" relatively less frequently describe the acts or the attitudes, both interpersonal and noninterpersonal, of *other* people; when they do describe their own interpersonal attitudes or dealings with other people, they relatively more frequently characterize themselves as taking a submissive role, probably one which is also hostile. They also mention fewer negative noninterpersonal things about themselves while tending to focus more upon the noninterpersonal aspects of their lives in general. Similar to Pt.'s Silence, this latency-of-response measure tends to be negatively associated with amount of descriptive content and positively related to relative frequency of direct interaction with the interviewer, supporting the hypothesis that this distinction between description and interaction with the interviewer represents avoidance in the face of difficulty in communicating.

The similar nature of the content category correlates of Pt.'s Units and Pt.'s Adjustment suggests what might be termed an "outward" or "other-directed" orientation in those patients who speak a fewer number of times and also in those who speak with a shorter latency of response. Patients who speak more times and those who wait longer before speaking have content which focuses more upon themselves, and thus might be termed "inward" or "self-directed." This interpretation is supported by our recent finding that schizophrenic patients, who might be thought of as being at the extreme pole on a continuum of inward-directed vs. outward-directed orientation, speak a significantly greater number of times (but in shorter average utterances), and with much longer average latencies before responding, compared to normals (Matarazzo & Saslow, 1961).

Pt's Initiative

The more the patient shows temporal interactional initiative (speaks again following his own last utterance), the more he also shows a form of "initiative" in raising new topics (and the broader one might therefore infer his interests or concerns to be). A similar but nonsignificant trend is shown for the total number of different persons mentioned.

Pt's Quickness

These results are supported by the finding that another temporal variable has similar correlations with the number of topics and number of persons mentioned. Unlike Pt.'s Initiative, however, Pt.'s Quickness is similar to Pt.'s Silence in being related significantly to the relative amount of descriptive content vs. interaction with the interviewer. Thus Quickness seems to have two components: one, the *readiness* to communicate in patients who take the initiative *rapidly,* a covariation which is similar to that found for Silence; and secondly, a component which, like the relationship found for Initiative, is related to the broader range of concerns (more people and more topics) of these same patients (with the shorter Quickness durations).

Pt's Dominance

This is directly related to the relative frequency with which the patient talks about people other than himself as well as to the relative concern he shows for the noninterpersonal feelings and behavior of others. Particularly striking is the finding that the more *dominant* the patient is in his temporal interview *behavior,* the more he describes himself in *content* as dominant-positive (e.g., teaching, helping, advising, protecting, etc.) in his attitudes and dealings with other people. Thus it seems that for the patient whose interpersonal style is described (in content) as more dominant, the interruption behavior on the part of the interviewer in Period 4 is animating and challenging, rather than defeating. The findings for Pt.'s Dominance are very similar to those for Pt.'s Units, the content correlates of which also emphasized relatively more discussion of others. However, patients with higher verbal output, as defined by Pt.'s Tempo, more frequently described themselves as dominant-*hostile* rather than dominant-*positive* in their own interpersonal roles.[5]

DISCUSSION AND SUMMARY

The results seem both encouraging in an exploratory study relating two quite dis-

---

[5] There is no relationship in this sample between Pt.'s Units and Dominance ($r = -.27$, not significant), while Dominance and Pt.'s Adjustment are negatively correlated ($r = -.45$). Pt.'s Adjustment is positively correlated with Pt.'s Units, however ($r = .45$).

parate phenomena of interview behavior, and suggestive in the new meaningfulness which they add to the Interaction Chronograph variables by indicating relationships which seem inherently plausible and internally consistent. They provide a foundation for an approach to personality which combines content and temporal variables, and suggest personality dimensions which, underlying as they do at least two quite different spheres of behavior, may be particularly pervasive and consistent.

Viewed as a whole, the data presented in Table 3 suggest that patients who speak less often, who are faster to respond, and more dominant in the interview (that is, who have fewer and hence longer Units, shorter Pt.'s Adjustments, and more Dominance in the interruption stress period) have interview content which is relatively more oriented towards other people and towards interpersonal interaction, with social roles which are relatively more frequently described by them as dominant, either in a paternalistic or a hostile fashion. On the other hand, the correlations imply that the more a patient loses or submits to interruptions, is hesitant in speaking, and is less active verbally, the more his content emphasizes his own noninterpersonal concerns rather than interaction with others, and the more submissively hostile is his self-described role with other people.

In conjunction with the results of other validity-oriented studies of interview behavior correlates (Hare, Waxler, Saslow, & Matarazzo, 1960; Matarazzo, Matarazzo, Saslow, & Phillips, 1958; Matarazzo & Saslow, 1961), the present findings are a beginning at describing the characteristics which suggest a significant and cohesive description of the patient and how he interacts with others, viewed both from the subjective (content-inferred) and objective (temporally measured behavior) levels of observation. The major implication of these results bears upon the degree of generalizability of the Interaction Chronograph constructs and hence has to do with their

concurrent (and, more remotely, construct) validity.

The correlations shown in Table 3 are small in the sense of accounting for relatively little of the variance, although respectable for complex personality variables. Further, the complete correlation matrix contained 336 r's (28 content categories vs. 12 Interaction Chronograph variables), of which 28 were significant at the .05 level or better. Since 17 would have been expected to be significant at this level by chance alone, a replication study is being undertaken to determine whether the present findings can be cross-validated with another sample of subjects. A number of hypotheses are suggested by the results of this validity-oriented study which can be pursued in future investigations if the present findings are borne out in the replication study.

REFERENCES

AULD, F., JR., & WHITE, ALICE M. Rules for dividing interviews into sentences. *J. Psychol.,* 1956, 42, 273–281.

BALES, R. F. *Interaction process analysis.* Cambridge. Addison-Wesley, 1950.

CHAPPLE, E. D. The Interaction Chronograph: Its evolution and present application. *Personnel,* 1949, 25, 295–307.

CHAPPLE, E. D., & ARENSBERG, C. M. Measuring human relations: An introduction to the study of the interaction of individuals. *Genet. psychol. Monogr.,* 1940, 22, 3–147.

FREEDMAN, M. B., LEARY, T. F., OSSORIO, A. G., & COFFEY, H. S. The interpersonal dimension of personality. *J. Pers.,* 1951, 20, 143–161.

GOLDMAN-EISLER, FRIEDA. Individual differences between interviewers and their effect on interviewees' conversational behavior. *J. ment. Sci.,* 1952, 98, 660–670.

HARE, A. P., WAXLER, NANCY, SASLOW, G., & MATARAZZO, J. D. Simultaneous recordings of Bales and Chapple interaction measures during initial psychiatric interviews. *J. consult. Psychol.,* 1960, 24, 193.

LENNARD, H. L. Concepts of interaction. Unpublished doctoral dissertation, Columbia University, 1955.

LUNDY, B. W. An investigation of the process of psychotherapy. Unpublished master's thesis, University of Chicago, 1950.

LUNDY, B. W. Temporal factors of interaction in psychotherapy. Unpublished doctoral dissertation, University of Chicago, 1955.

MATARAZZO, J. D., & SASLOW, G. Differences in interview interaction behavior among normal and deviant groups. In I. A. Berg & B. M. Bass (Eds.), *Conformity and deviation.* New York: Harper, 1961, in press.

MATARAZZO, J. D., SASLOW, G., & HARE, A. P. Factor analysis of interview interaction behavior. *J. consult. Psychol.*, 1958, 22, 419–429.

MATARAZZO, J. D., SASLOW, G., & MATARAZZO, RUTH G. The Interaction Chronograph as an instrument for objective measurement of interaction patterns during interviews. *J. Psychol.*, 1956, 41, 347–367.

MATARAZZO, RUTH G., MATARAZZO, J. D., SASLOW, G., & PHILLIPS, JEANNE S. Psychological test and organismic correlates of interview interaction patterns. *J. abnorm. soc. Psychol.*, 1958, 56, 329–338.

MURRAY, E. J. A content-analysis method for studying psychotherapy. *Psychol. Monogr.*, 1956, 70(13, Whole No. 420).

PAGE, H. A. An assessment of the predictive value of certain language measures in psychotherapeutic counseling. In W. V. Snyder (Ed.), *Group report of a program of research in psychotherapy.* University Park, Pa.: Pennsylvania State University, 1953.

PHILLIPS, JEANNE S. The relationship between two measures of interview behavior comparing verbal content and verbal temporal patterns of interaction. Unpublished doctoral dissertation, Washington University, 1957.

SASLOW, G., & MATARAZZO, J. D. A technique for studying changes in interview behavior. In E. A. Rubinstein & M. B. Parloff (Eds.), *Research in psychotherapy.* Washington, D.C.: American Psychological Association, 1959.

SNEDECOR, G. W. *Statistical methods.* (4th ed.) Ames: Iowa State College, 1946.

Patients' Expectancies and Relearning as Factors Determining Improvement in Psychotherapy[1]

JEROME D. FRANK
LESTER H. GLIEDMAN
STANLEY D. IMBER
ANTHONY R. STONE
EARL H. NASH[2]

INTRODUCTION

The problem of criteria of improvement in psychotherapy is a complex one which is far from adequately solved. Whatever the ultimate criteria prove to be, however, unless the patient feels better and functions more effectively, it would be difficult to maintain that psychotherapy had helped him. Relief of symptoms and improved social effectiveness, then, may be regarded as the least common denominators of therapeutic change(1).

The purpose of this paper is to present experimental data which elucidate some as-

Reprinted from *The American Journal of Psychiatry*, 1959, 115 (11), 961–968, with the permission of the American Psychiatric Association and the authors.

[1] Read at the 114th annual meeting of The American Psychiatric Association, San Francisco, Calif., May 12–16, 1958.

[2] . . . This paper grows out of research studies supported by the United States Public Health Service (M-532, C-2) and the Ford Foundation.

pects of symptomatic improvement and, to a lesser degree, of improvement in social effectiveness in psychiatric outpatients. A tentative hypothesis is presented concerning two factors which may contribute to the observed changes.

METHOD

The research population consisted of white psychiatric outpatients, diagnosed as having a psychoneurotic or personality disorder, other than antisocial personality or alcoholism and without organic brain disease. Their age range was 18 to 55; about two-thirds were women. These patients were assigned at random to one of 3 types of treatment: 1. Individual therapy one hour once a week, 2. Group therapy, in which patients were seen in groups of 5 to 8 for 1½ hours once a week, and 3. Minimal contact therapy in the continued treatment clininc (CTC) of the Phipps outpatient department where the patients were seen for no more than half an hour once every 2 weeks. Individual and group psychotherapy at Phipps focus on the resolution of the patients' current interpersonal difficulties, through discussion of relationships with other persons and feelings aroused by them. To this end, group therapy emphasizes patients' feelings and behavior towards each other in the group. The interviews in CTC focus on patients' symptoms and their alleviation.

The design called for 54 patients to receive at least 6 months of treatment; 6 in each type of treatment with each psychiatrist. Three psychiatrists, all in their second year of residency training, each conducted all 3 types of treatment. The final population of 54 "treated" patients contained 48 (89%) who had at least 4 months of treatment and 37 (68%) who had at least 6 months. No patient was included in the "treated" group who had less than one month. For comparison purposes, 23 patients who dropped out of therapy before their fourth meeting were included in the study.

The two major measures of improvement were a Discomfort Scale which consisted of 41 common complaints of psychiatric patients, each of which the patient was asked to rate on a four-point scale of the distress experienced; and a Social Ineffectiveness Scale, consisting of 15 categories of behavior involving the patient's interpersonal relationships[3](2, 3, 4). Each of these categories was rated by trained interviewers and observers on a six-point scale following observed interviews with the patient and a relative(5).

It is important to keep certain aspects of the experimental design in mind in evaluating findings. Patients were told at the start that they would be treated for 6 months, at which time their condition would be re-evaluated and further treatment would be available if necessary. The psychiatrists were asked to treat each patient for 6 months. One psychiatrist left the clinic at this time and the other two continued to see their patients. After the 6-month period various possibilities were open to the patients. Some continued with the same doctor in the same form of treatment. Others were switched to a different form of treatment, sometimes with the same doctor, sometimes with another doctor. Some sought treatment outside the clinic. Some stopped treatment altogether, or for a while and then returned for further treatment.[4]

The drop-outs, of course, did not continue with their original doctor. Some stopped treatment, others sought treatment from outside physicians. Some returned for treatment after a lapse of time. In short, the experiences of patients after the 6-month period were very heterogeneous, so that initial differences in the treatment experiences of the different groups would be expected to diminish with the passage of time.

Every effort was made to get patients to come back for their re-evaluations. With respect to the treated patients, our efforts were quite successful. Of 54, 53 returned for the one-year evaluation and 46 for the two-year evaluation.[5] We had much less

---

[3] The items on the Social Ineffectiveness Scale are: overly independent, superficially sociable, extra-punitive, officious, impulsive, hyper-reactive, overly systematic, overly dependent, withdrawn, intra-punitive, irresponsible, overly-cautious, constrained, unsystematic, sexual adjustment.

[4] Between the first and second re-evaluation, 6 months and 1 year after starting treatment respectively, 25 of the original 54 patients were still in the original design, *i.e.* receiving their original form of treatment with the same psychiatrist. An additional 12 had been in treatment with a different therapist or form of therapy, making a total of 37. By the third re-evaluation, 2 years after beginning treatment, these figures had dropped to 9 and 9 respectively, for a total of 18 patients still in treatment or 1/3 of the original population.

[5] Two additional treated patients, both of whom had individual therapy, who had left town by the time of the third re-evaluation, were mailed the Discomfort Scales, making a total of 48 scored on these measures.

success with the drop-outs, 15 of whom returned for the one-year evaluation but only 8 for the two-year evaluation.[6] As a result, the group of drop-outs who still had contact with the clinic at the one- and two-year re-evaluations may not be comparable with the initial group.

RESULTS

The results of this study are expressed in terms of changes in discomfort and social

─────────────

[6]. An Ineffectiveness Scale was filled out for one additional drop-out patient by means of a telephone interview, making a total of 9 scored on this measure.

ineffectiveness. These changes are expressed both in terms of relative frequencies of different types of change at each evaluation and in terms of mean scores. Since the therapeutic experiences of our patients could be controlled only during the first 6 months, results obtained at the first re-evaluation will be considered separately from the later ones.

1. Changes in Discomfort and Ineffectiveness at Six Months

Tables 1 and 2 summarize the changes in Discomfort Scale scores. Since these changes were found to be independent of the type of treatment patients received, the

TABLE 1

FREQUENCIES OF CHANGE FROM PREVIOUS SCORE ON DISCOMFORT SCALE AT SUCCESSIVE EVALUATIONS FOR TREATED AND DROP-OUT PATIENTS

		Improved		Same		Worse	
		N	%	N	%	N	%
1st Re-Eval. (6 months)	Treated (N = 54)	38	70	1	2	15	28
	Drop-Out (N = 23)	17	74	0	0	6	26
2nd Re-Eval. (1 year)	Treated (N = 53)	28	53	3	6	22	41
	Drop-Out (N = 15)	7	47	1	6	7	47
3rd Re-Eval. (2 years)	Treated (N = 48)	24	50	2	4	22	46
	Drop-Out (N = 8)	(4)	(50)	(0)	(0)	(4)	(50)

TABLE 2

MEAN SCORES ON DISCOMFORT SCALE INITIALLY AND AT SUCCESSIVE EVALUATIONS, FOR TREATED AND DROP-OUT PATIENTS

	Initial		1st Re-eval. 6 months		2nd Re-eval. 1 year		3rd Re-eval. 2 years	
	N	$\overline{X}$	N	$\overline{X}$	N	$\overline{X}$	N	$\overline{X}$
Treated	54	41.6	54	30.1*	53	28.6*	48	30.0*
Drop-Out	23	34.3	23	21.1*	15	26.3**	(8)	(26.5)

* Change from Initial Mean Score significant, $p < .001$.
** Change from Initial Mean Score significant, $p < .05$.

treated patients are handled as a single group. It will be seen from Table 1 that 70% of the treated patients showed a decrease in discomfort, as did 74% of the patients who dropped out of treatment within the first month and were first retested at 6 months.

As will be seen from Table 2, the same result holds for average discomfort scores. At the 6-month evaluation both treated and drop-out patients show a change which differs significantly from zero.

To see whether certain types of symptoms were more liable to change than others, two sub-scales were formed from the Discomfort Scale. One consisted of nine items which were thought clinically to reflect anxiety or depression. The other sub-scale of 16 items consisted of somatic symptoms. The results obtained for these 2 sub-scales are summarized in Table 3 which contains their weighted mean scores initially and at the time of the first evaluation. The sub-scales taken separately show the same trend as the total scale, but the anxiety and depression items were scored higher initially and changed more at 6 months than the somatic items. The greater liability of the former to change is in accordance with general clinical experience.

These findings suggest that the relief of

discomfort experienced by our patients was chiefly due to relief of anxiety and depression, and that it was produced by a factor common to all 3 forms of treatment used, which seemed to be equally potent regardless of the amount or type of treatment contact. Patients who left treatment before the fourth session showed an average drop in discomfort at least as great as those who stayed in treatment longer, and patients receiving individual, group or minimal contact therapy did not differ in their change scores on this measure.

The major results on the Social Ineffectiveness Scale, which is a measure of the patient's social functioning, are summarized in Table 4 which contains the relative frequencies of change at each evaluation, and Table 5 which contains the corresponding mean scores.

Table 4 shows that a higher percentage of patients improved at 6 months in group and individual therapy than in minimal therapy. They also improved more frequently than those who dropped out. Examination of the mean scores (Table 5)[7]

---

[7] It will be noted from Table 5 that patients who remained in group therapy tended to be less ineffective initially than those who remained in individual and minimal treatment, a finding discussed elsewhere (6).

TABLE 3

Weighted* Mean Scores on Anxiety-Depression and Somatic Sub-scales of Discomfort Scale

| | Weighted Mean Scores | | | |
| | Anxiety-Depression Sub-scale | | Somatic Sub-scale | |
	Initial Eval.	1st Re-eval. (6 months)	Initial Eval.	1st Re-eval. (6 months)
Treated Patients (N = 54)	1.63	1.07	.77	.61
Drop-out Patients (N = 23)	1.34	.77	.63	.44

* The sub-scales were weighted to make them comparable by dividing the sum total of the sub-scale raw scores by the total number of scorable items. Thus Anxiety and Depressive Score =

$$\Sigma A + D \text{ Scores} \over 9 \quad \text{and Somatic Score} = {\Sigma \text{Somatic Scores} \over 16}$$

TABLE 4

FREQUENCIES OF CHANGE FROM PREVIOUS SCORE ON INEFFECTIVENESS
SCALE AT SUCCESSIVE EVALUATIONS

| | First Re-Eval. (6 months) | | | | | |
| Treated (N = 54) | Improved | | Same | | Worse | |
	N	%	N	%	N	%
Group	14	78%	0	0%	4	22%
Individual	14	78%	1	5%	3	17%
Minimal	10	56%	0	0%	8	44%
Total	38	70%	1	2%	15	28%
Drop-Out (N = 23)	15	65%	1	4%	7	30%
	Second Re-Eval. (one year)					
Treated (N = 53)	Improved		Same		Worse	
	N	%	N	%	N	%
Group (18)	8	44%	0	0%	10	56%
Individual (18)	12	67%	0	0%	6	33%
Minimal (17)	10	59%	1	6%	6	35%
Total (53)	30	57%	1	2%	22	41%
Drop-Out (N = 15)	9	60%	0	0%	6	40%
	Third Re-Eval. (two years)					
Treated (N = 46)	Improved		Same		Worse	
	N	%	N	%	N	%
Group (15)	6	40%	2	13%	7	47%
Individual (16)	9	56%	0	0%	7	44%
Minimal (15)	11	73%	0	0%	4	27%
Total	26	57%	2	4%	18	39%
Drop-Out (N = 9)	(2)	(22%)	(1)	(11%)	(6)	(67%)

TABLE 5

MEAN SCORES ON INEFFECTIVENESS SCALE AT SUCCESSIVE
EVALUATIONS FOR TREATED AND DROP-OUT PATIENTS

	Mean Scores							
	Initial		Follow-up Evaluations					
			First		Second		Third	
			6 months		1 year		2 years	
Treated	N	$\overline{X}$	N	$\overline{X}$	N	$\overline{X}$	N	$\overline{X}$
Group Treatment	18	20.8	18	15.3	18	14.9	15	15.2
Individual	18	29.0	18	22.8	18	19.0	16	17.1
Minimal	18	26.1	18	25.1	17	23.0	15	20.1
Total Treated	54	25.3	54	21.1	53	18.9	46	17.5
Drop-Out	23	23.4	23	20.4	(15)	(18.2)	(9)	(20.4)

shows the same tendency. The mean ineffectiveness score of the combined population of patients receiving group and individual treatment showed a significantly
greater improvement than the mean of
those receiving minimal therapy, and also
than the mean of those who dropped out.[8]
Thus amount of improvement in ineffectiveness seems to be positively related to
amount of treatment contact. This finding
is in contrast to improvement in discomfort, which was independent of amount of
treatment.

2. Changes in Discomfort and Ineffectiveness After Six Months

As indicated above, after 6 months the
treatment experiences of the patients could
no longer be controlled, and at the time of
the third re-evaluation, 2 years after the
beginning of the study, only one-third were
still in treatment in the clinic. At this time
it was possible to re-evaluate approximately
85% of the original treated population, so
that it would seem safe to regard the results
as characteristic of the total treated group.
The same cannot be said for the drop-outs,
only about 35% of whom could be re-
evaluated after 2 years. After 6 months there
is no consistent pattern of change for the
group as a whole on the Discomfort Scale
(Table 1). On each re-evaluation subsequent to the first, about half of the treated
patients who returned improved, and half
became worse. Of the drop-out population,
those who returned for re-evaluations
showed precisely the same tendency. Similarly, after 6 months neither the treated patients nor the drop-out patients who returned showed any significant change in
the mean discomfort score (Table 2).

To determine whether continuation in
treatment had any effect on discomfort
scores after 6 months, at each evaluation
period patients who were still in their initial
type of treatment were compared with the

rest of the group with respect to change
from the previous evaluation. No differences in frequency of change or in average
change were found, suggesting that the
persistence of a lowered discomfort score
after the 6-months re-evaluation did not
depend on whether or not the patients remained in any particular form of treatment.

The findings on the Discomfort Scale at
6 months and at follow-up raise two questions: firstly, are they simply the result of
repeating the scale? secondly, how early
does the relief of discomfort actually occur?

With respect to the first question, it
might be argued that unfamiliarity with
the test and the setting aroused some anxiety on its first use, which was reflected in
heightened discomfort scores. The second
discomfort score could then be construed
as representing the patient's baseline of discomfort, which would explain why it
showed no consistent changes after the second testing. According to this view, the
discomfort score may have been unaffected
by the treatment contact throughout the
study, but dropped initially simply because
anxiety connected with administration of
the test itself was less on its repetition (7).

The alternative view, equally compatible
with the data, is that the relief of discomfort resulted from a feature common to all
forms of treatment, namely the patient's
belief that he was being helped. Activation
of this belief ordinarily would not depend
on the nature or length of the treatment.
It would start to operate as soon as patient
and physician met, and would not be affected in any consistent way by subsequent
length of treatment contact. Accordingly,
it would be expected to produce a certain
degree of relief immediately, which then
would stay relatively constant.

Since a placebo activates the expectancy
of help in many patients, it affords a simple
way of testing the effects of this attitude
(8,9). Twelve patients of the orginal population, who were having routine follow-up
interviews 2 to 3 years after their first con-

---

[8] $p < .01$ and $< .05$ respectively.

tact with the project, were given a 2 weeks' trial on placebo. These patients had complaints similar to their initial ones and expressed a desire for relief. No psychotherapeutic sessions were held during the trial of placebo. The Discomfort Scale used throughout this project was given at the beginning and at the end of the placebo administration period. A statistically significant drop in discomfort score occurred, which was of the same order of magnitude as that following the initial 6 months of psychotherapy. Since with these patients the drop in discomfort occurred between the third and fourth administrations of the scale, the factor of familiarity may be excluded as an explanation of the result(10).

If the initial drop in discomfort is a result of the patient's belief that he is being helped, it becomes of interest to find out how promptly this belief is activated. In our study, unless patients dropped out of treatment after the first month but before the sixth month, they did not receive the Discomfort Scale until 6 months after their initial contact. The small group of patients who left treatment between the first and sixth months received the second Discomfort Scale at the point they stopped. There are too few of these patients and the range of their scores is too wide to permit statistical analyses, but it is interesting that their mean change score is the same as that for patients evaluated at 6 months. This suggests that patients who showed discomfort relief at 6 months might have shown it earlier had they been tested.

The placebo study reported above showed a marked drop in discomfort at two weeks. In a current study, we give patients similar to those in this study a modified form of the Discomfort Scale twice in the same interview, once just before receiving a placebo, and again about one hour later. The scale is repeated the following week. We are finding that many patients show marked relief of discomfort even within an hour. The degree of relief does not appear to be increased by receiving the placebo for the subsequent week. This is consistent with the hypothesis that the diminution of discomfort is a response to the patient's expectancy of help, which presumably is often strongly activated early in his contact with the doctor.

It seems safe to conclude from these findings that the drop in discomfort observed at 6 months in this study probably would have been found much earlier had it been tested, and that it was not due to mere repetition of the test.

The findings on the Social Ineffectiveness Scale after 6 months differed from those with respect to discomfort in that the treated patients continue to show progressive improvement in effectiveness (Tables 4 and 5),[9] whereas they show no further changes, on the average, in discomfort.

Although patients who initially received different forms of treatment seemed to improve in ineffectiveness at different rates, the meaning of these differences cannot be interpreted, because of the heterogeneity of patients' treatment experience after 6 months.

3. Relationship between Changes in Discomfort and Ineffectiveness

It seems apparent that changes in discomfort in response to psychotherapy reflect, at least in part, a different process than changes in social ineffectiveness. Further evidence in support of this view is afforded by the product moment correlations between changes in these two measures. For the treated patients, these correlations are .37 $(p < .01)$ at the first re-evaluation, .23 $(p < .10)$ between the first and second re-evaluations, and .30

---

[9] For the treated patients as a whole the difference between the initial and the first evaluations is significant at less than .01; between the first and second, at less than .05; and between the second and third, at less than .10.

The drop-out sample shows a similar trend up to one year, then a reversal, but attrition is so great after 6 months that the findings are uninterpretable.

$(p < .05)$ between the second and third re-evaluations. They are positive, but low, and only one achieves adequate statistical significance.

DISCUSSION

These findings are consistent with the assumption that the effects of psychotherapy depend on 2 interrelated factors: 1. The potentiation and activation of the patient's favorable expectancies and 2. Changes in attitudes and behavior depending on specific situational influences. In shorthand fashion the latter may be summarized as the unlearning of faulty attitudes and relearning of better ones, though we believe that many processes besides learning in the narrower sense may be involved.

The potentiation of favorable expectancies results chiefly in relief of the patient's subjective distress, especially that part of it related to anxiety and depression. These may be viewed as manifestations of the patient's apprehensiveness about his condition, the so-called "processing" aspect of illness (11).

Although the existence of this effect is common knowledge, it is characteristically dismissed as of little theoretical or practical interest. Actually, little is known about the conditions in patient and situation determining its extent and duration (12, 13). Our findings suggest that it often occurs very quickly, and that its intensity is unrelated to the type or duration of treatment. This would be expected, since any form of activity by a person culturally defined as healer may activate a patient's belief that he is being helped. In this study mere sight of the doctor or the first interchange seems to have been sufficient.

Changes due to exposure to a social learning situation would be expected to appear in the patient's social behavior. Such changes would differ in at least 2 respects from those due simply to a patient's belief that he was being helped. They should be more gradual and the kind of change should be related to the kind of situation to which the patient is exposed. In this study it was found that change in social ineffectiveness tended to improve throughout the period of observation, and the amount of change at 6 months seemed related to the amount of therapeutic contact.

Although changes in discomfort and social ineffectiveness thus appear to represent different therapeutic processes, one would expect them to be related in at least 3 ways. First, the scales overlap slightly in that some items on the ineffectiveness scale—for example, hyper-reactivity—are also indirect measures of subjective distress. Second, the relief patients experience from their expectancy of help probably frees their spontaneity, enables them to mobilize latent assets, and in general creates more favorable conditions for learning. Third, as a patient, by functioning more effectively, gains more rewards and suffers fewer frustrations, he should feel more comfortable. The low positive correlations found between changes in discomfort and ineffectiveness are consistent with these considerations.

This relationship between improvement in discomfort and ineffectiveness may account for the fact that, contrary to the usual supposition, relief of discomfort is often persistent. In some of our patients it lasted for at least 2 years, even without continuing contact with a therapist. Symptomatic relief, based on the expectancy of help, probably improved the morale of these patients and so made it easier for them to change maladaptive behavior patterns, which, in turn, reinforced their symptomatic improvement, as described above.

Although experimental studies of psychotherapy have accumulated much interesting information as to effects of the therapist's behavior on the patient's responses, surveys have consistently failed to reveal any overall differences in improvement rates of different therapies (14). This may be due to failure to understand adequately and take into account changes produced by the factor common to all therapies—the patient's expectancy that the treatment will help him. Only as the parameters of these changes are defined and controlled can the specific effects of different forms of treatment, if there be any, clearly emerge.

SUMMARY

A group of psychiatric outpatients received either individual psychotherapy, group psychotherapy or minimal therapy for about 6 months. After 6 months the treatment experiences of the patients became increasingly varied. Patients were rated with respect to change in subjective discomfort and social ineffectiveness at 6 months and at regular follow-up intervals up to 2 years. It was found that at 6 months the average discomfort had markedly decreased, and that the decrease was the same regardless of kind or amount of treatment. Symptoms of anxiety and depression tended to be scored higher initially and to decline more than somatic complaints. Subsequent studies with these and similar patients showed that a similar drop in discomfort could be found within one week, or even in the course of a single interview.

A significant improvement in social ineffectiveness also was found at 6 months. It was significantly greater for patients who had received group or individual therapy than for those in minimal therapy or those who dropped out within 4 sessions.

After 6 months, improvement in discomfort was maintained but did not increase, whereas social ineffectiveness continued to improve throughout the observational period.

These results are consistent with the view that improvement in psychotherapy may be produced by at least 2 factors: 1. Non-specific expectancy of relief; 2. Relearning, which is related to the amount and kind of treatment contact.

BIBLIOGRAPHY

1. PARLOFF, M. B., KELMAN, H. C., and FRANK, J. D. Am. J. Psychiat., 111, 343, 1954.
2. Ibid.
3. KELMAN, H. C. and PARLOFF, M. B. J. Abnorm. and Soc. Psych., 54, 281, 1957.
4. FRANK, J. D. Problems of Controls in Psychotherapy as Exemplified by the Psychotherapy Research Project of the Phipps Psychiatric Clinic, paper presented at the Conference on Research in Psychotherapy, Division of Clinical Psychology, American Psychological Association, April 1958. In press.
5. FRANK, J. D., GLIEDMAN, L. H., IMBER, S. D., NASH, E. H., and STONE, A. R. AMA Arch. Neurol. and Psychiat., 77, 283, 1957.
6. NASH, E. H., FRANK, J. D., GLIEDMAN, L. H., IMBER, S. D., and STONE, A. R. Internat. J. Group Psychother., 7, 264, 1957.
7. JACOBS, A. and LEVENTER, S. J. Abnorm. and Soc. Psych., 51, 449, 1955.
8. WHITEHORN, J. C. Am. J. Psychiat., 114, 662, 1958.
9. ROSENTHAL, D. and FRANK, J. D. Psychol. Bull., 53, 294, 1956.
10. GLIEDMAN, L. H., NASH, E. H., IMBER, S. D., STONE, A. R., and FRANK, J. D. AMA Arch. Neurol. and Psychiat., 79, 345, 1958.
11. BEECHER, H. K. J.A.M.A., 159, 1602, 1955.
12. FRANK, J. D. The Dynamics of the Psychotherapeutic Relationship, 1. Determinants and Effects of the Therapist's influence, Psychiatry. In press.
13. ROSENTHAL, D. and FRANK, J. D. Op. cit.
14. APPEL, K. E., LHAMON, W. T., MEYERS, J. M., and HARVEY, W. A. Long Term Psychotherapy, in Psychiatric Treatment, Proceedings of the Association for Research in Nervous and Mental Disease, 1951, Baltimore: Williams and Wilkins Co., 1953.

Reinforcement in a Therapy-like Situation Through Selective Responding to Feelings or Content[1]

IRENE E. WASKOW

This study is concerned with a simple type of learning that may occur early in psychotherapy. The general hypothesis is that a therapist may, by selective responding, reinforce those verbalizations that he considers important. The specific hypothesis being tested is that selective therapist responding will function as a reinforcer of the feeling or content aspects of a patient's communications.

Although there are many references in the theoretical literature to learning that occurs during psychotherapy (see Shoben, 1948, 1953 for review), only two research-

Reprinted from *Journal of Consulting Psychology*, 1962, 26 (1), 11–19, with the permission of the American Psychological Association and the author. Note 2, containing information about the author's affiliation, has been omitted.

[1] This paper is based on a PhD dissertation at the University of Wisconsin. The author is indebted to Barclay Martin under whose supervision the research was conducted, to David Grant and Carl Rogers who served on the research committee, and to Vilma Ginzberg and Tom Tomlinson who served as raters.

ers have rigorously studied events in therapy within a learning framework. Murray (1956) demonstrated increases or decreases in content areas which were encouraged or discouraged by a therapist and Dittes (1957) interpreted his results as extinction of fear connected with making embarrassing sex statements in therapy. Both of these researchers obtained their data from recordings of normally conducted psychotherapy sessions. In order to relate clearly the behavior of the therapist to the learning of the patient, in the present study the therapist's behavior was manipulated and its effects on patient behavior investigated.

Manipulation of the experimenter's behavior and the study of its effect on the subject's learning have been commonly employed by experimental psychologists. Of special relevance here are studies of verbal conditioning, in which the experimenter attempts, through selective responding, to reinforce a particular class of verbal responses. Most of these studies (see Krasner, 1958, for review) have demonstrated an increase in the frequency of the reinforced response class. Many writers have compared the procedures in these studies to the events that take place in therapy and Krasner (1955) has specifically emphasized the value of using the verbal conditioning paradigm to investigate variables in psychotherapy. The inference here is that the therapist may selectively respond to particular patient verbalizations. The experimental conditions in most studies of verbal conditioning differ radically, however, from those which obtain in psychotherapy. For example, many of these studies have utilized only simple responses of "umhmm" or "good" as reinforcing stimuli; the verbalizations reinforced have frequently been grammatical categories such as plural nouns or the choice of "I" or "we" from among six pronouns in beginning a sentence; and the experiments have generally been conducted in an experimental laboratory situation.

A few studies have approached the therapy situation more closely, by using more complex categories of reinforcing behavior, e.g., agreement with or paraphrasing of a response (Verplanck, 1955), or by reinforcing response classes more relevant to therapy, e.g., hostile responses (Binder, McConnell, & Sjoholm, 1957; Buss & Durkee, 1958), family as opposed to non-family memories (Quay, 1959), and self-references (Adams & Hoffman, 1960; Rogers, 1960). Several experiments reported since this study was undertaken have specifically dealt with the reinforcement of "feeling" responses. Levine (1958) attempted to reinforce expressions of feeling in fairly free interview situations, and Salzinger and Pisoni (1958, 1960) conditioned affect responses in both normals and schizophrenics in a situation closely resembling a traditional diagnostic interview.

In the present study, the verbal conditioning paradigm was used in a laboratory situation as closely as possible resembling psychotherapy. Accordingly, the experimenter introduced the study to student volunteers as a therapy-like experience. The class of reinforcing stimuli was reflection of certain aspects of the subjects' communications, a technique utilized at times by many therapists. It was hypothesized that such reflection would fulfill Skinner's (1953) criteria for a reinforcing stimulus. The response categories reinforced, the feeling as opposed to the content aspects of subjects' communications, have been emphasized in both theoretical and research writings of client centered orientation (Rogers, 1942; Seeman, 1954), and are of relevance to the widely held view that expression of previously punished feelings in the presence of a nonpunishing therapist is essential for new learning to occur in therapy (see, e.g., Dollard & Miller, 1950).

METHOD

The therapist selectively responded to different types of material in each of three experimental groups. In one group (Group F), she responded to references to the subjects' feelings and attitudes, in another (Group C), to the descriptive and intellectual content of the communication, and a third group (Group FC), to a combination of feelings and content.

Subjects

Thirty-six subjects were used, 12 in each of the experimental conditions. The experimenter asked students in discussion sections of an introductory psychology course to serve in the experiment for points which might improve their grades. They were told that the experiment involved research in psychological interviewing and psychotherapy and they were asked to volunteer only if they were interested in and felt that they could profit from a therapy-like experience. This procedure was used in order to obtain subjects at least minimally motivated for psychotherapy. Of the volunteers only those who had scores in the upper two thirds of a scale of manifest anxiety (Hein-

eman, 1953) were asked to come for preliminary interviews, since topics they would
deal with might more closely resemble
therapy material. A volunteer who was
currently in psychotherapy was dropped.

Preliminary Interview[3]

In the preliminary interview, lasting 15
minutes, the experimenter first assured subjects of the confidentiality of the tape recordings and then instructed them to:

. . . pretend that you are having your first
visit at a counseling center and . . . discuss
things that you think you might talk about if
you had gone to such a center for help, telling
something about yourself and about matters
that you have been thinking about or that have
been troubling you, and so on.

Subjects were asked to talk into the
microphone, and the experimenter then
left the room, so that there could be no
accidental differential reinforcement during
this preliminary interview.

The experimenter later listened to the
taped interviews and assigned each a global
rating on a seven-point scale, in which a
rating of 1 was given to interviews with
major emphasis on the feelings of the subject, 4 to interviews with equal emphasis
on feelings and content, and 7 to interviews
with major emphasis on content. The position of the subjects was largely toward the
content end of the scale. The 36 subjects
were ranked according to these ratings and
then assigned to twelve triplets, ranks 1–3
in one triplet, ranks 4–6 in the next, etc.
Subjects within each triplet were randomly
assigned to the three conditions, with the
restriction that each group contain 10 of the
30 female subjects and two of the six
males. With subjects in the three groups

---

[3] GSRs were recorded for all interviews, but
will not be discussed in this article. Although the
therapist's impression was that subjects were generally not very concerned about the GSR recordings, there is no data to support this impression
and it is possible that they may have influenced
the results.

matched for initial level of expressing feeling and content, any differences among the
groups due to differential reinforcement
might be expected to emerge clearly.

Experimental Sessions

Each subject was seen for four experimental interviews, two a week for 2 weeks.
These sessions extended over a 6-week
period, with four matched triplets seen
during each consecutive 2 weeks. The experimenter functioned as therapist and conducted all of the 30-minute interviews. All
interviews were tape recorded. At the beginning of the first interview, subjects were
told to consider this their first session and
to talk about the same types of things they
were asked to discuss during the preliminary interview, the only difference being
the presence of the therapist. If possible,
no further instructions were given throughout the interviews. At the beginning of
each, the therapist said she would like to
continue as before. Occasionally, during an
interview, a subject could not proceed. Only
general suggestions were made at such
times, such as "Any other things you've
been thinking about?" and "Maybe something that's troubled you in the past?"
Such suggestions occurred only once or
twice for most subjects.

The therapist attempted to respond
whenever a subject paused at the end of a
sentence or group of sentences concerning
one topic. The chief technique used was
a reflection of the subject's communication:
the therapist attempted to mirror, in her
own words, some aspect of what the subject
had said. This type of responding, in both
F and FC groups, is similar to what has
been called "reflection of feeling" in the
client centered literature (Bergman, 1951).
In the FC group, the therapist's response
included content as well as feelings, while
in the F group only feelings were reflected.
Although the therapist's reflections were
largely based on the subjects' explicit verbal
statements, she also responded to feelings

indirectly expressed through voice tone and through facial and bodily movements. The therapist's responses to subjects in the C condition were similar to what has been called "restatement of content" (Snyder, 1945).

Following is an illustration of the way in which the therapist might have responded to the same subject communication in each of the three conditions.

Subject: Sometimes my father yells at my mother—over just about nothing. But, boy, can he get mad. And I don't like it one bit when he does that.

Therapist:

F: You really get upset about that.

FC: You feel real upset when you father gets mad at your mother about things that don't matter.

C: Sometimes your father gets real mad and yells at your mother about little things.

Aside from the manipulation of the variable being studied, the therapist attempted to keep conditions as similar as possible for all three experimental groups. Since examination of early pilot interviews had suggested that the theapist sounded less interested and less warm in the C condition than in the others, she continued pilot work until it appeared that this variable was held constant. The therapist also attempted to maintain a constant frequency of responding in the three conditions, and an analysis of variance of the number of responses in each interview revealed no significant differences among the three groups. According to the therapist's retrospective account, the FC condition seemed most similar to psychotherapy and was quite easily implemented. Responses in the C condition often seemed superficial and those in the F condition sometimes seemed to distort the subject's meaning due to the separation of feelings from the context in which they appeared.

At the end of the fourth interview, subjects were given a questionnaire, which they were asked to return to the mailbox of "another psychologist interested in subjects' reactions to the experiment." The major purpose of the questionnaire was to assess, in various ways, the subjects' awareness of the selective responding by the therapist. Subjects were asked, e.g., which of several areas they thought should be stressed in therapy, what areas had actually been stressed in their sessions, etc.

Finally, the experimenter held a 5-minute interview with each subject, in which the subject discussed his hypotheses about the purpose of the experiment.

Rating of Interview Material

Ratings of the subjects' responses were made directly from the tape recordings. A subject response was defined as any communication which was surrounded by two therapist responses. Brief interruptions during a therapist's response were not rated. A list of rules for classifying responses, which had been developed in pilot work, was used for guiding decisions in difficult instances. Each response was classified as predominantly F, FC, or C or, when necessary, one-half credit was given to F and FC or to C and FC. These ratings sometimes depended on more than the simple presence or absence of words denoting feeling, since tone of voice was also taken into consideration. No inferences were made, however, about underlying emotional states, and interpretation of results must be limited to the conditioning of explicit expressions of feeling.

The therapist rated all interviews, listening to an entire tape and classifying each response as it was completed. Parts of an interview were replayed only if they could not be heard clearly or if listening was interrupted. A second rater, an advance graduate student in clinical psychology, rated 24 of the interviews for an estimate of interrater reliability. The 24 interviews were randomly selected except for the restrictions that they include two each of the first, second, third, and fourth interviews in each of the three conditions and that there be not more than one interview per subject. As a check on the objectivity of the ratings, the second rater heard only the subjects' statements and was not aware of the experimental condition in which a subject was placed. The interrater reliability of the F-FC-C profiles for the 24 interviews, as estimated by Mosier's formula (Guilford, 1954), was .81.

For testing the consistency of the therapist's responding in the three conditions, 36 10-minute segments were extracted from the interviews. These included one segment of an interview with each of the 36 subjects, and each condition was represented by a segment from the first, second, and third 10-minute periods of each of the four interviews. The therapist's responses were categorized by a graduate student, who had previously practiced making such categorizations with the therapist, as focusing predominantly on feeling (F), content (C), or feeling combined with content (FC), and the percentages of F, FC, and C responses were computed for each segment. For the entire sample of 12 segments in the F condition, the therapist made 77% F, 22% FC, and 1% C responses. In the FC condition, she made 84% FC, 14% F, and 2% C responses, and in the C condition, 88% C and 12% FC responses. In 34 of the 36 samples, the therapist responded most frequently with the response called for by the experimental condition. In one FC sample, she responded predominantly with F responses, and in one F sample, with FC responses.

RESULTS

In order to test for changes in the F-FC-C profiles of subjects over interviews, the analysis of variance applied was a trend test (Grant, 1956) analyzed so as to reveal differences in profiles (Block, Levine, & McNemar, 1951). Since the data departed to some degree from the distribution characteristics of normality and homogeneity of variance, a probability level of .01 was stipulated for accepting a result as significant. The results of the analysis are presented in Table 1 and the mean percentages for the three groups over interviews are plotted in Figure 1.

The significant interaction between categories and groups tends to support the major hypothesis: the subjects in the different experimental conditions did produce different patterns of responses in the F, FC, and C categories. Three Duncan range tests (Duncan, 1955) were used to compare the means for the groups in the three categories. Although the groups did not differ

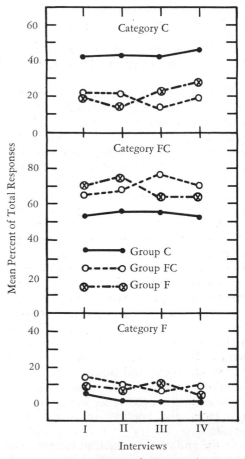

Fig. 1. Mean percentages of responses in categories F, FC, and C for three groups over interviews.

TABLE 1

ANALYSIS OF PERCENTAGE OF RESPONSES IN F, FC, AND C CATEGORIES FOR F, FC, AND C GROUPS OVER INTERVIEWS

Source of variation[a]	df	MS	F
Between means			
Categories	2	12.3276	222.52*
Groups × categories	4	.6621	11.95*
Between individual means	66	.0554	
Between linear trends			
Categories	2	.0285	1.86
Groups × categories	4	.0296	1.93
Between individual linear trends	66	.0153	
Between quadratic trends			
Categories	2	.0313	3.19
Groups × categories	4	.0077	—
Between individual quadratic trends	66	.0098	
Between cubic trends			
Categories	2	.0023	—
Groups × categories	4	.0222	2.06
Between individual cubic trends	64[b]	.0108	
Total	286[c]		

[a] No differences possible among treatment groups, since F, FC, and C scores must sum to 100% in all interviews for all groups.
[b] Degrees of freedom reduced by two, because missing values estimated for one interview (Cochran & Cox, 1950).
[c] Requirement that three scores sum to 100% results in loss of one degree of freedom for each interview, thus total df reduced by one third.
* Significant at .01 level.

significantly in the percentage of F responses they made, Group C made a significantly higher percentage of C responses and a significantly lower percentage of FC responses than did either of the other groups. There were no significant differences between groups FC and F and no significant trends over interviews. Thus, although Group C had a greater relative amount of C throughout the experiment, there were no consistent changes in the percentages in different categories over the four interviews. The only other significant finding was the higher overall percentage of FC responses. Even in Group C, FC responses continued throughout the interviews to constitute more than 50% of the total responses.

Since differences in the percentage of C responses appeared as early as the first interview, an analysis was performed to see whether an increase in C responses in the C group could be found within the first interview. The interview was divided into sixths according to the number of responses made and a trend analysis identical to the one cited above was performed. The results of this analysis are presented in Table 2 and the mean percentages of F, FC, and C responses for sixths of the first interview are plotted in Figure 2. Within the first interview, significant results were again found for the difference between categories and for the category-group interaction. In addition, the component of the difference between quadratic trends which may be attributed to the group-category interaction was found to be significant. Thus, although

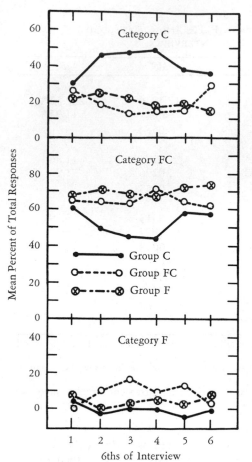

Fig. 2. Mean percentages of responses in categories F, FC, and C for the three groups during the first interview.

the C responses made by the C group did not increase in a linear fashion, they did show an increase during the first part of the first interview, with a reciprocal decrease in FC responses, and it is the initial increase which seems responsible for the higher level of C responses found in the first interview for the C group. Examination of the graphs plotting sixths of the other interviews suggests that the percentage of C responses for the three groups remains fairly stable within each of the interviews following the first one.

There appeared to be no general aware-

ness of the material being reinforced. Subjects in the three groups did not differ significantly (Friedman's test in Siegel, 1956), in the extent to which they believed different types of material had been stressed in the interviews. Also, no subject was able, when questioned at the conclusion of the experiment and after administration of the questionnaire, to state correctly the purpose of the experiment or even to approach an adequate explanation.

DISCUSSION

The major hypothesis of this study was partially supported. Selective responding to the content aspects of subjects' communications did result in a higher percentage of content responses. An increase in C responses for the C group took place within the first third of the first interview and the higher level was maintained throughout the rest of the interviews. Thus, reflection of content did function as a positive reinforcer. This finding demonstrates the occurrence of verbal conditioning in a situation closely resembling psychotherapy, in that the experiment was described to subjects as a therapy-like experience and the response class reinforced and the class of reinforcing stimuli were relevant to psychotherapy.

The successful reinforcement of content responses within the first interview leads to an interesting speculation: may such reinforcement early in therapy by some information-oriented therapists cause difficulties in their later attempts to focus on patients' feelings? To help answer this question, it would be necessary to obtain extinction as well as learning data, preferably comparing extinction of C responses through nonreinforcement and through reinforcement of F or FC responses.

Although the C group showed successful conditioning, selective responding to feelings (F group) and to a combination of feelings and content (FC group) did not function as reinforcers. For the FC

TABLE 2

ANALYSIS OF PERCENTAGE OF RESPONSES IN F, FC, AND C CATEGORIES FOR
F, FC, AND C GROUPS OVER SIXTHS OF THE FIRST INTERVIEW

Source of variation[a]	df	MS	F
Between means			
Categories	2	16.3892	97.32*
Groups × categories	4	.9104	5.41*
Between individual means	66	.1684	
Between linear trends			
Categories	2	.0231	—
Groups × categories	4	.0223	—
Between individual linear trends	66	.0445	
Between quadratic trends			
Categories	2	.0377	1.46
Groups × categories	4	.2059	7.95*
Between individual quadratic trends	66	.0259	
Between cubic trends			
Categories	2	.0355	1.35
Groups × categories	4	.0160	—
Between individual cubic trends	66	.0262	
Residual	144		
Total	432[b]		

[a] No differences possible among treatment groups, since F, FC, and C scores must sum to 100% in all interviews for all groups.
[b] Requirement that three scores sum to 100% results in loss of one degree of freedom for each interview, thus total df reduced by one third.
* Significant at .01 level.

group, examination of the data of the second and third interviews suggests that possibly a slower and less striking conditioning occurred than for the C group, an effect not large enough to reach statistical significance. Since all groups had an initially high level of FC responses (between 60 and 70%), there may not have been much room for a significant increase in these responses to occur. Although the high level of FC responses throughout may seem to indicate willingness of subjects to deal with emotional material, the FC responses made were largely concerned with feelings about relatively conflict-free, conversational subject matter. The FC responses so clearly dominated the interviews that, even in the successfully conditioned C group, the increased percentage of C responses did not exceed the percentage of FC responses.

The F responses, in contrast to the FC responses, frequently dealt with personal and troubling feelings. Although the percentage of F responses was relatively low at the beginning of the experiment, thus allowing considerable room for increase, selective responding to feelings did not result in the predicted increase in these responses. Even those subjects with a relatively high initial level of expression of feelings were not successfully conditioned. In the only other study in which reflections of feeling were used in an attempt to reinforce expressions of feeling (Levine, 1958), there was a similar lack of reinforcing effects. Since Levine also failed to condition expressions of feeling with the use of an "umhmm" reinforcer, one might suspect a difficulty inherent in the class of responses being reinforced. Salzinger and Pisoni (1958, 1960), however, present contradictory evidence: they have successfully reinforced statements of affect by the use of such reinforcing stimuli as "umhmm," "yeah," and "I see." Differences between the Salzinger and Pisoni studies and the Levine "umhmm" condition will not be discussed here, since we are primarily concerned with the disparity between our results and those of Salzinger and Pisoni. There are several ways in which the present experiment differs from those of Salzinger and Pisoni. The responses reinforced in the Salzinger and Pisoni studies were defined as all statements beginning with "I" and "we" followed by an expression of affect. Thus, since the class of responses reinforced as well as the class of reinforcing stimuli was less complex and more clearly defined than that in the present study, the contingency between the reinforcing stimulus and the reinforced responses may have appeared more clearly and may, therefore, have been more effective. The response-reinforcement contingency in the present setting was, however, sufficiently clear for the reinforcement of C responses to occur.[4]

A more important difference between this study and the Salzinger and Pisoni experiments may lie in the nature of the reinforcing stimulus. The utterance of "umhmm" or "yeah" may have simple positive connotations for a subject and may thus result in an automatic reinforcement of the preceding subject verbalizations. The reflection of a feeling, however, may cause a subject to look at his feeling and to realize that another person is also aware of it. Within the context of the present experi-

mental situation, this procedure may have been somewhat unpleasant and anxiety arousing, especially since the student volunteers seemed to prefer chatting to dealing with troubled emotions. Thus, aversive qualities of the reflection of feeling may have interfered with its proposed function as a positive reinforcer.

Under different conditions, reflection of feelings might function as a reinforcer of expressions of feelings. Recent studies (Mandler & Kaplan, 1956; Sapolsky, 1960; Sarason, 1958) have demonstrated the effects on verbal conditioning of such variables as subject personality, characteristics of the subject-experimenter interaction, and subjects' interpretation of the reinforcing stimulus. Manipulation of such variables within the context of the present study might lead to results different from those obtained. For example, individuals more similar to actual psychotherapy patients may have higher levels of expressing troubling feelings and more motivation to deal with them; they might, therefore, interpret the reflection of feelings as a positive stimulus. Also, as is probably the case in therapy, the therapist may first have to establish himself as a generally positive figure before he can successfully reinforce expressions of feeling. It is interesting to note here that Salzinger and Pisoni did have a 10-minute period of introductory questions in which the therapist reinforced everything the patient said.

In the present setting, selective responding to feelings did not function as a positive reinforcer. Thus, conditioning of subjects' verbal behavior in a therapy-like setting was not as easily achieved as one might predict on the basis of the verbal conditioning literature. In order to justify generalizations to psychotherapy from the learning literature, the complex variables which may influence learning in the therapy situation must be recognized and studied.

The finding that subjects were not aware of the selective responding to certain aspects of their communications is in agree-

---

[4] It is possible that the F condition differed from both the C condition and from Salzinger and Pisoni's procedure in having a longer latency of the therapist's responses. Although the therapist's impression is that the latencies were fairly constant in the different conditions, the recordings are no longer available for study of this variable.

ment with the frequent reports of lack of awareness in the verbal conditioning literature (see Krasner, 1958). The subjects in the present study seemed simply to accept the therapist's conduct as prescribed by a particular type of psychotherapy and were chiefly concerned with what they could find to talk about.

SUMMARY

This study tested the hypothesis that selective responding by a therapist would function as a reinforcer of content or feeling aspects of a subject's communications. Three experimental groups were utilized, one in which the therapist reflected feeling aspects of the subjects' communications (Group F), one in which she reflected a combination of feelings and specific content (Group FC), and a third in which she reflected content only (Group C).

The 36 student subjects had volunteered to participate in a therapy-like experiment. Triplets of subjects were matched for level of expressing feeling and content in a preliminary interview and were then randomly assigned to the three groups. Each subject was seen for four 30-minute experimental interviews spaced over a period of 2 weeks. An analysis of the therapist's responses indicated that the experimental conditions in the three groups had been established reliably.

The subjects' responses were categorized as consisting predominantly of feeling elements (F), content (C), or a combination (FC). An analysis of the ratings revealed a significant difference in the F-FC-C profiles for the three groups, due to a higher percentage of C responses, and a correspondingly lower percentage of FC responses, for the C group. No significant trends were found over interviews. In a separate analysis of the first interview, a significant difference was found in quadratic trends over sixths of the interview for the group-category interaction. An initial increase in the C responses for the C group appeared responsible for the overall

differences found. Thus the C group was successfully reinforced and the major effects of the reinforcement could be seen within the first third of the first interview. No significant differences were found between the F and FC groups and they showed no clear effects of reinforcement.

The questionnaire results and discussion with the subjects following the experiment suggested a lack of awareness by the subjects of the selective responding by the therapist.

The results for the content group constitute an extension of the verbal conditioning literature by demonstrating successful conditioning in a situation closely resembling psychotherapy. The lack of reinforcement in the F group suggests the presence in this setting of aversive properties in the reflection of feelings. The complex variables of the therapy situation must be considered and approached experimentally before generalizations are made from the verbal conditioning literature to psychotherapy.

REFERENCES

ADAMS, J. S., & HOFFMAN, B. The frequency of self-reference statements as a function of generalized reinforcement. *J. abnorm. soc. Psychol.,* 1960, 60, 384–389.

BERGMAN, D. V. Counseling method and client responses. *J. consult. Psychol.,* 1951, 15, 216–224.

BINDER, A., McCONNELL, D., & SJOHOLM, NANCY A. Verbal conditioning as a function of experimenter characteristics. *J. abnorm. soc. Psychol.,* 1957, 55, 309–314.

BLOCK, J., LEVINE, L., & McNEMAR, Q. Testing for the existence of psychometric patterns. *J. abnorm. soc. Psychol.,* 1951, 46, 356–359.

BUSS, A. H., & DURKEE, ANN. Conditioning of hostile verbalizations in a situation resembling a clinical interview. *J. consult. Psychol.,* 1958, 22, 415–418.

COCHRAN, W. G., & COX, GERTRUDE M. *Experimental designs.* New York: Wiley, 1950.

DITTES, J. E. Extinction during psychotherapy of GSR accompanying "embarrassing" statements. *J. abnorm. soc Psychol.,* 1957, 54, 187–191.

DOLLARD, J., & MILLER, N. E. *Personality and psychotherapy.* New York: McGraw-Hill, 1950.

DUNCAN, D. B. Multiple range and multiple *F* tests. *Biometrics,* 1955, 11, 1–42.

GRANT, D. A. Analysis-of-variance tests in the analysis and comparison of curves. *Psychol Bull.,* 1956, 53, 141–154.

GUILFORD, J. P. *Psychometric methods.* (2nd ed.) New York: McGraw-Hill, 1954.

HEINEMAN, C. E. A forced-choice form of the Taylor anxiety scale. *J. consult. Psychol.,* 1953, 17, 447–454.

KRASNER, L. The use of generalized reinforcers in psychotherapy research. *Psychol. Rep.,* 1955, 1, 19–25.

KRASNER, L. Studies of the conditioning of verbal behavior. *Psychol. Bull.,* 1958, 55, 148–170.

LEVINE, G. The effects of two verbal techniques on the expression of feelings. Unpublished doctoral dissertation, Columbia University, 1958.

MANDLER, G., & KAPLAN, W. K. Subjective evaluation and reinforcing effect of a verbal stimulus. *Science,* 1956, 124, 582–583.

MURRAY, E. J. A content-analysis method for studying psychotherapy. *Psychol. Monogr.,* 1956, 70 (13, Whole No. 420).

QUAY, H. The effect of verbal reinforcement on the recall of early memories. *J. abnorm. soc. Psychol.,* 1959, 59, 254–257.

ROGERS, C. R. *Counseling and psychotherapy.* Boston: Houghton Mifflin, 1942.

ROGERS, J. M. Operant conditioning in a quasi-therapy setting. *J. abnorm. soc. Psychol.,* 1960, 60, 247–252.

SALZINGER, K., & PISONI, STEPHANIE. Reinforcement of affect responses of schizophrenics during the clinical interview. *J. abnorm. soc. Psychol.,* 1958, 57, 84–90.

SALZINGER, K., & PISONI, STEPHANIE. Reinforcement of verbal affect responses of normal subjects during the interview. *J. abnorm. soc. Psychol.,* 1960, 60, 127–130.

SAPOLSKY, A. Effect of interpersonal relationships upon verbal conditioning. *J. abnorm. soc. Psychol.,* 1960, 60, 241–246.

SARASON, I. G. Interrelationships among individual difference variables, behavior in psychotherapy, and verbal conditioning. *J. abnorm. soc. Psychol.,* 1958, 56, 339–344.

SEEMAN, J. Counselor judgments of therapeutic process and outcome. In C. R. Rogers & Rosalind F. Dymond (Eds.), *Psychotherapy and personality change.* Chicago: Univer. Chicago Press, 1954.

SHOBEN, E. J. A learning-theory interpretation of psychotherapy. *Harv. educ. Rev.,* 1948, 18, 129–145.

SHOBEN, E. J. Some observations on psychotherapy and the learning process. In O. H. Mowrer (Ed.), *Psychotherapy theory and research.* New York: Ronald, 1953.

SIEGEL, S. *Nonparametric statistics for the behavioral sciences.* New York: McGraw-Hill, 1956.

SKINNER, B. F. *Science and human behavior.* New York: Macmillan, 1953.

SNYDER, W. U. Investigation of the nature of nondirective psychotherapy. *J. gen. Psychol.,* 1945, 33, 193–223.

VERPLANCK, W. S. The control of the content of conversation: Reinforcement of statements of opinion. *J. abnorm. soc. Psychol.,* 1955, 51, 668–676.

Selected Additional Readings

PROCESS

ANDERSON, R. P. Physiological and verbal behavior during client-centered counseling. *Journal of Counseling Psychology,* 1956, 3, 174–184.

AULD, G., & WHITE, A. M. Sequential dependencies in psychotherapy. *Journal of Abnormal and Social Psychology,* 1959, 58, 100–104.

BANDURA, A., LIPSHER, D. H., & MILLER, PAULA E. Psychotherapists' approach-avoidance reactions to patients' expressions of hostility. *Journal of Consulting Psychology,* 1960, 24, 1–8.

BERGMAN, D. V. Counseling method and client responses. *Journal of Consulting Psychology,* 1951, 15, 216–224.

BRAATEN, L. J. The movement from non-self to self in client-centered psychotherapy. *Journal of Counseling Psychology,* 8, 20–24, 1961.

BUTLER, J. M., RICE, LAURA N., & WAGSTAFF, A. K. On the naturalistic definition of variables: An analogue of clinical analysis. In H. H. Strupp & L. Luborsky (Eds.), *Research in psychotherapy.* Vol. 2. Washington. D.C.: American Psychological Association, 1962. Pp. 178–205.

DAVIS, S. E., & ROBINSON, F. P. A study of the use of certain techniques for reducing resistance during the counseling interview. *Educational and Psychological Measurement,* 1949, 9, 297–306.

DITTES, J. E. Galvanic skin response as a measure of patient's reaction to therapist's permissiveness. *Journal of Abnormal and Social Psychology,* 1957, 55, 295–303.

FRANK, G. H., & SWEETLAND, A. A study of the process of psychotherapy: the verbal interaction. *Journal of Consulting Psychology,* 1962, 26, 135–138.

GROSSMAN, D. An experimental investigation of a psychotherapeutic technique. *Journal of Consulting Psychology,* 1952, 16, 325–331.

HOWE, E. S., & POPE, B. Therapist verbal activity level and diagnostic utility of patient verbal responses. *Journal of Consulting Psychology,* 1962, 26, 149–155.

RAIMY, V. C. Self reference in counseling interviews. *Journal of Consulting Psychology,* 1948, 12, 153–163.

ROGERS, C. R., RASKIN, N. J., SEEMAN, J., SHEERER, ELIZABETH T., STOCK, DOROTHY, HAIGH, G., HOFFMAN, A. E., & CARR, A. C. A coordinated research in psychotherapy. *Journal of Consulting Psychology,* 1949, 13, 149–220.

ROSENMAN, S. Changes in the representations of self, other and interrelationship in client-centered therapy. *Journal of Counseling Psychology,* 1955, 2, 271–278.

SEEMAN, J. S. A study of the process of non-directive psychotherapy. *Journal of Consulting Psychology,* 1949, 13, 157–168.

SNYDER, W. U. An investigation of the nature of non-directive psychotherapy. *The Journal of General Psychology,* 1945, 33, 193–223.

SPIESMAN, J. C. Depth of interpretation and verbal resistance in psychotherapy. *Journal of Consulting Psychology,* 1959, 23, 93–99.

WINDER, C. L., FARRUKH, Z. A., BANDURA, A., & RAU, LUCY C. Dependency of patients, psychotherapists' responses, and aspects of psychotherapy. *Journal of Consulting Psychology,* 1962, 26, 129–134.

PROCESS RESEARCH—METHODOLOGY

BOOMER, D. S., & GOODRICH, D. C. Speech disturbance and judged anxiety. *Journal of Consulting Psychology,* 1961, 25, 160–164.

DIBNER, A. S. Ambiguity and anxiety. *Journal of Abnormal and Social Psychology,* 1958, 56, 165–174.

DITTMANN, A. T. The relationship between body movements and moods in interviews. *Journal of Consulting Psychology,* 1962, 26, 480.

GIEDT, F. H. Comparison of visual, content and auditory cues in interviewing. *Journal of Consulting Psychology,* 1955, 19, 407–416.

JAFFE, J. Verbal behavior analysis in psychiatric interview with the aid of a digital computer. In D. McK. Rioch & E. A. Weinstein (Eds.), *Disorders of Communication.* Baltimore: Williams & Wilkins, 1964. Pp. 389–400.

KANFER, F. H. Verbal rate, eyeblink, and content in structured psychiatric interviews. *Journal of Abnormal and Social Psychology,* 1960, 61, 341–347.

KANFER, F. H., PHILLIPS, J. S., MATARAZZO, J. D., & SASLOW, G. Experimental modification of interviewer content in standardized interviews. *Journal of Consulting Psychology,* 1960, 24, 528–536.

KRAUSE, M. S., & PILISUK, M. Anxiety in verbal behavior: A validation study. *Journal of Consulting Psychology,* 1961, 25, 414–419.

LACY, J. J. Psychophysiological approaches to the evaluation of psychotherapeutic process and outcome. In E. A. Rubinstein & M. B. Parloff (Eds.), *Research in psychotherapy.* Vol. 1. Washington, D.C.: American Psychological Association, 1959. Pp. 160–209.

LEARY, T., & GILL, M. The dimensions and a measure of the process of psychotherapy: A system for the analysis of the content of clinical evaluations and patient-therapist verbalizations. In E. A. Rubinstein & M. B. Parloff (Eds.), *Research in psychotherapy.* Vol. 1. Washington, D.C.: American Psychological Association, 1959. Pp. 62–95.

MOWRER, O. H. Changes in verbal behavior during psychotherapy. In O. H. Mowrer (Ed.), *Psychotherapy: Theory and research.* New York: Ronald Press, 1953. Pp. 463–545.

RAUSH, H. L., SPERBER, Z., RIGLER, D., WILLIAMS, J., HARWAY, H. I., BORDIN, E. S., DITTMAN, A. T., & HAYS, W. L. A dimensional analysis of depth of interpretation. *Journal of Consulting Psychology,* 1956, 20, 43–48.

TOMLINSON, T. M., & HART, J. T., JR. A validation study of the Process Scale. *Journal of Consulting Psychology,* 1962, 26, 74–78.

WALKER, A. M., RABLEN, R. A., & ROGERS, C. R. Development of a scale to measure process-changes in psychotherapy. *Journal of Clinical Psychology,* 1960, 16, 79–85.

WEINTRAUB, W., & ARONSON, H. The application of verbal behavior analysis to the study of psychological defense mechanisms: Methodology and preliminary report. *Journal of Nervous and Mental Diseases,* 134, 1962, 169–181.

SECTION 5 The Psychotherapeutic Relationship

This area of investigation could be considered as part of the study of the psychotherapeutic process, and it is sometimes difficult to decide whether a study should be included in that category or this one; in fact, one of the studies included in this section (Ashby, Ford, Guerney & Guerney) is meritorious largely because it represents an attempt to study many factors pertinent to psychotherapy in an integrated way. But the psychotherapeutic relationship seems an area important enough to warrant separate consideration.

Recognition of the importance of the relationship in psychotherapy developed for a number of reasons. One was an apparent equality of effectiveness of therapists holding very different theoretical viewpoints. This led to the question of whether a basic ingredient of psychotherapeutic effectiveness might lie elsewhere than in those aspects of the therapist's behavior which are determined by his theory of personality and of psychotherapy. Also, almost all schools of psychotherapy emphasize the importance of a warm, accepting, and permissive attitude on the part of the therapist and depend at least to some degree on positive feeling of the client toward the therapist. This has led some researchers to feel that a positive relationship is a necessary, and perhaps—in the context of discussion of personal problems—sometimes even a sufficient, condition to allow the emotionally disturbed person to move in the direction of better adjustment. At any rate, most therapists today would agree that the depth and type of relationship established between the client and therapist is an extremely important variable in psychotherapy.

Researchers in this area are seeking answers to such questions as the following: Do various theoretical orientations and various techniques of therapists have differential effects on the relationship that is formed? What sorts of personality factors and interests on the part of the therapist tend to be reflected in better relationships between therapist and client or in more successful therapy? What client personality traits or interests affect the relationship? How do certain client behaviors affect the behavior and feelings of the therapist toward the client? What effect do similarities and differences between the client and therapist have in the relationship established between them? What are the most important ingredients of the successful psychotherapeutic relationship?

We would also like to have the reader consider this area of research from a broader perspective. Since the work of Harry Stack Sullivan,[1] interpersonal processes and relationships have had a prominent place in the minds of mental health professionals and clinical researchers. The study of interpersonal perception, behavior, and attraction is a rapidly growing field.[2] Leary has put forth not only a functional theoretical base for research in this area, but a remarkable multilevel system for measuring interpersonal perception and behavior.[3] Adams has presented, in a different context, a view which could be regarded as an invitation to investigators of the psychotherapeutic relationship to broaden their perspectives: "The supposed complexity of personality and interaction between persons has been shown to be a purely semantic, verbal complexity, rather than a real complexity in actual fact. . . . All interpersonal behavior, both adaptive . . . and maladaptive, can be meaningfully categorized within one systematic frame of reference" (p. 194).[4]

Should not the study of the relationship in psychotherapy be viewed as a special case of this highly significant general area of psychological research? And does not the psychotherapeutic task present a remarkably appropriate and rich setting in which to study the interpersonal relationship? The answer is, of course, affirmative to both questions. But more, we think that in personality and clinical research a shift in emphasis is beginning away from nearly exclusive reliance on second-order data, as represented by paper-and-pencil tests, toward greater inclusion of the study and experimental manipulation of interpersonal behavior per se. Investigators such as Leary and Bales[5] have given us new general-purpose tools with which to do such research. Their predecessors, significantly, were those who studied the specific interpersonal verbal behaviors that occurred in psychotherapy as exemplified by Snyder, Bergman, and others

---

[1] See, for example, H. S. Sullivan, *The interpersonal theory of psychiatry* (New York: W. W. Norton, 1953).

[2] See, for various examples, R. Tagiuri & L. Petrullo, *Person perception and interpersonal behavior* (Stanford, Calif.: Stanford Univer. Press, 1958).

[3] T. Leary, *Interpersonal diagnosis of personality* (New York: Ronald Press, 1957).

[4] H. B. Adams, "Mental illness" or interpersonal behavior? *American Psychologist,* 1964, 19, 191–197.

[5] R. F. Bales, *Interaction process analysis* (Cambridge, Mass.: Addison-Wesley, 1950).

whose works may be found or are cited in Section 4 of this book. And they or their followers,[6] not by coincidence, are highly interested in the psychotherapeutic relationship. The ingenious study by Peter D. Russell and William U. Snyder represented in this section, and such works as those by Heller, Myers, and Kline and Sapolsky cited in the readings, might serve as paradigms not just for studying the psychotherapeutic relationship, but for the study of interpersonal behavior generally. Thus, research stemming from interest in the psychotherapeutic relationship may make a significant contribution to this area of general psychological knowledge.

[6] See, for example, H. H. Lennard & A. Bernstein, *The anatomy of psychotherapy* (New York: Columbia Univer. Press, 1960).

The Psychotherapeutic Relationship

G. GAIL GARDNER[1]

Psychotherapy has been variously defined. In this paper, it will refer to

a warm, permissive, safe, understanding, but limited social relationship within which therapist and patient discuss the affective behavior of the latter, including his ways of dealing with his emotionally toned needs and the situations that give rise to them [Shoben, 1953, p. 127].

Some writers on the subject of psychotherapy have focused on the "within which" aspects, citing numerous techniques as being more or less beneficial. Others have focused on the fact that psychotherapy is a relationship, and they have asserted that factors directly associated with this phenomenon contribute significantly to success or failure. This paper addresses itself to the validity of the latter assertion. The literature cited covers the period 1946–62.

CONCEPTIONS OF THE IDEAL THERAPEUTIC RELATIONSHIP

Since a relationship may be characterized in a myriad of ways, anyone who asserts that the relationship itself is important in

Reprinted from *Psychological Bulletin*, 1964, 61 (6), 426–437, with the permission of the American Psychological Association and the author.

[1] I wish to express gratitude to Allen E. Bergin, Rosalea A. Schonbar, and Laurance F. Shaffer for their helpful comments and criticisms during the preparation of this paper.

psychotherapy must state which sorts of relationship are desirable and which not. As Shoben (1949) pointed out, there is considerable agreement on this issue. The characteristics most frequently cited as desirable are the therapist's warmth, acceptance, permissiveness, respect for the patient, understanding, interest in the patient, and liking for the patient. Rogers (1957, 1959) made the additional stipulation that, in successful therapy, the patient must be able to perceive these therapist qualities, and he also asserted (Rogers, 1954) that the patient must like and respect the therapist.

A number of scales which have been constructed (Anderson & Anderson, 1954; Apfelbaum, 1958; Chase, 1946; Fiedler, 1950b; McClelland & Sinaiko, 1950; Sundland & Barker, 1962) for the purpose of defining the ideal relationship indicate that, while the factors cited above are the modal conception, agreement is far from perfect. Thus the issue is raised as to what factors are related to agreement with the modal conception.

Chase (1946) derived his scale from statements about counseling procedure which were endorsed by a majority of "expert" counselors. Counseling students' attitudes generally did not agree with those of the experts and did not correlate either with grades in the counseling course or with Army General Classification Test scores.

Chase concluded that acquisition of effective counseling attitudes was not related to scholastic achievement and probably was a function of actual experience in the counseling situation.

McClelland and Sinaiko (1950) refined the Chase scale and administered it to undergraduate and graduate psychology students. Comparisons within each of the two levels confirmed Chase's finding regarding scholastic achievement. Between-group comparisons, however, showed higher scores for the graduate students, and the authors concluded that training helped the students to acquire their instructors' attitudes. Of course this discrimination may have been more a function of self-selection of graduate students than of the training itself. Arbuckle (1956) found high agreement among graduate students' descriptions of the ideal counselor. In both studies, however, it is a moot question whether the graduate students actually believed in the attitudes they professed or merely were more adept at judging what answer was expected.

Fiedler (1950b), using a Q sort technique, found for seven therapists representing three schools that there were no significant differences in conception of the ideal therapeutic relationship between therapists of different schools, but that exprienced and inexperienced therapists of the same school did differ significantly from each other. He argued that ability to describe the ideal therapeutic relationship was a function of experience rather than of theoretical allegiance. Though Fiedler's evidence has often been cited as conclusive, it has not gone unchallenged. Apfelbaum (1958) criticized Fiedler's Q deck on the grounds that the items reflected extreme positions and thus tended to compel agreement among sorters, resulting in spuriously high intersorter correlations.

Behar and Altrocci (1961), using a scale constructed by Apfelbaum, asked nursing students to describe the ideal psychiatric nurse. Participation in psychiatric nursing courses seemed to produce high agreement, whereas actual experience with psychiatric patients did not. The authors concluded that they had refuted Fiedler's (1950b) hypothesis concerning experience, and that training instead was the critical variable. However, they failed to note that the high-agreement groups had had considerable experience with nonpsychiatric patients. Since it is quite doubtful that student nurses are taught to hold significantly different attitudes toward psychiatric patients as opposed to patients in general, the author's conclusions are questionable. The training and experience variables were not properly controlled in either this study or Fiedler's (1950b); thus the issue remains unresolved as to which contributes more to agreement on good therapeutic attitudes.

Sundland and Barker (1962) constructed a scale which did differentiate between therapeutic schools in terms of therapeutic attitudes. The criterion for item selection was that the items described points of controversy between schools; thus all that can be concluded is that the authors successfully validated their scale. In comparing their results to Fiedler's the authors recognized that different attitudes were measured, and they properly raised the issue of the extent to which differential responses to a scale may be a function of its content rather than of the persons responding. A related issue concerns the appropriate degree of specificity of items in an attitude scale. While everyone may agree that a therapist should be warm and accepting, there may be considerable disagreement as to what these terms actually imply. Sundland and Barker (1962) found, contrary to Fiedler's (1950b) results, that experienced and inexperienced therapists did not differ in their responses. But it must be noted that if a therapist is trained in a given school of thought, he does not need much experience to learn his school's position on the more controversial issues. Thus Fiedler's findings regarding experience and schools have still not been conclusively refuted.

Three studies (Anderson & Anderson, 1954; Fiedler, 1950b; Thomas, Polansky, & Kounin, 1955) noted that persons with no professional experience or training could describe the ideal therapeutic relationship about as well as therapists. Fiedler hypothesized that the therapeutic relationship may be only a variation of good interpersonal relationships in general.

Soper and Combs (1962), using a modification of Fiedler's (1950b) Q deck, found that teachers described the ideal teacher in much the same way that expert therapists described the ideal therapist. These data cannot be said to confirm Fiedler's hypothesis that the therapeutic relationship is only a paradigm of good human relationships generally, but they do support the notion of commonality among helping relationships, at least as described in Fiedler's terms by experts in the respective fields.

About the most that can be concluded from these various scales and samples is that the ideal therapeutic relationship may be as uniformly described as the scale provided permits. It is probably a variant of helping relationships in general and can probably be reasonably well described by anyone who considers it important. This latter hypothesis might explain the fact that Anderson and Anderson's (1954) patients were successful in the task while Behar and Altrocci's (1961) nonnursing students failed. Personal commitment to the significance of helping relationships may be a more pertinent variable than experience per se. Professional training does not seem to be especially relevant.

RELATIONSHIP FACTORS AND THERAPEUTIC CHANGE

We now consider studies in which aspects of the patient-therapist relationship are related to therapeutic change. The studies will be discussed in blocks according to the way in which the relationship variable is measured.

Therapist Ratings

It is difficult to obtain independent measures of the two variables under consideration. When one judges a helping relationship to be good in that it satisfies the conditions outlined above, one tends to experience a feeling of satisfaction which in turn acts as a set for perceiving progress toward therapeutic goals. Similarly, the converse is true. Even when one variable is measured alone, it is difficult not to get cues regarding the other. Given this inherent contamination, it only adds fuel to the fire to propose a design in which the same people rate both variables. The following two studies suffer from this error, and their results should be interpreted with caution.

Gorlow, Hoch, and Telschow (1952) studied therapy groups and found that the therapists had greatest liking for the most profited group. Since no statistical data were provided, it cannot be ascertained how strong the relationship was between liking and progress. Seeman (1954) found that therapist ratings of liking for their patients correlated .65 with therapist ratings of therapeutic success ($N = 23$). Retest reliability of the ratings was satisfactory. Since both ratings were made at the end of therapy, contamination is very likely. Therapist ratings of the degree to which the patient used his relationship to the therapist as a focus for therapy were not related to success. This finding casts doubt on the validity of notions to the contrary held by many therapists.

Snyder (1961) had significantly more positive affect toward his more improved patients. But the facts that his relationship and progress measures overlapped and that the patients were also his students suggest caution in interpreting these data and others from the same research to be reported below.

Two studies (Coons, 1957; Lesser, 1961) utilized projective and other personality tests to measure therapeutic change and thereby minimized the possibility of contamination. Coons (1957) found that a therapy group which focused on interaction showed significantly more improvement than either a group that stressed insight into psychological problems or a no-therapy control group. The latter two groups did not differ from each other. Coons concluded that interaction is the essential condition for therapeutic change. These findings contradict those of Seeman (1954). The difference may be due to the fact that Coons' patients were hospitalized schizophrenics and Seeman's were neurotics. Since withdrawal from interpersonal interaction is a major symptom of schizophrenia, whereas it may or may not be a central issue in neurosis, it seems entirely reasonable that measures of improvement would be more closely related to interaction in the former case than in the latter. The fact that Seeman's patients were in individual therapy and Coons' were in group therapy may also contribute to the difference in results.

Lesser (1961) found no relationship between therapists' ratings of their own empathic understanding and differences in patients' self-ideal discrepancies (Butler & Haigh, 1954) before and after therapy. It should be noted, however, that the number of hours of therapy varied from 3 to 12. For most patients in treatment for this short a period, even the most expert therapists cannot hope to effect significant changes in the more permanent personality constructs measured by the Butler and Haigh Q sort.

In all these studies, of course, the problems inherent in self-reports are relevant.

Patient Ratings

Studies in which patients made both judgments (Feifel & Eells, 1962; Grigg & Goodstein, 1957; Lipkin, 1948) also suffer from interdependent measures and must therefore be interpreted with caution. A patient who feels warmly toward his thera-

pist has more reason to judge himself improved; conversely, one who feels himself improved is more likely to have positive feelings toward his therapist, especially in retrospect.

Lipkin (1948) found that patients who mentioned the counselor's permissive attitude in posttherapy evaluations usually felt that it helped them to achieve insight into their problems. Though the length of treatment was no greater than that employed by Lesser (1961), the improvement criteria were much more situational; this difference probably explains the discrepant results. Grigg and Goodstein (1957), using a follow-up questionnaire, found that clients who felt a close relationship with their counselor reported significantly more favorable outcomes than did clients who felt a more distant relationship. Feifel and Eells (1962) obtained similar results.

Van der Veen (1961) utilized ratings by outside judges as the measure of improvement. He found significant positive correlations between patient ratings of the degree to which therapists provided a positive relationship and judges' process ratings.

A few studies have relied on test scores as the measure of progress in therapy. Lipkin (1954) measured therapy change by global judgments of Thematic Apperception Test protocols. He found that successful patients focused less than unsuccessful patients on their willingness to confide in the therapist, and when they did so focus, it was in a more positive way. The unsuccessful patients focused on mistrust. Lesser (1961) found no relationship between client ratings of therapist empathy and changes in self-ideal discrepancies. These negative results have been explained in the section on therapist ratings. Snyder (1961) reported a significant positive relationship between patients' attitudes toward the therapist and their classification as better or worse patients. Since, however, the measure of the two variables overlapped, the results are contaminated.

Ratings by Outside Judges

In studies in which judges rated both therapeutic change and the quality of the therapeutic relationship, it is not always clear whether or not the same judges made both ratings. Even if they did, these studies have merit over those described above in that the patient-therapist relationship is now rated by people who are not personally involved in the outcome of therapy.

Holt and Luborsky (1952) found that resident psychiatrists rated by their supervisors as successful were also rated as having better relationships with patients than were residents rated as unsuccessful. Unfortunately, the ratings were contaminated by the fact that the supervisors themselves had better relationships with the residents they judged to be successful. Luborsky (1952) noted that the successful residents were more flexible with respect to the range of behavior which they felt appropriate for their patients. Apparently the less successful residents tended to try to cast their patients into a preconceived mold. The finding that the successful residents had better relationships with ward personnel and fellow residents as well as with supervisors and patients lends some support to Fiedler's (1950b) hypothesis that good therapy relationships are not unique entities but rather instances of good relationships in general. Parloff's (1956) findings further support this notion.

Knupfer, Jackson, and Krieger (1959) noted the authoritarian nature of the relationship between the supervisor and the beginning therapist, and argued that supervisors' ratings may be heavily weighted with evaluations of the therapists' attitudes toward authority. Nevertheless, such ratings are probably more valid than the therapists' own ratings.

Van der Veen (1961) reported greater process-movement scores for clients whose therapists were judged to create better relationships. Truax (1961a) reported similar results and properly pointed out that caus-

ality had not been demonstrated. One study (Parloff, 1961), in which it was made clear that the judges of the relationship were different from the judges of therapeutic change, reported significant positive correlations between the two variables for patients in group therapy.

Two studies (Hiler, 1958; Parloff, 1961) relied on patient reports and behavior as the measure of change. Parloff (1961) noted a positive correlation between judged quality of the therapeutic relationship and patient reports of relief from symptomatic discomfort. In Hiler's (1958) study, therapists rated by staff psychologists as warm were better able to keep unproductive patients in treatment.

Truax (1961b, 1962) measured change by various test scores, including the Minnesota Multiphasic Personality Inventory (MMPI), and reported that, for two samples of schizophrenic patients, judged therapist empathy was positively related to improvement.

Three studies measured therapy change with a combination of ratings and test scores. Aronson (1953) reported no differences in improvement for clients of four therapists who were judged by their peers to have significantly different degrees of ability for warm interpersonal relationships. The fact that both therapists and judges were graduate students and that the judgments were not limited to therapist-patient relationships may have contributed to the null results. Truax (1961b), in a similarly designed study, obtained positive results for both neurotic and schizophrenic samples. His research differed from Aronson's primarily in that his relationship judgments were based on actual therapy sessions. Stoler's (1961) judges did not concern themselves with the therapists, but rather rated the likability of the patients on the basis of tape-recorded segments of therapy. Patients identified as more likable were more often identified as improved.

In evaluating all these studies, one must consider that, when there is little agreement as to the nature of improvement and no conclusive evidence that any form of change occurs as a result of psychotherapy, it seems premature blithely to examine the correlates of therapeutic change. Yet there seems to be no other appropriate course of action.

The evidence that the quality of the therapeutic relationship is a correlate of therapeutic change lies not in the conclusive results of any one study but rather in the repeated findings of a series of studies, most of which contain one or more serious defects. Methodology varies greatly, and absence of precise definitions often makes it difficult to discern whether the "good relationship" of one study contains the same elements as that of another study or different. In a sense, the diversity of procedure strengthens the force of the conclusion. Null results do not cluster in any one methodological cell, and, in all types of design, positive results occur far more frequently. Further support derives from the high agreement among different types of raters regarding the nature of the relationship between a given therapist and patient. Miller (1949) reported nonsignificant differences between the judgments of four raters with widely varying amounts of training. Parloff (1961) and Snyder (1961) reported correlations of .79 and .70, respectively, between patients' and judges' or therapists' descriptions of the patient-therapist relationship.

OTHER FACTORS RELATED TO THE PSYCHOTHERAPEUTIC RELATIONSHIP

Patient Variables

Diagnosis. Parloff (1961) found no correlation between initial patient evaluations and subsequent measures of the quality of the therapeutic relationship. Since the patients were all neurotic, the range of maladjustment probably was not very great. Hollingshead and Redlich (1958) reported an inverse relationship between patient maladjustment and therapist liking for patients

ranging over the whole gamut of disturbance. However, since maladjustment was also inversely related to social class, and since liking was positively related to social class, the results may be an artifact. Snyder (1961) indicated that the patients toward whom he felt most friendly were relatively more energetic, uninhibited, and suggestible. On the pre-therapy MMPI, these patients tended to be more schizoid and depressive.

Prognosis. Since diagnosis and prognosis are usually themselves related, it should follow that prognosis is correlated with therapists' affective attitudes. Strupp (1958, 1960) and Wallach and Strupp (1960) found this to be true. Strupp (1960) commented on "the ubiquitous but insufficiently realized effects of the therapists' attitudes as they permeate and color his clinical observations and judgments [p. 28]." Of course it must be realized that the direction of influence may also be the other way.

Motivation for Therapy. In three studies (Raskin, 1961; Strupp, 1960; Wallach & Strupp, 1960), therapists had greater liking for patients who evidenced a desire to change and improve. This is hardly surprising since motivation for therapy is usually a central consideration in making a prognosis. Wallach and Strupp inferred from their data that the patient's motivation probably influences the therapist's attitude only when the degree of maladjustment is not too great. Raskin (1961) noted that liking was more effective as a predictor of high- than of low-motivation ratings. Considering the correlational design of his research, the use of the word "predictor" seems inappropriate. Still the finding warrants further study.

Capacity for Friendliness. In two studies (Heller, Myers, & Kline, 1962; Snyder, 1961) therapists had warmer feelings for patients who were themselves more friendly.

Dependency. Heller et al. (1962) also noted that dependent clients evoked more interviewer friendliness than did more dominant clients. It seems that, at least for therapists judging clients at the outset of therapy, friendliness and dependency are interdependent variables. Presumably this would not hold true at the later stages of therapy.

Ethical Values. Snyder (1961) developed a warmer relationship with patients whom he rated as relatively more idealistic and altruistic.

Social Class. Hollingshead and Redlich (1958) observed that therapists' attitudes toward their patients were positively related to the patients' social class. This was true even when the range of maladjustment was curtailed by studying only the neurotic sample. The authors felt that therapists generally are unable to understand lower-class values and hence are less prone to like persons holding such values. Furthermore, the therapists' technical skill is threatened by the lower-class patient's tendency to demand that the therapist behave in an authoritarian manner.

Expectations Regarding the Therapist. Apfelbaum (1958) found that patients who expected a high degree of warmth from the therapist did not differ on pre-therapy MMPI scores from patients who expected a low degree, and that both these groups had more maladjusted MMPI scores than a group which expected a moderate degree of warmth. It could be hypothesized that therapists would have the most positive feelings for this middle group.

That therapist liking results from perceiving a "good patient" rather than the reverse was indicated by Strupp and Williams (1960) who found that two therapists' ratings of the following variables were all highly intercorrelated: patients' defensiveness, patients' capacity for insight, patients' motivation for therapy, patients' prognosis, and therapists' liking for the patients. When therapist liking was partialed out, there was no change in the magnitude of the other coefficients. Two writers (Fiedler, 1953; Truax, 1961b) reported contra-

dictory data. In each of these studies, a given therapist's attitudes were found not to vary across different patients. Homogeneity of sampling may account for the null results in both cases.

While it appears that warm relationships can best be established with "good" patients who are motivated for therapy, only moderately maladjusted, friendly, submissive, and who represent the middle or upper social classes, persons who do not fit into this category can sometimes be treated successfully. In order to raise this success rate, it would probably be fruitful to investigate which sorts of therapists are most capable of forming positive relationships with persons who are not good patients.

Therapist Variables

Personality Characteristics. Three studies (Ashby, Ford, Guerney, & Guerney, 1957; Brams, 1961; Fiedler & Senior, 1952) correlated a large number of therapist personality variables with measures of the quality of the therapeutic relationship. Positive results occurred no more often than would be expected by chance.

Holt and Luborsky (1952) reported that their successful psychiatrists—who maintained better patient-therapist relationships —were in the middle of the range on dimensions of control of affect and emotional impulsivity. Unsuccessful psychiatrists tended to be either impulsively expressive with their patients or overcontrolled with no expression of feeling. It may be that other therapist qualities have a curvilinear relationship with attitudinal variables and that their relevance has been refuted because only linear relationships were investigated.

Streitfeld (1959) found that ratings of self-acceptance (SA) and acceptance of others (AO) were not related to ratings of therapeutic competence. He concluded that, while general acceptance of others is not related to psychotherapeutic ability, acceptance of specific patients probably is related. The null results might also be explained by the fact that the therapists were all graduate students. Interestingly, therapists who obtained low scores on SA and AO rated their therapeutic ability similarly to the way in which their supervisors rated it, whereas this was not true for therapists high on SA and AO. The author suggested that high SA and AO therapists may be defensive and immature. A similar conclusion may be drawn from data reported by Fiedler and Senior (1952). Correlational techniques which are sensitive to curvilinearity may be most appropriate for studying the self-acceptance variable.

Familiarity with the Patient. Stoler (1961) found that raters who were familiar with patients' cases judged the patients as more likable than did raters reviewing the cases for the first time.

Ability to Predict Patient Behavior. A number of studies (Affleck & Garfield, 1961; Chance, 1959; Dymond, 1953; Fiedler, 1953; Luft, 1950; Melton, 1952) have found therapists' predictive ability to be quite poor and generally no better than that of persons who are not therapists. Correlations of this ability, such as it is, with relationship factors have variously been described as positive (Kahn, 1957), negative (Smith, 1960), and zero (Mellinger, 1956). Snyder (1961) reported positive but nonsignificant differences in his ability to predict questionnaire responses of his better and poorer clients.

Fiedler (1953) commented that therapeutic understanding refers primarily to making the patient feel understood and not to any objective diagnostic or predictive ability. The evidence is generally in support of his implication, namely, that predictive ability is not a relevant therapist variable.

Experience. Parloff (1956) reported that, for two experienced therapists, judges agreed that one created better therapeutic relationships than the other. Fiedler (1950a, 1951a) found that expert therapists were judged better able to approximate the ideal relationship than were novices. A major weakness in the study was that the judges could distinguish the experts—who were nationally known—from the novices on the basis of their voices. It is impossible to estimate the extent to which halo and "pitchfork" effects, respectively, were operating. Three other studies (Chance, 1959; McGowan, 1954; Strupp, 1958), in which this defect was avoided, obtained similar results. Hollingshead and Redlich (1958) found that inexperienced therapists tended more to dislike lower-class patients than did experienced therapists. It may be that the experience variable is most relevant in the case of patients who do not fit into the "good patient" category.

Therapist-Patient Similarity

Assumed Similarity (AS). This construct (Fiedler, 1951b) refers to the degree to which a therapist believes that his own personality is similar to his patient's personality. Hunt, Ewing, LaForge, and Gilbert (1959) reported a positive correlation between AS scores and the degree to which therapists liked their clients.

Real Similarity. Lesser (1961) found that similarity of self-concept between therapist and patient was not related to empathy scores. Vogel (1961) reported no correlation between judged quality of the therapeutic relationship and patient-therapist similarity on the California F Scale. However, there was a significant correlation between relationship ratings and similarity between patient and therapist ratings of the extent to which the therapist should behave in an authoritarian manner. It should be noted that, in this case, similar opinions would reflect complementary need patterns. Snyder (1961) also reported that patients with whom he had better relationships had need profiles (Edwards Personal Preference Schedule) which complemented, rather than reflected, his own. In this research also, *n* Dominance was the primary factor. Hollingshead and Redlich (1958) noted that therapists had more positive feelings toward patients whose social-class backgrounds were similar to their own.

Carson and Heine (1962) found a curvilinear relationship between therapist-patient similarity on the MMPI and therapeutic success ratings. That is, patients whose profiles were moderately similar to their therapists' were judged most improved. The authors reasoned that high similarity prevents the therapist from maintaining suitable distance and objectivity whereas high dissimilarity prevents him from being able to empathize with or understand his patient's problems.

These studies strongly support Levinson's (1961) thesis that patient-therapist similarity cannot be thought of as a unitary trait. Some similarities may facilitate good relationships and therapeutic progress, while others may be sources of impasses.

Technique Variables

Relative Importance of Relationship and Technique. Shortly before relationship variables came into vogue, Seeman (1949) studied reactions of clients who had been counseled by directive and nondirective methods. He found significantly different client reactions for pairs of counselors whose techniques were similar and nonsignificant differences where techniques were different. He concluded that some factor other than therapeutic method was producing differences in client reactions.

Fiedler (1950a, 1951a, 1953) rushed in to fill the vacuum, affirming Seeman's (1949) conclusion and stating that the therapeutic relationship is the critical variable in successful therapy. Fiedler (1953) commented, however, that a given technique might serve to make a therapist feel more secure and thus indirectly affect the course of therapy.

More recent research (Ford, 1956; Forgy & Black, 1954; Snyder, 1957) has placed technique in a somewhat more favorable light. These writers have concluded that relationship and success vary not as a func-

tion of technique alone but rather as a function of a particular therapist using a particular technique. They feel that the therapist and his method must be viewed as a single unit.

Strupp (1958) concurred that both relationship and technique factors are important in successful therapy. Interestingly, in a later article (Strupp, 1962), he was not so willing to commit himself and stated:

For some years it has been held that the quality of the therapeutic relationship is more basic to therapeutic success than the therapist's specific methods and techniques. . . . It may be predicted that the issue will remain alive for some time [p. 452].

Covariance of Relationship and Technique Factors. Two studies Aronson, 1953; Strupp, 1958) reported a negative correlation between the degree of warmth in therapists' attitudes toward their patients and the extent to which they used directive techniques. Apfelbaum (1958) studied patients' pre-therapy expectations of their therapists' behavior and reported a curvilinear relationship between the two variables. Therapists expected to be at the extremes of the warmth dimension were expected to employ directive techniques; therapists expected to exhibit a moderate amount of warmth were expected to be relatively more non-directive. The discrepancy between these data and those of Strupp (1958) and Aronson (1953) may be explained in two ways: either therapists do not exist who are warm as some patients expect or such therapists do exist but were not represented in Strupp's and Aronson's samples. Of course variations in measuring instruments may also account for the differences.

Throughout this paper, considerable weight has been given to methodological issues. It is indeed a pity that research findings must so often be questioned because of methodological defects. Not only the nature of the measurements but also the point at which they are made should be considered, especially in the case of patients' and therapists' self-reports. While time may dim the memory, it may also extinguish inhibitions and thus allow greater honesty as regards negative feelings and evaluations (Feifel & Eells, 1962).

REFERENCES

AFFLECK, D. C., & GARFIELD, S. L. Predictive judgments of therapists and duration of stay in psychotherapy. *J. clin. Psychol.*, 1961, 17, 134–137.

ANDERSON, R. P., & ANDERSON, G. V. The development of an instrument for measuring rapport. In, *Occasional papers in testing and guidance.* Austin: University of Texas, Testing and Guidance Bureau, 1954.

APFELBAUM, B. *Dimensions of transference in psychotherapy.* (Publications in Personality Assessment and Research, No. 2) Berkeley: University of California Publications, 1958.

ARBUCKLE, D. S. Client perception of counselor personality. *J. counsel. Psychol.*, 1956, 3, 93–96.

ARONSON, M. A study of the relationships between certain counselor and client characteristics in client-centered therapy. In W. U. Snyder (Ed.), *Group report of a program of research in psychotherapy.* State College: Pennsylvania State College, 1953. Pp. 39–54.

ASHBY, J. D., FORD, D. H., GUERNEY, B. G., JR., & GUERNEY, LOUISE F. Effects on clients of a reflective and a leading type of psychotherapy. *Psychol. Monogr.*, 1957, 71 (24, Whole No. 453).

BEHAR, LENORE, & ALTROCCHI, J. Agreement on the concept of the ideal therapist as a function of experience. *J. clin. Psychol.*, 1961, 17, 66–69.

BRAMS, J. M. Counselor characteristics and effective communication in counseling. *J. counsel. Psychol.*, 1961, 8, 25–30.

BUTLER, J. M., & HAIGH, G. V. Changes in the relation between self-concepts and ideal concepts consequent upon client-centered counseling. In C. R. Rogers and Rosalind F. Dymond (Eds.), *Psychotherapy and personality change.* Chicago: Univer. Chicago Press, 1954. Pp. 55–75.

CARSON, R. C., & HEINE, R. W. Similarity and success in therapeutic dyads. *J. consult. Psychol.*, 1962, 26, 38–43.

CHANCE, ERIKA. *Families in treatment.* New York: Basic Books, 1959.

CHASE, W. P. Measurement of attitudes toward counseling. *Educ. psychol. Measmt.*, 1946, 6, 467–473.

COONS, W. H. Interaction and insight in group psychotherapy. *Canad. J. Psychol.*, 1957, 11, 1–8.

DYMOND, ROSALIND F. Can clinicians predict individual behavior? *J. Pers.*, 1953, 22, 151–161.

FEIFEL, H., & EELLS, JANET. Patients and therapists assess the same psychotherapy. Paper read at American Psychological Association, St. Louis, September 1962.

FIEDLER, F. E. A comparison of therapeutic relationships in psychoanalytic, nondirective, and Adlerian therapy. *J. consult. Psychol.*, 1950, 14, 436–445. (a)

FIEDLER, F. E. The concept of an ideal therapeutic relationship. *J. consult. Psychol.*, 1950, 14, 239–245. (b)

FIEDLER, F. E. Factor analyses of psychoanalytic, nondirective, and Adlerian therapeutic relationships. *J. consult. Psychol.*, 1951, 15, 32–38. (a)

FIEDLER, F. E. A method of objective quantification of certain counter-transference attitudes. *J. clin. Psychol.*, 1951, 7, 101–107. (b)

FIEDLER, F. E. Quantitative studies on the role of therapists' feelings toward their patients. In O. H. Mowrer (Ed.), *Psychotherapy: Theory and research.* New York: Ronald Press, 1953. Pp. 296–315.

FIEDLER, F. E., & SENIOR, K. An exploratory study of unconscious feeling reactions in 15 patient-therapist pairs. *J. abnorm. soc. Psychol.*, 1952, 47, 446–453.

FORD, D. H. An experimental comparison of the relationship between client and therapist in a reflective and a leading type of psychotherapy. Unpublished doctoral dissertation, Pennsylvania State University, 1956. (*Dissert. Abstr.*, 1956, 16, 1490–1491.)

FORGY, E. W., & BLACK, J. D. A follow-up after three years of clients counseled by two methods. *J. counsel. Psychol.*, 1954, 1, 1–8.

GORLOW, L., HOCH, E. L., & TELSCHOW, E. F. *The nature of nondirective group psychotherapy: An experimental investigation.* New York: Teachers College, Columbia University, 1952.

GRIGG, A. E., & GOODSTEIN, L. D. The use of clients as judges of the counselor's performance. *J. counsel. Psychol.,* 1957, 4, 31–36.

HELLER, K., MYERS, R. A., & KLINE, LINDA V. Interviewer behavior as a function of standardized client roles. Paper read at American Psychological Association, St. Louis, September 1962.

HILER, E. W. An analysis of patient-therapist compatibility. *J. consult. Psychol.,* 1958, 22, 341–347.

HOLLINGSHEAD, A. B., & REDLICH, F. C. *Social class and mental illness.* New York: Wiley, 1958.

HOLT, R. R., & LUBORSKY, L. Research in the selection of psychiatrists: A second interim report. *Bull. Menninger Clin.,* 1952, 16, 125–135.

HUNT, J. McV., EWING, T. N., LaFORGE, R., & GILBERT, W. M. An integrated approach to research on therapeutic counseling with samples of results. *J. counsel. Psychol.,* 1959, 6, 46–54.

KAHN, R. K. Therapist discomfort in two psychotherapies. Unpublished doctoral dissertation, Pennsylvania State University, 1957. Cited by W. U. Snyder, Some investigations of relationship in psychotherapy. In E. A. Rubinstein & M. B. Parloff (Eds.), *Research in psychotherapy.* Washington, D.C.: National Publishing, 1959. P. 252.

KNUPFER, GENEVIEVE, JACKSON, D. D., & KRIEGER, G. Personality differences between more and less competent psychotherapists as a function of criteria of competence. *J. nerv. ment. Dis.,* 1959, 129, 375–384.

LESSER, W. M. The relationship between counseling progress and emphatic understanding. *J. counsel. Psychol.,* 1961, 8, 330–336.

LEVINSON, D. J. The psychotherapist's contribution to the patient's treatment career. Paper read at Conference on Psychotherapy Research, Chapel Hill, North Carolina, 1961.

LIPKIN, S. The client evaluates nondirective psychotherapy. *J. consult. Psychol.,* 1948, 12, 137–146.

LIPKIN, S. Clients' feelings and attitudes in relation to the outcome of client-centered therapy. *Psychol. Monogr.,* 1954, 68 (1, Whole No. 372).

LUBORSKY, L. B. The personalities of successful and less successful psychotherapists. *Amer. Psychologist,* 1952, 7, 337. (Abstract)

LUFT, J. Implicit hypotheses and clinical predictions. *J. abnorm. soc. Psychol.,* 1950, 45, 756–759.

McCLELLAND, W. A., & SINAIKO, H. W. An investigation of a counselor attitude questionnaire. *Educ. psychol. Measmt.,* 1950, 10, 128–133.

McGOWAN, J. F. Client anticipations and expectancies as related to initial interview performance and perceptions. Unpublished doctoral dissertation, University of Missouri, 1954. (*Dissert. Abstr.,* 1955, 15, 228–229.)

MELLINGER, G. D. Interpersonal trust as a factor in communication. *J. abnorm. soc. Psychol.,* 1956, 52, 304–309.

MELTON, R. S. A comparison of clinical and actuarial methods of prediction with an assessment of the relative accuracy of different clinicians. Unpublished doctoral dissertation, University of Minnesota, 1952.

MILLER, HELEN E. "Acceptance" and related attributes as demonstrated in psychotherapeutic interviews. *J. clin. Psychol.,* 1949, 5, 83–87.

PARLOFF, M. B. Some factors affecting the quality of therapeutic relationships. *J. abnorm. soc. Psychol.,* 1956, 52, 5–10.

PARLOFF, M. B. Therapist-patient relationships and outcome of psychotherapy. *J. consult. Psychol.,* 1961, 25, 29–38.

RASKIN, A. Factors therapists associate with motivation to enter psychotherapy. *J. clin. Psychol.,* 1961, 17, 62–65.

ROGERS, C. R. An overview of the research and some questions for the future. In C. R. Rogers & Rosalind F. Dymond (Eds.), *Psychotherapy and personality change.* Chicago: Univer. Chicago Press, 1954. Pp. 413–430.

ROGERS, C. R. The necessary and sufficient conditions of therapeutic personality change. *J. consult. Psychol.,* 1957, 21, 95–103.

ROGERS, C. R. Therapist-patient relationship. In E. A. Rubinstein & M. B. Parloff (Eds.), *Research in psychotherapy.* Washington, D.C.: National Publishing, 1959. P. 273.

SEEMAN, J. An investigation of client reactions to vocational counseling. *J. consult. Psychol.,* 1949, 13, 95–104.

SEEMAN, J. Counselor judgments of therapeutic process and outcome. In C. R. Rogers & Rosalind F. Dymond (Eds.), *Psychotherapy and personality change.* Chicago: Univer. Chicago Press, 1954. Pp. 99–108.

SHOBEN, E. J., JR. Psychotherapy as a problem in learning theory. *Psychol. Bull.*, 1949, 46, 366–392.

SHOBEN, E. J., JR. Some observations on psychotherapy and the learning process. In O. H. Mowrer (Ed.), *Psychotherapy: Theory and research.* New York: Ronald Press, 1953. Pp. 120–139.

SMITH, W. Social adjustment and interpersonal perception. In J. McV. Hunt (Ed.), *Interpersonal perception and interpersonal relationships in therapeutic counseling.* Technical Report No. 1, 1960, University of Illinois, ONR Contract Nonr-1834 (11), Office of Naval Research.

SNYDER, W. U. The psychotherapy research program at the Pennsylvania State University. *J. counsel. Psychol.*, 1957, 4, 9–14.

SNYDER, W. U. *The psychotherapy relationship.* New York: Macmillan, 1961.

SOPER, D. W., & COMBS, A. W. The helping relationship as seen by teachers and therapists. *J. consult. Psychol.*, 1962, 26, 288.

STOLER, N. Client likability as a variable in the study of psychotherapy. *U. Wisc. Psychiat. Inst. Bull.*, 1961, 1 (No. 11).

STREITFELD, J. W. Expressed acceptance of self and others by psychotherapists. *J. consult. Psychol.*, 1959, 23, 435–441.

STRUPP, H. H. The psychotherapist's contribution to the treatment process. *Behav. Sci.*, 1958, 3, 34–67.

STRUPP, H. H. *Psychotherapists in action.* New York: Grune & Stratton, 1960.

STRUPP, H. H. Psychotherapy. *Annu. Rev. Psychol.*, 1962, 13, 445–478.

STRUPP, H. H., & WILLIAMS, J. V. Some determinants of clinical evaluations of different psychiatrists. *Arch. gen. Psychiat.*, 1960, 2, 434–440.

SUNDLAND, D. H., & BARKER, E. N. The orientation of psycohtherapists. *J. consult. Psychol.*, 1962, 26, 201–212.

THOMAS, E., POLANSKY, N., & KOUNIN, J. The expected behavior of a potentially helpful person. *Hum. Relat.*, 1955, 8, 165–174.

TRUAX, C. B. The process of group psychotherapy: Relationships between hypothesized therapeutic conditions and interpersonal exploration. *Psychol. Monogr.*, 1961, 75 (7, Whole No. 511). (a)

TRUAX, C. B. Therapeutic conditions. *U. Wisc. Psychiat. Inst. Bull.*, 1961, 1 (No. 10c). (b)

TRUAX, C. B. Constructive personality change in schizophrenic patients receiving high-condition therapy, low-condition therapy, and no therapy. Unpublished manuscript, University of Wisconsin, Wisconsin Psychiatric Institute, 1962.

VAN DER VEEN, F. The perception by clients and by judges of the conditions offered by the therapy relationship. *U. Wisc. Psychiat. Inst. Bull.*, 1961, 1 (No. 10).

VOGEL, J. L. Authoritarianism in the therapeutic relationship. *J. consult. Psychol.*, 1961, 25, 102–108.

WALLACH, M. S., & STRUPP, H. H. Psychotherapists' clinical judgments and attitudes toward patients. *J. consult. Psychol.*, 1960, 24, 316–323.

Client Dependency and Therapist Expectancy as Relationship Maintaining Variables in Psychotherapy

KENNETH HELLER
ARNOLD P. GOLDSTEIN

The relationship and interactional aspects of psychotherapy, while long considered important, have received ever-increasing theoretical and experimental emphasis in recent years. Bordin (1959), for example, has stated:

The key to the influence of psychotherapy on the patient is in his relationship with the therapist. Whenever psychotherapy is accepted as a significant enterprise, this statement is so widely subscribed to as to become trite. Virtually all efforts to theorize about psychotherapy are intended to describe and explain what attributes of the interactions between the therapist and the patient will account for whatever behavior change results (p. 235).

Previous investigations of the psychotherapeutic relationship have frequently

been attempts to identify and interrelate client, therapist, and/or transactional variables which theoretically appear to be important dimensions of the therapist-client interaction. The present study, continuing in this direction, has focused upon client-therapist attraction as its major concern. This potentially significant dimension of the therapeutic relationship has been defined by Libo (1957), in a general sense, as "the resultant of all forces acting on the patient to maintain his relationship with the therapist." To implement this definition, he developed the Picture Impressions Test, a projective technique designed to call forth client verbalizations concerning feelings toward therapists and the therapy process. With client-therapist attraction defined in this manner, Libo (1957) demonstrated a significant relation between the magnitude of client attraction toward the therapist and certain clearly observable and therapy relevant, overt, client behaviors.

Reprinted from *Journal of Consulting Psychology*, 1961, 25 (5), 371–375, with the permission of the American Psychological Association and the authors.

There is evidence to suggest that the specific nature of these relationship maintaining forces acting upon the client may include such participant characteristics as client dependency and the therapist's expectations regarding a favorable therapeutic outcome. In a discussion of dependency in psychotherapy, Dollard and Miller (1950) note that therapy is often facilitated by initial client dependency. According to their formulation, the client brings to the therapeutic situation a desire to please the therapist, this desire being considered one of the main forces helping the client overcome the initial anxieties associated with therapy. As therapy progresses the client is expected to grow in independence, since he need no longer rely on pleasing the therapist as his only motivation for continuing in therapy.

The viewpoint that dependent clients become more independent after the successful completion of psychotherapy is also examined by another line of investigation. Studying the present-self and ideal-self descriptions of psychiatric patients, Fordyce(1953) found that those patients who described themselves as dependent stated that they would ideally like to see themselves as being more independent. Since Rogers and Dymond (1954) and others report that successful psychotherapy produces an increased congruence between present-self and ideal-self descriptions, it seems reasonable to expect that, after a course of successful psychotherapy, clients with pretherapy dependent self-descriptions should see themselves as growing independent.

The therapist's expectation of patient improvement, a second potentially important relationship maintaining variable, has been demonstrated by Goldstein (1960b) to affect significantly the amount of improvement the patient reports as having taken place and also the duration of psychotherapy. Kelley (1949), Rosenthal (1959), and Ulenhuth, Canter, Neustadt, and Payson (1959) have also demonstrated the potency of participant expectancies in two-person interactions.

Hypotheses

1. Client pretherapy attraction to the psychotherapist varies: (a) positively with client pretherapy dependency, and (b) positively with client over-therapy movement toward independence.

2. Client pretherapy attraction to the psychotherapist varies positively with the latter's expectation of client improvement.

METHOD

Two treatment conditions were utilized in the present investigation: therapy (experimental group), and no-therapy (control group). Thirty clients and 10 therapists participated. Most of the clients were undergraduates in attendance at the Pennsylvania State University who had sought psychotherapy at the University Psychological Clinic. Clients were randomly assigned to the two treatment conditions and the 15 clients in the experimental group were then randomly assigned to therapists. Each therapist met with his client(s) two times per week for individual, 50-minute sessions. The 15 control clients were placed on a waiting list and did not participate in formal psychotherapy during the 15 session duration of the investigation.

The 10 therapists employed in this study had all completed their formal predoctoral training in psychotherapy, including an approved internship. Eight therapists had yet to fulfill all the requirements for the PhD degree, while two had already received their PhD degrees. The therapists, all males, ranged in age from 24 to 37, with a median age of 32. When asked to describe their own orientation to therapy, none of the therapists expressed a strong preference for any particular "school" of psychotherapy. All stated that their approach would vary according to the client and the situation. The therapists were employed by either the Psychological Clinic or the Division of Counseling at Pennsylvania State University and usually saw clients as part of their regular clinical case load.

Measurement of Variables

Client-therapist attraction. As suggested above, client-therapist attraction was operationally defined as the client's score on the Picture Impressions Test. This projective technique consists of four cards depicting therapy-like situations to which the client is requested to respond in a manner analogous to TAT administration. Content analysis scoring (Libo, 1956) (e.g., Locomotion, Barriers to Locomotion, Satisfaction, etc.) was carried out independently by the authors with complete agreement occurring on 83% of the client stories. For each client, an attraction score was then determined by summing his scores for each of his four stories.

Dependent behavior. Dependent behavior was conceived of as the extent to which an individual prefers to have others prevent his frustration or punishment and provide need satisfaction (Fitzgerald, 1958). In order to narrow the definition of dependency even further, it was decided to concentrate on two aspects of dependent behavior described by Murray (1943) as Succorance and Deference. Measurement of dependent behavior occurred at two levels:

Self-descriptive dependency. To measure the extent to which clients attributed dependent behavior to themselves, the Succorance, Deference, and Autonomy scales of the Edwards Personal Preference Schedule (EPPS) (Edwards, 1954) were administered. Following the suggestion of several researchers (Bernardin & Jessor, 1957; Gisvold, 1958; Zuckerman & Grosz, 1958) a total self-descriptive dependency score was computed by summing the scores from the Succorance and Deference scales and subtracting from the sum the score from the Autonomy scale.

Overt dependency. A Situational Test of Dependency developed earlier by one of the authors (Heller, 1959) from a modi-

fication by Borgatta (1951) of the Rosenzweig P-F study (1947) was used in the current investigation. Borgatta developed a role-playing form of the P-F study in which the original paper and pencil situations were acted out by both examiner and examinee. Borgatta's evidence suggests that subjects react to the role-playing form of this test in a manner quite similar to the way in which they react to real, overt, threatening situations. The role-playing situations were further modified so that all the situations involved a degree of threat to the respondent. An additional modification was development of a forced-choice rather than an open-ended method of responding.

Therapist expectation. Therapist expectation of client personality change was generally defined as the feelings held by the therapist relating to the anticipated nature and intensity of his client's personality problems upon completion of the latter's psychotherapy. Operationally, this variable was defined (Goldstein, 1960b) as the difference between the therapist's ordering of personality problem Q sorts when he is instructed to sort them under two different orientations: (*a*) according to the status in which he, the therapist, expects his client's problems to be upon completion of psychotherapy; and (*b*) according to the manner in which he views his client's problems at the time of sorting, i.e., his present perception of his client.

The Picture Impressions, EPPS, and the Situational Test of Dependency were individually administered to all clients immediately prior to their first therapy session and immediately following their fifteenth session. If a therapy client dropped out of therapy before his fifteenth session, he was "post-tested" at the time of dropout. When this occurred, a control client who had been in the wait group for the same period of time as the experimental client had been in therapy, was also tested. The therapists completed their sortings after every 5 sessions for 15 sessions.

RESULTS AND DISCUSSION

The correlations, for both experimental and control clients, between pretherapy attraction and the dependency scores obtained pre- and posttherapy, as well as the resultant dependency difference score, are presented in Table 1.

The pretherapy correlations in Table 1 indicate a significant relationship between client's attraction and both self-descriptive and overt dependency. Those individuals who wrote stories to the Picture Impression cards indicating that they anticipated positive gratification from therapy, described themselves before therapy as more dependent according to the EPPS, and also acted more dependently on the Situational Test of Dependency. This finding lends support to the contention of Dollard and Miller that initial client dependence can act in ways that maintain the early stages of the psychotherapeutic relationship.

The hypothesized relationship between positive attraction to therapy and movement toward self-descriptive independence over therapy is also supported. Those clients who are positively attracted see themselves as becoming more independent as therapy progresses. Of additional interest is the fact that a distinction can be made between self-descriptive and behavioral changes toward independence. While the attracted clients saw themselves as becoming more independent, this relationship was not found on the overt behavioral measure. Behaviorally, the attracted clients in the experimental group were still dependent at the time of the posttherapy testing, i.e., after 15 sessions of psychotherapy. It appears that attracted clients may be set to see themselves as changing, although their interpersonal interactions remain relatively constant. The motivation for this change in self-descriptive dependency may well be the desire to please the therapist and thus say what they think the therapist expects or would like them to say. Working with a sample of psychotherapists who received their training at the same university as the therapists of the present study, Peterson, Snyder, Guthrie, and Ray (1958) have demonstrated that therapists of this training background show a great deal of atten-

TABLE 1

CORRELATIONS BETWEEN CLIENT PRETHERAPY ATTRACTION
AND DEPENDENCY

Pretherapy Attraction with:	All Subjects	Group Experimental	Control
Pretherapy			
EPPS dependency	.501***	—[a]	—
situational dependency	.491***	—	—
Pre-post difference			
EPPS dependency	—	−.774***	−.508*
situational dependency	—	−.189	.002
Posttherapy			
EPPS dependency	—	.065	−.009
situational dependency	—	.542**	.241

[a] Data obtained at this time preceded the assignment of subjects to experimental and control groups, hence pretherapy *r*'s were calculated across all 30 subjects.
 * Significant at .06 level.
 ** Significant at .05 level.
 *** Significant at .01 level.

tion to their clients when the latters' remarks demonstrate a preference to let others provide for the satisfaction of their needs. Should this differential between self-descriptive and overt behavioral test findings be corroborated in further research, serious doubt would be cast upon the common procedure of evaluating the effectiveness of psychotherapy by the *exclusive* use of self-descriptive measures.

Somewhat more puzzling is that the control clients, who received no formal psychotherapy, showed almost the same relation between attraction and self-descriptive movement toward independence. It should be noted that the control group *as a whole* showed no movement over therapy, either in the independent or the dependent direction. But still, when individual variation is considered, those in the control group who described themselves as becoming more independent over time were positively attracted toward therapy, while those who described themselves as becoming dependent tended to be those who were negatively attracted. The investigators can only speculate concerning the reasons for this relationship in the control group. Our present inclination is to view attracted clients as individuals who would interpret even minimal clinic contact (such as is involved in testing sessions) as benefiting them in some way.

A study by Barron and Leary (1955) appears to offer support for this contention. They state, with regard to wait-list control clients:

simply having committed oneself to participating in psychotherapy, and having had a reciprocal commitment from a clinic to afford psychotherapy, even though not immediately, represents a breaking of the neurotic circle. A force for change has already been introduced. In addition, the initial interview and the psychological testing may themselves be psychotherapeutic events, since during such sessions the patient makes some efforts to confront himself and his problems more objectively than he has in the past (p. 244).

A recent investigation by Goldstein (1960a) supports this finding.

Table 2 presents the correlations between therapist expectancy of client improvement, as obtained at five session intervals, and client pre- and posttherapy attraction, as well as the change in attraction over the course of therapy.

TABLE 2

CORRELATIONS BETWEEN CLIENT ATTRACTION AND THERAPIST EXPECTANCY

Variables correlated	r
Preattraction and:	
TE_5[a]	.427
TE_{10}[b]	.144
TE_{15}[c]	.199
Difference-attraction and:	
TE_5	.619*
TE_{10}	−.137
TE_{15}	.418
Postattraction and:	
TE_5	.535*
TE_{10}	−.162
TE_{15}	.096

[a] Fifth session therapist expectancy.
[b] Tenth session therapist expectancy.
[c] Fifteenth session therapist expectancy.
* Significant at .05 level.

These findings indicate a significant relation between the expectation of client improvement held by the therapist early in therapy, and both the change in client attraction over the course of therapy and the magnitude of client attraction subsequent to the fifteenth session. None of the other correlations presented in Table 2 reached accepted levels of significance.

In addition to offering partial support for the hypothesis that therapist expectancy is a relationship maintaining aspect of the psychotherapeutic interaction, these findings raise the question as to why this should only be the case with regard to the therapist's early expectations (fifth session), and not his tenth and fifteenth session anticipations of client improvement. A study by Good (1952) furnishes a basis for differentiating "early" and "late" therapist expectations, a differentiation which appears to shed light on the present study's findings. He states:

Support was found for the hypothesis that in a relatively novel situation, generalization effects chiefly determine the expectancy held by S, and that as S has more experience with the specific task, expectancies develop which are a function of this task (p. 99).

In the present study, the expectations held by the therapist at the fifth session regarding client personality change may be more a function of his perceived success and failure with past clients than his feelings concerning his present client's progress. By the tenth session, however, their psychotherapeutic interaction is less "novel" and the major determiner of the therapists' expectations may have shifted from generalization effects to task effects. Kelly (1955), Lennard and Bernstein (1960), and Rotter (1954) have also noted significant temporal shifts in therapist expectancies over the course of psychotherapy.

The basis for the failure of late-therapy therapist expectations to be relationship maintaining would appear to be an important question for further research.

SUMMARY

The present investigation attempted to determine the extent to which client dependency and therapist expectation of client improvement can be considered relationship maintaining variables in the psychotherapeutic interaction. Thirty clients undergoing psychotherapy at a University Psychological Clinic were randomly assigned to "therapy" and "no-therapy" conditions and the 15 "therapy" clients were randomly assigned to 10 therapists. The therapists, for the most part, were advanced graduate students in clinical psychology at the Pennsylvania State University. Testing,

on measures developed or modified for the current study, took place pre- and post-therapy for all clients and after every five sessions for the therapists. Results of the study indicated a strong positive relation between client pretherapy attraction to the therapist and: (a) both client self-descriptive and behavioral dependency before therapy and, (b) client self-descriptive, but not behavioral, movement toward independence over the course of therapy. A similar but less marked relationship occurred in control group clients, offering further evidence for the therapeutic nature of such nonspecific clinic contacts as the intake interview and psychological testing.

An unexpected finding was the relatively high degree of relation between pretherapy attraction in therapy clients and their *overt* posttherapy dependency, a finding at variance with that obtained on self-descriptive instruments. In addition to other implications, this finding suggests caution in interpreting results in psychotherapy research which are based solely on one level of measurement.

Finally, partial support was obtained for the hypothesis that favorable therapist expectation of client improvement can function to maintain the therapeutic relationship.

REFERENCES

BARRON, F., & LEARY, T. Changes in psychoneurotic patients with and without psychotherapy. *J. consult. Psychol.,* 1955, 19, 239–245.

BERNARDIN, A. C., & JESSOR, R. A construct validation of the Edwards Personal Preference Schedule with respect to dependency. *J. consult. Psychol.,* 1957, 21, 63–67.

BORDIN, E. S. Inside the therapeutic hour. In E. A. Rubenstein & M. B. Parloff (Eds.), *Research in psychotherapy.* Washington. D.C.: American Psychological Association, 1959. Pp. 235–246.

BORGATTA, E. F. An analysis of three levels of response: An approach to some relationships among dimensions of personality. *Sociometry,* 1951, 14, 267–316.

DOLLARD, J., & MILLER, N. E. *Personality and psychotherapy.* New York: McGraw-Hill, 1950.

EDWARDS, A. L. *Edwards Personal Preference Schedule: Test and manual.* New York: Psychological Corporation, 1954.

FITZGERALD, B. J. Some relationships among projective tests, interviews, and sociometric measures of dependent behavior. *J. abnorm. soc. Psychol.,* 1958, 56, 199–203.

FORDYCE, W. E. Applications of a scale of dependency to concepts of self, ideal-self, mother, and father. Unpublished doctoral dissertation, University of Washington, 1953.

GISVOLD, D. A validity study of the autonomy and deference subscales of the EPPS. *J. consult. Psychol.,* 1958, 22, 445–447.

GOLDSTEIN, A. P. Patient's expectancies and nonspecific therapy as a basis for (un)spontaneous remission. *J. clin. Psychol.,* 1960, in press. (a)

GOLDSTEIN, A. P. Therapist and client expectations of personality change in psychotherapy. *J. counsel. Psychol.,* 1960, in press. (b)

GOOD, R. A. The potentiality for changes of an expectancy as a function of the amount of experience. Unpublished doctoral dissertation, Ohio State University, 1952.

HELLER, K. Dependency changes in psychotherapy as a function of the discrepancy between conscious self-description and projective test performance. Unpublished doctoral dissertation. Pennsylvania State University, 1959.

KELLEY, H. H. The effects of expectations upon first impressions of persons. *Amer. Psychologist,* 1949, 4, 252. (Abstract)

KELLY, G. A. *The psychology of personal constructs.* New York: Norton, 1955.

LENNARD, H. L., & BERNSTEIN, A. *The anatomy of psychotherapy.* New York: Columbia Univer. Press, 1960.

LIBO, L. *Picture impressions: A projective technique for investigating the patient-therapist relationship.* (Department of Psychiatry Publication Series) Baltimore: Univer. Maryland Medical School, 1956.

LIBO, L. The projective expression of patient-therapist attraction. *J. clin. Psychol.,* 1957, 13, 33–36.

MURRAY, H. A. *Thematic Apperception Test: Pictures and manual.* Cambridge: Harvard Univer. Press, 1943.

PETERSON, A., SNYDER, W. U., GUTHRIE, G. M., & RAY, W. S. Therapeutic factors: An exploratory investigation of therapeutic biases. *J. counsel. Psychol.,* 1958, 5, 169–173.

ROGERS, C. R., & DYMOND, R. F. *Psychotherapy and personality change.* Chicago: Univer. Chicago Press, 1954.

ROSENTHAL, R. Research in experimenter bias. Paper read at American Psychological Association, Cincinnati, September 1959.

ROSENZWEIG, S. Rosenzweig Picture-Frustration Study, revised form for adults: Test and manual. St. Louis: Author, 1947.

ROTTER, J. R. *Social learning and clinical psychology.* New York: Prentice-Hall, 1954.

UHLENHUTH, E. H., CANTER, A., NEUSTADT, J. O., & PAYSON, H. E. The symptomatic relief of anxiety with meprobamate, phenobarbital and placebo. *Amer. J. Psychiat.,* 1959, 115, 905–910.

ZUCKERMAN, M., & GROSZ, H. J. Suggestibility and dependency. *J. consult. Psychol.,* 1958, 22, 328.

Client Perceptions
of Therapists:
A Study of
Therapeutic Relation

MAURICE LORR

An important feature of the therapeutic relationship is the client's perception of and feeling toward the therapist. This aspect of the relationship has become identified with Freud's term "transference." However, in defining transference, some investigators such as Apfelbaum (1958) emphasize the clients' "strongly held expectations regarding the personalities of their prospective therapists" gained prior to therapy. These expectations mould experience, creating misperceptions and inappropriate responses. Others like Snyder and Snyder (1961) regard transference simply as the character of the client's feeling and attitudes toward his therapist. The view taken by the writer is that the client brings to treatment certain well-established interpersonal reaction patterns. An individual's interpersonal behavior with significant others will be similar to the behavior he experienced in child-

Reprinted from *Journal of Consulting Psychology*, 1965, 29 (2), 146–149, with the permission of the American Psychological Association and the author.

hood, usually with his parents (Schutz, 1958, p. 196). When the client perceives his adult position in an interpersonal situation to be similar to his own position in his childhood relations, his adult behavior will be similar to his childhood behavior toward significant others. For example, the client may perceive and react to his therapist as though the latter were a rejecting parent, a competitive sibling, a nurturant protector, or a stern authority figure. The client's perception of his therapist will thus, at any stage of therapy, be a useful indicator of his interpersonal relation to his therapist.

In view of the importance of client perception of the therapist, it would be of considerable value to determine the major ways in which clients view their therapists. Accordingly, this study was designed to identify some of the principal dimensions of client perception of therapists. To this end eight constructs were hypothesized. Several concepts were drawn from Fiedler's (1950, 1953) conceptualizations of what constitutes a good therapeutic relationship. Other sources examined were Apfelbaum's

Q sort statements, as well as the concepts developed by Leary and his associates (Leary, 1957). The constructs postulated were the following: Directiveness, Nurturance, Understanding, Acceptance, Equalitarianism, Independence-Encouraging, Critical Detachment, and Hostile Rejection.

METHOD

An inventory of 65 statements was constructed and assembled. Each of the postulated constructs was defined by 4–10 statements descriptive of therapist behaviors. The patient indicated how often the therapist exhibited the behavior described (almost never, sometimes, usually, nearly always). The inventory was administered to 523 patients in individual psychotherapy in 43 veteran clinics in connection with a larger study of the correlates of length of psychotherapy. All patients had been in treatment at least 3 months but not more than 10 years. Approximately 50% of the sample were neurotics, 32% psychotics,

and the remainder, personality disorders and psychophysiological disturbances.

Responses to the statements were intercorrelated and ordered into a matrix on the basis of the hypothesized eight clusters. Examination revealed that three of the clusters were not distinguishable from the remaining five. As a consequence, the variables were reclustered entirely on the basis of their statistical properties. Five distinguishable orthogonal factors were extracted simultaneously by the multiple-group centroid method, with the highest correlation in a column as the communality estimate. The factor matrix was then transformed to oblique simple structure.

RESULTS

The results of the analysis are presented in Tables 1 and 2. The behaviors most substantially correlated with each factor are given in Table 1. Negative signs should be interpreted to mean that the behavior described occurred rarely.

TABLE 1

CORRELATIONS OF PERCEIVED THERAPIST BEHAVIORS WITH FACTORS

	r_{tv}
Factor A: Understanding	
Seems to know exactly what I mean.	.66
Seems to understand how I feel.	.61
Realizes and understands how my experiences feel to me.	.60
Understands me even when I don't express myself well.	.59
Misses the point I am trying to get across.	−.48
Has a hard time seeing things as I do.	−.47
Has difficulty understanding what I am trying to express.	−.45
Is protective of and really concerned about my welfare.	.43
Makes comments that are right in line with what I am saying.	.41
Factor B: Accepting	
Shows a real interest in me and my problems.	.66
Is easy to talk to.	.58
Acts as though we were co-workers on a common problem.	.54
Makes me feel that he is one person I can really trust.	.52
Is quick to praise and commend me when I am doing well.	.50
Gives generously of his time and energy to others.	.50
Understands my problems and worries.	.49

TABLE 1—*Continued*

CORRELATIONS OF PERCEIVED THERAPIST BEHAVIORS WITH FACTORS

	r_{tv}
Factor B: Accepting—*Continued*	
Shows a real liking and affection for me.	.47
Makes me feel free to say whatever I think.	.46
Seems to have a very real respect for me.	.45
Makes me feel better after talking about my worries with him.	.43
Relates to me as though I were a companion.	.43
Factor C: Authoritarian	
Is full of advice about everything I do.	.61
Tells me what to do when I have difficult decisions to make.	.59
Offers me advice on my everyday problems.	.54
Seems to try to get me to accept his standards.	.52
Expects me to accept his ideas and opinions.	.50
Tries to get me to think as he does.	.47
Makes me feel that I don't have to agree with him.	−.29
Tells me what I should talk about.	.28
Factor D: Independence-Encouraging	
Expects an individual to shoulder his own responsibilities.	.71
Thinks people should be able to help themselves.	.67
Encourages me to work on my own problems in my own way.	.51
Tries to get me to make my own decisions.	.47
Factor E: Critical-Hostile	
Becomes impatient when I make mistakes.	.46
Acts smug and superior as though he knew all the answers.	.45
Acts as though he were trying to outsmart me.	.41
Gives me the impression that he doesn't like me.	.37
Talks down to me as if I were a child.	.35
Ignores some of my feelings.	.32
Is critical and not easily impressed.	.32
Acts as though I were dull and uninteresting.	.29
Is a difficult person to warm up to.	.29
Seems glad to see the interview finished.	.28

TABLE 2

CORRELATIONS AMONG THERAPIST BEHAVIOR PATTERNS AS PERCEIVED BY CLIENTS

Therapist behavior	Factor				
	A	B	C	D	E
Understanding (A)	—				
Accepting (B)	.23	—			
Authoritarian (C)	.29	.25	—		
Independence-Encouraging (D)	.02	−.14	−.05	—	
Critical-Hostile (E)	−.25	−.44	.14	.17	—

Factor A, Understanding, is defined by behaviors that indicate the therapist understands what the patient is communicating and what he is feeling. The factor corresponds closely to Roger's (1957) postulated requirement for effective therapy. Factor B is the broadest of the five factors isolated. Interest, Nurturance, and Equalitarianism appear to play equal roles in definition of this factor, which is tentatively called Accepting.

In Factor C may be found those behaviors of the therapist relating to control. The client perceives the therapist as offering advice, direction, and assistance in reaching decisions. It should be noted that nurturant and supportive items correlate with Factor B and not with Factor C, which is labeled Authoritarian. The fourth factor, D, is relatively small but sharply defined. The pattern describes the postulated Independence-Encouraging construct. Every statement allocated to D correlated significantly only on D as predicted. The fifth factor, E, is labeled Critical-Hostile. The client perceives his therapist as critical, cold, impatient, and even competitive and disapproving.

The correlations among the factors (Table 2) indicate that on the whole the five factors are relatively independent. The small positive intercorrelations among factors Understanding, Accepting, and Authoritarian imply that a higher order factor common to the three could be demonstrated.

DISCUSSION

Rausch and Bordin (1957) in their discussion of the concept of therapist warmth present it as divisible into three more elementary notions called commitment, understanding, and spontaneity. Commitment refers to the degree to which the therapist seems willing to devote and lend himself to what the patient lacks. The concept of commitment appears to correspond closely to the factor of Accepting. Their concept of understanding refers to the therapist's ef-

fort to understand how the patient experiences himself and the world around him and appears to correspond to Factor A. The third element, spontaneity, is not clearly defined and appears not to have a correlative factor in the present study.

Fiedler (1950) envisages three dimensions in the therapeutic relationship. One is the therapist's ability to communicate with and to understand the patient. This variable is confirmed in Factor A, Understanding. The emotional distance which the therapist maintains toward the patient (close versus far), Fiedler's second variable, appears to be represented both by Critical-Hostility and Acceptance. The third Fiedler variable, the status of the therapist in relation to the patient (superior, equal, or subordinate), appears to be a composite variable. The attitude of superiority is reflected to some extent in the Authoritarian factor. The equalitarian tendencies are absorbed in Accepting, Factor B.

Apfelbaum (1958) in constructing his Q-sort items attempted to maximize intersorter variance. He constructed statements which were ambiguous enough to make the meaning given them a source of differentiating power. However, by and large, the items covered a wide variety of interpersonal expectations relevant to the psychotherapeutic situation. His procedures permitted him to discover only the principal themes that created difference among his three patient clusters, as he did not factor his Q-sort items. The themes suggested by the discriminating items were: warmth-nurturance versus coldness-indifference; directiveness versus nondirectiveness, i.e., independence-encouraging. The first theme may be seen to resemble the Accepting and Critical-Hostile factors. The second theme is represented here by the Authoritarian and Independence-Encouraging factors.

The factors identified thus correspond fairly well to those described by Rausch and Bordin, Fiedler, and Apfelbaum. But, do the dimensions isolated represent observed therapist behaviors or the expectations and distortions of the patient who made the ratings? The data do not permit such a question to be answered. The situation itself suggests the rating constitutes a complex amalgam of both sources of variance. However, it seems likely that the same dimensions are involved in either case. Dimensions of patient expectations will correspond fairly well to observed therapist behavior dimensions in therapy. Indirect support for this hypothesis is the Q-sort findings of Apfelbaum previously cited.

Of some interest are the relations of three ratings, obtained from patients and their therapists at the time of the completion of the inventory, to the inventory scores. As Table 3 shows, patient ratings of overall improvement and therapist judgments of patient satisfaction with treatment are positively correlated with the same factors. Patient ratings of therapist Understanding and Accepting are significantly associated with these two judgments. To a lesser extent the therapist improvement ratings are also associated with favorable perceptions of the patient. The results thus support the hypothesized importance of client views of their therapists.

TABLE 3

RELATIONS BETWEEN CLIENT AND THERAPIST RATINGS AND PERCEIVED
THERAPIST BEHAVIORS

Therapist behavior	Improvement rating		Judge client satisfaction
	Client	Therapist	
Understanding	.31	.19	.30
Accepting	.24	.16	.24
Authoritarian	—.16	—.03	—.19
Independence-Encouraging	.13	.08	.09
Critical-Hostile	—.19	—.06	—.08

Note.—Correlations greater than .13 are significant, $p < .02$.

REFERENCES

APFELBAUM, B. *Dimensions of transference in psychotherapy.* Berkeley, Calif.: Univer. California Publications, 1958.

FIEDLER, F. E. The concept of an ideal therapeutic relationship. *Journal of Consulting Psychology,* 1950, 14, 239–245.

FIEDLER, F. E. Quantitative studies on the role of therapists' feelings toward their patients. In O. H. Mowrer (Ed.), *Psychotherapy theory and research.* New York: Ronald Press, 1953.

LEARY, T. *Interpersonal diagnosis of personality.* New York: Ronald Press, 1957.

RAUSCH, H. L., & BORDIN, E. S. Warmth in personality development and in psychotherapy. *Psychiatry,* 1957, 20, 351–363.

ROGERS, C. R. The necessary and sufficient conditions of therapeutic personality change. *Journal of Consulting Psychology,* 1957, 21, 95–103.

SCHUTZ, W. C. *FIRO: A three-dimensional theory of interpersonal behavior.* New York: Rinehart, 1958.

SNYDER, W. J., & SNYDER, B. JUNE. *The psychotherapy relationship.* New York: Macmillan, 1961.

Counselor Anxiety in Relation to Amount of Clinical Experience and Quality of Affect Demonstrated by Clients[1]

PETER D. RUSSELL
WILLIAM U. SNYDER

In recent years increasing attention has been given to the behavior of the counselor in interview situations. Studies have been made investigating counselor personality, counselor techniques, and the relationship between counselor and client. These questions have practical significance for graduate programs in clinical psychology since they are relevant to the teaching of counseling methods.

In the present study the investigators attempted to examine the effect of a hostile

Reprinted from *Journal of Consulting Psychology,* 1963, 27 (4), 358–363, with the permission of the American Psychological Association and the authors.

[1] This study is based on a PhD dissertation conducted by Peter D. Russell at the Pennsylvania State University under the direction of William U. Snyder, Donald H. Ford, and Deno G. Thevaos. One of the tests used in the study was derived from scales devised by William U. Snyder, which had been based in part on previous work by Donald H. Ford and Oliver H. Bown.

or a friendly client demeanor upon counselor anxiety from the standpoint of relatively experienced and relatively inexperienced graduate student clinical psychology counselors. Two hypotheses were developed. First, it was proposed that student counselors, regardless of amount of experience, display greater anxiety in interviews with hostile clients than in interviews with friendly clients. The second hypothesis was that more experienced student counselors display less anxiety than less experienced student counselors in interviews with both hostile and friendly clients. These hypotheses were examined by means of four measures of the dependent variable of anxiety, i.e., palmar sweating, eyeblink rate, client-actor estimates of counselor anxiety, and judgments of verbal anxiety made by independent judges.

A review of the literature revealed that this was a relatively new area of consideration. Although there has been some theorizing, only a few experimental studies were found which explored the effects of hostile client affect on counselor anxiety. There were some investigations which utilized physiological measures, but only one report was found in which the counselors' palmar-sweating index had been employed, and this was only tangentially related to the current inquiry (Light, 1951). Using actors in the roles of clients, as in the present study, had been undertaken only once before to the investigators' knowledge (Kounin, Polansky, Biddle, Coburn, & Fenn, 1956). However, for that study the actor did not take an active role in the evaluation nor was the behavior of the counselors under scrutiny. Also, studies were reported which were concerned with speech patterns as an index of anxiety, but none of these inquired into counselor behavior. No investigations were found which directly related the counselor's level of experience to the anxiety produced in certain types of interviews.

Two studies have reported results relevant to those cited in the present investigation. Bandura, Lipsher, and Miller (1960), using analyses of actual therapy interviews (but not simulated interviews), found that therapists who typically expressed their own hostility in direct forms, and who displayed low need for approval, were more likely to permit and encourage their patients' hostility than were therapists who expressed little direct hostility and who showed high approval seeking behavior. Psychotherapists were more inclined to avoid hostility when it was directed toward themselves than when the patients directed their hostility toward others. The patients were more likely to drop the hostile topic, or to change the object of their hostility following therapists' avoidance reactions, than they were following the therapists' approach reactions.

Heller, Myers, and Kline (1963), in a subsequent study, copied in part after the present investigation, and employing client-actors in simulated therapy situations, have

demonstrated that dominant client behavior will evoke dependent interviewer behavior, and dependent client behavior will evoke dominant interviewer behavior. They also showed that hostile client behavior will evoke hostile interviewer behavior, and friendly client behavior will evoke friendly interviewer behavior. They were not able to demonstrate, as was the present study, that hostile client behavior will evoke anxiety on the part of a therapist.

METHOD
Design and Procedure

The design of the study randomized the order in which counselors participated. Two client-actors were each seen by half of a group of 10 more experienced counselors in their first interviews, and by the other half of the group in the second. The same procedure was followed for 10 relatively inexperienced counselors. Moreover, each of the two client-actors was seen in a friendly role 20 times and in a hostile role an equal number of times.

The two client-actors were chosen from a group of undergraduate males enrolled in a theatre arts course. It was felt that actors could assume the roles required most meaningfully. While having demonstrated acting proficiency, they had not appeared extensively in public roles where they might might have been observed by the student clinicians. The actors were chosen on the basis of lack of neurotic trends, similarity of physical appearance and age, and ability to take the required roles and play them spontaneously in a hostile and in a friendly manner. They were paid for their work, in order to maintain their interest in the project.

The actors underwent 10 hours of training to respond in interviews in two different ways: in a very friendly manner which was positive and helpful, and in a hostile and negative manner. They were quickly able to fill in the missing elements of their "background" stories when this seemed called for in the simulated counseling situation. While the spontaneity of the situation was maintained, their ways of presenting problems, information, and affect became quite constant. In a pilot study which was carried out, it was discovered that the actors were presenting somewhat extreme characterizations of the typical friendly or hostile client roles, so that the counselors of the pilot study were able to detect that the situations were somewhat exaggerated, and therefore not real counseling situations. Consequently the roles were made less deviant from the mean level of affect, and in the actual experiment itself, it was ascertained that none of the counselor-subjects detected the true character of the study, nor realized that the clients were actors.

The utility of the counseling paradigm which made use of actors who took the roles of clients was explored at some length. It was felt that this design had unique advantages for the study of counselor anxiety. It offers a compromise between the reality, but lack of control, of the study of real counseling, and the fine control, but lack of reality, of other analogues to a counseling situation, i.e., films or tape recordings. The use of actors role playing in what seems to be a normal counseling situation to the subjects, permits the manipulation of an independent variable which is uncontaminated by the fact that the counselor knows he is being studied or by other extraneous factors which are difficult to control. The counselor not only thinks that the client is real, but also that he is helping him. For the present investigation each subject was able to act as his own control for the study of the effects of hostility and friendliness due to the counterbalanced design, so the need for matching was eliminated.

Dependent Measures

Palmar sweating. Employing the revised method of Mowrer (1953), the fingerprint stain test of palmar sweating was administered before and after each interview following thorough handwashing. The densities of the stains were measured by means of an adaptation of Mowrer's apparatus which passes light through the stain onto a photoelectric cell. The counselors were told that this measure was being used on them in order to determine congruence of counselor-client feeling, a measure which was being considered for predictive ability regarding the extent to which marginally motivated clients would apply themselves in the counseling process.

In order to take into account possible influences on the amount of sweating, several new controls were employed. At the outset, stains were made for both index fingers. Where the stains appeared equally dark, the right index finger was used for subsequent measurements. In the cases where one print was perceptibly darker than the other, the finger producing the darker stain was used. This controlled for the possibility of peripheral nerve damage to an extremity (Cross, Dodds, & Knights, 1960) and consequent potential reduced sensitivity to tension changes.

Secondly, the counselors were allowed to rest for at least 15 minutes after coming to the experimental room so that they might become accommodated to the situation. This time was used to give the instructions. Also approximately 15 minutes of rest was given between post- and premeasures of the first and second interviews, respectively, in order to facilitate dissipation of any anxiety and concomitant physiological reactions. Temperature and relative humidity were measured continuously by means of hygrothermographs in both the counseling room and the monitor room where the palmar-sweating measurements were taken. Large changes in either might have affected the amount of sweating, but no significant variations were noted. Also, it seemed necessary to make sure that the counselors were not ill, since it is likely that fever might cause an increase in palmar sweating. In order to guarantee that there were no cases of fever or illness, this topic was brought up during the period before the first interview, and ruled out before the counseling began. Finally, hyperthyroidism can lead to an increase in palmar sweating (Walmer, 1961).[2] However this factor was adequately controlled by checking the pulse rate.

Eyeblink rate. By means of a concealed closed-circuit television system, blink rates of the counselors were observed and recorded during the second and fifth 5-minute portions of the half-hour interviews. A check on the accuracy of the investigator's counting of the number of blinks showed a very high degree of reliability of measurement.

"Client's" Scale of Counselor Anxiety. Following the completion of each interview while the counselor was having his postinterview stain test, the client-actor completed a scale rating the anxiety which the counselor had revealed in the interview. This scale consisted of 60 items selected from three sources: items modified from Snyder's (1961) *Client's Postinterview Attitudes Toward Therapy* scale and *Therapist's Personal Reaction Questionnaire,* and a group of 10 items prepared especially for the present study.

Judgments of verbal anxiety. This scale of criteria of verbal anxiety was developed from statements concerning counselor anxiety which appeared in the literature,[3] in addition to several criteria developed for the present study. These criteria were refined by being submitted to a group of five experienced and carefully trained judges who were doing full-time vocational counseling and psychotherapy in the Division of Counseling at the Pennsylvania State University. Those criteria which were adjudged "significant measures" by three of

the five judges, and for which the judges agreed upon the appropriate examples submitted to them, were compiled into a scale of 14 items. However, this scale was further modified by being submitted to a group of six other experienced judges, who were the ones who later did the actual rating of the interviews. Two new criteria which appeared relatively frequently enough in the pilot-study interviews were added to the original scale, thus making a total of 16 criteria for judging counselor anxiety which could be observed in the interview situation or protocols.

The sixteen criteria of counselor anxiety were the following:[4] direct statement of anxiety; asking questions or changing the subject; *interrupting; impersonal or premature interpretations; unnecessary reassurance; disapproval; intellectualizing, and not responding to client's feelings; introjection of references to the counselor's own experiences; *unfinished sentences; *repeating words or phrases; *stuttering; *blocking; poor voice quality, tremulousness, "cracking" voice, etc.; apologizing for some fault in counseling technique; inappropriate laughter; and other signs of anxiety.

Several of these signs of anxiety were not common among all counselors, but had a relatively high frequency of occurence in the protocols of particular ones. The starred items were common in all interviews.

Establishing Interjudge Agreement

The six judges spent approximately 12 hours in training as a group. During this period the meaning of each criterion and its application to sample interviews was discussed and clarified. It was required that an agreement of 88% be reached on each unit in the test sample before training was considered adequate.

Some question arises regarding the problem of controlling for interview identity

[2] J. D. Walmer, personal communication, July 15, 1961.
[3] See studies by Dibner (1956), Dollard and Mowrer (1947), Kauffman and Raimy (1949), Lasswell (1935), Sanford (1942), Zimmerman (1950), Mahl (1956, 1959), Boomer and Goodrich (1961) and Krause (1961).

[4] The starred items are those signs of anxiety occurring more frequently and more uniformly.

with regard to knowledge on the part of the judge as to whether the interview was a friendly or hostile one. It would be impossible, of course, to disguise this fact from the judges (who might also have guessed the identity of a few of the counselors). Some of the specific criteria of counselor anxiety which might be more influenced by this knowledge would be "direct statement of anxiety," "premature interpretations," "disapproval," and "apologizing for some fault in counselor technique." However, these were among the signs of counselor anxiety which occurred fairly infrequently, and therefore had relatively little effect on the score of counselor anxiety at which the judges arrived in each case.

Selection of Student Counselors

Two groups of 10 male student clinicians were drawn from the total poulation of clinical psychology graduate students. The 22 eligible students were evaluated for clinical experience in order to place them in the "more experienced" or "less experienced" group. Using a modification of Tirnauer's (1959) questionnaire, 13 types of clinical experience were taken into consideration in arriving at composite "clinical experience" rankings. The groups, as finally constituted, were also evaluated for general ability (using the Miller's Analogy Test scores) and age, since these factors might lead to the expected results if the experienced counselors were basically more capable and/or older. Ability, as defined by MAT scores, was not found to be a factor differentiating the two groups; the experienced group was, however, something a little over a half year older than the inexperienced group. This difference was not considered to be significant.

Judgments of Client-Actor Affect

The 40 interview typescripts were presented in an individually randomized sequence to three nonpsychologist judges.

They were asked to sort them into equal-sized piles in terms of client hostility or friendliness. The three judges performed this task without error, thus indicating that the client-actors had adopted clearly differentiable roles throughout the experiment.

RESULTS

The hypothesis concerned with the differential effects of hostility and friendliness on both the experienced and inexperienced groups of counselors was analyzed by means of the Wilcoxen matched-pairs signed-ranks test, while the Mann-Whitney U test was applied to the data in comparing counselor anxiety in terms of the levels of counselor experience.

As far as the comparison of types of affect was concerned, it was found that eye-blink rate, the "Client's" Scale of Counselor Anxiety, and the scores derived from the Judgments of Verbal Anxiety Scale revealed that hostile behavior on the part of a client-actor created more anxiety in the two groups of counselors than did friendly behavior. The levels of significance obtained were much greater than the level set in advance (.05 level) for rejection of the null hypothesis. Significance levels obtained were all at the .001 level for the more experienced counselors and better than the .005 level for the less experienced counselors. For the relatively inexperienced counselors, one individual from the group had results in the nonpredicted direction in each case. For both groups of counselors the trends for palmar sweating were in the expected direction, but were not statistically significant. Thus it could be said that the first hypothesis was supported.

The comparison between levels of counselor experience revealed that only one dependent measure significantly displayed the expected difference between groups of counselors. For the friendly interview, eyeblink rate indicated that the more experienced counselors were made less anxious by the client-actors' behavior than were the less experienced counselors. The total anxiety score from the Judgments of Verbal Anxiety Scale almost reached the .05 level of significance for this same type of interview. The results of the other dependent measures showed trends both in the predicted and nonpredicted directions for the two types of interviews. It may be concluded that graduate training and experiences did not seem to affect the degree of anxiety manifested by the counselors.

Paired relationships between the measures were computed by means of the Spearman "rho" correlation. Combinations of scales were also evaluated for interrelationship by means of the Kendall coefficient of concordance. For these correlations the two groups of counselors were combined. For the interviews with the hostile client-actor, eyeblink was found to be significantly correlated with the "Client's" Scale of Counselor Anxiety and with the total anxiety score of the index of judgments of verbal anxiety. None of the other paired comparisons of measures for either type of interview produced correlations indicative of a statistically significant relationship, nor did the group comparison of measures reveal significant intercorrelations.

DISCUSSION

The hypothesis stating that student counselors, regardless of experience, display greater anxiety in interviews with hostile clients than in interviews with friendly clients seems to be supported, at least as far as the present counselors were concerned. Regarding the failure to find significant differences in the predicted direction between the experienced and inexperienced counselors for both friendly and hostile interviews, it is felt that the indices might not have been sensitive enough to show existing differences. The supposition that there should be differences in reactions to both types of interviews, depending on the amount of clinical experience, still seems reasonable because the idea has at

least face validity, and there were more trends in the expected direction than the converse. Perhaps a more appropriate measure of experience would have been the amount of such experience which constituted work with hostile clients, specifically.

Increasing the size of the groups or extending the length of the interviews might help to distinguish between such groups from a graduate student population. Of even greater importance would be the selecting of therapist groups with a minimum of overlap between those with experience and those who were inexperienced.

Consideration of the relative value of the dependent measures as research instruments suggests that the palmar-sweating index is open to serious question as a meaningful research tool.

Eyeblink rate appeared to be quite useful for investigations of counselor anxiety. It not only discriminated very highly between types of client-actor affect for both counselor groups, but also reflected differences in direction for a particular type of interview.

The "Client's" Scale of Counselor Anxiety was also found useful, but certain modifications of the instrument appear to be necessary. The statement might be made that the differences obtained on this scale were due to biases of the actors. However, an evaluation of interactor agreement in the application of the scale suggests that the counterbalanced design should serve to randomize any consistent bias on the part of the client-actors. Additional items need to be constructed which would allow finer discriminations to be made at the nonanxious end of the scale.

Considering the Judgments of Verbal Anxiety Scale, there were high discriminating ability of the instrument between types of interviews, and high interjudge agreement achieved in using this scale. Perhaps certain individual criteria would prove to be more useful in specific contexts; however, removing some of these criteria might cause the scale to lose its differentiating ability. Increases in numbers of counselors or the length of interviews would be possible methods of improving the discrimination of this scale even further.

As far as the lack of demonstrated relationships among the indices is concerned, it can be maintained that this did not necessarily indicate that they were too unprecise to be of value. It is suggested that instead of the four apparently independent dimensions of anxiety having separate antecedents, they might be related to a single antecedent, viz., the mediating anxiety response.

REFERENCES

BANDURA, A., LIPSHER, D., & MILLER, PAULA E. Psychotherapists' approach-avoidance reactions to patients' expressions of hostility. *J. consult. Psychol.*, 1960, 24, 1–8.

BOOMER, D. S., & GOODRICH, D. W. Speech disturbance and judged anxiety. *J. consult. Psychol.*, 1961, 25, 160–164.

CROSS, R. L., DODDS, M. E., & KNIGHTS, E. M., JR. Sudomotor test. *M. D. med. News. Mag.*, 1960, 4, 65.

DIBNER, A. S. Cue-counting: A measure of anxiety in interviews. *J. consult. Psychol.*, 1956, 20, 475–478.

DOLLARD, J., & MOWRER, O. H. A method of measuring tension in written documents. *J. abnorm. soc. Psychol.*, 1947, 42, 3–32.

HELLER, K., MYERS, R. A., & KLINE, LINDA V. Interviewer behavior as a function of standardized client roles. *J. consult. Psychol.*, 1963, 27, 117–122.

KAUFFMAN, P. E., & RAIMY, V. C. Two methods of assessing therapeutic progress. *J. abnorm. soc. Psychol.*, 1949, 44, 379–385.

KOUNIN, J., POLANSKY, N., BIDDLE, B., COBURN, H., & FENN, A. Experimental studies of clients' reactions to initial interviews. *Hum. Relat.*, 1956, 9, 265–293.

KRAUSE, M. S. Anxiety in verbal behavior: An intercorrelational study. *J. consult. Psychol.*, 1961, 25, 272.

LASSWELL, H. D. Verbal references and physiological changes during the psychoanalytic interview: A preliminary communication. *Psychoanal. Rev.*, 1935, 22, 10–24.

LIGHT, B. H. Tension changes in patients undergoing psychotherapy. Unpublished doctoral dissertation, University of Illinois, 1951.

MAHL, G. F. Disturbances and silences in the patient's speech in psychotherapy. *J. abnorm. soc. Psychol.*, 1956, 53, 1–15.

MAHL, G. F. Measuring the patient's anxiety during interviews from "expressive" aspects of his speech. *Trans. N. Y. Acad. Sci., Ser. 2,* 1959, 21, 249–257.

MOWRER, O. H. *Psychotherapy theory and research.* New York: Ronald Press, 1953.

SANFORD, F. H. Speech and personality. *Psychol. Bull.*, 1942, 39, 811–845.

SNYDER, W. U. *The psychotherapy relationship.* New York: Macmillan, 1961.

TIRNAUER, L. Anxiety and the behavior of psychotherapists in an experimental setting. Unpublished doctoral dissertation, Pennsylvania State University 1959.

ZIMMERMAN, J. Modification of the DRQ as a measure of progress in counseling. Unpublished master's thesis, University of Chicago, 1950.

Empathy, Need to Change, and Improvement with Psychotherapy[1]

ROSALIND DYMOND CARTWRIGHT
BARBARA LERNER

There is a growing body of evidence indicating that improvement in psychoneurotic patients takes place concurrent with psychotherapy, but as yet little consensus concerning the factors responsible for such improvement. To the majority of writers in this field, improvement is a function of specific patient variables, therapist variables, and the interactions among them. However, different writers select different factors as accounting for the major portion of the variance in therapeutic outcome. Since the research evidence is most often unreplicated, or even contradictory, and since there are still large unexplored areas, one can pick and choose among the scraps and fashion a patchwork quilt after one's own heart or theoretic commitment.

Reprinted from *Journal of Consulting Psychology,* 1963, 27 (2), 138–144, with the permission of the American Psychological Association and the authors.

[1] The authors are pleased to acknowledge the very considerable help they received in clarifying the material in this paper from the critical reading of the manuscript by Ernest Haggard and Fred L. Strodtbeck.

Although the various schools of psychotherapy have different views as to what constitutes the necessary and sufficient conditions of the therapeutic process, the studies which compare the respective percentages of successfully treated cases have shown rather similar results for all theoretic approaches. This frequent finding suggests that some common elements exist among the vairous approaches to psychotherapy and, that they might very well be more significantly related to improvement than the elements on which the schools differ.

The evidence for two such common elements has been accruing slowly. The studies of Heine (1950) and Fiedler (1950a, 1950b) strongly suggest that one important therapist variable, independent of technique differences, is the therapist's ability to empathically understand his patient. A patient variable which is suggested by the work of Butler and Haigh (1954), Rosenthal and Frank (1956), Cartwright and Cartwright (1958), and Kirtner and Cartwright (1958), as one important to any form of verbal therapy, is the patient's initial recognized need to change. These two promising variables, *the therapist's empathy* and *the patient's need to change*, were selected to form the basic dimensions of this study. However, since we now feel that therapy depends not only on the qualities of the two participants but also on how these affect their relationship, this study attempted to tease out some of the interaction effects of these two major variables.

Part I of the study was undertaken with three primary hypotheses:

1. The degree of need to change on the part of the patient is directly related to improvement with psychotherapy.

2. The empathic understanding of the patient by the therapist is directly related to the degree of improvement in the patient with psychotherapy.

3. These two variables considered jointly will give a better prediction of outcome than either taken singly.

After analyzing the data relative to these hypotheses which had been formulated prior to the data collection, other questions arose concerning the interaction of additional variables with those selected for this study and with the dependent variable, improvement. Part II of this paper considers the sex of the patient in relation to the sex of the therapist, the "psychological distance" the therapist puts between himself and his patient, and the experience level of the therapist. These additional variables were explored to help clarify some of the interpersonal processes underlying the results obtained from testing the major hypotheses. This study, then, involves the consideration of five variables, some of their interactions, and their relation to improvement with psychotherapy. These five variables can be organized according to a threefold scheme: (*a*) patient characteristics independent of the particular therapist (recognized need to change), (*b*) therapist characteristics independent of particular patient (therapist's level of experience), and (*c*) characteristics dependent upon the particular patient-therapist pair (the therapist's empathy or

ability to understand the patient in his own terms, whether or not the patient and therapist are of the same sex, and the therapist's distancing of the patient).

METHOD

Sample

The subjects were 28 patients who voluntarily sought treatment at the Counseling Center of the University of Chicago.[2] Fourteen of the subjects were male, 14 female. They ranged in age from 19 to 43 with a mean age of 27.7. Although these patients were not formally diagnosed, according to their therapists' ratings on "severity of illness" they ranged from "very mild" to "near psychotic." Sixteen client-centered therapists were involved, and the case length varied from 6 to 116 interviews with a mean of 40.

Instruments

The two instruments in this study are referred to as Scale A and Scale B. Scale A provided the data for the improvement criterion and Scale B provided the measure of the patient's need to change, the measure of the therapist's empathic understanding of his patient, and the therapist's distancing of the patient.

Scale A was administered to the therapists on two occasions, after the second interview, referred to as the pretherapy rating, and after the last interview, for a posttherapy rating. The Improvement score was the sum of four components: three change scores between the pre-and posttherapy ratings of: (*a*) the patient's integration; (*b*) his kind of organization (defensive versus open); and (*c*) his present life adjustment. The fourth component of the Improvement score was the therapists' final rating of the

[2] No selectivity of patients was exercised. Each new applicant was requested to participate in the study until the quota of 30 subjects was reached. Two patients had not completed treatment at the time the data analysis was begun.

outcome of therapy. All ratings were made on nine-point scales.

Scale B differed in content for each subject. Each subject in a sense supplied his own items. This was done in an effort to insure that the scales would be highly personally relevant to each patient. The items were the personal constructs obtained by first administering Kelly's (1955) Role Construct Repertory Test to each subject. From these personal constructs which each patient introduced as constituting the important similarities and differences among the real people in his life, the first 10 discrete ones were selected. Scale B was then made up of the 10 items supplied by each patient arranged as five-point rating scales. On the first testing occasion following interview Number 2, the subject made various ratings of these items: (a) to describe himself as he is at present, and (b) to describe himself as he wants to be when therapy has been completed. The sum of the squared discrepancies between these two sets of ratings was used as the measure of his felt need to change on the 10 items of particular significance to him. The patient repeated this task at posttherapy to again describe himself as he was then.

Scale B was also the basis for the measurement of the therapist's empathic understanding of his patient. After the second interview the therapist was given a Scale B form containing the 10 items chosen by his patient. He then attempted to describe "the patient as he sees himself." The empathy measure was the squared discrepancy between the patient's self-description and the therapist's attempt to predict the patient's self-description. The therapist repeated this task at posttherapy time. This procedure was used to measure the therapist's empathic understanding after increased contact with the patient.

RESULTS
Part I

Hypothesis 1: The degree of need to change on the part of the patient is directly related to improvement. Table 1 shows that Hypothesis 1 is strongly supported.

The mean need to change score was much higher for the improved than for the unimproved group.

Hypothesis 2: The empathic understanding of the patient by the therapist is directly related to the degree of improvement in the patient with psychotherapy. Table 1 shows that there was no significant difference between the improved and unimproved cases on their therapists' ability to understand their pretherapy self-image. However, at the close of therapy, the therapists understood the self-image of the improved patients significantly better than they did those who were unimproved. Also there was a significant gain in the therapists' empathy score between the first (E_1) and second (E_2) occasions—but only

TABLE 1

MEAN SCORES ON PATIENTS' NEED TO CHANGE AND THERAPISTS' EMPATHY
FOR THE IMPROVED AND UNIMPROVED PATIENTS

Variables	Improved[a]	Unimproved[b]	t	df
Need to change	47.26	20.00	3.17**	26
Pre-T empathy (E_1)	15.93	16.69	—	
Post-T empathy (E_2)	9.40	14.46	2.24*	26

Note.—Since the Empathy Score is based on a D^2 measure, the lower the score the greater the empathy.
[a] $N = 15$.
[b] $N = 13$.
* $p > .02$.
** $p > .01$.

for the improved cases. This result showed that there was a significant relation between improvement and increased understanding. For those who were rated unimproved through therapy, the therapists made no significant gain in their understanding of them.

Perhaps the explanation of the relation between high posttherapy empathy and improvement is not the obvious one, that the therapist coming to understand his patient's own view of himself contributes to more and better therapeutic work being done. Perhaps, instead of the therapist coming to understand the patient, the patient is adopting his therapist's view of him. This alternate view might well account for the results. Such a change would make it easier for the therapist to predict how the patient "sees himself" and also possibly be valued as a growth in insight making it more likely that the case be rated "improved." We have, then, to test: do improved cases change so that their posttherapy self-description resembles the description the therapist made of them at pretherapy time more closely than their pretherapy self-description did. The chi square test here was significant in the opposite direction. At posttherapy, 11 of the improved cases descriptions of themselves were *less* like the therapists' pretherapy descriptions of them than they had originally been, and only 4 were more like them. For the unimproved group the reverse relationship was found, 9 cases were more like their therapists' pretherapy conceptions of them and only 4 were less like them. Improvement, then, goes with a patient change away from the therapist's early conception of him. Is the therapist's posttherapy conception of the patient then less like his pretherapy description and more like the patient's self-conception? The answer, given by a highly significant chi square, is yes for patients rated improved. The therapists of improved cases have changed their conceptions of the patients in ways that bring them closer to the patients' own view.

Perhaps the improved cases stayed longer and so these therapists had more contact time within which to improve their understanding. Actually, the improved cases had fewer interviews ($M = 37.33$) than the unimproved cases ($M = 43.69$, a nonsignificant difference). Thus neither a change to resemble the therapists earlier views nor the amount of contact alone accounts for the relation found here between improvement in therapy and increase in the level of understanding of the patient by the close of therapy.

Hypothesis 3: The two variables considered jointly will give a better prediction of outcome than either taken singly. By taking the two variables together, improvement and length of treatment, some interesting differences were revealed. Dividing the cases at the median by length into Long (25 or more interviews) and Short (less than 25), and into Improved (Improvement score 10 or greater) and Unimproved (Improvement score 9 or less) four subgroups were formed. Table 2 gives the means for these groups on the two measures.

Schematically, then, the relations between the variables were as follows:

Length improvement	Need to change	Empathy (E_1)
Short improved	High	High
Long improved	High	Low
Short unimproved	Low	Low
Long unimproved	Low	High

In terms of the joint consideration of the patient's need to change and the therapist's empathic understanding, several generalizations can now be offered.

Therapy is short when either of two conditions obtains. (*a*) Both the patient's need to change and the therapist's understanding of the patient are high. Although the mean number of interviews is small, these cases leave therapy with high improvement scores. (b) The patient's need to change and the therapist's understand-

TABLE 2

PATIENTS' NEED TO CHANGE, THERAPISTS' EMPATHY FOR FOUR IMPROVEMENT SUBGROUPS

Group	Patients' Need to change		Therapists' E_1		Therapists' E_2		Empathy change E_1-E_2
	M	Rank	M	Rank	M	Rank	M
Short Improved N = 8	56.62	1	12.37	1	10.12	2	2.2
Long Improved N = 7	36.57	2	20.00	4	8.57	1	11.4
Short Unimproved N = 6	17.66	4	19.83	3	18.16	4	1.6
Long Unimproved N = 7	22.00	3	14.00	2	11.28	3	2.7

ing of him are both low. These cases leave therapy in an equally short time but as unimproved.

Therapy is long, on the other hand, under two other conditions. (*a*) The patient's need to change is high but the therapist initially misperceives him. The high degree of patient motivation to change seems to be sufficient to keep him in contact long enough for the therapist to correct his misperception and come to see the patient in his own terms ($E_1 = 20.00$, $E_2 = 8.57$). These are long term cases but do eventually leave improved. (*b*) The therapist understands the patient's self-conception but the patient doesn't really want to change. The high understanding probably has sufficient reward value to keep the patient in contact but without the internal pressure to change or recognition that change is possible, he eventually leaves therapy unimproved.

Part II

Having reached this stage in the analysis, the study might well have been concluded. However, further questions kept occurring for which some clarification might be reached by searching the available data in new ways.

The finding that therapists varied in their level of understanding of their patients' self-conceptions after an exposure of only two interviews was not surprising. Nor was it surprising to find that some therapists, whose first attempts at understanding their patients were pretty wide of the mark, increased their understanding to a high level by the time therapy had drawn to a close. However, since there was a strong relationship between the therapist's ability to understand his patient's self-conception at the close of therapy and the outcome of the case, there was interest in discovering what characteristics of the relationship made the initial understanding either easy or difficult, and what characteristics were related to an improvement in understanding through time. The first of these characteristics to be investigated was the sex of the therapy pair.

Sex

Therapists obtained significantly higher empathy scores on the first occasion with patients of the opposite sex than with patients of the same sex. By the time therapy had been completed this difference no longer held. It seemed that the therapists had more initial difficulty understanding patients of like sex than of the opposite sex but that this handicap was overcome with time. (Therapists' empathy for clients of like sex did increase significantly $t = 2.37$, $p < .05$, df 13.) Perhaps therapists at the beginning of their contacts with patients of the same sex err in understanding by assuming that they are more like themselves than is warranted. This assumption of similarity would be less likely to occur with patients of the opposite sex, leaving the therapist freer from a projective set and more open to discovering how it is that the patient views himself.

Distance

In order to test the suggested explanation of the effect of the sex pairing on empathy, a distance measure was devised. First the actual similarity in the ratings that the therapist and patient each made to describe themselves was calculated. The squared discrepancy between these was called a measure of their "Real Similarity." Next the similarity of the therapist's description of his patient and of himself was calculated. The squared discrepancy between these two was called a measure of the therapist's "Assumed Similarity." The difference between the Real and Assumed similarity scores was used as a measure of the distance the therapist placed between himself and the patient. If he "assumed" more similarity than was "real" he was erring psychologically by bringing the patient closer to himself than was represented by the reality distance between their two self-ratings. These errors were scored with a positive sign and are referred to as errors in the direction of reducing the distance. If the therapist assumed less similarity than was real he erred in the direction of putting the patient farther from him than corresponded to the real difference in their ratings. These errors were scored with a negative sign and referred to as errors of increasing the distance.

Therapists on the first testing occasion reduced the distance with same-sex patients and increased the distance with opposite-sex patients. This tendency would seem to help to account for the finding of poorer initial empathy with same-sex than with opposite-sex patients. It appears from Table 3 that therapists potentially can understand patients of either sex equally well (E_2 12.00 and E_2 11.50) but that the initial assumption that the self-images of same-sex patients will be more like their own than in fact they are, temporarily delays the full operation of the empathic capacity. Although therapists also err initially with patients of the opposite sex by overemphasizing the differences between them, this negative distancing does not seem to interfere markedly with the empathy score. That is to say, therapists may incorrectly perceive the patient as very different from themselves and still perceive the way he sees himself reasonably accurately.

TABLE 3

SEX OF THERAPIST-PATIENT PAIRS AND EMPATHY, IMPROVEMENT, AND DISTANCING

Variables	Same Sex[a]	Opposite Sex[b]	t	df
E_1	20.21	12.35	2.278**	26
E_2	12.00	11.50	—	
$E_{1,2}$	8.21	.85	1.777*	26
Improvement	10.00	9.35	—	
Distancing	+ 5.21	− 6.42	2.211**	26

[a] $N = 14$.
[b] $N = 14$.
 * $p < .10$.
** $p < .05$.

TABLE 4

EFFECT OF DISTANCING OF SAME- AND OPPOSITE-SEX PATIENTS ON THE IMPROVED AND UNIMPROVED CASES

Sex pairing	Distancing		t	df	p
	Improved	Unimproved			
Same sex	+14.00	−6.50	2.594	12	.02
	N = 10	N = 4			
Opposite sex	−11.85	−1.00	2.893	12	.02
	N = 6	N = 8			
t	4.649	.797			
df	14	10			
p	.001	ns			

Distance, Sex, and Improvement

Now what is the effect of this initial distancing of same- and opposite-sex patients on their eventual therapuetic gain? Table 4 shows that the therapist's initial distancing of both same- and opposite-sex patients who were judged improved at termination was considerably more extreme than his distancing of those who were judged unimproved. Although both improved sex groups were subject to large distancing errors, these were in opposite directions. The same-sex patients who improved in therapy were initially seen by the therapist as more like himself than their own ratings would suggest. This reduction of distance seems to imply an immediate emotional acceptance of these people. In contrast, the same-sex patients who were subsequently rated as unimproved were held off emotionally at the beginning of therapy and seen by the therapist as more different from him than their own ratings placed them as being. For the opposite-sex patient the relationships were reversed. The opposite-sex patients who improved in therapy were early seen by their therapist as being very different from him—more different than their self-ratings showed them to be. This viewing the opposite-sex patient as very different seemed to imply a classification of, and insistence upon, the sex role distinction. The cross-sex patients who failed to

improve were not seen by the therapist as occupying a pattern distinct from his own. They were seen as being about as much like the therapist as their self-ratings showed them to be.

The really big difference was between same- and opposite-sex patients who improved. Same-sex patients who improved were early accepted by the therapist as very like him and opposite-sex patients who improved were early seen as very different.

Experience of the Therapist

The effect of the experience level of the therapist on distancing, empathy, and improvement was investigated next. Eight of the therapists were classified as more experienced, on the grounds of having handled more than five research cases prior to the present one, and eight were classified as inexperienced, having treated fewer than five. For five of the therapists the present case was the first one. The experienced therapists made distancing errors in both directions with about equal frequency. They were as likely to err in the direction of seeing more similarity than actually present as they were to see less. The inexperienced therapists, though, had a significant bias in the direction of the negative errors. Inexperienced therapists tend to see patients as less like them than the patients' own views show them to be. Perhaps what one learns as a result of experience in doing therapy is that nothing human is really foreign to us. Or perhaps it is that the new therapist is more open to threat and more easily made anxious by seeing patients as similar to himself and so does more defensive distancing.

Now to relate these various findings to improvement with psychotherapy, it appears that improvement was rated high for two groups of patients: same-sex patients treated by experienced therapists, and opposite-sex patients treated by inexperienced therapists. In both groups the therapists' posttherapy level of empathy (E_2) was high and the original distancing of the patient by the therapist extreme. The experienced therapist achieved high empathy and improvement with same-sex patients with whom the psychological distance was immediately reduced and the inexperienced therapist achieved high empathy and improvement with opposite-sex patients with whom distance was immediately increased.

DISCUSSION

The study shows that psychoneurotic patients have the best chance for a successful treatment experience with nondirective therapy, if they come to it with a high need to change, and meet a therapist who can accurately understand the way they see themselves. Some patients meet with therapists who have difficulty perceiving them in their own terms. If they have sufficiently high motivation to change they continue in therapy, and the therapist does come to understand more accurately how it is they see themselves.

For the therapist to improve his understanding in this way he must have more access to material relevant to the task. Presumably he misperceives originally because of barriers to this material, either in himself which distort his perceptions, or because of barriers in the patient which prevent him from revealing himself accurately. Barriers of both kinds are, in all likelihood, related to defenses against the potential threat involved in conscious recognition. If threat is reduced in the patient he would be more able to communicate personally relevant material to the therapist. This in turn would enable the therapist to base his view of his patient's self-image on a deeper understanding of him. If threat is reduced in the therapist he would be freer to perceive the patient's communications without distortions.

It would seem that the inexperienced therapist is the more open to threat in this situation than is the experienced therapist, and, in truth, it is he who tends to increase the distance with his patients. This in effect denies some of the similarity between himself and his patients which can be interpreted as a defensive maneuver to reduce his threat. This distancing might well be experienced by his patients as a message to the effect that "you are really very different from me." Such a message would probably raise the threat level of the same-sex patients but reduce it for opposite-sex patients. The experienced therapist who has less personal threat decreases distance between himself and his same-sex patients and conveys by this, "you are really much more like me than you think you are." This message from a prestigeful person of the same sex probably reduces the patient's threat level. This tentative explanation would account for the high improvement and final level of empathic understanding of the same-sex patients treated by experienced therapists and of the opposite-sex patients treated by inexperienced therapists.

REFERENCES

BUTLER, J. M., & HAIGH, G. V. Changes in the relation between self-concepts and ideal concepts consequent upon client-centered counseling in *Psychotherapy and personality change*. In Carl R. Rogers & Rosalind F. Dymond (Eds.), Chicago: Univer. Chicago Press, 1954. Pp. 55–75.

CARTWRIGHT, D. S., & CARTWRIGHT, ROSALIND D. Faith and improvement in psychotherapy. *J. counsel. Psychol.,* 1958, 5, 174–177.

FIEDLER, F. E. A comparison of therapeutic relationships in psychoanalytic, non-directive, and Adlerian therapy. *J. consult. Psychol.,* 1950, 14, 436–445. (a)

FIEDLER, F. E. The concept of the ideal therapeutic relationship. *J. consult. Psychol.,* 1950, 14, 239–245. (b)

HEINE, R. W. An investigation of the relationship between changes and the responsible factors as seen by clients following treatment by psychotherapists of the psychoanalytic, Adlerian, and non-directive schools. Unpublished doctoral dissertation, University of Chicago, 1950.

KELLY, G. *The psychology of personal constructs.* New York: Norton, 1955.

KIRTNER, W., & CARTWRIGHT, D. S. Success and failure in client-centered therapy as a function of initial in-therapy behavior. *J. consult. Psychol.,* 1958, 22, 329–333.

ROSENTHAL, D., & FRANK, J. Psychotherapy and the placebo effect. *Psychol. Bull.,* 1956, 53, 294–302.

Effects on Clients of a Reflective and a Leading Type of Psychotherapy[1]

JEFFERSON D. ASHBY
DONALD H. FORD
BERNARD G. GUERNEY, Jr.
LOUISE F. GUERNEY

With an Introduction by
WILLIAM U. SNYDER

INTRODUCTION

The four integrated studies described in the pages following this introduction are interesting in several respects. *First,* the design was unique. The researchers have compared a relatively nondirective method of treatment with a somewhat interpretive method, in order to determine whether one approach induces more resistance in the

Reprinted from *Psychological Monographs: General and Applied,* 1957, 71 (24) (Whole No. 453), with the permission of the American Psychological Association and the authors.

[1] This report constitutes an integration and condensation of four interrelated doctoral dissertations (1, 9, 16, 17) from the Pennsylvania State University. The studies were conducted jointly under the supervision of William U. Snyder, Leon Gorlow, and Alec J. Slivinske. William Ray served as statistical consultant for the studies.

client than the other, whether one produces more dependency, and whether clients with certain personality characteristics relate better to the therapist in one treatment-approach than the other. In order to make this comparison, training in the use of both treatment methods was given to 10 therapists. Then, during a time interval of one semester, almost all of the clients asking for help at the Psychological Clinic of the Pennsylvania State University were *randomly* assigned to these 10 therapists and to the two treatment conditions. Each therapist worked with four clients, using a nondirective approach with two and a more interpretive approach with two. Analyses of variance were completed on the data from the two samples. This design made possible a comparison of the two therapeutic approaches, a comparison of the therapists with each other, and an evaluation of the effects of a particular therapist using a particular therapeutic approach. Contributing to the strength of the design was the fact that the experimenters themselves did not act as therapists.

A *second* aspect of these studies that is of interest is that the investigators found it quite possible to classify client and therapist verbal behavior directly from the recordings, rather than from typed transcriptions of the interviews. In fact, they felt that their classifications were probably more accurate under these circumstances, since voice inflections were often crucial in determining how to code a particular response.

A *third* aspect of interest is some rather surprising reactions by the therapists. For example, in spite of the fact that all 10 therapists seemed quite willing to participate in the study, and the experimenters used considerable tact in working with them, some of the therapists did not observe the limits of the study. Four of them decided that "they knew best" and consequently deliberately used a different technique if they felt that it was in the best interests of the client. Although several explanations are possible, the one that seems most likely to the experimenters, in view of the information available, is that their personal needs were too strong for them to be willing to remain within the limits of the experiment. Three of the four were rather authoritarian in their relationship with their clients, and the fourth had a very strong need to be nonthreatening. Another thing that wasn't anticipated is that, although the therapists could learn quite satisfactorily how to play the roles required in each treatment method, this intellectual perception of what was expected of them did not necessarily take precedence over their personal needs to do what they thought best. A sociometric measure answered by fellow therapists, and used in the hope that it would provide an index of the stimulus value the thera-

pists held for their clients, proved not to be of value. The attempt to discover positive correlations between the therapists' personality characteristics and clients' behavior was unsuccessful. Nothing is as indicative of what a therapist will do in therapy as a recording of his actual in-therapy behavior! Another finding of interest concerning therapists is that clients seem able to relate satisfactorily not only to friendly, nonthreatening therapists, but also to authoritarian therapists who engender confidence. This matter of what therapist personality factors are conducive to an effective therapeutic relationship continues to be a challenging one. The writer has observed that, contrary to his former suppositions, it is possible for a therapist-in-training who has a number of personal problems to establish an adequate therapeutic relationship with some clients.

The writer would like to mention very briefly some of the results of the four integrated research studies. (a) The therapists consistently rated their clients as having improved more under an interpretive treatment than under the nondirective one. No other change variables reflected differences between treatments. The leading treatment produced more guarded verbal behavior. Since most therapists expressed a preference for an interpretive type of therapy, the researchers point out therapists' ratings may have been influenced by their therapy preferences. (b) Client pretherapy personality characteristics seemed to be more important in an interpretive therapy than in a nondirective one in the way they related to defensiveness during the early interviews of therapy. (c) The therapists differed in the amount of "guardedness" and/or "defensiveness" they engendered in their clients. Also, a particular therapist using a particular treatment method produced different effects in his clients in defensiveness. This suggests that for the beginning therapist a subtle interaction of personality characteristics and treatment methods is very important to the amount of defensiveness he produces in his clients. One might say we have known this all along. However, it is of value to have experimental evidence of this fact. We need to obtain more specific information about this tantalizing result. (*d*) The researchers observed that "openness" and "guardedness" in the client are interrelated and that the one type of response cannot be considered without reference to the other. In other words, when clients seemed really to be involved in therapy, they would state a problem, discuss it, and then, because it is painful to face oneself and modify one's self concept, they would become somewhat defensive or guarded. This sort of behavior seemed to occur in cyclical form. As a consequence, the researchers were led to the conclusion that perhaps resistance, or defensiveness, may be a "good" sign, in that it indicates that the client is really working on his problems. If he never gets into any real problems he has little need to be defensive. Of course, the "best" therapists would be those who would be able to keep this client defensiveness at a minimum and would not add to it through their own inept behavior.

Illustrative of how puzzling some results can be are the following findings. From some points of view it appeared superficially that the nondirective method produced more desirable results than the interpretive. For example, in the nondirective approach, there were larger percentages of client "openness" and "covert resistance" while the interpretive method had larger percentages of "dependency," "guardedness," and "overt resistance." Further, analysis of the "covert resistance" responses revealed that in the nondirective method 42% of these responses were so classified because the client had made long pauses, while in the interpretive method only 13% of "covert resistance" responses were due to long pauses. Also there were less "blocking" and "interrupting" in the nondirective than in the interpretive therapy. However, from another point of view the more

interpretive therapy seemed superior. For example, clients in the interpretive therapy tended to become more positive in their feelings toward therapy, as measured by a rating scale completed at the end of the fourth and again at the end of the eighth interview, whereas clients in the more nondirective therapy tended to become more negative or defensive. Also, therapists were able to hold clients in therapy better in the interpretive situation than in the nondirective one. Both therapies seemed to have certain aspects which produce favorable reactions in some clients.

Another puzzling result was in regard to the relationship between therapist personality and client "guardedness." If "guardedness" scores were considered independently, the lowest scores in this category were with therapists who were friendly, uncritical, and took a conversational approach, rather than focusing on client problems. Also, clients of "friendly" therapists tended to show more decrease in maladjustment scores, while clients of warm, accepting, but dynamically sensitive therapists tended to grow worse in adjustment, although this change was not statistically significant. It would appear, then, that the therapist who is friendly and uncritical and who does not focus as consistently on problems produces the least client "guardedness" and the greatest decrease in "maladjustment," while the therapist who is warm, accepting, but also aware of the client's problems and his motivation, produces more "guardedness" and more "maladjustment." The researchers in these studies chose to believe that the "guardedness" was a necessary concomitant of facing unpleasant facts about oneself, and that the seeming increase in maladjustment was a temporary one which would be replaced by a decrease in maladjustment as therapy progressed.

Lest the present studies should tempt the reader to make unwarranted generalizations, the writer would like to mention some limitations of the studies. First, although the two therapies were very different in some respects they were similar in others. The interpretive therapy was not extremely so, and the nondirective therapy was not completely "pure." Second, the treatment lasted only through one semester, with an average of about thirteen interviews. Third, the therapists were only moderately experienced. Fourth, the attitudes of the therapists were such that they appeared to have more confidence in the interpretive therapy than in the nondirective therapy. This lack of confidence could have influenced the effectiveness of the therapies in subtle ways.

The results of these four studies make us more aware than ever of the need for continued research on the nature of the relationship between the therapist and the client. We need to be able to identify the personality characteristics which enable a therapist to function in a maximally effective manner, and to delineate those techniques which will produce the most rapid and least painful progress for the client. It appears important to explore client and therapist interview behavior in relationship to therapeutic outcomes. In the writer's opinion such research will be more likely to be useful if it is based, at least in part, upon what actually happens in the therapeutic interview.

NEED AND STATEMENT OF THE PROBLEM

Over the span of years since the introduction of Rogers' *Counseling and Psychotherapy* (23), interest and research in the area of psychotherapy have constantly expanded (2, 3, 8, 10, 21, 25, 29, 31). However, the need for continued research and the development of more systematic theory is evident from our too limited knowledge of the therapeutic process. Recognizing the need for research on psychotherapy, and particularly the need for more comprehensive and better designed research, the writers set out to de-

velop a research project which incorporated a formal experimental design, which encompassed numerous variables related to the therapeutic process, and which involved more adequate samples of clients and therapists. The fundamental purpose of the project was to analyze many different variables and to assess their relationship to therapy. The list of problems investigated in this study follows.

Effects of Leading and Reflective Therapy

1. *Do pretherapy characteristics of clients relate differentially to the clients' reactions to a reflective and to a leading type of therapy?* An answer was sought in relation to each of the following client pretherapy characteristic variables: (*a*) need for autonomy, (*b*) need for succorance, (*c*) need for deference, (*d*) need for aggression, (*e*) tolerance-intolerance of cognitive ambiguity, and (*f*) defensiveness. The relationship of each of the preceding variables to client reactions to leading and to reflective types of therapy was explored with respect to (*a*) the therapeutic relationship as viewed by clients, and (*b*) the amount of defensive verbal behavior exhibited by clients in therapeutic interviews.

2. *Does clients' verbal behavior in therapy differ in a reflective and a leading type of therapy?* The client verbal behavior variables explored were (*a*) dependence, (*b*) openness, (*c*) guardedness, (*d*) covert resistance, and (*e*) overt resistance.

3. *Does the relationship between a client and his therapist differ in a reflective and a leading type of therapy?* The client relationship variables consisted of clients' subjective positive and defensive reactions to therapy and therapist. The therapist relationship variables consisted of the therapists' subjective positive and negative reactions to the clients and the therapy situation. An answer was sought at the fourth and eighth interviews.

4. *Do changes in clients through therapy differ in a reflective and a leading type*

of therapy? The client change variables investigated were (*a*) level of maladjustment, (*b*) anxiety, (*c*) defensiveness, (*d*) dependency, (*e*) positive attitude toward self, (*f*) positive attitudes toward others, and (*g*) therapists' evaluation of client changes.

Effects of Therapists as Individuals

1. *Are personal characteristics of therapists related to the effects therapists have on their clients?* The therapist personal characteristic variables investigated were (*a*) ability to enter the phenomenological field of another, (*b*) sympathetic interest, (*c*) acceptance of others, (*d*) social stimulus value, (*e*) need to aggrandize the self, and (*f*) aggression. The effects on clients which these characteristics might have were explored with respect to (*a*) clients' defensive verbal behavior in therapy interviews, (*b*) the client relationship variables, and (*c*) client changes in maladjustment through therapy.

2. *Are there differences among therapists in the way they affect clients' verbal behavior in therapy?* The client verbal behavior variables explored were (*a*) dependence, (*b*) openness, (*c*) guardedness, (*d*) covert resistance, and (*e*) overt resistance.

3. *Are there differences among therapists in the relationship they establish with their clients?* This question was explored with respect to clients' positive and defensive views of the relationship and to therapists' positive and negative views of the relationship at both the fourth and eighth interviews.

4. *Are there differences among therapists in the changes they produce in their clients during therapy?* The client change variables investigated were (*a*) level of maladjustment, (*b*) anxiety, (*c*) defensiveness, (*d*) dependency, (*e*) positive attitudes toward self, (*f*) positive attitudes toward others, and (*g*) therapists' evaluation of client changes.

Effects of the Interaction Between Therapists and Type of Therapy Administered

1. *Is client verbal behavior in therapy affected by the interaction of the therapist as an individual with the type of therapy he is employing?* The client verbal behavior variables explored were (*a*) dependence, (*b*) openness, (*c*) guardedness, (*d*) covert resistance, and (*e*) overt resistance.

2. *Is the therapeutic relationship affected by the interaction of therapists as individuals with the type of therapy being employed?* This question was explored with respect to clients' positive and defensive views of the relationship and to therapists' positive and negative views of the relationship at both the fourth and eighth interviews.

3. *Is the extent of change in clients through therapy affected by the interaction of therapists as individuals with the type of therapy they are employing?* The client change variables investigated were (*a*) level of maladjustment, (*b*) anxiety, (*c*) defensiveness, (*d*) dependency, (*e*) positive attitudes toward self, (*f*) positive attitudes toward others, (*g*) therapists' evaluation of change scores.

EXPERIMENTAL DESIGN AND PROCEDURES
Independent Variables

The effects of two independent variables were examined in this study. The first was the type of therapy administered and the second was the therapist as an individual. The type of therapy was manipulated by defining two families of therapist verbal responses.

Reflective Therapy

This family of responses included restatement of content, reflection of feeling, nondirective leads, and nondirective structuring responses. This therapy was built largely on the Rogerian approach (23, 24).

Therapists' behavior was guided by the following working hypotheses.

The therapist attempts to create a warm, acceptant, understanding, noncritical psychological atmosphere; to understand and accept the feelings which the client experiences as a result of his perception; and to communicate this acceptance and understanding to the client.

The therapist believes the client has within himself a capacity to understand himself and a capacity and tendency to reorganize himself. The therapist also believes that, in a warm, acceptant, understanding, and noncritical atmosphere, the client will reorganize himself at a rate and to a depth most appropriate for him.

It is necessary for the therapist to accept and clarify only those thoughts and feelings which the therapist believes are in the client's present phenomenological field. These thoughts and feelings must be strongly implied by the client himself, if they are not explicitly communicated either verbally or nonverbally. By consistently maintaining this role, the therapist enables the client to eliminate his need for defenses in the therapeutic situation, to recognize his conflicts, his emotional reactions and needs, and to bring about a self-reorganization of his patterns of perception and behavior.

Leading Therapy

The second family of responses was composed of directive leads, interpretations, directive structuring, approval, encouragement, suggestion, advice, information giving, and persuasion. The leading therapy was based largely on the approaches of Dollard and Miller (6) and Fromm-Reichmann (11). It was guided by the following working hypotheses.

The therapist attempts to create a warm, accepting, understanding, noncritical psychological atmosphere; to contrast the client's report of his situation and difficulties with an objective reality as the therapist deduces it; to formulate hypotheses about

the defenses which protect the conflicts; and to intervene in such a way that he helps the client understand the nature and function of the defenses. The therapist may then help the client in coping directly with underlying conflicts at a level which the therapist deems advisable and feasible within the limitations of time and the client's personal dynamics. He thus helps the client to become reoriented in terms of reality.

The therapist believes that the client has a capacity to learn new behavior patterns, but that this capacity is not being utilized effectively because the client's defenses, inappropriate reaction patterns, and fears prohibit his becoming aware of, and trying out, alternative patterns of perception and behavior.

It is necessary for the therapist to introduce, or direct attention to, factors not within the client's present awareness, in order to make the client aware of his defenses, to help him modify them or eliminate the need for them, to recognize his conflicts, emotional reactions, and needs, and to bring the client to adopt alternative patterns of perception and behavior.

Therapists

Therapists as individuals constituted the second independent variable. Ten therapists were used in this study. It should be noted that the authors did not participate as therapists. The therapists were all advanced graduate students ranging in age from 24 to 30 years. Six of the therapists had internship experience in a medical setting approximating one year or more. One had experience as a mental hospital attendant, caseworker, interviewer, and college counselor. One had approximately a year's experience with vocational and personal counseling in a university setting. Another had a year of experience with vocational and personal counseling in a university setting plus work in a school for delinquent girls under the supervision of a psychiatrist and a social worker. Another had worked three months doing casework in a settlement house. In addition, some had work experience in military, private, and public settings. They reported that their therapeutic biases were still in a formative stage, though at the time of the experiment all but one reported an inclination toward a leading type of treatment. All had had supervised experience in vocational and educational counseling in the Pennsylvania State University Psychological Clinic.

Prior to the beginning of the experiment, the 10 therapists had just completed a course in psychotherapy. In the course, they studied systems representative of both types of therapy. In addition, each person had carried two or more therapy cases under the supervision of an experienced clinical psychologist. The therapists also participated in a training program devised especially in preparation for this research. Through readings, practice with typescripts of previous cases, role playing, and discussions, the therapists were familiarized with the response families and given practice in their use. On the basis of the final role-playing session, all of the therapists were judged to be differentiating the two types of therapy.

A system for coding therapists' responses was devised and used to code responses from eight recorded interviews for each therapist. In a pilot study designed to demonstrate the reliability of the coding system, three of four judges coding independently agreed 92% of the time as to which of the response families a given response belonged. Three of four judges agreed 82% of the time that a given response belonged in one of 15 different categories. The coding system used was patterned after that of a previous research project (30). A criterion of approximately two-thirds of each therapist's experimental responses in the appropriate response family for all clients was established as the minimum acceptable differentiation of treatments. In addition, for a therapist to qualify, at least 60% of all his experimental responses had to be in the appropriate response family for each individual client. Six of the 10 therapists met the criteria. *Only these six therapists and their 24 clients are included in the principal statistical analyses of this study.* Some of the qualitative observations made in the study rest on all 10 therapists and their 40 clients. Table 1 shows the

TABLE 1

THE NUMBER AND PROPORTION OF THERAPISTS' RESPONSES IN EACH RESPONSE CATEGORY FOR EACH OF THE EXPERIMENTAL THERAPIES[a]

Response Categories[b]	Reflective Therapy		Leading Therapy	
	Number of Responses	% of Total Responses	Number of Responses	% of Total Responses
XCS	18	1.1	1	.1
XND	16	1.0	14	.7
XRC	547	34.4	168	8.6
XCF	509	32.1	123	6.3
XESCFD	35	2.2	54	2.8
XTR	30	1.9	52	2.7
XUN	36	2.3	36	1.8
XUNT	51	3.2	59	3.0
XDS	6	.4	32	1.6
XDL	155	9.8	880	45.1
XIT	130	8.2	358	18.3
XIF	39	2.4	99	5.1
XAER	11	.7	44	2.2
XSAP	3	.2	32	1.6
XDC	1	.1	2	.1

[a] Based on part or all of 10 therapists' responses on 40 records for each treatment.
[b] XCS—Nondirective structuring.
XND—Nondirective leads.
XRC—Restatement of content.
XCF—Clarification of feeling.
XESCFD—Ending contact, series, or free discussion.
XTR—Therapist reaction.
XUN—Unclassifiable.
XUNT—Unclassificable, recording unclear.
XDS—Directive structuring.
XDL—Directive leads.
XIT—Interpretation.
XIF—Information giving.
XAER—Approval, encouragement, reassurance.
XDC—Direct criticism.
XSAP—Suggestion, advice, persuasion.

distribution of responses in the 15 response categories for all 10 therapists. Clearly, restatement of content and clarification of feeling responses were emphasized in the reflective therapy, while interpretations and directive leads were emphasized in the leading therapy. If the nonexperimental categories of XESCFD, XTR, XUN, and XUNT (see Table 1) are excluded and the responses of the six therapists meeting the criteria are examined, 89% of their reflective therapy responses were appropriate to that therapy, while 81.5% of their leading therapy responses were appropriate to that therapy. The nondirective emphasis compares favorably with previous research describing the verbal pattern of Rogerian therapy (26, 29, 30). Research on leading treatment response-patterns is not available for comparison.

Dependent Variables
Client Variables

The major criteria used in selecting the client vairables were: (*a*) the measure had to have a logical and meaningful relationship to the therapeutic process; (*b*) the measure had to be obtainable without placing unreasonable demands on the client population; and (*c*) the measure should reasonably be expected to demonstrate differences between a reflective and a leading type of psychotherapy.

Client verbal behavior in therapy. Five main variables and one composite variable were based on clients' verbal behavior in the first four interviews. A tentative classification system based in part on previous research (4, 5, 15, 18, 19, 27) was devised by the four authors. A pilot study on nonexperimental recorded interviews produced several modifications of the tentative system. The coding rules were intended to identify responses reflecting general sets, rather than responses specific to individual therapists' statements. Descriptions of the verbal behavior summarizing the client verbal behavior variables follow.

1. *Dependence:* The extent to which the client asks the therapist for his opinions, advice, information, evaluation, and instruction, or demonstrates a need for structuring from the therapist.

2. *Openness:* The extent to which the client freely discusses his problems, his deviations from the "normal," his culturally frowned-upon traits, behavior, and motivations; and, in general, his willingness to expose himself to potential criticism and change; especially his willingness to discuss thoroughly those areas which seem most threatening. The client does this without at the same time qualifying, hedging, and engaging in defensive verbal maneuvers.

3. *Guardedness:* The extent to which the client exhibits wariness and hedging in regard to presenting and working on his problems, admitting faults, and exposing himself to potential criticism and change. This includes self-stimulated denial or minimization of his problems or his deviations from the "normal," and denial of culturally undesirable feelings, traits, and motivations. It also includes the need to justify himself or his actions to the therapist, and expectations of criticism from the therapist.

4. *Covert Resistance:* The extent to which the client manifests indirect or impersonalized criticism of the therapist or therapy. It includes blocking, delaying tactics, failure to recall or report things, changing the subject, and interrupting the therapist. It is resistance or hostility toward therapy, therapist, progress in therapy, or toward things which are thought of as being conducive to such progress. But the resistance is not directly expressed verbally; instead, other subtle escapes or hostilities are resorted to by the client.

5. *Overt Resistance:* The extent to which the client verbalizes criticism—in an open way—of the therapist or the therapeutic method. It includes personal and verbalized opposition to staying within the limits set by the particular kind of therapy which the client is receiving. This is verbalized un-

willingness as opposed to "inability" or failure per se.

6. *Defensiveness:* The sum of guardedness, covert resistance, and overt resistance.

A time interval was chosen as the unit of response so that reliabilty for each client response could be determined when the coding was done aurally from tapes and discs (all coding was conducted in this fashion). The unit of measurement, or the client "response" to be coded, was a 15-second interval of client verbal behavior. Every second of the interview during which the therapist was not talking was regarded as consisting of the client's verbal behavior. Each client response was coded in one of the experimental categories or in a "none" category. In this manner, all of the client's verbal behavior was classified. A client's score on a given variable was the percentage of all his responses which were so classified. In the opinion of the authors, the aural method of coding contained many advantages over typescripts.

The four authors were the coders in the reliability study. In addition to many hours of previous experience with the categorites, they underwent a training program of approximately 15 hours. Each coder simultaneously but independently classified client responses on four nonexperimental recorded interviews which were representative of the two experimental therapies. Of the 725 client responses on the records, 468 were classified by three or all judges as falling outside of the experimental categories. Thirty-five per cent, or 257 responses, were placed under one of the dependent variables

by two or more judges. In this combined task of locating and categorizing these experimental responses, at least three out of four coders were in agreement on 68% of the responses; at least half of the coders agreed 95% of the time. When coder agreement among the experimental categories alone is considered, excluding differentiation of an experimental from nonexperimental response from the data, all coders agreed on 81% of the client responses. Three or more of the coders agreed on 89% of the responses. These figures compare favorably with reliability studies reported in other investigations (15) in which client responses were coded from transcripts.

On the records classified for the experiment proper, the average client made 162 responses during the 45-minute interview. Of these, 52 (32%) were responses which fell under one of the dependent variable classifications. Table 2 shows the percentage of all client responses falling under each of the major client verbal behavior variables for the clients under the reflective therapy, the leading therapy, and these samples combined.

To obtain some information on the validity—in the sense of agreement with qualified opinion—and objectivity of the experimental coding, a Process Rating Scale was devised. This scale contained the summary descriptions of the five major client verbal behavior variables. Therapists were asked to rate on a five-point scale the extent to which each of their clients exhibited dependence, openness, guardedness, overt re-

TABLE 2

PERCENTAGE OF ALL CLIENT RESPONSES FALLING UNDER EACH OF THE
MAJOR CLIENT VERBAL BEHAVIOR VARIABLES

	Dependence	Openness	Guardedness	Covert Resistance	Overt Resistance
Reflective Sample	2.26	4.45	3.92	23.58	.63
Leading Sample	2.67	3.47	6.49	16.00	.72
Combined Sample	2.46	3.96	5.20	19.79	.68

sistance, and covert resistance. In order to maintain naivete the therapists were not given the scale until the close of the experiment. To make their rating more comparable in time to the experimental coding, they were asked to recall the behavior of their clients as it was in the *first four* interviews and rate accordingly. With 38 degrees of freedom, $\pm .31$ and $\pm .40$ are significant at the .05 and .01 levels respectively. The correlations of therapists' ratings with the scores obtained through coding were as follows: dependence .55; openness — .23; guardedness .03; overt resistance .59; and covert resistance .35. Considering the different nature of the types of measurement and the memory distortion that could have entered the ratings, these correlations seem to speak very well for the inherent power of the operational definitions and the reliability and objectivity of measurement in the experimental coding of at least three of the variables: dependence, overt resistance, and covert resistance.

Relationship: The Client Personal Reaction Questionnaire. This questionnaire (called the CPRQ hereafter), constructed by the authors, is composed of two 40-item scales.

One scale is intended to measure *defensive subjective reactions* to therapist and therapy. It includes items reflecting denial, distortion, withdrawal, justification, rationalization, projection, hostility, evasiveness, blocking of thought, blocking of speech, obscuring or confusing issues, anger, fear, criticism, resentment, and self-deprecation.

The second scale is intended to reflect *positive subjective* reactions to therapist and therapy, including a sense of progress, achievement, or accomplishment; feelings of identification and involvement with therapy and/or the therapist: feelings of "safeness" and/or security in the therapy situation; satisfaction of needs for acceptance, understanding, help, approval, respect, encouragement; and feelings of respect, admiration, confidence, and gratitude toward the therapist.

The two scales were constructed by having six advanced graduate students in clinical psychology write items to fit definitions for the two scales. Each of the items thus obtained was given a rating from one to four (poorest to best) by each of the four authors. Those items with the highest average ratings were included in the scale. These final items were further screened to avoid overemphasizing one type of reaction. Items which involved making judgments about therapist or therapy such as, "My therapist is well educated," were excluded. Only statements likely to elicit a subjective personal reaction were included, e.g., "My therapist is a nice guy."

Test-retest correlations were computed from data obtained in the experiment. Such correlations have treatment-effects intervening, but are still worth noting. The defensive CPRQ had a test-retest correlation of .79 ($p < .001$). The positive CPRQ had a test-retest correlation of .52 ($p < .01$). The positive and defensive scales obtained at two points in therapy corrleated — .35 ($p < .05$) at the fourth interview and — .31 ($p < .05$) at the eighth interview.

The Edwards Personal Preference Schedule. This test (7) measures 15 personality variables which have their origin in a list of manifest needs presented by H. A. Murray and others. Five needs from this test were used as client pretherapy characteristics. They were the need for deference, autonomy, succorance, dominance, and aggression.

Tolerance-Intolerance of Cognitive Ambiguity Test. This test by Siegel (27) consists of 20 pictures and 20 unrelated statements. Pictures and statements were both randomly selected by Siegel from different groups of magazines. The client was instructed to compare the statements with the pictures, and to indicate if he felt that any of the persons pictured made any of the statements. He was to match only those he felt were appropriate. The greater the tendency to associate statements with pictures, the lower was the tolerance for ambiguity.

The Mooney Problem Check List. The measures used from this test (20) were the total number of problems checked and the number of words used by the client in summarizing his problem. These two measures had served as measures of client defensiveness in a previous study (30). The assumption was made that the more restricted a client was in admitting and discussing problems, the higher was the level of defensiveness.

The Minnesota Multiphasic Personality Inventory. Six scales derived from the population of items on this inventory were used in the present study: Maladjustment Index (12), Taylor Anxiety Scale (32), Defensiveness Scale (13), Dependency Scale (22), Positive Attitude Toward Self Scale (14), and Positive Attitude toward Others Scale (14). These variables were intended to reflect the pre- to post-therapy changes.

The Therapist Posttherapy Rating Scale. This scale, developed by the present research group, was modeled after an earlier scale (33). It consists of 27 items, which reflect changes expected to occur in clients undergoing therapy. Items were selected by judges from a population of 77 items as being those most likely to reflect changes resulting from therapy.

Therapist Variables

The therapist-characteristic variables chosen for study were selected with several criteria in mind: (*a*) their relatively enduring nature, i.e., seeming unalterableness as a result of specific training; (*b*) their logical relationship to important aspects of prescribed therapist behavior; (*c*) their measurability; (*d*) their being relatively unbiased by the psychological sophistication of the therapists; (*e*) their objectivity of scoring.

Ability to Enter the Phenomenological Field of Another. This was defined as interest in learning about the internal frames of reference of others and being able to see how others perceive and feel in terms of these internal frames of reference. The Intraception scale from the Edwards Personal Preference Schedule, and a measure of role-playing ability devised by the authors were used to measure this variable. The latter measure was constructed by asking therapists to play the role of a client they know well, while a cotherapist played the role of a Leading Treatment therapist. The therapists understood this to be part of the training program. Ratings of the realism of the role played were assigned for three separate dimensions of role-playing ability. These dimensions were (*a*) the content, i.e. what the "client" talked about, (*b*) the reactions that the "client role-player" showed to the therapist's leads, (*c*) the affect which the role-player displayed while acting as client. Four judges assigned the ratings independently after practice in learning to make reliable judgments. A scoring guide was prepared defining five points for each dimension. Complete agreement was obtained among the four judges on 65% of the judgments, while 94% of the judgments were either in complete agreement or only one step removed from the consensus.

Sympathetic Interest. This was defined as a kindly interest in the activities and thoughts of others and was measured by therapists' scores on the Edwards Nurturance scale.

Acceptance of Others. This was defined as the willingness and/or ability of the therapist to understand and accept what the client has to say without feeling a need to evaluate, judge, or make criticism either openly, or in his own mind. The authors constructed a test called a Test of Clinical Judgment to measure this variable. It consists of items purported to be statements of beliefs, opinions, and values made by unidentified individuals. These items represent viewpoints deviant from those of this culture in general and those of psychologists in particular. However, the items do not express viewpoints so deviant as to warrant their necessarily being conceived of as pathological. Therapists were asked to classify the statements as being made by an adjusted or maladjusted individual. It was reasoned that those who classified fewer items as maladjusted would be those who were most accepting of the values of others. A pilot study with 30 clinical psychology graduate students supported the idea that the items intended to be ambiguous could be viewed as "adjusted" or "maladjusted." Six clearly pathological and six clearly normal statements were included as filler items to provide a frame of reference and as a kind of validity check. Twenty-eight of the thirty persons taking the test in the pilot group classified the filler items as intended by the authors, indicating that items clearly "adjusted" or "maladjusted" could be so classified.

Social Stimulus Value. This was defined as the favorable effect the individual produces on others with whom he has social contact. A sociometric measure devised by the authors was used for this variable. Therapists were asked to select the two most preferred and two least preferred members of their group in five different social situations which involved confiding threatening criticisms, personal friendship, cooperative work, professional supervision, and personal therapy. Scores were derived reflecting the degree of preference for each of the therapists.

Need for Aggrandizing the Self. This was defined as the need to make oneself important by gaining the attention, admiration, and awe of others. Therapists' scores on the Edwards' Exhibitionism scale were used to measure this need.

Aggressiveness. This was measured by the Aggression scale from the Edwards.

Relationship: The Therapist Personal Reaction Questionnaire. This questionnaire (called the TPRQ hereafter), constructed by the authors, is composed of two scales of 35 items each. One scale is intended to reflect Negative Reactions to therapy and client, and includes items reflecting feelings of hostility, resentment, criticism, superiority toward the client; feelings of doubt, discouragement, uncertainty, and failure in regard to progress and accomplishment with the client in therapy; feelings of anxiety, displeasure, discomfort, boredom in anticipation of or in the interviews; feelings of incompetence, inadequacy, ineffectiveness, lack of understanding, and inability to help both in regard to interview behavior and in the long run; feeling disliked, rejected, ridiculed, and pushed.

The Positive Scale reflects feelings of progress, achievement, and accomplishment with the client in therapy; feelings of identification and involvement with the client; feelings of comfort, pleasure, and anticipation in relationship to the interview hour; feelings of respect, admiration, sympathy, and affection for the client; and gratification of existing needs such as those for approval, respect, and therapeutic competence.

The construction of the TPRQ was identical to that of the Client PRQ previously described. Test-retest correlations were obtained by correlating a score obtained at the fourth interview with a score obtained at the eighth interview. The negative scale had a test-retest correlation of .85 ($p < .001$), while the positive scale had a test-retest correlation of .81 ($p < .001$). The positive and negative scales correlated $-.23$ ($p > .10$) at the fourth interview and $-.18$ ($p > .10$) at the eighth interview.

Clients

Most of the clients used in this study were young adults in their twenties whose symptoms were primarily neurotic in character. Each therapist had two clients in each treatment. Thus, there were 24 clients for the six therapists reported in this study. Seven of the clients were women and 17 were men. There were two women in the reflective and five in the leading therapy. The presenting symptoms often included some reference to unsatisfactory academic performance, since the sample consisted largely of university students. As therapy progressed, however, it was usually apparent that the academic problem was primarily symptomatic. Problems included inability to get along with peers or parents, feelings of inadequacy, sexual frigidity, homosexual impulses, unsatisfactory marital relationships, and disturbing emotions such as anxiety and depression. The intensity of problems ranged from mild to severe. The experiment was terminated at the end of the spring semester because many of the clients were leaving for the summer. The number of interviews completed at termination ranged from one to 23, with an average of 12.8. The fact that a considerable proportion of the clients continued their interviews after the experiment was terminated indicated that they had not completed their therapy at that point. The sample of clients described includes those who completed *four or more interviews* (In the part of this study concerned with client verbal behavior in therapy, there was no criterion of four interviews. The first four clients completing one or more interviews for each therapist were included. However, this sample differed from the former by only two clients so that the samples are almost identical.)

Procedures

Clients were randomly assigned to therapists and to the two therapies. Therapists met their clients in 45- to 60-minute interviews twice a week on nonconsecutive days. All interviews were recorded on discs or tapes. Before the initial interview, clients completed the MMPI, Edward's Personal Preference Record, the Mooney Problem Check List, and the Tolerance-Intolerance of Cognitive Ambiguity Test. After the fourth, eighth, fifteenth, and terminal interviews, clients and therapists completed Personal Reaction Questionnaires. After the client terminated therapy or the experiment was terminated, whichever occurred first, the client completed the MMPI again. In addition, several tests were completed by therapists early in the experiment.

Clients were never told they were participating in an experiment. They were informed that recordings and test data were used for research purposes. All procedures were handled as a part of regular clinic routine. It is the experimenters' impression that clients were unaware that two types of therapy were being used and no problems arose concerning the therapies. Therapists knew nothing about the variables or questions being explored until after the experiment was completed. Therapists reported experiencing considerable discomfort at the requirement of administering two different therapies. After the experiment, most felt they had benefited professionally from the experience.

Statistical Design

A double classification analysis of variance design was used in the present experiment. This design made it possible to evaluate differences between therapies, differences among therapists, and differences resulting from interaction effects of the two independent variables on the dependent variables. Correlations between pretherapy measures of clients and the dependent variables were not large enough to warrant analysis of covariance.

In the case of the client verbal behavior variables, a client's score on a given variable was the proportion of all of his responses which fell under that classification. The proportions were transformed to angles for the analyses of variance (28, p. 316).

Correlation procedures were used to relate client pretherapy personality characteristics to client reactions during therapy. Similar procedures were used to relate clients' reactions in therapy to therapist personality characteristics. A $p < .05$ was used as an acceptable level of significance.

RESULTS AND DISCUSSION
Client Pretherapy Characteristics

Tables 3, 4, and 5 report pairs of correlations between client pretherapy characteristics and three client therapy measures.

These correlations suggest that the more aggressive a client, the more verbal defensiveness will be manifested in the leading therapy. Although the correlation in the reflective therapy does not meet the criterion for statistical significance by itself, it is large enough to suggest the possibility that the more aggressive a client the less verbal defensiveness will be manifested in the reflective therapy (Table 3).

Clients who were less willing to discuss their problems on tests prior to therapy also tend to be more defensive in their verbal behavior in the leading therapy, while clients with less pretherapy defensiveness tended to be less defensive verbally in the leading therapy. The willingness to elaborate about problems on a test seemed not to relate to interview verbal defensiveness in the reflective therapy (Table 3).

TABLE 3

CORRELATIONS BETWEEN CLIENT PRETHERAPY MEASURES AND THE CLIENT VERBAL BEHAVIOR DEFENSIVENESS SCALE

Client Pretherapy Measures	Leading Therapy	Reflective Therapy	Significance of Difference between r's[a]	p
TICA[b]	−.36	−.10	.82	> .05
Deference	−.12	.09	.61	> .05
Autonomy	.41	−.01	1.31	> .05
Succorance	.02	−.33	1.05	> .05
Dominance	.14	−.06	.58	> .05
Aggression	.42	−.37	2.45	< .02
Mooney: Number of problems	−.28	−.10	.55	> .05
Mooney: Number of words	−.60[c]	.11	2.33	< .02

[a] Based on Fisher's z.
[b] Tolerance-Intolerance of Cognitive Ambiguity.
[c] $r = .444$ required to be significant at .05 level.

TABLE 4

CORRELATIONS BETWEEN CLIENT PRETHERAPY MEASURES AND CLIENT POSITIVE PERSONAL REACTION QUESTIONNAIRE AT THE FOURTH INTERVIEW

Client Pretherapy Measures	Leading Therapy	Reflective Therapy	Significance of Differences Between r's[a]	p
TICA	.38	−.05	1.31	> .05
Deference	−.17	.21	1.11	> .05
Autonomy	−.04	−.44	1.25	> .05
Succorance	.32	.01	.93	> .05
Dominance	−.24	.09	.96	> .05
Aggression	−.15	−.25	.32	> .05
Mooney: Number of problems	.22	−.27	1.46	> .05
Mooney: Number of words	.17	−.05	.64	> .05

[a] Based on Fisher's z.

TABLE 5

CORRELATIONS BETWEEN VARIOUS CLIENT PRETHERAPY MEASURES AND THE CLIENT
DEFENSIVE PERSONAL REACTION QUESTIONNAIRE, FROM THE FOURTH INTERVIEW

Client Pretherapy Measures	Leading Therapy	Reflective Therapy	Significance of Difference Between r's[a]	p
TICA	.29	−.09	1.14	> .05
Deference	.46[b]	−.28	2.30	< .05
Autonomy	−.52[b]	.18	2.22	< .05
Succorance	−.09	.12	.61	> .05
Dominance	−.04	−.24	.58	> .05
Aggression	−.09	.08	.50	> .05
Mooney: Number of problems	−.07	.35	1.28	> .05
Mooney: Number of words	−.22	.23	1.31	> .05

[a] Based on Fisher's z.
[b] $r = .444$ required to be significant at .05 level.

Deferent clients reacted with more subjective defensive reactions, and less deferent clients reacted with fewer defensive reactions in the leading therapy. There seemed to be no consistent relationship between the trait of deference and subjective defensive reactions of clients toward a reflective therapy (Table 5).

Autonomous clients tended to react with fewer subjective defensive reactions to leading therapy whereas less autonomous clients reacted with more defensive reactions. There seemed to be no consistent relationship between this trait and clients' reactions to the reflective therapy (Table 5).

It is worth noting that three correlations for the leading treatment sample were statistically significant while there were no significant correlations for the reflective treatment sample. This suggests that certain client reactions, at least during the first four interviews, are more predictable in a leading than in a reflective therapy. It is interesting to note also that the four significant differences in correlation involved measures of client defensiveness, one a behavioral measure of in-therapy resistance and the other a measure of the client's subjective reactions toward therapy. This suggests that defensiveness in a leading therapy is one

characteristic which is predictable from client pretherapy characteristics.

Differences Between Therapies

Twenty-one analyses of variance were completed. Table 6 reports these data. Only 2 of the 21 showed a statistically significant difference between the two therapies. The similarity of the effects produced on clients by the two therapies is a prominent finding in this area of the study. On the Therapist Posttherapy Rating Scale, therapists consistently rated clients in the leading therapy as showing more improvement than clients in the reflective therapy. This finding must be accepted with qualification, however, since all but one therapist expressed a preference for a leading type of therapy prior to the experiment. Their preferences may have affected their ratings. Clients' verbal behavior during the first four interviews was more guarded in the leading than in the reflective therapy. This suggests the leading therapy may have been somewhat more threatening. Guardedness will be considered in detail in the discussion of differences among therapists.

Although the levels of significance were not impressive, the consistency with which

TABLE 6

F RATIOS AND PROBABILITY STATEMENTS FOR THERAPY EFFECTS ON 21 VARIABLES
ON WHICH ANALYSES OF VARIANCE WERE COMPLETED

Variable	Reflective Mean	Leading Mean	F Ratio	p
Client Verbal Behavior Variables:				
Dependence	2.26	2.67	.26	$> .20$
Guardedness	3.92	6.49	4.92	$< .05 > .01$
Openness	4.45	3.47	.06	$> .20$
Covert Resistance	23.58	16.00	.62	$> .20$
Overt Resistance	.63	.72	.26	$> .20$
Defensiveness	22.6	21.0	.05	$> .20$
Relationship Variables:				
Defensive CPRQ—4th	206.5	213.1	.34	$> .20$
Defensive CPRQ—8th	214.0	197.3	1.98	$< .20 > .10$
Positive CPRQ—4th	312.6	333.9	.59	$> .20$
Positive CPRQ—8th	317.3	342.9	2.95	$< .20 > .10$
Negative TPRQ—4th	72.8	67.0	.47	$> .20$
Negative TPRQ—8th	74.8	61.3	1.85	$< .20 > .10$
Positive TPRQ—4th	101.8	97.3	.12	$> .20$
Positive TPRQ—8th	99.1	105.1	.28	$> .20$
Change Variables:[a]				
Maladjustment Index	+0.25	−6.09	.94	$> .20$
Dependency	+1.90	−2.35	.55	$> .20$
Defensiveness	+0.50	+0.05	.04	$> .20$
Positive Attitudes Toward Self	+0.35	+1.75	2.27	$< .20 > .10$
Positive Attitudes Toward Others	+0.70	+0.55	1.16	$> .20$
Taylor Anxiety Scale	+0.15	−0.45	.38	$> .20$
Therapist Posttherapy Rating Scale[b]	67.8	91.8	6.32	$< .05 > .01$

[a] All analyses were made on the *difference* between pre- and post-therapy scores except for the Taylor and Posttherapy Rating Scale where posttherapy scores were used. A decrease in score indicates a decrease in the trait measured.

[b] A higher score on the Therapist Posttherapy Rating Scale indicates a therapist judgment of greater improvement.

trends appeared between the fourth and eighth interview on the relationship measures is worth noting. The CPRQ suggests that clients tend to become more defensive in the reflective therapy and more positive in the leading therapy. Therapists tended to become somewhat more negative in their reactions toward clients in the reflective therapy.

Although statistically significant differences between the therapists were few, some trends in the data suggest that the two therapies may have somewhat different effects. Clients in leading therapy tended to become less defensive while clients in reflective therapy tended to become more defensive in their subjective reactions toward therapy. Leading therapy clients tended to show greater positive change in their attitudes toward themselves. Therapists tended to become more negative in their reactions toward clients in reflective therapy. Therapists were able to hold clients better in the leading therapy than in the reflective therapy, and rated clients in leading therapy as more improved. On the other hand, clients in the reflective therapy were less guarded and tended to exhibit less dependence and overt resistance, and more openness than clients in leading therapy. Covert resistance tended to be greater in the reflective therapy, due largely to a much greater number of client long pauses. Some other components of covert resistance, namely blocking and interruption of the therapist, were noticeably less frequent in the reflective therapy than in the leading therapy.

The writers had opportunities to observe some clients after they completed therapy. These observations indicated that improvements were made by clients in both types of therapy.

Several possible explanations may account for the fact that there were few statistically significant defferences between the therapies. The findings may mean that the leading and reflective therapies do not produce very different results. It is also possible that the two do produce different results but that differences did not show up because of the limited power of the experiment. The measures used may have been inadequate, or it may be that the variables themselves were not appropriate to demonstrate differences which actually exist.

Differences Among Therapists

Statistically significant differences among therapists appeared in 4 of the 21 analyses, as shown in Table 7. Three of the four differences appeared on the relationship variables. Therapists appear to produce differing degrees of subjective defensive reactions in their clients by the fourth interview, but these differences tend to disap-

TABLE 7

F RATIOS AND PROBABILITY STATEMENTS FOR AMONG THERAPISTS EFFECTS ON 21 VARIABLES FOR WHICH ANALYSES OF VARIANCE WERE COMPLETED

Variable	F Ratio	p
Client Verbal Behavior Variables:		
Dependence	.98	$> .20$
Guardedness	7.68	$< .01 > .001$
Openness	1.08	$> .20$
Covert Resistance	.86	$> .20$
Overt Resistance	.71	$> .20$
Defensiveness	.97	$> .20$
Relationship Variables:		
Defensive CPRQ—4th interview	4.22	$< .05 > .01$
Defensive CPRQ—8th interview	2.67	$< .10 > .05$
Positive CPRQ—4th interview	2.08	$< .20 > .10$
Positive CPRQ—8th interview	6.88	$< .01 > .001$
Negative TPRQ—4th interview	3.71	$< .05 > .01$
Negative TPRQ—8th interview	1.86	$< .20 > .10$
Positive TPRQ—4th interview	1.55	$> .20$
Positive TPRQ—8th interview	2.58	$< .10 > .05$
Change Variables:		
Maladjustment Index	1.17	$> .20$
Dependency	1.31	$> .20$
Defensiveness	.92	$> .20$
Positive Attitudes Toward Self	.26	$> .20$
Positive Attitudes Toward Others	1.67	$> .20$
Taylor Anxiety	1.57	$> .20$
Therapist Posttherapy Rating Scale	.39	$> .20$

pear by the eighth interview. On the other hand, differences in the degree of positive subjective reactions elicited from clients are not statistically significant until the eighth interview. From the clients' point of view, the defensive aspects of the relationship appear to develop earlier in therapy than do the positive aspects. Therapists differ in their negative reactions to their clients by the fourth interview but these differences tend to disappear as therapy progresses. Although not statisically significant, the data suggest that differences in therapists' positive reactions tend to develop as therapy progresses. From the therapists' point of view, the negative aspects of the relationship appear to develop more quickly than the positive aspects. Therapists also appear to differ among themselves in the amount of guarded verbal behavior they elicit from their clients during early interviews. There were no significant differences among these therapists in the changes produced in their clients on the client change variables investigated.

For ascertaining the relationships between therapists' personal characteristics and client reactions, Pearson product-moment correlations were computed between all the therapist variables and five of the client variables. The client variables were the fourth interview Positive and Defensive CPRQ, Guarded and Defensive verbal behavior in therapy, and the Maladjustment change variable. The values used for computing these correlations were the scores obtained by each therapist on each of the therapist characteristic variables and the mean scores of his four clients on the client variables. The correlations were computed using the total sample of 10 therapists. In those instances in which the correlation coefficients obtained were .30 or above, correlations were computed also for the sample of 6 therapists. None of the correlations met the criterion for statistical significance. This is not surprising since the extremely small samples provide very limited degrees of freedom and thus require

a correlation of .63 to be significant at the .05 level. However, six of the eight correlations computed using Edwards' Nurturance Scale yielded correlations of .40 or above, suggesting that the degree to which it is possessed as a quality by the therapist may have some real relationship to his clients' reactions in therapy. Similarly, the Test of Clinical Judgment, intended to reflect acceptance of the values of others, consistently correlated in the expected direction, although in magnitude the correlations were not statistically significant.

The experimenters feel that the main problem behind the failure to find significant relationships between therapist characteristics and client reactions lies in the approach taken. It is felt that the measures of therapist extratherapy behavior which were obtained were too far removed from their behavior in therapy. The writers now believe that a more profitable approach could be made by investigating therapists' behavior in the interview itself. At this stage of our knowledge it seems rather futile to continue with the investigation of "permanent" traits of therapists in the hope that they will relate to client behavior.

While none of the therapist personal characteristics studied related to differential reactions of clients, certain patterns of therapist interview behavior seemed to relate qualitatively to their clients' measured behavior. In the course of the investigation the experimenters listened to scores of interviews. From these interviews, the writers agreed that therapists could be grouped along the dimensions of *perceptiveness of client dynamics, threat to clients,* and *warmth and friendliness.* It should be made clear, however, that these groupings were relative only to the 10 therapists in this experiment. Characteristics attributed to each group are meant only to depict the principal ways in which members of the group differed from other therapists in the study. Table 8 presents data on selected variables for the three groups of therapists discussed below.

TABLE 8

MEAN SCORES FOR THE FOUR CLIENTS OF EACH THERAPIST ON SELECTED VARIABLES
GROUPED ACCORDING TO THE TYPE OF THERAPIST

	Conversational Therapists			Threatening Therapists				Friendly Dynamic Therapists		
	A	B	C	D	E	F	G	H	I	J
Guardedness	1.1	1.8	1.9	4.9	6.7	4.1	7.9	9.3	11.7	2.5
Openness	1.6	2.3	4.8	1.3	3.4	3.7	7.9	7.7	6.0	4.9
Maladjustment	15.8	10.3	14.5	.3	5.5	15.8	4.0	−5.3	2.5	−6.0
Anxiety	21.5	22.5	25.3	25.0	24.8	25.5	24.3	21.5	22.8	26.0
Dependence[a]	6.3	1.5	2.0	−5.5	4.0	3.0	−1.5	2.0	2.0	−1.5
Defensiveness[a]	2.0	−.3	−5.0	−2.0	−1.0	−4.0	0	−1.3	−2.8	0
Attitudes toward others[a]	1.0	1.0	2.0	0	2.0	2.5	1.0	−.5	−1.3	.3
Attitudes toward self[a]	3.0	.3	1.5	−.5	−1.0	1.8	.5	−.5	−.5	1.8
Positive CPRQ$_4$[b]	392.0	303.0	413.0	275.0	390.0	376.0	386.0	317.0	279.0	374.0
Positive CPRQ$_8$[c]	391.0	343.0	419.0	266.0	393.0	398.0	384.0	356.0	279.0	346.0
Defensive CPRQ$_4$[b]	186.0	246.0	172.0	229.0	202.0	209.0	203.0	224.0	170.0	206.0
Defensive CPRQ$_8$[c]	195.0	208.0	185.0	243.0	211.0	178.0	204.0	208.0	170.0	212.0
Positive TPRQ$_4$[b]	107.0	71.0	93.0	101.0	90.0	87.0	108.0	122.0	95.0	100.0
Positive TPRQ$_8$[c]	114.0	60.0	91.0	98.0	96.0	92.0	96.0	125.0	109.0	107.0
Negative TPRQ$_4$[b]	79.0	35.0	62.0	58.0	70.0	46.0	78.0	81.0	92.0	75.0
Negative TPRQ$_8$[c]	74.0	36.0	68.0	65.0	63.0	48.0	77.0	76.0	83.0	74.0

[a] Scores represent the difference between pre- and post-therapy scores. Plus scores represent improvement.
[b] Fourth interview.
[c] Eighth interview.

Three therapists were characterized as friendly, nonthreatening, and nondynamic, and were labeled "conversational" therapists. They appeared to take the role of "friend to the client." These therapists tried to be as nonthreatening as possible. They tried to communicate to the client that they were on his side. Their therapy seemed to consist mainly of restating content in Reflective Therapy or being reassuring and supportive in Leading Therapy. There was no consistent plan for encouraging clients to discuss problem areas. In fact, "conversational" therapists seemed actively to avoid problem areas at times. One need apparently controlling their behavior was a strong need for approval and acceptance. Clients of these therapists were less guarded in their interview verbal behavior. Consistently, they showed a decrease on the Maladjustment Index of the MMPI

from pre- to post-therapy. Strong positive reactions toward the therapy and therapist were reported on the CPRQ, as well as generally low defensiveness reactions.

Four therapists were characterized as nonfriendly, threatening, and dynamically oriented. These were labeled "threatening" therapists. They tended to correct the unrealistic perceptions and plans of the client. Through the choice of words, tone, or inflection of voice, client thoughts and actions were directly or indirectly evaluated. These therapists seemed to imply that they "knew the correct answers" to the client's problems or soon would—that they were authorities. They seemed less concerned, or less aware, than the other therapists with the amount of threat involved in their statements. Their interpretations were sometimes quite extreme and without sound basis. They seemed to direct the discussion from one area to another impulsively. "Threatening" therapists tended to be more aggressive and challenging than other therapists. One need apparently controlling their behavior was a need to dominate and control the situation. Three of the four therapists who did not maintain adequate differentiation of the therapies were in this group. Scores for clients of "threatening" therapists were inconsistent from therapist to therapist. However, it is interesting to note that the therapist whose clients were the most defensive, and least positive, on the relationship measures, and least open in the interview, was one in the "threatening" group.

The remaining three therapists were characterized as warm, skillful, and dynamically oriented. These were labeled "warm, dynamic" therapists. While very warm, they tended to be always mindful of the business at hand. In the reflective therapy, they clarified and restated therapeutically relevant feelings or content without distorting the client's emphasis. In the leading therapy they consistently offered leads more pertinent to the client's dynamics and closer to the client's capacity for dealing with the problem. Although all 10 therapists were generally adequate, the "warm dynamic" therapists tended to approximate more closely the "ideal" therapist as he is frequently described in the literature. The personal needs of these therapists were less obvious and seemed to interfere less with the progress of therapy than the needs of other therapists. They tended to report both more positive and more negative personal reactions than the other therapists. The experimenters fully expected that clients of "warm, dynamic" therapists would earn the most desirable scores on the various measures. However, in virtually every instance their clients failed to do so. Moreover, on some variables they consistently earned the least desirable scores.

It is difficult to account for the apparent poor showing of the clients of the "warm, dynamic" therapists. Why did their clients apparently fail to respond in a manner which would reflect the warmth, acceptance, and skill extended to them? Similarly, it is difficult to account for the apparent superiority of the scores of clients of the "conversational" therapists. The only reasonable explanation seems to be that the variables concerned with client reactions to therapy are actually of a different nature than was originally conceived. It was expected, for example, that the absence of guarded behavior in the interviews would be indicative of a better relationship and greater progress. Noting that the therapists who appeared most skilled seemed to have clients who indulged in relatively more guarded behavior than other clients, a different concept of guardedness emerged. It was found that while clients of the "warm, dynamic" therapists were quite guarded, they were also quite open. In fact, the two kinds of behavior seemed to go together. The confession of an inadequacy, or a socially unacceptable feeling, was usually preceded or followed by guarded statements. It seemed that clients regularly experienced some anxiety in relation to such openness about themselves and needed to cling to some defense in order to allay their anxiety. Conversely, clients of "conversational" therapists showed little tendency to discuss their problems openly. Thus, they had little to be guarded about. The relationship between guardedness and openness seemed to reflect what was occurring in therapy far more meaningfully than either variable considered alone.

The pattern of client scores in relation to therapist interview behavior also seemed to help clarify the concepts of positive and defensive reactions on the relationship measures. Originally, it was thought that relatively high defensive reactions on the CPRQ would be present only in a threatening therapy. Defensiveness was thought to be detrimental to therapy. It is now felt that a certain amount of defensiveness is probably a necessary concomitant of problem solving arising from the internal resistance of the client to a more realistic evaluation of himself. Relatively high positive scores on the CPRQ were originally conceived of as an instrument to therapy. It is now believed that high positive scores may represent in part dependence on the therapist as an authority figure. This view arose from the fact that therapists assuming benevolent or threatening authority roles achieved the highest scores on the CPRQ at both the fourth and eighth interviews.

The change in maladjustment favored clients of the "conversational" therapists. However, the meaning of this change is not clear. From these data, it might appear that a highly positive relationship is the crucial condition for clients to improve in therapy. However, the writers suspect that the nonthreatening atmosphere created by the conversational therapists resulted in a temporary lessening of anxiety which produced changes in maladjustment scores. It seems more likely that a positive relationship is a necessary but not sufficient condition for effective therapy. As a result of consistent attention to dynamics in a friendly atmosphere, it seems reasonable to expect clients of friendly, dynamic therapists to become more aware of their problems and disturbing feelings. The increase in maladjustment scores at the time the experiment was terminated for such clients may reflect this increased awareness. If effective therapy continued, this trend might be expected to reverse itself and a decrease in maladjustment scores appear by the end of therapy.

The fact that the friendly, dynamic therapists reported more positive and negative reactions may reflect a higher degree of sensitivity to, and involvement with, their clients. These therapists were apparently more aware of their own reactions and consequently were able to control their own behavior more effectively during therapy.

On the basis of the scores obtained by the three types of therapists described, it is suggested that a more significant index of the effectiveness of therapy may be the relationship between guarded and open behavior. Similarly the relationship between clients' positive and defensive subjective reactions may be an index to a truly therapeutic relationship. If there is too much guardedness in relation to openness and/or too much defensiveness in relation to positiveness, therapy is probably not proceeding optimally. Low scores on guardedness with little openness may indicate that little problem solving is occurring. High scores on guardedness with little openness may indicate that the therapist is unduly threatening. High scores on positiveness with little defensiveness suggest that the relationship may be satisfying to the client but not necessarily therapeutic. It should be pointed out that these proposed relationships apply only to the early stages of therapy. In later stages the optimal relationships of these scores may be quite different.

Differences Resulting from Interaction of Therapist with Therapy

Three of the 21 analyses revealed statistically significant interaction F ratios as indicated in Table 9. These differences appear in the analyses of the client relationship measures. The personal qualities which therapists invested in each of the therapies affected the degree of defensive reactions of clients. Such effects are pronounced by the fourth interview and persist at least through the eighth interview. Client positive reactions tend to vary in the same way. By the eighth interview, differences in client positive reactions are clear-cut. However, therapist reactions do not show similar interaction effects. None of the client verbal behavior variables or variables intended to reflect change during therapy revealed any significant interaction effects.

Therapists interacting with the therapy they are administering apparently create different effects in the positive and defensive aspects of the relationship from clients' points of view. The defensive aspects of the relationship tend to become less related

TABLE 9

F RATIOS AND PROBABILITY STATEMENTS FOR INTERACTION (THERAPIST $\times$ METHOD) EFFECTS ON 21 VARIABLES FOR WHICH ANALYSES OF VARIANCE WERE COMPLETED

Variable	F Ratio	p
Client Verbal Behavior Variables:		
Dependence	1.60	$> .20$
Guardedness	2.12	$< .20 > .10$
Openness	.38	$> .20$
Covert Resistance	1.09	$> .20$
Overt Resistance	.64	$> .20$
Defensiveness	1.15	$> .20$
Relationship Variables:		
Defensive CPRQ—4th interview	7.92	$< .01 > .001$
Defensive CPRQ—8th interview	6.61	$< .01 > .001$
Positive CPRQ—4th interview	2.98	$< .10 > .05$
Positive CPRQ—8th interview	9.56	$< .001$
Negative TPRQ—4th interview	.99	$> .20$
Negative TPRQ—8th interview	.40	$> .20$
Positive TPRQ—4th interview	.73	$> .20$
Positive TPRQ—8th interview	.21	$> .20$
Change Variables:[a]		
Maladjustment Index	1.22	$> .20$
Dependency	.79	$> .20$
Defensiveness	.16	$> .20$
Positive Attitudes Toward Self	.87	$> .20$
Positive Attitudes Toward Others	.48	$> .20$
Taylor Anxiety Scale	.60	$> .20$
Therapist Posttherapy Rating Scale	.42	$> .20$

[a] All analyses were made on the difference between pre- and posttherapy scores except for the Taylor and Posttherapy Rating Scale where posttherapy scores were used.

to therapists as persons but remained related to the interaction of therapist with the type of therapy administered. On the other hand, the positive aspects of the relationship become more clearly related to therapists as individuals as well as to therapists interacting with the type of therapy administered as therapy progresses.

Inspection of the raw data suggests an explanation of these changes. On the defensive CPRQ, total means for each therapist tend to converge toward the total mean for all therapists between the fourth and eighth interviews. At the same time, the difference between the reflective and leading treatment means for each therapist tends to become greater between the fourth and eighth interviews. This suggests that as therapy progresses clients tend to react more selectively to their therapists' behavior. Changes on the positive CPRQ result primarily from changes in the error term in the F ratios. At the fourth interview, the error term accounts for about one-third of the total variability, while at the eighth interview it accounts for only about one-eighth of the total variability. In other words, the scores of pairs of clients for each therapist in each treatment condition became more alike between the fourth and eighth interviews, while differences among averages of the scores for each therapist and each therapy tended to remain the same. This suggests that clients' subjective reactions tend to become less influenced by their habitual interpersonal sets and more by factors within the therapeutic situation.

A generalized fear of intimate interpersonal situations may be one of the more important of these sets. As this generalized fear is diminished, the client becomes more discriminating in his reactions. Because the client is reacting more discriminatingly to the stimuli within the situation, a more favorable set of circumstances for therapeutic change would appear to be developing.

Several factors may be related to these interaction effects. Therapists' training and experience may influence the effectiveness with which they administer different therapies. In this regard, it is interesting to note that the two therapists with the most extensive training and experience with leading forms of psychotherapy obtained the highest defensive CPRQ scores in the leading treatment at both the fourth and eighth interviews. Therapists' own dynamics and personal value systems may relate to the way in which they make use of a type of therapy. The types of roles assumed by therapists may vary with the type of therapy offered. This study provides no strong clues toward determining which factors are significantly related to these differences.

General Discussion

This study indicates that clients' views of the therapeutic relationship depend on the interaction of the client's own dynamics, the kind of therapy administered, and individual characteristics of therapists. This idea has been discussed frequently in the literature. On the other hand, the idea that one type of therapy is good for all clients and that any therapist can be effective with a given type of therapy has also been suggested. The present data tend to support the former rather than the latter view.

The implications of these results seem of considerable importance. Extensive research is needed to define differential client reactions to different therapies and to differ-ent therapist characteristics. Research is also needed to define the client pretherapy characteristics related to differential client reactions, as well as research relating client reactions during therapy to therapeutic outcomes.

The consistently significant findings on client guarded or defensive verbal behavior and the client positive and defensive relationships measures also suggest that these measures are sensitive to some of the effects of therapy and therefore merit further study. This observation may have broader implications, however, for research in this area. If one wants to measure what happens in therapy, behavior in therapy or reactions to the therapy situation specifically may be one of the most sensitive areas of measurement.

This study clearly illustrates the value of multivariate experimental designs with measures taken at different times when studying as complex an area as psychotherapy. The writers firmly believe that major advances in the effective use of psychotherapy will come most quickly from carefully designed and executed research. Only in this way will therapists become able to administer therapy based on a body of verified knowledge rather than finding it necessary to rely primarily on individual clinical experience.

CONCLUSIONS

The view that a leading and a reflective type of therapy produce different effects on clients was slightly supported. During the first eight interviews, these therapies did not produce significantly different effects on the defensive or positive aspects of the relationship from the clients' points of view nor in the positive or negative aspects of the relationships from the therapists' points of view. The therapies did not differ significantly in the extent of defensive, dependent, open, covertly resistive, or overtly resistive verbal behavior elicited from clients during the first four interviews. The therapies did not differ significantly in the amount of client change during therapy in dependence, defensiveness, maladjustment, positive attitudes toward self, positive attitudes towards others, or anxiety. Of 21 variables explored, client guarded verbal behavior and the Therapists' Posttherapy Rating Scale were the only ones showing a statistically significant difference.

The view that pretherapy characteristics of clients relate differentially to client reactions to therapy in reflective and leading types of therapy is partially supported. There were differences between the two types of therapy in the manner in which pretherapy defensiveness, and pretherapy aggressive need related to verbal defensive behavior of clients in therapy. There were also differences between the two types of therapy in the manner in which pretherapy needs to be deferent and to be autonomous related to client subjective defensive reactions to therapy. None of the differences in the other 20 sets of correlations were statistically significant. The differences between treatments reflect the following findings. Clients who were more defensive when they entered therapy tended to behave more defensively when they were in leading therapy. There was no such relationship under reflective therapy. There were tendencies for clients who entered therapy with more aggressive need to behave more defensively in the leading treatment, and less defensively in the reflective therapy. Clients who entered therapy with more need to be deferent to others felt more defensive in the leading treatment. No such relationship was apparent in the reflective treatment. Clients who entered therapy with a strong need for autonomy tended to feel less defensive in leading therapy. Autonomy need seemed unrelated to defensive feelings in the reflective treatment.

The view that individual therapists create different effects on their clients independent of the type of therapy given is partially supported. Therapists in this study differed significantly in the defensive and positive feelings they elicited from their clients during the first eight interviews. They also differed significantly in the extent of guarded verbal behavior exhibited by their clients in the first four interviews. However, they did not differ significantly in the extent of defensive, dependent, open, covertly resistive, or overtly resistive verbal behavior elicited from clients in the first four interviews. They did not differ significantly in their view of the positive or negative aspects of the relationship during the first eight interviews. They did not differ significantly in the extent of change produced in their clients in maladjustment, dependence, defensiveness, positive attitudes toward self, positive attitudes toward others, or anxiety during the course of therapy. They did not differ significantly in their evaluation of the extent of change produced in their clients as a result of therapy.

The view that selected therapist characteristics are related to the kinds of relationships established, the amount of defensive or guarded verbal behavior elicited from clients, and the amount of change in adjustment produced in clients is not supported. Therapists' ability to enter the phenomenological field of another, sympathetic interest, acceptance of the value system of others, social stimulus-value to associates, need to aggrandize the self, and aggressiveness did not correlate significantly with any of the five dependent variables examined.

The view that the interaction of the therapist as an individual and the type of therapy he is employing affects clients is partially supported. The way in which therapists used or molded a type of therapy had effects upon clients. Clients felt significantly more defensive or more positive in one type of therapy with individual therapists than did other clients for the same therapist in the second type of therapy. For some therapists the increased defensive or positive feelings were in the leading treatment while for other therapists the reactions elicited were greater in the reflective treatment. The clients in this study did not differ significantly as a result of the inter-action effect (therapist × method) in the extent of guarded, defensive, dependent, open, covertly resistive, or overtly resistive verbal behavior which they manifested. They also did not differ significantly as a result of the interaction effect in the extent of change they exhibited in maladjustment, dependence, defensiveness, positive attitudes toward self, positive attitudes toward others, anxiety, or therapists' evaluation of change as a result of therapy.

REFERENCES

1. ASHBY, J. D. The effect of a reflective and of a leading psychotherapy on certain client characteristics. Unpublished doctoral dissertation, Pennsylvania State Univer., 1956.
2. BORDIN, E. S. The implications of client expectations for the counseling process. J. clin. Psychol., 1946, 2, 17–21.
3. BOWN, O. H. An investigation of thera-peutic relationship in client-centered psy-chotherapy. Unpublished doctoral disserta-tion, Univer. of Chicago, 1954.
4. CURRAN, C. A. Personality factors in coun-seling. New York: Grune and Stratton, 1945.
5. DAULTON, M. J. A study of factors relat-ing to resistance in the interview. Unpub-lished master's thesis, Ohio State Univer., 1947. Cited in F. P. Robinson, Principles and procedures in student counseling. New York: Harpers, 1950.
6. DOLLARD, J., & MILLER, N. E. Personality and psychotherapy. New York: McGraw-Hill, 1950.
7. EDWARDS, A. Manual, personal preference schedule. New York: Psychological Corp., 1954.
8. FIEDLER, F. E. Factor analyses of psycho-analytic, nondirective, and Adlerian thera-peutic relationships. J. consult. Psychol., 1951, 15, 32–38.
9. FORD, D. H. An experimental comparison of the relationship between client and therapist in a reflective and a leading type of psychotherapy. Unpublished doctoral dissertation, Pennsylvania State Univer., 1956.
10. FRANK, J. D. Experimental studies of per-sonal pressure and resistance. J. gen. Psy-chol., 1944, 30, 23–41.
11. FROMM-REICHMANN, FRIEDA. Principles of intensive psychotherapy. Chicago: Uni-ver. of Chicago Press, 1950.
12. GALLAGHER, J. J. MMPI changes con-comitant with client-centered therapy. J. consult. Psychol., 1953, 17, 334–338.
13. GALLAGHER, J. J. The problem of escap-ing clients in nondirective counseling. In W. U. Snyder (Ed.), Group report of a program of research in psychotherapy. State College, Pa.; Pennsylvania State Uni-ver., 1953.
14. GIBSON, R. A factor analysis of measuring changes following client-centered psycho-therapy. Unpublished doctoral dissertation, Pennsylvania State Univer., 1953.
15. GILLESPIE, J. F. Verbal signs of resistance in client-centered therapy. In W. U. Snyder (Ed.), Group report of a program of research in psychotherapy. State College, Pa.: Pennsylvania State Univer., 1953.
16. GUERNEY, B. G., JR. Client dependency, guardedness, openness, and resistance in a reflective and in a leading psychotherapy. Unpublished doctoral dissertation, Penn-sylvania State Univer., 1956.
17. GUERNEY, L. F. Differential effects of cer-tain therapist characteristics on client re-actions to psychotherapy. Unpublished doc-toral dissertation, Pennsylvania State Uni-ver., 1956.
18. HAIGH, G. Defensive behavior in client-centered therapy. J. consult. Psychol., 1949, 13, 181–189.
19. HOGAN, R. A. A measure of client defen-siveness. In W. Wolff and J. A. Precker, Success in psychotherapy. New York: Grune and Stratton, 1952.
20. MOONEY, R. L. Surveying high school students' problems by means of a problem check list. Educ. Res. Bull., 1942, 21, 57–69.
21. MOWRER, O. H. Psychotherapy, theory, and research. New York: Ronald Press, 1953.
22. NAVRAN, L. A rationally derived MMPI scale to measure dependence. J. consult. Psychol., 1954, 18, 192.

23. ROGERS, C. R., *Counseling and psychotherapy.* Boston: Houghton Mifflin, 1942.

24. ROGERS, C. R. *Client-centered therapy.* Boston: Houghton Mifflin, 1951.

25. ROGERS, C. R., & DYMOND, ROSALIND. *Psychotherapy and personality change.* Chicago: Univer. of Chicago Press, 1954.

26. SEEMAN, J. A study of the process of non-directive therapy. *J. consult. Psychol.,* 1949, 13, 157–168.

27. SIEGEL, S. Certain determinants and correlations of authoritarianism. *Genet. Psychol. Monogr.,* 1954, 49, 187–229.

28. SNEDECOR, G. W. *Statistical methods.* Ames, Iowa: Iowa State College Press, 1946.

29. SNYDER, W. U. An investigation of the nature of nondirective psychotherapy. *J. genet. Psychol.,* 1945, 33, 193–223.

30. SNYDER, W. U. *Group report of a program of research in psychotherapy.* State College, Pa.: Pennsylvania State Univer., 1953.

31. STRUPP, H. An objective comparison of Rogerian and psychoanalytic techniques. *J. consult. Psychol.,* 1953, 19, 1–7.

32. TAYLOR, J. A. A personality scale of manifest anxiety. *J. abnorm. soc. Psychol.,* 1953, 48, 285–290.

33. TUCKER, J. E. Measuring client progress in client-centered psychotherapy. In W. U. Snyder (Ed.), *Group report of a program of research in psychotherapy.* State College, Pa.: Pennsylvania State Univer., 1953.

APPENDIX

THE CLIENT'S PERSONAL REACTION QUESTIONNAIRE

Directions

During the process of personal counseling, people have many different feelings and reactions. We know that these reactions are sometimes negative, sometimes positive, and often mixed. Your responses to the following questionnaire will help us understand people's reactions to personal counseling. This will have nothing to do with your counseling. It will be *completely confidential.* Neither your counselor nor his superiors will be informed of your responses. Approximately 15 minutes are required to complete it.

There are five possible responses to each of the items in the questionnaire.

1 not characteristic
2 slightly characteristic
3 moderately characteristic
4 quite characteristic
5 highly characteristic

Put a circle around the responses most representative of your present feelings. Your feelings may have been different in the past and may be different in the future. We are interested in your feelings right now at this point in your counseling experience. Be sure to put a circle around *one* response for *each* item. Do not spend too much time on any one item.

Positive Items[1]

1. I'm pleased with my counselor's interest and attention.

2. I wish I felt as sure of myself in all social situations as I do here.

3. I like our sessions even when I can't think of anything to say.

4. I remember and "chew over" things that my counselor says.

5. I have a very warm feeling toward my counselor.

6. I wish I had some friends who were as understanding as my counselor.

7. I am usually eager to hear what my counselor has to say.

8. I often feel in a better mood after an interview.

9. I sometimes feel like letting my counselor know what a nice person I think he (she) is.

10. I wish I could feel other people respected and liked me as much as my counselor does.

11. I feel comfortable talking with my counselor.

12. This is one of the few situations I've ever been in that I didn't worry very much about what the other person thought of me.

[1] Grouped for the reader's convenience.

13. I wish I were more like my counselor.
14. I feel that my counselor regards me as a likable person.
15. Many of the things my counselor says just seem to hit the nail on the head.
16. I experience a certain relief after telling my counselor something.
17. My counselor's attitude gives me hope I can get something out of this.
18. I feel that the counselor really likes to spend the counseling session with me.
19. I feel my counselor is really anxious to help me solve my problems.
20. It's easier for me to talk with this counselor than with most other people.
21. I think I could criticize or get angry at my counselor and he (she) wouldn't resent it.
22. My counselor must be one of the best ones here.
23. My counselor's understanding of me is encouraging.
24. I usually feel the interviews have been worth while.
25. I really get "wrapped up" in what's going on in the counseling session.
26. I wish I had asked for this kind of help sooner.
27. I can talk about most anything in my interviews without feeling embarrassed or ashamed.
28. I wish I could spend more time with the counselor.
29. I am gaining more respect for psychology as a result of my experiences in counseling.
30. The things my counselor says and does give me confidence in him.
31. I seldom feel the counselor has misinterpreted what I have said or done.
32. I know the counselor understands me even when I don't express myself well.
33. I have the feeling here is one person I can really trust.
34. I would like to behave toward other people more like my therapist behaves toward me.
35. I look forward to talking with my counselor.
36. I feel sure that my counselor would take anything I could say or do without getting upset.
37. I'm pleased with the progress I've made since beginning these interviews.
38. I'm glad this particular counselor was assigned to me.
39. The counselor is a warm and friendly person.
40. I think my counselor really sympathizes with my difficulties.

Defensive Items

1. It would be helpful if I could write things down and bring them in to the counselor to discuss.
2. I doubt if many people get much help out of these interviews.
3. Sometimes the counselor seems to twist around the things I say to mean something different than what I intended.
4. It's hard for me to talk about myself.
5. I sometimes feel like calling this whole thing off.
6. I've told the counselor a lot but he (she) still hasn't given me much help.
7. It takes a long time in an interview for me to get started talking about important things.
8. It seems to me there should be an easier and quicker way than this to solve my problems.
9. Many of the things we talk about don't seem to be related to my problems.
10. I sometimes feel like leaving before the interview hour is over.
11. Sometimes after the counselor says something I just can't think of anything else to say for awhile.
12. I sometimes hesitate to tell my counselor what I am really thinking.
13. If I had someone else as a counselor, I would probably feel freer to discuss my problems.
14. These interviews seem like a waste of time to me.
15. Sometimes I feel like I'm being criticized during the interviews.
16. It doesn't make much difference to me whether my counselor likes me or not.
17. I frequently find it difficult to think of things to say.
18. I get irritated at some of my counselor's comments.

19. I spend very little time thinking about these interviews when I'm not here.

20. It was kind of unnecessary for me to start this counseling because my problems really aren't very major.

21. I just don't know what to do or say in the interviews that would help.

22. When I'm in the counseling session I sometimes forget things I had meant to tell my counselor.

23. If my counselor understood me better I could make more progress.

24. I try to justify my actions so the counselor will see why I behaved the way I did.

25. There are some things which I don't yet feel ready to go into with my counselor.

26. I feel a need to keep the conversation moving during the counseling hour.

27. I can't see where my counselor has done much to help me solve my problems.

28. I don't know exactly why, but I feel nervous about coming to the counseling hour.

29. Sometimes it's hard for me to pay attention to what the counselor is saying.

30. I know what my problems are, but I don't know what to do about them.

31. I carefully organize what I'm going to say in the next counseling session.

32. The counselor's looking at me all the time makes me uncomfortable.

33. I sometimes wish we were talking about something different than what we're talking about at the moment.

34. If I would take a couple of hours a week to think about these things on my own, I could probably accomplish as much as I do in these interviews.

35. I feel my counselor wants me to tell him a lot more than I am telling him.

36. I'm afraid to express my real feelings in these sessions.

37. I don't think I have as many problems as other people in counseling.

38. I sometimes resent the counselor's attitude toward me.

39. I sometimes feel like I'm being put on the spot.

40. I feel that my counselor has me classified or categorized as some kind of "case."

THE THERAPIST'S PERSONAL REACTION QUESTIONNAIRE

Directions

During the process of personal counseling, counselors have many different feelings and reactions. These reactions are sometimes negative, sometimes positive, and sometimes mixed. Leaders in various schools of therapy seem to agree that having varied feelings and reactions toward clients is not undesirable as long as the counselor recognizes and understands them. In fact, they may provide additional sensitive evidence about the meaning of a client's communications. We are interested in learning what these feelings are and how they change.

Your responses will have nothing to do with your counseling. They will not be made available in identifiable form to your supervisor or anyone else except the researchers.

There are five possible responses to each of the items in the questionnaire.

1 not characteristic
2 slightly characteristic
3 moderately characteristic
4 quite characteristic
5 highly characteristic

Put a circle around the responses most representative of your present feelings. Your feelings may have been different in the past and may be different in the future. We are interested in your feelings right now at this point in your counseling experience with this client. Be sure to put a circle around *one* response for *each* item. Do not spend too much time on any one item. The numbers may appear in different orders before each item, but they will always signify the same response. Some of the items are written comparing this client with other clients you have had. Try to respond to the items in terms of that comparison, if possible.

When you have completed the questionnaire, return it to the envelope and drop the sealed envelope in the box marked TESTS in the waiting room. The test *must* be completed before your next interview with this client.

Positive Items[2]

1. I like this client more than most.
2. I have a more warm, friendly emotional reaction toward this client than others.
3. I feel sure that this client would not want to change therapists if given the chance.
4. I am seldom in doubt about what the client is trying to say.
5. I think about this client more often between meetings than others.
6. This client seems to appreciate my efforts.
7. In general, I could not ask for a better client.
8. I'll miss having these interviews a little when the client decides to terminate.
9. I prefer working with this client more than others I've worked with.
10. If I rated all of the clients I've worked with so far in my career in terms of the satisfaction I've gotten out of them, this client would receive a high rating.
11. I think this client is trying harder to solve his (her) problems than others I've had.
12. I sometimes wish the therapy sessions with this client would not end so soon.
13. I am more confident this client will work out his problems than I've been with others.
14. I can usually find significant things to respond to in what the client says.
15. I think I'd like this client socially if I had met him first in that capacity.
16. We get into more important material than is frequently the case with other clients.
17. It's easier for me to see exactly how this client would feel in the situations he describes than it is with others.
18. I sometimes feel like congratulating this client for something he has done.
19. I'm usually more absorbed in what this client is doing or saying than with others I've had.
20. Responses to what this client is saying come more "easily" than with others.

21. We may have our ups and downs, but underneath it all I think the client has confidence in me.
22. Therapy with this client is a more rewarding experience for me than with many others I've had.
23. When things are not going well for the client I feel upset too.
24. I usually have a good feeling about interviews with this client.
25. I think I'm doing a pretty competent job with this client.
26. I think we have a pretty relaxed, understanding kind of relationship.
27. I feel more comfortable in the therapy sessions with this client than with others I've had.
28. I find it easier to understand and communicate with this client than with others.
29. As compared to others, I'm pretty "wrapped up" in this client and in trying to help him.
30. If I had to leave here for some reason before this client was finished, I'd try very hard to see that he was assigned to "just the right therapist."
31. I'm glad this particular client was assigned to me.
32. I get anxious about what to do or say with this client less frequently than with others I've had.
33. I look forward to my interviews with this client more than with others I've had.
34. Similarities between my own emotional experiences and some of this client's make me feel a little closer to him (her) than to others I've had.
35. Relationships like this are bright spots in my schedule.

Negative Items

1. I'm usually relieved when the interviews are over.
2. I can't get this client to open up.
3. I get pretty bored in some of these interviews.
4. Sometimes I get pretty tense during the interviews.
5. I seldom feel that we have accomplished something in the interviews.
6. I would like to be able to feel more warmth toward this client than I now feel.

---

[2] Grouped for the reader's convenience.

7. I don't feel the client is making as much use of therapy as he could.
8. I don't particularly enjoy my hour with this client.
9. I can't get close to this client.
10. I sometimes wonder if another therapist might not get further with this client than I.
11. I disagree with this client about some basic matters like religion, morality, etc.
12. It is really an effort to "stay with" this client.
13. This client "hits me where it hurts" sometimes.
14. I find it harder to remember what has been covered in previous interviews with this client than with others.
15. In comparison with other clients, I find it hard to get involved with this client's problems.
16. I feel in need of help with this case.
17. I can't seem to get very interested in this client.
18. I seem to tire more quickly when I work with this client than with others.
19. I sometimes feel "pushed" by this client.
20. Sometimes I feel pretty frustrated in our interviews.
21. I have to exert more self-control and self-restraint with this client than with most.
22. I doubt if any counselor could do much for this client.
23. I get pretty discouraged at times about this one.
24. I feel pretty ineffective with this client.
25. I prefer working with this client less than others I've worked with.
26. I can't help but be annoyed to some extent by some of this client's behavior.
27. I'm "flying blind" with this client.
28. Sometimes I resent the client's attitude.
29. It's hard to know how to respond to this client in a helpful way.
30. In comparison with other clients, it's hard for me to put myself in this client's place.
31. I am sometimes at a loss as to how to respond to this client.
32. I don't think this client will stand out in my pleasant memories of cases.
33. Sometimes I have to show more sympathy and acceptance than I really feel toward this client.

34. Sometimes I wish some other therapist had this client.
35. The hour often seems to be dragging on with this client.

CLIENT VERBAL BEHAVIOR CATEGORIES

General Rules

1. A client response is a client statement or 15 seconds of silence between two therapist statements. If a client's statement is longer than 15 seconds it is divided in 15-second units. The last part of a client statement between a previous 15-second portion and the time the therapist speaks is categorized even though it may be less than 15 seconds long, unless it is a pause.

2. The category "N" is used for the client only when there is nothing in the client's response to call for a classification anywhere else.

3. If a statement cannot definitely be placed in a category other than "N" because it is not complete at 15 seconds when the recording machine is stopped, put it in that "N" category. But its meaning is allowed to have bearing on the categorization of the next 15-second portion of the client's response. If, on the other hand, enough of the client's statement is heard to put it definitely in a category, do so even though the sentence may not be complete.

4. The same *sentence* cannot be categorized in two places (unless it is an Interruption, Blocking, or Change of Topic), but more than one category may be used for the same 15-second interval.

5. If in conflict between two or more categorizations of the same client sentence, place it where the least inference is required.

6. We are interested in the variables being measured here only as they are manifest in the counseling situation itself. Client statements which indicate only that the client is or has been, for example, guarded or dependent outside of the therapy hour do not fall under the Guardedness or Dependency categories here.

Dependency

Briefly defined, "Dependency" is the extent to which the client asks the therapist for his opinions, or advice, information, evaluation, instruction or demonstrates a need for structuring from the therapist. Also it includes the degree to which the client places responsibility for progress or outcome of counseling on the counselor rather than accepting it himself.

Statements to be categorized as Dependency are statements in which the client:

1. Asks for help, opinions, advice, solutions, information, judgments, evaluations, instructions from the therapist. Asking the therapist for elaborations on his statement is also included here.

2. Shows by his statement that he is putting the responsibility for providing the above-mentioned things on the therapist, or he puts the responsibility for progress or outcome of therapy on the therapist. This can be shown indirectly through such statements as "You won't be able to figure out what's wrong with me unless I keep talking."

Note: Statements pertaining to appointment time, and asking for cigarettes, match, etc. are not categorized here.

Rhetorical questions (e.g., "Did I tell you about . . .") are not categorized here. Some pause or other indication that the client expects an answer is necessary for client questions of this sort to be categorized as "Dependency."

On the other hand, there may be statements which are clearly questions being asked of the therapist, although they may not be put in question form. For example, "I wonder why that would be (pause)." If such a statement seems aimed at the therapist, it should be categorized as "Dependency."

The following statements are some examples to clarify the category of Dependency:

1. "I didn't expect this to be easy or direct, but it does enter my mind, just what can be accomplished here and how?" . . . D. If a similar statement had cast more doubt on the worth of the therapist or therapy a Covert Resistance categorization would be warranted in addition to a Dependency categorization.

2. Therapist: "She didn't want to." Client: "You mean my sister?" . . . N. A question which calls for clarification of an ambiguous therapist statement does not receive a Dependency categorization. If the therapist's statement is judged clear in meaning and the client nevertheless requests clarification this may receive a Covert Resistance categorization.

3. Therapist: "Maybe you could do some thinking about that." Client: "In what way?" . . . D. The client is asking for instruction.

4. "When do you think a person should start thinking about getting married?" . . . D. This is a request for therapist's opinion.

Openness

"Openness" is defined as: the extent to which the client freely discusses his problems, deviations from the "normal," his culturally frowned-upon traits, behavior, and motivations; and, in general, his willingness to expose himself to potential criticism and change, particularly his willingness to discuss thoroughly those areas which seem most threatening. He does this without at the same time qualifying, hedging, and engaging in defensive verbal maneuvers.

In a way this category is the opposite of the "guardedness" category. When the client's statement does not exhibit any guardedness in a discussion area in which a clinician would often expect a person to be guarded, the client's statement is categorized under "Openness." This category is meant to reflect the ability or willingness of a client to "open himself up" to the counselor; to expose himself to possible criticism, to expose himself to the prospect of modifying his self concept, without at the same time feeling the need to defend himself as he is to his own or to the counselor's eyes. A confidence in the therapist's understanding, noncriticalness and trustworthiness is presumed to underlie such openness; i.e., the statements that are considered "open" are not such as one would tell to one's critics or even new-found friends.

1. Unqualified[3] admission to a problem,[4] deficiency, inadequacy, undesirable characteristic, trait, behavior pattern or act, feelings or attitudes.

2. Unqualified statements pointing to personal deviation from the norm in a culturally or personally undesirable direction.

3. Unqualified statements that admit to possession of culturally or personally undesirable characteristics, traits, behavior, feelings, or attitudes.

Note: Simple acceptance of a therapist's statement placing the client in an undesirable light is not scored "Open." It is only when the client proceeds in such a way as to place his statement under any of the criteria listed above that his statement is categorized "Open."

A simple statement of a problem qualifies as an "Open" response if it is unqualified.

_____

[3] An admission to a problem is "qualified" when it is coupled with expression of uncertainty (e.g., "maybe," "perhaps," "probably," etc.; the term "I think," however, is not considered to indicate uncertainty). Qualification may also exist in any minimization of the problem in terms of the extent or severity of the problem. Such minimization is, of course, a different thing than clarification and specification, and the coder must make a decision as to whether the client is being cautious and guarded or merely giving some definitive information to his counselor. When the case is ambiguous to the coder he should not categorize it as "Openness" (or Guardedness) but as "None." A qualification must occur in the same 15-second interval as a statement in order for it to disqualify the statement as "open." If an admission is accompanied (i.e., in the same 15-second interval) by anything that calls for a Guardedness categorization it is not categorized as Openness. These categories are mutually exclusive in the same client response.

[4] The word "problem" is defined in the section on "Guardedness."

A description of a particular conflict is not necessarily "Open." But an unqualified admission of having important unresolved contradictions or irrationalities within oneself is categorized "Open."

The following statements are some examples to clarify the categorization of "Openness":

1. Client (speaking about husband or father): "As far as really deep feelings—I have none for him." . . . O. This is an unqualified admission to culturally unacceptable attitude or feeling.

2. "My conversational ability is pretty weak. I can't carry on a long continuous conversation." . . . O. This is an unqualified admission of an inadequacy.

3. Therapist: "That seems kind of contradictory." Client: "When I think about it, that's true; as far as things have gone in the past I have no reason to feel inferior." . . . O. The client accepts and *elaborates* upon therapist statement pointing to important contradiction or irrationality in client.

4. "Most of the time I'm worried about people—what they're thinking of me." . . . O. This is an unqualified admission of a psychological problem.

5. Therapist: "And you feel like he's thinking only of himself." Client: "Not exactly. I don't blame him particularly. I guess I do in a way. I don't want to, but I do. I want him to accept me and my needs." . . . O. This is an admission to a feeling toward which a personal distaste is made clear.

Guardedness

Guardedness is defined as the extent to which the client exhibits wariness and hedging in regard to presenting and working on his problem, admitting to faults, and exposing himself to potential criticism and change. This includes self-stimulated denial, or minimization, of his problems or his deviations from the "normal"; and denial of culturally undesirable feelings, traits, and motivations. It also includes the need to justify himself or his actions to the therapist and expectations or anticipations of criticism from the therapist.

A key question for the judge to ask himself in listening to a client's statement with reference to this category is whether the client is in any way engaged in "protecting" himself from potential criticism or potential change in his self concept. Some of the cues to listen for are presented below.

1. Statements denying, qualifying, minimizing, or belittling the extent of a problem or the existence of one.[5] The denial is not in response to a question or statement of the therapist or any other particular person.

2. Statements pointing to nondeviation from the "norm," "average," "everyone," "other," etc., either as a person in general or in some particular aspect of thought, feeling, or behavior (e.g., "I guess we all have a tendency to talk in circles."). If such a statement is purely descriptive and factual or is in the nature of a complaint, rather than being something which is *comforting to the client,* it does not receive a Guardedness categorization.

3. Statements denying possession of an undesirable characteristic, trait, feeling, attitude, or denying an undesirable act or motivation. This category is not used when the characteristic has been attributed to the client by the therapist or some specific other person.

4. Statements in which the client attempts to justify an act, thought, feeling, statement, etc. to the therapist. "Justify" here means to hold forth one's behavior as just, right, warranted; to declare oneself guiltless; absolve or acquit oneself; to at-

tempt to show satisfactory excuse or reason for something that is culturally or personally undesirable. The reason that is offered by the client is usually one that is primarily "outside" of the self, i.e., the undesirable thing is a result of the behavior of others or circumstances. This category does not apply if the client has been asked to justify himself by the therapist or some specific other persons.

5. A statement indicating that the client might be anticipating a critical or differing thought or statement from the therapist. (For example, "That's the way I think about it, you may think differently, I don't know"). Such phrases as "sound to you" or "look to you" from the client to the therapist should alert the coder to the possibility that such a statement is an anticipation of difference or criticalness between the client and the counselor.

Some such statements could serve to beat the therapist to the punch. "All this must sound foolish to you." Here the expectation by the client of a critical attitude on the therapist's part is overt. In some cases the anticipation of a critical attitude is only implied by the client's overt acceptance of the blame or faultfinding he expects from the therapist. He will thus make a statement taking fault or responsibility upon himself, while he is in reality rejecting the blame or criticism. Sometimes this takes the form of a much-qualified acceptance of a statement by the therapist or some other person which places the client in a bad light. Admitting to blame does not, of course, automatically indicate that the statement should be categorized as Guardedness. Such a statement may belong in the N or OP category depending on the way it is said and:

1. The extent of qualification. As a rule, in doubtful cases, do not categorize as G an unqualified statement accepting blame (e.g., "I'm being foolish.") Do not categorize as G a statement containing a single qualification (e.g., "Maybe I'm being foolish.") Do categorize as G such a statement which contains a plural number of quali-

---

[5] "Problem" is broadly defined here as anything which is culturally frowned-upon, *or* which bothers the client personally. To qualify under the latter the client must make his personal distaste clear. Physical symptoms or manifestations of problems (e.g., headaches, crying, sweating, shaking) stated only as a physical problem are not considered to fall under the difinition of "problem." But psychological symptoms (e.g., nervousness, feeling depressed, etc.) are considered to be "problems."

fications (e.g., "I guess maybe I'm being foolish.")

2. The nature of the elaboration on the statement that is found within the same client response. As a rule, in doubtful cases: (a) the latter part of the client's response is considered more important—if the acceptance of fault follows the blaming of outside circumstances or other people, it should probably not be categorized as G. On the other hand, if the blaming of outside factors follows self-blame, this should probably be categorized as G; (b) the more detailed and specific part of the client's response is considered more important and the vague, more general, part considered to be less important. Thus, if a client states he is at fault in some general way, but criticizes another person or a circumstance in a more specific way, the statement is likely to be a Guardedness statement.

Note: A simple rejection of a therapist's statement, whatever it may have been, is not categorized as G. It is only when the client proceeds in such a way as to place his statement under any of the criteria listed above that his statement is categorized as Guardedness.

The following statements are some examples to clarify the categorization of Guardedness:

1. "I wonder if I have any problems. Maybe it's just that I think I have problems. Maybe that's all there is to the whole thing." . . . G. This is minimization of the problem.

2. "I guess everybody feels that way about something." . . . G. This is self-stimulated pointing to nondeviation from the norm.

3. "I was proud of the medal, and I showed it to everyone, as every successful athlete would." . . . G. The client is pointing to nondeviation from the norm in regard to the culturally frowned-upon trait of pride.

4. "I don't like to visit my family because when I have too much work to do it bothers me." . . . G. This is justification.

5. Therapist: "You feel inferior to them." Client: "Maybe that's true. I don't know. Anyway, they kept talking about things with which I wasn't familiar, which I thought was very inconsiderate of them." . . . If the manner in which the statement is said is consistent with such a categorization, this doubly qualified acceptance is put in the G category as an overt acceptance of a therapist's statement placing the client in an undesirable light which is really emotionally rejected by the client.

6. Therapist: "You feel inferior to them." Client: "No, it wasn't that. It was just that they kept talking about things with which I wasn't familiar, which I thought was very inconsiderate of them." . . . N. A rejection of a therapist's statement placing the client in an undesirable light is not categorized G unless it also falls in one of the criteria listed for G.

Covert Resistance

Covert resistance is defined as the extent to which the client manifests indirect or impersonalized criticism of the therapist or therapy, also blocking, delaying tactics, failure to recall or report things, changing the subject, interrupting the therapist. It is resistance or hostility toward therapy, therapist, progress in therapy, or toward things which are thought of as being conducive to such progress. But the resistance is not directly expressed verbally; instead, other more subtle escapes or hostilities are resorted to by the client.

1. Long Pauses (LP): A 15-second "response" in which the client does not talk.

2. Short answer (SA): An unelaborated simple thought statement not longer than four or five words that is followed by a pause. This category is not used when the client's response is in reply to a question by the therapist which can be given a simple affirmative, negative, or factual answer.

3. Changing Topic (TC): Client initiated changes in the topic being discussed. The new topic is clearly unrelated to the

previous statements of the counselor or client. Client statements which serve to cut off a topic (e.g., "That's all I have to say about it.") are also included here.

4. Blocking (Bl): Incomplete sentences that are not the product of an interruption by the therapist. Retracing and rephrasing or fumbling of sentences. Pauses in mid-sentence (at least 5 seconds in length). Any statement of, or indication of, failure or inability to think or talk about something in particular or anything in general; inability to recall a word, situation, or example; inability or failure to give reasons or motivations; inability to give any label to one's own feelings, attitudes, or perceptions.

5. Interruption (Int.): Client interruptions or overriding of therapist's verbalizations. (Agreement inserted into a therapist's verbalizations with no intent to cut him off are not included here.)

6. Verbalization or intellectualization (V): Talking about minutiae or irrelevant details. *Abstract* discussions of politics, religion, etc. Such statements bear no discernible relationship to the client's problems as he has been expressing them in the interview. To qualify for a categorization here such a statement must take up a whole 15-second interval. However, if the client spends time grouping for an irrelevant detail his response is categorized here whether or not the whole 15 seconds is spent on irrelevancies.

7. Resistance toward therapy or therapist (Th): Indirect or disguised reference to the inadequacy of therapy or therapist. This includes indirect or subtle minimizations of the benefits being derived from therapy. These statements are not made with any reference to the client's own feelings or thoughts about therapy or therapist, or the client is not taking any definite stand or position in his statement.

Statements indicating unwillingness to abide by therapeutic limits or demands when this unwillingness is only *indirectly* expressed. Any reason—other than open admission of not wanting to do so—for not appearing on time. Indecision about attending the next interview without stating any desire not to.

8. Inability to understand (U): Client statements indicating feigned or real inability to understand the therapist when the therapist's statement is judged to be clear in meaning. Requests for clarification of such therapist statements are included here, but not requests for further elaboration (which are included in Dependence).

Note: A rejection of a therapist's statement or interpretation is not considered resistance, unless it also happens to meet one of the above criteria.

The following statements are some examples to clarify the categorization of Covert Resistance:

1. "I can't define how I felt in that situation." . . . CR, "Bl" (Blocking).

2. Therapist: "I wonder where they get that idea?" Client: "I don't know." . . . N. Client's inability to provide labels, motivations, etc., for *other* people is not considered resistance.

3. "If I could be hypnotized that would help." . . . CR. This is an indirect reference to inadequacy of therapy.

4. "And I was going to tell him off, so I went down there about two o'clock (pause), or was it three o'clock (pause), I think it was two o'clock, and I said to him," . . . CR. This is "Verbalization," grouping for irrelevant detail.

5. "Since I talked about this thing with you I felt much better in class than I had before, but I think that was because I was sitting somewhere else this time" . . . CR ("Th"). This is indirect minimization of the benefits being derived from therapy.

6. Therapist: "You felt uncomfortable in that situation." Client: "What did you say?" . . . CR. This is real or feigned inability to understand a clear therapist statement.

7. "I don't know if I'll be able to make it next time, I have an exam coming up." . . . CR ("Th"). Client gives reason, other

than not wanting to, for possibility of not coming to therapy session.

Open Resistance

Briefly defined, "open resistance" is the extent to which the client *verbalizes criticism*—in an open way—of the therapist or the therapeutic technique. *Also,* personal and verbalized opposition to staying within the limits set by the particular kind of therapy which the client is receiving. This is *verbalized unwillingness* as opposed to "inability" or failure per se.

This is resistance or hostility toward the same things as are mentioned in "covert resistance," but here these things are admitted by the client.

1. Criticism or negative attitudes about the therapist or therapy verbally expressed. Statements are frequently expressed in the form of doubts, sarcastic remarks, and only thinly veiled criticism of the therapy or therapist. These statements admittedly convey the thoughts of feelings of the client himself and the client is taking a stand about his opinions or doubts.

2. Open admission of unwillingness (not "inability") to talk, or discuss any particular area, or to follow the conditions and limits of the kind of therapy the client is receiving.

The following statements are some examples to clarify the categorization of Open Resistance:

1. "I can't see how this is going to help very much." . . . Op. Res.

2. "All that's been happening so far is I've been answering questions, when am I going to get some answers?" . . . Op. Res.

3. "Isn't there some way we could speed this business up?" . . . Op. Res.

4. "That's something I'd rather not talk about right now" . . . Op. Res.

5. "I'd like to take a break from this for a while. I'll call you again when I want another appointment if that's O.K. with you." . . . Op. Res.

The Test of Clinical Judgment

Directions

This is a test of your clinical judgment. It consists of statements made by all sorts of persons. Your task is to read each statement carefully and then make a judgment about the *emotional adjustment of the person who made the statement. Do not* evaluate the content of the statement itself.

If you can conceive of a statement as coming from an essentially normal person, place a check under the column marked "A." If you *cannot* conceive of the statement as coming from an essentially normal person, place a check under the column marked "B." Place one check in front of each statement.

"Normal" Filler Items[6]

1. Money can become an important thing in anyone's life when he's really short of it.

2. Farmers have as much common sense as other people.

3. The threat of pneumonia is much less marked today than it once was.

4. A person doesn't like to think that his home town has turned out to be a dump.

5. One of the roughest things about the military life is that you have to do so many apparently senseless things.

6. It's hard for most of us to realize what it is like to go for days without getting enough food.

"Abnormal" Filler Items

1. Little by little, drop by drop, the doctors drain the blood from you 'til you are completely bloodless.

2. The men in Moscow have mind machines which they use to control anybody they want to control.

3. Everybody should really shower 10 or 12 times a day to be absolutely sure that his body is free of killer germs.

4. It's because they've been so sinful that people's bodies start to rot inside and you can smell them.

---

[6] Grouped for the reader's convenience.

5. They should send all of the iceboxes and refrigerators to Alaska and everyone should go up there and live in one with his mother and father.

6. Everyone is doomed. Very soon now, the earth will open up and we'll all be swallowed into Hell.

Test Items

1. My life has been laid out for me and I can do no more than live it as has been planned.

2. Wives should be traded around at fairly frequent intervals. Otherwise things get boring.

3. You can usually tell whether a kid is going to turn out to be a bad egg or not and if he is you might as well lock him up right then. There wouldn't be nearly so many killings and things if we'd lock them up and get rid of them.

4. The ordinary person doesn't know what's good for him and what isn't. He needs to be pushed for his own good.

5. Don't try to tell me that most everybody wouldn't cheat on tests if they could get away with it. They're just too scared, that's all.

6. Rich people are generally sex perverts or free-lovers.

7. We women are useless for anything except bearing children and keeping house.

8. Good and evil are constantly battling for your soul as well as mine.

9. Old maids are frustrated old women who get so eager for sex that they practice a lot of perversions.

10. Have you ever heard of them putting a Morgan or Rockefeller in jail? You're damned right they don't. Only the little guys pay.

11. Survival of the fittest is the law of God. It is wrong for us to try to keep weaklings alive.

12. Only a woman can really understand how others feel about love. Men are such insensitive brutes.

13. If a man can't hold down an honest job, then I say let him starve.

14. I advocate celibacy. I feel that there's little place for sex in professional life.

15. It's the devil that makes people do bad things. He's the one who is behind all of the bad people.

16. Women who paint up their eyes and faces must be whores at heart.

17. All of this nonsense about not frustrating children will lead to no good. God meant for us to have to do things we don't want to do or he wouldn't have set things up the way he did.

18. No rich man could get rich without stepping all over a lot of people on the way.

19. If I know a person is dishonest, even once, I'll never trust him again.

20. Yeah, they make more money at their fancy desks than you do out here in the yard, but did you ever look close at them? They're soft and white all over—just like women. They're nothing but a bunch of fruits.

21. Getting the jump on the next guy so that you end up on top is the main thing about living in this world, the way it is.

22. It's dangerous to let young boys and girls get together by themselves. The first thing they'll do is start playing around with each other.

23. People who get sick should pray to God to forgive them for their sins. Sickness is God's way of punishing us for our wicked ways.

24. It's gotta be a pretty queer guy in my way of thinking who would ever knit anything.

25. They just fill kids' minds with a lot of fancy stuff at those colleges so that their old men aren't good enough for them anymore.

26. You get a wild kid—the only way to handle him is to break him. Otherwise he'll end up a crook or something.

27. Listen, take my advice. Don't be fooled by the soft, delicate appearance women make. They'd take over this world and make slaves of us men if we'd relax our control just one little bit.

28. They ought to open the floodgates and flood the whole damned South with everyone in it.

29. Don't talk to me about those clergymen, with their "holier than thou" attitudes. They'd lie, cheat, and steal just as much as anybody.

30. Parents always know what's right, so it's best not to do anything without first asking them.

31. Most college graduates are radicals, homosexuals, or troublemakers.

32. Girls who go around screwing with the boys ought to be whipped in public and made an example of.

33. Those people in the slums are basically weak in character and you'll never make them strong like good honest workers by giving them more parks and fresh air.

34. Every big corporation and most of the smaller ones have company spies mixed in with the workers.

35. You've really got to make a criminal suffer severely for his crime. Punish him until he has no spirit left. Then he'll be willing to do what is right.

36. Dancing and card playing are just as sinful as sex. Better a person should keep himself locked in his room than to indulge in these evils.

37. My mother always said to act like a lady at all times. She is right. I've found that if a woman lets her guard down for a minute that a "gentleman" will change to an animal, just like that.

38. Man is basically evil and at the most can do no more than to control the evil that is within him.

39. It's bad business letting women take over men's jobs. Why do you think that they hate to have them in mines and on ships? Do you think it's just superstition?

40. A child must learn who his master is. There's plenty of time for him to think and act for himself when he's an adult.

41. If you don't stop those people from talking with each other, you will soon find that they have formed some sort of conspiracy which you will have a hard time suppressing.

42. We should destroy criminals because they'll just produce more of their own kind.

43. I tell you it's bad to send 18-year-olds to the Army. They'll turn them out as killers, cynics, homosexuals—or worse.

44. Laborers are a bunch of greasy, dirty slobs.

45. If it was a matter of sacrificing some of my happiness to help out someone else, I wouldn't do it.

46. Who would criticize the President of the United States except Communists, homosexuals, extremists, and that sort.

47. Who do these women think they're kidding with all of their modesty and morals? They'd jump into bed with the first guy that asked them if they thought they could get away with it.

48. Killing dogs and monkeys is a horrible thing—no matter how much good they claim will come of it.

49. The big shots can get away with anything. But just don't let the little man step over the line.

50. Bachelors are like vicious animals waiting to pounce on any young girl they can and take advantage of her.

51. I don't see why we should tax the people who are smart enough to make out in order to take care of those who are too dumb or too damned lazy to take care of themselves.

52. When somebody does not enforce a rule, it adds one more bit of disorganization to things. It's things like that which create no end of trouble for everybody.

53. You gotta be a bigger crook than they are; that's the only way you'll get the respect of those big shots.

54. There is no such thing as a "white lie." Any deviation from the exact truth, no matter how insignificant it may seem, fosters evil.

55. Don't let 'em fool you with these "I want to help you" spiels. They got an angle and they just want to use you.

56. A woman who would work as a bartender must be nothing but a prostitute. What other reason would she have for taking a job like that?

57. A company union, ha! You know what that's for don't you? So that the bosses can run it and bleed you for all you're worth.

POSTTHERAPY RATING SCALE

Directions

In rating the client on each item of the scale, consider the difference between the way the client was when he entered therapy and the way he was at the end of treatment. Base your rating on the change that has occurred in the client within this interval.

On certain items you may feel that a client came into therapy with a behavior already incorporated as part of his usual behavior and that he has not changed in this particular area. On these items, clients will be rated as "remained the same." For example, a client may have been quite willing to discuss the significant aspects of his problems from the time he entered therapy, and he has made no change in this respect.

The scale consists of two kinds of items. Most of the items deal with behavior which is not specifically related to the counseling situation; however, certain items are based on the client's behavior in therapy.

On those items which are related to over-all or general behavior, your rating should reflect changes in the behavior and/or characteristics of the client which you feel are relatively permanent and which also apply to his behavior in situations outside of therapy. On these items indicate *only* changes which you feel the client has integrated into his general behavior.

On those items related to behavior in therapy, try to distinguish mere conformity to the demands of therapy from those changes which are real reorganizations of the client's attitudes, feelings, and motivations operating within therapy. Your rating should *not* be based on mere conformity.

In certain cases, you are asked to rate changes in the client's behavior in terms of whether they are realistic or appropriate. For example, if a client was too positive in his evaluation of other people, a more realistic position might have resulted from the client's developing a more critical attitude toward other people. If the client had been hypercritical of others, a more realistic position would be based on the extent to which the client may have become less critical of others.

Items

1. The client's perception of the problem as a function of his own behavior has:
   (*a*) become less realistic; (*b*) remained the same; (*c*) become slightly more realistic; (*d*) become moderately more realistic; (*e*) become considerably more realistic.

2. The client's placing of responsibility for his difficulties on others and/or environmental circumstances has:

   (*a*) become considerably more realistic; (*b*) become moderately more realistic; (*c*) become slightly more realistic; (*d*) remained the same; (*e*) become less realistic.

3. The extent to which the client perceives the problem merely in symptomatic terms has:
   (*a*) decreased considerably; (*b*) decreased moderately; (*c*) decreased slightly; (*d*) remained the same; (*e*) increased.

4. The client's feelings of discomfort in his everyday life have: (*a*) decreased considerably; (*b*) decreased moderately; (*c*) decreased slightly; (*d*) remained the same; (*e*) increased.

5. The client's expression of positive emotions when they are appropriate has:
   (*a*) decreased; (*b*) remained the same; (*c*) increased slightly; (*d*) increased moderately; (*e*) increased considerably.

6. The client's symptoms have:
   (*a*) become considerably less disturbing; (*b*) become moderately less disturbing; (*e*) become slightly less disturbing; (*d*) remained the same; (*c*) become more disturbing.

7. The client discusses feelings and attitudes which are relevant to the problem:
   (*a*) considerably more freely; (*b*) moderately more freely; (*c*) slightly more freely; (*d*) the same; (*e*) less freely.

8. The client's comprehension of important causal relationships between his symptoms and the underlying needs and conflicts has:
   (*a*) decreased; (*b*) remained the same; (*c*) increased slightly; (*d*) increased moderately; (*e*) increased considerably.

9. The client's avoidance of making decisions which would seem to be necessary before anything can be accomplished has:
   (*a*) decreased considerably; (*b*) decreased moderately; (*c*) decreased slightly; (*d*) remained the same; (*e*) increased.

10. The client's attitudes toward other people have:
    (*a*) become less appropriate; (*b*) remained the same; (*c*) become slightly more appropriate; (*d*) become moderately more appropriate; (*e*) become considerably more appropriate.

11. Concerning his ability to solve his problems, the client has:

(*a*) become less confident; (*b*) become no more confident; (*c*) become slightly more confident; (*d*) become moderately more confident; (*e*) become considerably more confident.

12. The client's understanding of his problems in terms of his own past experience has: (*a*) become considerably more meaningful; (*b*) become moderately more meaningful; (*c*) become slightly more meaningful; (*d*) remained the same; (*e*) become less meaningful.

13. The client feels his relationships with others have: (*a*) become less satisfactory; (*b*) remained the same; (*c*) become slightly more satisfactory; (*d*) become moderately more satisfactory; (*e*) become considerably more satisfactory.

14. The extent to which the client develops new plans for improving his situation has: (*a*) increased considerably; (*b*) increased moderately; (*c*) increased slightly; (*d*) remained the same; (*e*) decreased.

15. The client's feelings and attitudes toward himself have: (*a*) become considerably more appropriate; (*b*) become moderately more appropriate; (*c*) become slightly more appropriate; (*d*) remained the same; (*e*) become less appropriate.

16. The client's expression of negative emotions when they are appropriate has: (*a*) decreased; (*b*) remained the same; (*c*) increased slightly; (*d*) increased moderately; (*e*) increased considerably.

17. The client's view of his strengths and shortcomings has: (*a*) become less realistic; (*b*) remained the same; (*c*) become slightly more realistic; (*d*) become moderately more realistic; (*e*) become considerably more realistic.

18. The client's emotional reactions to other people and situations have: (*a*) become considerably more realistic; (*b*) become moderately more realistic; (*c*) become slightly more realistic; (*d*) remained the same; (*e*) become less realistic.

19. The client's understanding of his problems in terms of his own needs has: (*a*) become considerably more accurate; (*b*) become moderately more accurate;

(*c*) become slightly more accurate; (*d*) remained the same; (*e*) become less accurate.

20. The client's expectations for himself in the interpersonal aspects of his life have: (*a*) become less realistic; (*b*) remained the same; (*c*) become slightly more realistic; (*d*) become moderately more realistic; (*e*) become considerably more realistic.

21. The client's acceptance of responsibility for solving his problems has: (*a*) increased considerably; (*b*) increased moderately; (*c*) increased slightly; (*d*) remained the same; (*e*) decreased.

22. The client's perception of the meaning of the reactions of others toward him has: (*a*) become considerably less distorted; (*b*) become moderately less distorted; (*c*) become slightly less distorted; (*d*) remained the same; (*e*) become more distorted.

23. The client's meaningful emotional involvement as opposed to an intellectual approach to his problems has: (*a*) increased considerably; (*b*) increased moderately; (*c*) increased slightly; (*d*) remained the same; (*e*) decreased.

24. The client's attempts to avoid significant areas of discussion has: (*a*) increased; (*b*) remained the same; (*c*) decreased slightly; (*d*) decreased moderately; (*e*) decreased considerably.

25. The extent to which the client sees where his own characteristic ways of thinking, feeling, and behaving bear an important relationship to his problems has: (*a*) decreased; (*b*) remained the same; (*c*) increased slightly; (*d*) increased moderately; (*e*) increased considerably.

26. The client's understanding of his problems as resulting from interpersonal relationships with other people has: (*a*) become less realistic; (*b*) remained the same; (*c*) become slightly more realistic; (*d*) become moderately more realistic; (*e*) become considerably more realistic.

27. The client's attempts to try new ways of handling his problems have: (*a*) decreased; (*b*) remained the same; (*c*) increased slightly; (*d*) increased moderately; (*e*) increased considerably.

Effective Ingredients in Psychotherapy: An Approach to Unraveling the Patient-Therapist Interaction[1]

CHARLES B. TRUAX

The essential question to be asked about psychotherapy is "What do we as therapists do that makes for constructive personality change in our patients?" What are the essential effective ingredients in psychotherapy? It seems certain that not all of what happens actually contributes to the work of psychotherapy.

Psychoanalytic (Alexander, 1948; Halpern & Lesser, 1960; Ferenczi, 1930; Schafer, 1959), client-centered (Dymond, 1949; Jourard, 1959; Rogers, 1951; Rogers, 1957), and eclectic theorists (Fox & Goldin, 1963; Raush & Bordin, 1957; Shoben, 1949; Strunk, 1957; Strupp, 1960) have emphasized the importance of the therapist's ability to understand sensitively and accurately the patient's inner experiences. Also, they have stressed the importance of nonpossessive warmth and acceptance of the patient and have emphasized that the therapist be mature, integrated and genuine within the relationship. These three characteristics of the therapist behavior cut across the parochial theories of psychotherapy and can thus be considered as elements common to a wide variety of psychoanalytic, client-centered, and eclectic approaches to psychotherapy.

Halkides (1958) and Barrett-Lennard (1959) have attempted to investigate the importance of these three therapist behaviors (or conditions) in a university counseling center population. Their evidence suggests the relevance of these three therapist conditions for success with counseling cases, although a replication of Halkides' (1958) study by Hart (1960) failed at

Reprinted from *Journal of Counseling Psychology*, 1963, 10, 256–263, with the permission of Journal of Counseling Psychology, Inc., and the author. Note 2, containing information about the author's affiliation, has been omitted.

[1] The present findings are a part of an ongoing research program supported in part by NIMH Grant No. M 3496, and in part by a grant from the Office of Vocational Rehabilitation, No. RD-906-PM. This research was carried out with patients at Mendota State Hospital with the generous support of Dr. Walter J. Urben, Superintendent, and his staff. The total program of which this present report is a part, has been directed by Carl R. Rogers, Eugene T. Gendlin, and Charles B. Truax.

confirmation. Recent research has also indicated the relevance of these therapist-offered conditions to effective group psychotherapy with hospitalized mental patients (Truax, 1961).

PSYCHOTHERAPY WITH SCHIZOPHRENICS
Empathy

Now a body of empirical knowledge is developing which shows the relationship of these three therapeutic conditions to psychotherapy with schizophrenics. This research involves attempts to relate measures of the three therapist conditions derived from tape recorded psychotherapy sessions to measures of change in the patient's personality functioning derived from psychological pretests and posttests.[3] The evidence showing the relevance of accurate empathic understanding communicated by the therapist to personality growth in the patient will be considered first.

Our first step was the construction of a scale, the Accurate Empathy Scale (Truax, 1961a), on which trained judges could reliably rate the extent of empathic understanding by the therapist occurring in tape-recorded samples of psychotherapy. The scale was designed to measure a conception of empathy which involves the sensitivity to current feelings, and, the verbal facility to communicate this understanding in a language attuned to the patient's current feelings. At a high level of accurate empathy the message "I am with you" is unmistakably clear—the therapist's remarks fit with the patient's mood and content. The therapist's responses not only indicate a sensitive understanding of the apparent feelings but serve to clarify and expand the client's awareness of his feelings or experiences. This is communicated not only

by language appropriate to the patient, but also by the voice qualities which reflect the seriousness, the intentness, and the depth of feeling. At a low level of accurate empathy the therapist may be preoccupied with his own intellectual interpretation and, so, be less aware of the client's "being." The therapist at this low level of empathy may have his focus of attention on the content of what the patient says rather than what the client "is" during the moment and thus may ignore, misunderstand, or simply fail to sense the client's current feelings and experiencings. Indeed, the therapist may be accurately describing psychodynamics to the patient but a lack of empathy is shown in the use of language not that of the client. A lack of empathy is also shown when dynamics are presented at a time when these are far removed from the current feelings of the client. Thus "accurate empathy" has much in common with the "good" psychoanalytic interpretation.

To see if this conception of empathy was related to therapeutic progress in the initial stages of psychotherapy, four patients who showed clear improvement and four patients who showed deterioration on a battery of psychological tests after six months of therapy were selected. The 384 samples of tape-recorded psychotherapy were randomly selected from the first six months of therapy and then coded so that raters would not know whether a sample came from a test-improved case or a test-deteriorated case, or, from an early or a late interview.

The findings clearly indicated the relevance of accurate empathy to the kind of personality change occurring in the patient: the psychotherapy involving test-improved patients rated consistently higher on accurate empathy than tape-recorded psychotherapy with test-deteriorated cases ($p < .01$).

A second study involving 14 hospitalized schizophrenic cases and 14 counseling cases from the University of Chicago and Stanford University was completed using 112 samples of recorded psychotharapy from

---

[3] Brief mimeographed research reports of the individual studies reported here by the author are available at the Wisconsin Psychiatric Institute, University of Wisconsin.

early and late interviews. Analysis of this data indicated that accurate empathy ratings were significantly higher for the more successful cases than for the less successful ($p < .01$). Also, the positive relationship between accurate empathy and outcome of therapy held for hospitalized schizophrenics and for counseling cases. The same condition seemed relevant for both populations. The more successful cases received higher accurate empathy ratings, while the less successful cases have many more average and low accurate empathy ratings ($p < .05$).

More recently, trends in the levels of accurate empathy for schizophrenics covering a time span from six months to three and one-half years have been investigated. One 4-minute tape-recorded sample was taken from every fifth interview for each of 14 schizophrenic cases, giving a total of 358 samples to work with. Analysis of these data showed no tendency for therapists to systematically change over time in the level of accurate empathy offered to the patient. As predicted, however, the therapists of the more improved patients were judged to have offered significantly higher levels of accurate empathy throughout the course of therapy than was received by the unimproved patients ($p < .05$).

These studies suggest that the level of accurate empathy is indeed related to the outcome of constructive personality change. Thus the question of *who* is causing empathy to be high or low in therapy becomes crucial. Is it the therapist, or is it the patient who determines the level of accurate empathy that will occur in a given psychotherapy relationship?

One way of answering this question is to have a group of therapists see each member of a group of patients and have each patient see all therapists. If the level of accurate empathy is different for different patients, this would show that patients determine accurate empathy levels offered by the therapists. If the level of accurate empathy is different from different thera-

pists, this would show that therapists determine levels of accurate empathy. A study has been completed using data from a group of 24 patients living on one continuing-treatment ward where eight different therapists offered psychotherapy to all patients on a demand basis. From the tape recordings of all interviews, samples were selected in which the same eight therapists saw the same eight patients according to a balanced incomplete block design. This research design allowed us to find out if the therapists had an effect upon the level of accurate empathy and, separately, if the patient had an effect upon the level of accurate empathy.

Analysis of ratings indicated that different therapists produced different levels of accurate empathy when interacting with the same set of patients ($p < .01$). In sharp contrast, different patients did not receive different levels of accurate empathy when interacting with the same set of therapists ($p < .40$).

The data, then, suggest that it is the therapist who determines the level of accurate empathy. While it is likely that with extreme patients (such as comparing very talkative with very quiet patients) it would be possible to show effects on accurate empathy of patients, the present findings indicate that the therapist is primarily responsible for the level of accurate empathy occurring in psychotherapy.

In summary, these findings say that the level of accurate empathy occurring in the patient-therapist interaction is higher for more successful cases than for less successful cases; and that this relationship holds not just for outpatient neurotics, but also for severely disturbed schizophrenic patients; and that the therapist is the principal determinant of the level of accurate empathy offered in psychotherapy.

Unconditional Positive Regard

As a precondition for the therapist's ability to deeply and accurately sense the patient's current feelings and experiences and for the patient's ability to use this accurate empathy in the process of his own self-exploration and experiencings, the therapist's nonconditional warmth has seemed theoretically crucial. A scale (Truax, 1962) designed to measure the degree of nonconditional warmth has been devised for use with tape-recorded psychotherapy sessions. At its highest levels, unconditional positive regard involves only the condition that the patient talk of personally relevant material; the therapist is willing to share equally the patient's fears and hopes or achievements and failures, without placing conditions upon the warm acceptance of the patient's inner self. Briefly, unconditional positive regard requires a nonpossessive caring for the patient as a separate person with the inherent right and responsibility of self-determination.

In a study applying this scale of unconditional positive regard to the 358 samples of psychotherapy taken from every fifth interview with 14 schizophrenic patients, it was predicted that the therapists of the more improved cases would be rated as higher than those of unimproved or failure cases. This prediction was supported by the data which showed that samples from improved cases were consistently higher in unconditional positive regard than samples from unimproved or failure cases ($p < .05$).

Viewed in tandem, accurate empathy and unconditional positive regard intertwine in a logical fashion that suggests that the achievement of a high level of accurate empathy is dependent upon first obtaining at least a minimally high level of unconditional positive regard for the patient. To be deeply sensitive to the moment-to-moment "being" of another person requires of us as therapists that we first accept and to some degree unconditionally prize this other person. However, neither of these two conditions could function properly without the therapist being himself integrated and genuine within the therapeutic encounter. At high levels of self-congruence this means that the therapist does not deny feelings and that he be integrated within the therapy hour: it does not mean that the therapist must burden the patient with overt expression of all of his feelings—only that he not be ingenuine.

Self-congruence of Therapist

Self-congruence is not taken to mean only the element of self-awareness, but also the presentation to the patient of a real person in the encounter. There is always the temptation to present a facade, a mask of professionalism, or some type of confessional-professional screen; the temptation to be incongruent with the self or ingenuine as a person.

A scale (Truax, 1962a) has been developed to measure the degree to which this conception of therapist self-congruence occurs within tape-recorded therapeutic sessions. In a very recent study this scale of therapist genuineness or self-congruence was used on the 358 tape-recorded therapy samples taken from every fifth interview of the 14 cases described above. Analysis of the data showed a significant tendency for the therapist in improved cases to be rated higher in self-congruence during the therapeutic sessions than therapists in nonimproved or failure cases ($p < .05$).

It should be noted that the ratings on each condition under study were done "blind" in the sense that the judges were given coded samples so that they did not know whether the samples came from early or late in therapy, or from a successful or unsuccessful case. Also, the last three studies employed naive lay raters who had no systematic knowledge about psychology or psychotherapy and so would have few of the biased preconceptions often found in judges. They simply rated randomly coded 4-minute samples of psychotherapeutic interaction according to the specific definitions of the scales.

CONTROL STUDIES WITH SCHIZOPHRENICS USING ALL CONDITIONS COMBINED

Thus, the above studies seem strong evidence to support the theoretical view that each of these three therapist-offered conditions are related to constructive change in patients. Since all three conditions, however, are considered by theory to be essential ingredients for successful psychotherapy, research has been completed comparing therapy cases rated high on all three conditions with both control patients receiving no therapy and therapy cases rated relatively low on levels of accurate empathy, unconditional positive regard and therapist self-congruence.

A total of 14 schizophrenics receiving therapy, and 14 matched controls were selected for analysis of over-all change in psychological functioning. Patients had been randomly assigned to either therapy or control conditions and complete batteries of psychological tests had been given initially and later.

All accurate empathy, unconditional positive regard and therapist self-congruence ratings from the studies reported earlier, were examined and mean values computed. A total of eight patients were judged to have received relatively low levels. The hypothesis was that patients receiving high levels would show greater constructive personality change, while patients receiving low levels of conditions in therapy and the control patients would show less constructive personality change.

The initial test battery and the latest test battery for both therapy and matched control cases were given to two clinical psychologists[4] for a "blind" analysis of change in level of psychological functioning.

Primary emphasis was placed upon the Rorschach and secondary emphasis upon

the MMPI in the assessing of change although the total test battery included the Thematic Apperception Test, the Wechsler Adult Intelligence Scale, the Anxiety Reaction Scales, the Stroop Tests, the F Authoritarian Scale, the Q Sort, and the Wittenborn Psychiatric Rating Scales.

Patients receiving high levels of conditions showed an over-all gain in psychological functioning (mean change of 6.0 where 5.0 represents no change) whereas, patients who received relatively low levels of accurate empathy, unconditional positive regard and self-congruence showed a *loss* in psychological functioning. Control patients evidenced moderate gains. These differences proved statistically significant ($p < .05$).

In terms of number of patients at or above the median change ratings, the control group had a rough 50-50 split while *all* patients in the group receiving low levels of conditions were below the median. Those patients receiving relatively high levels of conditions from the therapist are six of the eight patients at or above the median of positive change in psychological functioning.

Thus the data suggest that high conditions facilitate constructive personality change as predicted. However, the findings also say that patients who received relatively low conditions showed negative personality change.

Another study with the same design was conducted to specifically check the relation between conditions offered in therapy and change in anxiety experienced by the patient. The Anxiety Reaction scale consisting of three factors of Interpersonal Anxiety, Somatic Anxiety, and General Anxiety had been administered to each patient both early and late.

The data of all three subscales show a clear tendency for those patients receiving high conditions to show a drop in anxiety level, while those patients receiving low conditions show an increase in anxiety level. The controls show almost no change.

---

[4] John V. Liccione, Chief Psychologist, Milwaukee Mental Health Center, and Marshall Rosenberg, Director of Clinical Services, Psychological Associates, Clayton, Missouri.

The differences between the three groups reached statistical significance on both the measure of interpersonal Anxiety and on the measure of General Anxiety ($p < .05$).

When the Q Sort for self data on the same patients was analzyed an even more disquieting finding appeared: the self concept of the patients receiving high levels of conditions and the self concept of the control patients receiving no therapy both show a slight tendency toward better adjustment from early to late, but the patients receiving low conditions in therapy show a significant change toward less well-adjusted self concept ($p < .01$).

Similar analyses were carried out on subscales of the MMPI, the F Authoritarian Scale, the Wittenborn Psychiatric Rating Scales, and the Wechsler Adult Intelligence Scale. Statistically significant differences ($p < .05$) in the direction of the hypothesis occurred on the Sum of Clinical Scales, the Depression Scale, the Psychopathic Deviate Scale, the MF Scale, the Schizophrenia Scale and the Social Introversion Scale of the MMPI. Statistically significant differences occurred on only three of the 14 submeasures of intelligence; in each case the low conditions group showed a decrease in intellectual functioning. Differences were not found to be statistically significant on either the F Authoritarian Scale or upon any of the subscales of the Wittenborn Psychiatric Rating Scales. The scores from each instrument did, however, tend to show a consistent pattern: the patients receiving high therapy conditions tended to show improvement either slightly greater than or equal to that of the no therapy control group, while patients receiving low levels of therapeutic conditions tended to show negative personality change.

A final study involved the Constructive Personality Change Index which uses items from early and late MMPI tests as the measure of personality change. On this measure the control group showed moderate positive changes, the low conditions therapy patients showed moderate negative

changes, and the high conditions therapy patients showed large positive changes in personality functioning ($p < .05$). Next the therapy patients were ranked on conditions received in psychotherapy and these rankings were compared with their Constructive Personality Change Index scores. The rank order correlation *rho* was computed between the ranking on all conditions combined and the Constructive Personality Change Index, yielding a correlation of .87 ($p < .01$). Rank correlations with each of the separate conditions ranged between .67 and .90 ($p < .05$).

The comparisons of patients receiving high and low conditions in therapy with control patients receiving no therapy has a special significance. If comparisons had been made only between the therapy cases and the control cases, there would have been no differences in outcomes and it would have been erroneously concluded that all psychotherapy was ineffective as a treatment procedure with hospitalized schizophrenics. This certainly raises the intriguing question of whether or not the studies that have reported no effect of psychotherapy with neurotics have made such conclusions because they have lumped together psychotherapy involving high conditions with therapy involving low conditions.

The unexpected finding that the change in personality functioning is largely negative when conditions are lower is a very sobering one. It seems to say that low conditions lead schizophrenic patients to become more disturbed. Psychotherapists have, perhaps naively, held to the belief that even when psychotherapy did not prove therapeutic, it at least did not facilitate negative change in personality functioning.

One possible interpretation of the negative change in the low conditions patients is based upon the observation that all psychotherapy focuses upon the malfunctioning or life-failures of the patient. When the therapist is sensitively and accurately able to understand the patient and communicates this understanding in a relationship involving both genuineness and nonpossessive warmth, then life-failures can be explored and attempts at new modes of living can be tried. However, when these elements are not sufficiently present in psychotherapy, we would expect that the schizophrenic patient is left only with a greater realization of his life-failures. This reinforced realization of malfunctioning combined with an inability to resolve life-failures could be expected to produce negative change in personality functioning.

It may very well be that a lack of these three conditions in the patient's environment is what led him to become schizophrenic in the first place. If so—and the reverse of accurate empathy, unconditional positive regard and self-congruence certainly fits with what we know of the Schizophrenogenic Mother—then the present findings with psychotherapy show that more poor conditions continue to make the patient worse, not better.

To summarize the research, the evidence seems to clearly point to the importance of accurate empathy, unconditonal positive regard, and congruence in successful psychotherapy with even the most difficult patient population—the hospitalized schizophrenic.

IMPLICATIONS OF THESE FINDINGS

What meaning might these findings have for the future of psychotherapy? The evidence does suggest possible future directions for research, for the training of therapists, and for the practice of psychotherapy.

These findings reflect the fruitfulness of focusing upon the therapy behavior of the therapist. The attempts to newly conceptualize and measure the complex concepts of accurate empathy, unconditional positive regard, and therapist self-congruence have led to more explicit definitions.

The task ahead for research, then, is to further specify the separate types of therapist behaviors and evaluate their relevance to successful outcomes. Thus, since it now appears that communication of a sensitive accurate understanding of the patient's current feelings and experiences is related to positive personality change, it becomes important to know *which* therapist behaviors among all those now labelled as empathic are doing the actual work of therapy. For example, is the tonal quality of the voice that the therapist uses to communicate his deep understanding a significant factor, or is it only the understanding? Does it matter whether the therapist uses the patient's own words to communicate his understanding? Is the understanding more effective when it is expressed concretely or abstractly?

Present research, then, in isolating therapist-offered conditions effective in successful psychotherapy leads to even more specific questions for future research aimed at clarifying what we as therapists do that produces constructive change in our patients.

The unexpected finding that when patients receive low conditions in therapy, they show negative personality change, would, if confirmed by future research, raise a host of very serious ethical and practical questions. Since very large sums of both public and private funds are yearly spent upon psychotherapeutic treatment, there is a pressing social need for research to further investigate the validity and generality of these findings—to test this out both with schizophrenic and neurotic populations, and to experimentally vary the conditions.

As the research evidence becomes more specific and solidly founded, it will be possible to rely less on the learning of general concepts and more upon the teaching of specific behaviors in training therapists for the practice of psychotherapy. Research rating scales can be directly applied to training programs. Tape-recorded samples of psychotherapy rated very high on accurate empathy, for example, can be selected to provide concrete examples for the beginning therapist.[5] Beyond this, rating scales such as the Accurate Empathy Scale can be used to rate samples of therapy from the trainee's own early cases. This will give the trainee immediate and concrete informational feedback about how well he is learning the practice of the concepts. Finally, by selecting random samples of actual tape-recorded cases seen by the trainee and then having them rated along research scales designed to measure the concepts that were taught, a more objective evaluation of outcomes of training programs can be made. This means that evaluations of how well a trainee has learned could be objectively based upon how he behaves in therapy instead of merely how well he remembers and can intellectualize the concepts.

While the present findings are only beginning attempts to specify therapist behaviors which lead to sucessful psychotherapy, they point strongly to the importance of the therapist's ability to understand sensitively and accurately the patient and to communicate this understanding in a language attuned to the patient's current feelings. They point strongly also to the importance of a relationship that involves both genuineness and nonpossessive warmth.

What might these consistent research findings mean for us as therapists? (1) As therapists, we might aim toward a more clear and sensitive awareness of the patient's inner being; towards a greater ability to deeply understand the patient's moment-to-moment feelings and experiencings and to thus make more accurate meaning out of the shifts in posture, the slight inflections in tone, or the empty silences. It would mean that as therapists we would concentrate less upon developing skill at highly intellectualized diagnostic formulations and more upon developing skill at the moment-to-moment diagnosis of the patient's "be-

ing." (2) As therapists we could allow ourselves to express more openly our deep caring for the *person* who comes to us for help: to do this unconditionally would be to set no conditions on the prizing of the person. (3) As therapists we can afford risking confrontation with the patient as a person rather than as an institution. Our open or nondefensive intactness, our human genuineness encourages the patient to also deeply "be" himself within the relationship.

Finally, these research findings might mean that when we are not able to offer these therapeutic conditions to a particular patient, then we would best serve the interest of that patient by helping him to find another therapist.

REFERENCES

ALEXANDER, F. *Fundamentals of psychoanalysis.* W. W. Norton, 1948.

DYMOND, ROSALIND. A scale for the measurement of empathic ability. *J. consult. Psychol.,* 1949, 13, 127–133.

FERENCZI, S. The principle of relaxation and neo-catharsis. *Internat. J. Psycho-Analysis,* 1930, 11, 428–443.

FOX, R. E., & GOLDIN, P. C. The empathic process in psychotherapy: A survey of theory and research. Unpublished manuscript, 1963.

HALKIDES, G. An experimental study of four conditions necessary for therapeutic change. Unpublished doctoral dissertation, Univer. of Chicago, 1958.

HALPERN, H., & LESSER, LEONA. Empathy in infants, adults, and psychotherapists. *Psychoanalysis Psychoanalytic Rev.,* 1960, 47, 32–42.

HART, J. T. A replication of the Halkides study. Unpublished manuscript. Univer. of Wisconsin, 1960.

JOURARD, S. I—thou relationship versus manipulation in counseling and psychotherapy. *J. Individual Psychol.,* 1959, 15, 174–179.

RAUSH, H. L., & BORDIN, E. S. Warmth in personality development and in psychotherapy. *Psychiatry: J. Study of Interpersonal Processes,* Vol. 20. No. 4, November, 1957.

ROGERS, C. R. *Client centered therapy.* Cambridge, Mass.: Riverside Press, 1951, 73–74.

---

[5] Such attempts are now underway at Wisconsin by Eugene T. Gendlin and Marjorie Klein, and at the Psychotherapy Center, University of Kentucky, by Charles B. Truax and Robert R. Carkhuff.

ROGERS, C. R. The necessary and sufficient conditions of therapeutic personality change. *J. consult. Psychol.,* 1957, 21, 95–103.

SCHAFER, R. Generative empathy in the treatment situation. *Psychoanalytic Quart.,* 1959, 28, 342–373.

SHOBEN, E. J., JR. Psychotherapy as a problem in learning theory. *Psychol. Bull.,* 1949, 46, 366–392.

STRUNK, O., JR. Empathy: A review of theory and research. *Psychological Newsletter,* 1957, 9, 47–57.

STRUPP, H. H. Nature of psychotherapist's contribution to the treatment process. *Arch. Gen. Psychiat.,* 1960, 3, 219–231.

TRUAX, C. B. The process of group psychotherapy. *Psychol. Monogr.,* 1961, 75, No. 14 (Whole No. 511).

TRUAX, C. B. A scale for the measurement of accurate empathy. *Discussion Paper,* No. 20. Wisconsin Psychiatric Institute, University of Wisconsin, September 26, 1961. (a)

TRUAX, C. B. A tentative scale for the measurement of unconditional positive regard. *Discussion Paper,* No. 23. Wisconsin Psychiatric Institute, University of Wisconsin, January 16, 1962.

TRUAX, C. B. A tentative scale for the measurement of therapist genuineness of self-congruence. *Discussion Paper,* No. 35. Wisconsin Psychiatric Institute, University of Wisconsin, May, 1962. (a)

Selected Additional Readings

BANDURA, A. Psychotherapist's anxiety level, self-insight, and psychotherapeutic competence. *Journal of Abnormal and Social Psychology,* 1956, 52, 333–337.

BETZ, BARBARA J. Experiences in research in psychotherapy with schizophrenic patients. In H. H. Strupp & L. Luborsky (Eds.), *Research in psychotherapy.* Vol. 2. Washington, D.C.: American Psychological Association, 1962. Pp. 41–61.

BORDIN, E. S. Inside the therapeutic hour. In E. A. Rubinstein & M. B. Parloff (Eds.), *Research in psychotherapy.* Vol. 1. Washington, D.C.: American Psychological Association, 1959. Pp. 235–247.

CARSON, R. C., & HEINE, R. W. Similarity and success in therapeutic dyads. *Journal of Consulting Psychology,* 1962, 26, 38–43.

CUTLER, R. L. Countertransference effects in psychotherapy. *Journal of Consulting Psychology,* 1958, 22, 349–356.

DANSKIN, D. G., & ROBINSON, F. P. Difference in "degree of lead" among experienced counselors. *Journal of Counseling Psychology,* 1954, 1, 78–83.

DITTMAN, A. T. The interpersonal process in psychotherapy: Development of a research method. *Journal of Abnormal and Social Psychology,* 1952, 47, 236–244.

FIEDLER, F. E. A comparison of therapeutic relationships in psychoanalytic, non-directive and Adlerian therapy. *Journal of Consulting Psychology,* 1950, 14, 436–445.

FIEDLER, F. E. Factor analyses of psychoanalytic, non-directive, and Adlerian therapeutic relationships. *Journal of Consulting Psychology,* 1951, 15, 32–38.

FIEDLER, F. E., & SENIOR, K. An exploratory study of unconscious feeling reactions in fifteen patient-therapist pairs. *Journal of Abnormal and Social Psychology,* 1952, 47, 446–453.

FRANK, J. D. The dynamics of the psychotherapeutic relationship. *Psychiatry,* 1959, 22, 17–39.

GOLDSTEIN, A. P. Therapist and client expectation of personality change in psychotherapy. *Journal of Counseling Psychology,* 1960, 7, 180–184.

GOLDSTEIN, A. P. Participant expectancies in psychotherapy. *Psychiatry,* 1962, 25, 72–79.

HARWAY, N. I. Some factors in psychotherapists' perceptions of their patients. *Journal of Consulting Psychology,* 1959, 23, 379–386.

HEINE, R. W., & TROSMAN, H. Initial expectations of the doctor-patient inter-action as a factor in the continuance of psychotherapy. *Psychiatry,* 1960, 23, 275–278.

HELLER, K., MYERS, R. A., & KLINE, L. Interviewer behavior as a function of standardized client roles. *Journal of Consulting Psychology,* 1963, 27, 117–122.

KRASNER, L. The therapist as a social reinforcement machine. In H. H. Strupp & L. Luborsky (Eds.), *Research in psychotherapy.* Vol. 2. Washington, D.C.: American Psychological Association, 1962. Pp. 61–95.

LENNARD, H. L. Some aspects of the psychotherapeutic system. In H. H. Strupp & L. Luborsky (Eds.), *Research in psychotherapy.* Vol. 2. Washington, D.C.: American Psychological Association, 1962. Pp. 218–237.

MENDELSOHN, G. A., & GELLER, M. H. Structure of client attitudes toward counseling and their relation to client-counselor similarity. *Journal of Consulting Psychology,* 1965, 29, 63–72.

PARLOFF, M. B. Some factors affecting the quality of therapeutic relationships. *Journal of Abnormal and Social Psychology,* 1956, 52, 5–10.

RUBINSTEIN, E. A. Analysis of self and peer personality ratings of psychothera-pists and comparison with patient ratings. *Journal of Consulting Psychology,* 1958, 22, 10.

SAPOLSKY, A. Effects of interpersonal relationships upon verbal conditioning. *Journal of Abnormal and Social Psychology,* 1960, 61, 241–246.

SNYDER, W. U. Some investigations of relationship in psychotherapy. In E. A. Rubinstein & M. B. Parloff (Eds.), *Research in psychotherapy.* Vol. 1. Washington, D.C.: American Psychological Association, 1959. Pp. 247–259.

STRUPP, H. H. The therapist's contribution to the treatment process: Beginnings and vagaries of a research program. In H. H. Strupp & L. Luborsky (Eds.), *Research in psychotherapy.* Vol. 2. Washington, D.C.: American Psychological Association, 1962. Pp. 25–41.

New Psychotherapy
Variants and
Research Methods –
Therapy and Methodology

Much of the recent research in psychotherapy concerns the specification and exploration both of new therapy approaches and of laboratory and computer methods to study the process of therapy. Interest has especially focused on (1) attempting to generalize laboratory findings with animals and normal subjects to people with complaints and symptoms, with the goal of creating an objective, scientific approach to behavior modification, and (2) developing techniques which maximize the use of the therapist's time and decrease the amount of time people spend in therapy, thereby in some way attempting to meet society's demands for mental health services. Contributing to this interest has been the changing view of psychopathology from one emphasizing an "illness" and "disease" model to one emphasizing maladaptive behavior, faulty communication patterns, strategies, and learning. Concomitant with this has been a greater flexibility and willingness on the part of therapists to develop and apply new theories and new techniques. More therapists than ever before see themselves in the role of formal or informal researchers rather than as practitioners committed to a fixed art.

There has been a resurgence of interest in, and application of, operant and classical techniques and theories. Investigators have placed special emphasis on the treatment of the maladaptive behaviors or symptoms directly, rather than exploring underlying causes (i.e., the symptom is the problem, not a superficial manifestation of some inner psychic conflict) and on employing a variety of techniques for specific symptoms (e.g., systematic desensitization for phobias, avoidance conditioning for compulsions, and operant conditioning for shaping and developing some minimum behavioral repertoire in autistic children and chronic schizophrenics). So far, though, research has focused on the specification of new techniques and has, generally, taken the form of case studies of individual patients. Lacking, with minor exceptions (e.g., in this book, Lang, Lazovik, and Reynolds), is the use of appropriate control groups, if any. And without control groups, definitive statements about the efficacy of one treatment over another cannot be made.

This criticism also applies to those therapists who make use of techniques involving the whole family. This approach has grown out of the recognition of the family as a major contributor to the origin and perpetuation of a child's problems, as well as a most powerful therapeutic agent. However, research in this area again suffers from lack of control groups, and, in addition, suffers from poorly defined techniques as compared to the relatively well-detailed specification of techniques in those approaches to therapy based on various learning theories.

Some ideas that are in the developmental stage might eventually have a substantial impact on the practice of psychotherapy, at least by tearing down emotional barriers and opening up new areas of exploration. One example is the systematic use of parents as therapeutic agents for their children, as in filial therapy. Another is the idea of using computer technology in the direct treatment of emotionally disturbed persons.

Along with the increasing application of general psychological principles and techniques to treatment has been their increasing use in the laboratory with a wide variety of subjects in attempts to determine the basic elements and ingredients in the process of intra- and interpersonal interaction and behavioral modification. There have been many well controlled studies manipulating experimenter, subject, and situational characteristics which have made frequent use of therapy analogues, especially verbal ones, and other forms of operant conditioning. As for their relevance to treatment per se, many of these studies have been criticized for their manipulation of "trivial" behaviors not directly relevant to the therapy interaction, their infrequent exploration of extinction and generalization effects, and the fact that multivariate, rather than single-variate, designs are needed to explore the extremely complex interactions between people.

Desensitization, Suggestibility and Pseudotherapy[1]

PETER J. LANG
DAVID LAZOVIK
DAVID J. REYNOLDS

Positive change in psychotherapy has often been attributed to the relationship established between therapist and client, in the context of treatment. This phenomenon has been variously described as transference, suggestibility, the "hello-goodbye," or placebo effect. Lang and Lazovik (1963) demonstrated that phobic Ss who were briefly exposed to desensitization psychotherapy showed a significantly greater reduction in fear behavior than did untreated controls. The present experiment is an extension of this work, specifically to determine if the obtained change can be assigned to placebo effects.

A psychotherapeutic placebo is not as readily developed as the control medication

Portions of this paper were presented at the Midwestern Psychological Association Conference, 1965, and are reprinted with the permission of the authors.

[1] This research was supported by Public Health Service Grant M-3880, from the National Institute of Mental Health. The authors would like to thank Drs. J. Geer, R. Miller, R. Romano and Jean Wilkinson, who participated as therapists in this project. Appreciation is also expressed to Lynne Norris and R. Wiater, who assisted in organizing the data collection and analyzing the results.

of drug research. Psychological treatment is usually more prolonged; it involves a more complex interpersonal relationship, and the distinction between placebo and clinically effective agent can be less clearly delineated. Furthermore, the institution of a long pseudo-treatment is generally impractical in the clinical situation. Not only is it wasteful of the patient's and therapist's time, but the necessary deception and delay of legitimate treatment can seldom be justified, and may be detrimental to the patient's future chances for cure.

These objections had considerably less validity in the experimental context considered here, which offered an opportunity to employ a stringent placebo control group. Ss used in this research displayed phobic reactions to nonpoisonous snakes of considerable intensity. They systematically avoided snakes or places such as zoos or camping trips where they might be found. These individuals behaved so "unrealistically" as to react with anxiety not only to snakes themselves, but to pictures of snakes, artifacts (a snakeskin belt), similar shapes, or the mere mention of the word. Nightmares concerning snakes were not uncommon in this group. Such statements, descriptive of their fear as the following have been recorded: "There's nothing in the world that I'm more afraid of than snakes." "I'm just weak when I see one." "I don't even want to look at them in books." In nearly all respects, except the degree to which the phobia is an omnipresent source of concern, this fear resembled those that patients themselves bring to the attention of psychiatrists and psychologists.

However, these Ss were not drawn from a clinical population, but were selected from among normal college Ss by a classroom questionnaire and subsequent interview (their frequency is approximately one or two per hundred students surveyed). They volunteered to participate in an experiment on psychotherapy. They were instructed that the procedures used might reduce or eliminate their fear, but that the main purpose of the project was a scientific evaluation of different therapy methods.

The advantages of working with this population are obvious. Treatment can be specific. The number of sessions may be arbitrarily controlled. The moral responsibility to choose the best treatment is not involved. As this phobia is not a central life problem and these Ss were generally more stable than patients, extratherapeutic incidents less frequently interfere with therapy process. Most important, the necessary rigor of experimental procedure can be closely respected.

As in all translations of natural events into a laboratory context, something is lost in vivacity. In this case, some of the subject characteristics mentioned above, the rigidity of procedure, are obviously differences from what is characteristically found in the consulting room. However, much can be gained in the exactness and clarity with which natural events are elucidated. Thus, the present study does not constitute a clinical test of desensitization therapy (clinical statistics have already been reported by Wolpe, 1958), but it is rather an attempt to illuminate through experiment the mechanism by which fear reduction is achieved in this method. Specifically, this research is designed to determine if placebo effects account for the positive results achieved by systematic desensitization therapy, and also to evaluate the overall contribution of suggestibility, as a personality trait, to progress in desensitization and post therapy fear reduction.

METHOD
Desensitization Therapy

The procedure has been described in detail elsewhere (Lazovik and Lang, 1960; Lang and Lazovik, 1963). Each S first experienced five training sessions. At this time an *anxiety hierarchy* was constructed —a series of 20 phobic situations graded from least to most frightening. S was also trained in hypnosis and deep muscle relaxation (Jacobson, 1938). Subsequently he participated in 11 desensitization sessions. During these meetings he was hypnotized and instructed to vividly imagine the scenes described in the hierarchy.[2] The scenes were presented one at a time, starting with the least frightening, and repeated until S no longer reported coincident anxiety. This desensitization occurred in the context of deep muscle relaxation, which is held to counter condition or "reciprocally inhibit" (Wolpe, 1958) the fear response. Sessions lasted approximately 45 minutes at the rate of one or two per week.

Pseudotherapy

An effort was made to involve S in a treatment procedure which was therapeutically neutral except for the therapist-client relationship. Because desensitization was to be evaluated, all procedures employed in that method were included in pseudotherapy. Ss first experienced the same five training sessions as in desensitization, followed by eleven pseudotherapy sessions. The procedure for each of these latter sessions was

---

[2] Six recently treated Ss experienced desensitization without hypnosis.

the same. *S* was first hypnotized and then told to relax deeply. During the first fifteen minutes of the therapy hours *S* was asked to imagine a series of scenes, which he had previously described as pleasant and relaxing. The last half hour was keyed to the hierarchy items. The items were taken in order during the course of therapy, and provided starting points for a discussion of non-anxiety evoking aspects of *S*'s life. The therapist generally behaved in a non-directive manner. However, he did attempt to prevent phobic responses from being made in the context of the therapy hour. It was held that the occurrence of phobic verbal behavior could lead to positive change, for the same reason that theory predicts it in desensitization, i.e., inhibition of anxiety by relaxation or comfort responses instigated by the therapist. Thus, the pseudo-therapist gently steered the conversation away from phobic or other sensitive material—in the main by reinforcing nonsensitive topics with nods and verbal signs of his attention, and failing to similarly reinforce comments directly pertinent to *S*'s fear. For example, if the hierarchy item concerned a black snake at the farm of an uncle, the developing conversation might concern farms or farm animals, or experiences with the uncle, whatever *S* spontaneously brought up that did not directly refer to his anxieties.

The theoretical orientation given these *S*s facilitated the pseudo-therapist's task. In the first session the following explanation of procedure was offered:

Perhaps if I impart a little bit of psychological theory to you, it will help you understand our next procedure. You have learned how to relax your muscles and this is going to be important in dealing with your fear. Previous research suggests that people with fears like yours have higher levels of automatic tonus than others. What this means is that all the vegatative systems, digestive, circulatory, as well as the neural and muscular systems tend to overreact. They overreact mainly because they actually start from a higher level of tonus. Some psychologists hold that if this generally high tonus level could be reduced, the way would be paved for a general reduction in specific fears.

What we hope to do in the rest of our sessions together is help you achieve a general lowering of the tonus levels. We will do this by first having you relax as you have learned to do. Then you will be hypnotized and even deeper relaxation will be achieved. To facilitate this process we will suggest pleasant scenes, from time to time, for you to concentrate on.

As you probably know, fears such as yours are often related to situations which seem unimportant. After you are comfortable, that is, deeply relaxed, we will want to begin a discussion with some of the items you used in the fear hierarchy. We will use these as starting points in our talks but plan to deviate from them. Our goal is to explore a number of areas of living, and produce a lowering of your overall tension levels. The theory holds that a person may overcome his fear if he obtains a better understanding of himself and learns to deeply relax.

*S*s participated eagerly. They came regularly and none discontinued treatment before the end of the experiment. Furthermore, no *S* reported that he suspected he was involved in a nonviable treatment. The therapists reported consistently close, empathic relationships with these *S*s, comparable or superior to those achieved during desensitization.[3]

Subjects

This research has been underway continuously since September, 1960, and the present report describes the total sample of 44 *S*s. Included are 23 desensitization

[3] Two factors probably helped considerably to insure that the pseudo-therapist was not unmasked: (1) Treatment was relatively brief; (2) metropolitan residents were being treated for a snake phobia. Therefore, *S*s had little or no contact with the phobic object outside of the experimental situation. If *S*s were treated for a more omnipresent fear over a longer time period, unfavorable feedback from the life situation might make the deception much more difficult to maintain.

subjects, 11 untreated controls, and 10 Ss who participated in pseudotherapy.[4]

All Ss were introductory psychology students at the University of Pittsburgh. They rated their fear of non-poisonous snakes as "intense," on a fear questionnaire, and were included in this research only if a psychological interview corroborated this statement. Ss who appeared to have impairing physical disabilities or latent psychosis (based on the psychotic scales of the MMPI or the clinical judgment of the interviewer) were excluded. None of the Ss in this study were being seen elsewhere bcause of psychological problems.

Assignment to groups was essentially random, although some pretreatment effort to balance control variables was made. A more elaborate description of the selection battery has already been reported (Lang and Lazovik, 1963).

Procedure

After the selection tests and interviews, all Ss were administered the Stanford Hypnotic Susceptibility Scale (SHSS), Form A (Weitzenhoffer and Hilgard, 1959). Subsequently all Ss except the untreated controls participated in the five therapy training sessions, after which SHSS Form B was administered. Fear intensity was measured both before and after the subsequent eleven desensitization or pseudotherapy trials. Untreated Ss were not seen, except for evaluation sessions.

The measures employed (Lang and Lazovik, 1963) were: The Fear Survey Schedule (FSS), FSS #38, an avoidance

[4] The untreated Ss and 13 desensitization Ss were described in a previous report (Lang and Lazovik, 1963). All desensitization Ss were combined as there was no significant difference between this 1963 group and Ss who have since participated, either in selection method or results on the major assessment variables. Change scores for the 1963 sample and all other subsequent desensitization Ss were, respectively: Avoidance test, .23 and .32; Fear Thermometer, 2.47 and 2.38; FSS #38, 1.38 and 1.44.

test, and the Fear Thermometer. The FSS is a list of 50 phobias that S rates on a seven point scale. Item #38 is the snake item. In the Avoidance Test S was confronted with an alive, tame blacksnake. He was invited to approach the animal, in a controlled setting. The closest point of approach to the animal provided the basis for his test score. If S held the animal, he achieved a score of 1; refusal to go to the test room and observe the snake yielded a score of 19. Immediately after this experience S rated his situational anxiety during the avoidance test on a 10 point Fear Thermometer (Walk, 1956). An open-ended fear interview provided additional qualitative information.

The experimenters in this research were all experienced psychotherapists. Most of the subjects were seen by two psychologists who have a full time psychotherapy practice. The same experimenters who saw the pseudotherapy Ss also treated desensitization Ss. Fear evaluation was conducted by an experimenter who participated in no other aspect of the procedure.

RESULTS

Mean fear behavior change scores from pre-test and post-test are presented in Table 1. The similarity of the pseudotherapy and no treatment means is readily apparent. T-tests yielded no significant differences between these groups for any measure of fear change (Table 2). Furthermore, the change score frequency distributions for the two groups were normal and overlapping. Pseudotherapy and no treatment Ss were therefore combined into a single control group for subsequent analyses.

Mean change scores for the combined control group and the desensitization group are presented in Table 1. Desensitization Ss showed significantly greater fear reduction than controls as measured by all three indices of snake phobic behavior. The ts are presented in Table 2 and desensitization and control frequency distributions are

TABLE 1

MEAN PRE TO POST TREATMENT CHANGE SCORES FOR ALL FEAR MEASURES

Group	Avoidance Test	Fear Thermometer	FSS #38	Fear Survey
Combined Control (N = 21)	−.03	1.14	.48	12.14
Pseudotherapy (N = 10)	.14	1.30	.40	12.50
No treatment (N = 11)	−.19	1.00	.54	11.82
Desensitization (N = 23)*	.27	2.43	1.41	18.64
(hierarchy items completed)				
15 or more (N = 13)	.47	3.58	2.31	23.77
less than 15 (N = 10)	.01	.89	.11	7.33

Note.—The avoidance test score is the percent change statistic previously described (Lang and Lazovik, 1963). All other change scores were simply the difference between pre and post tests. The correlations between initial performance and fear change for all measures were insignificant and inconsistent in direction.
* Data were incomplete for three Ss. The Fear Thermometer and FSS Ns are 22 and 21, respectively.

TABLE 2

T-TESTS OF MEAN FEAR CHANGE SCORES FROM PRE TO POST TREATMENT

Groups	Avoidance Test	Fear Thermometer	FSS #38	Fear Survey
Combined Control vs. Desensitization	2.57*	2.12*	2.19*	1.25
Combined Control vs. 15 or more	3.26**	3.44**	3.99***	2.52*
Combined Control vs. Less than 15	.14	.41	1.85	.41
Less than 15 vs. 15 or more	2.33*	3.28*	5.00***	2.26*
Pseudotherapy vs. No Treatment	1.67	.48	.58	.12

Note.—The desensitization group was subdivided into two groups on the basis of performance in therapy. "15 or more" and "less than 15" refers to the number of anxiety hierarchy items successfully completed by the group during desensitizing.
  * $p < .05$.
 ** $p < .01$.
*** $p < .001$.

illustrated in Figure 1. Except for the avoidance test the control sample yielded essentially normal distributions of fear change. The desensitization Ss have a primary modal score in the same interval as the controls, but the distributions are skewed positively or are frankly bimodal.

Progress in systematic desensitization is directly measured by the portion of the twenty item anxiety hierarchy completed in the eleven therapy sessions. Table 3 reveals that all measures of fear reduction are positively related to the number of hierarchy items successfully completed by each S. No pretest measure of snake phobic behavior correlated significantly with the

TABLE 3

PEARSON CORRELATIONS BETWEEN THE NUMBER OF ANXIETY HIERARCHY ITEMS SUCCESSFULLY COMPLETED DURING DESENSITIZATION AND MEASURES OF FEAR CHANGE AND THE STANFORD HYPNOTIC SUSCEPTIBILITY SCALE

Fear Change	r	SHSS Form	r
Avoidance Test	.40*	A	−.06
Fear Thermometer	.50*	B	−.03
FSS #38	.60**		
Fear Survey	.50*	Change	−.05

Note.—SHSS change is the difference between Forms A and B.
  * $p < .05$.
 ** $p < .01$.

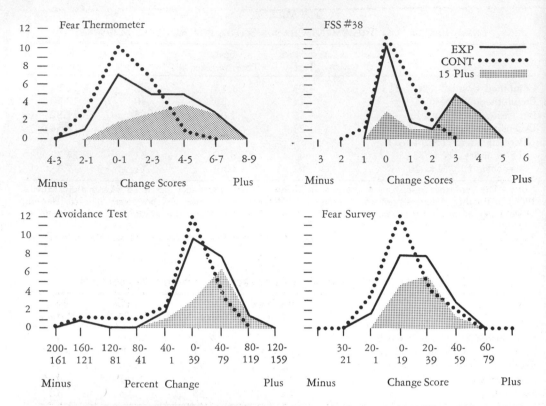

Fig. 1. Fear Change Score frequency distributions for the combined control (CONT) and desensitization (EXP) samples. The shaded area of the desensitization groups' distribution defines the Ss who successfully completed 15 or more anxiety hierarchy items.

number of items subsequently completed, although the first presentation of the FSS and items completed yielded an r of $-.435$ ($p < .05$). Number of items completed was wholly unrelated to any of the SHSS measures (Table 3).

A previous review of part of these data (Lang and Lazovik, 1963) suggested that while Ss who completed 15 items or more showed considerable positive change, Ss completing less than 15 showed no more change than untreated subjects. The current enlarged sample confirmed this trend. It may be noted in Table 1, that Ss completing more than 15 items have the highest average change scores for all fear measures. Furthermore, Figure 1 shows that the 15 plus Ss clearly account for the positive

skew of the distributions of experimental Ss. If the 15 plus group is eliminated, the remaining Ss are distributed normally around the control mode. These impressions were assessed by t-test, and the results are reported in Table 2: fifteen plus Ss show significantly more fear reduction than either controls or less than 15 Ss. The latter group was not superior to the control group on any change measure.

The correlations between the pretest fear measures and SHSS Forms A and B, and the difference score, are at the top of Table 4. Inspection of these coefficients reveals that only the avoidance test is significantly related to suggestibility. Correlations between fear reduction and the SHSS measures are listed in the bottom half of Table

TABLE 4

PEARSON CORRELATIONS BETWEEN THE
STANFORD HYPNOTIC SUSCEPTIBILITY SCALE
AND THE INITIAL MEASURES OF FEAR AND
FEAR CHANGE SCORES

Fear	SHSS Form		
Measures	A	B	Change
Total Sample (N = 44)			
(initial score)			
Avoidance Test	−.34*	−.47**	−.06
Fear Thermometer	−.14	−.22	.04
FSS #38	.10	.19	.11
Fear Survey	.00	−.10	−.13
Control Group (N = 21)			
(change score)			
Avoidance Test	.00	.12	.06
Fear Thermometer	.33	.46*	.15
FSS #38	.47*	.48*	−.02
Fear Survey	.29	.36	−.23
Desensitization Group (N = 23)			
(change score)			
Avoidance Test	−.16	.11	.28
Fear Thermometer	−.16	.18	.39
FSS #38	.07	.02	−.19
Fear Survey	.08	.07	.02

Note.—All correlational statistics were computed on the IBM 7090 at the University of Pittsburgh Data Processing Center.

* $p < .05$.
** $p < .01$.

4. It may be noted that avoidance test change is unrelated to suggestibility for either the desensitization or control S. For control Ss both the fear thermometer and FSS change are positively related to measures of suggestibility, and FSS #38 shows a tendency in this direction. There is no significant relationship between the desensitization group's SHSS scores and any fear change measure.

DISCUSSION

Desensitization Ss clearly showed a significantly greater decrease in phobic behavior than did controls; Ss whose therapeutic experience was restricted to a placebo relationship yielded no more positive change than did the untreated group.

These results imply that the reduction in fear following desensitization does not stem from a suggestion to change implicit in being "in therapy." Both placebo and desensitization Ss were asked to participate in a procedure which had fear reduction as a goal, and both groups spent equal time at this task. The findings also indicate that hypnosis, training in muscle relaxation, hierarchy building, and their continued use in a therapeutic context, do not in themselves produce change in fear behavior. Finally, the results suggest that the relationship which developed between experimenter and subject, with possible transference effects, was not in itself the vehicle of change.

The above inferences clearly depend on the extent to which the therapists kept their communications about goals the same for all Ss, and how well they succeeded in maintaining interpersonal relationships of comparable warmth and intensity with their client-subjects under both desensitization and placebo conditions. A number of factors argue that a high degree of comparability was achieved. The formal, experimental setting in which this research was carried out certainly assisted in this task. Each step of the procedure was defined, and a considerable portion of the therapist's communications with the S were read from a mimeographed program. Furthermore, it is unlikely that the therapists who saw most of the Ss in this study were personally committed to any outcome. They were paid for their participation, at the same rate per therapy hour regardless of the procedure administered, and they were involved in no other aspect of the experiment. It must also be mentioned that all Ss were seen by clinicians with considerable experience in interviewing and traditional psychotherapy, who would be well above average in their ability to meet the relationship requirements of the experiment. Finally, the post therapy interviews with the Ss, and discussions with the therapists, did not suggest that placebo Ss were less closely involved, nor did they yield Ss who doubted the fact that a true therapeutic procedure was being undertaken.

On the other hand, the possibility of error in procedure can never be completely discounted, and is best detected by independent attempts at replication. Furthermore, despite the fact that many of the same procedures were used in both placebo therapy and desensitization, the way they were used undoubtedly influenced the character of the experimenter-subject relationship. Unlike the pesudotherapy group, desensitization Ss received regular feedback concerning progress through the hierarchy. Clear-cut success experiences (as well as failures) were part of the therapeutic interaction. In this context, a good therapeutic relationship may be one in which the therapist has gained the properties of a reinforcer, and this capacity is in the service of a specific program of behavior change. Desensitization would then progress more rapidly if approval is given for the completion of items. The better the relationship, the more effective such reinforcement is likely to be. On the other hand, it should be pointed out that the completion of an item is in itself reinforcing and many Ss compliment themselves on their own progress. Thus, the quality of the relationship may be less relevant to a well motivated S's performance. These variables merit the continued attention of researchers.

While the desensitization Ss as a group showed considerable fear reduction, the change score distributions are skewed and some individual members changed no more than controls. The current experiment was limited to a brief 11 desensitization sessions, and it is, of course, possible that all Ss would have improved with a sufficient exposure. It is also possible that there are personality differences between those who profit and those who do not. As the sample size increases this contingency will be explored. In any event, suggestibility is clearly not one of the potential distinguishing traits. While a significant part of the control S's fear change is attributable to the SHSS no similar relationship between this scale and fear reduction was found for the experimental group. For desensitization Ss the positive effects of treatment were so overriding as to render undetectable any variance assignable to suggestibility.

All measures of fear change yielded high positive correlations with number of hierarchy items completed. Furthermore, Ss who completed at least 15 items showed significantly less fear than controls at the end of the experiment; Ss who failed to move this far along in the hierarchy were no different from pseudotherapy or untreated Ss. The correlations indicate that a general relationship exists between fear change and a measurable aspect of therapy process. It is unlikely that item 15 represents a "critical point" in this process. However, given the measures used here, the data suggest that the therapeutic task must be well advanced before effects clearly greater than those achieved by control Ss are observed.

As would be predicted by an S-R theoretical model, fears other than the phobia treated showed less marked reduction. The desensitization group as a whole yielded significantly greater change than controls on FSS #38; an analogous result was not obtained for the entire Fear Survey Schedule. Nevertheless, fifteen plus Ss did show a significant reduction on the FSS when compared either to control Ss or to the less than 15 group. These findings suggest that the treatment was specific, as intended, and when it was successful that fear reduction generalized positively.

These findings are inconsistent with some predictions from psychoanalytic theory. Fear reduction occurred without exploration of the phobia's dynamic background. Post treatment interviews revealed no examples of symptom substitution. Positive generalization of fear reduction was indicated, rather than an increase in other fears. Furthermore, a transference cure interpretation of the fear change is weakened by the failure to find marked placebo effects.

Although the relationship by itself was shown to be less effective therapy than client centered theorists have sometimes argued, this experiment does not constitute a test of that treatment method. A quasi-non-directive technique was employed in part of the pseudotherapy procedure, but its object was the opposite of client centered therapy, to avert affect laden statements rather than to encourage them. As was already suggested, theory would predict positive change in true client centered treatment for the same reasons as for desensitization. Advocates of the latter treatment hold, of course, that behavior therapy is more specific and systematic, and therefore faster and more thorough. The present experimental design offers an excellent setting for a test of this assumption. Now that the level of placebo changes is known the way is open for a meaningful, comparative evaluation of psychotherapies.

Both the limitations and the advantages of the subject population used in this experiment were mentioned at the outset, and they must be continually held in mind. However, the course of laboratory desensitization very closely followed the treatment process reported by clinical workers. Considerable success was achieved in eleven desensitization sessions, which compares favorably with the 11.6 average sessions per hierarchy reported by Wolpe (1958) for neurotic patients. Furthermore, many of the phenomena observed by the authors in clinical cases, and reported by others, were found with these experimental Ss. The systematic weakening of anxiety with repeated presentation of a hierarchy item was of course the typical result. However, Ss occasionally showed a perseveration of anxiety, and apparent summation with repetition, that presented all the difficulties that this situation creates when it occurs in a clinical case. Similarly, problems with visualization were frequently observed, as well as avoid-ance behavior when individual items were particularly upsetting. While these problems were undoubtedly fewer and less intense than would occur in clinical practice, they did not appear to differ in quality or kind.

Despite this apparent versimilitude, generalization to the clinic must be cautiously undertaken. Many issues are raised that need more intensive investigation. Nevertheless, the results obtained here encourage four important conclusions: (1) Simply being in a therapeutic context and relating to a therapist (even when all the trappings of desensitization—hypnosis, hierarchy building, relaxation—are included) does not in itself effect the important changes in phobic behavior achieved by systematic desensitization; (2) Successful desensitization is relatively independent of S's suggestibility; (3) Change in verbal and motor indices of fear behavior may be directly predicted from measurable events that occur during desensitization therapy; (4) The systematic desensitization of a specific fear generalizes positively to other fears. These findings are further presumptive evidence that desensitization therapy process conforms to its theoretical model, that it is an adapting out or systematic counterconditioning of fear responses to specific stimuli.

REFERENCES

LANG, P. J., & LAZOVIK, A. D. Experimental desensitization of a phobia. *J. abnorm. soc. Psychol.*, 1963, 66, 519–525.

LAZOVIK, A. D., & LANG, P. J. A laboratory demonstration of systematic desensitization psychotherapy. *J. psychol. Stud.*, 1960, 11, 238–247.

WALK, R. D. Self ratings of fear in a fear-invoking situation. *J. abnorm. soc. Psychol.*, 1956, 52, 171–178.

WEITZENHOFFER, A. M., & HILGARD, E. R. *Stanford Hypnotic Susceptibility Scale.* Palo Alto, Calif.: Consulting Psychologists Press, 1959.

WOLPE, J. *Psychotherapy by reciprocal inhibition.* Stanford: Stanford Univer. Press, 1958.

Conflict-Resolution Family Therapy

SALVADOR MINUCHIN

In basic science the interrelatedness between technique and theory and the way in which their development is mutually affected is clear. The development of new instruments expands our understanding of a particular universe, requiring new theories to explain the new facts; or, a new theory evokes the development of new techniques that allow refined exploration of its implications. This has not been, until recently, the course of psychoanalytic and psychotherapeutic theory and technique, wherein a large body of theory has been accompanied by limited exploration in the development of new techniques in therapy. My own recent experience, however, has been with a population that has forced me to turn to the exploration of new therapeutic techniques.

For the last five years, I have been working, at Wiltwyck School for Boys, with families who produce delinquent children.[1]

Paper presented at the American Psychiatric Association Regional Research Conference, Galveston, Texas, 1965, and reprinted with the permission of the author. Footnote reference symbols have been changed to numbers.

[1] Because as yet there is no system of diagnosis in the area of family therapy, we have no precise term to delineate this particular group of families. Throughout this paper, therefore, I refer to them as "multiproblem families," with the awareness that this term is purely descriptive and does not carry dynamic meaning.

These families are in the low socioeconomic group, mostly on welfare, and only 25 per cent of them are intact in the middle-class sense. They are sometimes composed of one or more transient males or a transient mother, at other times, a mother, her children and the children of her adolescent or young adult daughters; aunts are in maternal roles as frequently as are older siblings, and so on.

Psychologically these people are impoverished, rather than complex; their areas of experience are limited. Family themes are restricted, with emphasis on aggression, helplessness, abandonment, and nurturance. Role organization around family themes is narrow and stereotyped, and family members adhere rigidly to one another's expectations. Communication involves an unusually large amount of disconnected monologue, meaning being most often expressed through paraverbal channels. Since family members find it difficult to carry subject matter through to some conclusion, exchange of information is faulty. Interaction centers on the here and now, and transactions among members can shift abruptly from a high-pitched, emotional charge to passive disengagement. Consequently, these families are relatively helpless in the face of interpersonal tension, with very few tools for conflict resolution.

In spite of their needs, multiproblem

families have traditionally refused our therapeutic approaches and we have been compelled to search for approaches more adequate to this special population. Presently we have at Wiltwyck 60 families in treatment, and we have been experimenting with a variety of techniques for working with them. (Minuchin, Auerswald, King, and Rabinowitz, 1964). The technique to be described here has been used for the last year with 15 families at Floyd Patterson House.[2] Because this technique, *conflict-resolution family therapy,* is still being explored, we have too few cases in long-range therapy for complete evaluation of its effects. Yet, even at this stage it seems to be a promising new tool in the armamentarium of therapeutic techniques.

An explanation of the underlying theoretical assumptions of conflict-resolution family therapy is an essential first step in my description of the actual technique.

For the human being it is economical to develop certain short cuts in the organization of experience, namely, generalizations that allow such a cataloging of experiences that we need not always repeat anew the total process of perceiving and apprehending what we have already experienced. Although these generalizations may lead to distortions of individual situations, they compensate for such distortions by increasing our speed in organizing responses to new situations. Clearly, this blunts the familiar: people lose their ability to perceive not only nuances in known situations but also new elements embedded in familiar experience.

The blunting of our experience by mere familiarity is, of course, a complex phenomenon; it becomes infinitely more so within the immediate family. After all, the family insures the predictability of interaction among its members through precisely this process of generalization, which has been explained differently by different

schools of thought. There is agreement, nonetheless, that people do develop patterns of interpersonal responses and that knowledge of these patterns allows the therapist to predict with relative certainty the direction of behavior in similar circumstances. The more anxious a person is —the more his reactions tend to be affective only—the narrower and more predictable will be his range of interpersonal responses. There is also agreement that a neurotic person has a narrower than average range of perceptions and interpersonal activities. We could define a neurotic person, then, as one who in conflictual areas sees almost no alternative modalities of response, who perceives people along a narrow range of sterotyped categories, and who has very few roles available for interpersonal relationships. A neurotic person will play the part of Falstaff, say, even when a situation calls for Romeo or Othello.

Psychoanalytic schools emphasize that developmental processes in the midst of the family during an individual's earliest years orient him to a particular way of experiencing life; he then tends to handle new experiences through this set, modifying them if necessary, to make them fit his available molds. Implicit in this interpretation of human development is the idea that new learning can be handicapped by an overlearning of the previous experiential set, to the point that, for the neurotic person, new learning does not occur in emotionally charged areas.

Among the psychoanalytic schools, the existential movement holds that therapy should help the patient "find himself," rather than "strive" for success, achievement, or even understanding. The Zen Buddhist model of "interpretation," which creates an experience disregarding the intellectual understanding of the situation, has fascinated many existential analysts. In a similar vein, the modern theatre has moved toward a theatre of "experience." Playwrights of the "Theatre of the Ab-

---

[2] A half-way residence house of Wiltwyck School.

surd" (Esslin, 1961) have broken away from the plot, to experiment in creating an emotional experience in the audience. Familiar concepts are treated in such unusual ways as to shock the observer into recognizing—emotionally and cognitively—and experiencing anew something that has become stereotyped. Such a shock reaction to the familiar obliges the observer to encompass the concept in an emotional, rather than a logical, way. The meaning of recognition in this sense is to "cognite again" with the emotional connotation of the encounter.

Because experience, especially within the multiproblem family, tends to be cognitively undifferentiated and emotionally blunted, we need a therapeutic method through which we can foster in our patients a learning anew from their familiar experience. The existential analysts and the playwrights of the theatre of the absurd provide a clue to a means for helping multiproblem families encounter their own life and surroundings with new eyes. It is my view that the foregoing is relevant for psychotherapy in general; nevertheless, it seems particularly significant for the development of psychotherapeutic techniques for the multiproblem family.

In their interactions, members of these families seem to move from one extreme, enmeshment, to the other, abandonment. At the enmeshment pole, family transactions are characterized by a fast tempo of interpersonal exchange because multiproblem families tend to resolve tensions by action and because of their paucity of mediating processes between impulse and action. The resulting style of interpersonal relationship has a high degree of mutual enmeshment and fast shifts in both focus of transaction and affective tone. At the abandonment pole, family members seem oblivious to the effects of their actions on one another. Monologues, parallel play, and a variety of maneuvers of psychological and physical abandonment characterize this modality.

Neither extreme of interaction facilitates a differentiated experience of family transactions. Awareness of personal impingement and interpersonal causality remain global. A technique of family therapy adapted to this population must therefore *actively* frame interpersonal transactions around clearly *focused* issues and *direct* the attention of the participants to the nature of their mutual impingement. It could then foster among family members the capacity to observe interpersonal causality, as a stepping-stone for achieving change.

The technique of task-oriented family therapy directs family members to participate in familiar tasks under conditions that are different from, and sometimes the opposite of, their usual patterns of response. The family is seen once a week for one hour, usually by one therapist, sometimes by co-therapists. The majority of the 15 families had already undergone some variation of family therapy for six months to as long as two years prior to their introduction to this approach. (We have also explored the effects of this approach on a number of middle class families.)

The procedure during the session is as follows: The therapist first meets with the total family. During this initial period, he observes the free development of interaction among family members, deriving from this a diagnostic picture of transactional patterns. He then makes explicit the unstated forces ruling the transaction. He selects one area of conflict between some members of the family and addresses himself to these members, pointing out the nature of the conflict and their usual pattern in dealing with it. He points also to the pain-producing characteristics of this pattern. The therapist then instructs the family members involved to continue dealing with this conflict, but now he suggests that the interaction should occur within a different emotional context, for example, if the family members are involved in competitive interaction, he suggests cooperation.

The therapist then asks the other members of the family to join him behind a one-way mirror from where they can act as observers of the family subgroup transaction. The members of the family involved in the conflict remain alone in the original room, while the therapist directs and assists the rest of the family in their observations, so that they become more discriminating in their perception of a familiar transaction. Usually, the participant family members begin, at some point, to relate according to their former patterns and against the instructions of the therapist. The therapist may then instruct one of the observer family members to enter the room and try to change the situation towards the growth-encouraging lines that they have previously discussed.

If this new transaction follows the usual pattern, the therapist allows the process to develop, and then he may send another family member back into the room, or enter himself, to help the family members consolidate their understanding of what has happened. He points out the way in which the process has developed, and how their usual patterns of transaction inhibit the possibility for developing new patterns of isolation were expressed in an autofaction to the members. In this way, in a session lasting one hour, the exploration of one area of conflict may involve four or five different subgroupings within the family, the various members alternating between the roles of participant and observer.

As a partial example of this process, consider a family composed of a man whose self-derogatory image and feelings of isolation were expressed in an autocratic, critical relationship with spouse and children; a woman, whose dependency and helplessness reflected itself in an explicit acceptance of husband's dominance and an implicit coalition with the older son, encouraging him in a continuous rebellion against father; and their two sons, aged 14 and 12, who, caught between mother's overprotectiveness and father's unfailing perception of the negativity in their being, projected their confused identity in the home arena as well as in school through blind attack on their "pursuers."

During the session, the therapist pointed out to father that his attack on the elder son was accompanied by an explicit statement that he was helping his son, as well as by a less audible and more jumbled message indicating father's pain about his own helplessness. The therapist pointed out to the 14-year-old son that, although he seemed to want paternal acceptance, he could not trust that it would be forthcoming, and was continuously engaged in provoking his father and rendering him helpless, thus intensifying father's negative and critical responses toward him as father's only way of remaining a worth-while adult. The therapist then directed father and son to continue dealing with the issue in conflict, but gave them instructions on the modalities in which interaction should occur. He suggested that father should find positive areas in his son that he could highlight, and that the son should talk in such a way as to elicit his father's support.

In the observation room, the therapist, the wife, and the younger son observed how father and older son, after a feeble attempt to become engaged along the lines suggested by the therapist, again became involved in a power operation. The mother expressed her impatience with her husband's "preaching" and his rigid behavior, while the younger son pointed out that father wanted to teach his brother something worth-while. The wife expressed her feeling of wanting to be in the other room to stop the onslaught.

The therapist then pointed out to the wife how she and her husband were fighting through their son, leaving father and son isolated from each other and robbing them of all possibilities of developing a mutually satisfactory relationship. Her tendency was to empathize with the attacked child, label her husband the aggressor, and so intervene that she and her husband became involved in a heated argument, which "freed" and isolated the son. The therapist suggested to the wife that she should now go into the room and try to help the husband to support the son. Some minutes later, husband and wife were blaming each other, and the older son was isolated. After the process developed, the therapist intervened and helped the family members to re-examine their interactional patterns. In the next session, under similar conditions, the wife left the room, saying that, since she could not remain without intervening between father and son, at least she could remove herself and go to the observation room where she would not interfere.[3]

In general, the family members organize into supplementary and complementary subsystems which interrelate in ways that either hinder or enhance problem solving.

The therapist's work in a session entails the following:

1. Diagnosing family structure in relation to a salient conflict and recurrent interactions that impede the observing and problem-solving capacities of the participants.

2. Assigning participant roles to family members centrally involved in the conflict, and removing other family members from the situation.

3. Instructing the participant members in new and unfamiliar ways of dealing with the conflict.

4. Actively guiding the removed participants into the observer's role.

5. Identifying the kinds and forms of interpersonal and intrapersonal obstacles that emerge as the new problem-solving participation is attempted, and making inferences as to the defensive systems, both

inter- and intrapersonal, that block new growth.

6. Helping family members progressively integrate the observing role into their active participation in conflicting interaction.

There is a theoretical rationale for this type of therapy. In the first place, to become aware of one's manner of functioning, one must observe one's own actions. The ability to introspect (reflexive observation) develops in the child through his incorporation of the vigilant parental control and his need to tell the parenting figures what happens to him. This subjective process of observing myself and what I am doing involves, in the words of David Rioch (1963): ". . . a need to abstract myself from any commitment in order to be aware of it. In the state of commitment to another person, I have no sense of I. All other sensations become only guides useful or not in directing the course of interaction in which I am a part. . . . In the process of personal commitment we open our control to the messages from our vis a vis committing ourselves to the involvement and we expect and receive responses adequate to maintain the dialogue. . . . One cannot make observations when one is committed in personal involvement, but one can successively interact and successively abstract himself from the involvement recreating a concept of what must have happened."

Acting as a participant-observer, in effect, entails a paradox: to become an observer, one must stop participating, yet while one is participating, one cannot observe his participation because of the process of commitment. This paradox has been a problem for effective psychotherapy. Existential therapists are trying to help the patient experience without concerning himself with observing the new experience, whereas therapists generally have been trying to bring about an intellectually integrated interpretation and, at the same time, to maximize the affective experience of the

---

[3] I am aware that such a verbal description of an active intervening technique as this creates the impression of a controlling therapist dictating the movements of the patients as though they were objects. In the actual setting, however, there is the same quality of emotional commitment and human contact between family and therapist that characterizes other forms of therapy.

process. Ackerman has experimented with showing family patients filmed sessions of their own family. Other workers help families listen to their tape-recorded sessions. All such therapeutic devices aim at maximizing a person's ability to observe without handicapping his ability to participate. Our use of tasks also capitalizes on this principle, but the observation is of an "unfolding" process; moreover, it provides an artificial barrier against the strong habitual reaction of our patients. The one-way mirror maintains the emotional impact of interpersonal experience, while it contains impulsory discharge. This is our most serious problem with acting-out families. They are unskilled in introspection—in observing and evaluating their own actions—and require a therapy that centers on ways of making this process more available to them.

The questions, then, are these: How can we help the family patient to observe his own actions without, at the same time, stopping his participation or devitalizing his experience? How can we introduce introspection at the moment of interaction? The answer to these questions may be best provided by considering, first, what happens to the observing members of the family, then, the participant members.

The observer gets a look at the family conflict while he has no responsibility for participating. The one-way mirror acts as a semiporous membrane. The observer is still very much caught in the interaction. He is, as it were, still sitting in the other room in the empty chair, but he is, simultaneously, aware that his role has changed. Although he cannot influence what is happening to the participant members, he continues to be subjected to the impingement of their behavior. His impulse to react—in action, as is characteristic of this population—can be said to bounce against the mirror; thus it is delayed and, with the help of the therapist's questions, is channeled into verbal forms. The therapist, sitting near him, now engages him in a completely new function: he is invited to

join the therapist in the observation of the participant members' interaction. His role has changed from that of participant to observer, although he continues to feel involved in the interaction. With this change in role, there is a change in his relationship to the therapist, with whom he has become, in a sense, a peer in the observation.

This change from participant to observer is certainly not automatic. Parents and children of multiproblem families frequently respond to cognitive affective stress by defensive maneuvers of fast engagement. Interpersonal proximity is a time-honored way of escaping from conflict. A child caught stealing, for example, refuses exploration by attacking his sibling for not "minding his own business"; a mother's awareness of her helplessness is usually blocked by her multiple and erratic control maneuvers. Some mothers, when asked to observe the therapy of their children for a number of sessions, responded with increased anxiety in the observation room: the level of noise, the inability of the children to keep to the subject, the power operations that characterize their daily behavior—all had a powerful impact on the mothers *as if they were perceiving it for the first time.* "It's too emotional to observe," said Mrs. G., who had spent two years in conventional family therapy. To counter the use of fast engagement as a defensive maneuver that blocks differentiated perception of member interaction, we have made it part of our procedure that parents, at some point in therapy, remain in the observation room with a therapist for a number of sessions.

An example of the difficulty in assuming the observer role is the A. family, who came to therapy because of the delinquency of the older daughter. The family was composed of a mother, her two adolescent daughters by a former man, and her present husband, who was older and less educated than herself. The daughters complained that step-father was autocratic and punishing and did not listen to or understand them. The step-father complained about the loose behavior of American teenagers and the importance of filial respect; the woman interpreted the daughters and the husband to each other. It became clear that family structure was organized around at least two subsystems—the three females and the husband and wife—and that the husband felt excluded from the first subsystem as well as from the parenting function. When he was asked to observe the three females of his family in the observation room, he continued to engage polemically with his two daughters although he was aware that they could not hear him, and only after repeated efforts by the therapist could he disengage himself and become an observer.

The separation of one member from the system can sometimes highlight processes that would not otherwise appear. For example, the B. family, which has been in treatment for six months, consists of grandmother, and her five children. Symptomatology included three delinquent children and a suicidal mother with a history of three hospitalizations. The grandmother assumed all parental roles and relegated mother to the role of older sibling. The grandmother asked to observe how the family functioned in her absence. In the observation room, she looked impatient when one of the children began to drum on a chair while mother was talking with another sibling. The grandmother voiced her impatience to the therapist, pointing out that she would have stopped it right there. Some minutes later, the mother addressed herself to the child by engaging him with a question about his schooling, stopping the child's disruptive behavior. The therapist could then point out to the grandmother how her always being two minutes ahead of her daughter left her daughter unemployed as a mother.

In considering what happens to the participant members, it is well to remember that certain transactions between family members have become automatic. For example, a wife's request for help may characteristically bring the husband's response of resentful help. Perceiving this as control, the wife responds with refusal to accept help. This, in turn, elicits from her husband a sense of helplessness about contacting her and is followed by controlling anger. Such behavior can occur again and again in an automatically triggered, response sequence. The wife's manner of requesting help and the help the husband offers can sometimes hinge on a conversation that seems altogether unrelated to what is being transacted nonverbally. Though help is asked for and given, the tension lies in the pitch of the voice, the posture of the body, the muscles of the face. This transaction becomes automatic and the participants find themselves in their usual conflicting positions, unaware of how they got there. When we suggest in the task situation that the wife ask for help in a direct form and that the husband respond to her request without his usual controlling attitude, we are demanding their participation in a strange modality. We are demanding participation in a new form that eliminates the possibility of automatic responses and increases the awareness of participation.

The couple's assignment is being conducted in a situation of induced stress because the participants are aware that the rest of the family is observing them. A consciousness of being observed is an intermediary step in the process of introspection. The participant observes in himself what he assumes the unseen observer is focusing on. This sense of being observed brings the observer's role indirectly to the participant members as well. When people fail to operate along the lines of the assignment, there is a heightened awareness of the handicapping nature of the usual patterns of interaction, and certain patterns that have been ego-syntonic are seen as ego-dystonic. For example, while mother is in the observation room, children are asked to "talk to each other, one at a time, without 'ranking,' and looking for positives in each other." After the initial increase in noise that always accompanies this task, some of the siblings will take the lead in organizing the interaction, and when there is disruptive behavior, or when a sibling is derogatorily labeled (and this is very frequent), some of the children will attempt to reinforce the task by pointing at the mirror, stating that they should do better because mother and the therapist are observing them.

We have thus established distance from an automatic process by increasing awareness of the process itself. When we are working with a multiproblem family, we are introducing an almost unused psychological function. The observer becomes, as it were, internalized, and the process of introspection is fostered.

At some point in therapy, family members begin to respond with new nuances in their interactions. Because it first occurs in a clumsy and hesitant way, the other member often fails to take into account this "shadow of a change." It is then the function of the therapist to point out the new behavior. Unfortunately, therapists are often unskilled in perceiving new behavior that may first manifest itself largely in formal ways—a deference to another person's speech, a slight change in the tone of voice, a hesitancy before entering into the automatic response—and they must learn the art of spotting and supporting these new developments while they are still clumsily executed by the participant members.

When members of the family respond along growth-encouraging lines, it is important that the therapist reward or support these changes. However, the observing family members also reward the participants, and their reward is more significant for the crystallization of the change than is the therapist's support. When a change occurs and the family members solve a conflict in a new and different way, the reward lies in the actual resolution of the conflict, the mastering of the new pattern of inter-

action (although it may be temporary), and the emotional support of the family as a group.

Implicit in this conflict-resolution technique of family therapy is the idea that people can learn not only from a clear awareness of their neurotic conflicts but also by the mastery of alternative solutions to conflicts. The therapist must keep in mind that in order to produce change he must be alert not only to the areas of conflict and the ways in which the patient's character structure affect or handicap growth, but also to the possibility of increasing the patient's sense of mastery by offering him alternative ways of functioning and help in perceiving alternative solutions to conflicts. It is not uncommon to see a patient in psychoanalysis who, after having incorporated a thorough knowledge of the nature of his dynamics and the antecedents for his neurotic functioning, rejects old patterns of response, but nonetheless remains handicapped when it comes to selecting new ways of experimenting in life.

Devising the strategies of task assignment in conflict-resolution family therapy requires a clear understanding of individual dynamics and how these are manifested in family transactions, as well as in the family's patterns of communication. These strategies must be flexible, continuously responding to the changes the family is undergoing. At this point it should be emphasized that when we ask for an interaction in an unfamiliar modality, we are not attempting to break a habit by the simple formula of creating another; we are increasing the vivid awareness of hidden patterns and underlying motivations at the same time that we are offering experience in alternative ways of attacking a problem.

There are many analogies to describe the unusual role of the therapist in this technique. In some ways his role is more central than in traditional family therapy; in other ways, he is less central. In some ways he is like the director of a play, directing the family members to try to comply, pressuring them to seek other than their usual repertoire of interaction, demanding that they fulfill his expectations. He also plays his traditional role, interpreting underlying dynamics and teaching the family a new experiential language. In the observation room he gives direction to the perceptions and observations of the observing members; he also acts as the connecting link when a new member comes to the observation room, filling him on what has been going on. At the same time, because the family members are themselves participants and observers, and even in a sense therapists, when they come in to help family members correct their faulty transactions, the therapist's role is partially decentralized. When he is in the observation room, the participant family members are alone in the other room tackling the conflicting transactions by themselves; they are actually trying out in the therapeutic sessions, without the help of the therapist, new modalities of mutual interaction.

One final word of caution: conflict-resolution family therapy in the hands of an inexperienced therapist can lend itself to an authoritarian display of power and an artificial manipulation of people, and the only road for the development of meaningful tasks is deep understanding of family dynamics.

In conclusion, for the last year we have been using conflict-resolution tasks as a therapeutic focus, in combination with our three-stage technique (Minuchin, Auerswald, King, and Rabinowitz, 1964) and with conventional family therapy, and the clinical results with the conflict-resolution technique have been encouraging. Families that have been in treatment for a year and longer respond to the introduction of tasks with a sharpening of awareness of their dynamics; sessions become more focused; children's participation increases and the level of noise so prevalent in these families' interactions decreases; and concentration on one issue and verbalization around this is-

sue, framed by the task, become central. Also, the therapist's verbalization diminishes. Through failures in reaching multi-problem families, the therapist as well as the social scientist has focused attention on the special characteristics of this population and on the need for developing therapeutic techniques that take these characteristics into account.[4] The significance of conflict-resolution family therapy for the low socioeconomic population lies in the following:

1. It presents usual interaction framed as *interpersonal problems* and suggests that this problem has *concrete solutions* in the interpersonal realm.

2. The tasks are clearly *structured,* deal with *familiar* situations, are focused in the *here and now,* and compel family members to search for solutions through *interaction* among themselves.

3. The division of the family into subgroups—participant and observers—when working with large families, facilitates the differentiation of the transactions in family subunits, which are usually hidden in the erratic and multiple stimulation of the larger group. Having the nonparticipating members observe the interaction keeps the total family involved.

---

[4] Frank Riesman (1962) emphasizes low-income culture and expectations as follows:

TYPICAL THERAPEUTIC EMPHASES	LOW-INCOME CULTURE AND EXPECTATIONS
Do it yourself, change yourself, assume responsibility.	Desire for authority, direction.
Introspective, think-centered, word focus.	Preference for work, action (talk deprecated).
Unstructured, permissive.	Desire for structure and organization.
Stress on the past.	Focus on present.
Self-focus.	Emphasis on family and group.
Stress on resistance and transference.	Problem focus.
Symbolic, often circuitous, interpretations and explanations.	Desire for simple, concrete, objectively demonstrable explanations.
Intensive transference and counter-transference.	Desire for less intense relationships; preference for informal friendliness, respect, sympathetic, non-patronizing understanding.

In this connection, see also Basil Bernstein (1964).

4. Observation through the one-way mirror maintains the impact of the familiar impingement, delays or eliminates the discharge of the habitual response, and channels the impulse into verbal forms.

A new technique of family therapy has been presented. This technique was developed in working with the multiproblem family's whole pattern of interpersonal transactions and style of communication, which handicap traditional therapeutic approaches. The technique capitalizes on the possibility of separating family members into participants and observers, thereby fostering the development of introspection and increasing awareness of automatic interpersonal processes.

REFERENCES

BERNSTEIN, B. Social class, speech systems and psychotherapy. *British J. Sociol.,* March, 1964.

ESSLIN, M. *The theatre of the absurd.* New York: Doubleday, 1961.

MINUCHIN, S., AUERSWALD, E., KING, C. H., and RABINOWITZ, CLARA. The study and treatment of families that produce multiple acting-out boys. *Am. J. Orthopsychiat.,* 1964, 34, 125–133.

RIESSMAN, F. *Some suggestions concerning psychotherapy with blue-collar patients.* (Mimeographed) New York: Mobilization for Youth, 1962.

RIOCH, D. MCK. Communication in the laboratory and communication in the clinic. *Psychiatry,* 1963, 29 (3), 209–211.

Filial Therapy:
Description and Rationale[1]

BERNARD GUERNEY, Jr.[2]

The great and growing need for combating emotional problems demand that much research be done to increase the leverage of professionals' time in effective psychotherapy. New methods should be explored to combat emotional problems early in life. Once such problems become relatively fixed, even massive expenditures of professional time often later fail to be of use. Hobbs (1963), speaking of plans for the development of clinical psychology, states that,

clinical psychology should now reclaim its birthright and devote itself primarily to problems of children. Fully one-half of our resources for the conduct of research and the provision of serv-

ices should be invested in people under the age of twenty. Another one-fourth of our resources for research and service should be invested in adults who are identified primarily through their relationships with children [p. 3].

Also, there should be attempts to develop new methods which allow each hour of professional time (and each square foot of physical facility, if you will) to help more individuals, and help them as effectively or more effectively than traditional methods have been able to do. We again quote Hobbs (1963):

Much of the practice of clinical psychology as well as psychiatry is obsolete. A profession that is built on a fifty minute hour of a one-to-one relationship between therapist and client . . . is living on borrowed time. The only substantial justification for investing the time of a highly trained professional person in the practice of psychotherapy as we know it is the possibility of discovering new and more efficient ways of working with people who are in trouble [p. 3].

The filial psychotherapy proposed here represents an attempt to develop a new method incorporating both these goals. (In addition, taking a long-range view, the method may have potential as a preventa-

Reprinted from *Journal of Consulting Psychology,* 1964, 28 (4), 304–310, with the permission of the American Psychological Association and the author.

[1] This research was supported, in part, by a grant from the University Research Council of Rutgers State University and, in part, by Public Health Service grant MH-08653-01 from the National Institute of Mental Health.

[2] The author is very grateful to Louise F. Guerney and Michael Andronico for their counsel, and their services as Filial Therapists; and to Lillian Stover, Thomas Steinberg, and Louise Clempner for their assistance in organizing and screening the Filial Therapy groups.

tive measure and as a method of building a foundation in childhood for better mental health and self-realization in adulthood.)

The technique uses parents as therapeutic agents with their own children. While the approach outlined here is new, there are encouraging precursors to employing parents in this capacity. Freud (1959) states in *Analysis of a Phobia in a Five-Year-Old Boy,*

the treatment itself was carried out by the child's father. . . . No one else could possibly have prevailed on the child to make such avowals; the special knowledge by means of which he was able to interpret the remarks made by his . . . son was indispensable [p. 149].

Another precedent is reported by Moustakas (1959). He suggests that "play therapy" sessions be conducted in the home by parents of relatively normal children, and he describes the very positive experiences of some mothers and children in such "relationship therapy." One such experience is reported separately by Natalie Fuchs (1957). With the encouragement of her father, Carl Rogers, she undertook home play therapy sessions with her daughter, and achieved impressive results in overcoming a toilet-training problem. A third major precedent is the view, supported by illustrative material, of Dorothy Baruch (1949) that play sessions at home offer a way of fostering good parent-child relationships. The home play techniques recommended by Moustakas and Baruch are in the same Rogerian tradition as those used in Filial Therapy. The parents to which they refer were not necessarily dealing with children who were emotionally disturbed in the clinical sense, but neither did the parents have continued close instruction, supervision, and the opportunity to discuss the process in a group therapy situation, as is the case in Filial Therapy. Thus, we regard their favorable experiences as encouraging with respect to Filial Therapy.

NATURE OF FILIAL THERAPY

Filial Therapy involves the training of parents of young children (in groups of six to eight) to conduct play sessions with their own children in a very specific way. After training, parents continue to meet weekly with the therapist to discuss results, conclusions, and inferences about their children and themselves. The sessions between the parents and child take place at home. The parent begins the play sessions at 30 minutes once weekly. This may later be increased, as desired, up to 45 minutes and two or more times a week.

The manner in which the child's play sessions are to be conducted is intended first to break the child's perception or misperception of the parent's feelings, attitudes, or behavior toward him. Second, they are intended to allow the child to communicate thoughts, needs, and feelings to his parents which he has previously kept from them, and often from his own awareness. (This communication is mainly through the medium of play.) The children's sessions with their parents are thus meant to lift repressions and resolve anxiety-producing internalized conflicts. Third, they are intended to bring the child—via incorporation of newly perceived attitudes on the part of his parents—a greater feeling of self-respect, self-worth, and confidence. The techniques or methods to be employed by the parents to accomplish this are modeled as closely as possible after therapy techniques in the Rogerian tradition, as exemplified by the writing, for example, of Dorfman (Rogers, 1951, Ch. 6) and Moustakas (1953).

Parent groups consist of mothers and fathers, about equally divided, who are not spouses. Because of the unique problems presented by the approach, flexibility of the group therapist's approach is necessary. Instructional techniques are used, including demonstration play sessions conducted by the therapist, and role-playing techniques. But when exploration of parental feelings and attitudes is involved in the instruction and later discussions, the group therapist is relatively client centered. Intensive probing and interpretation are generally not used.

The therapy may be described in terms of three general stages:

Stage 1

The first part of Stage 1 consists of an explanation, in as simple and personally meaningful terms as possible, of the benefits to be derived for the child and for parent-child relationships from the period of free expression and self-direction described. This is described in terms of release from tension-producing inner conflict, freer communication processes from child to parent, giving the child a greater sense of self-direction, self-respect, and self-confidence. The goals of the sessions are interwoven with discussion of the specific techniques to be employed. Full attention is paid to the parents' feelings and reactions, rather than employing a straight didactic approach. The goals of the sessions are explained to the parents as follows:

1. The encouragement of complete determination of the activities of the child by the child, within certain specified, definite limits, such as no destruction of nonplay material, and no activities which would be physically painful to child or parent.

2. The development of empathic understanding on the part of the parent as to the basic needs and feelings the child is trying to communicate and express through his play.

3. The immediate communication back to the child that these needs and feelings are understood, and that he as an individual is fully accepted, whatever his feelings or thoughts may be.

4. The need of the child to learn to see and accept responsibility for his actions. This is represented in the sessions by an understanding, but completely firm, enforcement of the "limits," mentioned earlier, under which the sessions are run. In other words, the child is expected to learn that he and his feelings are accepted, but that certain overt acts are not tolerated, and when the child performs them he will immediately, and invariably, suffer the undesirable consequence. In the context of the sessions, this consequence is the termination of the particular session.

It is emphasized to the parent that specific techniques will be meaningless, or worse, if they are applied only mechanically and not as a reflection of a genuine attempt at empathy. However, specific techniques to aid them in accomplishing the above goals are taught. These are the traditional techniques of Rogerian therapy: structuring, restatement of content, and, with major emphasis, clarification of feeling. Several demonstration sessions by the therapist are conducted, with the parents behind a one-way screen. Normal children and the children of the parents in the group are used for the demonstrations.

In the second part of Stage 1, the parents attempt to play their session role with either another parent's child or their own before beginning at home. The therapist's and parents' observed sessions are discussed by the group to enhance the group's understanding of the role, and their mastery of it. The orientation at the beginning is a completely task-oriented one, designed to maximize motivation and minimize resistance. The therapist clearly differentiates the parent's general role from the session role, and parents are not especially encouraged to attempt any of these techniques outside the session. But the questions concerning this possibility are discussed. (It is felt that much of that kind of generalization which is desirable could take place without direct encouragement from the therapist.)

Stage 2

The second stage begins after about six to eight sessions. When the parents and the therapist feel they are ready, the parents begin their sessions at home with their own children. Each parent has been provided, usually at their expense, with about $25 worth of standard play therapy equipment, including a family of Flagg dolls, a "house" made out of a corrugated box with lines painted on it to delineate "rooms," a "Joe Palooka" puncho bag, rubber knife, clay, crayons, paper, tea set, etc. They conduct the play session in a room suitable for play activities, and arrange things so that they will be uninterrupted for the preset time of the session. Parents take notes following the sessions, according to a prescribed outline. When available, tape recordings of the sessions that the parents may make at home can also be used as a starting point for discussion.

Techniques always remain a pertinent area for discussion in the group sessions themselves, and the therapist is always willing to revert to methodological and, therefore, task-oriented discussion. However, at this point, the therapist endeavors to focus the parents' attention on their own emotional reactions in the sessions, as well as those of their children.

Final Stage

As the therapy succeeds sufficiently to suggest to the parent that there is no longer a need for help, this is discussed by the group, and the parent, of course, is free to terminate. If and when a group gets down to three or four people for this reason, or because parents drop out for other reasons, a group may be merged with another similarly diminished group.

RATIONALE FOR FILIAL THERAPY

The question may rightly be asked: "How can parents who presumably contributed heavily to the creation of the problem be agents who are now expected to make a major contribution to its solution? Will not asking these parents to interact with their children in emotionally laden, conflicted areas only worsen the problem?"

We would reply first that parents interact heavily with their children under any circumstances. What we are training them to try to do during their session is to accept and understand their problems better, and in the process to *avoid* interpreting their behavior to them, avoid punitive action, etc. It is hard to see how this can worsen the child's predicament. And, should the sessions not directly help the child, they may still serve a very valuable purpose as catalysts to meaningful discussion in the parents' group therapy sessions.

To further clarify the issues, the theoretical views and propositions underlying this approach are briefly summarized below:

1. With young children living with their families, the primary source of maladjustment can presumably be traced directly or indirectly to interpersonal relationships, past and present, within the family, and to the patterns of deprivation, conflict, and defense that these relationships have engendered.

2. Two complementary, traditional paths for resolving the difficulties of the child are: (a) a therapist working with the child individually, fulfilling deprived needs and resolving conflicts, and (b) a therapist working with the parent toward changing the network of family relationships that support and reinforce the child's maladjustment.

3. In 2a above, the child's therapist, using traditional play therapy techniques, is presumably effective for three primary, interrelated reasons: (a) because the therapist delivers affective supplies needed by the child, and revises the child's self-concept via his respect and concern for the child; (b) because the therapist, by permissiveness and understanding, can extinguish the anxiety associated with certain feelings and thoughts, thereby relaxing defenses and allowing for the working through of conflicts and previously repressed feelings; a process which, to complete the circle, further reduces overdeveloped defensive patterns; (c) because the

therapist serves, through all his interactions with the child, to correct the distortions (or, in terms of learning theory, overgeneralizations) that the child carries with him in his perceptions of other people. These distortions were based on his experiences within the family, and had served to perpetuate and reinforce his intrapsychic and interpersonal difficulties. (Note that from the point of view presented in 3a, b, and c, the therapist's permissiveness and understanding are paramount. Detailed knowledge of intrapsychic dynamics is viewed as playing a very secondary role; rather, permissiveness, understanding, interest, and concern create the climate under which the individual can work through and resolve his problems, see Hobbs, 1962).

4. In the method proposed, the parent's intimate involvement in the specific plan to help the child will mobilize the parent's motivation to be helped and, perhaps more important, to be *of* help. It is anticipated that this will eliminate much of the resistance that is encountered where the parent is not quite sure exactly what is going on in the treatment of the child; or worse, when despite reassurances to the contrary, the parent emotionally interprets the treatment plan as meaning that he has done something wrong and that the only way to aid his child is to yield up the child to a therapist who will try to correct the damage he has done. Under these circumstances, the parent sometimes unconsciously fears that the child's therapist is a rival. Many such parents probably never begin treatment. If they do, there is the danger—of which all child therapists are aware—of a parent terminating therapy at precisely the point where progress has begun with the child, because of this rivalry. The present approach, on the other hand, may be expected to give the parents the feeling that they are not necessarily a destructive force in the child's life, but that, in fact, their help is vital in aiding the child. It is expected that this will have the effect of enhancing motivation to undertake and continue treatment.

5. With very few exceptions, parents of nonpsychotic, young, emotionally troubled children, given a very *clearly defined* role to play for a *clearly limited* time of day, and given *corrective feedback* by the therapist and by other parents attempting to learn the same thing, may be expected to learn to play that role with the child reasonably successfully.

6. A parent's very difficulties in learning to play such a role may prove to be a valuable source of material for re-examination and eventual insight. Such difficulties may enable the Filial Therapist, other parents in the group, and the particular parent himself to quickly bring to the fore the particular values he adheres to in child rearing, his conception of the good parent, his areas of inflexibility and of inability to respond to the needs of the child. It is anticipated that this will be a catalytic force for group therapy of parents that will be of significant value.

7. The fact that the parent is experimenting regularly, even for short spans of time, with a new role, could well have the effect of weakening habitual negative patterns of interaction with the child. It may do so by making it apparent that behavior which previously seemed the only possible kind of response to a given behavior on the part of the child is but one of several alternatives. (For example, recognition of the child's feeling, accompanied by firm setting of limits, as an alternative to punitive remarks and actions.) It is expected that this will facilitate the parent's ability to change negative patterns of interaction with the child.

8. By attentively observing the child with the child's needs uppermost in mind, and by the child's increased freedom in expressing himself during the sessions, the parent is in a position to gain greater understanding of the child, from which the parent can in turn gain more realistic expectations and attitudes.

9. The degree of voluntary attention and devotion to the child's needs on the part of the parent should prove to be therapeutic, even if there is a degree of failure in fulfilling the exact requirements of the prescribed role that is greater than is anticipated. This is expected by virtue of the fact that the interest and attention will at least be there; which could lead to an increased sense of security, improved self-concept, and a reduction of hostility on the part of the child.

10. Every bit of success the parent achieves in successfully filling the prescribed role should have an effect many times more powerful than that of a therapist doing the same thing. Referring back to points 3*a, b,* and *c* above: (*a*) a relatively small amount of affection, attention, interest, etc., from the parent, directly, can be expected to be more therapeutic to the child than a large amount from a therapist or parent surrogate; (*b*) assuming some success in the parent's learning of the permissive and understanding role, anxiety should be much more easily extinguished in the presence of the precise stimulus (parent) under which it was originally induced than in the presence of a stimulus which only resembles it (therapist); the child should therefore proceed to lift repression and work through conflicts more quickly; (*c*) when discriminations are established by the child to the effect that the parent himself differs in behavior according to circumstances, overgeneralizations can be corrected at the source; moreover, the whole image of the parent can be reformulated in a much more positive way, allowing the child to make positive rather than negative generalizations toward other people.

11. To a greater extent than in any other form of therapy, with the possible exception of Family Group Therapy, this technique offers the parents an opportunity to learn attitudes and interpersonal techniques which can serve them in consolidating their gains after formal therapy has ended. Further, it may extend their ability to help all their children fulfill their potentials as persons maximally, rather than simply improve negative aspects of their personalities.

PRESENT STATUS OF RESEARCH IN FILIAL THERAPY

At the Rutgers University Psychological Clinic, two Filial Therapy groups are being conducted. One has been going for 10 months and the other for 8 months. A third recently has been started at the Hunterdon Medical Center. Thus, there is not enough evidence at the present time for any quantitative report of results. However, it seems appropriate to present certain qualitative observations, even at this time.

Without evidence to the contrary, one might predict that the play sessions would be emotionally barren and devoid of socially undesirable reference to members of the family. Such a view would be based on the assumption that the parent's presence would inhibit expression of such material, or that the parent-as-therapist would subtly steer the child away from such material. One might also assume that parents could not maintain objectivity and would react negatively in the play sessions to signs of their child's hostility toward them, and be more or less ashamed to discuss such material with one another.

Our experience does not support these assumptions as being generally valid in the context of the Filial Therapy situation. On the contrary, the parent's presence seems often to be a stimulus to "threatening" family-related content, particularly aggression, rather than an inhibiting factor; such themes seem to begin at least as quickly as in ordinary play therapy—frequently in the first or second session. And the parents—trained to assume some of the important attitudes and goals of therapists—welcome the opportunity to present socially unacceptable themes enacted by their children, especially when such themes involve family members. Although attempts to ignore or minimize *implications* of such material are not uncommon, some of the messages are clearly perceived, giving the parent a fuller understanding of the depth of the child's feelings and his own unique view of the world. (One mother, for example, said she and her husband had often commented on the absence of hostility in their daughter, but lately recognized that such hostility had been there all along, when the girl called the "bop bag" she was punching "mother" and then "father.") The excerpt given below from a mother's report of home sessions is presented not as being typical, but to illustrate the above points, and to show that it is not unreasonable to attribute therapeutic potential to the play session itself, in addition to the group therapy experience per se of the parents' therapy sessions.

The boy, Fred, is 7 years old. It must be noted first that his presenting symptoms were the antithesis of overt aggression, and the mother's behavior completely opposite that of a client-centered therapist. As described in the psychological report before therapy began:

Fred complains frequently of headaches . . . is a nervous child, eats poorly, is enuretic, bites his nails . . . has nightmares . . . is a persistent throat clearer, unhappy, quiet, easily offended, and has no real friends. He is afraid of physical aggression, generally complaining about this sort of behavior from his peers. He denies competition and hostility in himself. . . . Testing and interviewing indicate a directing, assertive mother always controlling and guiding, warning and protecting.

Notes written on the interpretive interview with the mother and father at about the same time stated,

Mrs. S. seems cold and rigid . . . she said she "flares up" about psychological matters—her worst arguments with her husband come when he tries to impart some psychological insight to her about the children. She also said playing with children runs against her grain and it is

something she would like to avoid. . . . Mrs. S. literally winced at the recognition that she would have to spend one hour a week playing with her child.

Nevertheless, in response to the argument that such feelings were all the more reason that she should undertake the task, Mrs. S. agreed to do so, and is one of those who now reports marked improvement in her ability to relate to the child and in the child's behavior.

The excerpt, from a tape recording of the group session, is Mrs. S's report to the group of two consecutive play sessions at about the eighth month of therapy:

He punched the "bop bag" on the head and said, "That's Sally [his 8 year old sister] . . . I have to kill her. Look how the blood rushes out of her head." I said, "Yes, it is really messy." . . . He said, "Look at her cute belly button." He was almost imitating people who admire Sally's looks. I run into this constantly; people always admiring Sally and nobody saying "Boo" about him. . . . [In the next session] he said to me "I will call out the spiders and tell them to put you in a web; the spiders are my mean friends . . . better yet, I'll get the ghosts to hang you! They will close your eyes and shut your mouth!" I said, "You want my mouth shut; you think I talk too much." He said, "Yes, you boss too much!" After a few minutes of this, he called me "Dad"; it was a Freudian slip —he was doing that all day today, too, oddly enough. . . . This ghost business, I just realized . . . it has come up once or twice before. He does want a light in the hall when he goes to sleep. Yet he has never directly said he is afraid of ghosts. . . . Do you think his Freudian slip was important? I think it was. I think he is angry at both of us.

The tone in which this was said was obviously not hostile, but reflected simple acceptance and understanding. She then went on to question how she could best clarify the feelings underlying the fact that when Fred pretends to stab her with the play knife he always turns the knife back upon himself.

In general, it can be said that parents'

motivation is high, most play their session role remarkably well, the children are responding with significant emotional release, including dynamic material, and a number of parents have reported great improvement. Thus, our experience has encouraged us to plan for quantitative studies of the Filial method. It has also prompted the present paper, since it has been demonstrated to our satisfaction that this method, or such variations of it as others may devise, is worthy of thorough exploration—exploration not only with the aim of increasing the leverage of professional persons and the physical resources at their disposal, but as another tool for increasing knowledge about the emotional and fantasy life of children, especially as it relates to parent-child interaction.

REFERENCES

BARUCH, DOROTHY W. *New ways in discipline.* New York: McGraw-Hill, 1949. Pp. 161–175.

FREUD, S. Analysis of a phobia in a five-year-old boy. In, *Collected papers.* New York: Basic Books, 1959. Pp. 149–289.

FUCHS, NATALIE R. Play therapy at home. *Merrill-Palmer Quart.* 1957, 3, 89–95.

HOBBS, N. Sources of gain in psychotherapy. *Amer. Psychologist,* 1962, 17, 741–747.

HOBBS, N. Strategies for the development of clinical psychology. *Amer. Psychol. Ass. Div. Clin. Psychol. Newsltr.,* 1963, 16(2), 3–5.

MOUSTAKAS, C. W. *Children in play therapy.* New York: McGraw-Hill, 1953.

MOUSTAKAS, C. W. *Psychotherapy with children.* New York: Harper, 1959.

ROGERS, C. R. *Client-centered therapy.* New York: Houghton Mifflin, 1951.

Therapeutic Person-Computer Conversation[1]

KENNETH MARK COLBY
JAMES B. WATT
JOHN P. GILBERT

A commonly stated goal of artificial intelligence is to enable computers to do what people do when the latter are behaving intelligently. One thing people do, which is often considered as evidence of intelligence, is carry on conversations in natural language. While everyday conversation has many purposes, the intent of therapeutic conversation characteristic of psychotherapy is to benefit a patient suffering from mental distress. Our aim in developing a computer program which participates in therapeutic conversation is ultimately to provide a type of psychotherapy for thousands of mental hospital or psychiatric center patients for whom there are no human therapists available.

The first program of this type was written by Joseph Weizenbaum of M.I.T.[2] His primary aim was to demonstrate how natural language could be handled by his list-processing language SLIP in an on-line time-sharing system. Our aim is to reproduce the performance of a therapist as closely as possible within the limitations of person-computer communication. The "conversation" involves a person typing on a teletype connected to a PDP-1 computer in turn connected to an IBM 7090. The person is asked to talk about his problems as he might to a therapist and to respond to the replies he receives typed back by the computer on his teletype and/or appearing as a visual display on an oscilloscope. A person can type in anything he wishes using any spelling and punctuation. He signals the end of his transmission by a slash and then receives a reply in the form of a natural language statement. The person responds to this statement and a continuous back and forth dialogue ensues. Although all communications are in written form, the dialogue has many properties of spoken conversation in that it is dynamic, demands an immediate reply and seeks to evoke as well as express. Examples of conversation are shown in Figure 1.

Reprinted with permission of the authors.

[1] Supported by Grant MH 06645-01, 02, 03 from the National Institute of Mental Health, and Grant NSF-GP 948 from the National Science Foundation.

[2] We are indebted to Joseph Weizenbaum of the Massachusetts Institute of Technology for many suggestions and to Michael Levitt, Computer Sciences, Stanford University, for the PDP-1 program required.

PERSON—GREAT. NOW LET'S TALK ABOUT YOU. MACHINES BUG ME./

PROGRAM—HOW DO YOU FEEL ABOUT A COMPUTER.

PERSON—COMPUTERS ARE MACHINES AREN'T THEY./

PROGRAM—WHAT ARE YOUR FEELINGS ABOUT THIS CONVERSATION.

PERSON—ITS LOUSY./

PROGRAM—IS THAT REALLY INTERESTING TO YOU.

PERSON—YES./

PROGRAM—KEEP GOING—YOU'RE DOING FINE.

PERSON—CARS COST TOO MUCH./

PROGRAM—LET'S TRY TO GET TO THE POINT OF YOUR PROBLEMS.

PERSON—CARS ARE MY CURRENT PROBLEM./

PROGRAM—PLEASE CONTINUE.

PERSON—WHAT KIND OF CAR SHOULD I BUY./

PROGRAM—IS THAT A QUESTION.

PERSON—YES, IT'S A QUESTION,. I KNOW WHAT YOU MEAN I THINK. CARS ARE NOT A PROBLEM TO ME REALLY. IT'S MY FATHER./

PROGRAM—YOU SAY YOUR FATHER.

PERSON—MY FATHER DOESN'T WANT ME TO BUY THE CAR./

PROGRAM—WHY IS IT YOUR FATHER DOESN'T WANT YOU TO BUY THE CAR.

PERSON—HE SAID I CAN NOT AFFORD IT./

PROGRAM—WHAT ELSE DID HE SAY.

PERSON—HE SAID I NEED MORE MONEY. HE IS NOT VERY BRIGHT./

PROGRAM—MM—HMM.

PERSON—HE WORKS HARD BUT DOESN'T GET ANYWHERE./

PROGRAM—TELL ME MORE ABOUT HIM.

PERSON—MY DOCTOR SAYS I SHOULD SEE A PSYCHIATRIST./

PROGRAM—YOU SAY YOUR DOCTOR SAYS YOU SHOULD SEE A PSYCHIATRIST

PERSON—I AM VERY DEPRESSED AND I HAVE BEEN DRINKING TOO MUCH./

PROGRAM—HOW LONG HAVE YOU BEEN VERY DEPRESSED

PERSON—ABOUT A YEAR. A YEAR AGO MY WIFE DIED. AT FIRST IT DIDN'T BOTHER ME. BUT THEN IT HIT ME. I COULDN'T BELIEVE SHE WAS DEAD./

PROGRAM—YES—GO ON

PERSON—I THOUGHT I SHOULD CHANGE MY WORK. SO I DECIDED TO GO BACK TO SCHOOL AND STUDY LAW. I WENT INTO BUSINESS JUST TO MAKE MONEY. I WAS REALLY INTERESTED IN LAW./

PROGRAM—YOU WERE REALLY INTERESTED IN LAW

PERSON—YES. SO WHEN I SOLD THE HOUSE AND MOVED TO PALO ALTO THEN TROUBLE STARTED. I BECAME A REAL ALCOHOLIC./

PROGRAM—IN WHAT WAY

PERSON—I DRANK EVERY DAY HEAVILY. TWICE I GOT THE DT'S. MY DOCTOR SAID I WAS HEADING FOR SKID ROW OR SUICIDE. THAT SCARED ME./

PROGRAM—UH—HUH

PERSON—I AM DESPERATE NOW. I CAN'T WORK, I HAVE THE SHAKES, I CAN'T SLEEP AND I FEEL LIFE HAS LOST ALL ITS MEANING./

PROGRAM—WHY CAN'T YOU

PERSON—I'M EITHER TOO DRUNK OR TOO HUNGOVER. AND I HAVE LOST ALL INTEREST IN IT./

PROGRAM—WHAT MAKES YOU FEEL YOU HAVE LOST ALL INTEREST IN IT

PERSON—IN THE MORNING I CAN'T GET OUT OF BED. I JUST DON'T WANT TO FACE THE DAY./

PROGRAM—WHY DON'T YOU

PERSON—IT HAS NO FURTHER INTEREST FOR ME. WITHOUT MY WIFE IT SEEMS POINTLESS./

PROGRAM—THAT IS INTERESTING

PERSON—WHY SHOULD I FEEL THIS WAY. I WAS ALL RIGHT AFTER SHE DIED. I KNEW SHE WOULD DIE./

PROGRAM—UH—HUH

PERSON—DO YOU THINK I AM A REAL ALCOHOLIC./

PROGRAM—I DON'T KNOW YET

PERSON—I THOUGHT I WAS NOT. I THOUGHT I COULD HANDLE IT. BUT MY DOCTOR SAYS I HAVE TO FACE THE FACT I AM AN ALCOHOLIC./

PROGRAM—APPARENTLY YOU HAVE SOME DOUBTS ABOUT IT

PERSON—YES, I DO./

Figure 1.   Sample of a Person-Program Conversation.

Details of the program will be given in a future publication. We shall confine this preliminary communication to a brief description of how the program works.

Sentences typed in by a person are stored in an array and at the end of transmission they are scanned for the presence of keys. A key consists of single or multiple words. Examples are the single "I," the couplet "YOU ARE" and the triplet "I DON'T KNOW." At the time of writing there are 275 keys in the program with the highest order n-tuple being triplets. Shortly we expect to expand the number of keys to several hundred including quadruplets, quintuplets, etc. The ability of the program to recognize keys serves three functions. The first is to trigger a response. For example, the key "I AM" can trigger the response "HOW LONG HAVE YOU BEEN." A second function is to provide the capability of substituting appropriate words for those found in the input sentences. For example:

PERSON—MY MOTHER DISLIKES ME.
PROGRAM—YOUR MOTHER DISLIKES YOU.

The third function of keys is to identify important topics such as parents in contrast to trivia about the weather.

Some keys trigger a response while others do not. At present there are a total of 167 responses which will be expanded to several hundred in the near future. Each key acting as a trigger has several potential responses, one of which is selected by a "reader" designed to choose the response most appropriate to that phase of the dialogue. There are two types of responses, one being a complete entity in itself, e.g., "IN WHAT WAY," while the second uses the input sentences by splitting them up, attaching a phrase in front of the key and changing key words to yield grammatically acceptable sentences. For example:

PERSON—MY FATHER DOES NOT UNDERSTAND ME.

PROGRAM—WHAT MAKES YOU FEEL YOUR FATHER DOES NOT UNDERSTAND YOU.

If input sentences do not contain keys, they trigger a response intended to steer the person away from no-key topics or to return him to previous topics in the conversation countered important.

A running count is kept of the frequency of appearance of keys. At the end of the conversation a table is printed out giving the total frequency of all keys. This table is useful to human therapists monitoring the therapy to determine what topics in the protocol concern a person the most, what concepts might be introduced into the program for the next session and how the program might be adjusted to fit a particular person or class of persons.

Thus far we have not tried the technique on actual patients. Participants in the conversations have been ourselves, friends, co-workers, relatives and others interested in joining in the experience. We are grateful for their help. Further research and development must be carried out before applying the technique to psychiatric patients.

Our intent is not to replace the psychotherapist, but to place one in environments where none are available or to utilize available therapists more efficiently by extending their abilities to monitor and regulate the therapy of dozens of patients instead of being limited to the current one-to-one patient-therapist ratio. One of the great practical problems in the treatment of mental illness is a simple manpower lack of therapists in mental hospitals and psychiatric centers. Most of those patients who could benefit from therapeutic conversation never have the opportunity because there are thousands of patients and only a handful of therapists in large psychiatric installations. When a patient does receive individual psychotherapy in these environments, it represents an inefficient use of the short supply of therapists because of the one-to-one requirement of conventional therapy.

The manpower shortage will not be relieved by any foreseeable increase in the number of therapists trained by medicine, psychology or social work. Other sources of therapists must be found and other types of therapists must be trained. Another alternative is to provide an opportunity for therapeutic conversation through the use of time-shared computers. The power of computers in extending the skills of a therapist is that, through time-sharing, dozens and perhaps hundreds of patients an hour can be treated. While the program itself lacks a cognitive model of the patient, the treatment can be both monitored and altered by therapists using cognitive models of patients according to their clinical judgments. Our attempt is to develop this computer alternative. With increasing experience in collaboration with therapists and patients, we hope to be able to provide large numbers of patients a type of individual psychotherapy using person-computer conversation.

Experimenter-Subject Psychotherapy: A New Method of Introducing Intensive Office Treatment for Unreachable Cases

CHARLES W. SLACK

This paper constitutes a report on a pilot study which is presently investigating a new method of introducing "unreachable" cases to psychotherapy. It must be considered a preliminary report. Only 11 cases (all male) have been involved in any way with the new method of treatment and only eight of the 11 should "count." Seven of the eight who "count" are delinquents who are still in treatment with the author and two of his associates as of March 1, 1959, and one was not a delinquent but a conscientious objector whose treatment was successfully completed in about 50 hours. Of the three who "don't count," one was a nondelinquent student whose treatment never really "got underway" in 15 hours

and who stopped coming because school let out. It can't be stated whether or not treatment would have been successful if continued. The remaining two were delinquents whose treatment was interrupted at the very beginning due to circumstances beyond our control. One boy committed a robbery on the night after his first two-hour interview, was caught and sent to reform school, and the other went to work after only two interviews and couldn't come at the available hours. Both stated that they would have continued if they could. The author has just started to resume treatment in the case of the boy who was in reform school.

All therapy reported on in this paper was done by the author, although most of the findings have been cross-checked by the experience of at least one other worker. All therapy was recorded on tape. All subjects involved in the project have had at least one thing in common—a high resistance to

Reprinted from *Mental Hygiene*, 1960, 44, 238–256, with the permission of The National Association for Mental Health, Inc., and the author.
 . . . This investigation was aided by grants from the Louis and Pauline Cowan Foundation and the Aaron Norman Foundation.

even the idea of going to a psychiatrist or psychologist for any reason whatsoever and especially for help with personal problems. In the case of two delinquents, psychotherapy had at one time been a condition of probation. They never showed up at the clinic where they were supposed to go. Others had had "run-ins" with psychiatrists and psychologists in prison and in reform school and all had a negative attitude toward the professions. *All stated that they would never have gone to a psychiatrist or psychologist and all had histories of active refusal to get professional help with personal problems.*

A sample of a small number of incompleted cases seen by a single individual is not much to go on in evaluating a therapeutic technique. However, the technique is primarily a technique for *introducing* treatment in otherwise unreachable cases. Such a method can probably be as well evaluated from cases in treatment as from completed ones. At any rate, the results so far are exceedingly encouraging. Although the number of cases is small, one must remember that they would all be definitely classified as unreachable. This makes the attainment of a therapeutic relationship in even a single case a noteworthy event. Eight or nine cases in a row may very well be a significant trend indicating the effectiveness of the method.

PSYCHOTHERAPY WITH "UNREACHABLE" CASES

Office practice of intensive psychothrapy and psychoanalysis has heretofore been almost impossible with so-called "unreachable" and involuntary cases. Two major reasons for this state of affairs are, first, the high cost of treatment and second, an extensive and intensive resistance to treatment, which includes the act of going to the therapist. Consequently, large and important groups of patients have gone without study and treatment by the intensive, individual, voluntary methods of psycho-

analysis and other depth or "reconstructive" therapies. There is no literature on this type of treatment with such groups as members of religious sects whose beliefs tend to preclude psychology and psychiatry, social deviants who do not wish to be "cured," transients such as gypsies and migratory workers. Others, such as adolescents, are so difficult to work with in office psychotherapy that psychoanalysis, for example, is often contraindicated.[1]

Among adolescents there is a group which needs intensive study and treatment in a most vital way. These are the law-breaking adolescents whose car thefts and gang wars are a major social woe. If it could be demonstrated that some adaptation of traditional intensive treatment was feasible with this group, the demonstration would stimulate interest and serve as a model for the reaching of other unreachable cases.

This paper is intended to describe the use of a new approach to psychotherapy which overcomes resistance and makes possible the conducting of office-type depth psychoanalysis and other forms of intensive psychotherapy with groups such as juvenile delinquents. Although the method does not solve the economic problem, it does not substantially increase the cost of treatment. If individual treatment could prevent crime in any significant way, it would probably pay for itself.

Unfortunately, there would appear to be little hope for the success of individual psychotherapy with delinquents. There is no way in which one can view the record and feel satisfied with the present situation. Healy and Bronner (1) achieved 50% cessation with intensive treatment. However since this was a "total push" effort involving school, home, and social agencies, and included intensive treatment of parents, the figure cannot represent child-treatment alone. (In another much more

---

[1] Freud, Anna, address delivered at Clark University, 1957.

recent study involving a control group, those receiving treatment committed slightly more delinquencies than those without treatment.)[2,3]

There is no need to go deeply into the failure statistics. Prevailing opinion among informed and experienced workers in the area seems to be that individual treatment is not going to prove a primary means of decreasing delinquency. Other methods which involve *going to* the delinquent and working with him in his natural group (street-corner working[4]) and total residential treatment[5,6] seem more hopeful. The trend toward street-corner working and total milieu treatment is not, of course, merely a response to the failure of individual treatment. These methods are valuable and successful in themselves. If individual treatment could be made successful, it could be used in connection with other techniques and might become the method of choice for those individuals who, for one reason or another, fail to readjust as the group acquires new norms. Such isolated individuals do not respond to positive group pressure and the group worker may find he is spending a great deal of time working with a single destructive member in order to prevent him from blocking the group's progress.

It is doubtful whether the poor results to date are representative of the effect which psychological treatment could have if certain very large burdens were lifted from the therapeutic endeavor. Perhaps psychotherapy with delinquents has oper-

ated under such handicaps that it cannot properly be called psychotherapy—except in the very rare cases where it "takes" for reasons not applicable to other cases.

In any attempt at treatment the therapist starts at a serious disadvantage. To the delinquent he is an enemy; he represents law and order and is presumed to be trying to convert his patient to the hated cause. Few delinquents come willingly to psychotherapy. The therapist has to convince them that he is friendly and truly permissive.

In view of these difficulties it is not surprising that therapeutic attempts frequently fail.[7]

In part, the trouble lies in misconceptions about the personality and function of the psychiatrist. Instead of viewing him as a person through whom to get help, the working class adolescent sees the psychiatrist as a person to be avoided at all cost. He is afraid of him and that fear is broad and deep.

Like I say, he asked me 'what are you in for?' He was a weird looking bastard—bushy—just like a regular guy you see in the movies—bushy hair—tight, kinky, bushy hair, thick thick glasses and a mustache like a weird looking bastard, man. His eyes look like they went right through you when you'd meet his stare. (*From tape-recording of delinquent subject No. 5.*)

They give you all kinds of needles in the head and fix wires to your brain. I would never go to one of them guys. I don't mind needles or nothin', but—have one of them creeps asking me questions? Later! (*From recording of delinquent subject No. 1.*)

The fear includes both superstitious and realistic elements. The psychiatrist cannot read minds, but he can lock you up without trial. He cannot turn you into a werewolf (as was done in the film *I Was a Teenage Werewolf*), but he can analyze the things you say and come to the conclusion that

[2] McCord, W., and J. McCord, *Psychopathy and Delinquency*. New York, Grune and Stratton, 1956.

[3] Powers, E. and Helen Witmer, *An Experiment in the Prevention of Delinquency: The Cambridge-Somerville Youth Study*. New York, Columbia University Press, 1951.

[4] Austin, D. M., "Goals for Gang Workers," *Social Work*, 2(1957), 4.

[5] Redl, F. and D. Wineman, *Control from Within*. Glencoe, Ill., Free Press, 1952.

[6] Weeks, H. A., *Youthful Offenders at Highfields*. Ann Arbor, University of Michigan Press, 1958.

[7] White, R. W. *Abnormal Personality* (2nd edition). New York, Ronald Press, 1956, pp. 392-393.

there is something wrong with you. Since the psychiatrist is often imagined to be a diabolically powerful person, his inability to render change in a short time may cause severe disappointment and resulting disillusionment.

. . . I've had times in there, one of the times when I went back I just went in the bunk and I laid down on the rack. I went into the cell and I laid down on the rack and just looked down and ran up and just grabbed ahold of the bars and I just wanted to rip them apart and got all choked up—I didn't cry, one time I almost did cry—I just flipped, though. I flipped my lid one time, I threw the table right at the cell and everything. The screw come up and asked me what was the matter—I told him 'Get out of here,' like that there. So then they sent the guy [prison psychologist] in to see me, some guy who asked me a whole bunch of questions: 'You got any strange habits?' and all this stuff. So I mean, how the hell do they expect you to feel in there? You tell them . . . then after a while you say what's the use of telling them guys. . . . (*From recording of delinquent subject No. 5.*)

In some ways it seems as though the entire "doctor-patient" relationship is inadequate.

But it is quite clear that the basic structuring of the physician's role in our society *did not come about through the application of theories of the ideal situation for psychotherapy.* It was a spontaneous, unplanned development of social structure which psychiatry has been able to utilize and develop, but which originated independently of its influence.[8]

The doctor-patient relationship is, after all, a very special transaction[9] with limits and requirements which involve going and coming, eating and sleeping, tone of voice in talking and obeying of certain commands —just to name a few. It takes years of con-

ditioning, cultural processing and even interested study in popular literature before the middle class child understands what doctors can and cannot do. We cannot expect the working class delinquent to respond to a treatment which begins only after a fairly realistic understanding of this situation develops. Why should a working class individual be expected to see the point of giving up so many hours of his life for a promise of some sort of vaguely defined help?

Spiegel (2) has mentioned the difference in time orientation between middle class American and working class Italian-American and Irish-American. The working class groups put very little emphasis on future time which includes such functions as scheduling and planning. Psychotherapy, basically a middle class institution, demands a high reliability of attendance from both doctor and patient.

Furthermore, there would appear to be a fundamental indignity involved in submitting one's self to examination in very personal areas. It must be proved to be worth it. The doctor, himself, might be living proof of its worth except for the fact that the juvenile delinquent patient has difficulty in identifying with the doctor. He can never be a doctor, is ignorant of his ways, and is suspicious of his motives. The gulf heightens feelings of inferiority which are further increased by those aspects of the treatment which encourage discussion of childish things. The process feels degrading to the patient. The doctor wants the delinquent first to realize that he needs help and then to come willingly to get it. To the patient, it seems as though someone is trying to make him think he is crazy or at least incapable of getting along on his own. The delinquent is extremely sensitive about his needs for attention, love, and help. He is not likely to sacrifice his hardwon pride by giving in to coming day after day when the very act of coming represents an admission of his emotional deprivation. The act of coming may also represent

[8] Parsons, T., *The Social System*. Glencoe, Ill., Free Press, 1951, p. 462.

[9] Miller, W., "Two Concepts of Authority," *American Anthropology*, 57(1955), 271–289.

hostility toward the parents, and some delinquents are very defensive about their parents, being fearful of losing what little support they have. Coming to treatment may also stand for a submission to the will of authority. If that authority makes no believable offer of tangible support, there is little point in offering one's self up to such a schedule.

Important as these reasons are, they are probably not as potent resistances in the single person as when combined with group pressure from other gang members. The individual delinquent gains much of whatever sense of identity he has from membership in the group with which he "hangs." Therefore, he can never be expected to perform an important series of actions which will run contrary to their standards of conduct.

I couldn't show my face back at the corner. They'd say are you buggy or what? That's why I never went. Naw, naw man, that don't go . . . they can't make a person go. They think they can but they can't. Not if he doesn't want to. (*Subject No. 3.*)

All in all, the therapist is in a most difficult spot when he tries to treat the involuntary juvenile delinquent patient. His job is not made much easier by the methods of coercion and persuasion which he has at his disposal to make the delinquent come. If the delinquent patient were to come regularly and voluntarily, many of his misconceptions about the therapist, his methods and motives would be straightened out in the treatment itself. If it were socially acceptable to the family and friends and contained tangible rewards or reinforcements, then treatment might proceed without the crippling handicaps now encountered. Instead, the method of coercing—of threatening the patient with prison or reform school for not coming—may even make matters worse. It can cast a dark shadow of open defiance over an already gloomy picture. Coercion may be of some use in those cases where a strong voluntary

basis is covered by a veneer of resistance. For example, the patient can say "I'm only going because I have to" and use this as a rationalization for committing a socially disapproved act. By and large, however, it is bound to be of limited value. You cannot force a person to be free; psychotherapy and coercion are antithetical.

The therapist who is treating a patient under coercion must, of course, go to great pains to separate himself from the forcing agent by protesting that it is not he, but the abstract law, who is responsible for the pressure. The therapist must convince the patient of the truth of a really weak argument. "I do not want to make you come; that is someone else's idea. I want you to come; that is my idea. Someone else thinks that you would change and that I'm going to make you do it and that is why they make you come. They are wrong, I cannot make you change, I can only help you to do what you want to do. And yet I let them do it," etc. The therapist and patient are never more than making the best of a very bad situation. Even if the therapist succeeds in separating himself and his hour from the resentment which surrounds it, the results are likely to be unsatisfactory. If the patient seems to be responding well during the hour, this does not mean that the benefits are generalized. The hour separated from the agency of its existence seems also to be separated from other things of life. Yet there is no method in common practice other than coercion which will bring the recalcitrant and unreachable patient into the office for the first few times. The patient must come once or twice before he can be persuaded to come again.

Persuasion itself may involve voiced or implied promise of infantile gratification or at least parental-like care. There is a hostile implication and an element of deceit in such "seduction." One promises what one does not intend to deliver. Of course, every patient has, to some extent, the wrong idea of what psychotherapy is until his treatment is completed. However, the therapist should not contribute to the misunderstanding by letting the patient believe that his infantile wishes can be gratified during treatment. When the patient discovers that they are merely going to be exposed, his resentment may preclude his experiencing the benefits of the understanding which results from that exposure.

This raises a most important point about the contribution of psychotherapy to reduction of juvenile crime. No method of treatment is going to be effective in cutting down the incidence of antisocial acts unless it contains a sure way to select the cases for treatment. A very high degree of selective effectiveness is required. It is obviously impossible to treat only those for whom a particular method happens to work. We need to be able to treat those who are doing or about to do the damage. Highly reliable techniques for spotting and getting into treatment those most "inflammatory" cases is a must, if individual treatment is to be more than an expensive game of skill.

All in all, there is a real need for another way of doing things. If the emotional climate which obtains in the successful treatment of more typical neurotic patients, say, of the middle class, could be approximated, then psychotherapy could have a chance. This does not mean that the external situation should be duplicated or that the same mechanisms should be used. To the contrary, major changes in the mechanics of the process must be made in order to achieve the same emotional atmosphere with the working class individual.

The method outlined and illustrated in this paper introduces some basic alterations in the mechanics of the therapeutic process in order to insure the attainment of an emotional setting suitable for good diagnosis and treatment. The alterations also necessitate the inclusion of research aims as an integral part of the individual psychotherapeutic process. Complete recording of sessions is possible, for example, even with patients who would otherwise be much too suspicious. On-the-couch free

association has been tried and is workable (although probably not the method of choice with delinquents) and such special techniques as psychodrama and group therapy may be possible although they have not yet been tried.

The method permits high selectivity of cases to be worked with in very intensive treatment, and is therefore expected to enable individual treatment to contribute toward the reduction of juvenile crime.

THE ROLE TRANSACTION

The therapeutic techniques to be described are founded upon and embedded within a role relationship which differs in a number of respects from the traditional one. Instead of working with a transaction based upon the relationship of the physician to his patient, we work with one based upon the relationship of an experimenter to his subject. Basically, the role pattern is derived from experimental psychology rather than from medical psychiatry. It is believed that the experimenter-subject transaction which belongs to the larger class of employer-employee relationships is better suited to psychotherapy with involuntary and "unreachable" groups than is the doctor-patient relationship which belongs to the larger class of professional relationships.

Of course, there are many different experimenter-subject relationships, just as there are many medical ones. The E-S relationship used in psychotherapy with delinquents is that which permits the greatest interaction and mutual exchange of information between the parties. It is not the restricted and distant or "objective" relationship which is very useful in the later stages of scientific work where a precise experiment is attempted and where uncontrolled factors of experimenter bias are removed. At that period of psychological research the experimenter must absent himself, as an unpredictable influence, as completely from the scene as possible, and no real relationship is formed. In the very early stages of research, however, it is not uncommon for psychologists of even the strictest behavioristic bias to sit down with the subject and listen very carefully to what he says about his experiences. At this point both the experimenter and the subject are phenomenologists and introspectionists, and although what is communicated is heuristic and cannot often pass for scientific fact, it is of the utmost utility as far as discovery is concerned. Finally, after an experiment has been run, it can do no harm to go over the whole thing with the subject. There may be some benefit in it for him as well as for the experimenter. Subjects usually want to know "How well have I done?" The postexperimental inquiry is a natural time to "feed back" knowledge of results to the subject. Often this information can be of use to him, and lead to an attitude change.[10]

In E-S psychotherapy the inquiry and evaluation part of the experimental session is lengthened, elaborated, and expanded into almost unrecognizable proportions. It becomes the main body of the experiment, may last years, and provides the structure of a relationship which can be as completely psychotherapeutic as circumstances such as the skill of the experimenter-therapist will allow.

During the time that the E-S relationship holds, the experimenter pays the subject for his services as information-giver. It is essential that the material provided by the subject be of real value to the experimenter independent of its therapeutic value to the subject. Recording of sessions, frequent diagnostic testing and evaluative procedures—indeed, anything which is instrumental to research or a research orientation—is highly suggested. The subject's cooperation is enlisted in the task of "find-

ing out about himself" and at any time he wishes, the experimenter is perfectly willing to spend as much time as is necessary in going over the subject's research protocols, playing back old tapes, talking about the purposes of research (becoming aware of things about people, especially one's self, of which one was ignorant, unclear, or unconscious).

It is important to note that a loose, rather than strict, scientific attitude toward the research is taken with the subject. The subject need not have obsessive concern for matters of differing research philosophy and methodology any more than the psychoanalytic patient should be burdened with the problems of warring factions within that movement.

The relationship allows for a great deal of 'give and take' as to which party is the primary beneficiary of the process of uncovering information. During the early days it is clearly not the subject-patient. He has not asked for help nor yet received it. Later, during those rare and beautiful moments of deep insight and resulting emotional freedom, it is clearly the subject who primarily benefits. After a transition period, a final treatment stage is reached in which the overwhelming emphasis of experimenter and subject is upon helping the subject to become a happier and freer individual. If the subject can afford it and feels it is worth it, he may stop being paid himself, or pay the experimenter.

What kind of research can go on in E-S psychotherapy? Obviously not all kinds fit into the pattern of activity usually called psychotherapy. Are research and treatment really similar enough to permit the therapist to go about both at the same time?

The answer to the latter question is both yes and no. Yes, with regard to the therapist's *actions,* and no, with regard to his *role.* The role of the doctor is quite different from the role of the experimenter; however, the experimenter may talk in the same manner and behave in the same way

---

[10] Cantril, H., *The "Why" of Man's Experience.* New York, Macmillan, 1950. See, for example, chapter 5. In general the transactional theory, of which Cantril is a leading exponent, is of great help in understanding the novel role relation. The implications of transactional theory for E-S psychotherapy will be discussed in a forthcoming paper.

as the doctor except for stating or implying a contractive agreement to treat.

With regard to treatment, the experimenter's position is something like this: he *wants* to help the subject and may tell him so from the very beginning. The subject may be told that he will be allowed and even encouraged to make use of any and all information available to him and the experimenter to make his life happier in any way he sees fit. The experimenter is under no formal obligation or role-demand to help the subject who is, of course, under no formal obligation to accept help or to change.

The therapeutic pattern of the interaction restricts the kind of research, of course, and limits it to the clinical case-study. It is obviously research into the attitudes and feelings of a single individual, and such results cannot easily be generalized.

We can take advantage of the fact that every therapeutic method yet devised, from hypnosis to non-directive technique, is also a research tool; there is no restriction imposed by the change from a research-centered to a patient-centered focus or back again. The experimenter and subject can continue to do many of the same things while looking at what they do from different points of view. The fact that not all research tools are treatment methods is no problem in view of the fact that all treatment methods are potential research tools.

In general, experimenter-subject therapy places great responsibility upon the experimenter to show the value of his ways to the subject. Real psychotherapy, wherein treatment is actually helping the subject, is not considered happening unless the experimenter and the subject both feel it is. Otherwise, for example, research may be in progress. Objective criteria may be brought to bear by either the experimenter or the subject, but in the end it is the subject who decides on his own criteria, whether he is being helped or not. On the other hand, experimenter-subject therapy places *little* or *no* responsibility for the subject upon

the experimenter in the manner of a physician's responsibility for his patient. The experimenter does not promise to take care of the subject—for example, does not give him advice, nor assume charge of his behavior. Furthermore, *there is no real obligation* upon the part of the experimenter to make the subject better in any way. The experimenter helps in every way he can, but makes no promise of cure and treatment and assumes no responsibility for them. If the subject gets better, he does it by himself, with the experimenter's help. It is necessary that nothing the subject can do will "reflect" upon the experimenter. The experimenter is the helper of the subject and not his keeper. Of course, every employer has responsibilities for his employees, including those involving his safety and well-being. The experimenter has, on the other hand, the added responsibility toward his subject in that there may be hidden dangers in any experiment procedure of which the subject is unaware. All in all, the responsibilities of the experimenter to his subject, like those of the employer to his employee, amount to a guarantee *to leave the individual no worse off at the end of his employment, due to conditions of employment, than he was at the beginning.* If the employer, in this case the experimenter, can help to make the employee-subject happier, healthier and more emotionally stable during the course of the job, this is all to the good.

The question comes up of deception on the part of the doctor-experimenter. Is he just fooling the patient and pretending to be his employer, when actually he intends to give treatment, and is he therefore using the experimenter role as a front for other, ulterior activities? The answer turns out in practice to be a reasonable one. If the experimenter is unwilling actually to give up his role as a doctor, then the business of paying the patient is just a ruse or a trick to get him to come. If on the other hand the therapist drops all pretensions at being a professional, considers himself in every way to be a scientist-employer, puts aside all claims at cure, tries to experiment instead of to treat, promises to study the subject instead of to change him, takes no responsibility for his actions and makes no guarantee except to do him no harm (and to pay him his wages or other benefits or reinforcements), then there is no deception involved.

In simplest terms, the E-S relationship is nothing more than a means of acquainting a person, first-hand, with what psychotherapy really means. After this he can decide for himself whether he wants to participate in it or not, and the decision can be made without the force of the prejudice which preceded that acquaintance. The subject comes to have a more realistic view of the process of treatment and along with it an ever increasing opportunity to help himself through that process. At all times the process is completely voluntary for the subject, who can quit his job at any time he wishes.

There are, no doubt, a number of workers, especially psychologists, who have come in contact with persons needing psychotherapy when those persons volunteered as subjects in psychological experiments. Subject motivation is not well enough understood at the moment to be able to say what part the unconscious desire to get help plays in the act of volunteering for experiments. The experience of professionals who may be doing both research and counseling in a university setting would lend support to the idea that there are a number of people who would volunteer for an experiment instead of going to the counseling bureau but *for essentially the same reason.* These people are looking for the answer to the question "Is there anything in it for me?" but for various reasons do not take the direct route.

Dr. Richard Alpert, now of Harvard University, reports that, while at Stanford University, he did psychotherapy with a number of former experimental subjects. In one study he interviewed some subjects

afterward to find out why their behavior displayed a rejection of the experimenter's instructions. After eight to ten interviews he concluded that these particular subjects were characterized by special problems in dealing with authority in general. When he informed these "deviant" subjects that he had what he wanted for research purposes, over half of them expressed the desire to continue the relationship without being paid. Some even offered to pay for further discussion of their personal problems. In two cases, quite effective long-term treatment ensued.

It is important to note that these subjects were individuals whose subgroup cultural values would not have permitted initiation of therapeutic contact through the usual channels.

The present author tried the same method with a middle-class individual who was a strong-stand conscientious objector. For the last 16 sessions of this subject paid the therapist a dollar an hour rather than the other way around. The treatment was accompanied by considerable attitude change including modification of the strong antiviolence position; the subject decided not to go to federal prison for his beliefs.

E-S PSYCHOTHERAPY WITH JUVENILE DELINQUENTS

E-S psychotherapy has been tried, so far, with a small number of delinquent subjects. The discussion which follows will be restricted to problems concerned with initiating therapy only. The question is one of getting and keeping the subject in the experimental-treatment setting. All other issues including those concerned with conducting and terminating treatment will have to go undiscussed for the present, as will the major question of whether any form of psychotherapy can cut down on crime. Proper experiments have yet to be done which would include control groups who get work and pay but no treatment.

Furthermore, the method outlined should be considered as a working model and not as a finished design. It is probably quite clumsy in many respects. It is not presented in order that it be followed to the letter but in order that it may be *departed from* and altered to adapt to local conditions.

SELECTING SUBJECTS

The subjects involved in the present study were selected on the basis of two criteria. First, that they were true "hard-core" delinquents with long records going back to early years and, second, that they were truly recalcitrant individuals noted for being "impossible to work with" and with histories of active refusal to go to treatment.

Subjects for E-S psychotherapy may be selected on the basis of *any* criterion, however. It might for example, be advisable to select on the basis of gang leadership, or troublesomeness to a group worker, or delinquency potential in younger children.

THE INITIAL CONTACT

Since E-S psychotherapy is a job and not a treatment, subjects are hired and not referred. The experimenter selects his own subjects on the basis of his own criteria and does not get referrals from other agencies such as the courts, settlement houses and schools. The experimenter may need cooperation from such agencies to supply him with *information* about his subjects in order that he can have independent evidence of their meeting his qualifications, but he does not need association with existing agencies. He may or may not be a part of a "team" approach, as he sees fit. He is in a favorable position to cooperate with other agencies but he does not *need* to do so. In doing psychotherapy with delinquents it is a definite advantage not to be associated with the police.

The initial contact is made through some responsible person who knows the subject[11] and who can arrange to be at a telephone at a time when the subject is also near by. The "contact" calls the experimenter and the experimenter asks to speak to the subject. The experimenter makes a proposition to the subject such as this one:

Miss B. [name of "contact," say a social worker] says that you might like to work for us a while. Maybe you have heard that some of the teenagers are getting jobs where they work for one or two hours a day at two dollars an hour (one dollar for younger kids). Would you like to hear more about it? Well, it's really a pretty easy job and most of the kids like it a lot. You can ask Billy S. (if possible, mention the name of a respected gang member) about it if you want to. You take tests and tell us about yourself. We are interested in finding out about the kids in the neighborhood. I can't explain too much about it—you have to see for yourself. It's not too hard, really, and you don't have to do anything you don't want to. You can quit any time if you want to, and if you don't like any of the work just tell us and we'll try to fix it up. The pay is good for the hours and you get paid every day, so that you can have a couple of extra dollars this way every day. There's no withholding tax taken out, and you get paid every day. If you want to have another job at the same time we can try to fix it so the hours are OK and you can have both. There is no obligation or anything, just come over tomorrow at 12:30 and you can see what it's like. (*Edited quote from experimenter's phone conversation.*)

The subject may inquire about bringing a friend.

You may come with someone you hang with if you want to and we can sign him up on our list, but he can't work now because we are all filled up.

The subject is then given directions for finding the lab.

[11] The author is very grateful to Miss Elsa Baldwin, director of the Cambridge Neighborhood House, for her assistance in acting as "contact" for our subject-patients.

The subject cannot be expected to arrive on time the first time. Several contacts may be necessary before he even comes at all. It may even be necessary for the contacting person to come with the subject on the first visit. As soon as the subject knows exactly how to get to the lab and knows what to expect when he arrives, his attendance should settle down to a predictable, although not immediately regular, schedule.

It is helpful to think of the act of attending as a whole which can be broken down into parts. First we want to get the subject *to come to the laboratory at any ime and for any reason.* As soon as the response of coming has occurred it should be rewarded or reinforced with payment. Immediate reinforcement is very important.[12] Next we wish to get the response of coming to occur within an hour or so of the correct time. The experimenter is not fussy if the subject be late or early. Only after the subject becomes dependent upon the money or other support is there an attempt to get him to come at exactly the right time. Lastly, we wish to get him to come for the right reasons—that is not just for the money but for the feeling of relief which is a consequence of the insight and help with problems.

THE FIRST HOURS ON THE JOB

It is very important that the subject be accepted warmly in every way on his visits. The subject is likely to be very sensitive to rejection. Secretaries and personnel other than the experimenter must cooperate to make him feel at home and wanted.

In the first hour, the experimenter elaborates further on the purpose of the research and requests the subject to give it a try. In explaining the purpose of the research the experimenter lets the subject know that he intends to offer help during the process. The subject can be told that

most other subjects get more out of coming than just the money and that any time he would like help with a problem not to hesitate to bring it up.

In the initial sessions and throughout the treatment the subject is provided with comforts which one might usually associate with the home. Food such as fruit, tea and coffee, as well as cigarettes and candy, are available and the subject is urged to partake. At times the subject may be given bonuses to get himself special articles of clothing, etc., or as in one case to help him send a package to his brother in reform school. The attempt is to create a nurturant atmosphere, although the experimenter must be careful to avoid a showy display of opulence. A single item such as an orange shared with the experimenter can be a very effective ice-breaker.

Hesitant at first, the subject will gradually come to use all the facilities. He may make it a point to take cigarettes upon leaving and will use the laboratory bathroom. One subject always interrupts his hour in the middle to use our toilet.

In general, whatever is done for the subject should be done with these thoughts in mind—the subject is basically a deprived individual, no matter what his protests to the contrary. However, he is very sensitive about it. Make no show of wealth before him. Do not offer him what you cannot give (seduction) and do not force too much on him all at once, since he may not be able to take it. Never give a gift which could seem like a bribe. Never tie strings to gifts and never make a gift if it will cause pride to suffer. Pride is ego-strength and must be conserved. Eissler (3) has specified the conditions for gift-giving to delinquents. The author has found his procedures excellent for use within the framework of E-S psychotherapy. According to Eissler, the gift should be given when it is least expected. The author has found that the gift need not be money, however; an unexpected football served as turning point in the treatment of one 17-year-old. It was

---

[12] Skinner, B. F., *Science and Human Behavior.* New York, Macmillan Co., 1953.

an ideal gift since it did not imply that the experimenter wanted the subject to "grow up and get a job," and it was wanted but not "needed" by the subject. On the other hand a gift of money to another subject to get his teeth fixed was a mistake since it did not serve to deepen the relationship and resulted in the subject's being put in the conflicting position of thinking he must present dire need in order to get a "hand-out." The subject did not use the money to get his teeth fixed since he was, at the time, afraid to go to the dentist. He felt he should lie to the experimenter about the use of the funds. Furthermore, later on the subject needed money for a gambling debt and pretended a physical complaint. He felt that the experimenter was a "live one" (soft touch). As he got to like the experimenter better he could no longer dismiss his faking as hard-blooded "conning" and thus felt guilty and ashamed at having to "suck around" for money. This was, of course, a transference of a pattern established at home with the mother and was eventually dealt with satisfactorily by interpretation. Interpretation could not be given, however, until the subject had an outside job and felt the resulting self-respect.

The Eisslerian gift and other similar techniques such as giving an allowance,[13] providing clothes, and so on, all have their place in treatment of delinquents, but they are rather special ways of deepening the interpersonal relationship and great care must be taken in their use. A 50-cent allowance, for example, may be just the thing in one case but much too "childish" in another.

None of these techniques can substitute for or should be confused with the salary paid in the E-S work relationship; they are entirely independent. The subject may be paid a salary *and* given an allowance, for example; these are two very different kinds of money.

E: Look, R——, you are giving all you earn to your mother, right?

S: Not all, I keep some. I got to buy clothes, you know, and [jokingly] I got to have booze money.

E: Well, I want you to have some money to spend on yourself just the way you want to. If you want to get a quart of beer with it that's okay with me, only just don't blow your top and get sent away. This is not pay for working. It's just an allowance from me. Every week I'm going to give you an extra 50 cents, only I want you to spend it on yourself and not give it away to anybody.

S: You don't have to do that.

E: I know I don't. I have to pay you because that's part of the job. But this is a gift, an allowance from me to you. I know there are 12 kids at home and there isn't enough to go around there. I got some money from the foundation, so it won't break me. The only thing is I want you to spend it on something you really want for yourself [Jokingly] For example buy a car, okay? (*Conversation with subject No. 6.*)

The subject is paid his salary at the end of each session. To start with, he will most likely spend or give the money away during the interim and return impecunious to the next session.

During these first hours the experimenter makes litle attempt to direct the conversation to emotionally laden areas. On the other hand, he does try to get at the facts as seen by the subject. He listens to the subject's "story" about how he is put upon by the police, by parents who are "on his back," and so on. The experimenter unconditionally accepts the emotional message of the subject, although he may register disbelief at some of the subject's attempts to "con" him. For example, the subject will often tell the experimenter "whoppers" about his skills at sports, sex, and crime. The experimenter may register mild disbelief or may accept the lies as truth, but should avoid giving the subject the impression that he (the subject) is being accepted

---

[13] Kaufman, Irving, "Three Basic Sources for Pre-Delinquent Character." *The Nervous Child*, II, 1(1955), 12–15. Kaufman reported privately to the author that he used a 50¢ allowance successfully with pre-delinquents.

on the basis of the lies. The subject should feel he would be accepted in any case.

We must remember that the subject is not a patient in the ordinary sense of the word. The subject has not come for treatment and may feel very strongly that he wants to work out any problems he has on his own without the help of the experimenter. The experimenter should always passively support these trends. There is no need in E-S therapy for the subject to admit that he cannot work out his problems by himself. Later on, if he really feels he is being helped, he will probably admit that the experimenter and his ways are valuable to him, but he does not have to accept the experimenter as a therapist until he really sees the point of it.

In the meantime, research goes on. The subject is paid to take diagnostic tests of a very intensive and complete sort. Long-term thematic apperception tests, for example, are given; in these tests the subject is asked to tell many stories about a single picture. We are in no hurry. The idea is to get as complete a picture of the subject as can be obtained; at the same time we are allowing the interpersonal relationship to mature and grow warmer.

During this period, the subject's suspicions regarding the experimenter and his motives are allayed. The subject begins to be familiar with the range of the experimenters' tools—to know which ones he likes and dislikes. The experimenter becomes an anticipatable object to the subject and vice versa. The subject gets to know, for example, that the experimenter never has any contact with the police and, on the other hand, the experimenter gets to know after the first few times that if the subject doesn't show up he is probably, say, at the beach and there's no need to worry, he will come in tomorrow as usual. Another more reliable subject may miss only when in jail. Sometimes it happens that the subject will come, in the beginning, for a few hours in a row and then not show up at all. This is because (a) the habit of coming is not firmly established, and (b) the

subject thinks that if he misses a few times he has lost the job. At this point the experimenter must go out of his way to let the subject know by letter, phone and telegram that his hour is still open for him.

Generally speaking, it has not been terribly difficult to get the subjects we want to come to work with us. Now that the treatment is socially acceptable on the corner (the teenagers jokingly refer to the author as the "witch-doctor") it is even easier. Actually we could fill up with cases who apply to us (through friends who are coming), but we have been interested in proving that we can get and keep in treatment those whom *we* select and contact on the basis of our criteria.

It has largely been a matter of persistence. The rules seem to be: Do everything you can to let the subject think the door is always open. Never let him feel that there is any such thing as a final act of staying away. If possible, arrange that the subject "have a lift" for a few times. Never give up. The problem of delinquent attendance is a very different problem from middle class attendance. It is sometimes assumed that, since the delinquent won't come to ordinary doctor-patient psychotherapy, he is incapable of forming deep interpersonal relationships. This assumption is unwarranted. If a middle class patient contracts to do and pay for psychotherapy and then fails to appear time after time, it is often a sign of the severity of the problem. If the delinquent subject says he will come every day at a certain time and then does not show up, it is usually merely a sign that he is not "shaped up" into the habit yet. In the middle class neurotic, attendance failure indicates a breakdown of control mechanisms; in the working class delinquent it merely indicates what we know already—he never learned to schedule his time (2).

THE FIRST INSIGHTS

Unlike patients who come in for help in traditional doctor-patient psychotherapy, subjects in E-S psychotherapy are not asking for help with emotional problems. They may have "a degree of tension, arising from incompatible personal desires or from the conflict of social and environmental demands with individual needs,"[14] but they probably don't recognize it as such or view the experimenter as a person through whom that tension might be reduced.

However, there is one type of complaint which the subject is likely to voice immediately. The subject beefs against society, solid citizens, police and government. He gripes that the police will not "get off my back," that he has done "bum raps," and so on. Even if the subject has the ego-strength to see the fundamental nature of his hostility and dependency upon his parents at the moment, these are presented as reality problems, and his main mode of defense is acting out. Anyone who has tried the approach of attempting to get the delinquent to see the error of his thinking will understand that it is almost impossible to plunge in and prove that his troubles are caused by his own attitude. And yet, surprisingly, this is just what the subject seems to expect and even, at times, desires. The subject expects that the experimenter will try to prove him wrong, and is often afraid that such might really happen. This implies that, at some unconscious level, the subject really wants to give in and be taken over by authority—that he wishes to surrender his will to greater power. Since the subject has had little adult attention to promote identification, he suffers from a strong fear of being a "nothing person."

S: You don't like it, you know? You resent that. I mean like, I mean if they had put me away right then and there for the attempted breaking and entering I would've said, well I'd be bitter that I was away, I'd say "them bastards," you know, and—like that, but still in the back of my mind I'd know that I did it and I'd know that I'd have to serve my time and I'd know that

---

[14] Rogers, C., *Counseling and Psychotherapy*. Boston, Houghton Mifflin Co., 1942, p. 76.

they wouldn't keep me in there forever, you know, that someday I'd hit the street. But being in there for something that you didn't do, or like that insolence charge, just sticking up, sticking up for your own mother and father, a person that calls them names, you know? That's it, then you look around and say "What the—— kind of a country is this?" you know? Even the Russians probably get treated better. Start thinking of all kinds of screwy things, if you had a chance to be a Communist or something, if the guy, if they ever let you out, you know, you'd probably be one and try to get even with them and——like that there. Think of weird things. I know I did, boy, I really hated them. Like I say, I was so——mad I was killing ants and naming screws after ants, naming ants after screws and torture the bastards. Something I look at now and I laugh, I say "What the—— was wrong with me?" you know? But I mean boy, you do some . . . and listening to the guys cracking up and going crazy and you're saying "I wonder, I wonder if that can happen to me?" you know, "I wonder who's next?" or this and that, you know? Gee, you get this sense, you just get a real sense that you're lost, that no one can help you, you know? You want to just get out and talk to someone or grab your mother and hug her or your father, and say, you know, say "Make them understand," you know, or something. You're just nothing, it's like not being, not being born, not even being alive, you're just there and that's it. Your body's there and your soul ain't or something. (*Subject No. 5.*)

The terrific fear of losing his identity makes him extremely wary of any situation where his pride, his strength, his stature or definiteness is likely to suffer. The experimenter and his lab are such a situation. On the other hand, the subject can get strength from the experimenter, he can benefit from his association with him. The subject deeply needs support and protection. This need is so great that the subject must always be on guard lest he be "conned" or "sucked in" due to his immense need for attention, love and support. This makes the delinquent subject an extremely suspicious person. He does not trust the experimenter to start with. After a while, however, the reliability of the experimenter's support begins to take effect. The subject discovers that, perhaps for the first time in his life, another individual has taken a sincere interest in him and proved it in concrete ways. Just the mere fact that the experimenter can be counted on to be on time and to devote time and money to the subject—to really deliver the promised goods —starts to work some change in the attitudes and behavior of the subject. He begins to skip hours less and less frequently and only with more reasonable excuses. The hour starts to become a very important part of the subjects's day; he moves other events around in order to show up on time. Furthermore, the subject is very likely to start giving indications of the development of that phenomenon *which is perhaps the single most outstanding feature of E-S psychotherapy—an extremely powerful, almost overwhelming positive "transference" or rapport with almost no negative manifestation.*

S: Do you, do you get many people? You got many people?

E: What do you mean by that? Well, I'd be glad to tell you. I would be. Only I would like to know why you want to know.

S: Why I want to know?

E: Yeah.

S: I just wondered. I mean I just wondered if there are many people that do this. I mean do you have many people in the day?

E: Do I see lots of people during the day?

S: Yeah.

E: Yeah, well at the moment I'm not seeing too many people. Sometimes I see more.

S: I just wondered how many people you know, were taking you know——

E: Why?

S: Hm?

E: Why?

S: I, it just, it just, just dawned on me that I wondered if you did that, if many people did it.

E: If many people do this?

S: Yeah.

E: You wonder whether what you're doing is——

S: Oh no, no.

E: ——something a lot of people do?

S: I just wondered if it was, you know, a big experiment—not experiment, but whatever you want to——

E: Yeah, big one—you mean lots of people?

S: Lots of people and lots of you guys, you know, people like you, doctors like you.

E: Oh, that's other doctors.

S: Yeah.

E: Yeah, lots of them do things similar.

S: I mean right now, in this——

E: In this particular one?

S: Yeah.

E: No.

S: Just you?

E: Just me, yeah.

S: You're from down south, huh?

E: No. Why? Do I sound . . . I mean I'm south of here.

S: Yeah.

E: But not——

S: No, I thought maybe, you know when you said the other day you didn't come from around here.

E: I come from——.

S: Oh, —— . . . lives in——. I have an aunt in——.

E: You want to know about me.

S: No, I just, I thought maybe you come from the south.

E: You want to know about me, you want to know how many other people do I see—like that, huh?

S: Nosy.

E: No. You know why? I bet why. Cause I helped you. All right? I think. I think I helped you. I wanted to help you. I thought I could.

S: You'd be surprised how much you did.

E: What?

S: You'd be surprised how much you helped me.

E: Yeah? How much?

S: A lot, a damn lot. More than I could help myself.

E: You needed somebody outside yourself.

S: It worked.

E: What?

S: It's working.

E: It is?

S: Yup.

E: Well how does it make you feel if it works?

S: It's like changing my whole way of thinking and living. Things I didn't, you know, care about—like that.

E: Any bad things about it?

S: All for the best, all for the better.

E: What about the idea of giving up your own way—do you have that feeling? Sometimes they have that feeling, you know? They don't want to——

S: It's changing, it's like changing the whole, my whole way of thinking.

E: How, what else could you describe about it?

S: Well, like things I thought were right before, you know, my way of thinking. I never believed in this stuff before.

E: What about now? You do. So there's something in it anyway.

S: I thought it was all horse——

E: Yeah.

S: Surprising. I mean it—like my brother was kidding me about it—he said they give you all sorts of needles, you know. I don't mind needles or anything like that. He talked about it as though they took you apart. [Laugh] I never believed in the stuff before, psychology or anything like that—I thought it was a lot of ——. I didn't think anybody could do that stuff. They can though. Used to read about it in books and stuff. A lot of marlarkey. (*Edited quote from subject No. 3.*)

This lack of hostility is probably a natural consequence of the fact that, in reality, the experimenter is in a much more powerful position in E-S therapy than is the doctor in doctor-patient psychotherapy. Subjects are loathe to bite the hand that feeds them, and become dependent upon the therapist for some financial as well as psychological support. This finding regarding the lack of negative feelings in the E-S in-interpersonal relationship needs greater validation with other experimenters and subjects, of course. At the moment we do not have enough cases to be asbolutely certain of either the finding or its cause. But, considering the extreme resistance and even open defiance shown by delinquents in traditional treatment, even two or three cases in a row with the opposite effect are impressive.

Once the transference has taken hold and attendance is really regular, the experimenter has a way to go before "therapy" can begin. He must give insight which is truly recognizable as such by the subject and which will therefore give the subject a clear idea of how the process of psychotherapy operates. The initial insights can be used as a model for future therapeutic work and the experimenter can use even a "shallow" interpretation as a prototype. When the situation becomes structured as a therapeutic one, the insight (and the attention and support of the experimenter) become reinforcers of the act of attending in and of themselves. The subject reports that he does not come "just for the money."

E: When you talk to me, does it remind you of anything? I mean is it like anything that happened to you? What's it like?

S: In a way it brings back a lot of things that happened, court and stuff, talking to the guy about the case, or the lawyers, —— like that there. But only here, I got a better chance to talk cause I'm doing the talking and you're doing the listening, and there, they were doing the talking and I'd have to do the listening. I'd be trying to put what I, how I felt about it, or what I thought about it, if I was getting screwed, I couldn't, you know, they'd be just talking back and forth, but here it's different. You got someone to listen, you know? I mean that's what it is, really, I mean you just, you want, you got this stuff built up and you want somebody to listen, you know, you want someone's opinion. What it is, in a way, you're feeling sorry for yourself and you want someone to tell you "Well yeah, you did get a raw deal," you know, that's what you want to know. I mean that's what I'd want to know, you know? Like I'm talking, like I explained the whole case about how I got —— up in the bottle deal, you know, how I happened to be standing in town, and here's a person—well it's no skin off your ass by me telling you this, you ain't gonna send me away or nothing. So you're gonna listen and you'll have your opinion, what you thought about it, and whether I was in the wrong or whether I shouldn't have been there or should've been there, who was right, or what, you know?

E: Yeah. Well how does it make you feel, after that comes out, then what?

S: Well it makes you feel better because you get this thing off your chest, and you're different from the people in court, I mean there everyone's, everyone's wrong, you got a record —like I say, everyone's wrong, you know? And you just like for, for instance, a change hearing someone say "Well Jeez, you did get a raw deal," you know. In other words, you understand, you know? what the hell I'm trying to tell you, or what I'm talking about. . . . Um, someone that understands. Someone that you talk to and you know what the hell, or get a good idea of what's going on, you know? Like I say, you ain't the one that's gonna put me away or anything. I mean if you could . . . that's what the feeling you get, if you could sit there and talk to the judge personally and . . . I mean like he just, you're another man. You're there, he doesn't know anything about you, the only thing he knows about you is your record. He doesn't try to figure out *why* you done these things or that you were a victim of circumstance or you happened to be there—he doesn't try to figure out them things, he just goes on the evidence that he's got against you and ——— like that there—in other words you're nothing. You just stand there and you wait to get sentenced. And you want to, something's inside of you saying "If you'd only understand, let me explain," you know, "let me explain," and you can't. You can't tell him, you get that feeling that you're just penned in, you can't talk to anyone. Or no one wants to listen to you, they figure you're no good, right away you know, and you try to explain, you try to say "Well look, I'm not no criminal, real criminal, I, I . . ." you know, "give me a break," or something like that there. Or "I didn't, how am I supposed to know what another guy's thinking. If he throws a bottle out the window—I didn't do it," you know, "what've you got me in here for, why am I being tried? You don't—let me talk to you, Judge, let me explain." But they don't ever give you no chance to explain. That's it, you know? And then you get in there and say "——— it, no one's gonna listen to my side of the story." Lot of times, boy, I was on the verge of just, "F———it," I says, "they got me . . ." (*Edited quote from subject No. 5.*)

SUMMARY

A method for introducing psychotherapy to unreachable cases has been presented with special reference to juvenile delinquents. The method has the following advantages over traditional techniques:

1. Selection of cases for treatment is possible.
2. Regular attendance is achieved.
3. Treatment can be done in one's office: the patient comes to the therapist.
4. A strong positive transference occurs with no negative aspects.
5. Recording of all sessions is possible.
6. Special techniques such as the couch, free association, may be used.
7. Cooperation in diagnostic testing is assured.
8. Procedure becomes socially acceptable to gang members.
9. Therapist does not play professional role in treatment, hence therapist need not be "doctor."
10. Subject does not play patient role and hence there is no stigma of mental illness attached.
11. Treatment is intensive and supportive.
12. There is no restriction regarding approach. Orthodox psychoanalysis, for example, is no doubt possible as is non-directive counseling.
13. Coercion and seduction are not used and subject has feeling of freedom.
14. Medical-type responsibility is not implied in the role relationship.
15. Subject need not admit he needs help in order for treatment to begin.

The method uses a special kind of experimenter-subject relationship as a vehicle through which to do psychotherapy. The major change is the payment of the subject-patient by the experimenter-therapist rather than the other way around.

ACKNOWLEDGMENT

The author is very much indebted to Dr. Andras Angyal for his consultation on some of the therapy represented in this paper. Many of the theoretical notions stated and implied in this paper derive directly from conversation with him.

REFERENCES

1. HEALY, W. and A. F. BRONNER, *New Light on Delinquency and Its Treatment.* New Haven, Yale University Press, 1936.

2. SPIEGEL, J., "Some Cultural Aspects of Transference and Countertransference." Mimeographed paper, Harvard University, 1958.

3. EISSLER, K. R., "Ego-Psychological Implications of the Psychoanalytic Treatment of Delinquents," *The Psychoanalytic Study of the Child,* 5. New York, International Universities Press, 1950.

Control of the Behavior of Schizophrenic Patients by Food[1]

T. AYLLON
E. HAUGHTON

Attempts to control the behavior of schizophrenic patients have relied heavily on the use of reinforcers such as candy, cigarettes, and money (Lindsley, 1956; King, *et al.*, 1957; Hutchinson & Azrin, 1961). To improve the limited effectiveness of these reinforcers, Lindsley (1956) studied the reinforcing characteristics of a wide range of stimuli. For example, he has used such reinforcers as religious pictures, auditory feedback, and music. These reinforcers have proved to be effective for some individuals, but not appropriate for general use. In research with humans, a powerful reinforcer is greatly needed which will have general application irrespective of such variables as age, intelligence, or psychological deficits. One such reinforcer is food.

The advantages of using food as a reinforcer are self-evident. Indeed, the control of psychotic behavior may be made more effective by making food contingent upon desired behaviors. Since most experimenters are keenly aware of the possibilities of food as a reinforcer one may well wonder why it has not been used. The most probable reason is the administrative difficulties encountered in controlling food in the patient's environment.

As part of a programmatic research in the development of techniques for the control of psychotic behavior, we attempted using food as a reinforcer. However, in the planning stages of this investigation, we learned that a number of schizophrenic patients refused food and required special treatments to prevent possible starvation. Therefore, attempting to use food as a reinforcer of general application seemed unreasonable. An inquiry indicated that "eating problems" were often regarded as

Reprinted from *Journal of Experimental Analysis of Behavior,* 5 (3), 1962, 343–352, with the permission of the Society for the Experimental Analysis of Behavior and the authors. Notes 2 and 3, containing information about the author's affiliations, have been omitted.

[1] This report is based, in part, on a 2-year research project conducted at the Saskatchewan Hospital, Weyburn, Saskatchewan, Canada, and supported by a grant from the Commonwealth Fund. Grateful acknowledgement is due to H. Osmond and I. Clancey of the Saskatchewan Hospital for making the research possible at this institution. The advice and criticisms of J. Michael, I. Goldiamond, and N. Azrin are also greatly appreciated.

symptoms of the patient's "mental condition." Many of these patients exhibited delusions or made peculiar statements regarding food. For instance, some insisted the food was poisoned, others claimed God forbade them to eat, and so on. Frequently, a "dynamic" interpretation was found in the patient's file to explain his refusal to eat. Other times, "psychotic intrusions" and lack of "reality contact" or "ego identification" were also advanced as explanations. All of these interpretations seemed to point to one conclusion: eating problems can be modified only if the patient's mental state is modified first.

Refusal to eat is observed in most mental hospitals. The treatment varies from hospital to hospital, and, indeed, from ward to ward. Often, a patient requires only a personal "reminder," such as when the nurse[4] looks for the patient at mealtimes and lets him know that he had better go to the dining room to eat. Other times, the nurse takes the patient by the hand to eat. If the patient complains of the food being poisoned, the nurse may ingest a few spoonfuls and say, "Look, I'm eating the same food you have; you can see it is not poisoned." If the patient's eating behavior remains unaltered, spoonfeeding, tubefeeding, intravenous feeding, and electroshock treatments are often used. Although the patient may start eating after any or all of these treatments, many patients do so only for short periods of time. Those patients who require "constant supervision" are regarded as chronic eating problems.

Such considerations form the background for the problems concerning the schizophrenic's eating behavior. Clearly then, we had to first determine if food alone would control normal eating behavior in schizophrenic subjects, including those patients known as chronic eating problems. Only

then could we proceed to study the effects of food as a reinforcer.

THE EXPERIMENTAL WARD AND CONTROL OVER THE REINFORCEMENT

This study was conducted in a mental hospital ward, to which only authorized personnel were allowed access. The dining room was the only place where food was available, and entrance to the dining room was under full experimental control. Water was freely available at a drinking fountain on the ward. None of the patients had ground passes or jobs outside the ward.

EXPERIMENT 1: CONTROL OF NORMAL EATING BEHAVIOR OF SCHIZOPHRENIC PATIENTS BY FOOD

Subjects

The Ss were 32 female patients in a mental hospital. Seven of these patients were selected solely because they were regarded as eating problems and because they were able to walk. Before they were admitted to the experimental ward, these patients had been spoonfed, tubefed, or given electroschock therapy when they refused to eat. The remaining 25 patients were selected at random from a population of longstanding schizophrenic patients. The median for continuous hospitalization for all patients was 20 years. The median age for the group was 54 years. The diagnostic categories for the patients were: 30 schizophrenics, 1 mental defective, and 1 patient suffering from involutional depression.

No medications were given to 28 of the 32 Ss during the investigation. Phenothiazine derivatives were administered to 4 patients.

Procedure

The traditional treatments for eating problems were discontinued. Patients were no longer coaxed, reminded, led, or es-

---

[4] As used in this paper, "nurse" is a generic term, including all those who actually work on the ward (attendants, aides, and psychiatric and registered nurses).

corted to eat. They were not spoonfed, tubefed or subjected to electroshock therapy.

In order to bring eating behavior under the sole control of food, the nurses were kept away from the patients at mealtimes. In so doing, the social reinforcement in the form of attention and sympathy for refusal to eat was removed. If the patient was to eat a meal, she had to walk into the dining room without any coaxing, persuasion, or guidance from the nurses. To insure objectivity of recording, the response recorded was "entering the dining room." Eating invariably followed this response; therefore, the terms eating and entering the dining room are used interchangeably.

At mealtime, a time interval of 30 min was allowed for the patients to be admitted to the dining room. Patients were not told of the time limit. A nurse called the meal and opened the dining room; and at the end of the 30-min interval, the door was locked and no patients were allowed to enter.

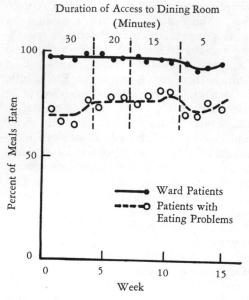

Fig. 1. The unassisted eating by mental patients. All assistance, persuasion, and spoonfeeding at mealtimes were removed. Following meal call, access to the dining room was gradually reduced from 30 min. to 20, to 15, and, finally, to 5 min.

Results

The eating problems of the schizophrenic patients were eliminated. As Fig. 1 shows, the patients with eating problems showed a low percentage of meals eaten upon the removal of all assistance for taking meals. These patients maintained a stable percentage of eating when access to the dining room was limited to 30 min. After 4 weeks, only 20 min of access to the dining room was allowed. Under this reduced access time, the patients still maintained a stable eating behavior. Even when only 15 min of access time was allowed, the patients continued eating their meals. The time limit for entering the dining room was then reduced further to 5 min. Only under this stringent requirement did the patients show a slight temporary drop in the percentage of meals eaten. The rest of the ward patients showed a similar stability in the percentage of meals eaten, and also a slight drop when the time limit for access

to meals was lowered to 5 min. The main difference between these two groups of patients lies in the overall percentage of meals eaten.

The eating behavior of two patients differed somewhat from that of the rest of the patients. One patient stopped eating for 7 days, and then was given milk, concentrated protein, and multivitamins intermittently. In time, she was maintained on a fluid diet of 1200 to 1500 calories per day, and received this at the same time other patients received medications. She was kept on this regimen for 110 days, so that she lost 18% of her body weight. Thereafter, she started going to the dining room. Another patient who suffered from obesity stopped eating for 15 days, drinking only water during this time. At the end of this fast, she had lost most of her excess weight (15% of the original weight). At this time, she resumed going to the dining room with all of the other patients.

Discussion

These findings demonstrate that the control of the eating behavior of schizophrenic patients by food alone is feasible. Even patients who fasted for long periods eventually came under the control of food.

Of course, the development of normal eating in schizophrenic patients did not occur immediately. Initially, patients engaged in a wide range of behaviors directed at seeking encouragement and physical assistance from the nurses. For example, some patients went as far as the dining room door but remained standing there, as if waiting for the nurse to ask them in. Other patients waited in a similar expectant manner for as long as 25 min before going to eat. Often, the patients informed the nurse that they had not eaten and solicited encouragement to do so. For example, one patient said to a nurse, "I haven't eaten yet today, should I go eat now?" When confronted with these behaviors, nurses made no comment, of course. Instead, they acted as if they had not noticed the patient's efforts to obtain help. Since the nurses did not force the patients to eat, several patients arrived late for the first few meals. Because none of the help-seeking behaviors commanded attention from the nurses, they gradually disappeared.

In contradiction to the psychiatric theories, warnings, and cautions of the ward and professional staff, these findings show that psychotic patients will eat and will do so without assistance. Indeed, this assistance appeared to produce whatever eating problems existed. This finding is made more significant considering that seven patients were selected because of a long history for being helped to eat. Most patients ate about 90 percent of the available meals; but the patients with eating problems ate about 70 to 80 percent. Except for the difference in the percentage of meals eaten, all patients learned to eat unassisted.

The eating behavior of two of the patients took somewhat longer to come under the control of food alone. One patient who fasted for 15 days had a 17-year history for requiring "personalized" help to eat. She had refused to eat unless the head nurse personally took her to the dining room for every meal. Since the patient's "requirement" to eat could not always be met (the head nurse had days off), she intermittently allowed others to take her to the dining room to eat. The other patient who fasted for 7 days had required some degree of persuasion and coaxing to eat for the past 3 years. Although both patients stopped going to the dining room for varying periods of time, they resumed eating without persuasion, coercion, or the use of electroshock treatment. Despite their failure to eat, both of these patients were maintained in excellent health.

The fact that these patients were not only able to eat their meals without assistance, but, in addition, learned to meet the temporal demands was a revelation to the nurses. However, when the 5-min limit was introduced, the nurses were extremely wary about the advisability of such a move. The main objection was that it was such a short time interval that only with a watch could the patient succeed in going to meals on time. Because the patients were given no information whatever about the time limit, the nurses regarded this 5-min interval of time as one that would be extremely difficult for the patients to meet.

Neither psychiatric diagnosis nor body weight were related to the development of eating problems. For example, some schizophrenic as well as mental defective patients had a history of eating difficulties. Likewise, a subject weighing over 200 pounds had a long history of refusing to eat, and so did a subject of 75 pounds. Fears concerning the imminent danger of starvation in lightweight subjects were unfounded. Both heavy and lightweight Ss eventually ate when refusal to eat was no longer followed by social reinforcement.

These results lead to two conclusions: 1) problem eaters are actually encouraged

(shaped) by their social environment to refuse food; and 2) food is a sufficient reinforcer to control normal eating behavior of
schizophrenic patients.

EXPERIMENT II: CONTROL OF THE MOTOR BEHAVIOR OF SCHIZOPHRENIC PATIENTS BY FOOD

Subjects

After we had proved that patients will
eat, we were now in a position to use food
as a reinforcer in the development of
motor responses.

In order to increase the generality of our
findings about the control of normal eating
by food, 6 patients regarded as feeding
problems were added to the previous
group. This addition made a total of 38 patients, 13 of whom were selected because
of a history of refusing food. The median
length of hospitalization for these 6 patients was 16 years; their median age was
49 years. All 6 Ss were diagnosed as
schizophrenic. One S received barbiturates,
and the other 5 Ss received no medication.

Procedure

The patients were required to drop a
penny into the slot of a collection can to
gain entrance to the dining room. In addition, access to the dining room was limited
to 5 min from the time of meal call. The
development of the coin as an S^D for entering the dining room was begun by having
a nurse distribute a penny to each of the
patients congregated outside the dining
room door at mealtime.

In anticipation of difficulty, some shaping was used in this experiment. The first
day of Experiment II, the 5-min access to
the dining room was increased to 10 min
per meal. However, after the second day,
the time interval was again reduced to, and
maintained at, 5-min. The nurses also used
verbal shaping on the first day. The nurse

told the patients, "Give this penny to the
nurse when you go to eat." When the dining room door was opened, another nurse
stopped the patients at the door with,
"Drop the penny in the collection can,
please." (The nurse pointed to the can
placed outside the dining-room door.)

Results

All patients learned the motor response
required to obtain food reinforcement. Figure 2 shows that both the original patients
and the new ones added for this experiment showed a gradual development of the
motor response. The segment of Experiment I immediately preceding Experiment
II is included here by way of comparison.
In the transition from Experiment I to Experiment II, the behavior of the original
patients shows a temporary drop followed
by a nearly complete recovery. The motor
response of the new patients reached a level
comparable with that of the original pa-

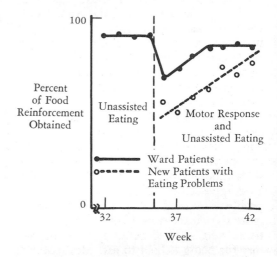

Fig. 2. When an additional requirement (motor response is added to the requirement of meeting a
time limit to obtain food reinforcement, the percentage of food reinforcement obtained initially decreases. As the response develops, the percentage of
food reinforcement obtained increases to approximately its previous level.

tients. The difference between them is less than 10%.

Discussion

Irrespective of the patient's history concerning eating, all patients learned the motor response. The acquisition of motor behavior was gradual for both the original and new patients. Initially, patients displayed behaviors which suggested the difficulties in developing the penny as a discriminative stimulus.

The first day, a few patients took the penny; others simply shrugged and went away; some refused the penny; and still others did not acknowledge the nurse's presence. During Experiment I, patients learned that failure to find the dining-room door open led to missing that meal. However, in Experiment II, patients were excluded from the dining room although the door was open. Without the penny, the patients missed the meal. As a result, the penny became the S^D for admission to the dining room.

Up to this point, little verbal interaction was observed among the patients. However, during the first 2 weeks of this experiment, the verbal interaction reached a relatively high frequency. The content of these verbal interactions was largely circumscribed to events associated with meals. For example, some patients asked how to get pennies. Others commented on their having been too late to eat. Once, a patient helped another to eat by "lending" her a penny.

The behavior of picking up a penny and dropping it in a slot was at first viewed with alarm by the nurses. Several arguments were offered to support their fears. It was suspected that patients would lose or throw away their pennies, or, worse yet, eat them. Because of their long period of hospitalization, the patients were regarded as "incapable of knowing" what the pennies were intended for. In addition, dropping a penny in a slot was considered a difficult task for patients who hallucinated so much that their symptoms would interfere with the completion of the task. Another argument was that patients would hoard pennies at the risk of starving rather than part with them. These fears were unfounded. All patients learned to execute the motor responses in the desired manner.

EXPERIMENT III: CONTROL OF THE SOCIAL BEHAVIOR OF SCHIZOPHRENIC PATIENTS BY FOOD

Subjects

Once we had proved that schizophrenics can be conditioned to execute a nonsocial motor response, we became interested in exploring the extent to which we could control social responses. The purpose of this experiment was to determine whether schizophrenics could be conditioned to cooperate with one another when the reinforcer is food.

Two patients who had been in Experiments I and II were excluded from Experiment III. The first patient was excluded because of a broken bone which required that she leave the ward; the other patient was transferred to another ward for routine tuberculosis check-up. Seven more patients with a history for being helped to eat were added for this experiment. This addition made a total of 43 patients, 20 of whom were selected because of a history of refusing food.

For the 5 years preceding admission to the experimental ward, all seven additional patients were assisted regularly to eat their meals. Five of these patients had been given a food tray on the ward at mealtime. The food tray was placed on a table in front of the patient while a nurse sat with her to supervise her eating. Because these patients had eaten under these circumstances, the nurses had not regarded them as eating problems. The other two patients had been taken by the hand to the dining room to eat, and were intermittently spoon-fed until they started to eat by themselves.

The median length of hospitalization for the seven additional patients was 21 years; their median age was 55 years. Five patients were diagnosed as schizophrenic, and two were diagnosed as mental defective. Only two of these patients received medication: one received a phenothiazine derivative; and the other, barbiturates.

Procedure

In Experiment II, all patients learned to execute the motor response that admitted them into the dining room, e.g., obtaining the penny from the nurse and dropping it into the slot. After the penny was established as the S^D for admission to the dining room, the next step was to make receipt of the penny dependent upon a cooperative response between two patients.

For the present experiment, a device was designed which functioned upon the coordinated effort of two people; thus, the term "social response." The device consisted of a table with one doorbell button at each end and a red light and buzzer in the middle. When the two buttons were pressed simultaneously, the light-buzzer came on. When only one was pressed, the light-buzzer remained off. Since the buttons were $7\frac{1}{2}$ ft. apart, one person could not press both of them at the same time.

To allow sufficient time for the proper execution of the social response, the device was available for the 5 min immediately preceding the meal call, and also during the 5-min duration of access to the dining room. Verbal shaping was used the first week to facilitate learning the response. The instructions used to shape the patients were minimal; e.g., "Push the button and see what happens," or "It takes two people to make the buzzer go." When two patients pressed the buttons, the light-buzzer came on and the nurse handed a penny to each "partner."

This social response enabled the patients to obtain the coin, but did not allow them free access to the dining room. Admission to the dining room required that the patient also insert the penny into the slot. Hence, the social response was required in addition to the motor response.

Results

The original patients, as well as the new ones added for this experiment, learned the social response necessary to obtain the coin; when they inserted the coin into the can, they had access to food reinforcement.

Figure 3 shows that after the 1-week period of response shaping, both groups

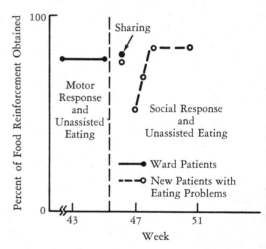

Fig. 3. When an additional requirement (social response) is added to the requirement of meeting a time limit and making a motor response, the percentage of food reinforcement obtained initially decreases. As the response develops, the percentage of food reinforcement obtained increases to approximately its previous level. Development of the social response required some shaping.

showed a gradual development of the social response. Again, in the transition from one behavioral requirement to another, an initial temporary drop in the behavior was observed. Only one patient failed to develop the social response. This patient continued paying for meals by finding pennies, and even dimes, which she exchanged for pennies. Since the S^D for entering the dining room was paying a penny, the nurse admitted her to eat.

Discussion

This experiment clearly demonstrates the feasibility of exacting co-ordinated social behavior from chronic schizophrenic patients in a hospital.

The response of the seven patients added for Experiment III followed the same general trend observed previously with eating problems. During the first few meals, the patients typically stayed away from the dining room, as if waiting for the nurse to come to get them. Next, the patients were observed gradually nearing the dining-room door, sometimes too late for the meal. By the second or third day of not eating, the patient entered the dining room after making the appropriate responses.

Verbal shaping was used only during the first week, but many patients neither acknowledged the nurse's presence nor followed the minimal instructions. Because patients were not allowed to enter the dining room without first inserting a penny, most went immediately to the table where patients were pressing the buttons. Some patients tried pressing the button in the absence of a "partner." Since nothing happened, a few banged the table, others walked away, and still others remained pressing the button until someone managed to press the opposite button. In a short time, there were two lines of patients, one behind each button.

The social responses necessary to gain access to meals produced other related responses. These were largely verbal responses directed to patients or to the nurses. Verbal behavior among patients centered about giving or receiving mutual help and information regarding the execution of the social response. The following are typical examples of this behavior. One patient approached another and asked her,

"Why don't you go to dinner? You can go to dinner by asking the nurse for a penny." The patient who had been spoken to got up and went to the nurse. On another occasion, a patient directed another to the table and instructed her, "Come on, lady, push the button; it takes two." The patient pushed the button as requested, and both obtained their penny and went to eat.

Verbal responses directed to nurses also occurred in the context of the experimentally produced social responses. For example, one patient asked the nurse, "Is this some kind of new game, what are we supposed to do?" On another occasion, a patient was pressing the button repeatedly in the absence of a partner. At this point, a patient observing this situation told the nurse, "I'll help her now if she will help me sometime," and she proceeded to press the button. Both patients obtained their pennies and hurried to the dining room.

The results of this experiment were very suprising to the staff. Because virtually all of the patients were regarded as chronic, and "out of reality contact," it seemed useless to expect them to be aware of each other. Because many patients exhibited hallucinations, *e.g.*, gesticulating and talking incessantly in the absence of a visible audience, it seemed unreasonable to the staff to expect these patients to interrupt their psychotic symptoms in time to engage in the social response demanded in this experiment. Finally, the experiment was regarded as so stressful for the patients that a "wave" of eating problems, particularly among those with a long history of such behavior, was anticipated. None of these apprehensions was supported by our results. By the deliberate, controlled scheduling of consequences, the patients learned the appropriate responses. However, unscheduled, or uncontrolled, consequences will shape the behavior of patients and staff just as effectively. Two incidents in this experiment illustrate this.

As mentioned previously, one patient was able to find the coins required for entrance to the dining room. Because inserting the coin into the slot was the sole determiner for the admittance to the dining room, she did not have to learn the social response.

Another example is that of the nurses who learned to admit the patients into the dining room upon hearing the click of the coin when it was inserted into the slot. This resulted in the occasional use of slugs, and other small metallic objects. However, this cheating by a few patients was quickly eliminated by the staff's intermittent request to see the penny before it was inserted into the slot. The moral of this story is that consequences, whether they are scheduled or not, will shape the responses of patients and staff effectively; therefore, great care must be taken not to develop a response adventitiously.

SOME NUTRITIONAL ASPECTS ASSOCIATED WITH TEMPORARY FASTING

None of the Ss in this investigation became either medically or behaviorally handicapped as a consequence of the experimental procedures.[5]

The manipulation of food as the reinforcer was not attempted until there was unequivocal evidence of the safety of carrying out this experimental procedure. By careful and continuous observations of the Ss' behavior in and out of the dining room, sudden changes in their physical condition were prevented.

Basic nursing skills such as taking temperature, pulse, and weekly weights were sufficient to screen those Ss whose bodily condition required further attention. In a few cases, blood samples and urine specimens were obtained at regular intervals for medical examination. Because of the poor eating behavior of eight patients, supplementary vitamins were administered, and only one patient required a special diet to make up for a possible vitamin deficiency. (See Experiment I.) There is a 10% difference between the meals eaten between the start and conclusion of this investigation. The reason for this slight difference is largely that some patients attended meals fewer times; but when they did, they ate as much as they could. Because the amount of food that patients ate at one meal was not controlled, a few patients could afford to eat only once a day or every 2 days. During the 12 months of this investigation, 64% of the total group missed one full day of meals. Although close to 50% of the patients had a history of refusing food, only 20% of the 45 patients missed as many as 5 days of meals. Typically, patients resumed eating after 2 to 5 days of fasting. The most significant clinical aspect of these experimental procedures is the finding that 98% of the patients will take an adequate diet without any assistance. The other 2% were easily cared for through vitamins.

These results have implications for eating problems in general. First, hospital personnel have emphasized regularity of eating, and, as a consequence, have shown the patients an unusual concern with food. Moreover, in doing so, hospital personnel have tended to demand more regularity in eating from patients than one would from normals. A great deal of unnecessary physical and social coercion has been brought to bear whenever the patient has refused food. Paradoxically, there has been little concern with keeping accurate records of the patient's eating behavior. The absence of records of eating behavior has made it difficult for hospital personnel to know what the eating characteristics are for each patient. Although most hospital personnel would not allow the patient to miss more than 1 or 2 days of meals, it is clear that

---

[5] The medical consultant for the ward was J. Horbaczewski, M.D. His close contact with the procedures on the ward insured that this investigation be carried out under strict medical supervision.

patients can maintain excellent health despite their poor eating behavior.

WEIGHT AS AN INDEX OF EATING

Patients were weighed every 4 weeks, and some, as often as once a week. The mean weight of the patients before Experiment I was 138 pounds, with a median of 128, and a range of 75 to 241 pounds. A comparison of their weights over a 6-mo period showed less than a 10% difference in weights before and after Experiment I. In the opinion of the ward's medical consultant, the small loss of weight was essentially of excess weight.

A comparison of the patients' weights over a 6-mo period before and after Experiments II and III indicated that 4 out of 45 patients lost more than 10% body weight.

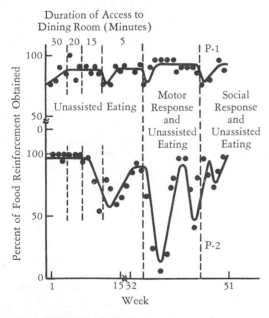

Fig. 4. Individual records of two patients. The top record (P-1) shows the typical effects of adding behavioral requirements to obtain food reinforcements. The bottom record (P-2) shows a high degree of variability seen in a few cases.

In the same period, two patients gained more than 10% body weight.

BEHAVIOR OF INDIVIDUAL PATIENTS

Figure 4, P-1, shows the typical effects of restricting access to meals by a time limit, plus the addition of motor and social responses. This record shows the characteristic drop in the level of responding each time that more complex behavior was required to obtain food reinforcement.

The patients' eating behavior also showed some variability. Because the experimental conditions were programmed for the whole group, in some instances a behavioral requirement was introduced at a time when an individual's behavior was not yet stable. (See Fig. 4, P-2.) Also, this variability occurred in part because the amount of food that patients ate at one meal was not controlled. Some patients went to eat fewer times; but when they did, they ate as much as they could, returning to the food counter several times during each meal.

DEVELOPMENT OF RESPONSE CHAINS

During Experiments II and III, the behavior of going into the dining room was only the final link in a chain of responses. The required responses included obtaining the coin, inserting it in the collection can, and entering the dining room. Sometimes, one or more links of the chain of responses was missing. For example, some patients obtained the coin from the nurse but either lost or misplaced it. A few times, patients exhibited the necessary chain of responses, but stopped short of entering the dining room. For example, upon being stopped for not inserting a penny in the collection can, one patient said, "Why do I have to do that, I'm the Queen." But because she was not allowed to enter the dining room, she finally inserted the penny. Never again did she make reference to being a Queen as an attempt to gain access. Another patient insisted, "I can't put the penny in." Consequently, she missed that meal; but at the next meal, she could and did "put the penny in."

Such omissions and distortions of the desired chain were drastically reduced during the experiment. Admission to the dining room was dependent solely upon the appropriate response. In time, inappropriate responses to the situation became rare.

DISCUSSION

Leaving patients alone at mealtimes served to withdraw the social reinforcement provided by the nurses for refusal to eat. This procedure was suggested by a previous investigation (Ayllon, 1960). In that study, a patient who had been helped to eat for 16 years was left unaided at mealtimes. After refusing food for 3 days, the patient started to eat on her own, without being persuaded, coaxed, or induced to eat, by any of the traditional methods. The major findings of that study were confirmed here.

During the first few meals, the patients typically stayed away from the dining room, as if waiting for the nurse to come to get them. Next, the patients were observed gradually nearing the dining-room door, sometimes too late for the meal. By the second or third day of not eating, the patient engaged in the appropriate responses preliminary to entering the dining room and eating unassisted. One conclusion is inescapable: refusal to eat, and verbal behaviors associated with it, may be conditioned through social reinforcement. Indeed, a wide range of behavioral responses may be made to increase or decrease through social reinforcement in such forms as attention or sympathy (Ayllon & Michael, 1959).

The eating behavior of schizophrenics can be controlled solely by food. This generalization also applies to extreme cases, as in-

dicated by the two patients who stopped eating for 1 week and as long as 2 weeks. Under normal hospital conditions, these patients would have been tubefed or given electroshock therapy after 2 to 3 days of refusing food. After 1 year of this work, all of the patients, including those who had a history for being helped to eat, were taking as good or better a diet than they had before this study. What is most significant is that they soon learned to do so without any assistance whatever.

These findings indicate that food is indeed a powerful reinforcer which may be used experimentally and therapeutically to develop or strengthen a wide range of normal behaviors. Contrary to the fears manifested by various psychiatric personnel, the patients were able to learn all the responses required in order for them to eat.

Medication, severity of illness, length of hospitalization, and age were not significantly related to the acquisition or maintenance of the behaviors studied. Likewise, a subnormal IQ presented no great problems in establishing the desired performance. The three mental defective patients in the group learned the behavioral responses quickly, and their performances were characteristically stable compared with those of schizophrenic patients.

A significant finding concerned the patients' verbal behavior. When patients encountered difficulties in securing their daily food, their verbal behavior increased notably. There was seldom any verbal interaction at mealtime when the patients were merely required to meet a time limit for access to the dining room. However, a large number of remarks and comments among patients occurred when access to meals was made contingent upon the motor and social responses. Two aspects of this verbal behavior are noteworthy. First, these verbalizations were usually appropriate to the situation. Second, these verbalizations took place only under stressful conditions. Typically, the patients' verbal behavior occurred during the first 2 weeks of each experimental change. Subsequently, very little verbal interaction was observed. This particular aspect of verbal behavior was also noticed by Azrin and Lindsley (1956) in an early experiment on cooperation in normal children.

REFERENCES

AYLLON, T., and MICHAEL, J. The psychiatric nurse as a behavioral engineer. *J. exp. Anal. Behav.*, 1959, 2, 323–334.

AYLLON, T. Some behavioral problems associated with eating in chronic schizophrenic patients. Paper read at American Psychological Ass., Chicago, September, 1960.

AZRIN, N. H., and LINDSLEY, O. R. The reinforcement of co-operation between children. *J. Abnorm. and Soc. Psychol.*, 1956, 52, 100–102.

HUTCHINSON, R. R., and AZRIN, N. H. Conditioning of mental-hospital patients to fixed-ratio schedules of reinforcement. *J. exp. Anal. Behav.*, 1961, 4, 87–95.

KING, G. F., MERRELL, D. W., LOVINGER, E., and DENNY, M. R. Operant motor behavior in acute schizophrenics. *J. Person.*, 1957, 25, 317–326.

LINDSLEY, O. R. Operant conditioning methods applied to research in chronic schizophrenics. *Psychiat. res. Repts.*, 1956, 5, 118–139, 147–153.

Problems in Living,
Psychotherapy Process Research,
and an Autoanalytic Method[1]

BERNARD G. GUERNEY, Jr.
GARY E. STOLLAK

Reviewing recent literature in the realm of psychotherapy research, Colby (1964) concluded that "chaos prevails." He cited Chassan's (1962, p. 615) observation that the conventional approach to such research has thus far failed as "a direct consequence of the relatively small number of patients available even in 'large' clinical studies, together with the general lack of homogeneity to be found in even quiet small groups of patients."

A second, related, consideration that has inhibited the progress of research in psychotherapy has been the ethical dilemma presented by the need to serve clients with problems on the one hand, and the demands of scientific investigation—such as "no treatment" controls—on the other.

Reprinted from *The Journal of Consulting Psychology*, 1965, 29, 581–586 with the permission of the American Psychological Association and the authors.

[1] Preparation of this paper was facilitated by grants from the University Research Council of Rutgers, The State University, and the Indiana University Foundation.

This conflict has also inhibited exploration of new techniques for fear that they might not work and therefore be unfair to those seeking help.

A third constraining factor, and the last with which this paper will deal, stems from the fact that psychotherapy researchers have largely ignored the study of some of the fundamental elements or components of psychotherapy. This is due in part to the reasons mentioned above, partly because to do so calls into question cherished beliefs, and partly because ways of isolating such variables for systematic study have not been easy to conceptualize. We are referring to the general failure of researchers to come to grips with such questions as the following: What factors exist in the therapy situation other than those derived from specific personality theories that might be influencing the client's progress? For example, what is the effect of the explicit or implicit *suggestion* made to the client that a particular procedure will help him become a more adequate person? What is the salutary effect, if any, of merely having a person who will regularly listen to one talk about his problems, even if the listener is not a trained psychotherapist, or even if he says nothing at all? To generalize: which of the variables present in traditional psychotherapy are really inert and which are really active, and in what ways? What variables must be considered in setting up adequate control groups for psychotherapy studies? As Colby (1964) points out and Hobbs (1962) exemplifies, the old beliefs are being seriously called into question. Now that we have looked at Medusa's face, can anything be done, experimentally, to unsnarl the snakes? Maybe the snakes even can be milked, and the product put to beneficial use.

In the realm of personality theory, the concept of "normality" has long been a controversial one (e.g., Shoben, 1957). Recently, Szasz (1960, 1961) proposed substitution of "problems in living" as a more accurate and useful term than "mental illness." Adams (1964) similarly proposes that "both adaptive (normal) and maladaptive (abnormal) can be meaningfully categorized within one systematic frame of reference."

It appears to the present writers that this controversy and these new proposals are highly relevant to the problems faced by researchers in psychotherapy, and that much personality, and particularly psychotherapy-process researchers, by unthinkingly accepting a "mental illness" analogue too often have limited the power of their investigations unnecessarily, and have artificially divorced their research from general psychology. Not allowing distinctions between "normal" and "neurotic" to confine one's research activities with respect to "psychotherapy,"[2] should do much to overcome the above-mentioned difficulties and have a generally heuristic effect. A rationale for psychotherapy research along these lines will therefore be presented along with

[2] To be consistent with the view presented here, a new term conveying the meaning of "psychoassistance" would probably be more appropriate.

a description of a methodology that is consonant with it. The problems in living orientation does not directly lead to the last two points in the rationale. Rather, these points simply have to do with the application of experimental methodology to psychotherapy research. But acceptance of the first six points in the rationale allows one to conceive of actually putting such methodology into practice, and therefore makes the last two less painful to contemplate and commit oneself to.

RATIONALE

1. All individuals have intra- and interpersonal problems. That is, all of us, each in our own eyes, have problems of feeling too much or too little in certain ways; working too hard or not hard enough; pleasing others too much or too little; being over-controlled or under-controlled, etc.

2. Such problems are dynamic and changing rather than structurally fixed and static. This is not to say that there are not repetitions and, in fact, often predictable patterns, to these problems. It is to say that new circumstances give rise to new problems and different forms of old problems. All of us are continually engaged in the process of solving intra- and interpersonal problems.

3. There is no hard and fast line separating "neurotic" from "normal." Rather, there are patterns of more or less success in solving these problems. In fact, whether due to semantics, to the incomplete state of the diagnostic art, or some absolute reality, it is not very rare for a person to move from one classification to another in his own eyes and the eyes of those around him, and probably—had they been studying him in good times as well as bad—the eyes of professional diagnosticians.

4. The person usually regarded as "neurotic" may be viewed as someone who habitually solves a great many such problems somewhat less well than will the majority of his peers; or he may solve only

a few very important problems at a particular point in time far less well than the majority of his contemporaries. Such people may be the ones who have the most to gain from psychotherapeutic procedures. But all people probably can benefit somewhat from some type of psychotherapeutic assistance at any time.

5. An understanding of the therapeutic process might be advanced significantly by studying the spontaneous, unaided efforts of people to solve life problems and to understand themselves better under a task orientation similar to psychotherapy, with particular emphasis on disruption and difficulties connected with such efforts.

6. Traditional psychotherapy may be viewed as one particular set of conditions under which life problem solving processes and the changing of related learning sets may be facilitated—or, as is scientifically equally relevant—retarded; e.g., hypnotic suggestion, alcohol, and varying types of conditioning, group situations, or interpersonal climates.

7. The traditional experimental paradigm is an appropriate one for studying conditions that facilitate life problem solution. This necessitates the careful delineation and specification of the conditions—in broad or narrow terms, depending upon the nature of the problem—to the extent that the experimenter can demonstrate that he has in fact created the conditions specified, and so that others can replicate what he has done. Particularly desirable would be experiments that would study how such conditions, including various therapeutic techniques interact (a) with each other, (b) with the personal characteristics of those administering them when they are interpersonal in nature, and (c) the personality characteristics and problem-solving abilities and disabilities of the client.

8. Our ability to pursue genuine experimentation and to analyze the effects of various therapeutic procedures will be severely handicapped unless the more "active" ingredients of psychotherapy are compared to the *presumably* "inert" or less powerful variables; or the latter are at least held constant while the former are manipulated. This means investigations that consider the effects of variables such as the following: (a) mere instructions to subjects to think and talk about their problems, feelings, etc.; (b) the time and place allotted for this purpose; (c) the explicit or implicit suggestion to the subject, or his own expectation, that the procedures performed will be beneficial; (d) financial arrangements; (e) the knowledge that another person is or is not listening to the subject's efforts; (f) the physical presence or absence of a listener.

DISCUSSION OF RATIONALE

What implications does this way of looking at things have for the psychotherapy researcher? It means that in posing questions as to how a certain variable—e.g., reflection of feeling, interpretation, or, more globally, say, "client-centered therapy"—affects individuals, one does not assume that the variable must be investigated only with a population seeking professional help for critical personal problems. Rather, anyone interested in increased adequacy or better self-understanding, or even in volunteering for a study in "free association" or "interpersonal relationships," can be regarded as legitimate subjects. Such a view has led, for example, to the increasing use of therapy analogues and quasi-therapy laboratory studies with normal subjects. (See, for example, Kanfer & Marston, 1964, and Waskow, 1962).

Certainly, there may be differences between the reactions of such groups and a group of people disturbed enough by their problems to face the stigma and the cost of getting professional help. Moreover, one might also expect differences among the groups selected according to each of the various motivations mentioned in the example given above. It seems clear, though, that any group of subjects and/or clients exposed to therapeutic or quasi-therapeutic procedures will contain individuals differing with respect to the degree of problem and/or the level and kind of motivation they bring to the situation. In any case, the researcher must define his population according to as many relevant variables as he can, and limit his conclusions to the population represented. If not right from the start, then eventually, such subject-variables themselves must be studied systematically in relation to the independent variables in a much more precise way than is represented by the distinction between "sought help" and "volunteer." In establishing the meaning of such parameters, one will doubtless want to use subjects with a wide rather than a narrow range on the variable in question, and a wider range will be available if we do not limit ourselves to "patients."

What are the heuristic advantages of rejecting the reasoning that in psychotherapy we are dealing with "ill" persons that require treatment procedures appropriate only to that "illness," and instead regarding these techniques as pertinent to all people with problems in living and, therefore, to a greater or lesser extent, to all people? Most importantly, on a theoretical level, it seems likely to stimulate the reformulation of our psychotherapy research questions in terms more consonant with general psychology.

On an operational level, the first advantage is that it opens the way toward the use of large samples to be studied or for the selection for study of more homogeneous groups from larger parent populations. This allows for more powerful experiments, and thus more adequate tests of hypotheses. It also allows the use of more complex experimental designs permitting the study of variables not just in terms of their independent effects, but also in terms of their interaction with other simultaneously studied variables. This is of great importance in studying something as complex and multi-determined as the process of changing emotional and behavioral patterns.

Perhaps even more important than numbers alone, however, is the greater willingness to make use of experimental procedures. It may be that findings from studies with subjects not requesting help will often require confirmation under conditions with those individuals seeking help. But this seems to be a final stage appropriate to the time when we know much more about how different experimental methods affect various types of people and bring about emotional and behavioral modifications.

Such a rationale also is likely to be heuristic by challenging one to formulate questions appropriate to people in general and not just in conformity to standard notions about the clients with which we have been accustomed to working in the past. It prompted the writers, for example, to ask: If individuals are constantly engaged in solving a stream of life problems, how do they go about doing it? More specifically, and closer to the psychotherapy situation, how do individuals explore their internal feelings and their overt actions in areas of concern to them when they are asked to do so and left to their own devices? Does an individual have a consistent style or pattern under such circumstances? Do some individuals, for example, concern themselves with their socially or personally unacceptable attributes, while others do not? Do some characteristically pay more attention to their feelings? Do some tend to orient themselves to the past, while others orient themselves to the future? Do some individuals seem to be very much engaged in defending themselves from an imaginary critic, while others seem less concerned with potential criticism? Do some find themselves repeatedly blocked, while others are able to speak freely? and so forth.

It seems likely that individuals will show some reasonably stable difference along such dimensions that could be studied systematically. Developmental patterns and sex differences might be investigated. And verbal behavior during problem solving could, of course, be studied in relation to traditional personality measures or psychiatric categories. Such studies conceivably could lead to additional dimensions for ordering observations about people. These dimensions might be more useful to the therapy researcher than standard paper and pencil tests, since they would be based on a process and task more similar to the psychotherapeutic one.

The area that might be of greatest interest to the psychotherapy researcher is that concerned with the difficulties that arise in life problem solution or in self-exploration, as might be demonstrated by hesitations, incomplete thoughts, or other criteria related to the problems of the particular individual, to conventional tests, or even to specific problems introduced by the researcher. Probably one of the most important of such difficulties would be akin to repression. In terms of a life problem solution orientation, this perhaps would be behaviorally demonstrated by an inability to hold the relevant questions, or the relevant feelings, or the relevant impulses necessary to the solution of the problem long enough in mind; a tendency to leave-the-field and concern oneself with nonpersonal or irrelevant material. In his research, the experimenter probably would be particularly interested in those conditions or techniques that brought relevant responses or content into the phenomenological field and held them there.

Briefly, we have asked acceptance for the following view: that the "emotionally disturbed" should be placed on the same specified *continua* of ability and motivation to solve life problems as others, rather than viewed as members of a specifically crippled (but otherwise poorly defined) class; that all individuals are confronted with a constant *stream* of problems that are solved either more or less adequately at any point in time; that psychotherapy be viewed as one of many conceivable conditions affecting the individual's style of approach and

solution of such problems. If these be valid ways of looking at neurosis and psychotherapy, then new possibilities arise for systematic and well-controlled studies of processes affecting the exploration or resolution of emotional and behavioral problems that do not present the practical, moral, and ethical dilemmas usually encountered in psychotherapy process research.

THE AUTOANALYTIC METHOD

Elements of what we here call the "autoanalytic" method have been used for relatively short duration, or for special purposes, by a number of investigators (Colby, 1961; DiMascio & Brooks, 1961; Lowinger & Huston, 1955; Martin, Lundy, & Lewin, 1960; Stollak & Guerney, 1964; Weintraub & Aronson, 1962). The authors are currently conducting work with the technique over a long time span with a population of college men and women, unselected except by virtue of their being unpaid volunteers. As it has been conducted in practice, the subject sits in a chaise lounge, alone in a relatively bare room, and talks into a tape recorder for half an hour, twice a week, for many months. In essence, the method consists of simply instructing the client to think aloud about what comes to his mind, particularly his feelings and particularly those things having to do with the emotional stresses and strains arising in his day-to-day life or his past, his interpersonal relationships, and areas of satisfaction and dissatisfaction with himself, or with the goal of coming to understand himself better and possibly changing himself for the better in accord with his own desires. The subject is left entirely on his own. In some ways, this resembles free association. The need for a different term arises first from the fact that the instructions do give the subject a frame of reference and goal orientation. Secondly, this task is accepted by the subject as something that he does at length and over a long period of time. This latter condition is met in orthodox psychoanalysis, but the difference there is that the therapist usually is present and the subject very definitely expects some eventual feedback. Here, he is talking to and for himself alone.

In a study now under way, Ss were checked in and out at appointed times by the experimenter, and a phone call of inquiry was made if they did not attend, and missed sessions were made up. Otherwise, the subjects had no special interaction with the researcher. Under these conditions, 17 of 18 males and all of 18 females completed 20 sessions. (At that time they were told that the experiment was over, but they could continue coming if they wished. About a third chose to continue!)

Many types of variables, from the physiological to various kinds of classification of form and content, should be helpful in illuminating the process of life problem solution. Such dependent variables will be related to each other and could also be related to various traditional personality dimensions, feelings, and attitudes, including any pre-post change after a long period. For example, the authors are currently coding the tapes of the above Ss for variables such as Openness, Guardedness, Discusses Self (Positively, Negatively, or Neutrally), Discusses Others (Positively, Negatively, or Neutrally), Blocking, Positive Feelings, Negative Feelings, Insight, etc. (The coding is done directly from the tapes, using 15 second intervals for standardization purposes.) Such variables will be related to certain preresearch personality dimensions, replies to questionnaires about feelings associated with particular sessions, and to change across many sessions. As can be seen from the above list, certain of the variables easily can be preconceived as having a facilitating effect on life problem solutions and adjustment. But a far-off goal of such research would be to determine whether such relationships actually can be demonstrated.

The autoanalytic situation as a talking situation is conceived as having certain ad-

vantages, compared to doing the same kind of thing via written media—mainly greater spontaneity, productivity per unit of subject time, and appropriateness over a wider range of population. But the greatest advantage of the technique is apparent when one considers its use as a control, or a base line condition for studying variables that affect life problem solution processes; i.e., psychotherapy variables. The method easily permits variation of structuring, suggestions, presession experiences and feedback, and studying their differential effects. The Ss' experience within the sessions similarly could be systematically varied by subjecting them, for example, to various tpes of in-session feedback, such as their relistening to their own productions or the comments of others on their previous productions. Of particular interest is the capacity of the technique to control and provide a base rate comparison for: (a) the presence of a "therapist" as a simple listener; (b) the effects of suggestion (i.e., the implication that going through such a process will prove beneficial); (c) type of interaction (e.g., talking in the presence of a liked or disliked peer, male or female therapist); and (d) specific kinds of control feedback and stimuli (e.g., praise, clarification of feeling, interpretation, directive leads).

Using subjects who have not come for help, but who attempt what are traditionally psychotherapeutic tasks, has been very helpful in permitting the writers to deal with some otherwise "unworkable" problems of manipulation and control necessary to experimental investigation of variables of interest to investigators of the psychotherapeutic process.

REFERENCES

ADAMS, H. B. "Mental illness" or interpersonal behavior? Amer. Psychologist, 1964, 19, No. 3, 191–197.

CHASSAN, J. B. Probability process in psychoanalytic psychiatry. In J. Scher (Ed.) Theories of the mind. Glencoe, Ill.: Free Press, 1962. Pp. 598–618.

COLBY, K. M. On the greater amplifying power of causal-correlative over interrogative inputs on free association in an experimental psychoanalytic situation. *J. nerv. ment. Dis.,* 1961, 133, No. 3, 233–239.

COLBY, K. M. Psychotherapeutic processes. *Annu. Rev. Psychol.,* 1964, 15, 347–370.

DiMASCIO, A., & BROOKS, G. W. Free association to a fantasied psychotherapist, a case report. *Arch. gen. Psychiat.,* 1961, 4, 513–516.

HOBBS, N. Sources of gain in psychotherapy. *Amer. Psychologist,* 1962, 17, 741–747.

KANFER, F. H., & MARSTON, A. R. Characteristics of interaction behavior in a psychotherapy analogue. *J. consult. Psychol.,* 1964, 28, 456–467.

LOWINGER, P., & HUSTON, P. E. Transference and the physical presence of the physician. *J. nerv. ment. Dis.,* 1955, 121, 250–256.

MARTIN, B., LUNDY, R. M., & LEWIN, M. H. Verbal and GSR responses in experimental interviews as a function of three degrees of "therapist" communication. *J. abnorm. soc. Psychol.,* 1960, 60, No. 2, 234–240.

SHOBEN, JR., E. J. Toward a concept of the normal personality. *Amer. Psychologist,* 1957, 12, 183–189.

STOLLAK, G. E. & GUERNEY, B. Exploration of personal problems by juvenile delinquents under conditions of minimal reinforcement. *J. clin. Psychol.,* 1964, 29, 279–283.

SZASZ, T. S. The myth of mental illness. *Amer. Psychologist,* 1960, 15, 113–118.

SZASZ, T. S. The uses of naming and the origin of the myth of mental illness. *Amer. Psychologist,* 1961, 16, No. 2, 59–65.

WASKOW, I. Reinforcement in a therapy-like situation through selective responding to feelings or content. *J. consult. Psychol.,* 1962, 26, 11–19.

WEINTRAUB, W. & ARONSON, H. The application of verbal behavior analysis to the study of psychological defense mechanisms: methodology and preliminary report. *J. nerv. ment. Dis.,* 1962, 134, No. 2, 169–181.

Computer Analysis of Content in Psychotherapy[1]

NORMAN I. HARWAY
HOWARD P. IKER

We are exploring a method for analyzing the words used during treatment interviews to see whether the data of psychotherapy can themselves generate a yardstick of "meaning" which is consistent across the changes in psychotherapy and against which various words and concepts can be displayed in order to determine changes. The association in time of the different concepts expressed in patients' speech is one of the guides used by psychotherapists to determine the psychological meaning of patients' references. To the extent that this represents one valid dimension of meaning, it should be possible empirically to examine such associations, to see which concepts, persons, objects, affects, and actions occur together within a reasonable time period with minimal *a priori* assumptions. Assuming that the individual word, perhaps the most easily defined unit of speech, represents a psychologically useful segment of analysis, then temporal associations among words can be readily investigated and the underlying structure, if such exists, displayed.

A central issue then is the extent to which the associations among words during the interview carry information as to the content of the interview. If the proposed procedures prove feasible, we should be able to examine the associative structure of the patient's and therapist's speech at different points in time and also to compare the structure for the patient with that for the therapist. Our purpose, in this report, is to describe briefly our approach to this problem, our methods and the possible advantages of computer analyses in examining psychotherapy. This is a preliminary report and we are not yet in a position to report on specific applications.

Almost all existing content analysis systems for interview data depend on *a priori* classifications. The usual procedure is to develop a system or schema which one asks a number of judges to apply in evaluating the raw therapeutic interview presented to them. This has been the main approach, at varying levels of complexity, of the majority of process studies of psychotherapy. The judges attempt to classify or rate seg-

Reprinted from *Psychological Reports*, 1964, 14, 720–722, with the permission of Southern Universities Press and the authors.

[1] Supported, in part, by a grant from General Research, Support Grant No. 1, GS 103, National Institutes of Health.

ments of the interview in terms of such variables, for example, as "discomfort-relief (Dollard & Mowrer, 1947), "disapproval and criticism" (Snyder, 1953), "sex, erotic feelings or motives" (Dollard & Auld, 1959). Such classifications require judges or raters and are time consuming and tedious. The underlying counting and integrating take place in an unspecified way inside the judge. As the advent of sound-recording methods permitted detailed, complex, and leisurely study of the raw verbal production in the psychotherapeutic interview, so developments in computer capabilities allow systematic and thorough investigations at simple levels of content analysis, e.g., frequency of usage and frequency of association of words.

A judge, as a measuring instrument, has characteristics which are as complex as the interview data under investigation. He imposes his own standards of judgment on the data, operates at low speed (restricting the amount of data he can handle), and his reliability must be established anew with each classification system or shift in sampling. In comparison, a computer is an instrument with specified, predetermined, communicable, and replicable characteristics capable of operating at high speeds and thus allowing extensive sampling.

To examine the associative structure of the interviews, a factor-analytic approach is being utilized. The basic idea is to intercorrelate the frequency of occurrence of each word spoken within a prespecified time segment with every other word spoken during that time segment across all segments comprising the total verbal output. In order to examine such associations two criteria have to be satisfied. One is theoretical and the other is practical. The theoretical criterion is the necessity for maximizing the variance of the frequency of occurrence for each word across all time units in order to allow a reasonably precise correlational analysis. The second criterion limits us to a maximum of 130 variables (in our instance, words) as a function of internal

storage capacity of the University's IBM 7074. The need to satisfy both of these criteria has resulted in the WORDS system.

We have punched, on IBM cards, transcribed psychoanalytic interviews divided into 1-min. segments. As some 900 or more different words may occur in a single interview, it was necessary to devise methods for reducing to the 130-word computer input. A series of computer programs condense, edit, and combine different forms of the same word. These procedures help to satisfy the criteria indicated in the preceding paragraph without discarding the majority of words spoken in the interview. Additional programs order, sort, count, collate and list all words with their exact frequencies, including zero, for all segments. The total programming system (the WORDS system) is composed of 11 different programs under the control of a monitor. At present, we are analyzing successive 1-min. segments across 5 to 10 consecutive interviews. Time units of different lengths, in multiples of 1 min., can be easily obtained by altering control parameters within the system. The frequency of occurrence of each different word within each segment is correlated with every other word across all the segments. The resulting 130 by 130 matrix is then factor-analyzed.

In the initial development of the WORDS system, the 80th and 222nd psychoanalytic interviews were chosen at random from a total population of over 300 such interviews for use as pilot data for testing and developing the system. As a result, both interviews have been completely worked by the system. Although intended only for testing purposes, the results of this analysis were themselves of interest. In reduction to 130 different words, we were concerned with possible loss of meaning. To assess this possibility, one of the WORDS programs allows a "rewriting" of the interview with the words remaining. We subjectively have been impressed with the extent to which the original content of these two interviews is adequately represented by just 130 words; indeed, some of the "meaning" (affect and dynamics) seems even clearer than in the original statement. Equally important, the correlation matrix deriving from the interviews also made a great deal of clinical sense when compared with the content of these therapeutic hours. Finally, the factor analysis and rotation of this matrix yielded a set of factors the large majority of which made excellent sense as major *themes* within the interviews under analysis. Because of the widely disparate times at which the interviews were chosen and because of the fact that certain of our rules and procedures have changed, we cannot logically present these various analyses in any meaningful way. Nevertheless, the fact that the method operated as well as it did with the kind of data, inadequate by our present standards, with which it was presented has suggested enough merit in the approach for us to continue it as a major programmatic research effort.

REFERENCES

DOLLARD, J., & AULD, F., JR. *Scoring human motives: a manual.* New Haven: Yale Univer. Press, 1959.

DOLLARD, J., & MOWRER, O. H. A method of measuring tension in written documents. *J. abnorm. soc. Psychol.,* 1947, 42, 3–32.

SNYDER, W. U. (Ed.) *Group report of a program of research in psychotherapy.* State College: Pennsylvania State College, 1953.

Experimental Treatment of Neurotic Computer Programs[*]

KENNETH MARK COLBY

An academic question is one which is supposed to be of little consequence. An academic lecture may or may not meet this requirement. While this is often an occasion to survey our field and to scold one another for our deficiencies and while I, too, have a number of things to exhort about in psychiatry and psychoanalysis, I have chosen another alternative, as indicated by the title of this address. I would like to talk about something today which may be of little consequence but which is really too new to have its consequences decisively evaluated.

One purpose of scientific and professional meetings such as this is, to quote Scrip-

Reprinted from the *Archives of General Psychiatry,* 1964, 10, 220–227, with the permission of American Medical Association and the author.

* Presented as the Academic Lecture at the Western Divisional Meeting of the American Psychiatric Association and the West Coast Psychoanalytic Societies, Sept. 27, 1963.

These studies were supported by Grant MH 06645-01, 02 of the National Institute of Mental Health and Grant NSF-GP 948 of the National Science Foundation.

I would like to express my gratitude to my collaborator in these investigations, John Gilbert of the Center for Advanced Study in the Behavioral Sciences, Stanford, Calif.

ture, "to hear or tell of some new thing." The computer simulation of psychotherapy is indeed new and I am honored to be granted the distinction of this opportunity to discuss it with you.

As a technical term, the word "simulation" is perhaps an unhappy choice since it is easily confused with its everyday usage, connoting the negatively evaluated synonyms of feigning or sham pretending. But among those developing the approach of computer simulation the term means to represent, to model a complex real-life situation in the form of a program, the conceptual instrument, which can be tested on a computer, the technical instrument. A program attempts to capture the essences of some problem-laden and untractable reality and to represent them in a symbolic form which becomes experimentally manageable. As a technical instrument of great speed and information-processing power, a computer carries out in compressed time a large number of processes commanded by the program so that an investigator can quickly obtain answers to the questions he is asking.

This type of inquiry is in the tradition of searching for useful understanding through model construction. By "model" I do not mean a complete replica such as a model house, nor an empirical interpretation of a calculus nor a formal mathematical model. A computer model is a type of theory which attempts to explain a class of observable phenomena by referring to relations between hypothesized entities and processes. The model simply does not copy the real world but embodies our *ideas about* the real world. The advantage of computer programs for modeling real-life situations involving human behavior is that they can do justice to the complexity of the subject matter. A program approaches the problem of simplifying ill-defined, immensely complex situations by making explicit in an easily agreed-on objective language a group of processes which could account for some of the observed events. These processes are made up of hypotheses and simplifying assumptions which attempt to account, not for the entire range of observables in the real-life situation, but for those aspects of it which are considered of cardinal significance. Into this system of processes one can introduce independent variables under varying initial and intermittent conditions. One can thus freely play with the program in a way which cannot be done in the real-life situation it simulates.

Rather than continue listing these merits of computer simulation, let us consider its application to a complex situation we are all familiar with, namely the psychotherapeutic session. Psychiatrists grapple with the class of problems it presents every working day and have been doing so for a long time. Yet much of what goes on in the clinical dyad remains a mystery. Research in psychotherapy has utilized naturalistic, experimental, and actuarial approaches with a small yield thus far to the practitioner. What the practitioner needs is more powerful methods of effecting change in individual patients. Except for polishing certain skills for selected patients there has been little advance in psychotherapy for thirty years. We are now developing better

notions regarding the ontogenesis of neurosis but our understanding of the influence and change process in therapy remains limited.

At the clinical level, then, we would like to increase our abilities to modify neurotic processes through the exchange of semantic messages between therapist and patient. At the basic science level of social psychology we want to understand how persons influence the belief systems of other persons. And at the basic-basic science level we would like to understand how to solve problems of extremely complex social and biological systems. It is the failure of conventional research methods to fulfill these desires that leads us to attempt novel approaches, to widen the scope of inquiry, to strike out in new directions, to try something like computer simulation.

How does one go about writing programs which simulate the treatment of neuroses by psychotherapy? As yet we do not know the right way to go about it but I shall describe one such attempt. This program is not yet fully satisfactory according to criteria we have for such attempts (1), but it might be viewed as a prototype not only of a more adequate program but also of a whole family of anticipated improvements. The program is too large to describe here in its entirety so I will confine myself to a brief description of some of its entities and some of the processes they take part in.

The program represents a particular neurotic process, namely anxiety and indecision in relations to men. As I will elaborate on in a moment, the data are taken from notes and tapes of a particular woman patient whom I had in treatment for about three years. The output from the system, and by "system" I shall be referring to the program running on the computer, consists of simplified English sentences. The program is written in SUBALGOL, which is Stanford's version of BALGOL, and runs on an IBM 7090. The sentences in Fig 1 have been edited to yield their counterparts in natural language. Each sentence should be

System Output
In Natural Language

PROGRAM: FATHER IS INDIFFERENT TO ME.
            MOTHER SAYS FATHER ABAN-
            DONED US.
            FATHER PREFERRED SISTER.
            I AVOID FATHER.
            SISTER ADMIRED FATHER.
            I FEEL TENSE NOW.

THERAPIST: YOU ADMIRE FATHER.

PROGRAM: NO.
            I DO NOT ADMIRE FATHER.
            I ADMIRE AL.
            MOTHER OUGHT NOT ADMIRE
            AL.
            MOTHER DETESTS FATHER.

Fig. 1.

looked at as analogous to a single statement
made by a patient or, more often, as a para-
graphic or even chapter theme which in
real-life would serve as a topic around
which a large number of other redundant
sentences saying much the same thing
would be clustered. As you can note the
program emits one sentence after another,
the therapist intervenes with a statement,
and the program responds with another
group of sentences.

Every sentence consists of a subject, a
verb, and an object, in that order. In the
simplified version of English which the system uses there are only two parts of speech,
nouns and verbs, and an order rule which
determines their function. One could get by
with just nouns and an order rule, but the
result was esthetically too unpleasant even
for us. Subjects and objects can have adjec-
tival modifiers and verbs have modifiers
indicating whether the tense is past, present, or future.

A compound sentence is one in which
the subject or object can be unpacked and
therein is found another sentence, as for
example in the sentence (Fig 1) "MOTH-
ER SAYS FATHER ABANDONED US"
the subject is "MOTHER," the verb
"SAYS" and the object is the sentence

"FATHER ABANDONED US." Verbs
can be compounded by using two sentences
having the same subject and indirect objects are represented also by combining
two suitable sentences.

Thus the system can express anything
that can be expressed in sentence form in
natural language. It may be a bit monotonous to read strings of sentences all having
the same unyielding format. But we are not
trying to replicate the generation of natural
language sentences with all their syntactical
and grammatical flexibility. We are only
trying for semantic accuracy. We feel the
meaning of the systems' output sentences
captures the meaning of sentences uttered
by the patient.

All the words which appear in output
sentences are stored in a dictionary (Fig
2). The dictionary consists of a two-dimen-
sional array or matrix. At the moment it
contains 257 words. Looking at a row in
this matrix, say location 72, we see that the
first cell is occupied by an English word.
Every word is actually the name of a class
or category which has instances or synonyms. "MEN" is a class having instances
while "FATHER," which in this system refers to a specific person, has only himself
as an instance and is thus a primitive term.

The third cell of a row location contains a
number which indicates whether or not the
word can be used as a verb. The fourth cell
contains a plus or minus number signifying
an evaluation valence. Thus "MEN" has a
value of −10 since they were negatively
evaluated by this patient. The fifth cell contains a number which represents a location
on another matrix, the substitute matrix
(Fig 2) which in turn gives a list of the
instances of this class, if it is a noun, or a
list of synonyms if it is a verb. From the
sixth cell on, the cells contain locations of
words in the dictionary which make up a
property list of this particular word. For
example, the property list of "FATHER"
consists of the location of the words MEN,
OLD, RICH, etc. Notice that "FATHER"
has the property of belonging to the class

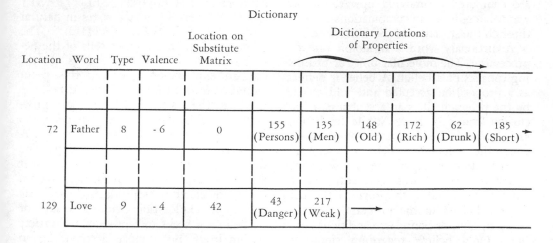

Dictionary

Location	Word	Type	Valence	Location on Substitute Matrix	Dictionary Locations of Properties					
72	Father	8	-6	0	155 (Persons)	135 (Men)	148 (Old)	172 (Rich)	62 (Drunk)	185 (Short) →
129	Love	9	-4	42	43 (Danger)	217 (Weak) →				

Substitute Matrix

Location	Dictionary Source	Location of Anonym List	Dictionary Locations of Instances or Synonyms			
42	129 (Love)	51	122 (Like)	13 (Approve)	2 (Accept)	-5 (Adore)
61	135 (Men)	0	72 (Father)	92 (Harry)	7 (Al)	
51	94 (Hate)	42	53 (Dislike)	169 (Reject)	-224 (Abhor)	-47 (Detest)

Fig. 2

"MEN." Each dictionary term has potentially an upward categorization, that is, it may be an instance of a super-ordinate class, and a downward categorization in that it may have instances. Verbs are organized into synonym hierarchies cascading downward from strong to weak forms. Each verb may thus have an upward stronger synonym and a downward weaker synonym. In the case of verbs there is also an associated antonym list to be found on the substitute matrix. Some nouns have stored antonyms while for others an antonym is computed depending on the context. All words are members of one or more lists, some of which are stored while others are computed by moving upward, downward, laterally, or in combinations of these through the structure of the dictionary.

A dictionary word is an atomic unit for processing. The molecular unit for processing consists of a belief. A belief is defined as a proposition accepted and held as true by the program. It is an acceptance, a conclusion from experience. While the dictionary represents the schematization of experience, the accepted beliefs represent the thematization of experience. Those themes which the patient was repeatedly and intensely concerned with provided the data for the beliefs in the program. Two circumscriptions or boundary conditions apply here. Only beliefs regarding significant persons, including the self, are represented. Not all beliefs regarding these persons are represented but only those which, in our judgment, appeared to be crucial or essential. At the moment, the starting belief list consists of 105 beliefs.

Beliefs are stored in a matrix (Fig 3). Sentences output by the system stem from the linguistic parts of a belief. Cells 9 through 15 represent the word content in that each cell number gives the dictionary location of the word involved. When printed out in output, this particular belief would yield the sentence, in the system's short version of English: "SELF (PAST) LOVE FATHER," which states in natural language: "I LOVED FATHER." The other numbers in the other cells of the belief represent various weightings, levels, etc, an explanation which at this point would lead us off into too much detail.

When the system is activated and processing begins, beliefs are grouped into complexes according to relevance criteria. A complex consists of a list of beliefs. The first action postulate of the system is that it strives to express its beliefs. The system maintains itself by reproducing itself. By activation, exploration, and expression of its beliefs it seeks to reproduce the variety within itself. But there is a second action postulate which is prepotent and demands that the system maintain itself through self-reproduction in an integrated form. This is a safety principle which states that severe conflict, since it is devisive, disintegral, and paralyzing to decision and ultimately to action, constitutes a danger which must be avoided.

From the flow diagram of Fig 4 we see that processing a complex consists of taking each belief on the complex list, matching it against all the others in the complex in a search for conflict and then sending the original belief or its created substitute

	1	2	3	4	5	6	7	8
Location	Complexity	Balance	Degree of Acceptance	Location of Reasons	Mark	Level and Sign	Residual Charge	Fixed Charge
64	0	1	5000	29	0	+1	3600	7000

	9	10	11	12	13	14	15	
Location	Subject Modifier	Subject	First Verb Modifier	Second Verb Modifier	Verb	Object Modifier	Object	
64	0	179 (Self)	0	153 (Past Tense)	129 (Love)	0	72 (Father)	

Fig. 3. Patient's belief matrix.

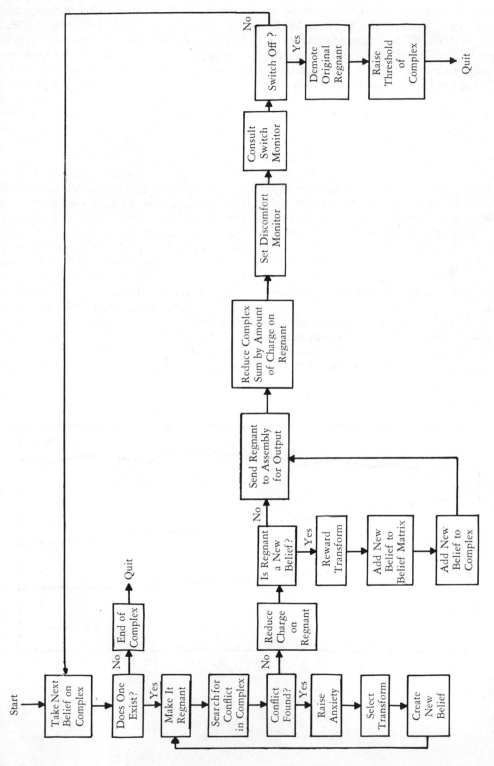

Fig. 4. Flow diagram for processing a complex of beliefs.

along for eventual output of its word content in the form of a sentence. Conflict is defined in terms of command-countercommand, eg, "I WANT X"—"I MUST NOT WANT X" and there are various degrees of conflict. When conflict is found, anxiety is raised. Here the term "anxiety" is being used in its theoretical sense of a danger signal rather than in its observational sense. The anxiety level in the system is an index of how greatly the system's integrity is threatened. When faced with conflict, the regnant, ie, the belief which the system is trying to throughput, cannot be expressed and a substitute belief must be created. For example, if the regnant is "I ADMIRE FATHER" and it runs into conflict with the counter-belief "I MUST NOT ADMIRE FATHER," the system transforms the subject, or verb, or object or combinations of these. The resultant new belief represents a distortion of the regnant.

To illustrate, at low levels of anxiety an attempt is first made to find a suitable substitute for the object. Using the dictionary, a search is made for a three-degree analog to FATHER, namely an object having three properties in common with FATHER. Suppose JOE satisfies these criteria, then the belief is constructed "I ADMIRE JOE." The new belief now becomes the regnant and again a search is made through the complex for conflict. If no conflict is found the new belief is throughput for eventual output expression. When expressed it would represent a cryptophor, a disguised and distorted metaphor of the belief it substitutes for. If conflict is found, anxiety is raised again and the new belief discarded, and an attempt is made to construct another one from the original regnant. Thus a defensive transform can fail, with a resultant rise in anxiety in two ways, (1) through failure to find an analog and, (2) an analog is found but conflict still exists between the newly created belief and some other belief in the complex. When a transform fails, others are tried until eventually a suitable substitute is constructed and can be expressed.

A transform which succeeds in creating a satisfactory new belief is rewarded by being given a greater proportion of the "anx-

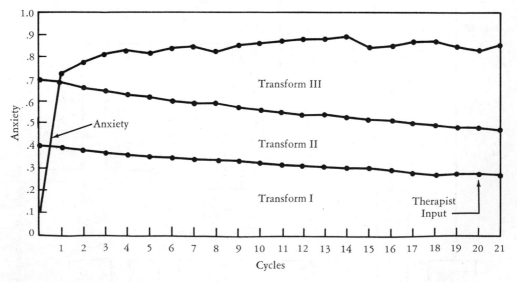

Fig. 5

iety space" to handle. In the system the range of anxiety is fixed or normalized between 0 and 1. When a given transform is rewarded the others are consequently demoted (Fig 5). Over time, a repeatedly successful transform gains a larger and larger area. Thus a preferred style or rigidity develops in that a transform becomes used disproportionately often and other transforms, potentially in the system, gets squeezed out.

Observing the output or macroprocesses of the system, there are four properties of its behavior which are characterized as neurotic. It maintains in general a high level of anxiety, it has repeated episodes of anxiety attacks, it becomes automatic and rigidly stereotyped over time, even in the face of novelty, and its output of information contains many incongruities and contradictions. One other interesting output property is that it blocks or avoids in response to pertinent therapist input.

At the level of microprocesses "inside" the system, what is neurotic is the severity of conflict and the manner in which it is temporarily dissolved through a distortive mode rather than by accommodative or integrative modes. Distortive transforms result not in resolution of conflict but in the maintenance of a disintegral state containing misconceptions and misbeliefs. Anxiety is temporarily reduced but at the cost of distorted misbeliefs (particularly regarding the self) and vulnerability to return of the conflict state.

As another illustration of the type of process the system carries out, consider the flow diagram of Fig 6 which shows the responses to input. In making "therapeutic inputs" we are trying to modify the behavior of the system in a way which simulates the way a therapist attempts to influence a patient. At the moment we are experimenting with different inputs under the same initial conditions. One of the advantages of treating a neurotic program is that one can go back in time and start over. This virtue of reiterability is unfortunately lacking in clinical and experimental stiuations with persons.

We want to try out a large number of alternatives and follow out their remote consequences. Since the system operates in compressed time we should be able to study a large number of outcomes which would be impossible to achieve in real life and in real time.

One of the weaknesses of the program at this time, which we are trying to remedy, is that it cannot correct itself. That is, it has no way of bringing evidence to bear on its distortions in an attempt to modify them. We are now attempting to include self-corrective processes which simulate those healthy processes which a patient brings to therapy. A patient seeks relief and variety through change. He not only has ways of defending by avoidance but also ways of contending by facing conflicts and working on them.

To turn now to more general aspects of this type of investigation, what we are trying to do is to develop a method consisting of three steps. The first step consists of collecting the cardinal facts and inferences of psychotherapeutic interactions. The second step consists of representing this data and hypotheses regarding its processing in the form of a computer program which can then be experimented with. The data, eg, the dictionary and beliefs, are idiosyncratic and unique to an individual patient, while the processes, eg, avertiveness, repression, and distortion in the face of anxiety, are assumed to be general. The third step will consist of taking back to the real-life situation what we have learned from the artificial experimental situation and applying it to persons. At the moment we are at least a couple of years away from carrying out the third step. One of the skills one acquires in writing and testing computer programs is that of postponement of deciding what *not* to do next. Not everything can be a problem all at once or one becomes swamped by the enormity of the task. First we must generate and accumulate a lot of experience

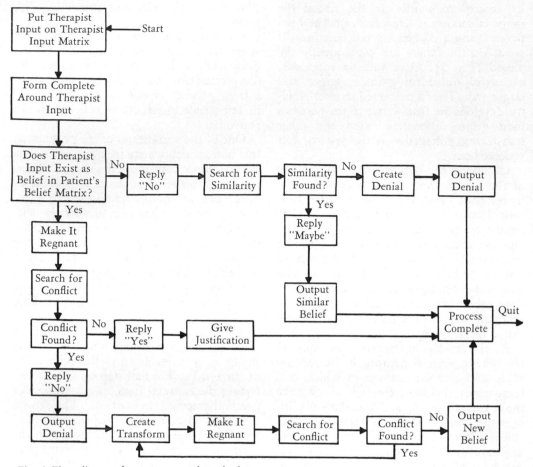

Fig. 6. Flow diagram for response to therapist input.

with the first two steps and especially the second, writing neurotic programs, because it has so much to say about the kind of data to be collected. Data are not the "givens" of nature but the "takens" and they are taken according to some decision criteria.

The criticisms of the approach should be familiar to you since they are the criticisms which are applied to all approaches to problems. One could assert that the hypothses are questionable, the postulates are naive, the boundary conditions are too narrow (or too wide), there is too much (or too little) structural detail in the model, there are better ways of solving the empiri-

cal problem, and the data are unreliable. I have no easy answers to these objections but I do have a suggestion regarding the data-reliability problem. Selecting the essential beliefs and inferring the crucial conflicts through clinical judgment may well yield data of low inter-judge reliability. But there is another way of using a computer which might help us here. With the development of a device which can learn through practice to recognize a given patient's voice, data could be taken directly from tapes of interviews, categorized as is done in a program known as the General Inquirer (2) and frequency counts made of the categories. This would give us statistical measures of what themes the patient is dealing with at below-chance or above-chance frequency.

Suppose we increase the reliability of the data. How do we know the model of the processes is correct? We are not ready to answer that question yet because we are not ready to ask it. The match with nature, the degree of correspondence between the model and reality remains untested. Ideally, experimenting with the program should yield predictions which have points of contact with observations in the real-life situation. A computer can be viewed as a single gigantic hypothesis consisting of thousands or statements. Before one can test a hypothesis one must first formulate it. We are at the stage of trying to learn how to formulate such extremely complex hypotheses.

Besides being interested in a better understanding of the processes of person-on-person influence, a practitioner of psychotherapy might wonder about eventual practical applications of such computer programs. One way to use them would be in difficult cases or at moments of impasse. Experiments on a suitable program might aid a therapist in discovering an optimal strategy for changing the patient's belief system in certain areas. A therapist as decision-maker is sometimes faced with a problem-situation which is too much for his information-processing capacity. A man-machine combination could significantly augment a therapist's ability to understand and to influence. We know from years of clinical experience that the most significant obscurity and chief technical problem in psychotherapy is the resistance to change. Attempts to change generate resistance to change. We need to understand more, not only how beliefs are generated, maintained and changed, but how they resist change and become so impervious to external social influence.

Another practical application might involve using neurotic programs as a training device. As it is now we simply start off the beginner in psychotherapy with live patients and it is often difficult to tell who is the more distressed by this experience. Preliminary practice with an artificial system, towards which the ethics of hurting do not apply, might be a helpful educational aid. Incidentally, during training we could tell who is the more effective therapist, at least with the artifact, because we could judge who effects the same system the most from the same starting conditions.

In sum I have been describing the strategy of a new laboratory and experimental method, giving a single example. The central methodological question is—Is the method suited to the empirical problem? It seems to me that conventional research methods for studying the problem of social influence, whether in psychotherapeutic or other contexts, are beginning to bog down. Methods and models have failed to come to grips with the chief complaint of investigators in the behavioral sciences, namely an inability to deal with elusive symbolic complexity explicitly. Theories in the form of conventional prose, mathematical equations, or statistical statements are not complicable enough to live up to the complexity of human behavior. Complexity itself is a methodologic rather than ontologic category. The models of behavioral processes we have at present are too abstract and too oversimplified. In approaching complexity one must always simplify but to over-simplify loses purchase on what we consider to be significantly human about persons, ie, that they process, exchange, and transform symbols. If we view a person as a large, complex, idiosyncratic, subtle, sensitive, dynamic, evolutionary, holistic, versatile symbol-processing system, why not use a system with similar properties such as a computer to represent him in these respects. This is what the excitement is about—we feel we now can begin to do justice to the complexity of the subject matter.

Prior to just a few years ago we had no such aid. We were confined to representing our ideas in prose and crude diagrams whose dynamics were impossible to analyze verbally. We could not follow out all the implications of what we were saying, and it was difficult to test the consistency and independence of our axioms. Now we have a tool which can in a few seconds or a few minutes work out thousands and millions of consequences.

We will have to use computers in a manner different from the way in which they are now being used in physics, mathematics, and engineering. But it has always been the case that a new technical instrument must be reconstituted and adapted to the problems of a particular subject matter. A computer is an interesting, exciting, and challenging new thing in the world and that may be justification enough to experiment with it. The ultimate test for us in psychiatry will be its usefulness in coping better with clinical problems. For the time being all we can do is work at it and wait and we shall see.

REFERENCES

1. COLBY, K. M.: "Computer Simulation of a Neurotic Process," in *Computer Simulation of Personality*, Tompkins, S. S., and Messick, S., editors, New York: John Wiley & Sons, Inc., 1963.

2. STONE, P. J.; BALES, R. P.; and NAMENWIRTH, J.: *Behav. Sci.*, 7:1, 1962.

Application of a Computer System of Content Analysis to Therapy-Analogue Interviews[*]

GEORGE PSATHAS
CHARLES CLEELAND
KENNETH HELLER

INTRODUCTION

One of the major problems confronting those interested in doing research on the psychotherapeutic process is the reduction of vast amounts of verbal data for analysis. Picking one or two sessions for intensive examination has been one approach, but there are many drawbacks involved in sam-

Reprinted by permission of the authors.

[*] A briefer version of this paper was presented at the meetings of the Midwest Psychological Association, May, 1965. It is a partial report of a research project, Content Analysis of Interaction in Psychotherapy, supported by a grant from the USPHS, National Institute of Mental Health, MH 08665-01. Computations were done with support provided by the Washington University Computer Center under National Science Foundation Grant G-22296.

We are grateful to Philip J. Stone who made the General Inquirer system available and generously provided consultation and assistance. We also wish to acknowledge the contributions made by Peggy Rothman and Dave Bridger.

pling small segments of the treatment of a given individual. Some investigators have analyzed many protocols for a given patient during his treatment, but the amount of coding and scoring necessary in such a large undertaking has generally operated to reduce efforts of this sort to a small number of sessions and patients. It would be an obvious advantage if methods of computer data processing which would illuminate the important features of content and interaction in therapy sessions could be applied to such studies.

This paper reports an exploratory attempt to apply the General Inquirer, a computer system of content analysis (Stone, et al., 1962) to a series of therapy-analogue interviews (Heller, 1963; Heller et al,. 1964) in which the interviewer's behavior was varied in order to determine the effects on the subject's behavior. Our purpose is to examine in detail the results of one specific output produced by this system, tag tallies, to determine the extent to which reliable interpretations can be made from statistically significant differences revealed in the analysis.

The General Inquirer system is described most completely in a paper by Stone, *et al.* (1962) and applications of the system in subsequent publications (Stone and Hunt, 1963; Stone, Dunphy & Bernstein, 1965; Psathas, 1965; Colby *et al.*, 1963; Colby & Menchik, 1964; Stone, *et al.*, in press). The system was designed for the content analysis of spoken or written verbal materials. After the text has been punched on cards, numerous clerical operations can be done automatically and reliably by a large, general purpose computer (IBM 7090-94 and/or 1401). First, the program will look up each text word in a stored dictonary and assign to it a "defining" category (tag); second, it will tally all words assigned to a given tag-category of the dictionary for any designated unit of text length (e.g., total document or some segment, by originator or recipient of the words, etc.). Third, the tag tally is reported by raw frequencies as well as proportions, i.e., the number of times a particular tag was applied divided by the total number of words in the text. Fourth, a leftover list of all text words not found in the dictionary is produced. Examination of this list can suggest revisions of the dictionary to include words that have been omitted and which occur with substantial frequency. It is also possible to determine what proportion of all text words are found in the dictionary.

The present dictionary contains approximately 3500 entry words drawn primarily from the Thorndike and Lorge (1944) list of frequently used words. Since the computer system chops word endings such as -e, -ed, -s, -ly, and -ing and also removes double letter endings (e.g. kiss, kissing, kisses and kissed are all reduced to "kis") thereby reducing many words to their root word, the actual number of words identified is estimated to be three times the figure

mentioned. Using this system in analyzing various texts, conversational as well as written sources, approximately 92–98% of the total text words (excluding proper names) have been tagged.

The system is sufficiently flexible that the investigator may compile his own dictionary of defining tags and insert it into the system. Thus, specific dictionaries as well as the general one reported here can be used.

The list of defining tags used in the present study, the Harvard Third Psycho-Sociological Dictionary (henceforth called the Harvard Third Dictionary), is presented in Table 1. First order tags, only one of which can be assigned to an entry word, refer to the "usual and explicit meaning of the word in standard usage." These are further divided into subgroupings such as Persons, Groups, Physical Objects etc.

Second-order tags refer to the "significant connotative and implicit meanings" of words with one part of the list having reference to sociological contexts and the other to psychological themes. More than one second-order tag can be applied to a word.

Since the tags, as assigned to entry words, represent the "theory of meanings" used by the constructors of the dictionary, it is important that the dictionary be examined is some detail so that users of the system can understand how the specific list of entry words which are assigned to a particular tag give that tag its "meaning" in the practical sense of "within the present dictionary." An illustration is provided in Table 2 where all words tagged Bad, a first order tag, are listed and Table 3 which contains the second-order tag, Sex-Theme. A sample section of the dictionary listing entry words in one column and defining tags in adjoining columns is presented in Table 4.

Text can be punched for analysis with or without syntax or special coding. Syntax coding, in our usage, will refer to a classification of subject, object and verb in a

TABLE 1

First Order Tags

Persons
  01 self
  02 selves
  03 other
  04 male-role
  05 female-role
  06 neuter-role
  07 job-role
Groups
  08 small-group
  09 large-group
Physical-Objects
  10 bodypart
  11 food
  12 clothing
  13 tool
  14 natural-object (natural-obj)
  15 non-specific-object (non-spec-obj)
Physical-Qualifiers
  16 sensory-ref
  17 time-ref
  18 space-ref
  19 quantity-ref
Environments
  20 social-place
  21 natural-world
Culture
  22 ideal-value
  23 deviation
  24 action-norm
  25 message-form
  26 thought-form
Emotion
  27 arousal
  28 urge
  29 affection
  30 pleasure
  31 distress
  32 anger
Thought
  33 sense
  34 think
  35 if
  36 equal
  37 not
  38 cause
  39 defense-mech
Evaluation
  40 good

  41 bad
  42 ought
Social-Emotional-Actions
  43 communicate
  44 approach
  45 guide
  46 control
  47 follow
  48 attack
  49 avoid
Impersonal-Actions
  50 attempt
  51 get
  52 possess
  53 expel
  54 work
  55 move

Second Order Tags

Institutional-Contexts
  56 academic
  57 artistic
  58 community
  59 economic
  60 family
  61 legal
  62 medical
  63 military
  64 political
  65 recreational
  66 religious
  67 technological
Status-Connotations
  68 higher-status
  69 peer-status
  70 lower-status
Psychological-Themes
  71 overstate
  72 understate
  73 sign-strong
  74 sign-weak
  75 sign-accept
  76 sign-reject
  77 male-theme
  78 female-theme
  79 sex-theme
  80 ascension-theme (ascend-theme)
  81 authority-theme (auth-theme)
  82 danger-theme
  83 death-theme

TABLE 2	TABLE 3
BAD (COMPLETE LIST)	SEX THEME (SELECTED LIST)
AWFUL	ADVENTUR
BAD	AFFAIR
BADLY	ANIMAL
BITTER	APARTMENT
CHEAP	ATTACH
COARS(E)	ATTRACT
CRUDE	ATTRACTIV
DETERIORAT	BEACH
DREADFUL	BED
FALS(E)	BEDROOM
HIDEOU(S)	.
HORRIBL(E)	.
IMPERFECT	.
IMPERFECTLY	MARITAL
INCONVENIENT	MARRI
INCORRECT	MARRIAG
INFERIOR	MARRY
INVALID	MASTURBAT
LOUSY	MASTURBATION
MEAGR(E)	MAT
MEDIOCR(E)	.
MEDIOCRITY	.
TERRIBL(E)	.
UGLY	SEX
UNATTRACTIV(E)	SEXUAL
UNFAIR	SEXY
UNFORTUNAT(E)	SHEET
UNFORTUNATELY	SLEEP
UNSUITABL(E)	.
UNWORTHY	.
USELES(S)	.
VIL(E)	SWUNG
VULGAR	TENDER
WORS(E)	TONGU
WORST	TOUCH
WORTHLES(S)	TREAT
WRONG	WAIST

sentence by inserting a subscript after the word. Special codes can be used to identify persons, particularly for clarifying indefinite personal pronouns such as "he," "they," "them," etc. A sample of coded text is presented below as it would appear on IBM punch cards. The meaning of subscript code numbers and letters is explained below the sample.

KHO3AFEO1   OK. AH, FIRST HE/1S
            STARTED/3B OUT HAD/3B A

LITTLE BIT (AMOUNT) OF PROBLEMS/5 TALKING/3B TO THE COUNSELOR (COUNSEL/5MNH). TO ME/5P, HE/1S SEEMED/3B VERY WORRIED/3B ABOUT HIS/5S GRADES/5, +HE/8S WAS NOT SURE/9 HOW THEY (GRADES/1) WERE COMING/3B ALONG, + THEY (GRADES/1) WERE COMING/3B ALONG BADLY. HE/1S HAD/3B A GIRL/5FNE BACK HOME.

Syntax Coding

Subject	/1
Verb	/3
Object	/5
Indirect Object	/5
Attributive Object	/8
Attributive Verb	/9

Special Codes

Time of action
- A past action
- B present action   used only for verbs
- C future action

Persons
- P patient or interviewee, subject in the interview
- S subject in the tape-recorded case
- M male
- F female
- MF Person(s) who could be either or both (e.g. parents)
- N non-family persons
- J family of procreation members
- R family of orientations members
- H higher status persons
- E equal status persons
- D lower status persons
- T interviewer or therapist

The General Inquirer system is also a retrieval system, i.e. the text can be searched automatically until specified patterns of word usage or tags are found. The unit for retrievals is the sentence.

Thus, it is possible to utilize words and/or sentences as the basic units of analysis. The tag tally uses the word as the unit. Retrieval programs utilize the sentence as the unit. To illustrate retrievals examples of sentences in which particular tags occurred will be given.

THE DATA

Heller presented subjects, undergraduate psychology majors, with a standard case study narrated on tape by an actor portraying a college student seeking guidance for personal problems. Immediately after listening to the stimulus material, subjects were asked to participate in a 15-minute interview, with one of four different types of interviewers. Subjects were given the following instructions:

TABLE 4

SAMPLE SECTION OF ALPHABETICAL LIST OF ENTRY WORDS AND DEFINING TAGS

DEFINING TAGS

(Second-Order Tags Precede First-Order)

Entry Words		
COVER	SIGN-ACCEPT	GUIDE
COW	FEMALE-THEME	NATURAL-OBJ
CRACK	FEMALE-THEME	SPATIAL-REF
CRASH	ASCEND-THEME, DANGER-THEME	DISTRESS
CRAWL	SIGN-WEAK	MOVE
CRAZY	SIGN-WEAK	DEVIATION
CREAM	FEMALE-THEME	FOOD
CREAT	ARTISTIC TECHNOLOGICAL SEX THEME	WORK
.	.	.
.	.	.
.	.	.
CUSTOM	COMMUNITY AUTH-THEME	ACTION-NORM
CUSTOMER	ECONOMIC	NEUTER-ROLE
CUT	SIGN-REJECT DANGER-THEME	ATTACK
DAILY	OVERSTATE	TIME-REF
DAMAG		ATTACK
DANC	RECREATIONAL SEX-THEME	MESSAGE-FORM

1. As a starter for the *first five minutes* you should remember and report as much about the tape as you can. (Description condition)
2. For the *next five minutes* you should discuss how you would solve the situation on the tape. (Solution-Proposal condition)
3. For the *last five minutes* you should talk about yourself—about how you seem different or like the person on the tape. (Identification condition)

Attempting to vary interpersonal behavior along the dimensions of activity (Active vs. Passive) and affect (Friendly vs. Hostile), Heller devised interviewer roles and trained graduate students in speech and theatre as interviewers. Heller's description of the four roles devised is as follows:

1. Active-Friendly interviewer (AF). This interviewer leads the interview by encouraging verbalization but not directing the content of the discussion. He is sympathetic, friendly and considerate of the interviewee. He is supportive and helpful. He speaks often, tends to be verbose, and uses non-verbal signs of approval.
2. Passive-Friendly interviewer (PF). This interviewer allows the interviewee to lead the interview. He is agreeable, friendly and interested. He is laconic but agrees readily when he does speak. He uses non-verbal signs of approval.
3. Active-Hostile interviewer (AH). This interviewer leads the interview by requesting verbalization but not by directing the content of the discussion. Although not in extreme form, he shows disdain, disapproval and lack of appreciation for the interviewee's approach to the task. He speaks often, tends to be verbose and uses non-verbal signs of disapproval.
4. Passive-Hostile interviewer (PH). This interviewer allows the interviewee to lead the interview. He is aloof and shows lack of interest. He is laconic but voices skepticism or disapproval when he does speak. He uses non-verbal signs of disapproval.

Twelve interviewers, three per condition, were trained in the four conditions, and each saw eight subjects in his condition. From Heller's original sample, two interviews were randomly selected from each interviewer for this study, 24 cases in all, six in each of the above conditions.

PROCEDURE

Our own use of the General Inquirer involved some special procedures. Instead of using the sentence, our basic unit was the *proposition* (Lennard and Bernstein, 1960) which is basically the same as the *actor-action* construction used by Fries (1952). It is defined as a "verbalization containing a subject and a predicate either expressed or implied." Special rules were constructed for the definition of propositions, and coders were trained in this procedure in preparing text for punching. It was this unit which was retrieved by the computer in all sentence retrievals.

Syntax coding, although not utilized in the data analysis presented here, was also done. Syntax was defined as follows: *who* is acting (the subject of the unit) *what* the action is (the verb), *what* is acted upon either directly or indirectly (the object). In addition, if the proposition represents action as seen or reported by someone other than the subject, or as modified by the subject, then the attributive subject, the attributive object, and the attributive verb were scored. For example, in the sentence "He said that he likes people," "He said" is an attributive part of the sentence and is coded in such a way as to indicate this.

Special person codes, mentioned above, were used to identify special features of this data, such as: time of action—past, present or future; persons—the subject, the interviewer, and the actor heard on the tape; the sex and the relationship of all persons named or referred to such as family or non-family members; the status of the person in relation to the subject in terms of higher, equal or lower.

The data were transferred from punch cards to tape. The dictionary lookup was accomplished with the General Inquirer on an IBM 7094. Subsequent operations, including tag listings, tag tallies, and retrievals were carried out on the IBM 1401. The tag tally program, generating both tag counts and index scores (which represent the frequency of occurrence of a tag divided by the total number of words in the text) automatically punches cards which then may be treated with standard analysis of variance programs. In the treatment of the data, an arcsin transformation was employed to normalize the distributions.

In the present exploratory stage of this type of study, an examination of the specific words contributing to the tag tallies is highly desirable. Sometimes the tags which show significant differences for a set of data do not "make sense" when examined in the context of sentences in which they occur. This has special relevance for the problem of defining or tagging entry words in the original dictionary construction. This problem is naturally greater when a general dictionary rather than one constructed specifically for therapy sessions is used since the "meanings" of words cannot be expected to remain constant in different subcultural contexts. At this stage, the only way to check the value of a given tag for a specific set of data is to examine the printouts of the sentences in which tagged words occurred. Our concern in this initial approach to the data was to see if the tag tallies, *in and of themselves,* could be used to generate meaningful statements about the data. Our assessment of meaningful results was facilitated by the fact that we were dealing with therapy-analogue sessions in which systematic differences between treatment conditions and the behavior of the subject in different phases of the interview could be expected. Heller's analysis of the same data provided some basis for comparing our results with other analyses.

Because our procedure involves an assessment of the validity of the Harvard Third Dictionary tags some mention must be made of at least two major assumptions which underlie the assignment of any tag to a given word. The first is that the word "naturally" belongs in the specific segment of social-psychological space to which it has been assigned in the construction of the Harvard Third Dictionary. The examination of this assumption necessitates a clinical judgment based on the particular set of data being analyzed. It is possible that words in the larger context of the "document" rather than sentences, are actually used in a consistently different manner than the denotative and connotative meanings assigned in the dictionary assume.

The second assumption is that the dictionary will be used with populations similar to those for which it was constructed. The reference population for this dictionary was a middle-class college group with generally middle-class values and modes of expression as described by Dunphy (1964). The subjects in the study analyzed here do belong to such a group.

These assumptions are considered in some of the procedures we followed. The actual words contributing to the tally on a tag were checked to see if special usage which deviates from the context of meaning established for the tag contributes a high proportion of the tagged words. This procedure might be thought of as establishing the reliability of the tag by testing for error. The word "well," for example, is included in the tag Good. If its use in the introjectory sense ("*Well,* I just don't know.") comprises a large number of the retrievals on the tag, interpretations that have reference to the definition of the tag Good in the dictionary construction would be misleading.

Most users of the Harvard Third Dictionary have used the frame of reference which underlies the theoretical construction of the dictionary in interpreting tag tallies. It is important to note that another way of looking at the data is possible. A direct empirical approach may be useful to those who have some reservations about the theoretical concepts used in constructing existing dictionaries and, for some reason, are not able to construct a dictionary for their own specialized use. With this procedure one notes the words that contribute heavily to a tag and interprets differences between treatments, time periods, or groups in the best manner for the data. New programs have recently become available to produce tallies for entry words automatically.

In the following sections, each tag showing a significant difference due to treatments or interaction between the experimental conditions will be evaluated with the above conditions in mind. The analysis of variance was used to test whether index scores for a single tag are significantly different due to:

1. the *activity* dimension (active or passive interviewer) or,

2. the *friendliness* dimension (friendly or hostile interviewer) or,

3. an interaction of these dimensions.

For each tag that showed statistically significant differences all sentences in which the tag occurred were retrieved. These retrievals were examined to determine what specific words might be contributing to the tag tally and whether the words, in the sentence context, actually fit the definition of the tag. This represents an attempt to assess the validity of the tag tallies before proceeding to interpret the differences. Actually, the processes of interpretation and validity testing go on simultaneously since significant tallies lead us to consider various interpretations which are then tested against the retrieval patterns. A completely "blind" interpretation based on the tag tallies alone is not yet possible though this is regarded as a future possibility once the problems of validity have been resolved.

Because some tags had zero frequencies for many subjects across as well as within conditions we decided to eliminate some of these tags from the analysis of variance to minimize the chances of obtaining results which were spurious. Our criterion for elimination was as follows: if zero frequencies occurred for half or more of the subjects within a phase of the interview, i.e. Description, Solution-Proposal or Identification, the tag would be excluded from the analysis of that phase. A tag was not eliminated if zero frequencies characterized one treatment in contrast to others.

In addition, two tags, 01 Self and 02 Selves, were excluded from the analysis because all or most entry words in these lists were assigned special person codes. These codes produce tallies and index scores in the same way that regular tags do and were included in the analysis.

RESULTS

In the presentation of results, specific tags will be examined to determine the extent to which reliable interpretations can be made of the statistically significant differences revealed by the analysis of variance. In view of the developmental stage of the computer system being used the results are not presented as tests of hypotheses concerning differences between conditions but rather as an effort to generate questions or hypotheses for later testing after dictionary revision has occurred.

Tables 5, 6 and 7 show that in the Description condition (first five minutes), 9 tags of 76 tested showed statistically significant differences at the .05 level or greater; in Solution-Proposal, 7 of 73 tested; and in Identification 14 of 74 tested. Since the number of statistical tests was three times the number of tags tested (2 treatment and 1 interaction effect) the number of statistically significant differences observed is not greater than chance expectation. However, since we are concerned with discovering patterns of differences that can be revealed by the Dictionary we chose to examine those tags which did show significant differences. In view of the small number of differences other starting points could be taken but, as indicated, our interest was in the interpretation of results based on tag tallies. Therefore, those tags which showed significant differences and which contain low rates of error are discussed.

In the Description condition, one tag, Anger, shows a difference in the same direction that the tag Distress does in the

TABLE 5

TAGS SHOWING SIGNIFICANT DIFFERENCES FOR DESCRIPTION CONDITION

Number and Name	Source	F
Physical Objects		
13 Tool	P > A	4.40*
Culture		
22 Ideal-Value	P > A	5.71*
24 Action-Norm	A > P	5.36*
25 Message-Form	Int.	6.64*
	AF > PH > PF > AH	
Emotion		
32 Anger	F > H	15.00**
Thought		
33 Sense	Int.	5.58*
	AH > PF > PH > AF	
Institutions		
60 Family	Int.	4.59*
	AH > PF > AF > PH	
57 Technological	H > F	4.53*
Status		
68 Higher-Status	H > F	9.81**

*P < .05
**P < .01
Total tags significant = 9
Total tags compared = 76

TABLE 6

TAGS SHOWING SIGNIFICANT DIFFERENCES FOR SOLUTION-PROPOSAL CONDITION

Tag Number and Name	Source	F
Persons		
03 Other	F > H	9.46**
Culture		
22 Ideal-Value	P > A	9.19**
Thought		
34 Think	Int.	5.71*
	AH > PF > PH > AF	
37 Not	Int.	14.21**
	PF > AH > AF > PH	
Social Emotional Actions		
43 Communicate	A > P	8.00*
Impersonal-Actions		
50 Attempt	Int.	8.61**
	PF > AH > PH > AF	
Psychological Themes		
75 Sign-Accept	H > F	5.28*

* p < .05.
** p < .01.
Total Tags significant = 7.
Total Tags compared = 73.

TABLE 7

Tags Showing Significant Differences for Identification Condition

Tag Number and Name	Source	F
Persons		
05 Female-Role	F > H	4.53*
07 Job-Role	F > H	7.43*
Culture		
22 Ideal-Value	Int.	11.30**
	PH > AF > AH > PF	
24 Action-Norm	P > A	4.67*
25 Message-Form	Int.	7.16*
	PH > AF > PF > AH	
Emotion		
31 Distress	F > H	4.47*
Evaluation		
40 Good	A > P	9.79**
41 Bad	P > A	6.64*
	H > F	4.48*
	Int.	4.60*
	PF > PH > AH > AF	
Impersonal Actions		
54 Work	Int.	9.44**
	PH > AF > AH > PF	
Institutions		
67 Technological	P > A	4.46*
	Int.	6.66*
	PH > AH > AF > PF	
Status		
68 Higher-Status	A > P	6.30*
Psychological Themes		
79 Sex-Theme	Int.	4.73*
	PH > AF > AH > PF	
Special Codes		
92 Family-Relative	A > P	9.27**
95 Males	A > P	4.52*

* $p < .05$.
** $p < .01$.
Total tags significant = 14.
Total tags compared = 74.

Identification condition, namely, significantly higher rates in the Friendly in contrast to the Hostile treatment. This suggests that rather than responding to the Interviewer with words that "fit" the treatment received (i.e. hostile words with Hostile treatment) there is instead a suppression or inhibition on the part of subjects. They may either feel freer to talk on Anger and Distress themes when treated in a friendly fashion or, in response to hostile treatment, suppress mention of topics of this kind.

Another tag that fits this interpretation, Sign-Accept in the Solution-Proposal condition, shows a higher rate in the Hostile in contrast to the Friendly treatment condition. Words such as "please," "like," and "support" contribute to this frequency.

"His parents were *supporting* his college education."

"But I *agree* with him breaking all ties with the hometown girl."

"And they (parents) just want to *help* him along."

"Why cannot I follow the guys and be *like* the rest of them?" (The use of "like" in a comparative sense does not fit the tag meaning but its frequency is low.) It is possible that subjects were making covert appeals for the interviewer to become less hostile or, inhibited in expressing hostile themes, focus instead on positive topics. However, exceptions to this interpretation are the higher rate for the Hostile condition on the tag Bad and the absence of any difference on the Hostile-Friendly dimension for the tag Good. This latter tag happens to have extremely high rates of error, however, in contrast to Bad which has little or no error. Thus, some tags show a consistent pattern when compared with each other and offer indications of a common "theme" characterizing conditions.

Intellectualizing kinds of behavior are indexed by high rates on the tags Think and Sense. These show significant interaction effects for the first two conditions (Description and Solution Proposal), both in the same direction, i.e. AH>PF>PH >AF. Words included under the Think tag which have the highest frequencies are "think," "know," "mean," and "solve" and for Sense "seem," "feel," and "see." The contrasting conditions, active-hostile and passive-friendly, show higher rates for these tags indicating that subjects are less direct in their communication. These words tend to be used most frequently in attributives i.e. "I think . . ." "I mean . . ." or in statements which indicate caution and qualification e.g. "It *seems* like teenagers always do," "He was beginning to *feel* that way," etc. Over 90% of the tally on the tag Think was caused by the attributive use of the word "think." The tag Not also fits this interpretation and shows interaction effects; PF and AH are both greater than AF

and PH respectively. Negation can be a way of defending and rationalizing as well as denying. These three tags may reflect an intellectualizing, rationalizing defense style by subjects in certain conditions.

It is noteworthy that almost all other interaction effects that are significant show these same two conditions, AH and PF, as being similar. For example, they are lower on Sex-Theme and Ideal Value in the Identification condition and Message-form in both the Description and the Identification condition, higher on the tag Attempt in Solution-Proposal and higher on Family words in the Description condition. Results such as this suggest the presence of additional common patterns for these two conditions which further analysis, particularly sentence retrievals, may reveal.

It was expected that the discussion of topics on Sex-Theme would be greater in the Friendly treatment condition. The actor on tape described several problems in relation to girls, dating, etc., and the subject in the Identification condition now has an opportunity to describe his or her own behavior in this area of activity. However, neither friendliness nor activity produce a consistent effect. The Passive-Hostile condition is one in which the high rate of sex words which was found was least expected. The next highest rate is in the Active-Friendly condition followed by AH and PF in that order. From the tag totals it is not clear whether subjects are, in fact, describing their own problems or merely repeating a description of the case. By far the largest number of tallies on this tag are for the word "date" with words like "love" and "sleep" also high.

"But we (boy and I) did *date* quite steadily."

"Well, he said that he was going to *bed* with her."

From this analysis, the interpretation that "friendliness" does not achieve greater success in having subjects talk about sexual topics is suggested.

The tag Message-Form contains words

referring to cultural forms for conveying information and meaning such as "book," "cash," "film," "grade," "lecture," "money," "music," etc. The actor reported problems dealing with school grades and courses, relationships with his parents involving the morality of certain behaviors and his obligations to his parents because of their financial support. Subjects in the PH condition tend to mention the word "grade" whereas those in AF mention "money," "dollar," and "grade." Both of these conditions are higher than the PF and AH, the latter being one in which "money" and "dollar" are not mentioned at all. Thus, some differential selection of topics occurs between Ss in these different treatment conditions. This result reveals one problem in interpreting tag tallies. Subjects may receive equally high totals on a tag while at the same time differing considerably in their usage of specific words which are included under the tag in question.

Of the tags which show statistically significant differences on the Active-Passive dimension certain patterns deserve comment. Action-norm is a tag which contains considerable error in the sense that the words included under it are not clearly consistent with the definition of the tag. The word "way" is a word with the highest frequency in this list and it has such varied uses that it does not convey a cultural form of taking action as do, for example, words like the following which are on this list; "assignment," "ceremony," "contest," "game," "marriage," "ritual," "traffic," etc. "Way" is often used in sentences like:
1. "... the way he explained it. ..."
2. "... from the way he talked. ..."
3. "... he should not act that way. ..."
4. "He does not know which way to turn. ..."

These usages involve idiomatic expressions referring to manner or style of speaking (1 and 2), standards of behavior (3) and direction or goal (4). For this reason no interpretation of the tag is made. Per-

haps another indication of the ambiguity in this tag is the fact that in the Description condition it is the Active treatment while in the Identification condition the Passive treatment which shows a significantly higher rate. This tag demonstrates how idiomatic uses of a particular word can introduce considerable variation of meaning. A mode of dealing with this issue is to incorporate idioms into the dictionary and provide different tag definitions for each.

The tag Ideal-Value contains words referring to cultural ideals and standards, e.g. "beauty," "courage," "kind," "liberty," "moral," "success," "tolerance," "worth," etc. In the Passive treatment significantly higher rates are found for both the Description and Solution-Proposal conditions but an interaction effect occurs in the Identification condition. This difference may reflect a withdrawal into "safe" topics and discussion of moral and ethical issues when subjects receive less stimulation and feed back from the interviewer. An alternative interpretation is that the subtle, indirect and implied disapproval in this condition stirs guilt about disapproved behavior. A detailed examination of specific sentences is a needed supplement to an interpretation based on the tags to determine whether a defensive style is in fact involved. It must be noted that in the Identification condition it is the PH condition which is highest on Sex-Theme, a topic which cannot be considered "safe," and at the same time shows a high rate on Ideal-Value.

The tag Communicate, which shows a significant difference with $A > P$ in the Solution-Proposal condition, contains 99 words, but only 12 were used by subjects in this experiment. Of these, four words, "tell," "said," "talk," and "say" account for 90% of the total. The subjects are referring primarily to the actor's failure to talk to others about his problems. They advise him to talk:
1. "maybe if he has a *talk* with ... a counselor ..."

2. "Maybe by *talking* to the parents
   ..."
3. "If he would stop and *talk* to them
   (parents) ..."
4. "He should try to *talk* to the girl
   too."

They also refer to things he *said*.

1. "He *said* he was not too sure about
   engineering."
2. "Like he *said,* his folks just ..."
3. "I know something else he *said*
   ..."

Thus, the subjects in the Active treatment seem to be more actively involved in giving advice. In order to confirm this interpretation the advice giving use of Communicate words would have to be separated from the mere description of what the actor said. This separation can only be done by combining tags (and/or words) in making discriminations between the different usages. This is an important and necessary next step to supplement the tag tally procedure.

In the Identification condition the special code tags Family and Males are higher for the Active dimension. This is most likely due to higher rates of talking about fathers (either his own or the actor's) by the subject. This result is significant because it indicates more involvement in the interview and a greater willingness to discuss his own relationship with his father in a direct manner as well as indirectly by reference to the actor's father. In contrast, Heller (1963) found a significant interaction effect for "family referents," defined as the subject's reference to his own family with $PH > AF > AH > PF$. Again, further specification is indicated in order to separate the two kinds of family references. The special coding referred to earlier allows for this possibility but retrieval procedures and theme analysis (Stone and Hunt, 1963), which involve more complicated procedures beyond tag tally operations, are necessary.

Several tags which show statistically significant results are not discussed here for various reasons. Tool, Technological and Good show high rates of error in retrievals, particularly instances in which the use of the word in the sentence context does not fit the meaning defined for the tag in the dictionary. Other tags not discussed are those which refer to persons (Female-Role, Job-Role, Other and Higher Status) whose relationship to the subject can be determined. Only words not assigned one of the special code tags would be classified on these tags which, thus, represent a residual for all less specific person references. In view of this fact and because the more reliable and specific special codes do not show any significant differences no interpretation of these latter four tags is attempted.

DISCUSSION

The analysis of tag tallies has revealed several meaningful patterns in the subject's behavior when treatment conditions are compared. Certain tags can be interpreted as indicators of intellectualizing, rationalizing defensive styles (e.g. Think, Sense, Not)! Other tags show differences between conditions which reflect the effects of interviewer styles in subject behavior (e.g. Anger and Distress higher in friendly treatment). However, in interpreting these results greater attention was paid to the methodological problems involved in the use of the General Inquirer which affect the validity of interpretations. Specific attention to these matters revealed problems which subsequent revisions of the dictionary and the computer system could incorporate and which would contribute to the improvement of its validity.

It must be noted that the analysis and discussion included only those tags which showed statistically significant differences on the analysis of variance comparing different treatment conditions. It is possible that if other tags had been examined and corrected for errors they would reveal interesting and meaningful patterns when conditions were compared. We have not exhausted the possible analyses that can be made on the basis of tag tallies. Rather than continue on this course, however, we felt it desirable to take stock of the problems that had been discovered and undertake revision of the dictionary.

The classification of errors in the assignment of words to particular tags directed our attention to major problems in dictionary construction and to the assumptions involved in it. In advance of an examination of the data it was not possible to tell whether the definition (tag) assigned to a word would accurately define the word as it is used in a specific body of text. Extensive and detailed examination of sentences and specific usages and the classification and calculation of types of "error" even after statistically significant results have been found would seem to be necessary. We could conceivably go through this stage and then, with new totals calculated, do the analysis of variance. The cost in time and effort of such a procedure would seem to defeat the initial purpose of an automated system of content analysis but at this time it is premature to assume an "errorless" classification system without determining, by a direct examination of the data, the amount of misclassification actually occurring.

The approach to a solution, compatible with reliance on a computer approach, seems to lie in a combination of dictionary construction, tests of its "goodness of fit" for particular sets of data, revision, retesting, and re-analysis. The examination of sentence retrievals provides the investigator with immediate feedback concerning the context of usage. The larger context of a paragraph or an entire interview can in fact suggest new "meanings" for earlier usages of words as well as presage emerging meanings as group culture develops. Thus, the interpretation of results and the discovery of new patterns of meaning which can be incorporated in subsequent dictionary revisions are procedures that go hand in hand.

We can foresee the possibility of individualized and automated dictionary construction such that meanings are assigned as they become clear through the usages made by a particular individual (or group) under study. A self-correcting and incrementing system would undoubtedly have to make some assumptions concerning when the frequency of a particular usage was sufficiently high to increase the set of definitions.

Nevertheless, the possibility must be faced that no pre-programmed system can completely capture the meanings of words as used by individuals in particular contexts. Even a self-correcting and incrementing system must rely on frequencies to determine which meaning is to be attached to a particular word in a given context since not all contexts can be anticipated and included in a finite dictionary. The reliance on frequencies can never completely eliminate error though programming features such as the inclusion of idiom definitions, context searches, and assignment of different definitions to the same word or idiom according to syntax and context will reduce many of the errors noted in examples given above. For interaction of the kind studied here the inclusion of nonverbal elements of communication, designated by appropriate coding, can increase the possibility of capturing some of the subtleties of interaction in therapeutic interviews.

Obviously, considerable work remains to be done before the promise of automated analysis of verbal interaction can begin to produce the results that computer systems foreshadow. Nevertheless, even the preliminary results presented in this paper offer some indication of the gains already achieved in computer systems designed for content analysis.

SUMMARY

This analysis has explored the feasibility of testing for differences between treatment conditions in a therapy-analogue interview using the results of tag tallies from the General Inquirer content analysis system. Though the tag tallies revealed only a few statistically significant differences some of these seemed to relate to theoretically meaningful differences between treatment conditions.

At this stage in the development of the General Inquirer it is still necessary to examine specific word counts under each tag and specific sentence retrievals in order to provide a check on the validity of interpretations. As the system develops and is tested on varieties of content, the possible range of applications and the feasibility of interpretations based on tag tallies alone will become clearer.

We have presented examples of several problems in the interpretation of tag tallies and shown how the actual words used and sentences in which the tag occurs can be examined to 1) indicate needed revisions of the dictionary, 2) to discover specific patterns of usage within a tag and 3) to indicate how interpretations based on tags can be supplemented or corroborated by utilizing the sentence retrieval feature of the same content analysis system.

REFERENCES

COLBY, B. N. & MENCHIK, M. D. A study of Thematic Apperception Tests with the General Inquirer System. *El Palacio*, 1964, Winter, 29–36.

COLBY, B. N., COLLIER, G. A. & POSTAL, S. K. Comparison of themes in folktales by the General Inquirer system. *J. of Amer. Folklore*, 1963, 76, 318–323.

DUNPHY, D. The evolution of two self-analytic groups. Unpublished doctoral dissertation, Harvard University, 1964.

FRIES, C. C. *The structure of English*. New York: Harcourt Brace, 1952.

HELLER, K. Interpersonal style in an interview analogue. Paper read at Am. Psychol. Assoc., Philadelphia, 1963.

HELLER, K., DAVIS, J. D., & SAUNDERS, F. Clinical implications of laboratory studies of interpersonal style. Paper read at Midwest. Psychol. Assoc., St. Louis, 1964.

LENNARD, H. & BERNSTEIN, A. *The anatomy of psychotherapy*. New York: Columbia University Press, 1960.

PSATHAS, G. Problems in the use of a computer system of content analysis, Paper read at Midwest. Sociological Society, April, 1965.

STONE, P. J., BALES, R. F., NAMENWIRTH, Z. & OGILVIE, D. The General Inquirer: a computer system for content analysis. *Behavioral Sci.*, 1962, 7, 484–497.

STONE, P. J. and HUNT, E. B. A computer approach to content analysis studies using the General Inquirer system, in *Am. Fed. of Inf. Proc. Societies Conference Proceedings,* Vol. 23, Spring Joint Computer Conference, 1963, 241–256.

STONE, P. J., DUNPHY, D. C. and BERNSTEIN, A. Content analysis applications at Simulmatics, *Amer. Beh. Scientist,* 1965, 8, 16–18.

STONE, P. J., DUNPHY, D. C. and OGILVIE, D. *The General Inquirer: A computer method of content analysis for the behavioral sciences,* in press.

THORNDIKE, E. L. & LORGE, I. *The teacher's word book of 30,000 words.* New York: Bureau of Publications, Teacher's College, Columbia University, 1944.

Selected Additional Readings

ABRAMSON, H. A. *The use of LSD in psychotherapy.* New York: Josiah Macy Foundation, 1960.

BERNE, E. *Games people play.* New York: Grove Press, 1964.

BINDMAN, A. J. Mental health consultation: theory and practice. *Journal of Consulting Psychology,* 1959, 23, 473–482.

BUCHWALD, A. M. Values and the use of tests. *Journal of Consulting Psychology,* 1965, 29, 49–54.

CUMMING, J., & CUMMING, ELAINE. *Ego and milieu.* New York: Atherton Press, 1963.

FAIRWEATHER, G. W. *Social psychology in treating mental illness: An experimental approach.* New York: John Wiley & Sons, 1964.

GEOCARIS, K. The patient as listener. *Archives of General Psychiatry,* 1960, 2, 81–88.

HARWAY, N. I., & IKER, H. P. Objective content analysis of psychotherapy by computer. Paper read at the 1964 Rochester Conference on Data Acquisition and Processing in Biology and Medicine, Rochester, N. Y., July 14, 1964. To be published in *The Conference Proceedings,* K. Enslein (Ed.). New York: Pergamon Press.

KAFFMAN, M. Short term family therapy. *Family Process,* 1963, 2, 216–234.

KING, G. F., ARMITAGE, S. G., & TILTON, J. R. A therapeutic approach to schizophrenics of extreme pathology: An operant interpersonal method. *Journal of Abnormal and Social Psychology,* 1960, 61, 276–286.

MANN, J. H. Experimental evaluations of role playing. *Psychological Bulletin,* 1956, 53, 227–234.

MURRAY, E. J. Direct analysis from the viewpoint of learning theory. *Journal of Consulting Psychology,* 1962, 26, 226–231.

PHILLIPS, E. L. Parent-child psychotherapy: A follow-up study comparing two techniques. *The Journal of Psychology,* 1960, 49, 195–202.

RIOCH, MARGARET, ELKES, CHARMIAN, FLINT, ARDEN, USDANSKY, BLANCHE S., NEWMAN, RUTH G., & SILBER, E. National Institute of Mental Health pilot study in training mental health counselors. *American Journal of Orthopsychiatry,* 1963, 33, 678–689.

SASLOW, G. A case history of attempted behavior manipulation in a psychiatric ward. In L. Krasner and L. P. Ullman (Eds.), *Research in Behavior Modification*. New York: Holt, Rinehart and Winston, 1965. Pp. 285–304.

SCHWITZGEBEL, R., & KOLB, D. Inducing behavior change in adolescent delinquents. *Behavior Research and Therapy*, 1964, 1, 297–304.

STOLLAK, G. E., & GUERNEY, B. Exploration of personal problems by juvenile delinquents under conditions of minimal reinforcement. *Journal of Clinical Psychology*, 1964, 20, 279–283.

STONE, P. J., BALES, R. F., NAMENWIRTH, Z., & OGILVIE, D. The General Inquirer: A computer system for content analysis. *Behavioral Science*, 1962, 7, 1–15.

ULLMAN, L. P., & KRASNER, L. Introduction. In *Case Studies in Behavior Modification*. New York: Holt, Rinehart and Winston, 1965. Pp. 1–63.

WOLPE, J. Behaviour therapy in complex neurotic states. *British Journal of Psychiatry*, 1964, 110, 28–34.

Subject Index

PRINTED IN U.S.A.